ABOUT THE AUTHOR

Tim Tranchilla is a traveler, writer, and diplomat. He has worked for 12 years in the United States Foreign Service, where he served for three years in Tel Aviv on assignment. That experience inspired this guidebook, the *BUCKET! Guide to the Holy Land*. Aside from Israel, Tim's lived in Mexico, India, Egypt, South Africa, and New Zealand. Tim holds a Bachelor of Arts in International Studies from Boston College focused on peace and conflict studies and the Middle East. He later completed a Master of Fine Arts in Creative Nonfiction Writing at The New School in New York City. His home base is Washington, DC. This is his first guidebook.

BUCKET! Guide to the Holy Land

A DIY Travel Planner to create a *Bucket List*-filled dream trip to Israel, Jordan, Palestine, and the Egyptian Sinai

TIM TRANCHILLA

BUCKET!

First published in the UK in July 2022 by
Journey Books, an imprint of Bradt Guides Ltd
31a High Street, Chesham, Buckinghamshire, HP5 1BW, England

www.bradtguides.com

Text copyright © 2022 Timothy Tranchilla
Photos copyright © 2022 Nestor Cerami
Edited by Chris Reed
Cover design by Ian Spick
Layout and typesetting by BBR Design, Sheffield
Maps by David McCutcheon FBCart.S
Production managed by Sue Cooper, Bradt & Jellyfish Print Solutions

ISBN: 9781784779566

British Library Cataloguing in Publication Data
A catalogue record for this book is available from the British Library
Digital conversion by www.dataworks.co.in
Printed in Turkey by Jellyfish Print Solutions

Paper used for this product comes from sustainably managed
forests, recycled and controlled sources.

To find out more about our Journey Books imprint, visit www.bradtguides.com/journeybooks

Contents

Acknowledgments — xix

Conventions — xx

What is BUCKET!? — 1

Enter: BUCKET! Guides — 1
BUCKET! Philosophy and Innovations — 1
How to Use this BUCKET! Guide — 4
Why Choose the Holy Land? — 6

PART 1 — HOW TO ITINERATE! — 7

Choose Your Method — 8

1. The In Situ Method — 8
2. The Stitch Method — 8
3. The Plug-and-Play Method — 9
4. The Non-Conformist Method — 9
5. The DIY Method — 10
6. The Itinerator! Method (online) — 10
How to Choose — 10

Understanding the Electives — 12

Structure of an Elective — 12
Rank — 12
The Holy Land BUCKET! List — 13
BUCKET!/Gold/Silver/Bronze/Pearl — 13
BUCKET! Scores — 14
Regions — 15
Anchor or Road Trip? — 16
Walks and Drives — 17
Themes and Categories — 17
Historical Eras/Periods — 18
Scales — 19
Finding Electives — 20

DIY Itinerator! — 24

Recording Electives 1: By Rank — 24
Time Needed — 25
Priorities — 26
Recording Electives 2: By Theme — 26
Days Needed — 27
Triage — 27
Rough Itinerary — 28
Recording Electives 3: By Region — 28
Routing — 30

Sleeping 30
Final Rough Itinerary 31
Travel Schedule 33

PART 2   TRIP PLANNING TO-DO'S **35**

Twelve to Six Months Before **36**
Do #1: Date It! 36
Do #2: Budg Et! 41

Six to Three Months Before **44**
Do #3: Fly It! 44
Do #4: Prepare For It! 46
Do #5: Sleep It! 48
Do #6: Reserve It! 53

Three Months to One Day Before **57**
Do #7: Money It! 57
Do #8: Pack It! 61
Do #9: Ready It! 62

PART 3   ARRIVAL AND ORIENTATION **65**
Do #10: Enter It! 66
Do #11: Transport It! 71
Do #12: Connect It! 75
Do #13: In Case You Need It! 76

PART 4   TODAY IN THE HOLY LAND **79**
Do #14: Eat It! 80
Do #15: Drink It! 93
Do #16: Beach It! 98
Do #17: Shop It! 100
Do #18: Late Nit! 107
Do #19: Last Min It! 109
Do #20: Bye-Buy It! 113

PART 5   BUCKET! (#1–3) AND GOLD ELECTIVES (#4–100) **117**
#1 Old City Jerusalem 121
#2 Petra 135
#3 Dead Sea 145
#4 Wadi Rum 155
#5 Tel Aviv 162
#6 Dome of the Rock 170
#7 Sea of Galilee 175
#8 Masada 182
#9 Church of the Holy Sepulchre 189
#10 Red Sea/Gulf of Aqaba 199
#11 Western Wall 205
#12 Temple Mount 210

#13 Akko 216
#14 Jerash 220
#15 Mount Sinai 225
#16 Modern Movement (Bauhaus Architecture) 228
#17 Israel Museum 232
#18 Church of the Nativity 235
#19 Madaba and the Madaba Map 241
#20 Qasr Amra and the Desert Palaces 244
#21 Dana Biosphere Reserve 247
#22 St. Catherine's Monastery 251
#23 Wadi Mujib and Mujib Biosphere Reserve 255
#24 Mount Nebo 258
#25 Caesarea 261
#26 Jericho and Hisham's Palace 266
#27 Bahá'í Gardens 271
#28 Makhtesh Ramon 274
#29 Nazareth and its Biblical Sites 279
#30 Jaffa 284
#31 King's Highway 288
#32 Citadel/Tower of David 292
#33 Capernaum and Tabgha 295
#34 Mount of Olives 299
#35 Yad Vashem 303
#36 Modern Amman 307
#37 Ancient Amman 310
#38 Biblical Tels 314
#39 Beit She'an 317
#40 Bethlehem 322
#41 Bethany-Beyond-the-Jordan 326
#42 Via Dolorosa 330
#43 Aqaba 335
#44 Jordanian Cuisine 339
#45 Umm Qais 341
#46 Tomb of the Patriarchs and Old Town of Hebron 345
#47 Jerusalem Walls and Gates 350
#48 Avdat 353
#49 Karak 357
#50 Ein Gedi 361
#51 Israeli Cuisine 365
#52 Jordan Trail 367
#53 Ras Mohammad 368
#54 Dahab 370
#55 Azraq Wetlands 371
#56 Tsipori 372
#57 Ajloun Forest 373
#58 Tsfat/Safed 375
#59 Megiddo 376
#60 Beit Guvrin and Maresha 378
#61 Nablus 381
#62 Golan Heights 382
#63 Tel Dan 385

#64 Beit Alpha 386
#65 Al-Aqsa Mosque 387
#66 Mea She'arim 389
#67 Mehane Yehuda Market 390
#68 Ramallah 391
#69 Jesus Trail 393
#70 Qumran 394
#71 Jerusalem Archaeological Park 396
#72 Jerusalem, New City 397
#73 Incense Route 399
#74 Ein Avdat 400
#75 Golan Heights Winery 402
#76 Ajloun Fortress 403
#77 ANU – Museum of the Jewish People 404
#78 Eilat 405
#79 Beit She'arim 407
#80 Banias 409
#81 Umm ar-Rasas 410
#82 Tel Aviv Nightlife 412
#83 Coral Beach 413
#84 Petra Kitchen 414
#85 Nimrod's Fortress 415
#86 Feynan Ecolodge 417
#87 Carmel Market 419
#88 Sharm el-Sheikh 420
#89 Tel Aviv Beaches 422
#90 Herodion 423
#91 Ramparts Walk 426
#92 Mount Zion 427
#93 Belvoir 429
#94 Western Wall Tunnels 430
#95 Tel Aviv Museum of Art 432
#96 Timna 433
#97 St. George's Monastery and Wadi Qelt 434
#98 Machneyuda 436
#99 Imperial Bar 437
#100 Dor HaBonim 438

PART 6   SILVER ELECTIVES (#101–250)   441

Abu Hassan 442
Akhziv Beach 442
Al-Ayoun Trail 442
Ancient Qatzrin 442
Apollonia 442
Argaman Beach 443
Argila/Hookah/Shisha 443
As-Salt 443
Banksy's Walled-Off Hotel 443
Bar'am 443
Basilica of the Annunciation 444
Battir Hills 444

Bedouin Tents and Coffee 444
Beit Sitti 444
Beit Yannai 445
Ben Yehuda Street 445
Bialik House 445
Bible Lands Museum 445
Bridge of Strings 446
Brown Beach House 446
Busi Grill 446
Café Culture 446
Camel Riding 447
Cardo 447
Carmel Hai-Bar 447
Carmel Winery 447
Church of St. Anne and the Pools of Bethesda 448
Church of the Transfiguration 448
City of David 448
Deir Quruntal 448
Design Museum Holon 448
Domaine du Castel 449
Dome of the Chain 449
Drummers' Beach 449
Ein Bokek 449
Ein Bokek Spa Hotels 450
Ein Hemed 450
Ein Hod 450
Ein Kerem 450
Elbabor 451
Elma Arts Complex 451
Fountain of Sultan Qaytbay 451
Gamla 451
Gan HaShlosha 452
George and John Tel Aviv 452
Hadassah Synagogue and Chagall Windows 452
Haifa 452
Halutza 452
Hamat Gader 453
Hamat Tiberias 453
Hammamat Ma'in Hot Springs 453
Herbert Samuel 453
Herziliya Beaches 454
Hezekiah's Tunnel 454
Hiking in Jordan 454
Hiking in the Negev 454
Hot Air Balloon Ride Over Wadi Rum 455
Hula Lake 455
Hummus 455
Israel National Trail 455
Jaffa Flea Market 456
Jewish Quarter 456
Jordan Archaeological Museum 456

Jordanian Hospitality 456
Kibbutz Lotan 456
Kibbutz Volunteer 457
King David Hotel 457
Korazim 457
Lag B'Omer at Moshav Meron 457
Little Petra 458
Lot's Cave 458
Mamilla Hotel 458
Mamshit 458
Manta Ray 459
Mar Saba 459
Mashya 459
Mediterranean Coast 459
Mitzpe Ramon 460
Miznon 460
Modern Israeli Cuisine 460
Monastery of Abu Ghosh 460
Montfort 461
Mount Arbel 461
Mount of Beatitudes 461
Mount Carmel 461
Mount Gerizim 462
Mount Gilboa 462
Mount Hermon 462
Mukawir 462
MUSA – Eretz Israel Museum 463
Museum of Bedouin Culture 463
Nahal Me'arot/Wadi el-Mughara 463
Nazarene Fusion Cuisine 463
Netanya 464
Neve Tzedek 464
Nitzana 464
The Norman Hotel 464
OCD 464
Palestinian Heritage Trail 465
Pastel 465
Pella 465
Petra by Night 465
Popina 466
Qasr al-Abd 466
Qasr Azraq 466
Qasr Kharana 466
Red Canyon 466
Rockefeller Archaeological Museum 467
Rosh HaNikra 467
Rothschild Boulevard 467
Royal Society for the Conservation of Nature (RSCN) 467
Sabich/Oved's 468
Sataf 468
Sea of Galilee Beaches 468

Sebastia-Shomron 468
Separation Wall 469
Shakshuka/Dr. Shakshuka 469
Shaumari 469
Shivta 469
Shobak 469
Shrine of Bahá'u'lláh 470
Sinai Trail 470
St. James' Cathedral 470
Stella Maris 470
Supreme Court of Israel 471
Suweimeh Spa Hotels 471
Tel Arad 471
Tel Ashkelon 471
Tel Aviv Port 472
Tel Aviv Tayelet/Promenade 472
Tel Beer Sheva 472
Tel Hazor 472
Tel-O-Fun Bike Share 473
Tiberias 473
Tulul Abu el-Alaiq 473
Tzfon Abraxas 473
Umm el-Jimal 474
Underwater Observatory 474
Uri Buri 474
Weizmann Institute of Science 474
Wild Jordan Center 475
Winery Tour 475
Wohl Archaeological Museum 475
Yatir Winery 475
Yehi'am 476
Yehudiya 476
Yemen Moshe 476
YMCA 476
Yotvata Hai-Bar 477
Zichron Ya'akov 477

PART 7   ELECTIVES BY THEME   479

Noteworthy   482
Spotlight 482
Adventure 484

Religion   487
Religions 487
Religious Figures 489
Holy Books 490
Houses of Worship (Extant) 493
The Sacred 496

Archaeology 499

Ruins by Period 499
City Conglomerates 512
Impressionable Historic Sites 514

Structure 517

Monuments 517
Architecture 518
Engineering 519

Nature 521

Geography 521
Life 524
Parks 526

Scenic 528

Vistas 528
Scenic Drives 530

Society 531

Government 531
Land 531
Cities 532
Towns 534
Cooperatives 535

People 536

Identity 536
Ethnic Groups 541
Community Celebration 544

Culture 545

Museums 545
The Arts 546

Active 548

Walks and Hikes 548
Land Sports 550
Water Sports 552

Leisure 554

Beaches 554
Water 555
Resorts and Holiday 556

Entertainment 557

Shopping 557
Amusement 558
Party 559
Sports 560

Food and Drink   **561**
Food 561
Wine 563
Drink 564

Accommodation   **565**
Stays 565

Organized   **567**
Participatory 567
Tours 569

PART 8   **ELECTIVES BY REGION**   **571**
A Jerusalem 575
B Greater Jerusalem 576
C West Bank 577
D Tel Aviv 578
E Mediterranean Coast 580
F Mount Carmel and Jezreel Valley 580
G Lower Galilee and Kinneret 581
H Upper Galilee 582
I Golan Heights 582
J Negev 583
K Dead Sea (Israel) 583
L Eilat and Arabah 584
M South Jordan 584
N Petra 585
O King's Highway 585
P Dead Sea (Jordan) 586
Q Amman 586
R East Jordan 587
S North Jordan 587
T Sinai 588
U Cross-Israel/Palestine 588
V Cross-Jordan 589
W Whole Holy Land 589

PART 9   **WALKS AND DRIVES**   **591**
A1 Jerusalem Old City: Main Sites 593
A2 Jerusalem Old City: Four Quarters 594
A3 Jerusalem Old City: Walls and Gates 598
A4 Jerusalem Old City: Jewish Quarter 600
A5 Jerusalem Hills: Zion/Olives/David 602
A6 East Jerusalem 605
A7 Jerusalem: New City and Neighborhoods ... 607
A8 Jerusalem: Government and Museums 611
B1 Greater Jerusalem 613
B2 Judean Hills 615
B3 Judean Hills Wineries 616

C1 Old City Bethlehem 618
C2 Southern West Bank 621
C3 Jericho and Wadi Qelt 623
C4 Northern West Bank: Ramallah Region 625
C5 Northern West Bank: Nablus Region 627
D1 Tel Aviv-Jaffa: Stroll the Promenade 628
D2 Jaffa 631
D3 Tel Aviv: City Center 633
D4 Tel Aviv: Rothschild and Southern Neighborhoods 636
D5 Tel Aviv: Architecture 638
D6 Tel Aviv: Food and Drink 641
D7 North Tel Aviv 649
D8 South Tel Aviv 650
E1 Haifa 652
E2 Akko 654
E3 Mediterranean Coast South 656
E4 Mediterranean Coast Central 657
E5 Mediterranean Coast North 659
E6 Central Israel Wineries 661
E7 Mediterranean Beaches 662
F1 Mount Carmel 664
F2 Jezreel and Gilboa 666
G1 Nazareth 667
G2 Central Galilee 669
G3 Sea of Galilee 670
G4 Jesus Sites in the Galilee 672
H1 Upper Galilee 675
H2 Galilee Panhandle 676
I1 Foot of Mount Hermon 678
I2 Northern Golan 679
I3 Southern Golan 681
J1 Northern Negev 683
J2 Southern Negev 685
J3 Incense Route 687
K1 Dead Sea (Israel) 689
L1 Eilat 691
L2 Israel's Red Sea and Egyptian Border 693
L3 Arabah Desert 695
M1 Aqaba 696
M2 South Jordan 698
N1 Petra Highlights 699
N2 Petra's Best Hikes 701
N3 Petra and Wadi Musa 703
O1 King's Highway 705
P1 Dead Sea Highway 707
P2 Christian Jordan 709
Q1 Ancient Amman 710
Q2 Modern Amman 713
Q3 Cultural Amman 714
Q4 Greater Amman 717
R1 Eastern Desert 718

S1 North Jordan 719
S2 Northwest Jordan 720
T1 Sinai on the Gulf of Aqaba 722
U1 North Israel Wineries 724
U2 Israel's 10 Best National Parks 726
V1 Jordan Parks and Reserves 728
V2 Jordan Pass 730
W1 Umayyad Castles 733
W2 Nabataean Ruins 734
W3 Cities of the Decapolis 736
W4 Crusader Castles 738
W5 UNESCO Sites 740

PART 10   ITINERARIES BY BUCKET!   **743**

Introduction 744
Itinerary Options 744

Time-Specific   **746**

Stopover/Layover 746
Three-Day City Immersions: Three Cities 746
Anchor Cities: Days 1–10 Priorities 750
Weekends: Fifteen Trips 751

High Score   **752**

BUCKET! Itinerary 752
Top Ten 754
High BUCKET! Scores: 7+ 755

More Superlatives   **758**

Most Popular 758
Complete Ruins 758
Most Entertaining 759

Country-Specific   **760**

Best of Israel 760
Best of the West Bank/Palestine 762
Best of Jordan 763
Best of the Sinai 764

Macro-Regions   **766**

A Jerusalem 766
B Greater Jerusalem 766
C West Bank 767
D Tel Aviv 767
E Mediterranean Coast 767
F Mount Carmel and Jezreel Valley 768
G Lower Galilee and Kinneret 768
H Upper Galilee 768
I Golan Heights 769
J Negev 769

K Dead Sea (Israel) 769
L Eilat and Arabah 770
M South Jordan 770
N Petra 770
O King's Highway 771
P Dead Sea (Jordan) 771
Q Amman 771
R East Jordan 772
S North Jordan 772
T Sinai 772
U Cross-Israel/Palestine 773
V Cross-Jordan 773
W Whole Holy Land 773

Off the Beaten Path   774

Israel and Palestine 774
Jordan 775

Thematic   776

Noteworthy 776
Religion 778
Archaeology 779
Structure 781
Nature and Scenic 782
Society and People 784
Culture 785
Active 786
Leisure 788
Entertainment 789
Food and Drink 790
Accommodation 791
Organized 792

Completists   795

Wonders of the World 795
UNESCO 795
Endangered 796
National Parks and Reserves 798

Cross-Genre   800

Community 800
Fine Arts 801
On the Road 802
Relaxation 803
Ancient History 804
Memorial 805
Gourmet 806
Modernity 807
Romantic 808
Under the Sun 809

Budget   **811**

Shoestring 811
Luxury 812

Companions   **813**

Kid-Focused 813
All Ages and Generations 813
Big Group Friendly 814

Time-Unlimited   **816**

Twelve Weeks 816
Slow Holy Land 818
Whole Holy Land Sprint: Gold 820
Whole Holy Land Crawl: Gold, Silver, Bronze 821
Regional Add-Ons 821
BUCKET! the World 823

Classic   **824**

Historic 824
Pilgrimage 825
Cinematic 827
Overland 827

Tailored   **829**

Local Tour Guides 829
Tourism Boards 829
Travel Agents and Specialists 830
Tour Operators 830
Cruises 832
Bus Tours 833

PART 11   ELECTIVES BY ALPHABET   **835**

LIST OF MAPS AND SITE PLANS

ELECTIVES

Top 100 Electives	118
Wadi Rum (#4)	156
Masada (#8)	184
Church of the Holy Sepulchre (#9)	191
Western Wall (#11)	206
Temple Mount (#12)	212
Jerash (#14)	222
Church of the Nativity (#18)	237
Caesarea (#25)	263
Hisham's Palace, Jericho (#26)	268
Basilica of the Annunciation, Nazareth (#29)	280
Beit She'an (#39)	318
Bethany-Beyond-the-Jordan (#41)	327
Via Dolorosa (#42)	331
Umm Qais (#45)	342
Tomb of the Patriarchs (#46)	346
Avdat (#48)	355
Karak (#49)	359
Megiddo (#59)	377
Beit Guvrin (#60)	379
Beit She'arim (#79)	408
Nimrod's Fortress (#85)	416
Herodion (#90)	424
Mount Zion (#92)	428

MICRO-REGIONS

Israel and Palestine	572
Jordan and Sinai	573
Jerusalem	574
Tel Aviv	579

WALKS AND DRIVES

A1 Jerusalem Old City: Main Sites	593
A2 Jerusalem Old City: Four Quarters	595
A3 Jerusalem Old City: Walls and Gates	598
A4 Jerusalem Old City: Jewish Quarter	601
A5 Jerusalem Hills	604
A6 East Jerusalem	606
A7 Jerusalem: New City and Neighborhoods	608
A8 Jerusalem: Government and Museums	610
B1 Greater Jerusalem	612
B2 Judean Hills	615
B3 Judean Hills Wineries	617
C1 Old City Bethlehem	620
C2 Southern West Bank	622
C3 Jericho and Wadi Qelt	624
C4 Northern West Bank: Ramallah Region	626
C5 Northern West Bank: Nablus Region	627
D1 Tel Aviv-Jaffa: Stroll the Promenade	629
D2 Jaffa	632
D3 Tel Aviv: City Center	634
D4 Tel Aviv: Rothschild and Southern Neighborhoods	637
D5 Tel Aviv: Architecture	640
D6 Tel Aviv: Food and Drink (key)	643
D6 Tel Aviv: Food and Drink (south)	644
D6 Tel Aviv: Food and Drink (north)	646
D7 North Tel Aviv	648
D8 South Tel Aviv	651
E1 Haifa	652
E2 Akko	655
E3 Mediterranean Coast South	656
E4 Mediterranean Coast Central	658
E5 Mediterranean Coast North	660
E6 Central Israel Wineries	661
E7 Mediterranean Beaches	663
F1 Mount Carmel	665
F2 Jezreel and Gilboa	666
G1 Nazareth	668
G2 Central Galilee	669
G3 Sea of Galilee	671
G4 Jesus Sites in the Galilee	673
H1 Upper Galilee	675
H2 Galilee Panhandle	677
I1 Foot of Mount Hermon	678
I2 Northern Golan	680
I3 Southern Golan	682
J1 Northern Negev	684
J2 Southern Negev	685
J3 Incense Route	687
K1 Dead Sea (Israel)	690
L1 Eilat	692
L2 Israel's Red Sea and Egyptian Border	694
L3 Arabah Desert	695
M1 Aqaba	697
M2 South Jordan	699
N1 Petra Highlights	700
N2 Petra's Best Hikes	702
N3 Petra and Wadi Musa	704
O1 King's Highway	706
P1 Dead Sea Highway	708
P2 Christian Jordan	710
Q1 Ancient Amman	711
Q2 Modern Amman	712
Q3 Cultural Amman	715
Q4 Greater Amman	716
R1 Eastern Desert	718
S1 North Jordan	720
S2 Northwest Jordan	721
T1 Sinai on the Gulf of Aqaba	723
U1 North Israel Wineries	725
U2 Israel's 10 Best National Parks	727
V1 Jordan Parks and Reserves	729
V2 Jordan Pass	731
W1 Umayyad Castles	732
W2 Nabataean Ruins	735
W3 Cities of the Decapolis	737
W4 Crusader Castles	739
W5 UNESCO Sites	741

Acknowledgments

A book of this size and scope could never have been completed alone. First and foremost, I want to thank my spouse, Nestor, who provided love and support throughout the many nights and weekends over seven years when I refused to leave my desk in order to inch closer to the finish line. Nestor was a huge contributor to the project; he took the photos, created graphics, designed the online worksheets, helped build the website, and performed countless other little tasks that he never signed up for. This may have been my crazy idea, but Nestor's contributions made this guide match the modern tone I was going for.

Six years into writing BUCKET!, I nearly gave up altogether. Trying to contract graphic designers, book layout designers, cartographers, publishers, editors, distributors, marketing companies, and a dozen other entities all independently was an impossible task I simply couldn't manage on my own. At just the right moment, Journey Books opened their doors and everything fell into place. My sincerest thanks to the Journey team, particularly Adrian Phillips at Bradt Travel Guides for taking on this project, Anna Moores for seeing it through to completion, Claire Strange for keeping track of it all, and all the lovely people who kindly helped introduce me to the book publishing industry. Most of all, I owe a large debt of gratitude to Chris Reed for creating a beautiful structure, a sense of balance and order, and a thoroughly researched and edited text that will hopefully keep this book relevant for many years to come.

Conventions

ELECTIVES This guidebook references sites and experiences (see *Understanding the Electives*, p. 12) in a unique way. Each recommendation is either a Gold, Silver, Bronze, or Pearl site. They are easily distinguishable by their styling:

- ★ Gold sites: **Old City Jerusalem (#1)**
- ★ Silver sites: ***As-Salt***
- ★ Bronze sites: Florentin (D4)
- ★ Pearl sites: *Druze Cooking Workshops (H1)*

CURRENCY Prices are listed in USD, unless specified. Israel and Palestine use the shekel, whose currency code is ILS. Unofficially, the code NIS (New Israeli Shekel) is commonly used. Jordan uses the dinar, whose code is JOD, often shortened to "JD." Egypt uses the Egyptian pound, EGP.

LANGUAGE Throughout the region, both transliterations and translations into English are used to identify place names on street signs, storefronts, maps, and elsewhere. For instance, a popular street in Tel Aviv may be translated as "King George Street" or transliterated from Hebrew to "Rehov HaMelech George [or Jorj]."

DIALING CODES You will need to add prefixes to the telephone numbers listed in the book. Callers must first dial "out" of their home country, then dial "in" to the destination country, and finally enter the number to call. The exit code from the UK (and many other countries) is 00, while from the US it is 011. Country codes are +972 for Israel; +970 Palestine; +962 Jordan; and +20 Egypt.

TIME ZONES
- ★ *Standard Time* The Egyptian Sinai, Israel, Palestine, and Jordan all use the same time zone: GMT/UTC +2 hours. This is also referred to as Eastern European Time or Israel Standard Time.
- ★ *Daylight Savings* Israel, Palestine, and Jordan recognize DST and are each GMT/UTC +3 hours for these six months, usually from the end of March to the end of October. Israel operates on Israel Standard Time (IST) and can switch to DST earlier or later than Jordan and Palestine.

WEBSITES Many regional websites are in either Hebrew or Arabic without English pages. To access these sites, we recommend you use a translation browser extension (Chrome has TransOver, for instance) or a translation app on your phone (try Microsoft Translator on the iPhone).

What is BUCKET!?

ENTER: BUCKET! GUIDES

BUCKET! is not just a guidebook, but a whole new way to think about travel planning. We offer a clear approach to putting together an itinerary, with dozens of improvements to the guidebook genre that will aid the modern traveler. This innovative resource is designed to help readers create you-focused experiences that would normally come by way of travel agents. Our guide helps you design your own trip: at your budget, on your time, and within your interests. We take you through each stage of the pretravel process to ensure you create a realistic travel plan with activities you're sure to enjoy – because you hand-picked them!

Our architecture is unique, with a more logical display of site data, integrated history and culture, practical tools, and dozens of intriguing ways to interact with the guidebook itself (see *BUCKET! Philosophy and Innovations*, below). BUCKET! highlights how we travel *today*: sampling food at street markets, taking Instagram-worthy photos, visiting national parks and UNESCO sites, sleeping in the coolest accommodations, splurging on that one crazy activity you've always wanted to try, and touring those once-in-a-lifetime bucket list sites you've been dying to see *forever*.

In short, we created a guidebook with the traveler in mind. Now let's go make your dreams come true.

BUCKET! PHILOSOPHY AND INNOVATIONS

Guidebooks haven't changed in decades. Sure, they're chockablock full of information, but thumb through any guidebook and you'll discover the same in each: a top-ten list, a couple of two- to four-week-long itineraries, and 800 pages of data sorted by city and region. In their essence, today's guidebooks are country-specific encyclopedias with travel tips sprinkled in. This format is overwhelming, outdated, and not user-focused.

The times have changed and we've created a guidebook to match. You'll soon be introduced to new concepts, such as **coverage**, **micro-regions**, **themes**, and **electives**. But there are broader, more structural changes that we want to draw your attention to first.

ELECTIVES

★ *Electives* Let's start with nomenclature. We call each of our individually ranked sites and activities an *elective*, because with every option you're electing whether to visit or not. We don't write about every single site, museum, gallery, restaurant, and hotel in town. Instead, we've limited it to the very best (see *Algorithms*, below).

★ *Algorithms* Traditional guidebooks contain thousands of listings. Ever had a problem narrowing down your trip options? Us too. To simplify the selection process, we invented an algorithm that awards every tourist site or activity in the Holy Land a score based on popularity, recommendation, and global recognition. We've only included sites that have at some point received special recognition

1

(star, thumbs-up, etc.). Merely being referenced in a guidebook was not enough to earn a place here.

★ *Rank* We then rank-ordered the results. The highest-scoring sites have received our most coveted global accolade: BUCKET! site status. The top 100 are our **Gold** sites, the next 150 are **Silver** sites, and another 350+ are **Bronze**. We also highlight our own personal favorites in 100+ **Pearl** sites.

★ *BUCKET! Score* BUCKET! scored each of our top electives on a scale of 1–10. We're consistent across all of our guidebooks; a "7 star" site would be comparable anywhere, whether in Mexico, India, or the Holy Land.

★ *BUCKET! List* We've begun designating sites to a global BUCKET! List – a moniker equivalent to a "Wonder of the World" – indicating a place of global significance that we purport should be added to every traveler's lifetime bucket list. These are the absolutely essential sites that every world traveler must experience before they kick the proverbial!

STRUCTURE

★ *Chapters* Nearly every other guidebook is divided into chapters by region: cities, states, districts, countries. But you'll never discover the hidden gems of Akko, Jerash, or Qasr Amra – all in BUCKET!'s Top 20 – if you're only reviewing the chapters on Tel Aviv and Jerusalem (the two places you've heard of). Old guidebooks aren't designed to help you answer these questions, so we've structured our guidebook differently.

★ *First, Rank* First, we put the highest-ranked electives up front. Our BUCKET! and Gold electives are listed in rank order. We recommend you thumb through each elective's "brochure" to learn what they have to offer, and whether you would like to add them to your travel plan.

★ *Then, Themes* Our electives are each cross-referenced in one or more themes. By reviewing the 15 major themes, you'll see electives that fall into a variety of categories within that theme, such as: long hikes, water sports, Crusader castles, cooking schools, spas, or beautiful structures. You'll very likely find a site you would not have considered otherwise.

★ *Finally, Regions* And should you find yourself stationed in a location with time to spare, we've got you covered: itineraries, walking tours, and road trips that collect and combine the greatest hits of a particular geographical area.

TRAVEL PLANNING

★ *New focus on travel planning* "Smart travelers plan" – that's BUCKET's motto. We've designed this entire guidebook around the premise that a little planning will increase your trip satisfaction exponentially. While other guidebooks give you the information but don't help you distill it, every part of this book has been written and designed to help you to create the most mind-blowing, fabulous, unforgettable, and realistic travel plan.

★ *Build your itinerary* Once you've narrowed down your favored electives, we build a plan to help you get there. A little forethought can have a massive impact on what you get to see and do: you don't want to come all this way and miss the Dome of the Rock because you showed up on a Friday or Saturday. Your plan needn't be a rigid, ten-point program of activities scheduled from 06.00 to midnight every day. It should be able to roughly answer: what do you want to see and will you have time to see it? We're laser-focused on answering those questions.

★ *The Itinerator* This DIY tool will guide you step by step in creating a personalized travel plan, with as much or as little detail as you like. We've included a simple version in Part 1, *How to Itinerate!*, with a more comprehensive version online (**w** buckettravelguides.com). In both, we offer simple exercises to get you interacting with the electives while tracking your choices using BUCKET!'s intuitive charts. We account for variables such as speed, pace, distance, budget, time of year, and transportation to create a comfortable and realistic plan. At the end of the process, you'll have a beautifully rendered schedule to use in-country.

★ *Plug-and-play itineraries* For those with less time/interest to plan, BUCKET! has curated more than 100 prefabricated but completely customizable itineraries divided logically by travel focus: regions, days available, special interests, and "best of," among other straightforward options.

★ *Self-guided walks and drives* Even if you aren't interested in an entire itinerary, you'll find our city walks and road trips a revelation. We've crafted dozens of self-guided tours in and around cities and regions that link together your elected sites with other hidden gems. Maps always included.

OTHER INNOVATIONS

★ *99% fewer hotel and restaurant recommendations* Without region-based chapters, we're free from the burden of including lodging and dining for *every single town*. Instead, we've included the most amazing lodging and dining *experiences*: unusual accommodation (mud huts! glamping!), luxe stays, famous chefs, Michelin-star dining, night markets, food stalls… all the top spots you don't want to miss.

★ *Worth the detour?* Well, is it? We'll tell you.

★ *Best strategy* How to get there, how long you need, when best to visit, what to do.

★ *Relevance* Not only does this approach reflect modern sentiment, but also means far fewer listings will go out of date.

★ *Extensive cross-referencing* Every time an elective is referenced, we'll direct you back to its location so you can easily find out more information. Look for markers such as rank (#1) and location (A1) tagged to the name of each elective.

★ *Context* History can be off-putting to those who get confused or bored by names and dates. In each of our electives, we've attempted to provide easy-to-absorb historical context under the headings *Context* and *BUCKET!pedia*. In our Top 50 sites, we also provide a digestible chronology of important events.

ONLINE RESOURCES Head over to **w** buckettravelguides.com for:

★ *Chronotours* These expanded walking tours take you on an indirect, nonlinear, non-obvious journey through time and place. Instead of going through the proverbial front door and walking clockwise like maps tell you to do, we approach points of interest in chronological order, starting at the oldest spot on site and criss-crossing through history. This technique provides greater context to the names and dates so often confused and discarded in historical sections of other guides. Chronotours for **Old City Jerusalem (#1)** and the **Church of the Holy Sepulchre (#9)** are already online, with more planned.

★ *Worksheets* Do you appreciate a little organization? Then you're going to love our set of worksheets which help you put all your thoughts in one place and keep you organized and on time.

HOW TO USE THIS BUCKET! GUIDE

This guidebook is meant to be read like, well, a book – from front to back. We think the best method to plan your trip is with a methodical approach, going step by step. But this isn't mandatory – you may find it most exciting to explore electives, themes, and regions by simply flipping through the book.

We've organized chapters into blocks of time when it would be ideal to start completing tasks, such as buying flights, booking hotels, or deciding on a restaurant. Each chapter is broken into bite-size chunks to make this manageable, some with activities or assignments to help you stay focused (completely optional).

Part 1: How to Itinerate! Learn the different ways you can use this guidebook, depending on your planning style. We provide an orientation to our electives system

CREATE YOUR ITINERARY *(see Part 1)*

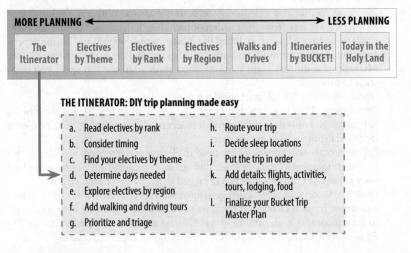

MORE PLANNING ◄────────────────────────────► **LESS PLANNING**

| The Itinerator | Electives by Theme | Electives by Rank | Electives by Region | Walks and Drives | Itineraries by BUCKET! | Today in the Holy Land |

THE ITINERATOR: DIY trip planning made easy

a. Read electives by rank
b. Consider timing
c. Find your electives by theme
d. Determine days needed
e. Explore electives by region
f. Add walking and driving tours
g. Prioritize and triage

h. Route your trip
i. Decide sleep locations
j. Put the trip in order
k. Add details: flights, activities, tours, lodging, food
l. Finalize your Bucket Trip Master Plan

PRE-PLANNING *(see Part 2)*

12–6 months before

0. The Itinerator, if applicable
1. Review the calendar
2. Prepare a budget

6–3 months before

3. Book plane tickets
4. Check documents
5. Research accommodation
6. Reserve your extras

3 months–1 day before

7. Sort your money
8. Pack for your trip
9. Get ready to leave

ARRIVAL

Day 0 *(see Part 3)*

10. Enter immigration
11. Coordinate transport
12. Connect with locals
13. Ready for emergencies

Day 1+ *(see Part 4)*

14. Eat everything
15. Drink everything
16. Lounge on a beach
17. Shop for gifts

18. Stay out late
19. Resolve any last-minute stuff
20. Begin your return home

while, for those of you wishing to DIY your trip, we provide a quick introduction to our *Itinerator!* system – a tool to help you build your dream trip.

Part 2: Trip Planning To-Do's Nine recommendations for every traveler to do before departing, broken down by time period.

Part 3: Arrival and Orientation This section covers immigration, customs, transportation, and other essentials for when you disembark the plane or cross over land borders.

Part 4: Today in the Holy Land Here we discuss food, drink, nightlife, and other information you will use after you've arrived. Think of this section as catering to more spontaneous decision-making, rather than preplanned activities (which is why it is not combined with *Electives by Theme*).

WAYS TO EXPLORE ELECTIVES

By rank *(see Parts 5 and 6)*

★ BUCKET! sites: #1–#3
★ Gold: #4–#100
★ Silver: #101–#250

By theme *(see Part 7)*

★ Noteworthy
★ Religion
★ Archaeology
★ Structure
★ Nature
★ Scenic
★ Society
★ People
★ Culture
★ Active
★ Leisure
★ Entertainment
★ Food and Drink
★ Accommodation
★ Organized

By region *(see Part 8)*

A	Jerusalem	L	Eilat and Arabah
B	Greater Jerusalem	M	South Jordan
C	West Bank	N	Petra
D	Tel Aviv	O	King's Highway
E	Mediterranean Coast	P	Dead Sea (Jordan)
F	Mount Carmel and Jezreel Valley	Q	Amman
		R	East Jordan
G	Lower Galilee and Kinneret	S	North Jordan
H	Upper Galilee	T	Sinai
I	Golan Heights	U	Cross-Israel/Palestine
J	Negev	V	Cross-Jordan
K	Dead Sea (Israel)	W	Whole Holy Land

Walks and drives *(see Part 9)*

★ 25 City Walks   ★ 49 Road Trips

Itineraries *(see Part 10)*

★ Time-Specific   ★ Completists
★ High Score   ★ Cross-Genre
★ More Superlatives   ★ Budget
★ Country-Specific   ★ Companions
★ Macro-Regions   ★ Time-Unlimited
★ Off the Beaten Path   ★ Classic
★ Thematic   ★ Tailored

Parts 5 and 6: Electives by Rank Electives are presented on the basis of overall ranking, with the highest-ranked sites having the most in-depth listings. **BUCKET!** (#1–3) and **Gold** sites (#4–100) appear in rank order in Part 5. However, there is little to distinguish between **Silver** electives (#101–250) in terms of rank, so these are listed alphabetically by name in Part 6.

Part 7: Electives by Theme Every elective has been allocated a primary **theme/ category label** in Parts 5 and 6, but many have multiple ways they can be categorized so this part cross-references them all across 15 broad themes.

Part 8: Electives by Region Each elective is listed in its corresponding region, from A: *Jerusalem* to T: *Sinai*, as well as our cross-regional groupings (U, V, and W).

Part 9: Walks and Drives We've created a series of **walking and driving tours** that correspond to our micro-regions. These tours collect Gold, Silver, Bronze, and Pearl electives located in that subregion and place them into an itinerary that can be completed in a day (or slow your pace to complete over multiple days). Each walk/ drive comes with its own map.

Part 10: Itineraries by BUCKET! For those of you that don't want to DIY your entire trip, or are looking for a little assistance to get started, BUCKET! offers more than 100 unique itineraries catering to a variety of travel styles, based on high ratings, rank, themes, budget, time, and other traveler-specific needs and wants.

Part 11: Electives by Alphabet This is a traditional index incorporating all the electives.

WHY CHOOSE THE HOLY LAND?

The Holy Land is magical. It is at once intoxicating, intimidating, and intense. You will fall in love deeply and immediately. From the tastes and smells to the sounds and sights, you have never experienced anything quite like this region of the world. Israel, Palestine, Jordan, and the Egyptian Sinai boast world-class historical sites, dining, beaches, nature, activities, and cultural opportunities. This land is also home to three of the world's greatest experiences: our BUCKET! electives, which we discuss more on p. 13.

BUCKET! has dedicated its inaugural book to the Holy Land because we believe it is best able to establish our identity and personality. We want to introduce independent travelers to fascinating locales that might otherwise seem too difficult to explore without a guide. We help to ease the fears of reluctant travelers by providing plenty of ready-made itineraries and DIY travel suggestions to minimize any discomfort with language or cultural barriers. Our more intrepid travelers will also find plenty of off-the-beaten-path alternatives to stay engaged and away from the tour-bus queues. We think everyone should experience this bucket-list region at least once in their lifetime. We hope you find BUCKET! to be your preferred planning tool and guide when crafting your own dream trip to the Holy Land.

Part 1

How to Itinerate!

Choose Your Method

As we get started, it's time to pick your path for building your itinerary: are you the type of person who wants to create their own travel plan from scratch (with guidance) or would you like to build from a ready-to-go itinerary that can be adapted based on your own needs, wants, and time? From lightest to heaviest prework, your methods include:

1. Don't plan anything: decide on site ("in situ").
2. Stitch together our city walks and road trips.
3. Customize one of our prefabricated, plug-and-play *Itineraries!*
4. Ignore our recommendations (you rebel) and just dive right in.
5. DIY by following our step-by-step guide.
6. Itinerate fully (online).

1. THE IN SITU METHOD

Prep-work None   *Hand-holding* Minimal

You don't actually need to do any prep-work to make use of this book. If you're flying to Israel and plan to spend time in Jerusalem and Tel Aviv, for example, you can easily open the book to the relevant elective you've happened upon and find history and information. Should you want to create a last-minute plan for your day, you have two good options: visit *Electives by Region* to piece together sites of interest, or follow along on one of the city walking tours in *Walks and Drives*. If you're looking for restaurant, bar, beach, or shopping recommendations, head to *Today in the Holy Land*.

WHAT TO READ The electives; *Electives by Region*; maybe a walking tour or two; *Today in the Holy Land*.

TIPS Keep in mind that several electives require advance booking; restaurants can book up on the weekend; and a rental car is recommended for most sites outside of Tel Aviv, Jerusalem, and Amman.

2. THE STITCH METHOD

Prep-work Minimal   *Hand-holding* Moderate

If you would like some recommended routes to help you navigate in and between towns, we of course recommend our *Walks and Drives*. Each creates a walking or driving path passing by every elective in that region – pick your preferred sites or visit all of them over a few days. There are food and activity recommendations for each micro-region tour, and information explicitly stating the total walking/driving time, difficulty, and distances. Should you wish, you can piece together a number of these trips to make a complete itinerary. We recommend how to prioritize walks and drives in *Itineraries by BUCKET!*

WHAT TO READ *Walks and Drives* (p. 591); the *Anchor Cities: Days 1–10 Priorities* (p. 750) and *Macro-Regions* (p. 766) itineraries; the electives in Parts 5 and 6 (cross-referenced in each itinerary).

TIPS We don't recommend an itinerary filled with activities from 06.00 to 22.00 every day of your trip, so pick and prune judiciously as you build your day's activities. The road trips in *Walks and Drives* are designed with a rental car in mind, rather than public transportation.

3. THE PLUG-AND-PLAY METHOD

Prep-work Minimal to moderate   *Hand-holding* Moderate to generous

Itineraries by BUCKET! are customizable travel plans that give you a solid foundation if you have specific needs or wants and are lacking the time/energy/will to design a trip from scratch. Think of it like dealing out the property deeds at the beginning of a game of Monopoly – the rules are the same, but the outline is preestablished to help you get into the game faster. The itineraries cover a variety of needs. Are you just wanting to see the highlights? Are you limited to a three-day trip? Do you only have weekends? Have children and/or older folks on the trip who need to go a bit slower? No problem. We have thoughts on these and many more contingencies, desires, and goals.

WHAT TO READ *Itineraries by BUCKET!*; the electives (referenced in each itinerary); *Walks and Drives* (referenced in some itineraries).

TIP If you want *more* hand-holding, look for itineraries related to time or high score. Later itineraries are more inspirational.

4. THE NON-CONFORMIST METHOD

Prep-work Your choice, minimal to extensive   *Hand-holding* Minimal

Dive right in. This book is organized in a way that hopefully requires minimal introduction to use. Open it up, poke around, and enjoy like you would your other favorite guidebooks. You'll still gain a lot from our new levels of organization. If you know exactly what you're looking for, you can use our easy-to-use indexes to find your electives, themes, regions, or itineraries of choice.

WHAT TO READ Whichever sections speak to your pre- and post-planning needs.

TIPS Choose your **Gold** sites, match your interests to **Silver** sites, and fit in nearby **Bronze** sites – that's the gist of how our DIY process works. Use the *Themes* to your advantage because they pair to your personal interests. Don't skip the walking/driving tours because these are the backbone of any trip, giving you a good overview of a region – you needn't visit every place, but we do recommend exploring beyond big cities.

5. THE DIY METHOD

Prep-work Moderate to all-inclusive   *Hand-holding* Moderate to generous

This is the bread and butter of the book. If you're looking for an action plan to turn a good vacation into a great one, we have created a step-by-step guide to help you to craft an itinerary you'll love because it includes all your favorite activities. We'll also keep you on track with your travel to-do's and help you make decisions about what to do after you arrive. You can be as casual or detailed as you like as you make your way through the itinerating section.

WHAT TO READ The first four parts of this guidebook, which are meant to be read in order – we recommend you start six months in advance, but you can pick up wherever you are in your travel planning journey, or work with a shorter deadline. Then use Parts 5 to 10 to build your itinerary.

TIP If you're looking to pair this exercise with easy-to-follow worksheets to keep you organized, head over to **w** buckettravelguides.com/diy-itinerator.

6. THE ITINERATOR! METHOD (online)

Prep-work Advanced to all-inclusive   *Hand-holding* Generous

The Itinerator! is a BUCKET!-designed, all-inclusive DIY tool that walks you through every step in creating a bucket list-rich itinerary filled with sites, activities, and adventures that best suit your tastes. You'll research, choose, and refine your electives with the aid of a number of useful worksheets and tracking tools, all available on our website for download. We'll walk you through our methodology for building your dream trip, ensuring you incorporate your interests, prebook when required, triage when necessary, guard your free time, and have a completely personalized and bespoke trip with all the kinks worked out so you can get to the business of enjoying yourself. You'll end up with a beautiful schedule you can print or refer to on your device.

WHAT YOU'LL NEED A printer, to have worksheets at your fingertips; some dedicated time; access to **w** buckettravelguides.com/diy-itinerator.

TIP If you want to dive into the worksheets without bothering with the instructions, start with the daily *Travel Schedule* (p. 34 and online).

HOW TO CHOOSE

How do you know which method of itinerary creation you will prefer? We think the best trip is the one you design yourself, but you may prefer recommendations. You can always start with DIY (or go the whole hog with the *Itinerator!*) and if you begin to get trip anxiety after only a few minutes, you can make a beeline to the prefabricated *Itineraries by BUCKET!* Here are a few scenarios and personality types to help you figure out which is your best course of action. Do any of these sound familiar?

★ *I can't fit it all in. Help!* DIY, baby! We're here for you! We can help you make time, plan appropriately, and conquer your bucket list.
★ *I don't like being bogged down by itineraries.* You sound like a more spontaneous traveler. Use our indexes to find the electives when you need them.

★ *I have ten days and a million ideas.* We can help you narrow your focus with our *Itinerator!* You'll set priorities, triage, scale back expectations, and come up with a comfortable pace to help you see the most important sites.

★ *I only have three days. I want to spend two days seeing Jerusalem, and then I'm open, but I'd like to get to the Dead Sea, Petra, Tel Aviv, Bethlehem, Nazareth, and the Sea of Galilee. And the Golan Heights.* In three days?!? This is, practically speaking, unattainable, and you're going to have to scale back this plan. We recommend you look at some of our three-day city immersions to get a feel for what is feasible in such a short amount of time.

★ *I want to see everything, but I don't need to spend all day at each place.* This is where our *Walks and Drives* come in handy. You can spend as much or as little time as you want at each location and move from place to place at your leisure. We've given you the maximum places you'd want to see in a day, but you can filter as you please.

★ *I'm sun-hungry. I want to focus on the beach, but I also know I should probably sightsee a little bit.* If your pace is slower, and you don't want a lot preplanned, you can probably zoom your way through the DIY module, or you can adapt one of our trouble-free itineraries, such as *Under the Sun* (p. 809).

★ *I have my grandpa and a couple of under-tens with me. How can I make this a worthwhile trip for everyone?* We have preestablished trips for families like yours, with ideas for kid-focused itineraries and activities that will please all ages. However, if everyone's a bit needy (e.g., grandpa likes historical museums and the kids like outdoor activities and you like the spa), you might need to DIY several itineraries, with points of overlap (breakfast/dinner/a couple of days) to make sure everyone stays happy.

★ *I can handle one museum for a couple of hours, and the rest of the time I really need to spend eating. Not a lot of walking.* You can DIY this by spending time with *Electives by Theme*. Pick your favorite categories (e.g., *Museums* and *Food*) and get planning!

★ *I just want to see the best.* That's doable! Check out our High Score itineraries.

As you can see, there's an answer for every scenario. If you'd just like to preview *Itineraries by BUCKET!* to see what matches your needs, you can skim the headings in the introduction of that chapter. We include alternatives depending on which airport you use, suggestions for where to sleep, and the minimum (and recommended) time needed to complete.

Understanding the Electives

Whether you're using one of our structured templates in *Itineraries by BUCKET!* or designing your trip from soup to nuts, you'll be making decisions about what to see or do in the Holy Land. Get ready: it's time to break into the electives!

So, what is an "elective"? An *elective* is a choice. Each of our electives are sites (e.g., Old City Jerusalem) or experiences (e.g., floating in the Dead Sea). Every elective is an option for you to add into your travel plan. Importantly, when we refer to *electives*, we're also referring to our guidebook entries.

STRUCTURE OF AN ELECTIVE

Our top electives each follow a logical template in structure:

★ *Brochure* Here, we give you a snapshot of the elective – highlighting all its best parts – to help you decide whether to add it to your schedule.

★ *Experiences* If you need a bit more information to go by, this section provides a checklist of the must-see sites and activities on site, with some secrets, tips, and special events.

★ *Itinerator!* Once you've decided to "elect" this activity, this section will help you to plug it into your schedule with relevant information about opening hours, timing (coverage/speed/pace), and distance from Anchor Cities. Because not everyone DIYs the entire trip, you may also prefer to use one of the highlighted *Walks and Drives* or *Itineraries by BUCKET!*

★ *Arrival Prep* These are things you need to do/know/bring/plan for before arrival.

★ *BUCKET!pedia* Once you're on site, this will provide you with a good amount of background to help you understand your surroundings and provide context to what you're seeing.

★ *Where to Next?* Choose your next adventure! We recommend similar electives and short-distance add-on opportunities.

Additionally, there are some concepts that may need further explanation, which we'll explain now.

RANK

Have you ever opened a guidebook and gone right to the "highlights" section looking for that area's best options? Or searched the internet for the top ten attractions in a major city? Scanned blogs for hidden gems? Of course. This is how we all figure out what to see, do, eat, drink, visit, listen to, or explore.

BUCKET! took this common practice and created a giant database of Holy Land recommendations. We scoured reviews, websites, listicles, guidebooks, best-of lists, globally recognized awards and nominations, newsletters, magazines, and word-of-mouth recommendations from bloggers, guidebook authors, journalists, and other seasoned travelers. We assigned points every time one of these sources found a site worthy of acknowledgment: a star or two, a "favorite," a thumbs-up symbol, a top-ten list, or stamp of approval. If the site was mentioned but not specifically recommended, no points – we were only looking for the best, after all. Once we tallied up all the points, we rank-ordered everything. This aggregate score gives a sense of each site's weighted importance as judged by the collective hive mind.

So are BUCKET!'s top 100 destined to be the most popular and most visited sites? No, not necessarily. Some of our electives are downright obscure, either because they were awarded points for their national status (perhaps as a UNESCO site or a national park) or because they are beloved by in-the-know travelers, without yet having hit the mainstream.

Will you agree with every ranking? No, probably not. (Nor do we! In fact, we let you know when this is the case: every elective from #1 to #100 has our own BUCKET! score and a section called *Worth the Detour?*) But instead of providing one person's opinion, this algorithm creates a global "best of" and allows you to pick and choose from the most highly regarded options throughout the Holy Land.

THE HOLY LAND BUCKET! LIST

As part of the BUCKET! brand, we're compiling a list of the world's absolute best sites and activities, which we've naturally deemed the **BUCKET! List**. This moniker could be compared to a "Wonder of the World" or World Heritage Site, indicating a place of global significance that we purport should be added to every traveler's lifetime must-see list. In our view, if you could only see or do one thing per trip, BUCKET! List electives would be worth the time, effort, and cost. In the Holy Land, we're in luck: within this small area are *three* of these world-class sites.

How does a site gain this most prestigious honorific? We've aggregated the rating from our Rank algorithm, our BUCKET! score, and the overall number of accolades. Three electives clearly rose to the top of the pack and can now proclaim to sit alongside the planet's most alluring, absorbing, impressive, and unusual spots on our (and your) global BUCKET! List. Without further ado, we introduce our inaugural BUCKET! List electives! [Drum roll, please.]

★ **Old City Jerusalem (#1)**: the most compact historical place on Earth; important to the three major monotheistic religions; a still-functioning city; glorious walls; millennia old; often controversial; archaeological center; place of remembrance; monumental sites.
★ **Petra (#2)**: rock-cut tombs; ancient ruins; healthy hikes; gorgeous scenery.
★ **Dead Sea (#3)**: buoyant water; mud baths; mineral pools; spa treatments.

We believe these three sites should be included in every trip to the Holy Land. You will soon see that Part 10, *Itineraries by BUCKET!* incorporates these sites whenever feasible. Thus, we spend a fair amount of time with these three sites; they are the first, longest, and most important electives in our guide.

BUCKET!/GOLD/SILVER/BRONZE/PEARL

In total, we uncovered more than 700 exceptional electives in the Holy Land for your consideration. We've categorized and tagged each one using a simple reference system to make searching and itinerary building easier.

★ *BUCKET!* electives are ranked #1, 2, and 3. These sites will always be in bold and followed by their rank, for example **Petra (#2)**.

★ *Gold* sites are ranked #4–100. The reference system follows the same pattern as BUCKET! electives, for example **Masada (#8)**.

★ *Silver* sites are ranked #101–250. Many of our hidden gems, off-the-beaten-path finds, and amazing sites worthy of your time can meanwhile be found here. These sites do not have an individual rank (as there's little difference between an elective ranked, say, #134 vs. #213). Rather, all Silver sites can be considered as "tied for 101st place." These sites appear in bold italics, for example ***Mar Saba***.

★ *Bronze* sites are those electives that ranked lower than 250, so we do not refer to their individual scores. These site names are followed by the micro-region tour in *Walks and Drives* where you can read further details about them, for example **Muslim Quarter (A2)**. If a site has a general location (U, V, or W), visit Part 8, *Electives by Region* or Part 11, *Electives by Alphabet* to find the site's description.

★ *Pearl* sites are unranked and can be considered just that: pearls. They're BUCKET!'s suggestion for unique places or experiences that haven't (yet) gained mass notoriety. These sites appear in italics followed by their micro-region location, for example *Bauhaus Center (D3)*.

BUCKET! SCORES

Alongside its rank, every elective also comes with a BUCKET! score. This was decided by the BUCKET! team and has nothing to do with global recognition – it's simply our honest assessment of an elective. The BUCKET! scale runs from 1 to 10, with our top score reserved for our distinguished BUCKET! electives:

1. Seriously terrible, dangerous, unwelcoming, or inappropriate for tourists; avoid.
2. Disappointing; BUCKET! does not recommend.
3. Site not recommended, but not *not* recommended.
4. Recommended by the hive mind, but BUCKET! wasn't sufficiently wowed to suggest everyone visit.
5. Good for enthusiasts.
6. Good for general audiences.
7. Great for enthusiasts.
8. Great for general audiences.
9. Must-visit for enthusiasts.
10. BUCKET! sites; must-visit for everyone; one of the world's best sites/experiences.

We consider our ratings to be *universal*. This means that we strive to make a 1 rating equivalent across all our guidebooks, just as we do with a 4, a 7, and a BUCKET! entry. The top-rated entries in each guidebook are places or experiences that we would recommend to anyone, from anywhere. In the instance a site is recommended for both enthusiasts (rating: 7) and general audiences (rating: 8), we go with the higher score.

We distinguish between "enthusiasts" and "general audiences" because not everyone is going to find every activity enjoyable. For instance, some people just don't like hiking so, obviously, the Jesus Trail is not going to be for them, no matter how wonderful.

BUCKET!'S TOP RATED As we've explained, BUCKET! electives have the highest rating of all sites, and are ranked the highest. But you might be interested to know: what else received a high BUCKET! score?

★ *BUCKET! electives* **Old City Jerusalem (#1)**; **Petra (#2)**; and **Dead Sea (#3)**.

★ *Rating: 9* **Church of the Holy Sepulchre (#9)**; **Israel Museum (#17)**; **Church of the Nativity (#18)**; *Abu Hassan*; *Modern Israeli Cuisine*; *Tzfon Abraxas*; and *Uri Buri*.

★ *Rating: 8* **Wadi Rum (#4)**; **Tel Aviv (#5)**; **Dome of the Rock (#6)**; **Masada (#8)**; **Akko (#13)**; **Caesarea (#25)**; **Bahá'í Gardens (#27)**; **Feynan Ecolodge (#86)**; **Tel Aviv Beaches (#89)**; *Hummus*; *Mediterranean Coast*; *Suweimeh Spa Hotels*; and *Tel Aviv Tayelet/Promenade*.

★ *Rating: 7* **Sea of Galilee (#7)**; **Western Wall (#11)**; **Jerash (#14)**; **Modern Movement (Bauhaus Architecture) (#16)**; **Qasr Amra and the Desert Palaces (#20)**; **Wadi Mujib and Mujib Biosphere Reserve (#23)**; **Jericho and Hisham's Palace (#26)**; **Makhtesh Ramon (#28)**; **Nazareth and its Biblical Sites (#29)**; **Citadel/Tower of David (#32)**; **Yad Vashem (#35)**; **Beit She'an (#39)**; **Bethlehem (#40)**; **Via Dolorosa (#42)**; **Jordanian Cuisine (#44)**; **Israeli Cuisine (#51)**; **Ras Mohammad (#53)**; **Dahab (#54)**; **Jesus Trail (#69)**; *Basilica of the Annunciation*; *Beit Yannai*; *Hot Air Balloon Ride Over Wadi Rum*; *Israel National Trail*; *Kibbutz Volunteer*; *Separation Wall*; and *Winery Tour*.

REGIONS

Though we've decided not to organize our guidebook into regional chapters, we haven't abandoned the concept of regions altogether – obviously you need to know where these electives are! Each of our electives has a designated region code with a letter and number, such as **A1**. The letter indicates the general region, or **macro-region** (A = Jerusalem, B = Greater Jerusalem, etc.), while the number indicates the subregion, or **micro-region**. In some cases the micro-region is a neighborhood, as with *A3: Jerusalem Old City: Walls and Gates*. Other times, it can be an entire swath of territory, for example *S1: North Jordan*. There are 26 macro-regions, from A to Z, starting with Jerusalem (A) and moving outwards in a logical direction. Israel has A–L, with the West Bank accounting for C. Jordan has M–S. We've only reviewed the historic holy region of Egypt, the eastern Sinai, which is covered in T. Broad regions and electives that don't fit neatly into one box are covered by U–W. Finally, there are three regions currently off-limits and not recommended (X–Z), which we don't cover in this guide.

A	Jerusalem	J	Negev	S	North Jordan
B	Greater Jerusalem	K	Dead Sea (Israel)	T	Sinai
C	West Bank	L	Eilat and Arabah	U	Cross-Israel/Palestine
D	Tel Aviv	M	South Jordan	V	Cross-Jordan
E	Mediterranean Coast	N	Petra	W	Whole Holy Land
F	Mount Carmel and Jezreel Valley	O	King's Highway	X	Gaza
G	Lower Galilee and Kinneret	P	Dead Sea (Jordan)	Y	Other Holy Land: Lebanon, Syria
H	Upper Galilee	Q	Amman	Z	Closed
I	Golan Heights	R	East Jordan		

Within macro-regions A–T there are 65 micro-regions. These *mostly* don't overlap with one another, though there are exceptions (e.g., *E7: Mediterranean Beaches* covers beaches referenced in E1–E5).

A1	Jerusalem Old City: Main Sites	A4	Jerusalem Old City: Jewish Quarter	A7	Jerusalem: New City and Neighborhoods
A2	Jerusalem Old City: Four Quarters	A5	Jerusalem Hills: Zion/ Olives/David	A8	Jerusalem: Government and Museums
A3	Jerusalem Old City: Walls and Gates	A6	East Jerusalem	B1	Greater Jerusalem
				B2	Judean Hills

B3 Judean Hills Wineries	E3 Mediterranean Coast South	L1 Eilat
C1 Old City Bethlehem	E4 Mediterranean Coast Central	L2 Israel's Red Sea and
C2 Southern West Bank	E5 Mediterranean Coast North	Egyptian Border
C3 Jericho and Wadi Qelt	E6 Central Israel Wineries	L3 Arabah Desert
C4 Northern West Bank:	E7 Mediterranean Beaches	M1 Aqaba
Ramallah Region	F1 Mount Carmel	M2 South Jordan
C5 Northern West Bank:	F2 Jezreel and Gilboa	N1 Petra Highlights
Nablus Region	G1 Nazareth	N2 Petra's Best Hikes
D1 Tel Aviv-Jaffa: Stroll	G2 Central Galilee	N3 Petra and Wadi Musa
the Promenade	G3 Sea of Galilee	O1 King's Highway
D2 Jaffa	G4 Jesus Sites in the Galilee	P1 Dead Sea Highway
D3 Tel Aviv: City Center	H1 Upper Galilee	P2 Christian Jordan
D4 Tel Aviv: Rothschild and	H2 Galilee Panhandle	Q1 Ancient Amman
Southern Neighborhoods	I1 Foot of Mount Hermon	Q2 Modern Amman
D5 Tel Aviv: Architecture	I2 Northern Golan	Q3 Cultural Amman
D6 Tel Aviv: Food and Drink	I3 Southern Golan	Q4 Greater Amman
D7 North Tel Aviv	J1 Northern Negev	R1 Eastern Desert
D8 South Tel Aviv	J2 Southern Negev	S1 North Jordan
E1 Haifa	J3 Incense Route	S2 Northwest Jordan
E2 Akko	K1 Dead Sea (Israel)	T1 Sinai on the Gulf of Aqaba

ANCHOR OR ROAD TRIP?

Now that you understand how we've broken down our regions, let's briefly discuss how you will begin putting together a trip that incorporates multiple regions. To do so, let's first decide what type of traveling strategy best suits you. We offer up three possible strategies: **anchor**, **road trip**, and **hybrid**.

1. ANCHOR By design, many travelers choose to spend a good chunk of their trip in one spot. This alleviates the need to pack a bag every night and spend countless vacation hours checking out/in, transiting between towns, and getting reacquainted. We call this strategy the *Anchor* because you drop your anchor in one town, then use it as a springboard for day trips in a radial arc of your choosing (say 200km) in any direction. We think this strategy makes a lot of sense – as long as you've based yourself in the right place! From our perspective, there are five recommended Anchor Cities, as listed below, along with the macro-regions that can be realistically visited within a day:

Jerusalem (A):	A–K
Tel Aviv (D):	A–K
Rosh Pina (H):	C (limited scope), E–I, S (limited scope)
Suweimeh (P):	O–S
Amman (Q):	O–S

What this means is that if you are anchoring in Jerusalem, you can visit any of the macro-regions from A to K as a day trip, starting and ending in Jerusalem. The West Bank (C), the Sea of Galilee (G), and the Negev (J) can all be visited in one day, if you choose.

Should they be? That's a different question, and depends on how much you want to see. Let's take an example: we recommend that you spend at least 8 hours at the Sea of Galilee. A drive from Jerusalem to Tiberias is 2 hours each way, making a

12-hour day in total. Does that sound enjoyable to you? It's doable, but might be pushing you to your maximum.

You can of course base yourself elsewhere: Akko (E), Nazareth (G), and Mitzpe Ramon (J) might be good bases if you have extensive travel plans nearer to those regions.

2. ROAD TRIP If your goal is to see a variety of places, another option would be to sleep in a new town every night or two. If you're a power mover, wanting to tick a lot of boxes, then you're probably ready to commit to a travel schedule. We at BUCKET! fall into this category (maybe you could have guessed). This style of travel caters to relaxed and hyper-planners alike. For those with flexibility in their schedule, moving every couple of days will afford you an opportunity to see every region the Holy Land has on offer, from the snow-packed mountains to the rocky and sandy deserts to the many glorious bodies of water. If you are on a tighter schedule, but want the same type of experience, we recommend using our *Itinerator!* in order to map out your trip so you can fit everything in.

3. HYBRID Alternatively, you can do a hybrid trip, staying in a few Anchor Cities and coordinating day trips from each. If you plan to visit Israel *and* Jordan, this is a great option for you. In our electives, we offer our perspective on what time to visit, which road trips you can use, distances to the Anchor Cities, and other details to help you decide on your home-base strategy.

WALKS AND DRIVES

Part 9 of this guidebook is dedicated to walking and driving tours:

★ *City walks* These are walking tours for our ten major cities, all of which can be completed in one day, but can equally be spaced out over several days to add more time for relaxation and/or further study.
★ *Road trips* These are driving tours which can be completed in 1–3 days on average, depending on where you start and finish (we give tips for this), how many electives you choose, the amount of time you want to spend in a car, your speed, pace, and group size, among other factors.

In total, BUCKET! has created 25 city walks and 49 road trips. Collectively, these tours incorporate all 700+ electives: every BUCKET!, Gold, Silver, Bronze, and Pearl elective referenced in the guidebook can be found in its corresponding micro-region tour.

THEMES AND CATEGORIES

Within each elective, themes and categories answer one of the most important pieces of information an unfamiliar traveler wants to know about a place: *What is it?* We've used 15 overall **themes** to cover the range of ways to describe what a site is: *Noteworthy*; *Religion*; *Archaeology*; *Structure*; *Nature*; *Scenic*; *Society*; *People*; *Culture*; *Active*; *Leisure*; *Entertainment*; *Food and Drink*; *Accommodation*; and *Organized*.

Each of these themes is then further broken down into **categories** which help narrow your search. Looking for food, museums, architecture, or shopping? You can find them under their respective themes. For instance, *Food* can be found under

Food and Drink, Museums under *Culture, Architecture* in *Structure*, and *Shopping* with *Entertainment*.

Do you like cultural activities? Open up *Culture* and scan for categories that might interest you. Are you thinking about a specific interest of yours, such as "beaches"? Scanning the chart at the start of Part 7, you'll find it under *Leisure*.

HISTORICAL ERAS/PERIODS

The history of the Holy Land is hardly uniform. If anything, the only shared experiences among its many peoples and cultures are the multitude of times the region has been conquered by foreign armies, adding yet another layer of culture, history, food, influence, language, and architecture. We've broken the historical time periods into five broad **eras**, each of which is further divided into **periods**, as shown in the table. The two italicized periods – *Herodian* and *Nabataean* – were uniquely important moments in the Holy Land that occurred in parallel with other overlapping periods. Each of the Gold electives is assigned any number of historical periods, corresponding to the time the site was active. Note that some electives, such as **Jordanian Cuisine (#44)**, do not have an assigned historical period.

Era	Period	Year
Prehistoric (before 1200 BCE)	Before humankind	pre-400,000 BP
	Proto-humans	400,000–50,000 BP
	Early human settlements	50,000 BP–8500 BCE
	Neolithic	10,200–4500 BCE
	Copper/Chalcolithic Age	4500–3300 BCE
	Bronze Age/Canaanites	3300–1200 BCE
Ancient Israel (1200–63 BCE)	Iron Age	1200–900 BCE
	Kingdom of Israel and Judah	900–586 BCE
	Babylonian	586–538 BCE
	Persian	538–333 BCE
	Greek	332–140 BCE
	Hasmonean	110–63 BCE
Roman/Byzantine (63 BCE–638 CE)	Judea	63 BCE–136 CE
	Herodian	40–4 BCE
	Syria Palaestina	135–395 CE
	Byzantine	395–638 CE
	Nabataean	312 BCE–663 CE
Islamic (638–1917 CE)	Rashidun	632–661
	Umayyad	661–750
	Abbasid/Fatimid	750–1099
	Crusader	1099–1187 (1291)
	Ayyubid	1187–1291
	Mamluk	1291–1517
	Ottoman	1517–1917
Modern (1917 CE–present)	Mandatory Palestine	1920–1948
	Independence and struggle	1948–1973
	Contemporary	1973–present

SCALES

Sites #1–100 each include the following scales to help you quickly assess key information about a site.

RUIN RATING (1–5) Our archaeological sites each have a ruin rating to help you determine how much imagination you're going to need to "see" the ancient site. Sometimes the ruins are rubble, and sometimes they're practically complete cities. The five ratings are:

1. *Needs excavation* Foundations of buildings; pottery shards; mostly one or two layers of stones; erosion or destruction leaves little to see; often prehistoric (e.g., **Nahal Me'arot**, **Halutza**).
2. *Limited excavation* Defined site; a few standing pillars or walls; site is known from stories or accounts (e.g., **Mount Nebo (#24)**, **Via Dolorosa (#42)**, **Megiddo (#59)**, **Korazim**).
3. *Small, well-defined site* A lot to see (and imagine); small to medium sites; clear site delineation (e.g., walls); several structures with clear purpose; easily identifiable; fortresses, castles, temples; small cities that have not been put fully back together (e.g., **Karak (#49)**, **Beit Guvrin (#60)**, **Beit She'arim (#79)**, **Nimrod's Fortress (#85)**).
4. *Sprawling site of interest* Medium to large site; historic; several grand monuments and points of interest; may represent different eras; may have parts still unexcavated and/or ongoing excavations (e.g., **Masada (#8)**, **Akko (#13)**, **Jericho (#26)**, **Umm Qais (#45)**, **Beit She'an (#39)**).
5. *Impressive and complete monument/site* Large city or monument; understood history; intact buildings (e.g., **Petra (#2)**, **Church of the Holy Sepulchre (#9)**, **Western Wall (#11)**, **Temple Mount (#12)**, **Caesarea (#25)**).

ENTERTAINMENT RATING (1–5) How much fun does BUCKET! (subjectively) think you might have at this elective? Are there things to entertain you, or is it dry (literally, figuratively) and boring? The entertainment scale provides a quick assessment of what you can expect from the elective:

1. *Not entertaining* Spiritual locations that are not kid-friendly; historic spaces that require your full imagination to appreciate (e.g., **Megiddo (#59)**).
2. *Discernible sites/activities* Little oversight or guidance; maybe a visitor center; one or two interactive activities; mostly static information; reading plaques; self-guided walks (e.g., **Jerusalem Archaeological Park (#71)**).
3. *Engaging* Activities available; tours; discussions; sound and light show; nearby shopping; food available (e.g., **Western Wall Tunnels (#94)**).
4. *Fully interactive* Kids and adults welcome; videos; displays; participatory activities; games; ample shops; good gift ideas; food options available (e.g., **Caesarea (#25)**).
5. *Sensory overload* Tons to see and do; great shopping; great food; caters for all ages (e.g., wine tasting, **Petra (#2)**, white water rafting).

INFORMATION RATING (1–5) The information rating will help you determine at a glance whether an elective is void of information or whether you'll be inundated with facts and history. Sites with low information ratings are good opportunities to seek out a local guide.

1. *Little to no signage* You either need a detailed guidebook or plan to hire a guide (e.g., **Megiddo (#59)**).
2. *Some signage/guides available* Many sites not labeled; general information on display; lacks context; maybe a brochure (e.g., **Jericho (#26)**).
3. *Learn with your eyes* Little signage, but not necessary; easy to navigate; site can be seen without being explained; use of a guidebook or guide will greatly increase your understanding (e.g., **Dead Sea (#3)**).
4. *Detailed brochure or mandatory guide* Proper sign placement; visitor center; video; museum; personal stories; site relevance (e.g., **Bahá'í Gardens (#27)**).
5. *Completely immersive experience* Interactive exhibits; engaging material; large, well laid-out museum; popular guides; context clear (e.g., **Israel Museum (#17)**, **Yad Vashem (#35)**).

POPULARITY RATING (1–5) How many people visit this site a year? We give our best guess (not all figures are available) so you know whether to expect a crowd.

1. *Off the beaten path* Fewer than 10,000 foreign visitors a year (e.g., lesser-excavated spots on **Incense Route (#73)**).
2. *Specialized interest* 10,000–100,000 foreign visitors a year (e.g., **Jerash (#14)**).
3. *Local gem* More than 100,000 domestic visitors a year, fewer than 25,000 foreign visitors (e.g., interiors of **Dome of the Rock (#6)** and **Al-Aqsa Mosque (#65)**).
4. *Popular* More than 100,000 visitors a year (e.g., **Akko (#13)**, **Israel Museum (#17)**, **Bahá'í Gardens (#27)**) *or* limited capacity and requires reservation (e.g., **Petra Kitchen (#84)**, **Machneyuda (#98)**).
5. *Famous* More than 1,000,000 visitors a year (e.g., **Old City Jerusalem (#1)**, **Tel Aviv (#5)**, **Petra (#2)**).

FINDING ELECTIVES

Most guidebooks organize their electives regionally – by city, state, or district – but we've opted not to organize our content this way. While location is an important way to find sites and activities, it shouldn't be the principal way, because this methodology places an outsized focus on big cities, and inadvertently prevents you from finding amazing sites that aren't on the trodden tourist trail. Instead, we recommend you employ a three-step process for finding electives of interest to you:

1. Research the region's best electives with *Rank*.
2. Explore electives that match your interests in *Themes*.
3. Add on nearby electives with *Region*.

ELECTIVES BY RANK Our top 100 electives – **BUCKET!** and **Gold** sites – are organized by rank, from #1 to #100, in Part 5. The better the ranking, the longer the entry. Our top ten sites go into great detail for each activity, providing all the important information you need to plan a successful visit. The top 50 sites are explored in depth and include the information you need to successfully navigate the three phases of trip planning:

1. *Deciding* During the development stage of your trip, you'll review the information under *Brochure* and *Experiences* to see if the site interests you. The electives ranked #51–100 are shorter, but will quickly help you evaluate whether to add these sites to your itinerary.

2. *Planning* Once "elected," you'll use *Itinerator!*, *Best Strategy*, and *Arrival Prep* to fit the elective into your schedule, choose the right time to visit, plan for how long to be there, and ensure you're prepared on arrival (advance purchase? modest dress?). You'll also engage with *Where to Next?* to find thematically similar, complementary, and nearby electives.

3. *On the ground* When you arrive, you'll use *Arrival and Orientation* (electives #1–10) and *BUCKET!pedia* to provide spatial and historical context to your visit.

We have opted to put our highest-ranked electives first for a number of reasons. When you skim a guidebook, the first thing a traveler wants to know is "what do I absolutely need to see?" We've made it very straightforward to help you find the most relevant and revered sites. Further, within each entry, we've included the elective's most salient selling points in *Elect Me!* Up front, we also explore: is it *Worth the Detour?*, the *Holy Land Relevance*, and any *Commendations*.

Silver electives are listed in Part 6, immediately following the Gold electives. These are listed alphabetically rather than numerically. Why? Because 100 electives are more than enough to choose from and the Silver electives are meant to be add-ons. No one will choose a Silver site specifically because it is ranked #134 or elect not to choose an activity because it's ranked #234.

Bronze and **Pearl** electives are embedded in Part 9 and directly integrated into the city walk or road trip applicable to that elective's micro-region. Each of these electives is explained briefly and you can choose to add in as many local options as you can fit in.

You might be thinking, "I won't have time to review more than 100 electives, or visit more than a handful, so why bother including more than that?" Which is a fine point. We don't expect you to review 700+ electives, or even all of the Gold electives. You may want to read all the way to 100, or stop after ten or 20. There's no right or wrong answer. But the whole point is that, by putting the best sites first, whenever you do stop reading you'll know that you'll have seen the most important material.

Once you've digested all you can, keeping note of your favorites (electives), you'll transition to *Electives by Theme*.

ELECTIVES BY THEME We believe that the best method for creating the most personalized experience is achieved by exploring themes of personal interest. As we discussed earlier, each theme is broken down into categories, and every elective is classified into one or more themes and categories.

As you read and assess the entries of the highest-ranked electives, you will find several references to themes and categories. Take, for example, **Western Wall (#11)**. You can review *Where to Next?* in the elective and see what themes/categories match your interests. Let's say you're interested in learning more about *Orthodox Jews*, or you want to see other *Iconic Structures*. You'll visit the themes of *People* and *Structure*, respectively, where you'll discover that **Mea She'arim (#66)** is a *Best Example* to learn about Orthodox Jews and **Dome of the Rock (#6)** is a *Best Example* for iconic structures. You'll be sure to plug both of those into your itinerary. Love Petra? Maybe you'll love other Nabataean ruins, day hikes, or sites with monumental architecture.

You can also *start* your research with *Electives by Theme*, finding your favorite themes and categories and discovering electives that correspond to your interests. Let's say you love scenic drives. Go to *Scenic* [theme] – *Scenic Drives* [category] and find out which electives best represent that category of sites: **King's Highway (#31)** and the **Golan Heights (#62)** are both listed as *Best Examples*, among others.

ELECTIVES BY REGION Some of you may be wondering, "What if I just want to know what there is to do in Jerusalem? Or near Wadi Rum? Or how to do the Negev?"

Our motive behind organizing BUCKET!'s electives in new ways is to convince travelers they are not bound to only one location. "I don't have a car, so I have to stay in Jerusalem" – it's just not true this day in age. You can take a bus! You can take a short flight! A train, a taxi! This entire region can be completed without a car (though it's honestly much easier with one), from **Mount Hermon** in Israel's north to the Eastern Desert in Jordan to Sharm el-Sheikh on the southern Sinai. You will be more restricted by time than by distance or transit. But you might be in Jerusalem for three days, and simply want to know what more there is to do in Jerusalem. There are a number of ways to find this information.

We begin by directing you to our third collation of electives: *Electives by Region*. Here we list each macro-region with all its electives, organized into micro-regions and displayed with their rank, BUCKET! score, and (for Gold electives) their corresponding categories. This will help you easily fill in any gaps in your schedule.

Secondly, each micro-region has its own corresponding **walking or driving tour**, explored in *Walks and Drives*. If you aren't interested in designing an entire regional trip of your own, use one of ours: you don't have to commit to the entire itinerary as they're completely customizable. Each can be walked/driven in one day (or less), though seeing everything in the region would likely take a few days.

Thirdly, we make locating a Gold or Silver elective's location easy, as we include its region code (A4, B3, D2, etc.) right at the beginning of the elective's entry. In the case of Bronze and Pearl sites, the elective is referenced *with* its location, for example Kuli Alma (D4). This system will help you determine whether two electives are near one another. Two electives that share a macro-region may not be within walking distance, but they should be easily reachable if visiting on the same day. We discuss this more in *DIY: Itinerator!*, but our guiding principle for building a multi-region itinerary is that each macro-region will require *at least one day to visit*. You might not spend all day at one elective or even in the one region, but practically speaking you wouldn't want to combine electives from two different regions in one day.

Our 15 highest-ranked electives represent 10 macro-regions, and only a few can be explored in the same day:

A	Old City Jerusalem; Dome of the Rock	K	Dead Sea; Masada
	(and Temple Mount); Church of the	L/M	Red Sea
	Holy Sepulchre; Western Wall	M	Wadi Rum
D	Tel Aviv	N	Petra
E	Akko	S	Jerash
G	Sea of Galilee	T	Mount Sinai

And there you have it. *Rank – Themes – Regions*. 1–2–3. This is the order in which we recommend you begin building your itinerary. For further guidance, we suggest you follow *DIY: Itinerator!* in the next chapter. (Alternatively, if you know exactly what you're looking for, you can visit *Electives by Alphabet*, which works like a regular index.)

WHERE TO NEXT? Each of the top 50 electives ends with a section called *Where to Next?* Here, we seek to direct you to other electives that might be of interest to you. Under *Thematic*, we list all instances when that elective is referenced in a theme or category in *Electives by Theme*. (Note: the *principal* theme/category is found under the *Brochure* heading.) Under *Complementary*, we offer other electives that we think you might enjoy based on your interest in this elective. This is a similar experience to searching through *Electives by Theme*, but with popular options for quick reference. Finally, under *Nearby*, we've listed any high-ranking electives in the vicinity, which you can cross-reference in *Electives by Region*.

DIY Itinerator!

We hope you're up for a complete DIY experience. We think that's how you'll get the most out of this experience. If you're using another strategy for itinerary creation, you can skip this chapter and move on to the *Trip Planning To-Do's*.

The process for DIY is straightforward and follows the previously mentioned threefold strategy of browsing electives **by rank**, then **by theme**, then **by region**. What follows is a shortened version of our online *Itinerator!* (**w** buckettravelguides. com/diy-itinerator). For worksheets and detailed explanations of each section, including printable worksheets and schedules, visit our website.

RECORDING ELECTIVES 1: BY RANK

Step 1 Print off the "Electives" worksheet from our website, or set up a sheet of paper like this:

	Elective name	(#)	Region	Time needed	Priority
1					
2					
3					
4					
5					
6					
7					
8					
9					
10					
11					
12					

Step 2 For each elective you choose during the process, fill in its name, rank, and macro-region.

Step 3 Start at Part 5 with our BUCKET! List electives. Read through each elective in its entirety. We recommend you visit all three. You will likely find other sites of interest during this first review. Record those as well, for review now or later.

Step 4 Go through as many Gold electives (#4–100) in Part 5 as you like. You can get right to the point and read the *Worth the Detour?* sections to decide whether this elective is for you. Our **BUCKET! Score** and **Theme/Category** may also help you make your decision. We recommend you read through all 100 electives, but that can be a large undertaking. Alternatively, you may want to review the first 10 or 25 electives, recording your selections, and then move on to *Electives by Theme*.

TIME NEEDED

Step 5 Now, let's record how much time you will need in the "Time Needed" column every time you find an elective. We recommend you base your estimate on how much you want to explore and learn, using our four *Coverage* concepts. "Introductory" looks will give you little more than a quick feel for a place. "Highlights" will give you enough time to visit the must-see parts of each site. "Comprehensive" indicates you're taking your time by hiring a guide, absorbing the site descriptions, and reading your guidebook carefully. "Exhaustive" indicates you'll be exploring every nook and cranny. Also, if the activity is outside normal "business" hours – early morning or evening – then you can write that here.

To save you some time, we've created the following chart which provides a rough approximation for how much time you should commit to our region's most popular destinations.

	Introductory	Highlights	Comprehensive	Exhaustive
Jerusalem, Old City	4 hours	1 day	3 days	5+ days
incl. Dome of the Rock, Temple Mount	30m	45m	1½ hours	2½ hours
incl. Church of the Holy Sepulchre	30m	45m	2 hours	3 hours
incl. Western Wall	15m	15m	30m	1 hour
Petra	4 hours	1 day	3 days	4 days
Dead Sea	30m	1 hour	6 hours	1 day
+ Masada	2 hours	3 hours	5 hours	8 hours
Wadi Rum	4 hours	1 day +overnight	2 days	3+ days
Tel Aviv	4 hours	1 day +beachtime	3 days incl. beachtime	4+ days
Sea of Galilee	4 hours	8 hours	2 days	3 days
Red Sea	2 hours	4 hours	3 days	5 days incl. scuba
Akko	2 hours	4 hours	8 hours	2 days
Jerash	1 hour	2 hours	4 hours	8 hours
Mount Sinai	4 hours hike	4 hours hike	6 hours: 4 hours hike + 2 hours St. Catherine's	2 days incl. overnight

If your speed is average, use the numbers as given, but halve them if your speed is fast (i.e., no extra stops for food, souvenirs, or photos), and double them if your speed is slow. For example, an introductory visit to Jerusalem is 4 hours, but 2 hours if your speed is fast and 8 hours for a slow group. Do your own calculations and record your estimated time needed as you work your way through the *Itinerator!* If there are any exceptions (e.g., the Western Wall Tunnels have set visit times with a tour guide), we will tell you in the elective.

The top ten sites all have their own *Coverage* guides. You'll want to review *Time Commitment* under electives #11–50 and *Best Strategy* in electives #51–100 to estimate the time you'll need.

PRIORITIES

Step 6 Make a quick assessment of how important the elective is to you in the "Priority" column. Using "+++" for essential electives, "++" for ideal electives, and "+" for if-there's-time electives. Eventually, you should end up with a list that looks something like this:

	Elective name	(#)	Region	Time needed	Priority
1	Old City Jerusalem	1	A	Highlights 1 day	+++
2	Petra	2	N	Comprehensive, speed × 2 = 1½ days	+++
3	Dead Sea	3	K or P	Highlights 1 hour	+++
4	Wadi Rum	4	M	Introductory 4 hours	+
5	Tel Aviv	5	D	Highlights 2 days (incl. 1 beach day)	+++
6	Dome of the Rock	6	A	no extra time	++
7	Sea of Galilee	7	G	Highlights 8 hours	+
8	Masada	8	K	Highlights 3 hours	+
9	Western Wall	11	A	no extra time	+
10	Akko	13	E	Introductory 2 hours	+
11	Jerash	14	S	Comprehensive 4 hours	++
12	Mount Sinai	15	T	4 hours hike	+

RECORDING ELECTIVES 2: BY THEME

Step 7 Now that we have an approximation for the amount of time we need, we're going to explore *Electives by Theme*. This is the bread and butter of our guidebook, because here's where you find all the electives that will speak to you as an individual.

In *Electives by Theme*, search through the 15 core themes to find your general areas of interest and then drill down to the categories that most appeal to your interests as a traveler. For example, you may not be a person who hikes normally, but if hiking is something you like to do when traveling, make sure to peruse *Active – Walks and Hikes* (p. 548).

Each category lists our recommendations for *Best Example* in the Holy Land. You can use those recommendations, but you can also go further by researching the complementary electives that also relate to this category. Remember: BUCKET! (#1–3) and Gold sites (#4–100) are located in Part 5 in numerical order, Silver sites (#101–250) are in Part 6 in alphabetical order, and Bronze/Pearl sites (#251+) are explained in their corresponding walking/driving itinerary in Part 9.

Add the name and macro-region for each additional elective added to your list. If your new elective is not a Gold site, and therefore does not have a numerical rank, you can record "S" for Silver or "B" for Bronze under the "#" column. In our continued example, we have a strong interest in food, bars, beaches, a wine tour, and we want to see a Crusader castle. So, in *Electives by Theme* we visit: *Food and Drink*

– *Food – Top Restaurants* (p. 561); *Entertainment – Party – Bars and Clubs* (p. 559); *Leisure – Beaches – Remote Beaches* (p. 555); *Food and Drink – Wine – Wineries* (p. 563); and *Archaeology – Ruins by Period – Crusader* (p. 510). After some research of the recommended electives, we have generated these additional options:

	Elective name	(#)	Region	Time needed	Priority
13	Tzfon Abraxas	S	D	evening	+++
14	Machneyuda	98	A	evening	++
15	Imperial Bar	99	D	evening	++
16	Kuli Alma	B	D4	evening	++
17	Dor HaBonim	100	E	4 hours	+++
18	Judean Hills Wineries	B3	B3	1 day	+++
19	Karak	49	O	2 hours	++

DAYS NEEDED

Step 8 We're now going to figure out approximately how many days you need in the Holy Land. To do that, we need to add up your total time commitments so far. Sites that are easiest to visit in the same day are identified by their **macro-regions**, which means that electives with the same macro-region letter can usually be combined into the same day trip, if desired. Let's return to your list and do some simple calculations:

1. Put your like regions together. Circle all your As. Star all your Bs. Whatever system works best for you.
2. Add up time *per macro-region*. For us, we have 2 hours planned in Akko and 4 hours at Dor HaBonim, which is 6 hours.
3. Consider your **pace**. How many hours of electives can you fit into one day? If you are a leisurely traveler (0–4 hours of activities per day, usually), and have 8 hours planned, either you need to plan on one busy day or you should record "2 days" to be safe.
4. Round each region's total time up to the next full day. 2½ days would be rounded to 3 days. Even 1 hour is rounded up to 1 day. In our example, we're assuming our pace is 8 hours of activities a day. We'll thus record "1 day" because we're rounding 6 hours up to the next whole day.
5. Add up the days.

Using our example, our time commitment by region is A: 1 day + evening; B: 1 day; D: 2 days + evening; E: 1 day; G: 1 day; K: 1 day; M: 1 day; N: 2 days; O: 1 day; S: 1 day; T: 1 day = 13 days. That means, in order to successfully see all of these electives, we'll need at least 13 days in the Holy Land.

TRIAGE

Step 9 Time to cull! If you know right away that you won't have enough time to see everything on your list, use your priority scale to eliminate some options. Review your lowest-priority electives (+) first. Use the "#" column to quickly find the elective in the guidebook and read more thoroughly about the site to determine if it still sounds like something you can't miss. Remove electives until you reach your maximum number of available travel days. In our example, let's assume we know that we can't exceed ten days of travel, but we have 13 days' worth of activities planned. We need to eliminate three days' worth of activity and remove the corresponding electives.

We wouldn't eliminate Masada (+) because it's easy to combine with the Dead Sea (+++). Same with the Western Wall (+) which is inside Old City Jerusalem (+++). We might instead consider eliminating Mount Sinai (+), Wadi Rum (+), the Sea of Galilee (+), or Akko (+) from this trip as they are all lower priorities and in their own regions, meaning they each require a one-day commitment.

ROUGH ITINERARY

Step 10 It's time to create a rough travel itinerary with the electives you've chosen, so you can begin to see your schedule take shape. Print off the "Regional Days" worksheet from our website, or use a new sheet of paper.

For each day of activity, you will assign *only one region*. We know Tel Aviv (D) needs two days, as does Petra (N), so we will assign two days to each of these macro-regions in the schedule. We're also only going to fill in electives up to the maximum number of electives you can manage per your *pace*. For us, we can commit to eight hours per day. Note that the "Days" column is simply a count of the total days in your itinerary. It does not refer to the sequential order of activities: we'll put each of these "days" in a logical order shortly.

Days	Region	Electives	Time needed	Tour	Route	Sleep	Order
1	A	Old City Jerusalem, Dome of the Rock, Western Wall, Machneyuda	1 day + evening				
2	B	Judean Hills Winery tour	1 day				
3	D	Tel Aviv	1 day				
4	D	Tel Aviv Beaches, Tzfon Abraxas, Imperial Bar, Kuli Alma	1 day				
5	E	Akko, Dor HaBonim	2 hours 4 hours				
6	G	Sea of Galilee	8 hours				
7	K	Dead Sea, Masada	1 hour 3 hours				
8	M	Wadi Rum	4 hours				
9	N	Petra	1 day				
10	N	Petra	½ day				
11	O	Karak	2 hours				
12	S	Jerash	4 hours				
13	T	Mount Sinai	4 hours				

RECORDING ELECTIVES 3: BY REGION

Step 11 Now that we have selected electives based on reputation and interests, our last foray into the electives will involve a deep dive into the regions you've selected, focusing primarily on micro-regions and their corresponding walking and driving tours, located in Part 9, *Walks and Drives*. Look for any time gaps in your schedule. If you have 8 hours of activities planned already, you probably don't want to add anything else. But if you only have a 2-hour activity planned, and you're willing to commit to a more aggressive pace, it's worth looking at that elective's corresponding micro-region tour. This could be a **city walk** or a **road trip**.

Several of our road trips incorporate thematic areas of interest, such as Crusader castles, regional wineries, and UNESCO sites. In our example, it looks like we have some room to add sightseeing activities on Day 7, the K day. Reviewing the **Masada (#8)** elective's *Brochure*, we see that this elective can be found in the micro-region of K1. Further in the elective, under *Day Tripping* and *Walks and Drives*, we find other options as well. We settle on the micro-region road trip and head to *Walks and Drives* to find the *K1: Dead Sea (Israel)* road trip (p. 689). There, you'll see that the Dead Sea and Masada – our two chosen electives that day – are both part of the same driving tour. Included in the same micro-region are Ein Gedi and Qumran, also Gold sites, which you can consider visiting while en route. In fact, there are a number of sites that might be of interest to you, including Bronze and Pearl electives (about which we provide brief overviews directly in the tour). If the K1 itinerary doesn't appeal to you, return to the **Masada (#8)** elective's *Itinerator!* to find other road trip ideas.

Step 12 As you work your way through the walks and drives, record them on your rough itinerary. Here's how we did it in our ongoing example:

Days	Region	Electives	Time needed	Tour	Route	Sleep	Order
1	A	Old City Jerusalem, Dome of the Rock, Western Wall, Machneyuda	1 day + evening	Walk: A1			
2	B	Judean Hills Winery tour	1 day	Drive: B3			
3	D	Tel Aviv	1 day D1: 2 hours D3: 2½ hours D4: 2 hours	Definitely D1 Promenade; Consider D3/D4			
4	D	Tel Aviv Beaches, Tzfon Abraxas, Imperial Bar, Kuli Alma	1 day				
5	E	Akko, Dor HaBonim	2 hours 4 hours				
6	G	Sea of Galilee	8 hours	Drive: G4			
7	K	Dead Sea, Masada	1 hour 3 hours	Some of Drive: K1 (2½ hours' drive time)			
8	M	Wadi Rum	4 hours				
9	N	Petra	whole day	Walk: N1 and N2			
10	N	Petra	½ day				
11	O	Karak	2 hours				
12	S	Jerash	4 hours	Consider: Drive S1			
13	T	Mount Sinai	4 hours				

ROUTING

Step 13 Time to decide routing. Are you going to do a day trip? Are you spending the night at the destination? Or are you visiting as a side trip on your way from point A to B? In order to find the most efficient routing for your itinerary, you have several options that we've already discussed. Using *Road Trips* to craft your day trips is the easiest option, as we've already done the work of figuring out what you can accomplish in a day, but if you're creating your own itinerary, use Google Maps (or your favorite mapping software) to plot your proposed itinerary and see if you can realistically accomplish your goals in one day.

In electives #1–50 we provide suggestions on whether to anchor or road trip. Our recommendation is to take advantage of **Anchor Cities** and use these as your base while you explore the Holy Land. Tel Aviv and Jerusalem are the best places to use as a base of operations, but other good Anchor City options include Rosh Pina in Israel's north, Suweimeh on the north shore of Jordan's Dead Sea, and Amman.

Under the "Route" column of your worksheet, indicate whether this is a day trip (like the Dead Sea) or a side trip (like Karak, where you can stop by on the way to Amman). You might find that a couple of your places can be combined together, as we did with our half-day for Petra and our half-day for Wadi Rum, opening up a whole day of extra activities to plan something else! You might also find that something in your itinerary is unrealistic, as we did with Mount Sinai, which cannot feasibly be done in one day (but might be possible with two – review the elective for more).

Once you've selected your strategy(ies) for how to create the route, you should document those decisions in your Itinerary.

SLEEPING

Step 14 In the "Sleep" column, you will make a best guess for where to spend the night. This will help to inform the order of your schedule in the next section. Let's look at our example again. For day trips such as the Judean Hills wineries and the Dead Sea, we're going to anchor in Jerusalem. At some point we'll move to Tel Aviv and anchor there too. Originally, we considered visiting Akko/Dor HaBonim and the Sea of Galilee as day trips from Tel Aviv, but since they are both in the north, we'll instead be anchoring for one night in Rosh Pina (note we scratched out Tel Aviv and added Rosh Pina on Day 5). We'll also be spending 2–3 nights in Petra, visiting Wadi Rum on the way in or out. Plus, we have two nights in Amman, with a day trip to Jerash (and/or *Road Trip S1*) in the mix. A useful tip to keep in mind is that if an elective takes more than 3 hours to reach by car, plan to spend the night nearby. Here's our example:

Days	Region	Electives	Time needed	Tour	Route	Sleep	Order
1	A	Old City Jerusalem, Dome of the Rock, Western Wall, Machneyuda	1 day + evening	Walk: A1		Jerusalem	
2	B	Judean Hills Winery tour	1 day	Drive: B3	self-drive from Jerusalem, 45m one way	Jerusalem	

Days	Region	Electives	Time needed	Tour	Route	Sleep	Order
3	D	Tel Aviv	1 day D1: 2 hours D3: 2½ hours D4: 2 hours	Definitely D1 Promenade; Consider D3/D4		Tel Aviv	
4	D	Tel Aviv Beaches, Tzfon Abraxas, Imperial Bar, Kuli Alma	1 day			Tel Aviv	
5	E	Akko, Dor HaBonim	2 hours 4 hours			~~Tel Aviv~~ Rosh Pina	
6	G	Sea of Galilee	8 hours	Drive: G4		Tel Aviv	
7	K	Dead Sea, Masada	1 hour 3 hours	Some of Drive: K1 (2½ hours' drive time)	day trip from Jerusalem	Jerusalem	
8	M	Wadi Rum	4 hours		combine w/Petra ½ day?	Petra	
9	N	Petra	whole day	Walk: N1 and N2		Petra	
10	N	Petra	½ day		combine w/Wadi Rum?	Petra	
11	O	Karak	2 hours		2 hours north of Petra, on way to Amman	Amman?	
12	S	Jerash	4 hours	Consider: Drive S1	day trip from Amman	Amman?	
13	T	Mount Sinai	4 hours		fly to Sharm, adds too many days?	Sharm el-Sheikh?	

FINAL ROUGH ITINERARY

Step 15 The last thing we'll do to the rough itinerary is to put the days in order. Remember: this is an art, not a science. In our example, we've made a number of changes to the itinerary based on the current plan. That's okay! Flexibility is key.

Days	Region	Electives	Time needed	Tour	Route	Sleep	Order
1	A	Old City Jerusalem, Dome of the Rock, Western Wall, Machneyuda	1 day + evening	Walk: A1		Jerusalem	1, 13–14?

Days	Region	Electives	Time needed	Tour	Route	Sleep	Order
2	B	Judean Hills Winery tour	1 day	Drive: B3	self-drive from Jerusalem, 45m one way	Jerusalem or Tel Aviv	3
3	D	Tel Aviv	1 day D1: 2 hours D3: 2½ hours D4: 2 hours	Definitely D1 Promenade; Consider D3/D4		Tel Aviv	4
4	D	Tel Aviv Beaches, Tzfon Abraxas, Imperial Bar, Kuli Alma	1 day			Tel Aviv	5
5	E	Akko, Dor HaBonim	2 hours 4 hours			~~Tel Aviv~~ Rosh Pina	6
6	G	Sea of Galilee	8 hours	Drive: G4		~~Tel Aviv~~ Rosh Pina	7
7	K	Dead Sea, Masada	1 hour 3 hours	Some of Drive: K1 (2½ hours' drive time)	day trip from Jerusalem	Jerusalem	2
8	M	Wadi Rum	4 hours		~~combine w/Petra ½ day?~~	~~Petra~~ Wadi Rum	12??
9	N	Petra	whole day	Walk: N1 and N2		Petra	11
10	N	Petra	½ day		~~combine w/Wadi Rum?~~	Petra	10
11	O	Karak	2 hours		2 hours north of Petra, on way to Amman	~~Amman?~~ Petra	10
12	S	Jerash	4 hours	Consider: Drive S1	day trip from Amman	Amman?	9
~~13~~	~~T~~	~~Mount Sinai~~	~~4 hours~~		~~fly to Sharm, adds too many days?~~	~~Sharm el-Sheikh?~~	n/a
13	Q	Amman	1 day	Walks: Q1/Q2/Q3	drive from Rosh Pina or Tel Aviv	Amman	8

In our continuing example for our 14-day trip, we're flying into Ben Gurion (equidistant to Jerusalem and Tel Aviv), so will be starting the trip in Jerusalem and spending **Day 1** there. **Day 2** will be spent on a road trip to the Dead Sea region. On **Day 3**, we are traveling to the Judean Hills, which is on the way to Tel Aviv, so we can either stay in Jerusalem one extra night or continue on to Tel Aviv. Once in Tel Aviv, we have **Days 4 and 5** covered. We've decided to sleep in Rosh Pina on **Day 6** after visiting Akko and Dor HaBonim. **Day 7** is filled with a long tour of the Sea of Galilee. Since we don't have any activities planned for Tel Aviv, we're choosing to stay in Rosh Pina an extra night and will leave the next morning for Amman. Having done research, we know that we can cross the border near Jerusalem and take a taxi to a rental car company. We've decided that our trip to Mount Sinai is too complicated and have instead added in a visit to Amman's sites on **Day 8**. On **Day 9**, we'll visit Jerash and possibly do the S1 drive. On **Day 10**, we'll drive south from Amman towards Petra, passing Karak along the way. The drive from Amman to Karak is 2 hours and from Karak to Petra is another 2 hours, plus our recommended time on site at Karak is 2 hours, so we likely won't have time to visit Petra on Day 10. That we'll do on **Days 11 and 12** (half-day), after which we leave for Wadi Rum and spend the night there under the stars. On **Day 13**, we'll drive back early to Amman to drop off the car, taxi to the border, and then head to Jerusalem (or Tel Aviv?) for our last evening. We depart from Ben Gurion on **Day 14**.

TRAVEL SCHEDULE

Step 16 Now that you've added tours, routing, and sleep options, it's time to create your final schedule. In our online *Itinerator!* (w buckettravelguides.com/diy-itinerator), we give you a template to keep track of all the important details for each of your travel days, or you can create one of your own like that shown overleaf. You should make note of your flights – particularly your arrival times – and begin plugging in the activities you have planned. You can do this however you like: in your online calendar, your daily journal, in a Word doc, TripIt, or whatever is your favorite way to stay organized. On our website, we've prepared a simple, printable schedule you can use, or try out the more comprehensive schedule designed for use with the online *Itinerator!*

ITINERATOR! TIPS

★ Keep your arrival and departure days activity-free. Inbound, you'll likely need to recover a bit from jet lag. Outbound, you don't want to be crossing borders or stuck in traffic trying to return on the day of your flight.

★ Ben Gurion is equidistant to Tel Aviv and Jerusalem, so plan to stay in either city on the front or back end of your trip.

★ You don't want to plan an international border crossing on the same day as your flight. Crossing times vary, but can take upwards of 3 hours. Borders can also close unexpectedly at any time. Give yourself a cushion, just in case.

★ Add "dates" and "days of the week" to your newly ordered travel "days." Why? You don't want to schedule a trip to the Old City on a Friday/Saturday if you want to get close to the Dome of the Rock, for instance.

★ Determine the best sleep locations before you book your lodging.

★ Don't forget about travel times! Each of our driving tours provides the travel time from prominent towns which needs to be added to the "driving time" calculation.

★ Don't wear yourself out. It's very easy to over-schedule. Consider booking only one or two things and then using *City Walks* to guide you to nearby electives.

★ Food is a major part of this culture. Research your options and get reservations to the hot-spot restaurants.

★ Reservations are required at a number of locations: **Petra Kitchen (#84)**, **Western Wall Tunnels (#94)**, *Petra by Night*, winery cellar doors, and some campgrounds, among other activities. We go over these in *Do #6: Reserve It!*

★ Car rentals are a good idea if you have a number of day trips in mind, but navigating rental car conditions can be tricky. Also, driving to the Palestinian Territories/West Bank is not allowed under Israel rental car agreements; nor is it possible to drive across the Israel–Jordan border with a rental car.

		Arrival day	Day 1	Day 2...
TIME	Date			
	Day of the week			
PLACE	Region of the day			
	Starting location			
	Sleep location			
	Lodging			
	Anchor vs. Road			
TRAVEL	Trip type			
	Transport			
	Travel time			
FLIGHTS	Flight number/routing			
	Arr./dep. time			
ALARM	Time at airport/on the road			
	Wake-up time!			
ELECTIVES	Day complete?			
	Morning			
	Time slot 1			
	Time slot 2			
	Time slot 3			
	Time slot 4			
	Evening			
	Alternative, if there's time			
TOUR	City walks			
	Day trips			
	Organized tour			
FOOD	Breakfast			
	Lunch			
	Dinner			
	Snack			
STOPS	Shopping			
	Quick stops			
BREAKS	Breaks			
	Other			

Part 2

Trip Planning To-Do's

Twelve to Six Months Before

DO #1: DATE IT!

First things first, let's pick a time of year you want to travel. You may have found cheap airfare that was too irresistible to pass up, but this chapter can still be useful for you – at least in terms of what to pack. We'll touch on holidays, climate, seasons, and tourism, before asking you to **narrow down dates**.

HOLY LAND HOLIDAYS Holidays can be an amazing time to visit the Holy Land as there will inevitably be something unique to do. **Islamic** and **Jewish holidays** can fluctuate in the calendar by a day or two, depending on the lunar cycle. The actual holiday is often not announced publicly until a week to a few days beforehand to ensure the authorities are following religious law. Jewish "days" begin at sundown. Thus, a religious holiday will begin the night before the stated holiday. For instance, Yom Kippur will begin on Tuesday, October 4, 2022 at sundown and continue until sundown, Wednesday, October 5, 2022. Christian holidays are not official public holidays in either Jordan or Israel, but are officially recognized days of observation. Many Christians will celebrate these days, while non-Christians will go to work. There are plenty of celebrations that take place during the holiday dates, and you can often participate in public festivities. However, some holidays (e.g., Ramadan and Yom Kippur) have specific rules for public behavior that you must follow, and it's important to be aware of these rules if your trip coincides with that holiday.

Jewish

★ *Tu Bishvat* Much like Arbor Day, this is a religious day in Israel where people plant trees and eat dried fruits and nuts.

★ *Mimouna* North African ("Maghreb") Jews celebrate the end of Passover by sharing a meal including leavened bread, which is strictly forbidden during Passover.

★ *Lag B'Omer* For those that don't take part in the pilgrimage, many people host bonfires on the beaches of Tel Aviv.

★ *Shavuot* One of the three Pilgrimage Festivals in the calendar year, when Israelis of antiquity would travel to the Temple in Jerusalem, and which is still observed by devout Jews today. The date recognizes the day when God revealed the Torah to the Israelites at Mount Sinai, and many will study the Torah.

★ *Tisha B'Av* The ninth day of the calendar month of Av, in Judaism this is a day of fasting while considering a number of horrors that have befallen Jewish people over the centuries, including the destruction of the two Temples.

★ *Yom Kippur (U)* Day of atonement in Israel, when everything shuts down, including stores, cars, and electricity, being the only day of the year when absolutely everything is blissfully empty and cities return to a calm state. Lots of people spend the latter part of the day wandering around highways and streets, which are all closed to traffic.

★ *Sukkot* A seven-day holiday when families build a temporary boxed structure outdoors in which they eat and sleep.

★ *Simchat Torah* A holiday immediately following Sukkot (above) that celebrates the love of the Torah with readings at night (which are normally prohibited).

- ★ *Sigd* Ethiopian Jews primarily celebrate this day, an Israeli public holiday, marking 50 days after Yom Kippur, and on which observants gather in Jerusalem to read the Octateuch (the Pentateuch plus three other books), pray, recite psalms, dance, and eat.
- ★ *Purim* Like a G-rated Halloween, with people of all ages dressing up to interpret the Jewish victory (represented by Esther and Mordecai) over Haman.
- ★ *Hanukkah, aka Festival of Lights* This minor holiday of eight days reflects the period in history when the Maccabees took back the Temple, purified it, and lit a menorah which miraculously burned for eight days despite there being oil sufficient for only one night. Today, people light menorahs, open presents, spin dreidels, and eat latkes and donuts.

Muslim
- ★ *Al Isra' wal Miraj* Also called Laylat al-Mi'raj ("Night Journey"), this commemorates Muhammad's journey first to "the farthest mosque" (now **Al-Aqsa Mosque (#65)** on Temple Mount) before ascending to Heaven, meeting several patriarchs and prophets, then returning to Earth.
- ★ *Ras Assanah al-Hijri* Islamic New Year, celebrated on 1 Muharram, when Muhammad began his migration (*hijra*) from Mecca to Medina in 622 CE.
- ★ *Mawlid al-Nabi* The Prophet Muhammad's birthday, celebrated by Sunnis on the 12th day of the month Rabi' al-Awwal.

Christian
- ★ *Holy Week* If you visit Jerusalem during Holy Week, you can take part in a number of interesting events, ceremonies, and processions. The week preceding Easter, Holy Week occurs from Palm Sunday, commemorating when Jesus entered Jerusalem, with morning mass at the **Church of the Holy Sepulchre (#9)** and an afternoon procession from historical Bethphage to Jerusalem through the Mount of Olives. Events continue on Holy Thursday, Good Friday, and Holy Saturday (with the Holy Fire Ceremony). Easter Sunday and Monday commemorate the resurrection of Jesus after his crucifixion. Several websites representing various sects provide updated lists of activities – try the Christian Information Centre at **w** cicts.org.
- ★ *Good Friday* The day when Jesus was crucified and died on the cross at Calvary (now in the **Church of the Holy Sepulchre (#9)**). Occurs during Holy Week (see above).
- ★ *Orthodox Easter* This is the same Easter that all Christians celebrate, commemorating the resurrection of Jesus Christ, but the Eastern Orthodox follow an older calendar created by Julius Caesar, the Julian calendar, rather than the Western calendar created in the 16th century CE, the Gregorian calendar.
- ★ *Christmas* Jesus' celebrated birthday, popular at the **Church of the Nativity (#18)**.

National days
- ★ *New Year's Day* A public holiday in Jordan, but not nearly as festive as in other parts of the world – no fireworks or public displays at midnight. New Year's Eve goes mostly unnoticed.
- ★ *Yom HaAliyah* "Aliyah" is Jewish immigration to the Holy Land, and this day ("yom" in Hebrew) is one to celebrate the importance immigration has had on the multicultural nation of Israel.
- ★ *Yom HaShoah* Holocaust Remembrance Day, and a reflection on the Jewish resistance movement during World War II.

SEASONAL TOURISM

	Festive holidays	Weather	No. of tourists	Hotel prices	Dead Sea	Red Sea	Med. Sea	Med. waves	Med. jellyfish
Jan	New Year's Day (Jordan)	rainy		$	18°C (65°F)	22°C (72°F)	19°C (66°F)	high	
Feb	Purim (Israel)	rainy		$	17°C (63°F)	21°C (70°F)	18°C (64°F)	high	
Mar		some rain		$	17°C (63°F)	21°C (70°F)	18°C (64°F)	medium	
Apr	Easter/Passover (Israel, Jordan); Al Isra' wal Miraj (Jordan)		busy	$$	18°C (65°F)	23°C (73°F)	19°C (65°F)	medium	
May	Independence Day/Memorial Day/Jerusalem Day/Shavuot (Israel); Ramadan begins (Jordan, Palestine)			$	21°C (70°F)	24°C (75°F)	21°C (70°F)	medium	
Jun	Eid Al-Fitr (Jordan, Palestine)		busy	$$	24°C (76°F)	26°C (79°F)	25°C (77°F)	low	
Jul		hot	busy	$$$	27°C (80°F)	28°C (82°F)	27°C (81°F)	low	may be jellies
Aug	Eid Al-Adha (Jordan, Palestine)	hot/humid	busy	$$$	28°C (83°F)	28°C (82°F)	29°C (83°F)	low	may be jellies
Sep	Rosh Hashanah/Yom Kippur/Sukkot (Israel); Islamic New Year (Jordan)		very busy	$$$	28°C (82°F)	27°C (81°F)	28°C (83°F)	low	
Oct	Simchat Torah (Israel)	idyllic		$$	26°C (79°F)	27°C (81°F)	26°C (79°F)	medium	
Nov	Prophet Muhammad's Birthday (Jordan)	some rain		$	23°C (74°F)	25°C (77°F)	23°C (74°F)	medium	
Dec	Christmas (Israel/Jordan)	rainy	busy	$$	20°C (69°F)	23°C (73°F)	21°C (69°F)	high	

★ *Yom HaZikaron* National Memorial Day (U) for Israel's fallen soldiers and those who have died in acts of terrorism.
★ *Yom HaAtzma'ut* Israel Independence Day, celebrated the day after Yom HaZikaron (above) and commemorating when Israel published its Declaration of Independence in 1948. This day is celebrated with Israeli military flight displays, with flyovers in the latest military planes.
★ *Labor Day* Celebrated in Jerusalem on International Workers' Day, May 1.
★ *Yom Yerushalayim* Jerusalem Day celebrates the Israeli victory in the 1967 war that brought East and West Jerusalem both under Israeli control.
★ *Eid al-Istiklaal* Jordan Independence Day, celebrated May 25, when the Hashemite Kingdom of Jordan replaced the Emirate of Transjordan in 1946.

Important notes
★ Jewish holidays start at sunset and continue to the following sunset. Thus, most holidays are two calendar days long. We've indicated the first day the holiday takes place, but note that festivities (if applicable) will not begin until sundown.
★ Muslim holidays are based on a lunar calendar that might shift a day or two. Individual countries will announce exact dates and public closures for Ramadan, Eid-al-Adha, and Eid-al-Fitr closer to the dates.
★ Much like in the West, holidays that fall on a holy day or weekend are often "observed" on the day preceding or following Shabbat (Friday night/Saturday)/ Jumu'ah (Friday).

WESTERN HOLIDAYS As you may have imagined, not too many people in the Holy Land celebrate **Christmas**. Israel is a Jewish state, while the Arabs who live in Palestine, Jordan, Egypt, and most Arab cities in Israel are primarily Muslim. There are some notable exceptions, and you will find some local celebrations in Nazareth, Bethlehem, and Jerusalem over the holidays, in addition to other towns. They are not, however, what you'd expect from European or American festivals – no Santas in malls or Christmas lights. The timing (December) means you will almost certainly miss out on enjoying the Mediterranean sun and Tel Aviv's white sandy beaches, as Christmas falls during the wintry, rainy season. You may consider going two weeks earlier, in the middle of December, as you'll likely save a boatload on airfare and hotel expenses. On the plus side, restaurants, museums, even workplaces are all open over Christmas! So you won't have any problem touring about.

The Jewish "**New Year**" is in September or October. Some secular Israelis (e.g., Tel Aviv) will celebrate with parties on the evening of December 31, but secular Israelis rarely need a reason to party. You won't find fireworks or big street festivals. Several clubs in Tel Aviv, Jerusalem, and Amman will host parties – possibly very pricey.

Many folks get their holiday in **August**. We hate to break it to you, but this is the worst month in the calendar year to visit Israel. Temperatures soar and humidity (dew point) is very high. Certainly, you can spend a lot of time on the beach and have a wonderful time, but if you have plans to go to Petra, Masada, the Negev, Red Sea, or any outdoor park (including all of Jerusalem's Old City) you'll be extremely warm and fatigued, and will need to plan accordingly. That said, August is hot in most northern-hemisphere places around the world. Your town isn't the only "most humid place on Earth" on the planet, you know!

FESTIVALS
★ *Religious* Several; see "Holidays" above.
★ *People and culture* Tel Aviv White Night (D3): once a year in the summer, everyone in the city stays up all night, walking the streets, going to parties and bars, eating,

listening to music and performances, and attending other organized group events. *Tel Aviv Pride Celebration (D1)* takes place in early June (see *LGBTQ*, p. 540), as does Jerusalem Pride.

★ *Food and drink* Jerusalem Beer Festival (late August).

★ *Music* Red Sea Jazz Festival (L1); Sacred Music Festival, aka Mekudeshet (B1); Oud Festival (A7); Abu Ghosh Vocal Festival, twice a year at Succot and Shavuoth (w agfestival. co.il/home/).

★ *Arts and crafts* Hutzot Hayotzer Arts and Crafts Festival (A7); Jerusalem International Arts & Crafts Fair (late August).

★ *Dance and theater* Israel Festival (A7); Fringe Theatre Festival (September in Akko).

CLIMATE **Summer** (May to August) is hot with 25–35°C (80–90°F) days. August is the most humid month. The beaches are packed and the sea temperatures warm, but the desert is scalding: Eilat, the Negev, and the Jordan Valley can reach 50°C (120°F), so hiking Masada after 10.00 or trails in the Negev can be very dangerous. Petra will be very warm for hikes by midday, so plan to leave early when it's cool. **Autumn** (September to November) is more pleasant with 20–25°C (70–80°F) days, with the occasional rain shower after Yom Kippur. **Winter** (late November to mid-March) is overcast if not rainy, though usually in spurts with periods of sunshine. It's never extremely cold in this area but the nights can get chilly especially in the Negev and Jordan deserts, and Jerusalem can see snow as it sits in the hills. Temperatures are 12–19°C (55–65°F) during the day and 5–10°C (40–50°F) at night. Israelis begin wearing parkas as soon as the temperature dips below 20°C (70°F), but it feels very mild if you're from a wintry climate. Mount Hermon in the Golan Heights has ski slopes. **Spring** (late March and April) is a short season, with pleasant, 15–20°C (60–70°F) days. The rains taper off in March, and everything starts to get hot and dry again in April.

Humidity can be a factor. June and September are typically muggy months, while July and August are nearly always muggy, each with several days that can reach oppressive levels. Unless you are on the beach, August is a miserable time to be in Tel Aviv, the coast, and Galilee areas, as the combination of humidity, heat, and the absence of tree shade can make being outside unbearable. On the plus side, if you like cooling off in the sea, much of Israel touches a body of swimmable water.

Winter is the **rainy season** in Israel (not so much in Jordan), lasting from November through March, and Tel Aviv sees the most rain out of all of our listed weather regions. Rain is often a reason for people to stay home. It doesn't usually last all day, though the sky might stay overcast. Be aware that many streets do not have proper drainage systems, and cars have little sympathy for walkers on sidewalks – you will get splashed. **Hamsin** are desert winds from the Sahara that occasionally plague the region with sandstorms of up to 140kph and extremely high temperatures. The air is unbreathable and the dust blocks out much of the light. It's considered unsafe to be outside during these storms, which can last a few days. They typically come in during the spring or summer but it's impossible to predict, so you needn't plan your trip around it. **Snow** is considered "freakish weather" in many parts of the country.

We've included **annual climate charts** in the entries for the BUCKET! electives (#1–3). For more charts, including Tel Aviv, Eilat/Aqaba, and Amman, visit our website (w buckettravelguides.com/climate-charts).

The coldest **seawater** months in all the seas are February and March. If you are planning a vacation that involves swimming, you might want to pick any other time. The biggest Mediterranean waves are in the winter months, but some waves can still be found summer mornings. December has the warmest water of the three big-wave months (December–February). **Jellyfish** (stinging) usually only arrive once a year – though it's hard to predict when – for anywhere from two to six weeks in June or July, typically.

SEASONAL TOURISM Keep in mind that *your* most ideal time might not allow you to do everything you may have planned. Sure, 20°C (70°F) degrees in March sounds blissful, but it's raining half of that month in much of Israel. The "Seasonal Tourism" table (p. 38) pulls together lots of seasonal data points: When is high season? When are the sunniest days? What are the major holidays?

PICKING THE BEST TIME TO VISIT **May** and **November** both hit the sweet spot of good weather, fewest tourists, cheapest hotels, warm-but-not-bathwater sea temperatures, decent waves, and no jellyfish. If you tend to be a more warm-weather-oriented person, **May** is the month for you – it can run quite a few degrees warmer than November. If you skew more towards cool weather, **November** is your month. If you don't mind crowds and have a more forgiving budget, **April**, **June**, **September**, and **October** are also lovely months throughout most of the region. If you want to lounge on the beach all day then **June**'s your month. The high holy days usually fall in **September** or **October**, normally gorgeous weather months. If you're thinking of coming during your winter/Christmas holidays then you'll probably need a jacket in some places, and maybe even a coat at night on the off-chance of snowfall.

DO #2: BUDG ET!

We've now looked at calendars and holidays and a variety of factors related to our most ideal time of year to travel and we've narrowed down our preferred time of the year to travel. We've considered coverage, pace, and speed, and have established the minimum number of days we need. Now, before we go and buy plane tickets to match those number of days calculated, we want to make sure we understand the monetary components of this trip. You should spend a little time **tracking prices** of airfares, hotels, rental cars, and any other variables that may go up and down the closer you get. After a month of tracking, you'll be able to make an estimated guess as to whether you should **book now or wait**.

AIR TRAVEL Airfare can be the biggest-ticket item if you're not a careful planner, but with a little research you can find some of the best-value travel deals for long-distance routes out there. If you're flying from Europe, you'll be able to find exceptional deals on budget airlines, and decent deals on the more reputable, older, mileage-club airlines.

Your best bet is always going to be to fly into **Ben Gurion Airport**, located between Tel Aviv and Jerusalem, in Israel. This is a notoriously strict and suspicious gateway, as you may have heard, but it is the most centrally located, and the one that most often has the best discounts for those flying from North America and Europe. Flying into Amman will often cost a couple of hundred dollars more, but would be much more convenient if you are planning a Jordan-based itinerary. For Asia-based origins, either Ben Gurion Airport in Israel or Amman International Airport in Jordan may work for you.

If coming from the **USA or Canada**, you have a few direct options. During the low season, you can find tickets for $600–800, maybe even slightly cheaper, from Miami, Washington DC, New York, and sometimes Chicago. This is absurdly cheap for how long you are in the air. As a general rule of thumb, routing through cities in Europe will afford you better deals. The West Coast is obviously more expensive, and adds 4–5 hours to the flight time (to say nothing of the layovers). If you're flying from **mainland Europe**, there are discount airlines galore. You can round-trip to Israel for $100–300 during low season, and maybe $100 higher than that during high season. **South America** is on the expensive side (southern/western hemisphere to the northern/eastern hemisphere), but you can find some great deals into/out of major cities in Brazil and Argentina – under $1,000 – which is less than the average cost to/from the USA for many South Americans.

If you're flying from **Asia**, it's much more expensive. Tickets from Bangkok, Shanghai, Hong Kong, and Tokyo typically range from $800 to $1,400 round-trip. The **Middle East**, though close, is equally difficult. Many neighboring countries don't fly directly to Israel, so you have to route through Amman, which we don't recommend unless absolutely necessary. Otherwise, you're looking at layovers in Amman or Istanbul, and tickets around the $400–600 mark. Local travel agencies might be able to find you a better deal on a charter, but it's a gamble. You can always take your chances overland if that doesn't work. **Oceania** costs a lot: the cheapest route is probably Perth to Amman for just under $1,000 but it's unclear how helpful that is for the masses: $1,200–1,700 is more typical from major cities.

TRACKING PRICES We highly encourage you to spend at least a few weeks – and up to a month or longer – tracking air prices before you make a commitment to purchase your tickets. There are several reasons for this:

1. The cheapest ticket is never really that cheap! There's always something missing from the final price, often biggies including luggage, seats, and food. This is a long flight – you don't want to starve. (We go more into these "extras" in *Do #3: Fly It!*)
2. Tracking airfares will take you no more than 5 minutes a day.
3. Airfare prices go up and down every day, and this often has to do with demand. Everyone buys their tickets on Sunday, costing $76 more than if bought on Wednesday or Tuesday!
4. Booking too far in advance can be disadvantageous also, with prices averaging $50 more. The ideal booking window is three weeks to four months in advance. Don't be in a rush to book!
5. Don't be tricked into long layovers and multiple stops to save a few bucks. This is a bucket-list trip. You don't want to start off exhausted.

Take the time to figure out how much you can afford to spend, do your research, then shoot for an airfare that meets your requirements (ideal time of year, minimum number of days, luggage, airline points, seats, etc.) while staying within budget. Once you have spent a while tracking, you'll have progressed through the next few chapters. We cover buying airfare in *Do #3: Fly It!*

COSTS The bottom line is that Israel is expensive, Jordan less so, and Egypt dirt cheap comparatively. Tel Aviv was ranked the world's most expensive city in the world in 2021 according to the Economist Intelligence Unit's annual Worldwide Cost of Living Index. Rent tends to be expensive, while groceries are slightly cheaper. Jerusalem runs 10–20% cheaper for most items, with the exception of alcohol, taxis, and many meats. At a national level, Jordan is cheaper than Israel, but Israel remains one of the most expensive places tourists can travel, ranked ninth most expensive in the world according to the World Economic Forum's *Travel and Tourism Competitiveness Report* in 2019. The average tourist spent $455 in-country. The idea that locals pay one price and tourists pay another (usually at a great premium) does exist in practice in the Holy Land, particularly at Old City tourist stands (where you'll have to bargain), in produce markets, and in Egypt. Restaurants tend to have the same prices for everyone, though if you don't see a menu, ask before you order. Also, like anywhere, you will pay more for food in touristy areas (e.g., the beachfront in Tel Aviv). Foreign food is pricey, as are hotels, nice restaurants, and gas. If you attempt to speak Hebrew, you *might* get a better deal, but if you have an accent it probably won't do you any good. Jordanians are more likely to be smitten with you if you try speaking Arabic. Bargaining is only allowed in markets where you don't see prices, but is not typical practice in restaurants, or even when ordering street food. Any sales tax is included in prices, so the sticker price is what you will owe.

According to w budgetyourtrip.com, the average cost of a trip to Tel Aviv – including accommodation, food, moderate drinking, some entertainment, transportation, water, and gratuities – is around $130 per person per day when staying in a hostel and dining modestly. Eating in nicer restaurants and staying in boutique hotels will set two people back about $565 per day (assuming double occupancy on the room, splitting a bottle of wine at dinner, etc.). Amman's mid-range options will cost a solo traveler around $90 per day, and a couple doing a higher-end vacation will spend closer to $200 per day. Obviously, your costs will vary depending on the type of trip you take. According to the Backpacker Index, Tel Aviv ranked 129th out of 137 international cities for cheap travel, costing $99.87 in 2020 for a dorm bed in a cheap (good) hostel, three beers, three basic meals, two bus rides, and visiting one touristy place per day. That's slightly more expensive than London or Copenhagen. Amman ranked 65th at $43.80 per day, similar to Cairo, Moscow, and Prague. In 2021, Israel ranked the seventh most expensive place to get a craft beer in the world (out of 177 countries), with the average pint of beer in a bar costing $11.59. Jordan was not far behind at #17 with the cost of a pint at $10.57. Egypt remains the cheapest at $3.50.

Six to Three Months Before

DO #3: FLY IT!

If you've been dutifully tracking air prices, calculated the minimum amount of time you need to visit your bucket-list electives, and have narrowed down the best combination of price, loyalty/points, and inclusions, then it's time to **book your airfare**.

TRAVEL DAYS Don't count your day of arrival or your day of departure when looking at flight itineraries. Meaning: if you have a ten-day trip in mind, you should count arrival day + ten additional days + departure day. Don't plan on getting much accomplished as soon as you get off the plane – you will likely have some jet lag. Same on the departure day: unless you are leaving late at night, don't try to cram activities into your final day. Use that day as a relaxing day to check out of your hotel, grab a bite to eat at your favorite place, and take a leisurely stroll if you have any time left.

Thus, when you're looking for tickets, you'll need to add *two* days to the search engine to account for those travel days; if your flight continues overnight, you'll need to add *three* days. For example, a "ten-day" itinerary would have you departing North/South America/Australasia on March 1, arriving on March 2, spending ten days from March 3–12 on the ten-day itinerary, and departing on March 13.

BOOKING AIRFARE *Spoiler alert*: we don't have any way of predicting the cheapest hour or day or season that will secure you the best chance at the best deal. Ticket prices are complex algorithms of demand, time of year, advance purchase, and luck. Sometimes you'll get a great deal, and sometimes you'll be stuck spending $1,600. To abate the final sticker shock, we recommend you spend time tracking prices, which we covered in *Do #2: Budg Et!* Once you're ready, it's time to take the plunge. Don't forget your **frequent flyer number**, **special meals**, and **TSA PreCheck/KTN number**, if applicable. And use the best **travel credit card** you've got to maximize reward points.

FLIGHT EXTRAS We also recommend you purchase your **flight extras** at the same time you make your booking. All of these will almost certainly be cheaper the earlier you buy: luggage, seat assignments, business class upgrades, food (if needed), insurance bundles, rental cars, and package deals. You will save significantly on the cost of extra **luggage** if you book before your flight. Review again the climate in *Do #1: Date It!* to properly evaluate how much luggage you will need. Overpacking could cost you a fortune; most airlines have a 24-hour cutoff time for prebooking extras such as luggage. And you don't want to be that person at the airport with their luggage strewn everywhere trying to shift around clothes so as to meet weight requirements: you're on vacation. Whether or not you booked a budget airline, check if you're authorized a **carry-on**. These days, it's anything but guaranteed. Also, if you're going on an overnight or long flight, do you really want a middle seat? If you've been tracking airfare, you'll have factored in **seat costs** into the overall cost of the flight. So prebook that aisle or window now.

AIRPORTS If you are flying from overseas, you have two principal airports to choose from: **Israel's Ben Gurion International Airport**, located roughly halfway between Tel Aviv and Jerusalem, and serving both nicely, or **Jordan's Queen Alia International Airport** in Amman.

There are a few regional airports you might want to consider, but by and large these market to very specific regional audiences. **Ramon Airport**, 18km north of Eilat, replaced Ovda and Eilat airports in 2019. It's the second largest in the country, after Ben Gurion. As it's roughly 3½ hours from Tel Aviv and Jerusalem, with limited connections, it's not a great option unless you're planning to rent a car. **Haifa Airport** has a few seasonal flights to Cyprus (Paphos and Larnaca) and Greece (Athens, Kos, and Rhodes) on Tus Air, but its primary purpose is to service Eilat flights. **Aqaba** has an airport that is not normally found on the international tourist map; however, budget airlines RyanAir, Wizz Air, and easyJet offer winter services to/from over a dozen European cities.

REGIONAL FLIGHTS If you decide you need internal flights, you can wait until closer to your travel dates to purchase, or you can buy them now. There aren't yet any money-saving air passes in Israel or Jordan. In most cases, if you want to fly between Tel Aviv and Amman or Tel Aviv and Eilat, you can buy those tickets separately on one of the airline websites we reference below. There are new routes being opened up between Ben Gurion Airport and Sharm el-Sheikh in 2022, and more routes are in the works to other countries as relations normalize between Israel and the region. One-ways (inside individual countries) are also fairly straightforward affairs.

AIRLINES *Important note: airlines and the tourism industry continue to experience significant disruptions due to the COVID-19 pandemic. This information could change at any time.* Plenty of airlines fly into Ben Gurion and Queen Alia, but Israel and Jordan only have one flag-carrying airline each. For Israel, that airline is **El Al** (meaning "skyward"). Jordan has **Royal Jordanian**, operated out of Queen Alia International Airport.

Non-stop According to w flightconnections.com, Royal Jordanian flies to 39 international destinations, including direct flights to Hong Kong, Bangkok, Montreal, New York, Detroit, and Chicago. El Al covers 53 destinations over 33 countries, with direct flights to East Asia, Europe, and North America.

Layovers For a variety of security-related reasons, Ben Gurion is not a "hub" for regional travel and you won't find yourself flying through Israel to get to another country. You *may* find yourself routing through Amman on your way elsewhere, though don't plan on leaving the airport unless you have a minimum of 8 hours to work with, as traffic is unpredictable and bad. If you do have time, visit our *Stopover/ Layover* itinerary (p. 746) for recommendations.

Stopovers Any stay longer than 24 hours on an international itinerary would be a "stopover." To do this in Israel or Jordan, you'd most likely be booking two one-way flights into and out of these two countries. The excellent information blog *Tourist Israel* has a running list of flights that connect to and from Tel Aviv (as well as approved city pairs) at w touristisrael.com/flights-to-ben-gurion-airport/.

CHECK-IN Note the check-in time of your flight. Some airlines will let you check in days in advance, while others only open up check-in 24 hours in advance. If you have *not* bought seats, you should set an alarm to check in as soon as the airline allows, so you can get out of a middle seat before it's too late.

DO #4: PREPARE FOR IT!

This part seems basic, and thus skippable, but it's the most important step! We need you to go get your **passport** and check the **expiration date**. You also need to do a little research on **visas**. Consider registering with your government (especially post-COVID, understand your government may be the only entity that can get you out of the country in an emergency).

CHECK YOUR PASSPORT This is not a joke! Go find your passport, for three reasons. First, can you find it? If yes, good! If you can't, then you need to get a new one! Aren't you glad you didn't wait? Second, is it still valid? If yes, great! If it's not still valid, you won't pay exorbitant fees and stress yourself out because you have to renew your passport two days before you jump on a plane. Third, if it is still valid, does it have at least a year of validity remaining? Many countries (and airlines) require six months' validity before letting you enter their country. *This can include transit and layovers.* If it's not valid for at least six months, do yourself a favor and renew now.

If you need a US passport, visit **w** usa.gov/passport. For more information on the six-month rule, visit The Points Guy's great website (**w** thepointsguy.com/2017/08/six-month-passport-validity-rule/). And be sure to review the traveler's checklist from the US State Department at **w** travel.state.gov/content/travel/en/international-travel/before-you-go/travelers-checklist.html.

DO YOU NEED A VISA?

Israel If your passport is not from the EU, Russia, US, South America, Japan, or most Oceania countries, you need to check for current rules. The Wikipedia page "Visa Policy of Israel" (**w** en.wikipedia.org/wiki/Visa_policy_of_Israel) has a consolidated list and links to find the appropriate consulate or government ministry site for updated guidelines. Passport holders from the countries with "visa free" travel to Israel receive a maximum of three months for tourism upon entry at no cost. Be aware that, if you are planning on volunteering, and your participation would constitute as paid "work" (a one-day archaeological dig would not qualify, for instance), contact your local Israel Consulate to find out if you need to apply for a special work visa (**w** mfa.gov.il/MFA/ConsularServices/Pages/ConsularServices.aspx).

Jordan The Wikipedia page "Visa Policy of Jordan" (**w** en.wikipedia.org/wiki/Visa_policy_of_Jordan) is useful, as is the Jordan Tourism Board's site (**w** international.visitjordan.com/page/4/VisasToJordan.aspx), which covers entrance fees, border crossings, visa fees, embassies, airports, and more. Most global citizens are issued visas on arrival if flying into Amman, which carries a fee of 40 JD for a one-month, single-entry visa. An exit fee also applies at 8 JD per person and 5 JD per vehicle. If you are part of a tour group, they will likely incorporate all these fees into your trip, or at least tell you to carry cash for exchange and payment at the border. If you are traveling by yourself, however, the most important takeaway about Jordanian visas is the **Jordan Pass** which covers the cost of Petra, dozens of other sites in Jordan, *and* a single-entry visitor visa! Buy this pass! See p. 60 for details. If entering Jordan without a visa, note that: Queen Alia airport and the Jordan River border crossing both issue visas on arrival; Wadi Araba crossing will issue a visa only for Jordan Pass holders; King Hussein border crossing does not issue visas; and Aqaba Airport issues visas to non-restricted countries, but restricted countries need a visa beforehand. More information can be found at **w** jordanpass. jo/contents/FAQs.aspx.

Egypt If you are only visiting the Sinai, most European Union, US, and Israeli citizens can receive a Sinai-only visa on arrival if entering through Taba (border) or Sharm el-Sheikh (via plane) and spending no more than 14 days. Egypt requires six months' validity on passports at time of arrival. Alternatively, organized and/or nervous travelers can book their visa in advance through Egypt's portal (**w** visa2egypt.gov.eg).

TRAVEL ADVISORIES
Many countries offer travel advice and travel advisories for dangerous regions, and several English-speaking countries have travel advisories for scenarios such as COVID-19. Check the security situation and review your country's recommendations for travel when considering travel to the following destinations, keeping in mind that the whole region is volatile and violence can erupt at any time. Travel advisories for **Israel and the Palestinian Territories** cover Gaza, including the border; West Bank, except Ramallah, Jericho, Bethlehem, and East Jerusalem; borders with Syria (east of Route 98), Egypt (including Highway 10), and Lebanon (Sheba'a Farms and Ghajjar); and Old City Jerusalem, where you should exercise caution. For **Jordan**, they comprise the border with Syria (excluding Umm Qais); border with Iraq; Highway 10 towards Iraq, east of Ruwayshid/Safawi; refugee camps; protests, which can get violent; and risk of terrorism. In **Egypt**, most countries have an advisory to avoid visits to North Sinai, to include bus trips from Cairo, due to kidnappings, terrorism, and the presence of militant groups, including Da'esh/ISIS. Many embassies recommend avoiding all parts of the Sinai, with the exception of Sharm el-Sheikh, which can be visited by air. Note, however, that a Russian plane was attacked and destroyed leaving Sharm in 2015.

VACCINES
Vaccines are not currently required for this part of the world. However, the introduction of COVID-19 to the travel landscape has changed how we fundamentally travel and enter countries, so make sure to follow rules as set forth by Israel's Ministry of Health (**w** gov.il/en/departments/guides/flying-to-israel-guidlines) and Jordan's Gateway2Jordan (**w** gateway2jordan.gov.jo). As of 2021, Egypt does not have a public-facing site for COVID information, so use **w** travel.state.gov or IATA's COVID-19 Travel Regulations Map at **w** www.iatatravelcentre.com/world.php.

REGISTER WITH YOUR EMBASSY
US citizens should enroll with STEP (Smart Traveler Enrollment Program) at **w** step.state.gov, which allows you to let the US embassy or consulate in (or nearest to) your destination country know that you're traveling overseas. What this means in practice is that you'll receive any alerts that the embassy/consulate sends, which can include updates about violence, severe weather, or travel restrictions in place. In practice, the US government cannot stop you from traveling wherever you choose, though the local government of course can. But, if you get in trouble or are accused of trouble, the consulate can serve as a point of reference to ensure you are receiving your rights under local laws. Also, if you have an emergency at home and a relative can't contact you, the embassy can get in touch with you to relay the information. If this sounds like Big Brother to you, Google "travel+enrollment" to read lots of pro-enrollment articles from non-government news organizations, such as Lifehacker and Condé Nast. Several other countries offer similar services, including Canada, New Zealand, Singapore, and Israel.

REGISTER WITH YOUR CREDIT CARD COMPANY Visit your credit card company's website to register your trip so your card doesn't get turned off for potential fraud as soon as you make an international purchase.

TIME ZONES Make sure you understand the time difference between the Holy Land and home. Israel, Jordan, and the Sinai are all in the same time zone, although daylight saving time can cause disruptions: Israel and Jordan observe daylight savings, but may change time on different dates, while Egypt does not observe daylight savings at all. The Holy Land is (generally): 11 hours behind Auckland; 9 hours behind Sydney; 6 hours behind Singapore; 2 hours ahead of Greenwich Mean Time; 7 hours ahead of Eastern Standard; and 10 hours ahead of Pacific Standard.

DO #5: SLEEP IT!

It's time to book your **accommodation**. If you're traveling to the Holy Land for less than a month (i.e., a couple of days to a couple of weeks), we recommend you book your lodging in advance. Accommodation in Israel is expensive, more so than many places in Europe. It rarely books up completely, but if you stand any chance of getting a deal, it's not on last-minute accommodation. By comparison, accommodation in Jordan is relatively inexpensive (usually half the price for comparable quality establishments) and can usually be booked closer to arrival. The exception is Petra: you likely want to book your Petra accommodation well in advance to secure the best price, closest location, nicest options, or a combination of the three. Holiday periods are the nightmare you imagine at most getaway locations: booking in advance probably won't help much, either, as hotels will have raised their prices accordingly. A "five star" hotel in Eilat over a holiday weekend will cost upwards of $600, whereas the same "five star" style hotel will cost roughly $150 in Aqaba (Jordan) and $75 in Taba.

HOW TO PICK A PLACE TO STAY We have a pretty simple way of helping you figure out what type of lodging to look for – pick the factor that is most important to you and visit its corresponding section below.

1. *Spend as little money as possible* Focus on our *Budget* options (below) – camping, field schools, or youth hostels.
2. *Meet people from the community* A Christian guesthouse, a kibbutz, or a volunteer farm are good *Community* options (opposite).
3. *Be immersed in a neighborhood scene* We recommend some kind of housing share – there are a variety of options, all explored in *Shared Space* (p. 50).
4. *Getting towels and linens changed daily* *Hotels* (p. 50) are for you – budget, boutique, and chain are all options.
5. *Feeling pampered* Check out the *Spa* and *Luxury* options (p. 51).
6. *Experiencing something unique* You might like Bedouin camping, tzimmers in the Galilee/Golan, an ecolodge in a biosphere reserve, or glamping in Wadi Rum, all in *Experiential* (p. 52). Also try *Unique* (p. 53) for a few more alternative options.
7. *Flexibility while on the road* Road trippers can visit *RV* (p. 53).
8. *Whatever is rated highest* See *Superlative Lodging* (p. 53).

BUDGET

Camping Traditional camping is popular and legal in Israel, while less organized (but still mostly legal) in Jordan. Apart from Wadi Rum and Dana, camping in Jordan is generally limited due to lack of options. Electives that involve camping are listed in

Accommodation – Campgrounds (p. 566) and *Accommodation – Experiential Lodging* (p. 565). Otherwise, there are nealy 100 campsites inside **Israel National Parks** (w parks.org.il/en/campgrounds/; 40–60 ILS per adult, 30–45 per child, including entrance and private caravan). There are also a number of **KKL** (Jewish National Fund) recreation areas throughout Israel that make for a great and easy setup, plus you'll be surrounded by good company. They do require you to register at least ten days in advance; you can probably get away with less, but still need to call (w kkl. org.il/eng/tourism-and-recreation/camping-picnic-sites/camping-sites/; free, but big groups have to pay for the import of chemical lavatories which requires prebooking). If you can read Hebrew, **Tiuli** is an excellent, well-organized website built for hikers which provides hiking paths and proximal campgrounds on an interactive map of Israel, with information about fees, toilets, electricity, and water for each (w tiuli. com; free). Note that camping wherever you please, or **wild camping**, is **allowed** in Israel but **not allowed** in Jordan. If it's wild, be prepared that there are no bathrooms, fire pits, or even waste bins, so you have to take everything with you when you leave (including used toilet paper – bring garbage bags).

Field schools The **Society for the Protection of Nature in Israel** (SPNI) offers accommodation, dining, and hiking tours in **field schools** in unspoilt regions throughout Israel, including Ein Gedi, the Golan, *Mount Hermon*, and Eilat (w natureisrael.org/ fieldschools). Booking in advance is required through the Teleteva reservation hotline (☏ +972 3 6388688; e teleteva@spni.org.il).

Youth hostels Most youth hostels in the region are associated with **Hostelling International**, a reputable international association of hostels (w hihostels.com/ destinations/il/hostels). The global **Hostelworld** (w hostelworld.com) also offers a variety of choice The **Israel Youth Hostel Association** (IYHA; w en.iyha.org.il) allows you to book a variety of hostel options around the country, while the English-focused website **ILH Israel Hostels** (w hostels-israel.com) contains lots of options throughout Israel, and includes options in Dahab and Sharm in the Sinai, as well as popular destinations in Jordan, such as Amman, Aqaba, Dana, Madaba, Petra, and Wadi Rum. The **Tourist Israel** blog/guide offers its recommendations, divided by region, in "Five of the Best Hostels in Israel" (w touristisrael.com/5-of-the-best-hostels-in-israel/3643/). The **Abraham Hostel** in Tel Aviv is quite popular and bookable on w abrahamhostels. com or sites such as w hotels.com and w booking.com ($25/night for dorm rooms).

COMMUNITY
Christian guesthouses The Christian Information Centre provides information on nearly 70 Christian guesthouses accepting travelers who are focused on quiet, meditation, and spirituality (i.e., you have to respect that monks, nuns, and priests all still live and work on the premises). Accommodation can be in monasteries, convents, or other religious houses, and the bedrooms are usually simple, sometimes with bunk beds, and can include half or full board. Guests of all religious persuasions are welcome. There are options throughout Israel – most do not have a website, but they do respond to email. For a complete list, visit w cicts.org and select "Accommodations" ($25–70/night, meals extra).

Kibbutzim For more information on the kibbutz movement, see *Society – Cooperatives – Kibbutzim* (p. 535). In short, kibbutzim are collective settlements of a few dozen to a few hundred people who typically live off of their own agricultural bounty, but have recently begun other ventures to support their communities; one of those activities is to lodge travelers. There are kibbutzim all over Israel. Most are on a compound and operate much like hotels. Some are simple and some fancy. Some kibbutzim specialize in family vacations (having focused their attention on tourism), and have created the concept of a "holiday village" which offers to provide entertainment – usually water and other sports – for all the family. Others specialize in religious visits or budget accommodation. Visit **w** booking-kibbutz.com for a good collection of kibbutz accommodations across the country ($75–100/person in low season, $100–250 in high season, but varies by region, time of year, and number of adults (price per person decreases if you add more to a room, but total room cost goes up)).

Volunteer/work If you feel like working to pay off the cost of your travels and want to get to know the culture while doing so, check out **Workaway** (**w** workaway.info/hostlist.html) and sort by country. There are dozens of volunteer opportunities working with social groups, tourism, building projects, and farms. More specifically, if you're willing to work on a farm for several hours a day, five days a week, you can get free room and board. This is a reputable, international organization with great opportunities to dig in (quite literally) and have an extremely localized experience. Join **WWOOF** Israel for more information on volunteering (**w** wwoof.org.il).

SHARED SPACE
House shares **Craigslist** has been popular in nearly every city in America for almost two decades, and many people have found apartments and rentals though its easy search function. It also has a vacation rentals page (**w** telaviv.craigslist.org/search/vac) which offers options in Tel Aviv, Jerusalem, Haifa, and the West Bank (not Jordan). **Couchsurfing** will set you up with locals who will let you stay in their place at dirt-cheap prices. Keep in mind you're heading into someone else's apartment – this can have its ups and downs, to say the least. Jerusalem and Tel Aviv each have listings (**w** couchsurfing.com/places/middle-east/israel/). **House sitting** may be an option, though listings are slim across many websites. There are a few open and completed assignments noted on Trusted Housesitters (**w** trustedhousesitters.com/house-and-pet-sitting-assignments/israel/tel-aviv/tel-aviv/), and **HomeExchange** lists nearly 200 people who are willing to trade you homes for a week or longer (**w** homeexchange.com). **Homestay** was established to help you find local families, though in Israel it's used more as a guesthouse finder. No bother – the housing is cheap, and you're usually met by the owner of the property who can give you insider tips (**w** homestay.com/israel). **Homeless** (**w** homeless.co.il) and **Yad2** (**w** yad2.co.il) are two popular Hebrew-language websites.

Apartment/house rentals The super trendy vacation rental site, **Airbnb**, is a popular option throughout major locations in Israel and Jordan, with plenty of options at a variety of price points, with accommodation ranging from shared spaces to furnished luxury villas. Another popular site, **VRBO**, or Vacation Rental by Owner (**w** vrbo.com), has nearly 1,500 listings throughout Israel, mostly on the Mediterranean coast. Jordan has significantly less (around 30 at the time of writing). If you'll be staying awhile, you can start your search with Secret Tel Aviv's "**Renting Apartments in Tel Aviv**" overview (**w** secrettelaviv.com/magazine/blog/renting-an-apartment-in-tel-aviv/).

HOTELS
Budget hotels **TripAdvisor** allows you to sort rankings in Israel or Jordan by "Best Value" and "Top Rated," then further divide by hotel class, location, and amenities.

Select "Budget" under the "Style" heading to limit for the best, cheap options. Similar services to refine your search are offered by w hotels.com, w booking.com, and w kayak.com – all offer last-minute options, as well. For only last-minute options, try w lastminute.com and narrow down by city, price, and star rating.

Boutique hotels "Boutique" hotels describe a typically small and stylish accommodation, sometimes without frills and sometimes luxurious. This is becoming more of a trend in Israel than in Jordan, though hotels in both countries are taking the hint and adding "boutique" to their name so make sure to do some research before committing to "X Boutique Hotel." Among our electives, the boutique hotels to seek out are: *The Norman Hotel* and *Brown Beach House* in Tel Aviv; *Banksy's Walled-Off Hotel*, Bethlehem; *Mamilla Hotel*, Jerusalem; Brown TLV (D4); Poli House (D4); Hotel Montefiore (D4); Lily & Bloom (D4); White Villa Hotel (D4); Brown Jerusalem (A7); Rothschild Hotel (D4); and Akkotel (E2).

Israeli brands Isrotel offers higher-end spa hotels including the Beresheet Hotel (J2), the Carmel Forest Spa Resort, and a half-dozen hotels in Eilat (w isrotel.com). **Fattal Hotel Chain** (w fattal-hotels.com) has 35 hotels in 14 regions of Israel, with their Leonardo, Herods, Hotel Rothschild 22, NYX, and U lines; Leonardo has an Advantage Club with 10% discount on bookings, free Wi-Fi, and late check-out. **Dan Hotels** (w danhotels.com) is the oldest hotel chain in Israel, with 18 prestigious hotels including the King David in Jerusalem and a variety of options with "Dan" preceding the hotel name. It offers "e-dan club" benefits, including discount on hotel rooms and on-site expenses. **Atlas Hotels** offers 16 boutique hotel options in Tel Aviv, Jerusalem, Haifa, Eilat and near Ben Gurion Airport, with discount rates on its website (w atlas.co.il/israel-hotel-deals). **Prima Hotels** has 14 hotels in seven locations, and its Prima Club gives 5% off online bookings and various other discounts (w prima-hotels-israel.com/prima-club).

International brands If you're looking to use or gain points, you'll find familiar faces (or lobbies) throughout the Holy Land. *Hilton* One Hilton in Tel Aviv and another in Suweimeh, Jordan on the Dead Sea. There's a DoubleTree in Aqaba. *IHG* Crowne Plaza, Intercontinental, and Holiday Inn have properties throughout Israel and Jordan. *Kempinski* Options for Jordan: Amman, Aqaba, and the Dead Sea (Ishtar). New to Tel Aviv: David Kempinski. *Mövenpick* Aqaba, Dead Sea, Petra, and a variety of Egyptian locations (including Taba). *Marriott* Renaissance, Sheraton, Luxury Collection (The Jaffa), Ritz-Carlton Herziliya, and Publica Isrotel in Tel Aviv. In Amman, there's a Marriott, Sheraton, St. Regis, and W. In Aqaba, a Luxury Collection (Al Manara) and Westin, a Marriott at the Dead Sea Suweimeh, and a Marriott in Wadi Musa/Petra.

LUXURY

Spa hotels Spa hotels are a craze in Tel Aviv and Jordan, with most of the chains (Dan, Herods, Isrotel, Crowne Plaza, Leonardo, etc.) offering luxury, spa hotel accommodations in a variety of locations, such as *Ein Bokek* (Dead Sea, Israel-side), Eilat, Jerusalem, and *Tiberias*. You can run a "luxury spa hotels in Israel" search on TripAdvisor which will give you a rank-ordering of the best in the country as rated by fellow travelers. The **Carmel Forest Spa Resort** is a favorite of Israelis. It's not cheap, but has a great location and a lauded breakfast (w isrotel.com; w booking.com). On BUCKET!'s list are: *Hammamat Ma'in Hot Springs*; the luxury hotel at *Elma Arts Complex*; the Beresheet Hotel (J2) in Mitzpe Ramon; and Efendi (E2) in Akko.

Luxury **Five Star Alliance** lists 17 four- and five-star luxury hotels in Israel and 12 sites in Jordan (**w** fivestaralliance.com). See *Accommodation – Highly Recommended* (p. 565) for a list of the acclaimed hotels among our electives (spoiler alert: they all qualify as "luxury" if they cost more than $200/night). Alternatively, use your favorite booking website and sort by the number of stars you are looking for.

EXPERIENTIAL

Bedouin camping This is like camping, but the tents and food are provided for you; many of the sites are located in Wadi Rum. Note that TripAdvisor shows them on the "specialty lodging" tab rather than under "hotels." The electives on BUCKET!'s list are: **Wadi Rum (#4)** and *Mamshit* tukul camping tent. Other popular options include Obeid's Bedouin Life Camp, Bedouin Lifestyle Camp, Rum Stars Camp, Wadi Rum Night Luxury Camp, and Wadi Rum Bedouin Camp (average $50/night).

Tzimmers/B&Bs A tzimmer (the name comes from the German word, *zimmer*) is a guesthouse, and Israelis love them. With more than 1,500 options, they can be found throughout Israel but are often hard to reserve because of unfriendly websites and a general lack of promotion. They are also not cheap, running hotel-standard prices. Tzimmers are usually located in beautiful, peaceful areas, surrounded by trees and hills. It's kind of a home-away-from-home, so you usually get the whole guesthouse. Occasionally, you may be sharing the space with the owner and get your own floor only. Sometimes food is included, but at the very least you'll get a functioning kitchen. If you're looking for budget options, this is not the place, but if you're looking to get away from city bustle, it just might do the trick. The **Tourist Israel** blog has a list of tzimmers in Israel (**w** touristisrael.com/hoteltype/zimmers-in-israel/), but the biggest collection can be found at the Hebrew-language site **w** zimmer.co.il and its sister English site, **w** zimmeril.com. It's not the easiest to navigate, sort, or quickly see the difference between places, but contains the vast majority of listings in Israel.

Ecolodges Both Israel and Jordan offer ecolodge options for the environmentally conscious traveler, but Jordan has the advantage. The most popular ecolodge in the region, and one of our electives, is **Feynan Ecolodge (#86)** in the Dana Biosphere Reserve, an hour north of Petra. Food and a variety of activities with Bedouin community members are included in your stay. If you plan to make a trip to Jordan based around nature reserves, the *Royal Society for the Conservation of Nature (RSCN)* offers accommodation in several of its biosphere/nature reserves. Most are open year-round, have private bathrooms, and offer gorgeous landscape views – visit **w** wildjordan.com/eco-tourism-section/lodging for more information on each site and to book. Desert Days, Negev Ecolodge, in Tzukim in southern Israel, uses solar panels for electricity and recycles water back to the desert, with reservations available on **w** booking.com. Also in Tzukim, Midbara offers ecolodge luxury in the middle of the desert in stark surroundings, but a homey atmosphere (**w** midbara. co.il; $200–400/night per room). For something more rustic, you could head to Nimrod's Fortress in the Golan and volunteer for building sustainable infrastructure for two to four weeks at the Nimrod Eco Lodge through GoEco (**w** goeco.org), a volunteer organization.

Glamping Glamour-camping, or **glamping**, has been adopted by several Negev and Wadi Rum sites to ease the burdens of camping by maximizing the luxury. Wadi Rum has really run away with the concept, with several options deep in the heart of the red sand desert. Our recommendations are Discovery Bedu (**w** discoverybedu.com;

$900/night per tent, including activities), Memories Aicha (w mlc.jo; $300/night per panoramic tent), and Wadi Rum Night Luxury Camp (w wadirumnightluxury.com; $250/night per bubble tent).

UNIQUE **Yurts** (large Mongolian teepees) are all the rage. Genghis Khan in the Golan is probably the most famous: check hostel websites for options. **Mud huts** are surprisingly just as popular and, given the lack of rain in the Negev, they tend to be in good shape for years and years: the w Israel21c.org blog recommends Kibbutz Neot Semadar, Essene Farm, and Khan Be'erotayim. For something completely different, the self-proclaimed "**smallest hotel in the world**," opened in 2011, is nothing more than a few blankets thrown inside a beat-up VW Beetle near **Shobak**. Nearby is a "lobby" with visitor cards, a souvenir shop, and a place the owners will serve tea (bookable on Airbnb; from 40 JD per night).

RV For a comprehensive guide to renting a camper van, or RV, in Israel, the Hebrew-language site w campingil.org.il has lots of information about the services offered at every campground with RV facilities. You can also find caravan rental options on Airbnb, though they might be stationary. Several articles that we found online cited the Hebrew-language LaOfek (w laofek.co.il) as a source of information, though there are a handful of other companies that offer the same services. Average price: $100/day. Important: you cannot cross international borders with car rentals, and you may not be allowed entry to Palestine without special permits and license plates, so it is important to discuss your options with your rental car dealer.

SUPERLATIVE LODGING Simply looking for the best hotels, as revealed by your favorite global critics? *Travel + Leisure*'s top five resort-hotels in the Middle East and Africa include the Beresheet Hotel (J2), while its top ten city-hotels in the Middle East and Africa include the Waldorf Astoria (A7), *King David Hotel*, and Four Seasons Hotel Amman. The Jaffa (D2) made *Condé Nast Traveler*'s **Hot List** for Best New Hotels in the World in 2019, the Poli House (D4) in 2017, and the *Elma Arts Complex* in Zichron Ya'akov in 2016. *The Norman Hotel* in Tel Aviv made *Condé Nast Traveler*'s **Gold List** in 2017, and *Mamilla Hotel* in Jerusalem in 2016. *Condé Nast Traveler*'s **Editors' Choice** for Favorite Hotels in the Middle East and Africa includes *The Norman Hotel* in Tel Aviv, which was also named Best Boutique Hotel by *Jetsetter Magazine* in 2015. *Jetsetter* also awarded *Brown Beach House* with a Best Design Award in 2016, while The Setai (D2) received "Best Pool Scene" in 2019.

BOOKING SITES For the easiest cancellation options, try w **booking.com**. The best reward program is at w **hotels.com** (buy ten, get one night free at the average rate of your previous ten night stays). Customer reviews are dominated by **TripAdvisor**, which also has an embedded booking aggregator tool. For the best deal, w **priceline. com** can get you a surprise hotel if you sign on to its Express Deal option: you find out the hotel once you commit the money (while receiving a heavily discounted rate).

DO #6: RESERVE IT!

Secure your **rental car**. Read the fine print to find out what you're going to need upon arrival, and whether insurance is suggested or required. Reserve your spot on any **activities that require reservations**, such as the **Western Wall Tunnels (#94)**, day tours, trips to **Petra (#2)** from Israel, or wine excursions. If you're thinking about **guided tours**, you need to make your reservations now: while some walking tours, for instance, can be booked in-country, other more elaborate trips might require several weeks' notice. For instance, a day trip to Petra would require coordination with a tour company, flight, borders, and hotel.

RENTAL CAR Renting a car for road trips within Israel or within Jordan is easy and is an invaluable time-saver. However, if you're just traveling within a two-hour radius it might not be worth the hassle and cost, in which case check out buses or get a quote for a taxi service.

You'll find most car rentals at the airports, just like anywhere else in the world. We recommend picking up your car from Ben Gurion Tel Aviv or Queen Alia Amman, but you can get cars in downtown Jerusalem, Tel Aviv, and Amman. There are also cars in Aqaba and Eilat, should you find yourself originating in those parts (or crossing the southern border). You can use your regular **driver's license** (or international driver's license), as long as it is in the Latin alphabet and was issued more than one year ago. **Prices** can be as low as $5/day, if you can find a decent deal. Sites can charge different fares for nationals of different countries, so if you're looking at an aggregator, make sure you indicate where you're from to get the corresponding price. Average prices hover around $20/day for an economy, four-door manual, no insurance included, picking up at Ben Gurion (Tel Aviv/Jerusalem) or Queen Alia International (Amman), dropping off at Ben Gurion. A three-day rental with those specs, assuming you have collision and theft coverage on your credit card (see below), would be about $56, plus fuel, liability insurance, and any other extras you may need/want (e.g., child seat, GPS). Plan a minimum of $100 for a car, and $200 if you're going to be using a lot of gas (average prices in Israel are very high, see *Driving*, p. 71).

Always read the **terms and conditions** of your rental car before you sign. This is NOT A JOKE! They are not long, and you will save yourself surprises when you get to the counter. Check for driver's license, extra fees, any required deposits, border fees, kilometer limitations, toll instructions, what happens if you get a flat tire, hours of operations (in case your flight is super early/late), etc. (If renting for a short period, you may only have 250km included. That's only 155 miles! Check the terms!) **Gas prices** obviously fluctuate all the time, so w numbeo.com is a great resource to do some calculations before your trip. At the time of writing, Jordan fluctuated between 2.65 and 3.79 JOD per gallon, averaging 3.16 JOD ($4.46). This is about 0.84 JOD ($1.20) a liter. In Israel, prices averaged 20.63–25.74 ILS per gallon, averaging 23.47 ILS ($6.89), or 6.20 ILS ($1.82) per liter. **Crossing borders** in a rental car is forbidden, and you will be turned around at the border and likely go through lengthy security questioning about what you're trying to pull. You cannot go to the Palestinian Territories or Jordan in a rental car from Israel, and vice versa. **One-way rentals** are possible (and cheap) in Jordan, but it's not recommended to enter and exit Israel from different borders, meaning you'll likely have to return to where you started anyhow.

When it comes to **insurance**, collision/damage waiver (CDW), theft protection (TP), and third-party liability are all compulsory. Your rental company will sell these at the pickup counter, or it may be included in the price of the rental. As a general policy, Visa and other credit cards do not cover Israel for CDW, which is what most people are referring to when they arrive to the rental desk and say, "No thanks, my credit card covers me." Chase Sapphire is one exception, though at time of writing it only covered CDW and TP, so you would still need to purchase liability insurance. With all other credit cards, then, assume you will need all three. For more information on car rental insurance, see w flightblitz.com/travel/car-rental-insurance-in-israel/.

DINNER RESERVATIONS As you've likely heard by now, modern Israeli cuisine is blowing up on the global scene. For such a laid-back culture, you'd think Israelis would be a bit more spontaneous with their dinner reservations. Au contraire! Popular restaurants book up weeks in advance, so planning to try your luck on a weekend will leave you trotting up and down the streets for hours. We recommend that you make the reservations in advance of your arrival. Unfortunately, there are no good reservation apps in Israel currently, so you'll have to either phone or go in person (don't worry, receptionists by and large speak English). Alternatively, you can ask your hotel front desk to call for you, but this will need to be done several days in advance. Restaurants will generally accommodate two table turnovers per evening, so you should plan on either an earlier (around 19.00) or later (around 21.00) sitting.

TripAdvisor and Google both have algorithms to figure out if a place is busy or open, and this usually works. Wannabe critics submit reviews on both sites and you can find good customer feedback that way. That said… can you get a table at one of these places without a reservation? Yes, if you work for it. You might initially be told "no," and then moments later the host/ess will concede "yes, but…" if you commit to departing within a certain amount of time (usually before the next sitting). You will be asked to leave promptly when the next party shows, so no dawdling.

In Jordan, the restaurant scene is much more casual. Some higher-end restaurants offer reservations via their websites or by calling, though most will accommodate you if you show up without a booking.

Eatwith (w eatwith.com) has a good following in Israel, offering up local kitchens, dining rooms, and small spaces to adventurous foodies looking for an intimate culinary experience. The prices can be high, but the experience will surely be unlike anything anyone else is doing. You can find Tel Aviv and Jerusalem events easily, along with a variety of other towns listed under Israel. Jordan, sadly, does not offer this service yet.

ACTIVITIES Israelis are mostly spontaneous travelers, but they'll make reservations for anything they know could get booked in advance (see *Dinner Reservations* above). Things you may want to consider booking in advance include: campgrounds; fancier restaurants; spas, B&Bs, and high-end hotels; winery tours; archaeological digs; volunteer opportunities; adventure sports and water sports during high season; once-in-a-lifetime-type experiences (e.g., a *Hot Air Balloon Ride Over Wadi Rum* or parasailing over the Dead Sea); tickets to big-name concerts; musical shows, or popular annual events (e.g., Israel Festival); cooking classes; hiking expeditions – unless part of a national park, sites will likely not have facilities set up for tourists, so bring your own water, supplies, and food; visits to some sites in the West Bank (e.g., *Sebastia-Shomron*, walking tours of Hebron, visiting refugee camps) require advance coordination with local authorities; visits to kibbutzim or moshavim that are not regularly open to tourists; bus tours; and certified tour guides and/or if you want detail beyond the basics.

In Jerusalem, activities requiring advanced planning are **Western Wall Tunnels (#94)** where guides are required, and visiting **Temple Mount (#12)** where times are limited. In Jordan, specifically, the cost-saving **Jordan Pass** discount card can only be bought in advance (see p. 60). If you're visiting Petra only for one day, you should plan your course of attack since the site is huge, *Petra by Night* is only available certain days of the week, and **Petra Kitchen (#84)** books up fast.

Luckily, the vast majority of experiences in Israel do not require a reservation, including: the vast majority of tourist sites; museums; national parks and reserves; movie theaters; casual restaurants; general guides in **Old City Jerusalem (#1)**, **Petra (#2)**,

Wadi Rum (#4), **Jericho (#26)**, and other popular sites, where you will find plenty waiting at the front entrance of a site.

Booking activities The best way to book activities is to start online, but be sure to compare prices to make sure you aren't getting ripped off: rates will vary significantly depending on what service you need. **Viator** (w viator.com) is part of TripAdvisor and offers a variety of tours, though some are exorbitantly priced. You can contact the vendor for more information, but be sure to read the fine print under "Important Info" so you understand the exclusions. **Get Your Guide** (w getyourguide.com) has fewer options, but is much cheaper than Viator. As the sites serve as repositories for guides and tours, prices will fluctuate based on the vendor. For more information on finding the right guide for you, check out *Itineraries by BUCKET! – Tailored* (p. 829).

DISCOUNT PASSES Discount passes are not as ubiquitous in this area of the world, so be sure to grab them if you qualify. The most important is the **Jordan Pass**, which will save you a ton of money – see p. 60 for more information.

DO #7: MONEY IT!

Next, we encourage you to research the economic situation in Israel and Jordan. You may find some other money-specific data useful, such as how much physical cash you will need to carry, whether you need a credit card with a chip, how to score discounts, and tipping protocol.

TRAVEL INSURANCE You are going to gloss over this part, so we'll write it in caps: MAKE SURE YOU ARE INSURED. If you get sick, how are you going to get medevac'd home? Can you afford $40,000 for a helicopter to fly you out? Can you afford a $10,000 outpatient bill for stomach flu, dehydration, a strange spider bite, or other traveler ailment? Take it from your author who worked as a consular officer in embassies around the world: people get sick *all the time*. It's true that insurance is a gamble, and there is a greater chance of not using it than using it, but one foreign hospital bill could cost more than all of the travel insurance you could possibly pay for in a lifetime.

It's imperative you **procure travel insurance prior to your departure date**, as most tour companies and cruise ships require proof of insurance prior to allowing you to board. Sometimes insurance is included with your credit card (e.g., collision damage waiver for your rental car, or lost baggage protection), but it is usually only base coverage and may come with a massive excess or deductible (i.e., the amount you must pay yourself before insurance kicks in). You can find several comparison tools online, such as w travelinsurance.com.

You could take a college course in understanding travel insurance policies, but a couple of good online resources explaining the basics are Rick Steves' coverage tips (w ricksteves.com/travel-tips/trip-planning/travel-insurance) and "Why You Should Consider Splurging for Travel Insurance" from *Condé Nast Traveler* (w cntraveler. com/stories/2015-08-06/why-you-should-consider-splurging-for-travel-insurance).

CURRENCY AND EXCHANGE RATES

Israel and Palestine Israel uses the Israeli Shekel (ILS) as currency, also called the New Israeli Shekel (NIS). This is written as "shekels" in English, but called "shkalim" in Hebrew, when pluralized. Much like there are 100 pence in a British pound, and 100 cents in a dollar, there are 100 agorot ("ah-go-wrote") in a shekel. Coins come in 10 agorot and ½, 1, 2, 5, and 10 shekels. Bills come in 20, 50, 100, and 200 shekel denominations but, as you can imagine, 200 is hard to change and should be avoided when possible. If you do end up with one or two, you can pay for large purchases, such as tour guides or expensive dinners, with 200s.

Over the last few years, the exchange rate from shekels to the dollar has hovered around 3.6, but this can spike during periods of bust and boom. From 2017 to 2018, and again in 2020, the rate was around 3.4, but was closer to 4.0 in 2015 and 2016, and dipped to 3.1 in 2021. As a consumer, the more shekels you get the better, so you're looking for the highest shekel exchange rate you can find. Think of it this way: if you are changing $100 at a rate of 3.46, you are getting 346 ILS for your $100. However, if the rate is 4.0, then you are getting 400 ILS. That's a difference of 54 ILS, which is nearly $16 at the 3.46 exchange rate. Obviously, the rate matters, but there is little you can do, other than visit several exchange facilities before settling on the one with the highest rate and lowest fee. A 3.5 exchange rate might seem difficult to calculate in your head, but just divide costs by three for a close approximation, so the 10 ILS *coin* is worth just over $3 (so pay attention when you pay for things!), the 20 ILS bill is worth around $6.50, 50 ILS around $16, 100 ILS around $33, and 200 ILS around $65.

Jordan Jordanian dinars (JD) are deceptive. They seem like they should be worth less than dollars (not because they are not beautiful, but because the country seems so much cheaper), but their currency is pegged to the dollar at a high rate, with 1 dinar actually worth about $1.40. This means when you eat in a restaurant, a meal totaling 20 dinars actually costs $28. In this sense, the dinar seems more like the euro or the British pound. One dinar is divided into either ten dirhams (think "dime"), 100 piastres or qirsh, or 1,000 fils. Coins come in ½, 1, 2½, 5, and 10 piastres, and ¼, ½, and 1 dinar, and bills come in 1, 5, 10, 20, and 50 dinars.

In practice, the dinar is mostly fixed to the US dollar at a rate of $1 = 0.709 dinar. This means that for every $100 you get nearly 71 dinars. This can be difficult to calculate for Americans, but the easiest way to remember is to equate 1 dinar to roughly $1.50, 2 dinars a little less than $3, 5 dinars around $7, 10 dinars around $14, 20 dinars around $28, and 50 dinars around $70.

Egypt Egypt uses the Egyptian pound (EGP), with a rate of roughly US$1 to 15 EGP, but British pounds and US dollars are accepted in many places in Sharm el-Sheikh.

GETTING/USING MONEY **Banks and ATMs** are both regular sights in Israel. Banks close early on Friday and holiday evenings, and are usually closed on Shabbat/Saturday. In Jordan, ATMs can run out of cash, and it's highly recommended to travel with cash, or exchange cash at one of the tellers at the border, if you're crossing from Israel. In Egypt, bring foreign currency and exchange in town. **Credit cards** are widely accepted. Chip cards are accepted, though not required (yet). **Changing money** is easy in Israel, and you can exchange money nearly everywhere – exchange agencies, post offices, banks, as well as airports and hotels, for a fee of course. If you use travelers' checks, then remember you'll need your passport, but they are not recommended in Jordan where you can find ATMs in most major cities. Cash is the better option here, as the country is not known for pickpocketing.

Israel does not place any restrictions on the quantity of money you can bring with you into the country (endless souvenir shopping!), and you can change up to $500-worth of shekels back to dollars without showing any paperwork at Ben Gurion airport, and up to $5,000 by showing your original foreign currency conversion receipts (so it doesn't seem like you earned a lot of money while you were in Israel). Jordan allows unlimited amounts of money to be imported into the country (declared), unless it's Israeli shekels, and then it's illegal. You can leave with up to 300 JD, and the same amount of other currency you declared when you came in.

You will be able to use **US dollars** in some tourist sites, such as souvenir stores in **Old City Jerusalem (#1)**, and when tipping drivers or tour guides. Other currencies may be accepted as well (14 world currencies in Israel, to be exact), though you will likely receive shekels or dinars in return.

CASH WITHDRAWALS You should use **ATMs in Israel** to withdraw cash. They are plentiful and likely have the best exchange rates (though you'll have to pay an ATM fee and whatever fee your bank charges). However, local banks will charge for cashing cashiers' checks, at a likely lower rate, so you won't save money coming "prepared" with travelers' or cashiers' checks. ATMs in Israel are not perfect, however, and can run out of cash. This is also particularly true of **ATMs in Jordan**. There are certainly plenty of banks, but the ATMs might not be stocked, particularly before holidays and weekends (Friday). **Petra** has very few ATMs. Make sure to exchange at least a little bit of cash when you cross the border, or plan to get money out at the airport upon arrival. Make sure the ATMs have the right logos: **Visa**, **Mastercard**, **AmEx**, **Cirrus**, or **PLUS**. **Citibank**, **Barclays**, and **HSBC** all have branches in Israel.

CREDIT CARD FEES With credit card charges, when prompted to either pay in your home currency (e.g., US dollars) or in local currency, you should always **pay in the local currency** because the conversion rates at your bank will almost always be better. If you want to pay with a credit card, but the company says they'll charge you 1–3% extra, should you use your credit card or pay in cash? As long as you're using a credit card with travel benefits, it's almost always smartest to pay with credit card, especially if you end up having to dispute the transaction (which you can't do with cash!).

As an example, let's do some quick math. Say a vendor wants to charge 1,000 ILS for a service, and will add 3% for credit cards. If you go to a seedy ATM with a terrible exchange rate (say, 3.2 ILS to $1), and you take out 1,000 ILS, you'll get the equivalent of $312.50, minus any bank fees (let's say $5). If you use your credit card, and you get the standard 3.4 ILS to $1, plus a 3% fee, then you'll be paying $294.12 for the service plus 30 ILS (3% fee) which is $8.82, for a total of $302.94. The credit card saves you almost $15, gives you a bit of added security, and possibly cash back or reward points for travel expenses.

Naturally, this figure is going to change a bit depending on the exchange rate. Our recommendation: pay with a credit card, one without a foreign transaction fee, one with rewards, and select "pay in local currency."

TRAVEL CREDIT CARDS If your credit card is worth its weight in gold electives, it will offer "no foreign transaction fees." Not sure? Check with your bank. Even if your bank's credit card doesn't offer travel rewards, we recommend you apply for a travel-specific credit card. Every year, The Points Guy offers up a ton of suggestions for which cards offer the best reward points (w thepointsguy.com/guide/best-rewards-credit-cards/), and w mint.intuit.com offers a similar service, offering you suggestions based on what you spend your money on. The **best all-around travel credit cards** would appear to be Chase Sapphire Preferred and Sapphire Reserve, American Express Platinum, and Capital One Venture Rewards. Some other possible benefits include: huge signing bonuses; elite status on airlines and at hotel groups; Global Entry/TSA PreCheck application fee credit; travel insurance; expense eraser; double or triple points for travel-related expenses; and airport lounge access. Whether or not the fees are worth it depends on how much you travel. If you travel less frequently, perhaps try the Capital One or Chase, which are under $100 a year and might even have "first year free" plus sign-up bonuses when you apply.

VAT REFUNDS In Israel, you can claim VAT on items worth more than 400 ILS. To do so, you need your entry visa (blue entry ticket), goods designated as "VAT Refundable" inside sealed bags, and the original receipts. It's not for the faint of heart. In Jordan, goods must be more than 50 JD and must not be food, accommodation, gold, or mobile phones. Visit *Do #17: Shop It!* (p. 100) for more information on VAT refunds.

DISCOUNT CARDS/PASSES Be sure to book the **Jordan Pass** (w jordanpass.jo) before you arrive. It is the premiere pass in the Holy Land, offering access to nearly every major site in Jordan (exceptions are the free/public sites of the **Dead Sea (#3)** and **Red Sea (#10)**). The pass is essentially all-inclusive, with two choices. First, you have to decide how many days you want to stay in **Petra (#2)** – one, two, or three – at 5 JD difference each (70, 75, and 80 JD, respectively). Second, you can add on **Bethany-Beyond-the-Jordan (#41)**, where Jesus was baptized for an additional 8 JD. You also save on the visa/tourist fee at the border if you stay at least three nights – which is a *huge* saving. The visa alone is 40 JD ($55). The Jordan Pass is worthwhile if you plan to visit two or three other sites and provides great savings if you plan on doing a week in Jordan.

Alternatively, you can visit Petra without the pass. Current prices are 50, 55, and 60 JD for one-, two-, or three-day visits, respectively. If you compare this with the Jordan Pass, you'll see that the Jordan Pass is the better deal if you plan on visiting any other sites in Jordan and/or you will be staying three or more nights. For Petra, if you're debating whether to get one or two days, definitely get two because there's enough to keep even those of modest interest busy and entertained over two days. And if you're debating between two and three, go with three – it affords you the most flexibility, allowing time to do *Petra by Night* one evening (supplemental cost), an all-day hiking experience the following day, and then a 06.00 sunrise jaunt to the Treasury on the third day. The price difference is only 5 JD, so better to be safe. Also included in the price are **Wadi Rum (#4)**, **Jerash (#14)**, **Ancient Amman (#37)**, **Madaba (#19)**, **Karak (#49)**, and the **Desert Palaces (#20)** – all of which should be on your bucket list!

The **Israel National Park Pass** (w parks.org.il/en/article/money-saving-tickets/) comes in three levels: Blue card (three sites over two weeks, 78 ILS); Green card (six sites over two weeks, 110 ILS); and Orange card (unlimited sites over two weeks, 150 ILS). All multi-site tickets include entrance to **Masada (#8)** and **Caesarea (#25)**, but not the *City of David* (Jerusalem Walls NP), nor the cable car at Masada. A variety of other types of cards are valid for one or two years, with discounts for bigger families (see w parks.org.il).

If you plan to spend a fair amount of time in Tel Aviv, and don't feel like walking the entire time, you can get to know the **Tel-O-Fun bikeshare system** (w tel-o-fun.co.il/en/), which has 2,000 bikes in over 200 stations. You'll have to pay an access charge (17 ILS per day, 48 ILS for three days, 70 ILS per week, or 280 ILS per year) and then the first 30 minutes are free, but thereafter you have to pay 6 ILS up to 60 minutes, increasing every 30 minutes.

The **Israel Museum** (w www.imj.org.il/en/content/ticket-info) offers discounts for seniors, students, children under 18, and disabled visitors. For everyone else, come back a second time within three months, save your ticket, and you'll get 50% off the next visit.

The **Jewish Quarter card** (w rova-yehudi.org.il/en/) gives you nine attractions for 100 ILS, including Hurva Synagogue (A4), both northern and southern **Ramparts Walk (#91)** tours, *Wohl Archaeological Museum*, Burnt House, and Zedekiah's Cave (A6), along with a pastry, parchment, and an audio guide.

Finally, flash a **student card** (half the time you can probably just say you're a student and you'll get the discount) at museums or when booking tours and you can get anywhere from 10% to 50% off. You can also get discounts on buses and trains if you're studying in Israel. See w egged.co.il/Article-794,1421-Students.aspx for more information.

TIPPING

Israel It is usual to add a 10–15% tip in restaurants, or a few shekels (usually 10+%) to a bartender, but check if a service charge has already been levied. Hotel baggage porters will expect small change, but the fancier the hotel, the higher you should tip (5 ILS is about $1.25). Hotel maids should be tipped 5–10 ILS per night at the beginning of the stay. Small change will be appreciated for deliveries, but there is no need to tip taxi drivers and it is not expected at spas. A tour guide should be tipped 15% and a tour driver half that amount (but don't combine the tips).

Jordan In restaurants, check if a service charge (10%) has already been added, and add 10% if not. Bartender will expect small change, hotel baggage porters 1–2 JD per bag, and hotel maids 2 JD per night at the beginning of the stay. Round up a taxi fare to the next JD, and give small change for deliveries. Spas will likely have a service charge, but otherwise a small amount is appreciated. A tip might be expected for tour guides, but let your travel coordinator do the arranging. If you've self-coordinated, you'll pay based on the length of the tour: something short, such as a camel ride, will be a pre-negotiated fare, but a scuba dive with guide for the whole day would be 5 or 10 JD, depending on the service. If multiple people are in attendance, pay 15–25 JD. Tip a tour driver half the amount that you're planning to tip the guide (but don't combine the tips).

Egypt Tipping is a big part of Egyptian culture. It's also likely that you'll be challenged for the amount you tip, which is part of the experience! Stick to the following amounts and politely refuse any requests for more. In restaurants, tip 10% regardless of whether there is a service charge, and give small change to your bartender. Hotel baggage porters should expect 3–5 EGP per bag, hotel maids 5–10 EGP per night, and hotel breakfast attendants 5–10 EGP per meal. No tip is necessary for taxi drivers, but have small change ready for deliveries and add 15% at spas. Tour guides really vary in Egypt, so if you're getting great service, consider a more European-size tip. If the person is merely walking you to a site, however, 50 EGP is probably sufficient. Tip a tour driver half the amount that you're planning to tip the guide (but don't combine the tips).

DO #8: PACK IT!

Need a bathing suit, new towel, travel container for your shampoo and sunscreen? Now's the time to buy those last-minute **travel essentials**. Get your bags ready: carry-ons, check-ins, and toiletries kit. Put your passport, visa, and vaccine history (if applicable) together.

PACKING FOR THE HOLY LAND The smartest packing list we've seen comes from SmarterTravel (**w** smartertravel.com/the-ultimate-packing-list/) and allows you to decide what's most important for your trip. It also has specific lists for beach vacations, cruises, and foreign trips. Remember, this region is: often hot; rarely rains; rarely dips below freezing; requires a bathing suit; offers tons of hiking opportunities; has some fancier restaurants, though suits are never required; and requires a fair amount of walking at tourist sites. You're going to want to *start* packing a week in advance. You don't have to pack everything, but you should start getting everything ready. Do laundry. Get out your packing cubes. Dust off your luggage. Then, no later than 24 hours in advance of your flight, you're going to do your real packing. Don't wait until you get to the airport to realize you've overpacked. Yes, Israel can be warm if you're going to the beach, and Jordan can be cold if you're camping in the desert, but you don't want to pack three suitcases of options either. Be wise – check out our tips for packing and getting organized so you can realistically anticipate your needs.

CLOTHES Time to pack! First things first, **check the weather**. And the climate (see our climate charts at **w** buckettravelguides.com/climate-charts). It's unlikely that it's going to rain. Yes it's possible you could be visiting on the two days a year it rains without stopping, but it really is rare. In **winter**, then, you'll need long sleeves and pants, maybe a jacket and umbrella, and sweaters in the evening. You likely won't need a coat, though it has been known to snow once every couple of years in Jerusalem, but you will need snow gear if you're going skiing on Hermon. In the **spring**, rain can continue until April or so, but sporadically. Most days will be very pleasant but maybe not Mediterranean-swim-ready, though lots of northern Europeans would disagree, so bring clothes for 70°F/20°C weather. Evenings are generally a bit cooler, but mild, and Jerusalem tends to be a bit cooler still. **Summer** gets progressively hotter and more humid towards August, with no rain. Shorts and T-shirts (or less) are popular in Tel Aviv; it's more conservative in Jerusalem and Jordan, though tourists will be in shorts. Even so, you'll need to be appropriately covered to get in religious sites. Finally, **fall** has beautiful weather (no rain yet), and is probably still okay for the beach as the water remains warm.

Types of clothes to consider are: beach/bathing suits; layers for cooler evenings; rain attire, if appropriate (particularly December to February); hiking gear (shoes, possibly a walking stick) if going to Negev or Petra for more than a day-walk; clothes to cover the shoulders and legs (men and women) and head (women); and possibly workout clothes for hotel or outdoor gyms. Nightclubs tend to be very informal, so you don't need anything special. Restaurants are also fairly casual, except in high-end luxury restaurants. Even the "modern cuisine" restaurants in Tel Aviv and Jerusalem will be pretty informal.

You will *not* want to shop in Israel or Jordan for everyday necessities, such as underwear and socks. Clothes in Israel are expensive, and there aren't any large department stores to get all your sundries.

APPS **Spotted by Locals** (**w** spottedbylocals.com/telaviv/) has guides to several dozen cities, including Tel Aviv, with curators who provide off-the-beaten-path and anti-tourist options for the rebels out there. Tips for bars, music venues, places to relax, snacks, and artsy venues will give you days and days of activities, and might just help you meet some locals. Free online, but $4 for each city guide. "Skip the tourist traps" says **Like A Local** (**w** likealocalguide.com), which has offline suggestions for Tel Aviv, while Jerusalem and Amman can be found on the website. **Viator** (**w** viator. com) offers plenty of day-trip tour options that you can peruse, see rankings, and get quick price quotes. If you can download in advance, then you can skip the data and roaming charges and still get hours of audio tour for the Old City in the **Jerusalem Audio Walking Tours** app.

DO #9: READY IT!

We know: a checklist buried in another checklist – tricky! But before you depart, use this final departure sheet to make sure you're ready to go! Get excited!

1. Completely pack your bags at least 24 hours before you leave for the airport. Do not leave it for the day you are supposed to leave. This gives your brain time to work out anything it's forgotten.
2. Set your out-of-office at work. Congrats! You're on vacation!
3. Check in for your flight.
4. Register the trip with your credit card companies to avoid fraud alerts.
5. Register the trip with your embassy in-country.

6. Leave your itinerary with family/friends.
7. Empty your fridge and take out the trash. Wash dishes and put everything away. Come home to a clean house.
8. Power down and unplug your computer, and any other electrical devices at home.
9. Turn off your air conditioning or heating, or set them so that it's not an icebox/sauna when you get back.
10. Drop your keys off with neighbor/friend to check mail/water plants.
11. Drop off your pet/children with caretakers.
12. Download books, movies, or games to your phone/device.
13. Charge your phone and a power bank, especially if your airline seat does not have a charger/outlet.
14. Set out all of your travel essentials: passport, (printed?) visa, wallet, headphones, neck pillow, eye mask, etc.
15. Take out your comfy airport/airplane clothes and fold them neatly on top of your dresser.
16. Prepack your toiletries kit – though you might need some things, leave everything you need on the counter. Don't put anything away.
17. Weigh your check-in and your carry-on. Are you under the maximum? Don't be that person at the airport trying to distribute 2kg from here to there.
18. If you're leaving early in the morning, set at least two alarms, five minutes apart. Put your alarm on the other side of the room so you have to get out of bed to turn it off.
19. Prebook your taxi to the airport (if needed), giving yourself at least two hours (small airport) to three hours (big airport or holiday) to work your way through departure protocols.
20. Turn off all lights, close windows, lock doors.

Part 3

Arrival and Orientation

DO #10: ENTER IT!

ISRAEL

Immigration It is true that some countries will not allow you entry if they find an Israeli stamp in your passport. Luckily, Israel has mostly phased out the passport stamp, in favor of a **blue entry ticket**. This paper ticket serves the same purpose as a visa: it lists your allowed period of stay, has your photo and passport number, and you must keep it until you depart the country. During your exit interview (unfamiliar to Americans, but normal for most other countries), you may be asked to present the visa/entry card to prove you are leaving the country. So don't lose it!

Upon entering, it's also possible that Israel may pull you aside for additional questioning. The only "trick" is to be prepared to answer basic questions about your travel. Immigration officials may ask you to show text messages from your phone, share your social media passwords, and provide names and details of anyone you plan on visiting – particularly if your plans take you straight to the West Bank. If you have something to hide, you'll get turned around: the Israelis protect their homeland ferociously and will not waste time trying to figure out what you are hiding.

If you are pulled aside, anecdotal stories indicate this process can take upwards of 4 hours, though some have stories of waiting an entire day. Most of the time, Israel will not keep you overnight. You'll usually be allowed to make a phone call. You may want to contact your **embassy**, who may in turn be able to contact your loved ones if you can't get hold of them yourself. Special note: your Embassy cannot help you gain entry/access to another sovereign nation. Every country decides its own security protocol and can turn away anyone it feels threatens the peace, sovereignty, or security of that nation.

If you are **denied entry**, you'll receive a letter with very little information, usually indicating that your denial was based on reasons related to security or immigrant intent, though it can be for any reason established by the immigration official at the port of entry. You will then likely board the next flight to the last location from where you entered Israel. Note that you will probably not get a ticket all the way back home: if you had a stopover in Europe, Turkey, or similar, they'll send you as far as the stopover point, and you'll have to work out with the airlines how to get home the rest of the way.

Those with **Palestinian heritage** may be denied entry at Ben Gurion, as all Palestinians are supposed to enter through Allenby Bridge. Even if you are not a Palestinian citizen or resident, if your parents or grandparents are on the Palestinian registry, and you have a *potential* claim to Palestinian nationality, you could also be on this registry and would be required to enter through Allenby via Jordan. This rule applies even to those with passports from countries without prearranged visa requirements, such as the USA and Europe.

Any **dual-national Israelis** entering Israel should be aware of the requirement that all Israelis **serve in the military**. You may be granted admission if you haven't completed this requirement, but if you are at or past military age, you will not be allowed to *leave* the country until you've completed the requirement or served a (not short) period in jail. If this might apply to you, you *must* request an exemption from your local Israel embassy prior to arriving in Israel.

A **Palestinian Areas Authority-only stamp** is issued for those who are *not* granted access to Israel or the shared city of Jerusalem. If you have any doubts about your eligibility to enter Israel, you should consult with the Israeli Embassy in your home country, or nearest country (**w** embassies.gov.il/Pages/IsraeliMissionsAroundTheWorld.aspx).

Customs For detailed information about customs requirements upon entry to Israel, visit **w** gov.il/en/departments/guides/guide-tourist-customs. There it lists the types of things you don't have to declare, and can use the green channel to sail through, including (one) tent, camping equipment, sporting equipment, (one) bicycle, personal computers, jewelry, musical instruments, and cameras. If you have any questions about importation of goods into Israel, try the government's Personal Import Guide (**w** gov.il/en/departments/guides/personal_import).

Ben Gurion Airport You'll first realize you are nearing Ben Gurion Airport about 45 minutes prior to landing. Flight regulations do not permit passengers to stand up on the plane while in Israeli airspace, so you'll hear a few announcements reminding you to stay seated. Unlike in the USA (but much like Europe), you don't have a **customs form** to fill out prior to arrival. Instead, you'll declare anything valuable in person before leaving the airport. When you land, you'll taxi briefly and should park at a gate in **Terminal 3**. If you are flying with a budget airline, you may park at the correct terminal, but without a gate. In this case, you'll all exit the plane and board buses that will take you to the terminal. Terminal 1 is used for processing departures but not arrivals, so if you do land at Terminal 1, again you'll be shuttled to Terminal 3. Terminal 2 doesn't exist any longer. This all means that Terminal 3 should be the only terminal you access. All taxis will pick up from there. There is **no duty free** upon arrival.

On arrival in the terminal, you will ascend escalators and begin walking towards immigration. Along the passage – often at the top of the escalators – are **security agents** who are looking for anything peculiar. Don't be alarmed if they stop you. If you are traveling alone, look flustered, or simply do not look Israeli, they may pull you aside to ask you questions before you've even gotten to immigration. This is a heavily militarized and risk-averse society, so they aren't taking any chances. Be honest and polite.

You'll continue down long corridors before reaching **immigration**. Israeli passport holders stand in the middle, and foreigners stand on the right (there are signs). Biometric passport entry options are for Israeli passport holders only, so foreigners need to stand in line to talk to an **immigration official**. Assuming you're successful, you'll get a three-month entry visa (at no cost) in short order. Lines can be quite long – 30 minutes or longer – but move quickly. Israel no longer stamps passports. Instead, you'll be given a **blue entry ticket** with your arrival information. You should keep this because it's your visa, and is needed for the electronic departure machines as you exit immigration.

Once past immigration, you can retrieve your **luggage**. Look for your carousel on the screens. If in Hebrew, just wait – they will change to English eventually. If your luggage is missing, there are kiosks to help you register any missing pieces. Following luggage, make your way through **customs**. If you have anything to declare (money over 100,000 ILS, for example), you'll follow the red signs. Nothing to declare, the green signs. There are a few seated customs officials who randomly pick travelers to screen. If you are selected, just put your bag on the conveyor belt and pick it up on the other side. There's no use arguing. The service industry is not well established in Israel, so do not expect a "please" or a "thank you."

Once through, you have entered the **arrival hall, or Level G**. Guests are not allowed to cross the barriers, so you will meet your waiting party past the mark on the floor. In this part of the airport, your options for **food** are limited. There is a coffee shop and a snack store. The arrival hall is the lowest floor. Here, and on every floor, there are **currency exchange** and **ATM machines** available for cash withdrawals. There is **free Wi-Fi**. In the arrivals hall, you can purchase a **Rav-Kav card** if you plan to take buses in Israel. If you're **renting a car**, the companies are located in the arrival hall, with cars parked in the garage across the street, usually the "Orchard" garage. More information can be found at w ifly.com/ben-gurion-airport/terminal-map.

You can organize a **VIP service** to fast-track your arrival through immigration, baggage, and customs – Tourist Israel organizes a convenient service through its website (w touristisrael.com/tours/vip-arrival-assistance-service-at-ben-gurion-airport/).

Ground transportation Once you've exited the airport at Arrivals (Level G), you have a few options. The airport provides explain its transport options at w iaa.gov.il/en/airports/ben-gurion/directions/directions-list/.

Train The train is located on the lowest level, Level S, below the arrival hall. It is fast and has free Wi-Fi, but you can wait upwards of an hour between trains. They go to Tel Aviv, the north, the south, and Jerusalem. The trip to Tel Aviv or to Jerusalem is less than 20 minutes, but the train leaves you on the outskirts of either city so you likely will still have to take a bus/sherut/taxi to get to your hotel, and is not the most convenient for those staying downtown. It is, however, cheap, with tickets approximately 16 ILS to Tel Aviv and 24 ILS to Jerusalem. A map can be found at w rail.co.il/en/pages/stationsnlines.aspx.

Shuttle As you leave the airport, the shuttle stops are right in front of you. For shuttles to Tel Aviv, there are bad reviews and high costs. At these prices, we recommend taking a taxi, which for two people costs the same as a shuttle, but with direct and immediate service. Public Bus 485 (17.50 ILS, cash only) provides an hourly service to Jerusalem every day except Shabbat. It stops at 218 Yafo/Jaffa Street, near the Jerusalem Central Station. TouristIsrael.com provides a great summary of the Hebrew-language bus site at w touristisrael.com/bus-ben-gurion-airport-jerusalem/20176/.

Sherut Right outside, you have the option of taking a shared taxi, or *sherut*, which will take you to Jerusalem or Haifa. They wait until ten people have filled before leaving, but can be much cheaper than a taxi. To Jerusalem, expect to spend 80 ILS.

Taxi Do not take a taxi from someone in the arrival hall – you will get ripped off. Lines are usually short and begin right outside the Arrival Hall doors on Level G. The queue begins next to the taxi kiosk. You can put your destination into one of the electronic kiosks to get an approximate fare. There are extras for luggage, additional persons, after-hours fares, etc. Taxis to downtown Tel Aviv should run to 120–175 ILS; to Jerusalem, around 200 ILS.

Rideshare apps You can now reserve cars from either Uber or Gett upon arrival at Ben Gurion. In theory, they're cheaper than those in the taxi line because Gett won a competition for the route. Uber is reportedly the same taxis as those in the taxi line.

Crossing to Israel from Jordan
Arriving via King Hussein (Allenby) If you've heard horror stories, you're not alone. The Mad Traveler (w themadtraveler.com) has compiled experiences from several travelers about crossing between the two countries into one blog entry, and updates regularly. First, you should understand that you will be going through two independent and separate border crossings (Israel = "Allenby"; Jordan = "King Hussein") Both countries have their own entry and exit protocols which you must

follow. While it should go without saying, it bears repeating that both countries are sovereign nations and have final say in who enters their country. Don't take the opening/closing times of the border checkpoints as gospel; both sides can close for any unforeseen reason. Here are the basic steps: on the Jordan side, you'll start by paying departure tax to Jordan, if owed. If you've stayed longer than one day, you will likely be asked to pay 10 JD exit tax. Leave your passport and board the bus to cross to Israel – your passport will be returned to you on the bus. You must then pay to board the bus and for any extra baggage (7.50 JD plus 1.50 JD for each bag). On the Israeli side, your bags will be scanned and searched. You'll then speak with an Israel immigration official, and if you require a visa, you'll present it now. If approved, you'll get a blue entry ticket, which equates to your passport entry stamp, and you can then change money at the exchange booth before the exit. Taxis and buses are waiting right outside to take you to Jerusalem, 50km away.

Arriving via Wadi Araba (Yitzhak Rabin) If you plan to exit Jordan via the Wadi Araba border crossing (near Aqaba, Jordan) and cross into Israel via the Yitzhak Rabin border crossing (near Eilat, Israel), you will need to pay departure tax to Jordan, if owed. If you've stayed longer than one day, you will likely be asked to pay 10 JD exit tax. Walk to the next window where you'll receive an exit stamp. Once finished, you can walk yourself to the Israeli border, which is allowed and takes only five minutes. Once at the Yitzhak Rabin crossing, your bags will be scanned and searched. You speak with an Israel immigration official and, if approved, you'll get a blue entry ticket, which equates to your passport entry stamp. You'll also have to get clearance from customs, which is in an unmarked booth next to the immigration officials. You can change money at the exchange booth at one of the last windows. Finally, there are taxis and buses right outside to take you to Eilat, 5km away.

JORDAN
Immigration and visa on arrival US citizens can visit **w** travel.state.gov or the US Embassy in Amman's webpage (**w** jo.usembassy.gov) for more information on entry requirements for Americans, though this information is subject to change at any moment. **Jordanian visas** can usually be obtained upon entry if flying into Amman or crossing at the Sheikh Hussein/Jordan River Border Crossing in this lesser-used point in the north of Israel and Jordan. Check to make sure your country is permitted on-arrival visas (**w** international.visitjordan.com/generalinformation/entryintojordan.aspx). At present, single-entry visas for one month are 40 JD, double-entry for two months are 60 JD, and multiple-entry visas for six months are 120 JD. Instead of a single-entry visa, you also have the option of purchasing a **Jordan Pass**, which grants access to Petra and dozens of sites around the country, and waives the single-entry visa fee. That's a no-brainer. The catch is you have to purchase this *in advance* and, to waive the visa fee, you have to stay a minimum of three nights, arrive via Queen Alia Airport, the Sheikh Hussein/Jordan River Border Crossing, or the Wadi Araba/Yitzhak Rabin Border Crossing and enter/exit from the same border point (see *Discount Cards/Passes*, p. 60).

Crossing from Israel Just like with Israel, remember crossing at a land border means you are dealing with two different sets of immigration officials. They don't communicate or coordinate, so don't assume that they know you're coming or that your paperwork will magically work in Jordan because it passed muster in Israel. Be courteous and patient, and if you are waiting an excessive amount of time (>1 hour), there's no harm in inquiring politely.

Arriving via Allenby (King Hussein) Jordan does *not* give entry visas at the King Hussein border crossing, so you must already have your visa in hand (the Jordan Pass visa fee exemption does *not* work here) to use this crossing. Though you might think this the most convenient tourist crossing point, this is the principal entry point for Palestinians. In practice, this means long lines, arriving early, and waiting for buses. Here's the procedure: on the Israeli side, your bags will be scanned and searched. Pay your exit tax to Israel, which is 179 ILS at the time of writing. Speak with an Israel immigration official to get out-processed. You should be prepared to present your blue entry ticket, and then you'll be given a pink exit card. You can change money at the exchange booth before the exit. This is a good idea, because ATMs aren't 100% reliable in Jordan. You'll board the bus to the Jordan side (7.50 JD plus 1.50 JD per bag), which won't leave until it's full so you may have to wait. Once you arrive at the Jordan side, you will pass through immigration/customs. As noted above, you must already be in possession of a visa. The scene will be chaotic and it may be difficult to understand what is going on, but the process is actually not that complicated. You just need to get your visa checked by an immigration official, who will stamp your passport. Once finished, there are taxis right outside to take you to Amman or Petra. They will cost a lot more than you might think (upwards of $50 to Amman, and more still to Petra), and be prepared to pay in cash/dinars.

Arriving via Yitzhak Rabin (Wadi Araba) If you wish to exit Israel at the Yitzhak Rabin border crossing (near Eilat, Israel side) and enter Jordan at the Wadi Araba border crossing (near Aqaba, Jordan side), you need a visa in advance. Visas are officially no longer offered upon arrival at Wadi Araba, but there are two exceptions: Israelis on a registered tour group (see w international.visitjordan.com/page/21/border) and **Jordan Pass** holders, which we recommend you carry (see above). That said, some tourists have reported obtaining visas for 40 JD at this border. Eilat is a long way from Jerusalem, so taking the risk is probably not worth it. You can park rental cars at the Israeli side, or you can take an expensive taxi from Eilat (you'll be initially quoted around 50 ILS, but bargain down because it's less than 10 minutes). The steps for exiting Israel and entering Jordan begin at Yitzhak Rabin. First, you can change money at the exchange booth at one of the first windows. This is a good idea, because ATMs aren't 100% reliable in Jordan. You'll also have to get clearance from customs and pay the exit fee. This unmarked booth is next to the immigration officials, but you'll be shooed to the right place if you can't find it. Right now, most foreigners pay 101 ILS but fees can change, so for the official price see w iaa.gov.il/en/land-border-crossings/yitzhak-rabin/fees/. You'll then speak with an Israel immigration official, and present your visa and/or blue entry ticket. If approved, you'll get a pink exit ticket. Your bags will be scanned and/or searched by customs. You can then take the 5-minute walk to the Jordanian border crossing. Don't forget to take your patience pill before arriving because this part can get frustrating, as windows are numbered strangely. You may have to go back to the same counter three or more times, and rules change all the time. Start at the visa window – officials will tell you which window is open that day. Pay attention to signage: those with the Jordan Pass will have certain requirements in order to get the visa fee waived. Once complete, there are taxis and buses right outside to take you to Aqaba (11km) for 11 JOD.

EGYPT
Crossing from Israel The Taba border crossing point is intended for Israelis and foreigners and can be accessed 24 hours a day. Taxis can be arranged from the

Taba border in advance through your hotel, or use a shared or private taxi waiting at the circle when you pass through the border. Fares for private taxis run about 400 EGP/$25 to Dahab (2 hours).

DO #11: TRANSPORT IT!

DRIVING Israelis and Jordanians both drive on the right-hand side of the road. The local driving style is not reckless: by and large, drivers are good and licensed in both countries. Most people drive around 80–90km/h on highways, which is a reasonable pace. Work days are Sunday through Thursday, with some people working a half-day on Friday. Evening rush hours can be brutal when driving south to Tel Aviv or east to Jerusalem, but Friday and Saturday are often blissfully free of cars. Be careful that you don't drive through an Orthodox neighborhood or your car may get stoned.

Roads in Israel are generally in excellent condition: potholes are rare, and speed bumps are only found in school zones. Major highways in Jordan are also good, though Google may lead you to believe that some slow, rural roads are actually highways. You'll also find plenty of speed bumps in Jordan, but few potholes. Lanes are medium-sized and comfortable enough for your car, but beware strange merges – you may find that roads suddenly become left-turn-only lanes with no warning. Locals will try to merge quickly back in when faced with the same dilemma.

Traffic lights are red, yellow, and green. Red and yellow together indicates that the light is about to turn green: you have about one second, and if your foot isn't already on the gas pedal, everyone behind you will let you know it. Before a light turns yellow, it will often flash green a few times. The essential driving rules are: NO right turn on red; U-turns are okay; use your blinker, but don't be offended if others don't; honking is permissible; and traffic signals are to be obeyed. In Israel, signs are generally in Hebrew, English, and Arabic. In Jordan, they are in Arabic and English.

Traffic police are practically nonexistent in Israel, but if you get in an accident they will show up if there are injuries. In Jordan, you may get flagged down by a police officer for a routine "check." Be extremely polite and friendly and you will hopefully not have to pay a bribe. Be aware of your speed limit in any event. You must have a passport in order to pass through checkpoints, and your car must also be allowed to enter. Rental cars are almost uniformly banned from crossing borders. Insurance, at the very least, is nullified, if you go from, say, Israel to the Palestinian Territories. Either way, you will need your passport, and rental/owner papers.

In Jordan, there are few rules and no parking meters. As long as your car doesn't block in anyone else, you can likely park there. However, in Israel, there are far more parking rules to be aware of. There are a few sidewalk norms: first, Israelis park on the sidewalk, but that does not mean you can. Second, be aware of the colors: blue and white stripes indicate there is a parking meter, which is usually free in evenings and on Shabbat; red and white stripes indicate a "no parking" zone; red and gray must be researched – check the signs (which are likely in Hebrew); red and yellow is for public transportation, and is also "no parking"; and no markings/no colors indicate free parking. Most street parking requires paying by app, or with exact change. In big building complexes (malls), you should be able to pay with a credit card or with high-denomination bills and receive change. There are several parking apps, and they vary by location. Some are only available in the Israel app store and/or are only in Hebrew, so you might be stuck when using a garage. Parking lots/garages provide ample places to park your car, many with kiosks that allow you to use a credit card. Closer to the beach means more expensive.

The World Health Organization reports that Israel recorded 333 fatalities in 2019, while Jordan had closer to 1,700 – that's 3.9 fatalities per 100,000 persons in Israel, and 17 fatalities per 100,000 people for Jordan. Seat belts and motorcycle helmets are mandatory in both countries. Mobile phone use is prohibited while driving, and random breath tests are carried out. Child restraints are required in Israel. The official speed limits for urban areas are 50km/h in Israel and 90km/h in Jordan; 80km/h and 120km/h respectively in rural areas; and 110km/h and 120km/h respectively on motorways. However, speed limits are not ubiquitously posted so they may be lower than you think. Roadside signs (and Waze) indicate when a speed trap is ahead. By law, you cannot drive in Israel or Jordan without insurance. There are three mandatory insurance clauses: collision/damage waiver, theft protection, and third-party liability. You must show proof of coverage for each before you can drive, or otherwise purchase local coverage (see *Rental Car*, p. 54).

Israel does not have access to gas lines from its wealthy oil-rich neighbors, so fuel prices are exorbitant – about $2/liter ($7/gallon). By contrast, in Jordan, prices are about $0.70/liter ($2.65/gallon). Gas stations are plentiful and easy to spot in Israel, less plentiful in Jordan (but they do have big buildings), and practically nonexistent in the West Bank. Most cars take 90 or 95 octane fuel at the pump. If you don't read Hebrew, you won't be able to use the Israeli credit card machine when paying for gas because it asks for your ID number (which tourists don't have) and license plate number, so it is best to pay the attendant first. Be aware that foreign credit cards may have a 200 ILS limit ($60) at the pump, while most car tanks need more than this to fill up.

Waze is by far the most used and useful of all traffic apps in Israel. It is an Israeli creation, headquartered in Herziliya Pituach, north of Tel Aviv, and although Google bought it in 2013, their results are still different. Users regularly post speed traps, police officers, vehicles on the road, haze, light/medium/heavy traffic, etc. It also offers options for avoiding Palestinian Territories, dirt roads, highways, and other routing options based on your needs. **Google Maps** has its limitations. It works in Israel, but the distance between sites in Jordan can be misleading, at best, and rerouting due to new roads is common. There's not really a good option yet there, so you'll need to find your inner yogi while driving in Jordan. Also, pay attention to road signs.

If you plan to spend a fair amount of time in Tel Aviv, and don't feel like walking the entire time, you can get to know the **Tel-O-Fun bikeshare system**, which has 2,000 bikes in over 200 stations (see p. 60). There are, of course, bike trails as well, which we cover in *Active – Land Sports – Biking* (p. 550).

BUSES

Israel Buses are a very popular form of transportation in Israel, with nearly 1 million people using them a day. They're equally popular for long-term travel between cities. The official government site is w bus.gov.il, while the best overview is at WikiVoyage (w en.wikivoyage.org/wiki/Public_transit_in_Israel). The two main **bus companies** in Israel are Egged (w egged.co.il/HomePage.aspx) and Dan (w dan.co.il). Egged operates everywhere, while Dan operates primarily in the greater Tel Aviv metropolitan area (Gush Dan). Haifa uses Superbus/Metronit and has three lines: red/blue/green (w metronit.co.il/pdf/english_brochure.pdf). Regardless, you can search for routes and schedules for all lines at w bus.co.il/otobusimmvc/en. Some trips can be booked online: for example, Egged's website lets you purchase tickets to Eilat and the Dead Sea region (Masada, Ein Gedi, various hotels).

The prepaid **Rav-Kav card** is used by most long-distance buses, and should be considered for anyone seeking to travel by light rail or inter-city rail. The card can be obtained from the airport right when you arrive, or from a train station, a Tourist Information Center, or a Rav-Kav Service Station (w ravkavonline.co.il/en/store/service-stations/). Only Israeli citizens are allowed to purchase a Personal Rav-Kav card, while tourists can purchase an Anonymous Rav-Kav, and save 20% on multi-trip tickets. Alternatively, if you are taking an inner-city bus, you may be able to purchase one directly from the driver for 10.90 ILS, which includes the cost of the card and the one-way journey. There must be enough credit on the card to cover your journey, so you can top up either at a service station, through the Rav-Kav Online app, the HopOn app, or through the website using a complicated USB card reader method.

On Dan, the standard fare is 5.90 ILS in the metropolitan areas of Haifa, Tel Aviv, Beer Sheva, and Jerusalem, with discounts for senior citizens, students, military, etc. It is worthwhile spending some time reading the English-language instructional pamphlet (w pti.org.il/docs/english.pdf), which explains zones, weekly and monthly passes, traveling between metropolitan regions, and creating "travel passes." Bus stops should be designated with a yellow flag and the bus number.

Only Haifa and Tiberias have lines that run on **Shabbat**, so your alternative options include sheruts in Haifa and Tel Aviv, and to/from the airport to Jerusalem. You may also find taxis in Jerusalem, and elsewhere.

It is worth remembering that sheruts (see below) run essentially the same routes as buses, but have fewer passengers, charge slightly less, and drive faster (but can take longer to fill up before departing).

Jordan Jordan doesn't abide by the same rules as Israel, and travelers are left without great information to map out their trips. You can certainly get bus timetables and routes, which are rarely followed, and may have you criss-crossing the country to get from one adjacent town to another (getting from Dana to Petra, for instance, might have you going first to Aqaba). Most buses only run once a day, and most long-distance buses will only leave in the morning. Fares are cheap and can be paid in cash to the driver. The most reliable and tourist-friendly bus company is **JETT**, with daily trips around the country (w jett.com.jo/en/schedule). Additionally, it offers round-trip journeys to many of the popular sites around the country, including to Petra from Amman, and to Bethany from Suweimeh. There's also a double-decker "red bus" in Amman that goes around town. More information can be found on the Visit Jordan website (w international.visitjordan.com/page/19/groundtransport.aspx).

SHERUTS Sheruts are a mix of taxi and bus. They look like yellow cargo vans; have designated waiting points, like bus stops, but can also be ordered in advance or hailed from the street; often have a similar numbering system to the bus lines so you know the route; and usually seat 10 people – you may have to wait for it to fill up before it leaves. The fare is 6 ILS for an inner-city service. The driver may not have change, though you can ask your fellow passengers if they can break bills – the driver will just continue driving while you sort it out. You have to tell the driver when you want to get out, just like on a bus. You can call a sheruts to pick you up and drop you off at Ben Gurion, and inter-city transport is also available: coordinate this with the driver, who will drop you off where you need to be, rather than at a bus stop.

TAXIS Most people will tell you that taxis in Israel are expensive, and they *are* – compared to other forms of transportation. If you're used to US or European prices, they are no worse, particularly if you use a taxi app such as Gett. In Jordan, you can hail yellow taxis from the street and they are cheap (a couple of dinars for most inner-city trips). If you're entering from the Aqaba border crossing, there are standard fares to popular attractions, and several cars will go there and back in the same day. Wadi Rum: 39 JD one-way, 55 JD return; Petra: 55 JD one-way, 88 JD return; Amman: 109 JD one-way; Dead Sea: 99 JD one-way.

It's still popular to hail taxi drivers. If you're staying in a hotel with a front desk, you can have them call you a taxi. Either way, always negotiate the fare before you get in the car (per car, not per person), or make sure the driver is using the meter. The meter will always give you the better fare, but tourists are often encouraged to agree to a flat rate. In a worst-case scenario, if you can't negotiate a fare, get out of the cab – don't let the driver start driving until you've settled on a fare. Ostensibly, taxis accept credit cards, but the machines go down all the time, leaving you stuck getting out money at an ATM if you aren't prepared. It is better to pay through an app if you can: use Gett or Uber in Israel, and Uber in Amman. Drivers' English is usually fair, but not great, so it is helpful if you can show on a map where you're going. They likely won't recognize building or street names in English, so you may want to find the name in Hebrew. Otherwise, taxis are generally safe with licensed cab drivers, so you'll be fine if you follow the guidance above: tourists may be ripped off, but they are rarely harassed.

SUBWAY The only city in the region with an active subway is Haifa. The line is called HaCarmelit (**w** carmelithaifa.com), and it has six stops on one line (one of the shortest in the world). The service runs frequently, is open on Saturdays, and takes only eight minutes to go from start to finish.

LIGHT RAIL Light rail is available in Jerusalem (**w** cfir.co.il/en/). The line is quite convenient, and connects to many major tourist sites in the city, including the Mehane Yehuda market, Central Bus Station, Mount Hertzl, and the Damascus Gate to the Old City. Payment and ticket validation must be made prior to boarding, either by purchasing a paper ticket from a station kiosk, using a prepaid Rav-Kav card, or by paying via app. In Tel Aviv, light rail (and some underground stations) has been under construction in for more than five years, with the first stations due to open in late 2022.

RAIL High-speed rail exists only between Jerusalem and Tel Aviv and started in December 2019 (**w** seat61.com/tel-aviv-to-jerusalem-by-train.htm) and offers one-way trips in 36–43 minutes (depending on the station), departing every 30 minutes and costing 22 ILS. You can use an app, a Rav-Kav card, or just buy at the station. Plan your journey at **w** rail.co.il/en. Regular passenger trains in Israel are frequent, of high quality, and service many parts of the country. Many locals will live in Haifa or Jerusalem and commute to Tel Aviv, for example, or vice versa. However, there are definite gaps in service. No railways connect any of the adjacent countries, nor any of the Palestinian territories (Gaza, West Bank). Several major tourist sites are not connected by rail: Eilat in the south, the Sea of Galilee and the Golan in the north, and the Dead Sea are not near any passenger lines.

Like the bus, the rail uses the Rav-Kav card. There are "flexible" tickets if you want multiple trips between two destinations and "integrated" tickets for combined bus and train travel, and you can also purchase single one-way tickets without a Rav-Kav card. Train tickets can be purchased either at a ticket booth (vendor) or at electronic ticket kiosks, and seats can be reserved in advance. Note that trains do not run on Shabbat or on Jewish holidays, so you will want to plan accordingly. Typical fares for regular-speed rail journeys are Tel Aviv to Haifa at 27.50 ILS one-way and 44 ILS return, and Jerusalem to Tel Aviv 20 ILS one-way and 32 ILS return. See w rail.co.il/en for full fare details.

There isn't a passenger rail option in Jordan or Egypt.

DO #12: CONNECT IT!

TOURIST INFORMATION CENTERS If you want/need advice, maps, or brochures, try a Tourist Information Center. Information usually comes in English, French, Russian, and Hebrew. Yes, these centers seem a bit antiquated, but most of their stuff is free and they can often point you in the right direction if you're stuck, lost, or decision-fatigued. You can find them in **Jerusalem** at Jaffa Gate (1 Jaffa Street/1 Omer Ben el-Hatab Street), and **Tel Aviv** has the Jaffa Information Center at the Clock Tower in Jaffa, the Boardwalk Info Center at 46 Herbert Samuel Street, and the Dizengoff Center inside the Dizengoff Mall. For elsewhere in Israel, w info.goisrael.com/en/tourist-information has options in Eilat, Nazareth, Haifa, Ashkelon, Tsfat, Netanya, Golan Heights, and others. Jordan doesn't have tourism centers, per se, but does have visitor centers in Petra, Wadi Rum, and a few other tourist sites. The official tourism agency for Jordan is w visitjordan.com, while Wild Jordan (w wildjordan.com) works in tandem with the *Royal Society for the Conservation of Nature (RSCN)*, a local nature conservancy project, and has an info center in downtown Amman.

WI-FI HOTSPOTS In Israel, there is free Wi-Fi everywhere. You can find it all over Tel Aviv and much of Jerusalem, and most museums, buses, malls, airports, hotels, restaurants and cafés have some Wi-Fi available, so you should be connected in no time. In Jordan, Wi-Fi is much harder to come by, so either plan to use it in your hotel or get a SIM card at the airport or in town.

SIM CARDS If you didn't prebook a SIM card, you still have plenty of options. There are a couple of places in the arrival halls of Ben Gurion and Queen Alia airports that sell SIMs for unlocked phones, though they can be pricey. Better, use the free Wi-Fi available and then wait until you can buy a SIM card in a downtown mobile shop. Jerusalem and Tel Aviv both have plenty of mobile phone shops selling SIMs with various call/data plans. Zain mobile shops can be found all over Amman.

MAKING CALLS The country code for Israel is +972, and for Jordan +962. When using a local SIM, drop the +9XX and add a zero before the first number (area code). Thus, if the phone number is +972 3 977 1111, and you have a local SIM, you would dial 03 977 1111. If calling from outside Israel, you dial your country's exit code then the number so, from the United States, for example, you would dial 011 972 3 977 1111.

If you're calling the USA with your local SIM, you have two options. First, if using a smartphone, you should be able to dial using just +1 (including the "+", which stands for "whatever is the appropriate exit code"). Otherwise, use the exit code for your carrier – 00 (Kod Gisha), 012 (Smile Tikshoret), 013 (NetVision), 014 (Bezeq), 018 (Xfone) – so you would dial 00 1 XXX XXX XXXX, or 013 1 XXX XXX XXXX, as appropriate. Jordan and Egypt are much simpler with just 00, so you would dial 00 1 XXX XXX XXXX. If you need more help, try w howtocallabroad.com – we use it all the time.

NEWS IN PRINT AND ONLINE There are tons of online and print news media for you to explore in Israel and Jordan. *Ha'aretz* is Israel's oldest daily newspaper, and the English edition of this paper is sold together with the *International New York Times*; it skews left. The *Jerusalem Post* is the oldest English-language newspaper, and is more centrist. The *Jordan Times* is a daily, English-language newspaper independent of the government. All three have an online presence. Israel's most popular paper, the Hebrew-language *Yedioth Ahronoth*, is available in English online as **Ynetnews** (w ynetnews.com); its journalism runs center-left. In addition to its regular reporting, the *Times of Israel* allows bloggers to contribute news. *Globes* provides financial reporting. Video-based news coverage is provided by w iltv.tv and w i24news.tv, while for audio-based news w tlv1.fm is progressive, like NPR, w israelnewstalkradio.com is an affiliate of FOX News, and w kan.org.il offers a one-hour English news digest every day.

TV HOT is of one of the more popular cable TV providers in Israel, and a running update of its channels, including languages, can be found at w anglo-list.com/english-list-hot-television-channels/. *The Forward* lists all the **Israeli TV shows** you can stream (w forward.com/culture/434533/your-guide-to-every-single-israeli -tv-show-and-movie-you-can-stream-right/).

PEOPLE-TO-PEOPLE The blog **Secret Tel Aviv** regularly updates group meet-up sessions for things like business networking and educational conferences, and for a variety of people wanting to meet other like-types, such as musicians, gamers, and runners (w secrettelaviv.com/tickets/categories/meetups). The same blog has an excellent article on secret places to meet people in Tel Aviv (w secrettelaviv. com/magazine/blog/places-to-meet-people-in-tel-aviv), and also carries start-up networking opportunity recommendations (w secrettelaviv.com/magazine/blog/newsletter/best-hi-tech-meetups-to-network-in-tel-aviv). A variety of options in tech, social, arts, and dozens of other categories can be found by searching for your city on w meetup.com (Tel Aviv, Jerusalem, and Amman currently have good representation).

DO #13: IN CASE YOU NEED IT!

EMERGENCY SERVICES

Israel and Palestine
Police: 📞 100
Ambulance: 📞 101
Fire department: 📞 102
Information (akin to 411): 📞 106

Jordan
Police: 📞 191
Ambulance: 📞 199
Fire department: 📞 199
Tourist police (complaints): 📞 196, ext 4661
Traffic department, accidents or
traffic problems: 📞 190
(NB If these numbers don't work, try 📞 911)

EMBASSIES/CONSULATES The times when citizens should contact their government for help in a crisis are: arrest or detention; death; loss of passport; emergency financial assistance; and options during a national disaster, pandemic, or war. You can also report the following, but you should probably start with the police: violent crimes; missing people; hospitalization; mental breakdown; and information about terrorism. Embassy emergency phone numbers in Israel are listed at w science.co.il/Embassies.php, with the five most common being:

USA: 📞 03 519 7575 (US Embassy Branch Office in Tel Aviv); 02 630 4000 (US Embassy in Jerusalem)
Russia: 📞 03 516 4019; 03 516 1525 (Embassy of Russia in Tel Aviv)

France: 📞 03 520 8500
Germany: 📞 03 693 1313 (during hours); 054 994 4724 (after hours)
UK: 📞 03 725 1222

In Jordan, the five most common embassy emergency phone numbers for non-Arab countries are:

US: 📞 +962 6 590 6000
Israel: 📞 06 550 3500
UK: 📞 06 590 9200

India: 📞 06 462 2098; 06 463 7262
Germany: 📞 06 590 1170

PHARMACIES In **Israel**, try searching for "Super Pharm" in your map app – there's bound to be one in your neighborhood. In **Amman**, you might want to get a cab to Remedy's Wellness Pharmacy (221 Mecca Street) or Oxygen Pharmacy near 6th Circle. There are also a number of Drug Center Pharmacies around town (w drugcenterjo.net). You can always ask your hotel concierge to direct you to the nearest location.

SIRENS/ROCKETS The Holy Land can be a dangerous neighborhood, so you need to be prepared in case violence escalates between Israel and Palestine or its neighbors. Rocket attacks from Gaza caused bystander deaths in Israel in 2014 and 2021. Israel responds with force, and many protesters and civilians have been killed by Israeli security in the Old City, East Jerusalem, the West Bank, and Gaza. This cannot be understated: avoid public areas – particularly the Old City – if tensions rise between Jews and Arabs. Should rockets be fired towards Israel, where most tourists are staying, follow these instructions from Israel's Home Front Command for what to do when you hear either an **alert siren** or an **explosion**.

If you're **in a building**: depending on the time available, close doors and windows; enter the building's identified protected space, underground shelter, or reinforced security room; residents of the top floor in a building of more than three floors without a protected space, shelter, or reinforced security room should descend two floors down and wait in the stairwell (stairwell floors are protected except for the ground floor and top two floors in buildings of more than three floors); residents of the top floor in a three-story building without a protected space, shelter, or reinforced security room should descend one floor down (the middle floor is protected in three-story buildings); civilians are requested not to be out in the building entrance area, since there is a risk of shrapnel and explosions as a result of missile landings in the area near the building.

If you are **outside**, enter the closest building, depending on the time available. If there is no building or cover/shelter nearby, or if you are in an open space, lie down on the ground and protect your head with your hands. If you are **in a vehicle**, stop at the side of the road, exit the vehicle and enter the closest building or shelter. If it is impossible to access a building, exit the vehicle, lie down on the ground next to your car, and protect your head with your hands. If it is impossible to exit the car, stop at the side of the road and wait 10 minutes.

Unless otherwise instructed, **after 10 minutes** you may leave the protected space. It is important to **stay away from any foreign objects or rockets** lying on the ground (in such circumstances, keep curious bystanders away and notify the police). **Continue listening to the instructions** issued by the media.

PUBLIC RESTROOMS You gotta go. No time to even read this section. Visit **w** pee. place/en or download **Flush** or **Toilet Finder** on the Google Play Store or iTunes App Store.

If you're on foot in Jerusalem, the **Old City** has public restrooms in several locations including right inside Jaffa Gate, on the left up the steps towards the Ramparts Walk entrance; at the Western Wall; inside the Dung Gate, near the entrance to the Jerusalem Archaeological Park; and throughout the market areas, look for signs marked "WC" for water closet, or public toilet.

In **Tel Aviv**, try the beaches – most of the commercial blocks on the beach have facilities, some with a small fee. In **Jaffa**, the big Hangar shopping complex has restrooms on the second floor. **Mehane Yehuda Market (#67)** in Jerusalem and Sarona Market (D3) in Tel Aviv each have a few restrooms to choose from.

Gas stations have bathrooms, as do **malls**. **Aroma** is the most ubiquitous coffee bar/restaurant and will have. **Hotels** may have, but might be tricky to find. **Bars and restaurants** will, but you probably have to be a patron. You can always ask.

Part 4

Today in the Holy Land

DO #14: EAT IT!

At BUCKET!, we don't actively review restaurants. Restaurants open and close. Who's to say whether a restaurant is just having a good or bad day when the travel writer popped in? Frankly, we think restaurant reviews in guidebooks are becoming more obsolete, to be replaced by crowdsourced reviews on sites such as TripAdvisor, Yelp, Google, and OpenTable.

That said, there are certainly dining establishments that deserve your attention. Rather than give you restaurants in every city and town, we've organized our food chapter differently. The region's most noteworthy restaurants – ones that have received so much acclaim as to merit an elective recommendation – are found in our *Food and Drink* theme (p. 561). There are a few specific food items which also warrant attention, but these are usually attached to a restaurant (e.g., shakshuka and sabich). We consider these to be electives because they are special enough to plan in advance and should be part of your schedule, if food is a priority category for you.

We use this section to discuss the food itself. We elaborate on the **Jordanian Cuisine (#44)** and **Israeli Cuisine (#51)** electives by providing a rich overview of the historical and cultural elements that have gone into those cuisines. Our section on religious customs discusses the unique personalities of the countries, as well as going over holidays and kosher/halal foods. And we give an overview of all the popular foods of the region – with a checklist so you can keep track of your progress!

REGIONAL CUISINE At their base, Arab cuisine and Israeli cuisine are derived from the same sense of place, and include a lot of the same types of local foods – salads, tahini, falafel, shawarma, lamb and chicken, fava and chickpeas, eggplant, pomegranate, figs, dates, nuts, parsley, za'atar, olive oil, olives, yogurt, and labneh. A variety of herbs, citrus, vegetables, and fruits are eaten uniformly across Israeli Arab, Israeli Jew, Palestinian Arab, Israeli Druze, Bedouin, Jordanian, and other Levantine peoples' cuisines. Pork is verboten in both the Muslim and Jewish tradition. Alcohol is also historically not allowed in Islam, but you will find beer and wine in Jordan, Palestine, and Israel, as well as the beloved drink, *arak*. Many of these ingredients translate into regional menus. Popular among all groups are the eminently recognizable dishes of falafel, pita, hummus, baba ghanouj, kibbeh, kebab, and shawarma.

Israeli/Jewish Cuisine (#51) Food in Israel is as diverse as the Jewish people of the world. This is not hyperbole – many Jews have lived in exile for millennia, and have not only passed on ancient traditions and recipes over the many hundreds/thousands of years, but they've also become part of their new national cultures. When Israel was still a dream in the late 1800s, and Jewish people around the world began migrating to the Holy Land, they kept their old traditions alive. This trend continued across waves of new immigrants that have arrived in the subsequent decades, on through the present day. Jewish people can be found all around the world, and today's Israeli cuisine represents a unique blend of ingredients and cooking styles, even in its most ubiquitous food. **"Modern Israeli cuisine"** has also been used to describe the new style of multinational, beautifully prepared, heavenly creations popularized in many new Tel Aviv restaurants and beyond. **"Jewish"** food (usually referring to the food eaten on special occasions) is discussed in *Jewish Holidays* (p. 85).

Ancient Jewish Based on archaeological evidence and written documentation as found in the Old Testament (Deuteronomy) and other biblical texts, there were seven foods primarily associated with the ancient Jewish people, all of which continue to have importance today: pomegranates, grapes, dates, figs, olives, barley, and wheat. Lots of other regular ingredients we see today have been around for eons, including various vegetables, nuts, meats, and cheeses.

Levantine This eastern Mediterranean cuisine combines multiple styles of food, often with similar principal ingredients but perhaps with dissimilar taste profiles. Turkish food is recognizable in Israel, with *baklava*, *kebab*, and *fattoush* salad being staple Middle Eastern menu items. Lebanese, Syrian, and Iraqi cuisines (all part of the Levant; see below) have also historically included *falafel*, *shawarma*, *baba ghanouj*, cucumber/tomato salads, lentil soup, *kibbeh*, *tahini*, strong black coffee (sometimes flavored), and *halva*.

Mediterranean (Sephardic) After the Jews were expelled from Spain and Portugal in the late 15th century, they resettled in north Africa and the eastern Mediterranean. In the former, they adapted the use of such ingredients as couscous, chickpeas, and pine nuts, seasonings such as saffron, cinnamon, rosewater, and cardamom, preparations such as stuffed vegetables, techniques such as preserved fruits, pickled lemons, and cured olives, and drinks such as *sahlab*, *malabi*, *arak*, and Turkish coffee.

Eastern European (Ashkenazi) This style of cuisine is most recognizable to Westerners familiar with "Jewish" cuisine, to include much of the recognizable holiday food such as gefilte fish, matzo ball soup, *challah*, *kugel*, *strudel*, *knishes*, and stuffed cabbage. Some unique ingredients include poppy seeds, beets, schmaltz, potatoes, honey, molasses, and liver.

Middle Eastern (Mizrahi) The Mizrahi people of Jewish tradition have perhaps contributed the least understood component to Jewish/Israeli cuisine, primarily because their cuisine is often reflected in that of the Sephardic and Levantine populations that lived nearby.

Yemeni Yemeni Jews have their own unique restaurants (or more often "stands" in markets), with dishes such as malawach and jahnoun, and condiments such as zhug. Check out *Breads and Fillings* (p. 86) for more Yemeni contributions.

Arab cuisine Navigating Arab cuisine can seem quite daunting, particularly as there are so many regional variants, and so many regions that lend their unique flair to the food they cook. This particular region of the Arab world is known as "the Levant," derived from the Italian for "rising" and referencing the rising sun in the eastern Mediterranean. Its food is thus "Levantine." While all of these cuisines might be described culinarily as "similar," including those of warring/neighboring Lebanon and Syria (the other two countries that make up the region), variances across the cultural/ethnic/religious groups mean they are not identical.

Jordanian Cuisine (#44) Jordan's national dish is called Mansaf (V), a lamb dish with rice or bulgur, cooked in fermented dried yogurt, called *jameed*. *Zarb* is a popular lamb-and-rice stew, prepared with raisins and nuts. Tomato sauce is a popular cooking ingredient in Jordan and can be found as the flavor base in many stews and vegetable dishes. Turkish coffee, a strong, unfiltered style of coffee, is the drink of choice (rather than "Arabic" coffee, which is filtered and brewed), along with hot mint tea. *Fuul* is mashed or whole broad beans which you collect from a giant clay pot and dress with tahini and other sauces.

Palestinian Palestinian cuisine is nearly as diverse as its people. Gazans (see below) live on the coast and eat differently than the inlanders in the West Bank, or the Arabs who live within Israeli borders. Those who live in the Galilee and the north use bulgur wheat for a variety of preparations, including *kubbi* (a mix of bulgur and meat), along with rice, chicken/meat skewers (shish kebab/*taouk*), and the traditional regional mezze (*hummus, baba ghanouj*, etc.). Meanwhile, those in the West Bank tend to have a mix of Galilee and Jordanian-style cuisines, eating *maqluba* and Mansaf (V), but the specialty is *musakhan*, a chicken roasted over taboon bread with onions, spices, and pine nuts and eaten with the right hand.

Gazan The publication of *The Gaza Kitchen: A Palestinian Food Journey* in 2013 opened the world's eyes to Gazan cooking. The authors discuss the variances found in Gazan cuisine compared to other Levantine food – for one, it's spicier and more herbaceous. Gazans are historically fishermen and continue to bring a delicious seafood element to their tables, including shrimp, calamari, and small fried fish. Some unique dishes include *rumaniya*, which is a pomegranate and eggplant stew, and *sumagiya*, which is a meat-based stew with *tahini* and *sumac* at its base. A salad called *dagga* combines tomato and dill with hot pepper.

Bedouin Bedouins are no longer the permanently free-roaming nomads they once were (though there are still shepherds and the communities still move around), but their cuisine remains hyper-local, meaning they primarily consume foods that are grown or foraged nearby. Today, they may make trips to the local town to buy bulk rice or coffee, for instance, but everyday cuisine centers around vegetables, rice, and the animals they rear. Dates are almost an entire food group to this community. Bedouins in Jordan have their own spin on *zarb*, which involves cooking a meat/vegetable stew in an underground pit – popular at campsites near Wadi Rum. Coffee is an important ritual, with many Bedouin communities having a resident coffee expert – someone who roasts the coffee, grinds the beans using a sophisticated and musical technique, and then serves the final product. Tea is often made from local plants. *Abud* is an unleavened bread, cooked in a firepit after being buried in ash and coals. *Markook* (or *shrak*) is also popular – another thin, unleavened bread cooked over a *saj* (like an upside-down wok). Meat and rice dishes are popular, and are often eaten in the community like Mansaf (V), with one hand from a big serving platter.

Druze The Druze style of cooking can be quite different, seeming like an interesting amalgam of Arab and Israeli styles, but with ingredients such as cinnamon, *baharat* and other spices, rice, grape leaves, a variety of wild greens, and locally pressed olive oil. The cooking tends to be seasonal, but centers around vegetables. Dishes can vary from vegetables-in-yogurt in the summer to bulgur/lentil-stuffed vegetables in the winter. Olive trees grow locally and many families preserve the olives themselves for later sale. Druze pita is a large, round flattened pita that seems more like tortilla, and is often covered with *labneh, za'atar*, and olive oil. Sesame cake is a nice dessert. You might also want to try Druze Cooking Workshops (H1) in the Galilee.

Galilee The locals of Nazareth and the Galilee have merged foreign cooking practices with Arab ingredients to create a uniquely **Nazarene Fusion Cuisine** (G1), which is quickly gaining renown.

Local The region does "local" very well. In Israel, food rarely travels more than a day before appearing in your grocery store or restaurant kitchen. Grocery items also are regularly covered in dirt and go bad in just a couple of days because of fewer pesticides and more natural farming practices. This is great news if you follow the "local," "seasonal," "fresh," and "raw" trends sweeping the world's culinary scenes.

Jordan – much like other countries in the Arab world – has adapted to its desert environment, meaning you'll find fewer vegetables on traditional menus, but there are still plenty of fruits and juice stands to keep your vitamins up. Hotel breakfasts will often have a grand smorgasbord of options and can cover the vitamin deficiency you'll inevitably feel after eating street falafel and shawarma for days (though those foods are delicious). Lots of the vegetables you'll see in Jordan are pickled in some manner, for preservation obviously, and then added to pitas or plates.

You will find lots of imported items in Israel, and to a lesser extent in Jordan. The cost will almost always come at a premium. We recommend that you stick to the Arab and Mediterranean food options, because you'll invariably get something local, seasonal, fresh, and better than whatever international cuisine options you find around.

FOOD PRACTICES AND SAFETY **Eating with your hands** is a regular practice. Israelis consider "breaking bread" to be a seminal tradition and one that involves physically touching food that you will pass along to the next person. Americans are notorious for not liking to touch things that other people have touched, so if you are a non-Jewish guest, you may or may not be expected to partake in this custom. You will look strange to locals if you try to eat your sandwich with a fork. **Jordanians only eat with their right hands**. The left hand is considered unclean as this hand is traditionally reserved for the toilet. In restaurants, you won't be bothered. On the street, exercise awareness that the right hand should be used to eat, shake hands, etc.

Drinking alcohol is generally considered verboten in Muslim countries, though you will still find Jordanian restaurants ready to serve beer, wine, and liquor. Drinking in public is not allowed or recommended. In liberal Tel Aviv, it's quite the opposite – you will get away with drinking in public, whether on the beach or on the street. The rules are very lax. Elsewhere in Israel, you should be careful about drinking outside establishments that permit it, with the exception of Purim (see *Jewish Holidays*, p. 85).

Tap water is considered safe for most Westerners in Israel. You should buy **bottled water** in Jordan, and skip any drinks prepared with **ice** on the street. In expensive restaurants, ice is likely clean, but if there are any doubts, skip it. All the same, bottled water is readily available. **Food-borne illnesses** are not unheard of in Israel and Jordan, but are uncommon. Street food and restaurant kitchens usually keep high standards of cleanliness, hygiene, and sanitation. Food stalls and restaurants may not be of the highest international standards, but use common sense – if it looks dirty, steer clear.

RELIGIOUS FOOD CUSTOMS
Shabbat In the Jewish tradition, *Shabbat*, or the Sabbath, is a time when families get together to have a meal. *Shabbat* starts at sundown on Friday and lasts until sundown on Saturday. The meal usually takes place on Friday night and can involve a variety of traditional foods, which of course vary by family as Jews come from all around the world. The next day (Saturday)'s morning and afternoon meals are also considered important. Jews break bread with one another, usually with two loaves of *challah*, or braided bread, which is blessed at the beginning of the meal. Wine is also traditional, and part of the blessings. A fish or meat main course are customary,

DEFINITION OF KOSHER In Talmudic times, scholars laid out very specific rules for food preparation and eating. Today, these ancient rules are still observed and applied to modern foods. Kosher foods are not different from regular food or groceries; they are merely food products that have gone through a review process by Jewish religious authorities and are determined to be in accordance with religious law. Pork and shrimp are famous examples of foods that are forbidden under kosher laws and cannot be eaten by kosher-practicing people. Although modern products, such as Cheez-Its cheese crackers, may not be mentioned in religious texts, their ingredients, production, and handling technically make them kosher.

DEFINITION OF HALAL Similar to kosher, halal is any object or action that falls under the rules of Islamic law. This can include, but is not limited to, food. Likewise, it has a certification process for food bearing the label "halal." *Haram* are acts forbidden under halal rules, such as eating pork.

FOOD TASTE There's no difference between the way kosher/halal food tastes versus non-kosher/non-halal food. This misconception likely derives from wine. In the olden days (25 years ago!), wine was boiled to meet kosher laws, and the Israeli product was universally agreed to be terrible. These days, many wineries now employ religious employees specifically to keep the product kosher by using kosher ingredients, such as authorized yeast, and having part of the product handled only by religious employees. Israeli wine produced today is terrible no longer, thank goodness!

CERTIFICATION Foods deemed either halal or kosher will have a label, and restaurants will have a halal sign or a certificate of kashrut (the state of being kosher) hanging in the window, like a TripAdvisor rating! Muslim country restaurants all tend to abide by halal laws and may not have halal displayed in the window, though you do normally see this certification in non-Muslim cities.

HALAL VS. KOSHER The two systems are very similar, as both use ancient religious texts to set dietary standards. Pork is prohibited in both sets of laws, while fish is permitted. One major difference in kosher laws is the separation of meat and dairy, which does not exist under rules of halal. Alcohol is prohibited in Islam, whereas it is allowed if kosher under kashrut laws, so you will find many Orthodox Jews drinking wine. Debates continue to rage today about whether newly introduced foods meet religious requirements.

KOSHER PRODUCTS There are three categories of food products: meat, dairy, and *parve*. Meat and dairy products cannot be served at the same meal, even on separate plates. Parve includes neutral foods that can be eaten with either meat or dairy, which includes fish and eggs.

KOSHER FOR PASSOVER Kosher laws are even more strict over the Passover holiday, and require a special packaging label (usually a "K").

with *gefilte fish* being a popular choice. The Ashkenazi and Sephardi cultures have a traditional stew, called *cholent/chamin*, which mixes meat, potatoes, barley, and beans. Chicken soup is also common. In the Yemeni tradition, *jachnun* is served on Shabbat morning, a sweet dough presented with crushed tomatoes, hard-boiled eggs, and *zhug* (hot sauce). If you're invited for a Shabbat meal, you'll want to make sure your gift – whether food or wine – is kosher.

Jewish holidays The thing most people recognize about **Passover** is that you will find no leavened bread. The *kashrut* rules dictate no food of any kind with *chametz*, or a leavening agent (sich as yeast). *Matzo/matzah* is very popular at this time, eaten plain or with accompaniments as a cracker. The **seder** meal is served on the first night of Passover. The six items which make up a seder plate are bitter herbs (such as horseradish or romaine), *charoset* (a fruit paste), *karpas* (vegetable in brine), shankbone, and a hard-boiled egg. On the side are three matzah. Exactly four cups of wine are also served. **Shavuot** historically occurred at a time when milk was plentiful, and dairy foods take center stage over these days. For **Rosh Hashanah**, sweets are popular, including apples and honey, honey cake (*lekach*), or *challah* with raisins and honey. *Gefilte fish* is universally despised, but this is its day to shine. On **Yom Kippur**, Jews fast for 25 hours, and all restaurants are closed. The dish *holishke*, a cabbage meat roll, is prepared on **Sukkot** and **Simcha Tora**. *Sufganiyot*, or giant jelly donuts, are very popular around **Hannukah**. **Latkes**, or potato pancakes, are known as *levivot* in Hebrew, and also eaten at this time. **Tu B'shvat** is a lesser-known holiday that recognizes ecology, and Israelis will eat dried fruits and nuts to celebrate. Finally, on **Purim**, everyone likes *hamantashen* (Yiddish), or *oznei Haman* (Hebrew), which are triangle-shaped pastries with poppy seed (traditional) or some other nut or fruit preserves. Drunkenness is also quite common at Purim.

Arab holidays During **Ramadan** – a month in the Islamic calendar lasting 29–30 days – Muslims will fast from sunset to sundown. *Suhur* is the morning meal (if eaten before sunrise) and *iftar* is the evening meal. Dates are usually consumed first, to break the fast, followed by a cold drink of carob, tamarind, licorice, or apricot juice. Lentil or *freekeh* soup usually comes next, followed by *mezze* (sides/salads) and a variety of mains. Typical foods such as *fattoush*, *tabboule*, *ful medames*, and *kanafeh* are served. Stuffed squash is popular, called *kousa mahshi*. *Qatayef* is a typical Ramadan dessert, a pastry filled with nuts or cheese. Dessert can also include *zalabieh*, or *awamat* in some regions, which are fried dough balls in syrup.

BREAD AND FILLINGS *Pita* is made from white or wheat flour, flat, and has a naturally occurring pocket in which to stuff other ingredients, making it the perfect container for your many sandwich desires. (Disclaimer: Israeli pita is the best pita in the world.) There are a few variations: *Druze pita* is long and thin and looks like a tortilla, and is heated on a inverted dome like naan. Often eaten with labneh and za'atar, it's found in Jerusalem, Haifa, Galilee, and other places near the side of the road. *Laffa*, or *Iraqi pita*, is a larger, single flatbread (i.e., no pocket) baked in a taboon oven and used as a wrap. *Lavash* is a thin, unleavened flatbread baked in a tandoori oven, also used as a wrap. *Injera* is the bread of Ethiopia, made from teff flour, tangy, and used to scoop Ethiopian food. *Markook/shrak* is unleavened flatbread, similar to pita, but long and thin and cooked over an upside-down wok called a *saj*.

Known as *börek* in Turkey – the likely origin of this flaky phyllo (or puff pastry) delight – *bourekas* can be found throughout the Holy Land. Everyone has their favorite *bourekas* stand. These tiny delights can be eaten at any time of the day, but in moderation – they aren't healthy by any stretch. Popular fillings (and shapes) include salty cheese (round), spinach (triangle), and mashed potatoes (square), topped with sesame seeds.

Besides bourekas, there are lots of other types of savory breads. *Challah* is a braided bread usually eaten on the Sabbath in Jewish tradition. *Ka'ak* is an Arabic word for "cake," and these traditionally refer to oblong bagel-like bread rings, but less dense, and topped with sesame seeds and served with *za'atar*. They're popular as a street food all over Jerusalem. *Non* is much like a bagel without a hole (originating from Bukhara, Uzbekistan/Tajikistan). Four breads of Yemeni origin are found throughout Israel. *Jachnun* is a sweet dough served with crushed tomatoes, hard-boiled eggs, and *zhug* (hot sauce). *Malawach* is a fried bread in a pancake shape, served with the same toppings as *jachnun*. *Kubane* is monkey-bread like brioche, rolled in butter/margarine, and served with grated tomatoes. *Lachoch* is similar to Ethiopian *injera*, made with wheat flour and pan-fried, then served with *zhug* and eggs.

SANDWICHES Falafel: either you love it or you looooooove it. A deep-fried dough mixture of chickpeas (fava beans in Egypt) as the base, and secret spices that vary the flavor ever-so-slightly from shop to shop, this staple provides just the right balance of satiety, comfort, and cost. Most eat it in a pita pocket, but you'll find some variations throughout the region – in expensive restaurants, on plates perhaps, or wrapped in a *laffa* or *lavash*. There are falafel shops everywhere. Truly everywhere. In Israel, a falafel sandwich can cost you anywhere from 5 ILS to 45 ILS, depending on whether you get a plate of food to accompany it (alternatively, you can just shove the toppings into your pita pocket and save the plate), how respectable is the chain, and how close is it to tourist attractions. The latter is usually the most important factor in price and quality. A good price for falafel would be 15–20 ILS for a single order, takeaway/no plate. In Jordan, falafel is ½–1 JD. Places vying for the best falafel in the Holy Land: Falafel Gabai (D3), **Miznon**, *Falafel Hazkenim (E1)*, Al-Quds Falafel (Q2), and Hashem Falafel (Q2).

Sabich is an Israeli pita sandwich, likely invented by Iraqi Jews. The ingredients are all veg-friendly: fried eggplant, hard-boiled eggs, sometimes chips/fries or boiled potatoes, veg salad, hummus, and tahini, with options of *amba* (sour mango pickle) and *zhug* (Yemeni hot pepper). Average price: 15 to 20 ILS. One of our Silver electives specializes in this sandwich: **Sabich/Oved's**.

Shawarma was brought to the Middle East by the Turks, it is presumed, a couple of hundred years ago, and it's been a favorite ever since. Essentially, the dish consists of roasted meat shaved from a rotating spit, eaten in pita or other wrap, and accompanied by the same ingredients you'd get with *falafel*. Shawarma can be made from almost any meat: beef, chicken, lamb, and turkey are popular, as are mixes. Shawarma in Israel is typically made from turkey meat, though there are a few respected versions that focus on lamb and/or veal. The average price is 30 ILS, but can go up in fancier or more touristy places, and down in ramshackle places.

Shnitzel (also spelled *schnitzel*), is a pounded-flat chicken breast (sometimes turkey), breaded and fried, and eaten on a plate or in a pita. It sells anywhere from 20–50 ILS, depending on the size and the fanciness. Jerusalem mixed grill, or *Me'orav Yerushalmi*, is an offal-lover's dream, though if you don't know what offal is, don't ask and don't bother looking it up. The offal is mixed with lamb and lots of spices and served in a pita with salads – you know the drill. "*Kebab*" you probably recognize, and goes by several names, including *shish ta'uk* and *shashlik*. *Merguez* is a spicy sausage. Silver elective **Miznon** serves a meat-in-pita sandwich with a cult following.

Tzfon Abraxas and Ha'achim are both known for their unique takes on kebab. At M25 (D3), try the *arayes*.

PLANT-BASED **Vegans** can get by well in Israel and Jordan. The diet permits the consumption of *hummus, falafel,* and *tabbouleh,* a salad of parsley, bulgur wheat, tomatoes, mint, and onion, plus a lemon/olive oil dressing. Also popular is *tahina/tahini,* a ground and liquified sesame seed spread. A **vegetarian** diet can add *sabich* (contains eggs), *bourekas* (cheese and sometimes meat, so check!), and *masabacha* (often cooked with butter and served with hard eggs). In addition to Middle Eastern, **Ethiopian** is reliable for vegetarians. In fact, it is mostly vegan (though not completely; be careful about ordering the raw meat!) and usually contains various legume-based mixes, such as lentils and split peas, as well as vegetable-centric portions, such as potatoes, carrots, and spinach. Instead of pita, Ethiopians consume their cuisine with a sour, spongy, teff flour-based utensil you'll either love or hate – *injera.* In case you didn't already know, these foods are **not vegetarian-friendly**: *shawarma, shnitzel, kebab, shashlik, kibbeh,* and "mixed grill" or *me'orav yerushalmi* are all members of the meat family.

Mezze is the word for a small plates served alongside one another on Middle Eastern tables before the main courses arrive. Some restaurants will serve more than 20 mezze before even bringing you a menu! (Try Jaffa's Old Man and the Sea (D2).) There are almost always staples, but you will find something familiar and something foreign at each meal. Hummus and eggplant-based dips are ubiquitous, as is a type of bread: *pita, taboon, lavash,* or Druze-style pita. Often, *labneh,* a hot sauce, and various salads are presented. *Tabbouleh* is popular in both cultures and is made of bulgur wheat, tomatoes, onion, and tons of parsley, with olive oil/lemon. You'll occasionally find pomegranate used instead of tomato. *Baba ghanoush* has an eggplant base and is mixed with *tahina* and olive oil. *Kibbeh* is a ball made of bulgur wheat, onion, and minced meat, cooked in a stock, sometimes deep-fried. There are dozens of other dishes you'll find at a mezze, with a focus on avocado, potato, beets, eggplant, hummus, cabbage slaw, carrots, celery, pickled vegetables, radishes, cucumbers, onions, peppers, chard, tomatoes, cheeses, lentils, and wheatberries, all with a unique sauce or herb accompaniment.

In Israel (less so in Jordan), you will find **salad** at nearly every meal. In fact, you will almost always have the option of stuffing your falafel/shawarma/shnitzel pita sandwich with a big serving of cabbage slaw or Israeli salad, or some other big helping of veg. The traditional Israeli Breakfast (U) will typically have several salads – greens, vegetables, lettuces, herbs, and/or grains. "Arab salad" or "Israeli salad" is a chopped salad of cucumber and tomato, usually with bell pepper and raw onion, garnished with parsley, mint, or other herbs, dressed with lemon juice and/or olive oil. But variations abound. And to be clear: Arab salad = Israeli salad – it's the same salad! Both cultures have their own interpretations within the culture, and within restaurants, so don't be fooled by nomenclature. Each will claim to be the founder, but it's a Levantine salad belonging to both cultures (and others). Sometimes you'll even see "Jerusalem salad," which is like a Greek salad, with feta, olives, cucumber, tomato, pomegranate, and *za'atar.*

What to drizzle over your *falafel* or *sabich*? *Tahina/tahini* is a ubiquitous ingredient made of toasted sesame seeds, ground into a viscous, light brown nut butter. Used on everything, it also serves as a base for lots of sauces. You'll see it on practically every menu, from starter to the base of a $50 meat or fish dish. *Amba* is a sour pickle made of mangoes and vinegar, mustard, chili, fenugreek, salt, and other special spices – also good on everything. *Zhug,* or *skhug,* or *sahawiq,* is a hot sauce made from fresh hot peppers, mixed with coriander, garlic, pepper, cumin, cardamom and/or other spices. Recipes vary. When a vendor asks if you want "kharif" (meaning "spicy") this is usually the condiment. *Matbucha* includes cooked tomatoes, garlic, onion, and bell peppers, to accompany bread, veg, and hummus. *Harissa* is a hot pepper paste mixed with garlic, coriander, oil, and an interesting spice like rose or saffron. *Muhamarra* is another hot pepper dip, made of ground walnuts, breadcrumbs, peppers, olive oil, salt, and lemon juice, sometimes with pomegranate molasses. *Dukkah* is more Egyptian, but can be found in some Jordanian restaurants, as well as Gaza. It's a dry dip made from ground hazelnuts, sesame seeds, coriander, and cumin, and served with olive oil and fresh bread. Variations on *dukkah* include nigella and pumpkin seeds.

This region consumes a lot of whole **wheat-based grain** products, though some cultures have found comfort in the less nutritious, but cheaper, white rice. *Freekeh* is made from the roasted and sun-dried seeds of durum wheat and used in soups and stews throughout the Arab world, often with lamb. *Bulgur* (*burgul* in Hebrew) is a dried, cracked wheat. Nutty, with a high nutritional content, it can replace rice in many recipes. It's often mixed with meat to make kofta. *Israeli couscous*, or *ptitim*, is unrelated to its namesake couscous (which is not popular in this region), which is made of semolina. *Ptitim* is a processed wheat product, rarely made at home, with much larger ball shapes, and occasionally shows up on restaurant menus. Arab names for similar products include *moghrabia* and *maftul*. **Rice** is a mainstay in many cities and cultural traditions, and will often be served as an accompaniment to fish or meat dishes. *Zarb/quzi* is a rice dish of the Levant made of lamb, vegetables, raisins, and nuts. **Lentils** are regularly used in stews and soups. *Mujadarra* is a rice and lentil dish smothered in sauteed onions. Fresh fava beans are a treat and abundant in this region. Chickpeas are served in a variety of forms, including falafel, hummus, in salad, and as mezze. Beans are relatively expensive and used less frequently in this region.

The word "**hummus**" is derived from the Arabic word for "chickpeas" but the dish is claimed by Jews and Arabs alike. Hummus is a bean mash, usually composed of chickpea (but sometimes fava), tahini, lemon juice, and olive oil. Salt, garlic, paprika, *za'atar* and other ingredients are to taste. There are lots of topping options, including mushrooms, pine nuts, olives, ground meat, onions, and various herbs. It can be eaten at any meal, and can be treated as a meal itself. Most commonly, it's eaten with pita as the dipping utensil. Pickles, onions, parsley, Arab/Israeli salad, and hot sauce are all popular condiments to accompany hummus and pita. Hummus is also regularly used as a spread. Popular variations include *masabacha* (or *mashawsha*) which is similar, but has more of an earthy, whole-chickpea vibe. Then there's *fuul*, which is made with fava beans and has a wholly different taste, but is often served alongside hummus. There are several regional restaurants that specialize in hummus, called *hummusiyas*. The whole town of Abu Ghosh, home to the **Monastery of Abu Ghosh**, is filled with restaurants claiming to supply the best hummus in Israel. **Abu Hassan** (aka Ali Karavan) offers the "triple" – a winning combination of fuul, hummus, and masabacha.

Spices are as ubiquitous as sauces, and best eaten when used in great quantity over a baked pita or other bread. They're also good toppers for hummus. And make great gifts! *Za'atar/hyssop* is usually a fine powder mixture of oregano, thyme, and marjoram, plus sesame and sometimes sumac. It's a medium-strength spice used in dipping oils or sprinkled over bread and labneh. *Baharat* is made from black pepper, coriander, cinnamon, cloves, cumin, cardamom, nutmeg, and paprika, though regional variations will include mint, rose, dried black lime, or saffron. It's a strong spice used while cooking or stewing meats or heavy vegetables. *Sumac* is purple in color and lemony in taste, and the ground fruit of the sumac plant. It's from the same family as poison sumac, but is not poisonous! It's a light spice often added to salads, vegetables, and bread.

ANIMAL-DERIVED One important, standout egg-based dish that requires its own acknowledgment is **shakshuka**. It is a simple dish comprised of tomatoes and eggs, herbs, maybe spinach, and lots of spices – all in a hot pan. And it's not an exclusively breakfast dish; some of the famous locations don't open until lunch. Check out **Shakshuka/Dr. Shakshuka** in Jaffa.

Levantines eat a lot of **dairy**. There are certainly a fair number of imports, but Israelis themselves tend to focus on a few familiar types: *feta* and *bulgarit* (a variation of feta) salt-brined cheeses. They can be made from cow, sheep, goat, or a mix of milks. *Tzfat* is similar to feta, but made of sheep's milk. There are a variety of Negev Goat Farms (J2) where you can sample dozens of styles of cheese made from the milk of local goats in the Negev. *Labneh*, or strained yogurt (sometimes called "Greek yogurt"), is a popular mezze addition in Arab restaurants, but Jewish Israelis eat it with frequency also, often smothered in olive oil. *Gavina levana*, called *quark* in Europe, is a fresh style of white, saltless, un-aged strained and set milk. It's high in protein and eaten as yogurt (without flavor) throughout Israel. In Jordan, goat's milk is used to make a yogurt called *jameed*, used in the Jordanian dish Mansaf (V).

MEAT If you're ordering **seafood or fish** in Jordan, the name on the menu will probably be recognizably English, whereas in Israel you will more likely find transliteration. The most common varietals include: *barbunia* (red mullet), *buri* (grey mullet), *denis* (sea bream), *faridah* (red snapper), *forel* (trout), *levrak* (sea bass), *lokus* (grouper), *mushte* (St. Peter's fish, or tilapia), and *musar* (red drum). Fish with the same name in English and Hebrew include cod, bass, anchovy, tuna, salmon, mackerel, herring, hake, sole, and sardine. *Chraimeh* is a popular fish stew made of firm, white fish (such as grouper) braised in a spicy red sauce. And because you've always wanted to know: *gefilte fish* is made by molding pieces of ground, white fish (such as carp) into balls and cooking them in broth. Considered the best fish restaurant in Israel, if not simply the best restaurant overall, don't miss **Uri Buri**.

Chicken is probably the most consumed of the meats, with lamb being the largest consumed "red meat." Meals that contain chicken include *shnitzel*, one of Israel's most consumed platters. *Shish taouk* is chicken shish kebab, or grilled chicken skewers. *Maqluba* is made by Arab and Druze people, and involves cooking a stew of layered vegetables, chicken, and rice in a giant crockpot, and then inverting the pot directly onto a platter. *Musakhan* is a Palestinian specialty of chicken cooked atop a taboon bread with spices.

In the **beef and lamb** camp, you'll find *kibbeh* (sometimes *kubba*), a baked oblong ball formed of bulgur, onion, and lamb or beef served as part of a mezze platter. *Kofta* is a type of meatball, made of beef, chicken, fish, lamb, or (rarely) vegetarian and prepared with onion, spices, and cooked in a tomato sauce. Mansaf (V) is Jordan's national dish of lamb and rice. *Merguez* is a spicy red sausage made of beef or lamb. *Shashlik*, or skewers, or *shish kebab*, are cubes of meat grilled on a metal skewer. Jordanians also eat goat. Famous Israeli chef Yotam Ottolenghi (cookbook author of *Jerusalem*, *Plenty*, *Plenty More*, etc.) recommends *Rachmo*, outside Mehane Yehuda Market, for kubba soup, a dish of braised beef wrapped in a bulgur/semolina dough dumpling and consumed in broth.

DESERTS AND SNACKS   A number of **traditional desserts** eaten in certain regions are very common, though may be unfamiliar to foreign travelers. *Kanafeh* is a specialty of Nablus, and is a pastry made of white cheese, topped with semolina and a sugar syrup with rose water. It's incredibly popular. *Mutabak* is phyllo dough wrapped around nuts or goat's cheese and then covered in sweet syrup and confectioner's sugar. *Baklava* goes by several names, including *bourma* which is phyllo surrounding chunks of cashew or pistachio, *ballorieh* which is surrounded by stringy, sugary dough, and *basma* which is kanafeh-covered pine nuts and cashews, among others. Pick what looks most appealing, as there will be dozens of options. *Halva* contains roasted and ground sesame seeds turned into *tahina*, to which a sugary syrup is added (note: this is the Israel/Palestinian way – *halva* can be any kind of nut butter, or even flour-based such as wheat/semolina). Pistachio, chocolate, and almond-filled varieties are common. *Rugelach* is similar to a croissant, but made with sour cream or yeast leaveners and filled with poppy seeds, chocolate, fruit, or nuts, among other fillings. It can be found in most bakeries. *Malabi* is a milk pudding (like blancmange) thickened with cornstarch, flavored with rosewater and topped with pistachios and syrup (date/sugar): there are many Israeli preparations for this Turkish original. Finally, don't skip the *babka*, a chocolate-swirled yeast cake.

If you're looking for a post-dinner sweet that's a little more recognizable, you still have options. Ika Cohen (**w** ikachocolate.com) has won numerous medals in international chocolate competitions: the first in 2012 for a lemon praline bonbon, and several gold and silver medals for ganache and pralines made with *za'atar*, *kefir lime*, and tamarind. Bruno Chocolate (**w** brunochocolate.com) won two silver medals: for a halva and cream praline and another called "Mumbai Crunch." Worth seeking out! Ice cream and gelato fans will find shops everywhere. While in the Middle East, you might want to sample a local flavor: perhaps pistachio, *malabi*, or a seasonal fruit. Anita (D4) is the most famous of the gelato places, landing on our electives list.

If **savory snacks** are your thing, look out for *bamba*, a peanut snack in the shape of a Cheeto, replete with dust like a Cheeto, but peanut butter-flavored. Bisli is a wheat snack in a variety of interesting flavors, such as barbecue, grill (that's different than bbq!), taco, falafel, onion, and pizza. In the **chocolate** camp, we have Krembo, a milk-chocolate-covered marshmallow with a cookie base, usually in vanilla flavor, but also in mocha. These are legendary. Milky is the most popular brand of chocolate pudding with whipped cream. Mekupelet is a flaky chocolate bar, similar to Cadbury Flake.

FOOD MARKETS   One important note about "**farmers' markets**": just because food is sold *outdoors* does not mean the vendor is the farmer, the producer, or anyone other than an individual grocer who sells food in the open air rather than in a store. Most of the products you will see in **Carmel Market (#87)** and **Mehane Yehuda Market (#67)** have come from far away (though usually within Israel) and are sold by small-business owners. You can always feel free to ask where the product came from – almost everyone speaks English. The *Tel Aviv Port* hosts a farmers' market on Fridays at Hangar 12 at Namal Tel Aviv, outside under the tent (⊕ 09.00–about 15.00 Fri). The Jaffa Port Market also hosts a farmers' market (⊕ 09.00–14.00 Fri).

The Sarona Market (D3) is an extremely popular **food hall**. With nearly 100 vendors and stalls selling everything from wares to books to bottles to foodstuffs, Israelis congregate here every day of the week, with pathways usually jammed full of people eating, chatting, and trying to maneuver around the crowds. If you're looking to sample the wide variety of foods available in Israel in one central location, this place tops most others. You'll find raw bars, ramen noodles, curry, burgers, bagels, chocolate, sandwiches, hummus, breakfast places, coffee, and an assortment of ethnic foods, along with a whole slew of shops that specialize in perhaps just one thing, such as *halva*, herbs, olives, nuts, or one particular type of dessert. Inside the **Tel Aviv Port** (Mon–Fri) you'll find a cramped but cute space, offering fresh produce, little plates of food, shops with wine, meat, fish, coffee, and homemade goods such as jam. The Jaffa Port Market offers significantly less than its peers, and has a harder time attracting permanent vendors, but you can still find hummus shops and mezze places in and among its stalls, though Old Man and the Sea (D2) with its 20 mezzes and fresh fish offerings tends to be the prime attraction here. On Fridays, the Dizengoff Mall hosts a variety of homemade stalls and stands offering up an eclectic, but exciting and popular, selection of tasty lunch treats. Shuk Tzafon (North Market) is a northeastern addition to the ranks of giant food halls such as Sarona and Namal, with 30 stores and restaurants in a big, open space near the Bnei Brak train station.

No matter where you're staying, be it the Holy Land, Madagascar, Siberia, or Easter Island – you should always plan to take a stroll through the local **outdoor market** (*shuk/souk*) during your visit. The sights and smells will likely immediately influence your understanding of the culture, food, and people. From recognizing ingredients that you order in a restaurant, sampling a local delicacy, talking with locals, hearing music, seeing people old and young, poor and rich, all shopping together – markets are always a memorable experience. **Mehane Yehuda Market (#67)** is perhaps Jerusalem residents' most beloved marketplace. With hundreds of stalls selling all kinds of food and wares, people from all walks of life converge here for their necessities. At night, the market reinvents itself into a hip locale with bars and restaurants. **Carmel Market (#87)** is Tel Aviv's largest market, with lots of food stalls, grocery items, small restaurants, and tasty bites to sample. Levinsky Market (D4) is known as a spice market to Tel Aviv tourists, though there are a variety of other products, including halva, dried fruits, nuts, and other culinary treats.

There are several popular chains of **grocery stores/supermarkets**, some of which you will find in downtown areas. If you're staying in an Airbnb, or a hotel with a kitchen, you'll definitely want to find a real grocery store: you can ask your front desk to point you in the direction of the closest. SuperCofix is cheap! Tiv Taam is open every day, including Shabbat. Mega and Shufersal have the widest selections.

There are **convenience stores** (*makolet*) on every block in Israel, so if you're looking for a quick snack, that's all you'll need. They usually have soft drinks, ice cream, snack chips, that kind of thing. AM:PM is the most ubiquitous chain of convenience stores, and probably the most convenient outside of an actual grocery store. Most are open 24/7 and Shabbat. Gas stations are also usually stocked with junk food, cold drinks, and the normal fare you'd find in an American gas station (not European). Note that many other convenience stores are closed on Shabbat.

RESTAURANTS If you're interested in the very best restaurants in the region, we have a quick list for you in *Food and Drink - Food - Top Restaurants* (p. 561). You can also follow along on our very own food tour in *D6: Tel Aviv: Food and Drink*.

FOOD CHECKLIST We want you to experience the maximum the cultures of the Holy Land have to offer. If you're game, keep track of how many different foods you've tried on your trip, and hopefully this list will inspire you to learn more, try more, and enjoy more!

Cuisines

- [ ] Israeli
- [ ] Jordanian
- [ ] Palestinian
- [ ] Gazan
- [ ] Bedouin
- [ ] Druze
- [ ] Modern Israeli
- [ ] Nazarene Fusion

Jewish holidays/Shabbat

- [ ] Seder
- [ ] Matzah
- [ ] Challah
- [ ] Cholent/Chamin
- [ ] Lekach
- [ ] Holishke
- [ ] Sufganiyot
- [ ] Levivot
- [ ] Oznei Haman

Arab holidays

- [ ] Iftar
- [ ] Kousa
- [ ] Qatayef
- [ ] Zalabieh/Awamat

Bread

- [ ] Pita
- [ ] Druze pita
- [ ] Laffa
- [ ] Lavash
- [ ] Injera
- [ ] Markook/shrak
- [ ] Bourekas
- [ ] Challah
- [ ] Ka'ak
- [ ] Non
- [ ] Jachnun
- [ ] Malawach
- [ ] Kubane
- [ ] Lachoch

Sandwiches

- [ ] Falafel
- [ ] Sabich
- [ ] Shawarma
- [ ] Me'orav Yerushalmi

Sauces/dips

- [ ] Tahina
- [ ] Amba
- [ ] Zhug
- [ ] Matbucha
- [ ] Harissa
- [ ] Muhamarra
- [ ] Dukkah

Grains/legumes

- [ ] Freekeh
- [ ] Burgul
- [ ] Ptitim/moghrabia/maftul
- [ ] Zarb/quzi
- [ ] Mujadarra

Beans

- [ ] Fresh fava
- [ ] Hummus
- [ ] Masabacha
- [ ] Fuul

Spices

- [ ] Za'atar
- [ ] Baharat
- [ ] Sumac

Dairy/egg

- [ ] Shakshuka
- [ ] Bulgarit
- [ ] Tzfat
- [ ] Labneh
- [ ] Gavina levana
- [ ] Jameed

Fish

- [ ] Barbunia
- [ ] Buri
- [ ] Denis
- [ ] Faridah
- [ ] Forel
- [ ] Levrak
- [ ] Lokus
- [ ] Mushte
- [ ] Musar
- [ ] Chraimeh
- [ ] Gefilte

Chicken

- [ ] Shnitzel
- [ ] Shish taouk
- [ ] Maqluba
- [ ] Musakhan

Red meat

- [ ] Kibbeh
- [ ] Kofta
- [ ] Mansaf
- [ ] Merguez
- [ ] Shashlik
- [ ] Shish kebab
- [ ] Kubba soup

Traditional desserts

- [ ] Kanafeh
- [ ] Mutabak
- [ ] Baklava
- [ ] Bourma
- [ ] Ballorieh
- [ ] Halva
- [ ] Rugelach
- [ ] Malabi
- [ ] Babka

Snacks/candy

- [ ] Bamba
- [ ] Bisli
- [ ] Krembo
- [ ] Milky
- [ ] Mekupelet

DO #15: DRINK IT!

WINE

History Wine is nearly as old as the Holy Land. In fact, references to wine can be found throughout the Old Testament, and as early as the ninth chapter of Genesis (the first book), when Noah is written to have planted the first vineyard. Wine appears throughout the Bible – references to growing techniques, storage methods, its value in trade, and its use in ceremony are referenced over multiple periods of time. Similarly, archaeological record confirms the importance of the wine industry for at least 1,000 years, as wine presses, clay pots, and storage caves are continuously being unearthed over many eras. It is now known that the wine of the ancient era was nothing like our own. Though production was similar – biblical accounts even seem to reference how wine quality is improved by elevating grapevines on a trellis – the taste was far different. Today, winemakers add particular cultures to wine, have better methods of preparation and storage, and 2,000 more years of experience in understanding how to handle grapes from vine to glass. Then, flavor was pretty experimental with lots of different types of additives to mask any harsh flavors. Honey, seawater, lime, pepper, and herbs were all used to improve quality.

Wine has nearly always played an important role in religious ceremonies. The Jewish Mishnah, written between the 1st and 2nd centuries CE, tells of the importance of drinking four cups of wine on Passover, a tradition that lives on to this day. Another Jewish holiday, Purim, celebrates the freedom of Jews from massacre by an ancient Achaemenid (Persia) king. Since at least Talmudic times, Jews have commemorated this moment by getting blind drunk, as it was written in the Talmud to drink until you can no longer tell the difference between the two main characters in the story.

In ancient times, wine was usually stored in amphorae (ceramic carrying vessels), covered with a natural oxygen deterrent (olive oil), and sealed with pine wax for long-term storage. Grapes were dried before being juiced, creating a higher-sugar/higher-alcohol wine, similar to the sweet wine process of wines from Italy and Greece. Cork was introduced in the 3rd century BCE. Oak barrels were mandated by the Roman Empire in the 3rd century CE, but glass bottles were not introduced until the industry came back to Israel almost 1,400 years after it left.

When Islam ushered in a new, less alcohol-tolerant era in the 7th century CE, wine production ceased. The Crusaders tried to reintroduce the industry in the 12th and 13th centuries, but it did not stick. Only when Jews returned from Europe – where wine continued to play a major role in life and ceremony – did they also bring back vines to the Holy Land. It is believed that Rabbi Itzhak Schorr established the first winery of modern times in the Holy Land. German Templars established an agricultural collective at Sarona (in the present-day neighborhood of Sarona in downtown Tel Aviv) and created the first wine factory in the region. Baron Edmond de Rothschild of France was famous for funding early Holy Land entrepreneurs. He helped finance several of the first Jewish-run wineries in the region, including wineries in Rishon Letzion and **Zichron Ya'akov** (still a wine town). At that time, most wine was produced for sacramental (*kashrut*) purposes. The modern wine revolution did not occur until many years later, with the consensus being that it kicked off with the establishment of the **Golan Heights Winery (#75)** in 1983, Israel's first highly regarded winery. Trained in California and using California root stock, then mimicked by other regional wine growers throughout the next few decades, the industry not only took off once again but has since gained international renown.

Grapes There are a few *unique* grapes to the region, some of which may be recognizable to an oenophile, but may be a new experience for you to try. Carignan is surprisingly the second-most grown grape in Israel, and Colombard, Argaman, and Muscat of Alexandria are also among the top ten most planted grape varietals. Viognier is well regarded. Most of these grapes are used in red table blends.

When the Israeli wine industry really took off in the 1980s, it was because vineyard owners transitioned from lesser recognized varietals to the so-called "noble" varieties, such as Riesling, Merlot, and Cabernet Sauvignon. Recently, though, experimentalists have been playing with local/wild varietals in the hope of creating new and successful styles. (Note: all of these are difficult to find.) Bittuni is a light-bodied red wine (unusual for Israeli reds, which trend heavy), mixed by Recanati. Dabouki – maybe the wine of Jesus? – is a white wine with melon-forward notes. When Marawi (or Hamdani) and Jandali are mixed together, the harshness from the one ancient varietal mixes well with the boringness of the other, and many are very excited about the prospect of this true Palestinian grape (grown in the West Bank). Recanati produces this blend under the name "Marawi." Cremison is a dark red wine, with strawberry aromas and flavors, and some tannin, produced by Cremisan in the West Bank.

Rosé wine is a thing! There's a good article on the many types of Israeli rosé at w winesisrael.com/en/4334/the-wine-of-the-mediterranean/. Your author also published a wine tasting note for an Israeli rosé in Jennifer Simonetti-Bryan's *Rosé Wine: The Guide to Drinking Pink* (available on Amazon).

Wineries Wine in Israel continues to garner international recognition year after year. Some of the most **highly regarded wineries** today include Clos de Gat Winery (B3), Flam Winery (B3), *Yatir Winery*, *Domaine du Castel*, **Golan Heights Winery (#75)**, Lewinsohn, Margalit Winery (E6), and Tzora Winery (B3). Carmel, Barkan, **Golan Heights Winery (#75)**, Teperberg 1870, Arza (majority sacramental wine), and Zion bottle close to 75% of all wine in Israel. **Golan Heights Winery (#75)**, Vitkin, Dalton, and Tulip were all favorably reviewed in 2015 by *Food & Wine* (w foodandwine.com/articles/israeli-wine-on-the-front-lines). **Boutique** wineries deserve attention: though they comprise less than 10% of total wine production, they make up more than 80% of Israel's wineries. There are boutiques everywhere, and their style is remarkably casual – you can often walk right in the front door and find a friendly person ready to introduce you to their product. (It's still best to call in advance, though.)

Wine tours If you are looking to set up a wine tour, you can either set up your own itinerary and self-drive (difficult, plus someone has to be designated driver) or you can organize a van tour. We have a number of listed wineries as electives, and you can get more information by contacting these venues directly. One option for creating your own itinerary would be to select two or three wineries in the same region, spacing them 2–3 hours apart. We've given you a head start with three driving tours you can customize as you see fit (or wherever you can get a booking), in three different regions. For the Judean Hills, see *Road Trip B3*; for central Israel, see *Road Trip E6*; and for Galilee/Golan, see *Road Trip U1*. Additionally, Israel has a popular route in the desert, an untraditional wine-growing region, called the Negev Wine Route (J2).

Alternatively, you can use a tour company. They will likely quote you a price that includes pickup and dropoff at your hotel, the cost of the car, driver, and guide, tasting fees, and a few stops along the way. Not included are tips (expected) for both the guide and driver, cost of lunch, and any extras you buy, of course. Expect to spend $50–100 per person, but the more people, the cheaper the overall price, as they will likely be able to accommodate up to 8–10 people in a van, and you're paying for the whole thing regardless of how many people come. You also may want to make a multiday adventure, in which case you'll have to double the price and factor in the cost of hotel.

Israel Wine Tour (w israelwinetour.co.il/tour-schedule/) is a great company with good predetermined tour options, including to the Judean Hills, Carmel/ Shomron, Negev, and Golan Heights. They actually tell you which wineries, too, which is surprisingly rare to find on the webpage itself. it also has kosher, evening, and multiday tour options. **My Israel Wine Tours** (w myisraelwinetours.com) combines history with wine, taking in one or two wineries along with a number of other stops on thematic or regional tours, which are presented nicely on its website. **Israel Wine Journeys** (w israelwinejourneys.net/wine-tour-in-israel) can help set up your day or multiday visit, with recommendations for three wineries, four wineries plus lunch, or overnight. **igoogledisrael** (w igoogledisrael.com/wine-tours/#ninja -popup-24599) has three tours to choose from, to the Judean Hills, to Shormon (*Zichron Ya'akov* region), and the Golan Heights.

Brands If you are in a wine store and simply looking for some reliable, mid-range brands, you actually have plenty to choose from. Easy-enough-to-find winemakers that should be available in your everyday corner store include Carmel, Clos de Gat, Dalton, *Domaine du Castel*, Flam, Galil Mountain, *Gamla*, Hermon, Pelter, Recanati, Tabor, Tishbi, Tulip, Vitkin, Yarden, and Yatir. If you are looking for table wine, something cheap, or *avoiding* bad-cheap, try Barkan, Binyamina, Carmel, Segal, or Teperberg.

Wines We don't recommend specific bottles – the vintages change every year, after all – but *Wine Spectator* does have rankings from 2016 (w winespectator. com/wines/list/id/53573): anything ranked 90 and above around the $30 mark is going to be a great find. *The Tower* recommends 13 Israeli wines that it claims will change your perspective of what Israel has to offer dramatically (w thetower. org/article/thirteen-israeli-wines-that-will-change-your-worldview/) – newer vintages could constitute a fun party game: have everyone bring a bottle to share! The *Jerusalem Post* has a "sip this" list (w jpost.com/Israel-News/Culture/Sip-This -The-wine-list-451122); Israel21c has a great overview of the Judean Hills wineries (w israel21c.org/sip-the-wines-of-the-fabulous-judean-hills-terroir/); *Food & Wine* features five "great Israel wines" (w foodandwine.com/articles/israeli-wine-on-the -front-lines) and lists 12 wines to explore from the region (w foodandwine.com/ wine/the-12-israeli-wines-you-need-to-drink-to-be-an-expert).

Rankings and ratings Ratings vary by rater, but wine ratings will generally be scored on a 0–100 scale, although the lowest score is only ever 50. Wines above 85 are good/ above average; wines above 90 are superior to exceptional; and 95–100 are rare and usually expensive. For starters, no Israeli wine has ever scored 95 or above from an international rating organization (see below).

Daniel Rogov was a famous Israeli wine rater whose book *The Ultimate Rogov's Guide to Israeli Wines* set the benchmark for reviewing much of what the region has to offer. Although he died in 2011, he was very well respected and had a lot to say about the evolution of the Israeli wine industry, so his book remains extremely relevant and can still be found in print. His points system awards up to 5 points in visual appearance, 15 points to aroma and bouquet, 15 points for flavor and palate impressions, and 15 points for overall impression. The total combined score gets 50 added to it for a minimum score of 50 and a maximum of 100. He awarded 96 points to the Golan Heights Winery's Yarden 2006 wine, and 95 points to the same wine from 2007, as well as Margalit's Special Reserve Cabernet Sauvignon from 2008 and 2009. He has awarded several others 94 points and below, and his book is highly recommended if you are interested in sampling a variety of hard-to-find and as yet globally unrecognized gems.

As mentioned above, *Wine Spectator* reviewed dozens of Israeli wines in its October 2016 issue. Tzora's Misty Hills Judean Hills 2013 wine scored top marks, at 93 points. Another Tzora wine, the Tzora Judean Hills 2014, scored 92 (the second-highest score), with six other wines scoring 91 points. Robert Parker's *Wine Advocate* has awarded three wines 94 points: Alexander Amorolo 2011, Clos Du Gat Sycra Muscat 2006, and Castel Grand Vin 2013. *Wine Advocate* also marveled at Château Golan in a subsequent issue.

The wine blog w winesisrael.com has a number of very good articles from Adam Montefiore, including a good review of the rise in international renown as told from the perspective of wine rankings (w winesisrael.com/en/4219/on-the-map/) and the story of Robert Parker and Mark Squires' history with Israel wine (w winesisrael. com/en/3991/the-worlds-no-1-critic/). Two wine critics created *The New Israeli Wine Guide* based on ratings from blind tastings (w tniwg2014.files.wordpress. com/2014/02/the-new-israeli-wine-guide-2014-eng1.pdf), and also produced *The New Israeli Wine Guide Top 10 Reds and Top 10 Whites* (w kishorit.org.il/ sites/default/files/files/the-new-israeli-wine-guide-preview-2014(1).pdf), in which two wines scored 92 points: the Mourvèdre 2012 from Château Golan (red) and the Shoresh 2013 from Tzora (Sauvignon Blanc, white).

According to *Wine Enthusiast* magazine, Recanati's 2011 Reserve David Vineyard Cabernet Sauvignon is the highest-rated Israeli wine, earning 94 points and garnering a "Best of the Year 2015" from the same magazine, ranked #100 in the Top Cellar Selections of 2015. The Dalton 2014 Alma Red ranked #63 in the magazine's "Enthusiast List" of 2017, scoring 93 points, and Jerusalem Wineries produced a 2013 Shiraz called Premium 3400 which scored 93 points and ranked #92 in the roundup of best wines of 2015. Barkan's 2016 Reserve Cab Sauv received 92 points and was rated #58 in the Top 100 Wines of 2019.

Hugh Johnson's Pocket Wine Book lists both Clos du Gat and Flam Wineries of Israel as four-star wineries, the highest recognition available. **Yatir** and **Castel** are both listed as three- to four-star wineries.

Quality Now, a question: you're in a restaurant and the waiter/sommelier hands you an international wine menu. Should you order **Israeli wine** or something else, if given the option? *No question: the Israeli wine!* Better bargain, great quality.

Same question, but in **Jordan**. There, you should order Jordanian wine, first, because there is no Israeli wine and, secondly, it's interesting to say you've tried it, even though it's limited in production and is not of the same quality.

In terms of **good vintages**, 2014, 2016, 2018, and 2019 were all considered good recent years. For you spenders or collectors, 1976, 1979, 1985, 1989, 1990, 1993, 1995, 1997, 2000, 2003, 2004, 2005, 2008, 2012, and 2013 were all exceptional years.

Price Does price represent quality? No. Some cheap wine is palatable and some $20 wine is undrinkable. To put a number on it, 95% of Israeli wine is drinkable, if sometimes heavy. If you can spend $15 on a bottle, it will be fine, maybe very good. Every year, Studio Ben Ami hosts a Best Value Competition for wines up to

79 ILS in price. In 2020, **Golan Heights Winery (#75)** scored four gold medals, while Barkan Winery (Israel's largest) received three. In 2019, Tabor Winery (G2) won nine medals. Winners in individual grape categories can be found at w winesisrael.com/ en/5532/best-value-2020/, or Google "best value Israel wines [20XX]." The *Times of Israel* published an article on all the major bulk-produced/cheap Israeli wines on the market, which has been popular since its publication in 2014 (w blogs.timesofisrael. com/the-2014-israeli-wine-bottle-etiquette-guide/).

BEER Beer (and alcohol) electives are covered under the *Food and Drink – Drink* theme (p. 564). If you're looking for cocktail bars or pubs, skip ahead to *Do #18: Late Nit!* (p. 107). For a ranking of beers from the region, look no further than w ratebeer. com/country/israel/101/ for Israel and w ratebeer.com/beer/country/jordan/106/ for Jordan: excellent is probably anything above a 4.0 score, but neither country meets that mark; Jordan has only one beer brand that scores above 3.0, which is Carakale; at the time of writing (rankings change frequently), Israel's Alexander/Mikkelier the Beer of Milk and Honey is #1 at 3.58, and Dancing Camel Doc's Green Leaf Party currently sits at #2 with 3.56.

The main local brands are **Goldstar** and **Maccabee**, which make up the largest share in Israel, at 60%. Dancing Camel is the largest microbrewer, while the Taybeh Brewing Company comes out of Ramallah (Muslim area!). Carakale is the main microbrewery in Jordan. Other **popular brand names**, with great reviews locally, are Alexander, Malka, and Jem's. Dancing Camel specializes in **seasonal beers**, producing a mint and rosemary blonde ale for "summertime in Tel Aviv," a wheat beer with Etrog lemon around Sukkot, and a pomegranate-flavored beer on Rosh Hashanah. Beer is not kosher for passover, so there are occasionally beers made from dates or chickpeas during this holiday. If you're not into beer, but you do like **cider**, then how about Buster's (B3) Dry Cider? They also make our electives' list for a place to visit, if you're interested in beers and breweries.

There are a few places where you can **sample** a variety of brews: if you're in Tel Aviv, Beer Garden in the Sarona Market (D3) has over 100 beers from 20 Israeli micro-breweries; the Jerusalem Beer Festival is a great option if you're in town in August; and the Beer Bazaar in **Mehane Yehuda Market (#67)** in Jerusalem and **Carmel Market (#87)** in Tel Aviv are also good options.

ALCOHOL Arak is the drink of choice in this region. It's a potent, anise-based drink in the style of sambucca, raki, and ouzo. Its alcohol content is usually 50% (or 100 proof), and it is traditionally mixed with two parts water to one part arak, which transforms it from a clear liquor into a milky-white liquid.

COFFEE Coffee exists in many cultures, and in the several cultures of the Middle East are no different. In Israel, the coffee is a bit more suited to the Western palate, so for the thick and dark Arabic/Turkish styles of coffee look to Muslim/Arab areas, such as Palestine and Jordan, and Arab cities/neighborhoods, such as Jaffa.

In Israel, there is no Starbucks: the closest equivalent to coffee-market dominator is **Aroma**. Found seemingly on every street corner, this chain offers good juices, breakfast, sandwiches, and salads in addition to its coffee collection. Other popular chains are Arcaffe, Cafe Hillel, CafeCafe, Cofix (5 ILS!), Cup O' Joe, and Ilan's, while so-called "third wave" coffee shops which roast their own Arabica beans include Cafelix, Mae Cafe, and Loveat. You'll also find a number of kiosks in Tel Aviv and other cities, with famous sites including Rothschild Coffee Kiosk and EspressoBAR.

In the Turkish tradition, coffee is served in a *finjan*. These pots are ubiquitous in the Arab areas, like Jaffa. Coffee electives can be found under the *Food and Drink – Drink* theme (p. 564). In terms of definitions: *coffee* usually means Turkish-style, i.e., thick, black, and short; *Nescafe* is exactly what you think it is, and the closest in style to an American black coffee; *Americano* is espresso with hot water; *cappuccino* (café hafukh) is espresso with steamed milk; *iced coffee* is a blended ice drink, not "iced coffee" in the American sense; *cold coffee* (café kar) is espresso and cold milk; *Arabic coffee* is usually flavored with cardamom and unsweetened; and *Turkish coffee* is unflavored and can be ordered sweetened or unsweetened.

TEA Tea is not super-popular in Israel, but it is growing. In Jordan, you will find Lipton everywhere. Some places to get your tea include the French, upscale chain Palais des Thés, or check out **Carmel Market (#87)** for loose-leaf.

JUICE Juice stands are ubiquitous in downtown Jerusalem and Tel Aviv. You'll see the various fruit options hanging from the rafters as you walk down busy pedestrian streets, side alleys, and market stalls. You'll even find them throughout the Old City. **Limonana** is perhaps the most ubiquitous – lemonade and mint; sometimes slushy, sometimes pure. You can get expensive versions in Aroma and cheap(ish) versions from sidewalk vendors, and it is popular in Jordan as well. Some places specialize in one particular style of juice. There are, for instance, **carrot juice** vendors outside **Carmel Market (#87)** in Tel Aviv selling cups for 5 ILS. In many Palestinian cities (and in Jordan), you'll find people selling **pomegranate juice**, which you can drink straight (intense) or cut with orange juice. Other flavors to look out for include **almond** and **tamarind**.

HOT/WINTER Sahlab is a popular drink made with ground sahlab orchid bulbs, hot milk, orange blossom, cinnamon, and vanilla, and topped usually with raisins, cinnamon, and coconut. Look for it in **Mehane Yehuda Market (#67)**, Abouelafia Bakery, Tmol Shilshom, Kadosh Café Patisserie, and any of Aroma Cafe's numerous locations.

DO #16: BEACH IT!

CHOOSING A BEACH With so many beaches to choose from, it could be hard to pick. But fear not: you need only answer a few simple questions. If you like being surrounded by people, want to be within walking distance of your hotel, or want lots of amenities: drinks, beach chairs, falafel shops, then stick with **Tel Aviv Beaches (#89)**, which have everything most travelers need. If you want a place where young kids can run around freely, then definitely stick to beaches with lifeguards, such as **Herziliya Beaches**, **Netanya**, or Palmahim (E3). If you want something gorgeous and less crowded, try **Dor HaBonim (#100)** or **Beit Yannai**, and review the *Leisure – Beaches – Remote Beaches* category (p. 555). Finally, if you prefer something way off the beaten path, then **Dahab (#54)** in the Sinai is a good option.

The Mediterranean has glorious, sandy beaches; the Red Sea has sand, though the water is the real draw; and the Dead Sea and Sea of Galilee are inland bodies of water with few waves and little sand (we go into much greater detail in *Leisure – Beaches*, p. 554). Water sports can be found practically everywhere, from windsurfing on the Sea of Galilee to snorkeling in the Red Sea, remote and popular beaches alike (see *Active – Water Sports*, p. 552).

A DAY ON THE BEACH You don't need to plan anything! Doesn't that feel great? Here's what you could do with your day:

- ★ Rent a lounge chair – usually 30–40 ILS. Comes with umbrella, chair, and cushion.
- ★ Order a few beers. If you're on an organized beach, the local restaurants will gladly serve you food or drinks.
- ★ Invest in a ping-pong set (no table) called *matcot* and start joining in the racket!
- ★ Run full speed into the water (in Tel Aviv). The breakers stop most of the waves and keep the water shallow.
- ★ Take a falafel break.
- ★ Reapply that sunscreen.
- ★ Walk up or down the promenade (Tel Aviv/Herziliya).
- ★ Rent a surfboard, or take a kiteboard (seasonal) or stand-up paddleboard class.
- ★ Watch the sunset.
- ★ Evening volleyball/matcot.
- ★ Take a nap.
- ★ Go for a jog.
- ★ Exercise on the many outdoor gym sets.
- ★ Join in the merriment at the beachside bars, which have theme nights to the late hours on Thursdays and sometimes Fridays.

LIFEGUARDS The official bathing season is centered around the summer months from May to October. Technically, beaches are only open when there's a lifeguard on duty, but in practice this means you're on your own if you wade out during any of the winter months. Lifeguards will use flags to indicate where swimmers can swim, and will whistle at you and yell through their loudspeaker if you don't abide by the rules! The hours of operation for most lifeguard stations is 07.15–16.45, though that extends by an hour in the month of June to 17.45. Will you get into trouble if you swim outside these hours? Or at a beach without a lifeguard? No, not really. Israelis are a "live and let live" kind of people, so you'll be left to your own devices. But understand that no rescue services will be available outside of these times.

FLAGS If you see flags on the beach, take note: *white flags* mean that you're allowed to swim anywhere; *red flags* mean that swimming is only permitted between the areas of the red flags due to dangerous sea conditions; *black flags* indicate that no swimming permitted; *purple flags* tell you there are jellyfish in the water; and *blue flags* are not a lifeguard label, but rather an indication that the beach meets certain indicators of water quality, safety, and cleanliness, among other factors (see below).

SAFETY Pay attention to *Lifeguards* and *Flags*, above. While **pickpocketing** may not be terribly widespread, it is still a good idea to have someone look over your things when you go into the water. It's not uncommon to ask the person sitting next to you to watch over your belongings if no one in your party is staying behind. If you do this, of course volunteer to do the same in return and don't stay out long. The **first rains of the season** usually come around Sukkot, washing away all the garbage that has been piling up in a city's drains for the previous six months. This makes swimming particularly rough, as there may be an inordinate amount of trash, oil, or even dead animals floating in the sea. **Rip currents** can catch you out, so avoid water where there are no waves breaking, as this tends to indicate that the water is being pulled back out to sea. That said, undertows can be found anywhere, so it's best to follow instructions from the lifeguard, particularly if you aren't a great swimmer.

JELLYFISH Jellyfish tend to find their way to the Mediterranean via the Suez Canal from the Indian Ocean every year, usually in June and/or July. The jellyfish season is not long, but it can be a bummer as swarms of stinging jellies travel all along the coastline in their millions. Weirdly, they also tend to be most active during a full moon (!), so checking a lunar calendar might be helpful. Though in Hebrew, there's a good website with maps showing where users have uploaded information about jellyfish, so if you're in town, you may want to avoid those beaches and look elsewhere (w meduzot.co.il/overview-map/).

WAVES Waves are at their prime from December to February, during winter. There can still be some unpredictable waves coming over the summer months, but if you're swimming when it's warm, the chances are the water is going to be calm. One of the most trusted sites for wave forecasting is w surfline.com, where you can get short-term weather reports including surf height, tide, and wind direction and speed; w windguru.cz offers a similar service, with live visual aids to help assess currents, temperature, cloud cover, precipitation, and even ideal times to be on the water.

BLUE FLAG The **Blue Flag Beach** program evaluates a number of characteristics of beaches and their seawater, including environmental management, water quality, education and signage, services, and safety. Countries enter into the program voluntarily, with the idea that clean beaches will promote tourism. Jordan has six Blue Flag beaches, with one marina, while Israel has 54 awarded sites, including all 13 of Tel Aviv's beaches. Egypt has not yet begun to participate. See w blueflag.global/all-bf-sites for more details.

PRICES Surprisingly, prices are standardized on all Tel Aviv beaches. You will find differing levels of service and price in other parts of the country, but the municipality at least tries to ensure tourists (and locals) aren't completely ripped off during their stay. If you visit the business (bar/restaurant/sport) directly rather than wait to get served on the beach, you can be assured of the following prices: beach chair 6 ILS/day; *reclining* beach chair 12 ILS/day; umbrella 6 ILS/day; pita with hummus 12 ILS; small bottle of water 7 ILS; and popsicle 5 ILS. Haaretz published a further list indicating that watermelon caps at 30 ILS, coffee at 5 ILS, beer at 21 ILS, french fries at 25 ILS, and meals at 60 ILS. Lockers are also available for 5 ILS.

BEACH SPORTS We cover water sports in great detail in *Active – Water Sports* (p. 552).

DO #17: SHOP IT!

GOING ABOUT IT

Haggling/bargaining Love it or hate it, if you want a good deal and you're in a local market with no listed prices, you're going to have to bargain. It works like this: you spend two extra seconds with a wood carving/rug/tchotchke and the vendor takes note, saying, how much are you willing to pay? You give a number, they say it's much too low and then quote you an unreasonably high number (which he knows is too high) and that's when the negotiation begins. Bear in mind these tips when deciding whether to buy something, be it a pear from a fruit market or a gold necklace in the Old City:

1. Consider how much the item is worth to you in your own currency. (That doesn't mean it's the price, but gives you a sense of when you should walk away.)
2. Convert the price into shekels or dinars.

3. Once you know how much you're willing to spend, and that you are interested in buying, ask for the price before touching the product. You don't want to fill a bag with two kilos of almonds and find out it costs ten times what you were expecting.
4. Don't like the price quoted? Bargain down.
5. Start with a price lower than what you were first willing to pay, because you're going to have to compromise somewhere in the middle.
6. Don't like how the conversation is going? Say "thank you" ("shukran" in Arabic; "to-dá" in Hebrew) politely, and walk away.
7. You can search around for lower prices. Many of the vendors buy from the same importers.
8. Wait, importers? Yes – check for "Made in ____" labels. Half the crafts (or more) in the Old City are made in China! Not sure where it originated? Ask the vendors – they know what they're hawking and will tell you bluntly, "That's Chinese junk, but this…"
9. For large items, credit cards are accepted in most venues, and are fairly safe. You may choose to forego credit card if the person tries to make a carbon or photocopy of the credit card before charging – that's an easy way for someone to steal your credit card number and should be avoided. If you're buying something worth less than $20, the vendor may not allow credit cards anyway, particularly if you're buying food.
10. If you're using cash, count it in advance and know how much change you need back. Tricky tricksters might forget to give you change. Happens everywhere.

The most aggressive merchants can be found in the Old City, but even their tactics are tolerable. Some will entice you to enter their store with a joke or a compliment: an "it's free to look!," and possibly a last-ditch attempt at a sale by plucking at your heart strings (a "please it's good luck for my first customer to buy something!"). All in all, the people in the Old City are pretty well-off vendors, and unless tourism has completely sunk for some reason (e.g., COVID-19), they normally fare well. The bottom line is if you don't like it, you don't have to buy it. Once you leave the store, they'll leave you alone.

VAT refunds "VAT" stands for Value Added Tax, for which the rate in Israel is 17%, and 16% in Jordan (technically a sales tax, but functions the same way). VAT works much like a state tax, and is levied on goods and services on top of your bill. As a foreigner, you are not obliged to pay this fee; however, in practice, the VAT is automatically included in the price of the good, which you'll have to pay for in full. You'll then collect a special tax receipt which can be reimbursed in the airport on your way out of the country. No food, drink, or tobacco are allowed for reimbursement as these are tax-exempt goods, so you were never charged VAT on them in the first place. Other goods or services exempt from taxes include: swimming, sports, and health facilities; many hotel services, such as laundry, television, telephone, and office services; personal car rentals; sightseeing transportation; domestic flights; and hospitalization. Jewelry has its own set of rules for purchases above 20,000 ILS, to include special packaging requirements. There are also VAT/duty-free trade zones, which eliminate VAT from all goods purchased in the economic incentive regions of **Eilat (#78)** and **Aqaba (#43)**.

To get any applicable reimbursement, you'll have to ask the merchant for a VAT refund invoice and tax receipt. Many stores will have a "VAT Refund for Tourists" sign in the window. In Israel, the goods must have cost more than 400 ILS ($125) per purchase, including VAT. You then need to present the fully completed VAT refund invoice, together with the goods, in its original unopened/sealed bag at the Milgam Municipal Services Ltd VAT refund desk at the airport. They have a counter before departure, so if you intend to put the goods in your checked luggage bring your passport, ticket, and goods to them here before you check your luggage in. After passport control, you can claim your refund (they want to make sure you are in fact leaving the country and not just skimping out on taxes). You *will* be required to pay a service charge, which varies according to how much you've spent, whether you are requesting cash or a refund to your credit card, and in what currency. In addition to Ben Gurion, you can claim your tax refund at any of the border terminals and the Ramon airport. Information on the Israeli VAT system can be found at w gov.il/en/departments/guides/vat-refund-guide-for-tourists.

The same routine applies in Jordan: pay the VAT, get your receipt, and then present it for reimbursement. Many stores are now asking the client to fill out a Tax Free Form that will automatically reimburse the client, though not immediately. Make sure you keep copies of everything.

You can't request refunds after leaving the country, so make sure to do so in advance.

Duty free There is one big duty-free store in **Ben Gurion**. It's operated by JR/DUTYFREE, and does not often have great deals. In **Queen Alia**, it's DUFRY. In both cases, we recommend against.

At Ben Gurion, it's nice to have the option of buying last-minute gifts, which can include Dead Sea mud and cosmetics, high-end wines and spirits, and other typical duty-free items such as perfume. However, Dead Sea products are obviously cheaper at the Dead Sea than at the airport, bottles of wine can be $10 more expensive than if you purchase them at a local store or at the winery itself, and most of the cosmetics, perfumes and candy are ridiculously overpriced. Even so, you are able to bring duty-free items with you on board the plane in addition to your other goods, so the benefits may outweigh the negatives if you don't want to pay for another checked bag, which can also be expensive. (Of course, *always* check with your airline to make sure that duty free is exempt from your hand luggage allotment, because some budget airlines might not honor this tradition.)

You can also find **duty-free stores** in some downtown areas of Israel, but they are probably not going to work for your short-term needs. They are also not very cheap. They require delivery, and often a two-week wait for clearing customs. Again, we recommend against.

PLACES

Markets In Jerusalem, the Old City **market** (souk) is arguably Israel's largest, with shops sprawling across most of the square kilometer of land, although it is better considered a mishmash of a bunch of discreet markets – the Muslim quarter varies markedly from the Christian side, which tends to cater to tourists, while the former handles many local clients. In Tel Aviv, **Carmel Market (#87)** is a bustling area for locals and tourists alike. The beginning of the market has a variety of vendors hawking clothes, electronics, Judaica, music, and other paraphernalia. Around halfway down, the food vendors begin, with lunch stalls, restaurants, produce stands, butchers, fromageries, and fishmongers. *Tel Aviv Port* on the far north end of the Tel Aviv beach strip houses a number of shops and restaurants, with an interesting food market which has great lunch options, gift ideas, and hosts a farmers' market on Friday. **Jaffa Port** has shops lining the waterfront along with restaurants and a Friday farmers' market. **Jaffa Flea Market**, or *Shuk HaPishpeshim*, is much beloved by Tel Aviv residents and runs across a few streets in Jaffa, with treasures found inside boutique shops, in covered vendor passageways, and on the street itself. **Akko (#13)** has a daily market which serves a mix of tourists and locals, offering hookahs, coffee, and other interesting goodies.

Malls Located just outside of Jerusalem's Jaffa Gate, Mamilla Mall contains lots of high-end retailers and recognizable brands, with a smattering of restaurants and cafés. Malcha Mall is one of the Azrieli brand malls (also found in Tel Aviv; see below), with over 200 shops south of the Old City. In Tel Aviv, Dizengoff Center (D3) has five floors and a bizarre structure, but it's still successful more than 30 years after opening, with all the recognizable stores you've come to expect from a mall, while Azrieli Center Mall has an H&M and other popular stores if you're desperate for global brands, Ramat Aviv Mall has Zara, Diesel, Pull&Bear, Desigual, Tumi, etc., and the Arena Mall on Herziliya's marina has over 100 shops to choose from. Elsewhere, Grand Canyon in Haifa is the largest mall in the north, with more than 200 shops; Kyrion Mall is big and popular, located between Haifa and Akko; and Eilat Mall offers VAT-free shopping (and an ice rink!). And of course you can find big, expansive malls in suburban neighborhoods such as Petah Tikva, Rehovot, Ramat Gan, Herziliya, and Rishon Letzion. All have their own giant facilities, in case you find yourself in those parts.

Shopping compounds Sarona Market (D3) in central Tel Aviv is an old German residential area, converted into a pedestrian center, replete with square blocks of land and cute old houses converted into stores and restaurants. There's also a big commercial food center that attracts thousands of people a day, and even more on the weekends. For a list of shops and food stalls, see w saronatlv.co.il/en/. Hatachana Train Station (D1) is an old converted train station in Tel Aviv which operated from 1892 to 1948. Today, it serves adults and kids alike, with plenty of boutiques, snack shops, activities, events, and entertainment.

Streets and neighborhoods In Jerusalem, **Ben Yehuda Street** is a tourist-centric pedestrian mall in downtown Jerusalem, with lots of souvenir shops, falafel shops, and loud foreigners (but useful gifts for Aunt Betty). In Tel Aviv, Sheinkin Street (D4) was once the trendiest street in Tel Aviv, but now caters to shops that can handle the high rents, though there are a few successful designers still perched along this road. Nahalat Binyamin (D4) has plenty of fabric and designer shops, with an arts and crafts fair two days a week. **Neve Tzedek** is the oldest neighborhood outside of Jaffa in Tel Aviv, and now known for its jewelry and clothing boutiques. In Amman, Rainbow Street (Q2) has lots of Jordanian-made souvenir purchases, including food items, rugs, ceramics, and handicrafts.

Outlets There is a clothing outlet mall in Herziliya, north of Tel Aviv, on Medinat Hayehudim 85, open every day, and with 35 shops. There's another near Ben Gurion Airport in Or Yehuda, called the Azrieli Or Yehuda Outlet, which is outdoors, has parking, and sells brands from the Azrieli malls at discount.

GIFTS AND SOUVENIRS
Common/local/special These gifts are your best bet, in our honest opinion. They are recognizable as *distinctly Holy Land*, within a decent price range, and will be easy to transport. Plus, they're ubiquitous, so you shouldn't have a problem finding them

if your trip is taking you through the Dead Sea, Jerusalem, Tel Aviv, or Amman, among other locales.

There are liquor stores everywhere in Israel, and grocery stores can also sell wine, so you really have a lot of options when it comes to finding **Israeli wine**. Now, picking a bottle… for that, we recommend you do some sampling yourself – and check out *Do #15: Drink It!* (p. 93) for more information on wine sampling. You can find junk **Judaica** anywhere, but for as close to real as you're going to get, try the Old City and ask the salesperson what is local versus what is foreign-made (Chinese). To choose from, you can have jewelry with your name in Hebrew, prints and posters of Hebrew scripts (usually biblical), chains, menorahs, yarmulkes (kippes), stars of David, hamsas (to ward off the evil eye), backdrops of the Old City skyline, and hundreds of other trinkets. For **Armenian pottery**, the Armenian quarter of the Old City has authentic shops still in operation, and they'll happily give you a demonstration and pack whatever you would like to take with you. Lots of Old City shops will sell **"olive wood" carvings** of Jesus, Mary, crosses, and biblical scenes, specifically the Christmas nativity scene. You can spend hours sifting through any of the hundreds of stores selling Bibles, rosaries, crosses, icons, and countless other pieces of **Catholic and Christian paraphernalia**. You can get a variety of colored **glass** objects, some of which are extremely lightweight. They are virtually indestructible (or so it is touted), moderately priced, and come in a variety of shapes, including wine glasses and lamps.

Lots of people will be hawking old Roman, Greek, and Jewish **coins**. The authenticity is hard to validate, so be careful before you make a high financial commitment to something merely because it looks old. There are lots of counterfeit items in Israel, including ones that proudly wield a "Made in China" sticker! You can do **spices** a few ways. First, you can buy in bulk from any of the masterful spice displays in towering conal shapes, but we'd recommend you consider that there *might* be bugs in those spices (moths have emerged more than once from our own spice collections). Second, you can buy a premade spice collection, though these often have been sitting for months or years. We recommend you look for small quantities of product, preferably packaged with a date, from the main shop display. Always check the expiration or manufacturing date, and if there isn't one: avoid. If you have an eye for **antiques**, you'll have much to admire in the Old City and Amman. There are plenty of fakes to wade through but, if you have the time, you can find gems from ancient eras just waiting to be discovered. At the extremely kitsch end of the scale, there are snow globes (yup, snow globes) to choose from, and generic items such as T-shirts, posters, magnets, and postcards, pretty much everywhere.

Dead Sea products You can purchase all sorts of products made of salts, minerals, and mud. Mud sachets can be purchased for roughly $5 and a variety of cosmetics can be purchased at reasonable prices, many at discount if you buy in bulk. Follow a few rules when buying mud:

1. Make sure you are buying from a place that sources locally. Check the packaging to make sure it's not being shipped from China. Yes, this is actually happening and, yes, you should actually check the packaging even if you are at the Dead Sea.
2. Before committing to a mud mask, make sure the mask is what you want. "Mask" might mean "skin mask" which is actually for all parts of your body except for your face. The attendants will usually key you in to what's what, but if they are busy, you should be reading the packaging.
3. You cannot take mud in your carry-on. Plan to check your mud in your luggage.

4. It is extremely cheap to purchase mud at the Dead Sea, and it is also recommended above purchasing elsewhere.

If you are visiting a public beach at the Dead Sea, there likely won't be any natural mud available. It's been mostly removed, which means you'll need to buy mud for personal use. You can do so from a local store and apply it liberally at the beach. It's not as free or natural as digging your own mud pit, but it's guaranteed to be smooth and rock-free, which is less irritating than the natural stuff.

Other Dead Sea products that you can also buy include **salts**, **cosmetics**, **toiletries**, and all sorts of **skin care items**, all made from locally sourced ingredients. Check labels to ensure you are buying local and natural. **Ahava** is the most popular brand, and its factory can be visited in Kibbutz Mitzpe Shalem, near the Dead Sea, about 12km north of Ein Gedi on Route 90. For **soap**, there are a couple of different routes you could go: olive oil soap made in Palestine, or you can seek out soap made from Dead Sea mud and/or minerals, for purchase at the Dead Sea (cheapest) or any mall in Israel, many hotels in Jordan and Israel, and duty-free shops in the airport, if you're desperate.

Artisanal goods   If you have space, you won't regret bringing back certain foodstuffs or bottled liquids to remind you of the fabulous time you're having in the Holy Land. You can't bring home fruit, vegetables, or herbs (transport of produce or meat is forbidden across most international borders), but you can stock up on spices, nuts, candy, or wine. Here are a few items you may want to consider (never to be bought in Duty Free, which will overcharge you royally).

Olive oil often comes in varying levels of potency, and is found all over. Small-batch vendors sell at outdoor markets, while larger (still local) vendors will have stands in markets such as Sarona or Mehane Yehuda; you can likely taste the brands in these bigger venues. **Za'atar**, **baharat**, and **sumac** are all unique spices you can buy and which we cover in *Do #14 Eat It!* under "Spices" (p. 88). For other spices, nuts, seeds, and legumes try **Mehane Yehuda Market (#67)**, **Carmel Market (#87)**, Levinsky Market (D4), or **Old City Jerusalem (#1)** for a variety of spice towers, nut packs, and the like.

Arabic coffee is not coffeepot coffee, and you need a special pot to get it close to perfect. You can use an espresso pot, the traditional *finjan*, or just boil the coffee with the water on a stovetop. If you're really dedicated to your new hobby, you can buy the *finjan*, the coffee, and a whole new serving set in the Old City. **Krembo** is a seasonal, boxed, chocolate-covered marshmallow treat that comes out only in the wintertime. **Halva** is a sweet/savory dessert made of sesame seeds and sweetener. Popular stores include Eli Maman in the Mehane Yehuda Market and Halva Kingdom in Sarona Market in Tel Aviv, but you can find it in every grocery store and outdoor market. **Pomegranate wine** is an alternative to the grape wine you know so well. Try Rimon Winery, which specializes in sweet pomegranates that can make this wine (which is for sale in wine shops, but also duty-free if you're desperate). It also has a visitor center in the Golan if you're interested. **Tahini**, or sesame paste, is a primary ingredient in making hummus. If you want a waking chance of creating hummus at home similar to the good stuff in the Holy Land, you'll need some decent tahini. You can visit a grocery store and just buy the most expensive brand. Or, you can do some research. **Dates** are seasonal, but the season is really "always." There are a number of varieties, at different price points, and some that come just around certain holidays. You may be surprised by how expensive they are, and how ornately some varieties come packed (try Medjoul, the "king of the date") but they are widely considered a prized delicacy.

Arts and crafts For little trinkets, you can go to **Old City Jerusalem (#1)**. However, you might be looking for something a little more personal. Extremely popular for handicrafts is the **Bezalel Arts Fair** on Fridays in downtown Jerusalem (A7). Running from Shats to Betsal'el streets between Ben Yehuda and King George, this little market sells lots of authentic options if the Old City isn't doing it for you. Running almost parallel to the Carmel Market in Tel Aviv is Nahalat Binyamin (D4), and on it the eponymous **Arts and Crafts Fair**, operating on Tuesdays and Fridays from late morning to mid-afternoon.

CLOTHING AND JEWELRY

Just walking around the streets, you probably wouldn't guess there's much of a **fashion** scene in Tel Aviv. Most folks wear T-shirts and sandals everywhere (even to restaurants). But boutiques and designer shops can be found throughout Tel Aviv. There are a few streets and neighborhoods good for fashionistas: Dizengoff Street in Tel Aviv has a number of boutiques, while Sheinkin Street (D4) hosts many famous Israeli designer shops. Similarly to the fashion shops and boutiques, you'll find plenty of **jewelry** stores all around town. The **Neve Tzedek** neighborhood and Dizengoff Street in Tel Aviv each have a high concentration of unique jewelry shops.

The largest fashion store chain in Israel, and most ubiquitous, is **Castro**. It's akin to H&M, with clothes for men and women. With more than 140 stores in several countries, it continues to dominate the market with its young, trendy, and affordable clothing lines. **FOX** clothing stores also claims to be the biggest, also with over 140 stores in a dozen countries. They have fashion lines for adults, teens, children, and babies. Their style is "basic casual." **Honigman** has women's fashion, as well as a children's store, and operates a teen/young adult store called **TNT**. Together, the company owns more than 150 stores around the country.

MAIL

Post Office Here are a few services provided in both Israel and Jordan by your friendly, neighborhood post office: stamps; currency exchange; Western Union wire transfers; withdraw cash (through debit or credit card, with fee); international calling cards; some SIM cards; fax; pay bills (if residing temporarily); package delivery; send domestic or international mail.

Postcards You can often get stamps at shops where postcards are sold in both Israel and Jordan. If not, the counter clerk will be able to tell you where to get stamps. Many hotels can provide this service also, or direct you to the post office.

Packages In Jordan, enter your product type and weight at w jordanpost.com.jo/en/calculate-postage to calculate your postage. In Israel, go to w israelpost.co.il, select English in the globe dropdown, and then select "Calculate Postage" on the new page. There, you can pick the delivery method, quantity, and weight in grams. There's a PDF chart on the website with all the Israel Post Mail rates. **DHL** is present in both Israel and Jordan. **FedEx** operates in Israel, and in Jordan through Synergy Express Inc. Neither operate in the Palestinian Territories.

Bookstores and paper If you're longing for a good bookstore, or a place that sells paper products (e.g., postcards, notebooks, and local knick-knacks and gifts), you have several options. A *Time Out* roundup of where to find the most unique gifts in Tel Aviv included three book/paper shops: Sipur Pashut (w sipurpashut.com/english/), The PhotoHouse (D3) (w thephotohouse.co.il), and *Bauhaus Center (D3)* (w bauhaus-center.com). In best-of lists for Israel more generally, The Little Prince, Halper's Bookstore, and Bookworm (all in Tel Aviv) feature regularly, as do the Good Book Shop on Rainbow Street (Q2) and Books@Cafe (Q2) (both in Amman) for best-of lists in Jordan.

DO #18: LATE NIT!

BARS There are quite literally hundreds of bars to choose from in Israel, but Jerusalem and Tel Aviv are the cities with the best scenes, with Tel Aviv particularly representing the vast majority of the best-reviewed and most diverse style of bars in the region. We've rounded up the top 20 bars to have made a noteworthy dent on the tourist and local blog pages. They are all in Tel Aviv unless otherwise indicated:

1. **Imperial Bar (#99)**: rated best bar in the Middle East and Africa by the World's 50 Best Bars, twice (HaYarkon St 66)
2. Kuli Alma (D4) (Mikveh Israel St 10)
3. Mike's Place (Retsif Herbert Samuel St 90; HaArba'a St. 14; Yafo St 33, Jerusalem; HaMayim St, Eilat)
4. Teder.fm (Derech Jaffa 9)
5. Spicehaus (Dizengoff St 117)
6. Jasper John's (Dizengoff St 190)
7. Sputnik (Allenby St 122)
8. The Block (Shalma Rd 157)
9. Bellboy Bar (D4) (Hotel B Berdichovsky, Berdyczewski St 14)
10. Aria Lounge (Nahalat Binyamin St 66)
11. Pasáž (Allenby St 94)
12. 223 (Dizengoff St 223)
13. Abraham's Hostel (Levontin St 21)
14. Abraxas Bar (Lillenblum St 40)
15. Double Standard (Dizengoff St 247)
16. La Otra (HaYarkon St 66)
17. Beit Maariv (Derech Menachem Begin 51)
18. Gatsby Cocktail Room (A7) (Hillel St 18, Jerusalem)
19. Dalida (Zevulun St 7)
20. Hoodna (Abarbanel St 13)

You'll find a dozen more bars, restau-bars, clubs, and in-betweens next door or near these recommended options. Luckily, it's pleasurable weather almost all year, so you won't have a problem **bar-hopping** from one place to another until you find the right scene for you.

Tel Aviv neighborhoods can be broadly classified as follows: Allenby – gritty; South Tel Aviv – big warehouse clubs; Florentin – hipster, music; the area around Rothschild/Lillenblum/Nahalat Binyamin/Allenby – trendy, popular; Jaffa – hip, chill; *Neve Tzedek* – classy, upscale; Port – party, club; and Beach – tourist, party. In **Jerusalem**, many of the bars are scattered in and around **Mehane Yehuda Market (#67)** on Yafo and Ben Yehuda streets, where revelers pour out onto the streets most nights, despite what you may think of Jerusalemites.

Drink local! Refer to *Do #15: Drink It!* section on **Israeli wines** (p. 93) for more information. Many wine bars will allow you to drink a taste, a half-glass, or a full glass, all at different price points. A new trend in some wine bars are cards that allow you to dispense your own choice of wines from their automated machines, with dozens of wine bottles. This allows you to sample before committing to a full glass – or just sample all night. When it comes to **beer**, a pint is a pint, but a half-pint is a *hatzi* and a third of a pint is a *sleesh*. Several Israeli beers are equal in quality to, say, Budweiser or Miller Light (and cheap), but for something more sophisticated, try an Israeli or Palestinian microbrew.

When it comes to **clubs**, expect a queue if you're not on the guest list, so check club and promotion websites for prebooking options. Women will rarely have to pay for entry, but their male cohorts will. Guys, you stand a better/faster chance of entry the more women you have with you. Either way, consider dressing up. Tel Aviv is super casual, but if you're trying to get into an exclusive club, the front door people aren't going to take you seriously unless you look like what they want their clients inside to look like.

DATING/HOOKUP You Millennial? No need to show up randomly at a bar looking for love or fun like it's 2003 – the apps live in the Holy Land too!

Straight people	*LBGTQ*
Tinder Use it just like you would anywhere – swipe right/left for interested/not interested, respectively; reports indicate many people use it as a long-term dating app, rather than for one-night-stand purposes.	**Tinder** Hook-ups, new friends, advice.
	Grindr (men) Hook-ups, new friends, advice, same as in the USA.
	Atraf (men) Mostly hook-ups and/or meet-ups; a popular Grindr-like app in Israel.
JSwipe Same as Tinder, but for Jews. Same swipe idea, but you can screen for religiosity (i.e., how kosher, orthodox, etc.). Lots of English speakers. Requires subscription after free trial.	**Atraf Girls** (women) New friends, meet up at bars for Atraf Girls events; popular app in Israel for lesbians.
	Romeo Hook-ups, transgender-friendly.

NIBBLES

Street food It's late. But before you stumble home, you need to put some food in that belly, so here are some options. In **Tel Aviv**, you can walk down any main street and find an open falafel stand at pretty much any hour. *Miznon* (Ibn Gabirol 23 and King George 30; **f** miznon; ☺ until 01.00) has pita filled with all sorts of goodness, and vegetables to go along with them. **Tony Vespa** (Allenby 118, Rothschild 140, and HaArba'a Street 8; **w** tonyvespa.co.il/en/opening-hours/; ☺ HaArba'a until 04.00 Thu/Fri, other branches until 01.00 or 02.00) sells pizza by the slice and priced by the gram. For burgers, try **Agadir** (Nahalat Binyamin 2, Tel Aviv Port, Jerusalem, Herziliya, Eilat, and Haifa, among others; **w** agadir.co.il/BRANCHES; ☺ until 03.00 or 04.00 most nights, later on weekends); **Susu & Sons** (Dizengoff 166, Herzl 6, and Yefet 9; **f** susuandsons); **Ad HaEtzem** (Rothschild 31 and Ibn Gavirol 21; **w** adhaetzemex.co.il; ☺ until 03.00 or sometimes 04.30); **America Burgers** (Allenby 112; **f** america.burgers; ☺ until 00.00 or 01.00); or **Meat Bar** (Sderot Chen 52 and Sarona; **w** meatbar.co.il; ☺ until midnight). **Frank** (Ibn Gavirol 23; **w** franks.co.il/contact; ☺ until 02.00 most nights, 04.00 Thu/Fri) does hotdogs, **Dixie** (Yigal Alon St 120; **f** dixie.grillbar; ☺ 24 hours) has chicken wings and a variety of egg dishes, burgers, and more. For a deli there's **Deli Fleishman** (Hertzl 12; **w** delif.co.il; ☺ until 02.00, 04.00 Thu), and for a kebab go to **Jasmino** (Allenby 97; ☺ until 02.30, 05.00 Thu). If carbs are your thing, grab a croissant sandwich at **La Gaterie** (King George 97; **f** LaGaterieCafe; ☺ until midnight most nights) and find all kinds of bagels, burekas, and breads, stuffed and not, at **Abouelafia** (Yefet St 7 and Retsif Herbert Samuel 58; **f** abouelafia; ☺ 24 hours).

If you're hungry after drinking in **Jerusalem**, head to **Mehane Yehuda Market (#67)**, where the late-night eateries are concentrated (though things do start to close around midnight), or for French fries and other fast food there's **ChipSir** (Heleni HaMalcha 7; **f** chipsir; ☺ until 01.00).

Diners If you're looking for a sit-down experience, there are a few good diner options to let you catch your breath. **Benedict** has a midnight–08.00 menu at its Rothschild 29 location (**w** benedict.co.il/en) and **Moses** has branches in Jerusalem (Yitzhak

Rabin 10 at Cinema City) and Tel Aviv (Dizengoff 293, HaBarzel 26, and Rothschild 35), and several outside of town (**w** mosesrest.co.il/branch/; ⏱ 24 hours, late-night menu starts 23.30).

Dessert If your sweet tooth is aching at the end of the evening, you can try one of these post-12 ice cream/yogurt/gelato locales in the late-night capital, Tel Aviv:

Anita's Florentin St 3; ⏱ until 01.15, later Thursday–Saturday.

Cremerie de l'Eclair King George 53, ⏱ until 01.00, later Thursday–Friday.

Legenda Dizengoff 94; ⏱ until midnight, other branches earlier.

Vaniglia Ibn Gabirol 98; ⏱ until midnight or 01.00.

Gelateria Siciliana Ibn Gabirol 90 (⏱ until 00.30) and Dizengoff 170 (⏱ until midnight).

DO #19: LAST MIN IT!

NO PLAN? CHANGE OF PLAN? Haven't booked anything for tonight, or this weekend, but are thinking of maybe just winging it? Depending on what you need, you can find various resources to help.

Lots of **hotels** offer last-minute bookings. You can use any of your favorite booking sites to find options, though you're unlikely to find any great discounts or deals. Israel is too small a country – there just aren't that many hidden gems waiting to be snatched up. Pricey/modern **restaurants** will likely tell you they're all booked up on weekends. If you press, they might let you come early and sit at the bar. If you show up with a small party, they'll make you swear you can finish dinner in 90 minutes (sometimes 120) which is usually not a problem for Americans or time-wary Europeans, though the casual Mediterranean crowd might find that too stressful. Some **bars** require advanced reservations and don't take walk-ins. Several rooftop bars have guest lists; most of the hipster bars do not. Some of the **clubs** also have lists, or lines. Best to ask around and check socials to find out where you can go to avoid lines/waits/entry fees.

If you're in a popular destination (Tel Aviv, Jerusalem, Petra) and looking for an **activity/tour**, then you can wing it. If you're in a national park, you can also usually wing it. There are a handful of exceptions that require prebooking and/or guided tours.

Want to fly to Eilat? Or Petra via Eilat? **Flights** are not usually a problem as Arkia (**w** arkia.com) and Israir (**w** israirairlines.com), Israel's two domestic operators, both have last-minute discounts.

EVENTS CALENDARS There are several go-to destinations online where you can learn more about seasonal events, special exhibitions, timely concerts and shows, and other of-the-minute entertainment you might find interesting. *Time Out* is a worldwide entertainment magazine with dozens of blog articles and listicles each week (**w** timeout.com/israel/things-to-do). **Tourist Israel** is a great blog that always features up-to-the-minute recommendations for events in Israel, broken down by location and event type (**w** touristisrael.com/events/) and bloggers **igoogledisrael** have an events calendar as well (**w** igoogledisrael.com/event-calendar/). Cultural events sponsored by **Nefesh B'Nefesh** can be found on its events page (**w** nbn.org.il), and **KKL**, the Jewish National Fund, offers nature-based events on its site (**w** kkl-jnf.org/tourism-and-recreation/events/). Upcoming events in Jordan are compiled at **w** calendar.jo.

FREE! Here's the good news – there are tons of free options, and you don't have to look too hard to find them. Of our BUCKET! list items, two of the three are (or can be) free. **Old City Jerusalem (#1)** has tons of free sites, and is still a functioning neighborhood that you can walk into, look around, and spend nothing if you don't want to. Free sites include: **Dome of the Rock (#6)**, **Church of the Holy Sepulchre (#9)**, **Western Wall (#11)**, **Temple Mount (#12)**, **Via Dolorosa (#42)**, sites at **Mount Zion (#92)**, churches at the **Mount of Olives (#34)**, and dozens of other sites. (You do, however, have to pay for the **Citadel/Tower of David (#32)** museum, the **Ramparts Walk (#91)**, the **Western Wall Tunnels (#94)**, several sites in the *Jewish Quarter*, and the *City of David*.)

The **Dead Sea (#3)** has a few points for public access that are free. The easiest spot to approach the Dead Sea (safely) is at *Ein Bokek* on the Israel side (southern part of the Sea). You can (freely) enter the site, lay on the beach, and get in the water. You may still have to pay to rent chairs, buy mud, etc. There are nicer places from which to enjoy the Dead Sea, namely the spas in Israel and the hotels on the Jordan side, but these are not free. **Petra (#2)** is not free, no matter how you cut it. It's in fact the most expensive single site in Israel and Jordan, so see *Discount Cards/Passes* (p. 60) in order to figure out how to get the most bang for your buck.

Other popular spots that won't cost you anything in Jerusalem include **Yad Vashem (#35)**, which is one of the few free museums you'll find; **Mehane Yehuda Market (#67)** is free to enter, though not free to eat. Walking around Tel Aviv, **Jaffa (#30)**, **Carmel Market (#87)**, *Neve Tzedek*, *Rothschild Boulevard*, *Tel Aviv Port*, *Tel Aviv Tayelet/ Promenade*, HaYarkon park, Florentin, Sarona, etc. are all free to access, though you will probably not be able to stop yourself from spending money on food, drink, etc. **Tel Aviv Beaches (#89)** are all free (though parking can be expensive, and chairs are plentiful but not free, though inexpensive), as are most Mediterranean beaches (except when they are part of a nature reserve, such as Dor Beach). You can enter the **Red Sea/Gulf of Aqaba (#10)** at public beaches for free in Eilat and Aqaba, but unless you have your own snorkel/scuba gear, you're missing out on all the fun. You can rent (for a price) along the beaches.

The walking tour of **Baháʼí Gardens (#27)** is free, as is walking around **Akko (#13)**, though several of the sites are not free. Most of the sites along the **Sea of Galilee (#7)** circuit are churches, and do not have an entry charge (the exceptions are Kibbutz Ginosar (G3) and the "Jesus Boat" as well as nearby national parks). Camping is free, and so are the national trails: the **Jesus Trail (#69)**, *Israel National Trail*, and Israel Bike Trail (U).

Remember that you *will* need to pay for national parks (which includes **Masada (#8)**, **Caesarea (#25)**, **Megiddo (#59)**, **Beit Guvrin and Maresha (#60)**, etc.), most museums, and wineries (basically, because they aren't set up with information centers like in the USA, so you can only go in if you want to taste, which costs money).

QUICK STOPS Got some time to kill? We've got lots of suggestions for places you might want to consider if you've finished everything you came for, find yourself with some free time, and are currently without ideas. If you're visiting…

★ … **Old City Jerusalem (#1)**, you're surrounded by interesting sites: **Mount of Olives (#34)** to the east, *City of David* to the south, *Yemen Moshe* (the oldest neighborhood outside the city walls) to the west, and lots of shopping and food (including **Mehane Yehuda Market (#67)**) within a short walk of Jaffa Gate.

★ … **Masada (#8)**, then get to the **Dead Sea (#3)** (and vice versa). It only takes 15 minutes and there are changing booths on public beaches. **Qumran (#70)** can also be a 30–60-minute quick stop if you're heading back to Jerusalem after your trip to the Dead Sea or Masada, and you can see where the Dead Sea Scrolls were discovered.

★ … the **Western Wall (#11)**, then take the walkway to **Temple Mount (#12)** at the top to get an up-close view of the **Dome of the Rock (#6)**.

★ **Beit She'an (#39)** in the lower Galilee, you can tack on a few extra national parks – **Beit Alpha (#64)**, *Gan HaShlosha*, *Mount Gilboa*, **Belvoir (#93)**, and Ma'ayan Harod (F2) are all nearby.

★ … the big crater, or **Makhtesh Ramon (#28)** (accessible from *Mitzpe Ramon*), then you're also very near a couple of national parks, including **Ein Avdat (#74)** (hiking), **Avdat (#48)** (Nabataean Incense Route ruins), and Ben Gurion's desert home at Sde Boker (J2).

★ … **Bethlehem (#40)**, don't forget to see the *Separation Wall* – a reminder of the divided world in which we all still live.

★ … *Haifa* for the **Bahá'í Gardens (#27)**, then you can sneak over to **Akko (#13)**, which is a 30-minute drive and another well-integrated city (though it feels more Arab) with great dining options.

★ … *Zichron Ya'akov* for a winery or shopping day, then tack on a little history with a visit to the *Nahal Me'arot* caves, which provide a brief but fascinating overview of the history of humanity in the Holy Land. This quick stop is an under-appreciated UNESCO World Heritage site.

ALTERNATIVES Looking for alternatives to those popular destinations filled with people, lines, waiting, traffic, and reservations? We have some suggestions:

★ *Tel Aviv* Sick of Tel Aviv's beaches? Try **Herziliya Beaches** – they're equally (if not more) beautiful than those found in downtown Tel Aviv, and the sand is just as white and soft. However, these beaches can be just as crowded, particularly on the weekends so, if you're looking for seclusion, try visiting on a weekday. Or head further north to **Dor HaBonim (#100)** or south to Palmahim (E3) – both have a nominal fee.

★ *Jerusalem* Jerusalem not gritty enough for you? Have a stay in the West Bank – **Bethlehem (#40)** is only ten miles south of Jerusalem and **Ramallah (#68)** 45 minutes north.

★ *Eilat* Eilat hotels too expensive? We hear you. **Aqaba (#43)**'s prices – hotel, food, activities – will be roughly half of the price of Eilat, and Taba (T1) in Egypt will be about a quarter, meaning you can stay in a five-star resort in Jordan for less than $200 a night, and in Taba for less than $100.

★ *Galilee* **Tiberias** is boring (honestly), so stay in Rosh Pina (H2) instead – it has a much cozier, woodsy atmosphere.

★ *Petra* **Petra (#2)** can be overwhelming, filled with tourists, and your photos will be never be empty of people. *Little Petra*, however, with interesting monuments of its own, is often gloriously empty.

★ *Crusader castles in Jordan* **Karak (#49)** is the most popular Crusader castle in Jordan, but *Shobak* is nearby and equally spectacular.

★ *Craters* **Makhtesh Ramon (#28)**, or the Ramon Crater, is a popular destination for novice hikers in the Negev. Try your hand at *Little Makhtesh/HaMakhtesh HaKatan (J1)* or *Big Makhtesh/HaMakhtesh HaGadol (J1)* instead.

★ *Dead Sea resorts* Bummed out by the prices and quality of the Dead Sea resorts in *Ein Bokek*? Suweimeh in Jordan hosts a variety of higher-quality and cheaper alternatives, and will take you only 30 minutes to arrive from the Jordan–Israel border crossing.

★ *Wineries* Judean Hills Wineries (B3) tours all booked up? There are several wine-growing regions in Israel, and you can make a visit to a circuit of them in a day from just about anywhere (see *Food and Drink – Wine*, p. 563).

NEARBY OPTIONS Haven't planned anything, but want to get out of town for a few hours? You have several good options for last-minute day or half-day trip destinations, without having to jet too far.

Tel Aviv

★ *Apollonia* national park is 30 minutes north of town (near **Herziliya Beaches**) and contains an impressive Crusader castle.
★ **Caesarea (#25)** is about an hour's drive north and well worth a visit. If you miss the museum, movie, and any tours, you can run through the site in an hour or two.
★ If you're taking the train, you can be in Haifa in an hour. Hike up to the **Bahá'í Gardens (#27)** and take the English tour at noon, grab a falafel sandwich, then circle back.

Jerusalem

★ Drive to the south of the Old City and in just 10 minutes you'll pass through border security to get to **Bethlehem (#40)**. Manger Square is famous for its Basilica of the Nativity where you can see the purported spot where Jesus was born.
★ *Ein Kerem* is 30 minutes west of Jerusalem and hosts a large medical center where you can find a beautiful synagogue with stained-glass windows designed by artist Marc Chagall.
★ Abu Ghosh (B1) is right off of Route 1 and home to endless hummus restaurants, the city's specialty. There, you will also find the **Monastery of Abu Ghosh** and **Domaine du Castel** winery, both worthwhile destinations in their own right.

Haifa/Akko

★ If you're staying the night in one, visit the other. They are very different, though both interesting and mixed Arab/Jewish cities.
★ At the northernmost border of Lebanon, you'll find **Rosh HaNikra**, which hosts cave formations that have been carved by the sea.

Amman

★ Don't miss **Jerash (#14)**, the region's best Roman ruins, an hour north of the city.
★ You can also head east towards Iraq to see the famed **Desert Palaces (#20)**.

Dead Sea, Jordan

★ If you're staying in Suweimeh, you're near the baptism site of Jesus, at **Bethany-Beyond-the-Jordan (#41)**.
★ You can also swing to the top of **Mount Nebo (#24)** to gaze over the place where Moses is said to have died.
★ Or, you can venture a bit further to **Madaba (#19)**, the home of the Madaba Map, one of the oldest representations of Jerusalem.

Dead Sea, Israel

★ Nearby are **Ein Gedi (#50)** national park, with ample walking trails and waterfalls.
★ Also nearby is **Qumran (#70)**, the site where the Dead Sea Scrolls were discovered.
★ Swing by **Masada (#8)**, take the cable car, and run quickly around the top of the mountain to take in the majesty of this 2,000-year-old Jewish bastion.

Eilat
★ Head north to **Timna (#96)**, a child-friendly park filled with ancient copper mines.
★ Further still is *Yotvata Hai-Bar* where your kids can meet a variety of desert animals.

Of course, you also have a whole slew of preplanned options available to you in Part 9, *Walks and Drives*, and Part 10, *Itineraries by BUCKET!*

DO #20: BYE-BUY IT!

LEAVING You should plan to get to Ben Gurion and Queen Alia airports **three hours in advance** of your international flights. Yes, this is a recommendation, and everyone will tell you that you can do it in less. But these countries have strict security protocols, and if you happen to be the type of person who looks like they need extra questioning, then you could risk missing your flight because of your exit briefing.

Also, if you are **checking luggage**, there is an extra layer of security after you enter Ben Gurion. There are two baggage screening lines, and every person with baggage must pass through these *before* you go to the check-in counter (which will also have a long line). This extra step very frequently takes one full hour. If you are **not checking baggage**, you can proceed to the security check-in past the first major luggage screening. You should plan to arrive two hours in advance.

You should always do **online check-in**, when available. Depending on the airline, this might not be an option for you. Either way, you will need to print physical copies of your tickets to show to the various security attendants. Will they review telephones? Probably. Are they always Millennials? No.

If you're super fancy, you can pay through the nose for a **VIP express service** at Ben Gurion Airport to walk you quickly through security and then settle you into a fancy, members-only lounge. As part of the VIP service, you will also gain access to the exclusive Fattal Lounge. Check out w israelwelcome.com/vip-lounge for more information.

GETTING TO THE AIRPORT Getting to the airport is a pretty straightforward affair. If in Amman, just take a taxi, which should cost around 20 JD. Sariyah Express goes every half hour from Amman's North Station to the airport, for under 4 JD. Visit w sariyahexpress.com/airport-express and you can also catch it at some of the other stops (7th circle).

If in Jerusalem or Tel Aviv, you can hire a shuttle, use a private taxi, or take a bus or train. From Jerusalem, Bus 485 picks up at the Central Bus Station, runs 24 hours a day (except Shabbat), and is very inexpensive at 16 ILS. It takes an hour and runs on the hour. Taxis will cost around 250 ILS. Nesher Taxis (w neshertours.co.il/en/contact-us) is a shared shuttle that picks up on the hour, charges around 65 ILS, and goes straight to Ben Gurion. From Tel Aviv, you should just take a cab, which will cost you probably 120–180 ILS if you use the meter, and possibly much less if you're going when there's no traffic (early morning). You can also download the Gett app or other similar (see *Taxis*, p. 73) to prepay and order in advance (Hadar is the cheapest, at 115 ILS).

The train to Ben Gurion departs from only one station, so you still have to take a cab to get there since it's really not close to a hotel district, and then you'll pay only 14 ILS or so to drop you off right at the airport. It's a very quick ride – under 20 minutes – and departs every 20–30 minutes, except for Shabbat when it's closed.

BEN GURION EXIT PROCEDURES

Departures/Terminals 1 and 3 Ben Gurion has **TWO TERMINALS**: Terminal 1 and Terminal 3. Terminal 1 primarily serves budget airlines, but international airlines also depart from here so you check the IAA website (**w** iaa.gov.il/en/) to see from where you are departing if not written on your ticket.

International carriers will often have their check-in at Terminal 3 and then, once you've passed through all the screening, they'll have a shuttle bus take you to Terminal 1, where you'll already be screened and pass through the back entrance to your gate (it's obnoxious, but faster than the regular screening at Terminal 3, so the time you lose is a wash). Terminal 1 airlines include Pegasus, RyanAir, Wizz Air, Up, easyJet, and Arkia. These airlines are not exclusively at Terminal 1, however, so you should always check in advance.

If you plan to submit a VAT refund for goods you are checking in your luggage, you need to visit the Milgam VAT Refund counter in the third-floor check-in hall across from Information. You'll receive a stamped document that will need to be presented at a second Milgam kiosk located in the duty-free hall after you've passed through security.

Check-in, security, immigration

Terminal 1 Terminal 1 is a small terminal, so getting through security is usually a much faster affair. All of the same rules apply as in Terminal 3, but with shorter queues. There is a possible final step: boarding a bus to be taken back to Terminal 3. This is extremely obnoxious, but you will skip all the security and go straight to your gate. It's also reason why you should plan to arrive 3 hours early for your international flight.

Terminal 3 This is a very busy terminal with unique security protocols, which we've outlined below.
1. You're met by a guard at the door who will likely ask for your ticket and passport.
2. If you have bags to check, you proceed to the security line where you will be questioned by members of Israel's security apparatus. They'll ask who packed your bags, check what you did while you were in the country, and may have other questions as well. *If you don't have bags to check, proceed to #5.*
3. You may then be asked to send your luggage through a preliminary security screening.
4. Once complete, you go to the check-in counters, which are probably full. The process is usually long and stressful, to be honest. You'll leave your luggage with the check-in attendants once confirmed.
5. Once clear, you take your passport and boarding pass to the security gate. Your passport will have a barcode which will be scanned.
   - If you didn't check bags, your passport never received the barcode, and you will need to proceed to a separate security line on the right-hand side of the big glass doors for "Web Check-In" clients.
   - Security personnel will ask you personal questions about your time in Israel, who packed your bags, etc.
   - Once screened, you'll be sent to the big glass doors.
6. This part is easy – if you have the barcode sticker, they'll scan your passport and send you towards the metal detectors…
   - … unless you are singled out for additional screening, in which case you will be sent to a special line, which is like US "secondary" screening, but for outbound flights.

7. Next, you pick a random line for security screening, trying your hardest not to let people jump the queue. The lines tend to take an amorphous structure until right before they get to the X-ray machine, at which point there's a mad push to get to the front. Patience, you'll get through.
8. After that security screening, you go to your exit interview with immigration. If you have a biometric passport, you can use one of the photo scanners along the wall. There are usually attendants to assist you. Otherwise, you can stand in any open line to talk with an immigration official. You may be asked to show the blue entrance ticket you received upon arrival. When the attendant is finished, they will hand you a *pink* exit ticket, which you need to scan in order to enter the departure terminals.
9. Scan the pink ticket and be on your way! You can proceed to duty free, your coffee station, bookstore, or your departure gate.

Shopping/eating/duty free Ben Gurion has limited dining options, though Aroma has a large outlet (closed on Shabbat, unfortunately, when lots of people are traveling), which serves sandwiches, coffee, breakfast goods, and other specialties. There are a couple of coffee stands in the central rotunda, and you can also find book stores and a few tourist shops.

Duty free is very expensive, as it is everywhere, but you can find plenty of nice gifts for people, if you still need gifts. Options include the best Israeli wine, Dead Sea cosmetics and mud, halva candy, and the traditional options you can get in any duty free around the world (liquor, cologne, Toblerone). Note that liquid duty-free items (cologne, alcohol, etc.) purchased in Israel are now allowed in European Union stopover cities (this was previously not the case) as long as the items remain in the original sealed container with the original receipt.

Otherwise, Ben Gurion is nothing special.

QUEEN ALIA EXIT PROCEDURES Queen Alia Airport does not have the same complicated security procedures as does Ben Gurion Airport, but it is still a busy international airport with a functioning security apparatus, so do plan to arrive 3 hours early in order to successfully make it through check-in, security, and immigration. The airport has a Starbucks, some sit-down places, fast food (McDonald's, Popeyes), and a variety of grab-and-go type places. It does not have great options.

VAT REFUND We covered VAT refunds in *Do #17: Shop It!* (p. 100), which explains everything you will need to present in order to receive your refund.

AT THE GATE Some gates at **Ben Gurion** are hidden downstairs, so make note if you have a letter next to your gate number, which usually indicates banishment to a lower level. If you're flying with a budget airline, you'll likely have to take a shuttle to your plane. There's free Wi-Fi! **Queen Alia** has free Wi-Fi, and plenty of charging points.

LOUNGES Ben Gurion's **Dan Lounges** are located in Terminal 3, on Concourses B and C (⏲ 03.00–08.00, plus 13.00–midnight Sunday–Thursday, 13.00–18.00 Friday, 20.00–midnight Saturday). Strangely, the Dan Hotels website (which manages the lounges) claims they are open 24/7, though this is clearly not true. Several price combos can be unlocked with a Priority Pass membership, Lounge Club, Diners Club card, or Star Alliance Gold, and business or first-class passengers can also gain access (some with a fee). LoungeBuddy may also have an option for payment. Up to 320 guests can be accommodated in the two lounges. Reviews are not great.

Queen Alia offers two lounges, **Crown** and **Petra** (both ☉ 24 hours), which are 30–43 JD, or you can enter with Priority Pass.

EXIT PROCEDURES AT OTHER PORTS OF DEPARTURE For information on border crossings, reread *Do #10: Enter It!* (p. 66) for inbound and outbound travel at Allenby/King Hussein Border Crossing (near Jerusalem) and the Yitzhak Rabin/Wadi Araba Border Crossing (near Eilat). You can also enter/exit through the Jordan River/Sheikh Hussein border crossing near Beit She'an, which follows the same pattern of activity. Please note that Jordan issues visas upon arrival to many foreign tourists arriving from Israel only at the Wadi Araba and Sheikh Hussein borders, not the King Hussein crossing – review **w** international.visitjordan.com/page/21/bordercrossings.aspx for up-to-date information.

Part 5

BUCKET! (#1–3) and Gold Electives (#4–100)

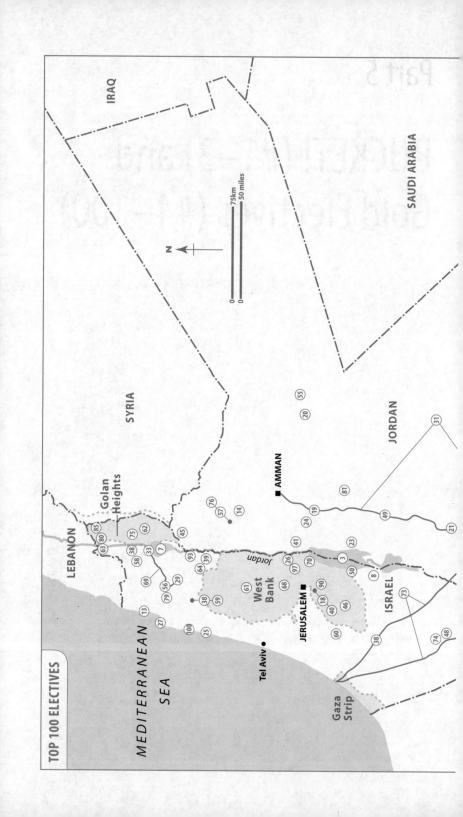

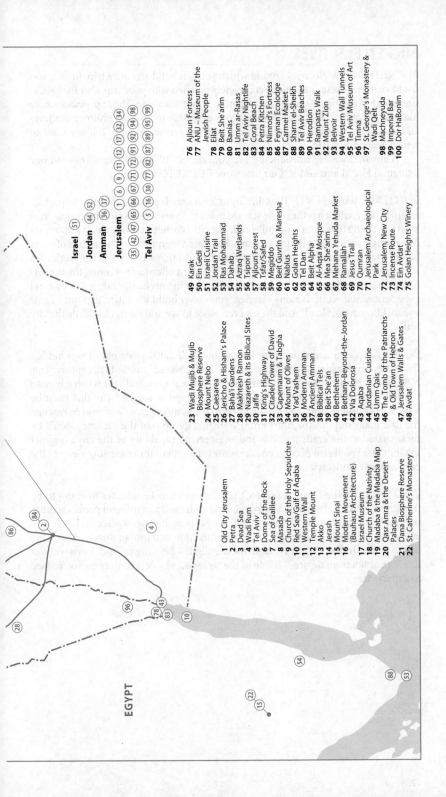

Israel ㊿

Jordan ㊸ ㊾

Amman ㊱ ㊲

Jerusalem ① ⑥ ⑨ ⑪ ⑫ ⑰ ㉝ ㉞
㉟ ㊷ ㊸ ㊽ ㊻ ㊼ ㊶ ㊱ ㊱ ㊳

Tel Aviv ⑤ ⑯ ㉚ ㉗ ㊷ ㊶ ㊵ ㊴ ㊳

EGYPT

1 Old City Jerusalem
2 Petra
3 Dead Sea
4 Wadi Rum
5 Tel Aviv
6 Dome of the Rock
7 Sea of Galilee
8 Masada
9 Church of the Holy Sepulchre
10 Red Sea/Gulf of Aqaba
11 Western Wall
12 Temple Mount
13 Akko
14 Jerash
15 Mount Sinai
16 Modern Movement
(Bauhaus Architecture)
17 Israel Museum
18 Church of the Nativity
19 Madaba & the Madaba Map
20 Qasr Amra & the Desert
Palaces
21 Dana Biosphere Reserve
22 St. Catherine's Monastery

23 Wadi Mujib & Mujib
Biosphere Reserve
24 Mount Nebo
25 Caesarea
26 Jericho & Hisham's Palace
27 Bahá'i Gardens
28 Makhtesh Ramon
29 Nazareth & its Biblical Sites
30 Jaffa
31 King's Highway
32 Citadel/Tower of David
33 Capernaum & Tabgha
34 Mount of Olives
35 Yad Vashem
36 Modern Amman
37 Ancient Amman
38 Biblical Tels
39 Beit She'an
40 Bethlehem
41 Bethany-Beyond-the-Jordan
42 Via Dolorosa
43 Aqaba
44 Jordanian Cuisine
45 Umm Qais
46 The Tomb of the Patriarchs
& Old Town of Hebron
47 Jerusalem Walls & Gates
48 Avdat

49 Karak
50 Ein Gedi
51 Israeli Cuisine
52 Jordan Trail
53 Ras Mohammad
54 Dahab
55 Azraq Wetlands
56 Tsipori
57 Ajloun Forest
58 Tsfat/Safed
59 Megiddo
60 Beit Guvrin & Maresha
61 Nablus
62 Golan Heights
63 Tel Dan
64 Beit Alpha
65 Al-Aqsa Mosque
66 Mea She'arim
67 Mehane Yehuda Market
68 Ramallah
69 Jesus Trail
70 Qumran
71 Jerusalem Archaeological
Park
72 Jerusalem, New City
73 Incense Route
74 Ein Avdat
75 Golan Heights Winery

76 Ajloun Fortress
77 ANU – Museum of the
Jewish People
78 Eilat
79 Beit She'arim
80 Banias
81 Umm ar-Rasas
82 Tel Aviv Nightlife
83 Coral Beach
84 Petra Kitchen
85 Nimrod's Fortress
86 Feynan Ecolodge
87 Carmel Market
88 Sharm el-Sheikh
89 Tel Aviv Beaches
90 Herodion
91 Ramparts Walk
92 Mount Zion
93 Belvoir
94 Western Wall Tunnels
95 Tel Aviv Museum of Art
96 Timna
97 St. George's Monastery &
Wadi Qelt
98 Machneyuda
99 Imperial Bar
100 Dor HaBonim

BUCKET! ELECTIVES

BUCKET! sites are electives around which you can build an entire trip. In fact, you could visit *only* these sites and be completely satisfied with your trip. Our BUCKET! sites are challenging, engaging, important, and awe-inspiring. They are places you've likely heard of before and have waited your entire life to visit. The history is always fascinating. Activities abound. There is beauty everywhere. You'll likely want to return again and again.

With that, we are introducing the concept of "BUCKET! Sites" here in our inaugural Holy Land Guide. Our first three BUCKET! sites are:

OLD CITY JERUSALEM (#1) The Old City of Jerusalem is perhaps the most important city in history, and it has the battle scars to prove it. Everywhere you turn, people have been traversing these lanes for millennia. The city is believed to be at least 3,000 years old, though settlements in this area may have been common for thousands of years before that. It is home to three of the most famous religious sites in the world. Yet it's more than just street-deep; in fact, one of its best offerings is visiting the tunnels hidden beneath the city. With picturesque walls, religious handicraft, a rich cultural experience, and some famous eateries, you could build an entire trip out of this square kilometer of land. And there's even more to see and do right outside the city walls.

PETRA (#2) Petra is unique from Jerusalem. Itself 2,000 years old, it was hidden from Western explorers for centuries, and "rediscovered" in the 19th century. This Nabataean city used Roman influences to sculpt monumental reliefs directly onto the soft red-rock valley walls creating an impression of a grand city that must be seen to fully understand. You will likely take 100 pictures before you've even reached the first main stop on the tour! From your first glimpse of the Treasury, you'll be mesmerized at the craftsmanship and engineering capability of the city's original inhabitants. You'll also need to endure some tough hikes for rewarding views of the carvings and landscape.

DEAD SEA (#3) The Dead Sea doesn't take longer than 15 minutes to enjoy, to be frank. But you can also spend all day, relaxing with mud and mineral pools, catching the sun's rays without the UV, all while setting foot at the lowest place on Earth. The landscape is gorgeous, with salt flats in one direction and Jordan directly across the massive lake. If that weren't enough, the highlight – buoying up and down without any sort of flotation device – is one of the strangest physical sensations you're sure to experience.

#1 Old City Jerusalem

BROCHURE

RATINGS		MACRO-REGION
BUCKET! Score	10/10	A: Jerusalem
Ruin	5/5	
Entertainment	3/5	**MICRO-REGIONS**
Information	3/5	A1–A4
Popularity	5/5	

TOP Considered one of the best cities in the world, with the best combination of sites, food, shopping, entertainment, choice.

COMMENDATIONS The Old City of Jerusalem and its walls were designated a UNESCO World Heritage Site in 1981 (listed as a Site in Danger). Jerusalem's walls and the *City of David* are national parks.

ESSENCE Jerusalem may just be the most important city in history, incorporating perhaps the most precious real estate on the planet. The history, politics, and shifts in power dynamics are fascinating. The city is referenced in the Old and New Testaments, as well as the Quran, and has great importance to the three Abrahamic religions (among several other minor religions). Jerusalem is the claimed capital for both Israelis and Palestinians, and is currently shared by both – not always successfully. The line that separates Muslim East Jerusalem from Jewish West Jerusalem runs right through the Old City, representing the very real boundaries between Israelis and Palestinians.

HOLY LAND RELEVANCE The Old City is home to several of the holiest sites in Islam, Judaism, and Christianity, including the **Western Wall (#11)**, **Temple Mount (#12)** (including the **Dome of the Rock (#6)** and **Al-Aqsa Mosque (#65)**), and the **Church of the Holy Sepulchre (#9)**.

ELECT ME! Jerusalem is a must for anyone even remotely interested in religious history. The history is accessible. You might not immediately recognize this building as Ayyubid or that wall as Ottoman, but you will know that you are walking through an historic city, and you'll see evidence of that everywhere. The cultural differences are not only noticeable, but occasionally stark. People of all orthodoxies walk the streets of this old city. It feels like a real, functioning city. People have been living, working, and playing here for 3,000 years! The walls are elegant, imposing, and impressive. They have defined the city for many centuries, and have shifted boundaries during the city's many sacks and sieges. It's fascinating to relive these changes (which we do in our *Old City Chronotour*, w buckettravelguides.com/old-city-chronotour).

WORTH THE DETOUR? Hopefully this BUCKET! site is more than just a detour for you, but if you're seriously short on time – then a resounding YES. Get inside the walls and thunder through its major attractions.

EXPERIENCES

CAN'T MISS The Old City contains several of the region's absolute best sites, all within its square-kilometer boundary. Including itself (#1), five of the Holy Land's top 15 sites are all within its walls. Here are all the Gold sites in and around the Old City: **Dome of the Rock (#6)**; **Church of the Holy Sepulchre (#9)**; **Western Wall (#11)**; **Temple Mount (#12)**; **Citadel/Tower of David (#32)**; **Mount of Olives (#34)**; **Via Dolorosa (#42)**; **Jerusalem Walls and Gates (#47)**; **Al-Aqsa Mosque (#65)**; **Jerusalem Archaeological Park (#71)**; **Ramparts Walk (#91)**; **Mount Zion (#92)**; and **Western Wall Tunnels (#94)**

SITES There is so much to see and do in Jerusalem that it's nearly impossible to create a comprehensive list. But don't worry, we tried anyway. Here are all the places awarded some kind of special recognition:

★ *Temple Mount* The raised platform hugging the easternmost wall of the Old City is called **Temple Mount (#12)**. Originally designed by King Herod in the 1st century BCE to hold the weight of his monumental Second Temple, both the Temple and several of the platform walls were destroyed by the Romans in 70 CE, leaving behind rubble, except for one remaining retaining wall. Having been banned from ascending to the Mount, Jews have since honored the **Western Wall (#11)** as the closest above-ground location to their sacred Holy of Holies (originally located on/near the peak of Mount Moriah) where they pray for the return of the Temple. Today, the most striking feature of this elevated space is the gold-domed edifice that crowns it. The stunning **Dome of the Rock (#6)** was built in the 7th century CE directly over Mount Moriah, the sacred and historic spot where it is believed that Abraham planned to sacrifice Isaac to God, where Muhammad ascended to Heaven after his Night Journey, and where once stood the First and Second Temples. In addition to the beautiful domed sanctuary, Temple Mount also holds **Al-Aqsa Mosque (#65)** – the third-holiest site in Islam – and lesser-known architectural gems the *Dome of the Chain* and the *Fountain of Sultan Qaytbay*.

★ *City walls* The walls of the Old City are spectacular. The **Citadel/Tower of David (#32)** museum tells the story of the city, while the adjacent **Ramparts Walk (#91)** allows you to climb to the walls' upper levels, ambulating above the city's famous gates. The whole perimeter is a dedicated national park called Jerusalem Walls.

★ *Christianity* Christian pilgrims will find some of the most important events in Jesus' life in the Old City, particularly the **Via Dolorosa (#42)**, marking the last moments in Jesus' life as depicted in the Stations of the Cross. The path starts in the Muslim Quarter, near the *Church of St. Anne*, which commemorates the spot where Mary was born. The route ends in the Christian Quarter at the **Church of the Holy Sepulchre (#9)**, a massive building that incorporates Golgotha, the hill where Jesus was crucified, and the cave in which he was buried.

★ *Archaeological sites* Visit **Jerusalem Archaeological Park (#71)** to explore the ruins of **Temple Mount (#12)**. See Byzantine-era streets along the *Cardo*, Jerusalem's principal street during ancient times.

★ *Jewish Quarter* See people of all orthodoxes in the *Jewish Quarter*, tour the four Sephardic Synagogues (A4), and have a coffee in Hurva Square (A4).

★ *Muslim Quarter* The Via Dolorosa starts here at the Monastery of the Flagellation (A2), near the Ecce Homo Arch (A2). The Mamluk dynasty left its mark on many buildings in this quarter.

★ *Armenian Quarter* Coordinate a trip to *St. James' Cathedral* and make time to stop by an Armenian pottery studio in the Armenian Quarter (A2).

★ *Mount of Olives* Located to the east of the Old City, the **Mount of Olives (#34)** houses a number of churches that represent important moments in the life of Christ. On the way, you'll pass a number of graves in the Kidron Valley (A5).

★ *City of David* The *City of David* contains ruins from Jerusalem's very first settlement, almost 3,000 years ago. Stomp through history on the wet tour of *Hezekiah's Tunnel*.

★ *Mount Zion* Opposite the southwestern wall of the Old City, **Mount Zion (#92)** contains King David's Tomb (A5), the Room of the Last Supper (Cenacle) (A5) (where Jesus had his Last Supper with his disciples), Schindler's Grave (A5) (Oskar Schindler of *Schindler's List* fame), and the Dormition Abbey (A5), where Mary died.

ACTIVITIES Place a note of prayer into the **Western Wall (#11)**; touch the ground on which the cross that carried Jesus stood at the **Church of the Holy Sepulchre (#9)**, then duck into the tomb where Christ's body was buried; enter the **Dome of the Rock (#6)** if you are Muslim, or on a super-exclusive tour; follow Jesus' final steps along the **Via Dolorosa (#42)** as it traces the Stations of the Cross from Jesus' sentencing by Pontius Pilate to his crucifixion and burial; scramble atop the Old City's western walls on the **Ramparts Walk (#91)**; buy pottery in the Armenian Quarter (A2); haggle for the best deals on religious paraphernalia, jewelry, clothing, and spices in any of the hundreds of shops throughout the Old City; and walk the residential streets of the Muslim Quarter to see how people live.

CAMERA *Most photographed* Jaffa Gate and **Tower of David (#32)**; **Dome of the Rock (#6)**; outside the westernmost walls (south of Jaffa Gate). *Best light* Dusk, when the sun glows off the white stones. *Best angle* Get up on the streets above the **Western Wall (#11)**; climb the steps and exit left for the best photos of the wall with the **Dome of the Rock (#6)** in the background. Keep in mind, tourists are not supposed to take photos of the wall, to keep from photographing worshippers. Feel a little better by being very far away (and thus not being able to identify individuals). *From up high* The **Ramparts Walk (#91)** gives you surprisingly great views of street life; the roof of the **Tower of David (#32)**; the Lutheran Church of the Redeemer. *Best long shot* The tourist car park on the **Mount of Olives (#34)** near the Pater Noster Church has the best view of the Old City. *Secret spot* In the Muslim quarter, there are a few commercial streets that lead right to the **Dome of the Rock (#6)**. Tourists can't enter **Temple Mount (#12)** from here, but the guards might allow you to snap a quick pic so you can capture a unique perspective of the gold dome.

SECRET With nearly 4 million tourists in 2019, there may seem to be few surprises left to be discovered, but you still can! We have dozens of lesser-known electives which you can explore on our walking tours. Also, see our notes on photo opportunities in *Camera* (above). And don't miss a hummus and falafel lunch at Abu Shukri or Lina's.

LUXURY More "regal" than "luxurious," check out *King David Hotel*. Otherwise, the Inbal, Mamilla, David Citadel, Waldorf Astoria, and American Colony will each stretch your pocketbooks.

SPECIAL EVENTS Palm Sunday Procession from the Mount of Olives into Jerusalem; Holy Saturday Holy Fire Ceremony at **Church of the Holy Sepulchre (#9)** (w sepulchre-candles.com); Jewish holidays at the Western Wall, such as Passover and Shavuot; Israel Festival in early summer (w israel-festival.org/en/); Jerusalem Festival of Light in early summer (w lightinjerusalem.com); Tower of David Night Spectacular on particular evenings (**w** tod.org.il/en/the-night-spectacular/); Sacred Music Festival, aka Mekudeshet (B1) in September (**w** en.mekudeshet.com).

MAPS See A1–A8.

ITINERATOR!

CALENDAR

	Rain (mm)	Sun (hours)	Temp				Dew
			C/F	Max	Avg	Min	
January	90	7	C	12	8	4	Dry
			F	54	46	39	
February	90	7	C	13	9	5	Dry
			F	55	48	41	
March	50	10	C	16	12	7	Dry
			F	61	54	45	
April	20	11	C	21	16	10	Dry
			F	70	61	50	
May	10	12	C	25	19	13	Dry
			F	77	66	55	
June	10	13	C	27	22	16	Comfy
			F	81	72	61	
July	10	13	C	29	23	17	Semi-humid
			F	84	73	63	
August	10	12	C	29	23	17	Humid
			F	84	73	63	
September	10	11	C	28	22	16	Semi-humid
			F	82	72	61	
October	20	10	C	24	19	14	Comfy
			F	75	66	57	
November	30	9	C	19	15	10	Dry
			F	66	59	50	
December	60	8	C	14	10	6	Dry
			F	57	50	43	

PEAK POPULARITY Religious holidays are obviously a big occasion here – all Muslim, Jewish, and Christian holidays tend to see a swell of crowds.

BEST SEASON This is an all-season type of place, though you're likely to enjoy it most if it's not steamy (August) or cold (December), unless you prefer that type of weather.

BEST TIME OF DAY Early morning when crowds are at their thinnest. Dusk is also beautiful as the sunset glistens off of Jerusalem's white stones.

DAYS/HOURS See individual sites.

CLOSED The Old City does not close, as it's a functioning city. Shops will open and close when tourists come, so if there are evening activities, vendors and food stalls will likely be open. Friday (Muslim day of rest) and Saturday (Jewish Shabbat) tend to be the most restrictive days to visit, with the *Jewish Quarter* being mostly closed on Shabbat and **Temple Mount (#12)** being closed on both days.

MORNING/EVENING You can visit **Temple Mount (#12)** as early as 07.30, the **Church of the Holy Sepulchre (#9)** even earlier (hours vary), and the **Western Wall (#11)** does not close. In the evening, you can experience sunset and a new city emerges at dusk. There are plenty of reasons to begin/end your day during off-peak hours.

TIME COMMITMENT To run through the principal sites, 4 hours. We recommend, at a minimum, visiting the sites listed in "Highlights" in *Coverage* below over the course of two days. There is so much to see, you can spend two more days just visiting our Gold and Silver sites. If you would like to take it slow to shop, read, learn, absorb, look, and take in museums, then you'll need at least two to three additional days.

SPEED RULES Apply: your speed is mostly up to you in the Old City. To avoid crowds and get quickly from one site to the next, take any of the back streets away from vendors. There are a few unpredictable or unavoidable queues: **Church of the Holy Sepulchre (#9)**, **Temple Mount (#12)**, and the **Western Wall Tunnels (#94)** – see their electives for details. **Slow groups** will likely take all day to see the main three sites; **casual groups** can do the principal sites in a half-day and tack on another activity (see *Coverage* below) in one busy day; and **fast groups** with power walkers, a good map, and some necessary preplanning can load a day with the main sites as well as a few afternoon activities.

COVERAGE

★ *Intro (4 hours)* **Dome of the Rock (#6)**; **Temple Mount (#12)**; **Church of the Holy Sepulchre (#9)**; **Western Wall (#11)**.

★ *Highlights (1–2 days)* *Intro* plus 2–3 of the following: **Citadel/Tower of David (#32)**; **Western Wall Tunnels (#94)**; **Via Dolorosa (#42)**; **Ramparts Walk (#91)**.

★ *Comprehensive (1½–3 days)* *Highlights* plus 1–5 of the following: Armenian Quarter (A2) (1 hour); Muslim Quarter (A2) (3 hours); **Jewish Quarter** (6 hours); Christian Quarter (1 hour); **Jerusalem Archaeological Park (#71)** (3 hours).

★ *Exhaustive (5+ days)* All of *Comprehensive*… or minus some sites, and add in time for shopping and meandering.

BASE Jerusalem is an Anchor City. While there are a few hostel options in the Old City itself, the neighborhoods of Nakhalat Shiva, *Yemen Moshe*, *Ben Yehuda Street*, or near **Mehane Yehuda Market (#67)** will all put you only 10–20 minutes' walk from the Old City. Staying in **Bethlehem (#40)** is complicated: it's very close in terms of distance, but commuting past security every day isn't ideal. Many of the suburbs are well connected via train.

ANCHOR CITIES Tel Aviv: 70km/1 hour; Amman: 230km/3½ hours (including border crossing); Rosh Pina: 200km/2 hours; Suweimeh: 240km/2¾ hours (including border crossing).

BEST STRATEGY Visitors should plan to take advantage of at least one of the three distinct strategies below (three of three is best) in order to take in the full majesty of the city.

1. You likely won't be able to stop yourself from heading straight to the famous sites. So let's do that. If you enter through Jaffa Gate, you can navigate your way down David Street past long strips of tourist shops (stopping, if you like) until you see signs for the **Church of the Holy Sepulchre (#9)** or the **Western Wall (#11)**. You may want to start the Christian sites with the **Via Dolorosa (#42)** – the path of Jesus' final moments – near Lions' Gate in the Muslim Quarter; the route ends at the Church of the Holy Sepulchre, where Jesus was crucified and buried. Then, head around to the Western Wall, the holiest site for Jews. Finally, go up the ramp by the southern exit (as you're walking towards Dung's Gate, on the left) to **Temple Mount (#12)**, where you can walk the grounds and gaze in awe at the **Dome of the Rock (#6)**. We go over this route in *City Walk A1*.

2. Take in the best views by getting to the highest viewpoints. There are a few ways to do this. Complete the **Ramparts Walk (#91)**, stopping at the **Citadel/Tower of David (#32)** for excellent city history along the way. Once complete, walk on the outside of the walls south towards **Mount Zion (#92)**. From here, you can see the *City of David*, the Kidron Valley (A5), and **Mount of Olives (#34)** across the valley. End on top of the Mount of Olives where the view is even more grand. The walls are explored in *City Walk A3*, while the Jerusalem Hills walk is covered in greater detail in *City Walk A5*.

3. Wander through each of the individual quarters – Armenian Quarter (A2), *Jewish Quarter*, Muslim Quarter (A2), and Christian – taking in each's sites. You can get a taste of all four quarters on *City Walk A2*, and explore the Jewish Quarter in depth on *City Walk A4*.

RELAXED PLANNING You can walk in through any of the Old City's gates and figure out where you're going: it's compact enough you'll likely run into all the main sites, or eventually find signs directing you (look above street intersections). Keep in mind, though, that this city was not designed in a grid, despite having four "quarters."

DAY TRIP OPTIONS You'll be able to see the highlights in one day, if you hurry. You can park in the Mamilla Mall parking garage, which affords direct access to the Jaffa Gate via an outdoor shopping center. Alternatively, there is street parking (look for blue and white lines for free parking), though this is harder to come by. Plenty of buses stop right outside the Old City.

CHRONOTOURS The *Old City Chronotour* (w buckettravelguides.com/old-city-chronotour) helps you understand the origins of the city and its strange evolution. The walls have changed a dozen times over the millennia. The original city wasn't even within the current city walls! How did this come to be? Join us for a walking tour through time.

The *Church of the Holy Sepulchre Chronotour* (w buckettravelguides.com/sepulchre-chronotour) takes you through four successive constructions of this monument, torn down and destroyed, then rebuilt atop the old. The current building can be hard to understand on your own, so let us help you gain perspective on the building and site's importance.

WALKS AND DRIVES A1, A2, A3, A4, A5, U2, W4, W5.

ITINERARIES The Old City appears in almost every one of the *Itineraries by BUCKET!*, including if you have time for *only one activity* while in the Holy Land.

ARRIVAL PREP

PREBOOK Only a few Old City sites recommend advance booking: the **Western Wall Tunnels (#94)**, occasionally the *City of David* activities, and the **Tower of David (#32)** night show.

TIPS There are a few "passes" that allow you access to several sites, all sold at the entrance to one of the sites. These include the **Ramparts Walk (#91)**, the *Jewish Quarter*, and several tour packages available online that combine several sites and the tour guide to accompany. See *Admission*, below.

CAUTION Always be completely aware of your surroundings. There are crazy people everywhere, but crazy people tend to flock to Jerusalem. Read **w** travel.state.gov's information on Jerusalem to best understand the current political environment and recommendations for travel. Use caution when entering/exiting through the Muslim Quarter gates of Damascus, Lions', or Herod: when violence mounts, the attacks on soldiers tends to take place at these three locations. The **Temple Mount (#12)** can be the site of quite sudden conflagrations, so be aware if a large number of police or angry-sounding protesters enter the premises. Most of the time, though, the safety measures in place are sufficient for the many millions of tourist visitors each year.

ANNOYANCES Swarms of people; popular bus/cruise stop with giant tour groups; haggling (if you don't like haggling); shopping in general is a nuisance if you don't like to be talked to while you're browsing.

CONSTRAINTS Wheelchair-bound people will have difficulty getting down the many steps, though there are ramps. Strollers are a nonstarter: you simply won't be able to maneuver with one, so plan to ditch it or come without kids.

OVERRATED Western Wall (#11) and **Dome of the Rock (#6)**. Do not read *too* much into this: they are incredibly important and magnificent sites and we've ranked and rated them highly. That said, for those with less knowledge about what to expect, you might find yourself a little underwhelmed. A little research will go a long way. Read our elective chapters or follow our *Old City Chronotour* (**w** buckettravelguides.com/old-city-chronotour) for a better understanding of the significance of these sites. The Western Wall is really just a wall where Jewish people pray. That's the gist of it. And the Dome of the Rock is presently closed to foreigners, so you're only viewing the building from the outside. Neither site requires more than 20–30 minutes to visit (5 minutes if you get bored easily). Most of the stops on the **Via Dolorosa (#42)** are hard to identify due to poor markings. Also, the Ecce Homo Arch (A2) is regularly referenced as a stop, but is hardly worth the effort as a site in and of itself.

BRING Shekels for street food and bazaar shopping; camera; if visiting **Temple Mount (#12)** (modest dress required), women need a shawl for shoulders and hair, while everyone must cover legs.

DON'T BRING Stroller (you'll regret it, even if you have a child – plan to carry your baby because the streets are too narrow and there are steps everywhere); backpacks filled with things – there is security everywhere; selfie stick – the city streets are too narrow to block traffic for photo opportunities; or inappropriate clothing.

DIRECTIONS The Old City is located on the western border of East Jerusalem. Highway 60 runs along the western border/walls of the Old City. Everyone knows the Old City, called "Ha'ir Ha'etikah" in Hebrew if taxiing from West Jerusalem.

PUBLIC TRANSPORT A number of buses (w egged.co.il) and the light rail run near the Old City. The Central Bus Station services the Damascus Gate directly (see *Caution* above).

PARKING The Mamilla parking lot across from the Jaffa Gate is an affordable, all-day option.

GPS-FREE Once you enter (greater) Jerusalem, you will begin seeing signs for "Old City" in English.

ACCESS There are seven well-known gates through which to enter the Old City: Jaffa, New, Damascus, Herod, Lions', Dung, Zion, and Tanner's.

BEST ENTRANCE Jaffa Gate is the easiest access point for the Old City. You can enter through any of the gates, but Jaffa Gate has the convenience of being the westernmost with lots of amenities for tourists. Just outside are coffee shops, a mall, a large parking garage, a bus stop, and a metro link, and it is also the end of pedestrian-friendly Yaffo Street.

BUDGET You can get away with spending very little here, as the city is free to enter. The few sites with entrance fees are reasonably priced, usually around $10. Street food is cheap. Handicrafts and souvenirs can (and should) all be bargained for.

ADMISSION Most everything in the Old City is free and open. The exceptions are the **Citadel/Tower of David (#32)** museum, the **Ramparts Walk (#91)**, *City of David*, some of the *Jewish Quarter* sites, and the **Western Wall Tunnels (#94)**. Special events, such as the Sound and Light show at the Tower of David, sometimes have an additional fee.

PAYMENT METHODS Credit cards should be accepted at most places, including sites, shops, and restaurants. For small transactions (such as lunch and gift shops), you'll likely need and want to pay with Israeli shekels just to speed up the process. Look for Visa/MC/AmEx stickers on the door.

RECOMMENDED GUIDE There are very few informational placards, so if you want to know a little history, then a tour guide is the way to go. If your preference is to learn with your eyes, you can't lose with our five walking tours. For a more detailed archaeological study, see *BUCKET!pedia* below.

VISITOR CENTER Just to the left after you enter through Jaffa Gate is an information booth, with free maps. Though not a formal visitor center, the **Citadel/Tower of David (#32)** museum – to your right as you enter at Jaffa Gate – will provide excellent background and historical perspective before you embark on a physical tour.

LANGUAGES English, as well as Russian, French, Spanish, German, Chinese… there are guides catering to every group. Though not all will be immediately available, English guides certainly will be.

TOUR GUIDE Signs are nonexistent, so if you are looking for help, you need to hire someone. Tour guides are readily available, and generally professional, and will approach you the moment you enter Jaffa Gate. To avoid the hassle, book your guide in advance. Private or group guides can be arranged through booking engines such as TripAdvisor or w viator.com, or directly from a guide list, such as can be found on w goisrael.com or w allaboutjerusalem.com. Sandemans (w neweuropetours. eu) offers free and paid tours of Jerusalem. Check out w viator.com for personalized walking tours, for which there are dozens of operators and independent guides.

APPS Search for "Jerusalem Audio Walking Tours" in your favorite app store. The Jerusalem Development Authority has created an app that has been translated into multiple languages.

EAT For a quick fix, we recommend good ol' hummus and falafel. Two worthy respites from the plethora of options are **Hummus Lina** near the **Church of the Holy Sepulchre (#9)** opposite the beginning of the **Via Dolorosa (#42)**, and Abu Shukri on Al-Wad Street next to the 6th station on the Via Dolorosa. Order labneh, hummus, and falafel. Pita and pickles will accompany. Yes, this will be more than enough to fill you!

SLEEP *King David Hotel* is famous, if you can afford the splurge. The **YMCA** has dorm rooms on the cheap. Both are in nearby neighborhoods.

BUCKET!PEDIA

AKA Capital of Palestine; Capital of Israel; the Divided Capital; the Shared Capital (one day?); City of Peace. *Hebrew name* Yerushalayyim. *Arabic name* Al Quds, meaning "the holy." *Historical name* Urušalima, meaning "foundation of the god Shalem" (a Bronze Age deity and later Canaanite god of dawn/dusk). The letters S-L-M that make up *Shalem* are the same foundation for *Salam* and *Shalom*, in Arabic and Hebrew respectively, both meaning "peace" and used in greetings. Jerusalem is thus sometimes referred to as the City of Peace. The city has also been known as Zion, which later became a moniker for Israel. *Size* The Old City is remarkably small for so much history – less than one square kilometer! *Population* c40,000. *Ethnic mix* 30,000 Arabs; >6,000 Christians (of whom maybe 500 are Armenians); 3,000 Jews. *Historical era* Ancient Israel to *Modern*. *Year founded* Unclear; the southeastern hill (*City of David*) has hosted residents since the Neolithic Period, and likely predates written records. *Years active* Jerusalem has been an organized city since at least 1000 BCE (possibly much earlier), though humans have been living in the area for at least 7,000 years.

CONTEXT The Old City is wrongly thought of as a static, historic place that's always existed inside these tall walls, but it was not always so. The borders of Jerusalem have been exceptionally fluid and have changed a dozen or more times over the millennia. Evidence of this can be seen in a number of closed portals and odd mismatched layers of bricks in the city's walls (indicating they were built in different periods). As is frequently cited, the city has been sacked and destroyed twice, sieged two dozen times, and attacked more than 50 times. It has four disproportionate quadrants: the Jewish, Muslim, Christian, and Armenian quarters. It contains the holiest Christian site (**Church of the Holy Sepulchre (#9)**), the holiest Jewish site (**Temple Mount (#12)**/ Foundation Stone), and the third-holiest Muslim site (Temple Mount, with **Dome of**

the **Rock (#6)** and **Al-Aqsa Mosque (#65)**), according to the individual religious traditions. While you are free to walk the four quarters, you will notice that Jerusalem remains a remarkably divided city, with tensions flaring constantly, and armed guards a reminder of the real threat felt and faced by both sides. Regional conflagrations can generally be traced to a spark in the Old City. The souvenirs here are the best in the country (do watch out for fake goods). The sites are top-notch and well worth any wait. The buildings are beautiful and the walls have been immaculately preserved. One could spend a lifetime exploring its alleyways, understanding its people, sampling its food, and imbibing its millennia of history. The Old City is tiny – less than a square kilometer – but filled with restaurants, sites, shops, cafés, and things to do. People still live here, too. It's important to remember that, as it can sometimes feel like Jerusalem caters exclusively to its tourist clientele, but it's home to many.

GEOLOGY Jerusalem sits atop Mount Moriah, whose highest point was leveled during the creation of **Temple Mount (#12)**. Mount Moriah is part of a series of hills that also includes the historic **Mount Zion (#92)** and **Mount of Olives (#34)**. Kidron Valley (A5) served as a geological buffer between Mount Moriah and the Mount of Olives, and is home to many ancient tombs. The Tyropoean Valley once separated Mount Moriah and the *City of David* from today's Mount Zion and the Christian and Armenian quarters. There are still long and tall staircases that reflect this natural history, for instance at the Western Wall Plaza and down David Street from Jaffa Gate.

ARCHAEOLOGY Jerusalem is a city of layers, and entire books have been written about its archaeological history. Jerusalem has a mishmash style, from buried early regional forms (now on display in museums) to Roman and Herodian styles, with later Byzantine and Islamic additions. If the architectural side of the city is of interest to you, you absolutely need a companion manual. There are more than 40 successive historical layers to be found in various parts of the city, which can be hard to decipher with the naked eye, so a good guide or guidebook is essential to understanding and recognizing the tiny differences: we recommend *The Holy Land: An Oxford Archaeological Guide*, which has tons of information, diagrams, and maps. The *Wohl Archaeological Museum*, the Davidson Center, and the **Tower of David (#32)** all provide excellent background on the many layers you can find, from Canaanite times to the Ottoman era.

ARCHITECTURE The Old City is an eclectic mix of 2,000 years of architectural construction and destruction. The current walls were renewed in the 16th century by Ottoman ruler Suleiman I, though they are built upon massive blocks laid in the times of the Hasmoneans, Herod, the Crusaders, and the Fatimids.

HISTORY (For a more complete account, read our *Old City Chronotour*, w buckettravelguides.com/old-city-chronotour.) Jerusalem has been inhabited since at least 2000 BCE, when the city was first referenced in Egyptian texts. But it's very possible that humans have been living on this small stretch of land for much longer than the written record, perhaps as many as 10,000 years. But when did Jerusalem become the important holy city it is today? At some point in the second millennium BCE, several local polytheistic religions synchronized to become **Yahwism**, the first religion to exercise a belief in only one god, Yahweh. Abraham, considered the patriarch of this religion, moved to the Holy Land on God's order to do so.

The forebears of this new monotheistic religion predate the archaeological record, but their stories live on in the holy texts of Judaism, Christianity, and Islam.

We know from the Bible and partially through the archaeological and religious record that an Israelite, David, became King of the United Kingdom of Israel and Judah and built his capital on the hillside just south of Mount Moriah. It was on Mount Moriah where the **Binding of Isaac** occurred, an event when God asked Abraham to kill his son Isaac in sacrifice and, upon Abraham's acquiescence, God spared the son. It was on top of this mountain that the covenant between Abraham and God was realized, and transitively the covenant between God and his followers (the Jewish people, but they wouldn't be named this until much later).

This city on the southeastern hill, just south of Mount Moriah, came to be known as the **City of David**. This is the location of the first era of the settlement we know as Jerusalem, and it was located completely outside of the present city walls. (It is important to remember that the present city walls are *modern*, dating to the 17th century, although they do at times follow the paths of older city walls, being built over Hasmonean or Herodian ruins.) Around 970 BCE, David's son Solomon ascended the throne. Atop Mount Moriah, King Solomon built the First Temple. This holy space was used to house the **Ark of the Covenant**, which contained the original stone tablets of the Ten Commandments, scribed by Moses.

Jerusalem would go on to have multiple foreign rulers over the next 1,000 years, minus a short period when Hasmonean Jews were again in control of the city, prior to Roman reign. Though the First Temple would be destroyed (its ruins have yet to be uncovered, but may be buried under the present Temple Mount), Herod I was appointed by Rome in 37 BCE and initiated a number of massive projects, including the construction of Caesarea, Herodion, and Masada, the leveling and expansion of Temple Mount, and the reconstruction of the Jewish temple.

Herod's Temple, which expanded and built upon the Second Temple, was not around long and would be destroyed by Rome in 70 CE, but its legacy remains powerful. As much of Temple Mount itself was destroyed along with the Second Temple, what remained was only the westernmost retaining wall. For centuries, Jews could only enter the city one day per year and were forbidden from approaching their former temple. Stories that the Jewish people would gaze upon the ruins of the Second Temple in great agony from the last remaining wall gave it the nickname of "Wailing Wall." Today, it's called the **Western Wall**, the holiest site in Judaism because it is the closest place to the Holy of Holies: the location on Temple Mount where the Ark of the Covenant was once housed.

The first Roman Emperor to convert to Christianity was Constantine, in 313 CE. Shortly thereafter, he would construct a monument to the spot (again, outside the city walls) where Jesus was crucified and buried. That church would become known as the Church of the Holy Sepulchre, but looked much different than today's church. (For more information, check out our *Church of the Holy Sepulchre Chronotour*, w buckettravelguides.com/sepulchre-chronotour.)

In 637 CE, Arabs from Medina took control of the city under direction of Muhammad, a prophet who claimed to be the last of the prophetic descendants of Abraham. Early Islamic rulers would construct Al-Aqsa Mosque and the Dome of the Rock on Temple Mount. The Dome of the Rock was situated directly over the rock where Abraham nearly sacrificed Isaac and the site of the two destroyed temples, causing a rift between the Jewish and Muslim peoples that would never be healed.

Though rulership changed hands many times, Muslims (but not necessarily Arabs) retained control of Jerusalem and the Holy Land for most of the next 1,200 years. The only break came in the 13th century CE when the Crusaders – Christian fighters from Europe – took control of the city for roughly 100 years, building a number of recognizable monuments, including a new Church of the Holy Sepulchre, the Cathedral of St. James, and the Church of St. Anne.

The Turkic Ottoman Empire started its 400-year reign in 1535 CE. Its crowning achievement is surely the present-day city walls which were restored and reimagined into the towering fortress-like walls which we see today. Most of the gates were also installed during Ottoman times.

After the Ottomans lost World War I, Britain took control of "Mandatory Palestine" until the creation of the Jewish state of Israel in 1947. At that time, Jerusalem was envisioned as a shared capital between Israel and Palestine. Peace was short-lived, however, as neighboring Arab countries immediately declared war on Israel. The Arab countries would lose that war, and another in 1967, but nonetheless Jordan was asked to broker peace; to this day, it has custodial control of Temple Mount. Since then, Jews have been prohibited from praying on Temple Mount.

CHRONOLOGY

4500–3500 BCE: Settlement established near Gihon Springs.

2000 BCE: First mention of city in Egyptian texts.

1850 BCE: Binding of Isaac (attempted sacrifice) occurs on Mount Moriah, present-day Temple Mount.

1000 BCE: Jerusalem inhabited by Jebusite people, city becomes known as Jebus.

1003 BCE: King David captures the area. Jebus becomes City of David. Biblical sources cite this period as the founding of the United Kingdom of Israel, though evidence is scant.

962 BCE: King Solomon builds the First Temple, called Solomon's Temple, on Mount Moriah.

586 BCE: Jerusalem is sacked by the Iraq-based Neo-Babylonian Empire. (Its king, Nebuchadnezzar II, built the Seventh Wonder: the Hanging Gardens of Babylon.) Citizens are exiled to Babylon. The First Temple is destroyed. No archaeological evidence of the temple has been discovered, though many believe evidence of the building is buried beneath the Temple Mount floor. (The Dome of the Rock and the other Muslim structures would have to be moved to conduct excavations, which is a nonstarter for religious and political reasons.)

539 BCE: King Cyrus of Persia defeats Neo-Babylonians. Allows Jews to return to Jerusalem from exile.

516 BCE: Building of Second Temple on Mount Moriah by Persian governor Zerubbabel.

332–116 BCE: Hellenistic (Greek) Period, run first by Ptolemaic (Egypt) Empire, then Seleucid (Syrian) Empire. Temple Mount is cleared and an altar to Zeus is erected. Jewish religion suppressed.

167–160 BCE: Maccabean revolt. Jewish priest Judah Maccabee leads a successful rebellion against the Seleucid Empire. Cleanses the Second Temple of false gods, now commemorated on Hannukah. Religious worship allowed, but Seleucids remain in control.

140–110 BCE: Independent Jewish rulers under the same Maccabee family gain semi-autonomous rule of Jerusalem. Named the Hasmonean dynasty.

110–63 BCE: Complete independence from Seleucids. Territorial conquest begins, expanding Hasmonean Kingdom throughout Israel and the Transjordan. Anti-Hasmonean Jewish rebels shelter in Jerusalem.

63 BCE: Hasmoneans are defeated by Roman Republic. First wave of Armenians (attempting to conquer region of Judea) arrives in Jerusalem.

37 BCE: Roman Senate appoints Herod I (aka Herod the Great) as the Roman vassal king of Judea.

36–4 BCE: Reign of Herod. He and family members convert to Judaism. Rebuilds and expands the Second Temple, to include massive construction on Temple Mount, including building retaining walls to keep the structure from collapsing. (The western side of the structure is all that's left today, the so-called Western Wall.)

5 BCE: Presentation of Jesus by Mary and Joseph 40 days after his birth at the Temple.

28–30 CE: Jesus conducts ministries in Jerusalem, including the Cleansing of the Temple and the miracle of healing a blind man.

30: Final days of Christ, or the Passion, including Palm Sunday (Jesus' entry into Jerusalem as Messiah), the Last Supper, the Crucifixion, Burial, and Resurrection. Followers are called Christians.

70: Siege of Jerusalem: Titus, son of the Roman Emperor, puts down the first anti-tax Jewish rebellion, destroying Herod's Second Temple on the Jewish calendar date of Tisha B'Av (the 9th of Av). (The last Jewish bastions are killed at Masada in 73.)

130: Emperor Hadrian visits a destroyed Jerusalem and rededicates it Aelia Capitolina. Builds a Temple to Jupiter on Temple Mount. Jews and Christians expelled.

313: Emperor Constantine converts to Christianity. Allows Christians to return to city.

325: Ban on Jews remains in place, but Tisha B'Av is the one day a year Jews can return, ostensibly to mourn the loss of their Temple.

335: Constantine builds first Church of the Holy Sepulchre on Calvary (aka Golgotha), the hill on which Jesus was crucified and buried.

614: Siege of Jerusalem. Sassanians (Persians/Iranians) take control of city, with assistance from Jewish leaders. Christians massacred. Church of the Holy Sepulchre burned. Most of the city is destroyed.

620: Muhammad takes his Night Journey to Jerusalem.

625: Al-Aqsa Mosque (on Temple Mount), then a small prayer house, is dedicated by Muhammad as one of the three holy mosques of Islam.

637: Another siege on Jerusalem, this time by the Arab Rashidun Caliphate (founded after Muhammad's death in 632). Byzantines leave. Christians and Jews allowed to worship.

636–1098: Succession of four Islamic caliphates: Rashidun (Medina-based), Umayyad (Damascus-based), Abbasid (Baghdad-based), and Fatimid (Tunisia, later Egypt).

691: Dome of the Rock constructed.

797 and 1030: Church of the Holy Sepulchre restored (destroyed in 1009).

1099–1187: European Christian Crusaders capture Jerusalem. Build a number of churches. Slaughter of Muslims and Jews.

1187: Sultan of Ayyubid dynasty, Saladin, takes Jerusalem from Crusaders.

1229: Crusades end. Christians abandon city. Muslims control their own sites.

1516: Turkish Ottomans begin regional rule.

1535: Ottoman leader Suleiman the Magnificent begins rebuilding walls around Jerusalem.

1860: Resident Jews build first neighborhood outside city walls, Mishkenot Sha'ananim, now part of Yemen Moshe.

1882–1903: First waves of Jewish immigrants arrive from Eastern Europe.

1897: First Zionist Congress meets in Europe. Jerusalem is described as capital of future Jewish state.

1917: Ottomans lose World War I. British Foreign Secretary writes Balfour Declaration announcing Palestine as future home of Jewish people.

1920: Nabi Musa riots spark initial conflagration between Jews and Arabs.

1947: UN declares Jerusalem a shared capital between independent Palestinian and Jewish states.
1948: Israel declares independence.
1949: Israel claims Jerusalem as its capital.
1951: King Abdullah I of Jordan is assassinated on Temple Mount.
1967: Arab neighbors attack Israel. Israel claims victory after only six days. As part of the peace agreement, Israel gives control of Temple Mount to the Jordanian Waqf. Jews banned from praying at Temple Mount.
1974: Jerusalem designates the Jerusalem Walls National Park, including the Old City walls and areas directly adjacent, including Mount Zion, City of David, and (controversially) parts of Arab neighborhoods.
1981: Old City Jerusalem is declared a UNESCO World Heritage Site.

WEBSITE w www.jerusalem.muni.il/en/.

MOVIES The Jerusalem IMAX movie provides an excellent bird's-eye view of the city and other sites in Israel, and is a marvel of cinematic beauty.

BOOKS Dense, but packed with history, is *Jerusalem: The Biography* by Simon Sebag Montefiore.

WHERE TO NEXT?

THEMATIC *BUCKET!* BUCKET! *Noteworthy* UNESCO; Wonders of the World; Endangered; Unique Experience *Religion* Judaism, Holiest Jewish Places; Christianity; Islam; Kings and Prophets and Saints; Jesus: Early Life; Jesus: Ministries and Miracles; Jesus: Death and Resurrection; Muhammad; Hebrew Bible/Old Testament; New Testament; Biblical Battlefields; Synagogues; Collections of Synagogues; Churches; Collection of Churches; Mosques; Pilgrimage *Archaeology* Bronze Age; Iron Age: Kingdom of Israel/Judah; Herodian; Roman; Byzantine/Christian; Ghost Towns; Walls; Historical Battlefields; Impressive Structural Remains *Structure* Iconic Structures; Architectural Styles *Nature* Earthquakes *Scenic* People-Watching *Society* Politics; Borders; Disputed; Principal Cities; Cool Neighborhoods *People* Jewish; Orthodox Jews; Arab; Ethnic Minorities *Active* Running and Free Exercise; Competition *Entertainment* Handmade; Souvenirs *Food and Drink* Street Food and Quick Bites *Organized* Guided

COMPLEMENTARY If you like layers of history, then check out *Archaeology – Ruins by Period – Tels* (p. 500). Many sites, such as **Jericho (#26)**, **Megiddo (#59)**, and *Tel Ashkelon*, require a good grip on historical context to best understand the importance a single site has played over the millennia. If you're going for a "wow" factor, check out the other two BUCKET! sites, **Petra (#2)** and the **Dead Sea (#3)**, and then also make your way around the country visiting UNESCO-designated areas – see the *Completists – UNESCO* itinerary (p. 795). Other impressive city ruins include **Jerash (#14)**, **Caesarea (#25)**, and **Beit She'an (#39)**.

NEARBY ELECTIVES Once you've finished the Old City, try **Jerusalem, New City (#72)**, including **Mea She'arim (#66)**, **Mehane Yehuda Market (#67)**, and **Machneyuda (#98)**.

NEARBY REGIONS Jerusalem has the most bang for your buck in terms of popular and well-regarded sites. Once you've completed the inside-the-walls walking tours, you can begin checking out the nearby sites which have played an even greater role in the history of Jerusalem, including **Mount Zion (#92)**, **Mount of Olives (#34)**, and the ***City of David***. Once you've completed those circuits, we go over a variety of additional electives in the city's eastern and western neighborhoods (*City Walks A6* and *A7*, respectively). If you're interested in the city's excellent museums, check out *Road Trip A8*: of particular note are the excellent **Israel Museum (#17)** and **Yad Vashem (#35)**.

#2 Petra

BROCHURE

RATINGS			MACRO-REGION
BUCKET! Score		10/10	N: Petra
Ruin		5/5	
Entertainment		5/5	**MICRO-REGIONS**
Information		3/5	N1, N2, N3, O1
Popularity		4/5	

TOP Best Nabataean ruins; most visited spot in Jordan.

COMMENDATIONS UNESCO World Heritage Site, 1985; New Seven Wonders of the World, 2000.

ESSENCE Heralded for its beauty, Petra is a 2,000-year-old Nabataean town (with clear Greco-Roman influences) containing dozens of monumental structures carved right out of the mountainside. It was lost to history for 700 years, adding to the allure and mystery of a hidden city in the red-rock desert.

HOLY LAND RELEVANCE The Nabataeans were an Arab people who gained some regional influence from the 1st century BCE losing independence to the Romans in 106 CE and the last Nabataean king fleeing. Petra residents remained until the rise of Islam in the 6th century CE, when the site was fully abandoned. They have a number of other sites, particularly in the Negev Desert along the **Incense Route (#73)**. Though Petra and the people who resided here (Horites/Edomites) are referenced in the Bible, the current site of Petra is mostly unaffiliated with religion or our "Holy" Land. One exception is a long walk that takes you to the purported tomb of Aaron, brother of Moses.

ELECT ME! You need only pass through the entryway (the Siq) and get a first glimpse of the Treasury to understand the majesty of seeing the facades of building-tall monuments etched into the red sandstone valley walls. A city carved out of rock – hidden for over a millennium – of this size and scope, designed with such stunning technological prowess, is a site like none other to behold. You will not be surprised why it has featured in so many mystery and adventure tales. The organic purples, oranges, and maroons on the rock steps and walls, developing by day as the light shifts in angle and intensity, are some of the most naturally beautiful phenomena you'll bear witness to.

WORTH THE DETOUR? Absolutely, though you're not really "detouring" here because it's quite out of the way: you will need to actively seek out Petra.

EXPERIENCES

CAN'T MISS The Indiana Jones view from atop the *Jabal al-Khubtha (N2)* mountain opposite the Treasury. It gives a glorious bird's-eye view of everyone's favorite monument inside Petra – and you just might end up with a unique perspective that few other travelers can say they worked for.

SITES At **ground level** (see *City Walk N1* for explanations): walk through the Siq and visit the Treasury, Roman-style Nabataean amphitheater, Street of Façades, royal tombs, Colonnaded Street, Great Temple, and Temple of Dushares (Qasr al-Bint). Ad-Deir, aka the Monastery (N2) competes with the Treasury for most stunning monument of Petra's many beautiful monuments.

ACTIVITIES Be the first to the Siq at 06.00 – you can do it! You won't regret getting up that early, promise (but pack a breakfast/lunch). Take a hike (see *City Walk N2*) to the High Place of Sacrifice (N2) (al-Madhbah, 2 hours), the Ad-Deir, aka the Monastery (N2) (2 hours), and *Jabal al-Khubtha (N2)* (the "Indiana Jones view" hike, 2 hours). Go on an extended hike (guides are usually required – inquire at the visitor's center) and discover Aaron's Tomb (Jabal Haroun), where Moses' brother was buried (a white mosque is distantly visible from several points in Petra – that's Aaron's tomb; 4–8 hours), or trek to Al-Beidha (**Little Petra**) and Al Beidha Village, a 10,000-year-old Neolithic village with extant structures (6 hours).

CAMERA *Most photographed* The Treasury itself, through the peekaboo window at the end of the Siq, with views of the Treasury, gets a lot of camera action. *Best light/time of day* Early afternoon, as the sun begins to set. The walls in Petra are tall, so the sun hides early and much of the site is cast in shade. *Best angle* The Treasury from any angle, really. *From up high* The High Point of Sacrifice. *Best long shot* Once you've reached the Monastery, keep walking past the monument to the farther hillsides, which have stunning views back to the Monastery and out over the desert wadi. *Secret spot* The view of the Treasury from above on the *Jabal al-Khubtha (N2)* (Indiana Jones view) path.

SECRET Be the first through the gates at 06.00 – it truly is worth it to have the Treasury tourist-free. Skip the horses at the intro: they are not really free as you will be strong-armed into tipping an exorbitant amount.

LUXURY The two nicest hotels in the area are both operated by Moevenpick. One is near the Petra entrance, the other is 5km south of Wadi Musa (Petra's town).

SPECIAL EVENTS Petra Kitchen (#84); *Petra by Night*.

MAP See N1–N3.

ITINERATOR!

CALENDAR

	Rain (mm)	Sun (hours)	Temp C/F	Max	Avg	Min	Dew
January	15	10	C	16	10	5	Dry
			F	60	50	42	
February	13	11	C	20	13	6	Dry
			F	68	56	42	
March	9	12	C	24	18	7	Dry
			F	75	64	45	
April	4	13	C	29	23	12	Dry
			F	83	73	54	
May	1	14	C	31	27	17	Dry
			F	88	80	63	
June	0	14	C	32	29	23	Dry
			F	90	84	74	
July	0	14	C	33	30	26	Comfy
			F	91	85	79	
August	0	13	C	33	29	26	Comfy
			F	92	84	79	
September	1	12	C	32	26	23	Comfy
			F	90	79	73	
October	3	11	C	29	20	16	Dry
			F	85	68	60	
November	6	10	C	24	14	10	Dry
			F	76	58	49	
December	11	10	C	20	11	6	Dry
			F	67	51	43	

PEAK POPULARITY This site is popular year-round, with fewer visitors from December to March. The spring months of April and May are busy, but have the best weather.

BEST SEASON Most will say spring and fall are the best times to visit, but you may like the winter if you enjoy hiking in the cold and visiting during off-season. The summer can be extremely warm, but it's usually a dry heat.

BEST TIME OF DAY Early mornings or late evening.

DAYS/HOURS Every day, 06.00–16.00 (last entry) in winter, to 18.00 in summer.

CLOSED Open all year.

MORNING/EVENING Petra opens at 06.00, and you'll want to be first out the gate one morning in order to get an unobstructed view of the Treasury at the bottom of the Siq entrance. Petra closes before dark, but you can visit in the dark of night on a *__Petra by Night__* tour.

TIME COMMITMENT One full day minimum. 2½–3 days in Petra will allow you to do all the best short hikes, go early one morning, go in the evening another night, while still going at your own pace.

SPEED RULES Apply: Petra easily accommodates folks of different speeds and mobilities. If you're a fast walker, you'll be able to get quickly through the Siq in the morning and to the summits of the hikes. The "roads" and steps are wide enough to allow for passing.

★ Siq: entrance to Treasury: 20 minutes to 1 hour (if on a tour).
★ High Point of Sacrifice, from starting point to the summit: 30 minutes (in shape, fast) to 1 hour (normal travelers) to 2 hours (slow groups with lots of stops). There are a lot of stairs. Descend around the back by a different path: 45 minutes.
★ Monastery from starting point to the summit: 45 minutes (in shape, fast) to 1½ hours (most walkers).

COVERAGE

★ *Intro (4 hours)* The Siq to the Treasury; Treasury to the Theatre; Royal Tombs, quickly.
★ *Highlights (1 day)* Intro plus one of the following: High Place of Sacrifice; Monastery.
★ *Comprehensive (1½–3 days)* Highlights plus 1–5 of the following: Morning at the Treasury; 1–2 additional hikes; Colonnaded Streets; Great Temple; Temple of Dushares.
★ *Exhaustive (4 days)* All of *Comprehensive* plus a long hike, perhaps to **Little Petra**.

BASE Your best bet is to stay in Wadi Musa, the town adjacent to Petra, for at least one night. The ticket price is discounted 40 JD if you stay at least one night in Jordan, which practically covers the hotel cost, especially if you are traveling with multiple guests. You'll likely use Petra as a stopover on the way north or south.

ANCHOR CITIES Suweimeh: 200km/3 hours; Amman: 240km/3¼ hours; Jerusalem: 50km/1 hour to Jordan border (plus about 1 hour at border), then 260km/3½ hours from border to Petra; Tel Aviv: 110km/1¾ hours to Jordan border (then as per Jerusalem), or 350km/4 hours to Eilat (plus about 1 hour at border), then 135km/2 hours from border to Petra.

BEST STRATEGY Petra is fairly remote, and best done over three to four days (including travel time) from Amman, Tel Aviv, or Jerusalem. Coming from Israel, you will of course have border issues to manage, in addition to the long drive. You cannot fly directly into Wadi Musa, but you can fly to Eilat to shorten the driving time to around 2 hours, plus border procedures. If you're so inclined, you'll want to add on **Little Petra**, which is a short taxi or drive away. **Wadi Rum (#4)** is a couple of hours east, if that's also on your bucket list.

RELAXED PLANNING There's only one entrance and one path to get to the Treasury, which is the first major site, so you can't get lost. Once past the Treasury, follow the paths down the only major thoroughfare and you'll run into most everything. You will need to keep your eyes peeled for the hike entrances.

DAY TRIP OPTIONS With a tour operator, you can arrange a same-day trip to Petra from Jerusalem or Tel Aviv, but it will be a long, incomplete day. You'll have to fly to Eilat, cross the border, spend more than 2 hours getting to the site, run through the Siq and probably one extension hike, before immediately heading back. It's rushed! If in Jordan, you can visit Petra from Aqaba, Wadi Rum, or the Dead Sea, but again they are long drives and you'll still be missing a lot. Stay the night.

WALKS AND DRIVES M2, N1, N2, N3, O1, V1, V2, W2, W4, W5.

ITINERARIES As a BUCKET! site, Petra makes lots of appearances here.

ARRIVAL PREP

PREBOOK Some might wonder why the **Jordan Pass** is so pricey; it's because of Petra. But the card is a great deal, giving you a discount on the Jordan visa if you stay three nights and allowing access to most of the country's other sites. The card comes in three flavors, and you merely select how many days you want to spend in Petra – each additional day costs a very reasonable $5 extra.

TIPS
★ If you're going only for a day from Israel, we strongly recommend you book a tour company that will coordinate everything for you. Yes, it will be costly, but Petra is a world-class site, and you don't want to spend half your day wandering around trying to figure it out – especially given complicated border crossings – and navigating the 2–4-hour journey to the site.
★ You can only enter the site once per day.
★ **Petra Kitchen (#84)** frequently books up. Definitely book in advance.
★ Also, *Petra by Night* requires a separate ticket, which you should coordinate on your first day.
★ You need an ID to get into the park. A passport may be required for non-cash payments.
★ If you're planning on buying tickets on arrival, note that the credit card machines don't always work. ATM machines in town don't always work either. Make sure you bring sufficient cash with you. The site will accept or exchange foreign currency.

CAUTION Gets very hot in the summer. You'll need lots of water. Below freezing in the winter at night.

ANNOYANCES Not great food options inside the park.

CONSTRAINTS Gravel walking paths. Gradual incline. Lots of steps (1–2 hours) to the best viewpoints.

OVERRATED The initial walk from the visitor center/ticket booth to the Treasury is just a taste of what you're about to see, but that's when many of the tour guides are going to stop and tell you the story of the place and its people. The best part actually begins once you leave the gravel road and enter the canyon between the mountain, at about the halfway mark. From here, it's simply gorgeous, and culminates with your first glimpse of the Treasury. Also, the short horse rides that are "included" in the ticket price aren't "free" at all because the folks who work with the horses expect a good-sized tip at the end of your ride, which can average $10 per person.

BRING Cash, layers (including a jacket for cold mornings), a hat, sunscreen, water, good hiking shoes and socks, a torch if you want to explore a bit, a good map, your best camera, and some non-meltable snacks. You can get tea and food along the way, but the food is expensive.

DON'T BRING Strollers: kids must be carried. Bags too (no suitcases).

DIRECTIONS Waze and Google Maps are useful. Cellphone service is spotty in the desert. The town is off King's Highway (Highway 35), with limited signage along the way. If coming from the south, you will pass a nicer Marriott and then a Mövenpick. Keep your eyes peeled for a small sign indicating the turnoff for Petra.

PUBLIC TRANSPORT Taxis are used to taking tourists from the Allenby/King Hussein and Yitzhak Rabin/Wadi Araba crossings to Petra. They should recognize your hotel name and may negotiate to take you back the same day. Buses visit Petra from Amman, but there are no direct buses from either border.

PARKING The site itself has a few parking spots nearby, but it's best to stay parked at your hotel and walk or taxi in.

GPS-FREE It remains difficult to find the town of Wadi Musa on your own. You will need to print a map. You'll need Arabic to read most street signs.

ACCESS Buy your tickets in Petra's Visitor's Center.

BEST ENTRANCE Walk downhill from the visitor center where you will find security.

ADMISSION If staying the night: one day 50 JD ($70); two days 55 JD ($77); three days 60 JD ($85). If you're not staying the night, one day 90 JD ($127). Tickets come in one-, two-, and three-day denominations. Two days is the most likely scenario and more economical than one day. Discounts: free for under-15s.

PAYMENT METHODS Have cash handy; credit card machines don't always work. No ATMs in park. Few in town.

RECOMMENDED GUIDE As always, supporting local is important. If you are interested in a guide, you can find good ones locally, or prebook. You should expect many guides to walk slowly, stop frequently, and leave you to do hikes on your own. If you are limited for time (less than a full day to explore), then skip the guide and run through the site on your own, taking in as much as you have time to see.

VISITOR CENTER The visitor center is very pretty, with modest displays and easily digestible exhibits. It's also where you purchase tickets. You can get a decent brochure here that gives an overview of each stop.

MAP You'll want a map: ask at the ticket counter as they aren't always given away automatically. Signs are missing from most sites and only basic directional signs are available. A few of the older maps have been scratched and defaced.

LANGUAGES Most of the guides speak English. The few available signs are in English.

TOUR GUIDE Plenty available for hire at the entrance. They don't like to take "no" for an answer. Prices negotiable: 10 JD/hour is reasonable. Since you'll be there for several hours, this can add up. 50 JD is the normal price offered at the visitor center. If you want a guide just to the High Place of Sacrifice or Monastery, you can hire them at the base of those climbs. There aren't any free group walking tours.

APPS The site promotes the Visit Petra app. It mirrors the clumsy website, but on the plus side it is free.

EAT Two Middle Eastern restaurants on site. The Basin is the nicer and is located at the end of the Colonnaded Street. Otherwise, eat a big breakfast at your hotel and take dinner in Wadi Musa. Restaurants in Wadi Musa are cheaper than hotel food: you can eat for under 10 JD.

SLEEP Just outside the entrance are multiple hotels, including Petra Guest House and the Mövenpick. You're technically not supposed to camp inside the site (many do, including Bedouins who still take residence there, despite efforts to relocate them), but there are plenty of legal Bedouin tent camp options a short drive away. The nice hotels in the region come at a premium, and food can be priced like Western restaurants. If you're on a budget, you can find basic hostels and hotels in Wadi Musa for $30.

BUCKET!PEDIA

AKA Rose City. **Arabic name** Al-Batra. **Historical name** Known as Raqmu by the ancient Nabataeans, and Rekem in the Dead Sea Scrolls. **Size** 264km² (102 square miles), which is big, but the principal sites are all within a 6km² area (2.3 square miles). Park entrance to Treasury is 20 minutes at a brisk pace. Several popular hikes are 2-hour affairs. **Population** Wadi Musa's population is roughly 17,000. **Ethnic mix** The residents from Wadi Musa are largely from the Layathnah Bedouin tribe. **Historical era** Mostly *Roman/Byzantine*, though began during *Ancient Israel: Greek*. We recognize a special *Nabataean* period. **Year founded/constructed** Unclear, but enters records in 312 BCE, with the site likely not being excavated extensively for several hundred years. **Years active** 312 BCE–663 CE.

CONTEXT Petra is gorgeous. It's an ancient town where the temples, stadiums, and many other major monuments were carved out of rock walls, rather than built from construction materials. (Though many sites in Petra were, in fact, built from quarried stone.) Because of the arid weather, the roughly 2,000-year-old site has been very well preserved. After the Byzantine collapse, Wadi Musa was home to two remote Crusader castles, but wasn't seen again by Western explorers for 700 years, until 1812. Some 300,000 people once lived in or near this area, with possibly up to 20,000 in Petra itself. Earthquakes over the millennia have caused the most destruction to the site, which continues to be excavated and explored.

GEOLOGY Petra sits in Wadi Musa, which means "Valley of Moses." To the west is the Aravah Valley, and the boundary between Israel and Jordan. Siq, the name of the entryway to the site, means "the shaft" and references the naturally narrow, eastern entrance to the ancient city. The mountains are made of sandstone, which erodes easily and explains the wind-carved passages of the Siq and the reason that Petra could be chiseled so meticulously. Additionally, the region was known to collect an unusual amount of water which, when channeled, could be stored in cisterns. There is a sophisticated series of aqueducts carved around the city center, including from the town of Wadi Musa, down the length of the Siq, into Petra town.

ARCHAEOLOGY This is a UNESCO site, and has several benefactors. Brown University faculty directed the 15-year excavation of the Great Temple. Current excavations include the Petra Garden and Pool Complex, Jabal Haroun, Qasr al-Bint, and other sites conducted by groups from France, Finland, the USA, Denmark, and Jordan. Only about 20% of the site has been excavated thus far. Archaeologists have only found evidence of Nabataean influence in the region from the 2nd century BCE when it (suddenly?) began to flourish. The Nabataeans quickly acquired a large network of land, taking control of a trade network that extended from Arabia to the Mediterranean. Much of the sale included incense and spice, earning the nickname of the **Incense Route (#73)**, now a series of mostly excavated Nabataean sites in Jordan and southern Israel. It's believed that Rome, and later Istanbul, shifted their trade routes away from land- to sea-based trade, causing a decline in the importance of way stations such as these. There's no clear answer as to what happened to the Nabataean people, or when they abandoned the site, but it coincided with the rise of Islam in the late 7th century. As the city laid in ruin for so long, it was long believed to have mortally suffered from the 363 earthquake, but construction appears to have continued in abundance for several hundred more years, as evidenced by the excavated churches behind the Winged Lion Temple, dating to the 5th and 6th centuries. Another earthquake in 551, as well as the rise of the post-Muhammad caliphate regional power, may have been enough to convince the locals to abandon the site. Except for a brief stint as home to a couple of nearby Crusader castles during the 12th century, Petra remained lost to the written record and was not seen again until a Western explorer, Johann Ludwig Burckhardt, tricked his Bedouin guides into taking him there in 1812. The site again entered the limelight, with archaeologists conducting excavations throughout the 20th century. But Petra remained undeveloped for tourism until the 1990s when financial support brought new life to Wadi Musa, and allowed for further excavation and reconstruction.

ARCHITECTURE The various spas, stadiums, churches, burial tombs, and temples, among other massive monumental structures, span almost 1,000 years of human settlement and reflect the construction and designs of a wealthy civilization. According to UNESCO, the site is a famous example where "ancient Eastern traditions blend with Hellenistic architecture." This is the site's greatest feature and most impressive and mysterious engineering feat: how did the Nabataeans cut these glorious facades into the rock face? This unique method was perhaps derived from similar traditions in Egypt (e.g., Abu Simbel) and India (e.g., Ellora and Ajanta Caves), though the Hellenistic styles were certainly unlike anything that had been attempted previously. It's now understood that the facades were chiseled from the top down, a few meters at a time, using scaffolding and hand-held tools. The architects would first smooth out the rock face to create a blank canvas before adding dimension. Once finished with the topmost lateral section, they would lower the scaffolding and begin the process on the next lower level. Check out w zamaniproject.org to see 3D renderings of each of the major monuments in Petra.

HISTORY The city of Petra, known colloquially as Raqmu, is perhaps several millennia old. Before Petra became the jewel of the desert, it was originally part of the Kingdom of Edom, referenced in the Bible as enemies of the Israelites. The original inhabitants, the Edomites, were eventually driven out in the 6th century BCE by nomadic Arabian tribes. One of these Arab Bedouin tribes in particular claimed the land in the coming centuries: the Nabataeans. In the 4th century BCE, this group would even defeat the colonizing Greek army, who had named this land "Petra," meaning "stone" in Greek. The site is first referenced in external accounts in 312 BCE, when its accumulated wealth made it prime real estate. As was confirmed on Greek scrolls uncovered in Petra, the city would be attacked by foreign invaders with some frequency.

Yet, with diplomacy and compromise, the Nabataeans would successfully capitalize on global trade routes that passed from the east (China/India) through Syria, then south to Arabian and Egyptian cities and ports. It wasn't long before the rise of the Kingdom of Nabataea, creating way stations and inns for continental merchants to spend the night while traveling on the multiday journey to the Mediterranean, Red Sea, or further. Petra became one of several posts on a route that has since become known as the Incense Route, highlighting the types of goods that were being transported through, including incense, spice, and silks. Petra would eventually grow in importance and prosperity, becoming heavily trafficked as a stop on the Via Regis, or King's Highway, during Roman reign.

The Nabataean kings used influences from centuries of interaction with world empires to craft their own unique take on city design. Irrigation, canals, dams, and cisterns were all part of the clever water management system devised by these desert inhabitants, who were able to control infrequent rainfall in order to maintain a year-round settlement. Interestingly, the Nabataeans carved their water systems directly into the mountainsides.

Their engineering genius would soon be channeled into monumental building works, to include rock-cut carvings that made exceptional use of the delicate red sandstone. As important persons passed away, temples would be built in their honor. History has lost the names and significance of these rulers, with glorious carved temples left to their lost memory. The Treasury (al-Khazneh) and the Monastery (ad-Deir) stand as two of the most impressive creations in Petra, utilizing hidden scaffolding, a top-down carving process, and exact measurements to trick the mind into believing the veracity of these buildings. By and large, they are just illusions, with shallow and long-vacant interiors. Any riches that were once buried or displayed on site have long since been looted.

The Nabataean kingdom would last nearly 500 years, peaking at a 20,000-strong population, before losing its independence to the Romans in 106 CE. In that year, the last Nabataean king either fled or was killed, and Petra was converted into a vassal state called Arabia Petraea. Over the next several hundred years, Petra's importance began to wane and its wealth slowly slipped away as trading paths began favoring sea routes, making Petra – in the middle of the desert – obsolete. Add to this a number of devastating earthquakes that made the land difficult if not impossible to rebuild, plus the rise of Islam in the region, and Petra was finally abandoned.

Crusaders built a few castles in nearby Wadi Musa which formed part of their castle frontier, including **Karak (#49)** and *Shobak*, but the city itself appears untouched. The Mamluks reference the site in the 1200s, but Petra doesn't show up again in written records until 1812, when a Swiss traveler, according to legend, dressed up as a Bedouin in order to "rediscover" the lost city. The site underwent a number of excavations in the 20th century, and continues to see major development. Maybe a fifth of the site has been excavated, and the surrounding towns continue to encroach on the land whilst trying to take advantage of the lucrative tourism industry. Travelers began seeking out Petra in earnest in the 21st century.

CHRONOLOGY

Neolithic era: Nomadic Arabian Bedouins settle near Petra.

6th–2nd centuries BCE: Nabataean tribes arrive, eventually displacing Edomite tribe. Egyptian, Greek, and Syrian influences on the Nabataean people. Establish way stations along famous trade routes.

4th century BCE–1st century CE: Kingdom of Nabataea rises. Theatre excavated. Treasury carved. Place of High Sacrifice and Tombs are established.

106: Rome, under Emperor Trajan, annexes Petra, possibly bloodlessly, naming the region Arabia Petraea. The final Nabataean king is believed to have died around the same time. Petra Roman Road built.

363: First major earthquake, centered on Galilee, much destroyed.

447: Urn Tomb is converted to a Christian church.

551: Second major earthquake; more abandonment.

663: Arabs conquer region; last inhabitants likely flee.

12th century: Crusaders build al-Wu'eira and al-Habis in Wadi Musa.

1276: Last reference to Petra (by Mamluks) until Western rediscovery.

1812: First reference to Petra by a Western traveler.

1985: Petra Bedouin relocated; designated UNESCO World Heritage Site.

WEBSITE w visitpetra.jo.

MOVIES Petra makes an appearance as the lost city in *Indiana Jones and the Last Crusade*, with the Treasury housing the Holy Grail. It's since showed up in a dozen other action films. Something more accurate, *Petra: Lost City of Stone*, is an hour-long documentary you can watch online.

BOOKS From 2000, *Petra: Jordan's Extraordinary Ancient City* has excellent reviews, and used copies can still be found on Amazon.

IF INTERESTED Search online for the original tourism plan for Petra, the Master Plan for the Protection and Use of Petra National Park, a USAID document from 1968, including the Bedouin resettlement plan, campsites, and other original ideas.

STREET VIEW Check out several of the sites on Google Street View.

WHERE TO NEXT?

THEMATIC *BUCKET!* BUCKET! *Noteworthy* UNESCO; Wonders of the World; Endangered; Unique; Exploration; Exotic/Wow *Religion* Burial *Archaeology* Nabataean Cities/Incense Route; Active Excavations; Impressive Structural Remains *Structure* Iconic Structures; Historic Monuments; Beautiful Structures; Impressive Feats *Nature* Geological Wonders; Mountains and Mounts; Earthquakes; Gorgeous Scenery *Scenic* Most Photographed *People* Bedouin *Active* Easy Hikes and Trails; Day Hikes; Tough Hikes; Long-Distance Walks; Competition *Organized* Guided

COMPLEMENTARY Other famous Nabataean ruins can be found at the "Incense Route: Desert Cities in the Negev" UNESCO site, which covers the amazing sites of **Avdat (#48)**, **Mamshit**, **Shivta**, and **Halutza** (all in Israel). **Little Petra** is part of the greater Petra complex and often done on a combined tour of (big) Petra. Mada'in Saleh in Saudi Arabia is the second-largest Nabataean Kingdom complex, also dating to the 1st century CE.

Jordan has a few other geological marvels: **Wadi Rum (#4)** is filled with the same red sandstone as Petra, but much has eroded into massive red sand dunes making it a stunning site. And don't forget the **Dead Sea (#3)** is here! Also a BUCKET! site, it's the lowest place on Earth and one of the saltiest seas. You can head there after Petra. Other great sites in Jordan from our top 25 include: **Dead Sea (#3)**; **Wadi Rum (#4)**; **Red Sea/Gulf of Aqaba (#10)**; **Jerash (#14)**; **Madaba and the Madaba Map (#19)**; **Qasr Amra and the Desert Palaces (#20)**; **Dana Biosphere Reserve (#21)**; and **Wadi Mujib and Mujib Biosphere Reserve (#23)**.

NEARBY ELECTIVES In and around Petra you'll find **Petra Kitchen (#84)**, *Little Petra*, and *Petra by Night*. Outside the city, use *Road Trip O1* to follow the **King's Highway (#31)** to *Shobak* (35km/40 miles), **Dana Biosphere Reserve (#21)** (55km/1 hour), and **Wadi Rum (#4)** (115km/2 hours).

NEARBY REGIONS *Road Trip M2: South Jordan* ends at Petra and includes **Wadi Rum (#4)**. *Road Trip O1: King's Highway* leaves from *Little Petra*, after you finish your Petra itinerary; you can divert at Dana and do *Road Trip P1: Dead Sea Highway* to end at the Dead Sea.

#3 Dead Sea

BROCHURE

	RATINGS		MACRO-REGIONS
BUCKET! Score		10/10	K: Dead Sea (Israel),
Ruin	n/a		P: Dead Sea (Jordan)
Entertainment		5/5	
Information		3/5	**MICRO-REGIONS**
Popularity		5/5	K1, P1

TOP Lowest spot on Earth! (*Note*: Despite its reputation, the Dead Sea is *not* the saltiest lake in the world – there are more salty lakes in Antarctica, Turkmenistan, Ethiopia, and Djibouti – but it is the most visited. Having said that, it is slightly saltier than the Great Salt Lake in Utah.)

COMMENDATIONS New Seven Wonders of Nature, nominated.

ESSENCE With a salinity level so high as to not support life, this body of water has earned the name "the Dead Sea." Accessible from Israel or Jordan, this is the lowest point on Earth at 430m (1,411 ft) below sea level. Swimming in its waters is one of the most bizarre experiences you're sure to encounter around the world.

HOLY LAND RELEVANCE Sodom and Gomorrah (not definitively identified but likely near the Dead Sea) are referenced in the Bible's Book of Genesis as two cities consumed by fire and brimstone for turning away from God. The same verses tell the story of Lot and his family who were informed by angels of the imminent destruction of their hometown, and explicitly told to march forward and not look back at Sodom upon their departure. Lot's wife disobeyed and was immediately turned into a pillar of salt (Genesis 19:26). Many centuries later, the Dead Sea Scrolls – some of the oldest extant biblical texts – were discovered in Qumran, near the lake's northwest side.

ELECT ME! There's much to love about this experience: descending along a gorgeous drive to the lowest place on Earth; taking a dip in the salt-dense sea; lathering yourself with mineral-rich mud; taking in the UV-less sun with its curative properties; admiring the beautiful vista of the sea itself and of the Jordanian mountains in the distance.

WORTH THE DETOUR? It's our most revered "experience" in all the Holy Land – so yes, we'd say that it's worth the trip!

EXPERIENCES

CAN'T MISS Entering the sea should be the culmination of a full Dead Sea experience. Start by covering yourself in mud. If you are visiting a popular entry spot, and haven't paid either a hotel or spa, then you'll have difficulty finding the once-ubiquitous black clay used as a skin exfoliant and polish. Do yourself a favor: buy a packet of cosmetic mud in one of the local shops before heading to the beach. (The packs also make great gifts, and are cheaper here than anywhere else.) Let it dry for 30 minutes, don't forget the obligatory photo, and wash the crust away to reveal your refreshed, baby-butt-soft, and mineral-enriched skin.

SITES **Highway 90** on the Israel side has great views all along the western rim of the Dead Sea. **Highway 31** in Israel starts where major toll road Highway 6 ends, and continues on a beautiful path through the Negev before ending at the Dead Sea, just south of **_Ein Bokek_**. Take the **obligatory photo** at the change-in-elevation signs on the descent from Jerusalem or Tel Aviv. **Giant sinkholes** showcase the danger of evaporation and the sea retreating. **Old water level signs** next to the highway show that some shore lines have retreated more than a kilometer in a few decades! **Salt farms** in the southern lake, which you can see as you drive south, collect minerals for industrial (plastics) purposes, water conditioning, and bath salts, among other uses. If you're lucky you might see **waves**! It's a strange phenomenon for a still, dying lake. _Dead Sea Panorama Complex (P1)_, located 8km south of the Kempinski Hotel, provides a good viewpoint on the Jordanian side.

ACTIVITIES Take a swim in one of the most buoyant lakes on Earth – you can't sink! Paddle around on your nonexistent raft: stomach-up is particularly fun, though watch your eyes and careful not to splash. Cake yourself in mud, either from a mud vat at a private beach or from one of the sachets you can buy at a cosmetics factory/store. Book a massage/spa package: check out any of the hotels listed in _Luxury_ (opposite) or at elective **_Ein Bokek Spa Hotels_**. AHAVA Dead Sea products are crafted just nearby, about 10 minutes north of Ein Gedi just off Highway 90: visit the shop and load up on some authentic souvenirs/gifts, always presented in nice packaging (but if you miss the visitor center, their products are sold everywhere, including the airport). Cure an ailment at a Dead Sea clinic: several medical spa clinics claim to treat a number of conditions, providing alleged relief (if temporary) of psoriasis (climate), arthritis (mud), skin ailments ("good" UV), respiratory ailments (water vapor), fibromyalgia (sulfur pools, black mud), and heart ailments, asthma, and cystic fibrosis (barometric pressure/high oxygen levels).

CAMERA Something waterproof (e.g., a Go-Pro could be fun, but watch the splashing), maybe with a case you can dirty up (due to muddy hands). *Most photographed* The ubiquitous shots of "reading a newspaper/book while floating" and "posing while covered in black mud." *Best light* On the Israel side, the sun sets behind mountains, which glows off the Jordan mountains in front of you – lovely. In Jordan, the sun sets as you are looking at the sea, which is blinding and terrible for pictures. Try mornings instead. *Best angle* From Israel, there are great views on top of **Ein Gedi (#50)** and **Masada (#8)**. *From up high* In Jordan, traverse the Dead Sea Panoramic Highway that winds to the top of the adjacent mountain that houses the *Hammamat Ma'in Hot Springs*. *Best long shot* **Masada (#8)** and **Mount Nebo (#24)**. *Surprise spot* The best views are from the Panorama Dead Sea Restaurant (decent food!) at lunch, and right after sunset when there's still a glow in the air.

SECRET *Ein Bokek* is the best public access point in Israel, and is legitimately free. Plus, it has the best setup: there are food and hotels nearby, as well as convenience shops to stock up on your Dead Sea goods. Technically, though, the southern part of the Dead Sea is not 100% natural: the water here is pumped in from the north lake for industrial mineral extraction. The southern area actually dried up in the 1980s, but the hotels stayed, so water is brought in for salt farming and to maintain tourism. For something more natural, look for cars parked on the side of the road about 5 minutes' drive north of **Ein Gedi (#50)** reserve. There's an unmarked access path to a free beach with hot water holes.

LUXURY In Jordan, the Kempinski is the nicest option, in Suweimeh. Near *Ein Bokek*, there are a number of high-end options, including Crown Plaza, Isrotel, Herod's, and Leonardo.

SPECIAL EVENTS In February, take part in the Dead Sea Marathon: 5km, 10km, 21.1km, 42.2km, and 50km options.

ITINERATOR!

CALENDAR

	Rain (mm)	Sun (hours)	Temp				Dew	Dead Sea temp
			C/F	Max	Avg	Min		
January	32	10	C	26	20	16	Dry	18
			F	78	69	60		65
February	29	11	C	30	23	16	Dry	17
			F	85	74	61		63
March	20	12	C	34	27	17	Dry	17
			F	93	81	63		63
April	8	12	C	39	32	22	Dry	18
			F	102	90	71		65
May	1	13	C	41	36	27	Dry	21
			F	106	97	80		70
June	0	14	C	42	38	33	Comfy	24
			F	107	101	91		76

	Rain (mm)	Sun (hours)	C/F	Temp			Dew	Dead Sea temp
				Max	Avg	Min		
July	0	13	C	42	39	36	Humid	27
			F	108	102	96		80
August	0	12	C	42	38	36	Very humid	28
			F	108	101	96		83
September	0	12	C	41	36	32	Humid	28
			F	105	96	90		82
October	5	11	C	39	30	26	Comfy	26
			F	103	87	79		79
November	13	11	C	35	25	20	Dry	23
			F	95	77	68		74
December	24	10	C	30	21	16	Dry	20
			F	85	70	61		69

PEAK POPULARITY The Dead Sea is famous, meaning it usually attracts a crowd, even midweek. But during off-season, especially at a nice hotel midweek (particularly on the Jordan side), you'll feel like you have the whole sea to yourself.

BEST SEASON Spring and autumn, like everywhere in Israel and Jordan. The summers can reach above 40°C/100°F but, because of the low UV exposure, it's not horrible to be outside. The water from the sea will likely be very tepid. Think: bathwater. In the winter, the water can be downright frigid.

BEST TIME OF DAY To get the most of any full-day spa experience, you'll want to start early. Weather-wise, there are rarely clouds here, so it's hottest from midday to late afternoon.

DAYS/HOURS In Israel, lifeguard stations are manned during daylight hours, seven days a week, in both winter and summer. Private hotels often have their own lifeguards with daytime hours of operation. For both countries, public beach access is 24/7.

MORNING/EVENING Yes, if you have a packed schedule, you can visit in the evening, after you check in at your hotel, or in the morning before breakfast.

TIME COMMITMENT You need at least 30 minutes (including changing time) for the most basic experience. Seek out mud, which adds another 30–60 minutes. With the spa and mineral baths, you'll need at least 3 hours. Many visitors in both Israel and Jordan spend the whole weekend on a hotel-spa package.

SPEED RULES Apply: *slow groups* should plan on spending the entire day at the Dead Sea, including transit times. In a pinch, you could do **Masada (#8)** in the morning and the Dead Sea in the afternoon, which will be a very full day. *Casual groups* can easily fit in Masada, and possibly a quick stop at **Qumran (#70)** for a busy day. *Fast groups* will probably follow the same itinerary as the medium groups, but can substitute a hike through **Ein Gedi (#50)** and/or a walk up to the *Masada's Snake Path (K1)* before ending with a dip in the Dead Sea.

COVERAGE

★ *Intro (30 minutes)* Jump in and out; skip all extras.
★ *Highlights (1–2 hours)* Head to a public beach; buy mud; lie out in the sun.
★ *Comprehensive (4–6 hours)* Visit a spa (includes sulfurous warm-water baths, a chlorinated pool, towels, showers, free mud, and private beach); don't forget lunch.
★ *Exhaustive (2–3 days)* Spend the weekend in a hotel-spa; relax!

BASE For cost reasons, we recommend day-tripping to the Dead Sea in Israel, using Jerusalem and Tel Aviv as anchors. On the Jordanian side, Suweimeh is an Anchor City on the Dead Sea and is home to the Dead Sea's nicest, most reasonably priced hotels.

ANCHOR CITIES Suweimeh: on the Dead Sea; Amman (to Suweimeh): 55km/1 hour. To Ein Bokek: Tel Aviv: 170km/2 hours; Jerusalem: 115km/1½ hours; Rosh Pina: 300km/3 hours.

BEST STRATEGY This depends on which side you enter. If you're on the Israeli side, we recommend spending a couple of hours in *Ein Bokek*, the free access point, unless you have a half- or full day, in which case splurge on one of the nearby *Ein Bokek Spa Hotels*. Due to unreasonably high costs, we don't recommend spending the night. That's not true for Suweimeh, Jordan's hotel district on the Sea. Plan to anchor in Suweimeh in lieu of Amman, and build in visits to the Sea every morning and evening if you like!

RELAXED PLANNING The most complicated part of the Dead Sea is finding a way to get to the water itself. On both sides, local people park on the side of the highway and walk to the shore. In Israel, this can be up to a kilometer, where you'll pass (and hopefully not fall into) dangerous sinkholes. For simplicity and safety, drive south until you get to the second lake and hotel district of *Ein Bokek*. Access to the beach is straightforward.

DAY TRIPPING Absolutely doable. You can arrange a number of day-long coach visits through a variety of tour companies. We like w touristisrael.com for information and tour setup. There are several electives you can add nearby if the idea of a day-long spa is not of interest – see *Nearby Electives* below.

WALKS AND DRIVES K1, P1, P2, U2, V1.

ITINERARIES Almost all of the itineraries in Part 10 include this BUCKET!-worthy experience.

ARRIVAL PREP

PREBOOK Not necessary for public beach access. Book your hotel-spa experiences in advance.

CAUTION

★ Mineral Beach and other popular access points in Israel have permanently closed due to thousands of dangerous sinkholes that have emerged in recent years. The holes have collapsed parts of the highway, beach pavilions, and (former) spas.
★ Big tour-bus stop.

★ Bring waterproof shoes (e.g., flip-flops). The "sand" is very rocky and scorching hot. Due to a lack of regular waves, this big still lake hasn't created any soft sand, so many people enter the sea with shoes on to avoid scrapes and burns. Don't worry: you can't lose them if they fall off – everything floats.
★ Don't shave the day you plan to enter the Sea. You'll thank us later.
★ Even minor cuts can cause serious discomfort in the Dead Sea.
★ Needless to say, don't get water in or near your mouth or eyes.
★ No splashing your friends! You'll regret it, guaranteed.
★ You can't sink, but you can still drown. No rough play!

ANNOYANCES If you visit a public beach, you're unlikely to find much remaining mud, if any. You can either take your chances by digging under adjacent rocks, or pop into one of the local convenience stores and purchase cheap, filtered, and packaged mud for your immediate use – or to bring home as gifts.

CONSTRAINTS Access into the water is not so easy.

OVERRATED The beach part. The beaches are not sand beaches! They are mostly densely packed salt, so don't go expecting to build sandcastles. The ground is both very hot on your feet and rock hard, so you won't want to lie down. Most people sit on lawn chairs and wear shoes.

BRING Bathing suit (changing rooms readily available); fresh water for drinking; a towel (for public beaches); flip-flops/water shoes for the many sharp rocks; lawn chair, but you can also rent/buy one.

DON'T BRING Sunscreen, for many people! UV is very low here, so you won't get scorched.

DIRECTIONS The entire Israeli side of the Dead Sea is located along Highway 90, with decent signposts. The entire Jordanian side is along Highway 65, or the Dead Sea Highway. A prettier, and more direct route from Tel Aviv is Highway 31, which connects from the 6. Driving to **Ein Bokek** will take 1½ hours (Jerusalem) or 2 hours (Tel Aviv) each way. Driving to one of the northern Dead Sea beaches nearer to Jerusalem will take 45m (Jerusalem) and 75m (Tel Aviv) each way. Suweimeh is 1 hour from Amman.

PUBLIC TRANSPORT Possible in Israel on the Egged buses. Plan your trip at w bus. co.il but be warned: times are not greatly convenient. Buses in Jordan are even less reliable and may involve multiple bus changes.

PARKING Plenty of parking at **Ein Bokek** and at hotels and spas, of course. For unmonitored access points, you'll need to find a place to park your car adjacent to the highway, but not on the shoulder (it's only a two-lane road). Looking for other parked cars is a good strategy.

GPS-FREE You can make do without GPS if you have a basic map.

ACCESS The Dead Sea is receding rapidly. Following this retreat, hundreds of large sink holes have begun to form in areas formerly under water. Thus, exercise extreme caution if you travel off the beaten path. Here are entry points in Israel you will pass from north to south: **Kalia** is closest to Jerusalem, so busy with the international crowd; **Neve Zohar**, a hot sulfur springs/public beach; **Biankini** (**w** biankini.co.il); **Einot Tsukim Nature Reserve**, where you can get a glimpse of the retreat of the Dead Sea; **Mineral Beach** (closed indefinitely, sinkholes); **Hot Springs** has natural hot water pools (unauthorized; 6km north of Ein Gedi Reserve; park on the side of Highway 90); **Ein Gedi Beach** (closed indefinitely, sinkholes); *Ein Bokek*, the most popular public-access beach; and *Ein Bokek Spa Hotels* – prebook and experience a luxe version, with freshwater pools and private access. From the Jordanian side, we recommend using your hotel's private beach, though there are public access points along the main highway.

BEST ENTRANCE If you're taking a bus or taxi from Jerusalem, then the best places to enter the sea are the north Dead Sea beaches of New Kalya (K1), Neve Midbar (K1), and Biankini/Siesta (K1), all three adjacent to the north side of the north lake. These require a nominal payment to the kibbutz that operates them. On the Jordanian side, there are a private access points, but we do not recommend them and prefer accessing the sea from Suweimeh hotels. Your Jordanian taxi driver may be able to guide you to a public-access spot (don't expect English language ability), but there won't be any services.

ADMISSION Depends on where you enter. In Israel, *Ein Bokek* is free; day passes to hotels (incl. lunch) can cost $80/day/pp. In Jordan, the best entry points are from hotels (40–50 JD; $55–70), though cheaper options ($20) can be found at Amman Beach.

PAYMENT METHODS Credit cards or cash in Israel. Cash in Jordan.

RECOMMENDED GUIDE Our guide is all you'll need.

VISITOR CENTER Jordan has two museums dedicated to the Dead Sea; the Museum at the Lowest Place on Earth, near *Lot's Cave* in Gawr as-Safi, has mediocre reviews. Better are the views from the Dead Sea Museum, at the Panorama Dead Sea Complex near the intersection of Hammamat Ma'in Street and Ma'in Street. Find Ma'in Street off the Dead Sea Highway about 8km south of the Kempinski Hotel Ishtar in Suweimeh. The museum is a further 9km along, sitting atop the adjacent Zara mountain range.

TOUR GUIDE You can hire same-day or multiday packages by group, bus, or with a personal driver from Jerusalem, Tel Aviv, Amman, and other destinations.

EAT There are several snack bars lining the public beaches, and mediocre restaurants in the hotels and spas. There's an Aroma Cafe (good sandwiches/coffee) near the McDonald's in *Ein Bokek*.

SLEEP *Ein Bokek* in Israel has a line of expensive, high-rise hotels with private beaches, spa facilities, pools, and restaurants. Suweimeh in Jordan offers a little more privacy, with hotels spaced out along the northern portion of the Sea, each offering the same amenities as *Ein Bokek*, but at much fairer prices.

BUCKET!PEDIA

Hebrew name Yam HaMelach ("the salty sea"). *Arabic name* Al-Bahir al-Mayyit ("the dead sea"). *Historical name* To the Romans, it was Palus Asphaltites, or the Asphalt Pool. *Size* 50km long and 15km wide at its maximum. The lake has decreased in length by 40% in only 50 years. Water levels have dropped 25m in the last 40 years alone. The water content has decreased from roughly 1,000km², before industrial chemical production began in the 1930s, to roughly 600km² today. Water levels continue to fall at a rate of 1m (three feet) per year. *Population* Small communities live on both sides. *Ethnic mix* On the western shore, the land north of Ein Gedi is technically part of the West Bank, but in practice the area is run by Israeli authorities as part of Area C. The border is unnoticeable. *Historical era* *Prehistoric* and *Modern*. *Year constructed* A formal tourism industry began in the 1960s. *Years active* The land has been active for millennia. The Bible talks of Sodom and Gomorrah, which were on the Dead Sea shores. Cleopatra visited for cosmetics. The last Jewish bastion was located across the way at Masada. The Dead Sea Scrolls were hidden here. Both Israel and Jordan began to use the Sea for agricultural purposes long before tourism set in in the 1960s, which has since created heavy hotel and spa demand.

CONTEXT The Dead Sea makes for a fantastic day trip with its multitude of interesting and unique characteristics. Visitors travel here to bathe/float in the waters, believing it to have healing qualities. The mud and air are also espoused as containing curative properties. It's usually hot, with high temperatures almost year-round, but it's rare to get a sunburn because of the low elevation and lack of UV penetration. Many hotels and spas provide private access to the Dead Sea's waters in both countries, and are worth the cost in order to get the best setup. Several come with chlorinated pools, mineral baths, and clean vats of mineral-rich clay/mud, which can be otherwise difficult to source on your own. Lots of souvenir shopping is available (for yourself or others) including inexpensive mineral salt, mud, and cosmetic products. The water in the Sea contains high levels of potassium, bromine, calcium, and magnesium. A variety of health therapies have arisen as a result of the region's elevation, climate, water, mud, and low levels of radiation.

GEOLOGY The Dead Sea is not technically a "sea," because it lacks access to a larger body of water. That classifies it more accurately as a lake. Because of the Dead Sea's physical recession (largely due to the diversion of water from the Jordan River and mining of the water for industrial purposes), it is no longer one lake but rather two adjacent bodies of water. The Dead Sea is the lowest place on Earth at 430m below sea level (and lowering!). Both Israel and Jordan have signs proclaiming the lowest point, but they are both roughly equally low. The lake is 304m deep, and is the deepest hypersaline lake in the world. It has variable salinity, but averages 33%, compared to the ocean's at 3.5%. No animals can survive in its waters, but bacteria and fungi have both been discovered. In 2010, researchers documented around 30 craters at the bottom of the Sea with a diverse array of bacterial life. It is believed that these bacteria may be able to tolerate both salt and fresh water, which is unknown among lifeforms today. In the north, both Israel and Jordan divert water from the Jordan River, which feeds the Sea, for industrial and agricultural purposes, which has further receded the total area encompassed by the Sea. Fresh groundwater has then been filling the empty aquifers where seawater once sat underground, dissolving the natural salts and creating massive sinkholes. Estimates vary, but somewhere between 1,000 and 5,000 sinkholes have formed over the last 30 years.

ENGINEERING In 1929, the Palestine Potash Company began the industrial processing of the Dead Sea, extracting potassium chloride (potash) and bromine, a chemical used in chemical manufacturing, as drilling fluid and in film. Now privatized, Israel Chemicals still generates very high revenue from processing minerals from the Dead Sea water. Jordan's Arab Potash Company also generates high income from this industry.

The companies first create salt evaporation pans before sending the product to on-site chemical facilities that turn the salts into usable product. The salts themselves are also used in several treatment therapies and cosmetic products.

Jordan, Israel, and the Palestinian Authority have agreed to develop a pipeline, called the Red Sea–Dead Sea Water Conveyance, which will pump water from the Red Sea to refill the Dead Sea, while also providing electricity and more usable water. The project, however, has been stalled for a decade.

ARCHAEOLOGY The Bible references several cities in the region, but few archaeological remains have survived. **Masada (#8)** is a Herodian fort on a nearby mountain plateau that has survived for 2,000 years. **Ein Gedi (#50)** contains remains of several periods of history, going as far back as the Neolithic Period and the first human settlements in the region. Perhaps the region's most famous discovery was the set of nearly 1,000 scrolls and fragments detailing biblical stories and texts dating as far back as the 3rd century BCE. These were discovered in the mid-20th century by Bedouin farmers in **Qumran (#70)**.

CHRONOLOGY

c3.7 million years ago: flooding from the Mediterranean aggregates layers of sand in the Dead Sea basin.

c2 million years ago: the continental African and Arabian plates brush crudely against each other, causing a rift that creates the Dead Sea, raising the area around it, and blocking inundation from the Mediterranean. The resulting large lake, Lake Lisan, stretches north all the way to the Sea of Galilee.

c26,000 years ago: Lake Lisan reaches its apogee, perhaps 250m above current levels.

c18,000 years ago: Lisan eventually loses its connection to the Sea of Galilee.

c10,000 years ago: Lake levels drop to about current levels, though the height has risen and fallen over the last 10,000 years.

c1000 BCE–100 CE: Dead Sea is referenced in numerous Bible verses related to ancient history, as are nearby locations: Ein Gedi, Jericho, Sodom, and Gomorrha.

c300 BCE–100 CE: Dead Sea Scrolls are written and stored in caves near Qumran, across from the Dead Sea.

1929: Palestine Potash Company founded.

1940s–1950s: Dead Sea Scrolls discovered.

1952: Dead Sea Works (later Israel Chemicals) replaces the Palestine Potash Company.

1953: Israel constructs Degania Gate Dam to collect water from the Sea of Galilee, diminishing the flow of the Jordan River.

1960s: Jordan also begins diverting water from the Jordan River, causing the level of evaporation to be greater than the amount of water replenishing the Dead Sea, leading to a shrinking Sea.

1964: First resort established near Neve Zohar.

1970s: Syria and Jordan begin diverting the Yarmouk River, which feeds the lower Jordan River.

1980/1992: Algal blooms color the Dead Sea red.

late 1980s: First sinkholes appear, predicted to be a result of the reduced water levels.

2010: Divers discover giant craters at the bed of the Dead Sea covered in bacterial life forms.

2013: Israel, the Palestinian Authority, and Jordan sign an agreement to transport water from the Red Sea, desalinate it, and repopulate the Dead Sea with it. (The project remains stalled.)

2015: Level of water is dropping by 1m (3 feet) per year. Since measurements began in 1927, the Sea is estimated to have dropped 40m (131 feet).

2050: The Dead Sea will evaporate completely if no action is taken.

WEBSITE No one official website.

ARTICLE Joshua Hammer, "The Dying of the Dead Sea," *Smithsonian Magazine*, October 2005 (**w** smithsonianmag.com/science-nature/the-dying-of-the-dead-sea -70079351/).

WHERE TO NEXT?

THEMATIC *BUCKET!* BUCKET! *Noteworthy* Endangered; Unique *Religion* Meditation, Yoga, and Quiet *Archaeology* Prehistory/Stone to Copper *Structure* Technological Advancement; Infrastructure *Nature* Geological Wonders; Geographical Superlatives; Desert; Gorgeous Scenery; The Great Outdoors *Scenic* Most Photographed; Scenic Drives *Society* Borders *Active* Swimming; Competition; Swimming *Leisure* Public/Popular Beaches; Sea Access; Thermal Waters; Spas and Massage; Peaceful *Entertainment* Souvenirs *Accommodation* Vacation Hotels/Resorts

COMPLEMENTARY If you are looking for more water activities, **Mediterranean Coast** will satiate you, with dozens of options to consider; the **Red Sea (#10)** offers excellent diving opportunities; and the **Sea of Galilee (#7)** shows you considerable history as you circumnavigate.

Other famous low places include: the Netherlands coastal provinces, which are 1–7 (3–23 feet) below sea level; Baku, Azerbaijan is the lowest capital city on Earth at –28m (–92 feet); Badwater Basin in Death Valley, California is 85m (–279 feet); and Laguna del Carbón in Argentina is the lowest spot in the Americas, at –105m (–344 feet). And also a salt lake!

And here are a few more salty lakes for you to visit: the saltiest body of water in the world is the Gaet'ale Pond in the Danakil Depression of Ethiopia at 43% salinity, while Lake Assal in Djibouti is 34% salinity; Antarctica has a number of salty lakes, with Don Juan (33%) likely being the saltiest; and the Great Salt Lake in Utah is 27% salinity.

NEARBY ELECTIVES *Israel* (all border the Dead Sea): **Masada (#8)**; **Ein Gedi (#50)**; **Qumran (#70)**. *Jordan* (distance from Suweimeh): **Madaba and the Madaba Map (#19)**: 35km/45 minutes; **Wadi Mujib and Mujib Biosphere Reserve (#23)**: 40km/30 minutes; **Bethany-Beyond-the-Jordan (#41)**: 17km/17 minutes; *Mukawir*: 40km/45 minutes.

NEARBY REGIONS Jerusalem (A) is an hour north/west of the Dead Sea. Technically, the Dead Sea in Israel sits in the West Bank (C), though it's completely controlled by Israel. The Aravah Valley/Desert (L) is just to the south of the Dead Sea on Israel's side, leading to Eilat. In Jordan, the Dead Sea is an hour's drive from Amman (Q) and is near the famed King's Highway (O).

#4 Wadi Rum

BROCHURE

RATINGS		MACRO-REGION
BUCKET! Score	8/10	M: South Jordan
Ruin	1/5	
Entertainment	3/5	**MICRO-REGION**
Information	3/5	M2
Popularity	4/5	

PRIMARY THEME/CATEGORY Nature – Parks – Gorgeous Scenery.

TOP Most beautiful natural scenery. Best spot for dark sky and stargazing. Best desert activities.

COMMENDATIONS UNESCO World Heritage Site: for its 25,000 rock carvings, 20,000 inscriptions, and 154 archaeological sites which trace the evolution of human-kind's history over the last 12,000 years; also for its iconic desert landscape, entered 2011. Also a Jordan Nature Reserve.

ESSENCE Famed red desert in southern Jordan, popular for sand activities, hiking, and overnighting in tents under the stars.

HOLY LAND RELEVANCE While not religiously related to the Holy Land, the Nabataeans who inhabited this land played an important role in the region, crafting **Petra (#2)** and building a number of sites, now marked on the **Incense Route (#73)**.

ELECT ME! If Petra is on your list, Wadi Rum is a short jaunt away and can be accomplished with one extra day (or even en route from Aqaba to Petra). It has a curious Martian quality with its red sand, and thus several movies (including *The Martian*) were shot here. You can easily organize a couple-hour day tour through the desert's most popular sites, or spend a few days hiking, riding horses or camels, or driving your own 4x4, among other activities. The activities are laid out for you upon arrival depending on how much time you have – the longer you have, the more you can explore the area. Overnighting is popular and for good reason: staying with Bedouins is a unique experience, as are the group tents, glamping quarters, firepit dinners, and stargazing. Don't miss the changing colors of light reflecting off the broad sand carpet at sunrise and sunset.

WORTH THE DETOUR? If you're spending more than a day in Jordan, absolutely. (If you've only got one day, just go to Petra.)

EXPERIENCES

CAN'T MISS Sunrise! Some outfitters will allow for a walk up one of the nearby peaks to watch the multi-hued arrival of the morning sun.

SITES There are a variety of routes your driver can take, depending on which sites interest you. Your individualized tour can be arranged either at the visitor center or directly with your campsite organizer (online bookings are recommended, though you needn't commit to the activities until you arrive). The **visitor center** is located next to Seven Pillars of Wisdom. Pay here, and organize jeep treks and register your own 4x4, if using. There is a big wall of options and you can add on as many stops as you like (for additional costs). There's also a museum, 10-minute video, and restaurant. Lawrence's eponymous book spoke of the **Seven Pillars of Wisdom**, the mountain which now bears its name. You can do a walk around it. **Lawrence's Spring** – where Lawrence of Arabia reportedly washed while camping here during

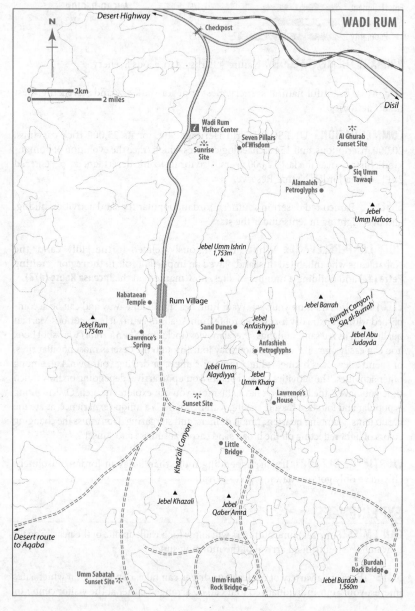

WADI RUM

Desert Highway

Checkpost

N

Disil

0 ——— 2km
0 ——— 2 miles

Wadi Rum
Visitor Center

Sunrise
Site

Seven Pillars
of Wisdom

Al Ghurab
Sunset Site

Siq Umm
Tawaqi

Alamaleh
Petroglyphs

Jebel
Umm Nafoos

Jebel Umm Ishrin
1,753m

Nabataean
Temple

Rum Village

Jebel Barrah

Burrah Canyon /
Siq al-Burrah

Jebel Rum
1,754m

Lawrence's
Spring

Sand Dunes

Jebel
Anfaishyya

Jebel Abu
Judayda

Anfashieh
Petroglyphs

Jebel Umm
Alaydiyya

Jebel
Umm Kharg

Lawrence's
House

Sunset Site

Khazali Canyon

Little
Bridge

Jebel Khazali

Jebel
Qaber Amra

Desert route
to Aqaba

Burdah
Rock Bridge

Umm Sabatah
Sunset Site

Umm Fruth
Rock Bridge

Jebel Burdah ▲
1,560m

the Arab Revolt in 1917 – is usually the first stop on a jeep tour. The **Rock Bridges** are three rock arches which you can climb above and over, with Jebel Burdah being very popular. When it comes to the **sand dunes**, best way to do it is hustle up to the top and then run screaming down. The people who built Petra have a couple of sites in the region, including the **Nabataean Temple** which was used to worship the goddess Allat. **Petroglyphs** are found in several spots, including Alamaleh, Anfashieh, Khaz'ali, and Lawrence's Spring.

ACTIVITIES There are tons of traditional **climbing** routes, though you'll need to get Bedouin permission unless hiking near Rum village. Lots of websites with mapped routes (**w** climbingjordan.com; **w** mountainproject.com; **w** 27crags.com) all include topos, pitches, distance, among other relevant information. Several activities can be organized at the entrance, or as part of a package if you're arranging a broader Jordan experience, including *Camel Riding*, **canyoning**, and **horse treks**. Desert trekking is often accompanied, meaning you will be followed by a jeep or the guide animals. There are a few legitimate hike paths, including to further-afield sites, such as the Jebel Burdah rock bridge. These will still require a guide. **Desert camping** is one of the highlights of a trip to Wadi Rum, but is not required. Usually included as part of a multiday/overnight package are your guide, activities, transport, usually dinner and breakfast, Bedouin shows, a mattress or tent or fancier outfit (*Glamping in Wadi Rum (M2)*), and free stargazing. You can book on **w** booking.com or other hotel sites. Price will increase if you require showers, toilets, *private* toilets, electricity, or tents.

CAMERA *Best shot* The whole dang place is a photographer's dream, but the land bridges and tops of rocks are the biggest draw. *Best light* Sunset.

SECRET You'll see little more than a few fuzzy petroglyphs at each of the "stops" on your jeep tour. But you're in it for the beauty. So don't feel like you absolutely must see Lawrence's Spring or any of the wadis if it'll prevent you from doing a longer trip to something more special (one of the land bridges, for instance). The entire region is beautiful, so just pick the stops that interest you.

LUXURY In addition to the **hot air balloon ride**, you can fancy it up with all-glass rooms (bubble hotels) in the desert, starting at $220 (much more in high season).

SPECIAL EVENTS Wadi Rum from above – **hot air ballooning** (from 130 JD per adult for 45 minutes), microlight aircraft (150 JD for 1 hour, you + pilot), ultralight aircraft (180 JD for 1 hour, you + pilot, leaves from Aqaba), or Diamond Aircraft (200 JD for 1 hour, 2 people + pilot, leaves from Aqaba): **w** international.visitjordan.com/Wheretogo/Wadirum.aspx.

ITINERATOR!

DAYS/HOURS The park is open to campers, so does not technically close. The Visitor's Center is where you can enter the site (🕐 08.00–18.00, closes occasionally for security reasons). If you are staying overnight, you can squeeze out more time in your day with a morning hike, and of course stargazing in the evening.

BEST TIME TO VISIT Spring and fall (high tourist season, of course), to miss the extremely cold winter nights (if staying overnight), and to avoid the extreme heat of the midsummer days. If you are visiting during summer, plan to depart on activities very early. If winter, expect freezing temperatures at night. Obviously most popular March–May and September–November.

TIME COMMITMENT You can get the gist of Wadi Rum simply by taking in the views from the visitor center, but it would be awfully silly to come this far and skip a jeep trip. Plan on a minimum of 1 hour for the quickest excursion, but 2–4-hour options are more common. Many stay overnight, and get up early for sunrise, so you may want to plan a full day and night. If you like hiking, you could stay several days. Also, keep in mind Wadi Rum is pretty far off the highway, so you'll need at least an hour to get there and back, from wherever you're coming from. Make sure to plan for driving times.

SPEED RULES Don't really apply. You're at the mercy of the Bedouin guides, who normally give you 30–60 minutes at a site, though you can ask to leave earlier. The whole point is to enjoy the natural environment, so rushing kind of defeats the purpose. If time is an issue, pick a shorter tour.

COVERAGE

★ *Intro* 1 hour for visitor center and walking around the sites nearby (no jeep needed), but hardly worth it if you've driven all the way here.
★ *Highlights* 2–3 hours includes a jeep tour to the most popular sites.
★ *Comprehensive* 1–2 days will include a full-day jeep trek to the principal sites, a camel ride (pay separately), overnight in a Bedouin camp, and a morning hike.
★ *Exhaustive* You can spend as many days here as you like, though most of the activities require a Bedouin guide to accompany you. Alternatively, you can arrange to be dropped off and picked up at specific times. Those looking to do rock climbing will want to plan longer trips. There are also walks between Wadi Rum and Petra that take three days, easily organized through a number of outfitters (check TripAdvisor).

BASE It makes the most sense to visit Wadi Rum on a road trip. Both Aqaba and Petra are near enough that you can run day trips, or stop by Wadi Rum between them, but none are considered Anchor Cities because they are not convenient from which to reach other sites. Best to rent a car and keep moving forward.

ANCHOR CITIES Amman (325km/4¼ hours) and Suweimeh (350km/4½ hours) are the two Anchor Cities in Jordan. They are too far for same-day round-trips, but you could travel from either on one day, spend the night, and return the following day.

BEST STRATEGY You can arrange a tour from Israel, Aqaba, or Wadi Musa, or drive yourself. Upon arrival, you will be escorted to your guide, if you don't already have one. The local Bedouin population wait in lines for the next tourists at the visitor center, much like a taxi service at the airport. You won't have much negotiating to do as the various options for jeep treks and camel/horse rides are written on a giant board just inside the main gates. The prices are per jeep (so bring a friend!) and can be bargained down a bit. There are a number of popular, predefined trips you can choose from, or you can coordinate your own itinerary with the driver, including the length of time and sites to visit. You'll then take a jeep/4x4 through the desert to Rum Village, get gassed up, and the journey into the desert begins.

WALKING ROUTES There are no easy walking routes for getting around. You'll have to hire transport to get to camp/activities/etc. There are a few short paths around the visitor center. For those on longer hikes, please note that cairns (stones piled up for navigation purposes) were laid by Bedouins and not tourists – the community asks you not to touch the stones in situ, nor create new cairns.

DAY TRIPPING You can organize a same-day return trip from either Aqaba (1 hour each way) or Petra/Wadi Musa (1½ hours each way).

WALKS AND DRIVES M2, V1, V2, W2, W5.

ITINERARIES High BUCKET! Scores: 7+; Off-the-Beaten-Path Jordan; Noteworthy; Nature and Scenic; Accommodation; Organized; UNESCO; Community; On the Road; Cinematic.

ARRIVAL PREP

PREBOOK Not necessary, and may even be possible to procure overnight camping space upon arrival, though we do recommend prebooking lodging (**w** booking.com or your preferred outlet – remember it's camping, not the Holiday Inn).

TIPS Wadi Rum is a desert, so Wi-Fi/credit card processing machines are mostly unavailable. Cash (JD) is recommended.

CAUTION Take all heat-related precautions – bring lots of water, sunscreen, hat, food – and don't assume you can procure goods and foodstuffs upon arrival.

REALITY CHECK When you do arrive, you'll feel like you're in a caravan of tourist vans heading into the desert – and you are. Once you get further out, the cars tend to disperse. The drivers/guides may try to wrap up the tour as quickly as possible. Or sometimes the opposite: they may be having tea far away from the jeep when you are ready to leave. Try to relax your Western time standards a bit. Jeep tours seem overpriced, but are a necessary evil if you're coming all this way.

CONSTRAINTS Beware of motion sickness as the jeep rides are very bumpy. For those with mobility issues, you'll be walking on sand, rocks, and mountains.

BRING Take cues from your guides and/or tour operator, but you'll want: water; hat; sunglasses; food for grill, if camping on your own; telescope (luxury item – you won't be able to fit this unless you have a porter and a private jet). If you're staying overnight, you'll need warm clothes; a flashlight; bug spray.

DON'T BRING Rolling luggage; things requiring electrical outlets or Wi-Fi to function; a lot of disposable things.

PUBLIC TRANSPORT Very limited – you will need to have a rental car or be part of an organized tour.

ACCESS The site is located along Jordan's Desert Highway (Highway 15), which starts/ends in Aqaba and continues north towards Maan (detour left to Petra). Signs will indicate when to turn toward the site. There's parking at the visitor center.

BEST ENTRANCE Wadi Rum Village.

ADMISSION Wadi Rum is cheap to enter (5 JD, children under 12 are free), but the entire experience can add up. A jeep tour for 2–4 hours will cost 20–40 JD, depending on what you're getting from the experience, the interaction with the guide, etc. A full-day jeep tour, plus overnight in basic accommodation, will be 60–80 JD. Camel rides are 10–20 JD. Camping can be anywhere from 25 JD (budget) to 200 JD (luxury). Tips are not required, but a small token of appreciation can go a long way – scale up the longer your trip.

RECOMMENDED GUIDE The driver is sufficient; no history guide needed. However, for solo hiking, a guidebook is essential. The most popular is Tony Howard's *Treks and Climbs in Wadi Rum*.

VISITOR CENTER The visitor center has limited informational material. Brochures are not regularly provided, but can be found online.

TOUR GUIDE Not exactly mandatory, but guides are recommended so you don't get lost in the huge desert expanse. Many of the "tour guides" act more simply as drivers, shuttling you from one location to another with little information about history or place. Don't expect them to be chatty if booked on site; English is widely understood, but speech is mostly limited. If a good guide is important, do research and book online in advance.

EAT Rations are very basic, so plan to bring and carry with you everything you need (food, water) if you are taking a long walk or drive. There is a basic restaurant at the visitor center, and another place to buy basics at Rum Village. If you're staying overnight, food is usually part of the package, which generally includes barbecue, some bread and salads, and continental breakfast in the morning.

SLEEP Lots of outdoor "bivouac" camping options; either bring your own tent or borrow one. Most places take cash and include a basic mattress, usually a tented toilet area (though some are more rustic), a blanket, and half- or full-board. Book on TripAdvisor or **w** booking.com. There are some glamorous options ("glamping") which should be arranged in advance.

BUCKET!PEDIA

AKA Valley of the Moon.　*Size* 720km^2.　*Population* In the hundreds.　*Ethnic mix* Several Arab Bedouin tribes.　*Historical era* Prehistoric: Neolithic to Roman/Byzantine: Nabataean.

CONTEXT "Wadi" means "valley" in Arabic, and Wadi Rum is the largest valley in Jordan. The burnt-sienna hue of the desert makes for a particularly impressive backdrop to the various sandstone rock formations jutting from the otherwise flat earth. This is the supposed site where T.E. Lawrence and Prince Faisal Bin Hussein made their base during the Arab Revolt during World War I. Today, the park is organized and operated by the resident Bedouin community, who provide all the park services you will need: transportation, long-hike guides, animal rides, dinner preparation, astronomers, etc. Their people have been living in this region for many generations, if not centuries.

GEOLOGY These sandstone mountains can reach above 1,700m in height. Where erosion has taken place, there are often big sand dunes (perfect for sandboarding!). The arch bridges were formed by wind erosion, removing the soft sand so just the hard rock remains.

ARCHAEOLOGY With roughly 12,000 years of human settlement, spanning from prehistoric times to the present day, the site does have historic value. Because of the harsh nature of the desert, there have not been large, permanent settlements – not that have been discovered, anyway. There are over 150 smaller archaeological sites, showing land use over several millennia. This area was a base of operations for the Nabataeans, a nomadic Arab tribe responsible for the grand architecture of Petra, Avdat, and other sites in the Holy Land during Roman rule. The evidence of human history comes from petroglyphs – tens of thousands spread throughout the park, carved onto the cliffs and harder rock material.

CHRONOLOGY

5th century BCE: Arabian and Nabataean tribes inhabit the land, using the rocks and shade for shelter, and inscribing/etching tens of thousands of drawings into the soft rock.

1917 CE: Lawrence of Arabia uses Wadi Rum as staging ground during the Arab Revolt in World War I.

1998: Jordan declares Wadi Rum a Protected Area.

2011: UNESCO declares Wadi Rum a World Heritage Site.

WEBSITE w wadirum.jo.

WHERE TO NEXT?

THEMATIC *Noteworthy* UNESCO; Nature Reserves; Exploration. *Archaeology* Prehistory/Stone to Copper. *Nature* Desert; Wadis; Birding; Gorgeous Scenery; The Great Outdoors. *Scenic* Earth Panorama; Sky; Sunrise/Sunset; Scenic Drives. *People* Bedouin. *Active* Adventure/Extreme Land Sports. *Accommodation* Campgrounds

COMPLEMENTARY For other **climbing activities**, check out the *Adventure/Extreme Land Sports* theme. **Timna (#96)** park also has good climbing opportunities. More things to do in **southern Jordan** include **Petra (#2)**, **Aqaba (#43)**, snorkeling/diving in the **Red Sea (#10)**, or consider *Road Trip M2*. If you like the **desert**, then Jordan has a ton of it! **Qasr Amra and the Desert Palaces (#20)** are an interesting addition to any trip to Jordan and can be done as a day trip (*Road Trip R1*). Israel has the Negev, too! You don't want to miss **Makhtesh Ramon (#28)**, another stunning geological oddity of the desert. And if you like ruins *and* the desert, you definitely don't want to miss the **Incense Route (#73)**, which pays homage to the various stops along the spice trade avenue from East Asia through to the Mediterranean port cities. These were created by the same Nabataeans who inhabited Wadi Rum.

NEARBY **Aqaba (#43)**: 77km/1¼ hours; **Petra (#2)**: 120km/2 hours.

#5 Tel Aviv

BROCHURE

RATINGS			MACRO-REGION
BUCKET! Score	▰▰▰▰▰▰▱	8/10	D: Tel Aviv
Ruin	n/a		
Entertainment	▰▰▰▰▰	5/5	**MICRO-REGIONS**
Information	▰▰▰▱▱	3/5	D1–D8
Popularity	▰▰▰▰▰	5/5	

PRIMARY THEME/CATEGORY Society – Cities – Principal Cities.

TOP City beaches; restaurants; nightlife; walking paths; relaxed attitude; accommodation.

COMMENDATIONS UNESCO World Heritage Site: White City of Tel Aviv – the Modern Movement, 2003. Tel Aviv is also in the UNESCO Creative Cities of Media Arts network.

ESSENCE Beaches, food, sun, fun, and hedonism.

HOLY LAND RELEVANCE Tel Aviv may very well be the most liberal city in all of Israel (arguably the Middle East) in terms of acceptance of different religions, ethnicities, languages, gender, sexual preferences, and appropriate outdoor attire. There are few things to see/do specifically related to the Holy Land within Tel Aviv's boundaries, but it provides a nice contrast to the history and religion you will encounter on the rest of your trip.

ELECT ME! Tel Aviv is a great Mediterranean beach town. It's very easy to spend weeks here, if you choose. The beaches have fine white sand, the water is warm and swimmable, and there are plenty of restaurants making it easy to lounge and drink beers or cocktails all day. The nightlife is easily the best in the country. The gay scene is prominent. There are a variety of family-friendly activities. If you're a foodie, you're in luck – this city is in its renaissance. Religious or not, Israeli or not, Jewish or not, this is the Middle East destination where you can be yourself, and you're welcome to be. It has a relaxed energy, where a typical weekend activity includes a stroll along the beautiful beach promenade. The weather in Tel Aviv is glorious for most of the year, so if you're looking for a Mediterranean beach spot that isn't (yet) hounded by millions of tourists at once, look no further.

WORTH THE DETOUR? Absolutely, as a counter to the intensity and sensory overload of Jerusalem, Tel Aviv makes for a wonderfully relaxing and entertaining part of any trip to the Holy Land.

EXPERIENCES

CAN'T MISS With a clear focus on architecture, history, culture, nightlife, beaches, and food (who wouldn't want that?), Tel Aviv's Gold sites are **Modern Movement**

(Bauhaus Architecture) (#16), **Jaffa (#30)**, **ANU – Museum of the Jewish People (#77)**, **Tel Aviv Nightlife (#82)**, **Carmel Market (#87)**, **Tel Aviv Beaches (#89)**, **Tel Aviv Museum of Art (#95)**, and **Imperial Bar (#99)**.

SITES

★ *Beaches* We have a whole elective dedicated exclusively to **Tel Aviv Beaches (#89)**.

★ *Streets for shopping* The *Jaffa Flea Market* (*Shuk HaPishpeshim*) has an eclectic variety of new and old. **Rothschild Boulevard** is for shopping, cafés, lazing about, and being seen. Sheinkin Street (D4) has great boutiques. Nahalat Binyamin (D4) has boutiques and bars.

★ *Architecture and art* **Modern Movement (Bauhaus Architecture) (#16)** can be found throughout the city and gives Tel Aviv its nickname of "White City"; Beit Ha'ir (D3) and **Bialik House**, an art museum housed in the former town hall showcasing Israeli art and architecture; Fire and Water Fountain (D3) at Dizengoff Square; and check out our *Modern Architecture* theme (p. 518) for several other Tel Aviv buildings.

★ *Jaffa* **Jaffa (#30)** is an old Arab city incorporated into Tel Aviv.

★ *Neighborhoods* **Neve Tzedek** is the oldest neighborhood outside of Jaffa, now with several boutiques and coffeehouses; Florentin (D4) is hip/cool.

★ *People-watching* Visit the huge HaYarkon Park (D7), **Tel Aviv Port**, Hatachana Train Station (D1), or Jaffa Port.

★ *Get out of town* Drive 20 minutes north to the **Herziliya Beaches** for beautiful sand in a more suburban feel; Rishon Letzion (D8) is a surprisingly big area with a great synagogue, history museum, and village park; Rishpon (D7) has cafés and a water park; in Ramat Aviv you can visit Kikar Levana/White Square (D8) and its tower to take in the panorama; and in Ramle visit the remains of the White Mosque (D8) and the Pool of the Arches/Al-Anazia (D8).

★ *Markets* **Carmel Market (#87)** is the area's most famous; Levinsky Market (D4) is found along a long corridor in Florentin with lots of food stalls and wholesale vendors; Sarona Market (D3) is in the trendy Sarona neighborhood and has a massive indoor space with dozens of food vendors and food-related shops (wine, fish, spices, etc.).

ACTIVITIES

★ Explore the **Tel Aviv Nightlife (#82)**: bars, clubs, restaurants, and music venues. **Imperial Bar (#99)** has racked up several awards, but just as popular are Kuli Alma (D4) and Butler Bar (D4).

★ Walk along the **Tel Aviv Tayelet/Promenade** from **Tel Aviv Port** to **Jaffa (#30)**, timing to catch sunset.

★ Taste delicious street food. Try *sabich*, an eggplant-based vegetarian pita sandwich, *shakshuka*, a tomato and egg breakfast, the world's best hummus at **Abu Hassan** in Jaffa, the internationally acclaimed cauliflower pita sandwich from **Miznon**, *rugelach* from Said Abouelafia in Jaffa, and *sufganiyot*, a huge jelly donut popular during Hanukkah. Anita (D4) has several interesting gelato flavors. And don't skip the falafel – try Falafel Gabai (D3) or HaKosem.

★ Reserve your table in advance for some of the country's famed **modern cuisine** at one of Tel Aviv's hip restaurants: **Tzfon Abraxas**, **Manta Ray**, **George and John Tel Aviv**, **OCD**, **Popina**, **Mashya**, **Pastel**, or **Herbert Samuel**. Or try one of the homier restaurant favorites, such as **Busi Grill** or **Old Man and the Sea (D2)** in Jaffa.

★ Take a short or long bike ride around town with the super-easy **Tel-O-Fun Bike Share**, then take a long coffee break at a local **café**.

★ Understand Jewish culture better at **ANU – Museum of the Jewish People (#77)** and/or the **MUSA – Eretz Israel Museum**, get an art fix at the **Tel Aviv Museum of Art (#95)** and **Design Museum Holon**, or study science at the **Weizmann Institute of Science**.

- ★ Stay in a boutique hotel near the beach, such as **The Norman Hotel**, **Brown Beach House**, Poli House (D4), or Brown TLV (D4).
- ★ Check out a show at the Cameri Theatre (D3) of Tel Aviv or the Suzanne Dellal Centre for Dance and Theatre (D4).
- ★ Buy some local gifts at The PhotoHouse (D3) or the *Bauhaus Center (D3)*.
- ★ Hire a guide or teach yourself a new Water Sport (D1): stand-up paddleboarding, kitesurfing, traditional surfing, and yachting are all popular options.
- ★ Pick up a game of Matcot (D1).

CAMERA *Best shot* A great spot is the top of **Jaffa (#30)**, looking towards the long stretch of beach. The Azrieli Center (D3) has an observation deck from its top floors, which is an okay vantage, but not a 360° view.   *Best light* Sunset every single day is glorious.

SECRET Whether or not you're into sports, in order to really fit in you need to learn Matcot (D1) (pronounced *maht-coat*) which is essentially ping-pong without a table, but a bit more aggressive, and you can't let the ball touch the ground. Cross the street at the beach to any convenience store and buy a set for cheap – they're usually right at the entrance. Or play with a stranger. Separately, jellyfish season is usually early July.

LUXURY New hotels are popping up all over. Look for The Jaffa (D2) ($600/night), The Setai (D2) ($400/night), **The Norman Hotel** ($600/night), or the Drisco ($300/night).

SPECIAL EVENTS Yom Kippur (U) (September–October); *Purim in Tel Aviv (D4)* (February–March); *Tel Aviv Pride Celebration (D1)* (June).

ITINERATOR!

DAYS/HOURS Many businesses are closed from sundown Friday to sundown Saturday (Shabbat), though you will find secular restaurants tend to stay open, as do some Russian grocery stores (Tiv Taam) and convenience shops. Everything is closed on Yom Kippur, no exceptions. But otherwise, Tel Aviv is another "city that never sleeps" with bars open all night long (usually until 04.00), and folks roaming the streets (and beaches!) until morning.

BEST TIME TO VISIT If you are coming for the beach, you want to come in the summer; it's glorious, although busy. The winter and spring can be too cold to get in the water. The fall is a great time, as the water is still warm, but the oppressive heat of July and August has passed. Religious holidays – Jewish and Christian – tend to see a peak in tourists: Passover, High Holidays (Rosh Hashanah and Yom Kippur), and Christmas.

TIME COMMITMENT If you're not into beaches, food, or fun, you can breeze through Tel Aviv in an afternoon. Otherwise, plan to spend at least one day and night. Ideally, stay three (you'll need one day to recover). While there aren't a lot of tourist sites, there's plenty to keep you relaxed and entertained.

SPEED RULES Don't apply, unless you're trying to time your city walks. Fast walkers can go from **Tel Aviv Port** to **Jaffa (#30)** in 45 minutes, regular pace is about an hour, and slow walkers are roughly 90 minutes.

COVERAGE

★ *Intro (2–4 hours)* Walk down the Tayelet (D1); wander through **Jaffa (#30)** (D2).

★ *Highlights (1 day)* *Intro* plus 1–2 of the following: participate in a Bauhaus Tour; stroll through **Carmel Market (#87)**; make a reservation at one of Tel Aviv's reputed restaurants; hit up a bar before or after dinner.

★ *Comprehensive (2–3 days)* *Highlights* plus 1–5 of the following: take in **ANU – Museum of the Jewish People (#77)** or **Tel Aviv Museum of Art (#95)**; plan to go out late one night, and sleep in the next day; complete one or more of *City Walks D3, D4,* or *D7*.

★ *Exhaustive (4 days–2 weeks)* All of *Comprehensive* plus: get to know the beaches (Hilton, Gordon Beach (D1), Jerusalem, Dog Beach, Metzitzim), streets (Sheinkin Street (D4), *Rothschild Boulevard*, Nahalat Binyamin (D4)), neighborhoods (Florentin (D4), *Neve Tzedek*, Sarona); and suburbs (Herziliya, *Rishon Letzion (D8)*, *Rishpon (D7)*, Ramat Aviv, Ramle, Giv'atayim, Bnei Brak).

BASE Definitely anchor here: it is very easy to get to the north, Jerusalem, the Dead Sea, and the Negev, all in day trips.

ANCHOR CITIES Jerusalem (65km/45–60 minutes); Rosh Pina (150km/90–120 minutes); to Jordan: Allenby Bridge border (100km/70–100 minutes), then factor in border crossing (1 hour) and time to get to Suweimeh (20km/25 minutes) or Amman (50km/1 hour).

BEST STRATEGY Tel Aviv is an Anchor City and our favorite base of operations from which to explore the country. From here, most every site within Israel can be reached in a day trip. That said, it's also expensive, so if costs are a concern you may want to consider offsetting some of your costs by either renting an Airbnb apartment with a kitchen or getting breakfast with your hotel room, and filling up until dinner.

Plan to make use of the walking tours. The "sites" in Tel Aviv are not obvious. It's certainly nothing like the **Old City Jerusalem (#1)**, which has monuments around every corner. You'll learn more about the city and its neighborhoods by following any or all of *City Walks D1–D6*. Each takes a couple of hours to half a day to complete, depending on your interest level. Combine two for a full day, or do one in the morning and spend the afternoon at the beach. Schedule at least one hedonistic day. Hit the beach, the bar, take up some water sports, eat yummy street food and rich restaurant food, and end the evening (or start the morning?) with a late-night dance club or bar. Plan a whole day (at least!) for relaxation purposes.

Take advantage of the Med. Swimming here is great, but calm waters mean ample opportunities for beginners to learn to surf, swim, kite surf, body surf, paddleboard, sail – you name it. And if the weather isn't great (unlikely), check out one of Tel Aviv's good museum options.

WALKING ROUTES *Tel Aviv Tayelet/Promenade* is pretty straightforward: you walk by the sea. *Rothschild Boulevard* has an Independence Trail to recount some of Tel Aviv's historic sites. The so-called Tel Aviv "Orange" routes are self-guided walking tours of the city, with explanatory signs plotted along the way, with maps available at the Tourism Info Offices.

DAY TRIPPING If you are only coming for the day, you should pull up right to the beach, pay the exorbitant fees ($20+) to park in a garage by the beach, and start your day eating breakfast along the water. There are some decent bakeries along the waterfront, or you can try *shakshuka*, *rugelach*, or *masabacha* from a hummusiya. Take a stroll through the city's pleasant streets, admiring the UNESCO-designated buildings, doing *City Walk D5*. Grab lunch at a market: *falafel*, *sabich*, *shawarma*… your choice. Spend the afternoon on the beach. Have some happy hour beers if you're not driving. Take a snooze, watch the sunset, eat an early fish dinner in Jaffa (<u>Old Man and the Sea (D2)</u> turns tables quickly) if you're hungry, before heading back.

WALKS AND DRIVES D1, D2, D3, D4, D5, D6, D7, D8, E7.

ITINERARIES Tel Aviv Immersion; High BUCKET! Scores: 7+; Most Popular; Most Entertaining; Nature and Scenic; Society and People; Organized; Endangered; Community; Fine Arts; Modernity; Under the Sun; Shoestring; Luxury; Kid-Focused.

ARRIVAL PREP

PREBOOK Popular restaurants should be reserved on the weekends at least a few weeks in advance. Hotels should be reserved several months in advance. The Bauhaus tour should be pre-reserved, as should any other group tours. Things do book up, especially during high season (summer/holidays).

TIPS Get around with the *Tel-O-Fun Bike Share*, with hundreds of places to park your bike around town.

CAUTION Violent crimes can occur at any time. Throughout 2015–2016, and again in 2021, Tel Aviv saw a spate of random violence (some say "terrorism," which is a loaded word we'll avoid), including gun and knife attacks, against civilians. Much of the violence is purposefully unpredictable. Make sure you always have a way to contact your group members if you get separated (phone, email, text). If you have phone access, you should plug in ☏ 100, the number for the police, and ☏ 101, the number for the local ambulance, operated by the Red Star of David (Red Cross equivalent).

REALITY CHECK Beaches and the Promenade can get very crowded on weekends (Friday/Saturday). Cigarette butts litter the sand. <u>Matcot (D1)</u> can be very distracting and loud. You might prefer your hotel's pool.

CONSTRAINTS Good news: *Tel Aviv Tayelet/Promenade* is disability-accessible! **Jaffa (#30)**, however, is not completely wheelchair-friendly.

BRING Beach gear, including swimsuit and beach towel; night-out clothes (restaurants are usually casual, but don't wear swimwear to a nice restaurant); city shoes for walking (no hills); umbrella (if visiting between November and March).

DON'T BRING Coats, even in the winter – the weather is very mild.

PUBLIC TRANSPORT Ample options if you are without a car. Bus lines travel all over the country: check w egged.co.il or w dan.co.il. Trains connect as far north as <u>Nahariya (E5)</u> on the coast, and as far south as Dimona, but tracks have not yet been constructed to reach the Sea of Galilee, the Dead Sea, or Eilat. A high-speed train between Jerusalem and Tel Aviv has recently opened and connects the cities in less than 30 minutes, faster than driving. Check w rail.co.il/en for timetables.

ACCESS Try to park close to the beach. There are big blue signs everywhere indicating parking garages – look for the ubiquitous "P."

BUDGET Tel Aviv is one of the most expensive cities in the world, recently ranked fifth among the World's Most Expensive Cities to Live according to *The Economist*. All that fun can cost a pretty penny. The beach is, of course, free. Everything else costs money. Tel Aviv matches New York prices, with coffee running around $4, a glass of wine costing $15, and a dinner at a mid-range restaurant costing upwards of $100 for two people. Dinners at the higher-end restaurants will cost closer to $150, including wine. Private rooms in a hostel will run about $80, while rooms in a boutique hotel will start at around $180, but average $250–300. Street food is one way to cut down on costs, with pita sandwiches usually $10 or less.

RECOMMENDED GUIDE There is an excellent series of DIY walking tours called DAY TOUR, available in multiple languages, for Tel Aviv and Jaffa, and on sale at tourist centers and **w** travelingisrael.com. You will want a guide for a Bauhaus tour, if you are interested in more than just facades. Some may appreciate a guide in **Carmel Market (#87)**, to get a better understanding of negotiation, different foods, and hidden gems. Find out more about guides in the *Organized* theme (p. 567) or at **w** visit-tel-aviv.com.

TOURISM INFORMATION OFFICES Two offices, one at 46 Herbert Samuel Street (two blocks south of Opera Tower on the beach) and the other in the main plaza in Jaffa near the clock tower. They have walking maps.

LANGUAGES Most people speak English. Locals speak Hebrew or Arabic, and you'll hear tourists speaking a hundred other languages.

GROUP WALKING TOURS Sandeman's New Europe offers free 2-hour tours of Jaffa (called the Tel Aviv tour). Plenty of other paid options.

SUPPLEMENTAL Into events? Check out *Time Out Israel* for the hippest lists and event calendars (**w** timeout.co.il/en).

EAT Before you leave, scroll through *Do #14: Eat It!* (p. 80) and the *Top Restaurants* category (p. 561) to identify which restaurant(s) you want to try, and make a reservation now. Falafel is delicious, but you'll want to set time to try some interesting Israeli street specialties too, as well as at least one nice restaurant.

SLEEP There are a ton of options at various price points, and Airbnb also has a fair selection. The average hotel night is Europe-prices-high.

BUCKET!PEDIA

Note See **Jaffa (#30)** for more on Jaffa's history.   *AKA* The White City.   *Hebrew/Arabic name* Tel Aviv-Yafo.   *Size* 52km².   *Population* 451,000 in city center (core); 3.9 million in metropolitan area (2018).   *Ethnic mix* 90% Jewish, but from all backgrounds, 5% Arab Christian and Muslim, 5% other.   *Historical era* Prehistoric: *Bronze Age* to *Modern* for Jaffa, *Islamic: Ottoman* to *Modern* for Tel Aviv.   *Year incorporated* 1909.   *Years active* **Neve Tzedek** was the first incorporated Jewish neighborhood outside of Jaffa, in 1887. Since then the city has continued to grow.

CONTEXT The first waves of immigrants started arriving in Israel in the late 1800s, when the Ottoman Empire (of Turkey) had already been loosely ruling the region for 400 years. Jews first began settling in and around the historic city of Jaffa, which had been a functioning port for thousands of years. Eventually, as Jews and Arabs began arguing over territory, Jews began to create neighborhoods outside the Jaffa city walls to accommodate the influx of new residents. In 1909, a number of these neighborhoods incorporated into the city of Tel Aviv. The city's first mayor, Meir Dizengoff, is emblazoned across squares and streets today and was instrumental in laying the city's first plan. Many of the original streets remain part of the city structure today: Herzl, Rothschild, and Lillenblum streets have all been around since the beginning.

By the 1930s, Tel Aviv was home to more than a third of all the Jews in British Palestine. The European Jewish immigrants brought their European sensibilities to the Holy Land, incorporating modern innovations such as picture theaters, recital halls, and electricity. Several architects came to Tel Aviv from Germany having studied a modern school of fine arts training, called the International Style, famous for having produced the Bauhaus art school. From 1933, more than 4,000 buildings were erected in the infamous Bauhaus style, many of which still stand today (in various states of repair). (Fast-forward to 2003 when UNESCO declares Tel Aviv a World Heritage Site for its vast collection of Bauhaus buildings.) From Israel's declaration of independence in 1948, there has continued to be a question surrounding the status of Jerusalem as the capital of Israel and of a future Palestine state. As a result, foreign relations have historically been conducted from Tel Aviv between Israel and other nations, though Tel Aviv is not the capital of Israel. Original plans placed Jaffa in Arab Palestine. After Israeli independence and the Arab–Israeli War, Israel annexed this part of the would-be Palestinian state and Jaffa became part of Tel Aviv. In 1950, the city officially became known as Tel Aviv-Yafo.

The city experienced a period of decline until the 1990s when two major things happened: a new wave of immigrants entered from the former Soviet Union, and the injection of new money in the technology sector, quickly turning Tel Aviv into a tech hub. Tel Aviv has not been without troubles: it was attacked repeatedly by Iraq during the First Gulf War, Prime Minister Yitzhak Rabin (who had orchestrated peace with the Palestinians) was assassinated in Tel Aviv in 1995, and the Second Intifada in the early 2000s brought a wave of suicide attacks against civilians.

Today, the city thrives and pulses with excitement. The city has been consistently recognized on global lists as one of the world's best food cities, with hip neighborhoods, great nightlife, great weather, great beaches, and being among the most LGBT-friendly.

ARCHITECTURE The city is noted for having the largest collection of Bauhaus architecture-style buildings in the world, earning it UNESCO World Heritage status.

CHRONOLOGY

c2000 BCE: Excavations in Jaffa in the 1970s reveal evidence of Egyptian towers and gates, visible today.

c2000 BCE (to present): Jaffa intermittently serves as a regional port, referenced several times in the Bible.

1470 BCE: Jaffa mentioned in Egyptian texts.

1887 CE: *Neve Tzedek*, the hip modern neighborhood, is founded as the first settlement outside of Jaffa walls. It's considered the first Jewish city, and a precursor of Tel Aviv.

1909: Official founding of Tel Aviv (name would come in 1910). Parcels of barren land are divided between 66 families in a lottery using colored sea shells.

1921: Riots between Arabs and Jews result in tens of thousands of Jews moving out of Jaffa and into Tel Aviv.

1933: Jews studying the Bauhaus style in Germany leave for Palestine following the rise of Nazism, translating this architectural style onto the blank canvas of Tel Aviv.

1947: The United Nations Israel–Palestine Partition Plan places Tel Aviv in the future Jewish state and Jaffa in the future Arab state.

1948: Following civil war and several months of siege, Jaffa falls in May, and Arab residents leave Jaffa.

1950: Tel Aviv incorporates several areas of Jaffa, and the government votes to consolidate the towns, renaming the city Tel Aviv-Yafo (Jaffa = Yafo).

1995: Israel's prime minister, Yitzhak Rabin, is assassinated while giving a speech in support of the Oslo Peace Accords. Plaza where he was killed is renamed "Rabin Square."

2003: UNESCO declares Tel Aviv a World Cultural Heritage Site for its collection of 4,000 Bauhaus buildings.

WEBSITE w visit-tel-aviv.com.

WHERE TO NEXT?

THEMATIC *Religion* Meditation, Yoga, and Quiet. *Structure* Modern Architecture. *Nature* Gorgeous Scenery; Parks. *Scenic* Sunrise/Sunset; People-Watching; Most Photographed. *Society* Principal Cities. *People* Jewish; Secular Life; Hipsters; LGBTQ. *Active* Walking Paths; Biking; Competition; Swimming; Adventure Water Sports; Running and Free Exercise; Surfing. *Leisure* Public/Popular Beaches. *Entertainment* Bars and Clubs; Vice; Nightlife. *Food and Drink* Culinary Capital; Coffee, Tea, and Coffeeshops. *Organized* Cooking School/Food Activities; Guided.

COMPLEMENTARY If you like the architectural angle of the Bauhaus structure, try: Beer Sheva (J1) for its Brutalist buildings; **Old City Jerusalem (#1)** and **Jerusalem, New City (#72)** for the "Jerusalem stone" which gives the city its unique color; staying in Tel Aviv, you'll find some awe-inspiring skyscrapers and other modern buildings (*City Walk D5*).

The beaches of Tel Aviv are glorious, but there's a whole coast full of beaches (and far fewer people). Aqueduct Beach at **Caesarea (#25)** has an actual ancient aqueduct on the beach. Just north of Tel Aviv, the great boardwalk-lined *Herzliya Beaches* have vast stretches of white sand, plenty of changing rooms, restaurants, and shops. **Dor HaBonim (#100)** has been named best beach overall many times.

Loving the TA nightlife, but wanting something a bit less obvious? *Haifa* has a very chill scene, **Ramallah (#68)** is where it's at in the West Bank, and **Jerusalem, New City (#72)** even has a few hipster watering holes.

NEARBY Everything is close, really. Within an hour, you can get as far east as Jerusalem (70km/1 hour), as far north as Haifa (95km/1¼ hours), and as far south as the Gaza border. It's not a huge country! The nearest Gold sites are **Caesarea (#25)** (57km/45 minutes), **Dor HaBonim (#100)** (75km/1 hour), and **Beit Guvrin and Maresha (#60)** (75km/1 hour).

#6 Dome of the Rock

BROCHURE

RATINGS		MACRO-REGION
BUCKET! Score	8/10	A: Jerusalem
Ruin	5/5	
Entertainment	2/5	**MICRO-REGIONS**
Information	3/5	A1, A2
Popularity	3/5	

PRIMARY THEME/CATEGORY Structure – Monuments – Iconic Structures.

TOP Most iconic site in the Holy Land.

ESSENCE One of the earliest examples of Islamic architecture, this gold-domed shrine with its stunning blue mosaic tiles is immediately recognizable, representing Islamic holy presence in Jerusalem.

HOLY LAND RELEVANCE The Dome of the Rock sits on perhaps the most sought-after real estate in the entire region – **Temple Mount (#12)**. Muslims and Jews alike believe this spot to be holy to their respective religions, and have been fighting for millennia for the right to pray here. The octagonal site encircles the peak of Mount Moriah, where Abraham was set to sacrifice his son Isaac, where the First and Second Temples once stood, and where Muhammad ascended to Heaven. Muslims consider Temple Mount to be the third most holy site in Islam, after Mecca and Medina. Jews consider the rock inside the shrine to be the holiest site in Judaism.

ELECT ME! No visit to Jerusalem is complete without ascending to Temple Mount and getting up close to the Dome of the Rock. You won't be able to enter unless Muslim, but the outside is worth the effort to see up close.

WORTH THE DETOUR? If you're not Muslim, you are limited to viewing just the exterior of the building, which is a shame, but still worthwhile. Try to visit on a weekday.

EXPERIENCES

CAN'T MISS The site only takes 15 minutes to see (longer if you want to take photos from every angle), so make sure you read on to learn what makes this shrine such an important part of history, and understand the religious significance, the architecture, and the history.

CAMERA *Best shot* The beautiful Persian tiles on the outer wall are gorgeous up close, the dome sparkles at all times of the day from every angle, but one of the most popular views with locals is from a small park on the **Mount of Olives (#34)** (requires a car, or longish walk uphill). *Best light* Times are limited; you're stuck with the hours available.

SECRET Several Arab markets in the Muslim Quarter wind their way down covered paths to Muslim-only entrances to Temple Mount. Unless Muslim, you won't be able to enter from here, but you should be able to take a wonderful shot of the gold dome from a unique angle.

ITINERATOR!

DAYS/HOURS To enter Temple Mount: Monday–Thursday, winter 07.30–10.30 and 12.30–13.30 Monday–Thursday; summer 08.30–11.30 and 13.30–14.30 (but times can change unexpectedly); closed Friday and Saturday, during periodic flare-ups, and during Ramadan.

BEST TIME TO VISIT Go midweek for the best chance of getting unobstructed photos. The site is usually busy due to limited hours of operation and being closed on two popular tourism days.

TIME COMMITMENT 20 minutes–1 hour for grounds; 2 hours for grounds plus prearranged tour.

SPEED RULES Your speed will depend on whether you're on a guided tour and whether you tend to take a lot of photos. It's a very photo-worthy building from all sorts of angles, and Temple Mount is quite big, which can take time.

COVERAGE

★ *Intro* If you aren't able to get to Temple Mount (timing/closed to public), you'll still be able to see the marvelous dome from various points in the Old City, as well as from Mount of Olives across the Kidron Valley.
★ *Highlights* We're talking 5–15 total minutes to circle the building.
★ *Comprehensive* Give yourself an hour to take in the edifice and take lots of pictures.
★ *Exhaustive* If you're Muslim, you can enter the interior, which brings about a whole new experience. Add an additional 30–60 minutes.

BASE/ANCHOR See **Old City Jerusalem (#1)**.

BEST STRATEGY Your best bet is to arrive early on a weekday, when you'll likely miss the hordes of tour groups who show up mid- to late morning. Make it one of your first stops: you can easily visit after a tour of the **Western Wall (#11)**. Most people visit these two sites, and the **Church of the Holy Sepulchre (#9)**, in one religiously inspiring day.

WALKS AND DRIVES A1, A2, W1.

ITINERARIES Jerusalem Immersion; High BUCKET! Scores: 7+; Complete Ruins; Religion; Structure; UNESCO; Memorial; Shoestring; Pilgrimage.

ARRIVAL PREP

PREBOOK No tickets required.

TIPS In order to enter the grounds, you need to be properly dressed. If you are wearing anything that shows legs or shoulders (and, for women, hair), you will be required to rent a shawl. The price is exorbitant for temporary use and looks/feels much like a tablecloth, which will be stapled around your legs and/or shoulders. Not the best for photos.

CAUTION Be aware of police presence, large congregations of angry-seeming men, and holy days, when violence can happen without warning. It is absolutely forbidden for non-Muslims to pray on Temple Mount. If Christians or Jews are caught praying, they will be removed.

REALITY CHECK You will be watched as you walk around. This is for your own safety.

CONSTRAINTS Wheelchair access now allows disabled visitors to get up close to the Dome.

BRING Passport (required); appropriate attire.

DON'T BRING Holy books: non-Muslim prayer is not allowed. Anything that can be construed as a weapon.

ACCESS The easiest and most reliable entry is from the Western Wall. If looking at the wall, you'll see a long ramp to the right of the ladies' section. Follow the ramp to ground level, near Dung Gate. You'll pass a security screening and some electronic signs in several languages indicating the entrance. There are other ways of getting to Temple Mount, through "gates." It's possible you may be able to go through one of these gates if you arrive early enough, but they are frequently closed, or only allow entry for Muslims. From any of the access points, you'll go through screening. You'll need a passport and your dress will be judged. See *Tips* above for more on dress.

ADMISSION TO DOME OF THE ROCK You can enter Temple Mount – free, no ticket required – but access into Dome of the Rock is limited to Muslims only. If you try to enter, you will be quizzed in Arabic. Though rare, you may be able to gain access through a special tour group registered far in advance.

RECOMMENDED GUIDE *BUCKET!pedia* read (below): 5 minutes.

TOUR GUIDE No free English tours available on site. Book a tour in advance. Unofficial guides will approach you as you enter the site, and you'll pay accordingly.

VISITOR CENTER There's no visitor center, and only one explanatory sign that has been weathered away by sun exposure.

EAT/SLEEP See **Old City Jerusalem (#1)**.

BUCKET!PEDIA

Hebrew name Kippat ha-Sela.   *Arabic name* Qubbat as-Sakhra.   *Size* Dome diameter 20.4m, each exterior octagonal side c18m long.   *Historical era Islamic: Umayyad.   Year finished* 692 CE.   *Years active* To present; this is one of the oldest extant versions of Islamic art and architecture in the world.

CONTEXT The Dome of the Rock is a shrine built by the Umayyad caliph Abd al-Malik in 692 CE, some 60 years after the death of Muhammad, the prophet of Islam. This makes it one of the oldest Islamic monuments anywhere in the world. Notably, it is not a mosque. The mosque, as referenced by Muhammad and in the Quran as the "furthest mosque" is neighboring **Al-Aqsa Mosque (#65)**, which also sits on Haram es-Sharif, or **Temple Mount (#12)**.

The exposed peak of Mount Moriah is known as the Foundation Stone. That spot has historical significance throughout Jewish, Christian, and Muslim texts and is associated with several key religious moments. For Jews, roots are even older, as this rock is considered to have produced the dust which God gathered to create Adam, as well as the site of the Binding of Isaac, when Abraham was tested by God who asked him to sacrifice his son Isaac atop the rock. For Muslims, the Mi'raj occurred here, when Muhammad ascended to Heaven on his Night Journey.

Herod built the Second Temple directly over the Foundation Stone, where the Ark of the Covenant was housed. It is possible Herod followed in the tradition of the First Temple, perhaps also built over the same location. Since at least Herod's time, the Foundation Stone has been the central point of Earth in Judaism, referred to as the Holy of Holies.

Following a failed Jewish uprising, the Romans destroyed Temple Mount and the Second Temple in 70 CE. The Romans erected a statue of their god Jupiter, but otherwise the site lay in ruins for several hundred years. Romans and Byzantines claimed ownership over the territory until the 7th century CE. A leader and prophet from the Arabian peninsula, Muhammad, had visited the site on his Night Journey, declaring it sacred to Muslims. He died in 632 CE, with a large following. Several Arab tribes banded together in his name to create an Islamic army that would go on to conquer the Near East, North Africa, and parts of Europe within only a few decades. Due to the religious significance of Jerusalem to Muhammad, the city – and particularly Temple Mount – were acknowledged as the third-holiest Muslim site in the world, after Mecca and Medina.

Under Umayyad Caliph Abd al-Malik's order, Temple Mount was identified as the site of a future mosque (which would become Al-Aqsa) and a glorious dome-capped shrine dedicated to Muhammad's Night Journey. That shrine, completed in AH 72 (691/92 CE) in the Islamic calendar, would be built over the Foundation Stone, where Muhammad ascended to Heaven, and thus became known as Qubbat al-Sakhrah, or the Dome of the Rock.

The site is not without a little controversy. The original Dome was initially considered to be a tasteless attempt at stealing away the attention drawn to Mecca. Al-Malik may well have built it merely to draw in followers from Palestine, and thus wanted a striking edifice as the symbol of Islam on top of a site that was venerated by many, rather than the historical site of Muhammad's ascension. To drive home the point, there is a Crusader-era building just north of the Dome of the Rock on Temple Mount that Muslims also acknowledge as the spot where Muhammad ascended to Heaven; it's even called Dome of the Ascension! Regardless, al-Malik rubbed some people the wrong way, and in turn a caliph from the Abbasid era some 100 years later rubbed out al-Malik's name on the "founder's inscription," replacing it with his own, perhaps making it the oldest inscription in the building, even if it was done in poor taste some 100 years after the building was actually founded.

Since the destruction of the Second Temple, Jews have not had regular access to the Foundation Stone and their Holy of Holies. Even today, in a Jewish state with Israeli military control over Jerusalem, the site is monitored by a neutral party: the Jordanian Waqf (a Muslim religious or charitable trust). After the Six-Day War in

1967, Jews granted the Waqf custodianship of the property in order to keep the peace. Jews were in turn banned from praying at or near the site. The **Western Wall (#11)** is now considered the closest location to the Holy of Holies, which explains the wall's significance.

ARCHITECTURE The Dome of the Rock stands today as one of the oldest examples of Islamic architecture in the world, and possibly the oldest extant Islamic building. Finished in 691/92 CE, this shrine is one of the most beautiful pieces of architecture in the world. Much of that has to do with the pleasing symmetry: an almost-perfect octagonal base with a central drum, upon which sits a grand dome.

The base of the structure is limestone, upon which are 3m-tall white marble panels inlaid with geometric patterns. Directly above is a layer of beautiful blue tiles (with white, black, yellow, and green colors interlaced throughout). The original tiles were weathered and worn by the time Caliph Suleiman I of the Ottoman Empire replaced them with Persian tiles in the 16th century. These too were eventually replaced with non-Persian facsimiles in a grand restoration project of the 1950s. Each octagonal side is set back with five windows adorned with stained glass. Above the windows are verses from the Quran. Other late additions included a crescent moon to the top and the construction of the adjacent *Dome of the Chain*.

The base of the dome is called the drum. The drum exterior tells in Arabic the story of Muhammad's Night Journey. The original dome collapsed in the 1016 earthquake and was rebuilt a few years later. It has since been repaired several times, including a replacement of its original heavy lead material with a gold-colored aluminum alloy. In 1993, that was covered with real gold leaf, famously donated by King Hussein of Jordan, who sold off one of his multi-million-dollar properties to pay for the addition.

The interior literally revolves around the Foundation Stone, with three ambulatories circling the large interior stone. The passage circumambulating the stone is currently blocked by a guard rail keeping visitors from accessing the site. It was once surrounded by a wrought-iron railing which is now in a museum, but the new barrier does prevent one from even being able to see the Stone. The Stone itself has been protected from visitors since the period of Crusader rule, when the Dome was turned into a church and saw the arrival of many pilgrims who believed the footprint in the southwest corner of the rock was made by Jesus. These pilgrims then took home pieces of the rock as relics, creating massive cuts in the stone that now make the sacred site look like a quarry. The top was later covered with marble to prevent further rock-robbers.

Inside, the walls are lavishly adorned with vegetable and floral motifs, Quranic verses, Arabic calligraphy, and the inscriptions of the lives of prophets and kings – Jesus, Saladin, and al-Malik, the founder – are each mentioned in texts adorning the interior walls. In the southeast corner is a cave which opens up underneath the rock and is referred to as the Well of Souls. It is mythologized that the souls of the deceased wait here for Judgment Day.

CHRONOLOGY
637 CE: Muslim conquest of Jerusalem.
692: Dome completed.
1099: Crusaders capture Jerusalem and convert Dome of the Rock into a church.
1187: City recaptured by Saladin and the Dome is converted back into a mosque.
1517–1917: Ottoman reign. Much renovation done, including placement of tiles on dome, mosaic work, and lavish decorations.

1967: Israel wins Six-Day War, but honor Muslim *waqf*, or trust, giving Jordan the responsibility of managing the site.

1993: King of Jordan sells one of his houses worth $8.2 million to pay for gold refurbishment on the dome to replace the copper dome.

2000: Tourists and non-Muslims are no longer able to visit Temple Mount due to security concerns at the start of the Second Intifada.

2003: Tourists return to Temple Mount, but Jews are restricted from visiting.

2015: Jews are again able to visit Temple Mount as part of US Secretary of State John Kerry's peace negotiations and updates to the status quo.

WHERE TO NEXT?

THEMATIC *Noteworthy* Unique. *Religion* Islam; Kings and Prophets; Muhammad; Quran; Pilgrimage. *Archaeology* Herodian; Islamic I (Umayyad). *Structure* Iconic Structures; Historic Monuments; Beautiful Structures; Skyline. *Scenic* People-Watching; Most Photographed. *Society* Borders; Disputed. *People* Arab.

COMPLEMENTARY Want to complete the best sites in Jerusalem? The **Western Wall (#11)** and the **Church of the Holy Sepulchre (#9)** complete the triumvirate. If you're interested in beautiful Islamic architecture, there are other impressive sites on Temple Mount: **Al-Aqsa Mosque (#65)**; the *Fountain of Sultan Qaytbay*, a Mamluk (15th-century) structure; and the *Dome of the Chain*, a prayer house built by the Umayyads at the same time as the Dome of the Rock.

NEARBY The site sits on **Temple Mount (#12)** and is within walking distance of all other **Old City Jerusalem (#1)** sites (*City Walks A1–A4*), as well as the surrounding hills of **Mount of Olives (#34)**, **Mount Zion (#92)**, and the *City of David*.

#7 Sea of Galilee

BROCHURE

RATINGS		MACRO-REGION
BUCKET! Score	7/10	G: Lower Galilee & Kinneret
Ruin	4/5	
Entertainment	2/5	**MICRO-REGIONS**
Information	1/5	G3, G4
Popularity	5/5	

PRIMARY THEME/CATEGORY Religion – Religious Figures – Jesus: Ministries.

TOP Christian Road Trip.

COMMENDATIONS Israel National Parks include: *Korazim*, Capernaum, Kursi (G3), *Hamat Tiberias*, and *Mount Arbel*. Plus one declared Nature Reserve: Majrase-Betiha/Bethsaida Valley (I3).

ESSENCE Called the "Kinneret" in Hebrew, the Sea of Galilee is famous for its biblical sites – particularly related to Jesus and his ministries – which surround this large freshwater lake and make for a great multi-stop road trip/day trip in northern Israel.

HOLY LAND RELEVANCE The Sea of Galilee drive is one of the highlights on a Christian tour of Israel, with nearly a dozen sites relating to Jesus' life and ministries, all within a few kilometers of each other. You'll also find great archaeological sites of ancient Jewish towns (remember, Jesus and his disciples were all Jews).

ELECT ME! If you grew up reading the New Testament, you'll recognize the names of many of the sites in this region. Even if you didn't, you still might appreciate the religious history.

WORTH THE DETOUR? Everyone should visit the north of Israel if they have time, stopping at a minimum in **Nazareth (#29)**, and ideally adding on a few sites we've listed. While the individual sites can initially seem underwhelming, it's the summation of the experience of visiting so many recognizable Christian places and events that make this such an interesting trip.

EXPERIENCES

CAN'T MISS The triumvirate of churches near Tabgha representing the Beatitudes, the Primacy of St. Peter, and the Loaves and Fishes.

SITES

★ *The Sea of Galilee* Also called the Kinneret, this body of water is associated with a number of events in the life of Christ, most notably when he walked on water, fed the multitude, and calmed a storm.

★ *Tiberias* Many tours will start here and head clockwise around the sea. There are ruins from the Herodian era in the southern part of the city on Mount Bernice/ Bereniki.

★ *Magdala Archaeological Park in Migdal/Magdala (He/En) (G4)* The birthplace of Mary Magdalene (originally "Mary of *Magdala*"), this recently uncovered city contains a 2,000-year-old synagogue, *mikveh* (ritual bath), and a large etched stone which is subject of much debate among archaeologists (visitor center opening soon: check w magdala.org for updates).

★ *The Ancient Boat in Kibbutz Ginosar (G3)* On display at the Beit Yigal Allon Museum is a 2,000-year-old boat, nicknamed the Jesus Boat, believed to be from the same time as Jesus' ministries in the region. It sunk in the Sea of Galilee and remained preserved in the mud for two millennia until a drought evaporated the coastline and revealed the boat in 1986. Guided tours can be booked through w yigal-allon-centre.org.il.

★ *Capernaum and Tabgha (#33)* In Capernaum: Ancient Synagogue; House of St. Peter; Monastery of the Twelve Apostles. In Tabgha: Church of the Multiplication of the Loaves and Fishes; next door, Church of the Primacy of St. Peter.

★ *Mount of Beatitudes* Believed location of Jesus' "Sermon on the Mount" where he spoke of the Beatitudes and the Lord's Prayer, among other important Christian teachings.

★ *Korazim* One of three ancient towns (including Bethsaida and Capernaum) that rejected Jesus' teachings. Now a national park known for its dolmens (burial stones) and ancient synagogue.

★ *Majrase-Betiha/Bethsaida Valley (I3)* Jesus cured a blind man at this place and other disciples hailed from here.

★ *Kursi (G3) and its Byzantine Church and Monastery* Another national park, famed for being the site where Jesus performed an exorcism on a man, casting his demons into a pig which then drowned itself in the Sea.

★ *Yardenit Baptismal Site on the Jordan River* Not the place where John the Baptist baptized Jesus (that is **Bethany-Beyond-the-Jordan (#41)**, in Jordan), but it is nonetheless where Christians go to get baptized today.

ACTIVITIES Bring a Bible and follow along; bring a pair of hiking shoes and walk in the steps of the prophets; watch the sunset.

CAMERA The **best shot** is from the top of *Mount Arbel*, looking out over the Sea.

EXTRA CREDIT If you're looking to add some other important Christian sites, you have options:

★ *Nazareth (#29) and Basilica of the Annunciation* Where Jesus grew up with Mary and Joseph. You can visit the church which celebrates when Mary was visited by the Angel Gabriel who exclaimed she would become the mother of the Son of God.

★ *Greek Orthodox Church of St. George at Kfar Kana (G4)* At the "Marriage at Cana" Jesus performed his first miracle of turning six jugs of water into wine at a wedding.

★ *Franciscan Church of the Transfiguration on Mount Tabor* Believed to be the location where Jesus is transformed into a radiant beam of light after going to a mountain to pray with his disciples.

SECRET Walk down to the beautiful seashore at the Church of the Primacy of St. Peter. Nearby *Mount Arbel* National Park has little religious significance, but stunning views of the Sea on clear days. Swim in the water: check out the *Leisure – Beaches* theme (p. 554) for more details about water fun around the Kinneret.

SPECIAL EVENTS Every summer, the Speedo Sea of Galilee Swim, the "largest amateur sports event in Israel," casts its participants on a 1.5 or 3.5km swim in the Sea. Check out w speedo.co.il for more information on this event, and others in the region. Also, *Tiberias* hosts a free 15-minute Sound and Light show on the southern promenade every evening at 20.30, 21.30, and 22.00.

MAP See G4.

ITINERATOR!

DAYS/HOURS Sites are open daily, usually 08.00–16.00/17.00, but can close for lunch and religious services.

BEST TIME TO VISIT Any time. Christian religious events, such as Easter and Christmas, can get very busy.

TIME COMMITMENT One full day to make the rounds. If you venture beyond the Jesus sites, you may need to add an additional day. Note: this does not include Lower Galilee parks, a full tour of Nazareth, Tsfat, the Golan, or any of the other close-by sites.

SPEED RULES At sites, rules apply. If you are self-driving, you can likely go twice as fast as those on a bus tour.

COVERAGE All Christian-focused trips to this region should start in Nazareth to see biblical sites there.

★ *Intro (2–4 hours)* Nazareth (start here); **Mount of Beatitudes**; Tabgha churches.
★ *Highlights (6–8 hours)* *Intro* plus: **Capernaum and Tabgha (#33)**; Jesus Boat at Kibbutz Ginosar (G3).
★ *Comprehensive (1–1½ days)* *Highlights* plus 1–2 of the following: **Korazim**; Magdala; Kursi (G3); Yardenit; views from **Mount Arbel** (nearby); **Church of the Transfiguration** (nearby).
★ *Exhaustive (2 days)* All of comprehensive, plus (if time): *Kfar Kana (G4)*; Tel Bethsaida (G4); Golan lookouts (Ophir Lookout (I3), Peace Vista (I3)); hot springs (**Hamat Tiberias**, **Hamat Gader**); **Tiberias**.

BASE For anchoring, we recommend using Rosh Pina, Tel Aviv, or Jerusalem. For road trips, you have a variety of options to continue your journey, including the Golan Heights (*Road Trips I1–I3*), Central Galilee (*Road Trip G2*), Upper Galilee (*Road Trip H1*), or the Galilee Panhandle (*Road Trip H2*).

ANCHOR CITIES Rosh Pina is located 15km/15 minutes north of Tabgha, **Mount of Beatitudes**, and **Korazim** on Highway 90. Tel Aviv to **Tiberias** is 130km/1½ hours each way. Jerusalem is 170km/2 hours to **Tiberias**.

BEST STRATEGY If you start your day in Tel Aviv or Jerusalem, start early. You'll want to begin in Nazareth, because it's the most important regional site, though a bit further west of the Sea. You can head next to **Tiberias** if you like, but it's not necessary if your purpose is to see Christian sites. Travel clockwise around the lake, beginning with Kibbutz Ginosar (G3) and the Ancient Boat, and continuing to whichever sites appeal to you. A day is usually sufficient to make the rounds, unless you're part of a slow group (and that's okay: spend the night in Rosh Pina). You may want a blend of archaeological (**Capernaum and Tabgha (#33)** or Kursi (G3)), modern church (Nazareth, Mount Tabor, and **Mount of Beatitudes**), historical (Ancient Boat), and biblical (Magdala, *Kfar Kana (G4)*, Tel Bethsaida (G4)) sites. Work your way back to where you started, often ending the day with a dip in the Sea at the Yardenit baptism site.

WALKING ROUTES See **Jesus Trail (#69)**. Also, bikers and walkers can circumnavigate the sea on the Kinneret Trail (G3).

DAY TRIPPING We recommend doing this in a day, starting very early. You won't be able to actively explore all dozen-plus sites in one day, so pick your favorites in advance.

WALKS AND DRIVES G3, G4.

ITINERARIES High BUCKET! Scores: 7+; Most Popular; Religion; Archaeology; Organized; UNESCO; National Parks/Reserves; Under the Sun; Big-Group Friendly.

ARRIVAL PREP

PREBOOK Not required.

REALITY CHECK This is a popular tour-bus stop.

CONSTRAINTS Many sites are wheelchair-friendly, particularly the big churches and museums/visitor centers.

BRING A Bible may come in handy; a car will allow you to set your own schedule.

PUBLIC TRANSPORT There are no direct trips by bus from central Israel to the Sea of Galilee sites. We recommend renting a car for the day or joining a tour group if renting a car is not an option.

ACCESS Access to each is easy. Some of the churches are private and may be closed unexpectedly. Parking is available and free.

ADMISSION Most of the sites have a nominal cost. Churches generally do not. National Parks are abundant in this area – consider the Israel Park Pass.

RECOMMENDED GUIDE Some might call your Bible the best guidebook of the region you can find. If you're without your own transportation, bus tours would be your best bet for historical and religious context. If you're driving yourself, each park gives a helpful brochure with map.

BUS TOURS Very popular option. If you choose to join a bus group (inquire with visitor centers, your hotel, or TripAdvisor), the stops will be preplanned and you likely will see fewer sites and spend longer on site than you need.

VISITOR CENTER There is not one center, but some sites have excellent information. The Ancient Boat museum has a great documentary, visual displays, and guided tours to answer all your questions. At the other end of the spectrum, the Tabgha churches are difficult to find, have no information on site, and are not promoted heavily.

EAT There are several restaurants right on the side of the Galilee road, though you may want to avoid any spot with giant tour buses; the service can go downhill quick. Restaurant Magdalena (in Magdala) has high-quality food with upscale décor. Tanureen, across the street, is a mob scene, but the food is also great.

SLEEP Many will stay in *Tiberias*, as it is outfitted for big groups, but if you're eager to sleep in the region you may find an evening in the resort town of Rosh Pina a bit more elegant, tranquil, and beautiful.

BUCKET!PEDIA

AKA Lake Kinneret.   *Hebrew name* Yam Kinneret (Kinneret Sea).   *Arabic name* Buhayrat Tiberia (Lake Tiberias).   *Historical name* During Islamic rule, it was Lake Minya, after the ruined Umayyad castle of Khirbet al-Minya.   *Size* 53km circumference, 21km long, 13km wide.   *Population* Tiberias is the largest city on the Sea, with roughly 45,000 inhabitants.   *Ethnic mix* Mostly Jewish; Arabs were

evacuated after the Arab–Israeli War of 1948.   *Historical era* *Roman/Byzantine.*
Year founded Tiberias: 18 CE; Capernaum: 2nd century BCE; Bethsaida: unknown/
discovery in question; Kursi: unclear; Korazim: unclear.   *Years active* Tiberias
may have been formed from the ruins of a previous city, but the new city was
built during the Roman era, and was named after Emperor Tiberius, who ruled
from 14 to 37 CE.

CONTEXT As you may have surmised by its size, the Sea of Galilee is not one static
location, but 50km of ancient and current settlements circling this important
freshwater lake. Much of the archaeology is intriguing and shows a clear connection
with Jewish and Christian religious records.

The Sea is perhaps most famous for being the setting of Jesus of Nazareth's
first series of ministries and the location of several miracles and Bible stories. It is
also here that he begins preaching, healing, and collecting disciples, marking the
beginnings of the early Church.

The Kinneret has always been associated with fishing. Several of Jesus' miracles
involve multiplying fish for the masses. The Church of the Multiplication of Loaves
and Fishes commemorates the feeding of 5,000 with five loaves of bread and two fish,
as told in all four Gospels. Around the time of Christ, many of the small villages that
circled the Sea were dedicated to fishing. In the 1980s, a fishing boat was pulled out
of the mud with much of the wood still preserved, and it's believed to coincide with
the time that Jesus conducted his ministries in the area (see *Sites* above).

Jesus' first miracle is associated with the Marriage at Cana, where, upon hearing
that a wedding party had run out of drink, Jesus transformed water into wine. Kfar
Kanna is the recognized location of this event. The Gospels of Matthew, Mark,
Luke, and John reference Capernaum as the center of Jesus' ministries, though Jesus
preached throughout the Galilee. The Sermon on the Mount is considered to be one
of Jesus' finest speeches, and the church at the Mount of Beatitudes commemorates
this event. Jesus preached in the Galilee somewhere between three and nine years.
He recruited disciples mainly from towns along the sea, particularly Capernaum,
whose ruins today include a converted church believed to have once been the home
of St. Peter, one of Jesus' disciples.

Bethsaida and Korazim are also referenced in connection to Capernaum, often
in a pejorative sense given that these three towns rejected Jesus' teachings, and he
cursed them to hell. Kursi is associated with the exorcism of demons from men into
swine (who scurried into the Sea and drowned), but nothing has been unearthed
yet that coincides with that story – though there is plenty of archaeological evidence
showing centuries of habitation. Magdala is synonymous with Mary of Magdalena,
one of Jesus' disciples, who is depicted in many colorful ways, from "prostitute" to
"Jesus' wife."

Eventually, Jesus' ministries would take him south through Judea and Perea to
Jerusalem, where he ultimately is captured by Roman authorities, tried for treason
against the state, and killed. The region of the Galilee continued to celebrate the life
and teachings of Jesus, and his congregation grew. Over the course of the next few
centuries, Christianity spread rapidly. Early Christians were Jewish, but later converts
came from all throughout the Mediterranean.

When Christ died around 33 CE, Judaism was facing an existential threat from
the Roman Empire. Ultimately, Rome sacked Jerusalem in 70 CE and the seat of
power of Jews shifted to the north, centering around the Galilee and the new town
of Tiberias. At the various archaeological sites around the Sea, remains of both
Christian and Jewish presence indicate the region was populated with both groups

for several centuries. Historical scholars tend to agree that Christianity in its more modern form took several hundred years to congeal before it ultimately split for good from Judaism in the 3rd or 4th century CE.

GEOLOGY This freshwater lake is the second lowest on Earth, after the Dead Sea. Its main source of water is the Jordan River, though underground springs also feed into it. The water line is an important agricultural marker in Israel. A low water level indicates a threat of drought, while the opposite indicates a possibility of flooding. The distances are not so vast: 208.8m below sea level is the upper marker, with 213m being the lower marker. The historic low is –214.87m, achieved in 2001.

ARCHAEOLOGY Confusingly, the archaeological record does not always support the written record. By reviewing the written record first, field researchers often identify several likely locations of as-yet-undiscovered biblical sites, then start digging until they find something. Much has been unearthed in the last 100 or so years in this way. As the levels of the sea rise and fall, there are new opportunities to find out what lurks beneath the lake. Several of the famous ancient churches of the New Testament were revered for many centuries, but fell into disrepair. They've since been expanded and surrounded by new, modern churches, which is the case for the Church of the Transfiguration, the Church of the Multiplication, and the Church of the Primacy of St. Peter, all built atop 4th-century CE church foundations.

CHRONOLOGY
c25,000 BCE: Sea of Galilee and Dead Sea are connected into one massive lake, Lake Lisan.
c17,400 BCE: Hunter-gatherers settle down next to the new Sea of Galilee. Animals, fruit, and vegetable remains have been found at a nearby site, Ohala II.
c17,000 BCE: Lake Lisan retreats, separating the two bodies of water.
c200 BCE: Capernaum established. Inhabited through Crusader era (11th century CE).
20 CE: Tiberias established, in honor of the Roman emperor of the time. It becomes an economic powerhouse through its fishing industry. The "Jesus Boat" is presumed to have been one of the famed fishing boats from this era.
30–33: Jesus' ministries.
135: Jews banished from Jerusalem. Many move north to the Galilee area.
741: Major regional earthquake destroys numerous towns, including Tiberias and Capernaum.
1909: Degania Alef – the first kvutza (communal agricultural settlement), and precursor to the kibbutz system – is established on the shores of the Sea of Galilee by Jews.
1924: Church of the Transfiguration completed, built atop 4th- and 12th-century churches.
1933: Church of the Primacy of St. Peter built on top of (and including parts of) a 4th century church, still visible today.
1938: Church of the Beatitudes constructed.
1939: Excavations begin of 4th- and 5th-century churches on site of present-day Church of the Multiplication of the Loaves and Fishes, which incorporates the floor plan of the 5th-century building.
1967: Israel wins the Six-Day War, capturing the eastern shore of the Galilee and the Golan Heights, leaving Israel with sole access to the Sea.
1986: A major drought exposes an ancient sunk fishing boat near Kibbutz Ginosar.
2015: Arsonists attack and heavily damage the Church of the Multiplication.

WEBSITE Israel Ministry of Foreign Affairs (**w** mfa.gov.il/MFA/IsraelExperience/
Religion/Pages/Christian-pilgrimage.aspx). Check the rising and falling water level
of the Kinneret (**w** forecast.israelinfo.co.il/kineret).

WHERE TO NEXT?

THEMATIC *Religion* Judaism; Christianity; Jesus: Ministries and Miracles; New
Testament; Collections of Churches; Pilgrimage. *Archaeology* Roman. *Scenic*
Sunrise/Sunset; Scenic Drives. *Active* Long-Distance Walks; Biking; Adventure
Water Sports. *Leisure* Sea Access; Fishing. *Organized* Multi-Stop, Self-Directed.

COMPLEMENTARY If you can't get enough New Testament, some other pockets of
biblical history include: **Old City Jerusalem (#1)**, including **Mount of Olives (#34)**; *Road
Trip P2: Christian Jordan*; or visit **Bethlehem (#40)** and **Nazareth and its Biblical Sites
(#29)**. Other great drives are: **King's Highway (#31)** through Jordan; **Golan Heights (#62)**;
and the **Incense Route (#73)**. If you think the path around the Sea is a gorgeous long-
distance walk, some other regional paths are: the **Jesus Trail (#69)**, visiting several of
the sites from this elective, but on foot; the *Palestinian Heritage Trail* takes you through
Bethlehem (#40), Jenin, Hebron (C2), **Nablus (#61)**, and **Jericho (#26)**; and the *Israel National
Trail* goes the extent of Israel, from *Mount Hermon* to **Eilat (#78)**.

NEARBY All within 50km, to the south are **Belvoir (#93)**, **Beit She'an (#39)**, **Beit Alpha
(#64)**, *Gan HaShlosha*, and *Hamat Gader*; to the west are *Mount Arbel*, **Tsipori (#56)**, and
Nazareth (#29); to the north are **Tsfat/Safed (#58)**, *Hula Lake*, *Tel Hazor*, and Rosh Pina (H2)
(Anchor); and to the east are **Golan Heights (#62)**, *Gamla*, **Golan Heights Winery (#75)**,
and *Yehudiya*.

#8 Masada

BROCHURE

RATINGS		MACRO-REGION
BUCKET! Score	8/10	K: Dead Sea (Israel)
Ruin	4/5	
Entertainment	3/5	**MICRO-REGION**
Information	4/5	K1
Popularity	5/5	

PRIMARY THEME/CATEGORY Archaeology – Roman – Judea.

TOP Most visited destination after Jerusalem.

COMMENDATIONS UNESCO World Heritage Site, 2001, and Israel National Park.

ESSENCE This fortified and self-sufficient town was built during the reign of King
Herod on a high mountain plateau overlooking the Dead Sea. It's well known for

marking the last stand of Jewish rebels in 73 CE who fought against the Romans, quarantined for years atop the mountain, then committed mass suicide rather than submit to Roman slavery.

HOLY LAND RELEVANCE Important to Jews as a reminder of their historical resistance to foreign powers. The site does not have particular religious significance.

ELECT ME! The views are incredible, the story is wild, the clifftop perch is perilous and pretty spectacular, the hike is exhilarating, and the cable car ride is a hit with all generations.

WORTH THE DETOUR? If you are a fan of Jewish history, or even just appreciate stories of Jewish resistance, this archaeological site is for you. For those on a day trip/weekend to the **Dead Sea (#3)** or **Ein Gedi (#50)**, you should consider adding it to your itinerary, as the site is impressive, especially given the history, mythology, and precipitous location.

EXPERIENCES

CAN'T MISS Walking down the cliffside to the Northern Palace where you'll get expansive views of the desert.

SITES **Masada Museum** has artifacts and history; the **Bathhouse** showcases Herod's impressive ability move water to even the most remote places – sauna, hot/cold rooms; the **Western Palace** contains frescoes, strangely in Greek style (one is of fruit); in the **Church**, by the Western Palace, check out the Byzantine structure and mosaics on the floor; the *mikvehs* are Jewish ritual baths; and the **water cisterns** are dug into the ground to prevent evaporation – you can descend into the largest one near the northernmost point on Masada.

ACTIVITIES The **cable car** requires minimal energy, but has a great view of the desert and sea as you ascend the mountain. *Masada's Snake Path (K1)* winds its way from the visitor center at the front entrance to the top (45–90 minutes). Many people ascend very early (04.00) to watch the sunrise. *Masada's Roman Trails (K1)* are the siege ramps built by the Romans to reach Masada from the west. It is a 15–30-minute ascent, but requires a 4x4 desert journey of several hours to reach the parking lot (not accessible from the Dead Sea entrance). **Paraglide** over Masada! There are a few outfitters – try Israel Extreme (**w** israel-extreme.com/activities/paragliding-israel/).

CAMERA *Best shot* Panoramic desert shots over the Dead Sea. *Best light* Sunrise views from Snake Path.

SECRET The southern end of the site gets very little foot traffic. There are also several hikes that reach the top via routes other than the Snake Path or Roman Ramp, including the Runners' Path, which is steep and tough, but less frequented. Also, everyone's looking for the "aerial" view of Masada from above, which you can't get to from Masada itself; achieve this via a strenuous hike to the adjacent Mount Eleazar.

SPECIAL EVENTS The **Sound and Light Show** (🕐 Tue/Thu, 19:30 winter, 20.30/21.00 summer) is only accessible via the Roman entrance or from Arad by Highway 3199 (arrive at least 30 minutes early). For **sunrise at Masada**, hike the Snake Path at 03.00

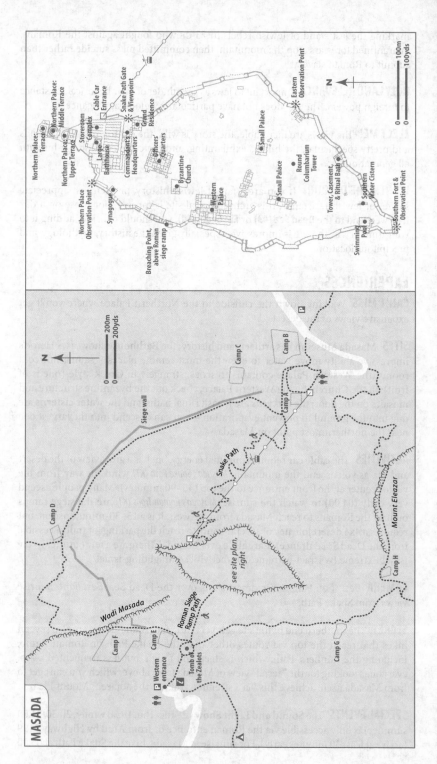

MASADA

Northern Palace: Terrace
Northern Palace: Middle Terrace
Northern Palace: Upper Terrace
Cable Car Entrance
Snake Path Gate & Viewpoint
Grand Residence
Storeroom Complex
Large Bathhouse
Commandant's Headquarters
Officers' Quarters
Northern Palace Observation Point
Synagogue
Byzantine Church
Western Palace
Breaching Point, above Roman siege ramp
Swimming Pool
Small Palace
Small Palace
Round Columbarium Tower
Tower, Casement, & Ritual Bath
Southern Water Cistern
Southern Fort & Observation Point
Eastern Observation Point

Siege wall
Camp B
Camp C
Camp A
Camp D
Snake Path
Mount Eleazar
Camp H
Wadi Masada
Camp F
Camp E
Roman Siege Ramp Path
Tomb of the Zealots
Western entrance
Camp G
see site plan, right

0   100m
0   100yds

0   200m
0   200yds

or 04.00 and watch the sunrise before the site opens. It's been a few years, but for **Opera at Masada** check **w** israel-opera.co.il/eng for any upcoming dates.

ITINERATOR!

DAYS/HOURS 08.00–16.00 daily, summer 08.00–17.00 Saturday–Thursday. The cable car closes early on holiday evenings. The Sound and Light Show starts at 19.30 in the winter, 20.30/21.00 in the summer. Hiking trails open one hour before sunrise.

BEST TIME TO VISIT Mornings can be busy with tour groups doing sunrise hikes, but early is required: the desert can quickly get above 40°C/100°F. During extreme heat, the Snake Path can close by 08.00. If you're not hiking, it's busy anyway. As the second most popular site in Israel after Jerusalem, it is normally crowded.

TIME COMMITMENT 2 hours minimum to take the cable car, walk quickly around the site, and descend. 2 hours driving time there and back from Jerusalem, or 4 hours from Tel Aviv. To fully enjoy the place, plan on staying at the site for 3–4 hours, depending on your stamina and how hot it is. The Snake Path affords another hour of strenuous activity, and to a lesser extent so does the Roman Ramp.

SPEED RULES Depending on the crowd level, it might not be as easy to move quickly through the site. The cable car may have lines. Otherwise, fast group/slow group speed rules apply.

COVERAGE

★ *Intro (1 hour)* Museum.
★ *Highlights (2–4 hours)* Skip the museum; take the cable car; self-paced walk around the site (highlights: Northern Palace, Synagogue, Western Palace, and Byzantine Church).
★ *Comprehensive (5–8 hours)* Highlights plus: museum; hire a guide; Snake Path (you can ascend on the ramp walk and take the cable car down, if you like); visit the southern site.
★ *Exhaustive (8+ hours)* All of *Comprehensive* plus: overnight camping on the Roman side (requires 4x4); ascend the Roman Ramp or the Runners' Path; Sound and Light Show.

BASE If you're anchoring in Tel Aviv or Jerusalem, you can easily make a day trip out of Masada and its surrounding sites. Approaching from Arad, you can make a road trip out of this by camping at the western entry campsite.

ANCHOR CITIES Jerusalem (100km/1½ hours); Tel Aviv (160km/2 hours); not ideal from Jordan.

BEST STRATEGY We recommend starting early (sunrise, if that sounds intriguing), hiking the Snake Path, touring the site, and descending via the cable car (for the views). You can have lunch on site, visit the museum, and then head south to **Ein Bokek** on the **Dead Sea (#3)** for another mind-blowing experience at a clean, free public beach.

WALKING ROUTES There are several to choose from: the Snake Path (from visitor center to peak) is the most popular and has an elevation of roughly 350m, taking around 45 minutes. The Roman Ramp is harder to access and a much shorter climb (c15 minutes), but less crowded. There are a few other access points for experienced hikers (w hike-israel.com).

DAY TRIPPING We recommend this as a day trip, including the **Dead Sea (#3)**, **Ein Gedi (#50)**, **Qumran (#70)**, and more, in *Road Trip K1*.

WALKS AND DRIVES K1, U2, W5.

ITINERARIES High BUCKET! Scores: 7+; Noteworthy; Archaeology; Nature and Scenic; Active; Endangered; National Parks/Reserves; Fine Arts; Ancient History; Memorial; Shoestring; Big-Group Friendly.

ARRIVAL PREP

PREBOOK Advanced reservations recommended for camping; register via e savit@npa.org.il.

TIPS There is no road linking the east and west entrance. Hiking paths open one hour before sunrise. If you're visiting any other National Parks, buy the Israel Park Pass, which gives you access to Masada and all other parks for 14 consecutive days.

CAUTION Temperatures can soar in the summer, and fatalities do occur. The Snake Path can close as early as 08.00 if it gets too hot. Bring a lot of water. Don't hike alone. There are pavilions to protect from the sun, but it is *hot*. That said, all ages visit here.

REALITY CHECK Always very busy with tour groups and buses. The site itself consists mostly of ancient dwellings, so there are not any monumental structures to focus on. Think: water cisterns, storage facilities, and bathhouses.

CONSTRAINTS Most of the site is wheelchair-friendly. There are accessible features for those with sight and hearing disabilities.

BRING WATER! (if you're hiking, this is a must); sunscreen; hat; comfortable shoes; your Israel Parks Card.

DON'T BRING Pets; food onto the mountain.

PUBLIC TRANSPORT Infrequent buses make this not the greatest option, but check w egged.co.il for timetables.

ACCESS Two very distinct entrances. The visitor center is easy to find off Highway 90. A second entrance is available from behind Masada, which is a 3-hour detour through the desert via 4x4 and has no cable car access, meaning you must climb the Roman Ramp to reach the site. Parking is available.

BEST ENTRANCE We recommend the Snake Path during moderate weather.

ADMISSION Entry: 31 ILS adults, 17 ILS children, or Israel Parks Card. Cable Car: 28 ILS adults, 14 ILS children one-way, 46 ILS adults, 28 ILS children return, no Parks Card. Museum only: 20 ILS. Sound and Light Show: 50 ILS.

RECOMMENDED GUIDE Tour guides will present in a theatrical style that a book simply cannot imitate, making them worth the investment. At the very least, watch the short film at the visitor center and read the park brochure, which has information about the three dozen or so individual sites on the mountain.

VISITOR CENTER There's a museum with a video, which plays on a loop – you may need to request English. Audio guides also available. Brochure at **w** parks.org.il.

EAT There's a restaurant at the base of the mountain.

SLEEP If you organize in advance, you can camp near the Arad/western entrance.

BUCKET!PEDIA

Hebrew name Metsada.   *Size* 400m above sea level, with dramatic cliffs on two sides, and 120m above where the Roman Ramp began. The top plateau is 550m × 270m. *Historical era Roman/Byzantine: Judea. Year founded/constructed* Possibly Hasmonean era, but all ruins begin with Herod in 35 BCE. *Years active* Inhabited through 73 CE.

CONTEXT Masada holds a place in Jewish folklore as one of the great sites of Jewish resistance against foreign oppressors in an attempt to salvage their Jewish state. It's unclear exactly when this site was first used as a fortress. The historian Josephus Flavius was the only known scribe who documented the Masada events, though he was not physically present for them. According to his notes, Masada hosted an earlier fortress built by the Jewish Hasmonean dynasty, possibly Alexander Jannaeus, who ruled through 76 BCE. Nothing has been found to substantiate this claim.

Rather, it was King Herod that fortified the site as a garrison and a winter palace, with storerooms and cisterns to provide food for months, if needed. In 66 CE, Jewish rebels ("Zealots") led by Eleazar Ben Yair fled Jerusalem for Masada and stayed there through 70 CE, when the last Jews in Jerusalem were expelled from the city and used Masada as their new staging grounds. During their residency, they built important Jewish holy sites, including one of the oldest synagogues yet discovered in Israel.

In 73 CE, Jewish troops came south to Masada to take over the only Jewish stronghold remaining in their province of Judea. The Roman commander Flavius Silva built military camps all around the mountain, still visible today. Flavius began the construction of a ramp to scale the western side of the mountain (the "Roman Ramp") while laying siege on the city. After several months, seeing their option as death or capture, Ben Yair reportedly convinced the nearly 1,000 residents to commit suicide by sword rather than be subjected to Roman slavery. As the Romans scaled the walls, they found a nearly empty site. Two women and five children were hiding in a cistern and explained what had transpired. The site was abandoned shortly thereafter, earning the site and its last residents a legendary status.

GEOLOGY Masada is part of a mountain block that was dislodged from the adjacent fault line, causing a "horst": an abrupt peak surrounded by wadis/valleys. Masada and the adjacent landscape is part of the Judean Desert, but the veinous land east of the site looking towards the Dead Sea is the sedimentary remains of high water levels from Lake Lisan, a giant lake that stretched to the Sea of Galilee 20,000 years ago.

ARCHAEOLOGY The entire complex was built in three phases by Herod in 35, 25, and 15 BCE. The most impressive portion is the cliffside palace, called the Northern Palace, which hangs down the northern wall and which has stunning views of the desert expanse. Also noteworthy are the massive water cisterns which kept nearly 1,000 people alive in the desert for years, even during a long war blockade. In 2016, domesticated barley seeds were found in a cave on the cliffside of Masada and dated to roughly 6,000 years ago.

Interestingly, human remains have not been found in great numbers at the site. Thus far, only 28 bodies have been discovered, of which 25 were found in an adjacent cave. Given that pig bones were found in the same area, it's also possible those bodies were not Jewish, but Roman soldier remains. The unanswered question: what happened to the 1,000 bodies? It's unclear. Without archaeological evidence, it's difficult to prove Josephus's version of events. We may never know how many people died, if suicide was their method of death, or whether the whole thing was a tale to foment more discord with the Roman overlords.

CHRONOLOGY

2nd century BCE: Possible founding by Hasmonean King Alexander Jannaeus.
35 BCE: First phase of Herod's fortress is built.
66 CE: Zealots relocate to Masada and encourage Jews to fight the Roman rulers.
70: Jerusalem is sacked by Roman armies, Second Temple destroyed, Roman garrison stationed at Masada is killed, and Jews from Jerusalem relocate to Masada.
73: Roman legion builds a ramp to reach Masada, which takes 2–3 months, after which they lay siege to the fortress. Legend says that almost 1,000 Jews killed themselves before the Romans arrived. Only 28 bodies have been discovered.
5th century: Byzantine monks live at the site, build a church.
1838: Having been lost to history for almost 2,000 years, the site is identified successfully by use of a telescope from Ein Gedi.
1842: First modern climbers reach summit.
1959: Excavations begin. Yigael Yadin leads 1963–65 expeditions (museum is named after him).
1969: Rabbinical court decides the remains of the 28 bodies found on Masada are Jewish and reburies them as Jews in a state ceremony.
2001: Masada declared a UNESCO World Heritage Site.
2007: Yigael Yadin Museum opens.

WEBSITE w parks.org.il/en/reserve-park/masada-national-park/.

WHERE TO NEXT?

THEMATIC *Noteworthy* UNESCO; National Parks; Unique. *Religion* Judaism; Oldest Synagogues. *Archaeology* Herodian; Roman; Byzantine/Christian; Historical Battlefields; Active Excavations. *Structure* Iconic Structures; Historic Monuments; Memorial; Impressive Feats; Infrastructure. *Nature* Geological Wonders; Mountains and Mounts; Desert. *Scenic* Historical Vantage; Earth Panorama; Sunrise/Sunset; Most Photographed. *People* Jewish. *Culture* Music. *Active* Tough Hikes; Adventure/Extreme Land Sports. *Accommodation* Campgrounds.

COMPLEMENTARY Other celebrated sites from Jewish history are the **Western Wall (#11)**; **Beit She'arim (#79)**; *Lag B'Omer at Moshav Meron*, to visit the grave of Rabbi Shimon bar Yochai. Other popular Israeli tourist attractions in the country are Tisch Family

Zoological Gardens (B1); **Caesarea (#25)**; **Banias (#80)**; **Ein Gedi (#50)** (next door). Other great expansive views are **Mount Sinai (#15)**, **Mount Nebo (#24)**, **King's Highway (#31)**, and **Nimrod's Fortress (#85)**.

NEARBY Follow *Road Trip K1* to catch all the best spots in the region.

#9 Church of the Holy Sepulchre

BROCHURE

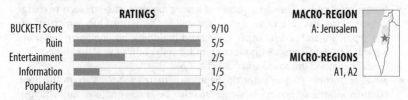

RATINGS			MACRO-REGION
BUCKET! Score		9/10	A: Jerusalem
Ruin		5/5	
Entertainment		2/5	**MICRO-REGIONS**
Information		1/5	A1, A2
Popularity		5/5	

PRIMARY THEME/CATEGORY Religion – Religious Figures – Jesus: Death.

TOP Most important site related to the life of Jesus.

COMMENDATIONS Included in the Old City of Jerusalem's UNESCO nomination.

ESSENCE The location of the crucifixion, burial, and resurrection of Jesus of Nazareth, a Jewish prophet and father of Christianity. Also the site of the last four stations on the **Via Dolorosa (#42)**.

HOLY LAND RELEVANCE Most significant site of Christendom, located a short distance from the **Western Wall (#11)** and **Temple Mount (#12)**, and site of pilgrimage for many of the world's Christians. The minor squabbles by religious sects over pieces of land in the Church serve as a microcosm of the broader territorial problems in the region.

ELECT ME! Forget the Vatican, this is the most important site in the world for Christian pilgrims. It's a moderately quick visit, if you skip the lines, and free. If you're Christian, it can also be a very powerful experience. The confluence of Christian sects sharing the space creates for an interesting visual experience.

WORTH THE DETOUR? Absolutely worth a visit. If you're not Christian, you might not need to stand in line to touch the rock or the tomb, but the Church is still a remarkable collection of history, architecture, and engineering. Catching a ceremony is always special.

EXPERIENCES

CAN'T MISS **Golgotha**, the rock upon which Jesus was crucified, and the **Ædicule**, which encloses the Holy Sepulchre, or tomb of Christ.

SITES

★ *Station 9* The final six Stations of the Cross are located at the Church. Station 9, "Jesus falls a third time," is found on the roof, above the entrance to the Ethiopian Monastery, accessible via the market on Beit HaBad Street.

★ *Ethiopian Monastery* A number of buildings cobbled together out of old Crusader ruins by Ethiopian communities who have no access rights to the Sepulchre itself. This small collection of churches – and their purposefully impoverished Ethiopian caretakers – can be accessed from the Parvis or the roof.

★ *Parvis: the Church's entryway* If looking at the front doors, directly behind you is the <u>Mosque of Omar (A2)</u>. On the left are three Greek chapels, inaccessible from here. On the right are a number of other chapels, not open to the public, save the door leading to the Ethiopian area and roof. The stairs to the right of the door lead to the Chapel of the Franks, also closed. Adjacent to the second-floor window above the front door is the "Immovable Ladder."

★ *Immovable Ladder* The consequence of having multiple religious sects in charge of one space. Because of an agreement called the Status Quo, which affects the Sepulchre and several other Holy Land buildings, no one party can move anything in the Church without consent from the other five shareholders. The ladder has stood unmoved since at least 1757.

★ *Stone of Unction* As you enter the Sepulchre, there's a stone slab on the floor, commemorated as the very stone where Jesus' body was anointed and wrapped after his death. In fact, this stone is a replica, placed in 1810. Worshipers bow down to pray on the stone and bless their holy articles. There's no real queue; inch your way in.

★ *Rock of Golgotha* Immediately to the right of the entrance are tall stairs leading to Golgotha, the hill where Christ was crucified. Visitors queue up to reach beneath the floor to touch the rock where the cross stood.

★ *Stations 10–13* Each of these stations mark Jesus' final moments as a mortal. All occurred on Golgotha, same as above. Stations 10, "Jesus is stripped of his garments" and 11, "Jesus is nailed to the cross," are venerated on the Catholic altar, to the right of the Greek display which honors Station 12, "Jesus dies on the cross," while Station 13, "Jesus is taken down from the cross and placed in the arms of his mother," is commemorated between the two with a statue of Mary.

★ *Chapel of Adam* Directly underneath Golgotha is a small chapel, traditionally believed to be the burial place of the first man, Adam. The cracks in the rock are said to have been caused by an earthquake immediately following Christ's crucifixion.

★ *Catholicon* Inside the Church are a number of chapels and churches. In the center is a grand Crusader-era (12th-century) construction called the Catholicon. As you leave the Chapel of Adam, walk towards the Holy Sepulchre tomb and you can view the high-ceilinged church opposite. Despite the "Catholic" name, it is used by the Greek Orthodox.

★ *Centre of the World* Located inside the Catholicon, this floor marker (occasionally covered by a religious apparatus) was once used by mapmakers to denote the center of the world. Don't forget to document yourself standing at the center of the universe!

★ *Syriac Chapel and Joseph of Arimathea's Tomb* On the outer edge of the room outside the Catholicon (the Rotunda Room), several tombs have been uncovered. It's believed that a rich Jew gave up his own tomb for Jesus, and upon his death was buried near Jesus' tomb, now the western edge of the Church.

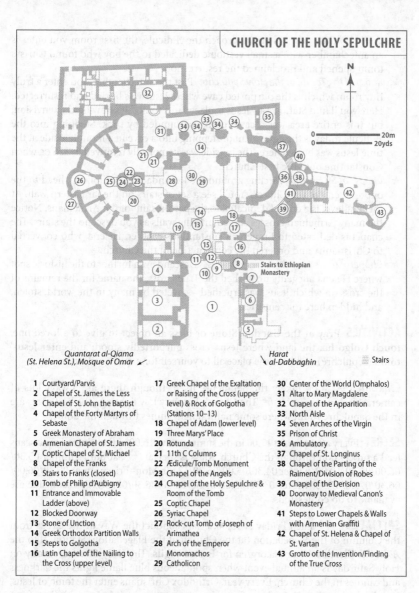

CHURCH OF THE HOLY SEPULCHRE

Quantarat al-Qiama
(St. Helena St.), Mosque of Omar

Harat
al-Dabbaghin

▓ Stairs

1 Courtyard/Parvis
2 Chapel of St. James the Less
3 Chapel of St. John the Baptist
4 Chapel of the Forty Martyrs of
   Sebaste
5 Greek Monastery of Abraham
6 Armenian Chapel of St. James
7 Coptic Chapel of St. Michael
8 Chapel of the Franks
9 Stairs to Franks (closed)
10 Tomb of Philip d'Aubigny
11 Entrance and Immovable
   Ladder (above)
12 Blocked Doorway
13 Stone of Unction
14 Greek Orthodox Partition Walls
15 Steps to Golgotha
16 Latin Chapel of the Nailing to
   the Cross (upper level)

17 Greek Chapel of the Exaltation
   or Raising of the Cross (upper
   level) & Rock of Golgotha
   (Stations 10–13)
18 Chapel of Adam (lower level)
19 Three Marys' Place
20 Rotunda
21 11th C Columns
22 Ædicule/Tomb Monument
23 Chapel of the Angels
24 Chapel of the Holy Sepulchre &
   Room of the Tomb
25 Coptic Chapel
26 Syriac Chapel
27 Rock-cut Tomb of Joseph of
   Arimathea
28 Arch of the Emperor
   Monomachos
29 Catholicon

30 Center of the World (Omphalos)
31 Altar to Mary Magdalene
32 Chapel of the Apparition
33 North Aisle
34 Seven Arches of the Virgin
35 Prison of Christ
36 Ambulatory
37 Chapel of St. Longinus
38 Chapel of the Parting of the
   Raiment/Division of Robes
39 Chapel of the Derision
40 Doorway to Medieval Canon's
   Monastery
41 Steps to Lower Chapels & Walls
   with Armenian Graffiti
42 Chapel of St. Helena & Chapel of
   St. Vartan
43 Grotto of the Invention/Finding
   of the True Cross

★ *Rotunda* Underneath the largest of the Church's domes, this room houses the
  Ædicule and Tomb. Due to restorations over the years, it's actually rare for
  the room to see much sunlight, though its original design likely had the room
  flooded with light. It now has a dark and chamber-like feel.

★ *Ædicule* The structure surrounding the Tomb was built in 1810 in a baroque
  Ottoman style, popular in the day. Over two centuries, the structure became
  badly damaged by neglect and earthquakes. Reconstruction was completed in
  2017 after $3 million of repairs. To access the tomb, visitors wait in a line that
  circles the Ædicule. The entrance is strictly controlled, with small groups granted
  access one at a time. Lines can take upwards of an hour.

★ *Chapel of the Angel* As you approach the Ædicule, the first room you enter is an antechamber with a small vestibule dedicated to the boy who found Christ's tomb opened and proclaimed the resurrection.

★ *Room of the Tomb, or the Holy Sepulchre* Past the antechamber, you enter a truly tiny room which is the purported cave where Jesus was buried and resurrected. Here you'll find Station 14, "Jesus is placed in a tomb." It's now hard to envision, but this entire area was a cave tomb, surrounded by rock. Stepping into the Ædicule today is the equivalent of stepping into a cave in a mountainside at the time Jesus was buried here. The hillside was completely removed in 326 CE when Constantine built the first Church.

★ *Chapel of St. Helena* Circling around the Rotunda and Catholicon, head to the opposite end of the Church. You'll see a set of stairs on the far eastern wall. At the first level is a chapel dedicated to the patron saint of the Armenians. Notice the many Armenian crosses carved into the walls as you descend the stairs. The chapel is dedicated to Emperor Constantine's mother, Helena, who converted to Christianity and ordered the construction of the Church.

★ *Chapel of the Invention of the Holy Cross* Descend even further to the historic spot where Helena allegedly unearthed the True Cross, the name for the remains of the cross on which Jesus was crucified – coveted by many in the world, stolen, and hidden here for centuries.

ACTIVITIES **Pray at the Unction Stone** or bless an object to give to a loved one; **touch Golgotha**, the land where Jesus' cross purportedly stood; and **enter Jesus' tomb** (sepulchre) and have the place all to yourself for a quick reflection.

CAMERA *Best shot* Likely the Sepulchre itself, though there are always lots of cameras flashing. *Best light* The Church has very low lighting. The best spots are in the Sepulchre room where some natural light shines through the dome.

SECRET Every afternoon at 17.00 in the summer, and 16.00 in the winter, Franciscans lead a procession through the Church. Mass is special (☐ Sat/Sun, summer 05.30/06.00/06.30/18.00, winter 04.30/05.00/05.30/17.00; Mon–Fri, summer 05.30/06.00/06.30/07.00/07.30, winter 04.30/05.00/05.30/06.00/06.30/07.15). Priests inside are available to do confessions.

SPECIAL EVENTS Each Friday at 15.00, Friars conduct the **Way of the Cross** from the Column of the Flagellation (at the Church of the Flagellation, Station 2) to the Ædicule. Check w custodia.org/en for **Easter Vigils**. The **Holy Fire Ceremony** on Holy Saturday is an annual event when spontaneous blue flame lights the darkness and candles in the Church. Every year, Orthodox Christians enter the tomb of Jesus, seal the door, and receive a flame from Heaven over the grave denoting the love from God and representing the resurrection of Jesus. Most denounce this tradition as superstition, though thousands of people cram into the Holy Sepulchre every year to bear witness to the "miracle."

ITINERATOR!

DAYS/HOURS Summer 05.00–21.00, winter 04.00–19.00, daily. Shorter holiday hours.

BEST TIME TO VISIT As early as possible, any day of the week. Skip weekends to avoid queues. Crazy at Easter.

TIME COMMITMENT Depending on the number of people, you may need several hours in order to see the entirety of the complex properly. During busy periods, it may take an hour to even enter the Church. Lines regularly form inside the Church to touch the ground of the crucifixion and separately to enter Jesus' tomb.

SPEED RULES Do not apply. The Church has a capacity of 8,000 visitors. If you happen to enter when it's empty, you'll be able to run through much faster, but more likely you'll be waiting in lines like everyone else.

COVERAGE
★ *Intro (30 minutes–1 hour, depending on lines)* Circling the site on your own.
★ *Highlights (1–2 hours)* *Intro* plus: standing in line at Golgotha; standing in line at the Tomb.
★ *Comprehensive (2–3 hours)* *Highlights* plus: our *Church of the Holy Sepulchre Chronotour* (w buckettravelguides.com/sepulchre-chronotour).
★ *Exhaustive (3–4 hours)* *Comprehensive* plus: hire a guide.

BASE/ANCHOR See **Old City Jerusalem (#1)**.

BEST STRATEGY There is only one entrance into the Church itself, so start there. We recommend the following route: have a look at the structure from the outside, enter and kneel at the Stone of Unction, climb the stairs to the location of Jesus' crucifixion, circle around the Ambulatory, stopping at any chapels of interest, descend the stairs to the Armenian chapels, then back up and around the Rotunda where you find Christ's Tomb, the Holy Sepulchre.

WALKING ROUTES The *Sites* (above) can be followed in order.

DAY TRIPPING This site will be part of any quick Jerusalem tour.

WALKS AND DRIVES A1, A2.

ITINERARIES Jerusalem Immersion; High BUCKET! Scores: 7+; Most Popular; Complete Ruins; Noteworthy; Religion; UNESCO; Memorial; Shoestring; Big-Group Friendly.

ARRIVAL PREP

PREBOOK Not necessary; free entry.

TIPS Many people bring religious articles, photos, or mementos to "bless" at the Stone of Unction.

CAUTION The quantity of people can be stifling and seemingly against fire regulations. Be careful on the ancient steps – they are not compliant with present-day safety codes.

REALITY CHECK The number of tourists visiting this site – particularly cruise day-trippers – is staggering. And there are pilgrims from all over the world. You may be surrounded by people who may not understand the concept of a queue. Be patient but assertive.

CONSTRAINTS The Church was built in the 1200s, so it's not easily accessible for persons with disabilities. There are steep steps to reach Golgotha and more steps to visit the basement rooms, though the Tomb is on ground level. For claustrophobes, know there are lots of places where you can feel uncomfortably enclosed, including the Tomb itself.

BRING Modest clothing; religious articles okay.

ARRIVAL See **Old City Jerusalem (#1)**.

ACCESS Enter the Parvis (main building platform/entranceway) through one of three paths: 1) through the Muristan (Christian Quarter); 2) while on the Via Dolorosa path (heading west from Muslim Quarter) descend the stairs to the Parvis; or 3) via the roof going down through the Ethiopian chapels, accessible from Beit HaBad Street/runs north to Damascus Gate.

ADMISSION No charge or security screening.

RECOMMENDED GUIDE *Church of the Holy Sepulchre Chronotour* (**w** buckettravel guides.com/sepulchre-chronotour).

VISITOR CENTER No visitor center or placards, but the recently updated website is chock full of information (**w** custodia.org/en/sanctuaries/holy-sepulchre).

EAT/SLEEP See **Old City Jerusalem (#1)**.

BUCKET!PEDIA

AKA Church of the Resurrection; Church of the Anastasis (Eastern Orthodox); Ecclesia Sancti Sepulchri (Latin). *Hebrew name* Knesiyat ha-Kever (Church of the Burial/Grave). *Arabic name* al-Qiyamah (Church of the Resurrection). *Historical name* The site where Jesus was crucified was known by two names: Calvary (Latin) and Golgotha (Greek). Both are derived from the same term, meaning "place of the skull," which is how the crucifixion mountain was known. The original building of 335 CE was the earliest to be known as the Church of the Holy Sepulchre – "sepulchre" meaning a rock-cut or stone-built room or monument to lay or bury a dead person. *Size* 180m × 100m, 4 "floors." *Historical era* Roman/Byzantine to Modern. *Year constructed* 325 CE, the year Constantine ordered its creation. Consecrated in 335. *Years active* 335 CE to present, almost continuously.

CONTEXT A bizarre amalgamation of buildings, chapels, points of historical interest, biblical references, and competing authority, this giant building might better be thought of as a shrine more than a church. Shared by six Christian denominations, including Armenians, Copts, Ethiopians, Franciscan (Catholic/Latin), Greek Orthodox, and Syriac Orthodox, each shares a piece of the collective whole. There are also communal areas, under the joint authority of Catholics, Greeks, and Armenians, which include Christ's tomb. You will likely see persons of religious orders either praying or administering their respective sites. The Greeks, for instance, are responsible for the presumed site of the crucifixion, and manage the candles and flow of people (not wonderfully). Despite, or perhaps because of, the various Christian denominations struggling for control, two Muslim families share responsibility of keyholders to the facility.

The building has undergone a number of significant changes over the last 1,700 years. It began as a site of pilgrimage for those seeking to visit the site of Christ's death and rebirth. The Roman emperor Hadrian rebuilt Jerusalem from the ashes of the 70 CE siege, constructing a pagan temple over the hills where Jesus was crucified and buried.

Christianity spread to Europe in the 3rd and 4th centuries CE, eventually becoming the religion of the Holy Roman Empire. At the request of his mother, Helena, Emperor Constantine I ordered the site of the pagan temple to be cleared and replaced with a basilica dedicated to Jesus. This first building was completed in 335 CE and was extended all the way to the Cardo Maximus – a much larger complex than the current building – containing an atrium that connected to the main street, a basilica, an open courtyard where Calvary was exposed, and then a rotunda with the tomb in its center (much as it is today).

When Jerusalem was sacked in the 7th century by Persians, the complex burned to the ground. Under Arab rule, later that same century, Christians were allowed to rebuild their church, and Muslims (who viewed Jesus as a prophet) allowed Christian worship. The Mosque of Omar stands opposite the building entrance in commemoration of Muslim mercy.

The building went through a number of disasters over the coming centuries, including many fires and ultimately the complete destruction of the Church by a crazed Fatimid caliph, al-Hakim, who from 1099 ordered the destruction of Jewish and Christian monuments throughout the Holy Land. This caused such outrage in Europe that it ultimately led to the independent financing of European crusaders, who arrived in waves to reclaim Jerusalem and the Holy Land from Arab invaders. Byzantine leaders worked with later Fatimid rulers to rebuild the Church, but the basilica was lost forever.

The Crusaders made the most extensive changes to the Church, focusing on the Rotunda and Tomb. Several chapels had been built adjacent to the Church, as well as the long colonnade, and the Crusader efforts enclosed these disparate pieces into one connected building. They capped it with a dome over the rotunda and another over the Catholicon, the giant room opposite the Ædicule, which was the original Crusader church, and which was built atop Constantine's basilica. Finally, the Crusaders added the bell tower. Most of what you see today is Crusader period, which ended in 1244.

Centuries of Arab rule left this site without any proper oversight. In 1757, Status Quo went into effect, freezing any decisions about changes to Jewish, Muslim, and Christian holy places until all parties were in agreement. Internally, this has meant that the Christian sites cannot be changed without the explicit agreement of Eastern Orthodox, Armenian, and Roman Catholic leadership, and to some extent the Syriac, Coptic, and Ethiopian communities. Outside, the "immovable ladder" is testament to the sheer difficulties in getting anything done under this arrangement; that ladder has not moved since 1757 because no party is allowed to move anything without the consent of the others.

The clash of styles is a result of a variety of decisions: In 1808, a fire destroyed the Rotunda and the dome collapsed, critically damaging the Ædicule. Seven of the pillars from the Constantine building had to be replaced, leaving just three of the original columns in the Rotunda – a different color than the rest. The Church has a feeling of being enclosed, which you get immediately upon entering. This is due to the wall behind the Unction Stone, which was originally built for temporary support during renovations. Upon completion of the work, the Greek community instead decided to embellish the wall with paintings. It now completely blocks the view of the massive Church behind it. The last good decision of the collective was to repair the Ædicule itself, which after 200 years was near collapse. The three sects monitoring the Sepulchre have since agreed to repair the floor of the Church as well as the foundation of the Tomb.

Today, this building stands testament to 1,700 years of history, at least four times when the building was completely renovated, and six denominations trying to keep the peace while catering to more than three million visitors each year. It truly is an astounding piece of work.

ARCHAEOLOGY How do we know Jesus was buried here? There's obviously little "proof" given that he got up out of the grave and walked out, right? The most logical answer is not based on archaeological proof, but tradition. Just as people today mark up walls and buildings with "[Your name] was here," so too did people thousands of years ago. Various graffiti marks have pointed to this location as the most likely and logical place for these events. Also, Jewish Christian followers would likely have been visiting these places on pilgrimages year after year. It makes sense that Hadrian would have situated his Temple of Venus and Statue of Jupiter to cover the religious sites of his conquered subjects, and Constantine would have removed those temples and placed his Church there, as did the successive generations.

Furthermore, Jesus is said to have been buried outside of Jerusalem's walls. At the time of his death, the walls did not yet include the "Christian Quarter" (which, of course, was not yet Christian). As a heretic, Jesus was led outside the city walls to be punished, matching this location. His Roman captors marched him to the top of "Skull Mountain," recognized as "a small hill that was close to a garden covering an abandoned quarry." The Greeks called this hill Golgotha and Latins called it Calvary, both meaning "skull mountain," and presumably shaped as a skull and easily recognizable to visitors. According to Scripture, his tomb was near other graves. This much is true: his tomb was found to be carved among other tombs dating from the 1st century BCE to 1st century CE, but the purported tomb of Jesus was newly cut and had been unused. When Constantine removed the pagan idolatry on site, he also cleared the land to make space for his church, removing many of these landmarks, but being careful to leave in place the exact hilltop where the cross stood at Golgotha (hence why you walk up tall stairs when you enter) and the rock upon which Jesus' body was lain in the tomb. The rest of the earth was cleared away, but Christian pilgrims have come continuously for two millennia to pay homage at this very location.

ARCHITECTURE There are three domes: the Rotunda, Catholicon, and Chapel of the Franks. The Church has been completely rebuilt several times. To get a sense of the various architectural styles and combinations, pay particular attention to: **Roman** columns in the Anastasis chamber; **Byzantine** walls; **Armenian** cross etches in the stairwell towards the Chapel of Adam; the **Ottoman**-style Ædicule, surrounding Christ's tomb; and the **Greek Orthodox** altar at Golgotha, wall behind the Stone of Unction, and ornamentation in the Catholicon.

CHRONOLOGY
33 CE: Jesus is crucified on Golgotha mountain. He is buried in a rock-cut tomb in a nearby garden. Three days later, according to tradition, Jesus rises from the dead.
130: Roman Emperor Hadrian declares the city of Jerusalem the new colony of Aelia Capitolina.
135: Hadrian creates temples honoring the Roman gods of Jupiter and Venus where Temple Mount and Jesus' tomb once stood, burying those sites under earth.
326: Roman Emperor Constantine places his mother, Helena (now St. Helena), in charge of finding holy relics in Palestine. At the site of the Sepulchre, she discovers

three crosses, attempts to perform miracles with all three, successfully heals a sick woman with one of them, and declares it to be the True Cross.

335: Having proclaimed tolerance for Christians in the Holy Land, Roman Emperor Constantine himself converts to Christianity and orders the construction of the Basilica and Church of the Holy Sepulchre, enclosing the sites of Golgotha, Jesus' tomb, and the location of the True Cross.

c542 CE: The **Madaba Map (#19)** is laid in Madaba, Jordan, now the oldest surviving map of the Holy Land, and Jerusalem in particular. This map has helped archaeologists understand the layout of the Roman/Byzantine city, and the grandiosity of Constantine's original Basilica.

614: The Byzantine Empire retreats from the Holy Land following a long debilitating war against the Persian/Sassanid empire. The Persians partially destroy Constantine's Basilica.

638: Muhammad's forces enter the Holy Land. The second Rashidun caliph, Omar ibn al-Khattab, quickly takes control of the city. He declares the Christian churches to be protected sites. (For this honor, a mosque was dedicated to Omar in 1193 directly across from the Church's southern entrance.)

746: An earthquake strikes the region, damaging the Church. Further earthquakes and fires cause severe structural damage to various elements of the overall building, causing periodic failure and collapse of the Basilica, Rotunda and dome, roofs, and doors over the following centuries.

1009: Caliph al-Hakim destroys what remains of the Constantine structure, with the exception of the Rotunda and the rock-cut tomb, which was perhaps unintentionally buried, mostly unharmed, under debris.

1012–48: Muslim rulers negotiate with Byzantine authorities to allow for Christian worship and small repair projects to be completed at the Church. A few chapels are added, and the Ædicule unearthed, though the majority of the site still lies in ruins. The former basilica and atrium are not seen again.

1099: In an attempt to free the Holy Land from Muslim control, the Latin Church embarks on its "First Crusade" (to be followed by several more waves). Only a few weeks after arriving, the Kingdom of Jerusalem is established by council from the site of the Church of the Holy Sepulchre.

1163: The Crusaders excavate the crypts, create chapels dedicated to the Calvary, design an ambulatory, build workers' quarters on the former site of the Basilica, rebuild the colonnade for the new dome, and cover the courtyard with a Romanesque style church and choir, now the Catholicon. The building has been transformed from a complex of four buildings into a whole structure, however disjointed it seems today.

1187: Not long after the completion of the Church, the founder of the Ayyubid dynasty Salah ad-Din (or Saladin) takes Jerusalem from the Crusaders. Among other things, he melts the church bells from the bell tower, which are not replaced until the 19th century.

1187, 1192, or perhaps earlier: Saladin entrusts two families with guarding the front door to the Church. The Joudeh family is responsible for keeping the keys to the building, while the Nuseibeh family (purportedly the oldest Muslim dynasty in Jerusalem) opens the front doors every morning and locks up every evening. It's possible this arrangement has existed since Muslims gained control of the city in the 7th century, but it's also possible the tradition didn't begin until the 16th century (the oldest contract dates to 1517), when records actually exist of these keys. The purpose for this tradition is not clear, but may have been to collect a visitor entrance tax. The families believe the 12-inch-long iron keys themselves are at least 800 years old. The tradition passes from father to son.

1192: Richard the Lionheart and Saladin sign a pact allowing for the return of Christian pilgrims to worship in the Church.

1244: Khwarazmian Turks take Jerusalem, slaughter monks in the Sepulchre, and allow the Church to decay.

1342: A papal bull enacted by Pope Clement VI (Custodia Terrae Sanctae) places the Franciscans in charge of the Sepulchre grounds and Church.

1517: Sultan Suleiman the Magnificent of the Ottoman Empire takes control of Jerusalem, allowing freedom of worship.

1545: Top-most level of the bell tower collapses.

1555: Limestone surface upon which Jesus was buried is covered by a marble slab in the Ædicule to prevent any further damage, graffiti, and tomb robbing.

1579: Miracle of the Holy Fire.

1622: Turkish rulers favorable to the Orthodox community allow Greek Orthodox adherents the right to claim jurisdiction over their holy places. Conflicts emerge between the Latin-Franciscans and the Greek Orthodox. They each begin staking claims to parts of the Church.

1719: Upper 2½ stories of the bell tower are removed due to lack of repairs over the centuries.

1757: Status Quo goes into effect, freezing any decisions about changes to Jewish, Muslim, and Christian holy places until all parties are in agreement. This extends to the Church. A ladder just above the Church's front door becomes the visual representation of this agreement, and has not been moved since.

1808: A major fire erupts and burns the entire complex severely, destroying seven out of the remaining ten 7th- and 10th-century columns in the Rotunda. The Rotunda's dome collapses and damages all but the interior of the Ædicule.

1810: Present Ædicule is constructed around the tomb. Following the fire, the exterior of the tomb is reconstructed in the then-contemporary "Ottoman Baroque" style, which we see today.

1853: Territorial divisions within the Church are solidified in another decree reaffirming Status Quo, halting any further changes to ownership or changes to the Church without unanimous agreement, and leading to the present-day divisions.

1927: A major earthquake puts the entire Church in danger of complete structural failure.

1947: The British erect a temporary steel frame to keep the building from collapsing. Other makeshift scaffolding is added around the interior, including the Ædicule.

1959: Partition groups finally decide on a mutually agreeable plan to restore the Church.

1964: Pope Paul VI – the first pope to have left Europe in centuries – conducts the first papal visit to the site.

2016: During repair work to the Ædicule, researchers remove the marble slab covering the tomb of Jesus, which had not been uncovered since 1555.

2017: Ædicule work is complete, after $3 million in repairs. New construction imminent to repair the foundation of the tomb and the floor of the Rotunda.

WEBSITE w custodia.org/en/sanctuaries/holy-sepulchre

WHERE TO NEXT?

THEMATIC *Noteworthy* Unique; Exotic/Wow. *Religion* Christianity; Jesus: Death and Resurrection; New Testament; Churches; Oldest and Ancient Churches; Burial; Pilgrimage; Ceremonies and Events. *Archaeology* Roman; Byzantine/Christian;

Crusader. *Structure* Impressive Structural Remains; Iconic Structures; Historic Monuments; Memorial; Skyline. *Nature* Caves/Grottoes. *Scenic* People-Watching. *Society* Disputed. *People* Ethnic Minorities; Holidays.

COMPLEMENTARY Some of the other most important churches in the region are: the **Basilica of the Annunciation** in **Nazareth (#29)**, where Mary was visited by the Angel Gabriel to inform her she would carry the son of God; the **Church of the Nativity (#18)** in Bethlehem, where Jesus was born; and the **Mount of Beatitudes**, where Jesus proclaimed his Sermon on the Mount and the Lord's Prayer. Other important sites from Jesus' life in Jerusalem are: **Mount Zion (#92)**, the site of the Last Supper; the **Mount of Olives (#34)**, where Jesus taught and slept during his trip between Jerusalem and Bethany; and the **Via Dolorosa (#42)**, which follows the path of Jesus' final moments, ending at the Church of the Holy Sepulchre.

NEARBY See **Old City Jerusalem (#1)**.

#10 Red Sea/Gulf of Aqaba

BROCHURE

RATINGS			MACRO-REGIONS
BUCKET! Score	▬▬▬▬▬▬	6/10	L: Eilat and Arabah;
Ruin	n/a		M: South Jordan; T: Sinai
Entertainment	▬▬▬▬	4/5	
Information	▬▬▬	3/5	**MICRO-REGIONS**
Popularity	▬▬▬▬▬	5/5	L1, L2, M1, M2, T1

PRIMARY THEME/CATEGORY Active – Water Sports – Snorkeling.

TOP Northernmost reef in the world; top regional dive spot; best snorkeling; warmest winters.

ESSENCE Three resort towns converge at the top of the Red Sea – Taba (T1) in Egypt, **Eilat (#78)** in Israel, and **Aqaba (#43)** in Jordan – and continue south along the Sinai peninsula. Each town has its own personality and activities, but the common denominator is the undersea reef environment.

HOLY LAND RELEVANCE Moses parted the Red Sea, according to Scripture, but this is not relevant or apparent on your dives in the coral reef.

ELECT ME! The beaches alone are pleasant enough, but do not rival those at Tel Aviv. This trip is for certified or wannabe divers and snorkelers, but also for families looking for a resort getaway in the winter since it never gets too cold.

WORTH THE DETOUR? Depends on where you go. The southern Sinai has great snorkeling, but is difficult to get to. In Israel and Jordan, the coral has seen better days. If you can get away from shore, you'll be rewarded with something particularly worthwhile. For the best snorkeling spots, you'll want to spend some money either visiting a private beach or paying a tour guide. The trash will bother many.

EXPERIENCES

CAN'T MISS **Ras Mohammad (#53)** is consistently ranked one of the best dive sites in the world.

DIVE SITES Aqaba offers the *Cedar Pride* shipwreck; the Seven Sisters (a sunk tank!); Rainbow Reef (good night dive); Gorgone I (famous for gorgonians, or Alcyonacea, giant sea fans); and Saudi Border (last stop before Saudi!). Sinai has *Blue Hole (T1)* (a semi-dangerous spot for diving with a number of deaths associated here, making it both a challenge and a draw); **Dahab (#54)**; **Sharm el-Sheikh (#88)**, including the Thistlegorm Wreck (one of the world's most famous wreck dives); and **Ras Mohammad (#53)**, possibly the best reef wall in the world.

SNORKELING SITES Eilat: **Coral Beach (#83)**; Princess Beach; Lighthouse Beach. Aqaba: South Beach (public access, very clear); Berenice Beach Club (private); Japanese Garden (very popular).

NON-WET OPTIONS *Underwater Observatory* in Eilat.

ACTIVITIES You'll want a waterproof diagram to identify the below – check with your hotel or with the guides where you rent equipment.

ANIMALIA Barracuda; Clownfish; Dolphins; Dugongs (closest relative is the sea cow); Fusilier; Grunters; Hawksbill Turtles; Humphead Wrasse; Manta Rays; Moray eels; Sergeant Major; Whale sharks.

PLANT LIFE Cabbage coral; Mangroves; Seagrass beds.

CAMERA *Best shot* Underwater, of course. Specifically, Seven Sisters and the Tank, as well as Cedar Pride are popular spots. Bring an underwater camera.

SECRET Diving is not that much cheaper in Taba (if at all), despite rumors to the contrary. Reputable places all cost about the same, whether you're in Eilat, Aqaba, Taba, Dahab, or Sharm. You can of course find great deals, to mean one of two things: it's low season and the center is desperate for customers, or it's a scam and you get what you pay for.

MAP See L2/M2.

ITINERATOR!

DAYS/HOURS Open all year. Early morning/evening dives possible.

BEST TIME Surface water temperatures are in the upper 20s°C/low 80s°F in the winter, and rise to the low 30s°C/low 90s°F in the summer. That makes it pleasant all year long. Underwater temperatures are usually 21°C, though can get down to 18°C in winter. One thing to consider is the amount of drift (choppiness) in the water, which will make snorkeling and diving more difficult. There is a fair amount of drift all year, but it's mildest on the coastlines. The summer has the lowest choppy days (50 reported days of calm a year) in Red Sea/Gulf of Aqaba waters. Spring is the busiest period.

TIME COMMITMENT Timing is completely up to you, but keep in mind that diving and snorkeling trips are either half-day or full-day scheduled trips. If you're looking for something more flexible, you can go to a public beach and rent snorkeling equipment. For diving enthusiasts, you can organize several days in a row of introductory dives or PADI recertification.

SPEED RULES This is meant to be a relaxing/fun trip, so by speeding through you're doing it wrong.

COVERAGE In a morning or afternoon, you could snorkel with rented equipment off the city shore. Most dive trips can be completed in one day, with two or three dives, costing $75–100, often including food. In two or three days, take an "Intro to scuba" course. In five days, get your Open Water certification in scuba.

BASE This has to be done on a road trip (or by flying to Eilat or Sharm), as it's very far from any of our Anchor Cities. Depending on which country you are spending more time in, plan to do all of your activities in that one country, without crossing borders. Why? Because you can't take car rentals to other countries.

ANCHOR CITIES Jerusalem to Eilat: 315km/3¾ hours; Tel Aviv to Eilat: 350km/4 hours; Amman to Aqaba: 330km/4 hours; Suweimeh to Aqaba: 280km/3¼ hours.

ANCHOR FLIGHTS Amman to Aqaba: tickets as low as $50, normally $150–180; Ben Gurion to Eilat: as low as $80, normally $150.

BEST STRATEGY If this is part of a bigger tour, you should base yourself out of either Eilat or Aqaba, but visiting both is not necessary. Consider Eilat if your primary goal is snorkeling. Consider Aqaba or Sharm if you have intentions to scuba.

DIVING TRIPS You can organize both shore-based diving trips and boat diving trips as half-day, full-day, or multiday trips, depending on how much you love the water. There are a dozen or so dive shops in Aqaba, and just as many in Eilat, so you have lots of options. Taba is smaller, but Dahab and Sharm el-Sheikh further down the Egyptian Sinai are both hotspots for water activities. Communicating with your preferred dive center beforehand is encouraged, as boats tend to leave in the morning and require payment in cash in advance. The boat captains are relaxed, but if you're running late they might leave without you and you'll wait until the next day. Most folks spend two or three days just doing dive trips. This will include lunch, several stops, and an underwater guide/refresher training. Keep in mind that your PADI license should be up to date but, if not, you'll get a refresher certificate at an additional price (though not a lot of additional guidance, frankly).

RELAXED PLANNING For all-day boat excursions, you'll likely leave by 09.00 and return between 16.00 and 18.00. Preplanned tours will leave much earlier.

DAY TRIPPING Can it be done? Yes. Should it be done? Probably not.

WALKS AND DRIVES L1, L2, M1, M2, T1.

ITINERARIES Most Entertaining; Off-the-Beaten-Path Jordan; Nature and Scenic; Active; Under the Sun; Luxury; Kid-Focused.

ARRIVAL PREP

PREBOOK We recommend you prebook dives to guarantee a spot. At the very least, do some research, contact the companies, and make sure they have availability. They're usually casual, unless it's busy season. Popular dive centers with good reputations in **Eilat** are Nautilus, Palamida, Shulamit, Manta Isrotel, and Deep Siam; in **Aqaba** Deep Blue, Aqaba International Dive Center, Coral Garden, and Ahlan; in **Taba** Red Sea Waterworld, and Aqua Sport, while hotels also organize excursions (Mövenpick and Taba Hotel are popular); in **Dahab** Scuba Seekers, Octopus World, H2O, Poseidon, Sea Dancer, Big Blue, Shams, Orca, and Penguin; and in **Sharm** Pyramids, Reef Oasis, Red Sea Elite, and Ocean College.

TIPS Check out **w** divezone.net for reviews of a variety of diving sites, while **w** scubadiving.com has lots of well-researched articles on specific sites and regions.

CAUTION Snorkeling requires a certain amount of physical fitness. Go with a guide if you haven't swum in a while or have never tried snorkeling. Dive trips are not the activity where you want to go with the cheapest vendor. All dive centers are not created equally. Diving is dangerous and requires good equipment. It's also expensive, so better to pay $200 for an excellent day of dives than $100 for a quick dip in a trashy reef with ill-fitting equipment.

REALITY CHECK You may not like your dive center! If you're planning a multiday trip, perhaps only sign up for one day: make sure the boat and equipment is in good condition, the captain is to your liking, and you feel safe. Chances are you can join the next day's boat once you get to know the captain.

CONSTRAINTS Etgarim in Eilat offers scuba for people with disabilities. The legal minimum age for diving is 10 years, and children 10–12 years old should have parental supervision.

BRING Coral reef and/or fish guide, if you're a birder of the sea; snorkeling equipment; bathing suit; sunscreen; lots of water; cash tips; underwater camera (case).

DON'T BRING Disposable things to the beach as there are few trash cans, and the few there are always full. Plan to take away everything you bring.

PUBLIC TRANSPORT If you have a car, you can drive to your dive center, but most centers will pick you up from your hotel, which might bring an additional charge.

ACCESS Parking available at the dive centers. Some of the beaches also have public parking, though it might not be monitored or official, so don't leave anything valuable.

ADMISSION The Red Sea is free and open at all **public beaches**. **Private beaches** often offer snorkeling equipment: rates vary, usually $10–20, which may include pool and towel rentals. **Snorkeling** is the cheapest option: you can rent the gear on private beaches ($5–15) or use what your hotel has in stock, then swim out to shore on your own. **Guided snorkeling** is possible too. Eilat and Aqaba cost $75 for a group of two including pickup, equipment, towel; Taba a bit more at Red Sea Waterworld, but includes lunch. **Introductory dives** (without certification) cost about $50 in Eilat, $70 in Aqaba, $40 in Taba, $35 in Dahab, and $40 in Sharm. For a **pre-certified diver**, a first dive is $60 in Eilat, $50 ($70 at night) in Aqaba, and $40 in Sharm. An entry-level **PADI scuba diver course** (2–3 days) is $300 in Taba, $320 in Eilat, $350 in Aqaba, $225 in Dahab, and $215 in Sharm. **Open water certification** (3–5 days) is $500 in Eilat, $380 in Aqaba, $560 in Taba, $325 in Dahab, and $350 in Sharm. There are generally discounts with more dives, and boat dives tend to be more expensive than beach dives.

RECOMMENDED GUIDE A boat guide is required for diving. For books, check out the *Red Sea Reef Guide* by Helmut Debelius, if you can get your hands on it, or *Coral Reef Guide Red Sea* by Ewald Lieske.

VISITOR CENTER There isn't one visitor center as this site straddles three countries, but there are tourism bureaus in each of the countries who can direct you.

EAT Plenty in towns, though boat tours will provide basic food and drink.

SLEEP See individual cities for eat/sleep options.

BUCKET!PEDIA

Nomenclature Technically, the Red Sea is an inlet from the Indian Ocean, while the Gulf of Aqaba is an inlet of the Red Sea. The Red Sea includes the main channel of water, the Gulf of Aqaba, and the Gulf of Suez (which is entirely within Egyptian territory). The Gulf of Aqaba has Egypt at its west, Saudi Arabia at its east, and Israel and Jordan each with small coastal territories at the top. For diving purposes, the names "Gulf of Aqaba" and "Red Sea" are often used interchangeably, though notably there are "Red Sea" dive sites that are not on the Gulf of Aqaba, such as Hurghada on Egypt's Gulf of Suez. *Hebrew name* Yam Suf (Reed Sea)/Mifratz Eilat (Gulf of Eilat). *Arabic name* Al-Bahr al-Ahmar (Red Sea)/Khalij al-Aqabah (Gulf of Aqaba). *Historical name* Erythraean Sea. *Size* The Gulf of Aqaba is 160km long, 24km wide at its widest, and has a maximum depth of 1,850m.

CITIES The three northern Red Sea towns of Taba (T1) in Egypt, **Eilat (#78)** in Israel, and **Aqaba (#43)** in Jordan are essentially one metropolitan area divided into three distinct pieces due to borders and regional/ethnic tensions. One can access the Gulf of Aqaba from any of these places. On the Sinai peninsula, **Dahab (#54)** and **Sharm el-Sheikh (#88)** are popular spots to organize diving trips.

COUNTRIES Egypt, Israel, Jordan, Saudi Arabia.

CONTEXT In referring to the Red Sea or Gulf of Aqaba, this elective does not focus on the region's cities, which are reviewed elsewhere. Rather, we're going underwater to the extraordinary reefs that line the shores of the Gulf of Aqaba and provide excellent snorkeling and diving opportunities. Because of human pollution, the corals just off the coast tend to be a bit sad, trashy, and bleached. Due to industry, tourism, and pollution, colorful fish are far fewer in numbers these days, but you will certainly see them and find them remarkable. Getting away from the city centers will increase the quality and quantity of sea life sightings. Diving opportunities abound, and there are plenty of places to get you certified, if you're starting from scratch. Further down the eastern coastline, you'll run into Saudi Arabia which is not set up for Western tourism and is not reviewed here. The Egyptian coast arguably offers the best options, including the best diving in the world according to many: the National Park of **Ras Mohammad (#53)**.

GEOLOGY The Gulf of Aqaba sits in the Dead Sea Transform, a series of faults that are driving the African and Arabian tectonic plates apart. The transform runs through the center of the Gulf and up through the Dead Sea and Sea of Galilee, dividing Israel and Jordan. Interestingly, both plates are actually moving in the same direction, but one is just moving faster. This fault system caused the land to slip below sea level, forging the Dead Sea as the lowest place on Earth. That same fault affects the Gulf, pushing the Sinai away from Saudi Arabia and creating a trench 1,850m deep. Meanwhile, the Gulf of Suez on the other side of the Sinai is wider but much more shallow, never measuring more than 70m deep. The Dead Sea Transform is the northern extension of the greater Red Sea Rift, which is also pulling Somalia apart from the rest of continental Africa and will likely create a separated landmass within the next ten million years.

ARCHAEOLOGY The port at Aqaba has been used since Egyptian times, connecting land-based trade routes with sea routes. **Timna (#96)**, just north of Eilat, contains a large copper mine from the Neolithic age.

WEBSITE Eilat's official site is w eilat.city/en; Aqaba's tourist center maintains w international.visitjordan.com/Wheretogo/Aqaba.aspx.

WHERE TO NEXT?

THEMATIC *Noteworthy* Exploration. *Archaeology* Shipwrecks. *Nature* Sea Creatures, Reefs, Aquarium. *Active* Swimming; Diving; Snorkeling. *Leisure* Public/Popular Beaches; Fishing.

COMPLEMENTARY A couple of other diving sites are **Caesarea (#25)**, with an underwater port, and *Rosh HaNikra*. Other interesting animal experiences in the area are *Aqaba Bird Observatory (M2)*, Dolphin Reef (L2), and *Yotvata Hai-Bar*.

NEARBY In Israel, **Eilat (#78)** has a number of sites, many related to the water; it's also about 30km south of **Timna (#96)** park. In Jordan, **Aqaba (#43)** is a 2-hour drive from **Petra (#2)** and an hour's drive from **Wadi Rum (#4)**. In Sinai, crossing the border at Taba is a straightforward affair, but the trip to **Dahab (#54)** is 140km/2 hours further south, **Sharm el-Sheikh (#88)** is 220km/3 hours, and **Ras Mohammad (#53)** is 250km/3½ hours.

MACRO-REGION A

Top **Old City Jerusalem (#1)** is our top site in the region, with dozens of attractions in its 1km² walls. Catch this view from the Mount of Olives – see *City Walk A5*.

Right The **Jerusalem Archaeological Park (#71)** will introduce you to the Second Temple period of Jerusalem.

Bottom The **Dome of the Rock (#6)** is perhaps the most recognizable building in the Holy Land, and it is indeed a stunner.

MACRO-REGION A

Top The **Church of the Holy Sepulchre (#9)** commemorates where Jesus died and was reborn.

Middle The **Mount of Olives (#34)** is the location of an ancient Jewish cemetery and several churches celebrating the life and death of Jesus and his mother, Mary.

Bottom left **Al-Aqsa Mosque (#65)** is the third-holiest site in Islam.

Bottom right **Mount Zion (#92)** hosts several important sites, including the Room of the Last Supper and King David's Tomb.

MACRO-REGION A

Top **Temple Mount (#12)** is the raised ground on which stands the Dome of the Rock and Al-Aqsa Mosque.

Right The **Citadel/Tower of David (#32)** is a museum highlighting the history of Jerusalem whose walls and ruins span more than 3,000 years of history.

Bottom The **Western Wall (#11)** is the holiest site in Judaism and regularly hosts hundreds of visitors at at time.

MACRO-REGION A

Top The incomparable **Israel Museum (#17)** houses the Dead Sea Scrolls, among other art and artifacts.

Left **Jerusalem, New City (#72)** transitions "Jerusalem" away from ancient history and into the modern era, with pedestrian boulevards, coffee shops, open markets, and shopping.

Bottom left **Mehane Yehuda Market (#67)** is Jerusalem's premier market, and good for tourists looking for unique food and gifts.

Bottom right **Yad Vashem (#35)** is Israel's hope-inspiring Holocaust memorial museum.

MACRO-REGION C

Top The **Church of the Nativity (#18)** was built over the purported site of the birth of Jesus, where visitors can touch the ground where Jesus was born.

Right **Bethlehem (#40)** at Christmastime in Manger Square.

Bottom At **St. George's Monastery and Wadi Qelt (#97)** you can visit cliff-hanging monasteries inhabited by monks since the 5th century.

MACRO-REGION D

Top **Tel Aviv (#5)** is the modern antithesis of Jerusalem – a city of beaches, restaurants, cafés, and modern architecture.

Left **Jaffa (#30)** is the old Arab center of Tel Aviv, now incorporated as one unit, but maintaining its own unique personality.

Bottom left The **Modern Movement (Bauhaus Architecture) (#16)** is a UNESCO World Heritage site recognizing the more than 4,000 buildings in the German-inspired style.

Bottom right The **Tel Aviv Museum of Art (#95)** hosts Israel's best collection of modern Israeli art.

MACRO-REGION E

Top **Akko (#13)** is a walled city filled with Crusader-era ruins.

Right **Dor HaBonim (#100)** is perhaps the nicest stretch of sand on the eastern Mediterranean.

Bottom The **Bahá'í Gardens (#27)** are a gorgeous, structured plan of gardens celebrating the founder of the Bahá'í religion.

MACRO-REGION F

Top **Beit She'an (#39)** has a long history, including serving as one of Rome's Cities of the Decapolis.

Middle left **Belvoir (#93)** is one of the excellently preserved Crusader castles peppered throughout the region.

Middle right **Beit She'arim (#79)** is a UNESCO site honoring an extensive network of Jewish catacombs and accompanying sarcophagi from the 2nd century CE.

Left **Megiddo (#59)** is the present-day namesake of Biblical Armageddon, location of the end of days, now an archaeological site.

MACRO-REGION G

Top left **Tsipori (#56)** is home to more than 40 Byzantine mosaics.

Top right **Nazareth (#29)** was the site of the Annunciation of Mary and childhood home of Jesus.

Right The **Sea of Galilee (#7)** has a number of pilgrimage sites celebrating the life and ministry of Jesus Christ. Baptisms are a regular occurrence on the Sea's shore.

Bottom **Tabgha (#33)** is the location of the Church of the Multiplication of the Loaves and Fishes, pictured here, commemorating the miracle performed by Jesus.

MACRO-REGION I

Top left **Nimrod's Fortress (#85)** was built by Arab rulers to defend against the Crusaders and has great views of the valley below.

Top right **Banias (#80)** has rare Greek ruins as well as a picturesque boardwalk through the forest to a gushing waterfall.

Left The **Golan Heights Winery (#75)** introduced the world to quality Israeli wine and continues to impress.

Bottom The **Golan Heights (#62)** are claimed by Israel, historically Syrian, and are unlike the rest of the country with cooler weather, greenery, and even a snowcapped mountaintop for skiing.

MACRO-REGION J

Top **Avdat (#48)** is the largest of the Nabataean ruins in the Negev.

Right **Incense Route (#73)** sites are sprinkled through the south of Israel and Jordan and mark the waypoints where traders used to rest their camels.

Bottom **Makhtesh Ramon (#28)** is a rare erosion crater unique to Israel, with plenty of great hikes on offer.

MACRO-REGIONS K AND L

Top left **Ein Gedi (#50)** is a desert oasis replete with hiking trails, tree cover, and great views of the Dead Sea.

Top right The **Dead Sea (#3)** is one of our three BUCKET! electives, offering an unforgettable water experience.

Middle **Masada (#8)** has ruins that commemorate the final staging ground of the Jewish resistance during the Roman–Jewish wars.

Left The **Red Sea/Gulf of Aqaba (#10)** is famous for its snorkeling and scuba and can be accessed from Taba, Eilat, or Aqaba in Egypt, Israel, and Jordan, respectively.

MACRO-REGIONS M AND N

Right Aqaba (#43) is Jordan's southernmost city and has several diving outfitters to explore the nearby reefs and shipwrecks.

Middle Petra (#2) is as mysterious as it is mesmerizing and deserves at least three days of your time.

Bottom Wadi Rum (#4) has an otherworldly landscape you can explore on foot or by jeep, with many choosing to stay the night in tents or glamping huts.

MACRO-REGION 0

Top The **Madaba Map (#19)** is the oldest map of Jerusalem yet found and is just one part of the sprawling series of mosaics found in the town of Madaba.

Left **Dana Biosphere Reserve (#21)** offers visitors nature galore: endemic animals and birds, wildflowers, a pristine desert landscape, and enticing day walks.

Bottom **Feynan Ecolodge (#86)** prides itself on its desert conservation efforts, while also incorporating local Bedouins who participate in all-inclusive activities such as tea ceremonies, cooking demos, and bush walks.

MACRO-REGIONS P AND Q

Right **Mount Nebo (#24)** honors the Biblical site where Moses is said to have died after leading his people from slavery and laying eyes on the Promised Land.

Middle **Ancient Amman (#37)** has a number of fascinating ruins right in the heart of its downtown.

Bottom **Modern Amman (#36)** showcases the food, culture, and activities of Jordan's principal city.

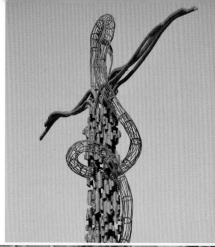

MACRO-REGIONS S AND U

Top **Jerash (#14)** contains arguably the best Roman ruins in the entire region.

Left **Umm Qais (#45)** is an off-the-beaten-path gem in Jordan's north.

Bottom The **Biblical Tels (#38)** are three UNESCO sites that each represent thousands of years of human history and whose discoveries continue to influence the historical record of the Holy Land.

#11 Western Wall

BROCHURE

RATINGS

BUCKET! Score		7/10
Ruin		5/5
Entertainment		2/5
Information		3/5
Popularity		5/5

MACRO-REGION
A: Jerusalem

MICRO-REGIONS
A1, A2, A4

PRIMARY THEME/CATEGORY Structure – Monuments – Historic Monuments.

TOP Holiest Jewish site.

HOLY LAND RELEVANCE The Western Wall is the holiest place in Judaism. It is the closest spot to the since-destroyed Second Temple's Holy of Holies room, the holiest spot on Earth (see **Temple Mount (#12)**), to which Jews are not permitted access due to ongoing struggles with Arab neighbors and the fact that it's covered by the Dome of the Rock. Jews have been visiting the Western Wall as a symbol of the Temple since the destruction of the Temple in 70 CE.

ELECT ME! The Western Wall is, not surprisingly, the westernmost wall – and nearly all that remains – of Herod's once-grand Temple Mount complex. The Wall is the holiest site in Judaism and the place to see Jewish culture and religion come together. It's a quick visit that is a must-see stop on all Jerusalem tours.

WORTH THE DETOUR? Yes, it's a must-see spot on any Old City tour.

EXPERIENCES

CAN'T MISS Peek into the Wall itself. You'll see hundreds of pieces of paper wedged between the stones. These are prayer notes. You can submit one, if you're inclined, but don't pull out any others!

Only men are allowed to enter on the left side of the Wall, where you can find a complimentary kippeh/yarmulke. Place it on the crown of your head to show respect, regardless of religion. You can return the kippeh as you leave. Women can also approach the Wall, but from the middle of the plaza, adjacent to the scaffolding holding up the pedestrian bridge to Temple Mount. Head and shoulder coverings are not provided, but are recommended. The women's side is separated from the men's side by a makeshift wall.

This is somewhere to people-watch. The ultra-religious/ultra-orthodox come to the Wall to pray and lament the loss of the Holy Temple. There are many types of dress and mannerisms depending on the sect.

SITES From left to right:

★ *Wilson's Arch* This arch is adjacent to the left/men's side of the Wall, inconspicu-ously serving as the entrance to a cavelike synagogue. It's actually the topmost part of a grand arch that once supported a street connecting the "Upper City" to

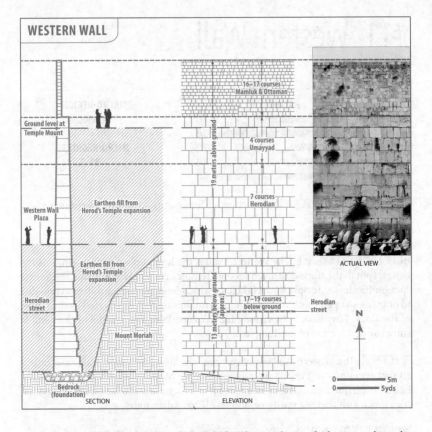

WESTERN WALL

16–17 courses
Mamluk & Ottoman

Ground level at
Temple Mount

4 courses
Umayyad

19 meters above ground

Western Wall
Plaza

Earthen fill from
Herod's Temple expansion

7 courses
Herodian

Earthen fill from
Herod's Temple
expansion

Herodian
street

17–19 courses
below ground

Herodian
street

13 meters below ground
(approx.)

Mount Moriah

ACTUAL VIEW

N

Bedrock
(foundation)
SECTION

ELEVATION

0 — 5m
0 — 5yds

Temple Mount. The rest is underneath the plaza and extends down to where the street level used to be (see **Western Wall Tunnels (#94)**). It was named after Charles Wilson who surveyed the site in 1865.

★ *Stone Courses* Surveying the Wall, you can count 28 courses (rows) of stones from the plaza to the top. The first seven are thick Herodian-era stones that were part of the Wall's original construction. The next four are from the Umayyad period, 600 years later. (Note that the ground level of present-day Temple Mount starts on the other side of the Wall from the third Umayyad course.) The next 17 courses have much thinner stones and were added by the Ottomans.

★ *Visitor entrance to Temple Mount* Access **Temple Mount (#12)** via the wooden platform on the southern end of the plaza. Walk towards Dung Gate and security will be on your left. Requires a passport and modest dress.

★ *Robinson's Arch* This feature can be seen from the **Jerusalem Archaeological Park (#71)** near the southwest corner of the Western Wall, or from one of the elevated platforms as you approach the exit. Halfway between the ground and the top of the Wall are the remains of a curved structure, now collapsed. The feature was named after Edward Robinson who determined this was once a great stone archway leading Jews from the "Lower City" up massive steps to the Temple complex above. All that remains is this broken arch.

★ *Western Wall Tunnels (#94)* Most interestingly, about 40% of the Wall is below ground and extends to the original street level. You're standing on an artificially raised platform high above the true ground! You can see the full extent of the Western Wall on this underground tour. Advance reservation necessary. Entrance is in the middle set of arches on the northernmost end of the plaza (not the Wall itself). Highly recommended.

SECRET Photos are not allowed on Western Wall Plaza. However, you can get a great shot of the Wall (while still being respectful of worshippers) by ascending the huge staircase on the northwest side of the plaza opposite the Wall, exiting left, and walking the back streets until you find an open plaza offering expansive views of the Wall and the Dome.

SPECIAL EVENTS Tisha B'Av (usually in July or August) is the traditional day revered for praying at the Wall, and gets tens of thousands of visitors. Passover, Sukkot, and Shavuot are also busy.

ITINERATOR!

DAYS/HOURS Always open.

TIME COMMITMENT Speed rules apply. You do not need to budget much time here unless you're going for long prayers. The whole experience of walking to the Wall and back (and even writing a note) will take 10–20 minutes. Note: timing does not include **Western Wall Tunnels (#94)**.

BASE Anchor from Jerusalem or Tel Aviv.

BEST STRATEGY The site is easy to find and navigate. Combine it with your **Temple Mount (#12)** entry, **Western Wall Tunnels (#94)** tour, and/or visit to the **Jerusalem Archaeological Park (#71)**. Also, if you want to avoid crowds and hit the major sites early, the Western Wall doesn't close and Temple Mount opens at 07.30, so you can see both of these sites before they are mobbed. The **Church of the Holy Sepulchre (#9)** also opens early, if you want to hit all three of Jerusalem's major sites early.

WALKS AND DRIVES A1, A2, A4.

ITINERARIES Jerusalem Immersion; High BUCKET! Scores: 7+; Most Popular; Complete Ruins; Noteworthy; Religion; Structure; UNESCO; Shoestring; Big-Group Friendly; Pilgrimage.

ARRIVAL PREP

PREBOOK Not necessary.

REALITY CHECK Be aware of your surroundings. Don't be disrespectful, loud, take photos without permission, pray without the appropriate attire, or attempt to visit the opposite sex's side. There is security everywhere and violaters will be dealt with swiftly and sternly. Photography is *not* permitted on the Shabbat. No playing with or talking on your phone on any day. No smoking. This is a popular tourist spot and can get very crowded.

BRING Your own head covering. (Men, if you need a kippeh, there are plenty to borrow.)

ACCESS There are four ways to enter the Western Wall Plaza, so it's difficult to miss. Each requires that you pass security, including screening of bags and bulky clothing items, similar to an airport screening.

ADMISSION Free. But special occasions (bar/bat mitzvah) require reservations.

RECOMMENDED GUIDE None required. For detailed background and tutorial on customs, you'll want a Jewish guide (ideally local). Set up in advance (w english. thekotel.org/tours/) or use a private service (w newjerusalemtours.com; free for basic, 120 ILS for expanded).

BUCKET!PEDIA

AKA "Wailing Wall" (now pejorative). *Hebrew name* Kotel HaMa'aravi (Kotel, for short). *Historical era* Roman/Byzantine: Herodian. *Year constructed* 19–4 BCE. *Size* The visible portion in the Western Wall Plaza is 57m (187 feet) long × 19m (62 feet) tall, though the entirety of the Wall (much of which is hidden behind buildings in the Muslim quarter) is 488m (1,601 feet) long. From its foundation to its top, the Wall is 32m (105 feet) tall.

CONTEXT The Western Wall is one part of a vast retaining wall, built by King Herod in 19 BCE, which was meant to physically support the weight of his monumental building projects on Temple Mount. Though a simpler "Second Temple" had already been built many centuries earlier (following the destruction of the First Temple) in 516 BCE, Herod had a grander vision. He decided to double the area of the mount, level the grounds, and create a masterful and renovated temple dedicated to God that was built over the Foundation Stone – the peak of Mount Moriah. This was where, according to biblical tradition, God created Adam from the earth, Abraham came to sacrifice Isaac, and where once stood the First Temple.

To complete this project, Herod built an entirely new platform that would serve as a retaining wall, to hold up the Temple, its sub-rooms and auxiliary buildings, and allowed the site to take a more deliberate rectangular shape. Without these retaining walls, the massive buildings would have sunk into the earth below. To create these new walls, Herod's engineers cut and shaped massive blocks of stone, precisely placing them next to one another without sealant, filler, or holes, and layered them 24 courses high. This was no simple feat: the largest stones weigh upwards of 500,000kg!

Herod completed the project and built his Temple, but his masterpiece wouldn't last. The Temple was destroyed when Rome sacked Jerusalem during the Roman–Jewish wars in 70 CE. The Romans not only destroyed the Temple, but also many of the other monumental structures present, including most of the retaining walls. Very little – except the Western Wall – remains from the Second Temple period. However, the Romans reportedly started their disassembly from the topmost layers. Many courses from the Western Wall were tossed to the valley floor below, with the lower layers becoming buried beneath the rubble. And they remained intact.

Over the following centuries, Jews were banned outright from visiting Jerusalem save for one day a year – Tisha B'Av – when Jews were permitted entry and wept for its loss, earning it the name of "Wailing Wall." Because the Temple had been destroyed, the Western Wall became the closest location in proximity to the Foundation Stone/Holy of Holies, where the Ark of the Covenant was kept in the Temple. The Romans removed all of that and had placed pagan statues atop Temple

Mount. These were replaced in 692 CE with the Arab arrival and their construction of the Dome of the Rock over the Foundation Stone, it being a central story in the narrative surrounding Muhammad's Night Journey to Jerusalem when he visited his prophet forefathers.

The Wall went through periodic changes over the centuries. Above ground, the bottom seven courses were the only original stones from Herod's time. The Umayyads added the four large middle courses, while the upper smaller courses were added during recent Islamic rule in the late 19th and early 20th centuries.

After the recapture of Jerusalem in 1967, Israeli leaders gave control of Temple Mount to a neutral Jordan, but chose to expose the Western Wall – the closest spot available to the Holy of Holies – from behind centuries-old buildings. To do so, they evacuated and leveled the Moroccan Quarter to make room for the Western Wall Plaza.

The plaza is now an open area for prayer, visits, remembrance, and celebration. Devout Jews regularly visit the Wall to read the Torah, chant, and write notes to God. These notes are placed in the cracks of the Wall, which you can see by visiting up close. Hasidic men can often be seen rocking back and forth while "studying." But you will witness all types of religious people wandering around, from secular to ultra-orthodox. You may even catch a religious ceremony – bar/bat mitzvahs are popular.

CHRONOLOGY

586 BCE: First Temple is destroyed.

516 BCE: Second Temple is constructed on Temple Mount.

19 BCE: Herod expands the Temple complex, and builds four retaining walls to support the growing number of buildings.

70 CE: Second Temple destroyed. Only Western Wall remains. Entrances dismantled, including Robinson's Arch.

135: Jews banned from Jerusalem.

4th century: Constantine permits Jews to visit the site once per year to weep.

637–692: Muslims conquer Jerusalem and build Al-Aqsa Mosque and the Dome of the Rock on Temple Mount, where they still stand, on top of what is believed to be the ruins of the Second Temple.

7th century: Umayyads add four courses on top of the remaining wall.

12th century: Moroccan Quarter established adjacent to the Western Wall with housing and narrow alleyways.

1866: Ottomans add an additional 14 layers.

1948: With Old City Jerusalem under Jordanian control following the 1948 Arab–Israeli War, access to the Western Wall is halted altogether for 19 years.

c1966: Before Israelis take control, a Muslim cleric has three courses added.

1967: Following the Six-Day War, Israel regains control over Jerusalem. Moroccan Quarter bulldozed to make way for Western Wall Plaza, a place for Jews to gather and pray.

WEBSITE Explore w english.thekotel.org for information on the site's history and to reserve for special events, such as bar/bat mitzvah.

WHERE TO NEXT?

THEMATIC *Noteworthy* Unique. *Religion* Judaism; Kings, Prophets, and Saints; Pilgrimage; Ceremonies and Events. *Archaeology* Herodian; Impressive Structural Remains. *Structure* Iconic Structures; Historic Monuments; Memorial; Impressive

Feats; Infrastructure. *Scenic* People-Watching. *Society* Borders; Disputed. *People* Jewish; Orthodox Jews.

COMPLEMENTARY For further understanding, visit the **Western Wall Tunnels (#94)** on the north end of the plaza (**w** english.thekotel.org/western_wall_sites/western_ wall_tunnels/); **Jerusalem Archaeological Park (#71)**; and **Temple Mount (#12)**.

NEARBY *Jewish Quarter* sites (*City Walk A4*), including the complementary sites, plus the *Cardo*, the Sephardic Synagogues (A4), the *Wohl Archaeological Museum*, and Hurva Square (A4). If you exit from Dung Gate, you're only a block from the *City of David*.

#12 Temple Mount

BROCHURE

	RATINGS		MACRO-REGION
BUCKET! Score	████████░░░░░	5/10	A: Jerusalem
Ruin	█████████████	5/5	
Entertainment	██████░░░░░░░	2/5	**MICRO-REGIONS**
Information	███░░░░░░░░░░	1/5	A1–A4
Popularity	█████████████	5/5	

PRIMARY THEME/CATEGORY Structure – Monuments – Historic Monuments.

TOP Holy spot for Jews and Muslims.

HOLY LAND RELEVANCE There is perhaps no place more relevant than Temple Mount when we talk about the Holy Land. Here, atop Mount Moriah, Abraham was called by God to sacrifice his son, Isaac. Solomon's Temple would later be built on this very spot, with the center called the Holy of Holies, the most sacred spot in Judaism. After the First Temple was destroyed, Herod's Temple (the Second Temple) was built here as well. Muhammad is said to have traveled here to visit the farthest mosque, which is what "Al-Aqsa" means. He ascended to Heaven from atop Mount Moriah, and after the destruction of the Second Temple by Romans in 70 CE, Muslims had a blank canvas to celebrate Temple Mount, and built the Dome of the Rock to commemorate the ascension.

ELECT ME! When visiting the **Dome of the Rock (#6)**, you're standing on top of Temple Mount, the elevated walled structure taking a large swath of the eastern part of Jerusalem, which also holds **Al-Aqsa Mosque (#65)** and other Islamic buildings. This is an essential stop on any tour of Jerusalem.

WORTH THE DETOUR? Given that you can't enter the two major sites unless you're Muslim, you may feel content with views from afar (**Western Wall (#11)**, **Mount of Olives (#34)**, or other high site), but you won't regret getting close to see the detailing of the tiles on the dome.

EXPERIENCES

CAN'T MISS **Dome of the Rock (#6)**, radiating spectacularly on top of Temple Mount.

ON TOP **Al-Aqsa Mosque (#65)**, a functioning mosque, built by the Umayyad dynasty in the 8th century CE, making it one of the oldest mosques in the world; *Dome of the Chain*, a possible model for Dome of the Rock, featuring a supreme interior ceiling with amazing tile work from the 13th century; *Fountain of Sultan Qaytbay*, a beautiful, 13m, carved *stone* dome dating from 1482 (the only exemplar outside Egypt).

ON WALLS **Western Wall (#11)** is the western retaining wall of the ancient Herodian structure, and the closest place Jews can get to the Holy of Holies, now the rock under the **Dome of the Rock (#6)**; **Western Wall Tunnels (#94)** provide a guided tour of ancient Jerusalem, seeing the absolutely massive foundation stones that were used to create Temple Mount; and **Jerusalem Archaeological Park (#71)**, just south of the Western Wall, covers ruins on and around the southern wall highlighting what Temple Mount once looked like and how it was accessed by Jerusalemites 2,000 years ago.

ACTIVITIES Help sort through excavated Temple Mount material at the *Temple Mount Sifting Project (A6)*, or leave a prayer note in the **Western Wall (#11)**.

SECRET Praying on Temple Mount is not allowed for Jews or Christians. If you are seen visibly praying or pulling out religious paraphernalia (e.g., a Bible), you will be approached or removed by Waqf authorities.

SPECIAL EVENTS Actually, avoid any special events happening on site. This is a site of frequent conflagration and you do not want to be mixed up in protests or religious fighting.

ITINERATOR!

DAYS/HOURS Sunday–Thursday, winter 07.30–10.30 and 12.30–13.30, summer 08.30–11.30 and 13.30–14.30, but times change frequently. Closed Fridays, Saturdays, and Muslim holidays. Everything limited during the month of Ramadan.

BEST TIME When open! Limited hours. You should arrive early if visiting on a Sunday. Long queues are not unheard of.

TIME COMMITMENT Speed rules apply. Given that **Dome of the Rock (#6)** and **Al-Aqsa Mosque (#65)** do not permit entry to non-Muslim guests, a visit to Temple Mount could be very quick indeed. To do a quick walk around the Dome of the Rock, you need only 10–15 minutes. If you want to circumnavigate the entire Temple Mount complex, plan on 30 minutes. Photos are permitted, so add an additional 10–15 minutes to capture your "photo of the year" winner. If you're on a tour, you could spend at least an hour learning about the site.

BASE Located in Anchor City Jerusalem.

BEST STRATEGY Structure your visit so you are in the Old City on a day other than Friday or Saturday (site closed). Also, go early: avoid the crowds; have the best chance of a tourist-free plaza in front of the Dome; skip the midday heat; visit before you go shopping as no religious paraphernalia is allowed.

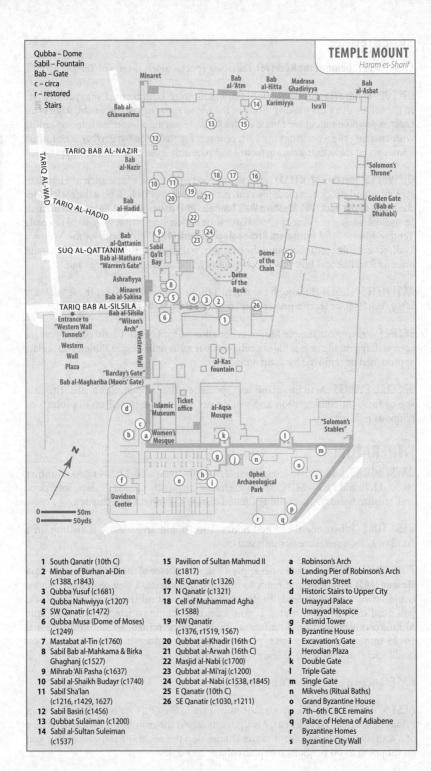

TEMPLE MOUNT
Haram es-Sharif

Qubba – Dome
Sabil – Fountain
Bab – Gate
c – circa
r – restored
▦ Stairs

Minaret
Bab al-'Atm
Bab al-Hitta
Madrasa Ghadiriyya
Bab al-Asbat

Bab al-Ghawanima
Karimiyya
Isra'il

TARIQ BAB AL-NAZIR
Bab al-Nazir

TARIQ AL-WAD
TARIQ AL-HADID

"Solomon's Throne"

Golden Gate (Bab al-Dhahabi)

Bab al-Hadid

SUQ AL-QATTANIM
Bab al-Qattanin
Bab al-Mathara "Warren's Gate"

Sabil Qa'it Bay

Dome of the Chain

Ashrafiyya
Minaret Bab al-Sakina

Dome of the Rock

TARIQ BAB AL-SILSILA
Bab al-Silsila "Wilson's Arch"
Entrance to "Western Wall Tunnels"
Western Wall Plaza

"Barclay's Gate"
Bab al-Maghariba (Moors' Gate)

Western Wall

al-Kas fountain

Islamic Museum
Ticket office

al-Aqsa Mosque

"Solomon's Stables"

Women's Mosque

Ophel Archaeological Park

Davidson Center

N

0 ——— 50m
0 ——— 50yds

1 South Qanatir (10th C)
2 Minbar of Burhan al-Din (c1388, r1843)
3 Qubba Yusuf (c1681)
4 Qubba Nahwiyya (c1207)
5 SW Qanatir (c1472)
6 Qubba Musa (Dome of Moses) (c1249)
7 Mastabat al-Tin (c1760)
8 Sabil Bab al-Mahkama & Birka Ghaghanj (c1527)
9 Mihrab 'Ali Pasha (c1637)
10 Sabil al-Shaikh Budayr (c1740)
11 Sabil Sha'lan (c1216, r1429, 1627)
12 Sabil Basiri (c1456)
13 Qubbat Sulaiman (c1200)
14 Sabil al-Sultan Suleiman (c1537)

15 Pavilion of Sultan Mahmud II (c1817)
16 NE Qanatir (c1326)
17 N Qanatir (c1321)
18 Cell of Muhammad Agha (c1588)
19 NW Qanatir (c1376, r1519, 1567)
20 Qubbat al-Khadir (16th C)
21 Qubbat al-Arwah (16th C)
22 Masjid al-Nabi (c1700)
23 Qubbat al-Mi'raj (c1200)
24 Qubbat al-Nabi (c1538, r1845)
25 E Qanatir (10th C)
26 SE Qanatir (c1030, r1211)

a Robinson's Arch
b Landing Pier of Robinson's Arch
c Herodian Street
d Historic Stairs to Upper City
e Umayyad Palace
f Umayyad Hospice
g Fatimid Tower
h Byzantine House
i Excavation's Gate
j Herodian Plaza
k Double Gate
l Triple Gate
m Single Gate
n Mikvehs (Ritual Baths)
o Grand Byzantine House
p 7th–6th C BCE remains
q Palace of Helena of Adiabene
r Byzantine Homes
s Byzantine City Wall

212

WALKS AND DRIVES A1, A2, W1.

ITINERARIES High BUCKET! Scores: 7+; Most Popular; Structure; Big-Group Friendly; Pilgrimage.

ARRIVAL PREP

PREBOOK Not applicable.

REALITY CHECK Because of turmoil, the Temple Mount is administered by Jordan. Jews are warned against entering the area. Non-Muslims are barred from entering the **Dome of the Rock (#6)** or **Al-Aqsa Mosque (#65)**. The whole site is frequently a locus of conflagration. Though most of the time it's quite peaceful, violence can erupt from seemingly nowhere. Exercise highest precautions when visiting.

Be on your best behavior: there are police everywhere. Respect the land. It's sacred to everyone. No graffiti, littering, spitting, etc. Modest dress. You will not be permitted access if your shoulders and knees aren't covered. Renting a shawl will cost you more than buying a shawl, and involves stapling a blanket around you (not comfortable ever, let alone when hot). Dress modestly, even on hot days.

BRING Passport is essential. Modest dress is also required or you will be forced to pay to cover up. Do *not* bring religious gear or accessories, including if you purchased some in the Old City.

ACCESS There are several access points to Temple Mount leading from side streets on the northern and western walls. These are for Muslims only. (Though you may be able to capture a photo if you ask the guard politely, stay your distance, and do so quickly.) Tourists must enter from the Western Wall Plaza, just south of the **Western Wall (#11)** and to the left. The large wooden platform leading up to Temple Mount should be your guide as to where to enter. Walk south from the plaza towards Dung Gate (not up the ramp that says "Exit") and the security gate will be on your left.

ADMISSION Free to enter, but you must present a passport and go through security screening.

RECOMMENDED GUIDE This is history-dense territory. If you're inclined, pick up an archaeology-focused book such as the *Oxford Archaeological Guide to the Holy Land*.

VISITOR CENTER There is a small museum on Temple Mount, but it has seen better days. There is no brochure and the plaques outside were bleached from the sun years ago.

BUCKET!PEDIA

AKA Haram es-Sharif ("the noble sanctuary"). *Historical era* Ancient Israel: Iron Age to Modern. *Year constructed* The current mount was built in the reign of Herod around 19 BCE. *Size* 36–37 acres (150,000m²).

CONTEXT First, terminology. The "Temple" refers to King Herod's Second Temple, while "Mount" refers to the top of Mount Moriah and what is called the Foundation Stone.

A thousand years before King Herod, though, there was the United Kingdom of Israel. This was a particularly relevant period of self-rule in Jewish history which began about 1000 BCE. King David defeated the local Jebusites who were living on the hill south of Mount Moriah (today, the *City of David*). David's son, Solomon, vowed to build a temple to honor God on the site where God was said to have gathered the dust of the earth to create Adam, and from where Abraham was to sacrifice Isaac before Isaac was spared. This spot became known as the Foundation Stone. It's believed that Solomon's Temple was built here and a sacrificial altar placed over this stone.

Solomon's Temple housed the Ark of the Covenant, a golden chest containing the original stone tablets upon which the Ten Commandments were scribed. The Ark was placed in a special room known as the Holy of Holies. As the name implies, this was the most important site in Judaism and the directional focus of all prayer.

Jews were exiled by the Babylonians from the Holy Land in 586 CE and Solomon's Temple was destroyed. No archaeological evidence has yet confirmed its existence, though it is widely believed to have been constructed on Mount Moriah. A few decades later, Persian rulers welcomed Jews back from exile and agreed to the construction of a new, simpler temple to replace the destroyed one. It stood there for centuries, despite a succession of foreign powers taking over Jerusalem.

Sometime around 20 BCE, King Herod of the Roman Empire ordered a massive expansion of the Second Temple on the same site. He was known for his incredible building projects and this site was to be like no other. Herod's architects designed a foundation with sturdy walls and countless tons of backfill that could support the weight of the buildings. Once filled in, Herod leveled the surface and built his Second Temple over the Foundation Stone. This new leveled surface became known as Temple Mount.

The new temple, called Herod's Temple, is referenced several times in the New Testament. It stood in its place until the end of the Jewish–Roman war of 67–70 CE, when the Roman Empire had had enough and sacked the city. (Herod had died many decades prior in 4 BCE.) Herod's Temple, or the Second Temple, was completely destroyed. Again, little evidence of its existence has been uncovered, so total was its destruction. Even the Temple Mount itself was partially destroyed, as can be seen today along the southern portion of the wall, with massive boulders still in situ from when Roman soldiers tried knocking the walls down with battering rams. The Western Wall now serves as proxy to the former Temple, as it is the closest location to the historic Holy of Holies.

Since 70 CE, Jews have not had regular access to Temple Mount. Beginning with Byzantine rule, Jews were only allowed to visit the former temple grounds from afar one day a year, on Tisha B'Av (the ninth day of Av). As Muslims took over the Holy Land following Muhammad's conquest of Jerusalem in 638 CE, the Muslim connection to Temple Mount became clear and long-lasting, with the construction of the grand Dome of the Rock and Al-Aqsa, now two of the holiest sites in Islam. The Dome of the Rock was built atop the same Foundation Stone that once housed the Ark of the Covenant and the Holy of Holies, the inner sanctum of the Temple. Since then, Jews continue to pray in the direction of the former (and future) Temple, which is to say Temple Mount. (Muslims once prayed towards Jerusalem, too, but this practice ended early on, and Mecca became the uniform direction of prayer.)

Fast-forward 1,200 years. After Israel's declaration of independence in 1948, Jerusalem remained in a state of flux. Israelis claimed Jerusalem as their capital, but it was not until 1967 that Israel defeated its Arab neighbors and established control of the Old City. Israel cleared out many buildings in the Moroccan Quarter, which backed up against the Western Wall. Jewish leaders created an open area, now

Western Wall Plaza, so Jews could again pray in the direction of the Holy of Holies, still located underneath the Dome of the Rock. Jewish law – rather than Muslim law – actually prevents Jews from getting close to the site lest they accidentally enter the area of the historic Holy of Holies (should it not be exactly where the Dome of the Rock today stands) and inadvertently desecrate the space. Despite its win, Israel handed over administration of Temple Mount to the Islamic Waqf of Jordan in 1967 in order to keep the peace, and that arrangement has stayed constant to the present day.

Palestinians view Jerusalem as an occupied capital. The United Nations recognizes Jerusalem as the capital of a future Palestinian state. Non-Muslims are not allowed to pray on the site, or they will be escorted out. Thus, few Jews are seen on Temple Mount, and even Christians are not permitted to bring religious items on site.

Little evidence exists of the First or Second Temple, unfortunately. A select few artifacts have been discovered that connect Temple Mount with that period of history from 1000 BCE to 70 CE. Muslims refuse any requests from Israel or external parties to conduct archaeological digs on their consecrated ground. That said, the governing Islamic Waqf has conducted a couple of minor construction projects that have led to middle-of-the-night truckloads of earth being dumped on land east of the city. Israeli officials promptly took possession of that soil and began excavations, sending a sharp rebuke to the Waqf for purposefully trying to erase Jewish history.

What is buried in Temple Mount, beneath the soil under Dome of the Rock and Al-Aqsa? It's hard to know and unclear if anyone will ever find out given the current political environment. The original retaining walls were 30m high, about 500m long, and about 300m wide. That's an awful lot of dirt to sift through. Who knows what treasures lie buried beneath the surface?

CHRONOLOGY

957 BCE: Site of First Temple, built by King Solomon, son of King David.

586 BCE: First Temple destroyed by the Babylonians under Nebuchadnezzar II (alternative Jewish dates: 832–422 BCE).

516 BCE: Persian governor Zerubbabel leads Jews out of captivity in Babylon and helps build a modest Second Temple on the site of the destroyed First Temple.

19 BCE: Herod constructs the Temple Mount with four massive retaining walls to handle the earthen fill that is required to level the mount and support the weight of an expanded Second Temple, its surrounding buildings, and waves of visitors.

70 CE: The Jewish–Roman War ends with the near utter destruction of Jerusalem, including the Second Temple and parts of its supporting structure.

135: Failure of the Kokhba revolt to return Temple Mount to Jews instead results in Jews being banished, save for one day a year: Tisha B'Av.

691: Dome of the Rock constructed on the cleared site of Temple Mount, at or near the site of the First and/or Second Temple.

1967: Israel captures Jerusalem in the Six-Day War. Declares Jerusalem its capital. To ease tensions, Israel asks Jordan to retain custodianship over Temple Mount.

WHERE TO NEXT?

THEMATIC *Religion* Judaism; Holiest Jewish Places; Islam; Kings, Prophets, and Saints; Jesus: Early Life; Muhammad; Hebrew Bible/Old Testament; New Testament; Ancient Manuscripts; Biblical Battlefields; Mosques; Oldest and Ancient Mosques; Other Holy Places; Pilgrimage. *Archaeology* Tels; Iron Age; Empires; Herodian; Roman; Byzantine/Christian; Islamic I; Impressive Structural Remains. *Structure* Iconic

Structures; Historic Monuments; Memorial; Impressive Feats; Infrastructure. *Society* Politics; Military; Borders; Disputed. *People* Arab. *Culture* Museum of Archaeology.

COMPLEMENTARY Follow along with *Old City Chronotour* (**w** buckettravelguides.com/old-city-chronotour).

NEARBY See **Old City Jerusalem (#1)**.

#13 Akko

BROCHURE

	RATINGS		MACRO-REGION
BUCKET! Score		8/10	E: Mediterranean Coast
Ruin		4/5	
Entertainment		4/5	**MICRO-REGIONS**
Information		5/5	E2, E5
Popularity		4/5	

PRIMARY THEME/CATEGORY Archaeology – Islamic – Crusader.

TOP Crusader city.

COMMENDATIONS UNESCO World Heritage Site, 2001.

HOLY LAND RELEVANCE The best historical site from Crusader history (11th–13th centuries CE) in the Holy Land.

ELECT ME! Ancient port and harbor, now with a pleasant walled old town to explore, and a healthy modern mix of Jews, Christians, Muslims, and Bahá'í. Come here for Crusader history and excellent food.

WORTH THE DETOUR? Absolutely. It's a big fortified city on the water with tunnels and underground chambers that are fun to explore. Plus, great food.

EXPERIENCES

CAN'T MISS The Subterranean Crusader City, which includes the Hospitaller Fortress/ Knights' Halls (E2). Interestingly, it was at street level during the Crusader era, but successive conquerors simply built on top of the ruins instead of removing them, paving over, and starting fresh.

SITES (explanations in *City Walk E2*): Citadel of Akko/Knights' Kingdom; Okashi Art Museum; Underground Prisoners' Museum; Treasures in the Wall Museum; Al-Jazzar Mosque (E2); Hospitaller Fortress/Knights' Halls (E2); Turkish Bath; Templar Tunnel; City Walls.

ACTIVITIES Browse the Sunday market; dine at *Uri Buri*, a delectable seafood restaurant right near the parking lot; and lunch at Hummus Said (E2) in the market, and fill yourself with perhaps the world's best hummus for only a few shekels.

SECRET Bahá'í holy places, including the *Shrine of Bahá'u'lláh*, are nearby. These gardens and temple are in the pristine Bahá'í style and part of the UNESCO World Heritage Site that includes the Bahá'í Gardens in *Haifa*. The Akko gardens are in fact the most important Bahá'í site in the world.

SPECIAL EVENTS Take a boat tour around the peninsula to see the city walls (check with boat captains, who leave when the boats fill; should be about 25 ILS). Walk around town at night, when everything is lit. Around Sukkot, the Fringe Theatre Festival takes over many of the sites (prebooked tickets are required to enter).

MAP See E2.

ITINERATOR!

DAYS/HOURS Most sites open 08.30–09.30 and close 17.00–18.00. Closed Jewish holidays.

BEST TIME Tends to be empty on Fridays, packed on Saturdays, moderate the rest of the week.

TIME COMMITMENT Speed rules apply. Expect 2 hours to walk the town, visiting the visitor center and Hospitaller Fortress/Knights' Halls (E2), and grabbing lunch at Hummus Said (E2) (if there's no wait and you eat quickly). Four hours will allow you a leisurely trip to all of the sites on the walking tour, and three-quarters of a day will allow you to add a visit to the *Shrine of Bahá'u'lláh* and one other local site, or add a sensory dining experience at *Uri Buri*. Spend the whole day and plan to eat well all day, visit the shrine, sleep in one of the great hotels (possibly), and/or drive to/from your preferred Anchor City.

BASE Overnighting on a road trip here is a luxurious affair; the good hotels are as nice as they are pricey. You can easily visit from Anchor Cities Tel Aviv (120km/1½ hours) or Rosh Pina (55km/1 hour).

BEST STRATEGY Akko is easy to visit on a day trip from Tel Aviv, or as a waypoint on the way to/from the Galilee/Golan. Old Akko is easy to figure out and you'll run into the major attractions.

WALKS AND DRIVES E2, E5, W4, W5.

ITINERARIES High BUCKET! Scores: 7+; Most Entertaining; Noteworthy; Society and People; Culture; Food and Drink; Organized; UNESCO; Endangered; National Parks/Reserves; Relaxation; All Ages.

ARRIVAL PREP

PREBOOK Not necessary (but see *Special Events* above).

REALITY CHECK Usually safe. Exercise normal cautions at night, if you are staying over. Parking can be a problem if you arrive on a weekend, but Fridays are typically empty (Arab religious day, so many businesses are closed).

ACCESS Park in the seaside parking lot on the southwestern tip of the peninsula which houses the walled Old Akko and meander on foot.

ADMISSION You can buy a comprehensive ticket (64 ILS) at the first site, the Templar Tunnels. There are other ticket options, which include removing the Turkish Bath, adding *Rosh HaNikra*, and a virtual-reality headset for 10 ILS.

RECOMMENDED GUIDE Most of the information is through visual and auditory aid (lots of videos/holograms), which are enough for the average visitor. If you want detailed history, there's a good museum, but the website's walking tours provide excellent detail (**w** akko.org.il/en/routes/).

VISITOR CENTER Located in the same complex as the Knights' Halls, the visitor center closes at 16.00 on Fridays and the day before holidays.

EAT *Uri Buri*: just really, really good seafood (in a country where seafood is not always great, honestly). Order *prix fixe*, or by the dish. Hummus Said (E2): dirt-cheap hummus place with a very limited menu, but satisfying, delicious hummus, pickles, pita, and water. Maadali (E2): tiny kitchen serving Palestinian tapas.

SLEEP Two highly regarded hotels here are the Efendi (E2) and Akkotel (E2), both five-star, beautifully modern, architectural buildings incorporating elements of Old Akko. The Efendi incorporated two 19th-century Ottoman palaces into its construction, which themselves were built over Byzantine and Crusader buildings. Akkotel actually incorporates the walls of Old Akko into its design and previously served as military quarters during the Ottoman era.

BUCKET!PEDIA

AKA Akka (Arabic); Acre (older English spelling); Ptolemais (to the Greeks). *Historical era* Primarily *Islamic: Crusader* to *Ottoman*. *Year founded* Unknown, possibly 5,000 years old. *Size* 13km². *Population* c50,000. *Ethnic mix* Jewish 65%, Muslim Arabs 27%, Christian Arabs 3%, other (Druze, Bahá'í) 5%.

CONTEXT In addition to being one of Israel's few functioning multicultural cities, Akko has done excellent work to preserve its older part, Old Akko, and keep it tourist-friendly without losing the natural town feel. The town is very easily done on foot. Individually, the town's sites are nice, if not exactly mesmerizing. However, taken together, they create an impressionable experience (thanks to many video enactments) of the ancient Crusader town of Acre. Within the town are synagogues and mosques, markets and restaurants, houses and people. The port is beautiful. The old walls look pristine – but that's because they're only 200 years old, as the Ottomans fortified them from the crumbling, thinner walls that came before. Excavations are under way to understand the much more ancient history of this city. Just outside the city walls is "Tel Akko," where archaeologists hope to better understand Akko's Phoenician history and the impact of Assyrian rule. Remains of the ancient sea harbor can be seen from the southern walls. Underwater surveys take place periodically to date these original fortifications and continue to place Akko throughout important moments in history, often because of its coveted natural sea harbor.

CHRONOLOGY

c3000 BCE: Possibly the town's first settlement.

15th century BCE: Akko mentioned in the curses of the kings of Egypt. Conquered by Tutankhamen III.

333 BCE: Occupied by Alexander the Great and settled by Greeks.

261 BCE: Ancient name of Akko is changed to Ptolemais.

c36 CE: St. Paul visits the first Christian communities.

66–68: During the Great Jewish Revolt, some 2,000 Jews are murdered in Akko.

640: City conquered by Muslims.

1104: City conquered by Crusaders during First Crusade. Used for its strategic location and port.

1187: City capitulated to Saladin of the Ayyubids.

1191: Richard the Lionheart (Third Crusade) takes the city back and declares it the capital of the Kingdom of Jerusalem (Crusader state).

1291: Mamluks defeat city, which is the last Crusader stronghold. Despite continued residency, city begins a state of disrepair over next 400 years.

1750: Daher el-Omar, a Bedouin, settles in the ruins and builds impressive walls.

1775: El-Jazer, an Ottoman ruler, continues the work (after executing el-Omar) of fortifying the walls.

1799: Napoleon attempts a siege of the city, but over two months is repulsed by Turkish and British fighters.

1840: Akko becomes the capital of the northern region of Palestine under the Ottomans. City shelled during Egyptian–Ottoman war of same year.

1918: Ottomans lose World War I; British move HQ to Haifa; Akko loses significance.

1948: Israel wins Arab–Israeli War, reclaims ownership of Akko.

2001: Akko declared a UNESCO World Heritage Site.

WEBSITE w akko.org.il/en/.

WHERE TO NEXT?

THEMATIC *Noteworthy* UNESCO; Endangered; Exploration. *Archaeology* Crusader; Walls; Historical Battlefields; Impressive Structural Remains. *Structure* Technological Advancement. *Nature* Earthquakes. *Society* Streets, Squares and Ports; Large Towns. *People* Secular Life; Arab. *Leisure* Fishing. *Food and Drink* Culinary Capital. *Organized* Cooking School/Food Activities; Digs.

COMPLEMENTARY You have quite a few Crusader-era castles to visit in the Galilee, including **Tsipori (#56)**, **Belvoir (#93)**, and **Beit She'an (#39)**, as well as *Montfort* and *Yehi'am*. More Crusader ruins can be found south along the coast at **Caesarea (#25)** and *Apollonia*. As an ancient city with a multilayered history and multiple sites to visit within Old Akko's walls, Akko has the most in common with **Old City Jerusalem (#1)**.

NEARBY Nahariya (E5) (11km/20 minutes), *Akhziv Beach* (15km/25 minutes), *Rosh HaNikra* (20km/25 minutes), and **Bahá'í Gardens (#27)** in *Haifa* (30km/30 minutes).

#14 Jerash

BROCHURE

RATINGS

BUCKET! Score	▰▰▰▰▰▰▱▱▱	7/10
Ruin	▰▰▰▰▱	4/5
Entertainment	▰▰▱▱▱	2/5
Information	▰▱▱▱▱	1/5
Popularity	▰▰▰▰▱	4/5

MACRO-REGION
S: North Jordan

MICRO-REGION
S1

PRIMARY THEME/CATEGORY Archaeology – City Conglomerates – Cities of the Decapolis.

TOP Roman ruins in the Holy Land.

HOLY LAND RELEVANCE Jerash was subject to most of the same waves of conquest and rulership as other major cities in the region, such as Jerusalem. Ancient Gerasa's history dates back to Neolithic man, continues through ancient Greek and Roman history (Jerash's heyday), and follows from Christian rule to Muslim to Christian and back again.

ELECT ME! Forget **Caesarea (#25)**, these are the region's most impressive Roman ruins. With far fewer crowds and covering a large area, you'll feel like you've discovered them yourself. Just an hour from Amman, this is a must-see site for any trip to Jordan. The ancient city, with its churches, temples to Greek gods, and Arab population is a good microcosm of this region's long and turbulent history.

WORTH THE DETOUR? Absolutely, and a no-brainer if you have the Jordan Pass.

EXPERIENCES

CAN'T MISS The unusual forum, built as an oval rather than a rectangle, with no other fora found like this in the Roman pantheon. Normally fora are the primary focus of a city, but likely the Temple of Artemis served as Gerasa's focal point.

SITES

★ *Hadrian's Arch* Gallant entrance, built in honor of Emperor Hadrian.

★ *Hippodrome* Chariot racing! 15,000-seater.

★ *Forum* The first big plaza you see after walking past the Hippodrome – a place from which to gaze upon the majesty of the whole site. It's in an oval shape, which is strange, and gigantic.

★ *Cardo Maximus* A 600m-long street with visible chariot tracks. All along would have been shops and buildings.

★ *Agora* A public meeting space, with excavated shops where the public bought food.

★ *Trio of churches* St. George, St. John, and Saints Cosmas and Damien, all three share a covered courtyard (atrium) and were built around 533 CE, with stunning mosaic floors.

- ★ *Nymphaeum* A lovely fountain to nymph gods, 2nd century CE.
- ★ *Temple of Artemis* The largest in Jerash as Artemis served as the patron goddess of Gerasa. Built around 150 CE but never completed. Impressive columns.
- ★ *Sanctuary of Zeus* Built atop an earlier temple, this sanctuary was finished in 166 CE, and destroyed later as evidenced by the columns strewn about the field.
- ★ *South Theater* Restored to host the Jordan Festival each year, seating up to 3,000 spectators, it was built at the end of the 1st century CE.
- ★ *South Gate* The entrance to Jerash from the 4th century CE, a duplicate of Hadrian's Arch, though smaller.

ACTIVITIES Watch a modern reenactment of a **chariot race** in the ancient hippodrome. Watch **Jordanian musicians** perform at the South Theater (daily, except Tuesdays). Participate in the **Jerash Festival**, held annually in the summer.

SPECIAL EVENTS The Jordan Festival takes place every summer in cities throughout Jordan. The **Jerash Festival** is one component of the Jordan Festival, and aims to celebrate local and international cultures through music and dance (**w** www.erashfestival.jo). The **Roman Army and Chariot Experience** occurs every day except Tuesdays (**w** jerashchariots.com; 12 JD adults, 2 JD children). The **Sound and Light Show Jerash** (20.00–22.00; 2 JD) plays in different languages on different evenings: contact the visitor center for more information.

ITINERATOR!

DAYS/HOURS Summer 07.30–19.00, winter 08.00–17.00. Evenings are occasionally open for the Sound and Light Show.

BEST TIME If visiting in the summer, try to arrive early or late due to the extreme heat and little shade.

TIME COMMITMENT Speed rules apply. In 2 hours, you can make a loop of the main sites: Hadrian's Arch, Hippodrome, Agora, Temple of Zeus, and South Theater, ending at the Temple of Artemis. Four hours offers time for a casual walk through all the city's sites.

BASE Anchor from Amman.

BEST STRATEGY Jerash is an easy day trip from Amman or the Dead Sea (Jordan side), or a long day trip from Jerusalem. The site itself is easy to navigate, though not so easy to find if self-driving, so pay attention to signs. Plan to spend several hours on site, though you can sprint through the highlights if you're short on time and headed to many places in one day. This is a good starting point for a round-trip from Amman to other sites up north (**Umm Qais (#45)**, **Ajloun Forest (#57)**, **Ajloun Fortress (#76)**). If you don't want to rent a car, there are same-day-return bus tours regularly leaving from Amman.

WALKS AND DRIVES S1, V1, V2, W3.

ITINERARIES Amman Immersion; High BUCKET! Scores: 7+; Off-the-Beaten-Path Jordan; Big-Group Friendly.

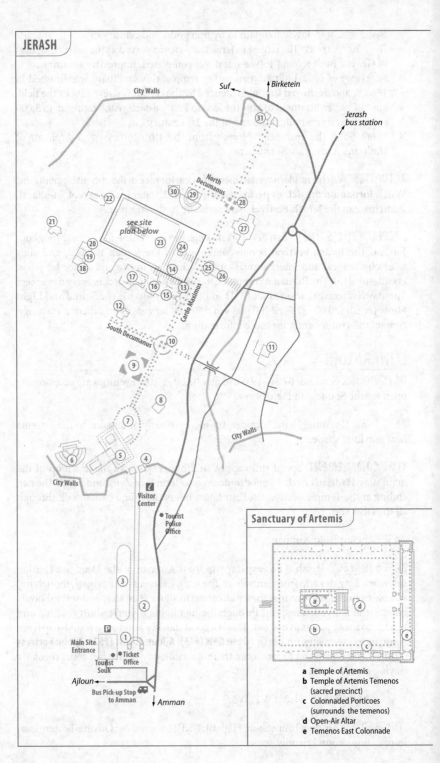

JERASH

City Walls

Suf → ← Birketein →

Jerash bus station

North Decumanus

㉛

㉚ ㉙ ㉘

㉒

see site plan below

㉓ ㉔

㉗

㉑

㉕

㉖

㉖

⑳
⑲
⑱

⑰ ⑯ ⑮

⑭
⑬

⑫

South Decumanus

⑩

⑪

Cardo Maximus

⑨

⑧

⑦

City Walls

⑥

⑤

④

City Walls

Visitor Center

● Tourist Police Office

③

②

ℹ

P
Main Site Entrance

① ● Ticket Office

● Tourist Souk

Ajloun ←

Bus Pick-up Stop to Amman 🚌

↓ Amman

Sanctuary of Artemis

a

d

b

c

e

a **Temple of Artemis**
b **Temple of Artemis Temenos** (sacred precinct)
c **Colonnaded Porticoes** (surrounds the temenos)
d **Open-Air Altar**
e **Temenos East Colonnade**

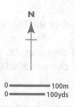

N

0 ——— 100m
0 ——— 100yds

▦ Stairs

1 Hadrian's Arch
2 Church of Bishop Marianos
3 Hippodrome
4 South Gate
5 Sanctuary of Zeus
6 South Theater
7 Forum (Oval Plaza)
8 Museum
9 Agora (Macellum)
10 South Tetrapylon
11 East Baths
12 Umayyad House
13 Nymphaeum
14 Stepped Street
15 Cathedral
16 Fountain Court
17 Church of St. Theodore
18 Church of St. George
19 Church of St. John the Baptist
20 Church of Saint Cosmas and
   Saint Damien
21 Church of Bishop Genesius
22 Synagogue-Church
23 Sanctuary of Artemis
24 Altar Terrace
25 Propylaeum Plaza
26 Byzantine Church
27 West Baths
28 North Tetrapylon
29 North Theater
30 Church of Bishop Isaiah
31 North Gate

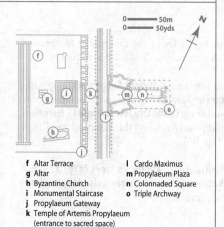

0 ——— 50m
0 ——— 50yds

N

f Altar Terrace
g Altar
h Byzantine Church
i Monumental Staircase
j Propylaeum Gateway
k Temple of Artemis Propylaeum
   (entrance to sacred space)
l Cardo Maximus
m Propylaeum Plaza
n Colonnaded Square
o Triple Archway

ARRIVAL PREP

PREBOOK Not necessary.

REALITY CHECK Sun-exposed and hot during midday. Bring lots of water. You may be asked for change or conversation from poor children while wandering the sites. Expect tour guides to try hard to win your dinars.

ACCESS The site is located in downtown Jerash. Follow signs for ruins once you enter the town. There is parking available on site.

ADMISSION 10 JD including Jerash Archaeological Museum, or free with Jordan Pass. Credit cards accepted, but have cash handy.

RECOMMENDED GUIDE These are ruins; as the name implies, you won't always be able to identify what you see. There are many colossal things to view within the site which will impress you without explanation, and if you're running through, you might be satisfied with just the visual aspect. But, for a bit of context, you'll need a guide. There are plenty who will approach you upon arrival. You needn't stick with the first person who accosts you. Ask for tour guide ID and go with the person whose English you understand best and negotiate the rate at the beginning – it should be around 20 JD.

VISITOR CENTER Yes, there is a visitor center, along with a museum that's included in the price. One can rent an audio guide, buy a guidebook, or obtain a map here. A brochure can be requested from the ticket booth, though they are not available 100% of the time.

EAT/SLEEP Head back to Amman.

BUCKET!PEDIA

AKA Gerasa; Antioch on the Golden River; one of the ten Cities of the Decapolis. *Historical era* Roman/Byzantine: *Judea* to *Syria Palaestina*.   *Year founded/ constructed* c4500 BCE, but the ruins date to the 1st and 2nd centuries CE, from Pompey through Trajan and Hadrian.   *Size* At its largest, the city was 800,000m² within its walls.

CONTEXT A shockingly impressive series of ruins in an unexpected location. The site is quite large so, even on busy days, the long colonnaded streets will keep you separated from big groups. Much of the site remains in good repair. The columns are wonderful and it's very easy to envision the city in its heyday, which is not true for many "ruins." There's a nice variety of Roman and Greek styles, and you'll recognize the hippodrome, theater, archways, and cardo. These are of excellent quality, and will tickle anyone who appreciates a nearly pristine ancient city.

CHRONOLOGY

Neolithic era (7500–5500 BCE): Possible human settlements in Jerash (two rare human skulls were discovered here in 2015).

331 BCE: Alexander the Great's forces found the city of Gerasa.

63 BCE: Conquered by Pompey.

90: Jerash absorbed into the province of Arabia (capital Amman, or Philadelphia).

1st to 2nd centuries: Principal construction period.

130: Emperor Trajan visits. Entry arch built in his honor.

450–611: Construction of churches, mostly out of pagan temples.

614: Persian invasion causes rapid decline.

749: Earthquake destroys much of the city.

1878: City is finally repopulated.

1925: Excavations begin, unearthing ancient Gerasa from a millennium's worth of sand that had accumulated, covering the site.

1981: Jerash begins hosting the Jerash Festival of Culture and Arts.

WEBSITE w international.visitjordan.com/Wheretogo/Jerash.aspx; w kinghussein. gov.jo/tourism3.html.

WHERE TO NEXT?

THEMATIC *Archaeology* Prehistory; Roman; Cities of the Decapolis; Impressive Structural Remains. *Structure* Historic Monuments. *Nature* Earthquakes.

COMPLEMENTARY Other Roman ruins in Jordan are **Ancient Amman (#37)** (specifically its Citadel), **Pella**, **Petra (#2)**, and **Umm ar-Rasas (#81)**, and in the wider region **Beit She'an (#39)**, **Caesarea (#25)**, Herod's buildings in **Old City Jerusalem (#1)**, **Herodion (#90)**, and **Masada (#8)**, including Roman camps surrounding the mount. Other Cities of the Decapolis to visit feature in *Road Trip W3*.

NEARBY **Ajloun Forest (#57)** (23km/40 minutes), **Ajloun Fortress (#76)** (25km/ 35 minutes), **Ancient Amman (#37)** (50km/50 minutes), **Umm Qais (#45)** (68km/ 1¼ hours), and the **Dead Sea (#3)** (94km/1½ hours).

#15 Mount Sinai

BROCHURE

RATINGS

BUCKET! Score		5/10
Ruin	n/a	
Entertainment		1/5
Information		3/5
Popularity		2/5

MACRO-REGION
T: Sinai

MICRO-REGION
T1

PRIMARY THEME/CATEGORY Religion – Holy Books – Hebrew Bible/Old Testament.

TOP Old Testament site.

HOLY LAND RELEVANCE Moses is a prophet in the Abrahamic religions of Judaism, Christianity, and Islam. The moral code that he received from God inscribed in stone was said to have been delivered atop Mount Horeb. Mount Horeb has not been conclusively identified, but is recognized by scholars as Mount Sinai. The Ten Commandments of God, written down by Moses, identified the basic ethical principles for the Israelites. The commandments form the basis of Jewish *halakha*, or law.

ELECT ME! Many tourists pay homage to Moses' self-imposed exile on Mount Sinai, where he waited 40 days to receive the Ten Commandments from God. Today, a hike to the top of the mountain is the quest. The real draw begins in the middle of the night when a caravan of cars departs from **Dahab (#54)** or Nuweiba on a 2-hour drive to the base, giving hikers plenty of time to summit the mountain in time to catch the sunrise.

WORTH THE DETOUR? If you're in the Sinai, it's a very popular day trip from any of the beach destinations. At time of writing, the Sinai is still considered dangerous according to many countries' travel warnings. If you understand the risks and decide to go, the overnight (sometimes) trip, the steep climb, the spiritual component, and the beauty of the sunrise/sunset overlooking the vast desert will certainly be a memorable experience.

EXPERIENCES

CAN'T MISS The summit, obviously, but also **St. Catherine's Monastery (#22)** at the base of the mountain.

SITES The **Chapel of the Holy Trinity**, a Greek Orthodox chapel built in 1934, is closed to public – it is said to contain the rock from which the Ten Commandments were inscribed onto tablets (called the "Tablets of Stone"); **Moses' cave**, where Moses waited alone for God's message those 40 days; and a functioning **mosque** at the summit.

ACTIVITIES Hike Siket El Bashait ("Camel Path," 2½ hours, moderate), or Siket Sayidna Musa (45 minutes–3 hours, steep) with its 3,750 steps to reach the summit, called the "Steps of Penitence." Both of these lead you to an amphitheater, the "Seventy Elders of Israel," named after the elders who accompanied Moses on his journey to "God's Mountain." From here, at Elijah's Basin (or Hollow), walkers take 750 more steps to the summit. You can also organize treks to nearby mountains, such as Mount Catherine, at the Mount Sinai trek office.

SECRET Get a good night's sleep. Eat breakfast. Then drive to **St. Catherine's Monastery (#22)** mid-morning and tour the facility before it closes at noon. Start your hike mid-afternoon and catch sunset instead. There will be far fewer people and you'll be able to see the path while hiking up. (Careful about midday hikes: the sun will be too hot.)

MAP See T1.

ITINERATOR!

DAYS/HOURS The mountain hike doesn't close, but you'll want to tack on a visit to **St. Catherine's Monastery (#22)**, which is only open mornings, 09.00–noon.

BEST TIME Most everyone makes the trek in the wee hours of the morning, which is when it's dark and cold. The busiest hours are in the middle of the night. If you're visiting in winter, go in the daytime. If in summer, go overnight.

TIME COMMITMENT The whole affair will likely take around 14 hours, door to door. If you leave at night (c23.00), expect to return mid-afternoon the next day. Speed will play a factor in how long it takes to ascend, which can be anywhere from 45 minutes to more than 3 hours. That said, if you're going for an event such as sunrise or sunset, rushing to the top won't matter very much, and it's coldest up there.

BASE There are guesthouses near **St. Catherine's Monastery (#22)**, but it's just as easy to depart from your hotel for a day trip from **Dahab (#54)**, Nuweiba, or **Sharm el-Sheikh (#88)**.

BEST STRATEGY Organizing a day trip is easy because everyone will be advertising this trip on the Sinai coast. You should absolutely use a tour guide to complete this circuit. We used to recommend a self-drive itinerary, but it's no longer safe. When you arrive at the base, you are required to hire a Bedouin guide whose job is to take you up the mountain safely via one of the two paths. We recommend afternoon ascents, but the midnight one is the more popular and highly regarded, albeit cold.

WALKS AND DRIVES T1.

ITINERARIES Noteworthy; Religion.

ARRIVAL PREP

PREBOOK You can reserve with a local tourism agency upon arrival at your hotel.

REALITY CHECK The Sinai has recently become a hotbed of terrorist activity aimed particularly at unsuspecting tourists. **Read your country's travel warnings** before deciding to travel. ISIS and other militant groups have taken refuge in the region.

Police convoys are sometimes set up to ensure stability in the region, so **your drive may take longer than anticipated** as the security apparatus does its best to keep you safe. It's always **cold and windy**, especially at the summit (it's a mountain!), so make sure you bring warm clothes any time of the year. It's **high elevation** with **uneven paths** – as you are climbing several thousand steps, keep in mind that limited medical care is available. This used to be a **popular tour stop**, but tourism decreased substantially once Egypt began having civil problems. However, when tourism is high, the mountain can get very crowded, particularly at sunrise. The chapel at the top of the mountain is regularly **closed**, so temper your expectations.

BRING Warm clothes; good walking/hiking shoes; water bottle; camera; tip money.

ACCESS The drive takes 2–3 hours, often leaving in the middle of the night in order to start the sunrise trek. Enter from the monastery and choose your preferred path: the Steps of Penitence (short and steep) or the Camel Path (gradual and longer).

ADMISSION Organize rates with your hotel or tour company before making the trek. You will likely need to tip your guide before you leave.

RECOMMENDED GUIDE Guides are required, so make sure you understand yours and feel comfortable with him. If you're wanting to take the stairs instead of the tourist/camel path, make sure you make that clear when booking.

VISITOR CENTER Not really, though you can use either **St. Catherine's Monastery (#22)** or the nearby village as a staging ground.

EAT Several restaurants at the base of the mountain.

SLEEP Camping occurs just below the summit at Elijah's Basin/Hollow. You can rent blanket and mattresses at the top, but cleanliness is a reported issue. You can also camp or hotel near **St. Catherine's Monastery (#22)** at the base of the mountain.

BUCKET!PEDIA

AKA Gebel Musa ("Moses' Mountain" in Arabic). *Elevation* 2,285m above sea level. *Historical era* Prehistoric: Bronze Age. *Years active* Unknown exactly when Moses visited, but he is estimated to have lived around 1500 BCE.

CONTEXT According to the books of Exodus and Deuteronomy, Moses first met God on Mount Horeb (now Mount Sinai). God revealed himself to Moses in a burning bush (where St. Catherine's Monastery currently sits) and commanded Moses to free his people from slavery. Upon Moses' successful return to the Mount, God proclaimed to Moses the Ten Commandments, a set of ten principal rules that became the moral code of Israelites and later Jews and Christians. God requested that Moses ascend Mount Horeb/Sinai in order to receive the commandments in written form. After 40 days of waiting, Moses received two tablets with the Ten Commandments etched in stone by the finger of God.

The story gets more complicated, as Moses descended the mountain to find his worshipers had instead begun worshiping a goat because he had taken too long, so Moses broke the tablets in a fit of rage. He then reascended the mountain, got two new tablets, and those tablets were the ones that went into the Ark of the Covenant in the Holy Temple in Jerusalem (First Temple). To this day, Mount Sinai remains synonymous with the Ten Commandments.

Today, the mountain is a place of reflection following a strenuous early-morning hike with the reward of a beautiful sunrise. It is not the highest peak in the Sinai, but sits next to Mount Catherine, which is the highest in Egypt.

WEBSITE w egypt.travel/en/attractions/mount-sinai-trekking.

WHERE TO NEXT?

THEMATIC *Noteworthy* UNESCO; Nature Reserves. *Religion* Judaism; Christianity; Kings, Prophets, and Saints; Old Testament; Quran. *Archaeology* Bronze Age. *Nature* Mountains and Mounts. *Scenic* Historical Vantage; Earth Panorama; Sunrise/Sunset. *Active* Tough Hikes. *Accommodation* Campgrounds.

COMPLEMENTARY More Old Testament sites: Abraham nearly sacrificed Isaac on Mount Moriah, now **Temple Mount (#12)**; Abraham and his clan are buried in Hebron at the **Tomb of the Patriarchs (#46)**; and **Mount Nebo (#24)** is where Moses laid to rest. Important Jewish sites: the **Western Wall (#11)** is the closest spot to Mount Moriah accessible to Jews today, and the **Tomb of the Patriarchs (#46)** in Hebron is one of Judaism's Four Holy Cities, along with **Old City Jerusalem (#1)**, **Tsfat/Safed (#58)**, and *Tiberias*. For the best of Sinai, follow *Road Trip T1* or our *Best of the Sinai* itinerary (p. 764).

NEARBY From **St. Catherine's Monastery (#22)** at the base of mountain, Nuweiba is 119km/2–2½ hours, **Dahab (#54)** is 129km/2–2½ hours, and **Sharm el-Sheikh (#88)** is 212km/2½–3½ hours.

#16 Modern Movement (Bauhaus Architecture)

BROCHURE

	RATINGS		MACRO-REGION
BUCKET! Score		7/10	D: Tel Aviv
Ruin		5/5	
Entertainment		2/5	**MICRO-REGIONS**
Information		4/5	D3, D4, D5
Popularity		4/5	

PRIMARY THEME/CATEGORY Structure – Architecture – Architectural Styles.

TOP Largest collection of Bauhaus buildings in the world. And if that's not enough, Bauhaus is considered by some to be the most influential school of thought in design.

COMMENDATIONS UNESCO World Heritage Site, 2003.

HOLY LAND RELEVANCE Tangentially related, this architectural movement coincided with waves of Jewish immigration that followed the rise of totalitarianism and ethnic and religious marginalization (and eventually genocide), leading to an exodus of Jews from Europe and the need for greater, bigger cities in Israel. Tel Aviv was a new, mostly empty city which benefited from the rapid influx in population from European immigrants and could incorporate and adapt the contemporary styles of the day upon this desert canvas.

ELECT ME! Tel Aviv carries the nickname "The White City" due to the more than 4,000 1930s-era Bauhaus-style buildings concentrated downtown. A UNESCO site dedicated to the Modern Movement (and not just Bauhaus), there are interesting buildings all throughout the city which can be seen on any of our Tel Aviv walking tours.

WORTH THE DETOUR? Tel Aviv is likely on your list of places to visit. If you have any interest in architecture whatsoever, it's absolutely worth a couple of hours of your time to learn what makes this city unique.

EXPERIENCES

CAN'T MISS Bialik Square with *Bialik House* and Beit Ha'ir (D3), plus *Rothschild Boulevard* for Bauhaus. Pagoda House (D4) is a popular stop for Eclecticism.

ARCHITECTURE IN THE INTERNATIONAL STYLE For **Bauhaus**, see below; **Eclectic** is when a building incorporates historic styles in an original way to create something new; from the 1950s, the **Brutalist** style prioritizes the building material (often concrete) over the aesthetic; and **Modernist** signifies innovative designs in construction with the idea that form should follow function.

BAUHAUS DESIGN FEATURES Block balconies; hard, 90° angles, but also wavelike angles; flat roofs; small, recessed windows; straight lines; purposeful absence of decoration; full shadows; staircases (spiral is important); asymmetry; and Eclectic styles.

STREETS AND REGIONS, CONCENTRATIONS OF BUILDINGS Bordering Allenby to the south, Yarkon to the north, the sea to the west, and Ibn Gabirol and Begin roads to the east, the principal area of interest comprises Bialik Street, *Rothschild Boulevard*, Dizengoff Street, Dizengoff Square, Shlomo Hemelech Street, and the Florentin (D4) neighborhood.

SECRETLY NOT PART OF THE UNESCO DESIGNATION, BUT ALSO FUN TO SPOT Postmodernist weirdness (Crazy House (D1), 2 Trumpeldor); contemporary (**Tel Aviv Museum of Art (#95)**, Peres Center, *Design Museum Holon*); funky skyscrapers (Meier on Rothschild (D5), Azrieli Sarona Tower (D5), Azrieli Center (D3)).

WALKING TOURS Check out *City Walk D5*. The Bauhaus Center at 99 Dizengoff offers English-language walking tours every Friday at 10.00, starting at the Bauhaus Center (80 ILS). If you can't make Friday, the Center also offers other languages at other times, and an audio tour option which you can rent for 80 ILS. The Tel Aviv

Tourist Information Office offers free Bauhaus tours every Saturday at 11.00 (no need to reserve in advance; meet at 46 Rothschild Boulevard, corner of Shadal Street), and Liebling Haus and the White City Center offer a variety of tours which can be customized for groups (**w** whitecitycenter.org/general-info).

MAP See D5.

ITINERATOR!

DAYS/HOURS Most of the buildings are residences and not open to the public. Those with visiting hours should have times posted outside. The Bauhaus Center is open 10.00–19.00 Sunday–Thursday, 10.00–14.30 Friday. Group tours start every Friday at 10.00 at the Center. The self-guided tour is available 10.00–15.00 Sunday–Thursday, 10.00–12.00 Friday, closed Saturday.

TIME COMMITMENT Speed rules apply. The self-guided walk or tour with the Bauhaus Center will take 1½–2 hours; doing both will take half a day.

BASE This site is located in Anchor City Tel Aviv.

BEST STRATEGY Schedule a tour with the Bauhaus Center and spend 1½ hours with an expert who can point out architectural points of interest. Then, when you're doing your *City Walk D3/D4* tours, cross-reference with *City Walk D5* to take in some other modern-style buildings with your newfound knowledge.

WALKS AND DRIVES D3, D5, W5.

ITINERARIES Tel Aviv Immersion; Complete Ruins; Noteworthy; Structure; Organized; UNESCO; Endangered; Fine Arts; Modernity.

ARRIVAL PREP

PREBOOK The Bauhaus Center recommends booking its tours in advance. You can pop in the day before or pay online.

REALITY CHECK Sourced from an architecture snob: there are more beautiful versions of Bauhaus buildings in the world. Many of the buildings are in various states of disrepair. Instead, you can find outstanding examples of Brutalist-style architecture throughout Tel Aviv, particularly among hotels along the beach. These concrete masses with their elemental repetitions cast very expressive shadows creating unique and beautiful patterns at different hours of the day.

BRING Street map, as identifying the buildings is tricky at first.

ACCESS You can see most of the building facades from the street.

ADMISSION There's no cost to look at buildings, but the tours cost money (80 ILS for Bauhaus Center's guided and self-guided audio tours).

RECOMMENDED GUIDE We recommend either of the two options with Bauhaus Center; being able to ask questions is always helpful when trying to understand art.

VISITOR CENTER Visit the Bauhaus Center for a tour, books, and historic photos. Museums in Bialik Square also offer historical information on the Bauhaus movement.

EAT/SLEEP See *City Walk D3*.

BUCKET!PEDIA

AKA The White City; Bauhaus Movement; International Style. *Historical era Modern*.

YEARS CONSTRUCTED 1920s for Eclecticism; 1930s for Bauhaus; 1960s for most Brutalist.

CONTEXT Bauhaus was an art school founded by Walter Gropius in the Weimar Republic, Germany, and later headquartered in Dessau and Berlin. Following the rise of Nazism and the closure of the school in Germany, a number of German Jewish architects left Germany for Palestine where they found an outlet for their stylistic movement in the new town of Tel Aviv (established in 1909). The local climate changed the traditional Bauhaus style a little, given the different weather, including extreme heat. Some elements were substituted for others: for instance, smaller, recessed windows took the place of large glass windows. Roofs were made flat for social spaces. Large, thick, layered balconies provide appropriate shade for the residents' balcony just below. Today, more than 4,000 buildings comprise the White City of Tel Aviv, with many clustered around the city center and the major thoroughfares of Dizengoff Street and Rothschild Boulevard. The name "White City" derives from the light-colored concrete, which is a recognizable hallmark along many streetscapes. The best way to get a sense of the style is to take a walking tour of the city, organized by the Bauhaus Center Tel Aviv.

WEBSITE Unofficially, **w** bauhaus-center.com.

WHERE TO NEXT?

THEMATIC *Noteworthy* UNESCO; Endangered. *Structure* Architectural Styles; Modern Architecture. *People* Jewish. *Organized* Guided.

COMPLEMENTARY For more Bauhaus try Weizmann House, **Weizmann Institute of Science**, Rehovot (greater Tel Aviv), or **Bonem House (A7)**, corner of Rambam and Arlosoroff Street, Jerusalem. For more Bauhaus in Jerusalem, read *Bauhaus: Jerusalem* by Ulrich Knufinke (**w** bauhaus-center.com/gallery-art-exhibition/bauhaus-jerusalem/).

NEARBY See **Tel Aviv (#5)**

#17 Israel Museum

BROCHURE

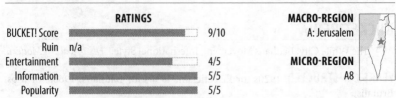

RATINGS			MACRO-REGION
BUCKET! Score	████████████	9/10	A: Jerusalem
Ruin	n/a		
Entertainment	████████	4/5	**MICRO-REGION**
Information	████████████	5/5	A8
Popularity	████████████	5/5	

PRIMARY THEME/CATEGORY Culture – Museum – of Archaeology.

TOP Museum in the region.

HOLY LAND RELEVANCE Contains nearly 500,000 objects of regional, religious, and historical significance. It's the best introduction to the Holy Land by way of a museum that you can find.

ELECT ME! Israel's premiere national museum, housing the Dead Sea Scrolls (A8), the Aleppo Codex, a replica of the Second Temple in Jerusalem, and sculpture garden, among other highlights. Whether or not you like museums, many of the individual pieces of the collection are engaging. Plus, there is art inside and out, the rotational exhibits are usually excellent, and the whole thing is interactive for kids and adults.

WORTH THE DETOUR? Absolutely, this is a world-class museum with an unbiased approach to the region's history. From prehistoric man to the dress of ethnic and religious groups, this museum admirably tackles a wide range of topics and never disappoints.

EXPERIENCES

CAN'T MISS The Dead Sea Scrolls (A8) are incredible, as is the building that houses them. Buried in a few caves for a couple of thousand years, Bedouin shepherds discovered seven scrolls at **Qumran (#70)** which led to a further discovery of almost 1,000 biblical texts spanning the 3rd century BCE to the 1st century CE, some of the oldest in the world.

SITES

★ *Shrine of the Book* The name for the building that houses the Dead Sea Scrolls (A8), the Aleppo Codex, letters from Simon Bar-Kochba, and **Masada (#8)** artifacts. The building is designed to mirror the earthenware where the scrolls rested all those years, even built partially underground.

★ *Second Temple Model* A large-scale 1:50 replica of the Second Temple period in Jerusalem, c66 CE, before the Great Revolt and its destruction by the Romans. An almost shocking level of detail which brings the Old City to life in a way that's nearly impossible to envision through text alone.

★ *Archaeology Wing* In seven chapters, tells the story of the Land of the Hebrews through a variety of interesting artifacts, organized chronologically from prehistory to the Ottoman Empire. Impressive side rooms on glass, coins, and the Hebrew language.

★ *Billy Rose Art Garden* A beautiful, outdoor space: Zen garden meets Western sculpture. James Turrell's *The Space That Sees* is memorable.

★ *Jewish Art and Life Wing* Follow the "synagogue route" through reconstructed Venetian, German (detail-painted Horb Synagogue), Indian, and Surinamese synagogues; over 200 illuminated Hebrew manuscripts.

★ *Fine Arts Wing* Includes the Lipschitz collection (thousands of artifacts collected from around the world) and the huge *The Boy From Tel Aviv*.

★ *Beit She'an Mosaic Floor* 5th–7th-century CE mosaic relocated from ancient Beit She'an showing the Ark of the Covenant.

★ Always interesting temporary exhibitions.

ACTIVITIES The Ruth Youth Wing contains interactive youth art activities (adult-friendly), or catch a kid-friendly, informative film in the Dorot Auditorium about living during the Second Temple period or the discovery of the Dead Sea Scrolls.

SECRET Save your ticket: repeat visitors can return within three months for half-price.

SPECIAL EVENTS There are special events going on all the time (w www.imj.org.il/en/events-list).

ITINERATOR!

DAYS/HOURS Open 10.00–17.00 Saturday, Sunday, Monday, Wednesday, and Thursday, 10.00–14.00 Friday and holiday eves, 16.00–21.00 Tuesday.

TIME COMMITMENT Speed rules apply. The grounds are huge (20 acres), so even a sprint through the most important places will take you at least a couple of hours. Better to plan at least half a day, though you could easily go over, especially if you eat lunch here. If you don't love museums, focus on one part (the sculptures or Dead Sea Scrolls) and plan on an hour or two.

BASE Located on the western outskirts of Jerusalem, you can do this from Anchor City Jerusalem, or on your way to Tel Aviv (65km/50 minutes).

BEST STRATEGY Can be done as part of *City Walk A8*, near **Yad Vashem (#35)** and government buildings, though you may experience museum fatigue by attempting too many educational sites in one day. Better idea: schedule an afternoon here after spending a few hours in the Old City.

WALKS AND DRIVES A8.

ITINERARIES Jerusalem Immersion; High BUCKET! Scores: 7+; Most Entertaining; Archaeology; Structure; Culture; Organized; Fine Arts; Ancient History; Modernity; Kid-Focused; All Ages; Big-Group Friendly.

ARRIVAL PREP

PREBOOK Can be booked online or in person. Discount tickets only available at box office.

REALITY CHECK With over 800,000 annual guests, this museum can get busy. It's a popular tour-bus stop. The Shrine of the Book is the busiest building in the complex, so plan to visit early or late. English-language tours are not every day – check the website first.

ACCESS Jerusalem bus lines 7, 9, 14, 35, 66, or line 100 from Tel Aviv Shapirim Junction Parking. If driving, parking is available for museum visitors, though somewhat limited. Keep your ticket for exit validation.

ADMISSION Adults 54 ILS (includes audio guide), students 39 ILS, children 27 ILS (free Tues/Sat), seniors/disabled/repeat visitors 27 ILS, Jerusalem residents 49 ILS.

RECOMMENDED GUIDE The audio guide is excellent, though frankly you could get by without it just by reading the well-written placards. If you have a particular area of interest, check out the events calendar, keeping in mind many are in Hebrew (w www.imj.org.il/en/events-list).

VISITOR CENTER Yes, upon entry, at ticket booth. Very helpful information desk. Also good brochure with map, and museum shop.

EAT Modern is a kosher meat restaurant located on site. Otherwise, there's a dairy café near the Model of Jerusalem.

BUCKET!PEDIA

Size 50,000m². *Historical era* *Prehistoric* to *Modern*.

CONTEXT This museum houses some of the most visually stunning, relevant, historically significant, moving, shocking, and memorable pieces of archaeology, anthropology, art, literature, and Judaica not only in the Holy Land, but truly in the world. You won't forget seeing the Dead Sea Scrolls. The Archaeology Wing will leave you exhausted, but beyond impressed. The museum ties together all the history of the region, of Jewish people, and of civilization as we know it in a gorgeous setting inside an architecturally appealing (building and landscape) space.

ARCHITECTURE Located on a hill overlooking West Jerusalem, the original **museum complex** was designed by Israeli architect Alfred Mansfeld in 1965. The collection was housed in a series of masonry buildings – a modern take on an Arab village. The entire complex was renovated in 2010 to the sum of $100 million. Designed by Armand Bartos and Frederick Kiesler, the **Shrine of the Book** opened in 1965 is the home of the Dead Sea Scrolls. The white onion-shaped roof was meant to resemble the cover of the clay pots in which the scrolls were found, and the interior reflects the environment of the caves in which the scrolls were kept safe. The outside pool literally reflects the building and sky. Across from the dome is a black wall contrasting sharply with the white of the Shrine, supposedly taken to symbolize the imagery of one of the Dead Sea Scrolls, *War of the Sons of Light Against the Sons of Darkness*. The **Billy Rose Art Garden** was designed by sculptor Isamu Naguchi with semicircular terraces housing contemporary sculpture over 20 acres.

WEBSITE w www.imj.org.il/en/.

WHERE TO NEXT?

THEMATIC *Religion* Ancient Manuscripts; Dead Sea Scrolls; Oldest Hebrew Bible. *Archaeology* Prehistory. *Structure* Modern Architecture; Beautiful Structures. *People* Jewish. *Culture* Museum of Art; of History; of Archaeology; of Science and Learning. *Organized* Guided.

COMPLEMENTARY Other highly ranked museums include **Citadel/Tower of David (#32)**, **Yad Vashem (#35)**, **ANU – Museum of the Jewish People (#77)**, and **Tel Aviv Museum of Art (#95)**. Learn about prehistoric humans at *Nahal Me'arot/Wadi el-Mughara*, **Ancient Amman (#37)**, and El Bariyeh's Shuqba/Natuf Caves (C5). For more Dead Sea Scrolls fanaticism, there's **Qumran (#70)** and *Jordan Museum (Q3)*.

NEARBY *Bible Lands Museum* (across the street), *Bloomfield Science Museum (A8)* (650m/ 8 minutes), and the Knesset (A8) (800m/10 minutes).

#18 Church of the Nativity

BROCHURE

RATINGS			MACRO-REGION
BUCKET! Score	▬▬▬▬▬▬	9/10	C: West Bank
Ruin	▬▬▬▬	5/5	
Entertainment	▬	1/5	**MICRO-REGION**
Information	▬▬	3/5	C1
Popularity	▬▬▬▬	5/5	

PRIMARY THEME/CATEGORY Religion – Religious Figures – Jesus: Early Life.

TOP Reason to visit Bethlehem.

COMMENDATIONS UNESCO World Heritage Site, 2012.

HOLY LAND RELEVANCE Birthplace of Jesus. Oldest functioning church in the world. Additionally, the place where the Bible was translated into Latin, making it available to the Roman masses.

ELECT ME! Site of the birthplace of Jesus, this cave-grotto beneath a series of churches going back to the 4th century CE is nearly always swarming with guests, but the wait to visit the underground caves is worth it. Believer or not, there's something intensely satisfying about waiting hours in line to pray (or reflect silently) on the spot where history's most revered religious leader was born.

WORTH THE DETOUR? You really can't beat free. It's a religious and historic relic, both as a building and a moment in time celebrated by people the world over on December 25. Touching the place where Jesus was born is a spiritual bucket-list item for many people.

EXPERIENCES

CAN'T MISS Obviously, the Grotto of the Nativity.

SITES

★ *Church of the Nativity* The building itself has been heavily fortified over the years, with thick-walled buildings surrounding the church. From Manger Square, you are looking at several buildings: St. Catherine's Church and two convents from the Greek Orthodox and Armenians.

★ *Door of Humility* The famed church door is only 4 feet high and requires one to bow upon entry. Its origin is less humble: this covered portal from the Ottoman era was meant to repel invaders rather than force you to genuflect.

★ *Grotto of the Nativity (c4 BCE)* Commemorated as the physical birthplace of Jesus, underneath the altar on the main floor, and accessible via the staircase to the right (left side is the exit).

★ *Altar of the Nativity* The little cove next to the grotto represents the altar where Jesus was placed at birth (replete with crib). You'll also find the Altar of the Adoration of the Magi opposite the manger scene.

★ *Constantine's 4th-century Basilica* In the main room, view a piece of the mosaic floor from Constantine's original basilica, beneath glass on the floor in the front nave.

★ *Columns* The 44 columns date to the 6th century, while the paintings that adorn them are from the 12th century and depict Crusader-era saints.

★ *Wall mosaics* The north and south walls contain mosaics dating to 12th century, depicting the provincial and ecumenical councils, as well as Jesus' genealogy.

ACTIVITIES For the Grotto, wait in line to reach the spot of Jesus' birth. Reach into the hole beneath the 14-pointed star to touch the purported stone slab upon which Mary gave birth. Mass is held every Sunday. Attend midnight mass on Christmas Eve, if you're up for it.

SECRET There are several other grottoes, which can be accessed through St. Catherine's Church next door. They are worth a visit for the historical context of the site: St. Joseph (commemorating the angel's appearance to Joseph), St. Paula (burial site), the Holy Innocents (commemorating the children killed by King Herod), and St. Jerome's study and tomb (1st–4th centuries CE).

SPECIAL EVENTS St. Catherine's hosts a midnight Christmas mass each year, broadcast around the world.

ITINERATOR!

DAYS/HOURS April–September 06.30–19.30, October–March 05.30–17.00. Sunday morning mass. Grotto closed Sunday mornings, but open in the afternoon.

BEST TIME Christmas season, if of interest to you. Otherwise anytime.

TIME COMMITMENT There isn't all that much to see and do, so 1–2 hours will give you plenty of time to explore the church, stand in line, and spend a little time in Manger Square. With 4 hours, add on the *City Walk C1* walking tour of Bethlehem. Speed rules generally do not apply, as it's hard to predict if you'll be waiting minutes or hours at the grotto, depending on tourist buses.

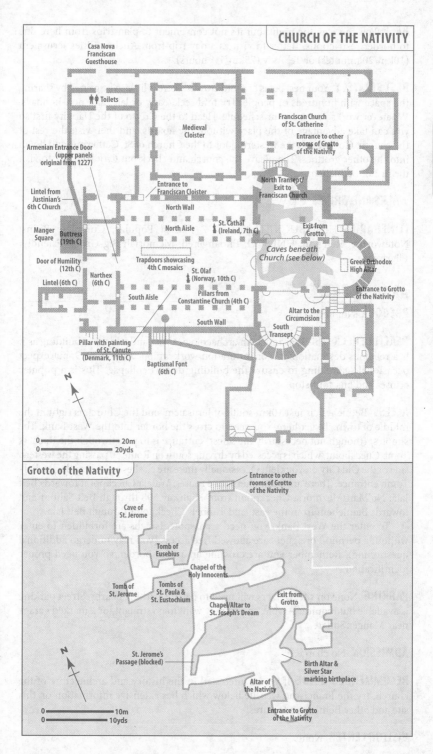

BASE You can stay the night, but it's not convenient to plan trips from here due to border restrictions. Better to visit as a day trip from Anchor Cities Jerusalem (10km/20 minutes) or Tel Aviv (75km/1¼ hours).

BEST STRATEGY Your best bet is to avoid crowds: there is little to be gained by sharing the space with hundreds of people. Try midweek, early or late, and non-holidays. Whatever works best for your schedule. Head to the Grotto of the Nativity first so you can take advantage of the place without the hoards, and then visit the rest of the church. Go through the western door to the Church of St. Catherine, and down into the other grottoes. Then leave the church and check out *City Walk C1* to visit the rest of Bethlehem.

WALKS AND DRIVES C1, W5.

ITINERARIES High BUCKET! Scores: 7+; Most Popular; Complete Ruins; Noteworthy; Religion; UNESCO; Endangered; Memorial; Big-Group Friendly; Pilgrimage.

ARRIVAL PREP

PREBOOK Not necessary.

REALITY CHECK This is as much an archaeological site and a historic building as it is a religious destination. Major restoration work wrapped up in 2019, but expect occasional scaffolding to ensure the building doesn't collapse. This is a popular cruise- and bus-tour stop.

ACCESS Bethlehem is just 10km south of Jerusalem, and the Church is right in the middle of town. To get here, you need to cross the border into the West Bank. The simplest (though not necessarily the safest) entrance is to pass through the Rachel's Tomb Checkpoint, which is accessed by driving south on Route 60 passing the western side of the Old City on your left. Occasionally there are clashes right near the Rachel's Tomb entrance. There are a few alternative routes: Walala Checkpoint towards Beit Jala; Nu'Man/Mazmoria Checkpoint from Highway 398 through Beit Sahour and towards Bethlehem from the east; and Tunnels Checkpoint through Beit Jala.

To enter the West Bank, you need a passport. Israelis are forbidden to enter without a permit. Foreigners are allowed free access (you may undergo additional questioning). Remember you are crossing an armed border, so you need proper identification.

PARKING None on site. Drivers will need to pay for parking nearby. Street parking is available but requires Arabic, so you may want to go straight for a marked garage near Manger Square.

ADMISSION No charge.

RECOMMENDED GUIDE If you're interested in the history and architecture of the church, try the Franciscan website below which has extensive information on this site and other Bethlehem features.

VISITOR CENTER None.

EAT Manger Square has a number of restaurants. Side streets contain typical Arab food, including shawarma and falafel.

SLEEP Lots of hotels offer deep discounts in order to attract tourists who would otherwise just spend the evening in Jerusalem. Unless staying at the novelty site, *Banksy's Walled-Off Hotel*, we also recommend sleeping in Jerusalem or Tel Aviv.

BUCKET!PEDIA

AKA Basilica of the Nativity.   *Historical era* Roman/Byzantine.   *Year constructed* Originally 339 CE and rebuilt in 540.   *Size* Basilica: 54m × 20m; grotto: 12m × 3m.

CONTEXT Upon converting to Christianity (and bringing the rest of the Roman Empire with him), Constantine I visited the Holy Land with the intention of marking the spot where Jesus was born with a basilica. After its pseudo-destruction by the Samaritans, Emperor Justinian created a much bigger church in its place, which is preserved in the shape we see today. Whereas most other churches in the Holy Land experienced irreparable damages following various conquests, the Nativity remained mostly untouched, save for the internal ornamentation. Today, the paintings and mosaics are faint versions of their former glory, keeping in mind the church is nearly 1,500 years old.

Religious or not, there is something spiritual, or magical, or powerful – whatever you call it – about standing (or kneeling) alone above the spot where Jesus was born. The rest of the church has plenty of history but, let's face it, most people come to descend the stairs to the cave grotto with the star marking the very spot where the Virgin Mary gave birth. It's important to remember that the church (much like the **Church of the Holy Sepulchre (#9)**) was built atop a network of caves where people used to live and work. The city of Bethlehem is now level, and feels like a city, but this used to be a series of cave-ridden hills where people sought shelter, shade, and even gave birth. As you descend the stairs, try to turn off the crowds and focus instead on the historical importance of this tiny room, just a cave in the hill in the desert of Palestine.

ARCHITECTURE The current structure is a collection of additions made over almost 2,000 years. The remains of the original 4th-century CE church are the nave and four rows of columns, as well as the original mosaic floor found beneath glass in the central nave. Interestingly, some of the material used in the original columns was reused in later-period construction. The three dome-covered semicircular "apsides" (plural of "apse") were built in the 6th century under Justinian. The wall mosaics high on the ceiling were introduced in 1160. Paintings on the columns date from the 12th century. The roof is from the 15th century. The entire complex was restored in the 19th century.

CHRONOLOGY

2nd century CE: Early Christian tradition places the site of Jesus' birth in a cave.
323: Emperor Constantine begins building the church on request of his mother, St. Helena, who came to supervise the works in 326.
339: Church dedicated and opened.
384: St. Jerome settles in Bethlehem and translates the Bible into Latin, later called the Vulgate. The room in which he wrote the Vulgate and his tomb are accessed by the stairs through St. Catherine's Church.

529: Samaritans revolt around the country, setting fire and wreaking carnage. The Church, among many sites, is destroyed.

540: Emperor Justinian renovates the site, leaving the base plan for what future versions of the Church would be built.

614: Persians conquer Holy Land and destroy every church but the Church of the Nativity. According to legend: because they saw the Three Wise Men in a mosaic, who were dressed in Persian clothes.

1347: Franciscans acquire possession of the Grotto and Church.

1517: Greeks and Franciscans begin long battle for custodianship of the Church.

1847: The 14-pointed star that marks the spot of Jesus' birth was mysteriously stolen; it was replaced in 1853, but not before starting the Crimean War (some say).

1857: Status Quo is formalized in the Treaty of Paris, ending the Crimean War, and granting rights to holy buildings in Jerusalem and Bethlehem to all religious communities with claims to the church, effectively eliminating any changes to the building(s) without consent by all parties.

1934: Original flooring discovered during renovations.

1948: Cloister of St. Catherine's Church rebuilt in present style.

2002: Palestinians take refuge in Bethlehem and hole themselves up inside the Church for 39 days, holding some 200 monks hostage.

2012: Declared a UNESCO World Heritage Site.

2019: Major restoration work completed. Site removed from UNESCO's List of World Heritage in Danger.

WEBSITE w custodia.org/en/sanctuaries/bethlehem.

WHERE TO NEXT?

THEMATIC *Noteworthy* UNESCO; Endangered; Unique. *Religion* Christianity; Jesus' Early Life; New Testament; Churches; Oldest and Ancient Churches; Pilgrimage; Ceremonies and Events. *Archaeology* Byzantine; Impressive Structural Remains. *Structure* Historic Monuments. *Nature* Caves/Grottoes. *People* Holidays.

COMPLEMENTARY Other monumental churches include the **Church of the Holy Sepulchre (#9)**, **Basilica of the Annunciation**, **Church of the Transfiguration**, **Monastery of Abu Ghosh**, **Mount of Beatitudes**, and **St. James' Cathedral**. Other famous places in Jesus' life are **Old City Jerusalem (#1)** (site of final teachings and death), **Sea of Galilee (#7)** (where Jesus conducted his ministries), and **Nazareth (#29)** (where young Jesus was raised).

NEARBY Solomon's Pools (C2) (5km/12 minutes), **Herodion (#90)** (11km/15 minutes), and **Battir Hills** (hire a driver, see *Road Trip C2*).

#19 Madaba and the Madaba Map

BROCHURE

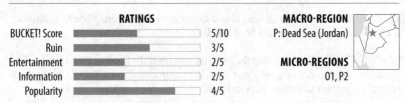

RATINGS			MACRO-REGION
BUCKET! Score		5/10	P: Dead Sea (Jordan)
Ruin		3/5	
Entertainment		2/5	**MICRO-REGIONS**
Information		2/5	O1, P2
Popularity		4/5	

PRIMARY THEME/CATEGORY Archaeology – Ancient Cities and Remains – Mosaics.

TOP Most important mosaic you'll likely ever see.

HOLY LAND RELEVANCE At the time of creation, the city of Madaba was under Christian governance. Jerusalem actually takes up only a small piece of the map, which covers a bird's eye view of Jericho, the Dead Sea, Karak, Hebron, and Bethlehem, all the way to Mount Sinai and the headwaters of the Nile near Cairo. It truly covers much of the Holy Land. Also, it has played a major role in identifying since-destroyed structures in the Old City, including the Nea Church.

ELECT ME! The mosaic of Madaba marks the earliest known depiction of Jerusalem on a map, providing a glimpse of the city's Byzantine layout. This, and dozens more mosaics, are available to visit in and around town, for those who fancy this ancient art style.

WORTH THE DETOUR? You can spend a long weekend visiting every mosaic in town, and this would be a wonderful exercise for a Byzantine mosaic buff. Otherwise, you can pop in to see the Madaba Map and be on your way.

EXPERIENCES

CAN'T MISS The Madaba Map at the Greek Orthodox Basilica of St. George.

OTHER SITES Archaeological Park I (contains the Church of the Virgin Mary and Hippolytus Hall); Archaeological Park II (contains The Burnt Palace); Madaba Museum; and the Church of the Apostles (the sea goddess Thetis/Thalassa is depicted here, along with a dedication to the 12 apostles).

ACTIVITIES Climb the church tower at the Shrine of the Beheading of John the Baptist for the best views of Madaba.

SECRET Play "I spy" – try to spot on the Madaba Map: the (disembodied) lion hunting the gazelle; the Church of the Holy Sepulchre; Bethlehem; the Nile Delta; and the Mediterranean.

ITINERATOR!

DAYS/HOURS 08.00–18.00 (opens later on Fri/Sat; closes early in the winter and on holidays).

TIME COMMITMENT Speed rules apply. The Church of St. George, which houses the Madaba Map, can take as little as 5 minutes. If you have a guide, 30 minutes is probably sufficient. There are other mosaics in town too, which take 2 hours total to visit.

BASE Anchor from the Dead Sea (35km/45 minutes) or Amman (37km/50 minutes). If on a road trip, there are plenty of hotels.

BEST STRATEGY Combine Madaba on a day trip from the Dead Sea or Amman, and circle through the regional religious sites. We recommend *Road Trip P2* to combine several important Christian sites in Jordan.

WALKS AND DRIVES O1, P2, V2.

ITINERARIES Culture.

ARRIVAL PREP

PREBOOK Not applicable.

REALITY CHECK The Madaba Map is a quick stop – 15 minutes is probably sufficient for most people. It makes sense to visit the other mosaics in town to make the trip worthwhile.

ACCESS Madaba is easily accessible via bus, taxi, and car.

ADMISSION Nominal cost to enter some of the sites, including the St. George Church – bring a few coins or small bills, as the price is usually 1–2 JD per person.

RECOMMENDED GUIDE A good map should suffice, though a tour guide can provide you with specific details about what you're looking at, and why the art is so impressive.

VISITOR CENTER Located on the same road as the Archaeological Park, this new site is open every day, including holidays.

EAT Haret Jdoudna and Jaw Zaman are both consistently ranked highly food, as are the Ayola Coffeeshop & Bar for snacks/drinks and Aswar Madaba Restaurant.

SLEEP Use your favorite booking site, but better to anchor in Suweimeh.

BUCKET!PEDIA

AKA City of Mosaics. *Historical era* Roman/Byzantine. *Year founded/constructed* Madaba is referenced in the Bible as part of Moab, so has existed for thousands of years, though its origin is unknown. The Madaba Map dates to the 6th century CE.

CONTEXT First referenced in the Old Testament's Numbers 21:30 as a Moabite town, the entire city is famous for one semi-large mosaic map excavated from a church floor. There are other nice mosaics in the region, but the one that bears the city's name (the "Madaba Map") contains the oldest extant depiction of the Holy Land, with Jerusalem at its center. The original map is estimated to have contained some 1.1 million pieces of glass and stone, all hand-laid. Based on the buildings built into the map itself, it's safe to guess the mosaic was created sometime between 542 and 570 CE. In the late 1800s, as the city was being resettled and rebuilt, a large number (possibly hundreds) of mosaic artworks were discovered, now visible in various churches and archaeological museums within the city.

CHRONOLOGY

840 BCE: Mesha Stele commemorates the Moabite victory over the Israelites, who later claim that Madaba residents will pay dearly.

106 CE: Becomes part of Roman province of Arabia.

451: City gains its own Christian bishop.

527–65: Roman Emperor Justinian orders the reconstruction of many churches in the area, including the St. George Church.

542–70: Estimated time of completion of the Madaba Map, given that Jerusalem contains the New Church of Theotokos, which was dedicated in 542, but various buildings known to have existed from 570 onward are not depicted.

749: Earthquake destroys Madaba; residents abandon site.

1872: European archaeologists begin forming excavation teams in the region.

1880: Christian families leave Karak to settle in the abandoned ruins of Madaba.

1897: Archaeologist Giuseppi Manfredi publishes the finding of the Madaba Mosaic Map. The world gushes.

1962: Archaeological Museum opened.

WEBSITE w international.visitjordan.com/Wheretogo/Madaba.aspx.

WHERE TO NEXT?

THEMATIC *Religion* Churches. *Archaeology* Byzantine; Mosaics. *Scenic* Most Photographed.

COMPLEMENTARY More amazing mosaics can be found at: **Mount Nebo (#24)**; **Jericho (#26)**; **Beit She'an (#39)**; **Beit Alpha (#64)**; and **Umm ar-Rasas (#81)**. Other Jesus sites in the region (*Road Trip P2*) include: **Mount Nebo (#24)**; **Bethany-Beyond-the-Jordan (#41)**; **Umm ar-Rasas (#81)**; and *Mukawir*.

NEARBY **Mount Nebo (#24)** (9km/13 minutes), *Hammamat Ma'in Hot Springs* (30km/ 40 minutes), **Umm ar-Rasas (#81)** (31km/40 minutes), *Mukawir* (34km/45 minutes), **Modern Amman (#36)** and **Ancient Amman (#37)** (36km/40 minutes), and the **Dead Sea (#3)** (40km/50 minutes).

#20 Qasr Amra and the Desert Palaces

BROCHURE

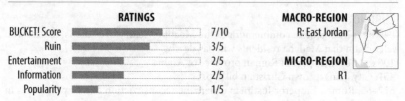

RATINGS		
BUCKET! Score		7/10
Ruin		3/5
Entertainment		2/5
Information		2/5
Popularity		1/5

MACRO-REGION
R: East Jordan

MICRO-REGION
R1

PRIMARY THEME/CATEGORY Archaeology – Islamic – Umayyad.

TOP Qasr Amra is the most impressive of the region's many Umayyad palaces.

COMMENDATIONS UNESCO World Heritage Site, 1985.

HOLY LAND RELEVANCE The Umayyads were the second Islamic caliphate following Muhammad's death and the subsequent expansion of the Arab empire. They built these palaces in the early 8th century CE, bearing depictions of people and secular life, which would soon become (and remain) taboo in Islamic art.

ELECT ME! These summer homes-slash-forts of the Umayyad caliphs of the 8th century CE really get you off the beaten trails, with several of the sites standing as mirages in the desert until you get up close. Like the Incense Route, you don't have to stop at every site, and only the most intrepid travelers will. But do pick a few – especially Qasr Amra, which continues to impress visitors with its provocative imagery (and Islamic art to boot!) on its very well-preserved frescoes.

WORTH THE DETOUR? In terms of obscurity, this is up there. For that reason alone, it might tickle your fancy. For those with a tight timeline, it might be too out of the way to justify the loss of an extra day.

EXPERIENCES

CAN'T MISS While Qasr Amra is the definite star here, the other **palaces** to see in the Eastern Desert (explanations in *Road Trips R1* and *W1*) are *Qasr Azraq*, *Qasr Kharana*, Qasr Burqu (W1), Qasr al-Mushatta (W1), Qasr al-Qastal (W1), and Qasr al-Hallabat/Hammam es-Sarah. The notable **murals** at Qasr Amra include: the first depiction of Heaven (with a zodiac and constellations); the Fresco of the Six Kings (of Spain, Byzantium, Sassanid Empire, Aksum (Ethiopia), and two others – possibly China, India, or Turkey), of unknown intention but possibly representing defeated kingdoms of Islam, or those that have paid respect to the Umayyads; and the bathing women, a very unusual depiction of unclothed women.

ACTIVITIES Do your research at the visitor center at Qasr Amra.

SECRET There are several sites way off the beaten path. Furthest afield is Qasr Burqu (W1), halfway to Iraq. There's an ecolodge on site with a variety of other activities including hiking, birding, and desert exploration.

SPECIAL EVENTS Bird migration is in May, including raptors such as eagles and vultures.

MAP See R1/W1.

ITINERATOR!

DAYS/HOURS November–March 08.00–16.00, April–May 08.00–17.30, June–October 08.00–18.30, during Ramadan 08.00–15.30.

BEST TIME The summer is excruciating; there is little cover and your car tires will be burning up in these desert outposts. Pick a cooler season. Given the remoteness of the sites, you may be the only ones around, so don't show up 5 minutes before closing time and expect to get in. Most of the palaces further afield have caretakers with keys – and they might go home early if it's been a slow day.

TIME COMMITMENT Speed rules apply. The fortresses themselves are not massive, so you can get through Qasr Amra in an hour, and the rest in 30 minutes each. It takes an hour each way to drive from/to Amman, but the more you see, the longer the drive. Our *Road Trip R1* itinerary is an all-day affair.

BASE Anchor from Amman to Qasr Amra (85km/1¼ hours) or Suweimeh (120km/1¾ hours). You can road-trip and stay in accommodation in Azraq or Burqu, or camp in several other desert locations.

BEST STRATEGY Unless you're an enthusiast, we recommend making this a day trip from Amman (the closest Anchor City) using *Road Trip R1* as a guide.

WALKS AND DRIVES R1, V1, V2, W1, W5.

ITINERARIES High BUCKET! Scores: 7+; Off-the-Beaten-Path Jordan; Noteworthy; Archaeology; Nature and Scenic; Organized; UNESCO; Endangered; National Parks/Reserves; Fine Arts; On the Road.

ARRIVAL PREP

PREBOOK Not necessary.

REALITY CHECK Though the borders are fairly well regulated, they are not impenetrable. You may wish to steer clear of anything near Jordan's non-Israeli borders, particularly Syria and Iraq. Most embassies advise against travel beyond the main sites. It's very hot: be prepared with water, clothing, sunscreen, and a summerized vehicle. Food is hard to come by outside of the Azraq area, so bring your own.

ACCESS Highways 30 and 40 make this an easy round-trip.

ADMISSION 3 JD per site, generally, though the Jordan Pass covers most of them.

RECOMMENDED GUIDE Start at the visitor center at **Qasr Azraq**. There's also a good amount of information at w kinghussein.gov.jo/tourism5.html.

EAT There is food in Azraq, but come prepared with rations because it's mostly empty out there.

SLEEP You can sleep in lodges at Azraq or Burqu, or camp in more remote desert areas with a guide. Inquire/book at w wildjordan.com.

BUCKET!PEDIA

AKA Quseir Amra; the Desert Castle Loop; the Umayyad Desert Castles/Palaces. *Historical era* Islamic: Umayyad. *Year constructed* Qasr Amra: early 8th century CE, likely just before 743 CE; the others were built between 660 and 750 CE, when the Umayyads held power.

CONTEXT In the early era of Islam, the Umayyad Caliphate of Damascus built a series of farmhouses, which today look and seem like castles, though in fact were used as respites from city life. These palaces may also have served as caravanserai (travelers' inns) for travelers, as their locations were strategically located along economic trade routes, and near important sources of water in the desert.

Qasr Amra was commissioned by a future caliph, Walid Ibn Yazid, prior to his assuming power. This holiday retreat home was part of a greater complex, the foundations of which are still visible in the building's surroundings. The famed frescoes are located on the ceiling inside the main reception room, with other frescoes aligning the walls of the adjoining hammam – one of the oldest Islamic hammams in the world. The art had not yet evolved the strict Islamic principles of avoiding exact depictions of humans and animals. Thus, one can find pictures of people hunting and bathing, among other activities, in a Byzantine style that would soon be prohibited in Islamic art.

CHRONOLOGY

300 CE: First Roman fortress built at the site of Qasr Azraq.
632: Muhammad dies; Rashidun Caliphate begins its expansion, taking most of the Middle East in rapid succession.
658: Civil war breaks out in the Rashidun Caliphate, and the Umayyad dynasty within the Rashidun group establish their own caliphate.
661: The Umayyads of Damascus gain control of the Islamic empire.
661–750: Umayyads build a number of desert castles, forts, garrisons, and summer retreat houses in present-day Jordan's eastern desert. Other castles from the same period exist in Syria, the Sea of Galilee, near Jerusalem, and outside Amman.
685: Abd el-Malik builds al-Qastal, believed to be the first of the desert castles, and later Qasr al-Hallabat and the adjacent Hammam es-Sarah. (He also orders the construction of the Dome of the Rock.)
700: Al-Walid I builds Qasr Burqu on site of a previous Syrian outpost.
711: Qasr Kharana is built on the site of a Roman/Byzantine building.
743: Walid Ibn Yazid assumes leadership as caliph for a short reign. Qasr Amra is attributed to him, though it was completed before he became caliph. He also commissioned Qasr al-Mushatta.
750: Umayyads lose power to the Abbasids, based in Baghdad.
1237: Mamluks reshape Qasr Azraq into its present formation.

1917: Arab revolt against the Ottoman Empire; Lawrence of Arabia uses Qasr Azraq as his headquarters.
1985: Inscribed onto UNESCO World Heritage list.

WEBSITE w kinghussein.gov.jo/tourism5.html.

WHERE TO NEXT?

THEMATIC *Noteworthy* UNESCO; Endangered. *Archaeology* Islamic I; Impressive Structural Remains. *Scenic* Scenic Drives. *Organized* Multi-Stop/Self-Directed.

COMPLEMENTARY Other contemporary castles are **Hisham's Palace (#26)** and Khirbet al-Minya (G3). Other Umayyad buildings are **Dome of the Rock (#6)**; Amman Citadel (**Ancient Amman (#37)**), **Al-Aqsa Mosque (#65)**, the *Dome of the Chain*, and the White Mosque (D8) of Ramle. Castles that are not Umayyad include **Ajloun Fortress (#76)** and **Nimrod's Fortress (#85)**, while *Qasr Azraq* is more noticeably Ayyubid than Umayyad.

NEARBY From Qasr Amra: **Azraq Wetlands (#55)** (26km/20 minutes), *Shaumari* wildlife reserve (35km/25 minutes), and the Saudi border (72km/45 minutes).

#21 Dana Biosphere Reserve

BROCHURE

RATINGS		MACRO-REGION
BUCKET! Score	6/10	0: King's Highway
Ruin	2/5	
Entertainment	2/5	**MICRO-REGION**
Information	1/5	01
Popularity	2/5	

PRIMARY THEME/CATEGORY Active – Hikes – Day Hikes (2+ Hours).

TOP Nature Reserve in Jordan.

COMMENDATIONS Jordan Nature Reserve.

HOLY LAND RELEVANCE You'll find a few ruins scattered about, but nature is the focus of this excursion.

ELECT ME! Dana is one of Jordan's six official nature reserves, and also its largest. It offers plenty for the outdoorsy type – animal and bird spotting, nature walks, beautiful desertscape, ancient rock towns, and surprising wildflower blooms. Inside the park is also the famed **Feynan Ecolodge (#86)**, one of only two residences that made such an impression on travel writers as to earn Gold status in this guide.

WORTH THE DETOUR? If your goal is one or two days of hiking, you're better off focusing on **Petra (#2)** or **Wadi Rum (#4)**. However, if you can give one or two days to

Dana, you'll find it's the best way of seeing both natural Jordan while simultaneously learning about Bedouin practices (coffee, foraging, cooking, hospitality).

EXPERIENCES

CAN'T MISS The best way of incorporating Dana hikes and Bedouin lifestyle is to stay in the **Feynan Ecolodge (#86)**, which incorporates the Bedouin community into its several daily activities.

ANIMALIA Endangered species include Sand Cat, Syrian Wolf, Lesser Kestrel, Spiny-tailed Lizard, Nubian Ibex, Spotted Eagle, Imperial Eagle, and the Syrian Serin, a bright yellow- and pale gray-feathered bird. Other notable species include Caracal (a medium-sized – 12kg – cat), Grey Wolf, Blanford's Fox, and Griffon Vulture.

FOLIAGE Acacia; Evergreen Oak; Mediterranean Cypress; Phoenician Juniper; Rocky Sudanian.

GEOLOGY Limestone; sandstone; granite; sand dunes.

GEOGRAPHY Mediterranean; Irano-Turanian; Saharo-Arabian; Sudanian.

HUMAN INHABITANTS Paleolithic; Egyptian; Nabataean; Roman; Arab.

PURCHASE Copper, silver, or bronze jewelry; candles; sun-dried fruit; goatskin leather goods.

WALKING TREKS Most require a guide and advanced planning. The **self-guided/ guided** routes are the Dana Village Tour (easy, 2km) and the Wadi Dana Trail (Dana Village to Feynan Ecolodge; moderate, 14km), while **guided** routes are the White Dome Trail (Rummana to Dana Village; moderate, 8km), Nawatef Trail (easy, 2km), Shaq al-Reesh Trail (moderate, 3km), Wadi Ghweir Trail (difficult, 16km), and Wadi Dathneh Trail (extremely difficult, 19km).

SECRET Bird-watchers can spend up to a month in the park – inquire with the authorities (w rscn.org.jo).

SPECIAL EVENTS Early spring for bird viewing and flower blooms; autumn for animal viewing.

ITINERATOR!

DAYS/HOURS Every day except during Ramadan, though guides are not always available.

BEST TIME For lodging, Dana Guesthouse and **Feynan Ecolodge (#86)** are open year-round, while the Rummana Campsite is only open from March 15 to October 31. Many of the hikes are only open during the same period. Early departures are welcome and best for avoiding the midday sun and for wildlife spotting.

TIME COMMITMENT Your timing will correspond to the various hikes you choose but, given the amount of time it takes to get to Dana, plan to spend at least one day.

If you're staying overnight, plan for two days, keeping in mind that morning activities (at Feynan) are worth sticking around for. Speed rules apply, if you're walking by yourself. If you're in a guided group, you're only as fast as your slowest member.

BASE You can reach Dana from Anchor Cities Amman (200km/2¾ hours) or Suweimeh (150km/2½ hours), though the distances mean you'll likely want to spend the night unless you're committed to a lot of driving and only a little bit of hiking. If you're on a road trip (such as *O1: King's Highway*), you can sleep in Dana before continuing south or north. **Petra (#2)** (60km/1 hour) is nearby.

BEST STRATEGY Booking in advance is essential here. Make a reservation at one of the three accommodations and also book your preferred hike – there are a number to choose from. We recommend staying at **Feynan Ecolodge (#86)** and partaking in their diverse course offerings, which vary but can include cooking lessons, coffee with Bedouins, stargazing, sunset walks, wadi exploration, and lots of educational opportunities to learn about the local people.

WALKS AND DRIVES O1, V1.

ITINERARIES Off-the-Beaten-Path Jordan; Nature and Scenic; Active; Organized; National Parks/Reserves; Community.

ARRIVAL PREP

PREBOOK Required if you want to do one of the longer hikes. Accommodation is best booked in advance.

REALITY CHECK Almost all hikes need to be coordinated in advance with the *Royal Society for the Conservation of Nature (RSCN)*, which runs the guesthouse and the information center. Its hours can be sporadic during low season, possibly closing as early as noon. Let them know you're coming in advance, even if not staying there. Hiking trails close during Ramadan, which will cause problems at the beginning of the season for the next few years. Ramadan shifts dates every year, but overlaps with the March 15 start date until 2026. Also, temperatures can soar above 40°C/100°F.

ACCESS The entrance to Dana is in two parts. Dana Village, where many of the trails begin and where the Dana Guest House and RSCN information center are located, can be found just north of Qadisiya Village on King's Highway (Highway 35) and just south of tiny Rashadiya. There are signs at the intersection. The other entrance is through Feynan which you can access from the Dead Sea Highway and which is the more direct access to **Feynan Ecolodge (#86)**, but less helpful for hikers.

ADMISSION 8 JD per day for entry to Dana, which includes the Rummana Campsite and Dana Village. Additional 10–20 JD applies to each of the hiking trails, and includes the cost of the guide, though not transportation to/from the start of the trails. These are payable to RSCN. Their prices for everything, including accommodation, food options, and coffee, are posted on Wild Jordan's website, listed below.

RECOMMENDED GUIDE **Feynan Ecolodge (#86)** will provide local guides who will greatly enhance your understanding of the region. Otherwise, work with RSCN for guided walks.

VISITOR CENTER RSCN runs the Dana Guest House and the information center that organizes trip bookings and guide hires. This is located in the village of Dana, only 2.5km off King's Highway. The online brochure is excellent for helping decide which hike to book.

EAT Nothing outside the small village and the lodging facilities. Bring your own camping and snack rations. You can source the basics, i.e., some sandwiches and water. The hotels may set up lunch packs for a price if you'll be gone for the whole day.

SLEEP RSCN runs the three recommended sites of Dana Guest Lodge (economy and deluxe rooms), the Rummana Campsite (tents), and **Feynan Ecolodge (#86)** (includes individual rooms plus board and all activities). There are several other hotel options in Dana catering to travelers.

BUCKET!PEDIA

Size 320km². *Historical era* Mostly *Roman/Byzantine*, but the ruins have not been extensively studied. *Year founded* Human occupation from 4000 BCE to present.

CONTEXT Though not the first nature reserve (that honor goes to **Shaumari**), it was the largest in Jordan when it was created in 1993. The site hosts much of Jordan's wildlife and plantlife, including half of all bird and mammal species that pass through, and a third of plants. Additionally, it covers four distinct geographical zones (see *Experiences* above), lending to its unique diversity. Lucky visitors may spot birds of prey, ibex, smaller desert cats, doglike carnivores (wolves, jackals, etc.), and small thorny mammals among the more typical desert reptiles and amphibians.

Dana is thus known for its walks, which marry interesting wildlife with gorgeous, mostly arid scenery. That doesn't mean there is no water – several trails pass through creeks and pools. There are only two trails that you can do on your own, an easy route from Dana Village or a long straight (downhill) hike to Feynan Ecolodge, which is about 14km and not recommended if you have a lot of luggage. (If that's you, just hire transport to pick you up.) The guided walks must be set up in advance and vary from 2 to 10 hours, and from easy to extremely difficult.

GEOLOGY You're walking through the great Rift Valley, which has occurred due to the African and Arabian plates rubbing side by side, dislodging the earth, creating the Dead Sea and the lowest point on Earth. Some of Dana sits below sea level.

WEBSITE w wildjordan.com/destinations/dana-biosphere-reserve.

WHERE TO NEXT?

THEMATIC *Noteworthy* Nature Reserves. *Nature* Animals, Zoo, Wildlife; Birding; Plants, Gardens, Farms; Gorgeous Scenery; The Great Outdoors. *Scenic* Earth Panorama; Sky. *Active* Easy Hikes; Day Hikes; Long-Distance Walks. *Accommodation* Campgrounds. *Organized* Guided.

COMPLEMENTARY Other great Jordan hiking sites are **Petra (#2)**, **Wadi Rum (#4)**, **Ajloun Forest (#57)**, the *Al-Ayoun Trail*, Wadi al-Dahik (R1), and Yarmouk Forest (S1). Other interesting lodging options in Jordan are **Bedouin Tents**, Burqu (R1) ecolodge, and *Glamping* *in Wadi Rum (M2)*. Other Jordan wildlife reserves are **Wadi Mujib and Mujib Biosphere Reserve (#23)**, the **Azraq Wetlands (#55)**, **Ajloun Forest (#57)**, and *Shaumari*.

NEARBY *Shobak* (27km/30 minutes), <u>Wadi al-Hassa (01)</u> (37km/45 minutes), **Petra (#2)** (55km/1 hour), **Karak (#49)** (88km/1¾ hours), and <u>Umm ar-Rasas (#81)</u> (150km/ 2 hours).

#22 St. Catherine's Monastery

BROCHURE

RATINGS		MACRO-REGION
BUCKET! Score	6/10	T: Sinai
Ruin	3/5	
Entertainment	2/5	MICRO-REGION
Information	4/5	T1
Popularity	2/5	

PRIMARY THEME/CATEGORY Religion – Holy Books – Ancient Manuscripts.

TOP Second-largest library of religious texts in the world, after the Vatican. Oldest continually operational library in the world. More than half the world's Byzantine icons are located here.

COMMENDATIONS UNESCO World Heritage Site, 2002.

HOLY LAND RELEVANCE The monastery was built at the base of **Mount Sinai (#15)** where Scripture says God spoke to Moses through a burning bush.

ELECT ME! Named after a young girl who was disembodied after caught proselytizing for Jesus in the 4th century CE, the monastery – built some two centuries later – has since carried her name, Catherine. The monastery contains priceless literary artifacts, including scraps and pieces from the world's oldest known Bible, the Codex Sinaiticus, written between 325 and 360 CE. In addition, it's believed to be the original site where Moses saw the burning bush, and a chapel and bush commemorate that occasion.

WORTH THE DETOUR? Quite off the beaten path, this stop is usually incorporated into a visit to **Mount Sinai (#15)** (or vice versa), though perhaps difficult to appreciate after a long night of hiking. With its large collection of biblical materials on display, this is an essential stop for bibliophiles.

EXPERIENCES

CAN'T MISS We'd say the Holy Bush, but it's often off-limits. The Codex Sinaiticus and Syriac Sinaiticus are worth seeking out for the sheer amazement that these documents still exist.

SITES

★ *Church of the Transfiguration* A 6th-century church with a descendant of the "burning bush" in the garden, and a mosaic of the transfiguration event, earning the church its name.

★ *Moses' Well* A spring that feeds water to the entire complex, and where Moses met his wife.

★ *Monastery Museum* Showcases the icons, including crosses and chalices, in addition to some prized and revered Bibles, codices, and manuscripts in the museum's library.

★ *Syriac Sinaiticus* From the 4th–5th centuries, containing the four Gospels of the New Testament in the ancient Syriac language.

★ *Early icons* This kind of religious art was frequently painted on walls, wood frames, or through mosaics, which are on display here dating back to the 6th century. Much was painted using colored beeswax. Seek out *Christ Pantocrator*, believed to be the oldest in the world done in the Pantocrator style.

★ *Art collection* Largest collection of Crusader icons from the 13th century.

★ *Palimpsest manuscripts* To save on expensive paper, ancient scribes used to erase and write over old texts. More than 160 pages of palimpsest material has been recovered, and scientists have since been able to decipher many of the believed-erased words.

★ *Ossuary* More than a millennium's worth of monk skulls are collected and displayed because the ground was unsuitable for burial.

ACTIVITIES Two climbing paths will take you to the summit of **Mount Sinai (#15)**. Gebel Katerina makes for a long (6-hour) hike with equally stunning but less touristed vistas.

SECRET Behind the iconostasis (gilded backdrop hiding the sanctuary, typical in the Orthodox tradition) in the main monastery is the Mosaic of the Transfiguration, the Chapel of the Burning Bush, and the relics (bones) of St. Catherine, which you'll need special permission to visit. (Inquire with a tour agency in advance to see if there are any special events permitting visitors.)

SPECIAL EVENTS Though the Feast of St. Catherine is recognized elsewhere by Eastern Orthodox and Catholic traditions on November 25, St. Catherine's Martyrdom Day is celebrated at the monastery on December 8. Interfaith services are planned on that day.

ITINERATOR!

DAYS/HOURS 09.00–11.30, perhaps opening a little earlier and closing a little later. Closed Fridays, Sundays, and Greek holidays.

TIME COMMITMENT Given the limited opening hours, you can't spend more than 3 hours here. If you don't like museums, tell your guide in advance that you want only an hour on site. Speed rules apply.

BASE Most people will do this on a road trip from **Dahab (#54)** (130km/2 hours), Nuweiba (110km/2 hours), or **Sharm el-Sheikh (#88)** (205km/3 hours), by hiring a driver. Self-drive is not recommended. You can also stay the night at the guesthouse – see *Sleep* below.

BEST STRATEGY Organizing a day trip can be done from any tour operator or hotel in the Sinai cities of Dahab, Nuweiba, and Sharm el-Sheikh. You will leave at 01.00 if you are taking the sunrise hike to Mount Sinai, so be prepared for an extremely early morning, unless you're prepared to camp at the summit. You'll usually descend the mountain in the late morning and end with a visit to St. Catherine's. Alternatively, you can visit St. Catherine's in the morning and ascend Mount Sinai for sunset.

WALKS AND DRIVES T1.

ITINERARIES Noteworthy; Religion; Society and People; Shoestring.

ARRIVAL PREP

PREBOOK Not necessary, unless staying in the guesthouse.

REALITY CHECK The Sinai has recently become a hotbed of terrorist activity aimed particularly at unsuspecting tourists. Read your country's travel warnings before deciding to travel. ISIS and other militant groups have taken refuge in the region. During periods of unrest, the monastery (and the town around it) have been known to close to tourists.

ACCESS Drivers will take you. Don't try to self-drive.

ADMISSION Nominal donation recommended. You must be dressed appropriately: no shorts and ladies must cover shoulders.

RECOMMENDED GUIDE Private guides are ostensibly not allowed on site, but guides with a preestablished relationship with the monastery who pre-organize will likely be permitted access. Otherwise, you can walk around or find a guide from the monastery.

VISITOR CENTER Much of the site is off-limits, so you'll have to follow the monastery's directions of moving from one space to the next.

EAT There is a café on site with limited options. You get dinner and breakfast if you stay in the monastery.

SLEEP The guesthouse must be booked in advance. Check the website for details, but phone for reservations (+20 69 3470 353). Includes dinner and breakfast; basic, but comes recommended.

BUCKET!PEDIA

AKA Sacred Monastery of the God-Trodden Mount Sinai (officially). *Historical era* Roman/Byzantine. *Year constructed* Work commenced in 542.

CONTEXT The oldest still-functioning monastery in the world, this 6th-century site built under the direction of Emperor Justinian I sits at the base of Mount Sinai (which offers rewarding hikes) at the supposed location where Moses spoke with God via a burning bush. This bush has been on the Christian tourist circuit for 1,500 years. The site also holds the rarest collection of liturgical materials outside of the Vatican.

St. Catherine's is named after a martyr of the 3rd century, St. Catherine of Alexandria, who at 18 years old converted hundreds of people to Christianity, was killed in public, and later inspired Joan of Arc.

CHRONOLOGY

305 CE: Catherine of Alexandria converts a number of pagans to Christianity and for this is martyred. Her body is brought to the peak of St. Catherine by angels.

325–350: Codex Sinaiticus is written.

383: First mention of the Holy Bush by Egeria.

542–65: Monastery and basilica built on the order of Eastern Roman Emperor Justinian. Walls date to this period. Complex granted autonomy.

6th century: Mosaic of the Transfiguration is created.

6th–7th centuries: Oldest panel icons are painted using encaustic technique.

623: Muhammad grants a protection on the Holy Monastery of Sinai.

11th century: Original refectory converted into a mosque.

1797: Napoleon conquers Egypt and places the monastery under protection.

1871: Bell tower added to the Catholicon.

1951: Library added.

1975: Cache of new material discovered after an earthquake.

WEBSITE w sinaimonastery.com.

WHERE TO NEXT?

THEMATIC *Noteworthy* UNESCO; Nature Reserves; Off-the-Beaten-Path. *Religion* Christianity; Kings, Prophets, and Saints; Ancient Manuscripts; Oldest New Testament Bible; Churches. *Archaeology* Byzantine; Mosaics; Impressive Structural Remains. *Nature* Mountains and Mounts. *People* Ethnic Minorities. *Culture* Museum of Home. *Accommodation* Campgrounds.

COMPLEMENTARY More ancient manuscripts can be seen in: the **Israel Museum (#17)**, which houses the Dead Sea Scrolls (A8); **Qumran (#70)**, near the Dead Sea, where the scrolls were found; and *Jordan Museum (Q3)*. There are no other UNESCO sites in Sinai, but elsewhere in Egypt are: Abu Mena, an early Christian city built over the tomb of the Christian martyr, Menas of Alexandria; historic Cairo; the Pyramids; ancient Thebes; and Nubian monuments. Other Greek monasteries are **St. George's Monastery (#97)**, *Deir Quruntal*, and *Mar Saba*.

NEARBY Nuweiba (119km/1¾ hours), **Dahab (#54)** (129km/1¾ hours), and **Sharm el-Sheikh (#88)** (212km/2½ hours).

#23 Wadi Mujib and Mujib Biosphere Reserve

BROCHURE

RATINGS		
BUCKET! Score		7/10
Ruin		1/5
Entertainment		2/5
Information		1/5
Popularity		2/5

MACRO-REGION
P: Dead Sea (Jordan)

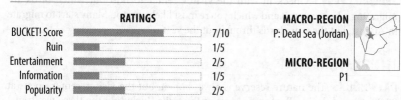

MICRO-REGION
P1

PRIMARY THEME/CATEGORY Active – Hikes – Wet Hikes.

TOP River hikes in Jordan.

COMMENDATIONS Jordan Nature Reserve (1987), Important Bird Area (IBA), and nominated by Jordan for UNESCO World Heritage status (2007).

HOLY LAND RELEVANCE The Mujib River, known as Arnon Stream in biblical times, is referenced several times in the Old Testament as the dividing waters between the Moabites and bordering tribes, including the Amorites, Gadites, and Reubenites.

ELECT ME! The Mujib Biosphere Reserve surrounds Wadi Mujib, a canyon that ends at the Dead Sea at more than 400m below sea level. Still active, this canyon gets seasonal water flows which provide life-giving essence to a variety of unique flora, fauna, and migrating birds as the water weaves its way towards the Dead Sea. Most tourists visit for the excellent hikes, particularly the 2-hour, wet'n'wild Siq Trail. Note: visitors must be 18+.

WORTH THE DETOUR? If you're not traveling with kids and like hiking, then this spot is for you! Plus, you'll get soaked – a bonus on hot days!

EXPERIENCES

CAN'T MISS You don't have to put in a whole day to have a great experience – schedule a couple of hours for the Siq Trail.

MAMMALS Caracal Cat; Nubian Ibex; Striped Hyena; Syrian Wolf.

BIRDS Arabian Babbler; Barbary Falcon; Bonelli's Eagle; Dead Sea Sparrow; Griffon Vulture; Imperial Eagle; Lesser Kestrel; Little Owl; Long-legged Buzzard; Sand Partridge; Tristram's Starling; White Stork.

WATER TRAILS The Siq Trail (easy, 2 hours, guide not required), Canyon Trail (moderate, 4 hours, guide required), and Al-Hidan Trail (moderate, 3 hours, guide required) all require actual swimming and are open from April 1 to October 31.

DRY TRAILS The Ibex Trail (moderate, 4 hours, guide required) runs all year, weather permitting, and the Malaqi Trail (moderate, 7 hours, guide required) runs from April 1 to October 31.

SECRET There are other activities in the canyon, including three rock-climbing paths and a dual zip line, which can be organized from the visitor center.

SPECIAL EVENTS Check in with the visitor center to find out which birds are migrating when you visit and which you're most likely to spot. Many start to migrate in August, but there are birds throughout the year.

ITINERATOR!

DAYS/HOURS The nature reserve is always open, but the visitor center opens at 08.00. Closed during Ramadan. Most of the trails (including the three wet trails) are closed November–March.

BEST TIME Spring and fall are busy. April and May have the lowest numbers.

TIME COMMITMENT You can do the Siq Trail in 2 hours, and in 4 hours you can finish most of the longer trails. Speed rules apply.

BASE If road-tripping, you can stay at the chalets (see *Sleep* below). Otherwise, do a day trip from Anchor Cities Amman (90km/1½ hours) or Suweimeh (40km/ 30 minutes).

BEST STRATEGY We recommend doing this as a day trip from Suweimeh, if you're staying at a Dead Sea resort. If not, and you're staying in Amman, you might want to spend one night in a chalet (see *Sleep* below) so you can add in the **Dead Sea (#3)** experience. Then build in as much time as you have for hiking, taking in the Siq Trail at a minimum. Go on a weekday to avoid crowds.

WALKS AND DRIVES P1, V1.

ITINERARIES High BUCKET! Scores: 7+; Off-the-Beaten-Path Jordan; Nature and Scenic; Active; Organized; National Parks/Reserves.

ARRIVAL PREP

PREBOOK Yes, register in advance at **w** wildjordan.com/content/booking.

REALITY CHECK Children under 18 not allowed. Extremely hot and dry temperatures most of the year. There are maximum group sizes, making weekend visits very difficult. Reserve in advance, if you can. Flowing water can be dangerous and cause injuries.

BRING Lunch, swimsuits, sunscreen, waterproof shoes, waterproof camera.

ACCESS Find the visitor center along the Dead Sea Highway, about 30km south of the Dead Sea hotel area in Suweimeh.

ADMISSION Each of the trails has a cost (**w** wildjordan.com/eco-tourism-section/rates): Siq and Ibex are 21 JD, Canyon is 31 JD, and Malaqi is 44 JD. Inquire at **w** wildjordan.com/content/booking for updated pricing on other trails.

RECOMMENDED GUIDE Some hikes require guides. For Siq, plan to take a guide unless you are in excellent physical shape.

VISITOR CENTER Yes, called the Mujib Adventure Center. Mujib brochures are available at **w** wildjordan.com/eco-tourism-section/brochures.

EAT Plan to bring everything you will need to eat and drink on a hot day. There is a café and restaurant at the park entrance. If staying at the Mujib Chalets, you can order a packed lunch or dinner.

SLEEP There are 15 double-room chalets to rent near the Mujib entrance and walkable to the Dead Sea. Book with Wild Jordan, below.

BUCKET!PEDIA

AKA Mujib; Arnon Stream; Mujib Nature Reserve; Mujib Biosphere Reserve; Wadi Mujib. *Historical era* Prehistoric: Copper Age. *Size* 212km²/82 square miles. *Elevation* From 900m above sea level to 396–420m below sea level (depending on who you cite).

CONTEXT Declared a nature reserve of Jordan in 1987, this region of mountains and valleys is known for its biodiversity thanks to its seven different water sources/tributaries. It flows heavily during the spring and summer, offering rivers and waterfalls through the more popular and wide canyons. Due to the abundance of water, the area is also an Important Bird Area, with migratory and resident birds providing a constant source of intrigue, particularly the big birds of prey. Originally set up as a breeding ground for the endangered Nubian Ibex, Mujib has also happily witnessed the mountain goat succeed in the region, with around 100 goats now registered in the reserve. Wild cats, hyenas, and other carnivores are resident. The Mujib region includes several walks with the potential to see rare mammals, though you'll have a much better chance of seeing plants and birds. Many of the trails end on the shores of the Dead Sea, so don't forget swimsuits.

WEBSITE **w** rscn.org.jo/content/mujib-biosphere-reserve-1; **w** wildjordan.com/destinations/mujib-biosphere-reserve.

WHERE TO NEXT?

THEMATIC *Noteworthy* Nature Reserves; Exploration. *Nature* Rivers, Lakes and Waterfalls; Desert; Canyons, Wadis and Makhteshim; Animals, Zoos and Wildlife; Birding; Plants, Gardens and Farms; Gorgeous Scenery; The Great Outdoors. *Scenic* Earth Panorama. *Active* Easy Hikes; Day Hikes; Wet Hikes; Experienced Hikers; Adventure/Extreme Land Sports; Adventure Water Sports. *Organized* Guided.

COMPLEMENTARY Other great 2-hour walks in Jordan are **Dana Biosphere Reserve (#21)**, **Ajloun Forest (#57)**, the *Al-Ayoun Trail*, and Yarmouk Forest (S1). Other wet hikes in the region are **Hezekiah's Tunnel**, **Yehudiya**, and Majrase-Betiha/Bethsaida Valley (I3). There are more birding sites at **Aqaba (#43)**, **Azraq Wetlands (#55)**, and **Hula Lake**.

NEARBY **Dead Sea (#3)** (30km/24 minutes), **Karak (#49)** (53km/53 minutes), **Modern Amman (#36)** and **Ancient Amman (#37)** (85km/1¼ hours), **Shobak** (135km/2 hours), **Petra (#2)** (166km/2½ hours), and **Aqaba (#43)** (242km/2½ hours).

#24 Mount Nebo

BROCHURE

RATINGS			MACRO-REGION
BUCKET! Score		5/10	P: Dead Sea (Jordan)
Ruin		2/5	
Entertainment		2/5	MICRO-REGION
Information		4/5	P2
Popularity		4/5	

PRIMARY THEME/CATEGORY Religion – Religious Figures – Kings and Prophets.

TOP The drive to Mount Nebo is consistently ranked one of the most beautiful road trips in the world.

HOLY LAND RELEVANCE In the Bible's Book of Deuteronomy, Moses spent a harrowing 40 years in the desert seeking the Promised Land. According to legend, Moses spent his final days atop Mount Nebo, viewing (but not entering) the expansive Promised Land before him.

ELECT ME! A sacred place on the biblical sites tour of western Jordan, affiliated with Moses' death, and providing a stunning panorama west towards Israel, with views of Jericho, the Dead Sea, Bethlehem, and Jerusalem on clear days. A 4th-century church commemorates Moses' final moments. Interesting mosaics are on view for visitors.

WORTH THE DETOUR? If you're not religious, this might not be for you. The mosaics are nice, but there are better ones in **Madaba (#19)** and **Umm ar-Rasas (#81)**. It does have a nice view, but it's not worth rearranging your whole schedule unless you're doing the *Road Trip P2* itinerary.

EXPERIENCES

CAN'T MISS That view, but also the drive to the top. Take it all in – the landscape is the whole point!

CHURCHES AND MOSAICS
★ *Memorial Church of Moses* This church was recently renovated into its traditional basilica style, incorporating a number of the older ruins it now covers, many of which have gorgeous mosaics.

★ *Sixth-century basilica* This contains perhaps the oldest of the mosaics. The mosaics here are portrayed along a grapevine motif, with swastika designs (pre-Nazi era, this was a positive symbol) and other geometric figures.

★ *Old Diaconicon Baptistery* A mosaic floor dates this church to August 531 CE. Hunting and pastoral scenes, with a number of native African beasts such as zebras, tigers, and lions.

★ *New Diaconicon Baptistery* Dating to 598 CE, with mosaics of flowers, animals, and geometrical figures.

★ *Theotokos Chapel* Dating to 604 CE, with mosaics of flowers and animals.

★ *The Brazen Serpent* An artistic representation by Giovanni Fantoni of a biblical story involving a brass serpent which God tells Moses to use to protect the Israelites against the real snakes that God had unleashed on Moses' enemies.

★ *Church of Saints Lot and Procopius* Located in Khirbet al-Mukhayyat, 2km away from Nebo, but on the same turnoff. Believed to be the town referenced in the Mesha Stele from the 9th century BCE. Contains a 560 CE mosaic with animals, hunting, fishing, and agriculture. Other sites in the area are in ruins.

ACTIVITIES Take in the sweeping view of the "Promised Land" from right outside the Church of Moses.

SECRET Skip the "ruined churches" in neighboring Hesban, Moses' Spring, and Khirbet Mukhayyat (except St. Lot, see above), which are too dilapidated to appreciate and too often closed.

SPECIAL EVENTS This is a working monastery and visitors are not allowed inside the monastery itself without permission. There may be special events happening simultaneously on holidays. Christmas Mass is popular. Reserve a mass/prayer for your group in advance.

ITINERATOR!

DAYS/HOURS Summer 08.00–18.00, winter 08.00–16.00.

BEST TIME You don't want to be blinded by the view, so sunset is actually not a great time to come. For the best camera shots, the morning is best. Also, the spring is pretty when the eucalyptus trees blossom.

TIME COMMITMENT As little as 15 minutes can be spent here, though on average guests spend 45–60 minutes. Speed rules apply.

BASE Best done on a day trip from Anchor Cities: Suweimeh (22km/30 minutes) or Amman (40km/1 hour).

BEST STRATEGY We recommend incorporating this site into a tour of other biblical sites in the region. It's not worth doing on its own.

WALKS AND DRIVES P2.

ITINERARIES Religion; Memorial; Pilgrimage.

ARRIVAL PREP

PREBOOK Mass, if inclined.

259

REALITY CHECK Popular tour-bus stop.

ACCESS Signage is not great for arrival. Leave Madaba's St. George Church on Palestine Street, which turns into Al Quds. It's a straight shot on this road all the way to Mount Nebo. Parking is available next to the site.

ADMISSION 2 JD will be requested upon entry.

RECOMMENDED GUIDE The museum has good explanations giving an account of the biblical and historical record.

EAT Plenty of restaurants here and in Madaba, some with views.

SLEEP Recommend to anchor in either Suweimeh or Amman.

BUCKET!PEDIA

AKA Siyagha ("the peak of the mountain") or Jabal Nebo in Arabic; Har Nivo (Hebrew). *Historical era* Roman/Byzantine. *Year constructed* Late 4th–late 6th centuries. *Elevation* 817m above sea level.

CONTEXT According to the Book of Deuteronomy, God instructed Moses to seek out Canaan, or the Holy Land. He told Moses that, upon seeing Canaan, he would not cross over. Rather, the land was sworn to his descendants: Abraham, Isaac, and Jacob. And thus Moses died at the age of 120, after 40 years of searching for the Promised Land, staring from the mountaintop at paradise below, unable to enter.

Is this where Moses died? Who knows. Moses, if he existed at all, lived in the 13th century BCE, some 1,700 years before a church was dedicated on this spot. That said, the sweeping view matches the biblical accounts, that's for sure. On clear days, you can see Jericho and Jerusalem, some 50km away.

The present-day site offers sweeping views of the valley below. They continue to astound. Do not skip the drive up to the site from the Dead Sea, which is equally spectacular. Try to go in the morning or at midday so you can actually look west – in the afternoon, the sun will be too strong and blinding to enjoy either the drive or photos.

On site, there is one recently renovated basilica that is supposed to take the form of the original basilica, which itself was built over the original 4th- and 5th-century buildings that were dedicated to Moses. In each of these ancient churches are interesting mosaics, done in a variety of motifs, with lots of winemaking, hunting, agriculture, and pastural practices emphasized.

While Moses' actual tomb has never been discovered, six tombs have been found carved into the bedrock below the floor of the present church. Debates remain about whether this is even the true Mount Nebo referenced in the Bible, though at this point does it matter? It's been recognized as the site for at least 1,600 years, with pilgrim tourists having visited the site as early as 394 CE. Another outstanding question is whether Moses' grave is not elsewhere. Jews and Muslims celebrate the site at Nabi Musa (C3) ("Moses' Tomb"), a site near Jericho.

Mount Nebo, however, still appeals. Christian, Jewish, and Muslim visitors will appreciate its significance given how important Moses is in the line of prophets. The view truly is spectacular. The drive is worth it alone. And there are several points of interest along the way.

CHRONOLOGY

Late 4th century CE: Egyptians are thought to have built a small church on the mountain where Moses is believed to have died.

394: first mention of a church commemorating Moses, made by Lady Aetheria, a Christian pilgrim touring the Holy Land. The site was thus already being visited by foreigners, lending some credence to the location.

Late 5th century: Church enlarged.

530s: Mosaics are lain on the church floor.

597: Church is rebuilt in the Byzantine basilica style.

604: Theotokos Chapel added as dedication to Mary, Mother of Jesus.

1932: Franciscans buy the site.

1935: First excavations.

2000: John Paul II visits the site.

2016: Site reopens after ten years of rehabilitation.

WEBSITE w montenebo.org; w custodia.org/en/sanctuaries/mount-nebo.

WHERE TO NEXT?

THEMATIC *Religion* Christianity; Kings, Prophets, and Saints; Old Testament; Churches; Burial; Pilgrimage. *Archaeology* Mosaics. *Structure* Memorial. *Nature* Mountains and Mounts. *Scenic* Historical Vantage; Earth Panorama.

COMPLEMENTARY For other biblical sites in Jordan, follow *Road Trip P2*. Other important Moses monuments are **Mount Sinai (#15)**, the *Church of the Transfiguration*, and Nabi Musa (C3). For more great sprawling views, try **Masada (#8)**, **Mount Sinai (#15)**, **King's Highway (#31)**, and *Mukawir*.

NEARBY **Modern Amman (#36)** and **Ancient Amman (#37)** (32km/45 minutes), *Mukawir* (35km/45 minutes), the **Dead Sea (#3)** (45km/50 minutes), and **Petra (#2)** (220km/2¾ hours).

#25 Caesarea

BROCHURE

RATINGS		MACRO-REGION
BUCKET! Score	8/10	E: Mediterranean Coast
Ruin	5/5	
Entertainment	4/5	**MICRO-REGION**
Information	5/5	E4
Popularity	4/5	

PRIMARY THEME/CATEGORY Archaeology – Roman – Herodian.

TOP Herodian structure in the region.

COMMENDATIONS Israel National Park.

HOLY LAND RELEVANCE Pontius Pilate, St. Paul, Origen, Rabbi Akiva, and other famous biblical characters and theologians have history at Caesarea. The Crusaders took the city during their religious conquest of Israel.

ELECT ME! An ancient Roman city built during the time of Herod perched just above the sea, Caesarea offers dramatic views of classical Roman structures, including an amphitheater, hippodrome, and aqueduct. The visitor center/museum is top-notch.

WORTH THE DETOUR? Absolutely. This is actually a great stop if you have limited time, as it's close to **Tel Aviv (#5)** and can be done quickly if need be. If you have no plans to visit other Roman or Crusader ruins, and will not be leaving Israel, this is your best chance to see the extent of Roman, Byzantine, and Crusader reach.

EXPERIENCES

CAN'T MISS It's rare to be able to visualize an ancient site, especially one that has been razed and recreated as much as Caesarea. Be sure to visit the Travel Through Time multimedia display, a worthwhile 10 minutes, so you can get a stimulating and visually orienting understanding of the park before you begin your journey.

SITES
★ *Roman Theater* A reconstruction of the original Herodian house, which seated upwards of 4,000.
★ *Herodian Hippodrome* Horseshoe-shaped theater for watching horse races and other sporting events 2,000 years ago.
★ *Crusader City* Mostly built in 1251 by King Louis IX of France. Walls here once stood 10m tall.
★ *Port of Sebastos* The grandest of the time, now submerged under the Mediterranean, but then a three-part port, with the old Straton's Tower harbor being the innermost ring, the middle portion a natural bay, and the outer basin the architectural marvel that gave Caesarea its great Roman reputation.
★ *Roman Aqueduct* Nice at sunset! The aqueduct is mostly buried under sand, though peeks out at the northern end of Caesarea.
★ *Byzantine Streets* Still being excavated, but you can make out some of the streets by their (formerly) colonnaded pathways.
★ *Hippodrome* In ruins, but once seated over 30,000 fans.

ACTIVITIES Tour the visitor center and engage with the interactive display, Travel Through Time. Climb to the top of the Tower of Time. Dive with Old Caesarea Diving Center to see the old Herodian port, now submerged, the highlight of the Underwater Museum at Caesarea. Night dives also available. Admire the *Ralli Museums (E3)* of Jewish Sephardic and Latin American artwork. Swing at Caesarea Golf Club, the country's only full-size golf course.

SECRET Don't miss Aqueduct Beach (E4), to which you can drive (3km/6 minutes) or walk (2km/25 minutes).

SPECIAL EVENTS Lots of concerts at the Caesarea Amphitheater (w touristisrael. com/concerts-in-caesarea/).

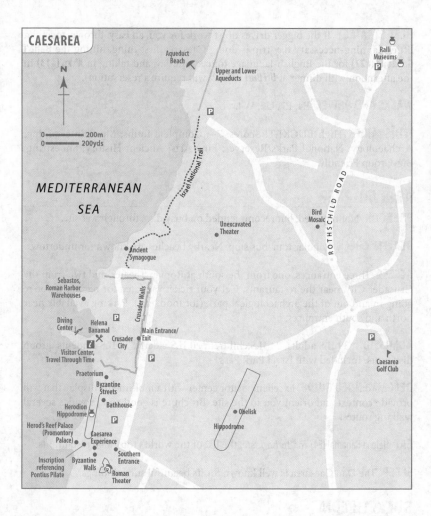

ITINERATOR!

DAYS/HOURS Summer 08.00–18.00, fall 08.00–17.00, winter/spring 08.00–16.00, 08.00–13.00 Friday and holiday eves, entrance closes 1 hour before closing.

BEST TIME There is not a lot of shade on site, so morning or afternoon is preferable to midday if visiting in the summer. Weekends are always busy, particularly because the site is open on Saturdays.

TIME COMMITMENT 1½–2 hours is enough time to stroll through the highlights and make a quick visit to the museum. In 4 hours, do the grand loop and visitor center. Add time for lunch. Speed rules apply.

BASE You can do this road trip on your way north from or south to **Tel Aviv (#5)** (60km/50 minutes) using *Road Trips E4, E7, U2,* or *W4* as guides. Otherwise, you can visit from Tel Aviv in one morning or afternoon.

BEST STRATEGY If the bigger drives don't work for you, an easy, thrown-together, little-planning-necessary day trip is doing Caesarea first thing, hitting the **Bahá'í Gardens (#27)** for the English-language tour at midday, and taking in **Akko (#13)** in the afternoon with dinner at *Uri Buri* (which will require a reservation).

WALKS AND DRIVES E4, E7, U2, W4.

ITINERARIES High BUCKET! Scores: 7+; Complete Ruins; Most Entertaining; Archaeology; National Parks/Reserves; Fine Arts; Ancient History; Shoestring; Big-Group Friendly.

ARRIVAL PREP

PREBOOK Not required, but recommended on busy days through website.

REALITY CHECK Popular tour-bus stop. Nearby beaches are known for undertow.

ACCESS Three entrances, one from the south at Roman Theater, and two from the Crusader City, near the restaurants. Get your ticket validated for reentry if you're going in and out of the archaeological park (for food, etc.). Parking available near north and south entrances.

ADMISSION 39 ILS adults, 24 ILS children, 20 ILS elderly, 34 ILS students, group discounts. Included with Israel Park Pass.

RECOMMENDED GUIDE Excellent visitor center with a multimedia display that will provide context and orient you to the site. Brochure is good and provides several walking routes.

EAT Helena Banamal (E4) made *La Liste*, the list of the world's top 1,000 restaurants.

SLEEP The Dan Caesarea is well known for its beautiful surroundings.

BUCKET!PEDIA

AKA Caesarea Maritima; Caesarea Palestinae; sits atop the ancient Phoenician site of Pyrgos Stratonos ("Straton's Tower"). *Historical era Roman/Byzantine: Herodian*, also *Islamic: Crusader* and *Ottoman*. *Year founded/constructed* Founded in 4th century BCE; buildings mostly date to Herodian period. *Size* 3.5km along the beach, a total of 31km², though the ruins represent only a portion of that space.

CONTEXT Caesarea was selected for its sea access and calm port waters, first in the Persian era in the 4th century BCE, and again during Herod's major reign. In honor of Augustus Caesar, who had gifted the site to Herod, it was named Caesarea. The site was built up by Herod to rival other Mediterranean ports, and now serves as a well-preserved (and restored) site representing multiple levels of history – from Herodian times through later Roman, Byzantine, and Crusader rule, with some noticeable Islamic influences. Caesarea has a decidedly winning view, particularly if you were a spectator at the theater or hippodrome during those early years.

Without a natural harbor, Herod decided to build an artificial port using completely new technology to transform 100,000m² of rough sea ground into a working base of operations. To create such a structure, the Romans invented a way to temper concrete underwater, which formed the basis for the mammoth breakwater port. The experiment worked, turning Caesarea into a maritime hub (called Caesarea Maritima) and making the port the largest in the eastern Mediterranean. The success ultimately converted Caesarea into a major city. Caesarea replaced Jerusalem as the capital of the Roman province of Judea, and maintained capital status as the province changed to Syria Palaestina and Palaestina Prima throughout the Roman and Byzantine years. By the 6th century CE, tectonic movement (and possibly a tsunami) had caused the jetties to be buried under at least 5m of sea, rendering the harbor useless.

Pontius Pilate, who famously sentenced Jesus to death, was based out of Caesarea. A piece of limestone on site is etched with an inscription bearing Pilate's name, which is the only piece of evidence, save the Bible, confirming the existence of the Roman prefect.

CHRONOLOGY

4th century BCE: Straton, ruler of Sidon, builds a port here, crafts a tower (now referred to as Straton's Tower), which was later the base for Herod's port.

22 BCE: Commissioned by Herod, construction begins on a grand port, the likes of which had not been seen before, and which enclosed some 100,000m^2.

6 CE: Caesarea becomes the seat for Roman governors. Pontius Pilate dedicates a temple on the port site; visitors can see Pilate's name engraved on a stone block.

66: Great Jewish Revolt begins in Caesarea when religious tensions rise between Jewish and pagan residents. After four years of fighting, the revolt ends with 20,000 Jews killed.

70: Destruction of the Temple in Jerusalem: 2,500 more Jews sacrificed, this time as part of the "entertainment" in Caesarea's theater.

130: Earthquake causes grave damage to the harbor.

135: After the Bar Kokhba Revolt, Romans torture and execute the famous Jewish sage Rabbi Akiva here.

c250: Origen wrote the Hexapla in the Theological Library of Caesarea, once housing 30,000 religious texts (the most at the time).

640: Site conquered by Arab armies, gradual decline in importance.

1101: Crusaders take over. Baldwin I at the helm.

1251: King Louis IX constructs the Crusader City.

1291: Mamluks destroy the site again. Sand dunes take the rest.

1878: Ottomans transplant a group of Bosnian Muslims here (their mosque remains) but the inhabitants abandon the site after the Arab–Israeli War of 1948.

1940: Kibbutz Sde Yom residents till the land and discover many ancient relics, the obvious indication an impressive city once stood here.

1950s–1960s: Extensive archaeological excavations.

1952: Israeli city of Caesarea established near ancient ruins.

1960: Divers discover an image of the ancient port, once in the shadow of three huge statues atop two massive towers. Remnants have not been discovered.

1961: Pilate Stone unveiled.

WEBSITE w parks.org.il/en/reserve-park/caesarea-national-park/.

WHERE TO NEXT?

THEMATIC *Noteworthy* National Parks. *Archaeology* Herodian; Byzantine; Shipwrecks; Impressive Structural Remains. *Structure* Historic Monuments. *Nature* Earthquakes. *Active* Surfing; Adventure Water Sports.

COMPLEMENTARY Other great national parks that are not Jerusalem are **Masada (#8)**, **Makhtesh Ramon (#28)**, and **Avdat (#48)**. For more spectacular Roman ruins, try **Jerash (#14)**, **Beit She'an (#39)**, and **Tsipori (#56)**. Other impressive sites on the Mediterranean are **Akko (#13)**, **Bahá'í Gardens (#27)**, **Dor HaBonim (#100)**, and *Rosh HaNikra*.

NEARBY Margalit Winery (E6) (6km/10 minutes), *Zichron Ya'akov* (14km/17 minutes), **Dor HaBonim (#100)** (21km/27 minutes), *Nahal Me'arot/Wadi el-Mughara* (23km/21 minutes), **Bahá'í Gardens (#27)** (43km/35 minutes), **Megiddo (#59)** (46km/40 minutes), **Tel Aviv (#5)** (53km/40 minutes), **Akko (#13)** (66km/50 minutes), and *Rosh HaNikra* (83km/1 hour).

#26 Jericho and Hisham's Palace

BROCHURE

RATINGS		MACRO-REGION
BUCKET! Score	7/10	C: West Bank
Ruin	4/5	
Entertainment	2/5	**MICRO-REGION**
Information	2/5	C3
Popularity	4/5	

PRIMARY THEME/CATEGORY Archaeology – Ancient Cities and Remains – Mound/Tels/Artificial Hills.

TOP One of the oldest cities in the world, it potentially has the oldest tower, walls, and stairways of any site in the world. Lowest city in the world.

HOLY LAND RELEVANCE The parable of the Good Samaritan takes place on the road to Jericho from Jerusalem. The prophet Elisha purified the water at Ein es-Sultan (today, Tel Jericho) and made it suitable for drinking. Jebel Quruntal, or the Mount of Temptation, can be seen in the distance with its cliff-hanging monastery, *Deir Quruntal*. This is said to be where Jesus was tested by Satan. Zacchaeus, a dishonest tax collector, also climbed into a sycamore tree in Jericho in order to see Jesus and repent. And John the Baptist was alleged to have received his own baptism here. The walls of Jericho are famous for having "come tumbling down" – a reference to Joshua's battle here.

ELECT ME! Famous for its superlatives: being one of the oldest and oldest continually inhabited cities in the world, for its "walls of Jericho," and its several biblical connections. More than 20 layers of ruins have been discovered, so this site is best considered as cross-temporal. Two popular spots here (different periods) are the cable car to the Mount of Temptation and a short drive to the Umayyad winter castle site called Hisham's Palace. Visits here are for archaeology and history buffs.

WORTH THE DETOUR? You need a fairly active imagination to make sense of the ruins. They are remarkably small, but the history is astounding when you consider that 20 different civilizations have lived here, and you can see pieces of each in successive layers of mud. Worth your time when considered in combination with *Deir Quruntal* and Hisham's Palace.

EXPERIENCES

CAN'T MISS Hisham's Palace is not located in Tel Jericho, but shouldn't be skipped. It represents a much different period (only 1,300 years ago vs. 11,000 years ago) but is easier to visualize.

SITES

★ *Tel es-Sultan* This is Tel Jericho, or the principal archaeological site (not to be confused with modern-day Jericho) highlighting 20 successive layers of history.

★ *Walls of Jericho* Dated to Neolithic period (8000 BCE), the walls were likely built for floods or defense.

★ *Tower of Jericho* 8.5m stone structure also from Neolithic period – one of the earliest stone structures in existence.

★ *Mount of Temptation* Dangling on the side of this mountain is *Deir Quruntal* (or Monastery of the Temptation), which hosts the site where Jesus was tempted by the Devil. Views and a cable car ride are further highlights.

★ *Hisham's Palace* Winter retreat of 8th-century caliph Hisham Ibn Abd al-Malik, and featuring the Tree of Life mosaic depicting gazelles and a lion.

★ *Tree of Zacchaeus* Sycamore tree more than 2,000 years old.

ACTIVITIES Take the cable car to the Mount of Temptation; walk the streets of Ancient Jericho; participate in an archaeological dig.

SECRET If you're really short on time, the six-pointed window-wheel at Hisham's Palace makes a nice photo opportunity, as does the Tree of Life mosaic, halfway through the route.

ITINERATOR!

DAYS/HOURS Tel es-Sultan/Hisham's Palace: 08.00–17.00 daily; *Deir Quruntal*: 08.00–16.00 Monday–Friday, 08.00–14.00 Saturday, closed Sunday.

TIME COMMITMENT Two hours is more than enough time in Tel es-Sultan, even reading all the placards. You can add in a trip to *Deir Quruntal*, which can be done in an hour, but many stop to enjoy the views. Hisham's Palace will add 1 hour including the introductory video. Speed rules apply.

BASE Anchoring from Jerusalem (25km/45 minutes) is ideal here, as it's the closest spot.

BEST STRATEGY Start early at Tel es-Sultan, before it gets too hot. Buy your tickets for Jericho and the cable car (or plan to walk). Once you've visited both sites, drive to Hisham's Palace (3km/7 minutes).

WALKS AND DRIVES C3, W1.

ITINERARIES High BUCKET! Scores: 7+; Archaeology; Ancient History; Pilgrimage.

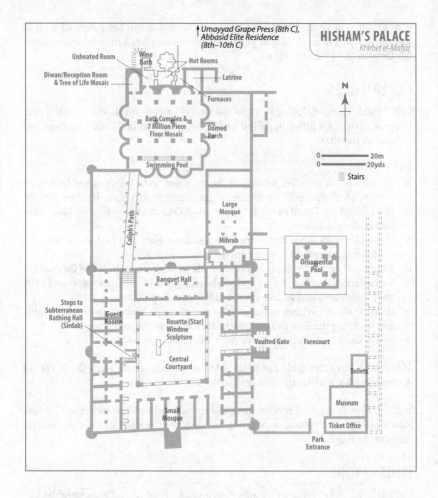

HISHAM'S PALACE
Khirbet el-Mafjar

↑ *Umayyad Grape Press (8th C),*
Abbasid Elite Residence
(8th–10th C)

Unheated Room

Wine
Bath

Hot Rooms

Diwan/Reception Room
& Tree of Life Mosaic

Latrine

Furnaces

Bath Complex &
7 Million Piece
Floor Mosaic

Domed
Porch

Swimming Pool

Caliph's Path

Large
Mosque

Mihrab

N

0 ——————— 20m
0 ——————— 20yds

▦ Stairs

Ornamental
Pool

Banquet Hall

Steps to
Subterranean
Bathing Hall
(Sirdab)

Guest
Rooms

Rosette (Star)
Window
Sculpture

Central
Courtyard

Vaulted Gate   Forecourt

Toilets

Museum

Ticket Office

Small
Mosque

Park
Entrance

ARRIVAL PREP

PREBOOK Jericho Cable Car.

REALITY CHECK Popular tour-bus stop. Jericho Cable Car to ***Deir Quruntal*** can book up, so buy tickets in advance.

BRING Passport to get through Israel/Palestine checkpoints.

ACCESS Drive to the end of Route 1 from Jerusalem and make a left at Route 90. The first major street (with big signs) is for Jericho (opposite Allenby Bridge) where you'll present your passport at border inspection. You will pass through the town of Jericho to get to Tel Jericho, near Ein es-Sultan. ***Deir Quruntal*** is on the cliffs at the end of Tel Jericho, but the Jericho Cable Car is near the entrance to the archaeological site (you can also hike the cliff).

ADMISSION 10 ILS adults, 5 ILS children.

RECOMMENDED GUIDE The placards do not have great content and are a bit sun-bleached. A guide can add context and point out the most prominent layers.

VISITOR CENTER Jericho has a Tourist Information Center, but it's not a museum. They will answer questions. There's a video at Hisham's Palace.

EAT Not famous food, but you can certainly find grub, particularly meat.

SLEEP Best bet is Jerusalem, though there are budget hotels here.

BUCKET!PEDIA

AKA Tel Jericho is known as Ariha in Arabic and Yeriho in Hebrew, but really Tel es-Sultan is the famous site; Hisham's Palace as Qasr Hisham (literal translation) at Khirbet al-Mafjar (ruins of Mafjar). *Historical era* Prehistoric: Neolithic to *Ancient Israel: Kingdom of Israel and Judah*, then *Roman/Byzantine: Byzantine* to *Islamic: Umayyad*. *Year founded* c9000 BCE.

CONTEXT Jericho is one of the oldest inhabited cities in the world, made famous for its mythical "walls." Today these walls are nothing more than layers of settlements buried in earthen sediment, but in 8000 BCE they were surely a novelty. Their discovery makes Jericho the "oldest walled city in the world," though it's difficult to say whether it was the first or just the oldest in our archaeological record (so far).

Jericho is a tel, or a multilayered excavation site. More than 20 different civilizations have laid claim to Jericho, and each has a layer of history on record helping to inform of their influence and association with the site. How it works is that a culture will abandon their homes for some reason: loss in battle, change in climate, earthquake, etc. The buildings that remain are either repurposed by the conquering nation, razed to the ground, or buried and built over. However, the foundations of buildings are often left intact and then built on top of. In this way, the new culture adds its own influence, stays on site for decades or centuries, is defeated, the buildings are again razed or repurposed, and the process repeats. The earth, pottery, coins, and other artifacts within help to date the various periods of history. In this way, more than 20 successive cultures are known to have made their mark on Jericho. The oldest discovery thus far dates to 9600 BCE when Natufian hunter-gatherer groups first settled permanently at Tel es-Sultan.

Up the road a bit is Hisham's Palace. This site was built several centuries after the abandonment of Tel es-Sultan, starting in 734 CE. The impressive winter hunting retreat of Caliph Hisham Ibn 'Abd al-Malik near Jericho, one of the final Umayyad Desert Castles, contains beautiful and complete mosaics, and once boasted impressive architecture. There is a model of the proposed site at the end of the walkabout. The site suffered irreparable damage from the 749 CE Galilee earthquake.

CHRONOLOGY

9000 BCE: At the beginning of the Holocene, or human epoch, some Natufian groups settled permanently in Tel es-Sultan, close to the Ein es-Sultan spring.
8000 BCE: Walls of Jericho erected, oldest yet discovered. Tower of Jericho constructed at same time and will remain world's tallest structure for more than 5,000 years.
7800–7500 BCE: First Jericho settlement abandoned.
6800 BCE: Second settlement begins. Burials of the dead, mud-brick architecture, and artistic statues and human representations. Of particular interest are real human

skulls whose jawbones were removed, eyes replaced, and the heads covered in plaster, then buried. This civilization lasts 2,000 years.

4500 BCE: Replaced with a new civilization, and a quick succession of waves of immigrants comes through.

3150 BCE: Several new walls built, obviously defensive, but the latter finds were found to be erected in haste, and poorly, likely indicating rapidly approaching enemy combatants.

2600 BCE: Bronze Age settlement by Amorites.

1900 BCE: Canaanites capture town.

1573 BCE: City abandoned for several centuries after major earthquake burns city.

1400 BCE: Wall of Jericho "destroyed" by Joshua and his fellow religious worshipers who blew horns at the wall until it fell.

10th–9th centuries BCE: City rebuilt by Hiel the Bethelite.

7th century BCE: Last major settlement, building over previous layers of town.

600–580 BCE: Babylonian exile; Tel es-Sultan abandoned for the last time.

2nd century BCE: Tulul Abu el-Alaiq, the Jewish/Hasmonean Winter Palaces, built near ancient Jericho to serve as new administrative capital in winter.

1st century CE: Abandoned with the departure of Roman troops and the dispersal of Jews after the Roman–Jewish wars.

4th century: Ericha, a new Jericho, is constructed during the Byzantine era in the region of present-day Jericho, with churches and synagogues.

659: Ariha (Arab name for Ericha) comes under Umayyad dynastic control. Earthquake in same year destroys Ariha.

734: Construction begins on Hisham's Palace by Walid Ibn Yazid for Caliph Hisham Ibn Abd el-Malik.

749: Site nearly complete, but destroyed and abandoned following the 747/749 Galilee earthquakes.

1867: First excavation of Tel es-Sultan.

WEBSITE w visitpalestine.ps/jericho-intro/.

WHERE TO NEXT?

THEMATIC *Religion* Jesus' Ministries and Miracles; Old Testament; New Testament; Biblical Battlefields. *Archaeology* Tels; Prehistory; Bronze Age; Herodian; Islamic I; Mosaics; Walls; Active Excavations. *Structure* Infrastructure. *Nature* Geographical Superlative; Desert; Earthquakes. *Scenic* Urban Landscape. *Society* Large Towns. *People* Arab.

COMPLEMENTARY Other oldest cities are: **Biblical Tels (#38)**, including **Megiddo (#59)**, *Tel Beer Sheva*, and *Tel Hazor*; **Old City Jerusalem (#1)**; **Tel Dan (#63)**; and *Tel Ashkelon*. Other Umayyad structures in Israel are: **Dome of the Rock (#6)** and **Al-Aqsa Mosque (#65)** on **Temple Mount (#12)**; Khirbet al-Minya (G3); and the White Mosque (D8) of Ramle. While in Palestine, don't forget to check out **Bethlehem (#40)**, the **Tomb of the Patriarchs and Old Town of Hebron (#46)**, **Ramallah (#68)**, and **Herodion (#90)**.

NEARBY *Deir Quruntal* (cable car on site at Tel es-Sultan), *Tulul Abu el-Alaiq* (3km/ 7 minutes), **St. George's Monastery (#97)** (5km/5 minutes), Qasr al-Yahud (C3) (15km/ 20 minutes), **Dead Sea (#3)** (25km/30 minutes); **Qumran (#70)** (28km/30 minutes), Inn of the Good Samaritan (C3) (28km/28 minutes), **Old City Jerusalem (#1)** (47km/45 minutes), and **Ramallah (#68)** (60km/60 minutes).

#27 Bahá'í Gardens

BROCHURE

RATINGS	
BUCKET! Score	8/10
Ruin	n/a
Entertainment	3/5
Information	4/5
Popularity	4/5

MACRO-REGION
E: Mediterranean Coast

MICRO-REGIONS
E1, E5, F1

PRIMARY THEME/CATEGORY Structure – Architecture – Landscape/Streetscape.

TOP Most beautifully landscaped gardens outside of Versailles.

COMMENDATIONS UNESCO World Heritage Site, along with other Bahá'í Holy Places in *Haifa* and the Western Galilee, 2008.

HOLY LAND RELEVANCE Many do not think of the Bahá'í when they think of the Holy Land, perhaps because the faith is comparatively new (19th century). Yet the two most holy sites for members of the Bahá'í Faith are found in **Akko (#13)** and *Haifa*. The Bahá'ís' Universal House of Justice, the nine members of which govern the religion, is based near the Gardens.

ELECT ME! These terraced gardens are Haifa's most famous tourist attraction. An easy day trip, they're also a marvel and a beauty. Hugging a sheer cliffside that ascends about 500m, their 450 plant species are aligned symmetrically and concentrically, in 19 circles that expand out from the Shrine of the Báb, one of the Bahá'í faith's revered leaders. Do visit and plan appropriately: tour guides are required, but are free and available at certain times each day. The walk goes downhill.

WORTH THE DETOUR? If you are in a hurry, you can skip the rest of Haifa. If you are only spending one day in the north, it would be better spent in the Galilee. But if you are taking a tour of the coast, or are planning a multi-stop itinerary in north Israel, the Bahá'í Gardens should rank high on your list of things to see.

EXPERIENCES

CAN'T MISS The English-language tour, so make sure you show up on time. Otherwise, you'll be taking pictures from behind a gate rather than in the garden itself.

SITES The spiritual leader's body rests in the **Shrine of the Báb**, the gold dome of which contains nearly 12,000 Portuguese tiles. You can visit the inside, shoes removed, silence a must. The **Inner Gardens** surround the shrine and can be approached without a guide. There are **19 concentric terraces**, a holy number in the Bahá'í religion. Neither the **Universal House of Justice** nor the **International Bahá'í Archives** are open to the public.

ACTIVITIES Taking the **Panorama Tour**. Count the **steps**: how many did you get?

SECRET A number of Baháʼí sites in the area make up the UNESCO designation, including the *Shrine of Baháʼuʼlláh* in **Akko (#13)** and 26 structures at 11 locations in Akko and *Haifa*.

SPECIAL EVENTS Check w bahai.ca/holy-days/ for annual holidays.

ITINERATOR!

DAYS/HOURS The English-language tour is every day at noon except Wednesday, but double-check as times can change. The grounds are open 09.00–16.00, but not all parts of the site can be visited. The shrine and inner gardens are only open 09.00–noon a few days a week (check website). Closed Baháʼí holy days and Yom Kippur.

BEST TIME All seasons (but summer will be hot). The gardens change foliage and are in bloom constantly, each season bringing new life and stunning visuals.

TIME COMMITMENT You can walk in and out of the gardens (there is security) to get a quick look, but highly recommended is the guided tour, which takes 1 hour. Speed rules don't apply with guide.

BASE Easy add-on for many road trips, and you can stop here or in Akko for the night. Or use Anchor Cities Tel Aviv (95km/1¼ hours) or Rosh Pina (80km/1 hour).

BEST STRATEGY Lots of good options. The Baháʼí Gardens can be done as a day trip from Tel Aviv, part of a whirlwind trip of the north, a stop on the way to the Galilee, or as part of a stay in Haifa itself.

WALKS AND DRIVES E1, E5, F1, W5.

ITINERARIES High BUCKET! Scores: 7+; Most Popular; Noteworthy; Structure; Nature and Scenic; Organized; UNESCO; National Parks/Reserves; Relaxation; Memorial; Under the Sun; Shoestring; Pilgrimage.

ARRIVAL PREP

PREBOOK Not applicable.

REALITY CHECK Popular tour-bus stop. Check the website for periodic closures of the shrine and gardens due to maintenance and cleaning. Can be dangerous when it rains! And wear modest dress.

BRING Clothes that cover your shoulders and knees – this is a holy place. Shoes with good traction in case of rain. In the summer, it's hot – sunscreen, hat, sunglasses. Cameras allowed, except in shrines.

ACCESS The tour starts at 45 Yefe Nof Street at the upper part of the gardens.

RECOMMENDED GUIDE To see the grounds you have to use their tour guides, who are excellent. English guides perform every day except Wednesday at noon (arrive 10 minutes early). First-come, first-served. Tour information (including language availability) can be found at w ganbahai.org.il/guided-tours.

VISITOR CENTER There's a hidden visitor center below Terrace 11.

EAT You can sip on water, but no other food or drink is allowed inside the site. There are some famous restaurants in *Haifa* and **Akko (#13)**: hummus places in both; Israeli and seafood places in Akko. See those electives for more information.

SLEEP You can stay in *Haifa*, if you wish, but **Tel Aviv (#5)** is a better bet. Two great hotels in **Akko (#13)** too.

BUCKET!PEDIA

AKA Terraces of the Baháʼí Faith; Hanging Gardens of Haifa. *Historical era* Modern. *Year founded/constructed* 1953 shrine; 2001 gardens. *Size* 200,000m².

CONTEXT The Baháʼí Gardens of Haifa are situated right downtown on a beautifully landscaped, terraced cliff. Nearly 100 gardeners are kept on staff full-time to maintain the lawns and manicure the plants. The symmetry is immediately noticeable, as is the care that goes into keeping these gardens pristine. Background on the Baháʼí faith is given during the free public tours which are equally fascinating. This, and other Baháʼí holy places in the area, were together declared a UNESCO World Heritage Site, though these are the most lavish and impressive. The gardens surround the Shrine of the Báb, the founder of the Bábi Faith, and the second most holy place in the Baháʼí religion (the first is the *Shrine of Baháʼuʼlláh* in Akko).

The first two leaders of the Baháʼí religion – Báb and Baháʼuʼlláh – lived, prophesied, and were imprisoned in Haifa and Akko, respectively. The religion began when the Báb proclaimed himself as a spiritual successor to Jesus and Muhammad. After he died, Baháʼuʼlláh took the mantle and his followers have since been known as Baháʼís, after his name.

The Baháʼís are monotheistic and believe in the same God as Jews, Christians, and Muslims. The principal tenets of the faith are prayer, work, marriage, a 19-day fast each year, a 19% tax tithe paid to the Universal House of Justice of the Baháʼí Faith, teetotaling, disengagement from partisan politics, and unity among all peoples, religions, and gender.

The gardens seek to be a quiet, contemplative place free from judgment or ill thoughts. The Shrine of the Báb serves to harmonize Eastern and Western architectural influences, while the gardens incorporate English, Indian, and Persian influences. Their design incorporates a terraced staircase, looping around 19 concentric circles which geometrically conform to the design putting the burial site of the forefather of the Baháʼí faith, the Shrine of the Báb, at the center of this stunning achievement in landscape design. There are some 450 plant types within the gardens, each selected for reasons of size and proportion to create a distinct look and style.

CHRONOLOGY

1819 CE: Siyyid Ali Muhammad Shirazi is born in Iran.
1844: Shirazi claims to be a messenger of God, calls himself Báb, meaning "gate" to the Hidden Twelfth Imam in Shiʼa Islam, gains a following, starts publishing, and later claims to be a manifestation of God. His followers are known as Bábis.
1850: Báb is executed in Persia.
1863: One of the Báb's followers, Baháʼuʼlláh, claims to be the manifestation of God, as foretold by Báb prior to his death.

1868–92: Baháʼuʼlláh imprisoned in Akko. Writes *Kitáb-i-Aqdas*, the central book of laws for Baháʼís, and writes treatises on unity in the divided world. Imprisoned for 24 years until he dies of illness.
1909: Báb's body is brought to Haifa.
1953: Shrine of the Báb constructed to serve as mausoleum.
2001: Gardens finished.

WEBSITE w ganbahai.org.il/visit-us.

WHERE TO NEXT?

THEMATIC *Noteworthy* UNESCO; Exotic/Wow. *Religion* Religious Minorities; Other Holy Places; Pilgrimage. *Structure* Historic Monuments; Landscape; Impressive Feats. *Nature* Parks. *Scenic* Urban Landscape; Most Photographed. *Organized* Guided.

COMPLEMENTARY Other Baháʼí sites of interest include the **Shrine of Baháʼuʼlláh**. Famous Baháʼí houses of worship elsewhere in the world: Wilmette, Illinois (oldest surviving Baháʼí temple); Lotus Temple, New Delhi, India; and the Baháʼí Temple in Santiago, Chile. The most far-flung is the Baháʼí House of Worship in Tiapapata, Samoa, and there are others in Sydney, Germany, Uganda, and Panama.

NEARBY **Mount Carmel** (17km/30 minutes), **Beit She'arim (#79)** (22km/26 minutes), **Akko (#13)** (26km/26 minutes); **Megiddo (#59)** (34km/34 minutes), *Akhziv Beach* (38km/38 minutes), **Dor HaBonim (#100)** (38km/37 minutes), *Rosh HaNikra* (43km/42 minutes), **Caesarea (#25)** (43km/34 minutes), and **Tel Aviv (#5)** (93km/68 minutes).

#28 Makhtesh Ramon

BROCHURE

RATINGS		MACRO-REGION
BUCKET! Score	7/10	J: Negev
Ruin	1/5	
Entertainment	2/5	**MICRO-REGIONS**
Information	4/5	J2, J3
Popularity	3/5	

PRIMARY THEME/CATEGORY Scenic – Vistas – Nature Panorama.

TOP Largest erosion crater (*makhtesh*) in the world.

COMMENDATIONS International Dark Sky Park, 2017; Israel Nature Reserve.

HOLY LAND RELEVANCE Several of the markers from the Nabataean **Incense Route (#73)** have been found in Makhtesh Ramon.

ELECT ME! Some call it Israel's Grand Canyon. The colors and vistas astound, while some of the hiking options are doable for even average or non-committed hikers (though you do have to appreciate/enjoy the desert). Also great for stargazing and fossil spotting.

WORTH THE DETOUR? This is worth at least a stop if you're on your way to **Eilat (#78)**. Otherwise, it's its own destination. If you're into desert hiking, it's a must-do. If you don't like the heat, and have no other desert adventures in your itinerary, it's too far out of the way.

EXPERIENCES

CAN'T MISS The visitor center for its views, hiking guidance, and a great 3D display of the crater.

GEOLOGICAL FORMATIONS

★ *HaMinsara, or The Carpentry Shop* Near the visitor center, these prismatic rocks with sawed edges were created from exposure to extremely hot lava.

★ *Giv'at Ga'ash (north end) and Karney Ramon (south end)* Extinct volcanos, now hills of basalt, the byproduct of volcanic eruptions cooled quickly above ground.

★ *Ammonite Wall* At the southern end of the makhtesh is this sheer rock face with spiral-shelled ammonite fossils embedded within. These octopus-like creatures with a shell lived some 80–90 million years ago when the Negev was covered by a vast sea.

★ *Shen Ramon, or Ramon's Tooth* Near the Ammonite wall is this black, magma-based rock looking like a jagged tooth jutting out of the earth.

EASY/MODERATE HIKES

★ *Albert Promenade* Easy, with a few hills, 2km/1–2 hours, from the visitor center through the geological garden and various exhibits, providing views of the Western Makhtesh at Camel Hill.

★ *The Prism/Carpentry Shop* Easy, some steps, maybe 30m, with parking in front of the hike start.

★ *Lotz Cisterns* Easy, 3 hours, footpaths.

★ *Saharonim Stronghold* Easy, 0.5km/1 hour, visit part of the **Incense Route (#73)**.

★ *Har Ardon* Moderate, 7km/2–3 hours, loop trail; this mountain is what gives the crater its heart shape on its eastern part.

★ *Saharonim to Parsat Nekarot* Moderate, 6km/2–3 hours, for views and fitness, popular.

LONGER DAY HIKES There are a bunch of options, especially if you have a car. The choice is going to depend heavily on weather and how much time you can spend outdoors. A number of hikes leave from the **Mitzpe Ramon** visitor center. We recommend you talk to a ranger, tell them how much time you have available, and they'll give you advice accordingly.

MULTIDAY HIKES There is a two-day hike, seeing the highlights, with camping (w negevtrails.com/cross-ramon-crater) and an eight-day hike, circumnavigating the whole crater, with camping (w negevtrails.com/ramon-crater-8-days-trek).

DRIVES The Ramon Colors Route in the eastern part of Makhtesh Ramon is a dirt road highlighting various geological points of interest.

275

OBSERVATION POINTS The **visitor center** has great views. **Albert Promenade** has plenty of views while walking, particularly up Camel Hill (Har Gamal). **Arod Lookout** is the westernmost point of the crater, near Mount Ramon (dirt road, all vehicles, opposite turnoff to Lotz Cisterns). Hike the mountains – you can do it! Stay in the Beresheet Hotel (J2) (expensive). If you're driving through the desert, you will actually cut through the crater on **Highway 40**, and there are several good turnout places to get photos.

ANIMALS Wild animals include Nubian Ibex, Onager (a local variety of wild donkey), Arabian Leopard, Dorcas Gazelle, and Striped Hyena. The Hai-Ramon Living Desert Museum (next to the visitor center) lets you see several indigenous creatures. There is also an Alpaca Farm (J2) (w alpaca.co.il).

BIRDS Eagles, kestrels, owls, and vultures.

ACTIVITIES **Astronomy Israel** provides a window (actually, a telescope) into the world of stars above you (w astronomyisrael.com). **Negev Jeep** gives tours of the region, along with history/biology/geology lessons (w negevjeep.co.il).

SPECIAL EVENTS Bedouin evenings nightly (see *Sleep* below) and stargazing activities (see *Activities* above).

ITINERATOR!

DAYS/HOURS Visitor center 08.00–16.00 Saturday–Thursday, 08.00–15.00 Friday (one hour later in summer); camping times not restricted. Closes during flash floods or extreme heat, but there is limited enforcement.

BEST TIME Midday is of course the hottest time of day and should be avoided (not possible if going on a longer hike). Summer should also be avoided, if possible, though some trails are notably open only during the summer.

TIME COMMITMENT Two hours affords a good look at the visitor center, chat with a ranger, and walk to Camel Hill. Four hours allows for a moderate hike and 6–8 hours for the longer hikes. Speed rules apply, to an extent. It's still the desert so you won't be as fast as you are under normal hiking conditions.

BASE This isn't the best anchor spot due to the remoteness, but if you are determined to see all of the desert, you certainly could do worse than stay in *Mitzpe Ramon* for a few days. There are plenty of interesting things to see, places to hike, and experiences to enjoy. You can start very early to make a day trip of it from Tel Aviv (210km/2½ hours) or Jerusalem (205km/2½ hours).

BEST STRATEGY Figure out how much time you have to spend in the park. Then, head to the visitor center, which is excellent, and coordinate your day-trip options with the rangers there. Assuming you have a car, there are a number of options within a short drive that give a variety of perspectives. Walk the Albert Promenade to Camel Hill for the northern view, and then pick one of the mountain hikes on either end to see the rest. Along the way, stop at one of the marked trails off Highway 40 to see interesting geological features.

WALKS AND DRIVES J2, U2.

ITINERARIES
High BUCKET! Scores: 7+; Noteworthy; Nature and Scenic; Active; Organized; National Parks/Reserves; On the Road; Shoestring; All Ages.

ARRIVAL PREP

PREBOOK Only required if: camping in Be'erot Campground; requiring a guide; planning to hike in the eastern corridor which is also a military zone.

REALITY CHECK People die every year from heat exhaustion, sun exposure, lack of water, etc. The park can close due to intense heat (rare), so call ahead if it's above 40°C.

BRING There is no potable water in the park (except at Be'erot Campground), so stock up in *Mitzpe Ramon* with what you need for the day/trip.

ACCESS Begin your journey at the visitor center. Especially if you're going on a longer hike, you want to register with the rangers so someone can find you in case of accident.

ADMISSION National Park Pass can save a lot of money here. Otherwise, the entry is 28 ILS per adult, 14 ILS per child. The campground is 55/40 ILS per adult/child with own tent or 80/65 ILS per adult/child to stay in the big tent camp on a mattress.

RECOMMENDED GUIDE Excellent brochure at the equally excellent visitor center. There are more detailed maps for off-roading (on foot or with wheels) adventure fans. Hikers should strongly consider purchasing the detailed/scaled Society for the Protection of Nature in Israel (SPNI) map.

EAT Few restaurants, mostly at hotels.

SLEEP Be'erot Campground can be reserved at w parks.org.il/en/camping/khan -beerot/. It's the only organized camping site in the crater. There are other campsites with no facilities (see visitor center). Free camping is not allowed. Or stay in a succah, a wood/stone hut providing peace and tranquility, with solar-powered shelters, shared breakfast, vegetarian meals (w succah.co.il).

BUCKET!PEDIA

AKA Ramon Crater.   *Historical era* Roman/Byzantine: Nabataean.   *Size* 40km long, 2–10km wide, roughly 500m deep.   *Population* **Mitzpe Ramon** is the only nearby settlement, with a population of roughly 5,000.

CONTEXT Makhtesh Ramon, or Ramon Crater, despite its name, is actually *not* a meteor crater. It's in fact the world's largest *makhtesh* – which is technically not even a crater. Rather, this geological feature is what happens when soft rock is eroded by water on a valley bed, and the surrounding harder rocks are not eroded. Those harder rocks retain their original height, creating a crater-like appearance when the soft rock in the middle of the valley all washes away. The feature is actually unique to the Negev and Sinai. The location is named after Ilan Ramon, the Israeli astronaut who died in the *Columbia* space shuttle disaster in 2003.

CHRONOLOGY

110 million years ago: This desert land was once covered with water – rivers, lakes, and seas. There was not yet a massive crater, just rolling land.

90 million years ago: A shallow sea fills the land and plentiful sea creatures fill the waters. When these animals die, their shells and bodies build up deposits on the seabed. After tens of millions of years, the seabed is nearly 0.5km thick with skeletons that have converted into limestone.

60–80 million years ago: Tectonic plate shifts along the Ramon fault cause the ground to swell upwards and split, separating the layers of sediment along the sea floor.

10–20 million years ago: Large rivers flood the area, depositing sediments from far-away places such as Saudi Arabia, while also wearing away the sandstone layer which has risen to the top layer of the ground due to plate tectonics.

… to today: The limestone layers can be seen broken in half on the north and south ends of the makhtesh, most visible from the Ammonite Wall. This wall used to be the seabed, but was gradually pushed upwards over time. The delicate sandstone layer beneath the harder limestone layer has eroded away leaving the crater we see today.

WEBSITE w parks.org.il/en/reserve-park/makhtesh-ramon-nature-reserve-and -visitors-center/.

WHERE TO NEXT?

THEMATIC *Noteworthy* Nature Reserves; Exploration. *Nature* Geological Wonders; Desert; Canyons, Wadis and Makhteshim; Animals, Zoos and Wildlife; Gorgeous Scenery; The Great Outdoors. *Scenic* Earth Panorama; Most Photographed. *Active* Walking Paths; Day Hikes; Tough Hikes; Long-Distance Walks; Experienced Hikers; Biking; Adventure, Extreme Sports. *Accommodation* Campgrounds. *Organized* Guided.

COMPLEMENTARY Other amazing short hikes can be found at **Dana Biosphere Reserve (#21)**, **Wadi Mujib and Mujib Biosphere Reserve (#23)**, **Ein Gedi (#50)**, and **Ein Avdat (#74)**. For more desert camping, try the Roman entrance at **Masada (#8)**, the tukul (Nabataean khan) in *Mamshit*, or Shkedi's Camplodge (K1). For more animals you can pet, see *Yotvata Hai-Bar* and the Negev Goat Farms (J2).

NEARBY Avdat (#48) (35km/30 minutes), Sde Boker (J2) (50km/45 minutes), Makhtesh HaGadol (78km/1¼ hours), *Shivta* (90km/1¼ hours), Beer Sheva (J1) (96km/1¼ hours), Makhtesh HaKatan (100km/1½ hours), **Eilat (#78)** (140km/1¾ hours), and the **Dead Sea (#3)** and *Ein Bokek* (150km/2 hours).

#29 Nazareth and its Biblical Sites

BROCHURE

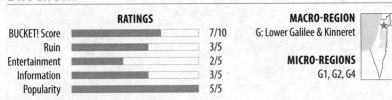

RATINGS

BUCKET! Score		7/10
Ruin		3/5
Entertainment		2/5
Information		3/5
Popularity		5/5

MACRO-REGION
G: Lower Galilee & Kinneret

MICRO-REGIONS
G1, G2, G4

PRIMARY THEME/CATEGORY Religion – Religious Figures – Jesus: Early Life.

TOP The Sea of Galilee gets the most attention, but Nazareth is arguably the most important biblical site in the north.

HOLY LAND RELEVANCE Jesus' childhood home, referenced in the Four Synoptic Gospels of the New Testament. There are a number of churches related to the Holy Family and His disciples.

ELECT ME! The home of Mary, mother of Jesus, and the place where Jesus "of Nazareth" spent his childhood, as referenced in the Gospels of the New Testament. Now home to a diverse array of churches from Christians of differing sects. The most impressive is the ***Basilica of the Annunciation*** which celebrates when the Angel Gabriel visited Mary to announce she would carry the Son of God. Also in town are various places from Jesus' family's life, including possibly Joseph's carpenter studio and a well attributed to Mary. This is an essential stop on a biblical tour of north Israel. Bonus: the food in Nazareth is delicious.

WORTH THE DETOUR? If you have an interest in Jesus sites, then this is an essential stop. Nazareth is only 2 hours from **Tel Aviv (#5)**, so if you are visiting the **Sea of Galilee (#7)** or the **Golan Heights (#62)** for other reasons, you should pop in quickly to the Basilica for a quick view of the Grotto area. Grab lunch at a fusion restaurant or falafel shop if you have time.

EXPERIENCES

CAN'T MISS If you only see one thing, it should be the ***Basilica of the Annunciation***.

CHURCHES

★ *Basilica of the Annunciation (Roman Catholic)* Church celebrating the Annunciation, when the Angel Gabriel declares to Mary that she will bear the son of God. Inside the church, in its lower level, is the Grotto of the Annunciation, at the back of which is the historic cave dwelling of Mary, where she saw Gabriel. Further layers of history are evidenced by the ruins of a Crusader-era church, a Byzantine-era church, a synagogue mosaic, and an 18th-century Franciscan church, which all combine under the roof of the 1969 church.

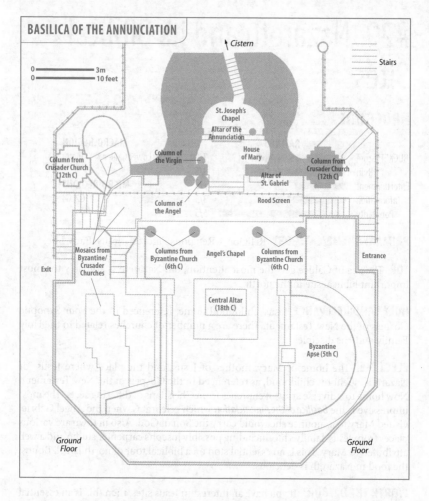

BASILICA OF THE ANNUNCIATION

Cistern

Stairs

0 ———— 3m
0 ———— 10 feet

St. Joseph's Chapel

Altar of the Annunciation

Column of the Virgin

House of Mary

Column from Crusader Church (12th C)

Column from Crusader Church (12th C)

Altar of St. Gabriel

Column of the Angel

Rood Screen

Mosaics from Byzantine/ Crusader Churches

Columns from Byzantine Church (6th C)

Angel's Chapel

Columns from Byzantine Church (6th C)

Entrance

Exit

Central Altar (18th C)

Byzantine Apse (5th C)

Ground Floor

Ground Floor

★ *Church of St. Joseph (Roman Catholic)* Supposed site of Joseph's carpentry shop.
★ *Church of St. Gabriel (Greek Orthodox)* Alternative site of the Annunciation as celebrated by the Orthodox community. Next to St. Gabriel, Mary's Well is recognized as the place where Mary drew water.
★ *Ancient Bathhouse* Next to Mary's Well, with water from the same source. Guided tours of the Roman-era ruins of this hammam cost 120 ILS for up to four people, or 28 ILS pp for five or more.
★ *Synagogue Church (Melkite Greek Catholic)* The synagogue where Jesus studied and prayed.
★ *Mensa Christi Church (Franciscan)* Where Jesus dined with his apostles following his resurrection, usually closed. See *Secret* (below) for entry requirements.
★ *Basilica of Jesus the Adolescent (Salesian-Catholic)* On top of a hill with good views.

ACTIVITIES The **Jesus Trail (#69)** goes from Nazareth to **Capernaum (#33)** over a 60km path, passing many religious spots. Experience life as it was lived during Jesus' time at **Nazareth Village** (w nazarethvillage.com). Next to the Basilica, the International Center of Mary of Nazareth (G1) is a museum and religious site inside a 1st-century CE home, with multimedia displays, an archaeological site, and history of Mary, the mother of Christ (w il.chemin-neuf.org).

SECRET To visit the Mensa Christi Church, get a key from the Guardian of the Convent, opposite the church at the first door in the alleyway. A donation to the church is expected.

SPECIAL EVENTS The town sets up a big Christmas tree and market in December. The Feast of the Annunciation is celebrated on March 25 each year. Mass occurs at various times throughout the week and year – see w custodia.org/en/sanctuaries/nazareth for updated timetable.

MAP See G1.

ITINERATOR!

DAYS/HOURS The Grotto is open 05.45–21.00, the rest of the basilica 08.00–18.00, and Joseph's shop/church 07.00–18.00. The archaeology museum is closed Sundays. Town open Shabbat.

BEST TIME Winter is particularly nice for the Christmas feel. Summer can get warm. The downtown is empty on Sundays, which means you miss most of the markets.

TIME COMMITMENT An hour is enough to do a quick round-trip of the city's main churches (follow *City Walk G1*), but a half-day will give you enough time to do a more complete tour, including lunch. If religious history inspires you, plan a whole day in Nazareth. Speed rules apply.

BASE You can use Nazareth as an Anchor City, but we recommend Rosh Pina (H2) (50km/50 minutes), which has a charming atmosphere. For road trips, this is the biggest city besides *Tiberias* (which we don't recommend) in the region east of the Mediterranean, from which you can spend weeks trying to see everything. Otherwise visit from Tel Aviv (100km/1½ hours) or Jerusalem (150km/2 hours).

BEST STRATEGY You should build in time at least for a visit to the ***Basilica of the Annunciation***, which is visually striking and an interesting church-in-a-church-in-a-church. But ideally you will tour about town, using *City Walk G1* as a guide. Then, sample one of the nice restaurants in town.

WALKS AND DRIVES G1, G2, G4.

ITINERARIES High BUCKET! Scores: 7+; Religion; Structure; Organized; UNESCO; National Parks/Reserves; Memorial; Big-Group Friendly; Pilgrimage.

ARRIVAL PREP

PREBOOK Not necessary.

REALITY CHECK Popular tour-bus stop, particularly Christian tours.

BRING Modest clothes: shorts and bare shoulders are not allowed.

ACCESS There are a variety of places to find parking near the ***Basilica of the Annunciation***, or try your luck with street parking. The sites are all next to each other. There may be security at the churches. Churches are free to enter.

RECOMMENDED GUIDE The Franciscans have included a ton of information at w custodia.org/en/sanctuaries/nazareth.

VISITOR CENTER The International Center of Mary of Nazareth (G1) is the de facto visitor center (see *Activities* above).

EAT Excellent, locally sourced cuisine, with an international twist. Al-Reda Cafe, Diana, and Tishreen are popular, higher-end choices. Hummus places abound as well, such as al-Sheikh and Imad's Hummus. And sweets exist in and among all this – try Al-Mokhtar Sweets, Mahroum Sweets, and Al-Sadaqa for knafeh, baklava, and other local desserts.

SLEEP The Fauzi Azar Inn gets lots of mentions. Pilgrims can stay at the Casa Nova next to the Basilica.

BUCKET!PEDIA

AKA an-Nasira (Arabic); Natzrat (Hebrew); Natzrath (Aramaic).   *Size* 14km².
Population 77,500.   *Ethnic makeup* Primarily Arab (a Jewish town called Old Nazareth was formally declared in 1974), with 69% Muslims and 31% Christians.
Historical era Roman/Byzantine: Judea.   *Year constructed* Sites have various dates; present Basilica is from 1969.

CONTEXT Nazareth is a town of mostly Arab Muslims, which is an interesting contrast to its Christian identity, but not unexpected: the town has been inhabited by Arab Muslims for most of the last 1,500 years. The various religious sites have been constructed and razed over multiple periods, from Roman times through the early Arab period. After a long stretch lost to history, the Crusaders came to highlight the importance of the Grotto, but their tenure was short-lived and the next 700 years would see the site under Muslim rule.

Many of the city's earliest examples of altars, shrines, or churches are dedicated to the event known as the Annunciation. The early life of Jesus, and much of Mary's life, are documented as occurring in Nazareth, though little has been discovered in the archaeological record.

The Basilica of the Annunciation highlights a number of small but interesting churches that have all been incorporated under the large-roof basilica that was built over the site of Mary's childhood cave home. Nearby is the studio where Joseph worked, but that site has been recognized only since modern times.

City Walk G1 offers a good roundup of the churches that have sprung up over time from the various Christian denominations. Don't forget that this is a functioning city with its own unique contribution to the culinary world: Arab fusion. Check out *Eat* above for recommendations.

CHRONOLOGY
Origin: unknown, but inhabitants have been in the region since at least the Bronze Age.
2nd century CE: village first referenced in an ancient inscription.

380: Traveler Egeria notes that the Grotto of the Annunciation contains an altar.

570: The Pilgrim of Piacenza talks of two churches on the same spot (one may have been a synagogue, of which part of a mosaic still remains).

638: Arab Muslims assume control of the region.

670: Pilgrim Arculf mentions two substantial churches, including St. Joseph's and one that incorporates the Grotto. The synagogue was gone by then. Mosaics from that church are on display.

1102: A visitor to Nazareth, Saewulf, says the village of Nazareth is in ruins, but states the monastery is beautiful.

Late 12th century: Crusaders build one of the finest churches in the region atop the ruins of the Byzantine church.

1178: Christians removed from Nazareth after Crusaders lose control of the region.

1263: Sultan Babars destroy all Christian sites in the region.

1620: Franciscans allowed to return and establish a monastery.

1730: Begin reconstruction of a church on the site of the Annunciation. The central altar in the church dates to the Franciscans' 18th-century church.

1918: British grant certain autonomy to the 8,000 mostly Christian residents of Nazareth.

1948: Nazareth incorporated into the new state of Israel.

1955: Work begins on present Basilica.

1969: Basilica opens as the largest church opened in the Holy Land in almost a millennium.

WEBSITE w custodia.org/en/sanctuaries/nazareth; w nazarethinfo.org.

WHERE TO NEXT?

THEMATIC *Religion* Christianity; Jesus' Early Life; New Testament; Collections of Churches; Pilgrimage. *Archaeology* Bronze Age; Roman. *Society* Large Towns. *People* Arab. *Food and Drink* Culinary Capital. *Organized* Cooking School/ Food Activities.

Complementary More Jesus sites: **Sea of Galilee (#7)**, **Mount of Olives (#34)**, **Bethlehem (#40)**, and **Mount Zion (#92)**. Other big churches: **Church of the Holy Sepulchre (#9)**, **Church of the Nativity (#18)**, *Mount of Beatitudes*, and *Church of the Transfiguration*. Other great Arab restaurants not in Nazareth: *Elbabor* (Arab-Israeli cuisine in Umm el Fahm), *Uri Buri* (seafood in Akko), and Fakhr el-Din (Q2) (fancy in Amman).

NEARBY **Tsipori (#56)** (9km/17 minutes), *Kfar Kana (G4)* (10km/18 minutes), Mount Tabor (17km/34 minutes), **Beit She'arim (#79)** (23km/30 minutes), **Megiddo (#59)** (25km/25 minutes), *Tiberias* (30km/30 minutes), **Beit She'an (#39)** (37km/36 minutes), *Haifa* (44km/40 minutes), and **Tsfat/Safed (#58)** (60km/60 minutes).

#30 Jaffa

BROCHURE

RATINGS

BUCKET! Score	▬▬▬▬▬▬▬▬	6/10
Ruin	▬▬▬▬	2/5
Entertainment	▬▬▬▬▬	3/5
Information	▬▬▬▬	2/5
Popularity	▬▬▬▬▬▬	5/5

MACRO-REGION
D: Tel Aviv

MICRO-REGIONS
D1, D2

PRIMARY THEME/CATEGORY Society – Cities – Cool Neighborhoods and Quarters.

TOP Reminder that Israel is not solely Jewish. Also, best combination of port, shopping, and dining.

HOLY LAND RELEVANCE Jaffa has several mentions in the Bible, which references a city opposite the territory of the Tribe of Dan, who had inherited coastal land in middle Canaan around 1000 BCE (Joshua 19). In the New Testament, St. Peter resurrects the widow Tabitha in Jaffa (Acts 9–10). Let's not forget that this is the spot where Jonah is said to have departed for Tarshish before being swallowed by a whale (Jonah 1–2)! Jaffa has been an important port city in the Holy Land region throughout much of history.

ELECT ME! Jaffa, or Yafo as it's known in Hebrew and in the city name, has been an important port city and Arab bastion for at least 4,000 years. It was formally integrated to become "Tel Aviv-Yafo" in 1950, but it retains its unique neighborhood character. Jaffa is recognizable by its tall clock tower standing guard atop Jaffa Hill, and has the best view of Tel Aviv's glorious beaches. Jaffa is a place to soak up an Arab (and hipster) vibe, but also a place to rent a sailboat, dine al fresco, shop in a flea market, or stay in a swanky hotel.

WORTH THE DETOUR? Certainly visit if you are spending multiple days in **Tel Aviv (#5)**, either on a walking tour or for one of its fine restaurants.

EXPERIENCES

CAN'T MISS There are four essential restaurants to try. Work them into your schedule!

SITES (explanations in *City Walk D2*): View of Andromeda's Rock; Kedumim Square; St. Peter's Church; House of Simon the Tanner; Zodiac Fountain; Ramses Garden; Suspended Orange Tree; *Ilana Goor Museum (D2)*; port area; and **Jaffa Flea Market** (Shuk HaPishpeshim).

ACTIVITIES _Abu Hassan_ has hummusiyas of the highest quality; **Shakshuka/Dr. Shakshuka** is a morning (or anytime really) staple; Old Man and the Sea (D2) – order fresh grilled fish, get 20 salads free; and Said Abouelafia Bakery (D2) is a bakery with unmatched options – try the babka.

SECRET Nazi war criminal and Holocaust organizer Adolf Eichmann was captured in 1960 by Mossad agents and interned in the old Jaffa police station, now the glorious Setai Hotel across from the Jaffa Clock Tower.

SPECIAL EVENTS Weekly arts market near the flea market. Also, down Olei Zion are a number of art studios, galleries, and artsy bars with weekly/monthly shows. Try Cuckoo's Nest, Magasin III, Beit Kandinof, Galerie Charlot, and Gordon Gallery (further afield).

MAP See D2.

ITINERATOR!

DAYS/HOURS Information Center open 09.30–18.30 Sunday–Thursday, 09.30–16.00 Friday and Saturday. Otherwise, this is a neighborhood, so places open and close at their normal business hours. Lots of late-night activities.

TIME COMMITMENT Two hours for *City Walk D2*, or 4 hours for the walk plus visits to sites, including meal(s) time. Speed rules apply.

BASE Tel Aviv-Yafo (=Jaffa) is an Anchor City. If you're visiting just for the day, Jaffa is a good part of town to visit, aside from the beach.

BEST STRATEGY We recommend *City Walk D2* on one of the days you spend in Tel Aviv. Make sure to plan a meal (or two) around the trip.

WALKS AND DRIVES D1, D2, D6.

ITINERARIES Tel Aviv Immersion; Most Popular; Nature and Scenic; Society and People; Culture; Entertainment; Organized; Community; Fine Arts; On the Road; Ancient History; Under the Sun; Shoestring.

ARRIVAL PREP

PREBOOK Not necessary, except for restaurants on weekends.

REALITY CHECK Popular tourist area. Restaurants can get booked up. Try off-hours; they generally don't close between services. To be frank: the history and archaeology are only moderately interesting.

BRING Cash for the market.

ACCESS Not easy to find parking. Better to walk in. No entrance fees.

RECOMMENDED GUIDE There's a great little guidebook called *Day Tour Tel Aviv/ Jaffa* for sale at the Jaffa Information Center. There are also free tours offered every day, which you can schedule through **w** tel-aviv.gov.il (10.00 Wednesday, meet at clock tower). Sandemans also does a free tour (tips expected; **w** neweuropetours. eu/sandemans-tours/tel-aviv/free-tour-of-tel-aviv/).

VISITOR CENTER The Information Center is located in Kedumim Square, up the stairs from the port area.

EAT Plenty of stalls to buy food inside the Jaffa port market area, including falafel, fish, sandwiches, and pizza. On side streets, there are a number of famous restaurants (see *Activities* above).

SLEEP Airbnb has become popular in Jaffa. Lots of new, fancy hotels along the beach facing Tel Aviv, including The Setai and The Jaffa.

BUCKET!PEDIA

AKA Jaffa is pronounced *Yafo* in both Hebrew and Arabic. *Population* 46,000. *Ethnic makeup* Estimated at 30,000 Jews, 16,000 Arabs. *Historical era Prehistoric: Bronze Age* to *Modern: Contemporary*. *Year founded* Unclear, possibly 10,000 years ago.

CONTEXT Jaffa is the oldest part of Tel Aviv-Yafo, with 10,000 years of possible human habitation. Excavations are still under way to literally unearth the various periods of human presence, including its oldest recorded period as an Egyptian vassal state, some 4,000 years ago. The city has changed hands from Egyptian to Jewish to pagan to Christian to Arab, and back and forth many times throughout the ages. As a city, it was only passed by Tel Aviv in population in the mid-1920s. Though majority-Jewish now, the city was once part of the original design of Mandatory Palestine in the UN Partition Plan. Following the war of 1948 which established the Israeli state, Jaffa and Tel Aviv were merged into one, as they remain today. The name Tel Aviv-Yafo is often shorted to just "Tel Aviv" but the formal name recognizes the importance of Jaffa in the history of this area. Jaffa retains an Arab charm and influence, with many of its interesting sites to do with its Arab history.

Most people today tour Jaffa not for its history but for its ambience. It simultaneously has a cosmopolitan and ancient feel. The port area has been redone several times and now contains a number of fine restaurants, stores, shopping, and leisure places. The boardwalks are lovely. People stroll casually along the pedestrian-only streets. The hill upon which the clock tower rests is the highest point in the region and provides an unparalleled view of the Mediterranean Sea, the gorgeous beaches and promenade, and the greater Tel Aviv skyline. This alone makes the visit worthwhile.

CHRONOLOGY

18th century BCE: Ramses Gate Garden ruins shows evidence of Egyptian control in the region at this time.
14th century BCE: Jaffa (then Yapu) referenced for the first time in the historic record in the Egyptian Amarna Letters.
13th century BCE: Entrance gate to Pharaoh Ramses II palace, placed in Ramses Garden.
10th century BCE: King Solomon reportedly uses Jaffa port to ship in cedar wood from Lebanon (Tyre) to construct the First Temple in Jerusalem (Ezra 3).
3rd century BCE: Inscription to Ptolemy IV found at the Jaffa excavations in Kedumim Square.
66 CE: During the Jewish Revolts, the Roman army kills 8,000 men in Jaffa. City sacked.
11th century: Crusaders revitalize town, but falls back into disrepair during Mamluk and Ottoman eras.
1654: Church of Saint Peter completed.
18th century: Walls added to surround Jaffa.

1799: Napoleon captures the town in the Siege of Jaffa in a battle against the Ottoman Empire. Several thousand killed.

1820: Jewish khan established, bringing Jews back to the town.

1865: Jaffa lighthouse constructed; decommissioned in 1966.

1866: First people move outside the Jaffa walls.

1870s: Walls are destroyed, aiding the quick expansion of the city.

1900: Clock tower built.

1909: Tel Aviv established.

1917: British conquer region and build a customs house at the port.

1921: Jaffa riots.

1930s: Port expanded.

1948: Jaffa, being a primarily Arab town, surrenders to Israel after the Arab–Israeli War. Arab residents flee.

1950: Tel Aviv and Jaffa merge into a single city, Tel Aviv-Yafo.

1961: Jaffa Museum opens in the Old Saray Building (soap factory).

WEBSITE w oldjaffa.co.il.

WHERE TO NEXT?

THEMATIC *Religion* New Testament; Mosques. *Archaeology* Bronze Age; Active Excavations. *Scenic* Most Photographed. *Society* Cool Neighborhoods; Streets, Squares and Ports. *People* Secular Life; Hipsters; Arab. *Active* Adventure Water Sports. *Leisure* Fishing. *Entertainment* Markets; Handmade; Bars and Clubs. *Food and Drink* Street Food and Quick Bites; Culinary Capital. *Organized* Cooking School/Food Activities.

COMPLEMENTARY What else was going on before Israel was Israel? Chronologically: *Nahal Me'arot*, **Timna (#96)**, **Megiddo (#59)**, *Tel Beer Sheva*, and *Tel Hazor*. Other great foodie spots are: **Akko (#13)**, **Mehane Yehuda Market (#67)**, *Nazarene Fusion Cuisine*, **Rothschild Boulevard**, and Levinsky Market (D4).

NEARBY On foot: *Hatachana Train Station (D1)* (900m/12 minutes), Kuli Alma (D4) (2km/27 minutes), **Carmel Market (#87)** (2.1km/27 minutes), Simon Peres Center for Peace (2.3km/30 minutes), Dizengoff Square (3.3km/45 minutes), Sarona Market (D3) (4km/50 minutes), and Hilton Beach (4.4km/55 minutes).

#31 King's Highway

BROCHURE

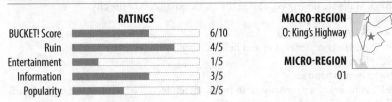

RATINGS			MACRO-REGION
BUCKET! Score		6/10	0: King's Highway
Ruin		4/5	
Entertainment		1/5	**MICRO-REGION**
Information		3/5	01
Popularity		2/5	

PRIMARY THEME/CATEGORY Scenic – Vistas – Scenic Drives.

LENGTH 300km.

TIME TO DRIVE 6+ hours.

TOP Driving tour in the region; lots of stops along the way.

HOLY LAND RELEVANCE First referenced in the Bible's Book of Genesis as the route a coalition of kings used to attack another allied group of kingdoms, thus earning its name. During the Exodus, Moses requested permission from the Edomites for his people to use the King's Highway, but they were refused passage. Many successive generations have used the path as a trade route from Syria in the north to Arabia in the south. Their identities can still be distinguished at various stops along the path, particularly the Nabataeans (for Petra), Byzantines (mosaics), and Crusaders (castles).

ELECT ME! Besides passing along some of the best-known sites in Jordan, including **Petra (#2)**, **Karak (#49)**, *Shobak*, **Aqaba (#43)**, **Madaba (#19)**, and the **Dana Biosphere Reserve (#21)**, it's also a gorgeous drive. The drive takes you along the Rift Valley clifftop with majestic views of the great arid valley basin (sloping to the **Dead Sea (#3)**) below.

WORTH THE DETOUR? It's a great multiday trip, as we've tried to highlight. If you are limited on time, you don't have to stop everywhere. Your priorities are of course **Petra (#2)**, and then **Karak (#49)** and **Madaba (#19)** or **Umm ar-Rasas (#81)**, plus **Dana Biosphere Reserve (#21)** if you have time. Thus, this route could potentially lead you through several places on your bucket list. Plus, those views!

EXPERIENCES

CAN'T MISS The chance to drive on your own. Driving in Jordan is not difficult and the ability to stop where you want is a worthwhile luxury. So… rent a car (or a car with driver) for this trip.

SITES All can be found in *Road Trip 01*, which goes south–north. The fuller version of the "highway" started in Egypt and ended in Syria. The route was approximately: Heliopolis, Egypt → Suez, Egypt → **Aqaba (#43)** → **Petra (#2)** → *Shobak* → **Dana**

Biosphere Reserve (#21) → **Karak (#49)** → **Madaba (#19)** → **Ancient Amman (#37)** → **Jerash (#14)** → Bosra, Syria → Damascus, Syria → Resafa, Syria.

GREAT VIEWPOINTS Grand Canyon, near Mujib Dam; Wadi Mujib Panorama, near Mujib Dam; **Karak (#49)** castle, from atop; hikes in **Dana Biosphere Reserve (#21)**, which you'll have to organize in advance, but the Dana Guest House also has good introductory views to the nature reserve; **Mount Nebo (#24)**, if you detour off Highway 35 at **Madaba (#19)**, taking Al Quds Street west 10km; and "Petra View," which is not a view of Petra but rather the red rock landscape that makes Petra famous, about 22km south of Petra on the way to Aqaba.

SECRET If you detour from Dhiban to **Umm ar-Rasas (#81)**, there are signs along the road directing you to more stunning viewpoints.

SPECIAL EVENTS See individual sites.

MAP See O1.

ITINERATOR!

DAYS/HOURS See individual sites; highway open 24/7.

TIME COMMITMENT If you go straight through, it will take you a minimum of 6 hours due to all the twists and turns. If you stop at each of the sites, including **Petra (#2)**, you can do the whole thing in three days, flying through, including one full day and two nights at Petra. If you want to spend time at sites, you'll need at least two days for Petra and two for **Dana Biosphere Reserve (#21)**. The rest can be done as side trips on a one-directional road trip. Speed rules don't apply to the road itself, which can be fast in places, and slow in others. Traffic is usually light in the middle, but heavy towards Madaba and Amman.

BASE This is a classic road trip. You don't want to anchor from any of these sites or anywhere in between, as this is a one-way route that takes the better part of a day to drive straight through (without stopping). Stopping in **Petra (#2)**, **Dana Biosphere Reserve (#21)**, and Amman are your best bets, and **Karak (#49)** if you must.

BEST STRATEGY If combining Jordan with Israel, you'll enter from either Jerusalem or Eilat. Given that you must exit from the same location, you can choose to do the King's Highway itinerary (*Road Trip O1*) as half of a round-trip, and then return via the Dead Sea Highway (P1), including the BUCKET! site of the **Dead Sea (#3)**.

WALKS AND DRIVES O1.

ITINERARIES Nature and Scenic; Organized; On the Road.

ARRIVAL PREP

REALITY CHECK Carry your passport when you travel. You may encounter an unanticipated roadblock where police officers ask for your identification and car papers. You should absolutely identify as a tourist, smile, and be polite. Hopefully you will just get waved through, but if you have problems, make sure you have your Embassy's phone number in your emergency kit. Also, speed bumps may not be marked. Drive slowly through towns. Two-way roads mean it's easier to get stuck behind trucks.

BRING A full gas tank – only a few gas stations in the major towns along the route.

ACCESS From Amman, the highway becomes more rural and scenic after Madaba. At the other end, the highway loses its charm shortly after Petra.

ADMISSION The highway is free; the sites are not. See individual entries. Also, buy the Jordan Pass, which covers most of these sites.

RECOMMENDED GUIDE A good map.

VISITOR CENTER Nothing specifically for King's Highway, though the sites themselves have either a visitor center or guides near ticket booths to provide guidance.

EAT You can stock up on snacks in Wadi Musa (Petra) on the road, but the towns in between Amman and Aqaba are small. You'll be able to find local cuisine, but might be best to pack snacks and lunches on the days you'll be on the road.

SLEEP Depending on how many nights you plan to spend doing King's Highway stops, you can incorporate some of the nice lodging into the stay. **Petra (#2)** has some good options. Dana has the **Feynan Ecolodge (#86)**. There aren't great options from Karak north, until Amman, but we actually prefer swinging west and staying in Suweimeh, an Anchor City, which is on the Dead Sea and has a number of nice hotels.

BUCKET!PEDIA

AKA Via Regis; Via Traiana Nova; Jordan Highway 35. *Historical era* Ancient Israel: Iron Age to Islamic: Crusader. *Year founded* Unclear, but in use since antiquity.

CONTEXT Historically, the King's Highway ran from Heliopolis in present-day Cairo, Egypt to Resafa in Syria. It wasn't always a "highway" per se, having only been paved in the mid-20th century. Rather, it was a series of way stations for traders passing spices, incense, food, and marketable goods that arrived from the east to Arabia, Egypt, and the Mediterranean.

The route has changed hands multiple times over the millennia, usually corresponding to whoever had control over the territory. Moses was famously turned down for passage on the King's Highway by the Edomites and Ammonites, who controlled different parts. The Moabites also contributed to the passage of goods through their territory, while the various tribes maintained independence in the second millennium BCE.

The Nabataeans were responsible for the construction of Petra around 200 BCE from where they controlled their expanse of land west to the Mediterranean and south through Saudi Arabia, and used the path (called the Incense Route) to get goods north to Syria and south to Arabia.

The Romans' capital was in Bosra in southern Syria, so their capture of the Nabataean region at the turn of the millennium secured their continued use of the road, ending at their port in Aqaba. Centuries later, Christian pilgrims used this route when building churches at biblical sites. Their work can be seen today in Madaba and Umm ar-Rasas.

The region was conquered by Muhammad's armies in the 7th century CE, but the Crusaders gained a Christian stronghold in parts of Israel and Jordan again during the 12th century. They put guard posts at Amman, Karak, Shobak, and Aqaba to monitor foreign armies along the King's Highway route.

Eventually, the road lost its relevance with more direct land and sea routes. The individual sites along the route were pulled together by the advent of the national highway system in Jordan. Today, the road feels much less like a *highway* between sites given its rugged and skinny appearance, and more like a country road. All the more reason to take it slow and enjoy. The sites are spectacular, but the journey there isn't too shabby either.

CHRONOLOGY

5000–3000 BCE: Wadi Jadid dolmen field created.

4500 BCE: Feynan started developing copper mines, which the Romans added on several thousands of years later.

2000 BCE: Road already in use to transit goods from Syria to Arabia.

1500 BCE: Moses denied passage on King's Highway by Edomites and Amorites.

200 BCE: Petra constructed by Nabataeans.

7 BCE: Khirbet et-Tannur constructed by Nabataeans.

300 CE: Qasr Bashir constructed by Romans.

Mid-6th century: Madaba Map created by Byzantine-era pilgrims.

5th–8th centuries: Umm ar-Rasas reaches zenith with mosaics constructed by Byzantine-era pilgrims.

629: Battle of Mu'tah. Muhammad loses to Byzantine Empire.

1115: Shobak Castle built by Crusaders.

1142: Karak Castle built by Crusaders.

WHERE TO NEXT?

THEMATIC *Archaeology* Bronze Age.   *Scenic* Earth Panorama; Scenic Drives. *Organized* Multi-Stop/Self-Directed.

COMPLEMENTARY Other great road trips: **Incense Route (#73)** (*Road Trip J3*); *Road Trip E7: Mediterranean Beaches*; Golan Heights (*Road Trips I2 and I3*).

NEARBY **Dead Sea (#3)**: 87km/1½ hours to Suweimeh from Karak; **Wadi Rum (#4)**: 265km/3½ hours from Karak.

#32 Citadel/Tower of David

BROCHURE

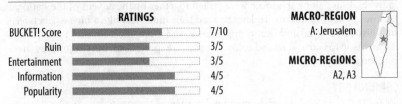

RATINGS			MACRO-REGION
BUCKET! Score		7/10	A: Jerusalem
Ruin		3/5	
Entertainment		3/5	**MICRO-REGIONS**
Information		4/5	A2, A3
Popularity		4/5	

PRIMARY THEME/CATEGORY Culture – Museum – of History.

TOP Place to get educated on the history of Jerusalem.

HOLY LAND RELEVANCE Interestingly, the religious significance is almost exclusively in its name. The structure has no connection with King David, nor anything during the time period of David's reign (10th century BCE). Early Christians and Muslims misinterpreted writings from historian Josephus Flavius and understood the Phasael Tower at the Citadel to be correlated with King David from the Song of Songs 4:4. In fact, it dates to Herod's time (37 BCE, some 1,000 years later). Although still a hypothesis, many scholars posit that Pontius Pilate – a government official – must have stayed in Herod's Palace at the Citadel when he visited Jerusalem to conduct the trial of Jesus of Nazareth. If true, this would make the Citadel the actual First Station of the Cross (the Praetorium), as opposed to the site venerated by Christians in the Muslim Quarter near Lions' Gate. This theory certainly complicates the veracity of sites along the **Via Dolorosa (#42)**!

ELECT ME! The Citadel, aka the Tower of David, is a marvelous fortress-turned-museum that impresses you immediately upon arrival at the Jaffa Gate. The museum enriches your Old City experience by providing a succinct and palatable summation of the history of this most fascinating city. While the exhibitions are done very well, the site itself is equally impressive and attractive, with proper explanations of the many layers of history and their relevance. This is also the springboard for the southern portion of the **Ramparts Walk (#91)**, and has one of the best views of the city.

WORTH THE DETOUR? Absolutely – before you dive head-first into the layered city of Jerusalem, it's beneficial to have a bit of context. There is a lot of history to absorb and this museum does a great job of distilling it down to basics.

EXPERIENCES

CAN'T MISS The 16m² model underneath the site and the views from the top of the Tower of David/Phasael.

WALKING TOUR The site is designed to move traffic in a forward direction: Moat → Tower of Phasael → Hasmonean Wall → Minaret → Mosque.

SITES

★ *Moat* Remains of a quarry from First Temple period (7th century BCE), steps from Herod's palace (1st century BCE), and a special entrance dating to Kaiser Wilhelm II of Germany (1898 CE) are part of this dry moat.

★ *Tower of Phasael* One of three towers built during Herodian times (1st century BCE) and the only one left standing. Partially destroyed after the Crusader period, and rebuilt by Mamluks: the smaller stones on top date to the Mamluk period (14th century CE). Note: this is the tower you pass as you enter and not the tower with the minaret.

★ *Hasmonean Wall* During the period of the Hasmonean (Jewish) dynasty (2nd century BCE), Jerusalem was surrounded by a series of defensive walls. This was the first of three of those walls.

★ *Minaret* Ottoman period, built in 1635. When Westerners arrived in the 19th century, they presumed this to be the famed Tower of David and the name was adapted to the entire site.

★ *Mosque* Origins in the Mamluk period (1310), but renovated during the Ottoman period (1531).

★ *Model of Jerusalem* Constructed in 1873 by a Hungarian bookbinder, Stefan Illes, this map of Jerusalem at 1:500 in the 19th century CE, right when people started moving outside the city walls, is a gem. Accessible by stairs from the inner site gardens.

★ *Kishle* Separate portion of the museum, on the southern wall, underground in an old prison.

SECRET The site has nearly a dozen periods of history jumbled together, making it difficult to make sense of what you're seeing. Download the audio guide to walk chronologically through the site and through Jerusalem's history to make sense of it all.

SPECIAL EVENTS Every evening, there is a "Night Spectacular" which allows viewers to experience an interactive show highlighting the history of Jerusalem with sounds and lights as you walk through the site. There's also a "King David Night Experience" blending art and history, plus tons of temporary exhibitions each year (**w** tod.org.il/en/events).

ITINERATOR!

DAYS/HOURS 10.00–16.00 Monday–Wednesday and Saturday, 10.00–18.00 Thursday, 10.00–14.00 Friday, closed Sunday. Parts may be closed during restoration (began 2020). There are two sound and light shows which play most evenings.

BEST TIME Weekends (Fri/Sat) are busy; tours are not available on holidays or eves.

TIME COMMITMENT Two hours is enough to get the most out of the museum. You'll need an evening slot for the night show, but it only takes an hour. Speed rules apply.

BASE Located in the Anchor City of Jerusalem.

BEST STRATEGY If you have two days in Jerusalem, this site should absolutely be added to your list of places to visit. Depending on what kind of learner you are, you may appreciate the information before (to prepare yourself) or after seeing

Jerusalem's other sites (for context). When you reserve your tickets, you can book a combo pass allowing you access to both the site and the show. You won't be able to see the site in the short 30 minutes you'll have once the light show begins.

WALKS AND DRIVES A2, A3.

ITINERARIES High BUCKET! Scores: 7+; Culture; Entertainment; Organized; Ancient History; All Ages; Big-Group Friendly.

ARRIVAL PREP

PREBOOK Yes, on website, book tickets for discount.

ACCESS At the Jaffa Gate, turn right and go up the stairs at the big tower.

ADMISSION 40 ILS adult, 30 ILS student, 20 ILS senior/disabled, 18 ILS child. The Night Spectacular is 65 ILS extra. 80 ILS for museum and night show combined tickets, and 65 ILS for senior/student/child. Membership cards exist for annual passes.

RECOMMENDED GUIDE The site has good explanations, but if you are an aural absorber of information, join the English tour (included in the price; 11.00 Sunday–Thursday). Hebrew language tours are Tuesdays at 10.30.

BROCHURE/AUDIO GUIDE At the entrance, you'll get a brochure to set you in the right direction. You can also download an audio guide to listen to as you walk around in lieu of a guide.

EAT/SLEEP See **Old City Jerusalem (#1)**.

BUCKET!PEDIA

AKA "Tower of David" and "Citadel," interchangeably. *Size* Tower height is 773m. *Historical era* Ancient Israel: *Kingdom of Israel and Judah* to Islamic: *Ottoman.* *Year constructed* Unclear, probably 2nd century BCE.

CONTEXT Archaeological studies have found evidence of usage of the site as early as the 8th century BCE, though most of the above-ground portions of the site first date to the Hasmonean era. Jerusalem expanded outwards in the 2nd century BCE, when the Jewish Hasmonean kings reigned. The First Wall was constructed to protect the new settlements. Herod, at the end of the millennium, added three towers to the wall – Mariamne, Hippica, and Phasael – the latter of which is the only one left standing, though the higher-level stones are from successive periods of domination. The Romans, at war with rebellious Jews in 70 CE, destroyed Jerusalem, but left the towers standing as a marker of the power they overtook. Byzantine pilgrims visited in the 4th century and incorrectly associated the Tower of Phasael to the biblical residence of King David (still undiscovered, but believed to be in the City of David, to the southeast of the present city walls). The name "Tower of David" has been hard to shake since. When the Crusaders attacked in 1099, the walls stood, and the Muslim rulers were escorted out without further destruction. Much of the city would be destroyed at the end of the Crusader reign, including much of the Citadel.

The Mamluks in the 14th century saw value in the site and refortified many of the towers and walls. The Ottomans ruled the region for 400 years (to 1918) and used the site to station their soldiers, adding a minaret to the top of their own mosque. That minaret (plus flag) earned the epithet "Tower of David" when Westerners visited in the 19th century. The name was expanded to include the entire site of the Citadel, which is now also known as the Tower of David Museum.

CHRONOLOGY Will be explained on your tour.

WEBSITE w tod.org.il/en/.

WHERE TO NEXT?

THEMATIC *Archaeology* Empires. *Structure* Skyline; Urban Landscape; Most Photographed. *Society* Disputed. *Culture* Museum of History; of Archaeology. *Organized* Guided.

COMPLEMENTARY More important spots on the walls of Jerusalem are **Temple Mount (#12)**, **Jerusalem Walls and Gates (#47)**, and the **Ramparts Walk (#91)**. More top views of Jerusalem are **Mount of Olives (#34)**, *YMCA*, Haas Promenade (B1), and Lutheran Church of the Redeemer (A2). The best museums in Jerusalem are **Israel Museum (#17)**, **Yad Vashem (#35)**, and **Western Wall Tunnels (#94)**.

NEARBY Jaffa Gate (150m/2 minutes), **Church of the Holy Sepulchre (#9)** (400m/ 6 minutes), **Western Wall (#11)** (650m/10 minutes), and **Temple Mount (#12)** and **Dome of the Rock (#6)** (1km/15 minutes).

#33 Capernaum and Tabgha

BROCHURE

RATINGS		MACRO-REGION
BUCKET! Score	5/10	G: Lower Galilee & Kinneret
Ruin	3/5	
Entertainment	2/5	**MICRO-REGIONS**
Information	2/5	G3, G4
Popularity	5/5	

PRIMARY THEME/CATEGORY Religion – Religious Figures – Jesus: Ministries.

TOP Collection of biblical sites from Jesus' ministry period.

COMMENDATIONS Israel National Park.

HOLY LAND RELEVANCE There are quite a few references to Capernaum in the Bible. The Gospels of Matthew, Mark, Luke, and John all reference the site in various passages. It was there that Jesus performed a number of miracles, including healing the sick and feeding the masses. Four of his 12 apostles are said to have been from Capernaum. A home-turned-church in the park is recognized as the home of Apostle Peter, now Saint Peter, one of the first leaders of the Church.

ELECT ME! These sister sites are represented under the banner of one national park and both represent important moments in the life and times of Jesus Christ and his apostles. If you've done the **Sea of Galilee (#7)** loop, you've already visited these two sites. If not, and are looking for an easy and quick introduction to Jesus' life in the Galilee, these are the two most evocative sites along the sea.

WORTH THE DETOUR? Definitely for the Christian tourist. For the less religiously minded, they are probably not worth their own day trip, unless combined on the Sea of Galilee loop or passed on the way to/from the Golan.

EXPERIENCES

CAN'T MISS Ancient Synagogue or Tabgha's churches.

CAPERNAUM Capernaum was the center of Jesus' ministries, proximal to the hometowns of many of his disciples, and the location where Jesus performed a number of miracles, including the healing of a paralytic.

★ *House of St. Peter* The remains of a house where it's believed Jesus' disciple Peter lived, as his name was found inscribed on the walls along with "Lord" and "Jesus" among other indicators. In the 4th century the house was converted to a church (verified by Christian pilgrim accounts) and in the 5th century the church was expanded to become an octagonal basilica in the Byzantine style.
★ *Church of the Twelve Apostles* Pink domes with murals inside where ancient Capernaum once stood.
★ *Ancient Synagogue* With a basilica-style design, this 4th-century synagogue is believed to have been quite grand. It was possibly built atop an earlier religious structure from the 1st century where Jesus preached.
★ *Pier* Sail in!

TABGHA Contains two churches particularly dedicated to important moments in Jesus' ministries: the **Church of Multiplication of Loaves and Fishes**, which commemorates the story of the same name where Jesus takes a limited amount of fish and bread and feeds 4,000–5,000 (differing accounts); and the **Church of the Primacy of St. Peter**, Jesus' fourth appearance after his crucifixion where Jesus multiplies fish (again) and asks Peter to feed his sheep, after which Peter atones for his sins, having thrice denied Jesus. Other nearby sites are Job's Spring, The Hidden Waterfall, Nur Spring, Tel Kinarot, Kinar Spring, and Job's Cave.

ACTIVITIES Walk to Tabgha along the new promenade (3.5km), or sail into Capernaum's new dock from *Tiberias* or Ein Gev.

SECRET The church's exterior aesthetics do not accurately represent what you'll find inside.

SPECIAL EVENTS Public and private ceremonies are held on site.

ITINERATOR!

DAYS/HOURS 08.00–16.00 Saturday–Thursday, Friday 13.00–15.00 summer, 08.00–15.00 winter. Closed holidays. Closes early holiday eves. House of St. Peter is often closed.

TIME COMMITMENT Two hours is enough time to see both sites at a quick clip, driving between Capernaum and Tabgha, while 4 hours gives enough time for the 7km round-trip walk between the two. Speed rules apply.

BASE Works well on a road trip, anchoring from Rosh Pina (H2) (18km/18 minutes) or camping on the Galilee shore.

BEST STRATEGY We recommend using *Road Trip G4* to visit the religious sites around the Holy Land, starting with the Jesus Boat at Kibbutz Ginosar (G3), followed by the ***Mount of Beatitudes***, Tabgha, and Capernaum, with further sites optional depending on time.

WALKS AND DRIVES G3, G4, U2.

ITINERARIES Most Popular; Religion; Pilgrimage.

ARRIVAL PREP

PREBOOK Not necessary.

REALITY CHECK Popular tour-bus stop. Modest dress expected.

ACCESS Two entrances if driving: enter via Tabgha or via the national park entrance at Capernaum further east on Highway 87. Nominal fee to visit the sites. National Park Card works from Capernaum entrance.

RECOMMENDED GUIDE The placards should be sufficient. A more elaborate visitor center is under construction. Brochure available at Capernaum.

EAT Migdala has a number of good restaurants, 10km south.

SLEEP Rosh Pina (H2) is an Anchor City. ***Tiberias*** has accommodation options.

BUCKET!PEDIA

AKA Capernaum is Kfar Nahum in Hebrew; Tabgha was originally Heptapegon ("seven springs") in Greek, later shortened to al-Tabigha in Arabic and Ein Sheva ("Spring of Seven") in Hebrew. *Historical era* Ancient Israel: *Hasmonean* to *Roman/Byzantine*, then *Islamic: Crusader*. *Year constructed* Likely during Second Temple period.

CONTEXT The multi-millennial site provides an interesting survey of Jewish and Christian life over 1,200 years. The ancient fishing village is famous as the place where Jesus gathered many of his apostles, performed miracles, and left in a dramatic episode, cursing the town. The current site is famous for the House of (Saint) Peter, which was memorialized by a church, now displayed as an archaeological site and a modern memorial. There are remains of an opulent 4th-century CE synagogue built in the octagonal-basilica style of the Byzantine. This makes sense when keeping in mind that the first Christians were Jewish and are considered today to have been a hybrid religion, the Judeo-Christians. This later synagogue may have been built atop another, even more ancient, 1st-century CE structure, possibly the location in the Bible where Jesus cast out demons. Dating has proven difficult because anachronistic pieces (e.g., coins from the 5th century CE) have been found underneath presumably older sites. It's possible these churches and synagogues have been uprooted multiple times over the centuries.

A new promenade takes walkers to Tabgha along the coast of the Sea of Galilee where visitors see two churches. The Church of the Primacy of St. Peter commemorates the fourth appearance of Jesus following his resurrection and his attributing the Peter with a leading role among his apostles. Nearby, the other church commemorates Jesus' miracle of multiplying two fish and five loaves of bread to feed thousands. Scripture says the event occurred near the seven springs (see *AKA* above), so this could in fact be the right site. A chapel was erected here in the 4th century and mosaics from the original church are still visible, though the church was lost to time for 1,300 years. The church was badly vandalized by arsonists in 2015, luckily not damaging its 5th-century mosaics.

CHRONOLOGY

2nd century BCE: Jewish settlement on shore.

30–33 CE: Jesus' ministries in Capernaum and the Sea of Galilee.

4th century: Village reaches its zenith as an important waypoint on the Roman trade route, the Via Maris. Earliest version of Church of the Multiplication on site, now buried underneath present floors.

5th century: Mosaics laid in Church of Multiplication as part of church expansion.

613 and 638: Persian invasion and Islamic takeover, at which point the town, synagogue, and churches are all destroyed.

Mid-7th century: Town shifts eastwards (now covered by the Greek Orthodox Church).

749: Galilee earthquake destroys site and surrounding towns.

11th century: Unclear if the Crusaders ever found this site, but their impact was minimal if they did.

13th century: Pilgrim shares that the village was abandoned and despicable.

1887: Land purchased by the Greek Orthodox.

1968: St. Peter's House discovered during excavations.

1990: Modern church built over St. Peter's House.

2015: Arsonists attack Church of the Multiplication.

WEBSITE w parks.org.il/en/reserve-park/kfar-nahum-capernaum-national-park/.

WHERE TO NEXT?

THEMATIC *Noteworthy* National Parks. *Religion* Judaism; Christianity; Kings, Prophets, and Saints; Jesus' Ministries and Miracles; Jesus' Death and Resurrection; New Testament; Collections of Churches; Pilgrimage. *Archaeology* Roman; Byzantine; Active Excavations. *Nature* Earthquakes. *Active* Walking Paths.

COMPLEMENTARY Other famous Jesus sites in the Galilee are **Sea of Galilee (#7)**, **Nazareth and its Biblical Sites (#29)**, **Jesus Trail (#69)**, *Church of the Transfiguration*, and

Mount of Beatitudes. Other non-Jesus sites in the Galilee are **Beit She'an (#39)**, **Tsipori (#56)**, **Beit Alpha (#64)**, **Belvoir (#93)**, and *Mount Arbel*.

NEARBY *Mount of Beatitudes* (4km/5 minutes), Kibbutz Ginosar (G3) (8km/9 minutes), *Korazim* (9km/9 minutes), *Tiberias* (16km/18 minutes), **Tsfat/Safed (#58)** (24km/ 26 minutes), *Tel Hazor* (27km/25 minutes), and **Nazareth and its Biblical Sites (#29)** (48km/45 minutes).

#34 Mount of Olives

BROCHURE

RATINGS			MACRO-REGION
BUCKET! Score		6/10	A: Jerusalem
Ruin		2/5	
Entertainment		2/5	**MICRO-REGION**
Information		1/5	A5
Popularity		5/5	

PRIMARY THEME/CATEGORY Religion – Houses of Worship – Collections of Churches.

TOP View of Jerusalem.

HOLY LAND RELEVANCE There are many passages in the Bible and Mishnah related specifically to the Mount of Olives. Jews believe this is the place God will redeem the dead when the Messiah comes (i.e., the Last Judgment), and thus many Jews have chosen to be buried here. Jesus passed through here on his way to Bethany many times. And the Lord's Prayer, the prayer in the garden of Gethsemane, and Jesus' ascension to Heaven all occurred here.

ELECT ME! There are several things to see and do at the Mount of Olives. As this is an important Christian site, there are a number of churches here, all built in a variety of styles. Several claim to be the purported Garden of Gethsemane, where Jesus was arrested before being tried and ultimately killed. Additionally, there is a massive Jewish graveyard with at least 70,000 tombs, in use for 3,000 years. At the top of the mount is the most sweeping and majestic view of the Old City.

WORTH THE DETOUR? If you only have a day in Jerusalem, you can probably squeeze it in, but you'll need a car to get to the best vista point. The religious sites are fine, but not absolutely necessary unless the purpose of your trip is Christian religious focused.

EXPERIENCES

CAN'T MISS Observation point opposite the Seven Arches Hotel.

WALKING TOUR You can start either at the Mount of Olives Information Center (if you want a map of the graveyard) or at the Church of All Nations.

1. *Church of All Nations/Basilica of the Agony* The present-day church (1924) sits atop a 12th-century Crusader church, which itself was built over a 4th-century Byzantine basilica destroyed in the 746 earthquake. The historical spot marks where Jesus is said to have prayed in Gethsemane before being arrested by Roman authorities and sentenced to death. Note the gold mosaic facade.
2. *Tomb of the Virgin* Located at the base of the Mount of Olives (Gethsemane), the rock-cut tomb is located in the Church of the Sepulchre of Saint Mary, at the crossroad of Jericho and Mansuriya Streets. Tradition labels this as the burial cave of Mary and Joseph. (Note that some Christian traditions put Mary's death near Ephesus, Turkey.)
3. *Grotto of Gethsemane* Site where Jesus was betrayed, and later arrested, by Pontius Pilate. Also contains an ancient oil press. Return to street, walk up Mansuriya Street and enter the Garden on your right.
4. *Garden of Gethsemane* Jesus prayed here before being arrested and tried by the Romans. Now known for the olive trees on site which are said to date to before Jesus' time, perhaps with root stock as old as 2,300 years. However, the present trees are from the 12th century. Exit on the tiny road with tall walls and start walking uphill. Beware of cars.
5. *Church of Mary Magdalene* Russian Orthodox church on the Mount of Olives, visible by its distinctive onion-shaped gold domes and dedicated to Mary Magdalene, one of Jesus' disciples and the first person to see Jesus after his resurrection. Two Russian saints are buried here (🕐 10.00–noon, Tuesday/Thursday).
6. *Dominus Flevit* In this Franciscan church, Jesus wept when faced with the vision of a future destroyed Jerusalem. The chapel is in the shape of a tear, symbolizing when Jesus wept.
7. *Tomb of the Prophets* The last three minor prophets of the Old Testament – Haggai, Zechariah, and Malachi – are purportedly buried here. This is hard to prove since the above-ground graves date to the 1st century BCE/CE, while the prophets lived 500 years earlier.
8. *Viewpoint* Climb the hill and head across the car park towards the Seven Arches Hotel, where you're afforded one of the best views of Jerusalem.
9. *Church of the Pater Noster* Jesus taught the Lord's Prayer in a cave on the Mount of Olives. The first Christian Emperor, Constantine, requested that a church be built on the very spot. Early Christian travelers visited that church, and it existed until the Muslim invasion. The Crusaders rebuilt it, but it again fell into disrepair. The current church was never completed – a testament to the messy history, perhaps.
10. *Church of the Ascension* Originally centered around a footprint attributed to Jesus, the site is now venerated by many faiths as the location of Jesus' ascension to Heaven. The original plan of this church was a circle with an open roof – it is now a covered octagon. Built in 392 CE, and reconstructed during Crusader times, it has been under Muslim control since Saladin in 1200. If you're visiting without a guide, knock to enter.

EXTRA CREDIT

11. *Russian Church (Tower) of the Ascension* Continue from the Pater Noster Church and you'll reach this notable four-story tower with a belfry where John the Baptist's head was discovered in the 4th century CE. It also has a lovely view from the top! Only open Tuesday/Thursday for a couple of hours before lunch.

12. *Bethphage* A bit further up the road from the Tower of the Ascension is Bethphage, the site from which Jesus entered Jerusalem with his disciples. That said, no one knows quite where the historic Bethphage was.

13. *Bethany* If you continue even further, you'll get to Bethany, or El-Azariya, where Jesus raised Lazarus from the dead. You can visit Lazarus' tomb with a bit of work. Get a key from the local shopkeeper to descend into the tomb.

MORE TOMBS TO SEEK OUT Eliezer Ben Yehuda (revived the Hebrew language, now spoken by 5 million people); Menachem Begin (sixth prime minister of Israel and founder of Likud party).

SECRET Best shots from the car park come in the morning, to keep the sun from obstructing as it moves west in the afternoon.

SPECIAL EVENTS On Palm Sunday, Christians march in procession from the Mount of Olives to the **Church of the Holy Sepulchre (#9)**. Also, Jewish burial ceremonies can be arranged at the visitor center.

MAP See A5.

ITINERATOR!

DAYS/HOURS Most of the sites are open 08.00–noon and 14.00–17.00, with some variance. The Church of Mary Magdalene is only open 10.00–noon Tuesday/Thursday.

BEST TIME Tuesday morning and Thursday morning provide the right confluence of time to see everything when open.

TIME COMMITMENT Two hours should be sufficient for most people, despite the many stops. If you're part of a bigger group and/or are walking with slower folks, plan for 4 hours. Speed rules apply.

BASE In Anchor City Jerusalem.

BEST STRATEGY Mount of Olives has a bunch of sites to jet in and out of so, if you're a list-checker, make sure you plan to visit on Tuesday or Thursday morning, when everything is open. If you're an able and fast walker, you can combine this with the *City of David*, walking through the Kidron Valley (A5), and end at **Mount Zion (#92)** (see *City Walk A5*).

WALKS AND DRIVES A5.

ITINERARIES Jerusalem Immersion; Most Popular; Religion; Structure; Active; Memorial; Shoestring; Big-Group Friendly.

ARRIVAL PREP

PREBOOK Not necessary.

REALITY CHECK Popular tour-bus stop. Beware pickpockets. Modest dress required.

ACCESS You can walk in or drive, though parking is hard to come by and the streets are incredibly narrow.

ADMISSION All sites are free, but you will likely be hounded for tips in at least a few places, so bring change.

RECOMMENDED GUIDE A tour guide is recommended here as the signage is based on whatever the church groups have on display. If you're in a hurry, you can walk around with our basic overview. If you want something in the middle, use the excellent Franciscan Custodia website (w custodia.org/en/sanctuaries/gethsemane).

VISITOR CENTER Yes, on Derech Jericho just opposite Kidron Valley and below Gethsemane on the main road. It has maps and can help you find graves.

EAT Eat before you come: there are cafés, but the best food is in the Old City or near **Mehane Yehuda Market (#67)**.

SLEEP See **Old City Jerusalem (#1)**.

BUCKET!PEDIA

AKA Har ha-Zeitim (Hebrew); Jabal al-Zaytun (Arabic); also Olivet in biblical tradition. *Height* 818m. *Historical era* Ancient Israel to *Modern*. *Year founded* Unclear, but has been used as a burial ground for 3,000 years.

CONTEXT Part of the Judean Mountain ridge, along with Mount Scopus and the Mount of Corruption, the Mount of Olives is famous for a number of reasons. First, for the many interesting churches that can be spotted from across the valley at various points in the Old City. (Indeed it's even more interesting looking back the other direction.) Second, there are a number of scenes in biblical history that took place in or around this mount, and the churches were established to represent those moments. Third, as a Jewish burial site, with 70,000–150,000 burial graves that stretch back three millennia. And, finally, for the best view in town. The Mount of Olives is referenced several times in the Bible, both Old and New Testaments.

RELIGIOUS CHRONOLOGY

King David flees from his son, Absalom (2 Samuel 15:30).
King Solomon, David's son, erects false idols upon the Mount to honor his wives who come from neighboring (polytheistic) tribes (1 Kings 11:7).
King Josiah destroys the many idols built up on the Mount (2 Kings 23:13).
Prophecy proclaims God will split the Mount in two (Zechariah 14:4).
When the resurrection comes, God will start with the bodies on the Mount (Zechariah 14:4).
Jesus rides into Jerusalem from Bethany (Matthew 21, Mark 11, Luke 19, John 12).
Jesus teaches to his disciples and predicts the destruction of the Temple (Matthew 24, Mark 13, Luke 21).
Jesus spends his last night in Gethsemane and is arrested (Matthew 26, Mark 14, Luke 22, John 18).
Jesus ascends to Heaven from the Mount of Olives (Acts 1:9–12).

WEBSITE w mountofolives.co.il/en/information-center/; w custodia.org/en/sanctuaries/gethsemane.

WHERE TO NEXT?

THEMATIC *Religion* Judaism; Christianity; Kings, Prophets, and Saints; Jesus' Ministries and Miracles; Old Testament; New Testament; Collections of Churches; Burial; Pilgrimage; Ceremonies and Events; Memorial. *Scenic* Urban Landscape; Historical Vantage; Most Photographed. *People* Jewish.

COMPLEMENTARY Other important Jesus sites are **Sea of Galilee (#7)**, **Nazareth and its Biblical Sites (#29)**, and **Bethlehem (#40)**. Other major churches are **Church of the Holy Sepulchre (#9)**, **Church of the Nativity (#18)**, *Basilica of the Annunciation*, *Church of St. Anne*, and *Church of the Transfiguration*.

NEARBY Kidron Valley (A5) (500m/7 minutes), **Old City Jerusalem (#1)**, Dung Gate exit (1km/15 minutes), *City of David* (1km/15 minutes), and **Mount Zion (#92)** (2km/25 minutes).

#35 Yad Vashem

BROCHURE

RATINGS

BUCKET! Score		7/10
Ruin	n/a	
Entertainment		4/5
Information		5/5
Popularity		5/5

MACRO-REGION
A: Jerusalem

MICRO-REGION
A8

PRIMARY THEME/CATEGORY Structure – Monuments – Memorial.

TOP Arguably, the best (and most uplifting) Holocaust museum in the world.

HOLY LAND RELEVANCE The museum tells the story of the Jewish Holocaust of World War II, when six million Jews from Europe were murdered (along with many other cultural minorities, including gays, Roma, and the disabled). After the war, the United Nations came together to map out the boundaries for a Jewish state in Mandatory Palestine, leading to the establishment of Israel in 1947.

ELECT ME! Despite natural comparisons to other Holocaust museums around the world, Yad Vashem is truly a unique experience. You may already know the story in its gruesome entirety, but the ultimate message here is of hope and survival. Many exhibits relate to resistance, uprisings, successful attempts in reaching the Holy Land, the establishment of Israel, and the many that aided Jews in finding safety. The murdered are not forgotten, with dozens of individual stories being highlighted throughout the journey. The viewer follows a chronological path through the museum, learning about the Holocaust (called "Shoah" in Hebrew) and taking one's own pace to discover and explore the many interactive multimedia displays. The new museum, built in 1993, is a beautiful edifice, and the architecture and layout make for a very pleasing experience (as much as that is possible, given the circumstances).

WORTH THE DETOUR? If you're planning a cultural day outside of the Old City in Jerusalem, absolutely. It is much different than other Holocaust museums, and worth a visit. That said, there are other Holocaust museums in the world. So if you are short on time, focus on **Old City Jerusalem (#1)** first. Then if you have time for only one museum, pick between this and the **Israel Museum (#17)**.

EXPERIENCES

CAN'T MISS The Hall of Names and the mountaintop views.

MUSEUMS INCLUDED The Holocaust History Museum; The Art Museum; The Exhibitions Pavilion; The Learning Center; The Visual Center; The Synagogue; The Archives.

GALLERIES IN THE HISTORY MUSEUM The World that Was; From Equals to Outcasts; The Awful Beginning; Between Walls and Fences; Mass Murder; The "Final Solution"; Resistance and Rescue; The Last Jews; Return to Life; Facing the Loss.

SECRET Most people only visit the main exhibit halls of the museum. But the museum and center's resources are endless. You can visit the Reading Room inside the Archives, watch films in the Visual Center, listen to lectures asking big questions about the Holocaust, attend speaking events, and research names online. All of these things might seem obvious, but how often will you get the chance to meet a Holocaust survivor? Or hear from Holocaust experts? Take advantage.

SPECIAL EVENTS Visit w yadvashem.org for more information.

ITINERATOR!

DAYS/HOURS 08.30–17.00 Sunday–Thursday, 08.30–14.00 Friday and holiday eves, closed Saturdays and Jewish holidays.

TIME COMMITMENT 2–4 hours, depending on how much you read. Longer if you explore the adjacent museums and exhibitions. Speed rules apply.

BASE In Anchor City Jerusalem.

BEST STRATEGY If you're planning a day on Mount Herzl, note that Yad Vashem opens earlier than most of those sites, so you may want to start here. It will likely be crowded most of the day, so prebook your tickets to ensure you minimize wait times.

WALKS AND DRIVES A8.

ITINERARIES Jerusalem Immersion; High BUCKET! Scores: 7+; Most Popular; Most Entertaining; Structure; Organized; Memorial; Modernity; All Ages; Big-Group Friendly; Pilgrimage.

ARRIVAL PREP

PREBOOK Recommended, but not required (w forms.yadvashem.org/reservations).

REALITY CHECK Popular tour-bus stop. Often very crowded.

ACCESS Parking is available for 28 ILS, or you can take a taxi/light rail/bus/sherut/shuttle to Mount Herzl. Then make your way to the Mount of Remembrance, across the street. Admission is free, but entries are timed.

RECOMMENDED GUIDE The museum provides satisfactory explanation in the form of video, print, and visuals. Guided tours are available, and you can submit a reservation through the online reservation system at **w** yadvashem.org/visiting/private-tour.html.

EAT Yad Vashem offers a kosher meat cafeteria with hot meals, and a kosher-dairy coffee shop.

SLEEP This is an easy trip from any hotel in Jerusalem.

BUCKET!PEDIA

AKA The World Holocaust Remembrance Center ("Yad Vashem" means "memorial/monument and a name"). *Size* 45 acres/18 hectares. *Historical era Modern: Mandatory Palestine* to *Contemporary*. *Year constructed* Established in 1953 by the Knesset; new museum complex opened in 2005.

CONTEXT The Holocaust Museum, Yad Vashem, was created in 1953 through the Israeli Parliament in order to document and educate visitors about the horrors of the Holocaust, and the six million Jews that were exterminated in camps throughout Europe. But this museum has another purpose: to research and find stories of survivorship. For every destroyed community, there was a resilience that followed from those that moved elsewhere and told their community's stories. For every armed guard seeking to do irreparable damage, there was a Jewish person or ally who risked their life to save others. For every act of evil against strangers, there was an act of kindness in helping strangers. This museum tells those triumphant stories, despite the overwhelming loss. There was death – a lot of it – and that is not glossed over here. But there is something encouraging and uplifting about the stories that rarely get told and the persons that rarely get named.

Thus, we find the purpose: remembrance, as the name suggests. The Archives, Library, and Visual Center each contain more material than you could possibly digest in one visit, or 100 visits. Those with a particular interest in Holocaust studies should do their research on the very informative website prior to arriving so you can plan your day. The external building is something of an architectural marvel. Architect Moshe Safdie designed the new museum structure – a 180m prism which cuts through a mountain – to bring in light through one long skylight. Both ends of the building hang precariously over the ledges of the mountain, offering stunning views of the valleys below. This $100 million construction took a decade to build and does not disappoint. The views are part of the reflection and experience.

With more than a million visitors per year, this museum is second only to the Western Wall in terms of annual visitors. It will invariably be crowded, so try to visit during non-peak hours (weekdays) and book in advance.

CHRONOLOGY

19th century CE: Pogroms (ethnic massacres, usually of Jews) in Europe lead Jews to seek out a new homeland, choosing the Holy Land.
1882: First settlement in Ottoman Palestine. Established Rishon Letzion.

1882–1903: First Aliyah, or immigration wave, of Jews to Palestine, coming mostly from Eastern Europe.

1897: World Zionist Congress in Basel, Switzerland where Theodor Herzl calls for the establishment of a "legally secured homeland in Palestine."

1917: Ottoman Turkey loses in World War I, and Great Britain captures its territory in the Holy Land, including Palestine and Transjordan. The Balfour Declaration by the British Government guarantees a home for the Jewish people in Palestine.

1918: Germany is defeated in World War I, with many blaming Jews for the political surrender.

1920s: Rise of anti-semitism across Europe. Immigration closed to Jews in most countries.

1933/34: Adolf Hitler becomes Chancellor and soon Führer of Germany.

1933: Dachau opened as the first concentration camp, ostensibly for "political prisoners."

1933: Jewish business boycott in Germany. Jewish lawyers disbarred. Jewish doctors forced to resign.

1935: Nuremberg Laws, with marriages between Jews and Germans forbidden. Other European countries follow suit. Estimated population of Jews in Europe: 9.5 million.

1938: Kristallnacht, a pogrom in Germany in which Jewish businesses were destroyed and 30,000 Jews were taken to concentration camps. Roughly half of the German Jewish population (500,000) leaves Germany.

1939: Germany invades Poland, home to more than 3 million Jews.

1941: Germany invades several countries in Europe, begins sending Jews to concentration camps.

1942: Germans devise the Final Solution, a plan to kill all Jews.

1933–45: Two-thirds of the Jewish population of Europe, some six million Jews, die in the Holocaust genocide. This period of history is referred to as Shoah ("catastrophe") in Hebrew.

1945: End of World War II. Estimated population of Jews remaining in Europe: 3.8 million.

1948: Declaration of the state of Israel. Population of Israel: 806,000.

1949: End of Arab–Israeli War, with Israel taking control of the Arab areas designated as Palestine by the United Nations. Nearly 400,000 Jews migrate to Israel.

1952: Jewish population in Israel doubles in four years to 1.6 million.

1953: Yad Vashem established by an act of the Knesset, Israel's Parliament.

WEBSITE w yadvashem.org.

WHERE TO NEXT?

THEMATIC *Religion* Judaism; Memorial. *Structure* Modern Architecture; Beautiful Structures. *People* Jewish. *Culture* Museum of Culture. *Organized* Guided.

COMPLEMENTARY Best museums: **Israel Museum (#17)**, **Citadel/Tower of David (#32)**, **ANU – Museum of the Jewish People (#77)**, and **Tel Aviv Museum of Art (#95)**. Other modern art buildings: **Tel Aviv Museum of Art (#95)**, and *Design Museum Holon*.

NEARBY Mount Herzl (300m/3-minute walk), Herzl Museum (A8) (500m/5-minute walk), **Israel Museum (#17)** (4km/10-minute drive), Knesset (A8) (4km/10-minute drive), *Supreme Court of Israel* (4km/10-minute drive), *Hadassah Synagogue and Chagall Windows* (7km/15-minute drive), and **Old City Jerusalem (#1)** (9km/30-minute drive).

#36 Modern Amman

BROCHURE

RATINGS

BUCKET! Score		5/10
Ruin	n/a	
Entertainment		3/5
Information		1/5
Popularity		4/5

MACRO-REGION
Q: Amman

MICRO-REGIONS
Q2, Q3

PRIMARY THEME/CATEGORY Society – Cities – Principal Cities.

HOLY LAND RELEVANCE Amman – and Jordan as a whole – received a large wave of Palestinian refugees following the 1948 Arab–Israeli War and the 1967 Six-Day War.

ELECT ME! If you're a fan of cities, you'll like Amman. There's the ancient part, which we discuss in the following elective, but there's a modern sensibility too which pairs interestingly with the traditional, Muslim, and Arab side. It's more relaxed, safe, and accessible than many other Arab cities, with bars, clubs, nice restaurants, and interesting museums to explore.

WORTH THE DETOUR? The city is chaotic and has its charms, but it's the least enticing of the three big regional cities (**Tel Aviv (#5)** and **Jerusalem, New City (#72)** have much more on offer), there are better ruins in Jordan (**Jerash (#14)**, **Petra (#2)**), better places to sleep (**Dead Sea (#3)**), and nature is really a draw elsewhere (**Wadi Rum (#4)**, **Dana Biosphere Reserve (#21)**). That said, it's hard not to find your way to Amman if you are in Jordan. And particularly if you are visiting from another Arab city, you may find it positively blissful!

EXPERIENCES

CAN'T MISS Rainbow Street, which has bars, shops, hostels, food, and travelers.

SITES Raghadan Palace (King's court); Books@Cafe (Q2) (most famous spot in the city?); *Wild Jordan Center* – book a trip to the Jordanian wilds; Khalid Shoman Foundation/Darat al-Funun (Q2) for contemporary art or Jordan National Gallery of Fine Arts (Q2) for artifacts; mosques of different styles – Abu Darwish Mosque (Q3) (Circassian), Grand Husseini (pink), *King Abdullah I Mosque (Q3)* (huge), and just inside the Roman amphitheater are two little gems – Jordan Folklore Museum (Q3) and the Jordan Museum of Popular Traditions (Q3).

ACTIVITIES **Cooking school** at *Beit Sitti*; eating **falafel** (which is better: Al-Quds Falafel (Q2) or Hashem Falafel (Q2)?); **fine dining** at Fakhr el-Din (Q2); shop at the **Al-Balad market** for gold, spices, nuts, daggers (good luck getting through customs), keffiyehs (red and white checkered headdress worn by Jordanian men), brass teapots, salts/cosmetics from the Dead Sea, and olive wood; and get a soak in at the Al-Pasha Turkish Bath (Q3).

SECRET Easily put together this tour by combining *City Walks Q2* and *Q3*.

SPECIAL EVENTS Check out **w** calendar.jo.

MAP See Q2.

ITINERATOR!

DAYS/HOURS Many businesses close on Friday afternoon, the weekly holiday. Most mall shops, grocery stores, and restaurants stay open.

BEST TIME Summers are hot, like everywhere in the Middle East. It can snow in the winter, with January/February being the wettest period of the year.

TIME COMMITMENT Four hours minimum to breeze through our two walking tours together, without stopping anywhere. One or two full days to get a complete picture (including the **Ancient Amman (#37)** sites). Speed rules apply.

BASE Amman is an Anchor City, but you can also get here from Suweimeh on the Dead Sea (55km/over an hour).

BEST STRATEGY If you have one day, we recommend tackling *City Walks Q2* and *Q3* in the order they're presented: ancient ruins, then Rainbow/Wild Jordan/museums, then markets/baths/mosques. With any remaining time, try *Road Trip Q4* on the outskirts of town.

WALKS AND DRIVES Q2, Q3, Q4.

ITINERARIES Amman Immersion; Off-the-Beaten-Path Jordan; Society and People; Culture; Food and Drink; Relaxation; Shoestring; Cinematic.

ARRIVAL PREP

REALITY CHECK Traffic is ever-present. Very few good directional street signs. Construction is always ongoing, meaning lots of detours.

ACCESS It's easiest to orient yourself if you start near the Amman Citadel. There is some street parking around town, but taxis are cheap and you don't have to deal with parking meters or attendants who "watch" your car.

RECOMMENDED GUIDE A friend would be helpful here – someone who could show you local restaurants and bars and their favorite shops. Barring that, you can try a meet-up app (no guarantees there, it's a Muslim country). Or local recommendations on Culture Trip (**w** theculturetrip.com/asia/jordan/amman/).

VISITOR CENTER The ***Wild Jordan Center*** promotes the nature reserves and other sites in Jordan, but there isn't a good visitor center, per se, to Amman. The Jordan Tourism Board heavily promotes its website for all information (**w** international.visitjordan.com).

EAT Besides the better-known restaurants listed above, you can find a variety of falafel and shawarma stands across town. Rainbow Street offers the best international selection of food, while a car will afford you the opportunity to head into wealthier neighborhoods with a quieter ambiance. More options in the itineraries.

SLEEP The Rainbow Street district is called Jebel Amman, and there are a number of good hotel options there. Downtown also has lots of hotels, many in the budget category.

BUCKET!PEDIA

AKA Nicknamed "The White Pigeon" for its limestone facades. *Historical era Islamic: Ottoman* to *Modern: Contemporary. Year founded* After centuries of abandonment, the city was reinhabited in 1878 by Circassian farmers and exploded in population throughout the 20th century.

CONTEXT Amman is a healthy mix of antiquity and modernity, with ruins from the Classical era sitting right next to mosques, restaurants, and all sorts of new construction, giving the whole city an eclectic feel. It's an easier introduction to the Middle East – the people are friendly, the food is good, and there is enough to keep you busy for a day or two.

CHRONOLOGY

747: Ancient Amman destroyed by an earthquake. Mostly abandoned.

1878: Hundreds of Circassians begin to leave their Caucasus state of Circassia after defeat and annexation by Russia following the Russo–Circassian War, settling in Jordan. Their first established village is in Amman, the long-abandoned town.

1881: In a survey of the city, British officials note that Amman is used primarily for livestock grazing by local tribes, but the Roman ruins are among the most impressive of the territory that was then called Syria.

1921: Amman declared capital of the new Emirate of Transjordan.

1946: Jordan granted independence. Amman remains capital.

1948: Declaration of the state of Israel.

1948–49: Arab–Israeli War, which the Arab states lose. Israel declares victory. Jordan annexes the West Bank and Egypt takes Gaza. Arabs from new Israel state begin moving to Jordan, and Amman in particular.

1952: Population of Amman has quintupled to over 100,000.

1967: Six-Day War ends with Israel annexing the West Bank, Gaza, the Sinai, and the Golan. Mass exodus of Palestinian refugees to Jordan.

1970: Population swells fivefold again to more than 500,000.

1991: 200,000 Palestinians forced out of Kuwait due to Yasser Arafat's allegiance to Saddam Hussein.

1994: Israel–Jordan Peace Treaty signed.

1998: Population of Amman reaches 1 million.

2018: Population passes 2 million.

WEBSITE w international.visitjordan.com.

WHERE TO NEXT?

THEMATIC *Religion* Islam. *Archaeology* Impressive Structural Remains. *Structure* Historic Monuments. *Society* Politics; Principal Cities. *People* Arab. *Food and Drink* Culinary Capital.

COMPLEMENTARY Other Arab culinary capitals: **Akko (#13)**, *Nazarene Fusion Cuisine*, Abu Ghosh's hummusiyas (B1), and Hebron (C2). Other regional capitals: **Tel Aviv (#5)**; **Ramallah (#68)**, and **Jerusalem, New City (#72)**.

NEARBY **Jerash (#14)** (54km/1 hour), **Dead Sea (#3)** (55km/1 hour), **Petra (#2)** (240km/ 3 hours), **Wadi Rum (#4)** (322km/4 hours), and **Aqaba (#43)** (330km/4 hours).

#37 Ancient Amman

BROCHURE

RATINGS			MACRO-REGION
BUCKET! Score		6/10	Q: Amman
Ruin		4/5	
Entertainment		2/5	MICRO-REGION
Information		2/5	Q1
Popularity		4/5	

PRIMARY THEME/CATEGORY Archaeology – Roman – Judea.

HOLY LAND RELEVANCE The name "Amman" is derived from the 10th-century BCE Kingdom of Ammon which ruled the Transjordan region, and is referenced throughout the Bible as fighters against the Israelites. This ancient civilization was based in Rabbath Ammon, or present Amman. Most of the historically relevant sites in Amman proper are from the Roman Empire, which held dominion over the region for nearly 700 years.

ELECT ME! Amman's Roman ruins are surprisingly integrated into the downtown districts, almost as though the old and new cities have always been integrated. But they haven't: **Modern Amman (#36)** dates only to the 19th century, but its ruins are some 2,000 years old and sat unattended in the desert for millennia before becoming home to waves of immigrants. Most visitors to Jordan will pass through Amman, as it makes an easy way station and is also the location of the airport. If this is you, don't miss out: the handful of ruins here are very photogenic and needn't take long to explore.

WORTH THE DETOUR? If your trip has you passing through Amman, the ancient sites are priority #1. If you are debating a visit, know there are better ruins in Jordan at **Petra (#2)**, **Jerash (#14)**, and even **Umm Qais (#45)**.

EXPERIENCES

CAN'T MISS Citadel Hill.

SITES

★ *Jordan Archaeological Museum* On Citadel Hill, this site provides plenty of context.

★ *Citadel* With its impressive melange of cultures represented on this one tiny hill, Amman's Citadel showcases almost continuous occupation and rule from the Bronze Age to the beginning of Islamic rule. Once dominated by a hulking Hercules (a hand is all that remains of a 13m tall statue, near the museum), the 12m tall **Temple of Hercules** was inaugurated in 166 CE, the same era as the Roman Theater down the road; the few remaining columns were erected upon rediscovery. The larger of the two **Byzantine Churches** on site is from the 6th century with minor reconstruction; the smaller is older and in poor shape, but perhaps represents one of the earliest churches in the region. The entrance to the Umayyad (mid-8th century) area is known as the **Monumental Gateway** and consists of an ornate stone entrance with a massive (reconstructed) dome leading to an Umayyad administrative building. Beyond is a cistern, courtyard, Roman-era street, and mosque.

★ *Roman Theater* Down the hill from the Citadel is this 6,000-capacity theater, restored and lovely, with the Jordan Folklore Museum (Q3) and the Jordan Museum of Popular Traditions (Q3) on site.

★ *Roman Odeon* Next-door, baby theater, 500-person capacity.

★ *Nymphaeum* A public fountain dating to the 2nd century CE, not functioning.

★ *Jordan Museum (Ras al-Ein)* 1.2km west of the Nymphaeum, this is the largest museum in Jordan and contains the 'Ain Ghazal statues (perhaps the oldest in history) and the Copper Scroll from the Dead Sea Scrolls.

SECRET If you want to make the whole day walkable, start by taking a taxi to the Citadel and then walking downhill to the theater area, rather than the other way around.

SPECIAL EVENTS The Roman Theater hosts a number of events each year.

ITINERATOR!

DAYS/HOURS Summer 08.00–18.30, winter 08.00–16.00, April/May 08.00–17.30, Ramadan 08.00–15.30. Many things close on Fridays and close early (15.30) during Ramadan.

TIME COMMITMENT 1–2 hours for Citadel Hill and the Roman theaters, using taxis; 4 hours doing the whole thing on foot, plus walking to the Nymphaeum and Jordan Museum. If you like museums, most of the day. Speed rules apply.

BASE Amman can be an Anchor City; however, if your time in Jordan is limited, stay in Suweimeh (55km/55m) at the **Dead Sea (#3)** to tick off that bucket-list item.

BEST STRATEGY Skip midday if heat is an issue. Regardless, start early at the top of Citadel (08.00) and then make your way through *City Walk Q1*, ending at Jordan Museum. Pick up a combination of *City Walk Q2* and *Q3* sites in the same day for a very full day of walking and a good roundup of Amman's greatest hits.

WALKS AND DRIVES Q1, V2, W1, W3.

ITINERARIES Amman Immersion; Big-Group Friendly.

ARRIVAL PREP

PREBOOK Not necessary.

REALITY CHECK Heat warning. Steep hills. Uneven pavement.

BRING Small bills/coins to pay for entrance fees to sites, unless you have the Jordan Pass (which we recommend you book in advance via the website); hat/sunglasses; good walking shoes.

ACCESS Self-parking at the Citadel and in front of the Roman Theater, but you'll need to pay (tip) someone to watch your car.

ADMISSION 1–2 JD each, so just get the Jordan Pass, which pays for the visa, **Petra (#2)**, and 40 other sites in Jordan.

RECOMMENDED GUIDE The *Jordan Archaeological Museum* and the *Jordan Museum (Q3)* provide all the context you will need.

EAT Have a big breakfast at your hotel. After your morning walk, head to Rainbow Street for falafel (e.g., Al-Quds Falafel (Q2)), a restaurant, or café.

SLEEP See **Modern Amman (#36)**.

BUCKET!PEDIA

AKA Rabbath Ammon (Ammonite period, 13th century BCE); Philadelphia (during Ptolemaic/Greek times). *Size* 1,680km² (650 square miles). *Historical era* Prehistoric: Neolithic to Islamic: Umayyad. *Year founded* 'Ain Ghazal was founded c10,000 years ago.

CONTEXT Amman is probably one of the oldest settled cities in the world. The 'Ain Ghazal site (visits not currently allowed) produced a treasure trove of materials, including a few dozen human statues that are now on display in the Jordan Museum. This early human art confirms a sophistication of culture in this region that continued for millennia. For much of its history, the site of the Amman Citadel – Jabal al-Qal'a – has been the epicenter of the town, and the capital of the territory. Its name comes from the Kingdom of Ammon, referenced in the Book of Genesis in the Old Testament, reflecting the age of the city.

The current site of Citadel Hill has an impressive number of ruins, though they make little sense out of context, so a trip to the Jordan Archaeological Museum on site is a must, at least to piece together what you're looking at after you've seen it. The sites on the hill represent several thousand years of human habitation, and the three main sites of the Temple, Palace, and churches are successive ruling powers, but from different parts of the world, with different religions, languages, and cultures. The history on the hill is quite eclectic. There are other ruins throughout the city, but none more regal than the Roman amphitheater just down the hill in the downtown area. Another smaller theater and a public fountain dating to the same era are nearby.

Amman passed through the hands of successive powers over the next 1,000 years. After the Umayyads, the site fell into disrepair. The Abbasids, Crusaders, Ayyubids, Mamluks, and Ottomans all likely based soldiers or administrators in Amman, but the city saw a rapid decline in importance before it was completely abandoned by residents. Archaeological surveyors noted in the 1880s that the city was empty save for some animals grazing on the pastures among the hills of ruins. Not until

Circassians repopulated the region in the late 19th century did Amman begin to reclaim its status in the world.

CHRONOLOGY

7250 BCE: 'Ain Ghazal is one of several sites in the Fertile Crescent where Neolithic people settle to farm cereals and grains.

6200 BCE: Environmental collapse, likely due to climate change.

2250 BCE: Bronze Age. Rock-cut tombs appear on Jabal al-Qal'a.

1200 BCE: Jabal al-Qal'a, now Citadel Hill, becomes capital of the Kingdom of Ammon.

800 BCE: Ammonite Palace constructed on Jabal al-Qal'a.

246 BCE: City renamed Philadelphia after Ptolemy Philadelphus, an Egyptian ruler who rebuilt the city.

63 BCE: Roman reign. Region becomes part of Syrian province.

106 CE: Philadelphia joins the Decapolis League. Joins Provincia Arabia. Roman Theater, Odeon, Nymphaeum, and Temple of Hercules built.

324: Byzantine period begins. Earliest church on Jabal al-Qal'a may date to this period.

6th century: Larger of the Byzantine churches built on Citadel Hill.

635: Arab armies conquer region. City becomes known as Amman.

735: Umayyad Palace, mosque, residences, audience hall, throne chamber, and cistern all date to this period.

749: The first of a series of earthquakes over the next two centuries that would leave the area in ruins.

WEBSITE w international.visitjordan.com.

WHERE TO NEXT?

THEMATIC *Archaeology* Early Human Settlements; Prehistory; Bronze Age; Iron Age; Empires; Roman; Byzantine; Islamic I; Cities of the Decapolis. *Active* Competition.

COMPLEMENTARY Other impressive Roman ruins: **Jerash (#14)**, **Caesarea (#25)**, **Tsipori (#56)**, and **Beit She'an (#39)**. Other Cities of the Decapolis: **Jerash (#14)**, **Beit She'an (#39)**, **Umm Qais (#45)**, and *Pella*.

NEARBY **Madaba (#19)** (37km/45 minutes), **Jerash (#14)** (50km/50 minutes), Suweimeh/**Dead Sea (#3)** (60km/1¼ hours), **Azraq Wetlands (#55)** (100km/1½ hours), **Umm Qais (#45)** (120km/2 hours), and **Petra (#2)** (230km/3¼ hours).

#38 Biblical Tels

BROCHURE

RATINGS		
BUCKET! Score		6/10
Ruin		2/5
Entertainment		1/5
Information		2/5
Popularity		2/5

MACRO-REGION
U: Cross-Israel/Palestine

MICRO-REGIONS
F1, H2, J1

PRIMARY THEME/CATEGORY Archaeology – Ancient Israel – Iron Age.

TOP Tels.

COMMENDATIONS UNESCO World Heritage Site, 2005; Israel National Parks.

HOLY LAND RELEVANCE Megiddo is the present name for biblical "Armageddon" which was prophesied as the site of a battle at the end of days. Founding Father Abraham and sons lived in Beer-sheba (*Tel Beer Sheva*, which is just outside present-day Be'er Sheva). The Book of Kings mentions Hazor as an Israelite city fortified by King Solomon (son of David, builder of First Temple).

ELECT ME! These settlement mounds (tels) are the best-preserved examples of Bronze and Iron Age cities referenced in the Bible. The concept of a tel is fascinating: civilizations building on top of the remains of the ones that came before. Over time this adds enough debris and dirt to create actual hills with layers of civilization compressed one top of another, much like the fossil record found in rock layers (strata). Archaeology buffs will love this.

WORTH THE DETOUR? These sites are interesting if you have some context, but that means you're going to be doing some independent research. The sites themselves are each national parks and UNESCO sites, so there is plenty to absorb (albeit static reading) via brochures and placards. The ruins take a lot of imagination and the sites could defensibly be called "boring." These are good visits for archaeologists. Religious tourists likely won't find **Megiddo (#59)** very spiritual, though it is historically relevant.

EXPERIENCES

CAN'T MISS If you've got time for only one: **Megiddo (#59)**.

SITES Megiddo (#59), the most impressive and recognizable (the name means "Armageddon"); *Tel Beer Sheva*, the home of Abraham; and *Tel Hazor*, the largest of the three.

SECRET There are more than 200 other tels in Israel, but they don't come with the UNESCO moniker. Check out *Complementary* below for other (perhaps closer) options.

SPECIAL EVENTS There are a number of organization that coordinate 1–4-week digs in which you can participate.

ITINERATOR!

DAYS/HOURS Summer 08.00–17.00 Saturday–Thursday, 08.00–16.00 Friday, winter 08.00–16.00 Saturday–Thursday, 08.00–15.00 Friday, closed holidays.

BEST TIME Most of these sites are out in the open and require walking. For your own enjoyment, try to schedule a visit for when it's not uncomfortably warm.

TIME COMMITMENT Two hours is more than enough time to see each site; however, they are not adjacent to each other. Two are in the Galilee (50km apart) and the third is in the south/Negev. Attempting to visit all three in one day would not be advisable. Speed rules apply.

BASE Include these as side trips on your driving tours or your DIY road trips. **Megiddo (#59)** is 87km/1¼ hours from Tel Aviv. *Tel Hazor* is 12km/10m from Rosh Pina. *Tel Beer Sheva* is 120km from Tel Aviv and Jerusalem at (c1¼ hours if using toll road).

BEST STRATEGY You could possibly drive to each of the sites in one day, but this isn't realistic nor would it be enjoyable. Better to work them into your other trips planned to the north and south. Check out our drives below.

WALKS AND DRIVES F1, H2, J1, W5.

ITINERARIES Noteworthy; Archaeology; UNESCO; Ancient History.

ARRIVAL PREP

PREBOOK Not necessary.

REALITY CHECK Little shade. Not good sites for youngsters. Hilly.

BRING Hat, sunscreen, water.

ACCESS Parking available at all sites.

ADMISSION 14 ILS (Tel Beer Sheva), 22 ILS (Tel Hazor), and 28 ILS (Megiddo), or use your Israel Park Pass.

RECOMMENDED GUIDE Brochure and/or guide, as context is imperative to getting anything out of these sites.

VISITOR CENTER There's a visitor center at Megiddo and Tel Hazor has a museum, requiring prearrangement. And all three have explanatory brochures with maps and walking routes.

EAT Megiddo has basic food, but you'll want to plan to eat elsewhere or bring a lunch.

SLEEP Not recommended to stay here – no services and better options within an hour's drive.

BUCKET!PEDIA

AKA Tel Megiddo is also known as Har Megiddo (or Mount Megiddo). Har Megiddo when put together sounds a lot like the ancient and biblical name of this town: Armageddon. Beer Sheva means "Well of the Oath" or "Well of the Seven," named after Abraham's covenant with Abimelech to let him keep his self-dug water well in this location, cementing their connection and ties to this land. Hazor likely means "gathering place" or "village." *Historical era* Prehistoric: Bronze Age to *Ancient Israel: Kingdom of Israel and Judah.* *Year constructed* Megiddo inhabited in the Neolithic period; Tel Beer Sheva perhaps was constructed in the Chalcolithic era; Tel Hazor in the early Bronze Age.

CONTEXT The three sites that make up the UNESCO-designated "Biblical Tels" are scattered throughout Israel – in the lower and upper Galilee, as well as the Negev, but are the best preserved of the 200 or so historic tels (prehistoric settlement mounds) in Israel. Through the very minimalist remains, archaeologists have been able to uncover the development of human history, including the establishment of community, the collection of water, and the development of complex tools.

The three sites were collected together by UNESCO for their importance in understanding Canaanite and Israelite history, but the nomination went a step further in saying the sites met four specific criteria: 1) similar human values shared regionally by way of alliance and trade and showcased by a similar architectural style that married Hellenistic, Assyrian, and Egyptian styles; 2) representing the Canaanite and Israelite civilizations of the late Bronze and Iron Ages; 3) continued reference in the biblical record; and 4) the influence these cities had on understanding history.

CHRONOLOGY

6000–5000 BCE: Megiddo home to earliest human settlement discovered so far.

3000–4000 BCE: Beer Sheva settlement begins.

3000 BCE: Hazor settlement begins at the acropolis.

19th century BCE: Hazor mentioned in Egyptian texts.

1750 BCE: Hazor becomes a site for waves of immigrants, and an expanded city with fewer fortifications takes shape on the lower hill. Moat, glacis, and ramparts added to strengthen the city's defenses.

1468 BCE: Megiddo referenced in Ancient Egyptian inscriptions as loser in spoils of war. At this time, Megiddo had been part of an alliance of cities that rebelled against Egypt. Egypt collected a bounty from the site, including thousands of horses, indicating the grandeur of the ancient city.

14th century BCE: Hazor is largest city in Canaan and at its largest extent.

1230 BCE: Hazor destroyed in a fire, likely by Israelite enemies.

12th century BCE: Beer Sheva settlement begins anew, after a 2,000-year break.

1150 BCE: Megiddo's Canaanite palace and much of the city destroyed.

10th–9th centuries BCE: King Solomon or other contemporary Israelite king builds a new city on top of the ruins of Megiddo.

9th century BCE: Beer Sheva extends fortifications to include a 4m wall, earning status as a center in the Kingdom of Judah.

9th century BCE: Hazor rebuilt and doubled in size, though only on the upper hill. City regularly used as a stop on trade routes.

8th century BCE: Megiddo reaches its greatest extent, and serves as the staging ground for battles between Judah and Israel.

8th century BCE: Beer Sheva reaches its greatest extent.

732 BCE: Megiddo and Hazor captured by Assyrian King Tiglath Pilesar III who destroys all the cities of the Galilee.

701 BCE: Beer Sheva destroyed by King Sennacherib in Assyria's assault.

5th century BCE: Beer Sheva incorporates a fortress built by Persians, but rest of site left mostly in ruins.

2nd century BCE: Megiddo hill abandoned for nearby village.

1st century BCE: King Herod builds a fortress at Beer Sheva.

2nd century CE: The last structure is built at Tel Beer Sheva – a diamond-shaped fortress. City is finally abandoned and a new city is constructed nearby, at the site of modern-day Beersheva.

2005: The three sites are designated by UNESCO as World Heritage Sites.

WEBSITE w whc.unesco.org/en/list/1108; w parks.org.il/en/reserve-park/tel-hazor-national-park/; w parks.org.il/en/reserve-park/tel-megiddo-armageddon-national-park/; w parks.org.il/en/reserve-park/tel-beer-sheva-national-park/.

WHERE TO NEXT?

THEMATIC *Noteworthy* UNESCO; National Parks. *Religion* Judaism; Old Testament; Biblical Battlefields. *Archaeology* Tels; Prehistory; Bronze Age; Canaanite; Iron Age; Active Excavations.

COMPLEMENTARY Other famous tels: **Jericho (#26)**, **Tel Dan (#63)**, *Tel Ashkelon*, and Tel Gezer Archaeological Project (B2). Other important ancient biblical cities: **Old City Jerusalem (#1)**, **Jericho (#26)**, **Tomb of the Patriarchs and Old Town of Hebron (#46)**, *City of David*, and Tel Lachish (B2).

NEARBY Megiddo is nearest to **Nazareth (#29)** (25km/30 minutes). Tel Hazor is near Rosh Pina (H2) (Anchor) and **Tsfat/Safed (#58)** (20km/25 minutes). Tel Beer Sheva is near Beer Sheva (J1) (8km/15m), unsurprisingly.

#39 Beit She'an

BROCHURE

RATINGS		
BUCKET! Score		7/10
Ruin		4/5
Entertainment		3/5
Information		4/5
Popularity		4/5

MACRO-REGION
F: Mount Carmel & Jezreel Valley

MICRO-REGION
F2

PRIMARY THEME/CATEGORY Archaeology – City Conglomerates – Cities of the Decapolis.

TOP Roman ruins in Israel (sorry, **Caesarea (#25)**).

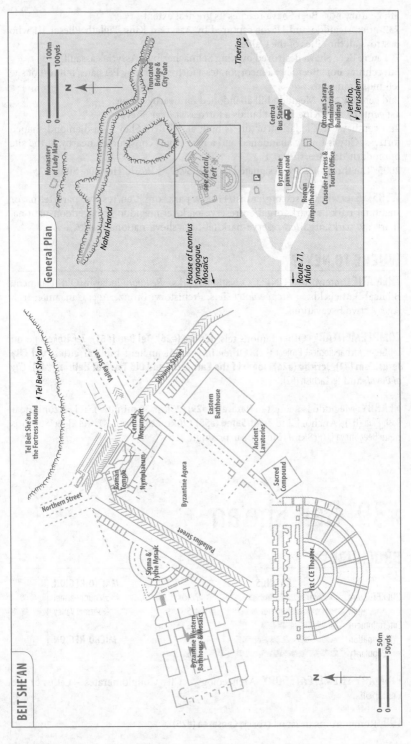

BEIT SHE'AN

Tel Beit She'an, the Fortress Mound

Tel Beit She'an

Valley Street

Sylvanus Street

Northern Street

Roman Temple

Central Monument

Nymphaeum

Eastern Bathhouse

Byzantine Agora

Ancient Lavatories

Palladius Street

Sacred Compound

Sigma & Tyche Mosaic

Byzantine Western Bathhouse & Mosaic

1st C CE Theater

N

0   50m
0   50yds

General Plan

Monastery of Lady Mary

Nahal Harod

Truncated Bridge & City Gate

N

0   100m
0   100yds

House of Leontius Synagogue, Mosaics

see detail, left

P

Byzantine paved road

Roman Amphitheater

Crusader Fortress & Tourist Office

Central Bus Station

Ottoman Saraya (Administrative Building)

Tiberias

Jericho, Jerusalem

Route 71, Afula

COMMENDATIONS Israel National Park.

HOLY LAND RELEVANCE Beit She'an was one of the ten Cities of the Decapolis (W3) in Roman times. Practically everyone in Holy Land history has lived here at some point: there are visible remnants from Chalcolithic peoples, Egyptians, Canaanites, Assyrians, Romans, Greeks, Byzantines, Arabs, Crusaders, Mamluks, and Ottomans. In the Bible, Book of Samuel 1, the Philistines attached Saul's body to the walls of Beit She'an.

ELECT ME! A partially reconstructed city that has existed for millennia, but really came to its own during the Roman era and whose most impressive ruins rival many of the better-known sites in the region (**Caesarea (#25)**, **Umm Qais (#45)**, **Ancient Amman (#37)**). It also contains a tel with successive layers of civilization (much like the **Biblical Tels (#38)**) on the strategically located hill above the Roman town, allowing for excellent views.

WORTH THE DETOUR? It's a phenomenal site with extremely impressive ruins, interesting history, some reconstructions that make the old town easier to visualize, great vistas, an intriguing layout, and a palatable history due to the preponderance of sites belonging to Roman times. If you're going to the Galilee, this is worth a visit – we'd even recommend skipping **Caesarea (#25)** if it means you can squeeze this in.

EXPERIENCES

CAN'T MISS The best view of the ruins are from the summit of the tel.

SITES **Tel Beit She'an**, the great hill at the back of the site, with more than 20 layers of history starting with the Neolithic period and continuing to modernity; 7,000-seat **Roman theater**, 1st century CE, three tiers (only one survives); **reconstructed colonnade**, 150m long, 4th-century CE renovations were the latest; **public latrine** with 57 toilet seats; **mosaic floor** in the Western Bathhouse; and **Tyche mosaic** in the Sigma.

SECRET There are a number of sites outside the main site which might be worth a visit: the Monastery of the Lady Mary (reserve in advance), a Crusader fort, a triple-vaulted bridge called "the truncated bridge," and a 6,000-seat Roman hippodrome.

SPECIAL EVENTS She'an Nights is a sound and light show that projects history right onto those old Roman streets.

ITINERATOR!

DAYS/HOURS Summer 08.00–17.00, winter 08.00–16.00, Friday closes 1 hour earlier, holiday eves closes at 13.00. Entrance closes 1 hour prior. Closed on holidays.

BEST TIME Midweek it will likely be empty. Summers will make the hike to the tel a bit more difficult.

TIME COMMITMENT Two hours if you stick with the bottom layers/Roman ruins. If you hike to the top of the hill, add another 30–45 minutes to hike and explore. Visiting any of the exterior sites will add 15–30 minutes each. Speed rules apply.

BASE You'll want to road trip through this section, possibly tying in other regional sites (see *Road Trip F2*). **Nazareth (#29)** (37km/40m) is a good spot to lay down.

BEST STRATEGY In an ideal world, you'd have time to visit all of the Galilee and Golan, but given that most travelers don't have four or five days exclusively set aside for Israel's north, we recommend adding this site to any trip of two or more days. Start at **Nazareth (#29)**, circle the **Sea of Galilee (#7)**, and then head south the next day. Beit She'an is the most important site of the lower Galilee/Gilboa region.

WALKS AND DRIVES F2, U2, W3, W4.

ITINERARIES High BUCKET! Scores: 7+; Off-the-Beaten-Path Israel and Palestine; National Parks/Reserves; Cinematic.

ARRIVAL PREP

PREBOOK Not necessary.

REALITY CHECK Underrated. No access to the tel other than on foot.

ACCESS The park is in the town of Beit She'an, with signs directing to the park from the entrance of the town.

ADMISSION 28 ILS adults, 14 ILS children, free with National Park Pass.

RECOMMENDED GUIDE The entrance map/brochure has enough detail to suffice.

VISITOR CENTER Yes, right outside the Roman ruins. Gift shop, brochure, limited dining.

EAT There are snacks and water at the visitor center. For good food, drive north a bit to **Nazareth (#29)**.

SLEEP Near the park, HI Beit She'an gets many mentions.

BUCKET!PEDIA

AKA Scythopolis (or Nysa-Scythopolis) and Beisan (Arab rule).   *Size* Current city: 7km²; park: 370 acres/1.5km².   *Population* Peak 30,000–40,000 inhabitants in the 5th century CE.   *Historical era* Prehistoric: *Neolithic* to *Islamic: Ottoman*, but principally *Roman/Byzantine*.   *Year founded/constructed* Prehistoric founding, but became one of the Cities of the Decapolis in 63 BCE.

CONTEXT As can be seen with the Biblical Tels, Jericho, and similar sites, Beit She'an contains successive styles, parked one on top of another. The most visible culture is Roman, located on the lower/flatter side of the hill, though Byzantine enhancements only enriched the space.

Today, the archaeological remains of lower Beit She'an are a testament to the grandeur of this city for over 700 years. Beginning with Roman occupation, the base of the site was transformed into a glorious city replete with columns, mosaics, the familiar cardo and decumanus streets, an amphitheater, and hippodrome. Byzantine influencers added public spaces (agora), bathhouses, fountains (nymphaeums), and churches.

The hill at the back of the lower city, or Upper Beit She'an, was inhabited for several millennia. The Romans built a temple to Zeus on the hill, while the Byzantines built a church. By then, this artificial hill would have already reached the height it is today.

Ultimately, the site succumbed to Mother Nature. The earthquake of January 18, 749 (or 746: dating is unclear) was nearly total. According to the Modified Mercalli Intensity (MMI) scale, the earthquake had a destructive force of 11 on a 12 scale, meaning few if any structures were left standing. Though impossible now to measure, the magnitude was likely around 7.0, which was enough to devastate many of the Decapolis cities and kill thousands as far away as Jerusalem. Beit She'an never recovered its former glory. Lucky for the visitor, it's been nearly returned to that former glory.

CHRONOLOGY

5th millennium BCE: Likely first settlement at Beit She'an, on present-day tel.

16th–12th centuries BCE: Regional administrative capital for Egyptian rule.

1150 BCE: Beit She'an destroyed by fire (?); Egyptians leave site.

1100 BCE: Canaanite city constructed.

1000 BCE: Beit She'an incorporated into Israelite Kingdom. Biblical text indicates that King Saul dies in battle at Beit She'an against the Philistines, who hang his body on the walls.

732 BCE: City falls to Assyrians, destroyed by fire.

3rd century BCE: Greeks name new city on the site Scythopolis, possibly after the Scythian people who settled there from Ukraine and South Russia.

2nd century BCE: Hasmonean Jewish Kings take over and the region becomes Jewish.

63 BCE: Roman rule begins and the city is named one of the Cities of the Decapolis.

66 CE: Jewish residents are killed and banished following the Bar Kokhba Revolt.

330–634: Byzantine period. The city reaches its zenith at nearly 40,000 inhabitants, mostly Christian (today's city has 20,000). Several of the park's sites date to this period.

634: Second caliph of the Rashidun Caliphate defeats Byzantines and takes over city, renaming it Beisan.

749: Devastating earthquake leaves site in ruins.

1099: Becomes part of the Crusader's Latin Kingdom of Jerusalem; fortress built.

WEBSITE w parks.org.il/en/reserve-park/bet-shean-national-park/.

WHERE TO NEXT?

THEMATIC *Noteworthy* National Parks. *Archaeology* Prehistory; Bronze Age; Byzantine; Crusader; Cities of the Decapolis; Mosaics; Impressive Structural Remains. *Structure* Historic Monuments. *Nature* Earthquakes.

COMPLEMENTARY Competing Roman ruins: **Caesarea (#25)**, **Capernaum (#33)**, **Ancient Amman (#37)**, **Tsipori (#56)**, *Bar'am*, and *Korazim*. Other Cities of the Decapolis: **Jerash (#14)**, **Ancient Amman (#37)**, **Umm Qais (#45)**, *Pella*, and Abila (S1). For the best sites in the Gilboa/Lower Galilee region, see *Road Trip F2*.

NEARBY *Gan HaShlosha* (6km/8 minutes), **Beit Alpha (#64)** (8km/11 minutes), **Belvoir (#93)** (20km/22 minutes), **Nazareth (#29)** (37km/38 minutes), and *Tiberias* (40km/ 42 minutes).

#40 Bethlehem

BROCHURE

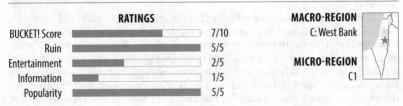

RATINGS		MACRO-REGION
BUCKET! Score	7/10	C: West Bank
Ruin	5/5	
Entertainment	2/5	**MICRO-REGION**
Information	1/5	C1
Popularity	5/5	

PRIMARY THEME/CATEGORY Religion – Holy Books – New Testament.

TOP Christian site in Palestine.

COMMENDATIONS "Church of the Nativity and the Pilgrimage Route in Bethlehem" is a UNESCO World Heritage Site for Palestine, added 2012.

HOLY LAND RELEVANCE Jesus Christ, God's only son according to the Christian faith and one of Islam's prophets, was born to Jewish parents, Mary and Joseph, in Bethlehem.

ELECT ME! Site of David's crowning as King of Israel. Birthplace of Jesus. Famous for the **Church of the Nativity (#18)**. Chief tourist engine for the Palestinian Authority.

WORTH THE DETOUR? Unless you are religious/spiritual, you may find Bethlehem a bit disappointing. The grotto is little more than a kneeling nook for a quick prayer where Jesus was born. If this is your thing, by all means – make the trek. As far as the rest of Bethlehem goes, there are things to see and do, but the **Church of the Nativity (#18)** and the *Separation Wall* are really the only true highlights.

EXPERIENCES

CAN'T MISS Church of the Nativity (#18), with the basement cave grotto where Jesus was born.

PILGRIMAGE ROUTE Manger Square is the main square of town, upon which the **Church of the Nativity (#18)** sits; Star Street is where Joseph and Mary historically walked at Christmas; and Damascus Gate is the historical gate of the town.

OTHER SITES (explanations in *City Walk C1*: Milk Grotto; Shepherds' Fields; Rachel's Tomb; Solomon's Pools; Aida Refugee Camp (C1); Church of St. Catherine; and *Separation Wall*, the literally and figuratively divisive barrier that keeps Palestinians and Israelis separated, and is covered with graffiti, some of which is from famed artist Banksy.

SECRET There are a number of Banksy artworks throughout town. See *City Walk C1* for a walking guide.

SPECIAL EVENTS Christmas in Bethlehem is of course a special time. The **Church of the Nativity (#18)** hosts a midnight mass. Manger Square has a tree and decorations, though don't expect much by way of holiday shopping. This is still a Muslim town in a hot country, which you will notice when it's 24°C/70°F degrees outside and the call to prayer rings out from the nearby mosque every couple of hours!

MAP See C1.

ITINERATOR!

DAYS/HOURS This is a city; most of its sites don't close or follow business hours.

BEST TIME Christmastime is obviously the most seasonal time to visit. If you are planning on coming during Christmas, expect to wait hours in line to see the grotto in the **Church of the Nativity (#18)**.

TIME COMMITMENT A breeze through the center of town is easily doable in an hour or two, assuming the line at the **Church of the Nativity (#18)** isn't too great. You can take longer walks, have a bite in a restaurant, and explore some of the suburbs over the course of a half- or full-day walking tour. Speed rules apply while walking; less for churches, where queues can delay you.

BASE Anchor from Jerusalem (10km/30 minutes) or Tel Aviv (75km/1¼ hours) for day trips.

BEST STRATEGY If you're planning a bigger trip to Palestine, start here and do our full tour. If you have limited time, or want a getaway from Jerusalem for a morning or afternoon, plan to at least visit the **Church of the Nativity (#18)**.

WALKS AND DRIVES C1, C2, W5.

ITINERARIES Most Popular; Noteworthy; Religion; UNESCO; Community; Memorial; Pilgrimage.

ARRIVAL PREP

REALITY CHECK Popular tour-bus stop. Periodically closed due to violent outbreaks. Passport required.

ACCESS You absolutely must carry a passport. If you are Israeli, it is forbidden to enter the Territories without a permit (and vice versa). Foreigners are allowed free access (you may be asked to send your belongings through a scanner), but you are crossing what is effectively an international border, so you need proper identification.

The simplest (though not necessarily the safest) entrance is to pass through the Rachel's Tomb Checkpoint, accessed by driving south on Route 60, which passes along the western side of **Old City Jerusalem (#1)**. Occasionally, there are clashes right near the Rachel's Tomb entrance. If so (but Bethlehem itself is deemed safe to travel), there are a few alternative routes: Walala Checkpoint towards Beit Jala; Nu'Man/Mazmoria Checkpoint from 398 through Beit Sahour and towards Bethlehem from the east; or Tunnels Checkpoint through Beit Jala and into Bethlehem.

You can take an Arab bus from the Old City's Damascus Gate, or an Egged bus from Jerusalem's Central Bus Station. If you are driving, street parking is available, but can be confusing as the machines are in Arabic. You may wish to park in a parking facility.

ADMISSION This is a city, so there is no charge to enter. The majority of the sites are religious in nature and do not have a fee, but you may be asked to provide a monetary donation.

RECOMMENDED GUIDE If walking/hiking is for you, check out the book *Walking Palestine: 25 Journeys into the West Bank*, with four walks around Bethlehem. Few of the sites come with explanations, so you'll likely also want a briefer. Use our guide or join an official tour (**w** visitpalestine.ps/tours-programs/).

VISITOR CENTER There is a gift shop in Manger Square. Visit Palestine, the tourism information center online, has a good Bethlehem brochure at **w** visitpalestine.ps/bethlehem-intro/.

EAT Hummus meals at Afteem are popular, as is Fawda Restaurant (reservation only) at the Hosh al-Syrian Guesthouse, hookah at Rewined, and café fare at The Singer Café.

SLEEP There are a few hotel options in Bethlehem, which are much cheaper than the equivalent in Jerusalem. Hosh al-Syrian and the **Banksy's Walled-Off Hotel** are the best bets.

BUCKET!PEDIA

AKA Beit Lahm ("House of Meat" in Arabic); Beit Lehem ("House of Bread" in Hebrew/Aramaic); House/Temple of Lehem/Lakhmu (a Canaanite god). *Size* 10km². *Population* 30,000. *Historical era* Roman/Byzantine. *Year founded* 1400 BCE.

CONTEXT First mentioned in the Egyptian Amarna Letters from 1350 BCE, Bethlehem began as a waypoint on the trip from Syria to Egypt for many travelers. Rachel, wife of Jacob and daughter-in-law of Abraham, died in childbirth on this same route to Hebron, where her gravesite is now located. According to the Books of Matthew and Luke, Mary and Joseph traveled to Bethlehem where Mary gave birth in a small cave, which has since been venerated by generations of pilgrims and religious authorities. New Christian convert and Roman Emperor Constantine and his mother, Empress Helena, commissioned the building of the Church of the Holy Sepulchre in Jerusalem and the Church of the Nativity in Bethlehem around 326 CE. Despite having suffered damage from a Samaritan revolt in 529 CE, a new church in its present form began to take shape thanks to Emperor Justinian shortly thereafter.

After a series of more than a dozen different rulers over the next 1,400 years, it wasn't until the 1990s when tourism really started to boom in Bethlehem, greatly increasing the socioeconomic status of its town members who benefited from tourism: hotels, restaurants, and shops grew as numbers increased. Two to three million visitors were expected by 2000, but unfortunately Bethlehem became a staging ground for the Palestinian uprising called the Second Intifada which lasted from 2000 to 2005. Palestinian militants holed themselves up in the Church of the Nativity, holding monks hostage, and tourism sank. Some 20 years later than predicted, the town is finally starting to see travelers in excess of 1 million. That said, the rescission of Israeli control in 1995 and the construction of the Separation Wall in 2005 has kept out many Israeli and Arab tourists. The UNESCO declaration of the Church of the Nativity in 2012 as a World Heritage Site in Danger also brought attention to the dilapidated and decaying state of that historic building, which has since been restored and removed from the "Endangered" list. That said, the wall is a continuous reminder of the violence that can strike at any time and the difficulties that will continue to exist for a city and its people whose access are cut off by walls.

CHRONOLOGY

4 BCE: Approximate date of Jesus' birth in Bethlehem.

136 CE: Hadrian builds a shrine to Adonis atop the site of the venerated Christian grotto.

339: Grotto-cave of Jesus' birth made the center of a new church, commissioned by Emperor Constantine.

384: St. Jerome arrives from Rome to review all versions of the Bible in order to create the Vulgate, a new translation based on Greek and Hebrew.

386: St. Paula founds a monastic community, which exists to the present day (after some breaks throughout history).

527: Bethlehem experiences major prosperity at time of Emperor Justinian.

637: Mosque of Omar built in honor of the Second Caliph of Islam who promised Christian access and security of the Church of the Nativity.

1100: Baldwin I, the first Crusader King of Jerusalem, is crowned in Bethlehem.

1263: Walls of the city are demolished with arrival of Mamluks, who took the town following the Ayyubid–Crusader compromise. Christians banished.

1831: Palestine returns to Egyptian rule.

1834: Muslim quarter of Bethlehem destroyed by Egypt in retaliation for the murder of an Egyptian loyalist.

1841: Ottoman rule resumes. Population dives as many emigrate due to poor economic conditions.

1857: Status Quo agreement grants rights to holy sites in Bethlehem to all religious communities.

1947: In the United Nations accord on Palestine, Bethlehem is considered part of Jerusalem and is to be administered by the UN, rather than Palestinian authorities.

1948: Jordan captures the town and refugee camps are established, including Dheisheh and 'Aida.

1967: Israel takes control of city after Six-Day War.

1995: Israel withdraws from Bethlehem following the Oslo II agreement.

2000: Tourism boom. Monthly average of 90,000 visitors.

2002: Church of the Nativity is used as the bunker for Palestinian militants fighting against Israel during the Second Intifada. The building suffers a fair amount of damage. Bethlehem tourism takes a dramatic plunge.

2002–2005: Construction of the Separation Wall during the Second Intifada, ostensibly to protect Israelis from suicide bombers.

2019: Tourism numbers soar, with more than 1 million pilgrims visiting during the Christmas holiday season.

WEBSITE There is good official historical and religious information at **w** bethlehem-city.org/en and **w** visitpalestine.ps.

THEMATIC *Noteworthy* UNESCO. *Religion* Christianity; Jesus' Early Life; New Testament; Collections of Churches; Mosques; Pilgrimage; Ceremonies and Events. *Archaeology* Roman. *Structure* Historic Monuments. *Scenic* Most Photographed. *Society* Streets, Squares and Ports; Large Towns. *People* Arab.

COMPLEMENTARY Most important sites in Jesus' life: **Old City Jerusalem (#1)**, **Sea of Galilee (#7)**, **Nazareth (#29)**, and **Mount of Olives (#34)**. Other UNESCO sites in Palestine: **Tomb of the Patriarchs and Old Town of Hebron (#46)** and *Battir Hills*. Most populous Palestinian towns: Gaza City, **Old Town of Hebron (#46)**, and **Nablus (#61)**.

NEARBY **Herodion (#90)** (5km/10 minutes), **Old City Jerusalem (#1)** (10km/30 minutes, depending on traffic and border crossings), *Mar Saba* (12km/25 minutes), and **Old Town of Hebron (#46)** (21km/30 minutes).

#41 Bethany-Beyond-the-Jordan

BROCHURE

RATINGS		MACRO-REGION
BUCKET! Score	5/10	P: Dead Sea (Jordan)
Ruin	1/5	
Entertainment	1/5	**MICRO-REGION**
Information	2/5	P2
Popularity	2/5	

PRIMARY THEME/CATEGORY Religion – Religious Figures – Jesus: Ministries.

TOP Most likely location of Jesus' baptism.

COMMENDATIONS UNESCO World Heritage Site, 2015.

HOLY LAND RELEVANCE Christianity essentially developed on the Jordan River. Today, you will mostly have to use your imagination, as the ruins are scant. But you will pass on the tour the (perhaps arbitrary) spots where Elijah ascended to Heaven, John the Baptist preached, the five apostles initially met, and where Jesus was first baptized in the waters of the Jordan. The name "Bethabara" appears on the **Madaba Map (#19)**.

ELECT ME! Here is the site where history (and Jordan) tells us that Jesus was baptized by John the Baptist. It's a strangely guarded site which requires a guide, with little more than some stone ruins in swampy land to see, but lots to ponder. The site was filled with landmines until the 1994 peace treaty between Jordan and Israel, when numerous sites of importance were discovered, including baptism pools, five churches from different periods, a monastery, and monastic caves. One of the most interesting bits is the sliver of water that separates Jordan from Israel/Palestine, with armed guards on both sides to ensure no unwelcome visitors. Today, many visit here (more on the Israeli side) for their own baptismal ceremonies.

WORTH THE DETOUR? If you're doing the important-Christian-sites loop, then it's a must. If you're just interested in seeing the spot, you should know that the waters of the Jordan don't penetrate the region as they once did (they are diverted heavily for agricultural use), and the ruined buildings sit amid stagnant water – it's not the prettiest of sites. You can't do a self-baptism either. Plus, you'll be walking around on a platform at the pace of your guide and fellow walkers. Keep all of that in mind.

EXPERIENCES

CAN'T MISS The Jordanian baptism site, which is the likelier of the candidates for the location of Jesus' baptism. Other locations are celebrated at Qasr al-Yahud (C3) and Yardenit.

SITES A few drawings indicate that **Elijah's Hill** (also known as Tel el-Kharrar, as well as Jabal Mar Elias) is the site where Elijah ascended to Heaven. At the **John the Baptist Spring**, it's believed the famed baptism likely took place. The **Churches of St. John the Baptist** are the remains of three sets of churches which historically marked the location of Jesus' baptism. Depending on the time of year, the water levels of the **Jordan River** vary.

ACTIVITIES For those looking for an immersion experience, see *Special Events* below. You can participate less formally on the Israeli side in two locations: Qasr al-Yahud (C3) at the same spot on the river and Yardenit in the Galilee.

SECRET You can visit the site remotely! Google Maps Street View will take you around the site.

SPECIAL EVENTS You can be formally baptized by the official Baptism Site Commission – you must give at least two days' notice (**w** baptismsite.com). In January, visit for Epiphany/Theophany.

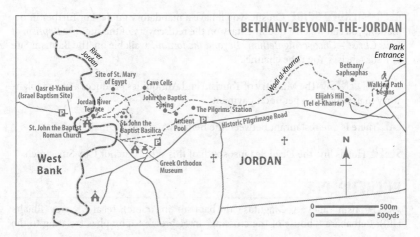

ITINERATOR!

DAYS/HOURS 08.00–18.00 daily. Site closes 1 hour earlier during Ramadan, and 2 hours earlier in winter.

BEST TIME There's about 2km of walking, half-shaded, so midday visits will be warm.

TIME COMMITMENT You'll be walking with a group, so the minimum time you should plan is 2 hours, though it might be 3 hours. Speed rules do not apply due to the mandatory tour.

BASE Anchor from Suweimeh (20km/20m) or Amman (55km/1 hour).

BEST STRATEGY There's a guided circuit, which you will be obliged to follow on bus and foot. Plan about 3 hours including waiting for the next shuttle, the tour, and getting in/out.

WALKS AND DRIVES P2, W5.

ITINERARIES Off-the-Beaten-Path Jordan; Noteworthy; Religion; UNESCO; Pilgrimage.

ARRIVAL PREP

PREBOOK Entrance: not necessary; private baptism: two days' notice via email or phone per website (see *Special Events* above).

REALITY CHECK Popular tour-bus stop. Don't try to be funny and cross the river. There are armed guards! And don't wander off from the group.

ACCESS Once you arrive, you'll join a queue waiting for a shuttle to fill. No private vehicles allowed. The more people that arrive, the less time you'll have to wait for the shuttle, so it actually helps to arrive on a busier day.

ADMISSION 12 JD, but if you book the Jordan Pass you can add Bethany for 8 JD. Free for children under 12. Shuttle bus and guide are included in the fee.

RECOMMENDED GUIDE On site, you'll have a mandatory guide. For further information, you can watch a documentary on the rediscovery of the site, *The Baptism of Jesus Christ – Uncovering Bethany Beyond the Jordan*, available on The Baptism Site of Jesus Christ's YouTube channel.

VISITOR CENTER The Ministry of Tourism and Antiquities produces a nice, explanatory map which you get upon payment.

EAT There is one restaurant between the Bethany site and the main highway.

SLEEP Hotels line the Dead Sea just south of this site at Anchor City Suweimeh.

BUCKET!PEDIA

AKA Baptism Valley; Al-Maghtas ("the baptism" in Arabic); Tel al-Kharrar (Elijah's Hill); Bethabara ("house of the crossing" in Hebrew); Saphsaphas (relating to the monastic caves on site). *Size* 3–5km². *Historical era* *Roman/Byzantine.* *Year constructed* Church of John the Baptist: c500 CE.

CONTEXT For religious pilgrims (or even lapsed Catholics and other Christians) this site offers a chance to visit another important location in the life of Jesus Christ – the place where John (the Baptist, or the Baptizer) baptized Jesus. This event is commemorated in eastern Christian traditions as Epiphany, on January 6 (Gregorian) or January 19 (Julian), depending on which calendar each Church uses.

Baptism perhaps began as a riff on the *mikveh*, a ritual cleansing in a pool in the Jewish tradition. John the Baptist practiced water cleansing and had baptized Jews in the Jordan River. According to the Gospel of Mark, John used baptism to forgive sin and prophesied that someone would follow him that would baptize with the Holy Spirit rather than with water. Enter Jesus, whom John baptizes in the Jordan River, after which the skies open and the Holy Spirit enters Jesus. From the beginning, baptism was a principal sacrament of Christians.

Scholarly tradition puts the site of the baptism on the far side of the Jordan River. But due to inconsistencies in the historical record, the name and location have been contested throughout history. The name "Bethany" refers to two places in the Bible: a town near Jerusalem from where Lazarus rose, and the site of the baptism. The baptism site – with only two mentions of its location in the Gospel of John – is referred to as "Bethany beyond the Jordan." The classical and modern interpretation of this statement indicates the historic town was located on the east side of the Jordan River. This fact has been disputed since at least the 3rd century and continues to draw consternation from Palestinian officials who claim there is no written evidence the site was in present-day Jordan. An early scholar, Origen, specifically noted there was no known "Bethany" east of the Jordan and instead opted to change the name to Bethabara, meaning "place of crossing." This same name, "Bethabara," appears on the **Madaba Map (#19)** from the 6th century, but confusingly on the west side of the river. Following the Muslim conquest in the 7th century, much of the Byzantine worship in the Holy Land ceased, and focus shifted to the western side of the river at Qasr al-Yahud (C3). Both Qasr al-Yahud and Bethany-Beyond-the-Jordan (called al-Maghtas by Arabs) were pilgrimage sites and staging grounds for war over the centuries. Not until Israel and Jordan signed their peace accord in 1994 did archaeological studies and tourism return. John Paul II formally commemorated al-Maghtas as the site recognized by the Holy See in a visit in 2000. Given the congregation of churches and recognition of al-Maghtas throughout history, it's likely that the correct spot is indeed east of the river.

CHRONOLOGY

500 CE: First (?) church is built near the venerated site of Jesus' baptism by John the Baptist, taking his name.

6th century: Marble steps are built, descending into a cruciform pool for visitor baptisms using the Jordan River water.

670: Arculfus of France writes of a vaulted church.

c670: Following the Muslim conquest of the region, reverence shifts to the western bank of the Jordan River (Qasr al-Yahud).

8th century: Epiphanius writes of a large church at the site, possibly the basilica that was built atop the foundation of the previous church(es).

1106: Abbot Daniel writes of an extant small chapel with an altar.

1967: Israel regains Qasr al-Yahud, but this and al-Maghtas remain militarized and the sites stay off-limits to tourism.

1981: To support baptismal activity at an alternative site, the Israeli government opens the Yardenit Baptism Site on the northern Jordan River in the Galilee.

1994: Israel and Jordan sign peace accord and clear both sides of the river of land mines, opening the sites up for future tourism ventures.

2000: Pope John Paul II visits al-Maghtas and recognizes the site as the location of Jesus' baptism.

2011: Qasr al-Yahud reopens.

2015: UNESCO declares al-Maghtas (and not Qasr al-Yahud) a World Heritage Site.

WEBSITE w baptismsite.com.

WHERE TO NEXT?

THEMATIC *Noteworthy* UNESCO; Unique. *Religion* Christianity; Kings, Prophets, and Saints; Jesus' Ministries and Miracles; New Testament; Collections of Churches; Pilgrimage; Ceremonies and Events. *Society* Borders.

COMPLEMENTARY Other Baptism locations: Qasr al-Yahud (C3) (Israel, east of Jericho) and Yardenit (beginning of the Jordan River as it leaves the Sea of Galilee). Other Christian sites of interest in Jordan: **Madaba (#19)**, **Mount Nebo (#24)**, **Umm ar-Rasas (#81)**, and *Mukawir*.

NEARBY **Dead Sea (#3)** (20km/20 minutes), **Mount Nebo (#24)** (36km/45 minutes), **Madaba (#19)** (45km/50 minutes), and **Modern Amman (#36)** and **Ancient Amman (#37)** (54km/1 hour).

#42 Via Dolorosa

BROCHURE

RATINGS		MACRO-REGION
BUCKET! Score	7/10	A: Jerusalem
Ruin	2/5	
Entertainment	2/5	**MICRO-REGIONS**
Information	1/5	A1, A2
Popularity	5/5	

PRIMARY THEME/CATEGORY Religion – The Sacred – Pilgrimage.

TOP Walking tour (procession, really), per Christian visitors.

HOLY LAND RELEVANCE As the final moments in Jesus' life, this is a major site (or series of sites) for Christians.

ELECT ME! Believed to mark the path that Jesus took on his final walk to death, after being tried and convicted, where he carries his cross, is crucified, and buried.

Long a path for pilgrims to follow in the same footsteps, the tradition is followed to this day, with markers denoting the "stations" for each of the 14 moments leading to Jesus' death.

WORTH THE DETOUR? For interested parties, Via Dolorosa should be included as the precursor to your visit to the **Church of the Holy Sepulchre (#9)**. If you're not familiar with the Stations of the Cross, it can be skipped or discovered casually. The stops are not well signposted and the stations are difficult to both find and interpret amid the throngs of Jerusalem visitors and residents who are not paying attention.

EXPERIENCES

CAN'T MISS The **Church of the Holy Sepulchre (#9)**. Otherwise, if you commit to the walk, may as well do the whole thing – it's only 600m long.

CURRENT STATIONS

1. *Jesus is condemned to die by Pontius Pilate* Location: inside the current madrasa/boys' school, Madrasa el-Omariyya, near the Lions' Gate on Lions' Gate Street.
2. *Jesus receives the cross* Location: this station is located across the street, at the Monastery of the Flagellation. Interesting fact: modern theologians believe that the sentencing by Pontius Pilate would likely have taken place in Herod's Palace, located in the southwest of the city. Regardless, commemoration continues to take place here.
3. *Jesus falls for the first time* Location: adjacent to the Polish Catholic Chapel (built by Armenians from Poland), at the corner of the Via Dolorosa and Tariq al-Wad

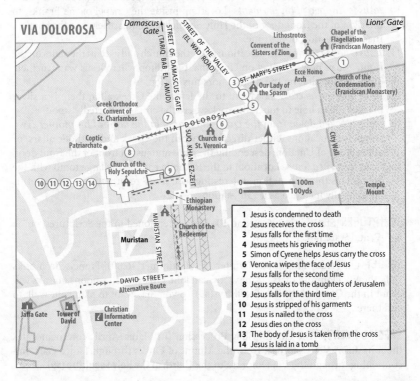

street. Interesting fact: the three falls are actually not recorded in any of the four Gospels.

4. *Jesus meets the Virgin Mary, his mother* Location: Armenian Catholic Patriarchate/Church of Our Lady of the Spasm, built in 1881, also on Tariq al-Wad. Interesting fact: also not referenced in any of the Gospels, but is part of popular tradition.

5. *Simon of Cyrene helps Jesus carry the cross* Location: Chapel of Simon of Cyrene, a Franciscan church built in 1895 on Tariq al-Wad and Tariq al-Saray.

6. *Veronica wipes Jesus' face* Location: "VI" is written on the door of the Church of the Holy Face and St. Veronica. Interesting fact: according to legend, the cloth on which Veronica wiped Jesus' face miraculously revealed the imprinted image of His face.

7. *Jesus falls for the second time* Location: Souq Khan es-Zeit and Via Dolorosa. Interesting fact #1: in the 13th century, the idea arose that this station represented the spot where Jesus' death announcement was posted. At the time of Jesus' death, this station would have marked the limits of the city walls, and thus this spot would be where outsiders would have read the announcement, placing Golgotha outside of the Old City walls, as Scripture indicates. Interesting fact #2: inside the chapel (if you can get in) is one of the original columns from the Byzantine Cardo (main street) of 6th-century Jerusalem.

8. *Jesus speaks to the daughters of Jerusalem* Location: Monastery of St. Caralambos on Aqabat al-Khanqah Street. Interesting fact: per tradition, Jesus stated, "Daughters of Jerusalem, weep not for me but for yourselves and your children."

9. *Jesus falls a third time* Location: go up the stairs and follow Aqabat Dair al-Sultan to the end. You're on the roof of the **Church of the Holy Sepulchre (#9)** at this point.

10. *Jesus is stripped of his garments* Location: inside the Chapel of the Franks, to the right of the front door of the Holy Sepulchre (staircase leads to the chapel). Inaccessible most of the time.

11. *Jesus is nailed to the cross* Location: enter the church and ascend the stairs on the right. You're now standing on Golgotha, the hilltop where Jesus was crucified. The Catholic altar on the right honors this station.

12. *Jesus dies on the cross* Location: to the left at the Greek altar, there is a silver marker with a hole to touch the rock where the cross purportedly stood.

13. *Jesus is taken down from the cross and placed in the arms of his mother* Two competing locations: either directly between the Greek and Catholic altars, or at the Stone of Unction, descending the steps and just in front of the front door.

14. *Jesus is laid in a tomb* Location: in the Rotunda room – the large tomb with the long line is the 14th station. Interesting fact: Jesus' resurrection (same spot) is occasionally included as a 15th station.

SCRIPTURES
Stations 1, 2, 5, 8, and 10–14 are mentioned in the Scriptures, but 3, 4, 6, 7, and 9 are not.

SECRET
On Friday afternoons (winter 15.00, summer 16.00), Franciscan monks walk the Via Dolorosa in its entirety. You can join. On other afternoons, monks will chant in the **Church of the Holy Sepulchre (#9)**, so you may want to plan your walk to end there.

SPECIAL EVENTS
The Good Friday Procession (in March/April) commemorates the long-form Via Dolorosa, from the Mount of Olives through Lions' Gate and continuing through the Via Dolorosa to the **Church of the Holy Sepulchre (#9)**.

ITINERATOR!

DAYS/HOURS Varies. The walk is outside, so does not have an operating schedule. The chapels along the route are not on regular schedules. The **Church of the Holy Sepulchre (#9)** is open most days 05.00–19.00.

BEST TIME Holy Week is the time when the street gets the most attention each year. But visiting any time of the year is recommended. The streets are today filled with vendors, so there is no good/bad time to visit. You may want to shop while you walk, in which case the middle of the day is fine. Most of the path is covered.

TIME COMMITMENT You can run through the Via in 20–30 minutes if you don't enter the chapels, which are not open regularly. If you'd like to gain access, you may have to wait until a larger group or tour guide contacts the chapel guardians to open the front doors. Separately, the **Church of the Holy Sepulchre (#9)** is a site that takes at least an hour, and often longer on first visit, if planning to stand in line to pray at the sites of the crucifixion and burial.

BASE Located in Anchor City Jerusalem.

BEST STRATEGY It's easy enough to add this short walk into a quick tour of Jerusalem. Ideally, you'll start at Station 1 upon leaving **Temple Mount (#12)** and end your walk, as prescribed, at the **Church of the Holy Sepulchre (#9)**.

WALKS AND DRIVES A1, A2.

ITINERARIES High BUCKET! Scores: 7+; Most Popular; Religion; Memorial.

ARRIVAL PREP

PREBOOK The (free) walk does not require reservation, but is not done the week after Easter or Christmas.

REALITY CHECK Popular tour-bus stop. Stops can be hard to find on your own.

ACCESS Having difficulty finding the stations? Try **w** biblewalks.com/ViaDolorosa for photos to orient you. No fee.

RECOMMENDED GUIDE A map is essential to spot the station markers, but there is little more than a Roman numeral to signify the location. A guide would provide more background on the city during Roman times, alternative versions and locations of the stations, and the difference between traditional and scriptural stations, but is not required.

VISITOR CENTER There is no visitor center or brochure. There is a new archaeological museum, the Terra Sancta Museum, located at Station 2, which helps with context (15 ILS).

EAT/SLEEP See **Old City Jerusalem (#1)**.

BUCKET!PEDIA

AKA Latin for "Way of Sorrows" or "Way of Suffering." *Length* 600m (2,000 feet). *Historical era* Roman/Byzantine: Judea. *Year founded* 33 CE, the year Jesus is believed to have died.

CONTEXT In Christianity, the last moments in Jesus' life are documented as a series of events, called stations. The Via Dolorosa marks nine of these stations, from the site of the former Antonia's Fortress (now an elementary school) to the Church of the Holy Sepulchre, where the final five stations took place. Roman in design, though it doesn't seem apparent now, the street was originally one of the main routes through the city – the *decumanus maximus* – which ran perpendicular to the north–south cardines in Aelia Capitolina (as Jerusalem was called during the Roman era).

The current path of the Via Dolorosa was only set in the 18th and 19th centuries, and has taken a number of circumnavigating routes around town (much like the walls of Jerusalem!) over the years. This has understandably not been without controversy. Scripture doesn't specifically define the site of Jesus' trial, which was once considered to be Antonia's Fortress and which still today marks the first station. Newer scholarship indicates the site was more likely Herod's Fortress, where Pontius Pilate normally resided when visiting from his base of Caesarea. That's now located at the Citadel/Tower of David Museum near Jaffa Gate, on the opposite side of the Old City. According to Jerome Murphy-O'Connor, this more likely route would have gone from the present-day Citadel, east down David Street, turning left at the end, and left again to the Holy Sepulchre. This would dramatically change the entire route of the Via Dolorosa, displacing all but the last five stations. Thus it's unlikely to change anytime soon. The route is mostly symbolic anyway.

The walk itself is not very well defined, so you need a map. The Via is actually a series of connected streets, mostly filled with vendors. Given the context, it's often startling to see station numbers in their current locations ignored and oddly unexploited.

CHRONOLOGY (courtesy Murphy-O'Connor)
5th–6th centuries CE: Byzantine-era pilgrims walk from Mount of Olives to Gethsemane through Lions' Gate to Golgotha. No further stops.
8th century: Gethsemane to the House of Caiaphas on Mount Zion, up to the Temple Mount, then over to the Church.
14th century: Franciscans create their own walk for pilgrims, starting at Mount Zion to the Sepulchre through Lions' Gate to Gethsemane and the Mount of Olives, then back to Mount Zion through the Pools of Siloam. This circular route impressed upon European pilgrims a route covering Jesus' final hours.
15th century: Stations of the Cross become popular throughout Europe as visual representation of the same tour for believers back home.
17th century: Fourteen stations becomes the standard in Europe, while Jerusalem residents count only eight (they would soon reconcile at 14).
18th century: Via Dolorosa route becomes fixed, though several stations weren't marked until as late as the 19th century.

WEBSITE Nothing specifically for Via Dolorosa, but the Custodia Terrae Sanctae has custodial rights to several of the sites. More information can be found at w custodia.org/en/sanctuaries/flagellation.

WHERE TO NEXT?

THEMATIC *Religion* Christianity; Jesus' Death and Resurrection; New Testament; Burial; Pilgrimage; Ceremonies and Events. *Society* Streets, Squares and Ports.

COMPLEMENTARY Other walks of Jesus' time: **Mount of Olives (#34)** and **Jesus Trail (#69)**. We recommend our *Church of the Holy Sepulchre Chronotour* (w buckettravelguides. com/sepulchre-chronotour) to accompany your visit.

NEARBY All **Old City Jerusalem (#1)** sites are within close walking distance.

#43 Aqaba

BROCHURE

RATINGS		
BUCKET! Score		4/10
Ruin		1/5
Entertainment		3/5
Information		1/5
Popularity		4/5

MACRO-REGION
M: South Jordan

MICRO-REGION
M1

PRIMARY THEME/CATEGORY Active – Water Sports – Diving.

TOP Dive spot in the Taba/Eilat/Aqaba region.

HOLY LAND RELEVANCE The country of Jordan is a relatively new creation (20th century). The city of Aqaba (formerly Ayla) is much older, with influences from many of the great empires of the region, including the Edomites, Nabataeans, Byzantines, Mamluks, and Ottomans.

ELECT ME! Aqaba is the easiest gateway to dive the **Red Sea/Gulf of Aqaba (#10)**. It's also an easy base for quick visits to **Petra (#2)** and/or **Wadi Rum (#4)**. The border here is much easier to navigate than Allenby Bridge.

WORTH THE DETOUR? Not really. The city itself is not the greatest tourist attraction and the downtown leaves much to be desired. You don't need to lose a day here, unless you're a diver. Jordan is the best option of the three cities on the Gulf of Aqaba for scuba. That said, the coast of Egypt has the best diving in the region (flight required). For everyone else, just cross the border here and head straight for your final destination. Better to spend your time under the stars in **Wadi Rum (#4)** or making the most of your time at **Petra (#2)**.

EXPERIENCES

CAN'T MISS Dive sites, mostly covered in **Red Sea/Gulf of Aqaba (#10)**.

HISTORICAL SITES **Aqaba Church** was constructed in the 3rd century, and is considered to be the oldest known purpose-built church. The **Medieval Ayla excavation area** is uncovering a Muslim town from 650–1100 CE. **Aqaba Castle** was built by Crusaders, and repurposed by the Mamluks.

ACTIVITIES **Aqaba Archaeological Museum** displays artifacts and information about the Ayla dig, next to the site. **Jordanian Cuisine (#44)** is rich in seafood, hummus, and kebabs. Go2Jordan has a good map and summary of each of the **dive sites** to the south of Jordan (w your-guide-to-aqaba-jordan.com/aqaba-dive-sites.html). Most sites are located in the Aqaba Marine Park, to the south of city center, running to the border with Saudi Arabia. Use a diving boat for **snorkeling**, or hire equipment from your hotel or a private enterprise along the coast. Go birding at the **Aqaba Bird Observatory**. For something more organized, try w naturetrek.co.uk for 10-day Jordan itineraries with an avian focus. It is easy to rent a **glass-bottom boat** from the town's main promenade, or ask your hotel. Swim at the South Beach (M2), which has free entrance and sandy beaches. The Marine Science Station Aquarium (M2) is a drier way to see the sea, south of town.

SECRET Shhh… check out *City Walk M1* and *Road Trip M2* for a quick overview and itineraries.

SPECIAL EVENTS Souk by the Sea every Friday.

MAP See M1.

ITINERATOR!

DAYS/HOURS Half- and all-day boat rides for snorkeling and diving expeditions leave around 08.00. City doesn't close.

BEST TIME Not summer. Average high for June to August is 39°C/103°F.

TIME COMMITMENT You needn't spend any time in Aqaba at all, and just head straight for **Wadi Rum (#4)** or **Petra (#2)**. But if you are here to dive then you'll need at least one day, planned in advance. If you find yourself here anyway, follow our day trip guidelines, spend one night, and get on the road early the next morning. Speed rules apply, except for diving trips.

BASE We don't recommend Aqaba as a staging ground. Rather, plan to road-trip through Jordan.

BEST STRATEGY Most of the full- and half-day diving trips leave in the morning, around 08.00, so you'll want to book at least a day in advance. Or email/call to coordinate ahead of time.

WALKS AND DRIVES M1, M2, V2, W2, W4.

ITINERARIES Active; Under the Sun; All Ages.

ARRIVAL PREP

PREBOOK Diving expeditions and boat rides to Pharaoh's Island (Egypt) should be booked in advance.

REALITY CHECK Beaches are crowded, dirty, and not well regulated. The corals are mostly bleached in the public areas due to human trampling and trashing. Even the private beaches are looking the worse for wear. The reefs are suffering from human pollution, particularly in the public beach area. Diving is mostly unregulated, though you are required to go with a dive shop and be "certified." Female travelers may feel uncomfortable at Aqaba's public beaches. While Jordanians are used to foreigners, many Arab women here are clad head to toe, even in the water.

BRING Consider your own snorkeling equipment, though it can be rented. Diving equipment will be provided.

ACCESS Easy enough from the border. Follow the signs from the airport (if self-driving), making a series of right turns until you're on Al-Hussain Bin Ali Street which leads right downtown.

ADMISSION If you've bought a Jordan Pass (discount on visa, **Petra (#2)**, and most tourist sites), Aqaba Museum and Aqaba Castle are included.

BUDGET Public beaches: free; private club/beach: 10 JD, full day, including towels; mid-range restaurant: 12 JD ($15); upper-end hotel during busy season: $200/night (average); upper-end hotel during low (summer) season: $100/night; snorkeling equipment for the day: 5 JD; half-day diving: 60 JD; full-day diving: 90 JD; beginner open-water (2–5 days) course: 290–420 JD.

RECOMMENDED GUIDE For kids, consider a colorful waterproof guide to the coral reefs for a fun underwater spotting game.

VISITOR CENTER Aqaba Tourist Information Center right off Ayla Circle.

EAT There's plenty of range. Falafel/shawarma places line the promenade. Mid-range places specialize in fish, but you can also find international cuisine here.

SLEEP Accommodation is inexpensive, so we recommend you go for a high-end hotel.

BUCKET!PEDIA

AKA Elath by the Edomites and Judeans, Aelana or Aela by the Romans, and Ayla by the Arabs until about the 13th century CE. *Size* 375km². *Population* 150,000. *Historical era* Prehistoric: *Chalcolithic* to Modern: *Contemporary*. *Year founded* 3500 BCE.

CONTEXT The city of Aqaba began its long 5,500 years of existence as a Chalcolithic settlement and has been occupied almost continuously since. In an interesting twist of fate, the city was historically called Elath (or Eilat), then Aelana, and Ayla from the same derivation, and eventually 'Aqabat Ayla meaning the "pass of Ayla." This was shortened to Aqaba in the Middle Ages. In 1947, when Israel gained access to the Red Sea, it decided to build a city on the gulf using the historic name Eilat. Aqaba has of course retained its newer name, despite all along being the original Eilat (Ayla).

While the history is interesting, the ruins are nothing much to look at and are not set up for tourists, save for the small downtown Ayla site. There's great opportunity here, but it seems the town would rather market the city to beachgoers, building resorts and artificial marinas on the west side of town rather than excavating any more land. The town is pleasant enough for a stroll, but there is little to keep one busy for much longer than a day. The site serves as a good jumping-off point for trips to diving wrecks.

CHRONOLOGY

3500 BCE: Chalcolithic settlement, copper mining, located at Tel Hujayrat al-Ghuzlan and Tel al-Magass.

13th century BCE: Edomites, a biblical kingdom that ruled much of the area between the Dead Sea and the Red Sea until about the 2nd century BCE, control Elath.

8th century BCE: City develops on the gulf. Ruins at Tel el-Kheleifeh.

3rd century BCE: Nabataeans (builders of Petra and Incense Route) use Elath as part of their trade route.

2nd century CE: Roman Emperor Trajan sets Aela/Aelana as the end of the Via Nova Traiana stretching to Bosra.

293–303: Aqaba church built.

630: Muslims conquer Aela first, call it Ayla, and use it as a staging ground for further conquests. Some building materials contain Christian iconography, showing Muslims repurposed some of the earlier Byzantine buildings.

1068: Earthquake splits the city of Ayla literally in two.

1116: Crusaders build their castle/fort.

1517: Mamluks renovate castle.

1917: T.E. Lawrence captures the city from the Ottomans in World War I.

1925: Aqaba becomes part of Transjordan.

1975: Sharif Hussein Bin Ali Mosque built.

WEBSITE w aqaba.jo.

WHERE TO NEXT?

THEMATIC *Religion* Oldest/Ancient Churches. *Archaeology* Prehistory; Bronze Age; Shipwrecks. *Nature* Sea Creatures, Reefs and Aquaria; Birding. *Society* Borders; Other Main Cities; Large Towns. *People* Secular Life; Arab. *Active* Swimming; Diving; Snorkeling. *Leisure* Public/Popular Beaches. *Accommodation* Vacation Resorts and Hotels.

COMPLEMENTARY Better diving: **Ras Mohammad (#53)**. Cheaper resort: Taba (T1). More interesting sleep options: **Wadi Rum (#4)** for camping/glamping. Better archaeology: **Petra (#2)**.

NEARBY **Eilat (#78)** (15km/1½ hours, depending on crossing times), **Wadi Rum (#4)** (70km/1 hour), and **Petra (#2)** (126km/1¾ hours).

#44 Jordanian Cuisine

BROCHURE

RATINGS		MACRO-REGION
BUCKET! Score	7/10	V: Cross-Jordan
Ruin	n/a	
Entertainment	3/5	
Information	3/5	
Popularity	5/5	

PRIMARY THEME/CATEGORY Food and Drink – Food – Cuisine.

TOP Honors for food choices in the Holy Land.

HOLY LAND RELEVANCE There's nothing particularly spiritual about the food, but you might have a revelatory moment while eating it!

ELECT ME! Like European cuisine or Asian cuisine, each Arab country has its local nuances and preferred dishes. Jordanian cuisine closely resembles the Levantine cuisine of Lebanon, Syria, and Palestine, but it also takes cues from the Circassian, Iraqi, and Armenian populations that have settled here, bringing in a variety of dishes from its recent immigrant history. Jordanian food is a great entry point to Arab cuisine and widely revered. If you visit Jordan, you will likely be forced into it, but we recommend you plan your trip around food instead of the other way around.

EXPERIENCES

CAN'T MISS The national dish is Mansaf (V), made of lamb cooked in a fermented yogurt sauce (derived from *jameed*, a dried goat's milk), accompanied by bulgur or rice. One eats this dish with the left hand behind the back and the right hand as a pinch-claw to scoop the food, absolving the need for utensils. Vegetarians, your "can't miss" is *fuul*.

ON THE MENU

★ *Big Jordanian breakfast* Savory goodness, including *fuul*, hummus, bread, olives, cucumbers, tomatoes, pastries, *labneh* (thick, strained yogurt), and bread. One must try *fuul* for breakfast, baked in a giant clay pot and ladled into bowls with a giant spoon. The dish consists of long-cooked fava or broad beans, slightly mashed with lemon juice and olive oil, and with any/all of the following toppings: tahini, cumin, chili, salt, onion. It's extremely filling and a must for bean-lovers.

★ *Starters* Also known as *mezze* (a collection of small dishes, served hot or cold), these generally include *kibbeh* (ground meat and bulgur with local spices), falafel, hummus, baba ghanoush, Arab salad, *labneh*, olives, pickles, *tabbouleh* (cracked wheat with parsley and tomato), and pita or taboon bread.

★ *Soup* Jordanians like to begin a meal with soup, usually lentils/*adas* (though freekeh can be substituted) cooked with vegetables and chicken stock.

★ *Sandwiches* Falafel and *shawarma* are ubiquitous, budget-friendly, and delicious.

★ *Mains Maqluba* is a rice dish cooked with meat and vegetables in a large pot, flipped upside-down dramatically onto the table, and then served with a yogurt/tahina sauce. *Zarb* is a meat and rice dish cooked in an oven buried in the sand. The meat can be lamb or chicken. It's prepared with vegetables, raisins, and nuts. *Mujadarra* is veg-friendly, and mixes lentils, rice, onions, and spices. *Galayet* is meat with stewed tomatoes.

★ *Dessert Knafeh* is a popular dessert, a goat's cheese and phyllo pastry soaked in rosewater syrup. The Egyptian dessert *Umm Ali* makes an appearance in most confectionaries, as does *muhallabiyeh* (pudding with almonds) and *maamoul* (semolina cookies). *Baklava* and *halva* can be found everywhere too.

★ *Drinks* Arab or Bedouin coffee (cut with cardamom), strong Turkish coffee, and tea with mint are widely consumed.

★ *Alcohol Arak* is a hard liquor with an anise flavor. Jordanian wine is gaining in popularity and quality.

SECRET If you're squeamish, you're in luck – the food is not "weird" to Western standards.

SPECIAL EVENTS Consider the presentation, which is half the fun and part of the adventure. Watching a Bedouin man perform his elaborate coffee ritual or a hiking guide bury your dinner in the sand should be considered quintessential Jordanian experiences.

ITINERATOR!

BEST STRATEGY Our recommendation is that you purposefully incorporate food into your trip plans. And should you already have plans to visit the below, then you're halfway there. Bon appetit!

★ International breakfast in either **Petra (#2)** or Anchor City Suweimeh on the **Dead Sea (#3)**. Skip the Western fare! Go straight for the Jordanian section and serve yourself an energy-filled portion of fuul, labneh, hummus, pickles, and other delectables.

★ Bedouin cookout in **Wadi Rum (#4)**: most people will incorporate an overnight into their plans, but that's not altogether necessary. You can, in fact, book a dinner without having to camp. Inquire with any of the popular campgrounds. You'll likely get some combination of zarb or barbecued lamb, *galayet*, chicken skewers, rice, hummus, olives, tabbouleh, and eggplant dips. If you do book the overnight, you'll get a traditional breakfast as well.

★ You have several goals in **Modern Amman (#36)**. **Restaurants**: treat yourself to higher-end fare. Fakhr el-Din (Q2) is the most well known and widely regarded restaurant. Sufra, Shams al-Balad (Q2), and Al-Kitkat (Q2) are all in the neighborhood around Rainbow Street and equally worthy – their menus are extensive and reflective of the broad cuisine. **Sandwiches**: competing for best falafel are Hashem Falafel (Q2) and Al-Quds Falafel (Q2), but another famous sandwich comes from Salah Addin Bakery with your choice of filling in the sesame-seed-crusted *ka'ak* bread. **Sweets**: Habiba is perhaps the most revered, with a dozen outlets, and several near the highlights (across from Hashem Falafel (Q2)). Zalatimo is just as popular with even more options.

★ Cooking school at **Petra Kitchen (#84)** or *Beit Sitti*, often consisting of three-course meal preparation, with the main usually being maqluba, accompanied by soup and/or vegetables and rice.

★ **Feynan Ecolodge (#86)** in the **Dana Biosphere Reserve (#21)** is an all-inclusive ecolodge experience, with cooking classes, home-cooked meals, and visits with the local Bedouin community where you can partake in the elaborate coffee rituals.

WALKS AND DRIVES Piece together our day trips. Start in Amman, head to Suweimeh on the Dead Sea, then south to Dana, on to Petra, and finally Wadi Rum. You could do *City Walk Q2* and *Road Trips P1, O1, N3,* and *M2* in your own time, eliminating anything that doesn't fit your schedule.

ITINERARIES There are several ways to put together an itinerary for a food-focused trip. Add in **other highly recommended electives** with our *High BUCKET! Scores: 7+* (p. 755), *Food and Drink* (p. 790), or *Shoestring* (p. 811) itineraries. A number of tour agencies have **food-forward trips**, including Intrepid (w intrepidtravel.com/uk/jordan/jordan-real-food-adventure-124473) and On the Go Tours (w onthegotours.com/nz/Jordan/Jordan-on-the-Menu-8-days). A DIY version could have you flying into and spending two nights in Amman, one night at the Dead Sea, two nights in Petra, one night in Dana/Feynan, and one night in Wadi Rum before circling back to Amman.

WHERE TO NEXT?

THEMATIC *People* Arab. *Food and Drink* Cuisine; Coffee, Tea, and Coffeeshops.

COMPLEMENTARY See **Israeli Cuisine (#51)**; *Road Trip D6: Tel Aviv Food and Drink*; the *Food and Drink – Food* theme (p. 561); and *Do #14: Eat It!* (p. 80).

#45 Umm Qais

BROCHURE

RATINGS

BUCKET! Score	6/10
Ruin	4/5
Entertainment	2/5
Information	2/5
Popularity	2/5

MACRO-REGION S: North Jordan

MICRO-REGION S1

PRIMARY THEME/CATEGORY Archaeology – City Conglomerates – Cities of the Decapolis.

TOP Most off-the-beaten-path destination in the top 50.

HOLY LAND RELEVANCE The Gospels indicate this may be where Jesus exorcised demons from two men into two pigs, which then dove off a cliff into the sea. Jews lived in this area until the great revolt of 66 CE, when many were killed publicly and unabashedly. Today, it's a place where expatriate Palestinians come to view the sweeping view of the land where they once lived; many visit on Fridays to share stories.

ELECT ME! Umm Qais is the present-day name of the ancient Greek and Roman Decapolis city Gadara. Visitors can mosey among the interesting and expansive ruins while admiring the beautiful view at a point near where three countries converge.

WORTH THE DETOUR? If you're a history buff, then you'll appreciate the ruins and the view. If you're interested in Roman ruins, **Jerash (#14)** has the best ones in the region and they are closer to Amman. Umm Qais is out of the way, so consider a visit if you are spending five or more days in Jordan.

EXPERIENCES

CAN'T MISS The sweeping view, with visuals of surrounding Jordan and the Yarmouk Forest (S1), the **Sea of Galilee (#7)**, the Israel–Jordan border, the Israel–Syria border, the contested **Golan Heights (#62)**, and *Mount Hermon* in the distance.

RUINS (starting at car park)
★ *City Walls* As you go, pay attention to how the walls have larger limestone courses at the base; these were built in ancient times. The smaller black basalt stones above were added by the Ottomans.
★ *Ottoman Village* This 18th-century village was built atop the Greek and Roman acropolis and includes Bayt al-Malkawi and Bayt Heshboni, two restored Ottoman-era houses.
★ *Bayt er-Russan* Formerly used as the Ottoman Governor's residence, now the site's museum with a famous headless statue of the city's patron goddess, Tyche.
★ *North Theater* Behind the museum, the ruins of this theater were likely used in the construction of other buildings.
★ *Tombs of Chaireas, Germani, and Modestus* Behind the Ottoman Village is a series of burial chambers with adjacent sarcophagi.
★ *Decumanus Maximus* The central thoroughfare of ancient Gadara.
★ *Octagon Church* The black basalt columns are all that's left of the original 6th-century Byzantine-era church.

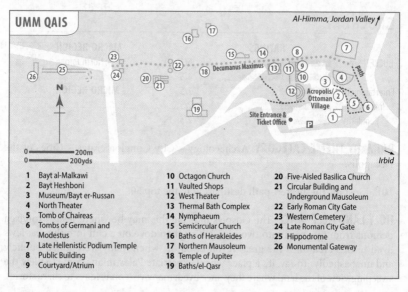

UMM QAIS

Al-Himma, Jordan Valley

Decumanus Maximus

Acropolis/ Ottoman Village

Site Entrance & Ticket Office

Irbid

0 — 200m
0 — 200yds

1	Bayt al-Malkawi	10	Octagon Church	20	Five-Aisled Basilica Church
2	Bayt Heshboni	11	Vaulted Shops	21	Circular Building and
3	Museum/Bayt er-Russan	12	West Theater		Underground Mausoleum
4	North Theater	13	Thermal Bath Complex	22	Early Roman City Gate
5	Tomb of Chaireas	14	Nymphaeum	23	Western Cemetery
6	Tombs of Germani and	15	Semicircular Church	24	Late Roman City Gate
	Modestus	16	Baths of Herakleides	25	Hippodrome
7	Late Hellenistic Podium Temple	17	Northern Mausoleum	26	Monumental Gateway
8	Public Building	18	Temple of Jupiter		
9	Courtyard/Atrium	19	Baths/el-Qasr		

- ★ *Vaulted Shops* A series of commercial shops along the Decumanus.
- ★ *West Theater* Constructed in black basalt, this 1st-century theater has a well-preserved upper level with great views of the sweeping valley.
- ★ *Thermal Bath Complex* Remains of a hot-water bathing structure built during the 4th century CE.
- ★ *Hippodrome* Now rocks, possibly never completed.

SECRET The best views are from various points along the Decumanus, particularly near the Nymphaeum and at the West Theater.

SPECIAL EVENTS Palestinian families visit in droves on Fridays.

ITINERATOR!

DAYS/HOURS June–October 08.00–18.30, November–March 08.00–16.00, April–May 08.00–17.30, Ramadan 08.00–15.30. Museum closed Tuesdays.

BEST TIME Spring, for wildflowers, but otherwise the elevation makes it perfectly pleasant any time of the year. Fridays are busy. Early evening is nice for the sunsets.

TIME COMMITMENT The site is bigger than you'd expect, so plan on spending at least 2 hours in addition to the drive. Longer if you meander, eat, and gaze out over the beautiful vistas. Speed rules apply.

BASE We recommend completing this as a day trip unless you have a desire to see more of the north of the country (check out *Road Trips S1, S2,* and *R1*) from Amman (120km/2 hours) or Suweimeh/Dead Sea (115km/2½ hours).

BEST STRATEGY Umm Qais is a great site, but far removed. If you're heading north, you can see **Jerash (#14)** too before heading back to Amman/Suweimeh. Or spend less time on site (1 hour each, say) and do a sampling of several northern sites.

WALKS AND DRIVES S1, V1, V2, W3.

ITINERARIES Off-the-Beaten-Path Jordan.

ARRIVAL PREP

PREBOOK Not necessary.

REALITY CHECK For fear of heights, know you're on solid ground, without sheer cliffs. Long drive needed to get here. If doing this as a day trip, expect at least one or two issues: there are lots of surprise speed bumps, slow cars, one-way passes, and car-oblivious people on the "highways" from Umm Qais back to Amman or Suweimeh.

ACCESS Straight shot on Route 65 from Suweimeh; big car park available and just off the main Umm Qais town road.

ADMISSION 5 JD adults, free for kids under 12 and disabled, or free with Jordan Pass.

RECOMMENDED GUIDE Signs are limited, so have your guidebook handy, or buy a brochure from the ticket booth. You can also hire a guide at negotiable rates. Note: during low season, the guides may hound you until you cave (but they'll tire out once you start going up the hill).

VISITOR CENTER Located at the entrance. The site museum is worth a visit.

EAT The Resthouse in the Ottoman Village is a popular stop with a nice view.

SLEEP Irbid is the closest town with broader options, but we recommend heading back to Amman or Suweimeh.

BUCKET!PEDIA

AKA Gadara (Greek). *Historical era* Ancient Israel: Greek to Roman/Byzantine: Judea, then Islamic: Crusader to Ottoman. *Year founded* 7th century BCE (?). *Size* The city walls are 3km in circumference.

CONTEXT A destroyed city from antiquity, important to both Greeks and Romans, this former member of the Greek Decapolis, and later the Roman Decapolis, enjoyed prosperity from the 3rd century BCE to the 1st century CE, though continued to be a seat of power for the Romans until the Muslims conquered in 636. In 749, the second big regional earthquake laid the place to waste, and the city was abandoned for centuries before the Ottomans built atop some of the main ruins.

CHRONOLOGY

330 BCE: Town bursts onto the scene with its resident creative artists, including Menippus, a Cynic satirist whose work influenced scholars such as Lucian and Varro.
198 BCE: Seleucids (Greek empire in Western Asia) defeat the Ptolemies (Greek kingdom of Egypt) for control.
98 BCE: Hasmonean (Jewish) King Alexander Jannaeus wrests control and destroys city.
64 BCE: Roman general Pompey regains control and rebuilds site.
30 BCE: Herod begins reign, which is tumultuous as the locals preferred the Roman Empire. He severely punishes the resident Jewish population so much there is a regular spate of suicides to escape his wrath.
66 CE: At the end of the Jewish Revolt, Roman Emperor Vespasian destroys site and kills all men and boys.
636: Gadara comes under Muslim control following the Battle of Yarmouk.
749: Earthquake devastates city. Not to be resettled until 19th century.
18th–19th centuries: Ottomans use site as residence and girls' school.
1990s: Excavations begin on Decumanus and surrounding sites.

WEBSITE w international.visitjordan.com/Wheretogo/UmmQays.aspx.

WHERE TO NEXT?

THEMATIC *Religion* Christianity; Cities of the Decapolis; Impressive Structural Remains. *Structure* Historic Monuments. *Nature* Mountains and Mounts; Plants, Gardens and Farms. *Scenic* Earth Panorama.

COMPLEMENTARY Nearby Decapolis cities: **Jerash (#14)**, **Ancient Amman (#37)**, *Pella*, Abila (S1), and Beit Ras. Jordan's other top 50 sites: **Petra (#2)**, **Dead Sea (#3)**, **Wadi Rum**

(#4), **Jerash (#14)**, **Madaba and the Madaba Map (#19)**, **Qasr Amra and the Desert Palaces (#20)**; **Dana Biosphere Reserve (#21)**, **Wadi Mujib and Mujib Biosphere Reserve (#23)**, **Mount Nebo (#24)**, **King's Highway (#31)**, **Modern Amman (#36)**, **Ancient Amman (#37)**, **Bethany-Beyond-the-Jordan (#41)**, **Aqaba (#43)**, and **Jordanian Cuisine (#44)**.

NEARBY Irbid (30km/45 minutes), **Ajloun Fortress (#76)** (63km/1¼ hours), **Jerash (#14)** (73km/1½ hours), and **Modern Amman (#36)** (123km/3 hours).

#46 Tomb of the Patriarchs and Old Town of Hebron

BROCHURE

RATINGS		MACRO-REGION
BUCKET! Score	5/10	C: West Bank
Ruin	3/5	
Entertainment	2/5	MICRO-REGION
Information	1/5	C2
Popularity	3/5	

PRIMARY THEME/CATEGORY Religion – The Sacred – Burial.

TOP Hebron is one of Judaism's Four Holy Cities (along with **Old City Jerusalem (#1)**, **Tsfat/Safed (#58)**, and *Tiberias*).

COMMENDATIONS UNESCO World Heritage Site, 2017; Israel National Park.

HOLY LAND RELEVANCE In Genesis 23:1–20, Abraham's wife Sarah dies in the field of Machpelah in Hebron. She becomes the first person in the Bible to be buried when Abraham buys her plot in a cave on the Machpelah land. Abraham is later buried there, followed by his son Isaac and wife Rebekah, and their son Jacob and his wife Leah (Genesis 49:31). That site has been revered since. Before ruling all of Israel, King David first ruled Hebron. It remained an important site throughout antiquity.

ELECT ME! Hebron is an ancient city in modern-day Palestine (southern West Bank) which contains the grave of patriarch/prophet/leader Abraham, progenitor of the Abrahamic religions, and the graves of his family members. These are encased in tombs inside caves which cannot be visited, but can be viewed from within a large burial complex which has a Jewish and Muslim side. Visitors can see both sides for an interesting contrast in rituals and homage. Very popular local religious site.

WORTH THE DETOUR? The Israeli *Separation Wall* is shocking for its size and scope, while the manmade barriers in Hebron seem somehow more depressing. The synagogue and mosque are interesting, but you are not entering the caves or tombs, so this is more of a religious and historical spot. It is out of the way unless you combine with other southern West Bank sites.

EXPERIENCES

CAN'T MISS The perspective of seeing the site from both sides.

SITES The **Tomb of the Patriarchs** has separate Jewish and Muslim entrances; the **Caves of the Patriarchs** are off-limits to almost everyone (you can see two entrances inside the building, one near Abraham's cenotaph and another near the mihrab in the mosque); **Tel Rumeida** is ancient, biblical Hebron, which predates Old Town Hebron by 1,000–2,000 years; **Deir al-Arba'in** is a former mosque in Tel Rumeida encompassing the Tomb of Ruth and Jesse, the great-grandmother and father of King David, respectively; **Terebinth/Oak of Mamre**, the location where God appeared to Abraham, is now a dead tree inside the Old Town; the **Tomb of Abner**, a war general to kings Saul and David, the **Tomb of Othniel Ben Kenaz**, Israel's first biblical-era judge; and the **former market** in the H-2 area, a spooky, empty street, now abandoned due to lack of commercial opportunities for Arab residents.

ACTIVITIES There are several guided tours to choose from, including the popular Dual Narrative Tour which provides both Muslim and Jewish perspectives (see *Recommended Guide* below).

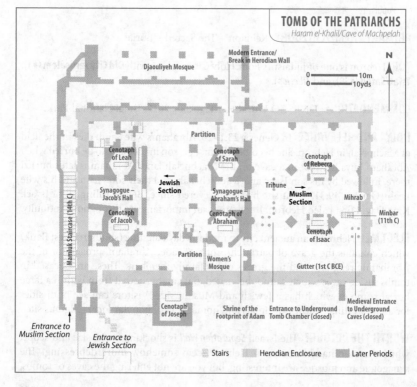

SECRET Other tombs in Hebron get less attention, including the Tomb of Abner, the Tomb of Ruth and Jesse, and further afield the Tomb of Lot.

SPECIAL EVENTS The sites are visited by throngs at various times of the year. Each side – Jewish and Muslim – is opened to members of the other faith over 10 days a year for specific holidays. On Shavuot, Jews visit the Tomb of Ruth and Jesse.

ITINERATOR!

DAYS/HOURS Open daily 04.00–21.00 winter, 04.00–22.00 summer. May closed to visitors during Muslim ceremonies, though visits to Jewish side are allowed.

BEST TIME Choose if you want a chaotic experience (potentially dangerous) during a ceremony or a tamer experience on a non-holiday.

TIME COMMITMENT Two hours is sufficient to see the Cave and surrounding sites. Speed rules apply.

BASE Road trip is recommended from Jerusalem (40km/50 minutes).

BEST STRATEGY Understandably, time is limited, and Bethlehem is both closer and has more recognizable sites, so you might feel like skipping. If you want to pack all of the southern West Bank into a day, you can do so without booking a tour and self-guide through the Cave and Tomb in a few minutes.

WALKS AND DRIVES C2, W5.

ITINERARIES Off-the-Beaten-Path Israel and Palestine; Religion; Entertainment; UNESCO; Endangered; Memorial; Pilgrimage.

ARRIVAL PREP

PREBOOK Dual Narrative (and other professionally guided) tours (see below).

REALITY CHECK Occasional epicenter of violent outbursts (rare) by both sides. Be cognizant of the heavy military presence.

BRING Passport to pass through to the West Bank if coming from Jerusalem or Israel; dress is modest, but if you don't have a head covering (kippeh or scarf) one will be provided.

ACCESS From the Israeli controlled H-2 side, access is relatively straightforward. You can pass to the Arab side by going through security. Bring your passport. No fee.

RECOMMENDED GUIDE There is a popular tour that presents Hebron from both a Palestinian and an Israeli perspective, called the Dual Narrative Tour. You'll speak with both sides to hear how regular people deal with living in a divided city, and get a tour of the Tomb, as well as other important sites in Hebron (w abrahamtours. com/tours/hebron-tour/).

EAT The street food in Hebron is widely regarded by Palestinians. Qedra is a popular meat and rice dish. Falafel and shawarma are staples. Sweets are also popular, such as baklava and knafeh.

SLEEP Recommended to stay in Jerusalem.

BUCKET!PEDIA

AKA al-Haram al-Ibrahimi ("Tomb of Abraham" in Arabic); Me'arat ha-Machpelah ("Cave of the Double Tombs" in Hebrew); the town is also known as al-Khalil in Arabic. *Historical era Prehistoric: Chalcolithic* to *Modern: Contemporary.* *Year founded* Perhaps 3500 BCE.

CONTEXT Hebron is the largest city in the West Bank, and home to Jews and Muslims, both of whom have lived here for millennia. As such, Hebron is a town divided, but holy to both due to its location as the burial ground of the founding father of the Abrahamic religions, Abraham. Abraham and his progeny are important not just to Jews but also to Christians and Muslims, as well as to the Bahá'í, Druze, Samaritans, and others.

As referenced in Genesis, Abraham purchased the "field of Machpelah before Mamre, now Hebron" after his wife Sarah passed away. Incidentally, this is both the first burial and the first commercial transaction recorded in the Bible (400 shekels for the plot). Abraham and other family members were eventually buried in the same location in sepulchers set in caves. Though the site has been venerated since antiquity, it was King Herod who built the first monumental (and enclosing) structure to commemorate the biblical ancestors. The caves once contained tombs of six members of Abraham's family, including himself, his wife Sarah, his son Isaac, Isaac's wife Rebecca, Isaac and Rebecca's son Jacob, and Jacob's wife Leah. The only matriarch missing is Rachel, Jacob's other wife, who is buried near Bethlehem.

The Old Town of Hebron, where the Tomb of the Patriarchs sits, dates only to the Greek and Roman era. Biblical Hebron is much older and sits to the west of the Old Town in Tel Rumeida, an archaeological park and residential neighborhood in H-2, the Israeli-backed part of Hebron. Within the Old Town are a number of tombs from the biblical period. Byzantine and Arab rulers developed and populated this area, recognizing the importance of the site. Over time the Tomb has been converted into a church and mosque and back again several times, most recently a mosque called the Ibrahimi ("Abraham") Mosque by Muslims. After Israel took control in 1967, half of the site became designated a synagogue, which now has its own entrance from the Old Town and is known as the Cave of Machpelah.

With roughly 250,000 Arabs and only a few hundred Jews in the town, it is the only shared city in the West Bank, and is heavily militarized as a result. The city has been host to all sorts of violence over the years. The separation of the town's people is one of the starkest visuals that visitors leave with.

CHRONOLOGY

c3500 BCE: Tel Rumeida settlement, some 200m west of Old Town Hebron, established in Chalcolithic era, possibly.

c2000 BCE: Abraham buys a burial plot for his wife Sarah.

1000 BCE: King David rules Hebron briefly before becoming King of Israel.

8th century BCE: Hebron becomes part of Judea.

586 BCE: City destroyed by Babylonians.

350 BCE: Hebron inhabited by Greeks, move town eastward to location of current "Old Town."

1st century BCE: Herod constructs an enclosure around the burial cave.

4th century CE (?): Byzantines convert Herod's structure into a basilica.

638: Umayyads convert basilica into a mosque.

1100: Crusaders convert back into a church.

1260: Mamluks convert back into a mosque.

12th–15th centuries: Mamluks create the urban structures and design of the city that continue today, later aiding in the site's designation by UNESCO.

1929: Hebron Massacre, where 67 Jews are killed during an insurrection. Hundreds more are saved by their Arab neighbors.

1948: Following Israel's creation, Hebron becomes part of the Jordanian West Bank.

1967: Israel occupies the West Bank, including Hebron, but resists settlers moving back.

1972: Kiryat Arba, a Jewish settlement, is established just outside of Hebron.

1979: Squatters begin to take over formerly Jewish buildings in downtown Hebron.

1984: Tel Rumeida in downtown Hebron is occupied by Jewish settlers.

1994: Jewish resident/settler kills 29 Muslim worshipers and injures more than 100 others before being beaten to death. Building split in two with Jews and Muslims not allowed to visit the other side.

1997: All of Hebron is split in two. H-1 is controlled by Palestinian Authority while H-2 is under Israeli military control, specifically in the areas where Jewish settlers have created homes, including Tel Rumeida, Deir al-Arba'in, and the Old Town of Hebron. Tomb of the Patriarchs/Abraham's Mosque sits across the dividing line to allow access for both parties, albeit from separate entrances.

2000–03: Second Intifada. Hebron Palestinians placed under curfew, lasting several years.

2017: UNESCO inscribes Old Town Hebron and the Cave of the Patriarchs into the list of World Heritage Sites in Danger under the state of Palestine.

WHERE TO NEXT?

THEMATIC *Noteworthy* UNESCO; Endangered. *Religion* Judaism; Holiest Jewish Places; Christianity; Islam; Kings, Prophets, and Saints; Old Testament; Quran; Mosques; Oldest/Ancient Mosques; Burial; Pilgrimage. *Archaeology* Prehistory; Bronze Age; Iron Age; Herodian. *People* Jewish; Arab.

COMPLEMENTARY Other Jewish Holy Sites: **Old City Jerusalem (#1)**, **Tsfat/Safed (#58)**, and *Tiberias*. Other Muslim Holy Sites: **Temple Mount (#12)**.

NEARBY **Herodion (#90)** (35km/40 minutes), **Bethlehem (#40)** (50km/1¼ hours), and **Old City Jerusalem (#1)** (60km/1½ hours).

#47 Jerusalem Walls and Gates

BROCHURE

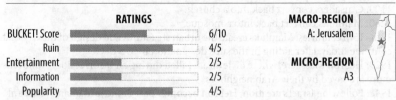

RATINGS		MACRO-REGION
BUCKET! Score	6/10	A: Jerusalem
Ruin	4/5	
Entertainment	2/5	**MICRO-REGION**
Information	2/5	A3
Popularity	4/5	

PRIMARY THEME/CATEGORY Archaeology – Ancient Cities and Remains – Walled Cities.

TOP City walls in the region.

COMMENDATIONS Israel National Park; part of the nomination for UNESCO World Heritage Site of Jerusalem, 1981.

HOLY LAND RELEVANCE These walls and their location have changed many times over the millennia. As an example, Jesus is known to have been crucified outside city gates on Golgotha, a hill that has since been incorporated into the **Church of the Holy Sepulchre (#9)** and is now within the Old City walls. At various times, the *City of David*, **Mount Zion (#92)**, and parts of East Jerusalem were all surrounded by walls, since destroyed or removed. The history of the walls tells the history of the city, and often simultaneously the stories of the conquerors and the vanquished.

ELECT ME! The walls of Jerusalem are striking. They are tall, majestic, and glistening. Passing through one of the gates feels like entering a medieval theme park – but they are real gates to enter a real city! Most everyone has Jerusalem on their bucket list and we would encourage you to incorporate one of the *Ways to Visit* below into your travel plans.

WORTH THE DETOUR? Absolutely worth the energy to climb the walls and see the city from above.

EXPERIENCES

CAN'T MISS Standing on top of the walls near Jaffa Gate.

WAYS TO VISIT
* ★ *Ramparts Walk (#91)* There is a north and south walk, both of which are included on the same ticket.
* ★ *Citadel/Tower of David (#32)* The museum incorporates walks in and among the walls.
* ★ *Jerusalem Walls and Gates (#47)* This national park incorporates the exterior walls and gates, as well as the **City of David**.
* ★ *Jerusalem Archaeological Park (#71)* The southern city walls merge with the south wall of Temple Mount highlighting the ruins of the Second Temple period.

★ *Temple Mount (#12)* Mostly concerned with the buildings atop, but Temple Mount forms parts of the eastern and southern boundaries of the walled city.
★ *City Walk A3* 1–3-hour self-guided tour of the city walls, passing all eight active gates, and several closed ones.
★ *Old City Chronotour* Criss-cross through time and space with our self-guided walk of the Old City where we start at Jerusalem's beginning and visit the most important sites chronologically (**w** buckettravelguides.com/old-city-chronotour).

GATES **Jaffa** (west) is the most common tourist entrance gate, providing access to **Citadel/Tower of David (#32)**, visitor center, and David Street (shopping); **New** (north) provides access to New City Jerusalem; **Damascus** (north) is a massive gate with direct access to the main thoroughfare, Beit HaBad Street; **Herod** (north) is the East Jerusalem entrance, providing access to Muslim Quarter (A2); **Lions'/St. Stephen's** (east) is near the first Station of the Cross on the **Via Dolorosa (#42)**; **Golden** (east) has been closed for centuries; **Dung** (south) provides access to the **Western Wall (#11)**; and **Zion** (south) is the exit to **Mount Zion (#92)**.

SECRET There's a ninth gate not on Google, called Tanners' Gate, opposite the Dung Gate, which was opened in 1990 and provides access to the *Jewish Quarter*.

SPECIAL EVENTS Sound and light shows are occasionally projected onto the city walls, particularly when there are art installations, such as the Israel Festival or Festival of Light.

MAP See A3.

ITINERATOR!

DAYS/HOURS Ramparts: 09.00–16.00 winter, 09.00–22.00 summer, 09.00–14.00 Fridays and holidays. The sites with tickets tend to close early on Fridays and may be closed on Saturdays. Ramparts North is closed Fridays. Ramparts South is closed Saturdays. Check individual sites.

TIME COMMITMENT To walk quickly around the exterior, plan 90 minutes for the 5.5km walk. **Ramparts Walk (#91)** will likely add at least 1–2 hours, but keep in mind it only covers half the walls. Speed rules apply.

BASE Located in Anchor City Jerusalem.

BEST STRATEGY At a minimum, we recommend walking at the base of the walls on *City Walk A3*. If you have time to delve deeper, plan to visit the **Citadel/Tower of David (#32)** and do both sides of the **Ramparts Walk (#91)**. The **Jerusalem Archaeological Park (#71)** has a great museum, but the ruins require some imagination.

WALKS AND DRIVES A1, A3, U2.

ITINERARIES Structure; Active; UNESCO; National Parks/Reserves.

ARRIVAL PREP

PREBOOK Not usually necessary, but you can book tickets online.

REALITY CHECK Steep climbs from the eastern valley to the southern walls if doing the whole circuit. Damascus and Herod's gates are occasionally focal points of violence against Israeli police. Routes are not disability-accessible.

ACCESS From any gate, except Golden. Jaffa is the most common and where you get tickets.

ADMISSION Free to enter **Old City Jerusalem (#1)**. Additional costs for **Ramparts Walk (#91)**, **Citadel/Tower of David (#32)**, and **Jerusalem Archaeological Park (#71)**.

RECOMMENDED GUIDE Self-guided.

VISITOR CENTER The Citadel and Jerusalem Archaeological Park sites both fill this role.

EAT/SLEEP See **Old City Jerusalem (#1)**

BUCKET!PEDIA

AKA The gates have had various names throughout the years. *Historical era* Ancient Israel: Hasmonean to Islamic: Ottoman. *Year constructed* Mostly 16th century, though there are Hasmonean (2nd century BCE) and Herodian (1st century BCE/CE) foundation stones.

CONTEXT The city walls have undergone millennia of change. Experiencing this evolution gives you a great perspective on how the city evolved over time. If you're interested in archaeology or history, consider using our *Old City Chronotour* (**w** buckettravelguides.com/old-city-chronotour) to explore the full extent of Jerusalem's changes throughout history.

CHRONOLOGY

1003 BCE: City of David established on the site of the conquered Jebusite city, Jebus. Walls built around the new city.

c950 BCE: King Solomon expands the city walls to include Mount Moriah (Temple Mount).

721 BCE: Hezekiah builds walls to the west of the City of David and Temple Mount to ward off an attack from the Assyrians (see Broad Wall in the Jewish Quarter).

586 BCE: Neo-Babylonians lay siege to Jerusalem, destroying the walls.

445 BCE: Nehemiah builds new walls around Temple Mount and the City of David.

164 BCE: Construction begins on the First Wall, or Hasmonean Wall, around the Upper Hill, including Mount Zion.

34 BCE: Herod constructs Temple Mount, to fortify the ground upon which he built the Second Temple. The foundations of Herod's walls can be seen on the southern and eastern borders of the city. Herod also builds his palace on the western border, near Jaffa Gate. At least one of the towers was incorporated into the site, now part of the Citadel.

70 CE: Written accounts of Jerusalem around the time of King Herod discuss a Second Wall (encompassing Damascus Gate, but not yet the Sepulchre) and Third Wall (expanding well beyond the northern border of today's walls). They've yet to be identified definitively. Reports indicate they were destroyed during the Jewish Revolt.

638: Arab rulers begin to enclose the city in walls again, extending as far south as Mount Zion and City of David with northern, eastern, and western walls that match today's locations.

975: To more easily defend the city, the Fatimid caliphs shorten the city walls, removing Mount Zion and the City of David. The shape is what we recognize today.

1187: Ayyubid leader Saladin fortifies the walls, adding several defensive towers.

1219: Ayyubids destroy all the walls in a spiteful move towards the Crusaders who are at their doorstep.

1535: Ottoman leader Suleiman the Magnificent restores the walls, making them taller and gallant. He runs out of money and lops off Zion and City of David.

16th century: Damascus, Jaffa, Zion, Lions', and Dung gates added.

1875: Herod's Gate added.

1887: New Gate added.

1981: Jerusalem and its walls added to UNESCO World Heritage list.

WEBSITE w pami.co.il/en/Tour%20Sites/; w tod.org.il/en/visitor-info; w generationword.com/jerusalem101/4-walls-today.html.

WHERE TO NEXT?

THEMATIC *Noteworthy* UNESCO; National Parks. *Archaeology* Walls; Historical Battlefields; Active Excavations; Impressive Structural Remains. *Structure* Iconic Structures; Historic Monuments; Landscape; Beautiful Structures; Skyline; Infrastructure. *Nature* Earthquakes. *Society* Borders. *Active* Walking Paths; Running and Free Exercise.

COMPLEMENTARY Other famous walls: **Western Wall (#11)**, **Temple Mount (#12)**, **Akko (#13)**, **Jericho (#26)**, and **Megiddo (#59)**.

NEARBY See **Old City Jerusalem (#1)**.

#48 Avdat

BROCHURE

RATINGS		MACRO-REGION
BUCKET! Score	6/10	J: Negev
Ruin	3/5	
Entertainment	3/5	**MICRO-REGION**
Information	4/5	J2
Popularity	2/5	

PRIMARY THEME/CATEGORY Archaeology – City Conglomerates – Nabataean.

TOP The best of the Nabataean desert towns on the **Incense Route (#73)**.

COMMENDATIONS Part of UNESCO World Heritage Site for Incense Route, 2005; Israel National Park.

HOLY LAND RELEVANCE The Nabataeans were a powerful tribe of Arab commercialists who controlled much of the Negev and its important trade routes from the Mediterranean to the deserts of Jordan and Saudi Arabia. It was an independent nation from its inception in the 4th century BCE through to annexation by the Romans in the 2nd century CE, though it continued to do business through to the Byzantine era before being swallowed in importance and uniqueness in the greater Arab conquest of 636.

ELECT ME! After **Petra (#2)**, this site was the most important Nabataean way station on the Petra–Gaza trade route. There are a number of towns in the desert to explore, but this is the most grand, with upright walls, pillars, artwork, and buildings that require less imagination to understand, making this an excellent introduction to the **Incense Route (#73)** for those with limited time to explore the whole thing.

WORTH THE DETOUR? The site pales in comparison with Petra, so don't expect anything similar. It is a well-preserved site, but is in a remote area. Definitely worth a visit if you're heading to **Makhtesh Ramon (#28)** or driving to **Eilat (#78)** (as it's right off the highway).

EXPERIENCES

CAN'T MISS An introduction to the site at the visitor center, making sure to stay for the 10-minute video.

SITES (in order of visiting)
- ★ *Roman Burial Cave* There are nearly two dozen burial niches inside this cave-tomb, with interesting cosmic Greek reliefs carved into the entryway.
- ★ *Roman Villa* As you enter and before you park, make sure to stop at the observation point with the Roman Villa – noticeable by its two recreated arches over one of the roofs. There you'll find stunning views over Avdat Valley.
- ★ *Late Roman Tower* Possibly designed to be earthquake-proof, this tower remained standing when many of the surrounding buildings collapsed. An inscription indicates it was built around 294 CE. Great views, particularly of the main street and quarter from the late Roman period.
- ★ *Pottery Workshop* Three rooms dedicated to local craftsmanship during the middle Nabataean period, of which Avdat was a manufacturing center.
- ★ *Acropolis* The **Fortress** contains a wine press and a chapel, and was once used as the principal location for gathering of the town's residents. **St. Theodore's Church** was named after the city's patron saint, and the **North Church**, with a baptistry in the shape of a crucifix, is used as the town's cathedral. On the western end of the Acropolis is a **Nabataean Temple** dedicated to Obodas III, now with a popular observation deck.
- ★ *Byzantine Bathhouse* To supply the hot-, tepid-, and cold-water baths, water was collected from a 64m well.

SECRET Further afield beyond the fortress are the sites of the caravanserai and military camps where overnight visitors would rest their camels and pitch tents.

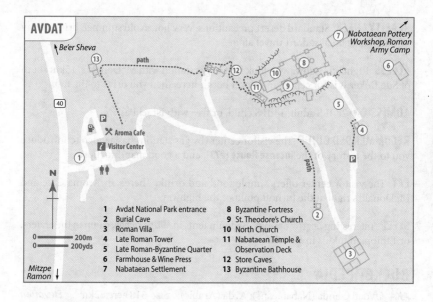

AVDAT

Be'er Sheva

path

7 Nabataean Pottery Workshop, Roman Army Camp

40

Aroma Cafe

Visitor Center

N

0 ———— 200m
0 ———— 200yds

Mitzpe Ramon ↓

1	Avdat National Park entrance	8	Byzantine Fortress
2	Burial Cave	9	St. Theodore's Church
3	Roman Villa	10	North Church
4	Late Roman Tower	11	Nabataean Temple &
5	Late Roman-Byzantine Quarter		Observation Deck
6	Farmhouse & Wine Press	12	Store Caves
7	Nabataean Settlement	13	Byzantine Bathhouse

ITINERATOR!

DAYS/HOURS Saturday–Thursday 08.00–17.00 early summer, 08.00–18.00 late summer, 08.00–15.00 winter, holiday eves closes 13.00.

BEST DAY/TIME The summer is excruciatingly hot – there's no shade, and it's in the middle of the Negev Desert. Thus, early morning is best, especially during the summer.

TIME COMMITMENT 1–2 hours to do the Acropolis, visitor center, video, and take lots of photos; 2–4 hours total to take in military camp, pottery workshop, bathhouse, Roman villa. Speed rules apply.

BASE Best to do this on a road trip, staying in **_Mitzpe Ramon_** (23km/20 minutes) for a night, tacking on other regional points of interest.

BEST STRATEGY If you're driving to **Eilat (#78)**, this is a good stopping point for lunch and a place to stretch your legs. Bonus that it's interesting! If you're a history fan, other stops along the **Incense Route (#73)** may also interest you. The site recommends a quick route for those with limited time, with further-afield sites that can be added if you have extra time.

WALKS AND DRIVES J2, J3, U2, W5.

ITINERARIES Off-the-Beaten-Path Israel and Palestine; Noteworthy; Archaeology; UNESCO; National Parks/Reserves; Cinematic.

ARRIVAL PREP

PREBOOK Not necessary.

REALITY CHECK Standard desert precautions: very hot, avoid summer, bring plenty of water, take breaks, don't travel alone.

ACCESS Right off Highway 40, look for the gas station with McDonald's, 15km south of Sde Boker. Visitor center and ticket booth here, then you drive to the top.

ADMISSION 28 ILS adult, 14 ILS child, or free with Israel Pass.

RECOMMENDED GUIDE The visitor center (by gas station) has a video to introduce you to the history of the **Incense Route (#73)**, and a good map/brochure.

EAT The visitor center offers simple food and drink. There's an Aroma Cafe and McDonald's right at the turnoff point of the highway.

SLEEP Interesting nearby options: Bedouin tents in *Mitzpe Ramon*, camp in the craters, or Ethiopian tukuls in *Mamshit*.

BUCKET!PEDIA

AKA Ovdat, Oboda (Nabataeans); Avda (Arabic). *Size* 518 acres/2km². *Elevation* 600m above sea level. *Historical era* Roman/Byzantine: Nabataean. *Year constructed* 4th century BCE, though little remains of the original site.

CONTEXT Today, the city of Oboda, or Avdat, is a large site of mostly Byzantine ruins in the middle of the desert. It was an important stop for camel caravans heading to the Gaza port with their spices and incense from Arabia and the Far East. While there were numerous stopping points along the route before landing on the Mediterranean, Avdat was one of the largest and most important, and is today one of the best preserved.

The city was founded some time in the 4th century BCE by Arab Nabataeans as a way station and commercial center for those traveling merchants. The city name, Avdat, is derived from the name of a revered Nabataean king, Obodas. The oldest buildings on site relate to the Middle Nabataean period, when King Obodas III ruled.

Around the time of Obodas III and his successor, Aretas IV, the city diversified economically, taking up animal husbandry and pottery craftwork. This was a good thing, because the town's focus as a trade route came to an end when warring Arab neighbors destroyed the town around 70 CE. Rome annexed Nabataea, including Avdat, in 106 CE and ceased use of the trade route, focusing energies on agriculture. A major earthquake struck the site in the 4th century CE, collapsing much of the Roman quarter.

The Byzantine reconstruction brought several new buildings, many of which survive today at the site, including a few churches in the Acropolis. Several hundred townspeople lived in caves and houses on the hillside nearby. The town was destroyed (again) during the Arab invasion of 636, abandoned, and suffered its final fate during an earthquake in the mid-7th century – much of the remains today are rubble from that earthquake.

CHRONOLOGY

4th century BCE: City founded, mostly used as a transient hub with few, if any, permanent structures.

29–28 BCE: Nabataean King Obodas III reigns. Avdat gains renewed interest.

70 CE: Leader Rabbel I sees the end of the line for the Incense Route and expands capabilities of site to include agriculture and production.

106: Roman annexation to Provincia Arabia, effectively ending the Incense Route, though it continued to serve Roman military purposes.

4th century: Pagan temples replaced by churches.

4th–7th centuries: Byzantine period sees Avdat at its most productive and expansive.

c636: Earthquake and Muslim conquest bring about a collapse of the town.

1807: First Western visitor.

1870: Site positively identified by researcher Edward Palmer.

1958: Excavations begin.

2005: Avdat declared a UNESCO site, along with other stops on the Incense Route.

WEBSITE w parks.org.il/en/reserve-park/avdat-national-park/.

WHERE TO NEXT?

THEMATIC *Noteworthy* National Parks. *Archaeology* Byzantine; Nabataean; Impressive Structural Remains. *Nature* Desert. *Scenic* Earth Panorama.

COMPLEMENTARY Other **Incense Route (#73)** sites: *Halutza*, *Mamshit*, *Nitzana*, and *Shivta*. More Nabataean ruins: **Petra (#2)**, **Wadi Rum (#4)**, and *Little Petra*.

NEARBY **Ein Avdat (#74)** (4km/5 minutes), Sde Boker (J2) (16km/17 minutes), *Mitzpe Ramon* (22km/17 minutes), *Mamshit* (48km/38 minutes), and *Shivta* (54km/40 minutes).

#49 Karak

BROCHURE

RATINGS		MACRO-REGION
BUCKET! Score	6/10	O: King's Highway
Ruin	3/5	
Entertainment	2/5	**MICRO-REGION**
Information	2/5	01
Popularity	2/5	

PRIMARY THEME/CATEGORY Archaeology – Islamic – Crusader.

TOP Largest Crusader castle in Jordan.

HOLY LAND RELEVANCE The town is referenced in the Old Testament. Karak town is also shown on the **Madaba Map (#19)**, surrounded by a big wall which is partially visible today.

ELECT ME! This seven-story Crusader castle holds lots of exciting spaces to explore – both excavated and not. The castle feels less like a museum than a cave, with its

357

many layers deep into the mountain. Karak Castle has a relatively short history. Built during the First Crusade, its legendary impenetrability lasted only until the Second Crusade when Saladin's forces took it in 1189.

WORTH THE DETOUR? If you're already traveling along the **King's Highway (#31)**, this is definitely a worthwhile stop.

EXPERIENCES

CAN'T MISS Ask permission at the ticket booth to visit the underground chambers. They're otherwise locked, but the groundskeeper will let you in if you ask.

SITES

★ *Impressive glacis* This artificial rocky slope, surrounding the castle, prevented invaders from using all but one side from which to attack the castle, giving the defenders the edge and making this castle one of the most difficult to penetrate.
★ *Underground rooms* Make sure you bring a headlamp if you're into exploration. Many tunnels are not lit, and the appeal of the place is getting to know its hidden nooks.
★ *Archaeological Museum* Located in the castle and set up to provide a short tour of the history of al-Karak the town via its anthropological record.
★ *Great views to Jerusalem* Provide evidence of the importance of this particular fort, which was able to signal to Jerusalem (Crusader Kingdom HQ) when attackers came in from Damascus.
★ *Two vaulted rooms* Beautiful architectural features in the lower level below the Lower Court.

SECRET The approach is impressive. As you drive in, you'll appreciate the size of the castle and its immense walls. Plan to stop along the road as you get closer to town.

SPECIAL EVENTS Occasional sound and light show, but does not operate regularly.

ITINERATOR!

DAYS/HOURS Daily 08.00–16.00 November–March, 08.00–17.30 April–May, 08.00–18.30 June–October, 08.00–15.30 Ramadan.

TIME COMMITMENT Two hours to give the site its worth, though can be rushed through in an hour or less if you stay only on the top level and ignore the museums; 3–4 hours if you're really into exploring. Speed rules apply.

BASE Road-trip along **King's Highway (#31)**, staying in Dana (70km/1¼ hours). If Karak town is where you end up, there are budget places to sleep in town.

BEST STRATEGY Most people who visit **Petra (#2)** and the **Dead Sea (#3)** or **Amman (#36/#37)** will need to pass through Karak on their journey, so we recommend you use this stop to stretch your legs.

WALKS AND DRIVES O1, V1, V2, W4.

ITINERARIES Archaeology; National Parks/Reserves; Cinematic.

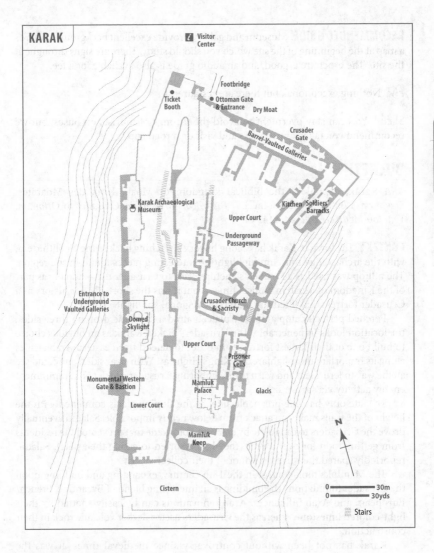

KARAK

Visitor Center

Footbridge

Ticket Booth

Ottoman Gate & Entrance

Dry Moat

Crusader Gate

Barrel-Vaulted Galleries

Karak Archaeological Museum

Upper Court

Underground Passageway

Kitchen

Soldiers' Barracks

Entrance to Underground Vaulted Galleries

Domed Skylight

Crusader Church & Sacristy

Upper Court

Prisoner Cells

Monumental Western Gate & Bastion

Mamluk Palace

Glacis

Lower Court

Mamluk Keep

N

Cistern

0 — 30m
0 — 30yds

Stairs

ARRIVAL PREP

PREBOOK Not necessary.

REALITY CHECK Acrophobics beware – the castle sits atop a sheer cliff. Site of an ISIS terrorist incident in 2016, though this seems to have been random.

ACCESS There are three approaches – from the <u>Dead Sea Highway (P1)</u>, from **King's Highway (#31)** to the south, and King's Highway from the north, all cutting through town. The castle is huge. Plus there are signs, so you'll find it. Tickets at the entry gate. Don't arrive towards the end of the day or you risk being turned away. Don't forget to ask for permission to see the lower levels.

ADMISSION 2 JD, or free with Jordan Pass.

RECOMMENDED GUIDE Museum and gallery provide excellent background. There's a map at the beginning of the site which you should study. There are signs throughout the site. The brochure is good, and an audio guide is also available for a fee.

EAT Nothing exceptional, but there are restaurants.

SLEEP You can stay overnight to avoid the throngs of tourists on buses, but we recommend you take your chances and visit on a road trip.

BUCKET!PEDIA

AKA Karak, capital of the biblical kingdom of Moab; Krak des Moabites. *Elevation* 1,000m above sea level. *Historical era Islamic: Crusader to Ottoman. Year founded/constructed* 1142 CE.

CONTEXT The town of Karak has a long history stretching back to the Neolithic era, with the archaeology museum highlighting interesting pieces found in the region. The hilltop was used as a fortified structure prior to Crusader use – notably as part of the Kingdom of Moab in biblical times – but it was the short 47-year history as a Crusader fortress that lifted Karak into the regional spotlight.

Perched perfectly atop a unitary plateau amid a dramatic drop on three sides, the location looks impenetrable. The Crusaders picked Karak as an obvious choice to build one of their largest fortresses in order to defend from eastern Arab armies along its important thoroughfare, the King's Highway. With clear skies, one could see all the way to Jerusalem and warn the neighboring Crusader district of any imminent enemy activity via smoke signal.

The site only has one pregnable side, as the sloping glacis combined with the height of the walls makes an attack from below nearly impossible. Saladin eventually drove the Crusaders to capitulate by creating a blockade that prevented the residents from getting food for over a year (they had resorted to eating their pets). Saladin reportedly spared their lives in honor of their collective grit.

The Mamluks took control in the 13th century, expanding and building upon the Crusader foundation. The building is an interesting blend of Byzantine, French/European, and Arab influences. Arab renovations can be easily spotted by their light-colored limestone, whereas the Crusaders used a darker volcanic rock in their construction.

Karak has not been without controversy since medieval times. It was the epicenter of Jordan's bread riots in 1996, and became the unexpected site of an ISIS terrorist attack in 2016.

CHRONOLOGY

1142 CE: Crusaders construct Karak Castle.
1183: Saladin attacks Karak, but is persuaded to cease hostilities until a wedding within the walls has taken place.
1184: Niceties over, Saladin attacks again, but Karak is saved by forces from Jerusalem.
1187: Saladin defeats Crusaders at the Battle of Hattin, severely depleting Crusader resources.
1188: Third siege takes more than a year and ends with surrender by castle inhabitants.
1263: Mamluks expand the site.
1840: Son of Muhammad Ali (the Governor of Egypt and Transjordan) destroys much of the castle, as locals were using it as a safe haven against his government.

1893: Castle used by Ottomans to house a local military garrison.
1996: Bread riots.
2016: ISIS attack kills three tourists.

WEBSITE w international.visitjordan.com/Wheretogo/Kerak.aspx.

WHERE TO NEXT?

THEMATIC *Noteworthy* Exploration. *Religion* Christianity. *Archaeology* Prehistory; Crusader; Impressive Structural Remains.

COMPLEMENTARY More Jordan castles: *Road Trips W1: Umayyad Castles* and *W4: Crusader Castles*. More great Crusader cities: **Old City Jerusalem (#1)**, **Akko (#13)** (best option), and **Caesarea (#25)**.

NEARBY **Wadi Mujib and Mujib Biosphere Reserve (#23)** (90km/1¼ hours), **Madaba and the Madaba Map (#19)** (113km/1½ hours), **Dana Biosphere Reserve (#21)** (135km/ 2 hours), **Shobak** (150km/1¾ hours), **Petra (#2)** (179km/2¼ hours), and **Wadi Rum (#4)** (260km/3 hours).

#50 Ein Gedi

BROCHURE

RATINGS		MACRO-REGION
BUCKET! Score	6/10	K: Dead Sea (Israel)
Ruin	1/5	
Entertainment	3/5	**MICRO-REGION**
Information	3/5	K1
Popularity	4/5	

PRIMARY THEME/CATEGORY Active – Hikes – Easy Hikes and Trails.

TOP Largest and best nature reserve in Israel.

COMMENDATIONS Israel Nature Reserve.

HOLY LAND RELEVANCE Ein Gedi is referenced multiple times in the Bible, including being described as the place where David hid when Saul's forces pursued him. Also inspired the writer of the Bible's Song of Songs.

ELECT ME! This oasis in the middle of the Judean Desert is host to two rivers – the Nahal Arugot and the Nahal David – as well as an ancient synagogue. An array of animals, flora, hikes, archaeological sites, and water features can be found here. Many visit for its proximity to the **Dead Sea (#3)**. If you want something a little more active to go along with a trip to the Dead Sea (and you don't feel like hiking up the cliffside at **Masada (#8)**) this is the place for you.

WORTH THE DETOUR? If you're hankering for a hike, this will scratch the itch. Popular with Israelis, but not an essential stop for foreigners unless your goal is hiking, in which case the long hike to the top of the desert plateau provides unmatched views of the desert and Dead Sea.

EXPERIENCES

CAN'T MISS The trail to David's Waterfall is suitable for most hikers, and the crowds prove the point.

ANIMALS Nubian Ibex (wild goat); Rock/Syrian Hyrax; Tristram's Grackle. Nighttime only: foxes, wolves, hyenas, Spotted Leopard (likely extinct).

PLANTS Acacia tree; Christthorn; Egyptian Balsam (perfume was made from this plant in antiquity); Giant Reed and Cattail; Maidenhair Fern; Moringa; Sodom Apple. Kibbutz Ein Gedi's Botanical Gardens contain 900 plants and over 1,000 species of cactus.

WALKING PATHS The **Lower David Stream** (well defined, easy, 1 hour) passes waterfall and pools, and leads to David Waterfall. The **Upper David Trail** (well defined, hard, 3–4 hours) passes Shulamit Spring, Dodim Cave at the top of the David Waterfall, and the Ein Gedi Spring. The **Tsafit Trail or Dry Canyon Trail** (hard, well defined, 4–6 hours) passes the Window Waterfall (without water), Ein Gedi Spring, and the lower David Spring. **Wadi Arugot** (off beaten path, medium, 2–4 hours depending on short or long track), goes to Hidden Waterfall or upper pools. **Field School to Mount Yishai** (very hard, 8 hours) goeas to Ein Gedi lookout via Ein Gedi Ascent to the lower David Stream Reserve. **Tel Goren to Wadi Arugot** (very hard, 7 hours) takes you down the Bone Hamoshavim Ascent ("extremely difficult"). The **Zeruiah Ascent** (very hard, 8 hours) goes from kibbutz Ein Gedi at the desert plateau to the top of the Essenes Ascent.

ANCIENT SETTLEMENTS There's a **Chalcolithic temple** (3000 BCE) near Shulammit's Spring; **Tel Goren** (7th century BCE) is an Ancient Israelite settlement; a **Roman-era synagogue with mosaic** (3rd century CE) is just off Highway 90 near the entrance; and a **Mamluk flour mill** (14th century CE) is next to Ein Gedi Spring.

SECRET Starting times are strict! You must begin any difficult trails by 08.00–09.00 (depending on the trail) and be registered at the visitor center. The medium-difficulty trails need to commence before noon. The easier hikes have a starting time of 15.00–15.30. All times one hour later during daylight savings.

SPECIAL EVENTS The **Shalom Marathon: Dead Sea Half Marathon**, aka the Ein Gedi Race, begins at the Ein Gedi Spa, 4km to the southeast. The **Ein Gedi Botanical Gardens** has a Night Tour (advance booking required; see **w** botanic-eingedi.co.il/en/botanic-garden-tours/ for dates).

ITINERATOR!

DAYS/HOURS Summer 08.00–17.00, winter 08.00–16.00, Fridays closes one hour earlier, holiday eves closes at 13.00. Wadi Arugot must be entered before 14.00. Reserve closes one hour before closing time.

BEST TIME Spring, winter, fall – the summer can be dangerously hot.

TIME COMMITMENT Minimum 2 hours to enter, visit the ancient synagogue, and do the hike to David Waterfall. Add any additional time based on your preferred hike. Speed rules apply. However, on the long hikes, fast hikers won't be able to shave the times in half, exactly.

BASE We recommend a road trip from Jerusalem (80km/1¼ hours). If you do want to stay the night and see more of the Dead Sea over a few days, there are hotels in **Ein Bokek** (30km/25 minutes).

BEST STRATEGY You have two options. You can spend an entire day in Ein Gedi, road-tripping from Jerusalem or Tel Aviv (early), incorporating a long hike and majestic views. Or you can do one of the easier hikes and add this into your Dead Sea day.

WALKS AND DRIVES K1, U2.

ITINERARIES Nature and Scenic; Active; National Parks/Reserves; On the Road; Romantic.

ARRIVAL PREP

PREBOOK Mostly no, but call ahead if you are worried about weather (sun/rain) when parts of the park close.

REALITY CHECK If there is a possibility of rain, floods can be quick and deadly. There's no food in the park. Bring a liter of water for every hour that you're hiking.

BRING Sun protection, lots of water, hiking shoes, binoculars.

ACCESS There's a main entrance right off the highway, and then two directions to get to the two different streams in the park, David and Arugot.

ADMISSION 28 ILS adult, 14 ILS child. Discount for seniors, groups of more than 30, and those wishing to visit only the synagogue.

RECOMMENDED GUIDE Make sure you take a map from the entrance. The easier walks are well signposted. Check with the rangers before you take off on one of the harder hikes. *Day Tour Ein Gedi* has good background and information on flora/fauna in the Ein Gedi region. If you want a complete guide just to Ein Gedi, check out *Hanan Eshel's Ein Gedi – Oasis and Refuge* for history, biology, and recommended walking trails.

EAT Note that eateries in this area are scarce. The spas and hotels have mediocre to bad restaurants. Also important to note: food is forbidden in Ein Gedi, so you have to eat *before* you start your hike.

SLEEP There is an international youth hostel and the Kibbutz Ein Gedi Hotel.

BUCKET!PEDIA

AKA Hebrew translation is "Spring of the Baby Goat/Kid"; biblically Hazazon Tamar. *Size* 14,350 dunams, or 14km². *Elevation* Base at c400m below sea level/ desert plateau at top of the fault escarpment c200m above sea level. *Historical era* Prehistoric: Chalcolithic to *Islamic: Mamluk*. *Year founded* 7th century BCE.

CONTEXT Ein Gedi has a sprinkling of archaeological sites related to its varied historical components, but the real draw here are the Judaean Desert hikes. Israelis love this park, though it does gets a fair share of tourists. The hike to David Waterfall is suitable for all ages and can get quite busy. The rush of water is quite surprising given the sheer lack of a water source anywhere in the region. This produces a green scene with a bit of canopy cover and even some wildlife sightings.

There are further scrambles up to the top of the mountain that will weed out the kids and the tour-bus types. Truthfully, you can make it to the top of the mountain without the strenuous 3–4-hour climb. As you leave the David Waterfall path (it's one-way), you'll see a sign leading you up a mountain, stating "for fit hikers" – which is true – but if you can manage a climb just to the top of the stairs (no small feat), then you will have a great panoramic view of the Dead Sea. You can continue to the springs and cave, or head back if you're short on time.

For those interested in longer hikes, you have plenty to choose from. There are 6–8-hour trips that will leave even fit hikers breathless, but the view of the Dead Sea from the desert plateau above will surely be worth the effort.

CHRONOLOGY

5000 BCE: Chalcolithic period temple on site attracts ancient religious pilgrims.
1000 BCE: David finds refuge in Ein Gedi when fleeing from King Saul's forces.
7th century BCE: Israelite settlement whose residents used irrigation for farming to grow dates and persimmon.
586 BCE: Destroyed by Babylonians.
2nd century BCE: New Jewish settlement built during Hasmonean period.
68 CE: Village destroyed following Jewish Revolt, before sacking of Masada, just south.
1st century: Members of the Essene sect of ascetic monks make Ein Gedi home.
3rd century: Ein Gedi rebuilt, synagogue built.
550: Village destroyed by fire and abandoned.
13th–14th centuries: Small village established near flour mill, but abandoned after short period.
1953: First permanent settlement in 600 years.
1956: Kibbutz established.
1959: Field school erected.
1971: Designated a nature reserve.

WEBSITE w parks.org.il/en/reserve-park/en-gedi-nature-reserve/.

WHERE TO NEXT?

THEMATIC *Noteworthy* Nature Reserves. *Religion* Old Testament. *Archaeology* Prehistory; Iron Age; Mosaics; Active Excavations. *Nature* Rivers, Lakes and Waterfalls; Mountains and Mounts; Forests and Green Parks. *People* Jewish. *Active* Easy Hikes and Trails; Day Hikes; Experienced Hikers. *Accommodation* Campgrounds.

COMPLEMENTARY Other great day hikes: **Petra (#2)**, **Dana Biosphere Reserve (#21)**, **Wadi Mujib and Mujib Biosphere Reserve (#23)**, **Makhtesh Ramon (#28)**, and **Ajloun Forest (#57)**. Other popular nature reserves: **Banias (#80)**, **Dor HaBonim (#100)**, *Gamla*, *Hula Lake*, and *Yehudiya*.

NEARBY **Masada (#8)** (20km/20 minutes), ***Ein Bokek Spa Hotels*** (30km/25 minutes), **Qumran (#70)** (35km/30 minutes), **Old City Jerusalem (#1)** (80km/90 minutes), and **Tel Aviv (#5)** (140km/2 hours).

#51 Israeli Cuisine

RATINGS			MACRO-REGION
BUCKET! Score		7/10	U: Cross-Israel/Palestine
Ruin	n/a		
Entertainment		4/5	
Information		3/5	
Popularity		5/5	

THEME/CATEGORY Food and Drink – Food – Cuisine.

HISTORICAL PERIOD *Contemporary.*

ELECT ME Israeli food is becoming a worldwide phenomenon. Drawing international notoriety with popular cookbooks such as *Jerusalem* and *Plenty*, Yotam Ottolenghi and Sami Tamimi brought Israeli-Palestinian-inspired food to kitchens around the world. Israeli chef Eyal Shani introduced the **Miznon** chain of Israeli street food into five global markets. With other famed Israeli chefs making inroads in markets from London, Paris, and New York to New Orleans, Philadelphia, Portland, and Atlanta, it's likely that you're already familiar with the cuisine. So why not taste it at its source?

Your foray into the cuisine can (and should!) include street food, restaurants, market goods, ingredients, bites, brunches, drinks, and special-occasion food. So important is food to your experience that we have written a whole section about it: *Do #14: Eat It!* (p. 80). There, you'll find food information based on cuisine, time of day, budget, and other metrics. Additionally, we go over all of the best food-related electives in the *Food and Drink* themes (p. 561).

CONTEXT From antiquity, the staples of the local diet have matched the climate and geology, and have consistently featured olive oil, bread, wine, legumes, cooked grains, fruits, and vegetables playing a central role, with eggs, dairy, fish, birds, and game showing up on special occasions, when available, or when in season. In fact, this diet is very similar to the modern Mediterranean cuisine and diet. The temperature in Israel is hot, so many of the fruits, vegetables, wine, and herbs that have become part of the farming culture in the past 100 years were selected for thriving in this hot climate. Many of the ingredients are local, seasonal, fresh, and delicious, and thus very little needs to be imported.

Influences on Israeli cuisine vary as much as the origins of the inhabitants of the state of Israel. Starting in the 1880s, waves of Jewish immigrants began to arrive in

Israel, first from Eastern Europe and then from all over the world, in order to build farming cooperatives, aka kibbutzim and moshavim. Since World War II, Israelis have come from more than 100 countries to settle in Israel and with them have brought a variety of food traditions. Naturally, there are Jewish styles of cooking that are usually found in the home, including recipes of Ashkenazi, Mizrahi, and Sephardic Jewish tradition. Much of the street food can be seen as paralleling several regional Middle Eastern, Mediterranean, and Levantine cuisines – think falafel, shawarma, and pita. Arab influence on Israeli cuisine has been there hundreds, if not thousands, of years.

In recent times, the cuisine has become considerably more international, modern, upscale (but still casual), and noteworthy. Today, you can find just about any global cuisine, from American hamburgers to Yemeni zhug. The restaurant scene is abuzz with new chefs cooking a "modern Israeli cuisine," a trend finding its way around the world.

WORTH THE DETOUR? Food is automatically going to be a part of your journey, so we'll doubly encourage you to make it a highlight. It's worth it! Sure, you can walk around eating falafel from street vendors and try your hand at any of the hundreds of restaurants available to you – and it will be delicious! But to get a true taste of Israel, you'll want to do some research in *Do #14: Eat It!* (p. 80).

BEST STRATEGY If you're spending a good amount of time in Tel Aviv, we recommend *City Walk D6*, which offers a DIY approach to creating a food itinerary. You can break it up over several days or define your whole trip with this style of food-first planning.

Otherwise, if you're working from a piecemeal (so to speak) strategy, you can pick what works to your palate/budget. Street food is meant to be quick and cheap (you might argue the latter point) and there are no shortage of options, from the ubiquitous falafel and shawarma to sabich and bourekas. Much of your sampling can be done in markets, with **Carmel Market (#87)** being the most famous. There you can also pick up spices for gifts, cheese and veg for picnics, and other local specialties. Arrange a cooking class to get to know some recipes intimately.

And don't forget to make restaurant reservations! Israel (Tel Aviv specifically) is home to 13 of the world's best restaurants, according to *La Liste*'s annual rankings (w laliste.com/en/laliste/world). Most require a reservation made at least a few days in advance (try the restaurant website, otherwise call). Trendier places will generally incorporate unique but local ingredients, a global cooking foundation, myriad influences, and a signature Israeli style. You won't want to miss out.

WALKS AND DRIVES D6.

ITINERARIES High BUCKET! Scores: 7+; Most Entertaining; Food and Drink; Shoestring.

SIMILAR ELECTIVES **Jordanian Cuisine (#44)**, **Machneyuda (#98)**, **Carmel Market (#87)**, and **Mehane Yehuda Market (#67)**.

#52 Jordan Trail

RATINGS		MACRO-REGION
BUCKET! Score	5/10	V: Cross-Jordan
Ruin	1/5	
Entertainment	2/5	
Information	1/5	
Popularity	1/5	

THEME/CATEGORY Active – Hikes – Long Walks.

HISTORICAL PERIOD *Contemporary*, but the sites span millennia.

ELECT ME If you're interested in hiking, there are few places that feel as uncharted as this new trail. Opened in 2017, it takes about 40 days to complete and passes through some 52 local villages over 650km, bringing tourism to rural communities throughout the country and introducing travelers to the famous hospitality of the Jordanian people. You needn't complete the whole thing nor walk alone; there are a number of options through a handful of tour operator who carry your luggage and organize your food and village accommodations. Along the way, you'll see some of Jordan's iconic sites, starting in **Umm Qais (#45)** and continuing through Ajloun, Salt, **Wadi Mujib and Mujib Biosphere Reserve (#23)**, **Karak (#49)**, **Dana Biosphere Reserve (#21)**, *Little Petra*, (big) **Petra (#2)**, **Wadi Rum (#4)**, and **Aqaba (#43)**. Though Jordan contains a number of biblical sites, this walk does not pass through the majority of them. Of note, though: new routes are being assessed annually.

CONTEXT Jordan has been criss-crossed over the millennia by travelers, merchants, religious worshipers, militaries, and foreign powers. Many of those wanderings have been on foot. **King's Highway (#31)** was a historic route leading from Syria in the north to the Red Sea in the south. The Nabataeans made use of the **Incense Route (#73)** by creating way stations in the desert to support travelers working their way west towards the Mediterranean. With the advent of adventure tourism, Jordan set out to marry its own history with the desire of people to see the otherworldly landscape of this glorious country.

Website **w** jordantrail.org. *Weather* Winter is cool/cold, with rare snow. February to April afford the ability to see Jordanian Wildflowers (S2). September to November is also good weather; June to September is too hot. *Time of year* Map to the weather, but be careful walking during Ramadan, which will limit the availability of supplies along the trail. *Packing* The Jordan Trail website provides a comprehensive packing list, with nods to dressing modestly, not using wood fires, and wearing non-cotton clothing due to the heat. *Route* The trip runs from **Umm Qais (#45)** in the north along the western side of the country south to **Aqaba (#43)**. *Day trips* Can be done on any of the sections. *Starting point* You can begin the trek where you like. If you join a group, it will provide location start information, and should provide transport from the airport. *Guides* Not required, but will surely add to the experience. The website lists a number of guides, escorts, and service providers, as well as languages spoken. *Prices* None, per se. The Bedouin experiences may require setup through a guide, including meals, which can cost $150–300 per person per day, all inclusive. Tour operators are still working these details out. *Fitness level* There are flat sections, but the vast majority requires good fitness to be outside in the heat, hiking in difficult terrain which includes steep climbs, scrambling, and elevation changes.   *Water* Is available in almost every day stop, but it's the desert, so you should plan to carry/drink 4–5 liters per day. *Maps* Boundary and elevation maps are available on the website in PDF, Google, GPS/GPX, and JPG. Not all sections are well marked, so solo hikers should bring GPS.

WORTH THE DETOUR? If you are interested in a long-distance hike that hits Jordan's highlights, this is for you.

BEST STRATEGY If you're short on time and have at least $150/day to spend on travel, you can get the best of all worlds: several days of hiking and camping, including Bedouin experiences, some meals, visits to **Petra (#2)** and **Wadi Rum (#4)**, hotels when you need them, a stay at **Feynan Ecolodge (#86)**, camel riding, and more. Plus, the tour company will organize luggage transport, which will make all the difference. Seek out Discover Jordan or Experience Jordan Adventures, both recommended by the Jordan Trail Association and TripAdvisor commenters.

Or, preferred: DIY your trip and save tons. We've got a *Best of Jordan* itinerary (p. 763) that might be up your alley if you want something semi-homemade.

ITINERARIES Shoestring.

SIMILAR ELECTIVES *Israel National Trail* and **Jesus Trail (#69)**.

#53 Ras Mohammad

	RATINGS	
BUCKET! Score		7/10
Ruin	n/a	
Entertainment		5/5
Information		2/5
Popularity		2/5

MACRO-REGION T: Sinai

MICRO-REGION T1

THEME/CATEGORY Active – Water Sports – Diving.

HISTORICAL PERIOD N/A.

ELECT ME This site is considered by some to be the best diving spot in the world. The coral reef ecosystem is diverse, with hundreds of species of coral, more than 1,000 fish species, various other sea creatures, and spectacular wrecks.

CONTEXT The Prophet Muhammad may have passed through here 1,400 years ago. A jagged cliff with the features of a face are said to resemble Muhammad, giving the place its name, the "Head of Muhammad" (Ras Mohammad). The site became Egypt's first declared natural protected area in 1983, became a National Park in 1986, and was awarded Green List status for sound management of marine ecosystems by the International Union for Conservation of Nature.

Region Encompasses 850km² and includes the islands of Sanafir and Tyran. *Climate* Average daily temperature of 18°C/64°F during winter months and 33°C/91°F during the summer months. Rain is rare, but usually falls only in winter. *Water temperatures* August is the warmest month at 29°C/84°F, but even the cooler months of February and March are not bad at 23°C/73°F. *Coral reef* More than 200 different species of coral, including more than 100 soft corals. *Big fish* Tuna, black tip shark, white tip shark, hammerheads, Napoleon wrasse, barracuda, grouper, whale sharks. *Marine animals* Rays, eels, turtles, dolphins. *Marine plants* Coral, mangroves. *Shipwrecks* Most shipwrecks will need to be visited on a day trip via boat, leaving early in the morning (3–4 hours away). The World War II-era SS *Thistlegorm* is touted as being the best shipwreck in the world, with a variety of artifacts to see underwater, including motorcycles, army trucks, tanks, and guns. Abu Nuhas is also a highly rated site with four wrecks in shallow water. *Diving* There's a variety of diving, including shallow, deep, and drift options. There are several spots from which to choose, depending on skill level and interest. Shark Reef, Yolanda Reef, Shark Observatory, Ras Ghozlani, and Anemone City are all popular and near one another. *Snorkeling* There are plenty of kid-friendly places to visit, including Jackfish Alley and Anemone City, which have less intimidating marine species and smaller but diverse and colorful reef fish.

WORTH THE DETOUR? For divers, absolutely. Aqaba is of course the easier option, and is adequate for most needs, but Ras Mohammad is among the world's best dive sites.

DAYS/HOURS 07.00–16.00 daily.

BEST STRATEGY The easiest access is by flying to **Sharm el-Sheikh (#88)** and hiring a boat from your hotel. There are other outfitters in town, but they more or less offer the same services. If you have a specific site you want to see, speak up, but Yolanda and Shark Reef tend to be the busiest and most respected. These trips will take all day.

WALKS/DRIVES T1.

ITINERARIES High BUCKET! Scores: 7+; Most Entertaining; Noteworthy; Nature and Scenic; Active.

SIMILAR ELECTIVES **Red Sea/Gulf of Aqaba (#10)**, **Aqaba (#43)**, and **Eilat (#78)**.

NEARBY **Sharm el-Sheikh (#88)** (36km/40 minutes).

#54 Dahab

RATINGS

BUCKET! Score		7/10
Ruin	n/a	
Entertainment		3/5
Information		1/5
Popularity		2/5

MACRO-REGION
T: Sinai

MICRO-REGION
T1

THEME/CATEGORY Leisure – Beaches – Remote Beaches.

HISTORICAL PERIOD *Contemporary.*

ELECT ME A gorgeous desert oasis on the bottom half of the eastern Sinai peninsula, where on clear mornings you can see Saudi Arabia and snorkel out on the extended shoreline. Excellent diving options abound on the nearby coral walls. Possibly the world's most dangerous diving spot, the Blue Hole, is also near. Windsurfing is popular as the water is flat and it's easy to learn. Many tour companies coordinate visits to **Mount Sinai (#15)/St. Catherine's Monastery (#22)** from here. Bedouins will take you on a jeep tour through the desert. Kitesurfing is an option too (best in September and October). Dirt-cheap sleeping options exist – literally a mattress on the sand for less than a dollar a night. If this "charm" is not for you, there are plenty of upscale hotels as well. The Sinai region is considered dangerous for tourists – read travel warnings.

CONTEXT Dahab has long been a fishing village. The Sinai was occupied by Israel after the Six-Day War, which Egypt lost, and Israel held onto it through 1982. At that time, Israelis visited Dahab in droves, and it began to grow as a tourist destination. In the 1990s, adventure tourists began to come and the town grew. It's become more and more popular since then, with a population today of around 15,000, roughly 14,500 more than a few decades ago.

WORTH THE DETOUR? Dahab is out of the way and doesn't work well for people on fixed schedules, unless you're staying in a resort. This place caters to spontaneity, relaxing, and doing whatever feels right that day. If you've got several days to chill, you will not be disappointed.

BEST STRATEGY Flying to **Sharm el-Sheikh (#88)** is easiest, then taking a bus or taxi. If you want to avoid hassle, either fix the taxi in advance or decide now on which bus to take based on your arrival schedule. Bargaining can be a hassle. Otherwise, if you want to taxi from **Taba (T1)** (140km/2½ hours), it'll cost about 1,000 EGP, plus Egypt visa/ entry fee. The whole point of Dahab is to relax, so plan to spend at least a few nights. For each of the following activities that interest you, add a day: windsurfing/kitesurfing; diving; **Mount Sinai (#15)**; desert hiking and/or camel riding; snorkeling or beach.

WALKS AND DRIVES T1.

ITINERARIES High BUCKET! Scores: 7+; Noteworthy; Society and People; Active; Leisure; Under the Sun; Shoestring.

SIMILAR ELECTIVES **Sharm el-Sheikh (#88)** is more upscale.

NEARBY __Sharm el-Sheikh (#88)__ (90km/1 hour), Nuweiba Beach Camps (T1) (70km/1 hour), and Blue Hole (8km/25 minutes).

#55 Azraq Wetlands

RATINGS			MACRO-REGION
BUCKET! Score		4/10	R: East Jordan
Ruin	n/a		
Entertainment		2/5	**MICRO-REGION**
Information		2/5	R1
Popularity		1/5	

THEME/CATEGORY Nature – Life – Birding.

HISTORICAL PERIOD *Contemporary.*

ELECT ME This wetland reserve has a 1.5km self-guided trail extending over wet and dry land, from which you can spot fish, some water buffalo, and most importantly birds – this is an Important Bird Area, though its bird numbers have plummeted over the past half-century. At the park, there are a number of hides allowing you to watch without being too intrusive. The rangers are enthusiastic and offer a longer walk at 3.5km to visit buffalo and birds. There are also a few bike trails.

CONTEXT The story of this wetland is tragic, actually. Decades ago, and for millennia before that, this area was a vast collection of pools and marshland, with a wide variety of native animals and so many migrating birds that they had been known to black out the sky. Unfortunately, the fresh water began to be tapped for irrigation and pumped for use in Amman and other cities in the 1980s and 1990s, rapidly and drastically dropping the natural level of the water beyond its ability to replenish. According to the RSCN, the current water levels are 0.04% of their previous size – a shocking statistic. Illegal pumping and a lack of experience are quoted as reasons behind the failure in achieving even a 10% rise in water levels from the lowest period in 1993, when no surface water remained. Much of the present water is pumped back in, rather than coming from natural sources. The types and counts of birds have also diminished, given the lack of water, and have largely rerouted through Israel. Sadly, this is a natural site in peril.

WORTH THE DETOUR? If you are into birding, you might find it worth your while in the spring or autumn, when birds are migrating through. Keep in mind that many of the migratory bird routes have shifted to *Hula Lake* in Israel with the disappearance of Azraq. Plop it in if you're doing our drive through the region. It's a good weekend respite from Amman. But otherwise, not necessary.

DAYS/HOURS 09.00–16.00 daily.

BEST STRATEGY If you're coming this way, plan to add in the other local sites, including **Qasr Amra and the Desert Palaces (#20)** and *Shaumari* wildlife reserve (across the street). Two hours max, but as little as 30 minutes needed.

WALKS AND DRIVES R1, V1.

ITINERARIES Off-the-Beaten-Path Jordan; Nature and Scenic; National Parks/ Reserves.

SIMILAR ELECTIVES This is the only wetland reserve, but Jordan has a number of other nature reserves. See *Road Trip V1* or the *Nature Reserves* category (p. 484).

NEARBY *Qasr Azraq* (5km/8 minutes), **Qasr Amra and the Desert Palaces (#20)** (25km/ 20 minutes), and *Shaumari* (drive around the air base (confusing) for 30km/25 minutes).

#56 Tsipori

RATINGS			MACRO-REGION
BUCKET! Score		5/10	G: Lower Galilee & Kinneret
Ruin		4/5	
Entertainment		2/5	**MICRO-REGION**
Information		2/5	G2
Popularity		2/5	

THEME/CATEGORY Archaeology – Roman – Judea.

HISTORICAL PERIOD *Greek* and *Hasmonean* to *Byzantine*.

ELECT ME This Israel National Park and archaeological park prides itself on its "Mona Lisa of the Galilee," a Byzantine mosaic in the Dionysus House on site, and one of more than 40 mosaics in the park. Tsipori is thought to be the birthplace of Mary, the mother of Jesus, as well as several famous rabbis, including Rabbi Judah Hanassi, who first codified the Jewish Mishnah here.

NAMES Several. Zippori and Sepphoris are the two names attributed to the city from the Roman and Byzantine periods, though it was briefly Diocaesaraea and Autocratoris. The Crusaders called the town Le Saforie and the later Arab village was called Saffuriya.

CONTEXT A site not referenced in the Bible, it was nevertheless an important place during that same period, serving as the administrative capital of the Galilee and a spiritual city for Jews during the Jewish King/Hasmonean period. Upon Roman conquest in 63 BCE, the already bustling town experienced renewed growth. Visit the Roman theater, dating to the 1st century CE under Herod Antipas (son of King Herod), which seated 4,500 and is today used occasionally for concerts. Interestingly, the town's residents did not rebel against the Romans during the Jewish Revolts, sparing their town from destruction. Jews from Judea traveled north following their banishment, beginning a new age of Jewish spiritualism. An excavated residential area dates to this period. For a short time in the 3rd century, the Sanhedrin too were located in Tzipori, before moving to *Tiberias* – long enough to draft one of the major works of Jewish oral tradition, the Mishnah. In the Byzantine period, the Christian community moved in, creating a multi-ethnic and ostensibly tolerant town. There was a certain synergy in creativity, as evidenced by a 5th-century synagogue with elaborate floor mosaics in similar styles to others found around town. In fact, the mosaics cover multiple periods: gods and goddesses, Hebrew and Aramaic text, Christian symbols, pagan revelry, a zodiac, and the Binding of Isaac. The Crusaders took over in the 12th century, using Tsipori to stage for the Battle of Hitting in 1187, a monumental battle of Crusader vs. Ayyubid armies, with the latter victorious. St. Anne's Church, commemorating the birth of the Virgin Mary's mother, was built during the Crusader period.

WORTH THE DETOUR? Mosaics are an important art form from the Roman and Byzantine era, and these are among the most complete, attractive, and numerous you can get at one site. If you go to Jordan, there are other more important sites at **Madaba (#19)** and **Umm ar-Rasas (#81)**, but, if you're staying in Israel and doing a trip to the north, it's worth a visit.

DAYS/HOURS 08.00–16.00 daily, closes 17.00 Saturday–Thursday in summer.

BEST STRATEGY Account for 1–2 hours to get through this site. Tsipori is near several other sites – notably **Nazareth (#29)** – and can be combined with several stops over one busy day.

WALKS AND DRIVES G2, U2, W4.

ITINERARIES Off-the-Beaten-Path Israel and Palestine; Archaeology; National Parks/Reserves.

SIMILAR ELECTIVES *Korazim*, **Beit She'an (#39)**, and **Belvoir (#93)** for Roman/Crusader ruins in the area; **Madaba (#19)** and **Umm ar-Rasas (#81)** for mosaics.

NEARBY **Nazareth (#29)** (11km/20 minutes), **Beit She'arim (#79)** (20km/20 minutes), and **Megiddo (#59)** (38km/30 minutes).

#57 Ajloun Forest

	RATINGS	
BUCKET! Score	▬▬▬▬▬▬▬	5/10
Ruin	n/a	
Entertainment	▬▬▬▬▬	2/5
Information	▬▬▬▬▬	2/5
Popularity	▬▬▬▬▬	2/5

MACRO-REGION
S: North Jordan

MICRO-REGION
S2

THEME/CATEGORY Active – Hikes – Day Hikes.

HISTORICAL PERIOD N/A.

ELECT ME Ajloun Forest Reserve offers a number of short and longer walking trails with opportunities to visit archaeological ruins, **Ajloun Fortress (#76)**, local communities (including a soap makers' guild), while passing interesting trees (pistachio! strawberry!), likely birds (it's an "Important Bird Area") and possibly animals (there is a breeding program for the locally extinct roe deer).

CONTEXT The Ajloun Forest Reserve was established by Jordan's ***Royal Society for the Conservation of Nature (RSCN)*** in 1987. At 13km² it's not huge, but the majority of the country is desert, with less than 1% of the country under tree cover. That makes this area a respite for flora and fauna, particularly since earning reserve status. One of the more successful programs involved reintroducing the roe deer back to its natural habitat after being driven away due to deforestation. There are porcupines, wolves, and foxes, hyenas, and a variety of ground mammals living in the area. See *Best Strategy* below for two self-guided walks. Additionally, RSCN guides can lead longer, full-day hikes of the reserve, visiting villages, the nearby **Ajloun Fortress (#76)**, or *Mar Elias Monastery (C2)* – lunch is usually included.

WORTH THE DETOUR? The hikes here are usually much more temperate than in other parts of the country because of the c1,000m sea-level advantage, bringing in cooler winds. If you're keen on hiking, but not on overheating, this is worth your time.

DAYS/HOURS 08.30–16.00 daily.

BEST STRATEGY If you're embarking on a tour of the northern sites in Jordan, plan to include this reserve, if only for the 1-hour hike before heading to the castle (also 1 hour). Options include visiting in springtime for **wildflowers**, including the Black Iris. If you want to camp, there are 10 **tent sites** available from March to November; the **Roe Deer Trail** (less than an hour, easy, self-guided) has good views and possible animal sightings, and takes you to an ancient wine press. If you have three hours, you can hit the **Soap House Trail**: you'll climb 1,000m, have a gorgeous view, and pass by a local village and purchase handmade soaps, foodstuffs, and silkscreens – all unique.

WALKS AND DRIVES S2, V1.

ITINERARIES Off-the-Beaten-Path Jordan; Nature and Scenic; Active; National Parks/Reserves.

SIMILAR ELECTIVES Other biosphere reserves include **Dana Biosphere Reserve (#21)**, **Wadi Mujib and Mujib Biosphere Reserve (#23)**, and **Wadi Rum (#4)**.

NEARBY **Ajloun Fortress (#76)** (11km/19 minutes), **Amman (#36/#37)** (74km/1½ hours), **Jerash (#14)** (23km/40 minutes), and **Umm Qais (#45)** (57km/1½ hours).

#58 Tsfat/Safed

RATINGS

BUCKET! Score		4/10
Ruin		3/5
Entertainment		3/5
Information		2/5
Popularity		2/5

MACRO-REGION
H: Upper Galilee

MICRO-REGION
H1

THEME/CATEGORY Entertainment – Shopping – Handmade.

HISTORICAL PERIOD *Crusader* to *Contemporary*.

ELECT ME You'll want to visit Safed ("Tsfat" in modern Hebrew) if you're interested in either Kabbalah or contemporary art. The town has a pleasant mix of archaeological sites, artist galleries, and 400-year-old synagogues, all on twisting pedestrian-only streets at the top of Israel's highest and coldest town. Come to buy art, tour the four famous synagogues, pay homage to the Kabbalists at the gravesite, or wander among the ancient Crusader castle ruins on the hilltop.

CONTEXT Tsfat's past goes back as least as far as the Crusaders, who built a fortress at the very top of the hill, now close to where tourists park. Their successors, the Mamluks, built a mosque and mausoleum, both of which survive. It was during Ottoman reign that the city began to grow and change. Following the 1492 expulsion of Jews from Spain, many found their way back to Israel. One famous resident was Rabbi Isaac Luria, who promoted Kabbalah, a form of Judaism that attempts to explain the Torah through mystical interpretations. Two of the famous synagogues – Ashkenazi Ari and Sephardic Ari – are dedicated to him and date to the 16th century. Another, the Caro Synagogue, is from the same period and relates to the author of one of the authoritative texts on Jewish law, the Shulchan Aruch. The oldest is Bana'a Synagogue, from the 15th century. Around 1640, the city became one of Judaism's Four Holy Cities (together with Hebron (C2), *Tiberias*, and Jerusalem), with Tsfat representing the element "air." It's easy to see why, it being the highest city in Israel at 900m. In 1837, an earthquake destroyed much of the town's historic buildings. Several of its ancient synagogues were rebuilt in the same place, but recognize the older foundings. After World War II and the establishment of the state of Israel, the city again began to draw Kabbalah worshippers, many of whom live in the town's artists' quarter. There, and in the alleys around the old city, are a variety of art studios and vendors where you can buy a wide array of hand-crafted gifts and Judaica.

WORTH THE DETOUR? If the terms "Jewish mysticism" or "artists' colony" appeal to you, then you'll likely appreciate this site. It has attractive streets, but is by no means a necessary stop on a short visit to the Holy Land.

BEST STRATEGY If you're passing through, plan for 2 hours, or more if you're into shopping. A walk through the Old Synagogue Quarter is a good idea (closed early Friday and all day Saturday) followed by a visit to the various art galleries. Also ranked highly: the Memorial Museum of Hungarian Speaking Jewry (H1).

WALKS AND DRIVES H1, W4.

ITINERARIES Entertainment; Pilgrimage.

SIMILAR ELECTIVES *Ein Hod* and *Zichron Ya'akov* both offer artist shopping areas.

NEARBY Rosh Pina (H2) (Anchor) (10km/17 minutes), **Nazareth (#29)** (60km/1 hour), **Capernaum and Tabgha (#33)** (23km/26 minutes), *Bar'am* (22km/25 minutes), and *Hula Lake* (40km/45 minutes).

#59 Megiddo

RATINGS		MACRO-REGION
BUCKET! Score	5/10	F: Mount Carmel
Ruin	2/5	& Jezreel Valley
Entertainment	1/5	
Information	1/5	**MICRO-REGION**
Popularity	4/5	F1

THEME/CATEGORY Archaeology – Ancient Cities and Remains – Tels.

HISTORICAL PERIOD *Neolithic* to *Babylonian*.

ELECT ME Besides being synonymous with the end of days and global annihilation, Megiddo – aka biblical Armageddon – is a UNESCO site, Israel National Park, and archaeological mound documenting at least 26 different layers of human history stretching back more than 6,000 years, and possibly even much older. Excavations have been ongoing for over 100 years and there are regularly grand revelations adding to the history of Israel from the period of the Canaanites and Israelites. Budding archaeologists and history buffs will likely find the site fascinating.

NAMES The site was known as Magiddu in its earliest references in the extinct Akkadian and Canaanite languages. In Ancient Hebrew, the city was referenced as Har Megiddo, with *har* meaning "mount." The Greeks referred to it as Ar-Magidd-on, which became Armageddon in modern translations. Thus our Megiddo = the biblical Armageddon.

CONTEXT The Book of Revelation in the New Testament talks of a final battle on Earth where the kings come together at Armageddon (Revelation 16:16). Megiddo had not been inhabited for over 600 years when Revelation was penned, believed to be in the 1st century CE. The importance of the site was perhaps not lost on the author "John," given that settlers called it home and garrison since at least 4500 BCE, and likely as far back as 7000 BCE, accounting for possibly 6,500 years of human habitation. Some 26 layers of settlements have been unearthed from a long swath of history.

The site's most significant remains date from the Chalcolithic period (4500–3300 BCE), showing the importance of the region during the Bronze Age (along with the sister sites of *Tel Hazor* and *Tel Beer Sheva*, the three UNESCO **Biblical Tels (#38)** sites). Megiddo served as the center of cult activity, with a number of

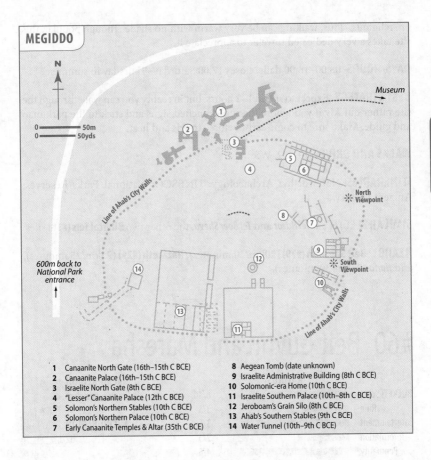

N

0 —— 50m
0 —— 50yds

Line of Ahab's City Walls

*600m back to
National Park
entrance*
↑

Museum

※ **North
Viewpoint**

※ **South
Viewpoint**

Line of Ahab's City Walls

1 Canaanite North Gate (16th–15th C BCE)
2 Canaanite Palace (16th–15th C BCE)
3 Israelite North Gate (8th C BCE)
4 "Lesser" Canaanite Palace (12th C BCE)
5 Solomon's Northern Stables (10th C BCE)
6 Solomon's Northern Palace (10th C BCE)
7 Early Canaanite Temples & Altar (35th C BCE)

8   Aegean Tomb (date unknown)
9   Israelite Administrative Building (8th C BCE)
10 Solomonic-era Home (10th C BCE)
11 Israelite Southern Palace (10th–8th C BCE)
12 Jeroboam's Grain Silo (8th C BCE)
13 Ahab's Southern Stables (9th C BCE)
14 Water Tunnel (10th–9th C BCE)

GOLD ELECTIVES · #59 Megiddo

on-site temples. One such temple, the Megiddo Great Temple, discovered in 2008, dates to the same era as the construction of the pyramids in Egypt and large cities in Mesopotamia, changing the narrative that the Levant was less innovative.

One of the most fascinating realities of Megiddo is that many of these "layers" are settlements, built one on top of the other, indicating that one society would collapse or be defeated by enemy armies, the town would be ransacked, leaving only foundational stones upon which the new denizens would build their town. After generations of habitation, and eventually centuries and millennia, you end up with an unintentional hill made of the remains of all the defeated towns that came before it – and are now buried under the previous. Often, the adjacent pieces of wall and buildings we see buried in the earth are historically anachronistic – foundations of constructions that never existed together, but were compressed to appear so.

WORTH THE DETOUR? This one is tough. The site is fascinating in theory, but in practice and in person the information is dense and difficult to grasp. Most of the visible ruins are no more than a layer of stone in the ground. There are few recreated sites to provide perspective (the entrance gate is one). Many of the 26 layers are marked in the dirt and not represented with excavated structures. This makes it very difficult for a layperson to visualize how the town might have looked at any moment in its history. This is purely an archaeological site, and nothing about it says "spiritual" or "religious." Plus, walking can be very warm with no shade. Though popular, this site takes a very dedicated traveler to appreciate it.

DAYS/HOURS 08.00–16.00 daily, closes 17.00 Saturday–Thursday in summer.

BEST STRATEGY Expect to spend 1–2 hours, but in reality you can walk through the site rather quickly if you ignore the sun-drenched signs and stick to the park map and guide. Make sure to come early, before crowds and heat.

WALKS AND DRIVES F1, U2, W5.

ITINERARIES Noteworthy; Archaeology; UNESCO; National Parks/Reserves; Ancient History.

SIMILAR ELECTIVES *Tel Hazor* and *Tel Beer Sheva*, the other two **Biblical Tels (#38)** sites.

NEARBY **Beit She'arim (#79)** (20km/20 minutes), **Nazareth (#29)** (25km/25 minutes), and *Haifa* (35km/30 minutes).

#60 Beit Guvrin and Maresha

RATINGS		MACRO-REGION
BUCKET! Score	6/10	B: Greater Jerusalem
Ruin	3/5	
Entertainment	3/5	**MICRO-REGION**
Information	2/5	B2
Popularity	4/5	

THEME/CATEGORY Structure – Engineering – Impressive Feats.

HISTORICAL PERIOD *Iron Age* to *Byzantine*.

ELECT ME This dual-city site is a popular stop between Jerusalem and Tel Aviv, and for good reason. For centuries, residents were carving into the soft chalky soil beneath these two sites in order to create a vast network of underground caves. Though people didn't live in the caves, per se, a lot of economic and customary activity occurred there, including religious ceremony, dove raising, and strategic hiding from warring neighbors. There are a number of above-ground portions, but it's the underground bits that bring crowds in droves.

CONTEXT A national park and UNESCO site commemorating the 3,500 man-carved underground rooms used over 2,000 years, beginning in the 8th century BCE, as well as the sister cities that existed above ground. The site began at Tel Maresha, which itself is what remains of the above-ground city that began in the Israelite period, some time perhaps in the 9th century BCE. Maresha is referenced in the Bible as being part of Judah, and in historical record as continuing to wield importance following the fall of the First Temple, when Jews and eventually Greeks moved to town. It was during the latter part of Greek/Hellenistic rule that many of the famous caves were dug, including the Columbarium, a dovecote where doves were raised for their excrement (used as fertilizer), eggs, and meat. You can see the tens of thousands of individual dove niches around "town" in various caves. The city of Maresha was eventually destroyed by Parthians/Iranians in 40 BCE and abandoned. There is little left of Maresha, but the view at the top of Tel Maresha is nice.

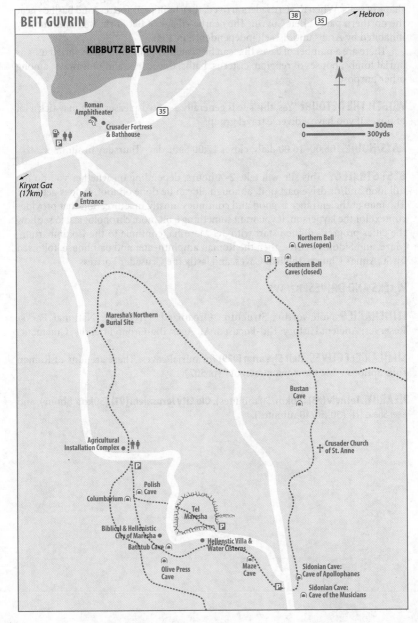

Beit Guvrin, another town nearby, became the most important regional site during the Roman period, as evidenced by the grand monuments built here, including the 3rd-century CE 3,500-seat amphitheater and 4,000m² bathhouse. It also earned the name Eleutheropolis, meaning "city of freed men." The transition from Rome to Byzantium brought more Christian influence in the region, which is when St. Anne's Church was built. The residents continued to quarry stone and marble for centuries, from the Byzantine era through Arab conquest of the region. The technique involved digging a hole and expanding outwards, giving the caves the shape of bells. When the Crusaders arrived, they built their fortress and basilica near the northern part of Beit Guvrin, The nearby village of Bet Jibrin was continuously inhabited by Arabs until Israeli independence in 1948.

There are a number of caves that can be visited, highlighting their varied uses as burial tombs, houses of religion, cisterns, baths, dovecotes, and hideaways, among other purposes.

WORTH THE DETOUR? Yes, this site is generally a crowd-pleaser, so it may tick a lot of boxes if you have a diverse travel group.

DAYS/HOURS 08.00–16.00 daily, closes 17.00 Saturday–Thursday in summer.

BEST STRATEGY This site will take 2–4 hours, depending on whether you do the full loop and/or drive part of it, although all can be done on foot. It does get busy. The map at the entrance is good and continues mostly in a direction that provides context for the layperson. If you want something a bit more chronological to see how the cities progressed, then start with Tel Maresha, continue to the Columbarium, Maze, and Sidonian caves, then the Roman amphitheater and bathhouse, followed by St. Anne's Church, the Bell Caves, and lastly the Crusader Fortress.

WALKS AND DRIVES B2, W5.

ITINERARIES Noteworthy; Structure; Organized; UNESCO; National Parks/Reserves; Ancient History; Kid-Focused; All Ages; Big-Group Friendly; Cinematic.

SIMILAR ELECTIVES **Beit She'arim (#79)** for burial caves. There are tons of Roman ruin options – see the *Roman* category (p. 507).

NEARBY **Tel Aviv (#5)** (80km/50 minutes), **Old City Jerusalem (#1)** (50km/1 hour), and Beer Sheva (J1) (50km/40 minutes).

#61 Nablus

RATINGS

BUCKET! Score	5/10
Ruin	2/5
Entertainment	3/5
Information	1/5
Popularity	3/5

MACRO-REGION
C: West Bank

MICRO-REGION
C5

THEME/CATEGORY People – Community Celebration – Local Community.

HISTORICAL PERIOD *Bronze Age/Canaanites* to *Contemporary*.

ELECT ME In addition to the Tel Balata Archaeological Park, famous inside are the Samaritan religious sect, its oily and oh-so-delicious kanafeh dessert, the olive oil soap factory for cheap souvenirs, and Nablus' still-functioning Turkish bath for relaxation. Religious sites include Joseph's Tomb, Jacob's Well, and nearby ***Mount Gerizim***.

CONTEXT Built atop the Canaanite/Israelite town of Shechem and the Roman town of Neapolis, Nablus sits between ***Mount Gerizim*** and Mount Ebal as an important Palestinian city with 125,000 residents. There is a ton of history to unpack here.

The city has been continuously inhabited for at least 5,000 years, and perhaps double that. The written record mentions a town, Shechem, in Egyptian Execration Texts (i.e., lists of enemies) from the 19th century BCE, and later in the Amarna Letters from the 14th century BCE as a center of the Canaanite people. Shechem is mentioned several times in the Old Testament, most notably as an early capital of the Kingdom of Israel around the 10th century BCE. The archaeological site of Tel Balata is believed to be ancient Shechem. During 8th-century BCE Persian rule, the Samaritan faith broke from mainstream Judaism and moved to Mount Gerizim to build its own temple. Samaritans have lived in Nablus since, though only 400 or so remain.

The city was believed destroyed by Rome during the first Jewish–Roman wars. A new city was built nearby, which Emperor Vespasian named "Flavia Neapolis." "Nablus," incidentally, is just the Arabic pronunciation of "Neapolis." The new city was often referred to as Little Damascus, and the Old City of Nablus today reflects a similar design structure to Jerusalem, with residents moving outside its walls 100 years earlier, in the 17th century CE. During the Ottoman era, many of the palaces and famous hammams became a regular part of city life. Nablus has continued to grow – eventually incorporating the ancient site of Shechem/Tel Balata – and is today the second largest in the West Bank, after Hebron.

WORTH THE DETOUR? Getting in can be difficult as it's in the middle of Palestine, and several sites have armed guards and close without warning. Due to the rental car restriction, you can't take a car from Israel into Palestine, so will likely have to hire a driver, which can get costly. But if you want to know Palestine, you can't miss Nablus.

BEST STRATEGY Depending on how much interests you, this site could take all day. If you have a lot planned (including neighboring ***Mount Gerizim***), plan an overnight, then work on *Road Trip C5* the next day. Get a good map and focus on your interests:

archaeology (Tel Balata, Sebastia), religious sites (Jacob's Well, Joseph's Tomb), local specialties (soap, kanafeh, cheese, olive oil), and recent history (the Old City, ancient palaces, Turkish baths).

There are a number of local specialties, not least of which is kanafeh, a sticky sweet dessert made of shredded wheat, cheese, and sugar. Al-Aqsa and Abu Sair are both sweet shops worth trying. The Nabulsi cheese by itself is also a treat. Castile soap is made from local olive oil and has been renowned for a millennium, with a number of factories available, with Albader perhaps being the most famous of them.

WALKS AND DRIVES C5.

ITINERARIES Off-the-Beaten-Path Israel and Palestine; Society and People; Entertainment; Endangered; Community; Relaxation; Pilgrimage.

SIMILAR ELECTIVES For Palestinian city feels: **Ramallah (#68)**, **Tomb of the Patriarchs and Old Town of Hebron (#46)**, and **Bethlehem (#40)**

NEARBY *Mount Gerizim* (3.5km/10 minutes), *Sebastia-Shomron* (35km/45 minutes), and Hiking in Jenin (C5) (45km/1¼ hours).

#62 Golan Heights

RATINGS

BUCKET! Score		6/10
Ruin		1/5
Entertainment		2/5
Information		1/5
Popularity		2/5

MACRO-REGION
I: Golan Heights

MICRO-REGIONS
G3, I1, I2, I3

THEME/CATEGORY Scenic – Vistas – Scenic Drives.

HISTORICAL PERIOD *Neolithic* to *Contemporary*.

ELECT ME Come to the Golan to visit the Druze and Alawite populations. Come for the luscious green scenery and take a respite from the heat suffocating the rest of the country. Excellent birding opportunities abound. There's the country's only ski slope at *Mount Hermon*. Excellent wine, impressive ruins, and beautiful expansive views round out the many reasons to make the very worthwhile trip to this region.

CONTEXT Golan cities are mentioned in the famed Amarna Letters (14th century BCE) while "Golan" is referenced first as a city in present-day Syria. The area of the Golan was part of the Kingdom of Israel, with the Tribe of Manasseh and the Tribe of Dan covering the area east of the Jordan River. The Tribe of Dan was centered at a town called Laish, now named after the tribe and called **Tel Dan (#63)**. Today, Golan is no longer a singular site or city, but representative of the whole region (whose name has changed names many times over the millennia). The region known as "Golan Heights" today encompasses 1,800km² of land in modern-day Israel and Syria, with Israel holding two-thirds of the territory.

The Golan Heights has been under Israeli occupation for 50 years, with no indication it will ever be returned to Syria. The UN views the annexation as illegal under international law. The Syrian civil war mostly drew attention away from the Golan during the 2010s, but missiles are still occasionally lobbed from Lebanon and Syria upon unsuspecting residents. Large zones are blocked off for military use and active land mines continue to be discovered from the 1967 war, when this area was a battlefield. Israelis started to construct residences in this sparsely populated district shortly after their victory.

The largest urban community is Majdal Shams, with around 11,000 people. There are four Syrian Druze villages: Mas'ade, Ein Qiniyye, Majdal Shams, and Buq'ata. There's also one Alawite community at Ghajar. Israelis make up just less than half the Golani population in more than 30 kibbutzim and moshavim. In total, less than 50,000 people reside in the Golan Heights. Most now have Israeli citizenship.

Much of the Golan remains controversial, although moderately peaceful. Residents of Ghajar have Israeli citizenship but live on either side of the Lebanese border. Another area, the Sheba'a Farms, is a tiny (22km²) stretch of land where the Covenant of the Pieces – the first covenant between Abraham and God – is believed to have taken place. Lebanon claims this portion as its own, but it remains disputed. The eastern border with Syria is demarcated by the United Nations and remains closed. Any territory within 5–10km of the Lebanese or Syrian borders is widely considered dangerous and/or off-limits according to third-party governments – exercise caution if you visit.

WORTH THE DETOUR? If you have only one day, and your interest is religious sites, then the **Sea of Galilee (#7)** has more immediately recognizable historical references. However, if you don't mind skipping the Jesus loop, or have an extra day, or prefer relaxation and/or outdoor activities to sacred places, then the Golan is right for you. Plus, because of its strange status of annexed/occupied land, it remains a must-visit for intrepid and box-checking travelers.

BEST STRATEGY You'll need a minimum of one full day to get there and back, no matter where you are. The entire region is large, so you'll need a car to see multiple sites. Public transport will get you to the center, but is then limited. If you have several days/weeks, you can explore a lot more on foot.

Without multiple days, you're going to have to make some decisions, as you cannot see all of the Golan's sites in one day. There are a few things you can eliminate off the bat. Don't like skiing? Nix *Mount Hermon*. Don't like hiking? Nix the streams. Don't drink? Skip the wineries. Pick what you like to do, and you can make your own road trip from the remaining bits.

TOWNS The largest of the four Druze villages, Majdal Shams (I2) is the one where they say residents yell to their Syrian relatives on the other side of the hill ("Shouting Valley"). Look out for the Druze flag. Kibbutz Merom Golan (I2) was the first settlement, established a few weeks after the 1967 Six-Day War. Ride a horse up a volcano. **Katzrin (Qatzrin)** is the largest town of the Golan, known for its mineral water. **Ramot** has lots of tzimmers, making it a good base of operations.

NATIONAL PARKS Nimrod's Fortress (#85) is the most impressive site in the region, built by the Ayyubids as a defense against the Crusaders, with Mamluk enhancements; *Mount Hermon* has ski and hiking trails; and Kursi (G3) is a Byzantine-era monastery.

NATURE RESERVES **Banias (#80)**, aka Hermon Stream, contains waterfalls and a Herodian city; **Tel Dan (#63)** is popular for its Israelite-period archaeological sites; *Gamla* boasts an impressive waterfall, vultures, and an ancient Jewish city that mirrored Masada in its ritual suicide when faced with defeat by the Romans; *Yehudiya* has hiking and birds; Meshushim Stream (I3)/*Yehudiya* have walking trails to ancient Bethsaida, hexagonal pools, and ancient dolmens; Tel Bethsaida (G4) is where Jesus performed numerous miracles; and Majrase-Betiha/Bethsaida Valley (I3) has wet hiking.

VINEYARDS **Golan Heights Winery (#75)**, the most highly respected vineyard in the country, produces the Gamla, Galil, Yarden, and Hermon brand wines; Château Golan Winery (I3) is near el-Al Reserve; and Pelter Winery (I2) is in Merom Golan.

RUINS *Ancient Qatzrin* was a Talmudic Jewish village (3rd–6th centuries CE); **Horvat Suşiţa** was the Decapolis city of Hippos; **Rujum El-Hiri** is a megalithic site with concentric rings (perhaps solar, burial, or religious) from around 3000 BCE, accessible from the Golan Trail (I2); and **Umm el-Kanatir** is a Byzantine-era Jewish village.

MUSEUMS Located in Qatzrin, **Golan Archaeological Museum** is a Golan lover's dream. And Golan Magic: there's an admission fee, but it provides an interactive and high-tech list of activities in the Golan.

VIEWS Mount Bental Lookout (I2) lets you see Quneitra, a Syrian town abandoned after 1973, and Golan Lookout/Tel Faher (I1) has trenches from the 1967 war. Follow *Road Trips I2* and *I3* for more.

ACTIVE Jordan River Rafting (I1).

PLANTS Springtime for wildflowers!

FRUIT *Picking Fruit (I2)* at Bustan Bereshit Bagolan: pick whatever is in season – cherries, berries, stone fruit.

WALKING TOUR The Golan Trail (I2) is a 130km walking trail from *Mount Hermon* to Ein Taufiq, in 15 segments.

WALKS AND DRIVES G3, I1, I2, I3.

ITINERARIES Noteworthy; Nature and Scenic; Society and People; Active; Organized; Community; On the Road; Romantic; Shoestring; Kid-Focused.

SIMILAR ELECTIVES The Golan is its own thing. There are similar electives to the those listed above, but there's nothing regional like the Golan Heights territory. It has a unique population, is sparsely populated, has an interesting cuisine, and a different weather and geography than the rest of Israel.

NEARBY The southern/western edge of the Golan is the **Sea of Galilee (#7)**. If you are staying in **Nazareth (#29)**, *Tiberias*, or another Galilee locale, you are well set up to have a full day in the Golan.

SUPPLEMENTAL w natureisrael.org/Golan.

#63 Tel Dan

RATINGS			MACRO-REGION
BUCKET! Score		5/10	I: Golan Heights
Ruin		2/5	
Entertainment		2/5	**MICRO-REGION**
Information		2/5	I1
Popularity		4/5	

THEME/CATEGORY Archaeology – Ancient Israel – Iron Age.

HISTORICAL PERIOD *Neolithic* to *Kingdom of Israel and Judah.*

ELECT ME The site encompasses Tel Dan as well as an outdoor recreational area, including a shallow bathing pool, some walks, and rolling brooks. The name recognition drives the crowds, though the site itself is quite small.

CONTEXT One of the 12 tribes of Israel, the Tribe of Dan was muscled out of its territory (near Jaffa) by the seafarer Philistines (today's Palestinians take their name from the same group). Upon regrouping, they moved north to a town called Laish, which the tribe attacked, defeated, and changed the name to "Dan." From here, they set up the northernmost outpost of the Kingdom of Israel, frequently referenced in the Bible as part of Israel's borders, i.e., "from Dan to Beersheva." On the eastern corridor, a massive 7m gate dating to the Canaanite period (c18th century BCE), which has been nicknamed "the Abraham Gate" due to a biblical story (Genesis 14) describing how Abraham traveled to Dan after rescuing his nephew, Lot. Another gate on site, called "the Israelite Gate," dates to the period of the Tribe of Dan and served as the entrance to the city. Right behind was a platform to greet guests, while also possibly used for ritual purposes. The site may also have been host to one of the two golden calves of the ancient kingdom once Judah split from Israel, in an attempt to provide a room for God to rival Solomon's Temple.

Several important historical pieces have been found on site. Most importantly, the Tel Dan stele, dating to the 9th century BCE during the Kingdom of Israel, references King David. This seems to be the earliest reference to the King of the United Kingdom. The city lost prominence when neighboring **Banias (#80)** rose to power.

WORTH THE DETOUR? Only if you're in the north and have a few days in the Golan. Tel Dan is too mythical and small to come all this way for on its own.

DAYS/HOURS 08.00–16.00 daily, closes 17.00 Saturday–Thursday in summer.

BEST STRATEGY One hour is likely sufficient, and we recommend you tack this site onto a drive of regional sites.

WALKS AND DRIVES I1.

ITINERARIES Archaeology; Nature and Scenic; Endangered; National Parks/Reserves.

SIMILAR ELECTIVES There are other Biblical Tels in the region: **Tel Hazor** is closest and **Megiddo (#59)** the most famous.

NEARBY **Banias (#80)** (5km/7 minutes), **Nimrod's Fortress (#85)** (12km/14 minutes), **Mount Hermon** (27km/40 minutes), **Hula Lake** (22km/32 minutes), **Tiberias** (67km/1 hour), and **Nazareth (#29)** (91km/1¼ hours).

#64 Beit Alpha

RATINGS

BUCKET! Score		4/10
Ruin		3/5
Entertainment		3/5
Information		4/5
Popularity		2/5

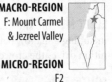

MACRO-REGION
F: Mount Carmel
& Jezreel Valley

MICRO-REGION
F2

THEME/CATEGORY Archaeology – Ancient Cities/Ruins – Mosaics.

HISTORICAL PERIOD *Byzantine.*

ELECT ME An easy stop in the Gilboa range near other popular sites, this ancient synagogue is best known for a massive, largely intact mosaic in the main hall. The jury is out about whether you're supposed to appreciate the mosaic for having survived this long or are allowed to giggle at the grade-school-level design.

CONTEXT This synagogue dates to the 6th century CE and the reign of Emperor Justinian. While the architecture is typical of the time, the most impressive piece is the largely intact mosaic that remains in situ. According to the narrative provided by the site, lesser-known (and possibly untrained) artists were hired to complete the mosaic, which led to its less-than-professional-looking designs.

The mosaic is rather large and has a raised visitor platform circling the piece. One of the end panels depicts the Binding of Isaac, the story from the Bible (Genesis 22) where Abraham brings his son, Isaac, to Mount Moriah to sacrifice him before God, only for God to spare Isaac once Abraham's loyalty is revealed. In the art, find Abraham on the right side holding the child above the fire; God is represented as a black circle and hand (stopping the execution); the ram in the middle is what was sacrificed instead. The two boys on the left had accompanied Abraham and Isaac on the journey.

The panel closest to the altar and Torah shrine shows the Ark of the Covenant, menorahs, lions, and other sacred objects. In the center is a zodiac wheel. The 12 months are represented and replete with Hebrew labels. Helios, the sun god in Greek literature, sits at the center of the circle, while the four women at the corners represent the seasons. The zodiac is an interesting thought experiment given that the symbolism was powerful enough to put in a synagogue, but none of the images are religiously Jewish, indicating there had been a strong convergence of Greco-Roman and Jewish culture at the time of the work's commission in the 6th century.

The synagogue wouldn't last long; it was destroyed in a late-6th-century earthquake. The mosaic was not discovered until 1928, by members of the local kibbutz.

WORTH THE DETOUR? While no means required, this site makes for an amusing 30-minute stopover if you happen to be in the area.

DAYS/HOURS 08.00–16.00 daily, closes 17.00 Saturday–Thursday in summer.

BEST STRATEGY It's a small site so 30 minutes is sufficient. But make sure to watch the video (it's in Hebrew, but they can play English subtitles) as it is remarkably amusing and provides excellent insight into why the mosaic looks so absurd.

WALKS AND DRIVES F2.

ITINERARIES National Parks/Reserves.

SIMILAR ELECTIVES For mosaics, try **Madaba and the Madaba Map (#19)**, **Umm ar-Rasas (#81)**, or **Beit She'an (#39)** nearby.

NEARBY **Beit She'an (#39)** (8km/10 minutes), **Belvoir (#93)** (29km/35 minutes), **Tiberias** (70km/1¼ hours), and **Nazareth (#29)** (35km/40 minutes).

#65 Al-Aqsa Mosque

RATINGS

BUCKET! Score		4/10
Ruin		5/5
Entertainment		1/5
Information		1/5
Popularity		3/5

MACRO-REGION
A: Jerusalem

MICRO-REGIONS
A1, A2

THEME/CATEGORY Religion – Houses of Worship – Mosques.

HISTORICAL PERIOD *Umayyad* to *Ottoman.*

ELECT ME A still-functioning mosque, built by Umayyads in the 8th century CE shortly after the **Dome of the Rock (#6)**, this is one of the oldest mosques in the world, the third-holiest site in Islam, and the place where Muhammad was transported on his Night Journey when visiting "the furthest mosque."

CONTEXT Many people think that the **Dome of the Rock (#6)** is a mosque, but the only mosque on site is Al-Aqsa, the massive construction at the southern end of **Temple Mount (#12)**. Constructed in 705 CE over an earlier Rashidun-era template, this mosque achieved its initial grandeur during the Umayyad Caliphate, but a series of earthquakes destroyed the original versions, to be replaced by the present-day building. It was finished by the Fatimid Caliphate in 1036 in early Islamic style. The original building's 15-aisle-and-nave design was decreased to seven, and the exterior gained its present look. The only parts of the earliest mosque still visible can be found in the mosaics high up in the drum and in the central arch.

Inside, the mosque has many dozens of fascinating pillars in a mix of succeeding empirical styles: Umayyad, Crusader, Ayyubid, and Ottoman. The Crusader period saw the mosque converted into the headquarters of the Templar Knights, the Catholic military order that reclaimed Jerusalem in 1099. The Fatimid construction was converted into horse stables, a church, a palace, and cloister. What's left of that period can be seen at the old Crusader dining hall, now split into the Islamic Museum and the women's prayer area. Saladin removed the Christian elements and reconverted the site for Muslim use. The Mamluks added structural integrity to the site, but the Ottomans did very little, instead focusing on the surrounding grounds of the Haram as-Sharif, or Temple Mount.

The building ultimately collapsed in 1937 following a series of earthquakes. It has not been without its controversy over the last century. The renovations from 1938 to 1942 removed much of what remained of the oldest parts of the building. New marble was donated by Mussolini to replace the interior columns. King Abdullah of Jordan was killed on site in 1951. In 1969, a fire set by a crazed Christian destroyed Saladin's wooden pulpit. And, in 1990, several dozen Palestinians were killed and injured when Jews attempted to lay the foundation of the "coming" Third Temple on site. In 2000, when Ariel Sharon visited the site accompanied by riot police, the First Intifada began, lasting some five years. The very existence of the site continues to instill great pride in Muslims and great resentment in many Jews.

Al-Aqsa's dome is a familiar sight – not the gold-plated one of "Dome of the Rock" fame, but the lead-plated one nearby (as can be seen from upper vantage points and high hills throughout greater Jerusalem). The mosque is 75m long and can hold up to 5,000 worshipers. Non-Muslim visitors are presently banned from entering, making this a difficult site to experience fully unless you are Muslim. Non-Muslim travelers can walk the perimeter.

WORTH THE DETOUR? Even if you can't enter, walking the **Temple Mount (#12)** grounds is absolutely relevant and necessary to understanding our BUCKET! site of **Old City Jerusalem (#1)**.

BEST STRATEGY We recommend our *Old City Chronotour* (w buckettravelguides.com/old-city-chronotour), but you can also visit **Temple Mount (#12)** on any *City Walks A1* and *A2*. Keep in mind that Temple Mount is closed Friday and Saturday.

WALKS AND DRIVES A1, A2, W1.

ITINERARIES Complete Ruins; Religion; Pilgrimage.

SIMILAR ELECTIVES Other important and/or ancient mosques in the region can be found in **Modern Amman (#36)**, **Tomb of the Patriarchs and Old Town of Hebron (#46)**, and **Bethlehem (#40)**.

NEARBY See **Old City Jerusalem (#1)**.

#66 Mea She'arim

RATINGS

BUCKET! Score	▓▓▓▓▓▓▓░░░	6/10
Ruin	n/a	
Entertainment	▓▓░░░	1/5
Information	▓▓░░░	1/5
Popularity	▓▓▓░░	2/5

MACRO-REGION A: Jerusalem

MICRO-REGION A7

THEME/CATEGORY People – Identity – Orthodox.

HISTORICAL PERIOD *Ottoman* to *Contemporary*.

ELECT ME A quick stroll through this neighborhood will open your eyes to the world of anti-modern, religious-right Jewish living. Mea She'arim provides a great visual perspective on how Orthodox Jews, mainly from Eastern Europe, have chosen to turn away from the modern world in pursuit of a strictly religious one.

Tourists are not welcome, per se, but can politely and very discreetly walk through the neighborhood, shop for Judaica (tchotchkes), and grab a bread pastry. All visitors must be respectful, quiet, fully covered, respect gender norms, stick to the main street, avoid Fridays and Saturdays, not drive, and refrain from taking photos. If you can handle that, stroll through – it's like visiting Lithuania or Poland in the 1870s.

CONTEXT Mea She'arim literally means "a hundred gates" or "hundredfold." The city name is derived from a verse in the Torah (Genesis 26:12) when Isaac reaped a bumper crop thanks to God's blessing. Tradition has it this was the verse of the week when the neighborhood was established. Founded in 1874 by a group of shareholders trying to flee the overcrowded and polluted streets of the Old City, the gentlemen built 100 apartments and surrounded the neighborhood with a wall.

Though much time has elapsed since those early days, you would be surprised to find that the people who live in the neighborhood look and act very similarly to those early settlers. This mostly Ashkenazi, ultra-Orthodox community speaks Yiddish instead of Hebrew, because Hebrew is considered God's language and should be spoken only in synagogue. The residents are mostly Hasidic, a subset of Haredi Judaism, and recognizable by their dress. Everyone here dresses conservatively and by sect. Male outfits have several variations often indicating their national origin, but generally consist of a long black coat, a head covering (from a basic kippeh to a shtreimel, the big fur hats), a beard and peyot – the hair curls hanging down the sides of the face. Women also wear black, skirts below the knees, stockings, and sometimes wigs, though a hair covering of any kind is acceptable. Large families are the norm. Men work or study, while women stay home to take care of the house and children. These residents live a more-or-less ascetic life – no television, limited technology, basic schooling, limited news, and little access to the outside world.

The Haredim have eschewed modernity in favor of a simpler way of life from yesteryear. Their very existence strikes many as odd, and even offensive, but most are perfectly happy to ignore the modern world in favor of religion and family.

WORTH THE DETOUR? Definitely interesting, though if you are an outspoken child of liberation movements with little tolerance for anti-modern sentiment, you should skip it.

BEST STRATEGY You don't want to spend too long because this is not meant to be a tourist attraction (read: no cameras), and these folks are just trying to live their lives without outside interference. Tourist groups aren't welcome, so travel in smaller numbers – no more than two or three people. The residents understand that they are viewed as an anachronism (though they believe the rest of the city to be the same) and will likely ignore you if you are polite, discreet, and follow the rules. Exercise caution, humility, and invisibility on Shabbat: Fridays and Saturdays. Driving here on the Sabbath will ensure rock-size dents in your vehicle from the rock-size rocks that the locals will be throwing at your doors and windows. You absolutely must wear the appropriate clothes to enter this neighborhood, or you will be aggressively asked to leave. This includes long pants, covered shoulders, very little skin, and head coverings. Men and women are requested not to walk together. There are "modesty posters" hanging in many parts of the neighborhood as a reminder.

WALKS AND DRIVES A7.

ITINERARIES Noteworthy; Community.

SIMILAR ELECTIVES *Jewish Quarter* and the **Western Wall (#11)** for more Jewish orthodoxy.

NEARBY Within walking distance are the **Old City Jerusalem (#1)**, **Mehane Yehuda Market (#67)**, Ethiopian Quarter (A7), Russian Quarter (A7), and Nakhalat Shiva (A7).

#67 Mehane Yehuda Market

RATINGS			MACRO-REGION
BUCKET! Score		6/10	A: Jerusalem
Ruin	n/a		
Entertainment		3/5	**MICRO-REGION**
Information		2/5	A7
Popularity		4/5	

THEME/CATEGORY Entertainment – Shopping – Markets.

HISTORICAL PERIOD *Mandatory Palestine* to *Contemporary*.

ELECT ME This market is the best place to fully digest the expansive food selection that Israel produces for local consumption. It's only a few blocks long and isn't competitive in size to similar outdoor European markets, but it sure makes up for it in selection. The vast diversity of ethnic Jewish and Arab (and other) peoples that have made a home in Israel all come together to celebrate their food traditions here, with food stalls, fresh produce, fish, bread, spices, dairy, meat, wines, and wares. It's remarkably clean for the number of people that shop here, and tourist-friendly.

CONTEXT The most popular market in West Jerusalem, Mehane Yehuda is well outfitted. There are excellent street food options, all clean and affordable. If you're cooking for yourself, you'll also find your standard fruits, vegetables, and herbs, and an often lovely assortment of fresh fish, international cheeses, and towering spirals of spices including za'atar, sumac, curries, and stock bases. You'll be able to find cheap souvenirs, from the aforementioned spices to a variety of package sellers. Right after work and on weekends, the place is shoulder-to-shoulder with traffic. Enjoy your chance to show off your Hebrew (you'll still get charged Western prices – bargaining works only minimally in the popular markets).

Preorder the Machane Yehuda Bite Card in order to sample the best of the market (w en.machne.co.il/category/the-machane-yehuda-shuk-bites-ticket). Follow along with the free audio guide app and get small portions of baked goods, hummus, juice, a beer, coffee or ice cream, and other specialties. There are also cooking classes that use ingredients sourced at the market (book through the same site).

WORTH THE DETOUR? Absolutely. Everyone has to eat. You need evening plans. Shop a little while you're at it. This spot ticks a lot of boxes.

DAYS/HOURS 08.00–19.00 Sunday–Thursday, 08.00–15.00 Friday, closed Saturday.

BEST STRATEGY You can run through in a few minutes – it's not a big market. But you should stay for lunch or dinner and a drink. The market changes the later in the evening you go, so best to stick around a while and count this as one of your evening activities. Everything's closed on Saturdays, though the restaurants will open in the evening. If you visit right before a holiday, all the better.

WALKS AND DRIVES A7.

ITINERARIES Jerusalem Immersion; Entertainment; Organized; Endangered; Community; Gourmet; Shoestring.

SIMILAR ELECTIVES **Carmel Market (#87)** in Tel Aviv.

NEARBY Ethiopian Quarter (A7) (1km/12 minutes), *Ben Yehuda Street* (900m/11 minutes), Russian Quarter (A7) (1.2km/15 minutes), Jaffa Gate (2km/22 minutes), Mamilla Mall (parking; 1.6km/19 minutes).

#68 Ramallah

	RATINGS			MACRO-REGION
BUCKET! Score			4/10	C: West Bank
Ruin			1/5	
Entertainment			3/5	MICRO-REGION
Information			1/5	C4
Popularity			2/5	

THEME/CATEGORY People – Ethnic Groups – Arab.

HISTORICAL PERIOD *Ottoman* to *Contemporary*.

ELECT ME The de facto capital of the West Bank, Ramallah would seem to be the center of confrontational politics. This may be true, but the city is actually more famous for its arts, culture, and nightlife, as well as being an economic engine for Palestine. Westerners will like Ramallah as it has a more relaxed civil code than other Palestinian cities, and is often viewed as the most liberal. Women can walk around without scarves, if desired, and there are generally more women outside than in other Muslim towns. Nightlife is popular here because alcohol is legal and readily available. Due to regular violent episodes, travelers are hesitant to venture here usually, but the city is remarkably well set up for tourists.

CONTEXT A truly Arab city, with both Christian and Muslim influences, Ramallah is actually one of the newer towns in the Holy Land. Though its origin hasn't been fully traced, it's likely the Crusaders were stationed here. Christians from Jordan moved here during early Ottoman reign. Yet the town didn't pass the 1,000 resident mark until roughly the 19th century. When Jordan administered the West Bank from 1949 to 1967, Ramallah doubled in size. Once designated as "Area A," after the Oslo Accords in the 1990s, it again saw a boom in activity. With roughly 40,000 residents today – still about 25% Christian – it continues to grow and expand with a busy downtown, historic center, popular nightlife, good restaurants, and cultural shows. As the headquarters of the Palestinian National Authority, it's also the current executive capital of Palestine – though Jerusalem is still the claimed capital of the Palestinian people.

WORTH THE DETOUR? Given you can't take a rental car into the West Bank, you'll have to bus or taxi in. If you want to see a truly mixed Arab city, this is a good one for foreigners, as it's both welcoming and empty of tourist dollars of late. If you only have limited plans to visit the West Bank, decide between here and **Bethlehem (#40)**.

BEST STRATEGY There are a number of sites to choose from, including the Yasser Arafat Museum (C4). Other important stops include: the produce market (*hisbeh*); the Old City with its mosques and churches; the tomb of Yasser Arafat; the Mahmoud Darwish Memorial (a Palestinian author-poet); the main thoroughfares from Al-Manara Square; walking around the Mukata'a, the HQ of the Palestinian Authority; the Dar Zahran Heritage Building highlighting Ramallah's history through art; eating kanafeh; and whiling away the night in a bar or nightclub!

WALKS AND DRIVES C4.

ITINERARIES Off-the-Beaten-Path Israel and Palestine; Entertainment; Community.

SIMILAR ELECTIVES **Nablus (#61)**, **Tomb of the Patriarchs and Old Town of Hebron (#46)**, **Jerusalem, New City (#72)**, and **Bethlehem (#40)** are all West Bank towns.

NEARBY **Old City Jerusalem (#1)** (18km/45 minutes), Taybeh Brewing Company (C4) (20km/35 minutes), *The Palestinian Museum (C4)* (14km/30 minutes).

#69 Jesus Trail

RATINGS			MACRO-REGION
BUCKET! Score		7/10	G: Lower Galilee & Kinneret
Ruin		1/5	
Entertainment		2/5	**MICRO-REGIONS**
Information		4/5	G2, G4
Popularity		1/5	

THEME/CATEGORY Active – Hikes – Long Walks.

HISTORICAL PERIOD *Judea.*

ELECT ME A nonprofit, volunteer-sponsored hiking trail established in 2007 which traces Jesus' journey from **Nazareth (#29)** to **Capernaum (#33)**. The hike passes many beautiful spots of scenery and historical points along a marked 65km trail. The group that created this trademarked journey also works as a tour operator, coordinating logistics including lodging, food, and luggage. Travelers can do self-guided or guided walks, with or without camping, on foot or bikes, and at your own pace.

CONTEXT The book *Hiking the Jesus Trail*, by one of the founders of the trail, David Landis, is indispensable. Average hiking time between Nazareth and Capernaum is four days, but the journey can be slowed down or sped up and there are a number of alternative routes.

The site passes through several of our elective sites, including **Nazareth (#29)**, **Tsipori (#56)**, *Kfar Kana (G4)*, **Mount Arbel**, *Migdala (G4)*, **Capernaum and Tabgha (#33)**, *Mount of Beatitudes*, and the **Sea of Galilee (#7)**.

The route takes you from Nazareth to Cana (15.5km) on the first day; then Cana to Lavi (13.9km); Lavi to Moshav Arbel (17.0km); and Moshav Arbel to Capernaum (18.5km). While there are some hefty climbs, most of the walk is downhill, having started at almost 400m in elevation in Nazareth and ending at 200m below sea level in Capernaum.

The Israel Ministry of Tourism is trying to create a similar route, the Gospel Trail, but it is not yet as well developed.

WORTH THE DETOUR? If you've got the time (four days), it just might be worth your while, particularly because the company handles all the logistical arrangements for you, so you can get to the business of enjoying yourself. If you are a fan of hiking and were planning on visiting the above places anyway, definitely consider doing the full four days of this unforgettable walk.

BEST STRATEGY There are a number of route options that can be accomplished in one day, including ascents of mountains along the trail and short walks between towns on the Sea of Galilee, but you can also piece together your own journeys. The book highlights options on the east coast of the Sea of Galilee, walking from Mount Arbel to Nazareth, from Tel Rekhesh to Mount Gilboa, and walking the Mount Yodfat Ridge. If you choose to walk the entire route, a one-way journey can be completed in a long weekend (four days). Tours can be arranged directly with the company (**w** jesustrail.com). Detailed maps are available in the guidebook and online.

WALKS AND DRIVES G2, G4.

ITINERARIES High BUCKET! Scores: 7+; Off-the-Beaten-Path Israel and Palestine; Noteworthy; Nature and Scenic; Active; Organized; Shoestring.

SIMILAR ELECTIVES *Israel National Trail*, **Jordan Trail (#52)**, *Palestinian Heritage Trail*, and *Sinai Trail*.

NEARBY Jerusalem to Nazareth is 150km/1¾ hours; Tel Aviv to Nazareth is 100km/ 1¼ hours. Capernaum to Rosh Pina is 18km/20 minutes and to Tel Aviv is 150km/ 2 hours.

#70 Qumran

RATINGS		MACRO-REGION
BUCKET! Score	5/10	K: Dead Sea (Israel)
Ruin	1/5	
Entertainment	2/5	**MICRO-REGION**
Information	2/5	K1
Popularity	4/5	

THEME/CATEGORY Religion – Holy Books – Ancient Manuscripts.

HISTORICAL PERIOD *Greek* to *Judea*.

ELECT ME If you're extremely curious to see the caves where the Dead Sea Scrolls were stored until Bedouins helped bring them to the attention of archaeologists and biblical scholars in 1947, you'll be delighted to find out that the site is just off the present highway at the north end of the Dead Sea in Qumran National Park. You can't enter the caves themselves, but there are vantage points to see them nonetheless.

CONTEXT In the latter half of the 1800s, Khirbet Qumran (as it's known in Arabic) was visited multiple times by archaeologists who were privy to the large cemetery and fort on site, one of many from ancient Judea.

In 1946, Bedouin shepherds fell into one of the caves (Cave 1) and discovered the first seven of what would be over 980 scrolls and fragments in situ. While they didn't understand their significance, the Bedouins did realize the value, and sold the scrolls to treasure hunters in the Middle East. At the same time, the Israeli War for Independence was breaking out and the location of the caves was lost to archaeologists, who also had a vested interest in making sure these pieces weren't damaged due to violence.

Of the seven first scrolls, one was the Great Isaiah Scroll, which was 1,000 years older than the oldest known version of the Book of Isaiah found previously. The other scrolls contained copies of biblical text, apocrypha (non-canonical texts), and Jewish law. It took two years to refind the first cave and ten years to get the original scrolls back – at which point they were now worth a considerable sum, creating a black market where forgeries became rampant.

An archaeological team began a full excavation of the Qumran hills in 1951, looking for more hidden scrolls in secret caves. In the next two years, five more locations were identified, some yielding hundreds of stored scrolls or fragments in remote hills. In total, 11 caves were identified over a seven-year period, with the greatest bounty coming from Cave 4 – visible now from Qumran National Park. Some 15,000 fragments covering hundreds of texts were found in the Cave 4 system alone. But it also contained the largest number of scrolls – more than 500 in total.

It's unclear which Jewish sect was responsible for writing and keeping these scrolls, and at which point they were abandoned, though archaeologists have long associated them to the Essenes – a regional Jewish sect well established from the 2nd century BCE to the 1st century CE, and lost to history after the revolt in 70 CE. Radiocarbon dating matches the cave findings to the same period. That said, several modern scholars now believe the scrolls may have originally been stored in the Jerusalem Temple and were stashed here during the Jewish Revolts and subsequent banishment from Jerusalem.

The scrolls had been preserved for around 2,000 years thanks to the arid conditions of the desert, the storage containers, low humidity, and their remote locations (preventing looting). Upon discovery, they became immediately vulnerable to contamination, deterioration, and novice preservation techniques. Today, they are stored in temperature-controlled facilities in the **Israel Museum (#17)**. A few of the scrolls on display are facsimiles while the originals have been removed for further preservation.

WORTH THE DETOUR? If you're interested in the scrolls, visit the **Israel Museum (#17)**. At the Qumran site, you'll learn the story of how the scrolls were found.

DAYS/HOURS 08.00–16.00 daily, closes 17.00 Saturday–Thursday in summer.

BEST STRATEGY This elective can be completed in 15 minutes if you simply walk to the viewpoint for Cave 4. For a better overview, plan an hour to watch the film, visit the museum, and walk the pathways around the site.

WALKS AND DRIVES K1.

ITINERARIES National Parks/Reserves.

SIMILAR ELECTIVES **Israel Museum (#17)** and the *Rockefeller Archaeological Museum* both have connections to the Dead Sea Scrolls, though only the former holds any today. *Jordan Museum (Q3)* in Amman also houses several scrolls, including the only Copper Scroll.

NEARBY **Ein Gedi (#50)** (34km/30 minutes), **Masada (#8)** (55km/45 minutes), *Ein Bokek* (67km/55 minutes), **Old City Jerusalem (#1)** (50km/1 hour), and **Jericho (#26)** (21km/20 minutes).

#71 Jerusalem Archaeological Park

RATINGS		MACRO-REGION
BUCKET! Score	5/10	A: Jerusalem
Ruin	3/5	
Entertainment	1/5	**MICRO-REGIONS**
Information	5/5	A2, A4
Popularity	2/5	

THEME/CATEGORY Archaeology – Roman – Herodian.

HISTORICAL PERIOD *Herodian to Umayyad.*

ELECT ME For those with a strong interest in archaeological history and wishing to find out more about **Temple Mount (#12)** and **Old City Jerusalem (#1)** in antiquity, this is a great stop. The Davidson Visitor Center provides a colorful, visual, and easy-to-comprehend explanation of how Jerusalem has changed over the ages. The site particularly looks at the ruins from the Second Temple period found on the southeast corner of Temple Mount (just south of the Western Wall).

CONTEXT One starts at the Davidson Exhibition and Virtual Reconstruction Center. This visitor pavilion provides an essential introduction to all the important Herodian-era archaeological finds at the Jerusalem Archaeological Park. There are a number of 3D, virtual reality, projected, simulated, and other high-quality visualization tools available for guests to fully appreciate the history of the site. Once you've finished with the museum, you can tour the grounds around the Temple Mount walls. The two most famous sites are Robinson's Arch and the Hulda Gates.

With the creation of the Second Temple atop Temple Mount, and the retaining walls around it, all that was needed was a staircase to bring the people to the temple itself. Robinson's Arch is all that remains of a massive structure that led to Temple Mount from the street below. The top of the stairs used to empty onto Temple Mount directly – the Ottomans added the further courses of small brick above the arch remains. Though it was built around 20 BCE, Robinson's Arch was named after a biblical scholar, Edward Robinson, who proposed in 1838 that the current eponymously named structure was the remains of a bridge that connected the staircase to the temple above. Until 1967, this area was covered in rubble. Tourists used to be able to touch the arch at ground level! Make sure to get a visual of the arch at the Davidson Center.

On the southern wall, there are two sets of gates: the Double Gate and the Triple Gate. Collectively they are known as the Hulda Gates after a description of Temple Mount in the Jewish Oral Torah, the Mishnah. These also date to the Second Temple period. The passageways behind the closed gates are a mystery as yet unsolved, as the sites are now used as Muslim holy spaces and archaeological activity is not permitted. Both sets of gates originally led up internal staircases to the ground level of Temple Mount. Today, only the right side of the Double Gate can be seen, as the rest is hidden behind an old Crusader fort (1129 CE). The Triple Gate also led to Temple Mount, but was disassembled and put back together again by the Umayyads, before being blocked off permanently in the 11th century CE.

Two other points of interest are here. The first is the western side of the wall, containing a paved street. This was in fact Jerusalem's main street during Herodian times. Secondly, as you walk north you'll come across huge blocks strewn across the walkway. These stones were purposefully dislodged from the Temple Mount walls during the Roman siege of 70 CE, and have been lying here for 2,000 years!

WORTH THE DETOUR? There's an additional cost of 30 ILS per person, so you'll want to have at least a passing interest in the site. The cost usually wards off big tourist groups. Even if you only have an hour for the museum, it's worthwhile for situational context.

DAYS/HOURS 08.00–17.00 Sunday–Thursday, 08.00–14.00 Friday, closed Saturday. Hours shift for daylight savings.

BEST STRATEGY Squeeze this site in whenever you can – ideally after visiting the **Western Wall (#11)** and before visiting **Temple Mount (#12)**. You'll get added perspective for both of those sites that will enhance your understanding of Jerusalem's history. Book guided tours in advance.

WALKS AND DRIVES A2, A4.

ITINERARIES Jerusalem Immersion; Archaeology; Big-Group Friendly.

SIMILAR ELECTIVES Both the **Western Wall Tunnels (#94)** and the **Citadel/Tower of David (#32)** provide a similar "wow" factor in understanding how this city once looked.

NEARBY All within 300m: **Western Wall (#11)**, **Temple Mount (#12)** entrance, *City of David*, and Dung Gate.

#72 Jerusalem, New City

RATINGS		
BUCKET! Score		6/10
Ruin		1/5
Entertainment		3/5
Information		1/5
Popularity		5/5

MACRO-REGION
A: Jerusalem

MICRO-REGION
A7

THEME/CATEGORY Society – Cities – Principal Cities.

HISTORICAL PERIOD *Ottoman* to *Contemporary*.

ELECT ME There are plenty of interesting places to explore outside the Old City's walls, including brilliant museums, colorful streets with wildly diverse residents, heads of state at work, the country's most famous market, pedestrian alleys, and plenty of interesting visuals.

CONTEXT We consider anything built outside the **Old City Jerusalem (#1)** walls to be part of the "New City," because no one lived permanently outside those walls until the mid-19th century. It was too unsafe! First and foremost, it's important to understand that the city is the point of central debate between the governments of Israel and the Palestinian Authority. Both sides claim Jerusalem as the capital. Arabs live primarily in "East Jerusalem," which includes most areas east of the Old City's walls. "West Jerusalem" is inhabited by those with Israeli citizenship, almost exclusively Jewish.

Today there are a number of neighborhoods to explore: **Yemen Moshe** includes the **YMCA**, **King David Hotel**, Montefiore's Windmill (A7), and Mishkenot Sha'ananim, the first settlement outside the Jerusalem walls in the 19th century; **Rehavia and Kiryat Shmuel** feature in our tour of architectural and historical buildings (see *City Walk A7*; the **City Center** contains the Ethiopian Quarter (A7), Russian Quarter (A7), Nakhalat Shiva (A7), **Ben Yehuda Street**, **Mahane Yehuda Market (#67)**, and **Mea She'arim (#66)**; the **Museum District** has **Yad Vashem (#35)**, *Bridge of Strings*, Herzl Museum (A8), *Bible Lands Museum*, and the exceptional **Israel Museum (#17)**; and the **Government Campus** is where you'll find the *Supreme Court of Israel* and Knesset (A8)

Some historical context is needed. As the Ottoman Empire waned in importance at the end of the 19th century, European powers began to regain an interest in the Holy Land, establishing diplomatic posts in Jerusalem. Foreign investment led to the construction of several buildings outside the walls of the crowded Old City, including a school, orphanage, a Russian pilgrim way station, and British government buildings. From 1860, disease and discomfort led a number of groups to look outside the confines of the historic city to create protected enclaves nearby. The first permanent settlement was in today's *Yemen Moshe* (est. 1892) at Mishkenot Sha'ananim, a Jewish residential neighborhood built with funding from Moses Montefiore in 1860.

Expansion continued under the British Mandate from 1917 until Israel's declaration of independence. As tensions continued between Jewish and Arab residences, the United Nations developed a plan in 1947 – never implemented due to the resulting war – that would keep Jerusalem as a shared capital, owned by neither party. Jordan annexed East Jerusalem in 1950, while Israel was responsible for administering the western neighborhoods, or new city. After the 1967 war, Israel declared its sovereignty over the entirety of Jerusalem, leaving East Jerusalem residents in a limbo status of "permanent residents" of Israel.

WORTH THE DETOUR? Certainly the museums are a superb way to spend your time, and those planning to stay longer than three days in Jerusalem would be wise to use at least one of the days exploring outside the Old City walls to get a feel for how Jerusalemites live.

BEST STRATEGY We recommend our three New City tours, starting with the museums (*Road Trip A8*).

WALKS AND DRIVES A6, A7, A8.

ITINERARIES Society and People; Culture; Entertainment; Organized; Under the Sun; Shoestring; Luxury.

SIMILAR ELECTIVES **Tel Aviv (#5)** is the other city with a variety of diverse neighborhoods to explore.

NEARBY As distanced from Yad Vashem, the furthest point west: *Hadassah Synagogue and Chagall Windows* (7km/14 minutes), Abu Ghosh's hummusiyas (B1) (14km/23 minutes), *Ein Hemed* (12km/18 minutes), *Sataf* (8km/13 minutes), and **Tel Aviv (#5)** (66km/50 minutes).

#73 Incense Route

RATINGS

BUCKET! Score		5/10
Ruin		1/5
Entertainment		1/5
Information		1/5
Popularity		1/5

MACRO-REGION
J: Negev

MICRO-REGIONS
J1, J2, J3

THEME/CATEGORY Archaeology – City Conglomerates – Nabataean.

HISTORICAL PERIOD *Nabataean.*

ELECT ME The Nabataeans (of **Petra (#2)** fame) created a network of towns and fortresses that can be visited in the Negev region of Israel. **Avdat (#48)** is the most famous of the sites on this route, but the entire passage provides a great tour of the southern desert, on foot or by car.

CONTEXT Four towns – *Halutza*, *Mamshit*, *Shivta*, and **Avdat (#48)** – were stations along the incense and spice trade routes of antiquity, linking Arabia with the Mediterranean. The "Incense Route: Desert Cities in the Negev" UNESCO site covers these four ruins, as well as four fortresses and two caravanserai, along the route from Petra to Gaza through which spice merchants passed in order to reach the Mediterranean, or vice versa. The entire collection of towns stretched some 2,000km and included majestic **Petra (#2)**, the most widely regarded of all Nabataean sites.

The Nabataeans were in charge of a great expanse of territory, connecting present-day Israel with Jordan and the northern parts of present-day Saudi Arabia, and benefited economically through their trade network and series of stopover towns allowing merchants a way to eat, sleep, cavort, and do business on their way to the Mediterranean, Egypt, or Arabia.

Fans of the Christmas story will surely be familiar with the tale of the Three Wise Men (or Magi) as told in the Gospel of Matthew. These men came from the east at the news of Jesus' birth, bearing frankincense and myrrh among their gifts for the child king. Not coincidentally, the Incense Route was largely a trading route for frankincense and myrrh. The remaining city ruins are testament to the influence these spices had in creating economic prosperity for its merchants and traders – and the city denizens who would host them on their global trade journeys.

Some of the towns retained their importance past the date of decline of the Nabataean empire and the movement of trade routes further north. *Mamshit* and Moa, for instance, are both referenced on the **Madaba Map (#19)** from the 6th century, some 300 years after the Nabataeans lost control of the region.

ADDITIONAL SITES *Fortresses* Kazra (in Makhtesh Ramon; ✛ 30°33′36″N 35°05′17″E; no road access); Nekarot (in Makhtesh Ramon; ✛ 30°34′45″N 35°00′48″E; no road access); Makhmal (in Makhtesh Ramon); Graffon (between Avdat and Makhmal; no road access). *Caravanserai* Moa Fort (near Kibbutz Tsofar off Highway 90); Saharonim (in Makhtesh Ramon). *Byzantine period* **Nitzana**, near the Egyptian border.

WORTH THE DETOUR? This is a route for die-hards. If you're in the area, visit **Avdat (#48)** or *Mamshit*.

DAYS/HOURS 08.00–16.00 daily, closes 17.00 Saturday–Thursday in summer. May vary by site. Rural sites may be open 24 hours or closed unexpectedly.

BEST STRATEGY You'll need a couple of hours to see **Avdat (#48)**, and another couple for *Mamshit*. The other sites can be breezed through, but driving and walking distances are substantial. If you're terribly interested in the historic value of the Incense Route (as UNESCO is), then visiting all ten of the designated sites will require at least two days (see *Road Trip J3*). If you are satisfied with visiting one or two, you have some options, starting with the best preserved of the sites: Avdat. You can combine the trip with an overnight in a Bedouin tent, a stay in Beer Sheva, or side trip on your way back to **Tel Aviv (#5)** from the **Dead Sea (#3)**. Alternatively, you can take a few days on your drive south from Tel Aviv to **Eilat (#78)**, stopping in *Mitzpe Ramon*, **Makhtesh Ramon (#28)**, Sde Boker (J2), **Ein Avdat (#74)**, and a few other off-the-beaten-path spots. While not recommended in summer, you can probably combine a few stops from the Incense Route with a few outposts on the Negev Wine Route (J2), some hiking in the craters, and a few national parks for a nice whirlwind trip of the region.

Mamshit has interesting lodging options, including sleeping in an Ethiopian tukul (350 ILS a night) or Bedouin tents (prices vary). There are sukkot options just outside *Mamshit* in the blissful emptiness (w succah.co.il).

WALKS AND DRIVES J1, J2, J3, W5.

ITINERARIES Off-the-Beaten-Path Israel and Palestine; Noteworthy; Archaeology; Organized; UNESCO; National Parks/Reserves; On the Road.

SIMILAR ELECTIVES **Petra (#2)** and *Little Petra*.

NEARBY From Mamshit: *Dimona (J1)* (9km/10 minutes), Sde Boker (J2) (40km/30 minutes), **Ein Bokek**, **Dead Sea (#3)** (62km/45 minutes), *Tel Beer Sheva* (53km/40 minutes), Beer Sheva (J1) (66km/1 hour), *Mitzpe Ramon* (75km/50 minutes), and **Makhtesh Ramon (#28)** (88km/1¼ hours).

#74 Ein Avdat

RATINGS			MACRO-REGION
BUCKET! Score		4/10	J: Negev
Ruin		1/5	
Entertainment		2/5	**MICRO-REGION**
Information		2/5	J2
Popularity		3/5	

THEME/CATEGORY Active – Hikes – Tough (short/steep).

HISTORICAL PERIOD *Byzantine* to *Nabataean*.

ELECT ME Perhaps getting a lift from its neighboring site – the Nabataean ruins of **Avdat (#48)** – Ein Avdat offers an outdoor experience canyoning in the Negev's Ziv Canyon with rewards of waterfalls at the end of its paths (but no swimming).

CONTEXT Ancient Nabataeans passed through Avdat and Ein Avdat on the way to Gaza from Petra (see **Incense Route (#73)**). Later, monks sought refuge in these wadi (canyon) caves during the Byzantine period, but abandoned their residences with the rise of Islam. Today, the site makes for a good wadi hike, passing waterfalls, caves, and a few other points of interest. The hike is particularly pleasant if visiting in the winter when the weather is cooler and the water holes and waterfalls are at their fullest.

WORTH THE DETOUR? Depends on how much time you have. Your time is best spent at **Makhtesh Ramon (#28)** and **Avdat (#48)**. If you have extra days, you can consider it, but we'd recommend further hiking in the makhteshim.

DAYS/HOURS 08.00–16.00 daily, closes 17.00 Saturday–Thursday in summer.

BEST STRATEGY There are two trails to choose from and two entrances to the park. If you have 2–3 hours, and two cars, you can do the one-way longer hike, which ends with a steep climb to the upper parking lot. Otherwise, start at the southern entrance and do the 1–2-hour loop hike. Note that you cannot descend to the wadi on the metal ladders – they're for climbing up only.

Both circuits allow walkers to see the waterfall and Ein Avdat pools when leaving from the northernmost parking lot. The waterfall is a 15m-tall chute, best during the rainy season. Near the river basin on the southern end is a poplar grove where a large number of Euphrates trees grow. At this point, the short-hike walkers turn around and head back to the car park. For those doing the one-way, you'll begin the steep climb via iron rungs stuck into the mountainside (fit hikers only). Along the way, you'll pass monks' caves and an ancient Byzantine tower before visiting a series of lookouts while walking towards the dry waterfall. As one can't descend from here, the walking path ends at the southern car park.

Along the way, there are a number of animals to look out for, including ibex and eagles. The brochure has details on other endemic species. As a warning, there is no eating or camping allowed in the park. Swimming is also prohibited.

WALKS AND DRIVES J2.

ITINERARIES Off-the-Beaten-Path Israel and Palestine; Nature and Scenic; Active.

SIMILAR ELECTIVES Try *Wadi Daraja (K1)* and **Masada (#8)** for more tough hikes nearby. **Ein Gedi (#50)** is also a good option.

NEARBY **Avdat (#48)** (4km/4 minutes), **Makhtesh Ramon (#28)** (26km/20 minutes), *Mamshit* (50km/38 minutes), and *Shivta* (52km/38 minutes).

#75 Golan Heights Winery

RATINGS			MACRO-REGION
BUCKET! Score	▮▮▮▮▮▮▯▯▯▯	6/10	I: Golan Heights
Ruin	n/a		
Entertainment	▮▮▮▮▯	4/5	**MICRO-REGION**
Information	▮▮▮▮▯	4/5	I2
Popularity	▮▮▯▯▯	2/5	

THEME/CATEGORY Food and Drink – Wine – Wineries.

HISTORICAL PERIOD *Contemporary.*

ELECT ME Visit the winery that started the wine craze in Israel. It's the winner of multiple international wine awards, including the New World Winery of the Year in 2012 from *Wine Enthusiast* and the Grand Gold Medal at the VINITALY 2011 competition.

CONTEXT In 1984, the year that the Golan Heights Winery's first vintage was released, few predicted that Israel would soon be penetrating the global scene. But this winery is often credited as setting a standard in quality and beginning a new era in international recognition of Israeli wines.

Robert Parker awarded the 2005 Yarden Gewürztraminer (a dessert wine) 93 points during his initial tasting of Israel wines in 2008. He thinks the Bordeau blends (Cabernet/Merlot) and the Syrah will be trademark wines for Israel in the future. In Daniel Rogov's *Ultimate Guide to Israeli Wine*, Golan Heights Winery is considered a five-star, world-class winery. He listed it as the best wine producer in the country (in the book's final edition in 2012) and Galil Mountain as the best value producer.

Yarden is consistently ranked among the best wines in the country, with the Bordeaux blend usually scoring high marks. Its high-alcohol Yarden T2 Touriga Nacional from 2014 was listed in *Food & Wine*'s "The 12 Israeli Wines You Need to Drink to Be an Expert" article. Rogov gives most everything from the Yarden label a score of 90+, with the Katzrin and Rom labels regularly scoring 95+.

Overall, Golan Heights Winery's brands include Golan, Yarden, Gilgal, Hermon, Sion, and *Gamla*. The winery is also the parent company of the smaller Galil Mountain Winery, a collaboration with the neighboring kibbutzim. The company's wines are all kosher but not pasteurized (*mevushal*), meaning there is a big difference between the boiled wines of yesteryear and today's impressive showings, courtesy of this forward-leaning brand.

WORTH THE DETOUR? Absolutely, if in the Golan. The tasting room is purpose-built for visitors, unlike most wineries in the country.

DAYS/HOURS 08.30–17.30 Sunday–Thursday, 08.30–14.00 Friday, closed Saturday.

BEST STRATEGY The winery has a variety of "wine experiences" which include tours of the vineyard, winery, cellar, and of course tasting rooms. All tours and special events must be booked in advance and can be booked online (**w** golanwines.co.il/en).

Walk-ins are allowed (tours are unlikely this way) and small or bulk purchases can be made in the shop.

WALKS AND DRIVES I2, U1.

ITINERARIES Most Entertaining; Food and Drink; National Parks and Reserves; On the Road.

SIMILAR ELECTIVES See the *Wineries* theme (p. 563).

NEARBY *Ancient Qatzrin* (3km/9 minutes), **Capernaum (#33)** (24km/24 minutes), **Nazareth (#29)** (70km/1¼ hours), and *Gamla* (16km/18 minutes).

#76 Ajloun Fortress

RATINGS			MACRO-REGION
BUCKET! Score		4/10	S: North Jordan
Ruin		3/5	
Entertainment		2/5	**MICRO-REGION**
Information		2/5	S2
Popularity		2/5	

THEME/CATEGORY Archaeology – Islamic – Ayyubid.

HISTORICAL PERIOD *Ayyubid* to *Mamluk*.

ELECT ME A uniquely Muslim castle, this well-preserved fort in the north of Jordan served to halt the Crusader expansion into Ayyubid territory. Today, it provides expansive and impressive views from the top.

CONTEXT The castle – also called Qal'at ar-Rabad – in its present form dates to 1184 of the Ayyubid period, towards the end of the first Crusader waves in the region. Built atop a monastery inhabited by a monk called Ajloun, the Ajloun Fortress (or Castle) served as protector of the Damascus–Cairo trade route. It was notably built less than 60km from the Crusaders' castle at **Belvoir (#93)**, which served as the Kurdish Muslim dynasty's point of resistance from further Crusader expansion. The southern part of Jordan had already been conquered by Crusader armies, who set up castles at **Karak (#49)** and *Shobak*, the former being about 150km south of Ajloun. The castle was never a battleground against the Crusaders, losing its strategic importance shortly after the Crusaders were defeated by Saladin's forces in 1187. The castle served in an administrative capacity through subsequent changes of leadership. Though invading Mongol armies attempted to destroy the castle outright, it has been rebuilt and restored over the years.

WORTH THE DETOUR? Only if you're doing a grand tour of Jordan's north.

DAYS/HOURS 08.00–19.00 daily.

BEST STRATEGY Don't forget your Jordan Pass for free entry, then have a tour of the site and make sure to capture views from the top.

WALKS AND DRIVES S2, V1, V2.

ITINERARIES Off-the-Beaten-Path Jordan; Archaeology.

SIMILAR ELECTIVES **Belvoir (#93)**, **Karak (#49)**, and *Shobak* are all Crusader castles from the same period. **Nimrod's Fortress (#85)** is the other famous Ayyubid castle.

NEARBY **Ajloun Forest (#57)** (11km/20 minutes), Dibeen Forest (S2) (18km/25 minutes), *As-Salt* (65km/1¼ hours), Yarmouk Forest (S1) (60km/1¼ hours), and **Umm Qais (#45)** (57km/1¼ hours).

#77 ANU – Museum of the Jewish People

RATINGS		
BUCKET! Score		5/10
Ruin	n/a	
Entertainment		4/5
Information		5/5
Popularity		4/5

MACRO-REGION
D: Tel Aviv

MICRO-REGION
D7

THEME/CATEGORY Culture – Museum – of Culture/Architecture.

HISTORICAL PERIOD *Kingdom of Israel and Judah* to *Contemporary*.

ELECT ME For those with or without Jewish heritage, this museum has created stimulating museum exhibits with visually striking displays. Much of the international collection was donated and each comes with its own incredible story.

CONTEXT After ten years and $100 million-worth of renovations, the new ANU (Hebrew for "we") – Museum of the Jewish People opened in 2021. Purportedly the largest museum dedicated to Jewry in the world, the museum formerly known as Beit Hatfutsot has been gifted all sorts of interesting historical artifacts and novelty pieces. Some of the collection includes Ruth Bader Ginsberg's iconic lace collar, a guitar from Leonard Cohen, and clips and memorabilia from famous Jews in film. There are other types of immersive experiences, such as an interactive Jewish cooking game, poetry and music recitals, and life-size displays of real people describing what it means to be Jewish. Some of the old displays survive, including 11 synagogue replicas from around the world. Kids have their own permanent exhibition in "Heroes," which tells the story of all kinds of people: notably not just military heroes or survivors of the Holocaust, but economists and scientists too, with plenty of female representation.

WORTH THE DETOUR? It's a very interesting museum, but you have to be in the mood for a museum. Those with Jewish ancestry or an interest in Judaica (you're in Israel, after all) will be particularly moved by the diverse exhibits.

DAYS/HOURS 10.00–17.00 Sunday/Monday/Wednesday/Saturday, 10.00–19.00 Tuesday, 10.00–22.00 Thursday, 09.00–14.00 Friday. The museum is located within Tel Aviv University in Ramat Aviv.

BEST STRATEGY Plan at least 2 hours here, though this will be greatly influenced by your speed and interest. It's further north, so you'll need a car or taxi.

WALKS AND DRIVES D7.

ITINERARIES Most Entertaining; Culture; Organized; Memorial; Modernity.

SIMILAR ELECTIVES **Israel Museum (#17)**, **Yad Vashem (#35)**, and **Tel Aviv Museum of Art (#95)** are all highly regarded museums.

NEARBY *MUSA – Eretz Israel Museum* (2km/6 minutes), HaYarkon Park (D7) (5km/15 minutes), *Herziliya Beaches* (12km/19 minutes).

#78 Eilat

	RATINGS		
BUCKET! Score			4/10
Ruin	n/a		
Entertainment			4/5
Information			3/5
Popularity			4/5

MACRO-REGION
L: Eilat and Arabah

MICRO-REGION
L1, L2

THEME/CATEGORY Accommodation – Stays – Vacation Resorts/Hotels.

HISTORICAL PERIOD *Independence and struggle* to *Contemporary.*

ELECT ME A modern resort town, often tacky, but with beaches, snorkeling, nightlife, and potential fun for the whole family. Eilat is the southernmost city in Israel and a 4-hour drive through the desert (or a short flight) from the Anchor Cities of Tel Aviv and Jerusalem. It's also the most expensive of the three Gulf of Aqaba towns; come for relaxation, but plan to spend money! The few activities here can fill a weekend. One other bonus: it's a VAT-free zone.

CONTEXT Eilat is referenced several times in the Bible as an important and lucrative port city which conducted trade with Egypt and its border states of Edom, Rephidim, and Midian. However, *that* Eilat (Ayla in Arabic) is located in downtown Aqaba, Jordan. This Eilat took its name from that ancient city, though is a completely modern invention. At 85km², this city with a population of 50,000 has grown quite a bit since its founding 70 years ago. The town is a post-independence creation set up initially as a port for Israel, but expanded due to copper mining (see **Timna (#96)**) and eventually tourism. Eilat regularly sees more than 2 million overnight visitors annually.

WORTH THE DETOUR? If you're planning on doing **Petra (#2)** going in and out of Jordan on the same day, your best bet is to spend the night in Eilat and cross first thing. If you've tired of hiking, you could do worse than a little fun in the sun in Eilat – though keep in mind that summers are a scorcher: above 40°C/100°F. The water is warm year-round, though the temperature range from December to February is only 10°C/50°F to 23°C/73°F. Humidity is usually low. Two things to note: the coral off the Red Sea is badly damaged, in large part due to the rapid rise of the Red Sea tourism industry. You will see fish, but not in the best conditions. It can also get extremely crowded with families and kids, particularly on Israeli holidays.

BEST STRATEGY Getting here is a bit of a struggle, so if your goal is Eilat, plan to spend at least the weekend. Make sure to book hotels well in advance.

ACTIVITIES **Beaches** include (from north to south) North (2km stretch), Mosh (most popular), Dolphin Reef (activity), Coral (protected reserve), and Princess (snorkeling, near Taba). **Glass-bottom boats** can be booked at your hotel (usually around $20). **Sailboats** cruise to Egypt ($100 pp full-day, but a bargain). **Bird-watching** can be done at the International Birding and Research Center (**w** ibrceilat.blogspot.co.il). Several local shops can offer courses in **kitesurfing** (waves are flat to choppy). **Scuba** can be found all along the waterfront, but is best at **Coral Beach (#83)**. **Snorkeling** is also all along the waterfront. For **parasailing** see **w** eilat.city/en/eilat-parasailing and for the **camel ranch** and treks see **w** eilat.city/en/camel-ranch. **Duty-free shopping** is everywhere – it's a duty-free zone. Save 17%! **Coral World Underwater Observatory** is a popular indoor/outdoor aquarium, and **Dolphin Reef** is a research station where you can swim with dolphins. Further afield, **Timna Valley Park** has walking trails, movies, and events.

EVENTS The **Red Sea Jazz Festival** takes place in the last week of August (**w** redseajazz.co.il), and the same organizers run the **Winter Jazz Festival**, usually in February. **Red Sea Classical Music Festival** is in winter, and, for bird lovers, **Eilat Spring Migration Festival** happens in March.

COSTS **Public beaches** are free, but you'll pay 20–30 ILS for beach chairs. You have to pay to visit a **private club/beach**, such as Coral Reef Beach (35 ILS adults, 18 ILS seniors/children); true private beaches are found at hotels for residents. A **mid-range restaurant** will set you back $20–25 per person (normally seafood), and an **upper-end hotel** will be $300–400 per night during the busy season and $250–300 per night during the low (summer) season. Bear in mind that hotels in **Aqaba (#43)** are much cheaper ($100–150/night) and Taba (T1) is cheaper still (under $100/night). **Snorkeling** equipment for the day is 40–60 ILS, while **diving** is $60 for a half-day, $120 for a full day, and $250–400 for a two- to five-day beginner open-water course. **Bird-watching courses** are 150 ILS for 2 hours, 220 ILS for 4 hours, 400 ILS for a full day, around $450 for three days, and around $800 for six days.

WALKS AND DRIVES L1, L2.

ITINERARIES Most Entertaining; Active; Accommodation; Organized; Relaxation; Romantic; Under the Sun; Luxury; Kid-Focused; All Ages.

SIMILAR ELECTIVES See **Red Sea/Gulf of Aqaba (#10)** for exploring the sea. **Timna (#96)** is the only historical site in the area.

NEARBY **Timna (#96)** (30km/25 minutes), **Yotvata Hai-Bar** (35km/30 minutes), **Red Canyon** (23km/23 minutes), Neot Smadar Winery (L3) (60km/45 minutes), and **Kibbutz Lotan** (53km/40 minutes).

#79 Beit She'arim

RATINGS		
BUCKET! Score		5/10
Ruin		3/5
Entertainment		3/5
Information		2/5
Popularity		2/5

MACRO-REGION
G: Lower Galilee & Kinneret

MICRO-REGION
G2

THEME/CATEGORY Religion – Sacred – Burial.

HISTORICAL PERIOD *Syria Palaestina* to *Byzantine*.

ELECT ME Both a National Park and a UNESCO site, this elective documents the resting place of the famous 2nd-century CE Jewish rabbi, leader of the Sanhedrin, and editor of the Mishnah (the oral Torah in Jewish tradition), Yehuda HaNasi. He was buried in the site's famous necropolis, with further catacombs being carved into the soft limestone over the next 200 years. Several of the burial cave systems are open for visitors and contain interesting sarcophagi and wall paintings from that era.

CONTEXT Meaning "House of the Gates" in Hebrew, the Arab village of Sheikh Abreik was finally identified in 1936 as the historic site of Beit She'arim, or Besara in Greek (from when it was founded). The site had long been referenced as the burial site for Jews following the expulsion from Jerusalem after the Roman–Jewish wars of the 1st century CE, but its location had never been confirmed. Following the death of Rabbi Yehuda HaNasi, who requested to be buried here in lieu of the **Mount of Olives (#34)** burial site in Jerusalem (which was then off-limits), many Jews chose to be buried near him at Beit She'arim. The town became a popular burial place for the next several centuries, before its destruction by a Roman governor in 351 CE.

More than 20 burial caves (technically "burial cave systems," as many rooms are interconnected) have been found on the site, with some dating to the 1st century CE, but most dating to the 2nd–4th centuries. Believed to be a vast necropolis network, only part of the site has been excavated. Many sarcophagi are still in situ, with inscriptions in Aramaic, Greek, Hebrew, and Palymyrian (a Syrian dialect of Aramaic). Several more are unexcavated, mostly because the graves are in poor shape and were victims of vandalism some time in the 8th–9th centuries.

WORTH THE DETOUR? Yes, worth a quick visit if you're doing a tour of Israel's north. If you're in a hurry, scurry to the Cave of the Coffins.

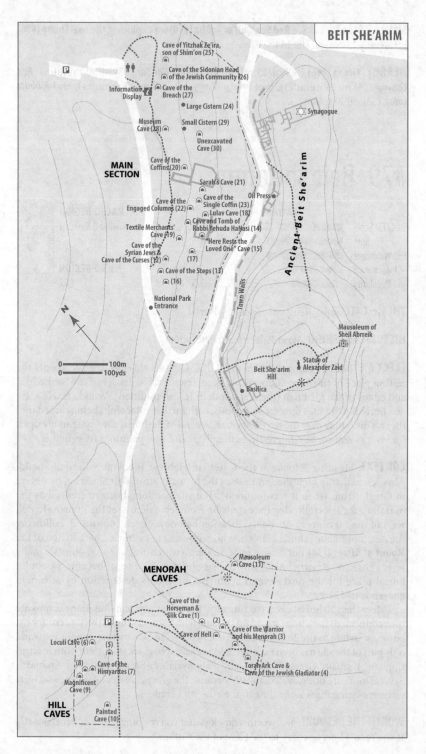

Cave of Yitzhak Ze'ira,
son of Shim'on (25)

Cave of the Sidonian Head
of the Jewish Community (26)

Information
Display

Cave of the
Breach (27)

Synagogue

Large Cistern (24)

Museum
Cave (28)

Small Cistern (29)

Unexcavated
Cave (30)

MAIN
SECTION

Cave of the
Coffins (20)

Sarah's Cave (21)

Cave of the
Engaged Columns (22)

Cave of the
Single Coffin (23)

Oil Press

Lulav Cave (18)

Textile Merchants'
Cave (19)

Cave and Tomb of
Rabbi Yehuda HaNasi (14)

Cave of the
Syrian Jews &
Cave of the Curses (12)

"Here Rests the
Loved One" Cave (15)

(17)

Cave of the Steps (13)

(16)

National Park
Entrance

Ancient Beit She'arim

Mausoleum of
Sheil Abrreik

Statue of
Alexander Zaid

0 ———— 100m
0 ———— 100yds

Beit She'arim
Hill

Basilica

Town Walls

Mausoleum
Cave (11)

MENORAH
CAVES

Cave of the
Horseman &
Slik Cave (1)

(2)

Cave of the Warrior
and his Menorah (3)

Cave of Hell

Loculi Cave (6)

(5)

Torah Ark Cave &
Cave of the Jewish Gladiator (4)

(8)

Cave of the
Himyarites (7)

Magnificent
Cave (9)

HILL
CAVES

Painted
Cave (10)

DAYS/HOURS 08.00–16.00 daily, closes 17.00 Saturday–Thursday in summer.

BEST STRATEGY Around 20 caves can be entered, though many are tiny. The most impressive of the bunch include the facade of the Rabbi Yehuda HaNasi cave, Cave of the Coffins (the largest, with nearly two dozen sarcophagi on site), and the Menorah Caves (1–4). Use the map provided on site to follow along the marked path and learn about the individual rooms. You'll need 2–3 hours.

WALKS AND DRIVES G2, W5.

ITINERARIES Off-the-Beaten-Path Israel and Palestine; Noteworthy; Religion; UNESCO; Endangered; National Parks/Reserves; Memorial; Big-Group Friendly.

SIMILAR ELECTIVES The **Old Town of Hebron (#46)** is home to the Cave of the Patriarchs. The **Mount of Olives (#34)** is the most famous Jewish burial ground, while nearby Kidron Valley (A5) has above-ground tombs. See the *Burial* category (p. 496) for more recommendations.

NEARBY *Haifa* (20km/25 minutes), **Akko (#13)** (35km/35 minutes), **Nazareth (#29)** (25km/30 minutes), and **Megiddo (#59)** (17km/22 minutes).

#80 Banias

RATINGS		MACRO-REGION
BUCKET! Score	4/10	I: Golan Heights
Ruin	2/5	
Entertainment	3/5	MICRO-REGION
Information	2/5	I1
Popularity	4/5	

THEME/CATEGORY Archaeology – Ancient Israel – Empires.

HISTORICAL PERIOD *Greek* to *Crusader*.

ELECT ME A pleasant hiking trail along an easy, elevated footpath through the forest, with a roaring waterfall as reward at the end. There are rare Greek ruins on site dedicated to the god Pan.

CONTEXT Also known as Hermon Stream Nature Reserve, this ancient city has undergone a number of name changes, including Banias for its Greek history and Caesarea Phillipi per the Romans. In fact, the Greeks knew the site as Panion, and later Paneas, as a dedication to the god Pan. Pan was the god of music and hunting, and from the waist down he was an anthropomorphized goat. The Seleucids controlled the area during the Hellenist period when the city appears to have been founded, and introduced Pan worship to the region, which stuck for several more centuries. There are various cutouts in the mountain indicating the niches where the shrines to Pan were once placed. At the base of a tall cliff, a temple to Pan was built onto a 70 × 40m ledge. The back of the temple is referred to as "the Cave of Pan" because the rear wall was once a cave, until the ceiling collapsed.

There is plenty more history here. According to Scripture, this is the location where Jesus is said to have told his disciple Peter that Peter was the rock on which Christianity would be built. Near the Springs Parking Lot are remnants of several other periods of history. The Palace of Agrippa dates to the late Herodians, specifically Agrippa II. A mosque in the south wall dates to the Mamluks. Little remains of the massive Crusader fortifications that once surrounded the town, but there are remnants of a Crusader wall.

Visitors are encouraged to go on foot (45 minutes) to the Banias waterfall, though you can drive to the Waterfall Parking Lot which saves a lot of time, but misses the nice walk. Truly, the site's main attraction is the Suspended Trail, a forest suspension bridge that hugs the cliffside next to the Hermon Stream and leads to a roaring waterfall, the most powerful in the country. No swimming, though.

WORTH THE DETOUR? This is a very popular site with locals. The archaeology is not clear to the lay visitor, so you'll need to pore over the provided brochure to understand the history. If doing a full tour of the **Golan Heights (#62)**, tack it on, but you needn't go out of your way unless you can't leave Israel without seeing its biggest waterfall.

DAYS/HOURS 08.00–16.00 daily, closes 17.00 Saturday–Thursday in summer.

BEST STRATEGY The site's history is interesting, but without reconstruction is hard to visualize. The walk along the Hermon Stream on the suspended bridge is nice, thus we recommend parking in the Springs Parking Lot and either having a second car waiting in the Waterfall Parking Lot at the end of the trail, or plan on a 2-hour hike round-trip. There's a picnic area for lunch.

WALKS AND DRIVES I1.

ITINERARIES Off-the-Beaten-Path Israel and Palestine; Archaeology; Nature and Scenic; All Ages.

SIMILAR ELECTIVES There are a number of nature reserves in the Golan and Galilee Panhandle nearby, including *Gamla*, *Hula Lake*, and *Yehudiya*.

NEARBY **Nimrod's Fortress (#85)** (6km/9 minutes), *Mount Hermon* (21km/30 minutes), **Tel Dan (#63)** (5km/7 minutes), and **Nazareth (#29)** (94km/1¼ hours).

#81 Umm ar-Rasas

RATINGS		MACRO-REGION
BUCKET! Score	5/10	O: King's Highway
Ruin	3/5	
Entertainment	2/5	**MICRO-REGION**
Information	1/5	01
Popularity	1/5	

THEME/CATEGORY Archaeology – Ancient Cities – Mosaics.

HISTORICAL PERIOD *Syria Palaestina* to *Abbasid/Fatimid*.

ELECT ME There are really two highlights at this UNESCO site: the grand mosaic floor at the Church of St. Stephen and an intact 14m-tall tower used by monks some time between the 3rd and 9th centuries CE as a place to live and pray in elevated isolation. There are 16 other churches at the main site; though mostly rubble, several have extensive mosaics on display showcasing incredible craftwork.

CONTEXT Possibly the biblical city of Mephaat, this UNESCO site was originally a Roman garrison camp used to guard the Via Traiana Nova, an offshoot of the ancient King's Highway. One of the inscriptions on the later Byzantine churches gives the name of the town as Kastrom Mefa'a.

Most of the site is not yet excavated. What is on display includes Byzantine mosaics, several ancient churches, and a tall tower. The floor mosaic in the Church of St. Stephen is the largest mosaic yet uncovered in Jordan. There were six artists involved in its creation and, like nearby **Madaba (#19)**, the tiles also reveal a map of the neighboring cities and towns. Interestingly, this map mosaic – and many of the artwork found inside churches of the same historical period – dates to 785 CE, well after Muslims had conquered the region. This shows that Christians not only remained present, but were tolerated for centuries.

On site, 16 other churches have been identified, many of which have their own mosaic floors, showcasing flora and fauna. Other portions of Umm ar-Rasas have been reconstructed, including a few noticeable archways, but be prepared for a lot of dust and debris. The mosaics have roof coverings for protection.

The other main feature of the site is the Stylite tower, located a mile north of Umm ar-Rasas, and the last of its kind left standing in the Middle East. These skinny, solid structures were built for ascetic Christian monks (as evidenced by the many Christian elements etched into the stone) to spend time in isolation high off the ground. At 14m, it's an excellent example of these well-documented, but poorly salvaged, buildings.

WORTH THE DETOUR? Yes, if you're ticking off UNESCO sites. Also yes if you're doing *Road Trips O1* or *P2* and considering a detour. If you are a die-hard Byzantine mosaic fan, consider as a day trip from **Amman (#36/#37)**.

DAYS/HOURS 08.00–16.00 daily; later in summer, earlier in Ramadan.

BEST STRATEGY At the very least, you'll want to see St. Stephen's Church and the Stylite tower, which won't take you more than an hour. The site contains minimal explanation. You'll want to hire a local guide if you're interested in the history.

WALKS AND DRIVES O1, V2, W5.

ITINERARIES Off-the-Beaten-Path Jordan; Noteworthy; Culture; UNESCO.

SIMILAR ELECTIVES **Madaba and the Madaba Map (#19)**.

NEARBY **Madaba and the Madaba Map (#19)** (30km/40 minutes), **Wadi Mujib and Mujib Biosphere Reserve (#23)** (11km/17 minutes), **Karak (#49)** (86km/1¼ hours), **Dead Sea (#3)** (63km/1¼ hours), and **Amman (#36/#37)** (77km/1 hour).

#82 Tel Aviv Nightlife

RATINGS			MACRO-REGION
BUCKET! Score	▰▰▰▰▰▰▱▱▱	6/10	D: Tel Aviv
Ruin	n/a		
Entertainment	▰▰▰▰▰▰▰▰▱	5/5	**MICRO-REGIONS**
Information	▰▰▰▰▰▱▱▱	3/5	D3, D4, D6
Popularity	▰▰▰▰▰▰▰▰▱	5/5	

THEME/CATEGORY Entertainment – Party – Nightlife.

HISTORICAL PERIOD *Contemporary.*

ELECT ME Tel Aviv offers something for everyone: young or mature; Jewish or not; LGBTQI or straight; casual or classy; music-, food-, or alcohol-focused. Lose the shoes while drinking beers on the beach, go full hipster in Florentin (or any of half a dozen other casual-chic neighborhoods), dance the night away at dingy warehouses, or while the night away at your favorite restaurant where the chefs are just as likely to join you for drinks at the end of the night shift. Tel Aviv's fun. It's really fun.

CONTEXT Over the last ten years, Tel Aviv has taken off as a center of entertainment and nightlife in the Middle East, if not the world. With its laid-back and tolerant attitude, most anything goes – even in this brazenly religious country, with staunchly conservative Jerusalem only 45 minutes away. Many of Tel Aviv's own neighborhoods and residents are deeply religious, but downtown is a different world, with beautiful weather year-round offering nightlife that literally spills out onto the city streets. Many bars and clubs don't open before midnight, so it's no surprise how the city earned its nickname, "The City That Never Sleeps."

Imperial Bar (#99) leads the way for craft cocktails, twice having earned the title of World's 50 Best Bars. Hipsters rule the roost with tons of places that simultaneously feel like a college garage party, your friend's basement apartment, and an underground club in New York City. Our top six bars in Tel Aviv worth exploring are Imperial, Bellboy Bar (D4), Kuli Alma (D4), Par Derriere (D4), Suramare (D4), and Butler Bar (D4).

The Spartacus Gay Travel Index ranks Israel as the 23rd most gay-friendly country for foreigners (largely thanks to Tel Aviv, it must be said) and Nestpick produced an index that put Tel Aviv as the fourth-best LGBT city in the world.

But don't just take our word for it: w hotels.com ranks Tel Aviv as one of the ten best nightlife destinations in the world, while *Fodor's* lists Tel Aviv among its top 20. *Thrillist* ranks it as 12th in the world for party cities and *CNN Travel* listed it as one of the best party cities globally.

WORTH THE DETOUR? Yes, because it's a complete 180° from the religiosity and archaeology and history you've been inundated with elsewhere around the country.

BEST STRATEGY There's a ton to go over here. Luckily, we do just that in Part 4, *Today in the Holy Land.* We go over eating, drinking, and after-hours entertainment in Do #18: *Late Nit!* (p. 107), with sections on bars, music, clubs, social connections, and food. Almost everything revolves around Tel Aviv.

Not everyone's idea of fun includes drinking. Tel Aviv caters to all nightlife types, and even comes with a world-class performing arts scene. Seek out itinerary ideas in the *Culture* themes (p. 545). We also have great suggestions in the *Fine Arts* itinerary (p. 801).

WALKS D3, D4, D6.

ITINERARIES Tel Aviv Immersion; Most Entertaining; Leisure; Entertainment.

SIMILAR ELECTIVES For a full report, see **Tel Aviv (#5)**. Combine with *Modern Israeli Cuisine*. Be sure to check out **Imperial Bar (#99)** and its ilk (see the *Entertainment* theme, p. 557) and "Bars" in *Do #18: Late Nit!* (p. 107).

NEARBY See **Tel Aviv (#5)**.

#83 Coral Beach

RATINGS			MACRO-REGION
BUCKET! Score	▬▬▬▬▬	4/10	L: Eilat and Arabah
Ruin	n/a		
Entertainment	▬▬▬▬	3/5	**MICRO-REGION**
Information	▬▬▬▬	3/5	L2
Popularity	▬▬▬	2/5	

THEME/CATEGORY Active – Water Sports – Snorkeling.

HISTORICAL PERIOD N/A.

ELECT ME This 1,200m coral reef is the most northerly in the world, one of the most densely populated, and the only coral in Israel. Snorkeling is the highlight here, with capped visitor numbers each day. Changing rooms, beach chairs, showers, bathrooms, and other amenities are available for those not wanting the underwater experience. Renting gear for snorkeling and diving is easy.

CONTEXT This nature reserve is one of the only places to get unobstructed views of coral in the **Eilat (#78)** area. The reserve extends 1.2km while the reef structure is much longer at 12km, and extends south to the Egyptian border.

The reserve makes it very simple to access the coral reef, including renting snorkeling equipment or organizing diving day trips. The water is amazingly clear making it easy to see the coral, sea grasses, and plethora of fish, sharks, octopi, eels, turtles, and other marine life. There are wading pools for small kids and bridges that allow visitors to see the coral and its life from above. There's plenty of beach, chairs for rent, and facilities for changing.

The area has only grown in popularity over the years and Israel understandably wants to profit from that. Yet there are signs that, despite the best efforts of the reserve, tourism in general is harmful to the reefs. Sunscreen damages coral, as do artificial light (from the streetlights), inexperienced divers, and people touching the coral. Multiply these harmful effects by millions of additional visitors per year (if government plans are achieved) and the reserve won't be hosting guests too much longer. The coral is already badly damaged in several places, though sea life continues to be plentiful.

WORTH THE DETOUR? No, you don't need to carve time out of your schedule specifically to see this beach unless you already have plans to be in **Eilat (#78)**. The reef is an interesting bonus in a trip to Eilat, but there are far nicer reefs in the world – and even in nearby Sinai (see below).

DAYS/HOURS 08.00–17.00 daily, closes 18.00 Saturday–Thursday in summer.

BEST STRATEGY The water is comfortable year-round. There is an entrance fee that limits the number of people coming in. There's a separate cost for renting snorkeling equipment. If you'd like to see the underwater life without actually getting into the water, try next door's *Underwater Observatory*. Or do both in the same day!

WALKS AND DRIVES L2.

ITINERARIES Nature and Scenic; Active; All Ages.

SIMILAR ELECTIVES See **Red Sea/Gulf of Aqaba (#10)**, **Aqaba (#43)**, and **Ras Mohammad (#53)**.

NEARBY **Eilat (#78)** (8km/13 minutes), *Underwater Observatory* (650m/2 minutes), and Taba (T1) (4km/10 minutes plus border control).

#84 Petra Kitchen

RATINGS		MACRO-REGION
BUCKET! Score	6/10	N: Petra
Ruin	n/a	
Entertainment	4/5	MICRO-REGION
Information	4/5	N3
Popularity	4/5	

THEME/CATEGORY Organized – Participatory – Cooking.

HISTORICAL PERIOD *Contemporary*.

ELECT ME Learn to cook Jordanian food! Located a block from the entrance to **Petra (#2)** in **Wadi Rum (#4)**, this restaurant/classroom lets you participate in a four-hour course preparing an authentic Jordanian meal, with mezze and mains, shared by everyone at a late dinner.

CONTEXT As though Petra weren't reason enough, this Jordanian cooking class tops off a day exploring the region's history with an exploration of Jordan's gastronomic contributions to the world food scene. Two courses are available. The most popular – so popular that it can book up weeks in advance, depending on the season – is the one-night course, which includes non-alcoholic drinks, a soup, several interesting mezze platters, and a vegetarian and/or meat main. You'll also get the recipes cooked that evening so you can recreate the meal at home. Additionally, there's a five-day workshop that includes shopping trips to local markets. Your cooking tutors will work out hotel and activity arrangements for you as well. Guests are responsible for performing pretty basic cooking techniques, though some may be unfamiliar due to the Levantine cooking practices. Chopping, mixing, and plating are typical responsibilities over the evening. This event has been featured on just about every news source available and is widely regarded.

WORTH THE DETOUR? If **Petra (#2)** is on your list, you won't have to detour. The rest of the food in **Wadi Rum (#4)** is fine, but this is a culinary experience you shouldn't miss.

DAYS/HOURS 08.30–23.30 daily; course begins at 18.00/18.30.

BEST STRATEGY Book in advance at **w** petrakitchen.com. If you wait until you arrive to check on availability, head straight to the restaurant to ask for any last-minute seats for the coming days. Same-day requests will likely not be possible. **Petra (#2)** can be exhausting, so make sure you save some energy for the evening.

WALKS AND DRIVES N3.

ITINERARIES BUCKET! Itinerary; Most Entertaining; Entertainment; Organized; Community; Gourmet.

SIMILAR ELECTIVES *Beit Sitti* cooking school in Amman is also popular. *Druze Cooking Workshops (H1)* in the Galilee are worth exploring too.

NEARBY The entrance to **Petra (#2)** is a 350m/5-minute walk.

#85 Nimrod's Fortress

RATINGS				MACRO-REGION
BUCKET! Score		6/10		I: Golan Heights
Ruin		3/5		
Entertainment		2/5		MICRO-REGION
Information		2/5		I1
Popularity		2/5		

THEME/CATEGORY Archaeology – Islamic – Ayyubid.

HISTORICAL PERIOD *Ayyubid.*

ELECT ME This castle is the most complete of all the medieval castles in Israel, and from its perch has stunning views of **Mount Hermon**, the Golan plains, and a flat view across to Syria. There are also secret passageways and nice sunset vantages.

CONTEXT Nimrod's Fortress has gone by several names, including Mivtzar Nimrod in Hebrew and Qal'at al-Subeiba ("Castle of the Large Cliff") in Arabic. Tradition ascribed the name "Nimrod" from the biblical story of a great hunter. It was finished in 1230 by the Ayyubid caliph al-Aziz 'Uthman (nephew of Saladin) in order to block

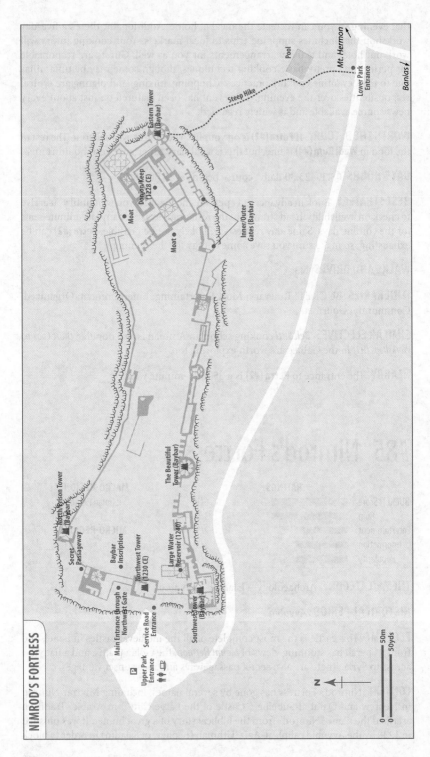

NIMROD'S FORTRESS

N

0 ——— 50m
0 ——— 50yds

Upper Park Entrance

Service Road Entrance
Main Entrance through Northwest Gate

Southwest Tower (Baybar)
Northwest Tower (1230 CE)
Large Water Reservoir (1240)
Baybar Inscription
Secret Passageway
Northwest Tower (Baybar)

The Beautiful Tower (Baybar)

Moat
Moat
Inner/Outer Gates (Baybar)
Donjon/Keep (1228 CE)
Eastern Tower (Baybar)

Steep Hike
Pool

Mt. Hermon
Lower Park Entrance
Banias

Crusader armies in the west from attacking Damascus (which lies only 60km away). In this way, it served its purpose, thwarting the Crusader attack of 1253 and nearly ending the European expansion through the region. Instead, the Mongols stampeded through in 1260, destroying the place. The Mongols' grip on the land didn't last; they experienced one of their first defeats at the hands of the Mamluk army, which pushed them out of the territory. The Mamluks took over Nimrod and expanded it, adding the circular towers in 1275. Inside the fortress, near the westernmost wall, there's a massive inscription some 1.35m tall and 6m wide documenting the date of construction – the largest of its kind in Israel. Once the Crusaders had left the Holy Land permanently, the castle lost its principal purpose and fell into disrepair. Over the centuries, it was irregularly used as a prison, then later served as a residence of shepherds and Druze.

WORTH THE DETOUR? It's in the far north, so no need to make a special trip unless you're a big castle fan. If you have plans to go to Golan, it's worth adding this impressive fortress into your itinerary.

DAYS/HOURS 08.00–16.00 daily, closes 17.00 Saturday–Thursday in summer.

BEST STRATEGY You need at least 1½–2 hours to hike and explore. The hiking route starts near the ticket office. We recommend doing the hike to the top if you have time, as the clifftop perch adds to the experience and understanding of the site's regional significance. That said, there are two other easy-access entrances: one with stairs by the northwest tower and the other on a service road for those with mobility issues – both a short distance from the parking lot. Don't miss ascending the eastern tower (four stories), called the *donjon* or keep, for the best views. The brochure includes a useful walking tour which explains the stages of growth of the site.

WALKS AND DRIVES I1.

ITINERARIES Off-the-Beaten-Path Israel and Palestine; Archaeology; National Parks/Reserves.

SIMILAR ELECTIVES **Ajloun Fortress (#76)** in Jordan is the other principal Ayyubid-era castle.

NEARBY **Banias (#80)** (6km/10 minutes), **_Mount Hermon_** (16km/26 minutes), and **Capernaum and Tabgha (#33)** (66km/1 hour).

#86 Feynan Ecolodge

RATINGS		MACRO-REGION
BUCKET! Score	8/10	O: King's Highway
Ruin	n/a	
Entertainment	4/5	**MICRO-REGION**
Information	5/5	01
Popularity	4/5	

THEME/CATEGORY Accommodation – Stays – Experiential Lodging.

HISTORICAL PERIOD *Contemporary.*

ELECT ME This mostly all-inclusive ecolodge in the **Dana Biosphere Reserve (#21)** is worth at least one night's stay. All food and activities are included in the price and they've incorporated several activities you might be interested in: desert hiking, meeting the local community, cooking Jordanian cuisine, getting off the grid, stargazing in dark sky country, and of course visiting the Dana reserve itself.

CONTEXT You may have heard of "ecolodges," which seek to offer various levels of comfort (from simple to luxurious) in obscure destinations using sustainable environmental and tourism practices. In reality, this can include any number of features, from limited electricity and water usage to incorporating local communities into activities. This particular ecolodge actively engages with the local Bedouin community, while maintaining full awareness in practicing "green" behavior so as to minimize environmental impact. Feynan is a joint venture between EcoHotels and Jordan's **Royal Society for the Conservation of Nature (RSCN)**, which is responsible for the care of Jordan's several nature reserves.

Located in Dana, guests are shuttled from a reception desk in the village of Feynan to the hotel (or you can hike in). Candles made by villagers light the way after dark and the stars at night are incredible. Part of the allure of the place is being removed from civilization for a short while. While there is Wi-Fi in the hotel lobby, there isn't elsewhere and you can turn off the world for a little bit (but check in if you absolutely need to). Electricity is all solar-powered, so charging is limited to the reception desk as there are no outlets in guest rooms. Food is vegetarian and delicious, and includes all meals for the stay. The chefs are all trained and hired locally, but are truly spectacular at their jobs. There are tons of delicious dining options, even for picky eaters, with the food focused primarily on the local cuisine – think falafel, fattoush salad, spreads, mezze, and other Jordanian and desert specialties. Cooking classes are a popular inclusion and offer basic lessons. Guests can purchase souvenirs crafted by some of the 500 Bedouin community members. Hiking options are varied and numerous, but heading off with a guide is recommended – even on the easy trails – as the knowledge of the indigenous people makes the experience so much more worthwhile. There are also several experiences integrating the local Bedouin community, including a delightful coffee-making ritual, application of eye makeup, and walking with non-English-speaking shepherds for a full day.

WORTH THE DETOUR? Given the number of activities you can partake in, and the rare chance to interact with locals in a small group atmosphere that doesn't feel exploitative, we think Feynan is a great option. Though more expensive than a normal hotel, it's well worth the cost given all that's included.

DAYS/HOURS Front office 09.00–17.00 Sunday–Thursday; check-in 15.00, check-out 11.00.

BEST STRATEGY If you're taking the multiday trip along the **King's Highway (#31)**, this makes for a well-timed stopping point. There are a number of ways to enter the park and reach the ecolodge, all of which are explored on the website. Spend at least a night, and longer if you want to take advantage of the hiking, quiet, and stars. Reservations are necessary (**w** ecohotels.me/Feynan).

WALKS AND DRIVES P1, O1.

ITINERARIES High BUCKET! Scores: 7+; Most Entertaining; Off-the-Beaten-Path Jordan; Noteworthy; Society and People; Food and Drink; Accommodation; National Parks and Reserves; Community; Gourmet.

SIMILAR ELECTIVES **Wadi Rum (#4)** offers great outdoor glamping experiences.

NEARBY Dana (within); **Petra (#2)** (63km/1¾ hours), **Shobak** (83km/2 hours), and **Dead Sea (#3)**/Suweimeh (170km/2½ hours).

#87 Carmel Market

RATINGS		MACRO-REGION
BUCKET! Score	6/10	D: Tel Aviv
Ruin	n/a	
Entertainment	3/5	**MICRO-REGIONS**
Information	3/5	D3, D6
Popularity	5/5	

THEME/CATEGORY Food and Drink – Food – Markets.

HISTORICAL PERIOD *Mandatory Palestine* to *Contemporary*.

ELECT ME This downtown food market in Tel Aviv is easy to peruse, has great street food, showcases the wild diversity of products available in this Mediterranean/desert country, and offers a perspective on the way people shop, bargain, and live… though it's also very touristy.

CONTEXT Tel Aviv's trendiest and probably largest outdoor market, the Carmel Market (or Shuk HaCarmel, in Hebrew) passes primarily down HaCarmel Street, though there are several offshoots (see a good map at w en.shuktlv.co.il/category/carmel-market-map). Vendors sell everything from cheese, produce, herbs, and various proteins to fast food, souvenirs, clothes, and wares.

There are a number of worthy food stops along the way. Several popular food stands include falafel at HaKitzonet, hummus at Hummus HaCarmel, Jerusalem mix sandwich at Bar Ochel, shakshuka at Shukshuka, meatwiches at M25 (D3), and bourekas at the boureka place. You can wash everything down with coffee, lemonade, fresh juice, beer, and other tasty beverages. Most vendors speak Hebrew, English, and probably some Arabic. Feel free to practice what you know.

Food tours are an option, too. Tourist Israel and Delicious Israel both run 3-hour tours which include sampling some obscure tastes you probably won't find elsewhere, such as etrog citrus, lahuh bread, and khat juice (a controversial Yemeni stimulant). Or go a step up and join a market tour/cooking class (f jonjonfoodtour).

The market makes for a great early morning adventure, but there are crowds all day long. It has a completely different vibe at night, when the shops close but the restaurants and bars spill out into the alleys. Note, though, the market is closed Friday afternoons and all day Saturday in observance of Shabbat.

WORTH THE DETOUR? Yes, this is a must-do in Tel Aviv on one of your days, takes as little time as you can spare, and incorporates lunch, which you needed to plan for anyway.

DAYS/HOURS 07.30–19.00 Sunday–Thursday, 06.30–2 hours before Shabbat Friday, closed Saturday.

BEST STRATEGY If you're staying for a week and shopping for meals, go early. That's when all the best produce is available and tourism numbers are low. For lunch, go anytime – the stands get started early. If you want to avoid midday traffic, you can also go at the end of the day, which is calmer and when you can find some good deals.

WALKS AND DRIVES D3, D6.

ITINERARIES Tel Aviv Immersion; Food and Drink; Organized; Community; Gourmet; Shoestring.

SIMILAR ELECTIVES Mehane Yehuda Market (#67) in Jerusalem is comparable in size and diversity. Other popular markets in Tel Aviv include Levinsky Market (D4), HaTikva Market (D8), Sarona Market (D3), *Tel Aviv Port*, and **Jaffa (#30)**, among others – check out the *Markets* category (p. 557).

NEARBY *Rothschild Boulevard* (850m/10 minutes), Trumpeldor Beach (1.2km/15 minutes), Dizengoff Square (1.3km/17 minutes), and Jaffa Clock Tower (D2) (2.1km/25 minutes).

#88 Sharm el-Sheikh

RATINGS		MACRO-REGION
BUCKET! Score	6/10	T: Sinai
Ruin	n/a	
Entertainment	3/5	MICRO-REGION
Information	3/5	T1
Popularity	4/5	

THEME/CATEGORY Accommodation – Stays – Vacation Resorts.

HISTORICAL PERIOD *Contemporary.*

ELECT ME This holiday resort area welcomes visitors looking for relaxation, some nightlife, and a posh atmosphere you'd be pressed to find elsewhere in Egypt. There are resorts stretching along the coastline at various price points. Sharm's real charm is found underwater: at diving sites. The famed **Ras Mohammad (#53)** national park is nearby, with boats heading out in droves every morning filled with snorkelers and scuba fanatics. It's also easy to coordinate trips to the trekking sites of **St. Catherine's Monastery (#22)** and **Mount Sinai (#15)**.

CONTEXT Sharm el-Sheikh is a resort town. Like other resort towns, quality varies. There are certainly plenty of two- and three-star hotels or Airbnbs that can save you money if you're on a budget, plan to dive a lot, or won't spend much time in your lodging. But the point of Sharm is to enjoy yourself so, for those looking to relax, we recommend splurging. You'll find there's little to do in town, but you can spend an afternoon strolling through the market and visiting Sharm's attractive mosque.

There are a number of high-end hotels, many of which have all-inclusive options. Beware of "five-star" hotels that cost less than $100. The Four Seasons is probably the nicest property in town, while the Royal Savoy and Rixos properties are less expensive and get high marks. Restaurants run the international gamut. Chinese, Indian, American, Italian – all are available, at good quality and decent prices.

Sharm became popular in the 1970s during the Israeli occupation of the Sinai, which was returned in 1982. The Egyptians continued to promote its glorious beaches, astounding underwater life, and laid-back attitude. The buildup of hotels over the last few decades has removed some of that carefree mindset as big properties have encouraged astounding growth. If you're looking for something quieter, check out **Dahab (#54)**.

Terrorism has been a concern for some time, with bombings in 2005 and an ISIS attack against a civilian plane in 2015 that killed more than 200 people. Several countries now recommend avoiding the Sinai altogether, though some make carve-outs for flying directly to Sharm (including the USA). The tourism industry has suffered greatly as a result. A pity, but we concur that travel should not include unnecessary risks/danger. Visit again once the situation in Egypt stabilizes.

WORTH THE DETOUR? If you're in Israel or Jordan, you have plenty of beach and resort options in **Tel Aviv (#5)**, **Eilat (#78)**, **Modern Amman (#36)**, the **Dead Sea (#3)**, and elsewhere, so you needn't make a special trip to Sharm unless you're a big fan of diving. If scuba is your passion, you'll want to coordinate a visit to **Ras Mohammad (#53)**. It also provides access to **Mount Sinai (#15)** and **St. Catherine's Monastery (#22)**.

BEST STRATEGY Getting to Sharm is a bit of a hassle as there are not many direct flights. That said, most countries recommend air transport to bypass the scattered terrorist cells located in the north of the Sinai. We recommend flying, even if you do get routed through Europe.

WALKS AND DRIVES T1.

ITINERARIES Nature and Scenic; Active; Accommodation; Relaxation; Romantic; Under the Sun; All Ages.

SIMILAR ELECTIVES **Eilat (#78)** and **Aqaba (#43)** for resorts and diving.

NEARBY **Ras Mohammad (#53)** (45km/45 minutes) and **Dahab (#54)** (90km/1¼ hours).

#89 Tel Aviv Beaches

RATINGS			MACRO-REGION
BUCKET! Score	▰▰▰▰▱	8/10	D: Tel Aviv
Ruin	n/a		
Entertainment	▰▰▰▱▱	3/5	**MICRO-REGION**
Information	▰▰▰▱▱	3/5	D1
Popularity	▰▰▰▰▰	5/5	

THEME/CATEGORY Leisure – Beaches – Public/Popular Beaches.

HISTORICAL PERIOD *Contemporary.*

ELECT ME **Tel Aviv (#5)**'s beaches are one of its best assets. The sand is golden and wide – perfect for lounging all day, playing sports, taking a nap after a swim, eating lunch, pitching a tent, you name it. As crowded as it gets, the strip is 13km long, so there's always a plot of sand with your name on it.

CONTEXT The Tel Aviv beaches are essentially one long strip of sand broken up by a few ports. There are 13 official beaches across the 13km running from Herziliya in the north to Jaffa in the south. Downtown, the Tayelet, or Promenade, provides a splendid walking path adjacent to the sand and extending from **Tel Aviv Port** to Jaffa Port.

Informally, there are even more named beaches, each with their own personality:

Extra credit (north)

1. *Tel Baruch* Long beach north of the **Tel Aviv Port** and the Reading Power Station; halfway to Herziliya (and the southernmost of the **Herziliya Beaches**, Hazuk); a bit stark with the barbed-wire fence on the opposite side; mostly empty; calm waves.

Downtown beaches (north to south)

2. *Metzitzim* Family beach, furthest north, shallow, lifeguards.
3. *Nordau Segregated Beach (D1)* Giant wall blocking off access to nonreligious people, except on Shabbat. Sunday, Tuesday, and Thursday are women only; Monday, Wednesday, Friday are men only.
4. *Dog Beach at Hilton* Small stretch of sand with a sign welcoming four-legged friends.
5. *Gay Beach at Hilton* On the north part of the Hilton sandbar, you'll find lots of speedos and rainbow umbrellas.
6. *Surf Beach at Hilton* South side of the Hilton sandbar, also a club beach with seats, a restaurant, and surfers passing by to ride the waves.
7. *Gordon Beach (D1)* The start of endless sand and tourist mania; this beach has several volleyball courts, all very busy; restaurants, bars, sundry shops.
8. *Frishman* Tons of chairs, restaurants, people, shallow water, sand for days, in front of the Dan Tel Aviv (hotel with rainbow-colored exterior).
9. *Bograshov* More endless sand; breakers keep the surf low.
10. *Trumpeldor* Quieter, no facilities, still lots of great sand.
11. *Jerusalem* Across from the famed Abuelafia bakery and various falafel stands (crossing the road); sand, sand, sand.
12. *Banana/Drummers' Beach* Surf beach with very popular drummers circle on Fridays.

422

13. *Dolphinarium and Charles Clore Park* Rocks, promenade, surf school, site of nightclub bombing.
14. *Charles Clore/HaMaravi* South of Charles Clore Park, thin stretch, near **Manta Ray** restaurant.
15. *Alma/Alma Dog* Last stretch before Jaffa, leash-free.

Extra credit (south)
16. *Givat Aliya/Ajami/Jaffa* Another 1.5km further south from Jaffa Port is this local beach, accessible from stairs.

WORTH THE DETOUR? Absolutely. This is quintessential Tel Aviv-Yaffo. Find your spot and make a day of it. The water is warm, the surf can be wavy or still depending on what you're seeking (look for breakers about 150m from shore, which "break" the waves to make the sea calm), and there are plenty of on- and off-shore activities. Or, choose to just people-watch and enjoy the great (nearly) year-round weather!

DAYS/HOURS 24 hours.

BEST STRATEGY To visit all of the beaches and surrounding sites, follow *City Walk D1*. Otherwise, we recommend parking somewhere near the middle of town (Opera Tower has public parking – expensive, but central). Hire an umbrella if it suits you. Grab a beer. Falafel for lunch. Don't forget *matcot*. And then enjoy yourself!

WALKS AND DRIVES D1, E7.

ITINERARIES High BUCKET! Scores: 7+; Active; Leisure; Relaxation; Romantic; All Ages.

SIMILAR ELECTIVES See the *Public/Popular Beaches* theme (p. 554).

NEARBY Much of **Tel Aviv (#5)** and **Jaffa (#30)** border the promenade.

#90 Herodion

RATINGS		
BUCKET! Score		5/10
Ruin		3/5
Entertainment		2/5
Information		2/5
Popularity		2/5

MACRO-REGION
C: West Bank

MICRO-REGION
C2

THEME/CATEGORY Archaeology – Roman – Herodian.

HISTORICAL PERIOD *Herodian.*

ELECT ME Near **Bethlehem (#40)**, this archaeological site commemorates the most important ruler in Judea since the breakup of the United Kingdom 1,000 years

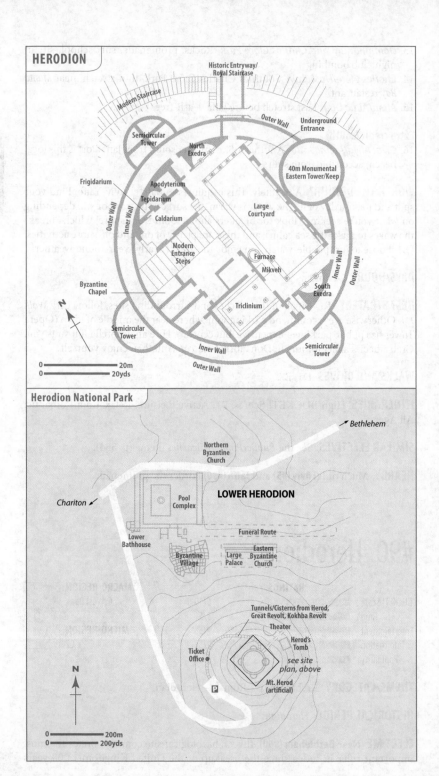

HERODION

Historic Entryway/
Royal Staircase

Modern Staircase

Semicircular Tower

North Exedra

Outer Wall

Underground Entrance

40m Monumental Eastern Tower/Keep

Frigidarium

Apodyterium

Tepidarium

Caldarium

Large Courtyard

Outer Wall

Inner Wall

Inner Wall

Outer Wall

Modern Entrance Steps

Furnace

Mikveh

South Exedra

Byzantine Chapel

Triclinium

N

Semicircular Tower

Inner Wall

Semicircular Tower

Outer Wall

0 20m
0 20yds

Herodion National Park

Bethlehem

Northern Byzantine Church

Chariton

LOWER HERODION

Pool Complex

Lower Bathhouse

Funeral Route

Byzantine Village

Large Palace

Eastern Byzantine Church

Tunnels/Cisterns from Herod; Great Revolt, Kokhba Revolt

Theater

Herod's Tomb

Ticket Office

see site plan, above

N

P

Mt. Herod (artificial)

0 200m
0 200yds

earlier: Herod I. He built this 750m conical hill as a perch for his palace. Later, as he sickened, he wanted a mausoleum built in his honor. You can visit Herod's first creation and perhaps his last resting place at Herodion, though controversy abounds whether his tomb is actually on site. A must for Herod fans!

CONTEXT Known as Herodion or Herodium, this Israel National Park is not to be confused with the period of time that we associate with the leader who was buried here, King Herod the Great, a Roman who was raised Jewish and whose dominion included Judea. The *Herodian* period, bearing his name, represents several decades of monumental construction projects at the turn of the millennium from about 40 to 4 BCE.

On the edge of the Judean Desert stands Herod's victory palace, which he built in 40 BCE to commemorate the defeat of oppositional Jews who had sided with his enemies. The conical hill became a symbol of his success where he later decided to build his palace/fortress. At the base of the hill he also established a small town dedicated to guests and the upkeep of the fortress. The star attractions were the palace and the great pool. Accompanying it were a variety of other buildings, including a stadium, gardens, theater, and several churches which were built later, around the 5th century.

In 2007, archaeologists believed they had located the as-yet-undiscovered tomb of Herod halfway up the hill, but this is in question as the tomb was far too modest for someone as powerful as Herod. And the body was missing. Playing devil's advocate, if in fact it were his tomb, it could have been desecrated by Jewish rebels – including the famed Bar Kokhba – during the Great Jewish Revolts of 71 and 135 CE.

Herod was a controversial ruler who died of an unknown disease that left him completely debilitated, but not before he was able to complete a number of monumental works. These included construction of **Masada (#8)**, **Caesarea (#25)**, and the **Tomb of the Patriarchs (#46)** in Hebron (C2), as well as a grand expansion of the Second Temple and development of today's **Temple Mount (#12)**.

WORTH THE DETOUR? The site's in ruins and there is no great mausoleum (though the undefined "Monumental Building" has been proposed as possibly Herod's mausoleum), but the views at the top are astounding, the engineering is wild, and there are some underground "escape tunnels" to explore (check with the ticket booth if locked). This could be a fun adventure, and it's close to **Bethlehem (#40)**.

DAYS/HOURS 08.00–16.00 daily, closes 17.00 Saturday–Thursday in summer.

BEST STRATEGY Head south from **Bethlehem (#40)**, plan 1–2 hours including the drive. Make sure to visit both the upper (fortress) and lower (palace) sites.

WALKS AND DRIVES C2.

ITINERARIES Off-the-Beaten-Path Israel and Palestine; Archaeology; Cinematic.

SIMILAR ELECTIVES Other Herodian buildings, listed above.

NEARBY Bethlehem (#40) (30km/35 minutes taking Highway 60), Jaffa Gate (32km/ 35 minutes), and Hebron (C2) (34km/40 minutes).

#91 Ramparts Walk

RATINGS

BUCKET! Score	6/10
Ruin	5/5
Entertainment	2/5
Information	1/5
Popularity	3/5

MACRO-REGION
A: Jerusalem

MICRO-REGION
A3

THEME/CATEGORY Scenic – Vistas – Urban Landscape.

HISTORICAL PERIOD *Ottoman.*

ELECT ME Surprisingly interesting without needing too much explanation, this walk begins in two places – to the left of the Jaffa Gate entrance, and then near the exit of the **Citadel/Tower of David (#32)** museum. A ticket will get you into both sides (which do not connect). You ascend to the top of the walls of **Old City Jerusalem (#1)**, and walk the perimeter. It sounds basic, but it's extraordinary, giving a bird's-eye view of tourists, shoppers, schoolchildren, people hanging clothes to dry, and other quotidian doings. Plus, you'll see the beautiful domes of **Temple Mount (#12)** and the **Church of the Holy Sepulchre (#9)**, among other recognizable sites. The path is remarkably well preserved and provides many panoramic views of Jerusalem, new and old.

CONTEXT "The Old City Jerusalem and its walls" are a UNESCO World Heritage Site, but the original nomination in 1980 did not reference the Ramparts Walk in particular (see **Jerusalem Walls and Gates (#47)**), That said, the Ramparts Walk is the best way to see the walls and gates up close.

The walk is split into two parts: a northern and a southern walk. The northern portion begins at Jaffa Gate (bathrooms at the top of the stairs). You can buy tickets right inside Jaffa Gate on your left. The north path runs clockwise from Jaffa Gate, passing New, Damascus, Herod, and Lions' gates for a total of about 2km. You must descend at Lions' Gate because visitors are not permitted to enter **Temple Mount (#12)** via its walls and ramparts, which form much of the eastern wall of Jerusalem.

The south Rampart Walk starts at the **Tower of David (#32)**, also near Jaffa Gate. You'll walk along the western and southern walls and gates, passing over Zion Gate and ending at Dung Gate in the *Jewish Quarter* near the **Western Wall (#11)**. Along the way, you can see a variety of architectural and archaeological sites from above – perhaps an easier way to visualize sites in ruin.

The walls as we see them today were completely redone during the reign of Suleiman the Magnificent of the Ottoman Empire from 1537 to 1541, although built atop older Hasmonean and Herodian foundation stones. Legend has it that Suleiman wanted the walls to extend to **Mount Zion (#92)**, but the empire ran out of money and the architects had to close the wall to its current location – for which he was furious and had the architects executed.

WORTH THE DETOUR? This activity involves a fair amount of climbing (no scrambling) up steep steps with little shade and some uneven footing (but with guard rails). A lot of the views are of rooftops and city life below. An absolute must for Jerusalem lovers.

DAYS/HOURS Ramparts North is closed Fridays. Ramparts South is closed Saturdays, and closes early Fridays. Otherwise 09.00–16.00 Sunday–Thursday.

BEST STRATEGY You'll need at least 2 hours to do both parts justice. Visit the ticket office just inside the gate entrance at Jaffa. You can descend at any of the gates, but you won't be able to reenter except at the points of origin (Jaffa Gate and Tower of David). The four northern gates can be sites of conflagration, so consider whether to continue the entire northern route to Lions' Gate if there has been recent strife between Palestinians and Israelis.

WALKS AND DRIVES A3; *Old City Chronotour* (**w** buckettravelguides.com/old-city -chronotour).

ITINERARIES Jerusalem Immersion; Complete Ruins; Active; UNESCO.

SIMILAR ELECTIVES **Jericho (#26)** has famous walls.

NEARBY The walls surround the entire **Old City Jerusalem (#1)**.

#92 Mount Zion

RATINGS			MACRO-REGION
BUCKET! Score		5/10	A: Jerusalem
Ruin		3/5	
Entertainment		1/5	**MICRO-REGION**
Information		1/5	A5
Popularity		5/5	

THEME/CATEGORY Religion – Sacred – Pilgrimage.

HISTORICAL PERIOD *Syria Palaestina* to *Mandatory Palestine*.

ELECT ME Arguably one of the most important parts of the Old City (but left outside the walls during 16th-century renovations), this hill to the southeast of the southern walls is home to King David's Tomb (A5), the Room of the Last Supper (Cenacle) (A5), the Dormition Abbey (A5) (where Mary died), and the Catholic cemetery which houses Schindler's Grave (A5) (Oskar Schindler of *Schindler's List* fame).

CONTEXT Today, Mount Zion refers to the "Western Hill" which is outside Jerusalem's current southern walls.

★ *Dormition Abbey (1910)* This basilica is recognized as the location where the Virgin Mary "fell asleep," or left her worldly body. The current building, built in 1910, has a 5th-century basilica, the Hagia Sion, as its foundational base. That building was drawn on the **Madaba Map (#19)**, but the building was destroyed by the Persians in 614. The Abbey of Our Lady of Mount Zion built a church atop those ruins, which was subsequently destroyed in the 13th century, before being

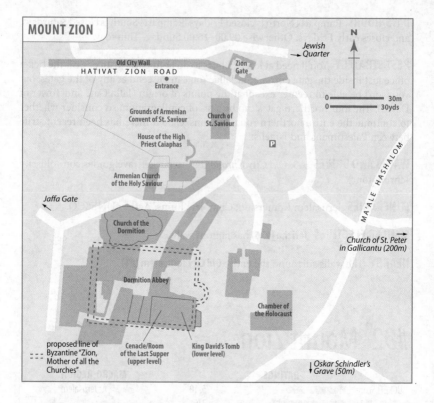

MOUNT ZION

Jewish Quarter

Old City Wall
HATIVAT ZION ROAD
Entrance

Zion Gate

N

0 — 30m
0 — 30yds

Grounds of Armenian Convent of St. Saviour

Church of St. Saviour

House of the High Priest Caiaphas

Armenian Church of the Holy Saviour

Jaffa Gate

Church of the Dormition

Dormition Abbey

Church of St. Peter in Gallicantu (200m)

Chamber of the Holocaust

proposed line of Byzantine "Zion, Mother of all the Churches"

Cenacle/Room of the Last Supper (upper level)

King David's Tomb (lower level)

Oskar Schindler's Grave (50m)

MA'ALE HASHALOM

uncovered in 1898 by German archaeologists. Mary's death has been placed in multiple far-away lands, including Turkey.

★ *King David's Tomb (380 CE?)* This tomb has a very questionable history. King David – of whom we know very little except what is written in the Bible – is said to have been buried on his Eastern Hill, now recognized as the ***City of David***, in his name. While theoretically possible that King David's grave was moved at some point in history, Mount Zion is certainly not the original burial place. The oldest elements of the building are no older than the 2nd century CE, which post-dates David's life by roughly 1,200 years. The tomb has not been surveyed or opened. Under Israeli control since 1967, it had long been a worship site for Muslims, who also consider David a prophet.

★ *Cenacle (380 CE?)* Located in the room above King David's Tomb, this proposed site of the Last Supper – Jesus' final meal with his disciples before being betrayed to the Roman authorities – is likely misplaced. There is little evidence to support the idea that the meal happened on this spot; the event is first attributed here in the 5th century.

★ *President's Room (1948)* The President's Room above the cenacle is the location where Jews could view the **Western Wall (#11)** and **Temple Mount (#12)** following Israeli independence, but were not allowed to enter the Old City while under Jordanian occupation. Israel's second president, Yitzhak Ben-Zvi, came once a year to pay homage to the Jewish holy sites, hence its name. Open Mondays midday.

★ *Oskar Schindler's Grave* In recognition of the contributions of the German Nazi Party member who saved 1,200 Jewish lives during the Holocaust, Oskar Schindler was buried in the graveyard outside.

WORTH THE DETOUR? Religious folks will surely find at least one of these stops of value. Despite the overwhelming evidence that none of the celebrated religious events actually occurred here, the site provides a nice place to reflect and continue the tradition of remembrance.

DAYS/HOURS Each site has its own hours. Most are open daily 08.00–16.00. Jewish sites close early on Friday, and are closed on Saturday. Dormition closes noon–14.00.

BEST STRATEGY Expect to spend 1–2 hours. Walking around is easy enough to figure out on your own.

WALKS AND DRIVES A5; *Old City Chronotour* (**w** buckettravelguides.com/old-city -chronotour).

ITINERARIES Jerusalem Immersion; Memorial; Pilgrimage.

SIMILAR ELECTIVES **City of David** and **Mount of Olives (#34)** are the other two neighborhoods of antiquity surrounding the Old City.

NEARBY Zion Gate (400m/6 minutes), Dung Gate (700m/11 minutes), and Jaffa Gate (900m/12 minutes).

#93 Belvoir

RATINGS		MACRO-REGION
BUCKET! Score	5/10	F: Mount Carmel
Ruin	3/5	& Jezreel Valley
Entertainment	2/5	
Information	2/5	**MICRO-REGION**
Popularity	2/5	F2

THEME/CATEGORY Archaeology – Islamic – Crusader.

HISTORICAL PERIOD *Crusader.*

ELECT ME The remains of a Crusader fortress sitting south of the **Sea of Galilee (#7)**, this is a remarkably well-preserved site with two concentric walls hiding the inner stronghold. Purportedly the most complete Crusader castle in the country.

CONTEXT Built near a Jewish settlement called Kokhava, Belvoir (meaning "good view" in French) has also been known as Kokhav HaYarden, taking the name of the ancient village and meaning "Star of the Jordan" in Hebrew, or Kaukab al-Hawa ("Star of the Winds") in Arabic. A noble family sold the property to the Crusader Knights Hospitaller in 1168, who immediately realized the inherent defensive qualities, the commanding views, and the proximity to the Jordan River – and built a massive fortress there. Within a few years, Saladin was at the doorstep (or moat, in this case) and a multi-year siege began that ended in a stalemate with the Crusaders retreating to Tyre. The Ayyubids feared Crusader retribution and tore down the walls and towers of the fortress, leaving the foundations. The Crusaders regained control of the territory for a short time in the 13th century, but the land fell under Muslim rule again shortly thereafter. The site would remain under rubble for almost 700 years. The site was excavated in 1966 by Israeli archaeologists, who miraculously found the castle mostly intact.

The (dry) moat of Belvoir was roughly 10–14m deep and 20m wide surrounding a fortification with two concentric walls. The outermost wall measured 100 × 100m and the inner wall was 50 × 50m, both with towers on the four adjoining corners. The two-story interior is where everyone lived, worked, prayed, and ate.

WORTH THE DETOUR? Castle fans will find this an interesting addition to the roster. The reconstruction is not complete, but there are several vaults and walls that have been put back together to give perspective. Best done as part of a tour of the region.

DAYS/HOURS 08.00–16.00 daily, closes 17.00 Saturday–Thursday in summer.

BEST STRATEGY Give yourself a good hour on site. For views of the Jordan River, **Golan Heights (#62)**, *Mount Hermon*, and **Sea of Galilee (#7)**, you can't miss the Dan Shomron lookout.

WALKS AND DRIVES F2, W4.

ITINERARIES Off-the-Beaten-Path Israel and Palestine; Archaeology.

SIMILAR ELECTIVES Other Crusader castles include *Montfort*, *Yehi'am*, **Karak (#49)**, and *Shobak*.

NEARBY **Beit She'an (#39)** (20km/23 minutes), **Beit Alpha (#64)** (29km/35 minutes), *Tiberias* (33km/38 minutes), **Nazareth (#29)** (40km/50 minutes), **Umm Qais (#45)** (50km/1 hour plus border control), and Sheikh Hussein Border Crossing (25km/25 minutes).

#94 Western Wall Tunnels

RATINGS		MACRO-REGION
BUCKET! Score	7/10	A: Jerusalem
Ruin	4/5	
Entertainment	3/5	**MICRO-REGIONS**
Information	5/5	A1, A2, A4
Popularity	4/5	

THEME/CATEGORY Structure – Engineering – Infrastructure.

HISTORICAL PERIOD *Herodian.*

ELECT ME The **Western Wall (#11)** has long been regarded as the holiest site in Judaism because of its close proximity to the Holy of Holies (the Foundation Stone, currently under the **Dome of the Rock (#6)** and inaccessible to Jews). The currently visible part of the wall is 60m long, yet the wall was (and is) eight times longer. Tours of the underground portion of the Western Wall are led by engaging and informative guides who give insight into the impressive engineering that went into the construction, as well as the way of life of the Jewish people who lived during this era. Highlights include massive vaulted spaces underneath the Muslim Quarter (A2), tight tunnels, the truly closest point accessible to the Holy of Holies site, as well as one of the world's largest building blocks.

CONTEXT To support the weight of a number of new buildings – including the creation of a glorious new Second Temple for the Jewish people – King Herod ordered the expansion and filling in of **Temple Mount (#12)**, which required huge fortification walls as support. Today's **Western Wall (#11)**, a 60m length of the original 488m-long wall, is a deceptively small portion of the full wall, hidden behind long-standing buildings and buried underground.

This subterranean tour gives a powerfully new perspective to the ancient city. Today, the Western Wall Plaza – from where you start this tour, by descending into vaulted chambers – feels like natural ground, but it's an artificial surface raised roughly 13m/43ft above the original earth. Measuring the height of the wall, the portion visible today is about 19m/62ft, a bit more than half of the wall's total height. Ground level during Herod's time was much lower, descending to the Tyropoean valley between Mount Moriah (Temple Mount) and **Mount Zion (#92)** in the west. Once Israel retook Jerusalem following the Six-Day War (1967), the Ministry of Religious Affairs began a 20-year excavation project that revealed 488 total meters of wall underneath current structures in the Old City.

On a tour of these tunnels, you'll descend to large underground chambers being supporting by large vaulted ceilings. The excavations demonstrate how Temple Mount is supported, from the design to the building materials, including a 570-ton foundation block that is one of the largest in the world. You can also learn about secret tunnels to Temple Mount (through Barclay's Gate and Warren's Gate), odd pools from unknown water sources, and the true spot closest to the Holy of Holies.

WORTH THE DETOUR? The tour is fascinating. Kids and adults tend to love it. It does require preplanning, as it regularly sells out.

DAYS/HOURS 07.20–late Sunday–Thursday, 07.20–noon Friday; reservation only Saturday evening.

BEST STRATEGY Note you can only visit with a certified guide, and you must prebook online at w thekotel.org/en/tours/western-wall-tunnels/ or by calling ☏ 972-2-627-1333. You'll need a printout of your reservation. The tour lasts around 75 minutes.

WALKS AND DRIVES A1, A2, A4.

ITINERARIES Jerusalem Immersion; Organized; All Ages.

SIMILAR ELECTIVES For a complete picture, group this with the **Western Wall (#11)**, **Temple Mount (#12)**, and the **Jerusalem Archaeological Park (#71)**.

NEARBY Access is from the Western Wall Plaza.

#95 Tel Aviv Museum of Art

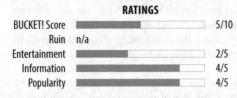

RATINGS

BUCKET! Score 5/10
Ruin n/a
Entertainment 2/5
Information 4/5
Popularity 4/5

MACRO-REGION
D: Tel Aviv

MICRO-REGIONS
D3, D5

THEME/CATEGORY Culture – Museums – Of Art.

HISTORICAL PERIOD *Contemporary.*

ELECT ME A broad sweep of modern art movements are represented at Israel's best art museum and the world's foremost collection of Israeli art. The building itself is worth a look as the architecture of the 2011 wing represents a futuristic nod to the **Modern Movement (Bauhaus Architecture) (#16)** and the "White City" of **Tel Aviv (#5)** in which it lives.

CONTEXT Founded in 1932, the Tel Aviv Museum of Art began as a center for modern and contemporary creativity, by Israelis and foreigners alike. The current site on Shaul HaMelech Boulevard was built in 1971, with the stunning Herta and Paul Amir Building opening to the public in 2011.

The Museum contains the largest representation of Israeli artists of any museum, with pieces curated from the last century, including from the New Horizons Group, the Expressionist Jewish artists, and Fauvists, among several other 20th-century movements. The Museum focuses intensely on new and contemporary works, but has equally collected an interesting assortment of European art, from its 16th–19th-century wing to its modern masters. There are a number of recognizable genres present, from surrealism and abstract art to Impressionism and Cubism. Picasso, O'Keeffe, Monet, Chagall, Dalí, Lichtenstein, Renoir, Pollock, Rothko, Kandinsky, van Gogh, and Klimt are among the recognizable artists present. There's also a unique collection of works by avant-garde Russian artist Alexander Archipenko. Other wings include design and architecture, drawings and print, and photography.

WORTH THE DETOUR? Fans of art will surely appreciate this modern collection. Fans of architecture will love the newest building with its otherworldly design and sharp edges.

DAYS/HOURS Noon–21.00 Tuesday and Thursday, noon–18.00 Wednesday, 10.00–14.00 Friday, 10.00–18.00 Saturday, closed Sunday and Monday.

BEST STRATEGY Plan 2 hours for the museum, though speed rules apply. You can buy tickets in advance at w tamuseum.org.il (regular price is 50 ILS).

WALKS AND DRIVES D3, D5.

ITINERARIES Structure; Culture; Fine Arts; Modernity.

SIMILAR ELECTIVES **Israel Museum (#17)** in Jerusalem, *Design Museum Holon*, the Tikotin Museum of Japanese Art (E1) in *Haifa*, and the *Ilana Goor Museum (D2)*.

NEARBY Rabin Square (D3) (1.1km/14 minutes), Sarona Market (D3) (850m/12 minutes), and the *Bauhaus Center (D3)* (1.2km/16 minutes).

#96 Timna

RATINGS			MACRO-REGION
BUCKET! Score		6/10	L: Eilat and Arabah
Ruin		2/5	
Entertainment		4/5	**MICRO-REGION**
Information		4/5	L3
Popularity		3/5	

THEME/CATEGORY Archaeology – Prehistoric – Bronze Age.

HISTORICAL PERIOD *Neolithic* to *Umayyad*.

ELECT ME Timna is a desert park with a variety of attractions for families, hikers, history buffs, and fans of geology. It also shows evidence of copper mining and smelting from as early as 5000 BCE.

CONTEXT What first brought Timna to notoriety were the 10,000 ancient copper mines discovered here in continuous use from the 14th century BCE to the 2nd century CE. Copper is a forged metal used by ancient people to develop weapons, tools, and basic objects to ease everyday tasks. It was such an influential developmental stage in human history that we often refer to the late Neolithic as the Copper Age, being the principal technology of the era (until tin was added to the mix to create bronze, and thus began the Bronze Age).

Timna had been mined for millennia – but the Egyptians turned the practice into a full enterprise. Their work was followed by the Bible's Midianites (son of Abraham and his descendants) who redecorated an earlier Egyptian temple purpose-built for the goddess Hathor into a temple for ritualistic purposes as yet identified. The Edomites, Nabataeans, Romans, and later Muslims all had a turn in exploiting this rich quarry, which had been mostly emptied out by the 7th century CE.

Within its 42km², Timna houses several attractions. The site sits roughly 30km north of **Eilat (#78)** in the middle of a multi-hued desertscape. Wind and water have eroded the soft rocks into some wild shapes. There are several examples of hoodoos, sometimes called fairy chimneys (like Turkey's Cappadocia), of various sizes and heights. As in the southwest USA, there are a series of natural arches, plus a site called Mushroom, a monolithic rock which teeters on a withered-away base. The most famous site is Solomon's Pillars, once thought to be smelting furnaces but in fact formed naturally. Rock carvings from the 14th century BCE round out the list of interesting sites.

There are more than two dozen walking trails, six bike trails, and an artificial lake with various activities, including free paddle boats. Night hikes are popular, as are making pottery and sand bottles, the reenactments of ancient times, mountain biking, archery, and more.

WORTH THE DETOUR? This site has benefited from an influx of funding, with a super-modern visitor center, multisensory visual displays, and a developed park complex (outside the National Park system). If you're already in the area and have half a day, it's worth a trip.

DAYS/HOURS 08.00–16.00 daily.

BEST STRATEGY Depending on how comfortable you are with walking in the desert, plan for at least half a day and up to a full day if you've got the time. With a car, you can explore more, as the site is big. It's a desert, so in summer months the longer hikes are not advisable.

WALKS AND DRIVES L3.

ITINERARIES Off-the-Beaten-Path Israel and Palestine; Archaeology; Nature and Scenic; Ancient History; Under the Sun; Kid-Focused; All Ages.

SIMILAR ELECTIVES *Ancient Qatzrin* in the Golan has a similar feel. The *Underwater Observatory* and Dolphin Reef (L2) are good family sites nearby.

NEARBY *Yotvata Hai-Bar* (8km/8 minutes), Amram's Pillars (L3) (19km/17 minutes), and **Eilat (#78)** (29km/23 minutes).

#97 St. George's Monastery and Wadi Qelt

	RATINGS		MACRO-REGION	
BUCKET! Score		5/10	C: West Bank	
Ruin		3/5		
Entertainment		2/5	MICRO-REGION	
Information		1/5	C3	
Popularity		2/5		

THEME/CATEGORY Structure – Engineering – Impressive Feats.

HISTORICAL PERIOD *Byzantine* to *Ottoman*.

ELECT ME There's a trio of activities to do and see in the Wadi Qelt, a desert between Jerusalem and Jericho. Many come for the cliff-hugging St. George's Monastery. There's also a Hasmonean-era synagogue, one of a series of royal winter palaces nearby. For adventure seekers, there is wadi-related fun, including cliff-face rappelling and hiking opportunities.

CONTEXT The Wadi Qelt, or Nahal Prat in Hebrew, is a valley following the Prat stream from Jerusalem to Jericho, carving a gulch in the landscape which has become part of biblical lore: the valley was the route where Jesus walked and told his parable of the Good Samaritan; where Joaquim wept over his wife's barren state only to be told by an angel of the birth of their child, who would become the Virgin Mary; and is associated with the popular phrase "valley of the shadow of death."

Such stories drew ascetic monks to these sites where they took refuge in the caves of the valley walls from around 420 CE, in commemoration of yet another biblical story where Elijah was fed only by ravens here, purportedly for 3½ years. The caves were formalized into a monastery in the late 5th century by John of Thebes, but gained notoriety from St. George of Choziba, a Greek monk, who would host weekend vigils – the only time the silent monks would leave their cells and communicate with others.

The Persians destroyed the site around 614 CE and killed the 14 resident monks, whose skulls are on display. There are two churches inside the tri-level monastery: Church of the Holy Virgin and Church of Saints John and George. The former is the principal prayer hall with doors dating to the Crusader reconstruction. The latter holds the oldest part of the original building, a 6th-century mosaic floor, as well as the tomb of St. George.

Crusader emperors attempted restorations, some of which can be seen today, but ultimately the site was abandoned and not refurbished until 1901. Today, it welcomes many visitors.

The rest of Wadi Qelt may be worth a gander if you are into hiking, with the valley ending at **Jericho (#26)** after passing a Hasmonean winter palace, *Tulul Abu el-Alaiq*.

WORTH THE DETOUR? Unlike other monasteries in the region, this one allows female visitors (and has since nearly its inception). The hike is steep, but the view is incredible. If you are visiting **Jericho (#26)** or heading to the **Dead Sea (#3)** from Jerusalem, it can be a quick visit.

DAYS/HOURS 08.00–11.00 and 15.00–17.00 Sunday–Friday, 0900–noon Saturday.

BEST STRATEGY The easier route is to drive and park in the upper parking lot, then walk 10–20m down to the monastery (you'll have to hike back up, and it's hot in the summer). Alternatively, you can walk in from Wadi Qelt, which is shaded if walking from the west (1–2 hours), but leaves much to be desired other than the occasional view of the monastery. Also, be careful of vendors who will try to force you to buy trinkets in order to ensure your car doesn't end up with flat tires. Don't forget modest dress – you will not be allowed entry if you are showing shoulders or knees. Women are allowed, but must be fully covered, as should men.

WALKS AND DRIVES C3.

ITINERARIES Off-the-Beaten-Path Israel and Palestine; Structure; Society and People.

SIMILAR ELECTIVES *Deir Quruntal* and *Mar Saba* are other famous monasteries in the West Bank, both also cliff-huggers.

NEARBY **Jericho (#26)** (5km/5 minutes), **Old City Jerusalem (#1)** (20km/20 minutes), and **Tel Aviv (#5)** (90km/1½ hours).

#98 Machneyuda

			MACRO-REGION
BUCKET! Score	████████░░	7/10	A: Jerusalem
Ruin	n/a		
Entertainment	███████░░░	3/5	MICRO-REGION
Information	███████░░░	3/5	A7
Popularity	████████░░	4/5	

THEME/CATEGORY Food and Drink – Food – Top Restaurants.

HISTORICAL PERIOD *Contemporary.*

ELECT ME The highest-ranked and -rated restaurant in the region, Machneyuda near the **Mehane Yehuda Market (#67)** in Jerusalem's western (new) city should be on every foodie's radar. It's also received an enormous number of accolades.

CONTEXT Machneyuda has taken the food world by storm, practically transforming the Jerusalem culinary scene, and creating stars of its trio of chefs. Assaf Granit, Uri Navon, and Yossi Elad have gone on to open up a number of other eateries, including two famous London joints: Palomar and The Barbary.

The restaurant has appeared in a myriad of "best-of" lists, including the World's 50 Best Discovery, *New York Times* (at least four times), *The Telegraph*, *Time Out*, *Condé Nast Traveler*, *Forbes*, *Frommer's*, *Food & Wine*, and *1001 Restaurants You Must Experience Before You Die*, just to name a few.

The scene is quite hip, with a no-BS attitude around the service or place settings, that's for sure. The food is distinctly Israeli, with most of the ingredients being sourced locally, but it's also unlike anything you will have tried before. The food isn't trying to be too fussy, which is what makes it all so enjoyable.

Expect tahini, labneh, za'atar, zhug, pickled onion, and yogurt – all recognizable Mediterranean and Middle Eastern ingredients. But you'll also find a global influence in these carefully crafted and locally sourced plates which reflects the multicultural heritage brought upon Israeli cuisine from a century of immigration and residents from more than 100 countries.

The menu is constantly changing, so don't expect to know what you'll find. You can check out a sample menu at **w** en.machneyuda.co.il. Stay open-minded and let your senses go for a wild ride (including your ears – the dining room is loud).

WORTH THE DETOUR? Absolutely, as you'll be in Jerusalem. Just don't expect to drop in – it's booked weeks in advance.

DAYS/HOURS 12.30–16.00 and 18.30–midnight daily.

BEST STRATEGY The tasting menu will put you back 295 ILS per person ($75) and is the clear way to go. Make sure to book as soon as you know dates for the Jerusalem portion of your trip.

WALKS AND DRIVES A7.

ITINERARIES Jerusalem Immersion; Food and Drink; Gourmet; Romantic.

SIMILAR ELECTIVES Check out more restaurants in our *Food and Drink* theme (p. 561).

NEARBY Jaffa Gate (2km/25 minutes) and **King David Hotel** (2km/25 minutes).

#99 Imperial Bar

RATINGS		MACRO-REGION
BUCKET! Score	7/10	D: Tel Aviv
Ruin	n/a	
Entertainment	3/5	**MICRO-REGIONS**
Information	3/5	D1, D6
Popularity	1/5	

THEME/CATEGORY Entertainment – Party – Bars and Clubs.

HISTORICAL PERIOD *Contemporary.*

ELECT ME If craft cocktails are your thing, look no further than this chic bar where the bartenders quiz you on your likes and mood to create a personalized drink just for you. (There's also a menu, and you can order classic drinks.) Named Best Bar in the Middle East and Africa in 2017, come for happy hour and stay for the evening.

CONTEXT The Imperial Craft Cocktail Bar, part of the Imperial Hotel in downtown **Tel Aviv (#5)**, just a block from the beach, has twice been rated by The World's Best team as one of the world's 50 best bars (2016–2017).

The food menu spans the global spectrum, much like the drinks menu, with small plates each made with high-quality and hard-to-find ingredients. Menus are subject to change, but Imperial has a Grand Tour collection of 14 global drinks, including La Vie en Rose (sparkling/refreshing/floral) dedicated to Kyoto, Seoul Searching (piquant/smoky/umami) from Korea, and the Andazi Daiquiri (rich/aromatic/fruity) ode to… Wakanda. For those who try each one, the bar has a prize for you.

The group behind Imperial also has La Otra (Mexican-Caribbean food and drink) next door, Imperial Red at the Isrotel in Kiryat Anavim (outside Jerusalem), and Bushwick TLV on Nahalat Binyamin, a nod to New York-style bars.

Drinks run to 55–60 ILS. Guests must be 25+. Happy hour runs from 18.00 to 20.00 and the bar stays open until you go home.

WORTH THE DETOUR? It's a classy cocktail bar, so you wouldn't roll up in beachwear and order a beer. But it's a very easy addition to your afternoon or evening.

DAYS/HOURS 18.00–last customer daily.

BEST STRATEGY Reservations are recommended (e reservations@imperialtlv.com or call). Given that it's not near other bars or restaurants, it's best to either start or end here. We recommend coming for happy hour and then moving to Rothschild, Florentin, Jaffa, or one of the other neighborhoods for dinner and (further) drinks.

WALKS AND DRIVES D1, D6.

ITINERARIES Gourmet.

SIMILAR ELECTIVES Check out the *Bars and Clubs* theme (p. 559), or "Bars" in *Do #18: Late Nit!* (p. 107).

NEARBY Trumpeldor Beach (150m/2 minutes), **Rothschild Boulevard** (1.7km/ 22 minutes), and <u>Kuli Alma (D4)</u> (1.8km/24 minutes).

#100 Dor HaBonim

RATINGS			MACRO-REGION
BUCKET! Score	▰▰▰▰▰▰▱▱▱▱	8/10	E: Mediterranean Coast
Ruin	▰▱▱▱▱	1/5	
Entertainment	▰▰▱▱▱	2/5	**MICRO-REGIONS**
Information	▰▰▰▱▱	3/5	E4, E7
Popularity	▰▰▰▱▱	3/5	

THEME/CATEGORY Leisure – Beaches – Remote Beaches.

HISTORICAL PERIOD *Bronze Age/Canaanites.*

ELECT ME Frequently described as Israel's best beach, Dor, the Canaanite Park to its north, and the Nature Reserve that surrounds it (HaBonim) combine to create a stunning Mediterranean experience.

CONTEXT The 4.5km strip of sand might be the most beautiful in **Tel Aviv (#5)**. It certainly has its proponents. The bay itself has the most inlets of anywhere else in Israel, a testament to the geological processes that have occurred over millions of years. There are also a number of sand dunes, with a very interesting history: they come from the Sahara and are deposited over Mediterranean waters, eventually washed ashore, and then blown inland to create the dunes present today. This process has been markedly slowed due to engineering projects in major waterways; the land was declared a nature reserve to protect it from future damage. Also of note are the many rocky inlets which create stunning channels and pools and provide excellent walking opportunities.

The beach itself is wide and sandy with a shallow surf and several points of interest on either the 2- or 4-hour hike along the sea. There's a shipwreck right off shore that sank a century ago when trying to deliver cement. It's a stunning center-piece where divers are known to observe the marine life that has flourished around it. Walking north along the rocky cliffs will provide excellent views before landing you at the ancient site of Tel Dor, a Canaanite settlement and harbor with minimal signage or reconstruction efforts (there's a museum in Kibbutz Nahsholim), leaving a beautiful set of natural ruins among an even more beautiful backdrop of rock, sea, and sand.

The site offers a designated campground that never gets too full, with showers and toilets, as well as a number of fire pits. The site can get very windy, and sand tends to blow, so be aware that you might need elemental protection if sleeping overnight.

WORTH THE DETOUR? Never that crowded, this elective is perfect for beachgoers seeking tranquility and beauty, free from commerce.

DAYS/HOURS Summer 08.00–20.00 daily; lifeguards 08.00–17.00 (longer in summer).

BEST STRATEGY There are no facilities at this nature reserve park, so you must bring everything you need (food/water) and leave nothing behind (trash, food, etc.) when you leave. There are a few places to park to avoid the small fees, but we encourage you to leave your car at the designated parking facility for HaBonim Nature Reserve in order to fund the cleanup and lifeguarding efforts of the Park Authority. Once locked up, it's a 10-minute walk to the dunes and beach.

WALKS AND DRIVES E4, E7.

ITINERARIES Off-the-Beaten-Path Israel and Palestine; Nature and Scenic; Leisure; National Parks and Reserves; Romantic.

SIMILAR ELECTIVES More beaches can be found in the *Leisure – Beaches* theme (p. 554), and don't miss *Do #16: Beach It!* in Part 4 (p. 98).

NEARBY **Caesarea (#25)** (22km/30 minutes), *Haifa* (25km/30 minutes), and **Tel Aviv (#5)** (73km/1 hour).

Part 6

Silver Electives (#101–250)

ABU HASSAN

BUCKET! Score 9 *Category* Quick Bites *Micro-region* D2

The great equalizer; if there's a place to bring Jews and Arabs to a communal table, this is it. This Jaffa mainstay – open since the 1970s – serves a line of people from morning until mid-afternoon when they run out of food. Staples are all that's on offer: creamy hummus, chunkier masabacha (hummus variety with whole chickpeas), falafel, ful, chips, and some condiments, spicy and pungent. Three outlets to choose, eat in (rustic) or takeaway.

AKHZIV BEACH

BUCKET! Score 5 *Category* Public/Popular Beaches *Micro-region* E5

One of the highest-regarded beaches in Tel Aviv, a national park, and an archaeological site. Once a Phoenician town, Tel Akhziv provides interesting Canaanite and Crusader ruins, but the city has existed since the Chalcolithic/Copper Age. Most of the ruins are from an abandoned Arab village, Az-Ziv. There are pleasant strips of beach all the way to **Rosh HaNikra**. Turtles lay eggs in the sand during July and August. Other animals of interest: starfish, octopi, sea urchins, and sea anemones. Ruin score: 3.

AL-AYOUN TRAIL

BUCKET! Score 5 *Category* Day Hikes (2+ Hours) *Micro-region* S2

Part of the Ibrahim al-Khalil Trail, this shorter, 12km day hike passes through the local villages of Orjan, Baoun, and Rasun, with lunch and dinner prepared by the villagers as options. Homestays are also possible. The hike includes a visit to a soap makers' collective, walking through orchards and vineyards, and a spring-forged valley. Guides are required. The Abraham Path Initiative can sort out details (**w** abrahampath.org).

ANCIENT QATZRIN

BUCKET! Score 4 *Category* Byzantine *Micro-region* I2

This Golan park highlights an ancient Jewish village that was active during the Byzantine period (also known as the Talmudic period). The village has been reconstructed to a much greater extent than regular archaeology parks, with a couple of houses built in their original style and filled with contemporary artifacts. A 6th-century synagogue is a highlight. The park comes replete with characters in costume explaining the history of the site. Ticket includes admission to the handsome Golan Archaeological Park which looks more broadly at the region and time period. Ruin score: 2.

APOLLONIA

BUCKET! Score 4 *Category* Crusader *Micro-region* D7

This site served the Phoenicians well from the 6th century BCE, with curious snails that produced a valuable purple dye. The site stayed active for centuries, changing its name regularly (Arshuf, Arsur, Sozousa). Crusader-era fortifications (c1241) are what remain today, including a large moat, grand fortress, and villa. The city was forcibly dismantled by its own residents who resisted the Mamluk siege for 40 days, ultimately losing. South of the site is the Sidna Ali Mosque, a 14th-century construction. Great views of Tel Aviv. Ruin score: 3.

ARGAMAN BEACH

BUCKET! Score 4   *Category* Public/Popular Beaches   *Micro-region* E2

A public beach opposite the bay from Old Akko, with great views of the walled city. Paid parking to visit, but the beach is large, sandy, and free. Lifeguards, toilets, showers. Drive from Old City in 5 minutes or walk the 1.5km from Old City. Note: not a Blue Flag beach.

ARGILA/HOOKAH/SHISHA

BUCKET! Score 5   *Category* Vice   *Macro-region* W

Extremely popular in Egypt, and readily available in coffeeshops and other establishments in Arab communities in Israel and Jordan, these waterpipes are used for smoking flavored tobaccos (apple, strawberry, watermelon, etc.). Note: contains nicotine. Also note: not healthy (but an interesting experience, and kind of tasty).

AS-SALT

BUCKET! Score 5   *Category* Architectural Style   *Micro-region* S2

This mountain town, once the local seat of the Ottomans, is of interest for its unique style of late-19th-century architecture, called Arab Eclecticism: sun-golden sandstone structures with arched windows and domed roofs. Simply walking about the city will give you a sense of the style and the interesting character of the period, but start at Abu Jaber Museum and As-Salt Archaeological Museum downtown and continue to Al-Hammam and Al-Khader streets.

BANKSY'S WALLED-OFF HOTEL

BUCKET! Score 5   *Category* Experiential Lodging   *Micro-region* C1

"Worst view in the world!" is the promise. Boutique hotel designed by international artist and troublemaker Banksy, who has thrown literal and figurative shade on the Israel–Palestine **Separation Wall** running next to his Bethlehem hotel. Get your Banksy souvenirs here! Plus, a piano bar, in-house residencies (read: famous people), a museum on Wall history, a Palestinian art gallery, a library to educate yourself, and a Wall*Mart. Various rooms, from budget to presidential suites (**w** walledoffhotel.com).

BAR'AM

BUCKET! Score 5   *Category* Roman   *Micro-region* H1

A grand facade still stands at a large, ancient synagogue in this Upper Galilee national park. Built by an as-yet-undetermined Jewish community believed to have lived here in the 4th century CE. The doors face south towards Jerusalem, as they do at sister sites **Korazim** and **Capernaum (#33)**. As you walk towards the synagogue, the ruins of Bar'am – a Maronite Christian community – lie in ruins, having been bulldozed by Israel in 1949 following the War of Independence in order to secure the Lebanon border. Ruin score: 2.

BASILICA OF THE ANNUNCIATION

BUCKET! Score 7 *Category* New Testament *Micro-region* G1

For at least 1,500 years, this Nazarene site has been associated with the Annunciation, the event when Mary was told by the Angel Gabriel that she would be the mother of God. Inside on the sunken ground floor lies a grotto where Mary purportedly lived. A Byzantine-era church commemorates this spot. Seven hundred years later, the Crusaders built a church over the ruins of the Byzantine church. The massive Brutalist-style basilica surrounding the archaeological ruins was opened in 1969. Layers upon layers! Ruin score: 1.

BATTIR HILLS

BUCKET! Score 4 *Category* Technological Advancement *Micro-region* C2

Recognized by UNESCO for its unique 4,000-year-old terraced hills amid a mountainous terrain, this region just south of Jerusalem (between Hebron and Nablus, but most visible near the present-day town of Battir) is impressive for the irrigation system invented to feed its planted grapevines and olive trees, as well as the farming capabilities used since antiquity in this difficult terrain. Organize a half-day hiking trip with w visitpalestine.ps. You can also self-guide, but don't miss the Palestinian perspective on the effects of land encroachment, particularly as it relates to Israel's controversial **Separation Wall**.

BEDOUIN TENTS AND COFFEE

BUCKET! Score 5 *Category* Coffee, Tea, and Coffeeshops *Macro-region* W

Sleep in a traditional goat-hair tent, drink coffee (three times!) with locals, and enjoy the serenity of the desert. Bedouins have lived in the region for thousands of years, and though once nomadic have since formed communities. Thus, you needn't drive around hours to find them: some hosts allow you to reserve in advance. Try Kfar Hanokdim in Israel or w bedouinhospitality.com for rustic and authentic group tents (or try a cave!) with dinner and breakfast options, camel and jeep rides, and hiking. Several Bedouin camping/glamping options in **Wadi Rum (#4)**.

BEIT SITTI

BUCKET! Score 5 *Category* Cooking *Micro-region* Q3

Cook a four-course Arab meal in downtown Amman at this popular-for-a-reason cooking school. Reserve in advance and pick your seasonal dish of choice, each of which comes with salad, a side dish, and dessert. Mujadarra, musakhan, mandi, maloubeh, and mutabbal are just some of the choices (that begin with M!). Classes can be arranged morning, lunch, or dinner. It has interesting homemade spices and condiments for sale, from olive oil and tahini to pomegranate molasses, sumac, and za'atar. Tons of good reviews. Plan for several hours for the full experience (w beitsitti.com).

BEIT YANNAI

BUCKET! Score 7   *Category* Public/Popular Beaches   *Micro-region* E4

Voted one of the world's 100 best beaches by World Beach Guide. Popular for all kinds of surfing, the lack of breakers (omnipresent in nearby Tel Aviv) mean a more ferocious current and tide, but the fun factor increases exponentially. The beach itself is part of the Alexander Stream National Park, so it's maintained by government resources and cleaner than other beaches, while also being less frequented thanks to its entrance/car fee. Camping is allowed in a separate, designated area.

BEN YEHUDA STREET

BUCKET! Score 6   *Category* Streets   *Micro-region* A7

A popular tourist stop, this West Jerusalem pedestrian mall is popular with locals and tourists alike. Called *mirachov* ("pedestrian street"), Ben Yehuda sits between the light-railed Jaffa Road and King George Street. Folks come for coffee, falafel, and souvenir shopping. Or just to people-watch. Closed Shabbat, reopens to much fanfare Saturday night. Bustling around Independence Day and Sukkot. Once described in the *New York Times* as one of "Five Places to Meet the World."

BIALIK HOUSE

BUCKET! Score 4   *Category* Museums of Home   *Micro-region* D3

Israel's "National Poet," Haim Nahman Bialik, built this house for himself in 1924, then a veritable castle. It later served as headquarters of the Hebrew Writers' Association, a library, and a museum. Today, the house showcases art while serving as a memorial and national archive. Many study the house as a prime example of a unique, blended architectural style using European and Arab influences which predates the Bauhaus revolution by a couple of decades. Part of Bialik Square, with several other buildings, including Beit Ha'ir (D3).

BIBLE LANDS MUSEUM

BUCKET! Score 5   *Category* Museum of Culture   *Micro-region* A8

This museum seeks to bring to life the people who lived in the historical Middle East (from Afghanistan to the Mediterranean, and from the Caucasus to Sudan) during ancient times. There are 20 galleries, ordered chronologically, tracing the journey of humanity from early civilizations, including Sumer, Egypt, and Babylon through to Canaan, the Persians and Greeks, and finally Roman-Byzantine times. A number of virtual tours of retired exhibitions are available at w blmj.org/en/.

BRIDGE OF STRINGS

BUCKET! Score 5 *Category* Beautiful Structures *Micro-region* A8

Also called the Chords Bridge, this striking bridge was designed by famous Spanish architect Santiago Calatrava (also responsible for the Athens Olympic Park, Turning Torso in Malmo, Auditorio de Tenerife, and World Trade Center Transport Hub in New York City) to bring visual imagery to the Jerusalem skyline. Opened in 2008, it carries the light rail as well as pedestrians. To enjoy this 160m-long, 118m-high, 66-chord structural beauty, start at the Jerusalem Central Bus Station and walk towards the neighborhood of Kiryat Moshe, or take the Red Line. Great for photographs.

BROWN BEACH HOUSE

BUCKET! Score 5 *Category* Highly Recommended Accommodation *Micro-region* D1

This contemporary boutique hotel is just one block from Trumpeldor Beach, right in the center of beach action. With its South Beach vibe and contemporary-chic décor, this hotel oozes cool. Many of the rooms have sundecks/balconies, and a few have jacuzzis. Rooms run on the smaller size. The breakfast was curated by Meir Adoni, one of the most famous chefs in Israel, and gets rave reviews. Plus, there are free bicycles and free gym passes. From $115 in low season, $225 average.

BUSI GRILL

BUCKET! Score 4 *Category* Top Restaurants *Micro-region* D8

Meat-lovers, this is for you. Opened in 1957, this contemporary kosher grill restaurant is located in the Petah Tikva neighborhood of Tel Aviv. The food caters to a modern Israeli palate. As the name implies, the highlights are the skewered meats grilled over charcoal. Busi recommends the spicy chicken and a foie gras and entrecôte special, but you'll find everything (kosher) from wings to liver, hearts, and beyond. Tons of sides: salads, soups, pickles, tahini/hummus. Alcohol is served. Family-friendly. Business lunch: 70 ILS.

CAFÉ CULTURE

BUCKET! Score 5 *Category* Coffee, Tea, and Coffeeshops *Macro-region* W

The importance of coffee to Holy Landers cannot be understated; it's a time for social gathering, relaxing, gossip, and observation. It's meant for sitting and enjoying rather than solely takeaway. Such is the rumor about why Starbucks failed in Israel (a badge of pride to all Israelis) as a takeaway-only shop. (Starbucks does exist in Jordan.) But European-style local espresso shops have penetrated the market and chains are now ubiquitous. Cappuccinos are most popular in Israel; Arabic coffee in Jordan. Check out *Do #15: Drink It!* (p. 93) for everything on caffeinated beverages.

CAMEL RIDING

BUCKET! Score 6   *Category* Animal Rides   *Macro-region* W

This is definitely an interesting experience you won't soon forget. There are options to ride a camel in **Petra (#2)**, **Wadi Rum (#4)**, and in parts of the Negev. The experience is quite extraordinary and is akin to riding a horse but you're much higher off the ground and the movement is much more pronounced – some might even say uncomfortable. Best advice: relax your body and go with the flow. Questions on ethics: camels are a domesticated animal; they're normally tame, so, if it spits or bites, it's being mistreated.

CARDO

BUCKET! Score 5   *Category* Byzantine   *Micro-region* A4

The "cardo maximus" was the main thoroughfare in Roman cities. Jerusalem was built with such an avenue, as depicted on the **Madaba Map (#19)**. The Cardo ran from Damascus Gate (evidence underneath the gate) to the Nea Church, which was destroyed in 614 CE. What remains visible today in the *Jewish Quarter* dates later, to Byzantine years. There are several prominent features: its 12.5m width; erected columns at the original street level; glass-covered shafts showing the original street; two arched storefronts built directly into the hillside. Ruin score: 2.

CARMEL HAI-BAR

BUCKET! Score 4   *Category* Animals/Zoos   *Micro-region* F1

The sister site to the *Yotvata Hai-Bar* wildlife reserve in Israel's Arava, this animal breeding center in the Carmel National Park outside Haifa seeks to breed, acclimatize, and eventually reintroduce endangered local wildlife into its native habitats. Note: the animals are caged. Visitors can get close to the fenced animals. On display: griffon vultures, endangered eagles, wild goats and sheep, mountain gazelle, Persian fallow, and roe deer.

CARMEL WINERY

BUCKET! Score 5   *Category* Wineries   *Micro-region* E4

Founded by Baron Rothschild in 1882, this is Israel's largest winery with production of over 15 million bottles a year, holding a market share of nearly half the total production in Israel. They also own *Yatir Winery*. Good reviews: Daniel Rogov deemed Carmel a five-star winery, while Hugh Johnson called it a two- to three-star winery. A visit to *Zichron Ya'akov*'s grand facility provides lots of history to go along with a tasting. Tours must be arranged in advance at w carmelwines.co.il/en/. Closed Saturdays and holidays. Adults only.

CHURCH OF ST. ANNE AND THE POOLS OF BETHESDA

BUCKET! Score 5   *Category* Saints   *Micro-region* A2

Several things of interest in this small site, including the Crusader-era Church of St. Anne which is spare but gorgeous. Its basement grotto is said to be where Anne (for whom the church is named) gave birth to Mary, mother of Jesus. Completed in 1138, it was one of the few buildings not destroyed by Saladin after he conquered the city. In the garden are various excavations, including the two Pools of Bethesda, proclaimed in the Bible to have healing properties. Ruin score: 3.

CHURCH OF THE TRANSFIGURATION

BUCKET! Score 5   *Category* Jesus' Miracles   *Micro-region* G2

Here, atop Mount Tabor, Jesus appeared before three of his apostles radiating in light and titled "Son" by a booming voice, cementing the relationship between earthly Jesus and heavenly God. Called the "transfiguration," this event is one of the five milestones in Jesus' life. The church commemorating the event was built in 1924 atop Byzantine and Crusader ruins. The Crusaders dedicated three grotto-chapels (still visitable) to the three prophets who appeared in the sky: Jesus, Moses, and Elijah. The views from the church are impressive. Ruin score: 1.

CITY OF DAVID

BUCKET! Score 5   *Category* Kingdom of Israel   *Micro-region* A5

This tiny strip of land to the south of the Old City walls once contained the Kingdom of Jerusalem. Some 3,000 years ago, King David conquered the territory from the Jebusites and claimed it for Israel. The City of David served as the seat of power for the Kingdom of Israel from the 10th century BCE until the Babylonians conquered the city in 586 BCE. The old city declined in importance as settlers moved closer to the Temple grounds. Today, the site includes **Hezekiah's Tunnel**, Siloam's Pool, and Warren's Shaft – water tunnels and pools referenced in the Old Testament. Ruin score: 3.

DEIR QURUNTAL

BUCKET! Score 4   *Category* Monasteries   *Micro-region* C3

North of Jericho, on the mountain also known as Mount of Temptation, a precariously placed Orthodox monastery visibly and dizzyingly hugs the cliffside. On the site is a cave where tradition says Jesus spent 40 days and 40 nights fasting while Satan/the Devil tempted him to break. This monastery dates to 1895 and centers around the rock where Jesus sat. It's easier to reach the summit these days – a cable car drops tourists off at the top for a hefty fee, or hike up in 15–30 minutes.

DESIGN MUSEUM HOLON

BUCKET! Score 5   *Category* Modern Architecture   *Micro-region* D8

Designed by architect Ron Arad, this contemporary art and sculpture museum opened in 2010 with the goal of educating the public on the importance of design in our lives. The red-hued building itself is a marvel, with curling layers of Corten steel that appear to have been bent at the designer's whim, so well built is the structure. Inside, there's a Materials Library with samples to touch and various collections and exhibits, all with a contemporary spin. 35 ILS; closed Sunday/Monday.

DOMAINE DU CASTEL

BUCKET! Score 5   *Category* Great Wine   *Micro-region* B1

A five-star (highest ranking) winery per Daniel Rogov, the Domaine du Castel winery is located in the Judean Hills at an altitude of 700m with an above-average rainfall, sloping hills, good drainage, low humidity, and soil of limestone, terra cotta, and clay. Four of its most award-worthy wines include: "C" Blanc du Castel, a 100% Chardonnay (French oak); the Bordeaux-blend Castel Grand Vin; the lower-priced Petit Castel (fruitier); and a tropical, beautiful rosé. Book tastings in advance (w castel.co.il/en/).

DOME OF THE CHAIN

BUCKET! Score 4   *Category* Other Holy Places   *Micro-region* A2

Built in 691 under the Umayyad reign, this prayer hall was built on **Temple Mount (#12)** shortly after the **Dome of the Rock (#6)** and **Al-Aqsa Mosque (#65)**. Possibly named after the chain that King Solomon suspended between Heaven and Earth, the exact origin and original function of this somewhat strange structure is unknown. There is no outer wall on the ground level; perhaps helpful for those looking to pass through to the afterlife on Judgment Day, believed to commence here. Ruin score: 5.

DRUMMERS' BEACH

BUCKET! Score 4   *Category* Music   *Micro-region* D1

At this stretch of sand just north of the Dolphinarium (also known as Banana Beach), all sorts of revelry can be found on Friday afternoons and evenings – dancing, capoeira, and especially drumming. Play with new friends as the sun sets. On non-Fridays, it's a bit more relaxed. Festivities are open to anyone with a passion for drumming. (While construction is ongoing, it's moved to the rocks opposite the beach at the Dolphinarium.) No fee.

EIN BOKEK

BUCKET! Score 6   *Category* Sea Access   *Micro-region* K1

On the southern lake (the manmade portion) of the **Dead Sea (#3)**, this resort town has sprung up with towering hotels and day spas. The main draw is safe, free, and public access to the Dead Sea. You can park near the outdoor malls, use changing rooms, and take freshwater showers – which you'll need after only 10–15 minutes in the salty water! No mud remains on site, so buy prepackaged mud from a mall vendor. The sand is virtually nonexistent (no waves), so bring something to sit on.

EIN BOKEK SPA HOTELS

BUCKET! Score 6   *Category* Spas   *Micro-region* K1

A spa/resort is an excellent option on a day trip to the **Dead Sea (#3)**. In *Ein Bokek*, roughly 1½ hours south of Jerusalem, you will find your traditional spa inclusions, such as massage and sauna. More interesting options include medical tourism (for skin, lung, and blood pressure ailments), sulfur pools, lathering in mineral-rich black mud, and swimming in saltwater pools. Options include: DMZ Medical Center at Lot, the Dead Sea Clinic, and the luxury hotels of Ein Bokek, including Herod's, Isrotel Neve, Lot, and Milos, as well as mid-range options such as Vert, Isrotel Ganim, Oasis, and Leonardo.

EIN HEMED

BUCKET! Score 4   *Category* Parks   *Micro-region* B1

An old Crusader fortress is the centerpiece of this green outdoor space with a big playground and picnic area. It serviced a farm, the ruins of which are also on site. Much of the water on site is engineered by man, including diverted spring water, ponds and reservoirs, and a spring that is entirely circular and recycled to prevent periods of desertification. Just outside of Jerusalem, this is a good family space, popular for concerts. Ruin score: 2.

EIN HOD

BUCKET! Score 4   *Category* Handmade   *Micro-region* F1

This colony/village outside of Haifa was founded in 1953 by Marcel Janco, a Dadaist who inspired artists to create a community. Today's 500+ residents regularly open their houses to the public to showcase pottery, sculptures, paintings, and other artistic feats. With less time, try the local art gallery or Janco Dada Museum – across the road from one another. The town art is mostly for sale, and there are technique workshops, readings, lectures, and concerts. Pre-coordination is a must; check with the Ein Hod Artists Village to book tours (**w** ein-hod.info).

EIN KEREM

BUCKET! Score 4   *Category* Pilgrimage   *Micro-region* B1

Birthplace of Saint John the Baptist, this is a popular site of Christian pilgrimage and Jerusalem escapism. Over the years, it has acquired a number of churches celebrating its association with both John and Mary, who visited when pregnant with Jesus. Pilgrims believe the village's water is still blessed after Mary drank from it. There are several convents and monasteries in town marking religiously significant moments, and a number of art galleries and restaurants too. Bus tours are very popular, but you can walk around solo. Ruin score: 1.

ELBABOR

BUCKET! Score 7   *Category* Top Restaurants   *Micro-region* F2

Yum. This Arab restaurant in the village of Umm al-Fahm is right off Highway 65 and makes for a perfect early or late lunch stop on the way in or out of the Galilee. Perfectly executed salads, fish, and meats that are truly a step above the same traditional foods you've eaten elsewhere. Stuffed lamb's neck is the specialty. For all this, you'll pay a small premium; it's Israel, and we say it's worth it. Comfortable for Israelis, Arabs, and foreigners. Featured on the documentary *The Search for Israeli Cuisine*.

ELMA ARTS COMPLEX

BUCKET! Score 5   *Category* Highly Recommended Accommodation   *Micro-region* E4

Formerly the Mivtachim Sanitarium, a convalescent home for unionists, the 1968 building is a Brutalist architectural stunner. Designer Yaacov Rechter won the Israel Prize in Architecture. Located close to **Zichron Ya'akov**. The Cube is a performance hall for diverse acts and Elma Hall is a 450-seater for classical performance and opera. The Art Center hosts a variety of festivals throughout the year. Painting and sculpture around the 100-acre property. Beautiful pool, spa, fitness center. Food gets high marks. Recently reopened after ten years of restoration. From $360.

FOUNTAIN OF SULTAN QAYTBAY

BUCKET! Score 4   *Category* Beautiful Structures   *Micro-region* A2

Often overlooked because of its proximity to the more widely recognized **Dome of the Rock (#6)**, this **Temple Mount (#12)** fixture was commissioned in 1482 CE by the Mamluk Sultan Qaytbay, hence the name. This public fountain (*sabil*) is an excellent representation of the Mamluk style of architecture, famous in Cairo, but seen in various buildings in the Muslim Quarter (A2) of Jerusalem. The alternating red and yellow stone pattern is called *ablaq* style. The dome is gorgeously decorated in arabesque design. Fountain still in use! Ruin score: 5.

GAMLA

BUCKET! Score 5   *Category* Parks   *Micro-region* I3

The Gamla Nature Reserve provides visitors to the Golan with lots of options. Start with griffon vulture-spotting, via a short trail to a bird-watching station with a great view. There's also the ancient city of Gamla from the Second Temple period atop a steep hill, with one of the oldest synagogues in Israel. There are walking trails along the Gamla and Daliot streams, including to the tallest waterfall in Israel at 51m. More than 700 dolmens (burial mounds made of boulders) from the Bronze Age can be found along the way to Gamla Waterfall. Ruin score: 1.

GAN HASHLOSHA

BUCKET! Score 5   *Category* Swimming   *Micro-region* F2

Also called Sakhne, meaning "hot pool" in Arabic, this national park is famous for its naturally warm pools. The waters stay at a constant temperature of 28°C all year round. The hot water comes from a thermal spring that feeds into each of the pools. The pools have been enlarged for the big groups that come on weekends with picnics and frolicking kids. Lifeguards, friendly fish, and shallow parts all available. Also on site is a reconstruction of one of Israel's pioneer camps from 1936, Tel Amal.

GEORGE AND JOHN TEL AVIV

BUCKET! Score 4   *Category* Top Restaurants   *Micro-region* D4

Located in the Drisco Hotel at 6 Auerbach Street, this modern Israeli restaurant just west of Florentin is under the direction of Chef Tower Tal whose focus is on the manipulation of ingredients through preparations: grill, pickle, smoke. There is a private dining room seating eight for a chef's table experience. Starters 70–110 ILS per course; mains 110 ILS (vegetarian) to 175 ILS; whole fresh fish and steak by the gram. Service is highly regarded. Reservations available online at w gandj.co.il/en/.

HADASSAH SYNAGOGUE AND CHAGALL WINDOWS

BUCKET! Score 5   *Category* Visual Arts   *Micro-region* B1

The site only takes a few minutes to visit, though is a bit out of the way (try *Road Trip B1*). Installed in 1962 in the Hadassah Medical Center's on-campus synagogue, these 12 beautiful stained-glass windows are a tourist attraction in their own right. Designed by the modern artist Marc Chagall, each window has a dominant color (though up to three colors were painted on each panel – a unique technique) and symbolizes one of the 12 tribes of Israel. They each measure roughly 11 × 8 feet.

HAIFA

BUCKET! Score 4   *Category* Other Main Cities   *Micro-regions* E1, E5

Visit Haifa for the stunning **Bahá'í Gardens (#27)**. Stay a little longer and you'll find plenty more to do. There's an alternative route up the mountain that provides stunning views, called the Path of 1,000 Steps. Haifa is known for its laid-back vibe and welcoming drinking holes. Check out *Falafel Hazkenim (E1)* for maybe the best falafel in Israel. Plus, sample the decent southern beaches, a famous Japanese art museum, and a couple of blocks that may remind you of old Europe at the German Colony.

HALUTZA

BUCKET! Score 3   *Category* Nabataean Cities   *Micro-region* J2

Among its sister sites of **Avdat (#48)**, *Shivta*, and *Mamshit*, this Nabataean city is perhaps the least developed. It was established in the 4th century CE on the route from **Petra (#2)** to Gaza. It reached its apex in the 6th century CE, but was abandoned by the 7th. The town contained churches, a bathhouse, and wine-production technology.

There's a Greek inscription of interest bearing the name of the town. Mostly covered in sand; 4x4 vehicle required. In military zone: caution; consider jeep tour. Visits on weekends only. Ruin score: 1.

HAMAT GADER

BUCKET! Score 4   *Category* Thermal Waters   *Micro-region* I3

A number of activities await at this almost-theme park in the Golan. Originally a Roman spa and first used in the 2nd century CE, visitors can walk through the ancient reconstructed ruins, including a 5th-century synagogue. There's a crocodile farm, petting zoo, pools, a fishing pond (eat what you catch), water park, and most popular: sulfur baths from underground hot springs at 42°C. Adults can enjoy massage, spa treatments, and restaurants. Camping or boutique hotel available (from 90 ILS, explore package deals at w hamat-gader.com). Ruin score: 1.

HAMAT TIBERIAS

BUCKET! Score 2   *Category* Thermal Waters   *Micro-region* G3

The 17 hot springs vary in temperature from 30°C to 60°C. Some can be entered (up to 40°C). There is also a 3rd–4th-century CE synagogue-in-ruins with Greek and Jewish mosaics dating across the building's generational history. Helios, the sun god, is center of a zodiac in a synagogue – odd, but similar to mosaics found at **Beit Alpha (#64)** and **Tsipori (#56)**. In 1780, a Turkish hammam was established on site and today there is a reconstruction that can be visited. No parking. Quick visit. Ruin score: 2.

HAMMAMAT MA'IN HOT SPRINGS

BUCKET! Score 4   *Category* Thermal Waters   *Micro-region* P1

Underground lava flows heat this resort's facilities at 264m below sea level, just east of the Dead Sea in Jordan, near Suweimeh (Anchor). Enjoy unique thermal waterfalls. Hot springs' water temperatures vary from 45°C to 60°C when they come to the surface, but are cooled to 30–37°C for the pools. Mud wraps, massage, body masks, Dead Sea salt treatments, and steam rooms are all available. Go for the day or stay the night; pools reserved for guests only 06.00–09.00. Rooms $200, including breakfast.

HERBERT SAMUEL

BUCKET! Score 5   *Category* Top Restaurants   *Micro-region* D7

Once the hippest business lunch in Tel Aviv, this Ritz-Carlton restaurant moved north to Herziliya where it has retained its high-end fine dining style in its new marina setting. Menu includes market salads with local ingredients, and fish and meat in a variety of modern preparations (starters 36–82 ILS, sides 36–66 ILS, mains 136–212 ILS). Renowned wine menu. Good for special occasions. Kosher. Reservations required.

HERZILIYA BEACHES

BUCKET! Score 6   *Category* Public/Popular Beaches   *Micro-region* D7

Leave the throngs of Tel Aviv for the residential enclave of Herziliya and its 7km strip of fine white sand. Popular beaches include Sharon, Acadia, and Zebulon, three of the seven options, each with lifeguards on duty. The stretch of beaches here is surrounded by cafés and clean changing rooms. Sports include kitesurfing, stand-up paddleboarding, and volleyball. Acadia, specifically, was recognized by Beach Inspector as a 2018 Best Beach for a Classic Holiday. The Herziliya Marina and Acadia are both Blue Flag beaches, recognizing their environmental stewardship. Disability-friendly.

HEZEKIAH'S TUNNEL

BUCKET! Score 6   *Category* Wet Hike   *Micro-region* A5

King Hezekiah once diverted his city's water source to block a siege from the approaching Assyrian army (2 Chronicles), carving a 533m tunnel beneath the 8th-century BCE *City of David* from Gihon Spring to the Pool of Siloam on the western part of the hill. According to history, the two engineering teams started at each end and tried to meet in the middle, with mixed results. With galoshes, visitors can now wade through the still-wet tunnels. Plan for 3 hours. Age 5+. Water reaches 70cm, water shoes required. Closed Saturday and holidays. Ruin score: 3.

HIKING IN JORDAN

BUCKET! Score 7   *Category* Day Hikes (2+ hours)   *Macro-region* V

There's a surprising amount of green and water in this otherwise arid country, whether you're hiking through dry wadis, red deserts, or river-cut canyons. There are a number of great options to explore in the *Walks and Hikes* theme (p. 548), but some of the best include **Petra (#2)** with its Monastery, High Place of Sacrifice, and Indiana Jones hikes (see *City Walk N2*). **Dana Biosphere Reserve (#21)**, **Wadi Mujib and Mujib Biosphere Reserve (#23)**, **Ajloun Forest (#57)**, and *Al-Ayoun Trail* all offer long day hikes. The **Jordan Trail (#52)** is a 40-day hike, with shorter options.

HIKING IN THE NEGEV

BUCKET! Score 5   *Category* Day Hikes   *Micro-region* J2

If you can make it past the heat, the lack of water, and minimal facilities, there is much to love in the great southern desert. The Negev is mostly a rocky desert with some interesting geological features. **Makhtesh Ramon (#28)** is the region's famous canyon (an erosion crater, actually), with short and long hikes, but there are other makhteshim to explore nearby. **Ein Avdat (#74)** has two good hikes, or the all-day Zin Valley Hike at its main gate. *Red Canyon*, Amram's Pillars (L3), and Black Canyon (near Amram's Pillars) are popular hikes on day trips from **Eilat (#78)**.

HOT AIR BALLOON RIDE OVER WADI RUM

BUCKET! Score 7   *Category* Above Earth   *Micro-region* M2

An unforgettable experience over an otherworldly landscape. Hot air balloon rides cost 130 JD for an hour in flight (2–3 total hours needed for the experience), paid in cash to the driver. Of course, flights are weather-permitting and usually try to be airborne by sunrise, so expect to arrive early. Contact the Royal Aero Sports Club of Jordan (w www.rascj.com). It also offers skydiving, ultralight aircraft, gyrocopters, and microlights in other parts of Jordan.

HULA LAKE

BUCKET! Score 6   *Category* Birding   *Micro-region* H2

The Hula wetlands were drained in 1951, which had a dramatic effect on the migration patterns of more than 200 species of birds that stopped here on their flights between Africa and Europe. In 1994, Israel flooded the empty valley (creating Lake Hula), which now serves as a nature reserve for the returning flora and fauna. Walk across a 600m-long "floating bridge" to observe birdlife (including cranes and pelicans), small mammals, and water buffalo. Rent bikes, golf carts, or take the "train tours" with stops to observe birds during peak migration periods (twice a year).

HUMMUS

BUCKET! Score 8   *Category* Food   *Macro-region* W

Universally loved, hummus is the quintessential Middle Eastern dish – neither Arab nor Israeli – with unclear origins but an overwhelmingly appeal. Chickpeas mixed with tahini, olive oil, lemon, and love. So popular is this dish that there are restaurants dedicated to it, called hummusiyas. Abu Ghosh has dozens of hummus shops. Akko, Jaffa, Jerusalem, Haifa, and Tel Aviv suburbs are filled with places considered "the best." Check out *Do #14: Eat It!* (p. 80) for more.

ISRAEL NATIONAL TRAIL

BUCKET! Score 7   *Category* Long-Distance Walks   *Macro-region* U

Over 1,000km in length, this path runs through Israel, avoiding controversial if not conflict zones, such as the Golan Heights and Palestine. Hikers follow the white-, blue-, and orange-striped markers bouncing from **Tel Dan (#63)** in the Galilee Panhandle to **Eilat (#78)** on the Red Sea. There's great information at w israeltrail. net, plus Trail Angels (helpers along the way, including kibbutzim; w shvil.fandom. com/wiki/INT_Trail_Angels). Maintained by Israel Trails Committee. One of *National Geographic*'s "World's 20 Best Hikes." Avoid summer (heat) and winter (floods). Water caches only necessary in Negev. Jacob Saar and Yagil Henkin's *Hike the Land of Israel: Israel National Trail*, aka the *Red Book*, has tons of maps. Plan for 40–60 days.

JAFFA FLEA MARKET

BUCKET! Score 4   *Category* Boutiques   *Micro-region* D2

The Jaffa Flea Market has been renewed and promoted for nearly a decade as a hip destination in its own right, with a wide assortment of antiques and secondhand clothes to go along with the trendy restaurant and bar scene. They say that one man's trash is another man's treasure, but there's a lot to sift through to find the treasure. Those with time and patience might just find a deal. Bargaining a must. Closed Saturday, but the restaurants and bars stay open. Also called the Shuk HaPishpeshim.

JEWISH QUARTER

BUCKET! Score 5   *Category* Orthodox Jews   *Micro-region* A4

Reclaimed by Israelis after independence, this area has been historically linked with Jewish residents probably since the time of King David, but at least since the Second Temple, as seen in exhibits at the Burnt House and the Herodian Houses. Four Sephardic synagogues and the Hurva Synagogue (1864) add to the religious character. Other points of interest include the Byzantine-era Roman **Cardo** and the **Wohl Archaeological Museum**. Of course, the **Western Wall (#11)** is its biggest draw. Synagogues closed Shabbat. Ruin score: 4.

JORDAN ARCHAEOLOGICAL MUSEUM

BUCKET! Score 4   *Category* Museum of Archaeology   *Micro-region* Q1

Located atop the Amman Citadel, this compact museum collects a wide swath of artifacts from across Jordan. Displays are ordered chronologically, from prehistory/ Paleolithic era through Islamic rule. Some of the earliest known statues (c6500 BCE) created by humankind were found at nearby 'Ain Ghazal and are on display here. Several coffins, skulls, pieces of glasswork, and clay figurines are on site. Once ranked higher, but much of the collection has moved to the glitzier *Jordan Museum (Q3)*.

JORDANIAN HOSPITALITY

BUCKET! Score 4   *Category* Meet Locals   *Macro-region* V

Jordanian hospitality received enough points to earn a spot on the podium, saying a lot for the culture! According to custom, your hosts will do anything to make your stay pleasurable. You can experience this first-hand in Bedouin tents or through coffee diplomacy in **Wadi Rum (#4)** or **Dana Biosphere Reserve (#21)**, particularly **Feynan Ecolodge (#86)**. (Keep in mind those are also businesses.) Hospitality also extends to city life, where a local may introduce themself at your dinner table and offer you tea or coffee. New friends and an experience you likely won't forget!

KIBBUTZ LOTAN

BUCKET! Score 4   *Category* Kibbutzim   *Micro-region* L3

Ecologically minded guest kibbutz in the Arabah Desert that offers temporary or longer stays, apprenticeships in sustainable development, interesting buildings made from recycled materials, bird-watching, shiatsu massages in warm-water pools, and other workshops. Home to the Center for Creative Ecology, where visitors and guests can learn how to engage in organic gardening, do a number of 2–4-hour workshops, go on a bird tour, or participate in a "green apprenticeship." Desert Inn with private bathroom around $80–120 per night.

KIBBUTZ VOLUNTEER

BUCKET! Score 7   *Category* Volunteer   *Macro-region* U

Volunteering in a kibbutz is a popular activity for young people (18–35) all over the world – Jewish or not – who have 2–12 months to devote to the communal lifestyle. You'll meet people from Israel and elsewhere, work hard on the farm, earn some travel money, learn a little bit of Hebrew, have your meals and housing paid for, with time off to travel the country. You'll interact with permanent kibbutz members who have fascinating perspectives on life in Israel that you can't readily find in big cities (w kibbutzvolunteers.org.il).

KING DAVID HOTEL

BUCKET! Score 5   *Category* Highly Recommended Accommodation   *Micro-region* A7

Since 1931, this five-star hotel has played host to an impressive array of leaders from around the world. Its architectural aesthetic leans towards European styling with local/Middle Eastern materials, including the pink limestone popular throughout Jerusalem. Originally a residence for royalty abdicating the throne, it later became the headquarters of the British administration and was bombed in 1946 by Zionists. Since 1958, it has been part of the Dan Hotel Group. Renowned for its history, location, service, and luxury. Some say "dated." From $300.

KORAZIM

BUCKET! Score 4   *Category* Roman   *Micro-region* H2

The ancient village of Korazim is one of the three "cursed cities" for having rejected Jesus' teachings as told in the Gospels of the New Testament. Today, the site gives testament to the large community that once lived here during Talmudic times. The construction comes from local black basalt, lending a dark (and hot) atmosphere to the still-under-excavation ruins. Evidence of olive oil production, a large synagogue, and other life during the first millennium on display at this Israel National Park north of the Galilee. Ruin score: 2.

LAG B'OMER AT MOSHAV MERON

BUCKET! Score 4   *Category* Holidays   *Micro-region* H1

Lag B'Omer is a complex Jewish holiday meant to represent a break in sadness over a variety of events attributed to this day – the death of kabbalist Rabbi Simon bar Yochai, the end of a plague, and the revelation of the mystical Zohar. In practice, Israelis spend the evening building bonfires and celebrating, which can be seen all throughout the country. Hundreds of thousands will also make pilgrimage to

Moshav Meron, the burial place of bar Yochai. Three-year-old boys get their first haircuts, weddings are allowed, and celebrants eat eggs and carob. (Caution: deadly stampede occurred in 2021.)

LITTLE PETRA

BUCKET! Score 5   *Category* Nabataean Cities   *Micro-region* N3

Siq al-Barid, or Little Petra, was possibly a **Petra (#2)** "suburb." Indeed, it's a smaller version of its grand Nabataean site neighbor, with a smaller area but fewer crowds. You can walk 4 hours over 14km to reach it from Petra itself (continue past the Monastery and follow signs), or you can drive 8km north of Wadi Musa. Popular spots include the four triclinia (dining rooms), the Painted Room (with a recently restored ceiling fresco from Hellenistic times), rock staircases, and panoramic views. Ruin score: 3. No fee.

LOT'S CAVE

BUCKET! Score 4   *Category* Old Testament   *Micro-region* P1

The Sanctuary of Agios Lot, or Lot's Cave, is the believed respite home of biblical Abraham's son, Lot, following his flight from the smoldering remains of Sodom and Gomorrah, destroyed for their residents' sinful behavior by a vengeful God. A Byzantine-era church was built to commemorate the cave where Lot lived with his daughters, who later intoxicated him to become pregnant, giving birth to Moab and Ben-Ammi, the forefathers of the Moabites and Ammonites: enemies of Israel from east of the Jordan. An inscription names Lot. Ruin score: 2.

MAMILLA HOTEL

BUCKET! Score 5   *Category* Highly Recommended Accommodation   *Micro-region* A7

Very close to the Old City Jaffa Gate, this modern hotel is a great option for a sophisticated traveler. Aiming to tie together a classic Jerusalem look with a sleek, clean, and inviting feel, the hotel also exhibits art by local artists. The rooftop restau-lounge has a panoramic view of the city, including the Old City walls. Also on offer are the Mirror Bar, a cosmopolitan cocktail bar, The Winery, and Happy Fish Restaurant. Swimming, spa, fitness, studio classes, and sundeck. From $360.

MAMSHIT

BUCKET! Score 5   *Category* Nabataean Cities   *Micro-region* J1

One of the four main stations on the **Incense Route (#73)**, Mamshit is the smallest but best preserved of the Negev Desert towns. The city was founded in the 1st century BCE. Greeks called the town Memphis; the Nabataeans may have used Kurnub, as Arabs do. The Arabian horse is believed to have been first bred here. Residents built two churches in the 4th century CE and, uniquely, wall fortifications. Don't miss the Nile Church mosaics. Outdoor markets. Sleep in an Ethiopian tukul (or "Nabataean khan") for something different – book through w parks.org.il. Ruin score: 3.

MANTA RAY

BUCKET! Score 5   *Category* Top Restaurants   *Micro-region* D1

Renowned seafood restaurant on the Tel Aviv beach on the south end of Charles Clore Park. Great views of the Mediterranean. Inside and outside seating. Early reservations recommended for prime seating. Dress is casual for many, but business meals are popular. Serving breakfast, lunch, and dinner. Breakfast is mostly eggs, yogurt, bagels – not fish (average 50 ILS). Lunch/dinner is mostly seafood (120 ILS). Separate vegan/vegetarian, dessert, and wine menus. Highlighted in *Condé Nast Traveler* and the *New York Times*; known by everyone local. Open 09.00–midnight.

MAR SABA

BUCKET! Score 5   *Category* Monasteries   *Micro-region* C2

This Greek Orthodox Monastery dates to 483 CE when founded by the Cappadocian monk, Sabbas the Sanctified (his relics/bones are on display). The monastery is a marvel: it appears to be slipping down the cliffside! Located halfway between the Dead Sea and Jerusalem, you'll need a car and the drive/views/colors are spectacular. Women are only allowed to enter Women's Tower at the front, annoyingly. Men can tour the monastery with an on-site monk. St. Sabas' five years of solitude were spent in a cave across the valley. Closed Wednesday and Friday. Ruin score: 3.

MASHYA

BUCKET! Score 5   *Category* Top Restaurants   *Micro-region* D1

Fine dining restaurant with a contemporary feel and Moroccan bent. Part of Israel's Modern Israeli movement. Every plate an Instagram pic. Breakfast, lunch, dinner menus. Breakfast is 108 ILS for a main and open buffet. Lunch/brunch has pasta, fish, and meat (94–152 ILS). Dinner is more diverse, with raw fish, salads, and hefty veg dishes (52–68 ILS) to accompany the meat/fish platters (88–168 ILS). Onza and Kitchen Market are part of the same group. Made *Condé Nast Traveler*'s Tel Aviv: Black Book and *La Liste*'s ranking of the world's best restaurants.

MEDITERRANEAN COAST

BUCKET! Score 8   *Category* Remote Beaches   *Micro-regions* E3, E4, E5

Beaches galore! From long, soft-sand beaches to rocky shores, the Israeli stretch of the Mediterranean has something for everyone. Every evening affords a beautiful sunset. Water sports are popular, including stand-up paddleboarding, surfing, and kitesurfing for beginners. Full disclosure: Tel Aviv is sufficient, unless you fear crowds. If so, go remote. You may be without lifeguards or wave breakers, so exercise caution and go frolic in the massive waves. If you have a rental car, you can be at a new beach every couple of kilometers. Review *Do #16: Beach It!* (p. 98).

MITZPE RAMON

BUCKET! Score 6 *Category* Experiential Lodging *Micro-region* J2

The town is your staging ground for **Makhtesh Ramon (#28)**. Visitor center for views or to prepare you for hiking with great exhibits on animals and geology. In town, an alpaca farm and archery range. If staying the night, two unique opportunities for lodging: the Beresheet Hotel (J2), a luxurious property straddling the crater; and high-end camping in darkness and silence with amazing night skies at Succah in the Desert, bookable through your favorite travel engine. Other lodging options vary from budget to the exotic to the luxurious.

MIZNON

BUCKET! Score 6 *Category* Quick Eats *Micro-region* D4

Celebrity chef Eyal Shani has received massive acclaim for his Miznon fast-casual chain, with two downtown locations in Tel Aviv (and branches in New York). Regularly changing menu, but always includes pita sandwiches with diverse ingredients. Forget your typical falafel – expect new tastes and sensations. The pita is one of the highlights! For carnivores: Hraime fish, minute steak, lamb kebab, rotisserie chicken all on rotation (38–48 ILS). Omnivores have mushroom, egg, chickpea, sweet potato, among other vegetarian options (23–34 ILS). World famous: whole roasted baby cauliflower. No reservations, expect long lines.

MODERN ISRAELI CUISINE

BUCKET! Score 9 *Category* Cuisine *Macro-region* U

Several world-recognized restaurants exist throughout Israel, but the hype centers on Tel Aviv where diners have dozens of choices, from casual to sophisticated. The modern style focuses heavily on vegetables and salads. Meat, chicken, and fish are often paired. Local ingredients are imperative. National origin is variable: could have French, Moroccan, Argentine, Thai, Georgian influences, but all comes together as distinctly Israeli. Expect giant charred vegetable mains, tons of regional olive oil, chutneys and pesto, drowned in tahini, dozens of salads with herbs as the "lettuce" mixed with pomegranate, date, fig, cactus, and fennel. Eggplant features heavily. Hummus is a category, not a dish. Background notes of pickles and olives. Kosher is optional. Molecular gastronomy occasionally makes an appearance. Local wines and beers to pair. With citizens from over 100 countries, Israeli cuisine has blossomed into something unique, modern, and exceptional.

MONASTERY OF ABU GHOSH

BUCKET! Score 4 *Category* Churches *Micro-region* B1

Monastery built around the semi-restored Crusader Church of the Resurrection of 1142, abandoned in 1187. Several of the original frescoes are literally de-faced from later Muslim rule. It sat for centuries, dilapidated, before being purchased by France in 1873 and given to the Mount-Olivet order of Benedictine nuns and monks. Gregorian chants, 850-year-old frescoes, and the underground spring in its crypt are highlights. Don't miss hummus restaurants afterwards. Closed Sunday/holidays.

May need to ring bell for entry. Check website for times (**w** abbaye-abugosh.info).
Ruin score: 1.

MONTFORT

BUCKET! Score 5   *Category* Crusader   *Micro-region* H1

Literally "strong mountain," the Crusader castle fortification was only in use for
40 years before Muslims gained control in 1187 and then abandoned it. Today, the
castle blends right into the forest landscape, with its towers and walls poking through
the surrounding greenery. A visit requires some moderate walking for around
45 minutes from Goren Park, across the valley, which is also where you get the best
photo shots. It's not the best-preserved castle (try **Nimrod's Fortress (#85)**), but does
make a nice walk. Ruin score: 3.

MOUNT ARBEL

BUCKET! Score 4   *Category* Historical Vantage   *Micro-region* G2

Panoramic views abound on top of this 380m mountain with views to the **Sea of
Galilee (#7)**, *Tiberias*, the Galilee plains, and the **Golan Heights (#62)**. Hiking trails take
you down the cliffside along the Arbel Spring to a ruined 2nd-century CE synagogue
(one of the world's oldest). Hike a simpler route to the Carob and Kinneret lookout
points for great views. This valley is home to one of the most important battlegrounds
in history: the Horns of Hattin, between the Crusaders and Saladin, the last time
Christians ruled the Holy Land. Ruin score: 1.

MOUNT OF BEATITUDES

BUCKET! Score 5   *Category* Jesus' Ministries   *Micro-region* G3

Recognized site where Jesus delivered the Sermon on the Mount, including some
of his most widely recognized teachings and recitable prayers: the Beatitudes
("Blessed are those…": Matthew 5:1–7) and the Lord's Prayer ("Our Father, who art
in Heaven…": Matthew 6:9–13). Today, a relatively modern church (1939, funded
by Mussolini!) stands on top of the mount to commemorate the sermon. Very
popular with church groups and pilgrims. Limited morning and afternoon hours.
Recommend to combine with other Jesus sites on *Road Trip G4*. Original church
across road from Tabgha churches (ruin score: 1).

MOUNT CARMEL

BUCKET! Score 4   *Category* Easy Hikes   *Micro-region* F1

This lush, green mountain just outside Haifa gets more rainfall than most other parts
of Israel, and makes for a great summer or winter hike. There are several dozen routes
to choose from, and four entrances. The park has a good brochure and map to help
you plan your trip. Within the park is the Hai-Bar Carmel Nature Reserve, where
you can visit a rehabilitation center for endangered animals. Places for picnicking
and camping. Two Druze communities here: Daliat el-Carmel and Isfiya, both busy
Saturdays. UNESCO Biosphere Reserve.

MOUNT GERIZIM

BUCKET! Score 4   *Category* Other Holy Places   *Micro-region* C5

Samaritans, a religious sect/offshoot of Judaism, believe this to be the site of the Holy of Holies (rather than Mount Moriah in Jerusalem), where Abraham was set to sacrifice his son, Isaac (see **Temple Mount (#12)**). A couple of hundred Samaritans live here. According to some, this is the oldest and smallest ethnically distinct religious community still in existence. Open Monday–Friday, but difficult to get to during troubled times, and closed on Samaritan Calendar New Year and Yom Kippur (differ from Jewish dates). Reserve a visit through w parks.org.il.

MOUNT GILBOA

BUCKET! Score 4   *Category* Scenic Drives   *Micro-region* F2

Mount Gilboa is where the Israelites, under their first king Saul, fought the Philistines 3,000 years ago. Less dramatic nowadays, the views from atop this 500m-tall mountain are nonetheless spectacular. Blanketed every spring in wildflowers, you'll want to visit the Mount Gilboa Iris Reserve. If hungry, two popular restaurants include The Gilboa Herb Farm and a bistro/wine bar specializing in local produce, Kimmel Restaurant. The Gilboa Scenic Road highlights biblical events. Hiking is also an option. Novice skiers enjoy the artificial ski slope. Ruin score: 1.

MOUNT HERMON

BUCKET! Score 5   *Category* Skiing   *Micro-region* I2

A ski resort in Israel? Indeed, at the highest point (2,200m) at the northernmost tip of the Israel-occupied **Golan Heights (#62)**. There are 45km of trails along 14 runs for skiers and snowboarders. Skiing is only possible during winter months when snowfall occurs, but you can hike or mountain bike the national park before 15.00 when it's warmer. Entrance, equipment, and ski pass is 415 ILS. Without equipment, 280 ILS. Private lessons are 300 ILS/hour. Other extreme sports/activities available. No public transportation. Book transport and tickets at w skihermon.co.il.

MUKAWIR

BUCKET! Score 4   *Category* Saints   *Micro-region* P2

Site of the beheading and martyrdom of John the Baptist in 32 CE. The spectacular view of the Dead Sea is about all that's left; the rest is left to the imagination as the ruins haven't been touched since they were abandoned. Originally the fortress of Machaerus, built by a Jewish Hasmonean king in 90 BCE, destroyed and rebuilt by King Herod to guard against trans-Jordan marauders. Like **Masada (#8)**, it was torn apart following the Jewish–Roman wars in 72 CE. Ruin score: 1.

MUSA – ERETZ ISRAEL MUSEUM

BUCKET! Score 5   *Category* Museum of Nationality   *Micro-region* D7

This museum of Israeli culture offers a diversity of exhibits related to objects or ideas as told from Israel's perspective, including coinage, the postal service, copper kilns, and photography. There are ten permanent displays on Israeli culture through time, and an archaeological site right in the middle of the property: Tel Qasile, a 12th-century BCE archaeological mound with an ancient wine press and oil press. The Baron Rothschild exhibit explores the man whose donations ultimately led to the creation of Israel. Planetarium. Closed Friday.

MUSEUM OF BEDOUIN CULTURE

BUCKET! Score 5   *Category* Museum of Culture   *Micro-region* J1

Located near Beer Sheva (J1) in the Joe Alon Center for Regional Studies, this museum offers exhibits on the Bedouins of the region as a way to preserve their rapidly disappearing traditions and by showcasing their wares, cloths, art, and tools. At the end, you get coffee and a conversation with a Bedouin representative in a tent. For those looking for a quick Bedouin experience, a couple of hours in this museum will provide you with history, culture, and an introductory meeting with Bedouin peoples.

NAHAL ME'AROT/WADI EL-MUGHARA

BUCKET! Score 5   *Category* Early Human Settlements   *Micro-region* F1

Take the "Prehistoric Man" trail to four caves (Tabun, Jamal, el-Wad, and Skhul) to see a progression of 500,000 years of prehistoric human activity. There are some distracting display figures, but the story is important enough to deem this a UNESCO site: evidence of the transition from hunting and gathering to animal husbandry and agricultural activities. Watch the audiovisual presentation in the cave at the end. There are longer walking trails for those interested in geology or local plant life. Ruin score: 1.

NAZARENE FUSION CUISINE

BUCKET! Score 6   *Category* Culinary Capitals   *Micro-region* G1

A combination of Galilean, Arab, and international flavors has turned this famous town into a foodie destination for in-the-know travelers. You may find traditional foods such as shakshuka cooked with bacon or chicken in pineapple curry (at Rosemary), seafood risotto with za'atar or chicken cooked with wheat berries and coffee (at Tishreen), cream with pistachio and pine nut or local leaves with red fruit salad (at Al Reda), lamb carpaccio and tartare or rotating preparations of seasonal salads/eggplant/tahini/vegetables (at Diana). Alcohol allowed. Prices from 80–100 ILS for mains. Reservations not usually required, unless holidays. Restaurants may close Sunday.

NETANYA

BUCKET! Score 4 *Category* Public Beaches *Micro-region* E4

Fourteen more kilometers of gorgeous stretches of sand await you. Poleg Beach is the southernmost option, with kitesurfing, paragliding, and stand-up paddleboarding options (along with regular surfing) available from tents near the entrance. The sand is fine, hot, and stretches for miles. Further north are more city-centric beaches, but not as crowded as Tel Aviv. Sironit Beach has a strong fan base. Day-trip here; not popular for hotels/restaurants, though there are certainly both.

NEVE TZEDEK

BUCKET! Score 4 *Category* Cool Neighborhoods *Micro-region* D4

The oldest neighborhood in Tel Aviv, established in 1887 (22 years before Tel Aviv itself, actually) this was originally the first town founded outside of Jaffa. Gentrification has made this a bit less grungy and student-filled, but art still prevails, with the Suzanne Dellal Centre for Dance and Theatre (D4) here, as do high-end boutiques, art galleries, and nice restaurants.

NITZANA

BUCKET! Score 3 *Category* Nabataean Cities *Micro-region* J2

Most of the remains here are from the Byzantine period or later, though it did originally serve as a trading post on the Nabataean **Incense Route (#73)** from the 3rd century BCE. 3.5km from the Egyptian border. Several churches and a huge fortress. Site was abandoned after the Muslim conquest. Nearby are the remains of a 19th-century CE hospital built by the Ottomans, which used the ruins for building materials. Look for a water tank that supplied trains passing through 100 years ago. Ruin score: 3.

THE NORMAN HOTEL

BUCKET! Score 5 *Category* Highly Recommended Accommodation *Micro-region* D4

"Five-star" luxury boutique hotel near **Rothschild Boulevard** in downtown Tel Aviv with a 1920s vibe, modern décor and amenities, and a rooftop infinity swimming pool. All-day bar The Library and fine-dining Alena (listed on *La Liste*'s World's Best Restaurants) are draws. Highly regarded breakfast included. Nespresso and iPads in rooms. Small fitness center. Recommended everywhere upon opening in 2014. High-end amenities. Fifty beautiful rooms from $600 per night.

OCD

BUCKET! Score 5 *Category* Top Restaurants *Micro-region* D4

An experiential restaurant, one of *La Liste*'s best in the world, and a destination for a foodie, with 16–20 courses served at each meal. Only 19 seats. With this kind of elaborate scheme, a little forethought is necessary: book in advance, make sure to indicate any preferences or allergies. Set courses only, but a remarkable variety:

carnivore, vegetarian, vegan, pescatarian, white-meat-free (!), lactose-free, and gluten-free. The menu changes with the seasons. Dinner 390 ILS, wine pairing 272 ILS. Credit card required at booking. Closed Saturday/Sunday.

PALESTINIAN HERITAGE TRAIL

BUCKET! Score 5   *Category* Long-Distance Walks   *Micro-region* U

Formerly the Masar Ibrahim Al-Khalil Trail, this 330km, 21-day sojourn from the north to the south of the West Bank seeks to introduce walkers to the diverse land, culture, and communities of the Palestinian people as the trail ventures from Jenin through Jerusalem and on to Hebron. Along the way, stay in family homes, Bedouin camps, or guesthouses. Record your journey with the trail's hiker passport. Local guides or tour operators (all on website) can help you plan, but the trail is well delineated for solo travelers at w paltrails.ps.

PASTEL

BUCKET! Score 5   *Category* Top Restaurants   *Micro-region* D3

This fine-dining French brasserie opened in 2014 with rave reviews about its architecture, winning Best Designed Restaurant. The restaurant attempts to match its cuisine to the stunning beauty of the space it inhabits. Pasta, seafood, and meat dishes incorporate a variety of ingredients and cooking styles, rather than hitting solely a French note. You'll find confit, scallops, tartare, and endive salads on the menu, as well as Marmite stock, Jerusalem artichoke cream, raw pheasant yolk, and blueberry raisins. Mains 100–200 ILS. Open daily, noon–midnight.

PELLA

BUCKET! Score 4   *Category* Cities of the Decapolis   *Micro-region* S2

Found on the Jordanian side of the Jordan River, this ancient town is quite possibly the most diverse archaeological site in Jordan, covering an almost complete narrative of history from Neolithic times (6000 BCE) to the present. Across a valley covering two tels, or hills, the site lacks signage or context, though archaeologists are impressed. The most visually representative ruins are of the columned Byzantine church. There are other important finds, visible at least at the foundation level, including residences and defensive walls. City of the Decapolis. Ruin score: 2.

PETRA BY NIGHT

BUCKET! Score 6   *Category* Ceremonies and Events   *Micro-region* N3

The experience of walking the Siq is often just a long (1.2km) precursor to the grand ah-ha moment of catching the first glimpse of the Treasury. That's what makes this candlelit walk in silence so amazing – you've likely already made the walk, but do so again quietly, with 1,500 candles, no heckling or tour groups, and see the starry sky. Ends with a show at the Treasury. Starts at 20.30 from the Petra visitor center. Operates Monday, Wednesday, and Thursday; 2 hours; 17 JD; no reservations.

POPINA

BUCKET! Score 5   *Category* Top Restaurants   *Micro-region* D4

French-style restaurant in **Neve Tzedek** founded in 2013 by famed chef and modern Israeli cuisine innovator Uriel Kimchi. One of *La Liste*'s top restaurants in the world. Good variety of small plates expected to pair together, each running from 80–120 ILS (caviar, veal, sea bass, etc. will cost a premium). Beautifully presented food. Kitchen in the middle of the restaurant to allow for conversations with the chef/staff. Tasting menu at 305 ILS for seven dishes. Large space. Vegetarian and vegan options. Open daily from 18.00. Reservations at **w** popina.co.il.

QASR AL-ABD

BUCKET! Score 4   *Category* Greek Empire   *Micro-region* Q4

Of all the castles in Israel and Jordan, most are Crusader (Christian), Umayyad (Muslim), or Hasmonean (Jewish). This is a rare Greek castle, built of monumental stone blocks, dating to the 2nd century BCE, some 1,000 years before the neighboring **Qasr Amra and the Desert Palaces (#20)** were built. There are interesting animal reliefs and carvings of lions. Possibly used as a pleasure palace. The building stands at its original height, being renovated to become a church during the Byzantine reign. An earthquake may have brought about its demise. Ruin score: 3.

QASR AZRAQ

BUCKET! Score 5   *Category* Ayyubid   *Micro-region* R1

The site began as a strategic base for Romans (3rd century CE), as it was near water which is today part of the **Azraq Wetlands (#55)** reserve. There's a mosque in the middle dating to the Umayyads (8th century CE). It was built up extensively by the Ayyubids in the 13th century, and later served as staging grounds for T.E. Lawrence ("Lawrence of Arabia") during the Arab Revolt in World War I. One of the castles comprising **Qasr Amra and the Desert Palaces (#20)**. Ruin score: 3.

QASR KHARANA

BUCKET! Score 5   *Category* Umayyad   *Micro-region* R1

A well-preserved structure from the early Muslim years, built by the Umayyads in the late 7th/early 8th centuries CE. Though often considered part of the **Qasr Amra and the Desert Palaces (#20)** group, it was probably not used as a castle because the fortifications aren't defensive. It more likely served as a meeting space, with some 60 rooms to house guests, many still intact, which can be explored over the two floors. Many of the architectural features and interior room designs remain visible. Ruin score: 3.

RED CANYON

BUCKET! Score 4   *Category* Easy Hikes   *Micro-region* L2

Only 2–4m wide in most places, this 2-hour hike near the Egyptian border (30km from **Eilat (#78)**) traverses a 150m-long ruddy-red (and purple and white!) sandstone canyon. There are a few trails: green is for families, while black is for experienced hikers and departs from the green in order to steeply climb to a panoramic viewpoint, and the red connects with the black to circle back to the parking lot. To enter the canyon, walkers must use ladders and rungs. 5km, 1½ hours.

ROCKEFELLER ARCHAEOLOGICAL MUSEUM

BUCKET! Score 5   *Category* Museum of Archaeology   *Micro-region* A6

Across from Herod's Gate in the Old City, this complement to the **Israel Museum (#17)** was opened in 1938 and was for decades the premier museum of Jerusalem. Inside are thousands of artifacts that were excavated during the British Mandate period. The collection organizes the pieces chronologically over the 9,000 years of human history represented. The building is lovely. Open 10.00–15.00 Wednesday, Thursday, and Saturday; free.

ROSH HANIKRA

BUCKET! Score 4   *Category* Geological Wonders   *Micro-region* E5

A one-way walking tour (complete with cable car ride from the top of the cliffs) offers an interesting look at the splashy grottoes that were formed from tectonic movement, as well as rain and sea erosion. The electric blue waters are gorgeous, kids like the trip, and there are biking and electric car options for getting around. You're just on the other side of Lebanon (no access) with a photo-worthy spot indicating so at the top of the cliff near the guards' tower.

ROTHSCHILD BOULEVARD

BUCKET! Score 6   *Category* Streets   *Micro-region* D4

Epicenter of Tel Aviv's financial businesses, wealthy elite, exercise fanatics, dog owners, idle coffeehouse patrons, and many buildings in the Bauhaus/International style – several of which have placards exploring the architectural history. Rothschild is Tel Aviv's (if not Israel's) most famous street, with pedestrian/bike areas right down the center. Running from *Habima Theatre (D4)* to *Neve Tzedek*, it makes for a great stroll with lots of fabulous people-watching opportunities. Stop for a coffee, stay for the afternoon.

ROYAL SOCIETY FOR THE CONSERVATION OF NATURE (RSCN)

BUCKET! Score 6   *Category* Parks   *Macro-region* V

Established in 1966 by Jordan's King Hussein, this group is responsible for overseeing the ten (and growing!) protected wildlife areas in Jordan. In addition to conservation projects, it also administers the *Wild Jordan Center* eco-tourism site and project. The RSCN has successfully reintroduced lost species to Jordan lands and has been a BirdLife partner since 1966. The RSCN owns **Feynan Ecolodge (#86)** in **Dana Biosphere Reserve (#21)** and works in the *Aqaba Bird Observatory (M2)*. Visit **w** rscn.org.jo for its latest projects and newest declared reserves.

SABICH/OVED'S

BUCKET! Score 5   *Category* Food   *Micro-region* D7

Sabich is a vegetarian sandwich that is anything but a salad-in-a-wrap. Comes with chunks of eggplant, egg, hummus, greens, cabbage, pickles, and various salsas drizzled on top – tahini, spicy, amba (mango) – all wrapped in a light and fluffy pita. Variations exist, with some including chips or fries in the mix. The most famous shop is debated, but likely Oved's Sabich in Givatayim, east of Tel Aviv downtown (3km/45 minutes' walk from Sarona Market (D3)). Check out *Do #14: Eat It!* (p. 80) for more recommendations.

SATAF

BUCKET! Score 4   *Category* Day Hikes   *Micro-region* B1

Beginning around 2500 BCE in the Jerusalem Hills, locals began implementing a terraced agricultural system for crops that didn't require irrigation – known as *ba'al* – such as olives, grapes, figs, and pomegranates. Much of the original design has been restored by the Jewish National Fund on the Sataf Nature Trail, offering 360° views as you meander along its moderately difficult, 2½-hour circular trail. There are several routes to choose from (including the Baal Trail) which pass ancient and more recent ruins, including the abandoned Arab village of Sataf.

SEA OF GALILEE BEACHES

BUCKET! Score 4   *Category* Public/Popular Beaches   *Micro-region* G3

This big lake – also called the Kinneret – is better known for its Jesus sites, but it has a number of water-based attractions to entice you as well. Just south of **Tiberias**, AquaKef Park near Ganim Beach has a water-based obstacle course while Gai Beach has a kid-friendly water park. Stay at Kibbutz Maagan or Kibbutz Ein Gev (G3) for two holiday resorts with private beaches. For public-access beaches and camping facilities, try Ein Gev Beach (2km north of resort) or Gofra Beach on the eastern shore. Or Bora Bora Beach north of **Tiberias** for a private, clean beach with amenities.

SEBASTIA-SHOMRON

BUCKET! Score 4   *Category* Byzantine   *Micro-region* C5

Ancient Shomron, or Samaria, is located about 12km north of **Nablus (#61)** and served as capital of Palestine during the late Iron Age, before its capture by Alexander the Great who added great fortifications. After the Hasmoneans destroyed the town in 107 BCE, King Herod rebuilt the city (the colonnade and amphitheater were his work) and gave it the name Sebastia. It houses a converted Byzantine-era church (now the Nabi Yahya Mosque) which once held the buried remains of John the Baptist. All visits must be coordinated in advance (☏ 09 9539222). Ruin score: 2.

SEPARATION WALL

BUCKET! Score 7   *Category* Borders   *Micro-region* C1

The West Bank Barrier, the Anti-Terrorism Fence, the security barrier – all names to describe the controversial 700km barrier that separates Israel and the West Bank. The wall continues to enrage Palestinians who can't move freely and have no state of their own, but is regarded by Israelis as essential to protect their own people from attack. This tension can best be felt near **Bethlehem (#40)** in a series of works graffitied by the UK artist Banksy. Famous works include *Girl Frisking Soldier*, *Flower Thrower*, and *Armored Dove*. See *City Walk C1*.

SHAKSHUKA/DR. SHAKSHUKA

BUCKET! Score 5   *Category* Food   *Micro-region* D2

If you haven't yet tried shakshuka, you'll be amazed at how a simple dish marrying eggs, tomato sauce, sometimes vegetables, and myriad spices can have a transformative effect when cooked together. A number of places specialize exclusively in shakshuka, but you'll find it on several breakfast menus. The most famous location is Dr. Shakshuka in Jaffa – with its Seinfeldian "Soup Nazi" feel – but explore others in *Do #14: Eat It!* (p. 80).

SHAUMARI

BUCKET! Score 4   *Category* Animals/Zoos/Wildlife   *Micro-region* R1

One of the **Royal Society for the Conservation of Nature (RSCN)**'s parks, Shaumari Wildlife Reserve was established in 1975 and today uses 22km² to breed animals endemic to the region which had since gone regionally extinct. Take a guided tour with knowledgeable staff in a safari jeep through this small reserve to see how the reintegrated fauna are doing, with eyes open for gazelles, ostriches, oryx, and onagers (wild donkeys). Bird-watching tower too. The visitor center is an excellent place to start.

SHIVTA

BUCKET! Score 5   *Category* Byzantine   *Micro-region* J2

Is Shivta more Nabataean or Byzantine? The jury's still out. The Nabataeans first settled here in the 1st century CE incorporating another stop on the **Incense Route (#73)** to Gaza. Shivta had a renaissance in the 5th century CE with more than 2,000 residents. Given its desert location, water collection was the primary activity to support its agricultural endeavors. The site gradually declined by the 9th century CE. There are excellent ruins here, including impressive churches, streetscapes, and a series of pools. UNESCO site. Ruin score: 4.

SHOBAK

BUCKET! Score 5   *Category* Crusader   *Micro-region* O1

Shobak, or Krak de Montréal, was a Crusader castle built in 1115 as part of the same line of defense as its sister site, **Karak (#49)**, some 100km to the north. It lasted one year longer than Karak before succumbing to Saladin's forces in 1189. The walls are interestingly from later Mamluk additions. Enveloped in emptiness, the castle piques interest for its unmissable hilltop location, remoteness, and many nooks and crannies to explore, including basement catacombs which purportedly contain Saladin's throne. Ruin score: 3.

SHRINE OF BAHÁ'U'LLÁH

BUCKET! Score 4   *Category* Landscape   *Micro-region* E5

One of the sites designated by UNESCO as part of the Bahá'í monuments in northwest Israel. This garden and shrine is located in Bahjí, just north of **Akko (#13)**, and is dedicated to the Divine Educator, Bahá'u'lláh, who died here in 1892 and whose remains are interred at the shrine. This is the Bahá'í "Mecca," towards which all Bahá'ís around the world pray, and the most holy place in the Bahá'í faith. On site is the Mansion of Bahjí where Bahá'u'lláh died. Opulent shrine, pristine gardens, total serenity.

SINAI TRAIL

BUCKET! Score 5   *Category* Long-Distance Walks   *Micro-region* T1

Voted best new tourism project in the world in 2016, this long-distance hiking trail (with shorter chunks you can complete) takes walkers through 550km of trails over some 52 days across the Egyptian Sinai peninsula. Along the way, hikers interact and stay with eight Bedouin tribes who volunteer as hosts. Most people hike with camels and a local guide, which is recommended given the terrain, lack of English, and to pay respect to the community who inhabit the land. It's a hot, desert climate with lots of mountain peaks, so even shorter hikes are for more experienced hikers; w sinaitrail.net is indispensable.

ST. JAMES' CATHEDRAL

BUCKET! Score 5   *Category* Churches   *Micro-region* A2

This lavish Crusader-era cathedral in the Armenian Quarter (A2) of Jerusalem's Old City incorporates a pair of 5th-century CE churches, each dedicated to a famously martyred "Saint James" – one an apostle of Jesus, the other a brother/relation of Jesus who became the first bishop of Jerusalem. In 1195 the site served as a hospice for Armenian pilgrims, and by the 17th century this cathedral became the seat of the Armenian Christian Church. Visits to the church are only permissible 15.00–15.40, during services, or with an Armenian guide. Ruin score: 5.

STELLA MARIS

BUCKET! Score 4   *Category* Kings/Prophets/Saints   *Micro-region* E1

The "Star of the Sea" monastery in Haifa – crowned by a lighthouse reflecting its name – serves as headquarters of the Carmelites, a Roman Catholic religious order whose focus is on contemplating service, prayer, and the community. The monastery surrounds the grotto/cave where Elijah the Prophet is believed to have taken refuge during the 9th century BCE (as told in the Book of the Kings). Open 06.30–12.30 and 15.00–18.00 daily. Cable-car up, or park. Visit the church, then descend to Elijah's Cave at the base of the hill. Ruin score: 1.

SUPREME COURT OF ISRAEL

BUCKET! Score 4   *Category* Politics   *Micro-region* A8

Established in 1948, the 15-member Supreme Court is the highest court of Israel. It's located near the Knesset (A8) in Givat Ram, the government quarter of Jerusalem. The court's two primary responsibilities are to hear appeals and to hear petitions against government authorities. The current President of the Supreme Court is Esther Hayut. The court manages an annual case load of roughly 10,000 proceedings. English-language tours leave every day at noon and discuss history, architecture, and the structure of the court and its building.

SUWEIMEH SPA HOTELS

BUCKET! Score 8   *Category* Spas   *Micro-region* P1

Just south of the town of Suweimeh on the Jordanian side of the **Dead Sea (#3)** is a series of luxury hotels that are our recommendation for how best to enjoy the Dead Sea. These hotels are moderately priced, but come with big rooms, great outdoor spaces, excellent breakfasts, and a slough of amenities to allow you time to pamper yourself. In addition to access to the Dead Sea (often by stairs, unlike on the Israeli side), mud tanks are often present, as are jet pools, freshwater and saltwater pools, indoor and outdoor facilities, and glorious views. All the hotels here come highly regarded: from the Holiday Inn on the least expensive side to the Crowne Plaza, Hilton, Marriott, Mövenpick, and the extremely posh and well-priced Kempinski Hotel Ishtar.

TEL ARAD

BUCKET! Score 4   *Category* Other Holy Places   *Micro-region* J1

Two ancient settlements are built on/around the archaeological mound of Tel Arad. In the lower section are the remains of a Chalcolithic/Early Bronze Age (3150–2200 BCE) era village. Up the hill, the remains of a Canaanite city (1200 BCE) include an ancient temple. The city contains the only House of Yahweh ever discovered, before Solomon's Temple in Jerusalem became the sole permissible worshiping house. Recently, cannabis was found in a hidden altar, showing Jews likely used psychotropic drugs for religious purposes. Ruin score: 3.

TEL ASHKELON

BUCKET! Score 4   *Category* Tels   *Micro-region* E3

A route along the Via Maris from Egypt to Syria, Ashkelon was an important way station through many successive civilizations. The first city, Tel Ashkelon, was founded around 2000 BCE during the Canaanite period and is referenced in the Bible (Samson/Judges). The site presents a variety of histories with its show-and-tell features, including a Roman basilica, Byzantine church, Fatimid walls, and Ottoman waterwheel, among other places of interest. The beach is open and there are hiking trails. Israel National Park. Ruin score: 2.

TEL AVIV PORT

BUCKET! Score 6   *Category* Ports   *Micro-region* D1

Developed as a new port for Tel Aviv in 1936, the Namal (Hebrew for "port") became derelict once the site became too small to manage container ships. It was closed in the 1960s before receiving a massive upgrade in the early 2000s. Old hangars were converted into restaurants, clothing shops, and bars. A wooden deck was built to emulate waves or sand and is filled with people ambulating at all hours. The space won a biennial landscape architecture prize in 2010 for best global design. There's an interesting indoor/outdoor food market that has great lunch spots and gift options, and hosts a farmers' market on Fridays.

TEL AVIV TAYELET/PROMENADE

BUCKET! Score 8   *Category* Walking Paths   *Micro-region* D1

The Tel Aviv Promenade, or *tayelet* in Hebrew, is the epicenter of the city in a lot of ways – from parks and obviously beach, to restaurants, sports, bars, workout equipment, volleyball courts, and falafel stands. The upgraded, pedestrian-friendly, and wide walkways are a perfect way to get from the *Tel Aviv Port* to **Jaffa (#30)** and any of the in-between stretches of glorious sand. Join hundreds every evening who sit on the steps to watch the sunset. A bike path runs just adjacent. Distance 6km.

TEL BEER SHEVA

BUCKET! Score 4   *Category* Iron Age   *Micro-region* J1

Scripture references a large desert city as the location where Abraham and Isaac settled after entering a covenant with King Abimelech: Abraham offered seven lambs in exchange for digging a well. The name "Beersheba" means "well of the oath" or perhaps "well of seven." Today, the site is testament to at least a dozen civilizations, from its many references in the Bible to destruction by the Assyrians to fortifications from Roman times. The modern city of Beer Sheva (J1) was built a few kilometers away. UNESCO site for **Biblical Tels (#38)**. Ruin score: 2.

TEL HAZOR

BUCKET! Score 3   *Category* Bronze Age   *Micro-region* H2

From the 18th century BCE until its destruction by Assyria in 732 BCE, this massive settlement in the Galilee Panhandle was one of the most important sites in the Holy Land, called the head of all Canaanite kingdoms in the Book of Joshua. Hazor was referenced in the Egyptian Amarna Letters and uniquely survived the Bronze Age collapse to maintain regional power. Visit Solomon's Gate, the Canaanite temple, and the underground water system. UNESCO site for **Biblical Tels (#38)**. Ruin score: 2.

TEL-O-FUN BIKE SHARE

BUCKET! Score 6   *Category* Biking   *Micro-region* D1

Thousands of bright-green bikes in hundreds of locations around Tel Aviv and Jaffa are available for your convenience and entertainment. Visitor passes are available for daily, three-day, or weekly access, plus annual subscriptions. Each ride is free for the first 30 minutes, 6 ILS each additional 30 minutes, cumulative. One bike at a time; 10-minute wait time after logging off. Dock in any station around town with a free spot available. Helmets encouraged but not required or included. Credit cards okay. \ *6070 with questions.

TIBERIAS

BUCKET! Score 2   *Category* Resort Locations   *Micro-region* G3

This seaside town has seen better days (or has it?). The **Sea of Galilee (#7)** makes a nice backdrop, but the city itself feels run down and depressing for a resort village. The Promenade is short. The draw would be water sports, but you can do these in multiple other places. There are a few small things on offer: the tombs of Maimonides and Rambam, but they are not set up as tourist attractions and do not feel welcoming or necessary. Stay in nearby **Nazareth (#29)**.

TULUL ABU EL-ALAIQ

BUCKET! Score 4   *Category* Herodian   *Micro-region* C3

Originally a Hasmonean winter palace, King Herod greatly expanded the complex to include three "winter homes" connected over the Wadi Qelt by a bridge. The kings and queens would swim in the grand pools constructed using advanced irrigation engineering techniques. Herod actually died here, before being moved to his tomb at **Herodion (#90)**. The buildings were built of mud brick, which didn't survive the earthquake of 31 BCE nor the Jewish Revolt of 70 CE, so there's little left to see here. Ruin score: 2.

TZFON ABRAXAS

BUCKET! Score 9   *Category* Top Restaurants   *Micro-region* D4

Tzfon (North) Abraxas is our pick for best restaurant in Tel Aviv. A celebrity chef institution, Eyal Shani long made this a must-eat restaurant for Telavivans. Reviewers sometimes complain about service or price – ignore them. You'll dine on butcher paper, eat almost everything with your hands, and get the food when it's ready. And yet it's chic and trendy inside. Menu is broken up not by course but ingredient (bread/vegetable/seafood/cow). Bottom line: it's beyond delicious, and you'll never look at cauliflower the same way.

UMM EL-JIMAL

BUCKET! Score 4   *Category* Byzantine   *Micro-region* R1

Close to the Syrian border, the present town of Umm el-Jimal arose out of the ruins of the multilayered historical town. That town began as a satellite of the neighboring town of Bostra, near the Via Nova. The monumental ruins in the part called al-Herri date to the Nabataean/Roman period. Later, the camp became a Roman military station before converting into a Byzantine and eventually Muslim Umayyad agricultural town. The ruins of more than 150 black basalt houses and 16 churches date to the 5th–7th centuries CE. Ruin score: 4.

UNDERWATER OBSERVATORY

BUCKET! Score 6   *Category* Aquaria   *Micro-region* L2

Two display halls are submerged 12m below the sea to provide a direct underwater glimpse at the extraordinary marine life located within the coral reefs in this marine park located in **Eilat (#78)** on the Red Sea. You can feed sharks, take a glass-bottom boat, and watch a pearl come out of a live shell. The site includes a rare fish display, a pool with 18 sharks, walruses, stingrays, and more. Advance booking required for Aquadome and Coral 2000. Entrance valid three days. Adult 105 ILS, child 85 ILS.

URI BURI

BUCKET! Score 9   *Category* Top Restaurants   *Micro-region* E2

Uri Jeremias, the chef with the long white beard who undoubtedly checks on every table to make sure they're content, is an unmistakable presence in his seafood restaurant and **Akko (#13)** in general (where he also owns the Efendi (E2)). At Uri Buri, you'll find the freshest seafood in the country, each dish prepared impeccably. Try the taster menu if you trust them – variable pricing depending on when you tell them to stop. For lighter fare, many dishes come in half-sizes. A couple of vegetarian/vegan options and alcohol.

WEIZMANN INSTITUTE OF SCIENCE

BUCKET! Score 5   *Category* Museum of Science and Learning   *Micro-region* D8

The Weizmann Institute is an active science lab, but the grounds include a visitor center with a number of technologically advanced exhibits to keep kids and adults alike interested. The Clore Garden of Science offers more than 80 outdoor interactive exhibits with the goal of fostering scientific curiosity in youth. A highlight is the hologram show where you control projected images by moving your body in different directions. Tour includes the original Weizmann House. Must prebook. Closed Friday and Saturday.

WILD JORDAN CENTER

BUCKET! Score 5   *Category* Meet Locals   *Micro-region* Q2

A downtown café, hotel, and information center that is owned by the *Royal Society for the Conservation of Nature (RSCN)*, whose responsibilities include the preservation of Jordan's nature reserves. Here, you can book tours and lodges at those parks. Located near Rainbow Street, this space has great views of Amman and the old city ruins and is a great meeting place, with breakfast, lunch, and dinner served 09.00–23.30. Daily special meals with traditional food for 10 JD. Studios with private bath for 73 JD.

WINERY TOUR

BUCKET! Score 7   *Category* Wineries   *Macro-region* U

In the 1990s, the **Golan Heights Winery (#75)** put Israel on the world map for production of quality, trophy-winning wines. Hundreds of large and boutique wineries have sprung up since then, in five distinct wine regions. Each region arguably deserves an entire weekend on its own – the Galilee/Golan, Judean Hills, Shimshon, the Negev, and Shomron. See *Road Trips B3, E6,* and *U1* for inspiration in setting up your trip. Touring wineries in Israel still feels intimate and warm, with most producers happy to tell you about the history of grape-growing in Israel, the family's background, and innovative cultivation techniques. Israel may not yet have its own signature character (which winemakers will tell you), but the wineries are still producing some eminently drinkable bottles. Book all tours in advance. Most wineries are closed Shabbat.

WOHL ARCHAEOLOGICAL MUSEUM

BUCKET! Score 5   *Category* Museum of Archaeology   *Micro-region* A4

Also called the Herodian Quarter, this underground museum showcases the ancient floors and walls of six upper-echelon family homes built during the Herodian/Second Temple period some 2,000 years ago. The whole city was burned and destroyed in 70 CE, burying many houses in ash and debris, and which were later covered over with streets and new houses. In these old houses, get a glimpse of how the wealthy lived: mosaic floors, mikvehs, furniture – much still recognizable today. Ruin score: 3.

YATIR WINERY

BUCKET! Score 4   *Category* Great Wine   *Micro-region* J1

Yatir is located at 900m above sea level where the climate is different from the Mediterranean climate of nearby wineries, with cold nights, cool mornings, and hot (dry) days. The soil is limestone. Its popular varietals include Viognier, rosé, Cabernet Sauvignon, Shiraz, and Petit Verdot, and its flagship bottle, Yatir Forest, regularly scores above 90 points. The "fundamental" brand is Mount Amasa, a red that combines its signature grapes with Malbec, Merlot, and Cabernet Franc. Hugh Johnson awarded the winery 3–4 stars. Must prebook tours; there's no visitor center.

YEHI'AM

BUCKET! Score 5   *Category* Crusader   *Micro-region* H1

This fortress includes several layers of history. Once a Byzantine-era village, the Crusaders used materials from that time to construct a well-protected feudal farm called Iudyn. The fortress was built in the mid-13th century CE, though was mostly destroyed by Mamluks in 1265 who left a tower and some inner walls, later restored by a local Bedouin leader in 1738. The tall outer walls and most of the present structure date to the 18th-century Ottoman period. Major battle in the War of Independence took place here. Ruin score: 3.

YEHUDIYA

BUCKET! Score 4   *Category* Easy Hikes   *Micro-region* I3

A popular hiking spot on weekends, this nature reserve has two entrances and nearly a dozen hiking routes. Use the park rangers wisely for advice on routes based on weather, time, and conditions (landslides happen). Some are water routes, up to 1m deep. The easiest route departs from the Yehudiya Forest parking lot and descends the canyon directly to a popular waterfall. You'll need advanced reservations for the Black Gorge. Each of the park's streams empties into the Kinneret: Yehudiyah, Zavitan, and Meshushim/Hexagonal Pools (which have a different entrance). Most are frigid snowmelt. Limited shade cover.

YEMEN MOSHE

BUCKET! Score 4   *Category* Cool Neighborhoods   *Micro-region* A7

This little neighborhood was the first Jewish settlement outside the Old City walls, established to avoid cholera spreading rampantly inside. Moses Montefiore spent time and money trying to convince Jews to move outside those walls; his neighborhood was finally established in 1892. Mishkenot Sha'ananim was the first housing block, and still exists today as a guesthouse for artists. Montefiore's Windmill is a landmark; it was designed as a flour mill, but never functioned. The resident houses are quaint and attractive and worthy of a stroll.

YMCA

BUCKET! Score 4   *Category* Urban Landscape   *Micro-region* A7

Yes, you can stay here, and many do for its mission of peace and unity for people of all cultures and nations. But it's best known for its panoramic tower-top views. Buy elevator tickets to the tower inside. Unfortunately, the visual aids have been sun-bleached and making out the names of places is difficult, though it is fun to see how the city has changed in the last few decades with new buildings and development where empty land once stood.

YOTVATA HAI-BAR

BUCKET! Score 4   *Category* Animals/Zoos   *Micro-region* L3

This desert wildlife reserve in the southern Negev just 35km north of **Eilat (#78)** was established to reintroduce endangered and endemic animals to their original habitat. Two animals have been restored successfully: the Arabian oryx (a type of antelope) and the onager, a wild ass. The breeding program also includes the addax (white or screwhorn antelope), caracal, desert cats, wolves, and ostrich. You'll need a car or jeep tour as the animals are not caged. Plan 2 hours; open all year.

ZICHRON YA'AKOV

BUCKET! Score 6   *Category* Handmade   *Micro-region* E4

One of the first towns established (1882) during the First Wave (*aliyah*) of Jewish immigrants from Europe. Many know **Carmel Winery** is located here, but the town is also known for its handicraft shops and art galleries. Visitors traipse along the Path of the Wine, a pedestrian mall with tourist-friendly restaurants, bookshops, art vendors, boutiques, and wine stores. Somek, Poizner, and Smadar wineries also in town. Near Tishbi Winery (E6) and Margalit Winery (E6). Very popular on weekends.

Part 7

Electives by Theme

CATEGORIES

Theme/Sub-theme		Category
NOTEWORTHY	Spotlight	UNESCO
		Wonders of the World
		Endangered
		National Parks
		Nature Reserves & Other Protected Areas
	Adventure	Unique Experiences
		Exploration
		Exotic/Wow
		Off the Beaten Path
		Quirky
RELIGION	Religions	Judaism
		Christianity
		Islam
		Religious Minorities
	Religious Figures	Kings, Prophets, & Saints
		Jesus' Early Life
		Jesus' Ministries & Miracles
		Jesus' Death & Resurrection
		Muhammad
	Holy Books	Hebrew Bible/Old Testament
		New Testament
		Quran
		Ancient Manuscripts
		Biblical Battlefields
	Houses of Worship (Extant)	Synagogues
		Collections of Synagogues
		Churches
		Collections of Churches
		Monasteries
		Mosques
		Other Holy Places
	The Sacred	Burial
		Pilgrimage
		Ceremonies and Events
		Meditation, Yoga, and Quiet
ARCHAEOLOGY	Ruins by Period	Early Human Settlements
		Tels (Multi-Period, Layered Cities)
		Prehistory/Stone to Copper
		Bronze Age
		Canaanite
		Iron Age: Kingdom of Israel/Judah
		Age of Empires: Babylonian, Persian, Greek, Hasmonean
		Herodian
		Roman
		Byzantine/Christian
		Islamic I: Rashidun, Umayyad, Abbasid
		Crusader
		Islamic II: Ayyubid, Mamluk, Ottoman

Theme/Sub-theme		Category
ARCHAEOLOGY (cont.)	City Conglomerates	Cities of the Decapolis
		Nabataean Cities/Incense Route
	Impressionable Historic Sites	Ghost Towns
		Mosaics
		Walls
		Shipwrecks
		Historic Battlefields
		Active Excavations
		Impressive Structural Remains
STRUCTURE	Monuments	Iconic Structures
		Historic Monuments
		Memorial
	Architecture	Architectural Styles
		Landscape
		Modern Architecture
		Beautiful Structures
		Skyline
	Engineering	Impressive Feats
		Technological Advancement
		Infrastructure
NATURE	Geography	Geological Wonders
		Geographical Superlatives
		Rivers, Lakes, and Waterfalls
		Mountains and Mounts
		Desert
		Canyons, Wadis, and Makhteshim
		Forests and Greek Parks
		Caves/Grottoes
		Earthquakes
	Life	Animals, Zoos, and Wildlife
		Sea Creatures, Reefs, and Aquaria
		Birding
		Plants, Gardens, and Farms
	Parks	Gorgeous Scenery
		Parks
		The Great Outdoors
SCENIC	Vistas	Urban Landscape
		Historical Vantage
		Earth Panorama
		Above Earth
		Sky
		Sunrise/Sunset
		People-Watching
		Most Photographed
	Scenic Drives	Scenic Drives

Theme/Sub-theme		Category
SOCIETY	Government	Politics
		Military
	Land	Borders
		Disputed
	Cities	Principal Cities
		Cool Neighborhoods
		Streets, Squares, and Ports
		Other Main Cities
	Towns	Large Towns
		Small Towns
	Cooperatives	Kibbutzim
		Moshavim
PEOPLE	Identity	Jewish
		Orthodox Jews
		Palestinians
		Secular Life
		Hipsters
		Refugees
		LGBTQ
	Ethnic Groups	Arab
		Bedouin
		Ethnic Minorities
	Community Celebration	Meet Locals
		Holidays
		Festivals and Events
CULTURE	Museums	of Art
		of History
		of Archaeology
		of Modern Times
		of Culture, Ethnicity, Nationality
		of Important Persons
		of Science and Learning
		of Home
	The Arts	Music
		Performance
		Visual Arts
ACTIVE	Walks and Hikes	City Walks
		Walking Paths
		Easy Hikes and Trails (under 2 hours)
		Day Hikes (2+ hours)
		Wet Hikes
		Tough Hikes (short and steep)
		Long-Distance Walks (2+ days)
		Experienced Hikers
	Land Sports	Skiing
		Biking
		Adventure/Extreme Land Sports
		Group/Team Sports
		Running and Free Exercise
		Competition

Theme/Sub-theme		Category
ACTIVE (cont.)	Water Sports	Swimming
		Diving
		Snorkeling
		Surfing
		Adventure Water Sports
LEISURE	Beaches	Public/Popular Beaches
		Remote Beaches
	Water	Sea Access
		Thermal Waters
		Fishing
	Resorts and Holiday	Spas and Massage
		Peaceful
ENTERTAINMENT	Shopping	Markets
		Handmade
		Boutiques (Clothing, Jewelry)
		Souvenirs
	Amusement	Amusement Parks
		Sky Activities
		Bars and Clubs
	Party	Vice
		Nightlife
	Sports	Sports
FOOD AND DRINK	Food	Cuisine
		Foods
		Top Restaurants
		Street Food and Quick Bites
		Culinary Capitals
	Wine	Great Wine
		Wineries
		Wine Regions
	Drink	Beer and Alcohol
		Coffee, Tea, and Coffeeshops
ACCOMMODATION	Stays	Highly Recommended
		Experiential Lodging
		Vacation Resorts and Hotels
		Campgrounds
ORGANIZED	Participatory	Volunteer
		Cooking School/Food Activities
		Petting Zoos and Animal Rides
		Digs
		Language School
	Tours	Food and Market
		Guided
		Multi-Stop/Self-Directed

Noteworthy

SPOTLIGHT

UNESCO With more than 1,000 sites inscribed on its **World Heritage list**, the United Nations Educational, Scientific, and Cultural Organization (UNESCO) is the foremost global program for identifying cultural and natural heritage sites of "outstanding value to humanity." Its mandate includes protecting and preserving these locations for future generations. Since 1972, countries party to the Convention Concerning the Protection of the World Cultural and Natural Heritage (of which there are currently 177) submit petitions to UNESCO to include their sites on the World Heritage list, and each year committee members of the Convention vote on the nominees. It has become fairly prestigious to earn the honor of the title World Heritage Site, and many of the newly inducted sites get funding to keep the site clean, informative, and free from vandalism or false narratives.

Jerusalem is an interesting admission because it was nominated by Jordan (which oversees the **Temple Mount (#12)**). Included are **Old City Jerusalem (#1)** and **Jerusalem Walls and Gates (#47)**, which we consider as two different sites in this book.

Israel's other sites include: **Masada (#8)**; **Akko (#13)**; **Modern Movement (Bauhaus Architecture) (#16)**; the **Biblical Tels (#38)** of **Megiddo (#59)**, **Tel Hazor**, and **Tel Beer Sheva**; the **Incense Route (#73)**; the **Bahá'í Gardens (#27)** and the **Shrine of Bahá'u'lláh** and its gardens in Akko; **Nahal Me'arot/Wadi el-Mughara**; **Beit Guvrin and Maresha (#60)**; and **Beit She'arim (#79)**.

Palestine's sites include: **Church of the Nativity (#18)** and **Bethlehem (#40)**; **Old Town of Hebron (#46)**; and **Cultural Landscape of Southern Jerusalem, Battir**.

Jordan's are: **Petra (#2)**; **Qasr Amra and the Desert Palaces (#20)**; **Umm ar-Rasas (#81)**; **Wadi Rum (#4)**; and **Bethany-Beyond-the-Jordan (#41)**.

And in the Sinai, Egypt: Saint Catherine area, to include **St. Catherine's Monastery (#22)** and **Mount Sinai (#15)**.

Israel, Jordan, Palestine, and Egypt each have a number of nominations pending on the Tentative List (sites are not removed from contention merely because they have not been acceded to the list on their year of submission), adding the potential for dozens more sites in the future.

WONDERS OF THE WORLD The "**Wonders of the World**" were seven recognized sites of the classical period that formed an early checklist, of sorts, for intrepid European travelers. The ancient Greeks seem to have been the ones who invented this scheme, and the original seven sites were mostly found around the Mediterranean and in parts of the Middle East. From that time, only the Great Pyramid of Cheops (or Khufu) remains.

In 2001, the New7Wonders Foundation hosted a contest of 200 extant monuments to create a list of seven modern icons that could compare to the seven of the ancient world. **Petra (#2)** was among its recipients.

In 2006, *USAToday* and *Good Morning America* created their own list in 2006, from a limited selection of judges, naming the **Old City Jerusalem (#1)** one of the world's new seven wonders.

ENDANGERED Part of UNESCO's designation highlights places that are at risk from war or violence, among other reasons. Called the **UNESCO World Heritage Sites in Danger**, we have a few in our region: *Battir Hills* for the separation wall dislocating farmers from their land; **Old City Jerusalem (#1)** for violence; the **Tomb of the Patriarchs (#46)** for susceptibility to violence; and Bethlehem/**Church of the Nativity (#18)** for unregulated tourism, obstructed views due to development, lack of repair, vulnerable roof, and industry/pollution.

Other groups have highlighted places "at risk." In *Frommer's 500 Places to See Before They Disappear*, from 2009, author Holly Hughes highlights a number of "fragile wonders" at risk of loss or destruction from human or natural elements. Included on her list of concern: **Petra (#2)** for excessive tourism; **Church of the Nativity (#18)** for decay; **Dead Sea (#3)** for evaporation; **Masada (#8)** for susceptibility to weather; **Akko (#13)** for decay; and **Old City Jerusalem (#1)** for development.

The **World Monuments Fund** is a nonprofit organization that has helped fund more than 600 projects in 90 countries under threat of being destroyed. In 1995, it established the **World Monuments Watch** to "identify imperiled cultural heritage sites and direct financial and technical support for their preservation." Included on the list for Israel are: Liftah (B1) for threats of development; **Modern Movement (Bauhaus Architecture) (#16)** in Tel Aviv for preservation and restoration; Old City of Lod (D8) for conservation and lack of tourism development; *Apollonia* for geological instability; **Beit She'arim (#79)** for erosion and lack of maintenance; German Colony (E1) for restoration issues (many of which have since been resolved); **Tel Dan (#63)** for conservation issues and exposure to the elements; and Ramle's White Mosque (D8) for lack of management and lack of conservation plans. In Jordan: Abila (S1) for lack of conservation, and looting; *Damiya Dolmen Field (S2)* for vulnerability to collapse; **Qasr Amra (#20)** for maintenance, crowd control, and site presentation; **Petra (#2)** for tourism maintenance; *Ain Ghazal (Q4)* for erosion and urban development; Jordan River Roman/Mamluk sites for misman-agement, erosion, pollution, and sewage issues; and *Khirbet et-Tannur (O1)* for looting. In Palestine: **Church of the Nativity (#18)** for susceptibility to earthquake, and a weak roof; Saint Hilarion Monastery/Tel Umm el-Amr for infrastructure issues and conflict in Gaza; *Battir Hills* for the separation wall; *Al-Qasem Palace (C5)* for decay; and Tel Balatah for development, weather, lack of maintenance, political unrest, and vandalism.

NATIONAL PARKS Declared national parks are often an indication of the value a country places on a particular swath of land. National parks in Israel and Palestine have been designated by the Israel Nature and Parks Authority, of which 36 are formally declared on the English-language pages of the website (w en.parks.org.il/map/): *Akhziv Beach*; *Apollonia* (Tel Arsuf); **Avdat (#48)**; *Bar'am*; **Belvoir (#93)**; Ben Gurion's Tomb (J2); **Beit Alpha (#64)**; **Beit Guvrin (#60)**; **Beit She'an (#39)**; **Beit She'arim (#79)**; **Caesarea (#25)**; **Capernaum (#33)**; **Ein Avdat (#74)**; *Ein Hemed*; *Gan HaShlosha*; *Hamat Tiberias*; Horshat Tal (I1); **Jerusalem Walls and Gates (#47)** and the *City of David* (combined national park); *Korazim*; Kursi (G3); Ma'ayan Harod (F2); *Mamshit*; **Masada (#8)**; **Megiddo (#59)**; *Mount Arbel*; *Mount Carmel*; **Nimrod's Fortress (#85)**; Palmahim (E3); **Qumran (#70)**; *Shivta*; *Tel Arad*; *Tel Ashkelon*; *Tel Beer Sheva*; *Tel Hazor*; **Tsipori (#56)**; and *Yehi'am*. Note that **Biblical Tels (#38)** and **Incense Route (#73)** also include several of the sites in this list. There are hundreds more sites listed in the Hebrew-language pages, highlighting far more nature reserves and national parks in Palestine.

Some of the undeclared sites (on the English page) that are perhaps worth exploring include: *Ein Kerem*; Emek Tzurim (A6); Eshkol (E3); Geder Beach (E7); HaYarkon Park (D7); HaSharon Beach (E7); Nahal Zalmon (H1); Nahal Refaim (B1); Nebi Samuel (C4); *Nitzana*; Sde Amudim (G2); *Sebastia-Shomron*; and Tel Lachish (B2).

Egypt and Jordan don't have any national parks per se, but rather each has declared protected areas as described in the following section.

NATURE RESERVES AND OTHER PROTECTED AREAS Nature reserves are also government-protected areas. As the name implies, this is to preserve some kind of plant, animal, historical, geological, or other special feature of a particular region.

In Israel, the following are part of the National Park system, declared as Nature Reserves: Ayun Stream (H2); **Banias (#80)**; *Carmel Hai-Bar*; **Coral Beach (#83)**; **Dor HaBonim (#100)**; Ein Afeq (E5); **Ein Gedi (#50)**; Ein Prat (C3); Einot Tsukim (K1); *Gamla*; *Hula Lake*; Majrase-Betiha/Bethsaida Valley (I3); **Makhtesh Ramon (#28)**; Meshushim Stream (I3); *Mount Arbel*; *Mount Carmel*; Nahal Amud (H1); *Nahal Me'arot*; Nahal Taninim (E4); Snir Stream (I1); Stalactite Caves (B2); **Tel Dan (#63)**; *Yehudiya*; and *Yotvata Hai-Bar*.

Additionally, these sites have received special recognition: Qasr al-Yahud (C3); Castel (B1); Inn of the Good Samaritan (C3); **Herodion (#90)**; *Mount Gerizim*; Nebi Samuel (C4); and Monastery of St. Euthymius (C3).

Jordan has designated the following as nature reserves: **Ajloun Forest (#57)**; **Azraq Wetlands (#55)**; **Dana Biosphere Reserve (#21)**; Dibeen Forest (S2); Fifa Nature Reserve (P1); **Mujib Biosphere Reserve (#23)**; *Shaumari*; **Wadi Rum (#4)**; and Yarmouk Forest (S1). The Burqu (R1) reserve is currently being set up, with a number of other reserves on a to-be-developed or proposed roster, including Dahek and Qatar.

Egypt's 30 designated sites are technically "Protectorates" which we've included under the Nature Reserves category. The following are in our region: **Ras Mohammad (#53)**, for its coral sea; St. Catherine (Katherine, with a K, in Egypt), which covers much of the southern Sinai, minus the coasts, and includes **St. Catherine's Monastery (#22)** and **Mount Sinai (#15)**; Nabq, the Gulf of Aqaba's largest coastal park, renowned for mangroves, gazelles, Nubian ibex, and coral reef; Abu Galam, also on the Gulf of Aqaba, is north of Dahab near the town of Dayayla, and includes undeveloped walks; Taba Protected Area, southwest of Taba (T1), contains several geological features, flora and fauna; and the Coast Marshes Area in Rafah, Ahrash, is 8km² of Mediterranean sand dunes near Gaza (not currently accessible).

ADVENTURE

UNIQUE EXPERIENCES Ever get tired of doing the same old thing? This area is filled with tons of interesting spots like you've never seen before. Here are a few of the unique finds, and how to find out more about them: **Old City Jerusalem (#1)** – perhaps the most important city in history; **Petra (#2)** – a city carved in rock; **Dead Sea (#3)** – lowest point on Earth with magical properties; **Dome of the Rock (#6)** – private tour, combined with **Al-Aqsa Mosque (#65)**; **Masada (#8)** – the last Jewish bastion before Roman defeat; **Church of the Holy Sepulchre (#9)** – where Jesus was crucified, died, and was buried; **Western Wall (#11)** – devotees and prayer notes; **Church of the Nativity (#18)** – walk into the grotto where Jesus was born; Baptism Valley at **Bethany-Beyond-the-Jordan (#41)** – dip into the waters where Jesus was baptized; **Dahab (#54)** – relaxing Sinai beach huts and resorts; **Golan Heights (#62)** – Israeli-owned, Syrian historically, Druze-occupied, and beautiful; **Mea She'arim (#66)** – dressing like the last 130 years never happened; **Jesus Trail (#69)** – much effort went into aligning off-the-beaten-path Galilee spots on day or multiday treks; **Feynan Ecolodge (#86)** – experience comfortable Jordanian hospitality and culture in the remote Dana Reserve; *Ein Bokek* – all that Dead Sea mud you get from around the world actually (maybe) comes from here; *Separation Wall* – graffitied wall telling the story of two peoples, still living opposite one another; *Israel National Trail* – month-long trekking from Mount Herzl in the far north to Eilat in the south; *Hot Air Balloon Ride Over Wadi Rum* – rolling red sand dunes as seen from the best vantage point; *Petra by Night* – walk the Siq in silence as you enter a candlelit ceremony at the Treasury; *Bedouin Tents and Coffee* – tradition and smiles plus coffee equals happiness; *Kibbutz Volunteer* – work your bones while getting a feel for the old communal farming lifestyle; *Camel Riding* – an experience you won't soon forget, unless you're used to riding in a saddle; *Banksy's Walled-Off Hotel* – hipster chic with views of the infamous wall; Yom Kippur (U) – in Tel Aviv, no engines means everyone plays in the streets and highways, though it's a much more somber day in Jerusalem; Ulpanim (U) – Hebrew language learning, on the ground; Archaeological Seminars Dig-for-a-Day (B2) – find historical treasures; Astronomy Israel (J2) – nothing but stars in the Negev Desert; Liftah (B1) – a ghost town right outside of Jerusalem; Holy Week in Jerusalem (A5) – watch as many Christian sects celebrate the life and death of Jesus Christ; *Powered Parachute Flight above Dead Sea/Masada (K1)* – can you even imagine?

EXPLORATION Do you or your kids like headlamps, flashlights, caving, exploring dark corners, and finding hidden gems? Check out this collection of sights for the explorer types: **Petra (#2)** – an ancient city hidden in between rocky walls, with short and long hikes to explore it; **Wadi Rum (#4)** – vast red desert, where you can hire a guide to off-road; **Red Sea/Gulf of Aqaba (#10)** – underwater exploration with vibrant coral and fish; **Akko (#13)** – there are lots of amazing parts of this city (on the ramparts, on the ground, below the ground) and it's amazing to find out how they connect; **Wadi Mujib and Mujib Biosphere Reserve (#23)** – unfamiliar water hikes; **Makhtesh Ramon (#28)** – hiking and camping are popular pastimes in this, the world's largest makhtesh crater; **Karak (#49)** – several eerie dark corners of this old Crusader castle to explore; **Golan Heights (#62)** – lush greenery in an otherwise dry part of the world; **Banias (#80)** – trek through the forest to various water holes; **Nimrod's Fortress (#85)** – obscured high in the forested hills, the trek to arrive here is impressive; **Timna (#96)** – Neolithic-era structures in this kid-friendly park; **Wadi Qelt (#97)** – walking through normally dry valleys, with ground-level views of the dangling monasteries above; *Israel National Trail* – get to know parts of Israel few have ever seen on this long trek; *Montfort* – Crusader ruins in the middle of the forest; *Mount Arbel* – ruins, caves, mountain, and a fortress to explore; *Red Canyon* near Eilat – climbing over and under big boulders and rock formations; *Rosh HaNikra* – it's fun to run in and around these water-filled caves; *Shobak* – another popular ancient castle option; *Yehudiya* – streams, gorges, pools, waterfalls, and canyons; Coloured Canyon (T1) – a popular rock formation near Nuweiba in the Sinai; Israel Bike Trail (U) – off-roading in the Golan; Wadi al-Hassa (O1) – a 40km valley in western Jordan terminating at the Dead Sea; Wadi Daraja (K1) – a challenging hike near Qumran by the Israeli side of the Dead Sea; Wadi Jadid (O1) – ancient dolmen fields about 10km south of Madaba in Jordan, Bedouin campgrounds, and desert pasturelands.

EXOTIC/WOW If you're in the mood for something that's going to blow your mind or impress your socks off, you may want to check out these: **Petra (#2)** – the first glimpse of the Treasury will leave you breathless; **Church of the Holy Sepulchre (#9)** – touching the ground where Jesus' cross stood, and where his tomb lay, is a Christian religious experience that moves many to tears; **Bahá'í Gardens (#27)** – meticulously designed and manicured lawns that will leave you in awe; **Dahab (#54)** – it feels like nowhere else you've ever been, with laziness, lounging, and beach huts for practically nothing; *Hot Air Balloon Ride Over Wadi Rum* – luxury bucket; *Mitzpe Ramon* – take a gander from a viewing platform overlooking the world's largest makhtesh crater; *Petra by Night*

– candlelit walk well worth the expense; *Separation Wall* – shockingly real, as is the disparity between life on both sides; *Blue Hole (T1)* – a revered diving experience; *Powered Parachute Flight above Dead Sea/Masada (K1)*.

OFF THE BEATEN PATH We know – just by including these, we're basically giving away their secret. But remember: this guidebook uses a hive mind, so the word is out to those in-the-know – and we're willing to share! If you like adventure, surprises, and few tourists, try: **St. Catherine's Monastery (#22)**; **Dahab (#54)**; **Ajloun Forest (#57)**; **Nablus (#61)**; **Golan Heights (#62)**; **Ramallah (#68)**; **Incense Route (#73)**; **Feynan Ecolodge (#86)**; *Shrine of Bahá'u'lláh*; *Tel Hazor*; *Little Petra*; *Bedouin Tents and Coffee*; *Red Canyon*; Camel Safari (T1); Freedom Theatre (C5); Majdal Shams and The Shouting Hill (I2); Palestinian Throne Villages (C5); Nuweiba Beach Camps (T1); Salad Trail (E3); Khirbet al-Minya (G3); Kibbutz Degania (G3); Mount Karkom (L2); Umm ar-Rihan Forest (C5); *Driving Through the Negev (J2)*; *Al-Qasem Palace (C5)*; *Old City of Lod (D8)*; *Khirbet et-Tannur (01)*; and *Damiya Dolmen Field (S2)*.

Each of the following was also a "recommended" site by someone, but for now we'll have to consider them "out of bounds" as they are surrounded by violence or extremely difficult to reach (e.g., Gaza): Krak des Chevaliers in Syria; Lebanon Mountain Trail in southern Lebanon; Sinai Camel Safari in the heart of the Sinai, where ISIS plays; and Tel Umm el-Amr, Anthedon Harbour, Jabaliya, and Gaza Port, all in Gaza.

QUIRKY If you're looking for something a little oddball, this might do the trick: **Dahab (#54)** – a hippie beach town in Egypt; **Mea She'arim (#66)** – a neighborhood in Jerusalem where Hassidic Jews dress like it's 1880; **Feynan Ecolodge (#86)** – homemade food, limited electricity, a telescope, interactive Bedouin activities, cooking workshops and more at this interesting all-inclusive; *Banksy's Walled-Off Hotel* – with picturesque views of a giant, ugly barrier wall; *Bedouin Tents and Coffee* – sit on rugs, hear the musical notes of coffee being ground, and listen to stories of the Bedouin life; *Kibbutz Volunteer* – if you've ever wanted to live on a commune, here's your chance; *Majdal Shams and The Shouting Hill (I2)* – born Syrians, now mostly Israeli, but separated from their families who live on the other side of the hill (now permanently closed, except for periodic controlled visits); *Akhzivland (E5)* – independent country?

Religion

RELIGIONS

JUDAISM Perhaps unsurprisingly, Jewish sites make up the greatest share of sites for any of our thematic collections. If you're interested in exploring one of the world's first monotheistic religions, you have plenty of options. There are opportunities to learn about Jews' diverse history in many of Israel's cities, national parks, archaeological sites, and small towns.

Best examples **Western Wall (#11)**; *Jewish Quarter*; and **Jerusalem, New City (#72)**.

Complementary **Old City Jerusalem (#1)**; **Sea of Galilee (#7)**; **Masada (#8)**; **Temple Mount (#12)**; **Mount Sinai (#15)**; **Capernaum and Tabgha (#33)**; **Mount of Olives (#34)**; **Yad Vashem (#35)**; **Biblical Tels (#38)**; **Tomb of the Patriarchs and Old Town of Hebron (#46)**; **Tsipori (#56)**; **Tsfat/Safed (#58)**; **Beit Guvrin and Maresha (#60)**; **Tel Dan (#63)**; **Beit Alpha (#64)**; **Mea She'arim (#66)**; **Qumran (#70)**; **ANU – Museum of the Jewish People (#77)**; **Beit She'arim (#79)**; **Mount Zion (#92)**; **Western Wall Tunnels (#94)**; *Ancient Qatzrin*; *Bar'am*; *Ben Yehuda Street*; *Bible Lands Museum*; *City of David*; *Gamla*; *Hadassah Synagogue and Chagall Windows*; *Kibbutz Lotan*; *Korazim*; *Lag B'Omer at Moshav Meron*; *Mount Gerizim*; *MUSA – Eretz Israel Museum*; *Tel Arad*; *Tel Beer Sheva*; *Tiberias*; *Yemen Moshe*; Goldstein Synagogue (A8); Hurva Square (A4); Khirbet Suseya (C2); Kidron Valley (A5); Nabi Musa (C3); Nakhalat Shiva (A7); National Memorial Day (U); Sde Boker (J2); Sephardic Synagogues (A4); Yom Kippur (U); *Dimona (J1)*; and *Purim in Tel Aviv (D4)*.

Holiest Jewish Places Since the 17th century, Jewish tradition has prized Jerusalem, Hebron, Tsfat, and Tiberias with the term "The Four Holy Cities."

★ *Jerusalem* The importance of Jerusalem – specifically **Old City Jerusalem (#1)** – supersedes that of the other three sites. It contains the Foundation Stone, where God created the Earth, where Abraham nearly sacrificed Isaac, around which the two Temples were believed to have been built (and the third to come), and which now sits underneath the Dome of the Rock (Rock = Foundation Stone). See also: **Temple Mount (#12)**.

★ *Hebron* The matriarchs and patriarchs are buried here at the Tomb of the Patriarchs. See: **Tomb of the Patriarchs and Old Town of Hebron (#46)**.

★ *Tsfat* Spiritual center of Kabbalah. See: **Tsfat/Safed (#58)**.

★ *Tiberias* Burial site of several important rabbis. The Talmud was said to have been composed here, and the Messiah will return here. See: *Tiberias*.

CHRISTIANITY Israel and Jordan may not be on many itineraries for casual Western Christian tourists but, if you've already seen Rome and the Vatican, the Holy Land is the next logical destination. Marking the Stations of the Cross – including the crucifixion, death, and burial of the Christian Lord, Jesus Christ – covers a ton. **Old City Jerusalem (#1)** offers a variety of holy places to choose from generally, including the nearby **Mount of Olives (#34)** and **Mount Zion (#92)**. Outside of Jerusalem, **Nazareth and its Biblical Sites (#29)**, **Bethlehem (#40)**, and the **Sea of Galilee (#7)** are all important locations to Christian tourists in Israel. In Jordan, there is no shortage of interesting options, and *Road Trip P2* is dedicated specifically to Christian Jordan.

Best examples **Sea of Galilee (#7)**; **Church of the Holy Sepulchre (#9)**; **Church of the Nativity (#18)**; *Basilica of the Annunciation*; and Holy Week in Jerusalem (A5).

Complementary **Old City Jerusalem (#1)**; **Mount Sinai (#15)**; **St. Catherine's Monastery (#22)**; **Mount Nebo (#24)**; **Nazareth and its Biblical Sites (#29)**; **Capernaum and Tabgha (#33)**; **Mount of Olives (#34)**; **Bethlehem (#40)**; **Bethany-Beyond-the-Jordan (#41)**; **Via Dolorosa (#42)**; **Umm Qais (#45)**; **Tomb of the Patriarchs and Old Town of Hebron (#46)**; **Karak (#49)**; **Megiddo (#59)**; **Nablus (#61)**; **Jesus Trail (#69)**; **Umm ar-Rasas (#81)**; **Ramparts Walk (#91)**; **Mount Zion (#92)**; **St. George's Monastery and Wadi Qelt (#97)**; *Bible Lands Museum*; *Church of St. Anne and the Pools of Bethesda*; *Church of the Transfiguration*; *Deir Quruntal*; *Ein Kerem*; *Haifa*; *Lot's Cave*; *Mar Saba*; *Monastery of Abu Ghosh*; *Mount of Beatitudes*; *Mukawir*; *Sebastia-Shomron*; *St. James' Cathedral*; Armenian Quarter (A2); Basilica of the Agony (A5); Church of Mary Magdalene (A5); Church of the Paternoster (A5); Dormition Abbey (A5); Ethiopian Quarter (A7); Garden Tomb (A6); International Center of Mary of Nazareth (G1); Kibbutz Ginosar (G3); Kinneret Trail (G3); Kursi (G3); Lutheran Church of the Redeemer (A2); Monastery of the Flagellation (A2); Nabi Musa (C3); Qasr al-Yahud (C3); Russian Quarter (A7); St. Catherine's Mount (T1); Tomb of the Virgin (A5); and *Church of the Ascension (A5)*.

ISLAM Jerusalem is the third-holiest city in Islam, after Mecca and Medina. Perhaps the most recognizable part of the Old City of Jerusalem – and the Holy Land in general – is the gold-roofed dome that sits atop historic Mount Moriah, where Muhammad ascended to Heaven. Nearby, Al-Aqsa is one of the world's oldest mosques.

Best examples **Dome of the Rock (#6)**; **Al-Aqsa Mosque (#65)**; and Museum for Islamic Art (A7).

Complementary **Old City Jerusalem (#1)**; **Temple Mount (#12)**; **Modern Amman (#36)**; **Tomb of the Patriarchs and Old Town of Hebron (#46)**; *Jordanian Hospitality*; *Fountain of Sultan Qaytbay*; *Dome of the Chain*; Muslim Quarter (A2); Nabi Musa (C3); Nebi Samuel (C4); and Al-Jazzar Mosque (E2).

RELIGIOUS MINORITIES Judaism, Christianity, and Islam get all the attention, but there are plenty of other religious cultures (or sects of those three) that also consider the Holy Land a spiritual homeland: **Bahá'í Gardens (#27)** – located in Haifa, these gardens are a marvel of architecture, engineering, symmetry, and landscaping; **Tsfat/Safed (#58)** – the mystical capital of Israel and the home to Jewish Kabbalah; **Nablus (#61)** – spiritual home of the Samaritans, a Jewish sect that separated from modern Judaism perhaps 2,500 years ago, and now numbers in the mere hundreds; **Wadi Qelt (#97)** – dangling from the cliffs of Wadi Qelt are a number of fascinating, hanging monasteries of the Greek Orthodox tradition; **Golan Heights (#62)** – Syrian Druze families still reside in this area, though separated from their Syrian families by likely permanent borders; *Mount Gerizim* – near Nablus, this is the holiest place of the Samaritans; **Akko (#13)** – considered the holiest place in the Bahá'í faith, the founder of which is buried in Akko at the *Shrine of Bahá'u'lláh*; Kfar Kama (G2) – village of Circassians; and *Druze Cooking Workshops (H1)* – a great way to learn more about this fascinating group of people.

RELIGIOUS FIGURES

KINGS, PROPHETS, AND SAINTS The Old Testament tells the story of God's creation of the world, but it also introduces readers to the great kings and prophets who were challenged by God and created legacies in the process: Abraham was to sacrifice Isaac, Noah had his ark, David slew Goliath, Jacob had 12 sons who became the "Tribes of Israel," and Moses received the Ten Commandments.

Some of the lesser-known locations include: Moses' final resting place at Mount Nebo; the childhood home of Mary, mother of Jesus, at the Church of St. Anne (named after Mary's mother); Elijah's cave at Stella Maris; the site where John the Baptist was beheaded at Mukawir; and a Nazareth museum dedicated to Mary and Christianity.

Best examples **Mount Sinai (#15)**; **Mount Nebo (#24)**; **Tomb of the Patriarchs and Old Town of Hebron (#46)**; *City of David*; *Tel Beer Sheva*; and *Church of St. Anne and the Pools of Bethesda*.

Complementary **Old City Jerusalem (#1)**; **Dome of the Rock (#6)**; **Western Wall (#11)**; **Temple Mount (#12)**; **St. Catherine's Monastery (#22)**; **Capernaum and Tabgha (#33)**; **Mount of Olives (#34)**; **Bethany-Beyond-the-Jordan (#41)**; **Mount Zion (#92)**; *Basilica of the Annunciation*; *Ein Kerem*; *Stella Maris*; *Mukawir*; Dormition Abbey (A5); and International Center of Mary of Nazareth (G1).

JESUS' EARLY LIFE Jesus' life is recorded in the New Testament. Jesus' birth story is perhaps the most popular story in the world, commemorated every year at Christmas. Jesus was born around 4 BCE to Mary, a virgin chosen by God to bear God's earthly son. Though married, Mary had not yet moved in with her husband, Joseph, which is why she was considered a virgin. The couple traveled from their hometown of Nazareth to Bethlehem for the birth. They presented baby Jesus at the Jewish Temple in Jerusalem, as was customary at the time, before moving back to Nazareth, where Jesus grew up. He grew up among brothers and sisters, but little is known of his childhood or teenage years.

In Bethlehem, you can visit the grotto where Jesus was born of the Virgin Mary, now a multilayered church with extensive repairs under way and a full history of its own. In Nazareth, visit Mary's childhood home, the location of the Annunciation (when Mary told by the Angel Gabriel that she was to carry the son of God), as well as Joseph's old work studio.

Best examples **Church of the Nativity (#18)**; and *Basilica of the Annunciation*.

Complementary **Old City Jerusalem (#1)**; **Temple Mount (#12)**; **Nazareth and its Biblical Sites (#29)**; and **Bethlehem (#40)**.

JESUS' MINISTRIES AND MIRACLES The first four books of the New Testament discuss Jesus as an adult, specifically his baptism, ministry, temptations, miracles, teachings, and interactions with disciples and laypeople. Jesus performed a number of miracles and conducted most of his ministries in the area surrounding the Sea of Galilee. This makes for a great day or weekend trip visiting the many sites.

Best examples **Sea of Galilee (#7)**; **Bethany-Beyond-the-Jordan (#41)**; *Mount of Beatitudes*; and *Church of the Transfiguration*.

THEMES Religion

Complementary **Old City Jerusalem (#1)**; **Jericho and Hisham's Palace (#26)**; **Capernaum and Tabgha (#33)**; **Mount of Olives (#34)**; **Jesus Trail (#69)**; *Deir Quruntal*; Church of the Paternoster (A5); Inn of the Good Samaritan (C3); Kursi (G3); and Nain (G4).

JESUS' DEATH AND RESURRECTION Jesus' final week before his death and resurrection are a central part of the Gospels. The majority of the events here take place in and around Jerusalem. The Via Dolorosa marks the last hours of Jesus' life, as he walked with his cross to Golgotha, site of his crucifixion and burial. The Church of the Holy Sepulchre houses these two locations: the hill of his death and the burial tomb where he was buried and rose again, three days later.

Best examples **Church of the Holy Sepulchre (#9)**; and **Via Dolorosa (#42)**.

Complementary **Old City Jerusalem (#1)**; **Capernaum and Tabgha (#33)**; **Mount Zion (#92)**; Basilica of the Agony (A5); and Monastery of the Flagellation (A2).

MUHAMMAD Muslims believe that Muhammad was the last prophet of God, following Abraham, Moses, Jesus, and others. Muhammad was the founder of Islam and conquered an enormous swath of land in the Arabian peninsula, including all of the Holy Land, by 637 CE. His teachings and customs still form the basis for Islam today, as do the messages Muhammad received from God, recorded in the Quran. **Old City Jerusalem (#1)** is the third-holiest city in Islam; **Dome of the Rock (#6)** on **Temple Mount (#12)** is where Muhammad ascended to Heaven on his Night Journey; and **Al-Aqsa Mosque (#65)** is traditionally viewed by Muslims as the "farthest mosque" where Muhammad traveled on the same Night Journey.

HOLY BOOKS

HEBREW BIBLE/OLD TESTAMENT The world of the Old Testament is much broader than our more specifically defined "Holy Land," encompassing present-day Turkey and Egypt, Persia, Syria, Armenia, and Iraq, among other places. The stories in the Bible predate modern humans, and had already been passed down for hundreds if not thousands of years before they were eventually written down. The Old Testament starts with the creation of all things, including the Earth and humans. The first of these, Adam and Eve, were the beginning of all humans to come. Their descendants included many of God's first believers, now considered prophets, including Noah, Moses, and Abraham. The Old Testament ends around the time of the Jewish return from captivity by the Persian king Cyrus, in the 5th century BCE.

Some of the most memorable moments of the Old Testament can be visited. **Temple Mount (#12)** is where Abraham offered to sacrifice Isaac, where King David created his city of God, and many other stories took place in or around Solomon's Temple. **Mount Sinai (#15)** is where Moses received the Ten Commandments. Hebron is the location where David was anointed the King of Israel and from where the Tribe of Judah governed the Kingdom of Judah.

Best examples **Temple Mount (#12)**; and **Mount Sinai (#15)**.

Complementary **Old City Jerusalem (#1)**; **Mount Nebo (#24)**; **Jericho and Hisham's Palace (#26)**; **Mount of Olives (#34)**; **Biblical Tels (#38)**; **Tomb of the Patriarchs and Old Town of Hebron (#46)**; **Ein Gedi (#50)**; **Beit Guvrin and Maresha (#60)**; **Tel Dan (#63)**; **Qumran (#70)**; **Mount Zion (#92)**; *City of David*; *Lot's Cave*; *Mount Gerizim*; *Mount Gilboa*; *Stella Maris*; *Tel*

Ashkelon; *Tel Beer Sheva*; Latrun Monastery (B2); Ma'ayan Harod (F2); Mount Karkom (L2); Mount Sodom (K1); and Tel Lachish (B2).

NEW TESTAMENT Considered by Christians as the second half of Scripture, following the Hebrew Bible and telling the story of Jesus Christ, the son of God. Events in the New Testament take place from the birth of Jesus Christ (told in four accounts, in slightly different variations) through the destruction of Jerusalem. Unlike the Old Testament, events in which took place over millennia, all events in the New Testament take place in the 1st century CE.

The most quintessential sites in the New Testament were referenced in the Jesus sections earlier – particularly Bethlehem and Nazareth. Bethlehem is the birthplace of Jesus and contains several other sites with biblical references, such as the Shepherds' Fields and the Milk Grotto. Nazareth is the home of Jesus, Mary, and Joseph, and includes sites related to their life.

Best examples **Sea of Galilee (#7); Church of the Holy Sepulchre (#9); Nazareth and its Biblical Sites (#29); Capernaum and Tabgha (#33); Mount of Olives (#34); Bethlehem (#40); Megiddo (#59); Mount Zion (#92);** and *Basilica of the Annunciation*.

Complementary **Old City Jerusalem (#1); Temple Mount (#12); Church of the Nativity (#18);** Jericho and Hisham's Palace (#26); **Jaffa (#30); Bethany-Beyond-the-Jordan (#41); Via Dolorosa (#42); Jesus Trail (#69);** *Church of the Transfiguration*; *Deir Quruntal*; *Mount of Beatitudes*; *Mukawir*; Basilica of the Agony (A5); Church of the Paternoster (A5); Inn of the Good Samaritan (C3); Kursi (G3); Monastery of the Flagellation (A2); Tel Bethsaida (G4); Nain (G4); *Bethany and Lazarus' Tomb (A5)*; *Bethphage (A5)*; *Kfar Kana (G4)*; Emmaus Nicopolis (B2); and *Migdala (G4)*.

QURAN The Quran (meaning "recitation") is the written recording of the divine guidance revealed to Muhammad by God through the Angel Gabriel over the course of 23 years and constitutes the basis for the Islamic religion. Muhammad was an orator, and the text of the Quran likely encapsulated his spoken words for the masses during his lifetime, but were finalized shortly after his death in 632 CE. The events in the Quran expound on biblical narrative and proclaim the messages that God revealed to Muhammad, believed by Muslims to be the last of God's prophets. The Quran contains 114 suras, of which there are more than 6,200 verses. The Quran should only be recited in Arabic, as its original language is believed to hold the true meaning of its words, which translation could never convey. Muslims who memorize the entirety of the Quran receive an honorific title. The first verse is "بِسْمِ اللهِ الرَّحْمَنِ الرَّحِيمِ" meaning "In the name of Allah, the Beneficent, the Merciful."

Complementary **Dome of the Rock (#6)** symbolizes the spot where Moses ascended to Heaven on his Night Journey; the Quran references a journey to the farthest mosque in Al-Quds, the Arabic name for Jerusalem. The Prophets Moses and Aaron are both connected to the Sinai peninsula and **Mount Sinai (#15)**, referenced in the Quran. Hebron is the site of the **Tomb of the Patriarchs (#46)**, honoring Abraham and his family who are venerated in Islam.

ANCIENT MANUSCRIPTS We've covered events from the various holy books, and now we're looking at the physical texts themselves. If you're interested in the actual vessel that housed those words originally, you'll find a number of ancient manuscripts in museums throughout the Holy Land.

The most famous, of course, are the Dead Sea Scrolls, found in Qumran, which we cover next. St. Catherine's is famous for being the oldest functioning library in the world, as well as hosting the largest collection of Christian manuscripts after the Vatican library.

Best examples **St. Catherine's Monastery (#22)**; and **Qumran (#70)**.

Complementary **Temple Mount (#12)**; **Israel Museum (#17)**; Dead Sea Scrolls (A8); and Jewish National Library (A8).

Dead Sea Scrolls The discovery of the Dead Sea Scrolls in **Qumran (#70)** in 1946 introduced roughly 1,000 new fragments of text, including some lengthy scrolls, to the very limited numbers of extant, ancient biblical texts. There are a few places to check out this collection of canonical and non-canonical documents. Aside from the two Silver Scrolls, the Dead Sea Scrolls from 300 BCE to 100 CE are the oldest existing pieces of biblical literature and religious manuscripts. The scrolls are widely considered of immense historical and religious significance and represent a range of times and languages, not to mention being "miraculously" preserved, and are now on display at the **Israel Museum (#17)** in Jerusalem and the *Jordan Museum (Q3)* in Amman.

Oldest Hebrew Bible The oldest nearly complete manuscript of the Hebrew Bible (Old Testament) is believed to be the **Aleppo Codex**. Written sometime in the 10th century CE, it was housed in a synagogue in Aleppo, Syria until 1947 when rioters started a fire and the book went missing for ten years. It reappeared in Israel with much of the Torah missing. Where are the missing pieces? Many believe them to be in a private collection. You can see the rest of the Codex in the **Israel Museum (#17)**.

The oldest fragments of the Hebrew Bible are believed to be the **Silver Scrolls**, found at the Ketef Hinnom site near the Menachem Begin Center just south of the Yemen Moshe neighborhood on the western side of Jerusalem (caves can be visited). The scrolls are written in an early version of Hebrew and contain verses from the Book of Numbers in the Torah. They date to the First Temple period, which is exceedingly rare. They've been preserved because they were inscribed onto silver scrolls, hence the name. See the Silver Scrolls in the **Israel Museum (#17)** and Ketef Hinnom.

Oldest New Testament Bible The earliest complete copy of the New Testament is the **Codex Sinaiticus**, named after its having been found in the Sinai in 1844. Written in Greek possibly as early as 330 CE, it contains parts of the Old Testament and all of the New Testament. The codex has been split between many homes, but continues to live in the region at **St. Catherine's Monastery (#22)**.

BIBLICAL BATTLEFIELDS The Bible tells the story of the struggles of God's children to build a nation that worshiped one God, abided by his covenant, and defeated the enemies of the state and religion. The Old Testament contains a wide variety of passages related to the successes and failures of the Israelites in securing territory from the surrounding pagan nations and establishing a monotheistic nation-state. The New Testament and Quran tell fewer war stories, though one of the most famous comes from the Book of Revelations, which foretells the "Battle of Armageddon," the end-of-days great war between good and evil.

One of the most epic battles, David versus Goliath in 1 Samuel 17, took place in the Ella Valley in the Judean Hills, now the site of Ella Valley Vineyards (B3).

In 1 Chronicles 11 and 2 Samuel 5, David marches on Jebus, the Jebusite stronghold, and declares it Jerusalem (archaeological evidence indicates this timeline doesn't make sense, as "Jerusalem" is referred to in the Amarna Letters of the 14th century BCE, but David ruled around 1000 BCE). The destruction of Jerusalem takes place in Matthew 24, Mark 13, and Luke 19–21.

Joshua 6 tells the story of the Israelites blaring their trumpets after the walls of Jericho fall (though scholars doubt the veracity of much of the Book of Joshua). Also in Joshua, chapters 7–8, the Israelites attack Ai, believed to be at et-Tell.

In Revelations 16 and 19, the Battle of Armageddon (aka Megiddo) takes place, pitting good vs. evil. It's set to take place at the end of days; several prophesied battles have already transpired, including a battle between Egypt and Canaan which is possibly the first recorded battle in history (at Karnak Temple, Egypt).

Complementary **Old City Jerusalem (#1)**; **Temple Mount (#12)**; **Jericho and Hisham's Palace (#26)**; **Biblical Tels (#38)**; **Megiddo (#59)**; *Church of the Transfiguration*; *Mount Gilboa*; Ella Valley Vineyards (B3); and *Et-Tell, ancient Ai (C4)*.

HOUSES OF WORSHIP (EXTANT)

SYNAGOGUES Synagogues are, understandably, found throughout Israel, but you wouldn't necessarily be able to spot them from afar because their purpose is, frankly, not to advertise their presence (unlike many churches and mosques which often attempt to be the most showy building in town). If you're interested in visiting a synagogue, here are some interesting and accessible options.

Best examples Ashkenazi Ari Synagogue (H1); Caro Synagogue (H1); Goldstein Synagogue (A8); Isaac Luria Synagogue (H1); Sephardic Synagogues (A4); *Belz Great Synagogue (B1)*; *Karaite Synagogue (A4)*; and *Rambam Synagogue (A4)*.

Complementary **Old City Jerusalem (#1)**; **Tsfat/Safed (#58)**; *Hadassah Synagogue and Chagall Windows*; Cymbalista Synagogue (D7); Hurva Square and Synagogue (A4); *Rishon Letzion (D8)*.

COLLECTIONS OF SYNAGOGUES Like Mount of Olives with its collection of churches, there are a few spots in Israel that host a group of synagogues together, of similar style.

Best examples **Tsfat/Safed (#58)**; and Sephardic Synagogues (A4).

Complementary **Old City Jerusalem (#1)**; **Jerusalem, New City (#72)**; and *Jewish Quarter*.

Oldest and Ancient Synagogues Synagogues have perhaps been around as long as Judaism, though the archaeological evidence is scant, perhaps because the building structures have historically not been grand or opulent. Many were also not purpose-built. It's difficult trying to decode whether a site was designed as a synagogue or merely repurposed as one, particularly 2,000 years after the building was constructed and all that remains is one layer of mud brick.

Synagogues are first referenced in the reign of Egyptian Pharaoh Ptolemy III, in the mid-3rd century BCE. Only eight synagogues have been discovered in the world that date to the time of the Second Temple period. Few existed in general, as no synagogues were allowed to offer worship services while the Second Temple was standing. Rather, synagogues were used as meeting halls. Because of the lack of adornments, it is difficult for archaeologists to definitively determine what counts as a true synagogue; a mystery remains as to whether the ancient synagogue on the Greek island of Delos is in fact the oldest synagogue in the world, whether it was Samaritan instead of Jewish, or even whether it qualifies as a synagogue – but for now it holds the title with an established date of c150 BCE. Ostia Synagogue, located in ancient Ostia, the seaport of Rome, is the oldest in Europe, dating from around 50 CE and in use through at least the 4th century CE.

Many of the time periods attributed to ancient synagogues are contested by archaeologists as fiercely as they are defended by archaeologists. Jews were building synagogues until the Romans besieged Jerusalem in 70 CE and the rest of the region by 73 CE. Jews were often sold into slavery and settled in regions around the world. Synagogues began to appear globally around the same time that churches started appearing, from the 2nd to 3rd centuries CE. What interests us here are those synagogues that predated the 70 CE Roman destruction of Jerusalem and Herod's Temple.

These are a few of the least-contested nominees for oldest synagogue in the world: *Khirbet Umm el-Umdan Synagogue (B2)* near the Latrun junction in Modi'in is an ancient synagogue dated to the Hasmonean period (2nd century BCE) by the Israel Antiquities Authority and in use through 132 CE; **Gamla** dates from the 1st century BCE, but possibly as late as just before 70 CE; **Masada (#8)** was destroyed in 73 CE, but excavators in the 1960s still found a small synagogue containing religious text; *Migdala (G4)* has been definitively dated to the Second Temple period, and part of the excavations included the Magdala stone containing perhaps the oldest representation of a Jewish menorah; **Herodion (#90)** is from 15 BCE, and was used until 70 CE, then again during the Bar Kokhba Revolt in 135 CE, but it is unclear when the synagogue was added; and Khirbet Badd 'Isa is a village from the Second Temple period with a synagogue and ritual bath, near Modi'in Illit.

CHURCHES Many people don't think of the Holy Land when they think of churches: with Israel being a Jewish state and the land having been ruled by Muslims for over 1,200 years, it's easy to forget that Christianity began here and continues to this day. There are old and new churches alike, many of which offer a panoply of architectural styles that reflect the global spread of Christianity over the millennia.

Best examples **Church of the Holy Sepulchre (#9)**; **Church of the Nativity (#18)**; *Basilica of the Annunciation*; **Church of St. Anne and the Pools of Bethesda**; *Church of the Transfiguration*; and **St. James' Cathedral**.

Complementary **Old City Jerusalem (#1)**; **Madaba (#19)**; **St. Catherine's Monastery (#22)**; **Mount Nebo (#24)**; *Monastery of Abu Ghosh*; *Mount of Beatitudes*; **Stella Maris**; Basilica of the Agony (A5); Church of Mary Magdalene (A5); Church of the Beheading of John the Baptist (P2); Church of the Paternoster (A5); Dormition Abbey (A5); Ethiopian Quarter (A7); Greek Orthodox Church of the Annunciation (G1); Holy Trinity Cathedral (A7); Latrun Monastery (B2); Lutheran Church of the Redeemer (A2); Monastery of the Flagellation (A2); Russian Quarter (A7); and *Old City of Lod (D8)*.

COLLECTIONS OF CHURCHES Several of our famous sites are well known because they house a number of well-regarded sites. The Mount of Olives, in particular, houses more than half a dozen famous churches to explore, ancient and modern.

Best example **Mount of Olives (#34)**.

Complementary **Old City Jerusalem (#1)**; **Sea of Galilee (#7)**; **Nazareth and its Biblical Sites (#29)**; **Capernaum and Tabgha (#33)**; **Bethlehem (#40)**; **Bethany-Beyond-the-Jordan (#41)**; **Jerusalem, New City (#72)**; **Umm ar-Rasas (#81)**; and *Ein Kerem*.

MONASTERIES Monasteries are buildings inhabited by monks or nuns – groups of people who have vowed to serve God (though there are other types of monks, e.g., Buddhist monks), have generally taken vows of chastity and poverty, and live their life helping others and practicing prayer. The residents of our favorite spots live in hair-raising, cliff-hugging monasteries.

Best examples **St. George's Monastery and Wadi Qelt (#97)**; *Deir Quruntal*; and *Mar Saba*.

Complementary *Monastery of Abu Ghosh*; *Stella Maris*; Dormition Abbey (A5); Ein Prat (C3); Latrun Monastery (B2); Monastery of St. Euthymius (C3); Monastery of St. Martyrius (C3); Monastery of the Flagellation (A2); *Monastery of St. Theodosius (C2)*; and *Mar Elias Monastery (C2)*.

Oldest and Ancient Churches The church building did not come about immediately. The oldest known church, called the **Dura-Europos Church**, was built inside a house in the early 3rd century in present-day Syria (note: may have been destroyed by ISIS). There were certainly many other early churches of this type throughout the region, though few have survived. Some others have been difficult to date because, prior to the quick accession of Christianity in the Roman empire, Christians still practiced in the Holy Land.

Two churches have been found in the region that potentially date to before Constantine's time. The **Aqaba Church** was discovered in **Aqaba (#43)** in 1998. It dates to the end of the 3rd century CE or beginning of the 4th and has been called the world's first "purpose-built" church. Though most churches from this period were destroyed after the Christian era, this one was likely saved due to its distance south of most Christian sites at the time. The **Megiddo Church** was found in **Megiddo (#59)** in 2005 and is tentatively dated to the end of the 3rd century. A large mosaic with the Christian symbol of a fish and reference to Jesus Christ are within.

More grand buildings entered in the early 4th century CE under Emperor Constantine (and later leaders of the Holy Roman Empire), though many have succumbed to earthquakes. That said, the grandest of all – those commissioned by Emperor Constantine – have retained at least portions of their original walls incorporated into the more recent constructs. **Church of the Holy Sepulchre (#9)** dates to 335 CE, while the **Church of the Nativity (#18)** in Bethlehem was completed in 339 CE. The grotto of the church where Jesus was born is still in use today, making it the oldest still-functioning church in the world.

A few sites elsewhere in the world may or may not predate these. **St. Thaddeus Monastery** in northwestern Iran was said to have been created as a tomb for the eponymous disciple of Jesus who preached in present-day Armenia and Iran. The original church was said to have been constructed in 66–68 CE, though little remains. Most of the "oldest" parts are dated to the 7th century CE. The **Etchmiadzin Cathedral** in Vagharshapat, Armenia was completed in 303 CE and may be the oldest cathedral in the world. The **Archbasilica of St. John Lateran** is the oldest of the papal basilicas and was consecrated in 324 CE, housing six papal tombs.

MOSQUES Whereas synagogues never put much value in exterior aesthetics, and while Christian churches have mostly (apart from the Sagrada Familia in Barcelona) ceased creating ostentatious designs, mosques can still find benefactors and architects to realize bigger and wilder creations. That's not the case in Israel, which is a Jewish country that controls much of what happens in Palestine. Jordan has a few modern mosques (see *City Walk Q3*), but they don't tend to rival those being built in the UAE, Saudi Arabia, and Pakistan. In the Holy Land, therefore, we're mostly looking at history, which means that the most important is Al-Aqsa, one of the oldest mosques in the world and destination on Muhammad's Night Journey, thereby making Jerusalem the third-holiest site in Islam.

Best examples **Al-Aqsa Mosque (#65)**; Abu Darwish Mosque (Q3); Al-Jazzar Mosque (E2); and *King Abdullah I Mosque (Q3)*.

Complementary **Old City Jerusalem (#1)**; **Temple Mount (#12)**; **Jaffa (#30)**; **Bethlehem (#40)**; **Tomb of the Patriarchs and Old Town of Hebron (#46)**; **Nablus (#61)**; *Sebastia-Shomron*; Beer Sheva (J1); and Khirbet Suseya (C2).

Oldest and Ancient Mosques Mosques were being built during the life of Muhammad and early examples can be found as far as Eritrea, India, and China in the 620s CE.

Before Muhammad's death in 632 CE, mosques faced Mecca and Jerusalem. Interestingly, the Masjid al-Qiblatain in Medina (623) has two qibla walls, one of which goes towards Jerusalem.

Al-Aqsa Mosque (#65) is likely the oldest mosque in our region, though little if any of the original building remains. According to the Quran, Muhammad went to Masjid-al-Aqsa, or the Farthest Mosque, on his Night Journey. The location of that destination has been identified as Jerusalem, so presumably a mosque existed there already. The first recorded structure called Al-Aqsa on **Temple Mount (#12)** was built by the Rashidun Caliphate and dates to around 637 CE, soon after Muhammad's death. (The Dome of the Rock, which is not a mosque, did not open until 691 CE.) That original structure was destroyed several times by earthquakes. The current structure was built by the Fatimids, repaired by every successive empire, and has been in constant used since 1035 CE. Al-Aqsa is considered the third-holiest site in Islam.

The foundation of a small mosque was recently unearthed in the Negev facing Mecca (meaning after Muhammad's death), making it one of the oldest mosques in the world and dating to the 7th or 8th century CE.

The **Tomb of the Patriarchs (#46)** in Hebron has undergone a number of changes over the years, first starting as a basilica during the Byzantine era and later being recommissioned as a mosque. The White Mosque (D8) was originally constructed of marble and finished in 720 CE by the Umayyads, but none of the original structure remains.

OTHER HOLY PLACES Not everything can be classified as a synagogue, church, or mosque, so we're rounding out our overview of significant holy places with an "other" category. *Tel Arad* is home to an extremely rare House of Yahweh. *Mount Gerizim* is the holiest site to Samaritans. *Dome of the Chain* is a Muslim prayer hall on **Temple Mount (#12)**.

Best examples *Dome of the Chain*; *Mount Gerizim*; and *Tel Arad*.

Complementary **Temple Mount (#12)**; **Bahá'í Gardens (#27)**; and **Mount Zion (#92)**.

THE SACRED

BURIAL The long period of human dwelling in the Holy Land means there are millennia of burial styles to visit, including crypts, mausoleums, megalithic tombs, sepulchers, sarcophagi, ohelim (a building housing graves of Hassidic rabbis), so-called "rock-cut tombs," shrines, and burial vaults.

Petra (#2) has some monumental (but empty) tombs to visit. Jesus was buried in a tomb now housed in the **Church of the Holy Sepulchre (#9)**. The patriarchs and matriarchs of Judaism can be found in their burial ground in **Old Town of Hebron (#46)**. Find a number of sarcophagi at **Beit She'arim (#79)** dedicated to the Jews who could not be buried in Jerusalem after its destruction in 70 CE. The **Mount of Olives (#34)** is a hillside filled with graves.

Best examples **Petra (#2)**; **Church of the Holy Sepulchre (#9)**; **Mount of Olives (#34)**; **Tomb of the Patriarchs and Old Town of Hebron (#46)**; **Beit She'arim (#79)**; and *Damiya Dolmen Field (S2)*.

Complementary **Mount Nebo (#24)**; **Via Dolorosa (#42)**; **Nablus (#61)**; **Herodion (#90)**; **Mount Zion (#92)**; **St. George's Monastery and Wadi Qelt (#97)**; *Gamla*; *Nahal Me'arot/Wadi el-Mughara*; *Sebastia-Shomron*; *Shrine of Bahá'u'lláh*; *Tiberias*; Ben Gurion's Tomb (J2); Garden Tomb (A6); Kidron Valley (A5); Latrun Monastery (B2); Nabi Musa (C3); Nebi Samuel (C4); Schindler's Grave (A5); Sde Boker (J2); Tomb of Queen Helena of Adiabene (A6); Tomb of the Virgin (A5); *Khirbet et-Tannur (O1)*; *Tomb of Maimonides (G3)*; *Tomb of Rabbi Akiva (G3)*; *Tomb of Rabbi Meir Ba'al Haness (G3)*; *Tomb of the Baba Sali (E3)*; and *Wadi Jadid (O1)*.

PILGRIMAGE
Pilgrimage has long been associated with spiritually significant travel. Global travelers have been visiting the Holy Land on pilgrimages for millennia, just as they do today. Every day, travelers from around the world follow along on the **Via Dolorosa (#42)** (literally "Sorrowful Way") as they retrace the last steps of Jesus before his crucifixion. **Mount Zion (#92)** remains a point of pilgrimage too, as home to religious sites including a (symbolic) Tomb of David, the site of Jesus' Last Supper (you know it from the famous painting by Leonardo da Vinci), and the Dormition Abbey where Mary the mother of Jesus is said to have died.

Best examples **Via Dolorosa (#42)**; **Mount Zion (#92)**; and *Ein Kerem*.

Complementary **Old City Jerusalem (#1)**; **Dome of the Rock (#6)**; **Sea of Galilee (#7)**; **Church of the Holy Sepulchre (#9)**; **Western Wall (#11)**; **Temple Mount (#12)**; **Church of the Nativity (#18)**; **Mount Nebo (#24)**; **Bahá'í Gardens (#27)**; **Nazareth and its Biblical Sites (#29)**; **Capernaum and Tabgha (#33)**; **Mount of Olives (#34)**; **Bethlehem (#40)**; **Bethany-Beyond-the-Jordan (#41)**; **Tomb of the Patriarchs and Old Town of Hebron (#46)**; **Tsfat/Safed (#58)**; **Nablus (#61)**; **Jesus Trail (#69)**; *Basilica of the Annunciation*; *Church of St. Anne and the Pools of Bethesda*; *Church of the Transfiguration*; *Deir Quruntal*; *Lot's Cave*; *Mount Gerizim*; *Mount of Beatitudes*; *Mukawir*; *Tiberias*; Church of Mary Magdalene (A5); Church of the Paternoster (A5); Garden Tomb (A6); Holy Week in Jerusalem (A5); Monastery of the Flagellation (A2); Nabi Musa (C3); and Qasr al-Yahud (C3).

CEREMONIES AND EVENTS
It's unlikely you consider yourself Jewish, Christian, and Muslim all at once, but that doesn't mean you can't participate in ceremonies of religious or cultural significance. Here are a few ways you can take part in some of those special moments. Notably, *Petra by Night* allows you to see Petra perhaps as the Nabataeans did thousands of years ago, by candlelight.

Best examples *Petra by Night*.

Complementary **Church of the Holy Sepulchre (#9)**; **Western Wall (#11)**; **Church of the Nativity (#18)**; **Mount of Olives (#34)**; **Bethlehem (#40)**; **Bethany-Beyond-the-Jordan (#41)**; **Via Dolorosa (#42)**; *Basilica of the Annunciation*; Holy Week in Jerusalem (A5); and Yom Kippur (U).

MEDITATION, YOGA, AND QUIET Yoga's a popular pastime everywhere, it seems, and Israel is no exception. Several types of yoga – Vinyasa, Mysore, Power, Prenatal – are available. A few options to research include: Beach Yoga (**f** BeachYogaTLV); Masada Sunrise Yoga (search **w** touristisrael.com); Desert Ashram (**w** desertashram. co.il); Deep Desert Israel (**w** deepdesertisrael.com/activities/outdoor-yoga/); and EllaYoga at the Tel Aviv Port (**w** www.ellayoga.com/en/namal).

Complementary **Dead Sea (#3)**; **Tel Aviv (#5)**; **Tsfat/Safed (#58)**; **Feynan Ecolodge (#86)**; **Timna (#96)**; and *Mitzpe Ramon*.

Archaeology

RUINS BY PERIOD

EARLY HUMAN SETTLEMENTS

Timeframe 1.4 million years before present (BP) – 10,200 before common era (BCE). The Levant (or eastern Mediterranean region, in historical terms) was a passageway and home to many successive generations of proto-humans and earliest human ancestors that left Africa beginning 1.4 million years ago.

So how long have humans lived in the Holy Land? Longer than you probably think! In fact, human ancestors have been found here spanning hundreds of thousands of years, including some of the very first proto-humans who were cave-dwelling hunter-gatherers from Africa.

Sites in our region span a number of times and cultures. This era represents the majority of the Stone Age, which is subdivided into eras representing specific tools in use. These are the cultures that archaeologists have discovered so far in our region:

★ *Lower Paleolithic* 750,000–250,000 BP: stone tools, hand-axes, domesticated dogs, control of fire. Local Culture/Complex: Acheulian, Acheulo-Yabrudian complex. Human species: proto-humans – *Homo habilis, Homo erectus*. Example: Qesem Cave, Tel Aviv (Acheulo-Yabrudian culture), 400,000 BP – oldest evidence of cooked meat; oldest flint knives discovered.

★ *Middle Paleolithic* 600,000–40,000 BP: flint tools. Local Culture/Complex: Mousterian culture. Human species: proto-humans – *Homo neanderthalensis, Homo heidelbergensis*. Example: Zuttiyeh Cave, Upper Galilee (Acheulo-Yabrudian culture), 300,000–200,000 BP – partial skull discovered of *Homo heidelbergensis*; viewable in the **Rockefeller Archaeological Museum**. Examples: Es-Skhul Caves, **Mount Carmel** (Mousterian culture), 120,000–80,000 BP, *Homo sapiens*; Qafzeh Caves, Lower Galilee (Mousterian culture), 100,000–90,000 BP, *Homo sapiens*; Kebara Cave, Carmel Range, 60,000 BP, *Homo neanderthalensis*.

★ *Upper Paleolithic* 50,000–20,000 BP: art, bone artifacts, fine flint blades, more advanced weapons (darts, harpoons, hooks). Local Culture/Complex: Jabroudian culture, part of Mousterian. Human species: emergence of *Homo sapiens*.

★ *Epi-Paleolithic* 20,000–10,000 BP: nomads, flint blades, big animal bones found at human sites. Local Culture/Complex: Natufian culture (12,500–9,500 BCE) – sedentary, leading to first agriculture. Human species: *Homo sapiens*.

In context/famous world examples Lucy – 3.2 million BP (*Australopithecus afarensis* – predates *Homo* genus); Omo Kibish sites near the Omo River – 195,000 BP – oldest discovered fossils of *Homo sapiens*; Cueva de El Castillo, Cantabria, Spain – 40,800 BCE – oldest cave paintings in Europe; Venus of Willendorf, Lower Austria – 28–25,000 BCE; and Lascaux Cave Paintings, France – 20,000 BP.

Best example **Nahal Me'arot/Wadi el-Mughara**. In the site of Nahal Me'arot and Wadi el-Mughara Caves, evidence of coexistence was found for the first time demonstrating that Neanderthals and early modern humans coexisted, in a period now known as Mousterian. Archaeologists also found evidence that hunter-gatherers began transitioning to a more sedentary, agriculture-based lifestyle during the Natufian era between 13,000 and 10,000 BCE.

Complementary **Ancient Amman (#37)**; Nahal Amud (H1); El Bariyeh/Wadi Khareitun/Nahal Teqoa (C2); Prehistoric Man Museum (I1); and Shuqba/Natuf Caves (C5).

TELS (MULTI-PERIOD, LAYERED CITIES)
Tels are artificial hills or mounds that occur when human populations build directly on top of abandoned cities. In many of these sites, construction took the form of mud-brick dwellings. Through abandonment, war, or disuse, the mud brick disintegrated, creating a sedimentary layer atop the city ruins. Future generations see the foundations of buildings and infrastructure already in place and decide to build directly on top of the old city layer. As time passes and these cities also become abandoned or destroyed, the layers continue to build. This cycle of build and decay can repeat over hundreds or thousands of years, aggregating dirt, buildings, and refuse, and eventually creating a layered hill whose buried contents are the compacted remains of all the civilizations that came before. There are dozens of tels in the Holy Land to visit – some famous, some renowned, and most still being excavated.

Best examples **Jericho and Hisham's Palace (#26)** and **Megiddo (#59)**. Jericho is famous for being the world's best-preserved (and perhaps first?) walled city, with perhaps the oldest synagogue in the world, great mosaics, and more than 20 successive layers of civilization. Megiddo is the historical Armageddon, a UNESCO site, and boasts some 26 layers to explore.

Complementary **Temple Mount (#12)**; **Biblical Tels (#38)**; **Tel Dan (#63)**; **Herodion (#90)**; **Tel Arad**; **Tel Ashkelon**; **Tel Beer Sheva**; Abila (S1); and Tel Gezer Archaeological Project (B2).

PREHISTORY/STONE TO COPPER
Timeframe 10,200 BCE – 3300 BCE. The advancement of human civilization is usually represented in three stages: the New Stone Age/Neolithic, the Copper Age/Chalcolithic, and the Bronze Age. These periods are broadly categorized by the tools used by the ancient civilizations of the time, with technological advancements more or less marking the categoric transitions. These are the cultures that archaeologists have discovered so far in our region:

★ *New Stone Age/Neolithic* 10,200 BCE – 4500 BCE. Accomplishments: use of wild cereals, farming begins, animal domestication, first walled cities, polytheism, trade, some pottery.
★ *Copper Age/Chalcolithic* 4500 BCE – 3300 BCE. Accomplishments: copper mining, smelting, far-reaching trade. Local Culture/Stage: Ghassulian (3800–3350 BCE).
★ *Bronze Age* 3300 BCE – 1200 BCE (see below, p. 502). Accomplishments: smelting copper and combining with tin to create bronze, year-round agriculture, invention of the wheel, writing system emerges, and the first centralized government.

The development of the world's first cities took thousands of years, and is not without its own controversy. What constitutes a city? Where was the first? When does a village become a city? When does a city become a civilization? Archaeologists continue to search and historians continue to theorize.

First cities The dates listed below relate to earliest known settlements, and not necessarily the rise of a "city" as we know it today – some may have had only a few dozen residents. **Jericho, Palestine** – c10,000 BCE, with population of 1,000–2,000 residents by 7000 BCE; **Damascus, Syria** – c9000 BCE; **Byblos, Lebanon** – c7000 BCE; and **Aleppo, Syria** – c5000 BCE.

First civilizations These are broad regional examples, but provide a Holy Land context, which often found itself under the power of foreign bodies. (* Indicates powers with extensive control over the Levant/Holy Land.)

★ *Egyptian (Nile Valley)* c3100 BCE – 30 BCE. Capital: Memphis; est. 6,000–30,000 population by 3000 BCE. Famous site: Pyramid of Cheops/Khufu (tallest of the Great Pyramids of Giza) – c2580 BCE, 230 × 230m long/wide, 145m tall.
★ *Sumerian (Tigris/Euphrates)* c3100 BCE – 1940 BCE. Eridu – possibly oldest true "city" in the world; founded in c5400 BCE; est. 4,000 population by 4000 BCE. Uruk – in 2800 BCE, had est. 50–80,000 residents. Famous site: Great Ziggurat of Ur – c2100 BCE, 64 × 45m long/wide, 30m tall.
★ *Akkadian* Controlled the Levant – 2234–2154 BCE. First empire, Semitic-speaking, Sumerian religion and region, based in Iraq – capital not yet discovered.
★ *Assyrian (Mesopotamia/Iraq)* 2500–612 BCE. The Neo-Assyrian Empire controlled parts of the Levant much later, in 9th century BCE.
★ *Minoan (Crete, Greece)* 2700–1450 BCE. Knossos, Crete – Europe's oldest city, founded in 7000 BCE, first palace from 1900 BCE, abandoned 1380–1100 BCE.
★ *Babylonia (Mesopotamia/Iraq)* 1894–1595 BCE. Babylon – possibly largest city in the world during ancient times, with it also being the first city to reach a population above 200,000 (in 600 BCE); founded in c2300 BCE, abandoned in 141 BCE. Famous site: Hanging Gardens of Babylon (from a later period).
★ *Hittites (Anatolia/Turkey)* 1600–1178 BCE.
★ *Mycenaean Greece (mainland and island Greece)* 1600–1100 BCE.

Best examples from the Stone/Neolithic Age Figurine from Berekhat Ram, Golan Heights (233,000 BCE) – perhaps the world's oldest piece of art, this volcanic rock was sculpted by early Stone Age hands; on display at **Israel Museum (#17)**; El-Bariyeh (El Bariyeh/Wadi Khareitun/Nahal Teqoa (C2)), Judean Desert, West Bank (100,000–10,000 BCE) – three caves show evidence of human habitation during this time, with the earliest use of fire in the region; *Ain Ghazal (Q4)*, Amman, Jordan (9000–6500 BCE) – a Neolithic site where nearly 200 small ceramic figurines were found (human and animal) dating to 7000 BCE; Atlit Yam, underwater off the coast of Atlit, Israel, approx. 6400 BCE – Neolithic village, submerged underwater (the coast was 1km west of its present-day location 10,000 years ago during the last Ice Age), with seven megalithic stone structures arranged in a semicircle, perhaps signifying the source of a water temple; and Sha'ar HaGolan, south of the Sea of Galilee at Kibbutz Sha'ar Hagolan (5500–5000 BCE) – an early permanent settlement, extensive art and artifacts on display at **Israel Museum (#17)**.

Best examples from the Copper/Chalcolithic Age Ghassulian cultural artifacts on display at **Rockefeller Archaeological Museum**; proto-Canaanite structures built at **Ein Gedi (#50)** and **Megiddo (#59)**; and *Wadi Jadid (Q1)*, with a dozen impressive stone burial markers from 5000–3000 BCE.

Complementary **Dead Sea (#3)**; **Wadi Rum (#4)**; **Jerash (#14)**; **Jericho (#26)**; **Ancient Amman (#37)**; **Biblical Tels (#38)**; **Beit She'an (#39)**; **Aqaba (#43)**; **Tomb of the Patriarchs** and Old Town of Hebron (#46); **Karak (#49)**; **Ein Gedi (#50)**; **Megiddo (#59)**; **Golan Heights (#62)**; **Tel Dan (#63)**; **Timna (#96)**; *Akhziv Beach*; *Pella*; and *Tel Arad*.

BRONZE AGE

Timeframe 3300 BCE – 1200 BCE. Not all world civilizations entered the Bronze Age at the same time. There are several important markers of this era, from the use of bronze technology to the development of writing systems, laws and administration, armies, religion, science, and hierarchical societies.

Though evidence is scant, later historical narratives attribute the early religious leaders and the emergence of monotheism to this region in the late Bronze Age:

c1800 BCE: Judaism emerges. Abraham is credited as the first believer in one God and the first patriarch of Judaism. He purchases the Cave of Machpelah in Hebron, later known as the **Tomb of the Patriarchs (#46)**, which houses tombs for him and his family members, who were later known as the patriarchs and matriarchs of the Jewish people.

c1550 BCE: Jerusalem. City of Jerusalem first referenced in the Execration Texts, which were Ancient Egyptian texts listing the enemies of the pharaoh.

c1250 BCE: Exodus. Moses leads the Israelites from Egypt through the desert, receives the Ten Commandments at **Mount Sinai (#15)**, and ends his journey in the land of Canaan. This exodus story has served as the foundational story of Jewish belief, with the Israelites being delivered from slavery by Yahweh in exchange for a moral code established through this Mosaic covenant. Shortly after the Exodus, Moses used a plan described by God to build the Ark of the Covenant to house the two stone tablets containing the Ten Commandments, since lost to history.

The same period corresponds to a rise in importance of certain tribal states, such as Canaan, and the establishment of a coalition of tribes that became the Kingdom of Israel. The Bronze Age cities in the Holy Land are: Beirut, Lebanon, c3000 BCE; Jerusalem (as Urušalima), early Canaanite period, c2400 BCE; Jaffa, Israel, c2000 BCE; and Hebron, Palestine, c1800 BCE.

Best examples **Timna (#96)**; *Tel Hazor*; and *Damiya Dolmen Field (S2)*. Timna Park, near Eilat, contains some of the oldest copper mines in the world, used as far back as the fifth millennium BCE, but primarily through the Bronze Age. Tel Hazor has an impressive temple. The Damiya Dolmens were erected between 3600 and 3000 BCE.

Complementary **Old City Jerusalem (#1)**; **Jericho and Hisham's Palace (#26)**; **Nazareth (#29)**; **Jaffa (#30)**; **King's Highway (#31)**; **Ancient Amman (#37)**; **Biblical Tels (#38)**; **Beit She'an (#39)**; Aqaba (#43); **Tomb of the Patriarchs and Old Town of Hebron (#46)**; **Megiddo (#59)**; **Beit Guvrin and Maresha (#60)**; *Akhziv Beach*; *Gamla*; *Tel Arad*; *Tel Ashkelon*; *Tel Beer Sheva*; Mount Sodom (K1); Prehistoric Man Museum (I1); and Tel Gezer Archaeological Project (B2).

CANAANITE
Canaan was a multi-ethnic civilization that comprised many of the groups attributed to the Holy Land during the Bronze Age, including the Ammonites (from where we get Amman), Edomites, Israelites, Moabites, Philistines (where we get Palestinians), and Phoenicians, among other tribes who emerge in the Iron Age. The Canaanites were a polytheistic people who succeeded the Chalcolithic period's Ghassulian culture. Their history is mostly reflected in archaeological findings of Ancient Egypt, of which it was a colony from 1600 to 1100 BCE, and from descriptions in the Bible.

The name "Canaan" appears in the Hebrew Bible more than any other location. Canaan is referenced as the land promised to Abraham and the Israelites by God. When Moses returned from exile, he looked out upon Canaan from Mount Nebo, where he died. Moses' disciple, Joshua, remembered in history as an Israelite spy, eventually led an army to defeat the Canaanite tribal authority.

c1450 BCE: Amarna Letters. Canaan is also referenced greatly in the Amarna Letters, a series of diplomatic correspondence from Egypt to neighboring kingdoms. Nearly 150 letters between local Canaanite kings and mayors were found, confirming an existing Canaanite culture outside of biblical texts. Most of the letters are in Germany or London; roughly 50 are at the Egyptian Museum in Cairo.

c1210 BCE: The Merneptah Stele. Sometimes referred to as the Israel Stele, this Egyptian Hieratic-language stele was written about Egyptian pharaoh Merneptah's victory over Canaan. First known reference to "Israel" and one of only four from ancient times. Not the greatest first reference, reading "Israel is laid waste and his seed is no more…"

c1200 BCE: Late Bronze Age collapse. The region, Canaan and its city-states were considered Egyptian vassals. As Egypt began to war with a still-mysterious and unidentified "Sea Peoples," we see the gradual decline in Egyptian power in the region. As Egypt warred with these Sea Peoples, many Canaanite cities were destroyed in the process. Within a few decades, nearly all the major Canaanite towns along the coastal region (Gaza, Ashdod, Ashkelon, Jaffa, Akko) as well as inland centers (Lachish, Beit Shemesh, Megiddo, Hazor) were raided and destroyed.

c1200–1000 BCE: Canaanite absorption. Gradual integration of the Canaanite culture by other regional denizens – the Philistines, Israelites, and Phoenicians. The Canaanite language, a subgroup of Semitic languages along with Aramaic (Jesus' tongue), separates further into Phoenician and Hebrew.

Best examples **Tel Arad**, capital of the Canaanite kingdom from 2950 to 2650 BCE; Tel Gezer Archaeological Project (B2) has extensive fortifications indicating its importance in the lead-up to the establishment of Israel; Nahariya (E5) has ruins of a citadel dating to c1400 BCE; and Nahal Refaim (B1), located in the Jerusalem Biblical Zoo, has the remains of a village culture that existed following the destruction of large urban areas such as Tel Arad and Megiddo by nomadic tribes.

Complementary **Biblical Tels (#38)**; **Megiddo (#59)**; **Dor HaBonim (#100)**; *Tel Ashkelon*; and *Tel Hazor*.

IRON AGE: KINGDOM OF ISRAEL/JUDAH

Timeframe 1200 BCE – 586 BCE. The Iron Age saw the introduction of iron tools and weapons to world civilizations. The traditional end to the Iron Age and beginning of recorded history generally coincides with the advent of writing. Another development was the first massive-scale world empires, either the Persian Achaemenid Empire or the Neo-Babylonian Empire. Elsewhere at this time were: Third Intermediate Period in Egypt (Dynasties 21–250); beginning of European Classical Antiquity (Carthage founded in 814 BCE; first Olympics in 776 BCE; Rome founded in 753 BC; Central and Eastern Europe dominated by the Hallstat culture, which trades with the Mediterranean; northern Europe still in the Bronze Age); Olmec society is the first major civilization of the Americas, developing in central Mexico around 1200 and continuing influence throughout the period; and the rise of Confucianism in eastern Asia/China. Zhou dynasty.

Major events (all dates estimates)

1050–930 BCE: Israelite Kingdom/United Monarchy. While the evidence doesn't completely corroborate the existence of a United Israel and Judah to form a great Kingdom of Judah, nonetheless tradition has that Saul, David, and Solomon oversaw the first great period in Israeli history during this time. Here we see the emergence of the Hebrew dialect, the foundation of the Jewish religion beginning with the Exodus, Moses receiving the covenant from Yahweh/God, and the elevation of Jerusalem as a central place of worship and politics, with King David first representing the Israelites and surrounding peoples under a unified government and unified Israel.

1002: Reign of King David. David, the third king of the United Israel and Judah, captures Jerusalem, establishes the *City of David*, and declares himself King of a United Israel. Conquers smaller states of Philistia, Edom, Moab, extending borders to Euphrates River, Red Sea, Mediterranean Sea, and Arabian Desert. Continues lineage through son, Solomon. Under grandson Rehoboam's reign, the kingdom splits in two.

970: Reign of King Solomon. Solomon, son of David, becomes the fourth king of Israel.

967: First Temple. According to the Hebrew Bible, the First Temple of Jerusalem was built during Solomon's reign on Mount Moriah, now **Temple Mount (#12)**. It housed the Ark of the Covenant, which held the Ten Commandments. This Temple has no archaeological evidence, only biblical references, as archaeological excavations on Temple Mount have never been completed.

930: End of United Monarchy. Upon Solomon's death, the United Kingdom splits and the kingdoms of Israel and Judah each have their own successive leaders. Jerusalem becomes capital of Judah. Bible is written down in present form, beginning with Psalms and early versions of the books of the 12 minor prophets.

930–722 BCE: Kingdom of Israel (Samaria). The ten tribes of the northern kingdom of Israel lasted until 722, when overtaken by the northern Neo-Assyrian empire. The population of Israel breaks up and scatters around the world, creating the Ten Lost Tribes of Israel.

701: Jerusalem under siege. Various walls crafted outside the City of David to defend the city, including the "Broad Wall," an 8m × 8m fortification visible in the *Jewish Quarter*.

930–587 BCE: Kingdom of Judah. The two tribes of the southern kingdom of Judah last until 587, when the Babylonians capture Jerusalem and send the Jewish people into exile.

587 BCE: Destruction of the First Temple. Struggle for regional hegemony pits Egypt vs. Neo-Babylonian Empire and destroys Jerusalem in the process. Temple and Ark of the Covenant destroyed. Leaders and Jews exiled/deported to Babylonia in Iraq. Evidence of the destruction has been found in the House of Bullae in the City of David and in archaeological digs at Sovev Homot Park on **Mount Zion (#92)**.

Best examples **Biblical Tels (#38)**; **Tel Dan (#63)**; *City of David*; and *Tel Beer Sheva*. UNESCO has awarded three tels – Megiddo, Hazor, and Beer Sheva – with World Heritage Status for their importance during the biblical period. Tel Dan is best known as the northernmost part of the Kingdom of Israel. Tel Beer Sheva was the home of Abraham and important to the United Monarchy and the Kingdom of Judah. Few realize that the *City of David* is the original Jerusalem, with fortifications built over the Jebusite city that came before it; this is where our journey in the Holy Land effectively begins.

Complementary **Old City Jerusalem (#1)**; **Temple Mount (#12)**; **Ancient Amman (#37)**; **Tomb of the Patriarchs and Old Town of Hebron (#46)**; **Ein Gedi (#50)**; **Megiddo (#59)**; **Beit Guvrin and Maresha (#60)**; **Timna (#96)**; *Akhziv Beach*; *Tel Arad*; *Tel Ashkelon*; Tel Bethsaida (G4); Church of the Beheading of John the Baptist (P2); Tel Lachish (B2); Zedekiah's Cave/Solomon's Quarries (A6).

AGE OF EMPIRES: BABYLONIAN, PERSIAN, GREEK, HASMONEAN

Timeframe 587 BCE – 63 BCE. In 587 BCE, the Kingdom of Judah fell to the Babylonians. Jewish leadership was exiled to Babylonia and the Jewish Temple was destroyed. After a nearly 50-year exile, Jews were again allowed to return to Israel, this time under Persian authority, and they were allowed to rebuild their Temple. The next 400 years saw successive leadership in the form of Persian, Greek, and Egyptian dynastic rule before Jewish people would revolt and once again regain independence.

Major events 586–538 BCE: Exile. Following Babylonian capture of Jerusalem and the sacking of the Great/First Temple, the leaders of the Jewish people were forced into exile in greater Babylonia where they would remain dispersed for nearly 50 years. Considered the first Jewish diaspora community. Some believe this is when the concept of Judaism as a monotheistic religion at last took shape. Old Testament Deuteronomistic books Joshua, Judges, Kings, and Samuel completed during exile period.

538–333 BCE: Achaemenid Empire. Cyrus of Persia, the king of the Achaemenid Empire, conquers region and allows the Jews in exile to return to Jerusalem. Purim originates under Persian rule.

515 BCE: Second Temple constructed. Building of a modest Second Temple is completed by Jewish groups, with Achaemenid approval. Built presumably on top of the remains of the First Temple at Mount Moriah, now **Temple Mount (#12)**. Old Testament Pentateuch books (Torah) written: Genesis, Exodus, Leviticus, Numbers, and Deuteronomy.

332–140 BCE: Greek Empires. Persian rule of the Holy Land ends when Alexander the Great of Macedonia reaches Jerusalem. The Holy Land territories undergoes numerous changes in governorship during Greek rule, from Alexander to Ptolemy (Egypt), to the Seleucid Empire (Iraq, run by immigrant Greeks). Job, Jonah, later Psalms, and Ecclesiastes likely written during this Hellenistic period. Examples: **Banias (#80)** and *Qasr al-Abd*.

167 BCE: Maccabean Revolt. The reigning Seleucid power attempts to turn the Second Temple into an interdenominational place of worship, specifically to include Greek gods. Tradition says a rural Jewish priest, Mattathias the Hasmonean, killed a Hellenized (or Greek-ified) Jew, and his family members began guerrilla warfare against other nonreligious Jews and members of the Seleucid army before ultimately capturing the Temple. No evidence of the Maccabees has yet been found. Hannukah commemorates the rededication of the Temple after the Maccabean victory and the removal of the Hellenistic ritual statues. Books of Maccabees written.

110 BCE: Independent Hasmonean kingdom. After gaining some freedoms from the Seleucids following their revolt, the Hasmonean dynasty of Judea (of which the Maccabees were in charge at the outset) gains complete independence in 110 with the collapse of the Seleucid Empire. Second period of Jewish independence in history. Capital is Jerusalem.

63 BCE: Roman Rule. The Roman Republic captures the Holy Land having conquered the Greek Empires.

THEMES

Archaeology

Best examples **Citadel (#32)**; **Banias (#80)**; *Qasr al-Abd*; and Kidron Valley (A5). Banias is named after the Greek god Pan and the site dates to the Ptolemaic period, gaining prominence in 200 BCE. Qasr al-Abd is a rare Greek castle. A trio of Hasmonean-era burial tombs can be visited in Kidron Valley. A Hasmonean wall and tower can be visited at the Citadel.

Complementary **Temple Mount (#12)**; **Ancient Amman (#37)**; **Nablus (#61)**; **Timna (#96)**; *Gamla*; *Mount Arbel*; *Mukawir*; and *Tel Arad*.

HERODIAN

Timeframe 40 BCE – 4 CE. Arguably, no one has had as great of an impact on Jerusalem and greater Israel/Palestine than King Herod, whose reign from 37 BCE to 4 BCE saw some of the most monumental building projects carried out, including the notable construction of **Temple Mount (#12)** and a greatly renovated and expanded Second Temple.

The Roman Empire conquered much of the Mediterranean, including the Holy Land in 63 BCE. The last Hasmonean ruler, Antigonus II, had led a multi-year siege against Roman forces, but Herod I ultimately prevailed and the region became a vassal state of the Roman Republic. Herod I, later Herod the Great, was proclaimed by Rome as "King of the Jews."

Herod had a controversial rule, and an infamous one. He is known for his massive, lavish building projects, including the construction now known as **Temple Mount (#12)**, which supported the Second Temple buildings and projects, and is recognizable today by the massive walls which held together the large amounts of fill that allowed for a flat "roof" on the top of the mount. The most famous remnant of this massive support structure is recognizable today as the **Western Wall (#11)**. He also constructed **Caesarea (#25)** using new and still-innovative approaches to underwater building, including hydraulic cementing. The last great Jewish outpost before complete Roman subjugation – **Masada (#8)** – was also a fortress built under Herod's direction. And we can't forget the eponymous **Herodion (#90)**, possibly his own tomb.

Besides building projects, Herod was known for his reign as a Jewish leader/usurper. He converted to Judaism, along with members of his family, though the jury is out on how pious he was. He is known to have killed members of his own family, incorporated Roman pagan statuary into Jewish sanctuaries (not allowed), and placed heavy taxes on the citizenry in order to afford the massive building projects, which arguably created jobs. He is less kindly referenced in the New Testament as a Roman king that was threatened by the arrival of a/the Jewish Messiah, and attempted to capture the infant Jesus. Joseph and Mary (Jesus' parents) would flee to Egypt before their capture and wait until after Herod's death before returning to the Holy Land, and specifically Nazareth, then outside Herod's son's control.

Thus his reign was controversial. Though he was regularly viewed as a despot, he publicly considered himself Jewish, expanded Temple Mount and the Second Temple (often called Herod's Temple), and believed himself to be King of the Jews – not a title he would have proudly accepted unless he legitimately respected the Jewish people, it could be argued. His enormous building projects around the Holy Land afford us the opportunity to be reminded of his short but important reign in the middle of the Roman Empire era.

Major events 73 BCE: Herod believed to have been born.
63 BCE: Pompey the Great conquers Jerusalem, putting the Roman Empire in charge of the Holy Land.

47 BCE: Herod's father appointed procurator of Judea by Julius Caesar. Herod later awarded governorship of the Galilee.

40 BCE: Herod declared King of the Jews and Judea by Roman Senate in Rome.

37 BCE: Herod defeats the last Hasmonean king, Antigonus II, and begins his rule over Judea.

4 BCE: Herod dies; his kingdom gets divided into three – one for each of his sons.

92 CE: Herodian dynasty ends; the kingdom dissolves and the region becomes incorporated into the broader Roman province.

Best examples **Masada (#8)**; **Caesarea (#25)**; **Jerusalem Archaeological Park (#71)**; **Herodion (#90)**; *Tulul Abu el-Alaiq*; and Zedekiah's Cave/Solomon's Quarries (A6).

Complementary **Old City Jerusalem (#1)**; **Dome of the Rock (#6)**; **Western Wall (#11)**; **Temple Mount (#12)**; **Jericho and Hisham's Palace (#26)**; **Tomb of the Patriarchs and Old Town of Hebron (#46)**; **Banias (#80)**; **Western Wall Tunnels (#94)**; *Mukawir*; *Sebastia-Shomron*; and El Bariyeh/Wadi Khareitun/Nahal Teqoa (C2).

ROMAN

Timeframe 63 BCE – 395 CE. The independent Hasmonean kingdom of Judea lost its (perhaps inevitable) battle with the Roman Republic in 63 BCE and was split into a number of districts. The first "King of the Jews" (that title later challenged by a certain leader of Christianity who emerges around 100 years later) had a controversial reign, but began construction projects on a massive scale, ostensibly in support of the Jewish people. Herod is discussed in the previous section.

Jesus of Nazareth was born in Bethlehem around the year 4 BCE, but his parents – Jews – faced persecution and moved around the region (Egypt, the Galilee) during Jesus' childhood. He became the principal figure of Christianity following his crucifixion by Roman authorities. Christianity would take 300 years before sufficiently impacting the Roman Empire enough to sway Emperor Constantine to allow its practice. Soon, Christianity was the state religion of the empire and Jerusalem became a center of Christian belief.

Meanwhile, Jews staged multiple uprisings before suffering severe defeats in three major rebellions throughout the region. Romans were responsible for the destruction of the Second Temple in 70 CE, and the last Jewish rebels were killed (or killed themselves) in 73 CE at Masada.

Eventually, the Romans faced a number of challenges on their territory, expanding and shrinking in size through wars of defense and aggression. In 330 CE, the Romans relocated their capital to Istanbul, then Constantinople (named after Roman Emperor Constantine, the architect of the capital move), though originally Byzantium, at which point the Roman era becomes known as the Byzantine era.

Famous people **Herod** (reign: 37 BCE – 4 BCE) – see previous section. **Jesus Christ** (c4 BCE – c30 CE) – Jewish leader, crucified by Romans, and honored as a Christian martyr, later to be the principal figure of Christianity. **Trajan** (reign: 98–117 CE) – the Empire reached its zenith under his command, and yet he's also known for overseeing an era of peace. He took over the Nabataean kingdom and established the Arabian province, or Arabia Petraea. **Hadrian** (reign: 117–138 CE) – though considered one of the five good emperors of Rome, his legacy in the Holy Land is having suppressed the Bar Kokhba Revolt and renaming "Judea" as "Syria Palaestina." **Simon Bar Kokhba** (rebellion dates: 132–136 CE) – led the third Jewish rebellion against the Roman Empire, called the Bar Kokhba Revolt. For three years, he acted as leader of the region, but was killed by Hadrian's forces in 135.

Major events 63 BCE: Roman rule begins. The Roman Republic captures the Holy Land having conquered the Greek Empires.

37 BCE: Herod. The Holy Land is broken up into Roman vassal states, and the Hasmonean dynasty comes to an end. Herod the Great established as King. Great epoch of monument, architecture, and city-building.

c4 BCE: Jesus born. Jesus, future religious figure of Christianity, born in Bethlehem.

c33 BCE: Jesus dies. Jesus is sentenced to die for claiming to be the King of the Jews, is crucified by Pontius Pilate, a Roman governor, and buried at Golgotha, now **Church of the Holy Sepulchre (#9)**.

66–73 CE: First Jewish–Roman War. Tensions between Romans and Jews flare up over taxation, ethnic tension, and use of the Jewish Temple. In 70 CE, Jerusalem's walls are breached by Roman armies and the Temple is destroyed. In 73 CE, the last of the Jewish rebels hold out in **Masada (#8)** before committing mass suicide ahead of the arrival of Roman forces.

106 CE: Nabataean kingdom incorporated into the Roman province, Arabia Petraea.

115–117 CE: Kitos War/Second Jewish–Roman War. A series of conflagrations among Jews living in the diaspora – Cyprus, Mesopotamia, and Egypt, among other places. Jews kill hundreds of thousands of local citizens before being defeated by Trajan's armies.

132–136 CE: Bar Kokhba Revolt/Third Jewish–Roman War. Jews under Simon Bar Kokhba lead a national rebellion against Roman leadership after the erection of pagan gods on **Temple Mount (#12)**. Hadrian silences the rebellion by 136 CE, several hundred thousand Jews are killed or sold into slavery, and Jerusalem becomes off-limits to the remaining residents. Hadrian renames the territory Syria Palaestina, removing any reference to Jews (Judea).

Best examples **Jerash (#14)**; **Ancient Amman (#37)**; **Tsipori (#56)**; and *Bar'am*. Jerash has perhaps the greatest ruins of any regional Roman city. In Amman, the Temple of Hercules, the Roman amphitheater, and the Nymphaeum are the city's most recognizable monuments, all dating to this period. Tsipori reached its peak in the Roman years. For something different, visit Bar'am, home to a Jewish community during Roman reign.

Complementary **Old City Jerusalem (#1)**; **Sea of Galilee (#7)**; **Masada (#8)**; **Temple Mount (#12)**; **Nazareth and its Biblical Sites (#29)**; **Capernaum and Tabgha (#33)**; **Bethlehem (#40)**; **Beit Guvrin and Maresha (#60)**; **Nablus (#61)**; **Beit She'arim (#79)**; **Banias (#80)**; *Cardo*; *City of David*; *Hamat Tiberias*; *Korazim*; *Tel Ashkelon*; *Tiberias*; Ancient Bathhouse of Nazareth (G1); Tel Bethsaida (G4); Jabotinsky Park (E4); Khirbet Feynan (O1); Kibbutz Ginosar (G3); Qasr Bashir (O1); and Tomb of Queen Helena of Adiabene (A6).

BYZANTINE/CHRISTIAN

Timeframe 311–638 CE (Byzantine period begins 395 CE). The Byzantine period begins with Constantine, who reigned from 306 to 337 CE. He ended the persecution of Christians, moved the capital of the Empire to Constantinople (Istanbul), and was baptized Christian upon his deathbed. He and his mother, Helena, commissioned the creation of the **Church of the Holy Sepulchre (#9)** at Golgotha, the *Church of the Ascension (A5)* on the Mount of Olives, the **Church of the Nativity (#18)** in Bethlehem, as well as

St. Catherine's Monastery (#22), to commemorate the holiest locations and moments in Christian history.

Major events 311–330 CE: Emperor Constantine decriminalizes Christian worship. Upon his orders and his mother's insistence, they create a number of churches sanctifying the life and death of Jesus.

365: Major earthquake strikes region, epicenter in the Galilee, leveling dozens of cities. Petra, Tsipori, and some Cities of the Decapolis are believed to have never recovered.

380: Constantine's successor, Theodosius, declares Christianity the Roman state religion with Jerusalem as one of five holy sees (or bishops' locations).

395: Empire divides into East and West. Palestine placed under Eastern Roman Empire control.

484–572: Samaritan and Jewish Revolts against Byzantine Empire. Series of five revolts over a century, with casualties on both sides, but the Samaritan population never recovers.

570: Muhammad, the central figure of Islam, is born.

614: Siege of Jerusalem by Sassanid Empire of Persia. True Cross captured.

629: Reconquered by Byzantine Emperor Heraclius.

638: Conquered again by Rashidun Caliph, ibn al-Khattab, an Arab leader of the new religion, Islam. Byzantine reign ends.

Best examples **Cardo**; **Sebastia-Shomron**; **Ancient Qatzrin**; **Shivta**; **Umm el-Jimal**. The Cardo was the principal north–south market street in Jerusalem during Roman-Byzantine times. Umm el-Jimal has some 15 church ruins, while Shivta and Sebastia also house interesting Byzantine churches. Ancient Qatzrin is a recreated Byzantine-era village.

Complementary **Old City Jerusalem (#1)**; **Masada (#8)**; **Church of the Holy Sepulchre (#9)**; **Temple Mount (#12)**; **Madaba (#19)**; **Caesarea (#25)**; **Capernaum and Tabgha (#33)**; **Ancient Amman (#37)**; **Beit She'an (#39)**; **Avdat (#48)**; **Beit Alpha (#64)**; **Incense Route (#73)**; Cities of the Decapolis (W3); Khirbet Suseya (C2); and Kursi (G3).

ISLAMIC I: RASHIDUN, UMAYYAD, ABBASID

Timeframe 638–1099 CE. Muhammad was born in 570 CE in Mecca, present-day Saudi Arabia. He was known to be a great leader of the Arab people, the successful general of an army that conquered much of Arabian peninsula before his death in 632 CE, and the founder of Islam. He is considered a Holy Prophet to Muslims.

Arab armies arrived in the Holy Land shortly after Muhammad's death during the reign of the second caliph of the Rashidun Caliphate. With it came Islam, a monotheistic religion following Judaism and Christianity which claimed Muhammad as the last prophet. This new Islamic and Arab empire gained huge swaths of territory in short order. Within a few decades, Muhammad's followers would take over much of the Middle East and North Africa. Jerusalem capitulated in 638, and Caesarea in 640, marking the end of Roman Empire rule in the Holy Land.

From Muhammad's death in 632 until the (relatively) short break with Christian Crusader rule, the Holy Land was ruled by a succession of Islamic caliphates: Rashidun, Umayyad, Abbasid, and Fatimid.

Major events 620 CE: Muhammad takes his Night Journey to Jerusalem, including Israh and Mi'raj (his ascension to Heaven to meet God).

622: The Islamic calendar is set to year 1 from the date of the *hijra*, when Muhammad and his followers moved from Mecca to Medina.

625: **Al-Aqsa Mosque (#65)** (on **Temple Mount (#12)**), then a small prayer house, is dedicated by Muhammad as one of three holy mosques of Islam.

632: Death of Muhammad. Rashidun Caliphate established in Medina. Small prayer house was established on Temple Mount and would become Al-Aqsa Mosque.

637: Another siege on Jerusalem, this time by the Arab Rashidun Caliphate (founded after Muhammad's death). Christians allowed to worship.

661: Sunni–Shia split, ending Rashidun Caliphate. Umayyad Caliphate forms with a base in Damascus.

691: **Dome of the Rock (#6)** constructed on Temple Mount, which has been undeveloped and in ruins for centuries. Jews and Christians are once again prohibited from worshiping on Temple Mount, now called Haram es-Sharif ("noble sanctuary"). They won't regain access until the Crusaders come in 1099.

750: Abbasids overthrow Umayyads, creating third caliphate to succeed Muhammad, centered in Baghdad.

797 and 1030: **Church of the Holy Sepulchre (#9)** restored. (It was destroyed again in 1009.)

909: Fatimid Caliphate, based largely in North Africa in the 10th–12th centuries, rules from Tunisia and later Cairo.

1009: Fatimids burn the Church of the Holy Sepulchre to the ground.

Road trip W1: Umayyad Castles.

Best examples **Dome of the Rock (#6)**; **Qasr Amra and the Desert Palaces (#20)**; Hisham's Palace (**Jericho and Hisham's Palace (#26)**); **Al-Aqsa Mosque (#65)**; and *Qasr Kharana*. Umayyad palaces are spread throughout Jordan and neighboring countries, and were used for hunting and winter lodges. Hisham's Palace is the grand Umayyad Desert Palace located on the west bank of the Jordan River – just north of Jericho, and part of that site.

Complementary **Temple Mount (#12)**; **Ancient Amman (#37)**; **Azraq Wetlands (#55)**; *Qasr Azraq*; Qasr al-Qastal (W1); Qasr al-Mushatta (W1); and White Mosque (D8).

CRUSADER

Timeframe 1099–1187 CE. The Crusaders were a series of Christian armies intent on reclaiming the Holy Land from Islamic control. The movement was extremely popular, and volunteers joined from all over Europe. The First Crusade was quite successful, and included the capture of Jerusalem in 1099. The Crusaders had a number of strongholds and built a number of forts in strategic locations throughout the Holy Land. They continued to have conflicts with a number of Muslim neighbors, including the Khwarazmians, Seljuks, Fatimids, and ultimately succumbing to the Ayyubids first, regaining territory, and then losing everything to the Mamluks.

Major events 1099 CE: The First Crusaders set out from Latin Christian European states to steal away control of the Holy Land from Islamic hands, particularly after the near complete destruction of the **Church of the Holy Sepulchre (#9)**. Upon their capture of Jerusalem, the Crusaders slaughter Muslims and Jews. The **Dome of the Rock (#6)** is turned into a Christian sanctuary and **Al-Aqsa Mosque (#65)** becomes the Crusader king's palace.

1113: Hospital in the Muristan (A2) gives rise to the Order of Knights of the Hospital of Saint John of Jerusalem, or the Knights Hospitaller, who defended the Holy Land and continued to care for the sick during the Crusades.

1138: *Church of St. Anne* erected.

1165: Armenians build *St. James' Cathedral*.

1170: Church of the Holy Sepulchre is reconstructed and expanded by the Crusaders, directly atop the church that was destroyed in 614 by the Persians, which itself was atop the ruins of Hadrian's temple from the 2nd century, above Golgotha and Jesus' burial cave.

1187: Saladin, founder of the Ayyubid dynasty, defeats the Crusaders at the Battle of Hattin and peacefully captures Jerusalem.

Road trip W4: Crusader Castles.

Best examples **Akko (#13)**; **Karak (#49)**; **Belvoir (#93)**; and *Shobak*. Much of the old city of Akko contains evidence of the Crusader period, including the Hospitaller Fortress, the Templar tunnel, and the walls (since rebuilt). Karak Castle had a short existence, but a lasting legacy, in this beautiful and sprawling site. Belvoir, or Star of Jordan, is a Sea of Galilee site famous for multiple Crusader battles.

Would-be best examples **Krak des Chevaliers** – had BUCKET! used this UNESCO site as an elective, it would have been ranked #32, but sadly modern borders have left it in tumultuous territory (Syria) and it won't be part of most people's travel plans for the foreseeable future; and **Beaufort Castle** is a Crusader castle in southern Lebanon with great views of Lebanon and Israel – it was occupied by Hezbollah for many years, shelled by Israel, and left in disrepair, unfortunately.

Complementary **Beit She'an (#39)**; **Tsipori (#56)**; **Golan Heights (#62)**; *Apollonia*; *Montfort*; *Yehi'am*; Castel (B1); Hospitaller Fortress/Knights' Halls (E2); and Muristan (A2).

ISLAMIC II: AYYUBID, MAMLUK, OTTOMAN

Timeframe 1187–1917 CE. The Crusaders lost control of Jerusalem in 1187, but wouldn't leave the region until 1291 after losing Akko. Saladin is one of the most famous Kurds, expanding the Ayyubid Empire and ultimately defeating the Crusaders. The Mamluks followed the Ayyubids and established a sultanate covering Egypt, Israel, and the Transjordan until losing sovereignty to the Ottomans of Turkey who held power in the Holy Land for 400 years until the collapse of the Ottoman Empire after World War I.

Major events 1187: Under Saladin's leadership, Jerusalem undergoes major renovations to its interior and exterior walls. Muslim sites also receive upgrades.

1219: With the threat of future Crusades on the doorstep, Ayyubid leader al-Mu'azzam Isa destroys all of the extant walls so the Crusaders will have a difficult time defending the city in the future. The Mamluks will exercise a similar strategy.

1229: The Sixth Crusade concludes with Christians regaining control of the city. As part of the agreement, Muslims gain control over their own sites. Indeed, the walls remain untouched for 400 years.

1244: Crusaders driven out of Jerusalem by Khwarazmian Tatars, a Turkic Sunni Muslim dynasty based in Central Asia and Turkey.

1291: Mamluk reign begins.

1517: Ottoman Empire (Turkey) begins regional rule, including Palestine.

1535: Ottoman leader Suleiman the Magnificent begins restoring walls around Jerusalem to their previous glory.

1757: Declaration of Status Quo of the Holy Land Sites by Ottoman authorities grants that nine sites (five of which are in Jerusalem, four in Bethlehem) shall not be changed without the expressed consent of all religious communities with interest in the site.

1860: Resident Jews build first neighborhood outside city walls, called Mishkenot Sha'ananim.

1881: Founder of modern Hebrew, Eliezer Ben-Yehuda, moves to Jerusalem.

1882–1903: First of several "waves" of Jewish immigrants (*aliyah*) arrive to Jerusalem. This group is primarily made up of Eastern Europeans.

1897: First Zionist Congress in Europe. Jerusalem is described as the capital of a future Jewish state.

1917: Ottomans lose World War I. British Foreign Secretary writes the Balfour Declaration announcing future home of Jewish people is in Palestine.

Best examples of Ayyubid works **Ajloun Fortress (#76)**; **Nimrod's Fortress (#85)**; and *Qasr Azraq*. Ajloun is an Ayyubid-era castle that controlled the northern Jordan valley against Crusader attacks. Nimrod is the other famous Ayyubid castle, with spectacular views and an enjoyable walk to reach it.

Complementary Khirbet al-Minya (G3) and Pharaoh's Island Citadel (T1).

CITY CONGLOMERATES

CITIES OF THE DECAPOLIS

Timeframe 323 BCE – 749 CE. The Cities of the Decapolis (W3) were a set of ten Greek cities (Deca + polis = 10 + cities), turned Roman, which kept their connection with the Greco-Roman culture despite periods of external rule (particularly Jewish).

The majority of the inhabitants of the Decapolis cities were not of Semitic origin. Further, they worshiped Greek gods, spoke Greek (later Latin), ate pork, and did not practice circumcision. Each of the cities functioned as an independent polis. The remains today show that each contained a Roman-style city plan, including the recognizable perpendicular thoroughfares (*decumanus* and *cardo*). There's also evidence that the cities were connected by a network of roads for trade, though the jury is out about whether they were a loose federation or league of city-states, or whether "Decapolis" was just a name ascribed to ten disconnected Greek towns in the southern Levant region.

City names and condition of ruins (if applicable) Canatha (Qanawat, Syria; ruin score: unknown); Capitolias/Dion (Beit Ras, Jordan; ruin score: 1); Damascus, Syria (ruin score: unknown); Gadara (Umm Qais, Jordan; ruin score: 4); Gerasa (Jerash, Jordan; ruin score: 4); Hippos (Horvat Suṣiṭa, Israel; ruin score: 2); Pella, Jordan (ruin score: 2); Philadelphia (Amman, Jordan; ruin score: 4); Raphana/Abila (Quwaylibah, Jordan; ruin score: 3); and Scythopolis (Beit She'an, Israel; ruin score: 4).

Major events 323–63 BCE: All Decapolis cities founded, with the exception of the extant Damascus.

80 BCE: Hasmonean king demolishes Pella for refusing to abide by Jewish customary laws (it was rebuilt shortly thereafter).

63 BCE: Roman conquest of Judean region over the Hasmonean Kingdom, a welcome turn of events for the Greek inhabitants of Decapolis cities. Start of the Pompeiian calendar.

161 CE: Popular ruins of Amman are built – Roman Theater, Odeon, Nymphaeum, Citadel.

451 CE: Christianity penetrates region and Decapolis cities begin taking Christian bishops.

636 CE: Muslim rule of region.

749 CE: Earthquake destroys Jerash, Beit She'an, Hippos, Gadara, Pella, and Abila, though all cities in the region experience severe damage.

Road trips W3: Cities of the Decapolis.

Best examples **Jerash (#14)**; **Beit She'an (#39)**; **Umm Qais (#45)**; and *Pella*.

Complementary **Ancient Amman (#37)**; Abila (S1); and Cities of the Decapolis (W3).

NABATAEAN CITIES/INCENSE ROUTE

Timeframe 312 BCE – 663 CE. The Nabataeans were a Bedouin people made up of Arab nomads and shepherds. Much of the history of the Nabataean people and their cities still remains a mystery. We have no records of the origin of the Nabataeans, the founding of **Petra (#2)** or many of the other cities, nor when exactly their lavish cities started to fall from favor. The Nabataeans spoke Aramaic, and wrote in a script very similar to Aramaic, now called Nabataean, but they either did not keep many written records, or the treasure trove has yet to be uncovered. We do know that the Arabic alphabet originated from the Nabataean alphabet, which came from Syriac, itself derived from the Aramaic alphabet.

Petra, as capital, was the convergence of several trade routes heading west from Asia and north from Arabia to the Mediterranean, where spices, incense (frankincense and myrrh were particularly popular), and other goods were distributed to the rest of the empirical lands. The **Incense Route (#73)** was perhaps the most well-known Nabataean trade route, which controlled access to the sea. Goods converged in the massive town of Petra before heading west through trading posts, caravanserai, fortresses, and other pit stops on the way to Gaza. Along the way, travelers would encounter **Avdat (#48)**, *Mamshit*, *Shivta*, and other sites which have since been honored with UNESCO World Heritage status.

The Nabataeans are referenced by a Greek historian from around 30 BCE, Diodorus Siculus, and the first Nabataean king is referenced in the Old Testament's Book of Maccabees. They worshiped multiple deities, similar to the gods found among tribes of the Arabian peninsula during this time. The Nabataeans had good relations with Rome until trade routes were rerouted through more northerly cities, dropping the importance of the Nabataean holdings some time in the 4th century CE. With influence from the Greco-Roman empires, the Nabataeans eventually transitioned to speaking Greek and practicing Christianity. Their culture was heavily influenced by Roman architecture, as can be seen in their greatest remaining accomplishment, Petra. Much of their history remains a mystery, though the grandeur of their constructions is easy to see even today.

Major events 312 BCE: First reference to the Nabataeans in written record – acknowledged as a tribe who fended off attack by the Greek/Seleucid colonial powers looking to plunder their wealth (thus implying they were already a powerful entity prior to this date, though no records exist).

168 BCE: First known Nabataean king, Aretas I, crowned.

93 BCE: King Obodas I (for whom Avdat is named) leads an army at the Battle of Gadara against the Hasmoneans, ostensibly to guarantee Nabataean trade routes to the Seleucids in the north and to Gaza on the Mediterranean.

86 BCE: King Obodas defeats the Seleucid army at the Battle of Cana.

9 BCE: Temple of Oboda built in Avdat (itself a trading stop since the 3rd century BCE) to bury and honor their new deity, King Obodas.

106 CE: Roman annexation of Nabataean kingdom. Name changed to Arabia Petraea. Use of Nabataean language wanes.

356 CE: Last known Nabataean inscriptions found in Saudi Arabia.

663 CE: Petra abandoned, likely due to changing trade routes and earthquake damage.

Road trip W2: Nabataean Ruins.

Best examples **Petra (#2)**; **Avdat (#48)**; **Incense Route (#73)**; *Mamshit*; and *Little Petra*.

Complementary *Halutza*; *Nitzana*; *Shivta*; and *Khirbet et-Tannur (O1)*.

IMPRESSIONABLE HISTORIC SITES

GHOST TOWNS For one reason or another, you have some spooky abandoned villages to see in our region (many can't be explored, unfortunately). At the Mount Bental lookout, you can look out over the Syrian border in the Golan Heights and see abandoned towns such as Quneitra, destroyed after the Yom Kippur War. Liftah, in Jerusalem, was a Palestinian town evacuated and later depopulated completely after the 1948 war between Palestinians and Israelis, and is now a nature reserve.

Complementary **Old City Jerusalem (#1)**; **Tsipori (#56)**; **Golan Heights (#62)**; *Battir Hills*; *Ein Kerem*; *Separation Wall*; Mount Bental Lookout (I2); Liftah (B1); Majdal Shams and The Shouting Hill (I2).

MOSAICS Mosaics were a distinctly Greco-Roman invention beginning around the 3rd century BCE, right around the time of Ancient Roman expansion. The art of mosaic involves taking small, colored pebbles, glass, or ceramic pieces and arranging them to create a design or picture. The Roman influence in the Holy Land incorporated this traditional design method into Roman and Byzantine – as well as Jewish and Christian – architecture.

Best examples **Madaba and the Madaba Map (#19)**; **Beit Alpha (#64)**; and **Umm ar-Rasas (#81)**. The most famous version is perhaps from Madaba, whose mosaic floor depicts the earliest map of the Holy Land, and Jerusalem in particular. Umm ar-Rasas is nearby in Jordan and holds preserved and mammoth mosaics. Beit Alpha is an ancient synagogue with a fabulous story and huge mosaic floor.

Complementary **St. Catherine's Monastery (#22)**; **Mount Nebo (#24)**; **Jericho and Hisham's Palace (#26)**; **Beit She'an (#39)**; **Ein Gedi (#50)**; **Tsipori (#56)**; *Hamat Tiberias*; *Lot's Cave*; *Mamshit*; Basilica of the Agony (A5); Inn of the Good Samaritan (C3); Khirbet Suseya (C2); Monastery of St. Euthymius (C3); and Monastery of St. Martyrius (C3).

WALLS What city has the oldest walls in the world? Or, more accurately, *defensive walls*? Jericho is the likely contender for the oldest walls in the world, and one of the oldest settlements during the Neolithic era, before the world's population expanded greatly, went to war, and began extensive building. But was Jericho even a city? Some have called it a "proto-city" for having an ill-defined governing structure. That said, the discovery of the Tower of Jericho from c8000 BCE almost certainly ensures that the walls surrounding Jericho were used for defensive purposes, and the tower used for watching enemies in the periphery.

Best example **Jerusalem Walls and Gates (#47)**. Walk at the base, circumnavigate, and view the Old City from atop its ancient walls. The aesthetic walls of today are primarily Ottoman (nearly 500 years old) with Hasmonean/Herodian base blocks.

Complementary **Old City Jerusalem (#1)**; **Akko (#13)**; **Jericho and Hisham's Palace (#26)**; *Tel Ashkelon*; and *Tiberias*.

SHIPWRECKS Harbors seem like a natural fit to this area of the world, with its extensive Mediterranean coastline, but the lack of islands, bays, and any major east–west all-year rivers has made this stretch of the Mediterranean a somewhat treacherous seafaring area, particularly when storms hit. There are several shipwrecks to visit, but our principal "wreck" is a regular fishing boat that sank in the Sea of Galilee around the time of Jesus. And check out **Red Sea/Gulf of Aqaba (#10)** if you like diving.

Best examples **Red Sea/Gulf of Aqaba (#10)** and Kibbutz Ginosar (G3).

Complementary **Caesarea (#25)**; **Aqaba (#43)**; **Ras Mohammad (#53)**; **Sharm el-Sheikh (#88)**; **Dor HaBonim (#100)**; *Haifa*; *Rosh HaNikra*; *Tel Ashkelon* and Nahariya (E5).

HISTORIC BATTLEFIELDS Interested in military history? Check out our sites for evidence of the brutal history that comes with several dozen hostile takeovers over the last three millennia.

Best examples Castel (B1).

Complementary **Old City Jerusalem (#1)**; **Masada (#8)**; **Akko (#13)**; **Jerusalem Walls and Gates (#47)**; **Herodion (#90)**; **Ramparts Walk (#91)**; **Belvoir (#93)**; *Apollonia*; *Gamla*; *Mount Arbel*; *Stella Maris*; Latrun Monastery (B2); and Muristan (A2).

ACTIVE EXCAVATIONS Many places in the Holy Land are still being excavated. If you like archaeology, there are several opportunities to participate in excavations yourself – check out our *Digs* category (p. 568).

Best examples **Petra (#2)**; **Beit Guvrin and Maresha (#60)**; and Tel Gezer Archaeological Project (B2).

Complementary **Masada (#8)**; **Jericho and Hisham's Palace (#26)**; **Jaffa (#30)**; **Capernaum and Tabgha (#33)**; **Biblical Tels (#38)**; **Jerusalem Walls and Gates (#47)**; **Ein Gedi (#50)**; **Megiddo (#59)**; **Jerusalem Archaeological Park (#71)**; **Umm ar-Rasas (#81)**; **Herodion (#90)**; **Mount Zion (#92)**; **Dor HaBonim (#100)**; *Cardo*; *Church of St. Anne and the Pools of Bethesda*; *Korazim*; *Mukawir*; *Tel Ashkelon*; *Tiberias*; Archaeological Seminars Dig-for-a-Day (B2); Cities of the Decapolis (W3); Kursi (G3); and Lutheran Church of the Redeemer (A2).

IMPRESSIVE STRUCTURAL REMAINS If you're looking for some places that will instantly wow you, look no further than the list below. Size sometimes does matter! Visits to any of these locations gives you the best bang for your buck (err, shekel/dinar). For more on structure, skip ahead to *Structure* below.

Complementary **Old City Jerusalem (#1); Petra (#2); Church of the Holy Sepulchre (#9); Western Wall (#11); Temple Mount (#12); Akko (#13);** Jerash (#14); **Church of the Nativity (#18); Qasr Amra and the Desert Palaces (#20);** St. Catherine's Monastery (#22); **Caesarea (#25); Modern Amman (#36); Beit She'an (#39); Umm Qais (#45); Jerusalem Walls and Gates (#47); Avdat (#48); Karak (#49); Beit Guvrin and Maresha (#60); Nimrod's Fortress (#85); Western Wall Tunnels (#94);** St. George's Monastery and Wadi Qelt (#97); *Basilica of the Annunciation*; *Little Petra*; *Mar Saba*; *Shobak*; and Hospitaller Fortress/Knights' Halls (E2).

Structure

MONUMENTS

ICONIC STRUCTURES The Holy Land contains some of the most recognizable, important, symbolic, and volatile sites on Earth – many of which are within just a few meters of one another – **Jerusalem Walls and Gates (#47)**, the **Western Wall (#11)**, and the **Church of the Holy Sepulchre (#9)**. **Petra (#2)** too has instilled a sense of hidden wonder in the many guests who walk the Siq to catch the first glimpse of the Treasury.

Perhaps none matches the **Dome of the Rock (#6)**, the symbol of Jerusalem and the Holy Land in general. Wrapped up in this building are decades of tension, the symbolism of Muslim influence in a Jewish country, and the competing themes of destruction and rebirth. Beyond what it represents, the Dome of the Rock is simply a stunning edifice.

Best example **Dome of the Rock (#6)**.

Complementary **Old City Jerusalem (#1)**; **Petra (#2)**; **Masada (#8)**; **Church of the Holy Sepulchre (#9)**; **Western Wall (#11)**; **Temple Mount (#12)**; and **Jerusalem Walls and Gates (#47)**.

HISTORIC MONUMENTS These large-scale structures symbolize the importance of a group of people, an influential event, or a significant period in time. Our picks are the connected sites of the **Western Wall (#11)** and **Temple Mount (#12)**, the former merely being the westernmost external wall of the latter. The Western Wall is all that remains of the great retaining walls that once served to support Temple Mount and Herod's Temple (aka the Second Temple), the great symbol of the Jewish people and epicenter of Jewish culture. Temple Mount was dismantled and mostly destroyed by the Romans in 70 CE. It was later built upon by ruling Muslim powers who also viewed it as a holy site. **Dome of the Rock (#6)** and **Al-Aqsa Mosque (#65)** have been there ever since. Since 1967, Jews have not been able to approach Temple Mount, so they pray at the Western Wall as the closest place to the Holy of Holies where once stood the Temple.

Best examples **Western Wall (#11)** and **Temple Mount (#12)**.

Complementary **Petra (#2)**; **Dome of the Rock (#6)**; **Masada (#8)**; **Church of the Holy Sepulchre (#9)**; **Jerash (#14)**; **Church of the Nativity (#18)**; **Caesarea (#25)**; **Bahá'í Gardens (#27)**; **Modern Amman (#36)**; **Beit She'an (#39)**; **Bethlehem (#40)**; **Umm Qais (#45)**; **Jerusalem Walls and Gates (#47)**; **Herodion (#90)**; *Little Petra*; *Separation Wall*; Montefiore's Windmill (A7); Tel Hai Fort (H2); and *Damiya Dolmen Field (S2)*.

MEMORIAL These sites or objects were constructed specifically to remember a person, group, or event. Our choice is **Yad Vashem (#35)**: if the idea of a Holocaust museum sounds depressing to you, check out this uplifting interpretation designed to reflect and honor the Jewish will and spirit, even amid the darkest of days.

Best example **Yad Vashem (#35)**.

Complementary **Masada (#8); Church of the Holy Sepulchre (#9); Western Wall (#11); Temple Mount (#12); Mount Nebo (#24); Mount of Olives (#34); Mount Zion (#92);** and Rabin Square (D3).

ARCHITECTURE

ARCHITECTURAL STYLES For being a young country, Israel has incorporated a number of unique looks into its aesthetic. One, the International Style movement which spawned Bauhaus, is glorified in thousands of buildings in Tel Aviv, earning it a UNESCO designation. .

The Palestinian Throne Villages were 24 villages that served as political centers during the Ottoman period in what is now the West Bank. Each had administrative responsibilities, and they were overseen by a sheikh who lived in a central palace. Each palace was unique, but all followed a similar style. Several can be visited today.

City walk D5: Tel Aviv: Architecture.

Best examples **Modern Movement (Bauhaus Architecture) (#16)** and Palestinian Throne Villages (C5).

Complementary **Old City Jerusalem (#1);** *As-Salt*; Deir Ghassaneh (C5); Mamluk Buildings (A2); and *Al-Qasem Palace (C5)*.

LANDSCAPE With its vast desertscape, "landscape" is not the first thing most people consider when they think of the Middle East. Unlike neighboring Jordan (which is beautiful in its own way), Israel benefits from a Mediterranean climate that brings in seasonal rains, offering the occasional floral bounty. In Haifa and Akko, the Bahá'í faith community has created several glorious gardens filled with breathtaking displays of serenity, symmetry, and seasonality.

Best examples **Bahá'í Gardens (#27)** and *Shrine of Bahá'u'lláh*.

Complementary **Jerusalem Walls and Gates (#47);** *Battir Hills*; *Rothschild Boulevard*; *Sataf*; and *Tel Aviv Tayelet/Promenade*.

MODERN ARCHITECTURE Its thousands of years of history have not stopped the Holy Land from embracing the modern. Particularly in Tel Aviv and Jerusalem, there are a number of state-of-the-art and visually striking buildings, works, and objects to inspire wonder. Below is a list of some of the more famous buildings and locations where modern architecture has begun to shine.

Best examples Shrine of the Book at **Israel Museum (#17);** new museum at **Yad Vashem (#35); Tel Aviv Museum of Art (#95);** *Design Museum Holon*; *Elma Arts Complex*; and Cymbalista Synagogue (D7).

Complementary **Tel Aviv (#5); Modern Movement (Bauhaus Architecture) (#16); Feynan Ecolodge (#86);** *Bialik House*; *Mamilla Hotel*; *Rockefeller Archaeological Museum*; *Separation Wall*; *Supreme Court of Israel*; *Weizmann Institute of Science*; *YMCA*; Ashdod Performing Arts Center (E3); Azrieli Center (D3); Beit Ha'ir (D3); Beresheet Hotel (J2); Beit Gabriel (G3); Beit Shmuel-Mercaz Shimshon (A7); Bonem House (A7); Brown TLV (D4); Consulate General of Belgium/Villa Salameh (A7);

Crazy House (D1); Dizengoff Center (D3); Hebrew University, Safra Campus (A8); Goldstein Synagogue (A8); Jerusalem Theatre (A7); Museum for Islamic Art (A7); Matcal Tower (D3); Opera Tower (D1); Pagoda House (D4); Ramot Polin Apartments (C4); Schocken Villa and Library (A7); Spiral Apartment House (D7); Tabor House (A7); and Yad Ben Zvi Institute for Judaeo-Arab Studies (A7).

BEAUTIFUL STRUCTURES We've discussed the modern. And there's the downright beautiful. (There will be overlap.) For photography buffs, this is a great list to start your journey. Of course **Petra (#2)** is stunning and the **Dome of the Rock (#6)** is beautiful from every angle. But we're highlighting some lesser-known gems: a Calatrava bridge in downtown Jerusalem and an oft-overlooked freestanding Mamluk structure on Temple Mount.

Best examples **Bridge of Strings** and **Fountain of Sultan Qaytbay**.

Complementary **Petra (#2)**; **Dome of the Rock (#6)**; **Israel Museum (#17)**; **Yad Vashem (#35)**; **Jerusalem Walls and Gates (#47)**; **Tel Aviv Museum of Art (#95)**; *Basilica of the Annunciation*; *Design Museum Holon*; *Dome of the Chain*; *YMCA*; and Church of Mary Magdalene (A5).

SKYLINE Every city has a skyline, sometimes designed and sometimes organically constructed. Some cities are so famous you can pick them out merely by their silhouette. That might not be our downtowns (yet), but there are some very noteworthy buildings that make for a fun game of name-that-skyscraper.

Tel Aviv Dan Tel Aviv (D1); Opera Tower (D1); Jaffa Clock Tower (D2); Azrieli Center (D3); Marganit Tower (D3); and Moshe Aviv Tower (D7).

Jerusalem **Dome of the Rock (#6)**; **Church of the Holy Sepulchre (#9)**; **Citadel/Tower of David (#32)**; **Jerusalem Walls and Gates (#47)**; *YMCA*; *Bridge of Strings*; Montefiore's Windmill (A7); Lutheran Church of the Redeemer (A2); and *Church of the Ascension (A5)*.

ENGINEERING

IMPRESSIVE FEATS There are so many impressionable sites in the region that we'd be remiss to not mention most everything on our list, but when it comes to these impressive feats of engineering, architecture, and physics, we can't help but be left speechless.

Beit Guvrin is an absolutely remarkable series of thousands of caves used for a variety of purposes – including raising doves, pressing oil, and burying the dead – underneath the twin cities of Maresha (dating to the First Temple period) and Beit Guvrin (from the Roman era through to the Crusaders).

Wadi Qelt is home to stunning cliffside monasteries, with St. George presenting as the most complete, if not also the most precariously situated, though it has remained stable since the 5th century CE (repaired in the 19th century).

Best examples **Beit Guvrin and Maresha (#60)** and **St. George's Monastery and Wadi Qelt (#97)**.

Complementary **Petra (#2)**; **Masada (#8)**; **Western Wall (#11)**; **Temple Mount (#12)**; **Bahá'í Gardens (#27)**; **Herodion (#90)**; **Western Wall Tunnels (#94)**; *Bridge of Strings*; and *Deir Quruntal*.

TECHNOLOGICAL ADVANCEMENT Some of our sites showcase human innovation, historically and in the modern era. Most impressive? UNESCO darling (approved shortly after submission), the Battir Hills are a series of stepped terraces designed for controlled irrigation farming via sluice gates during the Roman era, and are still used today in the region of Battir just outside of Bethlehem.

Best example **Battir Hills.**

Complementary **Dead Sea (#3)**; **Akko (#13)**; **Timna (#96)**; *Hamat Gader*; and *Nahal Me'arot/Wadi el-Mughara*.

INFRASTRUCTURE Here, we look at some of the elements of construction that propelled our area into the annals of history. We don't recommend you leave Jerusalem without a visit to the **Western Wall Tunnels (#94)**, where you can walk the streets of ancient Jerusalem, see the original walls of Herod's **Temple Mount (#12)**, and marvel at the construction that holds up the current city of Jerusalem from dozens of meters "below ground" – but from what is the actual ground level.

Best example **Western Wall Tunnels (#94).**

Complementary **Dead Sea (#3)**; **Masada (#8)**; **Western Wall (#11)**; **Temple Mount (#12)**; **Jericho and Hisham's Palace (#26)**; **Jerusalem Walls and Gates (#47)**; **Megiddo (#59)**; **Beit Guvrin and Maresha (#60)**; **Herodion (#90)**; **Ramparts Walk (#91)**; *Bridge of Strings*; *Cardo*; *Church of St. Anne and the Pools of Bethesda*; *City of David*; *Fountain of Sultan Qaytbay*; *Hezekiah's Tunnel*; *Separation Wall*; *Shobak*; *Tulul Abu el-Alaiq*; Ecce Homo Arch (A2); Pool of the Arches/Al-Anazia (D8); and Solomon's Pools (C2).

Nature

GEOGRAPHY

GEOLOGICAL WONDERS If you're interested in the wacky and wonderful ways the Earth creates beauty (and sometimes chaos), the Holy Land has some options for you. Some of the superlatives to be found here include: the lowest place on Earth, one of the saltiest bodies of water on Earth, beautiful beaches, lush hills, a mountain with snow, a vast desert, a unique series of craters, natural caves which transitioned humans to agriculturists, and forests. These are just some of the highlights of this compact, interesting, and diverse land.

The Dead Sea is impressively low and salty. Makhtesh Ramon is the largest erosion crater in Israel, and the world. At Rosh HaNikra, watch the lapping of the waves slowly erode this chalk cliff on the northern border with Lebanon.

Best examples **Dead Sea (#3)**; **Makhtesh Ramon (#28)**; and *Rosh HaNikra*.

Complementary **Petra (#2)**; **Masada (#8)**; *Hamat Gader*; *Little Petra*; *Red Canyon*; Amram's Pillars (L3); Coloured Canyon (T1); Mount Sodom (K1); Stalactite Caves (B2); *Blue Hole (T1)*.

GEOGRAPHICAL SUPERLATIVES The highest, the lowest, the first, the only. Let's go over some of the places that bring out the superlatives in our electives: **Dead Sea (#3)**, lowest place on Earth and one of the saltiest bodies of water; **Jericho (#26)**, oldest walled city on Earth; **Tsfat/Safed (#58)**, highest city in Israel; and *Mount Hermon*, tallest mountain in the region, and of the Anti-Lebanon mountain range.

RIVERS, LAKES, AND WATERFALLS Despite its desert setting, this region has a variety of water features of interest, particularly for those that are tired of the beach. There's kayaking in the Jordan River, water sports on the Kinneret/Sea of Galilee, and several national parks/reserves that revolve around oases, incorporating beautiful walks.

Wadi Mujib has a great (wet!) river walk. Gamla has a great river walk to a powerful waterfall. Kids and adults alike appreciate the naturally heated lakes/pools at Gan HaShlosha. And Hula Lake is the breeding ground for several bird species.

Best examples **Wadi Mujib and Mujib Biosphere Reserve (#23)**; *Gamla*; *Gan HaShlosha*; and *Hula Lake*.

Complementary **Ein Gedi (#50)**; **Golan Heights (#62)**; **Tel Dan (#63)**; **Ein Avdat (#74)**; **Banias (#80)**; **Timna (#96)**; *Tiberias*; *Yehudiya*; Ayun Stream (H2); Birkat Ram (I2); Ein Afeq (E5); Jordan River Rafting (I1); Kinneret Trail (G3); Nahal el-Al (I3); Nahal Taninim (E4); Wadi al-Hassa (O1); and *Wadi Daraja (K1)*.

MOUNTAINS AND MOUNTS The highest peak in the Levant region is Qumat as-Sawda in Lebanon, at 3,088m. Mount Hermon – a snow-capped peak in Lebanon, partly in the Golan Heights and serving as a ski resort from Israel – is 2,814m. Mount Catherine is the tallest peak in the Sinai at 2,629m, and the famed Mount Sinai can be found just adjacent at 2,285m. Jordan's tallest peak is Jabal Umm ad-Dami at 1,854m. Mount Nabi Yunis near Hebron is 1,020m and is the highest peak in Palestine. Mount Meron in the Galilee rounds out the list as the tallest place in Green Line Israel at 1,204m. Some of our more popular tourist destinations include Mount of Olives (826m), Mount Nebo (808m), Mount Zion (765m), and Mount Moriah/Temple Mount (740m).

Here are a few places where you can get your mountain hike/bike on! Try these mountainous zones: **Golan Heights (#62)**; *Mount Arbel*; *Mount Carmel*; *Mount Gerizim*; *Mount Gilboa*; *Mount Hermon*; Mount Karkom (L2); **Mount Nebo (#24)**; *Mount of Beatitudes*; *Deir Quruntal*; **Mount Sinai (#15)**; Mount Sodom (K1); Mount Tabor/*Church of the Transfiguration*; and St. Catherine's Mount (T1).

These popular hikes will take you through mountainous regions: Amram's Pillars (L3); Golan Trail (I2); Israel Bike Trail (U); *Israel National Trail*; **Jesus Trail (#69)**; Jordanian Wildflowers (S2); *Red Canyon*; *Sataf*; and *Wadi Daraja (K1)*.

These sites let you walk up the sides of mountains: **Ein Gedi (#50)**; *Mar Saba*; **Masada (#8)**; *Masada's Roman Trails (K1)*; *Mukawir*; **Nablus (#61)**; **Petra (#2)**; *Shobak*; **St. Catherine's Monastery (#22)**; **St. George's Monastery and Wadi Qelt (#97)**; and **Umm Qais (#45)**.

DESERT Some 75% of Jordan is desert. On the whole, the desert can be classified as part of the **North Arab Desert**, which extends into the neighboring countries of Iraq, Syria, and Saudi Arabia. Within the large desert, there are subdeserts with their own titles that define certain characteristics. The most famous in our group is the **Rum Desert**, from which we get Wadi Rum with its sandstone formations and hills of ochre sand. The **Eastern Desert** has water sources that have created animal sanctuaries, like at the Shaumari Wildlife Reserve. People have been living nomadically in these deserts for perhaps 10,000 years or more. The **Al-Harrah** basalt desert of Syria, Jordan, and Saudi Arabia contains thousands of rock drawings representing a wide swath of times and peoples (and has been nominated for UNESCO status).

The largest desert in Israel is the **Negev**, comprising the bottom half of the entire country. This is primarily a rocky desert, with a few sand dunes, some high plateaus, makhtesh craters, and the occasional rainfall. It's hot all year, but winter temperatures can get below freezing. The Negev continues across the border to the Egyptian Sinai, where it is known as the **Sinai Desert**. There's another popular desert area on the west side of the Dead Sea, known as the Judean Desert, which hosts Masada, Ein Gedi, and the Qumran caves.

Best examples **Wadi Rum (#4)**; **Wadi Mujib and Mujib Biosphere Reserve (#23)**; **Makhtesh Ramon (#28)**; **Ein Avdat (#74)**; **Timna (#96)**; and **Wadi Qelt (#97)**.

Complementary **Dead Sea (#3)**; **Masada (#8)**; **Jericho and Hisham's Palace (#26)**; **Avdat (#48)**; **Dahab (#54)**; **Azraq Wetlands (#55)**; **Qumran (#70)**; **Incense Route (#73)**; **Umm ar-Rasas (#81)**; **Feynan Ecolodge (#86)**; *Camel Riding*; *Hiking in the Negev*; *Hot Air Balloon Ride Over Wadi Rum*; *Israel National Trail*; *Little Petra*; *Mamshit*; *Mitzpe Ramon*; *Red Canyon*; *Yotvata Hai-Bar*; Al-Auja (C3); Astronomy Israel (J2); Beer Sheva (J1); Camel Safari (T1); Dead Sea Scrolls (A8); Israel Bike Trail (U); Jordanian Wildflowers (S2); Mount Sodom (K1); Negev Camping (J2); Negev Wine Route (J2); Neot HaKikar (K1); Rift Valley (V); Sde Boker (J2); Shkedi's Camplodge (K1); Wadi al-Dahik (R1); Wadi al-Hassa (O1); Wadi Ein Netafim (L2); Wadi Nasb (T1); *Dimona (J1)*; *Driving Highway 90 (K1)*; *Driving Through the Negev (J2)*; *Masada's Roman Trails (K1)*; *Wadi Daraja (K1)*; *Wadi Jadid (O1)*; and *Yeruham (J1)*.

CANYONS, WADIS, AND MAKHTESHIM Some definitions for common geological formations in the Holy Land: a **canyon** (aka gorge) is a deep and narrow depression in the land, usually formed by water, surrounded by steep sides; a **crater** is a collapse in the land from a meteor impact or a volcanic eruption; a **makhtesh** is a geological formation unique to the Negev and Sinai deserts where erosion creates a crater-like area, though it is technically not a crater; a **valley** is a depression in the land, usually formed by water, but less steep and deep than a canyon; and **wadi** is an Arabic word for "desert valley," typically dry except during rains.

Best examples **Wadi Rum (#4)**; **Wadi Mujib and Mujib Biosphere Reserve (#23)**; and **Makhtesh Ramon (#28)**.

Complementary **Feynan Ecolodge (#86)**; **St. George's Monastery and Wadi Qelt (#97)**; *Mitzpe Ramon*; *Nahal Me'arot/Wadi el-Mughara*; *Red Canyon*; *Yehudiya*; Coloured Canyon (T1); Shuqba/Natuf Caves (C5); Wadi al-Dahik (R1); Wadi al-Hassa (O1); Wadi Ein Netafim (L2); Wadi Nasb (T1); *Wadi Daraja (K1)*; and *Wadi Jadid (O1)*.

FORESTS AND GREEN PARKS This region of the world is filled with geographical diversity, and many will be surprised how green much of Israel is. Jordan and Egypt, too, have forested areas to complement their mostly desert environs. If you're trying to escape the heat or looking for ample green space for a family picnic, try:

Best examples **Ein Gedi (#50)** and **Ajloun Forest (#57)**.

Complementary **Golan Heights (#62)**; **Jesus Trail (#69)**; **Banias (#80)**; *Israel National Trail*; *Yehudiya*; Dibeen Forest (S2); HaYarkon Park (D7); Israel Bike Trail (U); Umm ar-Rihan Forest (C5); and Yarmouk Forest (S1).

CAVES/GROTTOES Caves can develop by any number of methods: water erosion, plate tectonics and earthquakes, wind, and organic and chemical decay. Due to the arid weather conditions in the region, caves have been instrumental in preserving the historic record in the Holy Land, from the first agricultural civilizations at Nahal Me'arot to the Dead Sea Scrolls at the Qumran caves.

Grottoes are a type of cave, which can be manmade or natural, whose origin comes from the Latin word for crypt. In a religious sense, grottoes are often used as sanctuaries or shrines and have been tied to a number of historical events, including the birth of Jesus.

Caves to explore **Beit Guvrin and Maresha (#60)**; **Banias (#80)**; **Timna (#96)**; *Nahal Me'arot/ Wadi el-Mughara*; *Mount Arbel*; *Rosh HaNikra*; *Lot's Cave*; Stalactite Caves (B2); and Shuqba/Natuf Caves (C5).

Grottoes to visit **Church of the Holy Sepulchre (#9)**; **Church of the Nativity (#18)**; *Basilica of the Annunciation*; *Church of St. Anne and the Pools of Bethesda*; *Stella Maris*; Church of the Paternoster (A5); and Garden Tomb (A6).

EARTHQUAKES Our region rests (un)comfortably between two major tectonic plates: the African plate and the Arabian plate. These two plates have been sliding against one another for the past several million years. Though both are moving northwards, the Arabian plate is moving at a faster pace than the African plate, which has caused some serious geological events, including several major earthquakes and creating a pull-apart basin, which is a depression in the land that forms when two plates undergo tension and cause the earth to sink. Around 18,000 years ago, the water that had filled this basin – running from the Sea of Galilee all the way to the Dead Sea, called Lake Lisan – lost its access to the sea and the water became a lake. The region began experiencing more desertification, and the Dead Sea dried up substantially. Over time, the lake retained its minerals and grew saltier as the water evaporated faster than the lake could be replenished.

This fault line, called the Dead Sea Fault, is one part of the longer Rift Valley (V), which extends from the Beqaa Valley in Lebanon down to Mozambique off the southern coast of Africa. It's hypothesized that this rift will eventually split the African continent into two pieces.

As you may have noticed, many of the famed sites of the Holy Land lie in ruins – this is often due to collapse from seismic activity and subsequent abandonment by the site's residents. Here are some of the major seismic events in recorded history and what they destroyed:

31 BCE: Joseph Flavius writes of an earthquake that killed 30,000 men.
363 CE: Petra, Sepphoris/Tzippori.
551: Further destroyed Petra.
749: Cities of the Decapolis largely destroyed – Beit She'an, Pella, Jerash, Hippos, Capernaum.
1033: Al-Aqsa Mosque, Tiberias.
1837: Safed Earthquake, 6,000+ deaths.
1927: Jericho Earthquake, lots of damage (Al-Aqsa, Church of the Holy Sepulchre, Nablus).

Many believe the Holy Land is long overdue for a massive earthquake. The last major earthquake struck the Galilee in 1847 and killed several thousand people.

Complementary **Old City Jerusalem (#1)**; **Petra (#2)**; **Akko (#13)**; **Jerash (#14)**; **Caesarea (#25)**; **Jericho and Hisham's Palace (#26)**; **Capernaum and Tabgha (#33)**; **Beit She'an (#39)**; **Jerusalem Walls and Gates (#47)**; **Tsipori (#56)**; **Tsfat/Safed (#58)**; **Nablus (#61)**; **Al-Aqsa Mosque (#65)**; **Beit She'arim (#79)**; *Ancient Qatzrin*; *Pella*; *Tiberias*; Cities of the Decapolis (W3); Rift Valley (V); and White Mosque (D8).

LIFE

ANIMALS, ZOOS, AND WILDLIFE The Holy Land sits at a convenient migration point for animals (and humans!). Historically, both temperate and tropical animals could be found in this part of the world. More recently, human civilization and the climate and land desertification have caused many of the bigger animals to become extinct or migrate elsewhere, including bears, leopards, cheetahs, and other region-specific species. Still, Israel and Jordan have each created wildlife reserves to preserve the land for its use by indigenous plants and animals. The Hai-Bars in Israel (Carmel in the north, Yotvata in the south) and Shaumari have all worked to reintroduce regionally extinct species back into their native habitats. Visit a range of antelope, big cats, ostrich, and other large animals.

Best examples **Carmel Hai-Bar**; **Shaumari**; and **Yotvata Hai-Bar**.

Complementary **Dana Biosphere Reserve (#21)**; **Wadi Mujib and Mujib Biosphere Reserve (#23)**; **Makhtesh Ramon (#28)**; **Azraq Wetlands (#55)**; **Ajloun Forest (#57)**; **Golan Heights (#62)**; *Camel Riding*; *Gamla*; *Hamat Gader*; *Hula Lake*; *Mitzpe Ramon*; *Mount Carmel*; Alpaca Farm

(J2); Gan Garoo (F2); Kibbutz Merom Golan (I2); Negev Goat Farms (J2); Safari Park (D8); Camel Safari (T1); and Tisch Family Zoological Gardens (B1).

SEA CREATURES, REEFS, AND AQUARIA With five major bodies of water adjacent, there is a surprising variety of sea life in the vicinity (notably, one – the Dead Sea – does not support life). Ras Mohammad in the Sinai is even considered by some to be the world's best diving spot (which you can check out in the *Diving* category, p. 552). The reef in the Red Sea is considered to be the northernmost coral reef in the world. Get a glimpse at the Underwater Observatory in Eilat.

Best examples **Red Sea/Gulf of Aqaba (#10)**; **Ras Mohammad (#53)**; and *Underwater Observatory*.

Complementary **Aqaba (#43)**; **Coral Beach (#83)**; *Hamat Gader*; Dolphin Reef (L2); and Marine Science Station Aquarium (M2).

BIRDING Birding fanatics know that the Holy Land is a landing point for many migratory birds. In fact, millions of birds from more than 300 species fly through Israel each year and upwards of 400 species fly through Jordan on their north–south adventure.

BirdLife International (w birdlife.org) has identified 18 sites in Jordan and 15 sites in Israel as Important Bird Areas (IBAs), meaning that the region meets one of four criteria: having either a regular presence of a globally threatened species; a restricted-range species; a biome-restricted species; or congregations of species of wetland or other seabirds. It has also listed the Levantine Mountains as an Endemic Bird Area (EBA), located in parts of Israel and Jordan, as well as Lebanon and Syria. These areas are defined as a place where at least two bird species are restricted to a migration range of smaller than 50,000km², meaning the birds are endemic to the area.

Additionally, there are several wetlands of importance as designated by the Ramsar Convention for the Conservation of Wetlands, which includes Hula Lake and the Ein Afek Nature Reserve in Israel and the Azraq and Fifa reserves in Jordan.

Best examples **Azraq Wetlands (#55)** and *Hula Lake*.

Complementary **Wadi Rum (#4)**; **Dana Biosphere Reserve (#21)**; **Wadi Mujib and Mujib Biosphere Reserve (#23)**; **Aqaba (#43)**; **Ajloun Forest (#57)**; *Gamla*; *Shaumari*; El Bariyeh/Wadi Khareitun/Nahal Teqoa (C2); Umm ar-Rihan Forest (C5); and Wadi Ein Netafim (L2).

PLANTS, GARDENS, AND FARMS With abundant wildlife comes a variety of types of plant communities. Israel recognizes some 19 principal plant communities (e.g., oak woodlands, steppe, desert, sand, and oases), while Jordan counts 13 (e.g., juniper forests, Aleppo pine, acacia, sand dune, mud flat, and tropical vegetation). Scientists have identified four principal contributing factors to the region's floral diversity: humans, climate, rock/soil, and the topography of the land. Indeed, the varied climate of Israel (from snow in the north to the desert sun in the south) has meant a wide variety of trees, plants, flowers, and other green life has found its way to this compact area.

Best example Iris Reserve (E4).

Complementary **Dana Biosphere Reserve (#21)**; **Wadi Mujib and Mujib Biosphere Reserve (#23)**; **Umm Qais (#45)**; **Azraq Wetlands (#55)**; **Ajloun Forest (#57)**; **Golan Heights (#62)**; **Belvoir (#93)**; *Mount Carmel*; *Mount Gilboa*; Dibeen Forest (S2); Ein Afeq (E5); Fifa Nature Reserve (P1); Horshat Tal (I1); Jordanian Wildflowers (S2); Negev Goat Farms (J2); Neot Kedumim Biblical Landscape (B2); Ramat HaNadiv (E4); *Picking Fruit (I2)*; *Scarlet South Festival (E3)*; and *Yeruham (J1)*.

PARKS

GORGEOUS SCENERY Some places just need to be seen to be believed. From the deserts of the Negev and Rum to the sandstone mountains to the stunning beaches and seas, there's a lot to fall in love with. Just shy of BUCKET! status, Wadi Rum has something for everyone in its remote corner of Jordan. Come for the gorgeous red rolling sand and strange rock formations, stay for the Bedouin camping, dark skies, petroglyphs, adventure sports, climbing, trekking, and horseback riding.

Best example **Wadi Rum (#4)**.

Complementary **Petra (#2)**; **Dead Sea (#3)**; **Tel Aviv (#5)**; **Dana Biosphere Reserve (#21)**; **Wadi Mujib and Mujib Biosphere Reserve (#23)**; **Makhtesh Ramon (#28)**; **Jesus Trail (#69)**; **Dor HaBonim (#100)**; *Hot Air Balloon Ride Over Wadi Rum*; *Israel National Trail*; and *Red Canyon*.

PARKS There are several places that administer parklands in the Holy Land. Visit our *Spotlight* categories (p. 482) for more details on the national parks, reserves, and UNESCO sites.

The **Israel Nature and Parks Authority** (w parks.org.il) is a government authority that has been responsible for the National Parks and Nature Reserves in Israel and the Palestinian territories since 1963, with the goal of protecting the country's natural and heritage sites. There are more than 60 parks and reserves in its system. The Keren Kayemeth LeIsrael – Jewish National Fund (**KKL-JNF**; w kkl-jnf. org) seeks to strengthen the bond between Jewish people and historic Israel. Since 1901 it has planted more than 220 million trees, built roads, water reservoirs, and recreational areas around the country. The Convention Concerning the Protection of the World Cultural and Natural Heritage established the **UNESCO World Heritage Site** program (w whc.unesco.org), now with more than 1,000 protected sites around the world. Israel has nine inscriptions making up 16 sites while Jordan has five UNESCO-designated cultural and natural sites. And the most impressive organization is the Royal Society for the Conservation of Nature (**RSCN**; w rscn.org.jo), which is responsible for protecting the nine (and growing!) protected wildlife areas in Jordan. In addition to conservation projects, it also administers the eco-tourism site and project Wild Jordan.

Our pick for best park? Gamla. This nature reserve has a bit of everything: Bronze Age dolmens, Israel's tallest waterfall, an early synagogue, Roman-era ruins, several walking paths, observation points, and a hulking vulture that nests here.

Best examples **Gamla** and **Royal Society for the Conservation of Nature (RSCN)**.

Complementary **Tel Aviv (#5)**; **Bahá'í Gardens (#27)**; **Golan Heights (#62)**; *Ein Hemed*; *Haifa*; *Hula Lake*; *Shrine of Bahá'u'lláh*; **Tel Ashkelon**; *Weizmann Institute of Science*; Eshkol (E3); HaYarkon Park (D7); Jabotinsky Park (E4); and *Rishon Letzion (D8)*.

THE GREAT OUTDOORS If you're just looking to get outside without much of a plan, you can certainly find plenty to keep you entertained in the following locations:

Best examples **Dana Biosphere Reserve (#21)**; **Wadi Mujib and Mujib Biosphere Reserve (#23)**; and **Golan Heights (#62)**.

Complementary **Dead Sea (#3)**; **Wadi Rum (#4)**; **Makhtesh Ramon (#28)**; **Azraq Wetlands (#55)**; **Ajloun Forest (#57)**; **Jesus Trail (#69)**; **Ein Avdat (#74)**; **Banias (#80)**; **Coral Beach (#83)**; **Feynan Ecolodge (#86)**; **Timna (#96)**; **Dor HaBonim (#100)**; *Akhziv Beach*; *Gamla*; *Hiking in the Negev*; *Hot Air Balloon Ride Over Wadi Rum*; *Hula Lake*; *Little Petra*; *Montfort*; *Mount Carmel*; *Mount Gilboa*; *Mount Hermon*; *Petra by Night*; *Red Canyon*; *Tel Aviv Port*; *Yehudiya*; *Yotvata Hai-Bar*; Amram's Pillars (L3); Astronomy Israel (J2); Camel Safari (T1); Dolphin Reef (L2); Golan Trail (I2); Haas Promenade (B1); Jordan River Rafting (I1); Jordanian Wildflowers (S2); Kibbutz Ein Gev (G3); Kibbutz Merom Golan (I2); Mount Sodom (K1); Negev Camping (J2); Rift Valley (V); Wadi al-Hassa (O1); Wadi Ein Netafim (L2); *Wadi Daraja (K1)*; *Wadi Jadid (O1)*; and *Yeruham (J1)*.

Scenic

VISTAS

URBAN LANDSCAPE There are some great spots from where you can view cities in their glory. Some involve elevators, some involve driving to the top of a tall hill, and some offer a bird's-eye view of the action below. The Ramparts Walk lets you peer down on Old City Jerusalem life in the Christian, Muslim, and Armenian quarters as you walk from Jaffa Gate either north or south along the tops of the spectacular old Ottoman walls. At the YMCA, buy a ticket (or stay the night) to visit the tower for a 360° view of Jerusalem, old and new.

Best examples **Ramparts Walk (#91)** and *YMCA*.

Complementary **Jericho and Hisham's Palace (#26)**; **Bahá'í Gardens (#27)**; **Citadel/Tower of David (#32)**; **Mount of Olives (#34)**; **Nablus (#61)**; **Jesus Trail (#69)**; *Deir Quruntal*; *Mount Gilboa*; *Wild Jordan Center*; *Yemen Moshe*; Azrieli Center (D3); Church of the Beheading of John the Baptist (P2); Haas Promenade (B1); Lutheran Church of the Redeemer (A2); and Kikar Levana/White Square (D8); *Church of the Ascension (A5)*.

HISTORICAL VANTAGE What did the previous generations see when standing on this very spot hundreds, if not thousands, of years ago? Each of the places below indicates a location in history that was used for scouting, protecting, or just taking in the views. At Mount Arbel, gaze down upon one of the most important battle sites in history, the Horns of Hattin. Mount Sinai provides picturesque views that would have captivated Moses, and Mount Nebo is where Moses last viewed the Promised Land.

Best examples **Mount Sinai (#15)**; **Mount Nebo (#24)** and *Mount Arbel*.

Complementary **Masada (#8)**; **Mount of Olives (#34)**; **Tsipori (#56)**; **Golan Heights (#62)**; **Jesus Trail (#69)**; **Ajloun Fortress (#76)**; **Nimrod's Fortress (#85)**; **Belvoir (#93)**; *Montfort*; *Mukawir*; *Shobak*; *Tel Arad*; Mount Bental Lookout (I2); Gadot Lookout (I2); and Golan Lookout/Tel Faher (I1).

EARTH PANORAMA Looking for sweeping vistas of Mother Earth? Check out the sites below. Or use KKL's scenic lookout map to find dozens of options as you plan your country road trip (w kkl-jnf.org/tourism-and-recreation/scenic-lookouts/map/). If you're going to pick one spot to peer out over nature, go with Makhtesh Ramon: the world's largest erosion crater, with stunning rusty-colored desert in a great expanse, as seen from Mitzpe Ramon or by hiking inside the makhtesh itself. Wadi Rum is also a stunner.

Best examples **Wadi Rum (#4)**; **Makhtesh Ramon (#28)**; and *Mitzpe Ramon*.

Complementary **Masada (#8)**; **Mount Sinai (#15)**; **Dana Biosphere Reserve (#21)**; **Wadi Mujib and Mujib Biosphere Reserve (#23)**; **Mount Nebo (#24)**; **King's Highway (#31)**; Umm

Qais (#45); Avdat (#48); Ajloun Forest (#57); Golan Heights (#62); Jesus Trail (#69); Ein Avdat (#74); Nimrod's Fortress (#85); Timna (#96); St. George's Monastery and Wadi Qelt (#97); *Battir Hills*; *Church of the Transfiguration*; *Gamla*; *Hiking in the Negev*; *Little Petra*; *Mar Saba*; *Mount Carmel*; *Mount Gilboa*; *Mukawir*; *Sataf*; *Underwater Observatory*; Mount Bental Lookout (I2); Beresheet Hotel (J2); Birkat Ram (I2); Einot Tsukim (K1); Kibbutz Ein Gev (G3); Ophir Lookout (I3); Peace Vista (I3); Camel Safari (T1); Snir Stream (I1); and Wadi al-Dahik (R1).

ABOVE EARTH Sometimes a 360° view just isn't enough. How about adding in some adventure sporting to your scenic flight? These two options will be experiences you'll never forget.

Best examples **Hot Air Balloon Ride Over Wadi Rum** and *Powered Parachute Flight above Dead Sea/Masada (K1)*.

SKY For those travelers who take an interest in the night sky, you can find information on solar and lunar eclipses at w timeanddate.com/eclipse/, or check your dates for meteor showers (w timeanddate.com/astronomy/meteor-shower/list.html). Below, Feynan has a telescope to view the night sky, while Astronomy Israel takes you deep into the Negev for that delicious dark-sky viewing.

Best examples **Feynan Ecolodge (#86)** and Astronomy Israel (J2).

Complementary **Wadi Rum (#4); Dana Biosphere Reserve (#21); Dor HaBonim (#100);** *Underwater Observatory*; *Petra by Night*; *Mitzpe Ramon*; and Wadi al-Dahik (R1).

SUNRISE/SUNSET We've got exquisite views at dawn and dusk. For sunset, anywhere along Tel Aviv's beachfront will provide a spectacular sunset, night after night. Mount Sinai is famous for midnight walks to catch the sunrise. And hang out in Jerusalem long enough to climb a tower as the sun starts to set to catch the glistening rays off the pink limestone.

Best examples **Mount Sinai (#15)**; *Tel Aviv Tayelet/Promenade*; and Twilight in Jerusalem (A2).

Complementary **Wadi Rum (#4); Tel Aviv (#5); Sea of Galilee (#7); Masada (#8); Nimrod's Fortress (#85); Timna (#96); Dor HaBonim (#100);** *Beit Yannai*; *Drummers' Beach*; *Haifa*; *Mediterranean Coast*; Negev Camping (J2); and Camel Safari (T1).

PEOPLE-WATCHING If you're up for a sit with a coffee while watching passers-by, we recommend Rothschild while in Tel Aviv and Ben Yehuda in West Jerusalem. To see the streetscape of the Old City from a secret vantage, don't miss the Ramparts Walk.

Best examples **Ramparts Walk (#91)**; *Rothschild Boulevard*; and *Ben Yehuda Street*.

Complementary **Old City Jerusalem (#1); Tel Aviv (#5); Dome of the Rock (#6); Church of the Holy Sepulchre (#9); Western Wall (#11); Mea She'arim (#66);** *Café Culture*; *Tel Aviv Port*; *Tel Aviv Tayelet/Promenade*; Florentin (D4); Hurva Square (A4); Nahalat Binyamin (D4); Nakhalat Shiva (A7); and Sheinkin Street (D4).

MOST PHOTOGRAPHED Any of these sites will put you in good company, as they are the most famous of sites and among the most photographed places – for good reason! We have two favorites. The first is Petra, whose first major surprise (the Treasury) is so stunning that you can't help but whip out your camera. The other is Mount of Olives, from where you get the best long view of the Old City in all its glory.

Best examples **Petra (#2)** and **Mount of Olives (#34)**.

Complementary **Dead Sea (#3)**; **Tel Aviv (#5)**; **Dome of the Rock (#6)**; **Masada (#8)**; **Madaba (#19)**; **Bahá'í Gardens (#27)**; **Makhtesh Ramon (#28)**; **Jaffa (#30)**; **Citadel/Tower of David (#32)**; **Bethlehem (#40)**; **Israeli Cuisine (#51)**; **Mehane Yehuda Market (#67)**; **Machneyuda (#98)**; *Ben Yehuda Street*; *Haifa*; *Tel Aviv Tayelet/Promenade*; and *Underwater Observatory*.

SCENIC DRIVES

Sometimes it's more about the journey… these routes allow for multiple stops, lots of breathtaking views, and a few noteworthy sites along the way.

On the King's Highway, drive along this ancient trade route in modern Jordan and visit Crusader castles, Roman mosaics, Nabataean cities, and biosphere reserves. And in the Golan Heights, our other favorite, you'll find a region unique in many ways, with lots of green space, snowy mountains in the north, Druze villages, several modern war sites, and famous wineries.

Be sure to consider the highways you pick as you drive from one region to the next, as there are some stunners.

Best examples **King's Highway (#31)**; **Golan Heights (#62)**; Dead Sea Highway (P1); *Driving Highway 90 (K1)*; and *Driving Through the Negev (J2)*.

Complementary **Dead Sea (#3)**; **Wadi Rum (#4)**; **Sea of Galilee (#7)**; **Qasr Amra and the Desert Palaces (#20)**; *Battir Hills*; *Mediterranean Coast*; *Mount Gilboa*; *Winery Tour*; *Yotvata Hai-Bar*; Jordanian Wildflowers (S2); Judean Hills Wineries (B3); Negev Wine Route (J2); and Wadi Nasb (T1).

Society

GOVERNMENT

POLITICS Both Israel and Palestine view Jerusalem as their capital. Israel's government campus is located just west of the Old City, near the Israel Museum. The Palestinian Authority is based in Ramallah in the West Bank, which at times has aligned itself with the Hamas government in Gaza, but these two entities are currently separate. Jordan's king sits in Amman, while the Sinai is part of Egypt whose president serves from Cairo.

The Supreme Court and Knesset in Israel can both be visited on tours, making them our choices here.

Best examples **Supreme Court of Israel** and Knesset (A8).

Complementary **Old City Jerusalem (#1)**; **Temple Mount (#12)**; **Modern Amman (#36)**; **Ramallah (#68)**; **Jerusalem, New City (#72)**; Beit Ha'ir (D3); and Russian Quarter (A7).

MILITARY A number of our sites deal with the military industrial complex. In Tel Aviv, the military still hold land right downtown near Sarona Market at HaKirya.

For those looking to immerse fully, converting to Judaism comes with a requirement to serve in the Israel Defense Forces (IDF). Called Tzahal, these are the armed forces of Israel, established in 1948 from the Haganah military group that fought for Israel's independence. Public service (either through IDF or another government-run program) is mandatory before university for both men and women. Non-Israelis can even sign up for short- or longer-term volunteer experiences.

Best example HaKirya (D3).

Complementary **Temple Mount (#12)**; **Golan Heights (#62)**; *Separation Wall*; Beit HaShomer Museum (H2); Mount Bental Lookout (I2); Clandestine Immigration & Naval Museum (E1); Gadot Lookout (I2); Tel Hai Fort (H2); *Dimona (J1)*; and Israeli Air Force Museum (J1).

LAND

BORDERS Borders are a major point of contention in this part of the world, always at the forefront of peace negotiations between Israelis and Palestinians, and something that people live and die to protect. Israel has fought multiple wars with its neighbors in the last 50 years to define its southern, eastern, and northern borders.

The United Nations does not recognize Israel's sovereignty over the West Bank or Gaza (collectively, Palestine), nor the Golan Heights (considered Syria). Nevertheless, Israel has exerted control over much of these territories via its powerful security apparatus.

The West Bank is often thought of as the home of Palestinians, but it has a large number of Jewish residents as well. Since 2005, Gaza has been self-administered.

Nothing symbolizes the separation between the two peoples greater than Israel's barrier wall, the *Separation Wall*, best viewed on a walking tour in Bethlehem, where

Banksy and other artists have expressed their opinion of the giant concrete block directly onto the wall itself.

Best example **Separation Wall**.

Complementary **Old City Jerusalem (#1)**; **Dead Sea (#3)**; **Dome of the Rock (#6)**; **Western Wall (#11)**; **Temple Mount (#12)**; **Bethany-Beyond-the-Jordan (#41)**; **Aqaba (#43)**; **Jerusalem Walls and Gates (#47)**; **Golan Heights (#62)**; **Eilat (#78)**; **Ramparts Walk (#91)**; *Mount Hermon*; *Rosh HaNikra*; Gadot Lookout (I2); Kerem Shalom (E3); Taba (T1); and Majdal Shams and The Shouting Hill (I2).

DISPUTED What *isn't* disputed in this area? Palestinians believe the entire country of Israel should comprise a future Palestinian state, though negotiations have tended to compromise on something much smaller. Israelis believe that the West Bank makes up historic Judea and Samaria and have gone almost as far as encouraging its citizens to take up residence in West Bank territory, considered by many countries and international organizations to be an illegal encroachment on Palestinian land.

Some of our Holy Land sites inhabiting disputed territories that you can still visit include: **Old City Jerusalem (#1)** – broken up into four quarters, the city also serves as the territorial distinction between Jewish West Jerusalem and Arab East Jerusalem; **Dome of the Rock (#6)**/**Temple Mount (#12)** – Jews are not allowed, though the Israeli military serves as security for the grounds, and Jordan is the custodian; **Church of the Holy Sepulchre (#9)** – control of this church is shared by six Christian denominations; **Western Wall (#11)** – the Moroccan quarter was bulldozed to create the Western Wall Plaza in 1967; **Bethany-Beyond-the-Jordan (#41)** – Israel claims its site, Qasr al-Yahud (C3), is contiguous with the baptism site of Bethany-Beyond-the-Jordan on the Jordanian side, a name attributed to the Book of John for a site located on the eastern bank of the Jordan River (present-day Jordan); *Separation Wall* – not following the never-implemented UN Green Line, this wall and border fence is subject of much debate due to its wild interpretations of Israeli territory; and **Golan Heights (#62)** – after more than 50 years of Israeli control, at which point is the site considered Israeli instead of Syrian?

CITIES

PRINCIPAL CITIES Our three main cities in the region are Jerusalem, Tel Aviv, and Amman. Not only are these the most populous centers in the Holy Land, but they're also each their own macro-region in our region groupings (see Part 8, *Electives by Region*). Below, we're going to discuss their population, the tourism industry, cost of living, biggest draws and problems, and we'll briefly discuss the economy based on international metrics.

Population The **Old City Jerusalem (#1)** is only a small part of what is today considered "Jerusalem." In fact, border walls, "Green Lines," and the Palestinian status make it difficult to classify where Jerusalem starts and stops. The Jerusalem District includes West Jerusalem (which we refer to as the "New City") and East Jerusalem (which we refer to as "East Jerusalem"), though the status of East Jerusalem is ever-controversial. Most countries recognize East Jerusalem as part of the West Bank, which is independent from Israel proper, albeit an unresolved point of contention between Israel and the Palestinian Authority. All-inclusive (if we are talking about metropolitan areas and not arbitrary boundaries), this district contained just shy of 1 million people in 2020. The area that Israelis occupy extends well beyond the Green

Line, the "Greater Jerusalem" line, and even past the "Metropolitan Jerusalem" line, going deeper and deeper into the West Bank each year.

The district of Tel Aviv is home to 1.35 million people, though the city itself houses only around 440,000. There are a number of established cities just outside of the Tel Aviv district, which could arguably be considered part of the greater Tel Aviv metropolitan area, called Gush Dan. When accounting for these districts, towns, neighborhoods, and smaller cities, then "Tel Aviv" hosts nearly half of the entire population of the country, with more than 4 million residents.

The last Jordanian census in 2016 counted more than 4 million people living in Amman, with a population in the entire country of Jordan of 9.5 million (30% are "guests," or refugees, including Syrians, Egyptians, and Palestinians). Of these 4 million, approximately 1.5 million are foreign guests.

Economies According to the Globalization and World Cities Research Network, which characterizes cities based on their connectivity to the global economy. Tel Aviv is classified as a Beta+ level city, with moderate links to the global economy. Amman is ranked Gamma, with small economic links to the world economy. Jerusalem does not classify on this scale, but is considered "Sufficient" with enough services to not be reliant on other world cities. On a separate index by the Brookings Institution in 2016, Tel Aviv was ranked as one of the world's "International Middleweights."

Tourism Israel saw a record 4.55 million tourists in 2019, up 11% over 2018, which itself was a record-breaking year. Jordan had 5.36 million visitors in 2019, also up from 2018 where it saw 4.9 million visitors. US citizens comprised roughly 865,000 of the 2019 Israeli visitors, while 191,000 visited Jordan. The subsequent years 2020 and 2021 will have been difficult due to COVID-19, but clearly Israel and the greater Holy Land have been identified as key spots on the tourist trail.

Cost of living and travel According to Numbeo (**w** numbeo.com), Tel Aviv is the 12th most expensive city in the world, above San Francisco and Tokyo. Compare this to Amman which is 261st out of 511 cities on the global index. An average meal for two people at a mid-range restaurant, according to the same index, places a three-course meal in Tel Aviv at $87.46, at $75.80 in Jerusalem, and $42.31 in Amman. In practice, these numbers are conservative in our estimation, with Israeli meals often costing more and Jordanian meals costing a bit less. The Budget Your Trip aggregator averages travel costs for a number of destinations around the world. Petra, for instance, averages 59 JOD/$83 per day for a mid-range stay; on the other hand, Amman, the biggest city, runs 40 JOD/$56 on average. Jerusalem averages 282 ILS/$82, while Tel Aviv's on the high end at 417 ILS/$122.

Biggest draws Tel Aviv is consistently ranked as one of the best beach cities, best food cities, and best gay travel destinations in the world. It's notorious for being laid back, hip, and popular for its nightlife and restaurant scene. Jerusalem is a much more diverse (if segregated) city, with tons of sites for all sorts of visitors. Amman, and Jordan in general, is inexpensive and under-appreciated, making it easy to explore without competition. Jordanians are warm and welcoming, and the country has managed to avoid cross-border conflicts with neighboring countries following the war with Israel in 1967.

Biggest problems Tel Aviv is one of the most expensive cities in the world, and its public transportation woes are legend in town. Jerusalem sees periodic flares of violence, from bus explosions and rammings to knife attacks and suicide bombers.

It's also an extremely divided city, with Jews living in the western portion and Arabs confined to the eastern part. Jordan tends to be a unique point of stability in a tumultuous Middle East region, driving millions of refugees to seek temporary cover there and creating constant challenges for the government and economy.

STREETS, SQUARES, AND PORTS Here are some of the more famous streets in our region. We recommend working them into your walking tours, or following our BUCKET! walking tours which will take you through the highlights. Don't miss Ben Yehuda Street in Jerusalem's New City, a pedestrian alley filled with life. Rothschild is Tel Aviv's most popular and elegant street, with cafés and Bauhaus buildings lining the boulevard. Tel Aviv's Port underwent an impressive renovation to increase foot traffic to its outdoor markets, restaurants, and shops. And Rainbow Street in Amman is every traveler's go-to for food and lodging.

Best examples **Ben Yehuda Street**; **Rothschild Boulevard**; **Tel Aviv Port**; and Rainbow Street (Q2).

Complementary **Akko (#13)**; **Jaffa (#30)**; **Bethlehem (#40)**; **Via Dolorosa (#42)**; **Haifa**; **Tel Aviv Tayelet/Promenade**; Haas Promenade (B1); Hurva Square (A4); Muristan (A2); Nahalat Binyamin (D4); Nakhalat Shiva (A7); Rabin Square (D3); Russian Quarter (A7); and Sheinkin Street (D4).

OTHER MAIN CITIES Though definitions can vary, we're counting a "city" as any settlement that houses more than 100,000 residents. Our favorite is Haifa. At only an hour from Tel Aviv, this Mediterranean coastal city in northern Israel has a laid-back vibe, proximity to a lot of green space (including the gorgeous **Bahá'í Gardens (#27)**), and some famous food establishments.

Best example **Haifa**.

Complementary **Aqaba (#43)**; **Nablus (#61)**; **Tel Ashkelon**; Beer Sheva (J1); Hebron (C2); and Rishon Letzion (D8).

TOWNS

LARGE TOWNS Technically, a "town" is any settlement with 1,000–100,000 residents. We've subdivided that further, to consider any large town to be a place with more than 10,000 residents. Here are some of the important ones in our region.

Israel **Akko (#13)** – Crusader ruins in the old town, great day trip; **Nazareth (#29)** – home of Mary, Joseph, and Jesus during childhood, with the towering *Basilica of the Annunciation*; **Tsfat/Safed (#58)** – spiritual center with Kabbalah mystics, a series of old but functioning synagogues, and artwork; **Eilat (#78)** – Red Sea resort town, very hot, good for long-weekend trip with swimming; *Tiberias* – main seaport on the Sea of Galilee/Kinneret; *Zichron Ya'akov* – artsy town with galleries, local wine, and gift shops; and Majdal Shams and The Shouting Hill (I2) – Druze village in the Golan Heights where residents shout across the hill to their family members on the Syrian side.

Palestine **Jericho (#26)** – best known for being one of the oldest cities in the world; **Bethlehem (#40)** – birthplace of Jesus and site of the Banksy art on the Separation Wall; **Ramallah (#68)** – major town just north of Jerusalem in the West Bank, with bars and nightlife; Dheisheh Refugee Camp (C2) – roughly 15,000 residents; and Jenin, a northern West Bank town popular for its Freedom Theatre (C5).

Jordan **Aqaba (#43)** – access to the Red Sea, cheaper alternative to Eilat; and ***As-Salt*** – home to Arab Eclecticism.

Sinai **Dahab (#54)** – laid back hippie stop on the Red Sea; **Sharm el-Sheikh (#88)** – ritzier beach town; and Taba (T1) – port city, cheaper option than Eilat or Aqaba, in Egypt.

SMALL TOWNS Thus, a "small town" is any establishment with c1,000–10,000 residents. Here are the electives that embrace their small-towniness enough to gain universal appeal.

Israel **Tsipori (#56)** – ancient ruins, synagogues, and galleries; ***Ein Hod*** – artists' town in Haifa district; ***Mitzpe Ramon*** – starting point for a trip into the Makhtesh Ramon erosion crater; Sde Boker (J2) – barely 1,000 people, this kibbutz was the last resting place of David Ben Gurion, now a museum to his home; Kfar Kama (G2) – Circassian village; and Ezuz (J2) – tiny tourist-friendly town near Egyptian border.

Palestine ***Mount Gerizim*** – home to a few hundred Samaritans; ***Sebastia-Shomron*** – town near Nablus next to the ruins of ancient Samaria-Sebaste; and Deir Ghassaneh (C5), famed for its Throne Village architecture.

COOPERATIVES

KIBBUTZIM The kibbutz is a type of community in Israel based on a shared economic model. Historically, this model has been based on socialism and agriculture, though in recent decades several kibbutzim have privatized and expanded to other industries, to include technology and manufacturing. Communities are usually tight-knit, with all members historically working for the collective profits to be shared equally among the members. Other collective activities include eating meals together and sharing in childcare responsibilities. The change in times has brought about a change in ideology, and the majority of kibbutzniks will now earn their own income but also share in the collective kibbutz earnings. By far the largest collective today is the Kibbutz Movement, with 230 kibbutzim located throughout Israel.

To experience kibbutz life, there's no better way than to get in and get dirty. Explore your options in the *Volunteer* category (p. 567). For visits, Kibbutz Lotan and Ketura – both in the south – each offer sustainable eco-tour options. Kibbutz Merom Golan and Ein Gev – communities in the north – provide more traditional weekend-away offerings.

Best examples **Kibbutz Lotan**; **Kibbutz Volunteer**; Kibbutz Ein Gev (G3); Kibbutz Merom Golan (I2); and Kibbutz Ketura (L3).

Complementary Kibbutz Degania (G3); Kibbutz Neot Smadar (L3); and Kibbutzim (U).

MOSHAVIM Moshavim are another example of collective farming in Israel. Whereas with kibbutzim the community members share in daily duties, earnings, and profits, in a moshav the sites are generally individually owned (though equal in size) with the profits going to the individual family owners, rather than the collective group. Depending on the type of moshav, the community will work together to purchase supplies, use farm labor, and market the sale of goods. The individual family unit has increased importance, so families eat together and raise their own children.

Options to visit Yad Hashmona (B1); Nahalal (G2); Rishpon (D7).

535

People

IDENTITY

JEWISH Who is a Jew? Who is Israeli? These are not simple questions. Jews are sometimes defined as an ethnic group, a religious group, and a cultural group. For the first time in millennia, more Jews live in Israel than in any other country. But nationality is not a defining feature, as there are millions of Americans who identify as *Jewish* but not necessarily *Israeli*.

Religiosity is also not a specific feature of being Jewish. Certainly, there are very religious Jews (see *Orthodox* below), but many Israeli Jews identify as secular, either not practicing regularly or not practicing at all. In their case, they may identify as culturally Jewish.

Israel is a country, recognized by the United Nations and most countries around the world. Israel considers itself the homeland of the Jewish people, and is a Jewish country, but it is home to more religions than Judaism (e.g., Muslims, Christians, and Bahá'í). The term "Israeli" includes all citizens of Israel, who needn't be Jewish, though the vast majority (roughly three-quarters) are Jewish. Around 2 million Israeli citizens living inside Green Line Israel or in East Jerusalem identify as Arab and hold Israeli citizenship.

Merely visiting Israel will afford you the opportunity to experience what it's like to be in a Jewish country. Yes, there are Jewish enclaves all around the world, but this is the only place on Earth where Jews have their own state and government, and it does feel different.

For perhaps the most succinct introduction to Jewish culture, try the Jewish Quarter, one of the four quarters in the Old City of Jerusalem. The Western Wall Plaza is usually filled with ultra-Orthodox, Orthodox, religious, secular, and foreign Jews mixing and observing.

Best example **Jewish Quarter**.

Complementary **Old City Jerusalem (#1)**; **Tel Aviv (#5)**; **Masada (#8)**; **Western Wall (#11)**; **Modern Movement (Bauhaus Architecture) (#16)**; **Israel Museum (#17)**; **Mount of Olives (#34)**; **Yad Vashem (#35)**; **Tomb of the Patriarchs and Old Town of Hebron (#46)**; **Ein Gedi (#50)**; **Israeli Cuisine (#51)**; **Tsfat/Safed (#58)**; **Golan Heights (#62)**; **Tel Dan (#63)**; **Beit Alpha (#64)**; **Mea She'arim (#66)**; **Mehane Yehuda Market (#67)**; **Jerusalem, New City (#72)**; **Golan Heights Winery (#75)**; **ANU – Museum of the Jewish People (#77)**; **Eilat (#78)**; **Carmel Market (#87)**; **Tel Aviv Beaches (#89)**; **Western Wall Tunnels (#94)**; **Tel Aviv Museum of Art (#95)**; *Ancient Qatzrin*; *Bar'am*; *Ben Yehuda Street*; *Bialik House*; *Bible Lands Museum*; *Café Culture*; *Carmel Winery*; *City of David*; *Hadassah Synagogue and Chagall Windows*; *Hamat Tiberias*; *Israel National Trail*; *Kibbutz Lotan*; *Kibbutz Volunteer*; *Lag B'Omer at Moshav Meron*; *Modern Israeli Cuisine*; *Mount Gerizim*; *MUSA – Eretz Israel Museum*; *Neve Tzedek*; *Rothschild Boulevard*; *Sea of Galilee Beaches*; *Tiberias*; *Yemen Moshe*; and *Zichron Ya'akov*.

ORTHODOX JEWS Orthodox Judaism is a conservative stream of Judaism which strictly observes Jewish law, or *halakha*. There are a few branches of orthodoxy, from the ultra-orthodox (*haredi*) to the Modern Orthodox movement. Both ends of the orthodox spectrum believe that Jewish law is binding and pure, as it has been interpreted from the Torah in oral and written contexts, specifically through the Talmud (the primary source of Jewish law). The groups differ in how much they are willing to accept the interpretations of the new world. Haredi communities believe in and practice the strictest of rabbinical interpretations, and segregate themselves from the modern world as far as possible in order to adhere to those values and regulations. In modern orthodoxy, believers attempt to integrate with the outside world under the constraints of rabbinical law in order to create a better world.

Hasidic Jews are a sub-denomination of Orthodox Judaism (specifically Haredi) and practice a type of spirituality that became commonplace in Eastern Europe in the 19th century CE. They often speak Yiddish and have their own style of dress. The men wear peyot, the long and curly sidelocks (sideburns), cover their heads at all times – often with brim hats, with some wearing fur hats on the Sabbath – and long black suits. Women are always covered past the knees and elbows, and their hair is either covered by a wig or scarf.

Kabbalah is a form of Jewish mysticism, its followers seeking to understand the spiritual universe through Jewish thought and teachings. It arose in the 12th century CE as a way to directly approach God (who is referred to as Ein Sof, or "without end").

Begun in the 19th century CE in Germany, the **Reform** denomination values ethics above traditions and does not regard the *halakha* as binding. Religious attire (to include kippeh/yarmulke for men) is not mandatory at all times. More progressive wings have embraced female rabbis, tolerance of LGBT communities, and looser observance of dietary restrictions.

Best examples **Mea She'arim (#66)** and *Jewish Quarter*. Your best bet to see Jewish orthodoxy is by taking a stroll through Mea She'arim. You'll find a large Haredi community in this West Jerusalem neighborhood. No cameras are allowed (and definitely no cars on Shabbat), but walking through will give you a superficial look at the life of Haredi people. For a more mixed community, look no further than the Jewish Quarter, where many of the above groups live and pray in close proximity.

Complementary **Old City Jerusalem (#1)**; **Western Wall (#11)**; and **Jerusalem, New City (#72)**.

PALESTINIANS

The name of the region known as "Palestine" may be older than written records. The region was called "Peleset" by Egyptian scribes from the Ramses III era around 1150 BCE, before Jerusalem was even founded. This name uses the same first four consonants of Palestine, so very likely correlates given that neither Hebrew nor Arabic employ vowels.

The actual term "Palestine" has been in use since at least the 5th century BCE, around the time of the Greek conquest of Jerusalem and the rest of the region. Indeed, the first known reference to this land as Palestine is from the Greek historian Herodotus, who references the "Syrians of Palestine" and the region of "Syria-Palestine" which went from Phoenicia (with its principal cities, Byblos and Tyre, in modern-day Lebanon) to Egypt, and as far east as the Jordan River valley. The Bible too (written over the coming centuries) references Philistines (in English variants, of course), a rough translation of ancient Hebrew that reads closer to "Palestines." Thus, Philistines and Palestinians are versions of the same term, though their meanings have evolved over the last 2,500 years.

Importantly, for thousands of years, there was no distinguishing characteristics of a Palestinian person, other than residence in the area of Syria Palaestina. When

Arabs conquered the region, its residents continued to be known as Palestinians, or a derivation of the word in the local dialect. When other Muslim tribes (Kurdish, Iranian) took over the region, the name stayed. In 1897, when the First Zionist Congress set out to draft its stated goals, the leaders stated that Zionism sought to secure a Jewish homeland "in Palestine." The *Jerusalem Post* has been a newspaper since 1932, but changed its name in 1950; it was previously known as the *Palestine Post*. During the British Mandate period from 1920 to independence, the area was known as Palestine E.I., where the E.I. stood for Eretz Israel (the land of Israel) – ultimately, the new country would drop the "Palestine" upon independence in 1948.

Once Palestinian Jews no longer used the title, taking on the new moniker of *Israeli* Jews, the term "Palestinian" began to reference those people in historic Palestine territory who had lost their land before or during the wars between Jews and Arabs in 1947, and later in 1967. The Palestinian National Charter of 1968 begins, "Palestine is the homeland of the Arab Palestinian people; it is an indivisible part of the greater Arab homeland, and the Palestinian people are an integral part of the Arab nation."

Notably, "Arab Palestinian" does not denote a specific religion, nor does anywhere else in the charter. Thus, it can include those Arabic-speaking persons who also lost land to the state of Israel, including Christians, Samaritans, and Druze populations. That said, there is nothing intrinsically different between, say, Palestinians from Gaza versus those who are living in exile in Jordan. Similarly, many Palestinians would agree they are Arab and share a history and cultural identity. Thus the term "Palestinian" has come to represent local Arab nationalism, though the group is ethnically indistinguishable from their Arab country neighbors.

A slight majority of Palestinians, or those with a claim to Palestinian nationality, today reside within the historic Palestinian homeland – be that Israel or any of the Palestinian territories. Those Arab residents of Palestine that agreed to recognize Israeli independence in 1948 were afforded Israeli citizenship. Today, those Palestinians and their descendants number more than 1.3 million and may self-identify as "Palestinian," "Arab," "Israeli," or a combination. (Of note, no Arabs except for new family members of Arab Israelis can become citizens of Israel. Still, the number of Arab Israelis continues to grow due to positive birth rates.) More than 4 million Palestinians live in "Palestinian territories," which implies the West Bank and Gaza. Though the Golan Heights were captured from Syria by Israel in 1967 and never returned, the Arab/Druze residents there were offered citizenship in exchange for loyalty to Israel. The Golan Heights are considered to be Israeli territory according to most Israelis.

The United Nations has identified more than 4 million Palestinian refugees whose families lost land from 1947 to 1967. Roughly half of the Palestinians who live outside of historic Palestine are in neighboring Jordan. Most are several generations removed from the 1948 declaration of independence, but still suffer from having been forcibly removed from their homes at the end of that war. Many have claimed Jordanian citizenship, though there is a sizable group of Arab leaders that refuse to take Jordanian citizenship in order to emphasize their determination to return to their ancestral home.

Today, Palestinians have a number of voices. Gazan Palestinians are ruled by a militant wing, Hamas, which has been deemed a terrorist organization by many Western states, including Israel and the United States. West Bank Palestinians back Mahmoud Abbas, leader since 2005 and the second president of the Palestinian National Authority, which has representation at the United Nations, though in non-member status only. As of 2020, only Palestine and the Vatican (Holy See) hold this unique status at the UN.

Road trip C2: Southern West Bank.

SECULAR LIFE In contrast to orthodoxy, there are many who live a secular lifestyle in Israel. The term "secular" can be interpreted in a number of ways. For some, it means keeping religion separate from daily life. Some secular Jews consider themselves culturally Jewish but do not claim any connection with the religion, though they may celebrate Passover and Hannukah, for instance.

Secularism in a political sense can also relate to the separation of church and state – as Israel is technically a secular state – and the desire to keep religion apart from civic life. The Basic Laws of Israel (similar to a Constitution) declare Israel a Jewish state with the freedom of religious practice for the country's other religious communities.

Secular Jews (*hiloni*) make up the largest chunk of the population of Israelis, at 43% as of 2018. The traditionalists (*masorti*) see themselves as neither secular nor orthodox, and are the next big chunk at 22%. The modern orthodox (*datii*) are 13% and the ultra-orthodox (*haredi*) are about 10%. In general, *hilonim* consider themselves Israeli before they consider themselves Jewish. To that end, *hilonim* by and large consider themselves "Zionists" (i.e., believe that the Jewish people have a state and homeland in Israel), whereas *haredi* populations primarily do not (though *masorti* and *datii* overwhelmingly consider themselves Zionists).

Best example **Tel Aviv (#5)**. By far, the best place to embrace the secular Jewish lifestyle is Tel Aviv, where people are very laid back in their attitudes towards dress, religion, diet, and activities on Shabbat.

Complementary **Akko (#13)**; **Jaffa (#30)**; **Aqaba (#43)**; **Eilat (#78)**; **Machneyuda (#98)**; **Imperial Bar (#99)**; *Ein Hod*; *Haifa*; *Neve Tzedek*; and *Zichron Ya'akov*.

HIPSTERS Young folks of the world, fear not. There are joints to satisfy all of your most hipster cravings. Whatever you're in the mood for, this is where to find it: **vegan food** is covered in *Do #14: Eat It!* (p. 80); Barberia has three **barber shops** in Tel Aviv and Haifa (**w** barberia.co.il); start your **thrift store** search in Shuk HaPishpeshim, Jaffa's popular flea market; for **bespoke cocktail bars** check out **Imperial Bar (#99)**; **coffee**, of course, is in *Do #15: Drink It!* (p. 93); take a **graffiti** art tour in Florentin (see *City Walk D4*); for **yoga** see the *Meditation, Yoga, and Quiet* category (p. 498); **bicycle rentals** are handled by *Tel-O-Fun Bike Share*; and for **Mary Jane** see the *Vice* category (p. 559).

Complementary **Tel Aviv (#5)**; **Jaffa (#30)**; **Mehane Yehuda Market (#67)**; **Jerusalem, New City (#72)**; *Drummers' Beach*; *Neve Tzedek*; Florentin (D4); and Kuli Alma (D4).

REFUGEES Jordan, Israel, Palestine, and Egypt each have their own unique refugee stories. In order to understand the situation better, let's first start with some definitions. **Asylum** is the act of being recognized as a refugee in order to receive certain guaranteed protections; an **asylum seeker** is a person who is being evaluated for asylum by another country and who must prove their country is dangerous (e.g., civil war) or engaging in persecution; a **migrant** is someone who seeks to move to another country voluntarily in order to improve their quality of life through work or family reunification; a **refugee** is someone who is forced to flee their home because of war or other violence, or because of persecution based on religion, gender, race, or another subgroup; a **refugee camp** refers to facilities meant to house, feed, and medically treat refugees temporarily; and a **stateless person** is someone who has no citizenship.

Jordan is home to some 750,000 refugees from nearly 60 countries. The vast majority are Syrian refugees, though there are large populations from Iraq, Yemen, and Sudan. Although 83% of refugees don't live in camps, the Za'atari (80,000) and Azraq (35,000) refugee camps continue to provide support to some of the largest numbers of Syrian refugees in the world.

According to the United Nations Relief and Works Agency (UNRWA) for Palestine Refugees, there are 5 million Palestinian descendants of the 1948 Arab–Israeli War who would today qualify for refugee status due to the 750,000 Palestinians who were displaced from their homes. More than 1.5 million people live in 58 Palestinian refugee camps outside of Israel but in other parts of the Holy Land region (including the West Bank and Gaza).

Israel has a much more strict view of taking non-Jewish refugees. This is the case with its Sudanese and Eritrean asylum seekers, the vast majority of whom have not been granted refugee status and have lived in limbo since 2006. The government continues to advocate for deportation while the Supreme Court tends to overrule those decrees to protect asylum seekers. As of 2019, there were approximately 55,000 refugees and asylum seekers in Israel.

Visit Aida Refugee Camp (C1) and Dheisheh Refugee Camp (C2). Near Jerusalem, there are two large refugee camps – Aida and Dheisheh – both of which offer visits to the public (it is not a tourist site, so try not to think of it as a "tour") to help you better understand the lives of the refugees who live there.

Complementary Freedom Theatre (C5) and Russian Quarter (A7).

LGBTQ Tel Aviv is often called the gay capital of the Middle East, or its "gay Mecca." Same-sex marriage is not legal, but homosexuality has been decriminalized since the 1980s. Interestingly, there aren't that many LGBT-specific clubs here, likely due to a combination of venues being gay-friendly or "open to everyone" and a tendency for clubs to host gay *nights*, rather than open as LGBT-focused. Check out **w** travelgay. com for a running list of gay-themed events. **Shpagat** on Nahalat Binyamin is easily the best LGBTQ bar in town, though tends to get male-heavy many nights. Tel Aviv hosts an international gay film festival each year, called **TLVFest** (**w** tlvfest.com). Also, lots of eye-candy, strutting, and posing can be found all day long at Hilton Beach, the notorious "gay beach" on the long Tel Aviv stretch of sand in front of the Hilton Hotel.

Despite its reputation as the epicenter of religiosity, Jerusalem has its own tiny LGBT scene. Its one gay bar, **Video Pub**, in the Russian Compound, has a devout following.

Tel Aviv Pride (**f** tlvpride) is a major event every June, and to a lesser extent (but growing) in Jerusalem. The Tel Aviv march/parade grows in size each year, attracting large international crowds, costumes, speakers, floats, big names, and even bigger dance parties. Tickets often sell out far in advance.

Homosexuality is legal in Jordan, although not practiced outwardly. Amman has a subdued LGBT scene, with no recognized "gay bars." That said, Rainbow Street (different connotation) has a number of restaurants, cafés, and pubs where gay people can feel comfortable. Check out Books@Cafe (Q2) for recommendations.

Time Out Israel has a dedicated section to LGBT happenings in Israel (**w** timeout. com/israel/lgbt). Like a lot of things these days, a lot of people find out about events through connections on dating apps. The *Jerusalem Post* includes LGBT news and stories regularly, collected on **w** jpost.com/tags/lgbt.

Complementary **Tel Aviv (#5)** and *Tel Aviv Pride Celebration (D1)*.

ETHNIC GROUPS

ARAB To be "Arab" can mean many different things to different people, and indeed the term is used in a variety of ways. The concept of "Arab" can connect people by nationality, such as when Syria and Egypt created the United Arab Republic, combining their two countries into one general Arab state from 1958 to 1961.

Not all Arabs live in an Arab country. Lebanon is a mixed-religion country. So is Israel, of course. Both are home to a large number of Arabs. So too are countries as far apart as Brazil (over 4 million), the United States, and France (over 3 million each).

The term "Arab" connects people who are ethnically Arab or from the Arab world. The latter tends to be its most common usage, and usually refers to people from the Middle East and North Africa. The Arab League is a loose confederation of 22 Arab countries, spanning from Somalia and Sudan to Mauritania and Morocco to Palestine.

"Arab" can also be a common marker for speakers of the Arabic language, though not all Arabic speakers are Arab. The governments of Israel, Eritrea, and Chad all claim Arabic as an official language, but none are officially Arab countries as registered in the Arab League.

The word "Arab" is often synonymous with "Muslim," which is also not a completely accurate assessment, though roughly 93% of Arabs are indeed Muslim. The remainder practice other religions, including Judaism, Christianity, and Bahá'í. To note, Muslims are not exclusively Arab either (e.g., Iranians are Persian, Turks are Turkish).

Arabs have been a recognized tribe (now much greater than that) since antiquity, with references first appearing in Assyrian records in the 9th century BCE. Their influence has not waned in the region over the last 2,500 years. The Nabataeans, of Petra fame, were an Arab tribe. Muhammad, too, was Arab. The Umayyad Caliphate of Syria, the Abbasids of Iraq, and the Fatimids and Mamluks of Egypt were all Arab dynasties of history.

It took around 1,500 years before Arab tribes unified, which only lasted a little over a century and took a massive war effort by Muhammad and his successors in the 7th century CE, in what turned into one of the world's fastest-growing and largest empires in history.

Outside of demographics, geography and politics, Arab people also see themselves as a unique cultural entity. Indeed, Arab influence has been felt throughout history in architecture, music, literature, mathematics, philosophy, art, medicine, and science.

So who or what is "Arab"? All of these things can lend themselves to Arab identity, though one needn't demonstrate mastery in every one to be "Arab." Like many identities, the definition of who is Arab often rests with the beholder.

If you're seeking a quintessential Arab experience while in the Holy Land, you needn't look far. Jordan and the Sinai are nearly 100% Arab, as is much of the West Bank, East Jerusalem, and Gaza. Even Israel counts 20% of its citizens as Arab. Visiting the Old City's Muslim Quarter, Jaffa in Tel Aviv, or ensuring you add Jordan to your trip will enrich your trip immensely, particularly if you are unfamiliar with Muslims or the Arab World.

Best example **Ramallah (#68)**.

Complementary **Old City Jerusalem (#1)**; **Dome of the Rock (#6)**; **Temple Mount (#12)**; **Akko (#13)**; **Jericho and Hisham's Palace (#26)**; **Nazareth and its Biblical Sites (#29)**; **Jaffa (#30)**; **Modern Amman (#36)**; **Bethlehem (#40)**; **Aqaba (#43)**; **Jordanian Cuisine (#44)**; **Tomb of the Patriarchs and Old Town of Hebron (#46)**; **Jordan Trail (#52)**; **Dahab (#54)**; **Nablus (#61)**; **Golan Heights (#62)**; **Al-Aqsa Mosque (#65)**; **Petra Kitchen (#84)**; *Argila/Hookah/Shisha*; *As-Salt*; *Haifa*; *Jordanian Hospitality*; Aida Refugee Camp (C1); Al-Auja (C3); Deir Ghassaneh (C5); Dheisheh Refugee Camp (C2); Freedom Theatre (C5); Jisr az-Zarqa (E4); and Khalid Shoman Foundation/ Darat al-Funun (Q2).

BEDOUIN Bedouins are a loose group of Arab tribes who live in the deserts of the Middle East and North Africa. Most are nomadic and practice Islam. They usually speak Arabic, though some in Israel speak Hebrew. Most have no rights to land ownership, but rather have an understanding with the government on their use of certain plots of land.

The Bedouins in the Negev are a bit different from those in other parts of the Middle East. This group has taken up a sedentary lifestyle following periods of government intervention from the Ottoman period through Israeli independence. Though many Negev Bedouins now consider themselves part of the Palestinian movement, this group was granted limited access to a sliver of their Negev land following the 1951 removal of Arabs from major parts of Israel. Their numbers vary wildly by statistics, but some 200,000 Bedouins are estimated to live in the Negev Desert, specifically the city of Rahat plus six other towns, as well as several dozen informal settlements.

The Negev Bedouins do not have much integration with the rest of Israeli society. Today, many are impoverished, though the government has implemented a number of welfare and development schemes to improve their living conditions. Still, birth rates are high. A quarter are believed to practice polygamy. These groups continue to focus their livelihood on agriculture and pastoralism (sheep, goats, and camels), even though they can't make money at a national or international level. School dropout rates are high. Many young Bedouins serve successfully in the Israel Defense Forces (IDF).

The Egyptian Sinai remains home to a number of Bedouin tribes, who remain partially nomadic but have relied heavily on tourism over the last several decades as a way of making ends meet and integrating with society.

Meanwhile, many Jordanians consider their ancestors to be of Bedouin stock, though only around 7% of the population was actually considered Bedouin according to a 2007 Jordanian census. Here, they also tend to combine the sedentary and pastoral lifestyles, setting up camps for several months at a time before moving to another location, and then perhaps back again in the following season.

Bedouin homes tend to be simple, easily packable, and movable. There is always space for guests, hot tea and coffee, and welcome carpets for sitting cross-legged on the ground. The Jordanian tents are recognizable by their black animal hair construction.

Best examples **Wadi Rum (#4)**; **Feynan Ecolodge (#86)**; *Bedouin Tents and Coffee*; *Museum of Bedouin Culture*; *Sinai Trail*. At Wadi Rum, Bedouins run the day trips and night programs. Stay in the middle of traditional Bedouin territory at Feynan, while engaging with Bedouin guides who introduce you to traditions, tea, villages, food, and nature. The museum in Beer Sheva concludes with conversation with a Bedouin representative. The Sinai trek lasts more than 50 days across 550km, staying with eight Bedouin tribes along the way.

Complementary **Petra (#2)**; *Jordanian Hospitality*; Beer Sheva (J1); and Sidreh-Lakiya Negev Weaving (J1).

ETHNIC MINORITIES Everyone is familiar with the two most common groups of people in the Holy Land: Arabs and Jews. But the Holy Land is not a story only of Jews and Arabs or Israelis and Palestinians. Several other groups have lived in the Holy Land for millennia, whose numbers are perhaps not as great but whose influence can be seen today in unique cultural facets.

Armenians As many as 10,000 Armenians could be living in Israel, with around 1,000 living in/around the Armenian Quarter in the Old City, where ceramic making is a local craft. The quarter has been welcoming Armenian Christians since the 5th century CE, and is now centered around the cathedral which dates to 1195. See **Old City Jerusalem (#1)**; *St. James' Cathedral*; and Armenian Quarter (A2).

Black Hebrews A group of African Americans arrived in Israel around 1970 claiming to be descendants of one of the Twelve Tribes of Israel and haven't left. They number about 5,000 and mostly live in Dimona (J1), where they practice veganism, polygyny, and biodynamic/organic food growing.

Circassians Muslims from the Caucasus region who mostly fled at the end of the 1864 Russo–Circassian War, sending millions into the diaspora. Only a few thousand live in Israel, with a much more sizable population in Jordan where they are famed for serving as guardsmen for the Jordanian king. See Kfar Kama (G2).

Druze Ethnically and religiously distinct from Arabs and Muslims, the Druze are Israeli citizens who speak Arabic and whose ancestors lived in the Levant, primarily around the Syrian/Israeli Golan Heights. They number about 120,000 Israelis. See **Golan Heights (#62)**; Majdal Shams and The Shouting Hill (I2); and *Druze Cooking Workshops (H1)*.

Ethiopians Also called Beta Israel, Ethiopians were assisted in immigrating to Israel during two major Israeli military operations: Moses (1984) and Solomon (1991). Most of the 125,000 Ethiopian Jews now speak Hebrew and practice traditional Judaism, while maintaining culturally unique qualities. See **Church of the Holy Sepulchre (#9)**; **Jerusalem, New City (#72)**; *Mamshit*; and Ethiopian Quarter (A7).

Greeks Though small in ethnicity count, Greeks lead the overall Greek Orthodox Church, which numbers half a million locally, of which 130,000 are in Jerusalem. See **St. Catherine's Monastery (#22)**; **St. George's Monastery and Wadi Qelt (#97)**; *Deir Quruntal*; and *Mar Saba*.

Russians Following the dissolution of the USSR, Russian Jews were finally allowed to emigrate and more than 1 million found their way to Israel. Most are Jewish, though some family members might not be. See **Jerusalem, New City (#72)**, and Russian Quarter (A7).

Samaritans With less than 1,000 members, this is our most endangered ethnic group and half live on Mount Gerizim, their spiritual homeland. Religiously distinct from Judaism, they're also an ethnically distinct group who claim direct ancestry to three Tribes of Israel: Benjamin, Ephraim, and Manasseh. See **Nablus (#61)** and *Mount Gerizim*.

Complementary Beer Sheva (J1) and Oud Festival (A7).

COMMUNITY CELEBRATION

MEET LOCALS The best way to get to know people is to integrate (if briefly) in their world. You can do this individually or by hiring a guide who can show you around and introduce you to local craftspeople, food markets and stalls, and even arrange cooking classes, hikes, or cultural performances.

The Palestinian village of Nablus packs a punch, with an historic downtown, unique foods like Nabulsi cheese, cultural centers, famous soap, and the dessert *kanafeh*. In Jordan, the ***Wild Jordan Center*** combines a cheap restaurant and hostel with a park ranger station. In general, Jordanians are famous for their niceties, and Bedouins in particular are revered for their warmth and generosity of spirit. Expect tea in many environments.

A note about the "Sabra" personality: the "sabra" is a prickly pear and is a common internal term for Israeli Jews who are comparatively tough on the outside, but sweet on the inside. It also references Jews born in Israel.

Best examples **Nablus (#61)**; *Wild Jordan Center*; *Jordanian Hospitality*

Complementary **Ramallah (#68)**; **Petra Kitchen (#84)**; **Feynan Ecolodge (#86)**; *Al-Ayoun Trail*; *Museum of Bedouin Culture*; *Royal Society for the Conservation of Nature (RSCN)*; *Winery Tour*; Al-Auja (C3); Deir Ghassaneh (C5); Kfar Kama (G2); Kibbutz Ein Gev (G3); Kibbutzim (U); Tel Aviv White Night (D3); Ulpanim (U); Zikra Initiative (P1); *Dimona (J1)*.

HOLIDAYS The original definition of *holiday* comes from the Middle English *hāligdæg*, meaning "holy day." The Holy Land is not lacking for holy days, that's for sure. Those listed below have gained substantial recognition and are worthy of planning your trip around. Check out the calendar in *Do #1: Date It!* (p. 36) for upcoming holidays over the next several years.

Complementary **Church of the Nativity (#18)**; *Lag B'Omer at Moshav Meron*; Holy Week in Jerusalem (A5); National Memorial Day (U); Yom Kippur (U); and *Purim in Tel Aviv (D4)*.

FESTIVALS AND EVENTS Although we've featured a number of festivals in other categories, here's a combined list of important festivals and events occurring around the region each year.

Best examples Tel Aviv White Night (D3); *Tel Aviv Pride Celebration (D1)*.

Complementary Holy Week in Jerusalem (A5); Hutzot Hayotzer Arts and Crafts Festival (A7); Israel Festival (A7); Oud Festival (A7); Red Sea Jazz Festival (L1); and Sacred Music Festival, aka Mekudeshet (B1).

Culture

MUSEUMS

There are so many different types of museum, and so many reactions to how an individual approaches a museum, that we felt it best to create a separate category for museums rather than distribute them to their individual places within the guide (i.e., history museums, art museums, castle museums, etc.). In this way, we hope to offer you a choice, with no surprises, as you create your itinerary.

OF ART
Best example **Tel Aviv Museum of Art (#95)**.

Complementary **Israel Museum (#17)**; *Bialik House*; *Design Museum Holon*; *MUSA – Eretz Israel Museum*; *Yemen Moshe*; Inn of the Good Samaritan (C3); Jordan National Gallery of Fine Arts (Q2); Negev Museum of Art (J1); and Tikotin Museum of Japanese Art (E1).

Consider adding some of these Pearl sites to your trip if you have scheduled to be in any of these regions Mishkan Museum of Art (F2); Mane-Katz Museum (E1); Ashdod Art Museum (E5); Ralli Museums (E3); The Herzliya Museum of Contemporary Art (D7); Sommer Contemporary Art Museum (D4); Ilana Goor Museum (D2); U. Nahon Museum of Italian Jewish Art (A7); and Ticho House (A7).

OF HISTORY
Best example **Citadel/Tower of David (#32)**.

Complementary **Israel Museum (#17)**; Clandestine Immigration & Naval Museum (E1); Hospitaller Fortress/Knights' Halls (E2); Museum for Islamic Art (A7); *Museum of Rishon Letzion (D8)*; and *Jordan Museum (Q3)*.

OF ARCHAEOLOGY
Best examples **Israel Museum (#17)**; *Rockefeller Archaeological Museum*; *Jordan Museum (Q3)*.

Complementary **Temple Mount (#12)**; **Citadel/Tower of David (#32)**; **Qumran (#70)**; *Jordan Archaeological Museum*; *Wohl Archaeological Museum*; Archaeological Seminars Dig-for-a-Day (B2); Hecht Museum (F1); Prehistoric Man Museum (I1).

OF MODERN TIMES
Complementary Atlit Detention Camp (E4); Beit HaShomer Museum (H2); Royal Automobile Museum (Q4); Tel Hai Fort (H2); The PhotoHouse (D3); Israeli Air Force Museum (J1).

OF CULTURE, ETHNICITY, NATIONALITY
Best examples **ANU – Museum of the Jewish People (#77)**; *MUSA – Eretz Israel Museum*; and *Bible Lands Museum*.

Complementary **Yad Vashem (#35)**; *Museum of Bedouin Culture*; Irbid Museum of Jordanian Heritage (S1); Jordan Folklore Museum (Q3); Jordan Museum of Popular Traditions (Q3); Memorial Museum of Hungarian Speaking Jewry (H1); Palestinian Heritage Museum (A6); Wolfson Museum of Jewish Art (A7); and *The Palestinian Museum (C4)*.

OF IMPORTANT PERSONS
Complementary Ben Gurion House (D3); Herzl Museum (A8); Sde Boker (J2); Yasser Arafat Museum (C4); Yitzhak Rabin Center (D7); *Menachem Begin Heritage Center (A7)*; and *Olympic Experience (D7)*.

OF SCIENCE AND LEARNING
Best example **Weizmann Institute of Science**.

Complementary **Israel Museum (#17)**; *Rockefeller Archaeological Museum*; Archaeological Seminars Dig-for-a-Day (B2); Children's Museum of Jordan (Q4); *Bloomfield Science Museum (A8)*; *Israel Children's Museum (D8)*; and *MadaTech (E1)*.

OF HOME
Best example **Bialik House**.

Complementary **St. Catherine's Monastery (#22)**; *Jewish Quarter*; *Weizmann Institute of Science*; Beit Ha'ir (D3); Ben Gurion House (D3); Sde Boker (J2); and *Bauhaus Center (D3)*.

THE ARTS

MUSIC From performance to orchestra to big vans blasting religious propaganda, there are all sorts of musical genres that visitors can elect. Lots of big names visit Tel Aviv and Jerusalem each year, but these cities and lots of small towns host as many styles of musicians as there are origins of Israelis. Check out w touristisrael.com/events/israel-concerts/ for background and upcoming listings. **The Sacred Music Festival**, aka Season of Culture and Mekudeshet Festival (w en.mekudeshet.com), has for ten years showcased a variety of soulful artists. The **Israel Philharmonic** (w ipo.co.il/en/) began as the Palestine Orchestra in 1936. The group has since gained international renown and performs regularly at the Charles Bronfman Auditorium in Tel Aviv.

Best example Sacred Music Festival, aka Mekudeshet (B1).

Complementary **Masada (#8)**; **Ramallah (#68)**; *Ben Yehuda Street*; *Drummers' Beach*; *Neve Tzedek*; HaYarkon Park (D7); Israel Festival (A7); Oud Festival (A7); and Red Sea Jazz Festival (L1).

PERFORMANCE You will find theater and dance in Israel and Palestine. Most beloved is the Israel Festival (w israel-festival.org/en/), a very popular, annual, week-long, 60-year-strong festival featuring music, theater, and dance.

Best examples Freedom Theatre (C5); Israel Festival (A7); Jerusalem Theatre (A7); and Suzanne Dellal Centre for Dance and Theatre (D4).

Complementary Cameri Theatre (D3); Fire and Water Fountain (D3); *Habima Theatre (D4)*.

VISUAL ARTS There is no shortage of things to gaze at in this part of the world, but what of it can be considered art? Let's start with the purposefully designed stained-glass windows in the Hadassah Medical Center Synagogue located in West Jerusalem. The beautiful colored glass was designed by artist Marc Chagall, while also providing a chance to visit a synagogue if you're otherwise unfamiliar.

Best example **Hadassah Synagogue and Chagall Windows**.

Complementary **Separation Wall**; **Ein Hod**; **Bialik House**; Florentin (D4); Hutzot Hayotzer Arts and Crafts Festival (A7); Israel Festival (A7); Khalid Shoman Foundation/Darat al-Funun (Q2); and Nakhalat Shiva (A7).

Active

WALKS AND HIKES

CITY WALKS If you're looking for a nice city walk, we've got you covered. See Part 9 for more than 20 walks through our major cities in the region, with seven in Jerusalem and six in Tel Aviv to keep you busy.

WALKING PATHS Below are a variety of easy walks on well-marked paths. The best would be the Tel Aviv Tayelet, or Promenade, which runs from the Tel Aviv Port to Jaffa Port for 6km.

Best example **Tel Aviv Tayelet/Promenade.**

Complementary **Tel Aviv (#5); Makhtesh Ramon (#28); Capernaum and Tabgha (#33); Jerusalem Walls and Gates (#47); Tel Dan (#63); Eilat (#78);** *Hula Lake; Mitzpe Ramon; Petra by Night*; Ein Afeq (E5); Haas Promenade (B1); and Kinneret Trail (G3).

EASY HIKES AND TRAILS (UNDER 2 HOURS) For easy- to medium-difficulty walks, you have a wide choice of options at Ein Gedi, where you can walk through a desert oasis, with most of the trails requiring only an average fitness. For those with more stamina, expend a little extra energy to reach great views of the Dead Sea. Yehudiya offers a dozen options for hiking, and there's really something for everyone. Mount Carmel is just outside of Haifa with a great big green park, replete with some easy hiking trails and picnic areas for an après-hike reward. The Red Canyon's a popular option outside Eilat.

Best examples **Ein Gedi (#50);** *Mount Carmel; Yehudiya; Sataf;* and *Red Canyon.*

Complementary **Petra (#2); Dana Biosphere Reserve (#21); Wadi Mujib and Mujib Biosphere Reserve (#23); Ajloun Forest (#57); Tel Dan (#63); Ein Avdat (#74); St. George's Monastery and Wadi Qelt (#97); Dor HaBonim (#100);** *Gamla; Hiking in Jordan; Little Petra; Mar Saba; Mount Gilboa; Nahal Me'arot/Wadi el-Mughara; Tel Ashkelon;* Kinneret Trail (G3); and Nahal Zalmon (H1).

DAY HIKES (2+ HOURS) If you've got more energy and are interested in longer day hikes, of medium to high difficulty, then you may be interested in the following. For tons of great hiking options, many of which require an adventurous spirit, check out w tiuli.com/tracks. Petra's two famous walks each take a couple of hours and can be combined into an active day, though there are several other walks there if you're doing a multiday trip. Dana Biosphere Reserve has a number of great hikes – some self-guided (if leaving from the visitor center), but many with the helpful Bedouin guides of the region to lead. At Ajloun Forest, choose between the Roe Deer Trail (see roe deer, naturally) and the Soap House Trail (purchase handmade soap, naturally).

Best examples **Petra (#2); Dana Biosphere Reserve (#21); Makhtesh Ramon (#28); Ajloun Forest (#57);** *Al-Ayoun Trail; Hiking in Jordan; Hiking in the Negev;* Ad-Deir, aka the Monastery (N2); High Place of Sacrifice (N2); and *Jabal al-Khubtha (N2).*

Complementary **Wadi Mujib and Mujib Biosphere Reserve (#23)**; **Ein Gedi (#50)**; **Nablus (#61)**; **Jesus Trail (#69)**; **Qumran (#70)**; **Feynan Ecolodge (#86)**; **Timna (#96)**; **Dor HaBonim (#100)**; *Little Petra*; *Lot's Cave*; *Mitzpe Ramon*; *Mount Arbel*; *Mount Carmel*; *Mount Gilboa*; *Mount Hermon*; *Sataf*; *Yehudiya*; Amram's Pillars (L3); Hiking in Jenin (C5); Majrase-Betiha/Bethsaida Valley (I3); Nahal el-Al (I3); St. Catherine's Mount (T1); Wadi al-Dahik (R1); Yarmouk Forest (S1); *Masada's Roman Trails (K1)*; and *Wadi Jadid (O1)*.

WET HIKES If you don't mind combining your hiking with your swimming, you might want to try Wadi Mujib and the Mujib Biosphere Reserve. With wet and dry trails, some seasonal, some requiring guides, and the possibility of seeing rare animals, plants, and even swimming to get through the trails, this place has everything. The entire biosphere is attractive, but the highlight is a soaked walk through the famous canyon, Wadi Mujib, to glorious pools.

Another great option for some family-friendly fun is the City of David system of ancient water tunnels just south of the Old City, Hezekiah's Tunnel. Built 3,000 years ago, water still flows fully and you will most certainly get drenched! Kids love it.

Best examples **Wadi Mujib and Mujib Biosphere Reserve (#23)** and *Hezekiah's Tunnel*.

Complementary *Yehudiya*; Majrase-Betiha/Bethsaida Valley (I3); and *Wadi Daraja (K1)*.

TOUGH HIKES (SHORT AND STEEP) This might not be a category you actively seek out, but it's probably good to know what you're getting yourself into. At Masada, you can take the cable car or brave one of the two entrances: Roman encampments from the western desert or the Snake Path at the main entrance, both of which are 30–60-minute steep hikes to the plateau top. At Ein Avdat, you'll find a variety of hiking trails of varying difficulties, indigenous Negev Desert plants, water holes, and rock art. (The steep ascent is between the two parking lots.) Wadi Daraja is filled with steep cliffs and rappelling.

Best examples **Ein Avdat (#74)**; *Masada's Roman Trails (K1)*; *Masada's Snake Path (K1)*; and *Wadi Daraja (K1)*.

Complementary **Petra (#2)**; **Mount Sinai (#15)**; **Makhtesh Ramon (#28)**; *Haifa*; *Montfort*; *Mount Arbel*; *Mount Hermon*; and *Red Canyon*.

LONG-DISTANCE WALKS (2+ DAYS) If hiking is your jam, then you have several great multiday options to choose from. Or don't choose, and enjoy all of them!

Best examples On the **Jordan Trail (#52)**, you'll walk 650km for 40+ days, broken up into eight chunks. The **Jesus Trail (#69)** takes you 65km from Nazareth to Capernaum in 3–5 days passing through a number of religiously significant towns. The *Palestinian Heritage Trail* is a 330km, 21-day, north–south sojourn of the West Bank. The *Israel National Trail* also runs north to south and covers 1,100km, though pieces can be done in day trips or 2–3-day chunks, while the whole thing will take 30–60 days, depending on pace. Egypt needn't be left out, as it too has its own *Sinai Trail*, a 550km, 54-day hike through eight Bedouin tribal towns, though 2–5-day trips are available.

Other good options are: Rift Valley (V), a 4–6-day trek from Dana to Petra (w wildjordan.com/eco-tourism-section/rift-valley-mountain-trek); the Golan Trail (I2), a 120km hike through the Golan Heights (which Israel Trail does not cover) over 5–8 days (w en.wikivoyage.org/wiki/Golan_Trail); the Sanhedrin Trail (G2), a 70km track (under development) from Tiberias to Beit She'arim with an accompanying app providing a virtual interactive element to the outdoor walk; and the Kinneret Trail (G3), which circumambulates the Sea of Galilee over 60km.

Complementary **Petra (#2)**; **Sea of Galilee (#7)**; **Dana Biosphere Reserve (#21)**; **Makhtesh Ramon (#28)**; **Golan Heights (#62)**; *Hiking in Jordan*; *Mitzpe Ramon*; and Hiking in Jenin (C5).

EXPERIENCED HIKERS Looking for some tough climbs? Much of Israel's trails are fairly easy, with well-marked paths, moderate distances between sites, free camping, and plenty of places to stock up on essentials. Here are a few things to note:

The **Golan Heights** are not completely mine-free. There are signs everywhere, but in case you're wandering through the country aimlessly, keep in mind that a few unexploded mines are still found every year from the war with Syria (remember, this land was governed by Syria until 1967). The **Negev** is a desert. You will need to be equipped for hot days and cold nights. The summers can get upwards of 40°C/104°F during the day and are often not safe for trekkers. The makhtesh hikes are steep in many places and require great fitness. **Masada**'s walking trails have been known to best a number of tourists due to the scorching desert heat and the hour-long uphill climb. **Jordan**'s off-roads are underdeveloped, which adds to the excitement, but should be attempted by experts only. People you meet will likely not be able to speak English, so a modest amount of Arabic is recommended if you plan to hike through villages.

All of the *Long-Distance Walks* above can be categorized as "experienced hikers only" unless you plan to go with a guide. Multiday hikes require much foresight and planning, physical fitness, and fortitude! Water may need to be cached along your track if going through long desert stretches.

These hikes, as referenced before, each require guides or equipment, or both:

Complementary **Wadi Mujib and Mujib Biosphere Reserve (#23)**; **Makhtesh Ramon (#28)**; **Ein Gedi (#50)**; **Jordan Trail (#52)**; *Palestinian Heritage Trail*; *Yehudiya*; and *Wadi Daraja (K1)*.

LAND SPORTS

SKIING The Holy Land countries rarely see snow, but the northernmost tip of Israel-controlled Golan Heights contains the southern point of the Anti-Lebanon mountain ranges. Atop the white-capped peak of Mount Hermon is a popular Israeli ski resort for those aficionados visiting in the winter.

Best example **Mount Hermon**.

Complementary **Mount Gilboa** and *Sandboarding in Wadi Rum (M2)*.

BIKING Bicycles can be hired to get around Tel Aviv through Tel-O-Fun. Similar rental options exist in most major cities in the region – ask your hotel or Google "bicycle rental [Jerusalem]." Mountain biking is quickly growing in popularity in Israel, with great weather, good tracks, and a lot of interest. Israel hosts the Epic Israel four-day mountain biking competition each year (w epicisrael.org.il/en/). Both w trailforks.com and w alltrails.com offer user-rated trails for your planning needs. Like the Israel Trail for walkers, the Israel Bike Trail (w ibt.org.il/en) traverses the country over 600km of marked bicycle trails.

Best examples **Tel-O-Fun Bike Share** and Israel Bike Trail (U).

Complementary **Tel Aviv (#5)**; **Sea of Galilee (#7)**; **Makhtesh Ramon (#28)**; **Golan Heights (#62)**; **Eilat (#78)**; **Timna (#96)**; *Neve Tzedek*; *Tel Aviv Tayelet/Promenade*; Al-Auja (C3); Amram's Pillars (L3); HaYarkon Park (D7); Kinneret Trail (G3); Neot HaKikar (K1); Mount Sodom (K1); Sugar Trail (C3); and *Ben Shemen Forest (B2)*.

ADVENTURE/EXTREME LAND SPORTS
There are a few places to brave danger and live life to its extreme – if you dare.

Rock climbing is growing in popularity. Check out **w** mountainproject.com for information on Israel's 40+ climbs and Jordan's 60+ climbs (with links to user-generated sites with technical grades and instructions on whether traditional or bolted climbs work best). There's a relatively recent guidebook written in 2015 outlining 15 of Israel's best climbs, available for purchase at **w** climbing-israel.com. Try Rock Climbing in Wadi Rum (M2); **Timna (#96)**; and Ein Prat (C3).

Rappelling, or abseiling, has its own admirers, and requires equipment, but in most cases can be done by kids and adults alike. There are many popular places in Israel and Jordan to partake in this activity, which you'll need to book in advance. Try **Qumran (#70)**; *Mitzpe Ramon*; the salt caves at Mount Sodom (K1); and Ein Prat (C3).

Canyoneering too can be done all over this region, with many involving combinations of hiking, rappelling, and wading through gushing water as you work your way through desert canyons. Try **Wadi Mujib and Mujib Biosphere Reserve (#23)**; Black Canyon in the **Golan Heights (#62)**; and Wadi Qumran (K1).

Off-roading vehicles, such as all-terrain vehicles, dirt bikes, and 4x4 jeeps, are welcome in Israel and Jordan. It's one of the most popular experiences in **Wadi Rum (#4)**; or you could also try **Masada (#8)**; **Makhtesh Ramon (#28)**; **Golan Heights (#62)**; and Wadi Nasb (T1).

Camel riding/racing is also a popular sport here – you can partake at **Wadi Rum (#4)** and Camel Safari (T1). Also at **Wadi Rum (#4)**, **sandboarding** involves using a snowboard to go down steep hills of sand. Goggles are recommended! Dror BaMidbar also offers lessons and boards for rent on a 30m sand dune near *Shivta*.

GROUP/TEAM SPORTS
If you're looking to meet some locals for a friendly match, head to **Tel Aviv Beaches (#89)** for some easy pickup volleyball games or a game of Matcot (D1).

RUNNING AND FREE EXERCISE
You needn't make too many advanced plans to get your jog on, but rest assured that you have plenty of options in the region. The *Tel Aviv Tayelet/Promenade* offers more than 5km (one-way) of beach and beauty, with extensions at both ends to take you south along the beach past Jaffa towards the Peres Center for Peace, and north through HaYarkon Park (D7), which itself has dozens of kilometres of trails. Along the Tayelet are a number of exercise blocks to allow for strength-building using basic outdoor gym equipment. Anywhere in **Tel Aviv (#5)** is a good option. Otherwise, take a jog down *Rothschild Boulevard* – you'll be in good company.

The **Old City Jerusalem (#1)** is a city-within-a-city that has paths circumnavigating the fortified **Jerusalem Walls and Gates (#47)** measuring some 4km with several descents and ascents. *Ben Shemen Forest (B2)* has dual-purpose trails for bike riders and trail runners. Nebi Samuel (C4), outside of central Jerusalem, also has running trails.

COMPETITION
There is a surprising number of annual competitions in this region given the typically hot climate, but winters can be cool and indeed a great time to host international running and biking events. If you're into making a trip out of a racing event, and are visiting in winter, you'll want to check out the following.

The very first marathon in Israel was run in 1977 in *Tiberias*, now called the **Tiberias Winner Marathon** and closing in on 50 years of this below-sea-level flat course. The **Jerusalem Winner Marathon** starts near the **Israel Museum (#17)** in West Jerusalem and continues towards the Old City, through the Armenian Quarter. Full marathon runners will head through East Jerusalem and several southern neighborhoods before ending back in West Jerusalem.

The **Tel Aviv Samsung Marathon** regularly handles tens of thousands of runners, with parts of the city shut down to accommodate the traffic. The event starts in HaYarkon Park (D7) and loops around downtown for the 5K and 10K; half- and full marathon runners will run largely along the beach before taking in parts of downtown. Tel Aviv also has an annual **10K Night Run**, with tens of thousands of runners and spectators cheering along the masses from 20.30.

Israel has a **Dead Sea Marathon** starting at *Ein Bokek* with various heats. Runners get to run on the dikes that serve as the border between Israel and Jordan. Further south, **Eilat (#78)** hosts the annual **Israman** competition, a full- and half-Ironman challenge considered to be among the world's most difficult, with 226km or 113km of relay or self swim, cycle, and run.

Jordan also has its own **50km Dead Sea Ultra Marathon** from Baptism Valley to the Dead Sea. There's also an annual **Wadi Rum Full Moon Desert Marathon** which has you running through sand at times under the glorious night sky. Camping options available, of course (**f** TREKSjo). The **Amman Marathon** has the traditional heats with runners passing **Ancient Amman (#37)**. Albatros Adventure Marathons organizes a **Petra Desert Marathon**, starting at the Siq (**Petra (#2)**).

WATER SPORTS

SWIMMING There is no shortage of swimming holes in this region, with five major bodies of water and lots of swimming venues inside each of the countries. You can swim in the calm waters all along Tel Aviv's coast thanks to the breakers that keep everything calm most of the year. For splashing in waves, head north or south along the Mediterranean coast where breakers are less common – but pick a beach with a lifeguard! Gan HaShlosha is the most popular non-sea-based water site, with year-round warm water in the natural swimming holes.

Best examples **Mediterranean Coast** and **Gan HaShlosha**.

Complementary **Dead Sea (#3)**; **Tel Aviv (#5)**; **Red Sea/Gulf of Aqaba (#10)**; **Aqaba (#43)**; **Dahab (#54)**; **Eilat (#78)**; **Coral Beach (#83)**; **Sharm el-Sheikh (#88)**; **Tel Aviv Beaches (#89)**; **Dor HaBonim (#100)**; *Akhziv Beach*; *Beit Yannai*; *Drummers' Beach*; *Ein Bokek*; *Ein Bokek Spa Hotels*; *Hamat Gader*; *Herziliya Beaches*; *Netanya*; *Rosh HaNikra*; *Suweimeh Spa Hotels*; *Tel Ashkelon*; *Tel Aviv Port*; *Tiberias*; *Yehudiya*; Beaches (U); Dolphin Reef (L2); Meshushim Stream (I3); Nahariya (E5); North Beach (L1); Palmahim (E3); South Haifa Beaches (E7); Taba (T1); and *Rishpon (D7)*.

DIVING World-class diving is within reach. The Red Sea/Gulf of Aqaba has great options for a quick trip, so be sure to check out that elective. If you have time, head to the Egyptian Sinai for some of the most famous and breathtaking spots. Ras Mohammad is an internationally recognized coral habitat with over 1,000 species of sea life to observe, just outside of Sharm el-Sheikh in the Egyptian Sinai. Just north, near Dahab, is the famous Blue Hole. Otherwise, Aqaba offers a number of dive shops to take you to reefs and sunken ships; try South Beach/ Berenice Beach.

Best examples **Red Sea/Gulf of Aqaba (#10)**; **Ras Mohammad (#53)**; and *Blue Hole (T1)*.

Complementary **Aqaba (#43)**; **Dahab (#54)**; **Coral Beach (#83)**; **Sharm el-Sheikh (#88)**; *Rosh HaNikra*; and South Beach (M2).

SNORKELING You needn't take a week-long diving course in order to see all the good fish. In fact, there's perfectly good snorkeling options just off the coast of the Red Sea towns of Eilat and Aqaba. Check out Aqaba Marine Park for the best city snorkeling options. The Coral Beach Reserve in Eilat is a nature reserve with beach and reef access.

Best examples **Red Sea/Gulf of Aqaba (#10)** and **Coral Beach (#83)**.

Complementary **Aqaba (#43)**; **Dahab (#54)**; **Eilat (#78)**; **Sharm el-Sheikh (#88)**; *Akhziv Beach*; *Underwater Observatory*; South Beach (M2); and Dolphin Reef (L2).

SURFING Surfers can be spotted all up and down the Mediterranean coast in Israel. There are plenty of options for new surfers, with options ranging from a same-day full course to surf schools, all accessible right on the beach in Tel Aviv, or at any of the major beaches further north. The sport is also accessible year-round, though the winter water can get cold. Waves are best in the winter, with 2–3m swells in parts of the country. Tel Aviv has manmade breakers that keep the swells at a minimum, which make it a great place to learn. Check out w magicseaweed.com for list of surfing conditions at dozens of beaches along the Mediterranean coast.

Best examples **Tel Aviv Beaches (#89)**, especially Hilton, HaMaravi, and Dolphinarium.

Complementary **Tel Aviv (#5)**; **Caesarea (#25)** (Arubot, Shonit, and Sdot Yam beaches); **Dor HaBonim (#100)**; *Beit Yannai*; *Haifa* (BackDoor and Casino at Beit Galim Beach, Sokolov Beach); *Herziliya Beaches* (Zvulun and Dabuch); *Mediterranean Coast*; *Netanya* (Kontiki and Sironit beaches); Water Sports (D1); Ashdod (Dromi Beach); and Ashkelon (Goote Beach).

ADVENTURE WATER SPORTS There are a variety of adventurous water sports to choose from, in addition to surfing. **White water rafting** can be experienced at Kfar HaGoshrim and Kfar Blum on the Jordan River. **Windsurfing** is a singles sport involving a surfboard with a sail attached; **kitesurfing** is also solo, with a rider stood upright on a surf board with a half-circle kite powered by wind pushing the harnessed rider along the waves. **Stand-up paddleboarding** is exactly as it sounds, but much harder than it looks, with strong core strength (and gentle water) needed to stay upright. **Sailing** obviously involves boats, and you can either learn how to do this yourself (check the American Sailing Association for a list of certified schools at w asa.com/schools/israel/) or rent a yacht with a skipper through Sailor Yacht Club (w sailor.co.il). **Kayaking** can be done on the Dead Sea and near Rosh HaNikra with guides, and **yachting** is an option from the Tel Aviv Marina if money is no object.

Complementary **Tel Aviv (#5)**; **Sea of Galilee (#7)**; **Wadi Mujib and Mujib Biosphere Reserve (#23)**; **Caesarea (#25)**; **Jaffa (#30)**; **Eilat (#78)**; **Sharm el-Sheikh (#88)**; **Tel Aviv Beaches (#89)**; *Beit Yannai*; *Ein Bokek*; *Hezekiah's Tunnel*; *Mediterranean Coast*; *Tiberias*; Jordan River Rafting (I1); Palmahim (E3); and Water Sports (D1).

Leisure

BEACHES

PUBLIC/POPULAR BEACHES Beaches!! How to choose? First, you have to pick a body of water. The **_Mediterranean Coast_** is usually the clear winner here, but there are some rocky beaches along the Dead Sea, some gems along the Red Sea, and a smattering of options we won't get into on various lakes and rivers (see *Sea Access* below). You can explore the **Dead Sea (#3)** and the **Red Sea (#10)** in their respective elective entries.

But when people think of "beaches" they are likely picturing the fine, white Mediterranean sand. Your next question: do you want to stay in Tel Aviv, or are you willing to drive a few hours to get an empty stretch of sand? If you're staying in **Tel Aviv (#5)**, you'll want to check out **Tel Aviv Beaches (#89)**. If you're willing to venture north or south, we recommend **_Akhziv Beach_**, **_Beit Yannai_**, **_Herziliya Beaches_**, South Haifa Beaches (E7), and **_Netanya_** as places with cities and resources available (read: changing rooms, lifeguards, etc.). Check out lesser-known gems (with fewer amenities) in the following section, *Remote Beaches*. Be careful of undertow in areas marked as dangerous and without lifeguards (but that's where you'll also generally find the biggest waves since these areas don't have breakers).

The travel blog sites Israel21c, Secret Tel Aviv, Go-TelAviv, Tourist Israel, The Culture Trip, *Time Out*, Travel Triangle, and I Googled Israel generally agree on the following list of great beaches (each site appears on at least two rankings):

★ In Tel Aviv, all 13 beaches make multiple lists. Those with the most votes were: Hilton (#1 overall) – the gay beach, a dog-friendly beach, and a place to see and be seen; Gordon (six votes) – the most happening strip of land with volleyball, cafés, and of course matcot; and Metzitzim (four votes) – the northernmost strip before the Tel Aviv Port area. Tied on three votes were Hatzuk North, Religious/Nordau, Frishman, Bograshov, Banana/Aviv/Drummers', Alma/Dog, and Ajami/Givat Aliya.
★ **_Akhziv Beach_**; **_Beit Yannai_**; and Aqueduct Beach (E4) (6 votes).
★ **Coral Beach (#83)**; **Dor HaBonim (#100)**; and Palmahim (E3) (4 votes).
★ **_Ein Bokek_**; Dolphin Reef (L2); and Mosh Beach on the Red Sea (3 votes).
★ South Haifa Beaches (E7); Jisr az-Zarqa (E4); Tel Baruch; **_Herziliya Beaches_**; **_Apollonia_**; Ein Gev and Gofra (**_Sea of Galilee Beaches_**); and New Kalya Beach (K1) (2 votes).

For information on surfing, see p. 553.

Finally, a note on *Group Fun at a Downtown Beach (D1)*: nothing will be quite as memorable as spending a full day with friends at a downtown beach. Grab falafel for lunch, a volleyball or matcot set for the afternoon, and keep the beers flowing for all-hours fun. Lots of people rent chairs or you can pitch your own towel/tent.

Complementary **Tel Aviv (#5)**; **Aqaba (#43)**; **Eilat (#78)**; **Sharm el-Sheikh (#88)**; **Tel Aviv Beaches (#89)**; *Akhziv Beach*; *Argaman Beach*; *Beit Yannai*; *Drummers' Beach*; *Ein Bokek*; *Herziliya Beaches*; *Mediterranean Coast*; *Netanya*; *Sea of Galilee Beaches*; Aqueduct Beach (E4); Bat Galim Beach (E1); Beaches (U); Dolphin Reef (L2); Gordon Beach (D1); Nahariya (E5); North Beach (L1); Palmahim (E3); South Beach (M2); South Haifa Beaches (E7); Taba (T1); and *Group Fun at a Downtown Beach (D1)*.

REMOTE BEACHES There are dozens of beaches to choose from on the ***Mediterranean Coast***, from the busy beaches of Tel Aviv which see millions of visitors each year to long stretches of sand without a soul to be found. If you prefer the latter, you have a lot to work with. First, skip the weekends. Second, skip the middle of summer. Shoulder-season weekdays are when you're going to find the emptiest and most glorious beaches.

The **Clean Coast Index** (w gov.il/en/Departments/Guides/clean_coast_program) is another way of evaluating beaches, this time specifically rating remote beaches by a cleanliness factor, scoring from Very Clean to Clean, Average, Dirty, and Very Dirty, where the number of plastic pieces determines the score. The Ministry of Environmental Protection in Israel rates their own beaches each year based on the same criteria. The index specifically evaluates "unauthorized" beaches that have no lifeguard presence and where swimming is (in theory) not allowed, accounting for 130km of the 185km in total of Mediterranean sand. On average, Israeli beaches score well, with some 70% regularly receiving scores of Very Clean or Clean. Each beach is measured over the course of several visits each year. The beaches scoring consistently highest (three scores of Very Clean) in 2020 (from north to south) were: South Akko, South Arsof, Tel Baruch, Bat Yam, Palmahim National Park (southern section), South Ashdod, and North Ashkelon.

Our recommendations are Dahab and Dor HaBonim. Dahab is a tranquil, cheap, hippie oasis on the Red Sea in the Egyptian Sinai. Dor is considered by some to be the most beautiful beach in Israel, which is stiff competition. But you'll have many off-the-beaten-path beaches to choose from outside the heavily trafficked Tel Aviv options.

Best examples **Dahab (#54)**; **Dor HaBonim (#100)**; and ***Mediterranean Coast***.

Complementary Atlit Beach (E4); Geder Beach (E7); HaSharon Beach (E7); Jisr az-Zarqa (E4); and *Solo Fun at a Wave-Filled Beach (E7)*.

WATER

SEA ACCESS Below are the main access points for the inland bodies of water, principally the **Sea of Galilee (#7)** and the **Dead Sea (#3)**. ***Tiberias*** is your best bet for arranging a trip on the Kinneret, while ***Ein Bokek*** provides free public access to the salty lake.

Best examples ***Tiberias*** and ***Ein Bokek***.

Complementary Biankini/Siesta Beach (K1); Neve Midbar Beach (K1); and New Kalya Beach (K1).

THERMAL WATERS There are a number of places which offer hot springs and mineral baths. Our pick is the Hammamat Ma'in Hot Springs near the Dead Sea in Jordan, with temperature-controlled waters and thermal waterfalls.

Best example **Hammamat Ma'in Hot Springs**.

Complementary **Dead Sea (#3)**; **Gan HaShlosha**; **Hamat Gader**; and **Hamat Tiberias**.

FISHING This area does not have a particular reputation for sport fishing, but there are some options for those looking for an under-appreciated spot for salt- or freshwater fishing. In Israel, there are three main spots: the Mediterranean, the Sea of Galilee, and the Red Sea. (Obviously, the Dead Sea is not a good spot to catch fish.) Much of the Mediterranean and Red Sea areas are protected marine conservation zones, and the Nature and Parks Authority has begun aggressively tackling (pun alert) unlicensed fishing vessels. Shore fishing is allowed, but licenses are still encouraged. The Israel Sport Fishing Association (w isfa.org.il) can help you with licensees. You'll find fishermen fishing off the walls of Jaffa and Akko, among other towns. Gaza, in particular, is a big fishing area.

Otherwise, rent a yacht and skipper from any of the major coastal cities – many of their websites are in Hebrew or direct people to call for more information. Book in advance unless you'll be on the coast for multiple days, in case the service is booked for several days ahead. There are also some lakes with fishing, including at Hamat Gader.

In Jordan, the government recognizes an uncontrolled recreational fish sector, so beware of any new regulations that local tour companies might forget to inform you about.

Complementary **Sea of Galilee (#7)**; **Red Sea/Gulf of Aqaba (#10)**; **Akko (#13)**; **Jaffa (#30)**; and *Hamat Gader*.

RESORTS AND HOLIDAY

SPAS AND MASSAGE The concept of a spa vacation has grown in popularity over the past 10–15 years in both Israel and Jordan. Options that regularly receive commendation from online blogs are: Carmel Forest Spa Resort; Cramim Resort and Spa, outside Abu Ghosh; Beresheet Mitzpe Ramon; Ritz-Carlton Herziliya; Herod's Eilat; Mitzpe Hayamim Rosh Pina; and David Intercontinental Tel Aviv. For self-care and skin treatments, head to the Dead Sea. *Suweimeh Spa Hotels* in Jordan offer the best options and its hotels are our favorites. In Israel, check out *Ein Bokek Spa Hotels*. For other recommended luxury and spa hotel options, see *Do #5: Sleep It!* (p. 48).

Best examples **Suweimeh Spa Hotels** and Hammams (Q3).

Complementary **Dead Sea (#3)**; **Nablus (#61)**; **Sharm el-Sheikh (#88)**; *Hamat Gader*; *Hammamat Ma'in Hot Springs*; Al-Pasha Turkish Bath (Q3); and Beresheet Hotel (J2).

PEACEFUL There's a lot of hustle and bustle in this region. Even on so-called "vacation," there always tend to be lots of people around (i.e., beaches in Tel Aviv; resorts on the Dead Sea or Eilat; sightseeing anywhere). Unfortunately, Tel Aviv's beaches are no place to find peace. The constant *plop, plop* from the matcot game played by everyone can be enough to drive you nuts. Rather, the mid-Mediterranean beaches are a better bet. Check out *Remote Beaches* above. Or head straight to **Dor HaBonim (#100)**, a glorious strip of sand you should have mostly to yourself.

The **Dead Sea (#3)** can be very peaceful, if you steer clear of public access points. Most people who pay for the experience at a hotel/resort are there to relax, though you can't be sure about big parties of kids or wedding parties, say. Even tranquil *Ein Bokek* tends to attract a crowd. Better, visit one of the *Suweimeh Spa Hotels* or *Ein Bokek Spa Hotels* midweek or off-season and find tranquility on a likely empty beach.

Small towns are usually a good bet. *Zichron Ya'akov* has the right feel of commercialism with a laid-back quality that is sometimes hard to find in this region.

Resort areas in Israel are often crowded. Sure, there are spa facilities (see above), but hotels tend to be loud. The super-relaxed town of **Dahab (#54)** is great to find a quiet place to read a book, drink a beer, or take a dip. You may even find solace at the resort town of **Sharm el-Sheikh (#88)** down the road.

Entertainment

SHOPPING

MARKETS One of our favorite pastimes is strolling through markets, or *shuks*. Not only do they provide great people-watching opportunities and often bite-size samples of local flavors, but the array of sights and smells is dizzyingly delicious. Mehane Yehuda in Jerusalem is small, but packs a big punch and converts from market into an after-hours food and drink strip. Carmel Market is the biggest and most famous in Tel Aviv, with clothing, electronics, produce, dairy, seafood, and meat for sale. The most coveted food stalls are at the southernmost end.

Best examples **Mehane Yehuda Market (#67)** and **Carmel Market (#87)**.

Complementary **Jaffa (#30)**; *Mount Gilboa*; *Tel Aviv Port*; *Zichron Ya'akov*; HaTikva Market (D8); Levinsky Market (D4); Muslim Quarter (A2); Sarona Market (D3); and *Dimona (J1)*.

HANDMADE If you're tired of the typical tourist trinkets, you might want to head to one of these places specializing in one-of-a-kind and handmade pieces. Mystical Tsfat is the city of Ḳabbalah, but also a city of art, with a number of art galleries selling beautiful pieces, as well as vendors selling all types of artistic Judaica. Zichron has wine and art.

Best examples **Tsfat/Safed (#58)** and *Zichron Ya'akov*.

Complementary **Old City Jerusalem (#1)**; **Jaffa (#30)**; **Ajloun Forest (#57)**; **Feynan Ecolodge (#86)**; *Ein Hod*; *Ein Kerem*; *Tel Aviv Port*; Armenian Quarter (A2); Hutzot Hayotzer Arts and Crafts Festival (A7); Jordan River Designs Showroom (Q4); Nahalat Binyamin (D4); Nakhalat Shiva (A7); Sheinkin Street (D4); *Hatachana Train Station (D1)*; and *Beit Jamal Monastery (B2)*.

BOUTIQUES (CLOTHING, JEWELRY) If you're looking for boutique or unique items (e.g., clothing and jewelry), try the Jaffa Flea Market, aka Shuk HaPishpeshim. You'll find old items and new, antiques, carpets, jewelry, secondhand clothes, fashion, and knick-knacks all set amid a cute area filled with cafés and restaurants.

Best example **Jaffa Flea Market**.

Complementary **Neve Tzedek**; *Tel Aviv Port*; Nahalat Binyamin (D4); Sheinkin Street (D4); and *Hatachana Train Station (D1)*.

SOUVENIRS If you're in the market for the best souvenirs, we recommend visiting *Do #17: Shop It!* (p. 100) so you can focus on that perfect gift for friends and family. Our top picks are the Old City, which sells all kinds of religious paraphernalia, cheeky T-shirts, jewelry, pottery, antiques, coins, you name it. The hassle factor can be quite high but, if you're a good bargainer, you're in for a treat. Remember: the first price is always going to be three times the value, or more, so start ridiculously low because you'll have to meet somewhere in the middle. Kibbutz Mitzpe Shalem is the home of Ahava Dead Sea products at bargain-basement prices. You can also buy them in Ein Bokek at any of the shorefront shops. Rest easy if you can't make up your mind: the Ben Gurion Airport has an excellent duty-free section you can take advantage of on your way out, including booze and perfume, but also Dead Sea mud products, high-end Israeli wine, and pomegranate wine, among other interesting products.

Best examples **Old City Jerusalem (#1)** and Kibbutz Mitzpe Shalem (K1).

Complementary **Dead Sea (#3)**; **Nablus (#61)**; **Mehane Yehuda Market (#67)**; **Carmel Market (#87)**; *Ein Bokek*; *Ein Bokek Spa Hotels*; *Zichron Ya'akov*; Armenian Quarter (A2); Hurva Square (A4); Hutzot Hayotzer Arts and Crafts Festival (A7); and Muslim Quarter (A2).

AMUSEMENT

AMUSEMENT PARKS There are several amusement parks (if you want to call them that) to choose from in the region. We're not talking about Disneyland or Six Flags, but they have their admirers. Water parks are popular with locals (in Rishpon, Tiberias, Tel Aviv, among others), but temper your expectations – none made our list. You'll find two major theme parks: Luna Park (Tel Aviv) and Superland (Rishon Letzion) offering rides for all ages, including roller coasters. Zoos and aquaria are also an option, which we cover in the *Life* categories (p. 524). Mini Israel is a fun activity, with shrunken versions of Israel's best sites.

Best example Mini Israel (B2).

Complementary **Timna (#96)**; *Ancient Qatzrin*; *Underwater Observatory*; Dolphin Reef (L2); and *Rishpon (D7)*.

SKY ACTIVITIES For fans of crazy airborne activities, you'll find a fair amount of options in the region.

★ *Tandem skydiving* Jump out of a plane while strapped to a professional at Paradive at Habonim Beach (**w** paradive.co.il), Israel Extreme in Akhziv (**w** israel-extreme. com/sites/achziv-drop-zone/), and SkyKef in the Negev (**w** skykef.co.il).

★ *Hot air balloons* Royal Aero Sports Club of Jordan offers balloon rides over Wadi Rum (**w** www.rascj.com), and Tourist Israel connects you to balloons in the Galilee (**w** touristisrael.com/hot-air-balloon-israel/1119/).

★ *Paragliding* A free-flying, non-motorized, winged-parachute-driven glider, usually done in tandem for new gliders: try Tel Aviv Paragliding Club (**w** isrpg. com). Experienced gliders with their own equipment can check out spots to glide at **w** paraglidingmap.com/sites/israel.

★ *Powered paragliding* Like paragliding, but in a motorized vehicle. Extreme Israel flies over Masada, Sea of Galilee, or Caesarea (**w** xn----zhcb4afbwe7a0dnem.co.il/ extreme-activities-in-israel), or try ◻ FreeFlightJordan for Jordan paramotors.

★ *Parasailing* More akin to waterskiing, as you're harnessed to a moving boat, but with the goal of sailing through the air via parachute. In Eilat, contact Kisusky (**w** kisuski.co.il; ✆ 072 392 2437).

★ *Bungee jumping* A company used to do jumps from the **Bridge of Strings** in Jerusalem, but no longer.

★ *Zip-lining* Travel speedily from one point to another via gravity and a suspension cable, to which you're harnessed. At over 400m, the longest zip line in Israel can be found at Deer Land in Gush Etzion (**w** deer-land.co.il).

★ *Helicopter rides* There are lots of options with either Israel Helicopters (**w** helicopter.co.il) or Israel Unlimited (**w** israelunlimited.com).

PARTY

BARS AND CLUBS Bars and clubs are covered extensively in *Do #18: Late Nit!* (p. 107), but a few of our stars actually made it to coveted elective (and near-elective) status, with several mentions by guidebooks and other Holy Land experts.

Twice named one of the World's 50 Best Bars, the craft cocktail bar in the Imperial Hotel Tel Aviv is likely to satisfy your alcohol-as-art cravings. Kuli Alma is easily the coolest spot in town – a high marker for trendy Tel Aviv.

If you're looking for a pub crawl to meet new people while taking the edge off, check out the Tel Aviv Pub Crawl (**f** BePartOfTheHeart) and Jerusalem Pub Crawl (**w** abrahamtours.com/tours/jerusalem-pub-crawl/). Dungeon Night Club is a fetish club in Tel Aviv that has a notorious international reputation.

Best examples **Imperial Bar (#99)** and Kuli Alma (D4).

Complementary **Tel Aviv (#5)**; **Jaffa (#30)**; **Ramallah (#68)**; **Jerusalem, New City (#72)**; **Eilat (#78)**; *Haifa*; *Neve Tzedek*; *Tel Aviv Port*; *Tel Aviv Tayelet/Promenade*; Bellboy Bar (D4); Butler Bar (D4); Florentin (D4); Gatsby Cocktail Room (A7); German Colony (E1); OTR (Q4); Par Derriere (D4); Petro (Q2); Suramare (D4); and *Jerusalem Nightlife (A7)*.

VICE Your centers of vice are **Tel Aviv (#5)** and **Ramallah (#68)**. Party culture is thickest, with the biggest mix of hip, casual, and young. Marijuana use is not rampant, but it's certainly available. Technically, cannabis possession is illegal in Israel, Palestine, Jordan, and Egypt. Use of the drug is of course discouraged by the governments, but enforcement is another matter. In Israel, the laws against possession may have weakened in recent years, but first- and second-time possession offenders are still levied hefty fines. In Jordan, first-time offenders can be sent to drug rehabilitation facilities. Keep in mind that first-time offenses for a foreigner using drugs could be deportation and a ban on return, so exercise sober thoughts before you knowingly decide to participate in illegal drug use, in private or public.

Smoking is illegal indoors in Israel, as well as in outdoor spaces where people are eating. Restaurants in Jordan (and to some extent Egypt) have designated smoking areas. The most popular regional vice is ***Argila/Hookah/Shisha***. As the preferred narcotic of choice in the region, many venues are specifically set up for lovers of the water pipe and its flavored tobacco.

NIGHTLIFE There's a lot of great nightlife options in many of the major cities in the region. For more information on late-night activities, check out *Do #18: Late Nit!* (p. 107). That said, you don't want to skip on Tel Aviv's nightlife, arguably the epicenter of nightlife in the Holy Land (and beyond). There are bars, restaurants, performances, dance venues, and lots of people happily meandering about until the wee hours. With decent weather all year round, nighttime is usually pleasant. And with minimal crime, most people feel comfortable to be out late (though exercise city-caution, like you would anywhere).

Best example **Tel Aviv Nightlife (#82)**.

Complementary **Tel Aviv (#5)**; **Mehane Yehuda Market (#67)**; **Ramallah (#68)**; **Jerusalem, New City (#72)**; *Haifa*; Tel Aviv White Night (D3); and *Jerusalem Nightlife (A7)*.

THEMES

Entertainment

SPORTS

In Israel, **basketball** could be considered the country's best sport, with the Maccabi (FOX) Tel Aviv Basketball Club having won a number of international titles over the years. Check out w maccabi.co.il for information and tickets. Their archrivals are Hapoel Jerusalem.

Football/soccer is, however, the country's most popular sport. Teams compete in Europe, and have had some success over the decades. Maccabi Haifa has won the most championships in the Israeli Premier League. Tickets can be purchased at the stadium before the show or through a discounter such as Leaan (w leaan.co.il). Football is also the most popular sport in Jordan, with several teams. Check out the Jordan Football Association (w jfa.jo) for matches and dates.

Jordan has won one **Olympic** medal as of 2020, in taekwondo, while Israel has won nine, with one gold (sailing), one silver (judo), and seven bronze in sailing, judo, and canoeing. The *Olympic Experience (D7)* gives access to Olympic stars.

Food and Drink

FOOD

CUISINE There are a number of recommended cuisines of which you should be aware in advance, in case you want to slot in time to experience those during your planning phase. Much more information can be found in *Do #14: Eat It!* (p. 80).

To give you a taste (ahem), both Jordanian and Israeli cuisines are highly regarded. In Jordan, there are great restaurants serving popular Levantine dishes, such as falafel, pickles, hummus, and olives, in addition to their distinctly Jordanian meat dishes. But there's also a distinct sense of place with the food over the course of millennia in this desert climate. For Israel, with people settling here from all over the world, the various foods of Jewish, Arab, European, Middle Eastern, Mediterranean, and many other peoples have combined into a kind of style of cooking that is distinctly Israeli. Visitors can experience this style in restaurants, markets, takeaway places, and all throughout the country. For something a bit more upscale, check out the elective on modern Israeli cuisine, a delectable foray into the blended cultures we just mentioned.

Best examples **Jordanian Cuisine (#44)**; **Israeli Cuisine (#51)**; and *Modern Israeli Cuisine*.

FOODS If we haven't made this clear: there are **very good food** options in these parts. The best examples are:

★ *Hummus*: there are entire establishments specializing in hummus called hummusiya. We promise these are worth your time! Check out *Do #14: Eat It!* (p. 80).
★ *Sabich/Oved's*: sabich is the famed sandwich in a pita (that's not falafel). Oved's in Giv'atayim is the most famous purveyor.
★ *Shakshuka/Dr. Shakshuka*: shakshuka is a delicious breakfast of tomatoes and eggs, most famous today at the Jaffa shop, Dr. Shakshuka.
★ Israeli Breakfast (U): a filling and robust meal, often served at hotels – though one can get a simpler affair from restaurants.
★ Mansaf (V): the national dish of Jordan, it traditionally includes lamb cooked in jameed (fermented, dry yogurt) sauce with various spices, served over shrak (large, thin lavash-like bread) with rice or bulgur.
★ Sufganiyot (D6): big jelly donuts eaten at Hanukkah.

TOP RESTAURANTS We've opted not to list restaurants and eateries in every city and town in the region in this guide. COVID-19 has had a grave effect on many in the hospitality industry, and, while those listed below represent the most beloved and/or revered, even these restaurants aren't impervious to economic troubles. We apologize if businesses move or close down. All the more reason why we've chosen to highlight only the establishments that have made a mark on the culinary world. In the following tables, we've highlighted all the restaurants that earned enough recognition to become their own electives. We've set them up so you can check them off as you go, or mark the ones of interest to you for further research. Note that the restaurants in Tel Aviv are all plotted on *City Walk D6*, while the others can be found in their indicated micro-regions.

THEMES

Food and Drink

Best examples **Machneyuda (#98)**; *Tzfon Abraxas*; *Uri Buri*; and *Elbabor*. Machneyuda rose to the top of the list as the best regional restaurant, while our personal favorite is Tzfon (North) Abraxas. A close second: *Uri Buri* (devastatingly destroyed in the 2021 uprising, but determined to reopen). Third place: *Elbabor*.

Complementary **Petra Kitchen (#84)**; Hotel Montefiore (D4); and Suramare (D4).

Tel Aviv

Restaurant	Cuisine	Micro-region
☐ M25	butchery	D3
☐ Yom Tov Delicatessen	deli	D4
☐ Tenat	Ethiopian	D4
☐ *Tzfon Abraxas*	farm-to-table	D4
☐ Claro	farm-to-table	D3
☐ *George and John*	fine dining	D4
☐ *Herbert Samuel*	fine dining	D7
☐ *Mashya*	fine dining	D1
☐ *OCD*	fine dining	D4
☐ Alena at The Norman	fine dining	D4
☐ Dallal Bakery	fine dining	D4
☐ Kitchen Market	fine dining	D1
☐ Toto	fine dining	D3
☐ Yaffo-Tel Aviv	fine dining	D7
☐ *Pastel*	French brasserie	D3
☐ *Popina*	French	D4
☐ *Busi Grill*	meat and grill	D8
☐ Ouzeria	Mediterranean	D4
☐ Turkiz	Mediterranean	D7
☐ Brothers/Ha'achim	modern Israeli	D3
☐ Dok	modern Israeli	D3
☐ HaSalon	modern Israeli	D7
☐ Port Said	modern Israeli	D4
☐ Social Club	modern Israeli	D4
☐ Meshek Barzilay	rustic vegan	D4
☐ *Manta Ray*	seafood	D1
☐ Milgo & Milbar	seafood	D4
☐ Old Man and the Sea	seafood	D2
☐ Anastasia	vegan café	D3
☐ Habasta	wine bar/food	D4

Jerusalem

Restaurant	Cuisine	Micro-region
☐ Majda	home-style	B1
☐ Ishtabach	Kurdish	A7
☐ Chakra	Mediterranean	A7
☐ Mordoch	Middle Eastern	A7
☐ Rachmo	Middle Eastern	A7
☐ Eucalyptus	modern Israeli	A7
☐ **Machneyuda (#98)**	trendy	A7

Mediterranean

Restaurant	Cuisine	Micro-region
☐ Maadali	Arab	E2
☐ Helena Banamal	fine dining	E4
☐ Hummus Said	hummusiya	E2
☐ *Uri Buri*	seafood	E2

Galilee

Restaurant	Cuisine	Micro-region
☐ HaBeit Be'einhud	Arab home-style	F1
☐ *Elbabor*	Arab/Israeli	F2
☐ Goats with the Wind	farm-to-table	G2
☐ Abu Ashraf	modern Arab	G1
☐ Magdalena	modern Arab	G4

Jordan

Restaurant	Cuisine	Micro-region
☐ Fakhr el-Din	fine dining Lebanese	Q2
☐ Shams al-Balad	local/seasonal	Q2
☐ Al-Kitkat	seafood	Q2

STREET FOOD AND QUICK BITES Food markets are a big draw for their vibrant smells and visual appeal, quick bites, and colorful cast of characters. Abu Hassan is the most famous hummusiya in Tel Aviv, with long lines in the morning. Miznon will knock your socks off with its unique pita sandwich combos. Oved's Sabich crafts a glorious eggplant-based pita sandwich in Giv'atayim, while Dr. Shakshuka is the Jaffa tomato/egg breakfast staple you didn't know you were missing.

Best examples **Abu Hassan**; **Miznon**; **Sabich/Oved's**; and **Shakshuka/Dr. Shakshuka**.

Complementary **Old City Jerusalem (#1)**; **Jaffa (#30)**; **Mehane Yehuda Market (#67)**; **Carmel Market (#87)**; **Jewish Quarter**; **Tel Aviv Port**; Abu Ghosh's hummusiyas (B1); Anita (D4); Beer Sheva (J1); Cafe Kaymak (D4); Falafel Gabai (D3); Hebron (C2); Levinsky Market (D4); Lina Hummusiya (A2); Muslim Quarter (A2); Sabich Frishman (D3); Said Abouelafia Bakery (D2); and Sarona Market (D3).

CULINARY CAPITALS A few cities are known specifically for their unique food or cuisine. Tel Aviv is the epicenter of modern Israeli cooking. Nazareth, surprisingly, has become known for its fusion of Israeli, Arab, and Galilean ingredients with international cooking styles. And if you haven't visited a hummusiya yet, go to Abu Ghosh, with its dozen restaurants specializing in, you guessed it, hummus.

Best examples **Tel Aviv (#5)**; **Nazarene Fusion Cuisine**; and Abu Ghosh's hummusiyas (B1).

Complementary **Akko (#13)**; **Jaffa (#30)**; **Modern Amman (#36)**; **Nablus (#61)**; **Jerusalem, New City (#72)**; **Modern Israeli Cuisine**; Amirim (H1); Deir Ghassaneh (C5); Fuheis (Q4); Hebron (C2); Kfar Kama (G2); and Negev Goat Farms (J2).

WINE

GREAT WINE We differentiate here between "wine" and "wineries" because not every winery has a customer-focused experience. That doesn't lessen the quality of their product! It can be difficult to find many of the best wines in regular liquor or grocery stores. For the following wines, we recommend either visiting the winery or looking for bottles from the winery on restaurant wine lists. *Food & Wine* features lists 12 wines to explore from the region (**w** foodandwine.com/wine/the-12-israeli-wines-you-need-to-drink-to-be-an-expert).

Best examples **Yatir Winery** and **Domaine du Castel**.

Complementary **Golan Heights Winery (#75)**; **Carmel Winery**; Carmey Avdat Farm Winery (J2); Château Golan Winery (I3); Clos de Gat Winery (B3); Dalton Winery (H1); Ella Valley Vineyards (B3); Flam Winery (B3); Galil Mountain Winery (H1); Margalit Winery (E6); Pelter Winery (I2); Recanati Winery (E6); Sea Horse Winery (B3); Tabor Winery (G2); Tishbi Winery (E6); Tzora Winery (B3); Vitkin Winery (E6)

WINERIES From the list below, you can put together a great set of wineries to visit on a day trip to any number of regions: Jerusalem Hills, Golan Heights, Negev, and beyond. For more on wines and wineries, visit *Do #15: Drink It!* (p. 93) or *Road Trips B3, E6,* or *U1.* No trip to the Golan would be complete without a stop at the Golan Heights Winery, the winery that put Israeli wine on the map. It has a great tasting room and a good central location from which to start and/or finish a broader wine tour.

Best examples **Golan Heights Winery (#75)**; **Winery Tour**; and **Carmel Winery**.

Complementary **Yatir Winery**; **Zichron Ya'akov**; Amphorae Winery (E6); Bulos Y Zumot Winery (Q2); Carmey Avdat Farm Winery (J2); Château Golan Winery (I3); Dalton Winery (H1); Ella Valley Vineyards (B3); Flam Winery (B3); Galil Mountain Winery (H1); Judean Hills Wineries (B3); Negev Wine Route (J2); Neot Smadar Winery (L3); Pelter Winery (I2); Recanati Winery (E6); Sde Boker (J2); Tabor Winery (G2); and Tishbi Winery (E6).

WINE REGIONS We go more in depth on how to tour wineries in the *Do #15: Drink It!* (p. 93), but there are several great regions to focus on when making your winery plans (and planning is a must – many wineries offering more intimate experiences are booked several weeks in advance).

Best examples **Golan Heights (#62)** and Judean Hills Wineries (B3).

Complementary **Battir Hills** and Negev Wine Route (J2).

DRINK

BEER AND ALCOHOL Wine might be the more historically relevant beverage of choice in the Holy Land (wine shows up in both Jewish and Christian religious services), but that doesn't mean Israel hasn't jumped on the microbrew bandwagon. **Buster's** in Beit Shemesh has its own brand of beer, as does **Taybeh** from Ramallah. Egypt and Jordan have their own national beers, which reward your wallet if not your taste buds. Jerusalem hosts an annual beer festival in August with more than 100 craft beers from Israel and overseas (**w** jerusalembeer.com/en).

Alexander Brewery is a Netanya facility using European malt and hops and purified Israeli water to create its unique blend, and won a Gold Award for its Alexander Black beer at the World Beer Cup (Friday-morning tours, book in advance). **Herzl Brewery** in south Jerusalem provides a tour of the brewing factory for groups of 10 or more. **Malka**: located adjacent to *Yehi'am* fortress, you can watch the brewing happen from glass windows while dining or drinking. **Srigim Brewery** in the Jerusalem Hills offers hour-long tours and tastings. The first microbrewer in Israel, the **Dancing Camel**, still has a solid following at its Tel Aviv establishment just south of Sarona. Tours available, there's a bar with eight taps, and it hosts music shows and classes.

Restaurants with craft beers on tap include: **Golan Brewery**, a big/busy restaurant in Qatzrin in the Golan with several of their own craft beers on tap; **Jem's** has a dozen beer gardens around Israel to choose from (**w** jems.co.il); and five of their own beers, plus a huge menu, make **LiBira Brewpub** a popular place near the Haifa port (**w** libira.co.il).

Best examples Buster's (B3) and Taybeh Brewing Company (C4).

Complementary **Mehane Yehuda Market (#67)** and **Carmel Market (#87)**.

COFFEE, TEA, AND COFFEESHOPS To those that drink it, coffee is not merely a beverage, but a lifestyle. That sentiment may be even truer in the Middle East, where social settings can at times require it. In Israel, the coffee scene resembles that of Western coffeehouses, while the Arab countries tend to have the Starbucks-type shops and more economical Arab-style coffeehouses. Either way, the café culture is what you're after – laid back, friendly, and usually combined with breakfast. Books@Cafe on Amman's Rainbow Road represents both styles well. Cafe Xoho is a great option in Tel Aviv.

Best examples *Café Culture*; Books@Cafe (Q2); and Cafe Xoho (D3).

Complementary **Tel Aviv (#5)**; **Jordanian Cuisine (#44)**; **Ramallah (#68)**; *Bedouin Tents and Coffee*; **Ben Yehuda Street**; *Jordanian Hospitality*; **Museum of Bedouin Culture**; *Neve Tzedek*; **Rothschild Boulevard**; **Wild Jordan Center**; Florentin (D4); German Colony (E1); Nakhalat Shiva (A7); and *Rishpon (D7)*.

Accommodation

STAYS

HIGHLY RECOMMENDED The following hotels have all received commendations not only from travelers but also from industry experts. Read *Do #5: Sleep It!* (p. 48) for specifics on types of lodging, lodging by budget, and other categories. Note: prices are subject to fluctuation – these are low-season rates, per night, two per room, available at time of writing.

Best examples **Feynan Ecolodge (#86)** – the accommodations are quite basic, but the Bedouin experience that comes with this hotel can't be beat (in Dana Reserve; $230); **Banksy's Walled-Off Hotel** – negatively highlighting the **Separation Wall**, this political statement of a hotel is also cute, interesting, and the best option in Bethlehem ($140); **Brown Beach House** – a contemporary boutique hotel just one block from the Tel Aviv beach, with a renowned breakfast, a South Beach vibe, and affordable price (from $115); **Elma Arts Complex** – a Brutalist architectural stunner in **Zichron Ya'akov**, now owned by Elma Hotels (from $360); **King David Hotel** – since 1931, this five-star hotel has played host to an impressive array of leaders from around the world (from $300); **Mamilla Hotel** – very close to the Old City, this modern hotel has great design, restaurant, and views (from $360); and **The Norman Hotel** – "five-star" luxury boutique hotel near **Rothschild Boulevard** in downtown Tel Aviv with a 1920s vibe, modern décor and amenities, and a rooftop infinity swimming pool (from $600).

Other hotels that have racked up awards, starting with the most recommended: Brown Jerusalem (A7), $240; Waldorf Astoria (A7), $500; Brown TLV (D4), $220; Hotel Montefiore (D4), $210; Poli House (D4), $250; Rothschild Hotel (D4), $200; White Villa Hotel (D4), $250; Lily & Bloom (D4), $230; Akkotel (E2), $160; Efendi (E2), $350; Beresheet Hotel (J2), $420; Isrotel Agamim (L1), $150; Glamping in Wadi Rum (M2), $150; Art Hotel (Q2), $76; and Intercontinental Jordan (Q2), $92.

EXPERIENTIAL LODGING The following lodging options provide you with a unique experience unlike anything else you'll be able to find in a typical hotel. We of course must again highlight Feynan Ecolodge. Set in the Dana Biosphere Reserve, this green ecolodge has become part of the local Bedouin community, offering walking, coffee, stargazing, cooking, and other great experiences included as part of the whole package.

Best examples **Feynan Ecolodge (#86)** and **Banksy's Walled-Off Hotel**.

Complementary **Dahab (#54)**; **Bedouin Tents and Coffee**; **Kibbutz Lotan**; **Mamshit**; **Mitzpe Ramon**; Beresheet Hotel (J2); Burqu (R1); Kibbutz Merom Golan (I2); Kibbutzim (U); Lutheran Guest House (A2); Negev Camping (J2); Nuweiba Beach Camps (T1); Sde Boker (J2); Shkedi's Camplodge (K1); Tzimmers (H2); and Glamping in Wadi Rum (M2).

VACATION RESORTS AND HOTELS There are several locations throughout the region that are set up specifically for your vacation needs. Eilat, for instance, is a holiday destination. At the southernmost tip of Israel on the Red Sea, this resort town is hot year-round, which makes it a lovely winter destination. Similarly, Sharm el-Sheikh, on the southeastern shore of the Egyptian Sinai, is known for its swanky resorts and proximity to swimming and diving holes.

Best examples **Eilat (#78)** and **Sharm el-Sheikh (#88)**.

Complementary **Dead Sea (#3)**; **Aqaba (#43)**; *Ein Bokek*; *Ein Bokek Spa Hotels*; *Hammamat Ma'in Hot Springs*; *Suweimeh Spa Hotels*; *Tiberias*; Burqu (R1); Kibbutz Ein Gev (G3); and Rosh Pina (H2).

CAMPGROUNDS Check out our section on camping in *Do #5: Sleep It!* (p. 48) (preplanning required). The following options are all electives with camping options. You may already be familiar with "glamping," or glamour camping, but it's essentially like sleeping outdoors without any of the uncomfortable bits. Wadi Rum has a number of options for those looking for a comfortable bed, hot shower, privacy, and luxury amenities – with tent covering or glass so you can see the stars.

Best examples **Wadi Rum (#4)** and *Glamping in Wadi Rum (M2)*.

Complementary **Masada (#8)**; **Mount Sinai (#15)**; **Dana Biosphere Reserve (#21)**; **St. Catherine's Monastery (#22)**; **Makhtesh Ramon (#28)**; **Ein Gedi (#50)**; **Golan Heights (#62)**; **Jesus Trail (#69)**; **Coral Beach (#83)**; **Timna (#96)**; **Dor HaBonim (#100)**; *Akhziv Beach*; *Beit Yannai*; *Church of the Transfiguration*; *Hiking in the Negev*; *Mitzpe Ramon*; *Mount Carmel*; *Sea of Galilee Beaches*; *Tel Arad*; *Tel Ashkelon*; *Yotvata Hai-Bar*; HaYarkon Park (D7); Horshat Tal (I1); Jordan River Rafting (I1); Nawatef Camp (O1); Negev Camping (J2); Nuweiba Beach Camps (T1); Rasoun Camping (S2); and Shkedi's Camplodge (K1).

Organized

PARTICIPATORY

VOLUNTEER There are a number of volunteer opportunities, if you have the time, commitment, and sometimes money, though there are also several paid/exchange opportunities. In fact, volunteering is one of our main recommendations in the region. Be it archaeology, ecology, refugee assistance, cultural immersions, farming, wine-growing, or tourism, there are a ton of ways to stay in Israel for a few months or longer, balancing work and play.

Kibbutz Lotan's Center for Creative Ecology offers a number of half-day workshops in sustainable development activities, including building domes, composting, gardening, and creating bricks. The **Jewish Agency for Israel** places Jewish volunteers in various settings, depending on your time, skills, age, and other factors (**w** jewishagency.org/get-involved-abroad/). **Nefesh B'Nefesh** has contact information and details on a variety of Israel volunteer opportunities, many of which do not have a religious component or requirement, if you are not Jewish (**w** nbn. org.il/sherut-leumi/sherut-leumi-organizations/). If you're interested in combining a tour of Israel and Palestine with cultural immersion, education, faith, language, and volunteerism, try the **Holy Land Trust**'s Summer Encounters – 30 days of a highly regarded, well-rounded experience (**w** holylandtrust.org/travel-experiences/summer-encounter). The **Palestinian Medical Relief Society** offers volunteers of many disciplines the opportunity to work in the West Bank and Gaza Strip (**w** pmrs.ps). Despite the low-budget aesthetic, the **iVolunteer** website has a number of popular and lesser-known opportunities (**w** ivolunteer.org.il/Eng/). For a nonpolitical/nonreligious option, if you have 6–9 weeks to commit, you can work at one of three **Abraham Hostels** in Tel Aviv, Nazareth, and Jerusalem. It's "volunteer" because you aren't paid for your 30 hours of work each week, but you do get free accommodation in a volunteer dorm room and free stays at the other two hostels. **GoEco** offers 2–4-week desert experiences volunteering in one of three south Negev locations: Yotvata Nature Reserve, Coral Beach Reserve, and Kibbutz Lotan (**w** goeco.org).

Best example **Kibbutz Volunteer**.

Complementary **Coral Beach (#83)**; *Yotvata Hai-Bar*; and **Kibbutz Lotan**.

COOKING SCHOOL/FOOD ACTIVITIES The best way to get to know a city might just be through its food, so what better task than a cooking class or a food tour? We highly recommend you book these in advance. Super-popular after a day of hiking is Petra's Kitchen. This cooking school offers nightly classes cooking Jordanian food over a three-hour lesson. Eat a feast at the end. Great fun! Beit Sitti is another great option for those with time in Amman.

Druze Cooking Workshops in the Galilee and Golan are spectacular. Druze families have opened up their homes and kitchens to introduce their locally sourced, tasty, and often healthful home-cooked cuisine. They also offer a foraging course where you pick wild greens before cooking them. Book through Galileat (**w** galileat. com). Also do an **olive oil sampling**, if you get a chance. Olive trees are abundant in this region, and they make some excellent olive oil. Dozens of options at w zait.galil. gov.il. **Tali Friedman** offers instructional courses in the Mehane Yehuda Market on selecting produce, oils, cereals, meats, and fish, and then the entire group cooks a meal together (w haatelie.com). Located in Bethlehem of Galilee (outside Nazareth, not to be confused with Palestine's Bethlehem), the **Spice Road Farm** hosts cooking workshops, lectures on organic farming practices, and sells dozens of varieties of spices and herbs (w derech-hatavlinim.co.il). Finally, there are a number of farms that host **fruit and vegetable picking** in the Golan Heights. Blogger Love Love Israel has the best running list of open farms and what they have on offer (w loveloveisrael. com/post/the-big-list-of-fruit-flower-and-vegetable-picking-places).

Best examples **Petra Kitchen (#84)**; *Beit Sitti*; and *Druze Cooking Workshops (H1)*.

Complementary **Tel Aviv (#5)**; **Akko (#13)**; **Nazareth (#29)**; **Jaffa (#30)**; **Mehane Yehuda Market (#67)**; **Jerusalem, New City (#72)**; **Carmel Market (#87)**; Levinsky Market (D4); and Zikra Initiative (P1).

PETTING ZOOS AND ANIMAL RIDES
We have a whole section on animals in the *Animals, Zoos, and Wildlife* category (p. 524), but these are the types of animals you can touch! We recommend riding a camel: although it is uncomfortable, and you should make sure you're supporting a camel that looks well cared for (not under-nourished), you will then join the club of camel riders everywhere.

Best example **Camel Riding**.

Complementary **Underwater Observatory** – dolphins, sharks, stingrays; **Hamat Gader** – petting zoo and crocodiles (not together); Camel Safari (T1); Dolphin Reef (L2); Alpaca Farm (J2); Kibbutz Merom Golan (I2) – horseback riding; Gan Garoo (F2) – kangaroos and wallabies gifted from Australia; and *Biblical Museum of Natural History (B2)*.

DIGS
If you have an amateur archaeologist in your family or friend group, they might appreciate participating in an actual dig. The Dig-for-a-Day option in Beit Guvrin is especially great for tourists, and families. If you have 3–4 weeks to devote, there are a variety of options each year at w mfa.gov.il/MFA/IsraelExperience/ History/Pages/Archaeological-excavations-in-Israel-2021.aspx. Most take place in June and July. You can also apply directly through the Biblical Archaeology Society (w biblicalarchaeology.org).

Best examples Archaeological Seminars Dig-for-a-Day (B2); Emek Tzurim (A6); Tel Gezer Archaeological Project (B2); and *Temple Mount Sifting Project (A6)*.

Complementary **Akko (#13)**; **Megiddo (#59)**; **Beit Guvrin and Maresha (#60)**; **Tel Dan (#63)**; **Timna (#96)**; **Dor HaBonim (#100)**; *Akhziv Beach*; *Apollonia*; *Tel Hazor*; *Tiberias*; Abila (S1); and Tel Lachish (B2).

LANGUAGE SCHOOL
For those wanting to learn a language (and have at least a month to spare), Israel has a lot of options. Known for its Hebrew immersion classes for new immigrants, ulpanim are language institutes that offer five months of subsidized classes to Jews who have recently made "Aliyah" to Israel (become a citizen). If this is you, you are likely already aware of the program as it's an integral part of the initiation for new Israelis.

Anyone looking to learn in a less rigorous or committed fashion can still attend private classes, often at the same institutions, but usually not with new immigrants. The blog SecretTelAviv has a great roundup of ulpans and other places to learn Hebrew (w secrettelaviv.com/magazine/blog/ulpan-places-to-learn-hebrew-in -tel-aviv). If grammar and rules make you hate language, you might appreciate a more conversation-focused course by the aptly named "This Is Not an Ulpan" (w thisisnotanulpan.com).

Arabic language instruction is available from a number of universities and institutes in Amman, Jerusalem, Ramallah, Nablus, and Bethlehem, among others. Culture Trip (w theculturetrip.com) has a great roundup of options in the West Bank and Amman for those looking to do longer-term training, starting at four weeks.

TOURS

FOOD AND MARKET The small but packed **Mehane Yehuda Market (#67)** has great market tours (w en.machne.co.il/category/tours-workshops). There are always great reviews for **TLVEG Tours**, which samples a variety of vegan restaurants and food on a walk through Tel Aviv (w betelavivtours.com/eng/TLVEG_Tours). In addition to their walking tours which comb **Carmel Market (#87)** and Levinsky Market (D4), **Delicious Food Tours** offers additional options to shop and then cook a variety of courses, visit wineries and breweries, or celebrate Shabbat (w deliciousisrael.com/delicious -walking-tours/). **Shuk TLV** offers three self-guided walking/eating tours of Tel Aviv markets, with six stops to give bites/tastes of the local goods. Options for "Bite Cards" include Carmel Market, Levinsky Market, and **Jaffa Flea Market** (w shuktlv.co.il). **Via Sabra** offers a dozen culinary tour options throughout Israel, including Nazareth, the Galilee, Haifa, and Akko in addition to Tel Aviv and Jerusalem. It offers a fabulous seven-day, all-inclusive $3,000 introduction to the best of the best Israeli cuisine, with reservations at some of our top restaurants, such as **Machneyuda (#98)**, *Uri Buri*, and *Elbabor*. Also part of the tour are foraging quests, Druze cooking instruction, and market tours (w viasabra.com).

GUIDED Guided tours are everywhere, and you'll notice them immediately when you enter **Old City Jerusalem (#1)**. See below the cities with easy-to-set-up guided tour options, while guided tours are specifically referenced in the entries for electives #1–#50.

Israel **Tanach Tiyulim** gets a lot of press (w tanachtiyulim.com/tiyulim.php). **Sandeman's New Jerusalem** offers tours in 18 cities, and promote its free 2-hour tour heavily everywhere. You'll see its red T-shirts throughout Tel Aviv and Jerusalem, where it offers both free tours and longer, more intimate paid tours. The free option in Jerusalem leaves twice a day from Jaffa Gate and visits the major sites over 2 hours. In Tel Aviv it tours Jaffa, leaving twice a day from the Clock Tower; the other tours are 2–3 hours and cheap (under $20; w neweuropetours.eu). **Abraham Tours** also has dozens of options, offering departures from Jerusalem, Tel Aviv, Nazareth, and Eilat to sites in the West Bank, Egypt, Jordan, various desert locales, and the Golan, among other more traditional Israel/Dead Sea/Petra destinations (☏ +972 (0)25660045; w abrahamtours.com/tours/). **Israel Photography Tours** in Jerusalem and Tel Aviv offer interesting 3- and 6-hour itineraries (w israelphotographytour.com/faq/).

Tel Aviv-Jaffa The **Bauhaus Center** offers the best and most educated tour of the White City, replete with examples from the more than 4,000 Bauhaus buildings in

Tel Aviv (80 ILS; English tour 10.00 Friday). If you like its tours, there are six others – three in Tel Aviv, in Jerusalem, Akko, and Masada – by reservation only. The **Tel Aviv Municipality** helps coordinate tours of the Tel Aviv Port (free; 11.00 Thursday), Sarona (11.00 Friday), and Downtown (11.00 Saturday) (w visit-tel-aviv.com/en/tel-aviv-global-tours/). The **Tel Aviv Greeter** program offers completely free (no tips either!) tours of the city with local guides. Booking needs to be done 3–4 weeks in advance (w telavivgreeter.com).

Jerusalem The **Jerusalem Municipality** offers free tours every Saturday, leaving from Safra Square at 26 Jaffa Street at 10.00. Official City of David tours can be booked and reserved at w cityofdavid.org.il/en/tours/city-david/city-david-tours-biblical-jerusalem. The **Western Wall Tunnels** also require a reservation (w thekotel.org/en/tours/western-wall-tunnels/). The **Israel Museum** has a calendar with available guided tours (w www.imj.org.il/en/events). Schedule your tour to **Yad Vashem** in advance (groups of six or more, required; w forms.yadvashem.org/reservations). For our Muslim readers, **a guided visit of the Dome of the Rock** interiors is a special experience. Unfortunately, entry is not permitted for non-Muslims.

Jordan Check out **Viator** for paid guides (w viator.com). Many tour operators run daily from Tel Aviv, Jerusalem, and Eilat to Petra, including **Abraham Tours** (see above). There are a number of other companies that run one- and two-day returns, with the latter often incorporating Wadi Rum, the Dead Sea, or biblical sites. (We don't think one day is enough in Petra, but it's better than zero days.) You'll want to call to confirm any bookings, as you shouldn't waste any time if you're planning last minute. Also try w petrafromisrael.com, w desertecotours.com, w ibookisrael.com, or w mantis-tours.com. We highly recommend the w touristisrael.com blog which also organizes tours, although it contracts with different vendors who often have mixed reviews on booking sites.

Complementary **Old City Jerusalem (#1)**; **Petra (#2)**; **Tel Aviv (#5)**; **Modern Movement (Bauhaus Architecture) (#16)**; **Israel Museum (#17)**; **Dana Biosphere Reserve (#21)**; **Wadi Mujib and Mujib Biosphere Reserve (#23)**; **Bahá'í Gardens (#27)**; **Makhtesh Ramon (#28)**; **Citadel/Tower of David (#32)**; **Yad Vashem (#35)**; **Western Wall Tunnels (#94)**; *Al-Ayoun Trail*; *Bible Lands Museum*; *Museum of Bedouin Culture*; *Royal Society for the Conservation of Nature (RSCN)*; Dheisheh Refugee Camp (C2); Camel Safari (T1); and Zikra Initiative (P1).

MULTI-STOP/SELF-DIRECTED A number of our electives are actually collections of great sites that require several days to do properly. Luckily, we've got you covered with **micro-region itineraries** that cover each of these collected sites: **Sea of Galilee (#7)** – *Road Trips G3 and G4*; **Qasr Amra and the Desert Palaces (#20)** – *Road Trips R1 and W1*; **King's Highway (#31)** – *Road Trip O1*; **Golan Heights (#62)** – *Road Trips I1, I2, and I3*; **Incense Route (#73)** – *Road Trip J3*; **Winery Tour** – *Road Trips B3, E6, and U1*; Cities of the Decapolis (W3) – *Road Trip W3*; and *Crusader Castle Hopping (W4)* – *Road Trip W4*.

Part 8

Electives by Region

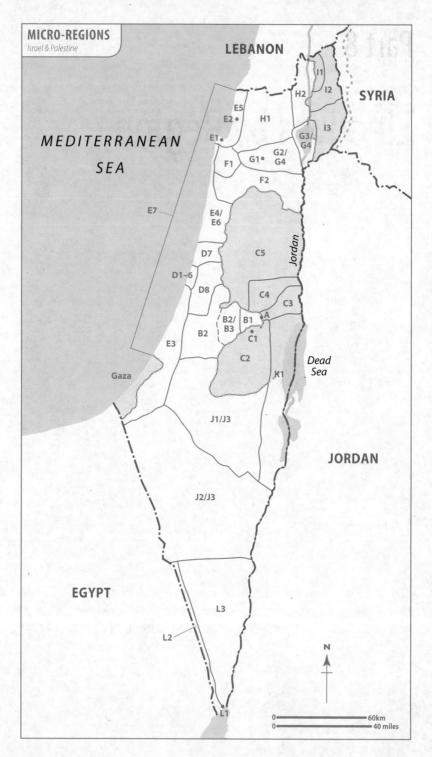

MICRO-REGIONS
Israel & Palestine

LEBANON

SYRIA

MEDITERRANEAN
SEA

I1
I2
H2
E5
E2
E1
H1
G3/
G4
I3
F1
G1
G2/
G4
F2
E7
E4/
E6
D7
C5
Jordan
D1–6
D8
C4
C3
B2/
B3
B1
A
B2
C1
C2
Gaza
K1
Dead
Sea
J1/J3
JORDAN
J2/J3
EGYPT
L3
L2
N
L1

0   60km
0   40 miles

572

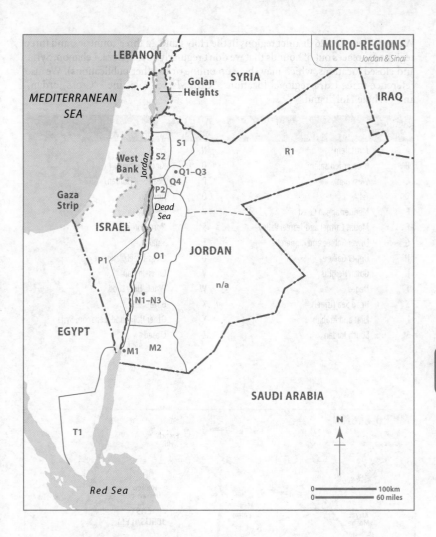

MEDITERRANEAN
SEA

LEBANON

SYRIA

IRAQ

Golan
Heights

West
Bank

Jordan

S1

S2

Q1–Q3
Q4

Gaza
Strip

P2

*Dead
Sea*

ISRAEL

JORDAN

R1

P1

O1

n/a

EGYPT

N1–N3

M1

M2

SAUDI ARABIA

N

T1

Red Sea

0 — 100km
0 — 60 miles

We have identified 26 distinct regions in the Holy Land, in three countries, and three regions for places out of bounds that we don't regularly cover (Gaza, Lebanon, Syria, and closed locations, which may show up online or in other publications). We also reference three extra-regional locations: "Cross-Israel/Palestine," "Cross-Jordan," and "Whole Holy Land."

Macro-region	Region	Macro-region	Region
A	Jerusalem	N	Petra
B	Greater Jerusalem	O	King's Highway
C	West Bank	P	Dead Sea (Jordan)
D	Tel Aviv	Q	Amman
E	Mediterranean Coast	R	East Jordan
F	Mount Carmel and Jezreel Valley	S	North Jordan
G	Lower Galilee and Kinneret	T	Sinai
H	Upper Galilee	U	Cross-Israel/Palestine
I	Golan Heights	V	Cross-Jordan
J	Negev	W	Whole Holy Land
K	Dead Sea (Israel)	X	Gaza
L	Eilat and Arabah	Y	Other Holy Land: Lebanon, Syria
M	South Jordan	Z	Closed

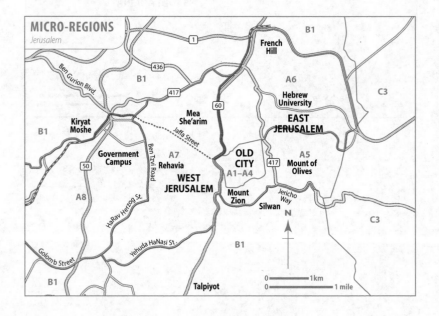

A JERUSALEM

GOLD

Rank	Elective	Theme	Sub-theme	Category	Micro-regions	BUCKET! Score	Time needed
1	Old City Jerusalem	BUCKET!	BUCKET!	BUCKET!	A1, A2, A3, A4	10	4 hrs–5+ days
6	Dome of the Rock	Structure	Monuments	Iconic Structures	A1, A2	8	20–60 mins (Muslims only)
9	Church of the Holy Sepulchre	Religion	Religious Figures	Jesus: Death	A1, A2	9	30 mins–4 hrs
11	Western Wall	Structure	Monuments	Historic Monuments	A1, A2, A4	7	10–60 mins
12	Temple Mount	Structure	Monuments	Historic Monuments	A1, A2, A3, A4	5	10–90 mins
17	Israel Museum	Culture	Museum	of Archaeology	A8	9	2 hrs–2 days
32	Citadel/Tower of David	Culture	Museum	of History	A2, A3	7	1–4 hrs
34	Mount of Olives	Religion	Houses of Worship (Extant)	Collections of Churches	A5	6	1–4 hrs
35	Yad Vashem	Structure	Monuments	Memorial	A8	7	1–4 hrs
42	Via Dolorosa	Religion	The Sacred	Pilgrimage	A1, A2	7	30 mins–4 hrs
47	Jerusalem Walls and Gates	Archaeology	Ancient Cities and Remains	Walled Cities	A3	6	90 mins–3 hrs
65	Al-Aqsa Mosque	Religion	Houses of Worship (Extant)	Mosques	A1, A2	4	5 mins–2 hrs (Muslims only)
66	Mea She'arim	People	Identity	Orthodox	A7	6	15–60 mins
67	Mehane Yehuda Market	Entertainment	Shopping	Markets	A7	6	5 mins–3 hrs
71	Jerusalem Archaeological Park	Archaeology	Roman	Herodian	A2, A4	5	1–2 hrs
72	Jerusalem, New City	Society	Cities	Principal Cities	A7	6	2 hrs–1+ days
91	Ramparts Walk	Scenic	Vistas	Urban Landscape	A3	6	1–3 hrs
92	Mount Zion	Religion	The Sacred	Pilgrimage	A5	5	1–3 hrs
94	Western Wall Tunnels	Structure	Engineering	Infrastructure	A1, A2, A4	7	1 hr 30 mins
98	Machneyuda	Food and Drink	Food	Top Restaurants	A7	7	2–3 hrs

SILVER

Elective	BUCKET! Score	Micro-region
Ben Yehuda Street	6	A7
Bible Lands Museum	5	A8
Bridge of Strings	5	A8
Cardo	5	A4
Church of St. Anne and the Pools of Bethesda	5	A2

Elective	BUCKET! Score	Micro-region
City of David	5	A5
Dome of the Chain	4	A2
Fountain of Sultan Qaytbay	4	A2
Hezekiah's Tunnel	6	A5
Jewish Quarter	5	A4
King David Hotel	5	A7

Elective	BUCKET! Score	Micro-region
Mamilla Hotel	5	A7
Rockefeller Archaeological Museum	5	A6
St. James' Cathedral	5	A2

Elective	BUCKET! Score	Micro-region
Supreme Court of Israel	4	A8
Wohl Archaeological Museum	5	A4
Yemen Moshe	4	A7
YMCA	4	A7

BRONZE

Armenian Quarter
Basilica of the Agony
Beit Shmuel-Mercaz Shimshon
Bonem House
Brown Jerusalem
Chakra
Church of Mary Magdalene
Church of the Paternoster
Consulate General of Belgium/ Villa Salameh
Dead Sea Scrolls
Dormition Abbey
Ecce Homo Arch
Emek Tzurim
Ethiopian Quarter
Eucalyptus
Garden Tomb
Gatsby Cocktail Room
Goldstein Synagogue
Hebrew University, Safra Campus
Herzl Museum

Holy Trinity Cathedral
Holy Week in Jerusalem
Hurva Square and Synagogue
Hutzot Hayotzer Arts and Crafts Festival
Ishtabach
Israel Festival
Jerusalem Theatre
Jewish National Library
Kidron Valley
King David's Tomb
Knesset
Lina Hummusiya
Lutheran Church of the Redeemer
Lutheran Guest House
Mamluk Buildings
Monastery of the Flagellation
Montefiore's Windmill
Mordoch
Muristan

Museum for Islamic Art
Muslim Quarter
Nakhalat Shiva
Oud Festival
Palestinian Heritage Museum
Rachmo
Room of the Last Supper (Cenacle)
Russian Quarter
Schindler's Grave
Schocken Villa and Library
Sephardic Synagogues
Tabor House
Tomb of Queen Helena of Adiabene
Tomb of the Virgin
Twilight in Jerusalem
Waldorf Astoria
Wolfson Museum of Jewish Art
Yad Ben Zvi Institute for Judaeo-Arab Studies
Zedekiah's Cave/Solomon's Quarries

B GREATER JERUSALEM

GOLD

Rank	Elective	Theme	Sub-theme	Category	Micro-regions	BUCKET! Score	Time needed
60	Beit Guvrin and Maresha	Structure	Engineering	Impressive Feats	B2	6	2–6 hrs

SILVER

Elective	BUCKET! Score	Micro-region
Domaine du Castel	5	B1
Ein Hemed	4	B1
Ein Kerem	4	B1

Elective	BUCKET! Score	Micro-region
Hadassah Synagogue and Chagall Windows	5	B1
Monastery of Abu Ghosh	4	B1
Sataf	4	B1

BRONZE

Abu Ghosh's hummusiyas
Archaeological Seminars Dig-for-a-Day
Buster's
Castel
Clos de Gat Winery
Ella Valley Vineyards
Flam Winery
Haas Promenade

Judean Hills Wineries
Latrun Monastery
Liftah
Majda
Mini Israel
Nahal Refaim
Neot Kedumim Biblical Landscape
Sacred Music Festival, aka Mekudeshet

Sea Horse Winery
Stalactite Caves
Tel Gezer Archaeological Project
Tel Lachish
Tisch Family Zoological Gardens
Tzora Winery
Yad Hashmona

C WEST BANK

GOLD

Rank	Elective	Theme	Sub-theme	Category	Micro-regions	BUCKET! Score	Time needed
18	Church of the Nativity	Religion	Religious Figures	Jesus: Early Life	C1	9	20 mins–2 hrs
26	Jericho and Hisham's Palace	Archaeology	Ancient Cities and Remains	Mounds/Tels/ Artificial Hills	C3	7	1–6 hrs
40	Bethlehem	Religion	Holy Books	New Testament	C1	7	1–8 hrs
46	Tomb of the Patriarchs and Old Town of Hebron	Religion	The Sacred	Burial	C2	5	30 mins–2 hrs
61	Nablus	People	Community Celebration	Local Community	C5	5	2 hrs–1+ days
68	Ramallah	People	Ethnic Groups	Arab	C4	4	2 hrs–1+ days
90	Herodion	Archaeology	Roman	Herodian	C2	5	1–2 hrs
97	St. George's Monastery and Wadi Qelt	Structure	Engineering	Impressive Feats	C3	5	30 mins–2 hrs

SILVER

Elective	BUCKET! Score	Micro-region		Elective	BUCKET! Score	Micro-region
Banksy's Walled-Off Hotel	5	C1		Mount Gerizim	4	C5
Battir Hills	4	C2		Sebastia-Shomron	4	C5
Deir Quruntal	4	C3		Separation Wall	7	C1
Mar Saba	5	C2		Tulul Abu el-Alaiq	4	C3

BRONZE

Aida Refugee Camp
Al-Auja
Banksy Art
Deir Ghassaneh
Dheisheh Refugee Camp
Ein Prat
El Bariyeh/Wadi Khareitun/ Nahal Teqoa
Freedom Theatre

Hebron
Hiking in Jenin
Inn of the Good Samaritan
Khirbet Suseya
Monastery of St. Euthymius
Monastery of St. Martyrius
Nabi Musa
Nebi Samuel
Palestinian Throne Villages

Qasr al-Yahud
Ramot Polin Apartments
Shuqba/Natuf Caves
Solomon's Pools
Sugar Trail
Taybeh Brewing Company
Umm ar-Rihan Forest
Yasser Arafat Museum

D TEL AVIV

GOLD

Rank	Elective	Theme	Sub-theme	Category	Micro-regions	BUCKET! Score	Time needed
5	Tel Aviv	Society	Cities	Principal Cities	D1, D2, D3, D4, D5, D6, D7, D8	8	4 hrs–4+ days
16	Modern Movement (Bauhaus Architecture)	Structure	Architecture	Architectural Styles	D3, D4, D5	7	90 mins–4 hrs
30	Jaffa	Society	Cities	Cool Neighborhoods and Quarters	D1, D2	6	1–4 hrs
77	ANU – Museum of the Jewish People	Culture	Museum	of Culture, Architecture	D7	5	1–4 hrs
82	Tel Aviv Nightlife	Entertainment	Party	Nightlife	D3, D4, D6	6	2 hrs–2+ days
87	Carmel Market	Food and Drink	Food	Stalls, Stands, and Markets	D3, D6	6	30 mins–2 hrs
89	Tel Aviv Beaches	Leisure	Beaches	Public/Popular Beaches	D1	8	1 hr–1+ days
95	Tel Aviv Museum of Art	Culture	Museum	of Art	D3, D5	5	1–4 hrs
99	Imperial Bar	Entertainment	Party	Bars and Clubs	D1, D6	7	1+ hours

SILVER

Elective	BUCKET! Score	Micro-region	Elective	BUCKET! Score	Micro-region
Abu Hassan	9	D2	MUSA – Eretz Israel Museum	5	D7
Apollonia	4	D7	Neve Tzedek	4	D4
Bialik House	4	D3	The Norman Hotel	5	D4
Brown Beach House	5	D1	OCD	5	D4
Busi Grill	4	D8	Pastel	5	D3
Design Museum Holon	5	D8	Popina	5	D4
Drummers' Beach	4	D1	Rothschild Boulevard	6	D4
George and John Tel Aviv	4	D4	Sabich/Oved's	5	D7
Herbert Samuel	5	D7	Shakshuka/Dr. Shakshuka	5	D2
Herziliya Beaches	6	D7	Tel Aviv Port	6	D1
Jaffa Flea Market	4	D2	Tel Aviv Tayelet/Promenade	8	D1
Manta Ray	5	D1	Tel-O-Fun Bike Share	6	D1
Mashya	5	D1	Tzfon Abraxas	9	D4
Miznon	6	D4	Weizmann Institute of Science	5	D8

BRONZE

Alena at The Norman
Anastasia
Anita
Azrieli Center
Beit Ha'ir
Bellboy Bar

Ben Gurion House
Brothers/Ha'achim
Brown TLV
Butler Bar
Cafe Kaymak
Cafe Xoho

Cameri Theatre
Claro
Crazy House
Cymbalista Synagogue
Dallal Bakery
Dallal Restaurant

MICRO-REGIONS
Tel Aviv

N

0 _____ 1km
0 _____ 1 mile

MEDITERRANEAN SEA

Port
HaYarkon Park
D7
2
20
D7

Marina

Dizengoff Street
Ibn Gabirol Street

D3/
D5–6
D1

CITY CENTER
HaKirya

Carmel Market

King George St.

Rothschild Blvd.

Sarona

Giv'atayim

D7

Allenby Street

D4/
D5–8

Rothschild

Neve Tzedek

Florentin

Kibbutz Galuyot Road

HaTikva

D8

Ben-Zvi Way

D2
Jaffa

20

D8

2

44

E3

Dan Tel Aviv
Dizengoff Center
Dok
Falafel Gabai
Fire and Water Fountain
Florentin
Gordon Beach
Habasta
HaSalon
HaTikva Market
HaYarkon Park
Hotel Montefiore
Jaffa Clock Tower
Kerem HaTeimanim/Yemenite Quarter
Kikar Levana/White Square
Kitchen Market
Kuli Alma

Leonardo Beach Hotel
Levinsky Market
Lily & Bloom
M25
Marganit Tower
Matcal Tower
Matcot
Meshek Barzilay
Milgo & Milbar
Moshe Aviv Tower
Nahalat Binyamin
Old Man and the Sea
Opera Tower
Ouzeria
Pagoda House
Par Derriere
Poli House

Pool of the Arches/Al-Anazia
Port Said
Rabin Square
Rothschild Hotel
Sabich Frishman
Safari Park
Said Abouelafia Bakery
Sarona Market
Sheinkin Street
Social Club
Spiral Apartment House
Sufganiyot
Suramare
Suzanne Dellal Centre for
    Dance and Theatre
Tel Aviv White Night
Tenat

The PhotoHouse	Turkiz	Yaffo-Tel Aviv
The Jaffa	Water Sports	Yitzhak Rabin Center
The Setai	White Mosque	Yom Tov Delicatessen
Toto	White Villa Hotel	

E MEDITERRANEAN COAST

GOLD

Rank	Elective	Theme	Sub-theme	Category	Micro-regions	BUCKET! Score	Time needed
13	Akko	Archaeology	Islamic	Crusader	E2, E5	8	2–8 hrs
25	Caesarea	Archaeology	Roman	Herodian	E4	8	2–6 hrs
27	Bahá'í Gardens	Structure	Architecture	Landscape and Streetscape	E1, E5, F1	8	15 mins–3 hrs
100	Dor HaBonim	Leisure	Beaches	Remote Beaches	E4, E7	8	1 hr–1+ days

SILVER

Elective	BUCKET! Score	Micro-region
Akhziv Beach	5	E5
Argaman Beach	4	E2
Beit Yannai	7	E4
Carmel Winery	5	E4
Elma Arts Complex	5	E4
Haifa	4	E1, E5
Mediterranean Coast	8	E3, E4, E5

Elective	BUCKET! Score	Micro-region
Netanya	4	E4
Rosh HaNikra	4	E5
Shrine of Bahá'u'lláh	4	E5
Stella Maris	4	E1
Tel Ashkelon	4	E3
Uri Buri	9	E2
Zichron Ya'akov	6	E4

BRONZE

Akkotel	Eshkol	Margalit Winery
Al-Jazzar Mosque	Geder Beach	Nahal Taninim
Amphorae Winery	German Colony	Nahariya
Aqueduct Beach	HaSharon Beach	Palmahim
Ashdod Performing Arts Center	Helena Banamal	Ramat HaNadiv
Atlit Beach	Hospitaller Fortress/Knights' Halls	Recanati Winery
Atlit Detention Camp	Hummus Said	Salad Trail
Bat Galim Beach	Iris Reserve	South Haifa Beaches
Clandestine Immigration & Naval Museum	Jabotinsky Park	Tikotin Museum of Japanese Art
	Jisr az-Zarqa	Tishbi Winery
Efendi	Kerem Shalom	Vitkin Winery
Ein Afeq	Maadali	

F MOUNT CARMEL AND JEZREEL VALLEY

GOLD

Rank	Elective	Theme	Sub-theme	Category	Micro-regions	BUCKET! Score	Time needed
39	Beit She'an	Archaeology	City Conglomerates	Cities of the Decapolis	F2	7	2–6 hrs
59	Megiddo	Archaeology	Ancient Cities and Remains	Mounds/Tels/ Artificial Hills	F1	5	1–3 hrs
64	Beit Alpha	Archaeology	Ancient Cities and Remains	Mosaics	F2	4	30–60 mins

Rank	Elective	Theme	Sub-theme	Category	Micro-regions	BUCKET! Score	Time needed
93	Belvoir	Archaeology	Islamic	Crusader	F2	5	1–2 hrs

SILVER

Elective	BUCKET! Score	Micro-region
Carmel Hai-Bar	4	F1
Ein Hod	4	F1
Elbabor	7	F1
Gan HaShlosha	5	F2

Elective	BUCKET! Score	Micro-region
Mount Carmel	4	F1
Mount Gilboa	4	F2
Nahal Me'arot/Wadi el-Mughara	5	F1

BRONZE

Gan Garoo
HaBeit Be'einhud

Hecht Museum

Ma'ayan Harod

G LOWER GALILEE AND KINNERET

GOLD

Rank	Elective	Theme	Sub-theme	Category	Micro-regions	BUCKET! Score	Time needed
7	Sea of Galilee	Religion	Religious Figures	Jesus: Ministries	G3, G4	7	2 hrs–2 days
29	Nazareth and its Biblical Sites	Religion	Religious Figures	Jesus: Early Life	G1, G2, G4	7	2–8 hrs
33	Capernaum and Tabgha	Religion	Religious Figures	Jesus: Ministries	G3, G4	5	2–4 hrs
56	Tsipori	Archaeology	Roman	Judea	G2	5	1–2 hrs
69	Jesus Trail	Active	Hikes	Long Walks (2+ days)	G2, G4	7	4 hrs–4 days
79	Beit She'arim	Religion	The Sacred	Burial	G2	5	90 mins–4 hrs

SILVER

Elective	BUCKET! Score	Micro-region
Basilica of the Annunciation	7	G1
Church of the Transfiguration	5	G2
Hamat Tiberias	2	G3
Mount Arbel	4	G2

Elective	BUCKET! Score	Micro-region
Mount of Beatitudes	5	G3
Nazarene Fusion Cuisine	6	G1
Sea of Galilee Beaches	4	G3
Tiberias	2	G3

BRONZE

Abu Ashraf
Ancient Bathhouse of Nazareth
Beit Gabriel
Goats with the Wind
Greek Orthodox Church of
    the Annunciation
International Center of
    Mary of Nazareth

Kfar Kama
Khirbet al-Minya
Kibbutz Degania
Kibbutz Ein Gev
Kibbutz Ginosar
Kinneret Trail
Kursi
Magdalena

Nain
Sanhedrin Trail
Sde Amudim
Tabor Winery
Tel Bethsaida

H UPPER GALILEE

GOLD

Rank	Elective	Theme	Sub-theme	Category	Micro-regions	BUCKET! Score	Time needed
58	Tsfat/Safed	Entertainment	Shopping	Handmade	H1	4	1–8 hrs

SILVER

Elective	BUCKET! Score	Micro-region
Bar'am	5	H1
Hula Lake	6	H2
Korazim	4	H2
Lag B'Omer at Moshav Meron	4	H1

Elective	BUCKET! Score	Micro-region
Montfort	5	H1
Tel Hazor	3	H2
Yehi'am	5	H1

BRONZE

Amirim
Ashkenazi Ari Synagogue
Ayun Stream
Beit HaShomer Museum
Caro Synagogue

Dalton Winery
Galil Mountain Winery
Isaac Luria Synagogue
Memorial Museum of Hungarian
　　Speaking Jewry

Nahal Amud
Nahal Zalmon
Rosh Pina
Tel Hai Fort
Tzimmers

I GOLAN HEIGHTS

GOLD

Rank	Elective	Theme	Sub-theme	Category	Micro-regions	BUCKET! Score	Time needed
62	Golan Heights	Scenic	Vistas	Scenic Drives	G3, I1, I2, I3	6	1–5+ days
63	Tel Dan	Archaeology	Ancient Israel	Iron Age/ Ancient Israel	I1	5	30 mins–2 hrs
75	Golan Heights Winery	Food and Drink	Wine	Wineries	I2	6	15 mins–2 hrs
80	Banias	Archaeology	Ancient Israel	Empires, Greek, Hasmonean	I1	4	1–4 hrs
85	Nimrod's Fortress	Archaeology	Islamic	Ayyubid	I1	6	2–4 hrs

SILVER

Elective	BUCKET! Score	Micro-region
Ancient Qatzrin	4	I2
Gamla	5	I3
Hamat Gader	4	I3

Elective	BUCKET! Score	Micro-region
Mount Hermon	5	I2
Yehudiya	4	I3

BRONZE

Birkat Ram
Château Golan Winery
Gadot Lookout
Golan Lookout/Tel Faher
Golan Trail
Horshat Tal

Jordan River Rafting
Kibbutz Merom Golan
Majdal Shams and The Shouting Hill
Majrase-Betiha/Bethsaida Valley
Meshushim Stream
Mount Bental Lookout

Nahal el-Al
Ophir Lookout
Peace Vista
Pelter Winery
Prehistoric Man Museum
Snir Stream

J NEGEV

GOLD

Rank	Elective	Theme	Sub-theme	Category	Micro-regions	BUCKET! Score	Time needed
28	Makhtesh Ramon	Scenic	Vistas	Nature Panorama	J2, J3	7	1 hr–2+ days
48	Avdat	Archaeology	City Conglomerates	Nabataean	J2	6	1–4 hrs
73	Incense Route	Archaeology	City Conglomerates	Nabataean	J1, J2, J3	5	2 hrs–2+ days
74	Ein Avdat	Active	Hikes	Tough Hikes (short and steep)	J2	4	1–4 hrs

SILVER

Elective	BUCKET! Score	Micro-region
Halutza	3	J2
Hiking in the Negev	5	J2
Mamshit	5	J1
Mitzpe Ramon	6	J2
Museum of Bedouin Culture	5	J1

Elective	BUCKET! Score	Micro-region
Nitzana	3	J2
Shivta	5	J2
Tel Arad	4	J1
Tel Beer Sheva	4	J1
Yatir Winery	4	J1

BRONZE

Alpaca Farm
Astronomy Israel
Beer Sheva
Ben Gurion's Tomb
Beresheet Hotel

Carmey Avdat Farm Winery
Ezuz
Israeli Air Force Museum
Negev Camping
Negev Goat Farms

Negev Museum of Art
Negev Wine Route
Sde Boker
Sidreh-Lakiya Negev Weaving

K DEAD SEA (ISRAEL)

GOLD

Rank	Elective	Theme	Sub-theme	Category	Micro-regions	BUCKET! Score	Time needed
3	Dead Sea	BUCKET!	BUCKET!	BUCKET!	K1, P1	10	30 mins–2 days
8	Masada	Archaeology	Roman	Judea	K1	8	1–8 hrs
50	Ein Gedi	Active	Hikes	Easy Hikes and Trails (under 2 hrs)	K1	6	2–8 hrs (hike dependent)
70	Qumran	Religion	Holy Books	Ancient Manuscripts	K1	5	15–90 mins

SILVER

Elective	BUCKET! Score	Micro-region
Ein Bokek	6	K1
Ein Bokek Spa Hotels	6	K1

BRONZE

Biankini/Siesta Beach
Einot Tsukim
Kibbutz Mitzpe Shalem

Mount Sodom
Neot HaKikar
Neve Midbar Beach

New Kalya Beach
Shkedi's Camplodge
Wadi Qumran

L EILAT AND ARABAH

GOLD

Rank	Elective	Theme	Sub-theme	Category	Micro-regions	BUCKET! Score	Time needed
10	Red Sea/Gulf of Aqaba	Active	Water Sports	Snorkeling	L1, L2, M1, M2, T1	6	2 hrs–5 days
78	Eilat	Accommodation	Stays	Vacation Resorts and Hotels	L1, L2	4	1–3 days
83	Coral Beach	Active	Water Sports	Snorkeling	L2	4	1–8 hrs
96	Timna	Archaeology	Prehistoric	Prehistory, Bronze Age	L3	6	2–8 hrs

SILVER

Elective	BUCKET! Score	Micro-region
Kibbutz Lotan	4	L3
Red Canyon	4	L2

Elective	BUCKET! Score	Micro-region
Underwater Observatory	6	L2
Yotvata Hai-Bar	4	L3

BRONZE

Amram's Pillars	Kibbutz Neot Smadar	North Beach
Dolphin Reef	Mount Karkom	Red Sea Jazz Festival
Isrotel Agamim	Neot Smadar Winery	Wadi Ein Netafim
Kibbutz Ketura		

M SOUTH JORDAN

GOLD

Rank	Elective	Theme	Sub-theme	Category	Micro-regions	BUCKET! Score	Time needed
4	Wadi Rum	Nature	Parks	Gorgeous Scenery	M2	8	1 hr–2+ days
10	Red Sea/Gulf of Aqaba	Active	Water Sports	Snorkeling	L1, L2, M1, M2, T1	6	2 hrs–5 days
43	Aqaba	Active	Water Sports	Diving	M1	4	2 hrs–1+ days

SILVER

Elective	BUCKET! Score	Micro-region
Hot Air Balloon Ride Over Wadi Rum	7	M2

BRONZE

Marine Science Station Aquarium	Rock Climbing in Wadi Rum	South Beach

N PETRA

GOLD

Rank	Elective	Theme	Sub-theme	Category	Micro-regions	BUCKET! Score	Time needed
2	Petra	BUCKET!	BUCKET!	BUCKET!	N1, N2, N3, O1	10	4 hrs–4 days
84	Petra Kitchen	Organized	Participatory	Cooking/Eating/Fruit-Picking	N3	6	4 hrs

SILVER

Elective	BUCKET! Score	Micro-region
Little Petra	5	N3
Petra by Night	6	N3

BRONZE

Ad-Deir, aka the Monastery   High Place of Sacrifice

O KING'S HIGHWAY

GOLD

Rank	Elective	Theme	Sub-theme	Category	Micro-regions	BUCKET! Score	Time needed
19	Madaba and the Madaba Map	Archaeology	Ancient Cities and Remains	Mosaics	O1, P2	5	5 mins–2 hrs
21	Dana Biosphere Reserve	Active	Hikes	Day Hikes (2+ hrs)	O1	6	1–3 days
31	King's Highway	Scenic	Vistas	Scenic Drives	O1	6	6 hrs–2+ days
49	Karak	Archaeology	Islamic	Crusader	O1	6	1–4 hrs
81	Umm ar-Rasas	Archaeology	Ancient Cities and Remains	Mosaics	O1	5	45 mins–2 hrs
86	Feynan Ecolodge	Accommodation	Stays	Experiential Lodging	O1	8	1+ days

SILVER

Elective	BUCKET! Score	Micro-region
Shobak	5	O1

BRONZE

Khirbet Feynan   Qasr Bashir   Wadi al-Hassa
Nawatef Camp

P DEAD SEA (JORDAN)

GOLD

Rank	Elective	Theme	Sub-theme	Category	Micro-regions	BUCKET! Score	Time needed
3	Dead Sea	BUCKET!	BUCKET!	BUCKET!	K1, P1	10	30 mins–2 days
19	Madaba and the Madaba Map	Archaeology	Ancient Cities and Remains	Mosaics	O1, P2	5	5 mins–2 hrs
23	Wadi Mujib and Mujib Biosphere Reserve	Active	Hikes	Wet Hikes	P1	7	2–4 hrs (hike dependent)
24	Mount Nebo	Religion	Religious Figures	Kings and Prophets	P2	5	15–90 mins
41	Bethany-Beyond-the-Jordan	Religion	Religious Figures	Jesus: Ministries	P2	5	2–3 hrs

SILVER

Elective	BUCKET! Score	Micro-region
Hammamat Ma'in Hot Springs	4	P1
Lot's Cave	4	P1

Elective	BUCKET! Score	Micro-region
Mukawir	4	P2
Suweimeh Spa Hotels	8	P1

BRONZE

Church of the Beheading of John the Baptist

Dead Sea Highway
Fifa Nature Reserve

Zikra Initiative

Q AMMAN

GOLD

Rank	Elective	Theme	Sub-theme	Category	Micro-regions	BUCKET! Score	Time needed
36	Modern Amman	Society	Cities	Principal Cities	Q2, Q3	5	4 hrs–2 days
37	Ancient Amman	Archaeology	Roman	Judea	Q1	6	1–6 hrs

SILVER

Elective	BUCKET! Score	Micro-region
Beit Sitti	5	Q3
Jordan Archaeological Museum	4	Q1

Elective	BUCKET! Score	Micro-region
Qasr al-Abd	4	Q4
Wild Jordan Center	5	Q2

BRONZE

Abu Darwish Mosque
Al-Pasha Turkish Bath
Al-Kitkat
Al-Quds Falafel
Art Hotel
Books@Cafe
Bulos Y Zumot Winery
Children's Museum of Jordan

Fakhr el-Din
Fuheis
Hammams
Hashem Falafel
Intercontinental Jordan
Jordan Folklore Museum
Jordan Museum of Popular Traditions
Jordan National Gallery of Fine Arts

Jordan River Designs Showroom
Khalid Shoman Foundation/
     Darat al-Funun
OTR
Petro
Rainbow Street
Royal Automobile Museum
Shams al-Balad

R EAST JORDAN

GOLD

Rank	Elective	Theme	Sub-theme	Category	Micro-regions	BUCKET! Score	Time needed
20	Qasr Amra and the Desert Palaces	Archaeology	Islamic	Umayyad	R1	7	4 hrs–1+ days
55	Azraq Wetlands	Nature	Life	Birding	R1	4	30 mins–2 hrs

SILVER

Elective	BUCKET! Score	Micro-region
Qasr Azraq	5	R1
Qasr Kharana	5	R1

Elective	BUCKET! Score	Micro-region
Shaumari	4	R1
Umm el-Jimal	4	R1

BRONZE
Burqu   Wadi al-Dahik

S NORTH JORDAN

GOLD

Rank	Elective	Theme	Sub-theme	Category	Micro-regions	BUCKET! Score	Time needed
14	Jerash	Archaeology	City Conglomerates	Cities of the Decapolis	S1	7	2–4 hrs
45	Umm Qais	Archaeology	City Conglomerates	Cities of the Decapolis	S1	6	2–6 hrs
57	Ajloun Forest	Active	Hikes	Day Hikes (2+ hrs)	S2	5	1–3 hrs
76	Ajloun Fortress	Archaeology	Islamic	Ayyubid	S2	4	30 mins–2 hrs

SILVER

Elective	BUCKET! Score	Micro-region
Al-Ayoun Trail	5	S2
As-Salt	5	S2
Pella	4	S2

BRONZE
Abila   Irbid Museum of Jordanian Heritage   Rasoun Camping
Dibeen Forest   Jordanian Wildflowers   Yarmouk Forest

T SINAI

GOLD

Rank	Elective	Theme	Sub-theme	Category	Micro-regions	BUCKET! Score	Time needed
15	Mount Sinai	Religion	Holy Books	Hebrew Bible/ Old Testament	T1	5	14 hrs
22	St. Catherine's Monastery	Religion	Holy Books	Ancient Manuscripts	T1	6	15 mins–3 hrs
53	Ras Mohammad	Active	Water Sports	Diving	T1	7	4–8 hrs– 3+ days
54	Dahab	Leisure	Beaches	Remote Beaches	T1	7	1–5+ days
88	Sharm el-Sheikh	Accommodation	Stays	Vacation Resorts and Hotels	T1	6	1–3 days

SILVER

Elective	BUCKET! Score	Micro-region
Sinai Trail	5	T1

BRONZE

Camel Safari	Pharaoh's Island Citadel	Taba
Coloured Canyon	St. Catherine's Mount	Wadi Nasb
Nuweiba Beach Camps		

Note Bronze and Pearl sites in macro-regions U, V, and W may not be referenced in a road trip. You can find their general descriptions on the page listed next to their name.

U CROSS-ISRAEL/PALESTINE

GOLD

Rank	Elective	Theme	Sub-theme	Category	Micro-regions	BUCKET! Score	Time needed
38	Biblical Tels	Archaeology	Ancient Israel	Iron Age/ Ancient Israel	F1, H2, J1	6	60 mins– 2+ days
51	Israeli Cuisine	Food and Drink	Food	Cuisine	U	7	2 hrs–5+ days

SILVER

Elective	BUCKET! Score	Micro-region		Elective	BUCKET! Score	Micro-region
Israel National Trail	7	U		Palestinian Heritage Trail	5	U
Kibbutz Volunteer	7	U		Winery Tour	7	U
Modern Israeli Cuisine	9	U				

BRONZE

Beaches (p. 554)	Kibbutzim (p. 535)	Ulpanim (p. 568)
Israel Bike Trail (p. 681)	National Memorial Day (p. 39)	Yom Kippur (p. 36)
Israeli Breakfast (p. 87)		

V CROSS-JORDAN

GOLD

Rank	Elective	Theme	Sub-theme	Category	Micro-regions	BUCKET! Score	Time needed
46	Jordanian Cuisine	Food and Drink	Food	Cuisine	V	7	2 hrs–5+ days
52	Jordan Trail	Active	Hikes	Long Walks (2+ days)	V	5	4 hrs–40+ days

SILVER

Elective	BUCKET! Score	Micro-region
Hiking in Jordan	7	V
Jordanian Hospitality	4	V

Elective	BUCKET! Score	Micro-region
Royal Society for the Conservation of Nature (RSCN)	6	V

BRONZE
Mansaf (p. 561)   Rift Valley (p. 524)

W WHOLE HOLY LAND

SILVER

Elective	BUCKET! Score	Micro-region
Argila/Hookah/Shisha	5	W
Bedouin Tents and Coffee	5	W
Café Culture	6	W

Elective	BUCKET! Score	Micro-region
Camel Riding	6	W
Hummus	8	W

BRONZE
Cities of the Decapolis (p. 512)   Qasr al-Mushatta (p. 733)   Qasr al-Qastal (p. 733)
Qasr Burqu (p. 733)

Part 9

Walks and Drives

WALKS AND DRIVES BY BUCKET!

We have two types of multi-stop tours for you to choose from: **city walks** and **road trips**. BUCKET! has developed walking tours for each of the region's major cities (Jerusalem, Bethlehem, Tel Aviv-Jaffa, Haifa, Akko, Nazareth, Eilat, Aqaba, Petra/Wadi Rum, and Amman) to give you an immersive introduction to the places where you're likely to spend the most time. BUCKET! also presents road trips for every micro-region in the Holy Land – no electives and no locations go unrecognized!

How do you find an elective's corresponding city walk and/or road trip? You'll find its tour options easily under the label *Walks and Drives* in the elective itself. If you've decided to visit **Karak (#49)**, for instance, you'll find it has several road-trip options, including O1, V1, and others.

You can follow each of these tours exactly, or pick and choose what suits you. You can also combine road trips and city walks to create your own half-, full-, or multiday itineraries. Tour stops can go in any direction or order, though we provide the most optimal itinerary for visiting each of the Gold, Silver, and Bronze electives in a given micro-region. We provide you with additional suggestions via Pearl electives – sites that are exclusively BUCKET! recommended. Other points of potential interest may also make an appearance as a detour. Collectively, the 74 trips highlight every one of the more than 700 Gold, Silver, Bronze, and Pearl electives.

Each tour lists the distance, walking/driving time, and completion time. Our walking tours also include the terrain you'll traverse and difficulty level. We offer estimated completion times, but you can equally expand these itineraries over several days. Your choice of coverage, pace, and speed will play a factor in how long you spend at each stop along the tour. Whether you're seeking an introduction, highlights, comprehensive, or exhaustive (see *Time Needed*, p. 25) overview of each site is completely up to you. You are welcome to poke your head in and out of most places, and stay longer at the electives you fancy most.

Our last tip: don't oversaturate your day. Four electives is usually the maximum number of sites one can comfortably manage without getting exhausted or overwhelmed: two in the morning, lunch, then two in the afternoon. Remember: pace and speed adjustments can accommodate faster or slower groups. You can go slow at half-speed, visiting one elective in the morning and one in the afternoon. Or go fast at 2 × speed, racing through four electives in the morning and four in the afternoon, eating packed hummus and pita in the car. The speedsters may tick off a lot of boxes, but are not going to be spending much, if any, time at each stop.

A1 JERUSALEM OLD CITY: MAIN SITES

Terrain Frequent steps, tight corridors for part
Difficulty (1–5) 2
Distance 2.6km
Walking time 45 minutes
Completion time 4 hours

Starting point Jaffa Gate (see **Jerusalem Walls and Gates (#47)**).

Tour stop 1 **Western Wall (#11)**.
At site **Western Wall Tunnels (#94)** – requires reservation.

Walk south towards Dung Gate; the wooden ramp to Temple Mount is on your left.

Tour stop 2 **Temple Mount (#12)**, specifically **Dome of the Rock (#6)**.
See **Al-Aqsa Mosque (#65)** (from the outside, unless Muslim).

At site **Fountain of Sultan Qaytbay**, **Dome of the Chain**.

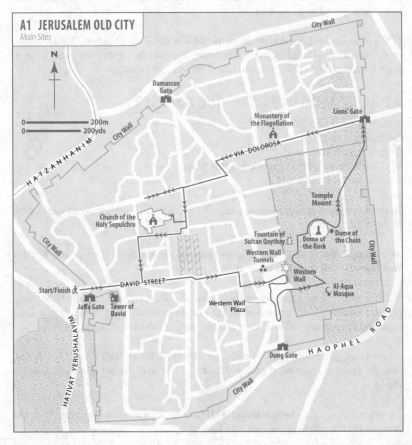

Though tourist entry is limited to one gate, you can exit Temple Mount from a number of gates. Exit on the northeastern wall near Lions' Gate and descend to the street, which is Via Dolorosa.

Tour stop 3 **Via Dolorosa (#42)**, Station #1 – *Monastery of the Flagellation.*
Note Via Dolorosa is itself a walking tour, and will end at the Church of the Holy Sepulchre. Follow directions in the elective, or:

Walk west on Via Dolorosa, pausing at the stations. You'll need to zig left onto Al-Wadi Street, then zag right back onto Via Dolorosa. The road ends at the Church.

Tour stop 4 **Church of the Holy Sepulchre (#9)**.

If you're ready to leave, you can depart from either exit south to David Street, then head west (turn right, ascending) to Jaffa Gate.

Ending point Jaffa Gate.

TIPS Temple Mount closes early and is only open Sunday–Thursday. The Church of the Holy Sepulchre closes late. Most other sites do not close. You can adjust your tour if you get off to a late start.

FOOD Abu Shukri is located on the corner of Wadi ha-Galil Street and Via Dolorosa, if you want a falafel lunch or snack. There are plenty of other restaurants, snack shops, juice bars, etc. throughout the Old City. You won't go hungry.

A2 JERUSALEM OLD CITY: FOUR QUARTERS

Terrain Some inclines
Difficulty (1–5) 2
Distance 5km, minimum
Walking time At least 1½ hours, but this is up to you
Completion time 12 hours

In this tour, you will see the same sites as in A1, but you'll get a more in-depth look at the old city.

Note **Temple Mount (#12)** and ***St. James' Cathedral*** require good timing, and **Western Wall Tunnels (#94)** require a reservation.

Starting point Dung Gate, on southern wall. If you are standing at Jaffa Gate (most popular entrance), walk south, with the wall to your left, then turn left past Zion Gate and keep going to Dung Gate (20 minutes), a vehicle entrance.

As you enter, go through security and descend to the Western Wall Plaza. Once inside, look for the wooden ramp (it's huge) leading to Temple Mount and walk towards the base.

Tour stop 1 Ascend to **Temple Mount (#12)** (and back to Muslim Quarter). It has the most restricted schedule, so visit here first.

N

0 ————— 200m
0 ————— 200yds

Damascus Gate

Church of St. Anne & the Pools of Bethesda

Lions' Gate

Muslim Quarter

Ecce Homo Arch

VIA DOLOROSA

El-Ghawanima Tower

Lina Hummusiya

Christian Quarter

VIA DOLOROSA

Abu Shukri

Temple Mount

Church of the Holy Sepulchre

Mosque of Omar

Lutheran Church of the Redeemer

Muristan

Fountain of Sultan Qaytbay

Dome of the Rock

Dome of the Chain

Western Wall Tunnels

Church of St. John the Baptist

Lutheran Guest House

Western Wall Plaza

Western Wall

Al-Aqsa Mosque

Jaffa Gate

DAVID STREET

The Cardo

Entrance to Temple Mount

Jewish Quarter

Citadel/ Tower of David

Wohl Archaeological Museum

Jerusalem Archaeological Park

Hurva Square

Armenian Quarter

Sephardic Synagogues

Start/Finish

Dung Gate

St. James' Cathedral

Muslim Quarter
Jewish Quarter
Armenian Quarter
Christian Quarter

See **Dome of the Rock (#6)**, **Al-Aqsa Mosque (#65)**, *Fountain of Sultan Qaytbay*, and the *Dome of the Chain*.

Optional tour stop *El-Ghawanima Tower*: situated in the northwest corner of Temple Mount, this stone minaret is one of four, the tallest, and dates to the Ayyubid period.

Exit at the northeast corner of the plaza, near Lions' Gate.

Tour stop 2 *Muslim Quarter*: the largest of the four quarters in the Old City of Jerusalem, it also has the most authenticity, with fewer tourists and more residents shopping in the range of stores offering prepared food, wares, and grocery items.

Note Veer off course here as much as possible. Walking down side alleys will lead you to all sorts of surprises – sometimes a great glimpse of the Dome of the Rock, sometimes a popular falafel stand, or spice vendor. Or maybe just gives you a slice of life – people do still live in the Old City, after all. You'll also be able to see…

Consider *Mamluk Buildings*: the Muslim quarter contains perhaps the greatest collection of Mamluk-period edifices and constructions, including several adornments on Temple Mount. An excellent companion piece is *Mamluk Architectural Landmarks in Jerusalem*, from the Old City of Jerusalem Revitalization Program (OCJRP), with identifying pictures and several walking paths (w ocjrp.welfare-association.org/sites/default/files/publications/altaawon2018final-compressed.pdf).

Visit **Church of St. Anne and the Pools of Bethesda**.

Visit **Via Dolorosa (#42)** Starting at Monastery of the Flagellation. A complex including the Church of the Flagellation, where Jesus was flogged by Roman soldiers, and the Church of the Condemnation and Imposition of the Cross, which symbolically represents the place where Jesus was sentenced to die by Pontius Pilate and made to carry his cross during the walk to the crucifixion point. Considered to be Station #1 of the 12 Stations of the Cross.

See Ecce Homo Arch: named after the Pontius Pilate speech condemning Jesus to death. This seemingly out-of-place arch on the Via Dolorosa once supported a bridge to the since-destroyed Antonia Fortress and Roman Forum, and was used to sack the city in 70 CE.

Walk west on Via Dolorosa to main shopping street, Al-Wadi, and turn left, then turn right back onto Via Dolorosa (it's a split street). Follow path of Via Dolorosa all the way to Church of the Holy Sepulchre.

Tour stop 3 Christian Quarter.

Visit **Church of the Holy Sepulchre (#9)**.

Optional tour stop Mosque of Omar: named after the Rashidun caliph who agreed to the capitulation of the city, but not to his praying in the most venerated Christian site, which he wanted to be left as-is. The mosque was built opposite the Church of the Holy Sepulchre to commemorate the steps upon which Omar prayed. The church's entrance has changed over the years, and thus so has the mosque, which is set to face the entrance. Thus, this mosque is not the original, though the intention is still nice.

Consider Lutheran Church of the Redeemer: a bell tower at this Christian Quarter church affords great panoramic views of the Old City from the top.

Consider Muristan: site of several iterations of hospices/hospitals from Roman times through the Ottomans, originally established to treat Christian pilgrims visiting Jerusalem, c600 CE. Now a shopping district.

Optional tour stop Church of St. John the Baptist: considered by some to be the oldest Christian church in Jerusalem. Like many others, this is a multilayered church. The original church dates to the 5th century, but was destroyed in 612 by the Persians. The remains sank and became the basement of the 11th-century (1040) church, which today is the basement chapel.

Visit **Citadel/Tower of David (#32)** museum: the best way to understand how the city has changed, plus great views.

Turn right as you're leaving the Citadel (away from Jaffa Gate) to enter the Armenian Quarter.

Tour stop 4 <u>Armenian Quarter</u>: south of David Street and west of Chabad Street in the Old City is where to find the Armenian Quarter. Home to the Citadel, St. Mark's Chapel, and **St. James' Cathedral**, as well as the oldest Armenian expat community in the world (4th century CE). Though Christian, they continue to have their own quadrant as ethnically and linguistically distinct from the Arab Christians of the Christian Quarter due to their long-standing history in the city. This quarter is famous for its intricate and beautifully styled tiles, ceramics, and pottery pieces, all hand-painted (if they're machine-made, look elsewhere). Most religious sites are only open during services and closed Sundays.

Visit **St. James' Cathedral**: only open 15.00–15.40, so time accordingly.

Tour stop 5 **Jewish Quarter**.

Note This is its own multi-stop itinerary (*City Walk A4*), which can take another day if explored completely.

Consider <u>Sephardic Synagogues (A4)</u>, <u>Hurva Square (A4)</u>.

Consider The **Cardo**, **Wohl Archaeological Museum**.

Visit **Western Wall (#11)**, **Western Wall Tunnels (#94)**, **Jerusalem Archaeological Park (#71)**.

Ending point Either Jaffa Gate or Dung Gate.

TIPS

★ This was designed as a tour to be completed after you've seen the main sites, but we've added the main sites for orientation and in case you have only one day. Ideally, you can combine this with the *City Walk A1* itinerary and break up those two schedules over two days.

★ This itinerary requires lots of exploring. We give you the basic sites within the four quadrants, but you'll have a much more enriching experience if you wander through all the back alleys and see what you can find.

★ If you are around for <u>Twilight in Jerusalem (A2)</u>, head to any of the high locations around town (note: not all locations will be open at all times), such as Ramparts Walk, Tower of David, Lutheran Church, Mount of Olives, or the roofs of Hashimi Hotel, Austrian hospice, Petra hotel, or Papa Andreas' restaurant, for twilight views of the Old City from above. Some may charge a nominal fee for the privilege.

FOOD <u>Lina Hummusiya</u> and Abu Shukri are both located near the Church of the Holy Sepulchre and vie for the title of best hummus in the city.

STAYS <u>Lutheran Guest House</u>: in the heart of the Old City, this hostel has small rooms, but very interesting stone architecture and a famous roof with dazzling views.

A3 JERUSALEM OLD CITY: WALLS AND GATES

Terrain Steep steps in places to reach viewpoints; mostly flat, but some change in elevation – down and up hills
Difficulty (1–5) 3
Distance 5.5km
Walking time 1¼ hours
Completion time 3 hours

Note There will seem to be some duplication of ground covered on this tour, but the perspectives are wildly different. You can start however you like: either circum-navigating the Old City first, or doing the Ramparts Walk north or south parts first.

Starting point Jaffa Gate. The Gate itself is Ottoman and originally dates to 1538, but the gate has been supplanted by a wide opening that allows cars to enter the Old City. This was planned by Ottoman authorities for the arrival of German Emperor Wilhelm II in 1898. The large entryway has remained open since.

Tour stop 1 **Citadel/Tower of David (#32)** museum – if you didn't visit the Citadel during *City Walk A2*, now is your chance. Great background, great views.

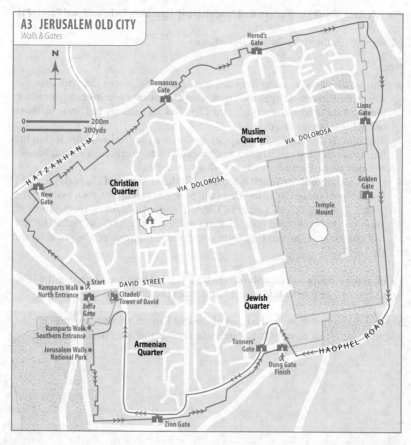

Tour stop 2 **Ramparts Walk (#91)** north entrance, near Jaffa Gate. The Ramparts Walk is its own walking tour, covering two sections on top of the walls, north from Jaffa Gate to Lions' Gate, and south from Jaffa Gate to just before Dung Gate. Both walks provide an excellent bird's-eye view of the Old City, with stunning views of the rooftops as well as a great perch from which to watch the hubbub of activity below.

The north portion of Ramparts Walk ends at Lions' Gate. You can descend there, and head back through the Old City, stopping at sites along the way, or walk the outside of the walls back to Jaffa Gate, following the latter half of this tour.

Tour stop 3 New Gate. Opened in 1887, corresponding to the period when Jews were moving outside the crowded walls of the Old City. The influx of residents in Jerusalem's new western neighborhoods influenced the construction of a direct entrance at this site.

Tour stop 4 Damascus Gate. This gate has a long history, having been used during Roman Emperor Hadrian's reign in 130 CE and constructed perhaps even earlier. The Crusaders cleared debris 1,000 years later and built a new entrance, using this gate as a standalone entrance into the Old City, but requiring the passage first through merchant shops. By 1537, the site was in disrepair and Suleiman I (the Magnificent) ordered the construction of new walls and gates to bring notoriety back to Jerusalem.

Tour stop 5 Herod's Gate. Known as the Flowered Gate, as well as Bab az-Zahra, relating to the Arab neighborhood and cemetery across the road, this gate was originally a minor entryway, rarely opened, and built during Suleiman's time in order to provide access to Arab neighborhoods. Around 1875, it acquired its enlarged gate with direct entrance.

Tour stop 6 Lions' Gate. On the eastern wall of the Old City is the Lions' Gate, or St. Stephen's Gate. The "lions" refer to the two beasts to the right and left of the entryway (lions are also the symbol of Jerusalem), though rumor has it these are actually panthers – the symbol of the Mamluks who briefly administered the city until their defeat by the Ottomans in 1517.

Tour stop 7 Golden Gate. Located on the eastern wall of Temple Mount, the Golden Gate was used from the 6th century to about the 9th, then fell out of favor with Muslims because of its association with the Kidron Valley and Mount of Olives. It was sealed and reopened only twice a year for ceremonial purposes by the Crusaders, before losing its purpose and being permanently closed in 1541.

Tour stop 8 Dung Gate. A once modest gate, widened in 1953 by Jordanians for cars (and now buses, being closest to the Western Wall), Dung Gate became a much more important entrance when Jaffa Gate was closed in the period between Israeli independence and its control of Jerusalem in 1967. The gate is called Bab Silwan, as it faces the Silwan neighborhood to the south of the city, as well as Bab Maghraba, referring to the old Moroccan/Moorish neighborhood that was demolished to create the Western Wall Plaza in 1967.

Visit Tanners' Gate. Named after the leather tanners who used to work near this gate, this pedestrian-only access point is near Dung and used for entry to the ***Jewish Quarter***. It was unsealed following excavations in the 1990s.

Tour stop 9 Zion Gate. Known by this name for its proximity to **Mount Zion (#92)**, this entrance leads to the Armenian Quarter (A2) and was erected in 1540.

Tour stop 10 **Jerusalem Walls and Gates (#47)**: as you walk around the Old City passing Jaffa, Zion, and Dung gates, you'll begin to see signs for the national park which indicate the history and architecture of the walls, before terminating at the *City of David*, the other part of the same national park.

Tour stop 11 **Ramparts Walk (#91)** southern entrance, ascending at the exit of the Citadel.

Optional tour stop **Jerusalem Archaeological Park (#71)** will introduce you to even more historic gates, including the Double Gate and Triple Gate, which led to Temple Mount in ancient times (both now sealed).

Ending point Dung Gate.

TIPS

★ The Ramparts Walk is broken up into two parts, but you can pay for both at once (along with a couple of other sites). You can also do this tour in the opposite direction, though the entrance for the Ramparts North walk is only at Jaffa Gate.
★ Keep in mind that the Ramparts Walk has few exits. This makes visiting other sites somewhat difficult. If you do exit, you can't reenter.
★ Choose this tour if you want great photos of Jerusalem's roofs.

FOOD Grab a quick falafel lunch near Jaffa Gate, in one of the restaurants in the Arab part of Jerusalem (*City Walk A6*) after you descend from the northern walls, or nearby in West Jerusalem (*City Walk A7*) after you finish the tour.

A4 JERUSALEM OLD CITY: JEWISH QUARTER

Terrain Mostly flat, on streets
Difficulty (1–5) 1
Distance 1.5km
Walking time 20 minutes, not including walking/standing time at sites
Completion time 6 hours

The *Jewish Quarter* is one of the four quarters of the Old City and has a number of sites of interest relating to Jewish and the city's 3,000 years of history.

Starting point Dung Gate, on southern wall.

Tour stop 1 **Jerusalem Archaeological Park (#71)**, aka The Davidson Center, The Ophel, or Ophel Archaeological Park.

At site Davidson Center, Hulda Gates, Robinson's Arch, Double Gate, Triple Gate.

Tour stop 2 **Western Wall (#11)**.

Tour stop 3 **Western Wall Tunnels (#94)**.

Tour stop 4 Burnt House. This ancient, buried house, replete with charcoal burns, appears to be from the Roman siege of the city in 70 CE.

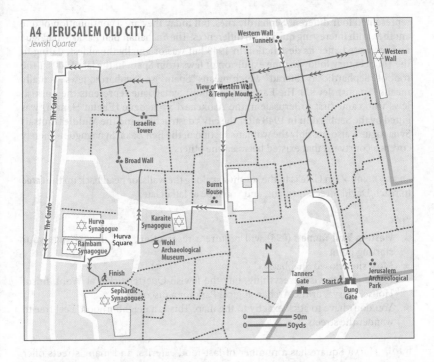

Tour stop 5 **Wohl Archaeological Museum**.

Optional tour stop *Karaite Synagogue*: possibly 8th century, though rebuilt, it's thought to be the oldest foundation of a synagogue, though the rest has been rebuilt.

Tour stop 6 Broad Wall. An 8th-century BCE wall which, when discovered in the 1970s, indicated the expansion of Jerusalem beyond the walls of the old **City of David** had occurred much earlier than originally thought.

Tour stop 7 Israelite Tower. This ancient tower contained arrowheads from the Babylonian destruction of Jerusalem in 586 BCE. Until this discovery, the sacking of Jerusalem had otherwise been theorized and documented in writing but never proved archaeologically.

Tour stop 8 The **Cardo**.

Optional tour stop *Rambam Synagogue*: built in 1267, believed to be the second-oldest synagogue in Jerusalem, and the only synagogue in Jerusalem for centuries. Closed in 1589, reopened in 1967.

Tour stop 9 Hurva Square and Synagogue. "Hurva" means "ruined," which is testament to the history of this spot. The current Hurva Synagogue, completed in 2010, is built over the ruins of two previous short-lived synagogues. The Hurva arch was officially erected in 1977.

Tour stop 10 Sephardic Synagogues: Four adjoining synagogues in the heart of the Old City which are still in use, but also serve as a museum. They may historically have represented four different Sephardic rites, but today they are a continuation of one another, with interesting quirks and differences. The Yochanan Ben Zakai Synagogue was renovated after its destruction in 1948 but was originally the oldest, dating to the 16th century following the expulsion of Jews from Spain in the late 1400s. (The root of "Sephardic" is "Sfarad" which means "Spain," so "Sephardic Jews" actually means "Spanish Jews.") The Eastern (Istanbuli) Synagogue represents the Turkish Jews who came first to Jerusalem, the Ashkenazi Synagogue (Eliahu Hanavi) was gifted by the Sephardim in 1948 after the city's destruction, and the Middle (Emtsai) Synagogue – also possibly the woman's section of the Ben Zakai Synagogue – merely covers a courtyard that existed between the others.

Ending point Zion Gate is to the southwest along the walls, or head back up the **Cardo** to reach David Street, turn left, and you'll be at Jaffa Gate.

TIPS
★ **Western Wall Tunnels (#94)** will require a reservation, and may change your starting point.
★ Most sites closed Shabbat.
★ If you plan to visit everything, buy the Jewish Quarter ticket at Wohl, Burnt House, Hurva, or the Archaeological Park for a discount.
★ You don't have to stick exactly to the map. This is a neighborhood. Feel free to wander the streets.

FOOD Hurva Square has a number of fast-food eateries, and many streets offer restaurants and street stands.

A5 JERUSALEM HILLS: ZION/OLIVES/DAVID

Terrain Steep hills. If you do **Hezekiah's Tunnel** (wet walk) then you also have to wade through water, though there's a dry route.
Difficulty (1–5) 3
Distance 5km
Walking time 1½ hours
Completion time 6 hours

Starting point From Zion Gate, walk south towards Mount Zion and the large multi-domed Dormition Abbey.

Tour stop 1 **Mount Zion (#92)**.

At site Schindler's Grave, Dormition Abbey, King David's Tomb, Room of the Last Supper (Cenacle).

Optional tour stop St. Peter in Gallicantu, a church commemorating the denial of Jesus by Peter. Visit for the great views of the Old City, City of David, and Silwan.

Tour stop 2 **City of David**.

At site Gihon Spring; Pool of Siloam.

Visit **Hezekiah's Tunnel**.

Tour stop 3 Kidron Valley. This valley is what separates the Old City of Jerusalem from the Mount of Olives, and is also known as the Valley of Jehoshaphat, where Judgment Day will occur with the coming of the Messiah. Today, the valley extends all the way to the Dead Sea.

At site The **Tomb of Benei Hazir** (2nd century BCE) is the burial site of a multi-generational priestly/rich family during the Hasmonean dynasty, replete with a variety of chambers for various members of the family. The **Tomb of Zacchariah** (2nd century BCE) is an unfinished tomb from the same period, with a pyramidal top on a Greek-inspired Ionic column base. It may be affiliated with the Benei Hazir family, rather than the anachronistic 7th-century BCE Zacchariah for whom it is named. The **Tomb of Absalom** (likely 1st century BCE) is attributed to King David's son, but is actually from close to 900 years later, when rich Jews would purchase ornate, monolithic tombs to coincide with their adjacent burial caves. Attribution has not been confirmed: the inscriptions relate to later historical periods and pious worshipers, not the buried.

Tour stop 4 **Mount of Olives (#34)**.
Note Mount of Olives is its own self-contained walking tour. Visit the elective for details.

At site Church of Mary Magdalene, Tomb of the Virgin, Basilica of the Agony, Jewish Cemetery, Church of the Ascension, Church of All Nations, Rehav'am Ze'evi Observation Point. Also the Church of the Paternoster, where Jesus possibly taught the Lord's Prayer.

Ending point Church of the Ascension, Mount of Olives (or continue to the two Pearl sites below): 40 days after his death, Jesus ascended to Heaven in front of 11 of his apostles, celebrated on Holy Thursday.

Optional tour stop Bethphage: near the Mount of Olives, this is the village from which Jesus rode into Jerusalem after raising Lazarus from the dead and was welcomed with open arms by Jerusalem residents. Palm Sunday processions often begin here and end in Jerusalem.

Optional tour stop Bethany and Lazarus' Tomb: in Al-Azariya east of Jerusalem, this is proclaimed to be the site of the Tomb of Lazarus, where Jesus raised Lazarus from the dead. Additionally, Jesus is said to have lodged here following his visit to Jerusalem, had dinner in the house of Simon the Leper, and traveled here with his disciples after his death before he ascended to Heaven.

TIPS

★ Churches closed Saturdays. Some have specific visiting hours (e.g., Church of Mary Magdalene: 10.00–noon Tuesday and Thursday).
★ Parking is not ideal on most of the Mount of Olives, with single-lane roads (two-way) and few street-parking options. However, the hills are steep. If you do drive to the top, you can generally find parking at the Reav'am Ze'evi Observation Point (great views) and near the top two churches.
★ If you're in town during Holy Week, particularly on Palm Sunday, join the procession from Mount of Olives to Jesus' crucifixion place.

FOOD You may need to detour into the Old City for the easiest and best options.

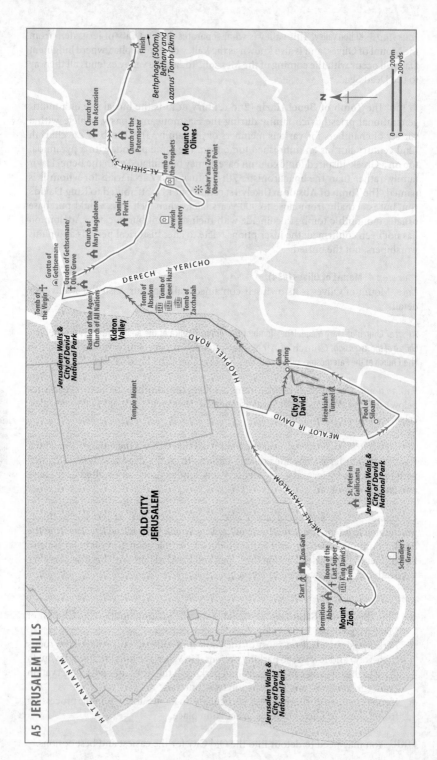

A6 EAST JERUSALEM

Terrain Moderate incline and descent, steps at sites
Difficulty (1–5) 3
Distance 5km
Walking time 1–2 hours
Completion time 4 hours

Starting point Damascus Gate, which marks the border of the 1949 Armistice Agreement Line.

Tour stop 1 Zedekiah's Cave/Solomon's Quarries is a massive limestone quarry underneath the Damascus Gate (whose weight caused the cave to partially collapse). The stones dug from here were purportedly used as Jerusalem building material, particularly the foundation walls and Second Temple. Though the caves were named after Zedekiah, a king in the 6th century BCE, and Solomon, the first King of the United Kingdom of Israel in 1000 BCE, it's unlikely this quarry dates as far back as their reigns. The dug rooms span well underneath the Muslim Quarter (A2). If you have purchased a **Jewish Quarter** pass, the site is included in the ticket.

Tour stop 2 Garden Tomb. Considered by some to be an alternative site of Golgotha and the Tomb of Jesus. Most archaeologists discount this notion, which emerged in the late 19th century as Christians of the time didn't know the walls of Jerusalem had moved and expanded many times, and that the present site of the **Church of the Holy Sepulchre (#9)** was once outside the old city walls. But that hasn't stopped throngs of tour buses from visiting this 8th–7th-century BCE rock-cut tomb just to the north of the Jerusalem walls. Closed Sundays. Takes only a few minutes to see the tomb.

Tour stop 3 Tomb of Queen Helena of Adiabene, aka Tombs of the Kings, although the latter name is a bit of a misnomer because there are no tombs and no kings are buried here. The sarcophagi are now all gone, but one was identified (shipped to the Louvre, where it sits today) as the tomb of Queen Helena, Kurdish royalty from a province called Adiabene and later a convert to Judaism.

Optional tour stop Palestinian National Theatre: aka Al-Hakawati, this theater troupe gained influence from the 1970s when Palestinian students of the Hebrew University decided to produce their own work, hire a director, and perform outside of school.

Optional tour stop American Colony Hotel: this glorious building and hotel, dating to the late 1800s and purchased from an Ottoman by an American couple building a commune, has catered to many famous clients over the years, claiming to be a neutral party in the Israel–Palestine conflict.

Tour stop 4 Palestinian Heritage Museum: three-story Ottoman building, on the grounds of the Dar Al-Tifl Al-Arabi Institution, including artifacts, weaving, a library, and an exhibit on the displacement of the Palestinians after 1948.

Tour stop 5 Emek Tzurim. Previous home of the Temple Mount Sifting Project. After Muslims completed earthen repair projects on Temple Mount, they dumped the dirt and debris in East Jerusalem. Israel declared the area a national park in 2000 and began sifting through the dirt, with the help of volunteers, for evidence of life

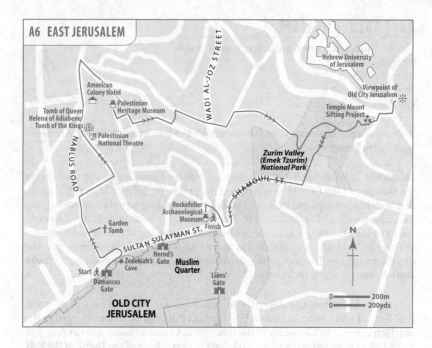

(Map labels:)
Hebrew University of Jerusalem
American Colony Hotel
Palestinian Heritage Museum
WADI AL-JOZ STREET
Viewpoint of Old City Jerusalem
Temple Mount Sifting Project
Tomb of Queen Helena of Adiabene/ Tomb of the Kings
Palestinian National Theatre
NABLUS ROAD
Zurim Valley (Emek Tzurim) National Park
SHAMOUIL ST.
Rockefeller Archaeological Museum
Garden Tomb
Finish
SULTAN SULAYMAN ST.
Herod's Gate
Zedekiah's Cave
Muslim Quarter
Start
Damascus Gate
Lions' Gate
OLD CITY JERUSALEM
N
0 — 200m
0 — 200yds

in ancient Jerusalem. Visitors now sift through excavated land from all over Israel. Plan 3 hours for the dig.

Optional tour stop *Temple Mount Sifting Project*: has been sorting through excavated material from the Temple Mount since 2005. Now located at Mitspe HaMasu'ot, next to Emek Tzurim. Two-hour experiences not to be missed for young archaeologists (**w** tmsifting.org/en/participate/).

Tour stop 6 **Rockefeller Archaeological Museum**.

Ending point Herod's Gate.

TIPS

★ This itinerary will give you a bit of history, a bit of Palestinian culture, a bit of Israel, some architecture, some religion, all on foot. If you want a more immersive cultural experience, there are a number of companies that can take you to refugee camps, Israeli settlements, for tours of the Separation Barrier, and historic Palestinian neighborhoods. Culture Trip has a good roundup (**w** theculturetrip.com/middle-east/palestinian-territories/articles/the-best-political-tours-of-the-west-bank/).

★ For a longer walk, you can continue north from the *American Colony Hotel*, passing the various embassies and consulates, then embarking on the huge Dan Jerusalem Hotel complex, walking through Hebrew University on Mount Scopus, catching some views, before connecting with Emek Tzurim. This will add another 2km/30 minutes of walking.

FOOD Grab some street food in East Jerusalem, or plan to eat before or after in the Old City or New City.

A7 JERUSALEM: NEW CITY AND NEIGHBORHOODS

Terrain Hills; mostly sidewalks
Difficulty (1–5) 2
Distance 8.5km
Walking time 2 hours
Completion time 4 hours

Note **Jerusalem, New City (#72)** is its own elective.

Starting point You can start at **YMCA** or Jaffa Gate. If the latter, walk south and cross the street, then head through the park and look for the large tower. It's about a 15-minute walk.

Tour stop 1 **YMCA**. Across the street is **King David Hotel**.

Tour stop 2 **Yemen Moshe** neighborhood.

At site **Montefiore's Windmill**: commissioned by Moses Montefiore, this mill, built in 1857, sits in the first Jewish neighborhood constructed outside the Old City's walls, Mishkenot Sha'ananim.

Optional tour stop **Menachem Begin Heritage Center**: the sixth prime minister of Israel, Begin founded the Likud party, negotiated peace with Egypt, and led the paramilitary Zionist group Irgun, among other noteworthy events. This museum tells his story.

Tour stop 3 **Museum for Islamic Art** (⏰ 10.00–15.00, 10.00–19.00 Thursday). Located in Jerusalem, this museum aims to link Arab and Jewish cultures through educational programming on Muslim civilization. Recent exhibitions include the Spread of Islam, the Art of Arabic Writing, Contemporary Iranian Posters, the Centrality of the Qur'an, and Technological Developments in Muslim Civilization.

Nearby The **Jerusalem Theatre**'s Center for the Performing Arts has multiple theaters and hosts more than 1,000 cultural events a year, including the Symphony Orchestra and the acclaimed **Oud Festival**, a celebration of the beautiful, lute-like stringed instrument, in November.

Tour stop 4 **Wolfson Museum of Jewish Art** (⏰ 09.00–15.00). A variety of Judaica in the Hechal Shlomo building for the Jewish Heritage Center in Jerusalem, with items going as far back as the Second Temple period.

Tour stop 5 Rehavia and Kiryat Shmuel.

En route **Consulate General of Belgium/Villa Salameh**: a gorgeous building with a complicated past. A wealthy Lebanese Christian, Constantine Salameh, bought the land from the Greek Orthodox Church after World War I. As was popular at the time, he constructed a building in the modern style (with Neoclassical elements) but wanted to design a house like no other before it. After independence in 1948, Israel reclaimed the land and locals fled from violence. He leased his property to his friend, the Belgian consul, and it has remained the Belgian consul's residence since then.

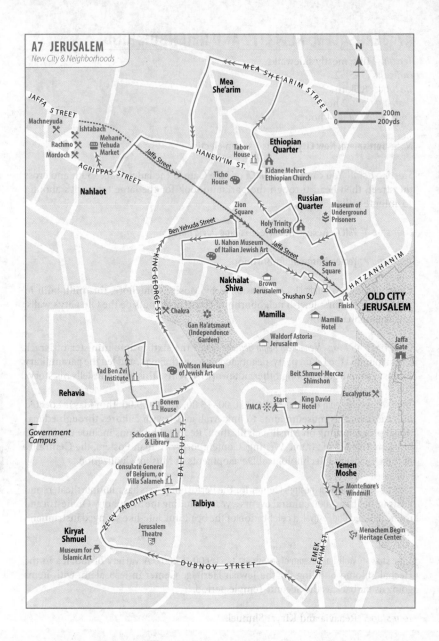

N

0 ——————— 200m
0 ——————— 200yds

JAFFA STREET

Machneyuda

Ishtabach

Rachmo

Mehane Yehuda Market

Mordoch

AGRIPPAS STREET

Nahlaot

Jaffa Street

HANEVI'IM ST.

MEA SHE'ARIM STREET

Mea She'arim

Tabor House

Ethiopian Quarter

Ticho House

Kidane Mehret Ethiopian Church

Zion Square

Russian Quarter

Museum of Underground Prisoners

Ben Yehuda Street

Holy Trinity Cathedral

U. Nahon Museum of Italian Jewish Art

Jaffa Street

KING GEORGE ST.

Safra Square

Nakhalat Shiva

Brown Jerusalem

Shushan St.

Finish

HATZANHANIM

OLD CITY JERUSALEM

Chakra

Gan Ha'atsmaut (Independence Garden)

Mamilla

Mamilla Hotel

Waldorf Astoria Jerusalem

Jaffa Gate

Yad Ben Zvi Institute

Wolfson Museum of Jewish Art

Beit Shmuel-Mercaz Shimshon

Eucalyptus

Rehavia

Bonem House

YMCA

Start

King David Hotel

Schocken Villa & Library

← Government Campus

BALFOUR ST.

Consulate General of Belgium, or Villa Salameh

Yemen Moshe

Montefiore's Windmill

ZE'EV JABOTINKSY ST.

Talbiya

Jerusalem Theatre

Menachem Begin Heritage Center

Kiryat Shmuel

Museum for Islamic Art

DUBNOV STREET

EMEK REFAIM ST.

En route Schocken Villa and Library: a collection of rare books that survived Nazi Germany's purge by way of an intense smuggling operation. The building is just as impressive.

En route Yad Ben Zvi Institute for Judaeo-Arab Studies: research center that once served as residence for two of Israel's former presidents.

En route Bonem House: now a Bank Leumi outlet, this is one of the rare Bauhaus buildings located in Jerusalem, and a stunning exemplar.

Tour stop 6 **Ben Yehuda Street**.

Optional tour stop **U. Nahon Museum of Italian Jewish Art**: Jewish art from Italy from the Renaissance period to the modern day.

Tour stop 7 **Nakhalat Shiva**: established in 1869, it's one of the oldest neighborhoods, and has been repurposed into a pedestrian-friendly series of streets with restaurants, shops, and outdoor cafés. There are a number of art installations that please the eye and make lovely Instagram shots. Two of the oldest synagogues in the city (including Nahalat Yaakov, which claims to be the oldest synagogue outside of the Old City walls) are located here.

Optional tour stop **Shushan Street**: when in Jerusalem, this is your hipster haven. Mazkeka gets lots of good reviews as an alternative music and arts venue/café.

Tour stop 8 **Russian Quarter**, aka Russian Compound. This section of Jerusalem most notably contains the barbed-wire-enclosed Moscovia Detention Centre, a prison, detention center, and interrogation facility, rendering the majority of this depressing quarter off-limits. An art school (called Bezalel) is currently under construction and the hope is that a new shopping and nightlife center will emerge again, as the city shut down the once-famous and seedy Soviet-style bars in 2006.

At site **Holy Trinity Cathedral**: this impressive church with its eight steeples was opened in 1872, during Ottoman reign.

Optional tour stop **Museum of Underground Prisoners**: located in the historic Russian Women Pilgrims Hostel in the Russian Compound, later converted into a prison by the British who jailed a number of political prisoners here, now part of the museum experience.

Optional tour stop **Ticho House**: a 19th-century home converted into a museum with works by Anna Ticho and other contemporary artists.

Consider **Tabor House**: built in 1889 by Protestant architect, Conrad Schick, and now operated by the Swedish Theological Seminary, this building is a fine example of Jerusalem architecture.

Tour stop 9 **Ethiopian Quarter**. West of the Old City, this little strip of territory is where, in 1888, an Ethiopian emperor purchased territory outside of the Old City's walls in order to build a church for his community. The elaborate and circular church, the Dabra Gannat, is the center of this quarter and worth a visit.

Tour stop 10 **Mea She'arim (#66)**.

Tour stop 11 **Mehane Yehuda Market (#67)**.

Ending point **Machneyuda (#98)**, hopefully.

TIPS

★ The whole Mehane Yehuda Market changes at night, if you make this an evening affair.

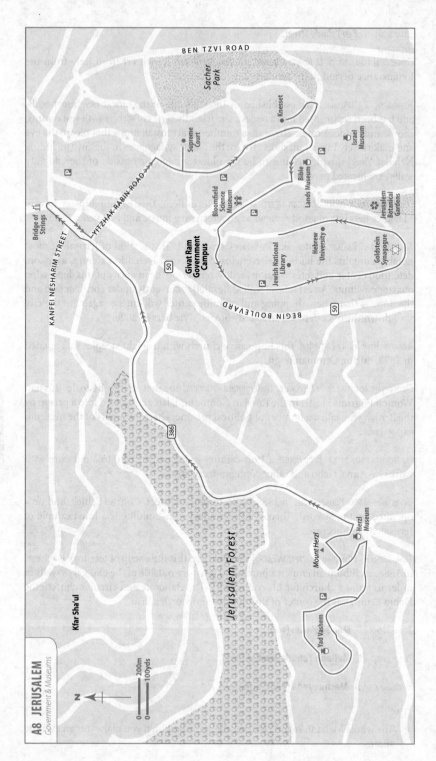

BEN TZVI ROAD

Sacher Park

Knesset

Supreme Court

Israel Museum

P

Bloomfield Science Museum

P

Bible Lands Museum

YITZHAK RABIN ROAD

Jerusalem Botanical Gardens

Bridge of Strings

Givat Ram Government Campus

KANFEI NESHARIM STREET

Hebrew University

Goldstein Synagogue

Jewish National Library

P

50

BEGIN BOULEVARD

50

386

Jerusalem Forest

Kfar Sha'ul

Herzl Museum

Mount Herzl

Yad Vashem

P

N

0   200m
0   100yds

★ If you want to end the tour back at Jaffa Gate, take Yafo Street from the market to Jaffa Gate, which adds another 25 minutes.

FOOD **Machneyuda (#98)** can be found close to the Mehane Yehuda Market, but book in advance. You have dozens of options at the market itself, or tons of options on the many streets in Nakhalat Shiva, along Ben Yehuda, or Yafo Street. Recommended restaurants include Mordoch, Ishtabach, Rachmo, Eucalyptus, and Chakra.

DRINK Gatsby Cocktail Room for happy hour. Don't miss *Jerusalem Nightlife*: while the Old City sleeps, West Jerusalem is awake and happening on Jaffa Street and the little alleys around Zion Square. Mehane Yehuda Market transforms into a hip hipster hangout after hours. You'll have to do some research to figure out what's best for you, as the bars are as varied as the origins of the city's denizens.

STAY **King David Hotel** is popular and regal, if expensive, and **Mamilla Hotel** gets a lot of press. Other popular: Waldorf Astoria, Beit Shmuel-Mercaz Shimshon, and Brown Jerusalem.

ACTIVITIES The Israel Festival is a week-long festival offering music, art, performance, and modern and classical dance in various locations around Jerusalem, but particularly the Jerusalem Theatre. The Hutzot Hayotzer Arts and Crafts Festival takes place over two weeks every summer in several venues just west of the Old City Jerusalem, where artists can sell their work, including everything from textiles and toys to paintings and jewelry, directly to the public.

A8 JERUSALEM: GOVERNMENT AND MUSEUMS

Distance 13km
Driving time 40 minutes
Completion time 2 days

Starting point From Jerusalem's Jaffa Gate: 7km/20 minutes; from Tel Aviv: 70km/50–90 minutes from downtown (very traffic-dependent).

Tour stop 1 Mount Herzl and Herzl Museum (⏲ 08.00–18.45). This museum explores the life of the famed Zionist from the late 19th century who promoted Zionism and pushed for Jewish settlement of Palestine.

Tour stop 2 **Yad Vashem (#35)** (⏲ 08.30–17.00), where you can visit the Dead Sea Scrolls at the Shrine of the Book.

Tour stop 3 Jerusalem Chords Bridge/*Bridge of Strings* – drive by, though you can walk on as well if you park nearby.

Tour stop 4 **Supreme Court of Israel** (tours in English at noon Sunday–Thursday).

Tour stop 5 Knesset (tours in English at 08.30, noon, 14.00 Sunday/Thursday). Israel's sole legislature (Parliament), this 120-member body dates its origin to the 5th century BCE and its members serve for four years (or less if dissolved by the prime minister). Tours are available Sundays and Thursdays, while visitors can view plenary debates Monday–Wednesday.

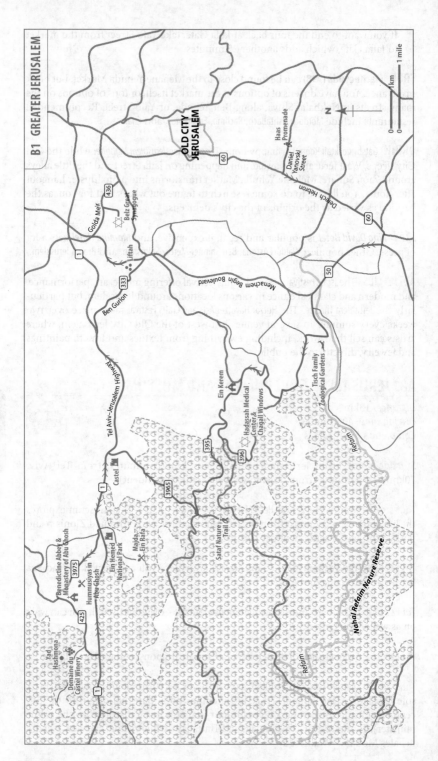

B1 GREATER JERUSALEM

OLD CITY JERUSALEM

Haas Promenade

Daniel Yanovski Street

Derech Hebron

Belz Great Synagogue

Golda Meir

Liftah

Ben Gurion

Menachem Begin Boulevard

Tel Aviv–Jerusalem Highway

Castel

Ein Kerem

Hadassah Medical Center & Chagall Windows

Satat Nature Trail

Tisch Family Zoological Gardens

Refaim

Refaim

Nahal Refaim Nature Reserve

Benedictine Abbey & Monastery of Abu Ghosh

Ein Hemed National Park

Hummusiyas in Abu Ghosh

Majda Ein Rafa

Yad Hashmona

Domaine du Castel Winery

1 km

1 mile

Tour stop 6 **_Bible Lands Museum_** (☉ 09.30–17.30).

Tour stop 7 **Israel Museum (#17)** (☉ 10.00–17.00) and the Dead Sea Scrolls.

Optional tour stop *Bloomfield Science Museum*: science-focused museum with lots of interactive exhibits popular with kids, as well as an IMAX.

Tour stop 8 Hebrew University, Safra Campus. Israel's Ministry of Foreign Affairs touts this campus for its unique architecture, including a white-domed synagogue facing Temple Mount (Goldstein Synagogue), the library inspired by Le Corbusier designs (Jewish National Library), and other architect-friendly buildings. Built in 1957 and winner of several architecture awards, the Goldstein Synagogue was built in a unique style, a sort of concrete bubble/dome, only 12 feet high with no windows. The Jewish National Library houses an enormous amount of Hebrew, Yiddish, and Ladino texts, plus a variety of Judaica relating to Israel, the Jewish people, and Judaism.

Ending point To Jerusalem: 6km/15 minutes to Mamilla/Jaffa; to Tel Aviv: 65km/45 minutes via Highway 1.

TIPS

★ Opening times are for days other than Friday and Saturday, when museums may be closed or have severely reduced hours. Always check websites for latest.
★ We've ordered the sites in the most logical sense to be sure to hit the sweet spot between hours of opening and availability of English-language tours.
★ You are unlikely to be able to fit all of this into one day, but you can certainly drop in on each site in one day. It's up to you to decide to see the parts that interest you.
★ If you like to take your time in museums, this itinerary is not for you. You can easily spend a whole day in the Israel Museum. Yad Vashem may be too depressing to spend all day, but can also take over much of your allotted program time.

FOOD The Israel Museum has the most variety: a high-end restaurant and several cafés.

B1 GREATER JERUSALEM

Distance 55km
Driving time 90 minutes
Completion time 3 days

Starting point From Jerusalem: 3km/10 minutes south of Jaffa Gate; from Tel Aviv: 75km/1 hour (plus traffic) via Route 1.

Tour stop 1 Haas Promenade. In south Jerusalem on Daniel Yanovski Street in the neighborhood of Talpiyot, this path is of higher elevation than the rest of the city, offering great views of the Old City, Dome of the Rock, Mount of Olives, and the villages packed together on the rolling hills.

Tour stop 2 Nahal Refaim. Plenty of green parks and hiking trails in this national nature reserve, following a river stream near the Tisch Family Zoo.

Tour stop 3 Tisch Family Zoological Gardens (⏲ 09.00–18.00). A zoo outside of Jerusalem with hundreds of animal species named in the Bible, including ibex and elephants.

Tour stop 4 **Ein Kerem**.

Tour stop 5 Hadassah Medical Center, **Hadassah Synagogue and Chagall Windows**.

Tour stop 6 **Sataf** Nature Trail.

Tour stop 7 Castel National Park. An old Crusader fortress that was used as a principal battle site during the 1948 Arab–Israeli War, was the first Arab site captured, and ultimately ensured Israeli control of the eastern edge of Jerusalem – now a national park.

Tour stop 8 **Ein Hemed** National Park.

Tour stop 9 Benedictine Abbey and **Monastery of Abu Ghosh** (⏲ 08.30–11.00 and 14.30–17.30, closed Sunday).

At site Abu Ghosh's hummusiyas. The tiny town of Abu Ghosh is home to more than a dozen hummus shops and restaurants specializing in the chickpea dish.

Tour stop 10 **Domaine du Castel** Winery (⏲ 08.00–17.00 Sunday–Thursday, by appointment only Friday, closed Saturday).

Tour stop 11 Yad Hashmona. Visit this moshav, just north of Castel Winery, which has a Biblical Garden where guides tell stories about ancient Israel and show a replica town.

Tour stop 12 Liftah. Depopulated Arab village after the 1948 Arab–Israeli War, preserved in time, now a nature reserve.

Optional tour stop Belz Great Synagogue: likely largest synagogue in the world, seating over 10,000

Ending point To Jerusalem: 5km/15 minutes south; to Tel Aviv: 65km/50 minutes via Route 1.

TIP Trip can be done in either direction, all in a circle.

FOOD Majda is excellent, in Ein Rafa near **Ein Hemed**, but requires a reservation. Or you may want to drop in on any of the hummus places in Abu Ghosh (see stop 9). Feel free to fit in lunch whenever you're ready, but an ideal time would likely be after Sataf, if you make that stop.

ACTIVITIES The Sacred Music Festival, since rebranded as Mekudeshet, seeks to be an annual, all-inclusive art and performance showcase presented in neutral spaces to bring together a diverse audience (w en.mekudeshet.com).

B2 JUDEAN HILLS

Distance 120km
Driving time 2½ hours
Completion time 2 days

Starting point From Jerusalem: 66km/1 hour; from Tel Aviv: 75km/50 minutes.

Tour stop 1 Tel Lachish. Destroyed by the Assyrians, this site was an important Israelite city, referenced throughout the Old Testament.

Tour stop 2 **Beit Guvrin and Maresha (#60).**

At site Archaeological Seminars Dig-for-a-Day. Real digs in Beit Guvrin National Park that are licensed by the Israel Antiquities Authority. Prices for a 3-hour dig in English or Hebrew are 110 ILS for adults and 95 ILS for kids 5–14. Private digs can be also be arranged for a flat fee. Check out **w** digforaday.com.

Optional tour stop *Beit Jamal Monastery*: a Catholic monastery for nuns and monks which sells pottery, wine, honey, and olive oil.

Tour stop 3 Stalactite Caves. This large cave at Soreq outside Jerusalem has a number of stalactites and stalagmites with amusing names such as "Snow White and the Seven Dwarves," "Romeo and Juliet," and "Elephant's Ears."

Optional tour stop *Biblical Museum of Natural History*: live exhibits and a petting zoo. By appointment only, age 7+ recommended, 50 ILS adults, 40 children.

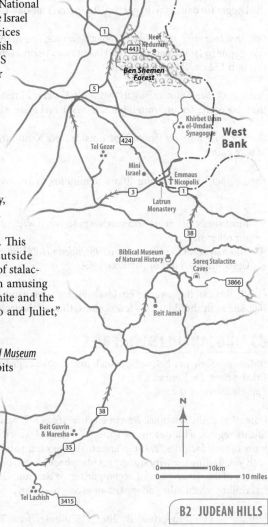

B2 JUDEAN HILLS

Tour stop 4 Latrun Monastery. A French Trappist monastery since 1890, now sellers of wine.

Tour stop 5 Mini Israel (🕐 10.00–17.00 Sunday–Thursday, 10.00–14.00 Friday; w minisrael.co.il/en). A park designed to allow you to see all of Israel in only a few blocks. With nearly 400 building models featuring the famous sites of the Azrieli Towers (Tel Aviv), the Western Wall, mosques, churches, and more.

Optional tour stop *Emmaus Nicopolis*: where Jesus appeared before two disciples after his death, dined with them, and, once they recognized him as Jesus, disappeared. In truth, the true location of Emmaus remains a mystery.

Tour stop 6 Tel Gezer Archaeological Project. A multi-year project that takes volunteers and students to work on this Bronze/Iron Age site. Coordinate with tour guide, Danny the Digger (w dannythedigger.com/tel-gezer/) for day-dig options.

Optional tour stop *Khirbet Umm el-Umdan Synagogue*: one of the oldest (if not the oldest) synagogue in Israel, dating to the Hasmonean period (2nd century BCE) and in use through 132 CE. Ruins in Modi'in.

Tour stop 7 Neot Kedumim Biblical Landscape. 625 acres of restored land used to recreate the flora of the region from biblical times. Israel Prize winner in 1994.

Optional tour stop *Ben Shemen Forest*: outside Neot Kedumim, this huge park has 32km of bike paths.

Ending point To Jerusalem: 40km/40 minutes; to Tel Aviv: 30km/25 minutes.

TIPS
★ Most sites close at around sundown, so you'll want to start early – we give times for other sites.
★ You may want to splice parts of *B3: Judean Hills Wineries* into this itinerary – try Clos de Gat Winery (B3) or Flam Winery (B3).

FOOD You can hop over to Abu Ghosh (B1) for some famous hummusiyas. En route, Beit Shemesh should have a few options, though they will be limited on Saturdays.

B3 JUDEAN HILLS WINERIES

Distance 65km, per below, but you'll likely make adjustments
Driving time 1½ hours
Completion time 2 days

Note Part of the Judean Hills Wineries elective: it's not Napa, and that's really the beauty of this region, with dozens of wineries, many of which will conduct tastings and tours of their facilities. Tastings are usually very intimate, with the sommelier seated with you, tasting the wines, and providing background on the growing methods and history of the winery, as well as comparison to New and Old World wines. The region has rolling, green hills and makes an excellent day trip.

Starting point From Jerusalem: 20km/25 minutes; from Tel Aviv: 55km/40 minutes.

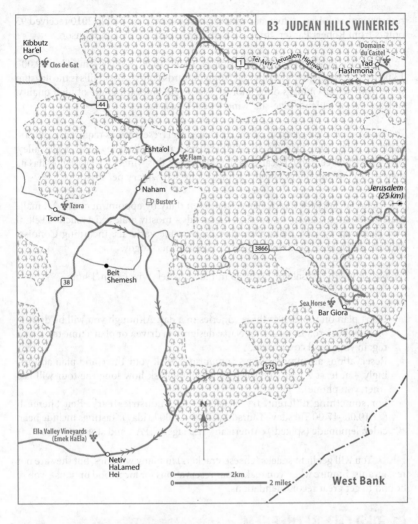

Tour option 1 **Domaine du Castel**, Abu Ghosh (reservations required; ⏲ 08.00–17.00 Sunday–Thursday, by appointment only Friday, closed Saturday; **w** castel.co.il/en/).

Tour option 2 Clos de Gat Winery, Kibbutz Harel (by appointment only; **w** closdegat.co.il). French barrels, mostly noble grapes, four collections (Sycra is the most prestigious), ranging from $30 to $80, plus some higher-end cellared vintages. Five-star winery in Rogov Guide.

Tour option 3 Flam Winery, Eshtaol (⏲ 10.00–17.00 Sunday–Thursday, by appointment only Friday, closed Saturday; wine tastings 70 ILS per person or 130 ILS including cheese pairing; **w** flamwinery.com). Family-run winery, best known for its reds – a high-end blend called Noble, and Cabernet Sauvignon, Merlot, and Syrah single-grape reserves. It has a budget-friendly blend called Classico, and rosé and white wines to round out the collection. A visit to the vineyard will take you through the delightful wine country. The tasting room is beautiful and tastings are intimate, with reservations required. A five-star winery, says Rogov; Flam Noble 2010 received 93 points from Robert Parker; three- to four-star winery says Hugh Johnson.

Tour option 4 Tzora Winery, Kibbutz Tzora (⊕ 10.00–16.00 Sunday–Thursday, 09.00–13.00 by appointment only Friday; w tzoravineyards.com). Misty Hills is the flagship wine from select vintages only. Shoresh is a single-vineyard grape of high quality. Judean Hills is a blend. Five-star winery per Rogov.

Tour option 5 Ella Valley Vineyards, Netiv Ha Lamed Hei (reservations required; ⊕ 09.00–16.00 Monday–Thursday, 09.00–13.00 Friday; e info@ellavalley.com; w ellavalley.com/en/visitor-center/). Located in the Ella Valley, this winery/events center has its own wine club and offers 1-hour tastings. Four-star winery per Rogov.

Tour option 6 Sea Horse Winery, Bar Giora (open daily by appointment only). Small-scale production, clever names on all the blends – mostly male artists such as Fellini and Hemingway. Also selling unique single-grape varietals, including Conoise, Muscat, and Grenache. Small producer. Five-star per Rogov.

Ending point To Jerusalem: 25km/35 minutes; to Tel Aviv: 65km/1 hour.

TIPS
★ Don't plan on more than three wineries in a day. Although you will be driving on hilly, back roads, this is not Napa: designate a driver, or plan a time to eat and regain your legal composure.
★ Reservations are almost always compulsory. Pick your three and plan accordingly – at least 2 hours between sites (though ask how long the tour will last when you phone).
★ For something different, try: Buster's, Sorek Industries Park, Beit Shemesh (⊕ 10.00–17.00 Tuesday–Thursday, 10.00–14.00 Friday). Tastings include beer, cider, lemonade (spiked!), American-style lagers, IPAs, and stouts.

FOOD You will get light snacks (cheese/crackers) in many wineries, but they are not restaurants. Inquire when you make your reservations for local food options – you're bound to get great recommendations.

C1 OLD CITY BETHLEHEM

Terrain Streets, mostly flat, though there are steps in some places (King David's Wells)
Difficulty (1–5) 2
Distance 9km
Walking time 2 hours
Completion time 4 hours

Note For more on how to plan your trip, see **Bethlehem (#40)**.

Starting point Manger Square.

Optional detour
★ *Tour stop A* Mary's Well, Beit Sahour. On their way to Egypt, the Holy Family visited this well for a drink – but the water was too deep. Mary performed a

miracle by making the water rise. Site is near The Well Restaurant and Bar. See w visitpalestine.ps for more information.

★ *Tour stop B* _Banksy Art_, Beit Sahour. The famous *Love Is In The Air, Flower Thrower* is located near a gas station/car wash in Beit Sahour near the Shepherds' Fields Apartments (h/t w notesontraveling.com).

★ *Tour stop C* Shepherds' Fields, Beit Sahour. Angels visited the land of the lowest caste, the shepherds (rather than the wealthy or priests), to announce the birth of Christ. There are multiple sites in Beit Sahour purporting to be the site of Shepherds' Fields. You can visit the Greek Church, the Catholic Church, and the Protestant sites.

★ Return to Manger Square.

Tour stop 1 Manger Square. The location of the Church of the Nativity, this is a pedestrian square with restaurants, a gift shop, and the sole mosque in Bethlehem, the Mosque of Omar. It's also the location of Christmas festivities in the city.

Tour stop 2 **Church of the Nativity (#18)**.

Tour stop 3 Chapel of St. Catherine. Next door to the Nativity, this Catholic church also sits above a network of caves. Named after the same St. Catherine as our elective in the Sinai.

Tour stop 4 Chapel of the Milk Grotto. By tradition, Mary was breastfeeding Jesus and a single drop landed on the floor of the cave, turning all the walls white.

Tour stop 5 Star Street. Included as part of the UNESCO designation for Bethlehem, this street charts the 1km journey from King David's Wells to the old Damascus Gate which was the ancient entrance to the city, near Manger Square. Several groups are attempting to revitalize this tiny street.

Tour stop 6 King David's Wells. These three cisterns on the site of the Catholic Action Center are said to be the location where King David's soldiers fetched him water during his time of thirst while in hiding from the Philistines. He was so grateful that he couldn't drink the water and poured it on the ground.

En route On Hebron Road, just south of the Bethlehem Museum, is a small sundry shop where you can see Banksy's *Girl Frisking Soldier* (for a nominal fee).

Tour stop 7 The **Separation Wall** and artwork. There is great graffiti art all along the Separation Wall, which winds in and out of different areas – some of which are inaccessible – but you can get a good feel along Hebron Street. There are also new murals around **Banksy's Walled-Off Hotel**, a Banksy institution.

Tour stop 8 Palestinian Heritage Center. Information on the cultural heritage of the Palestinian people. On the outside of the building is Banksy's *Armored Dove* painting.

Tour stop 9 Aida Refugee Camp. Near Bethlehem and the Separation Wall, this camp of 3,150 Palestinian refugees isn't a tourist site per se, but still welcomes visitors and volunteers. Check out w lajee.ps for volunteer opportunities. Seek out a guide if you want to do a tour. Hantourism (w hantour.ps/tours/bethlehem-sunday-reality-tour/) and Beyond Borders (w beyondborderstours.com) both offer comprehensive day tours.

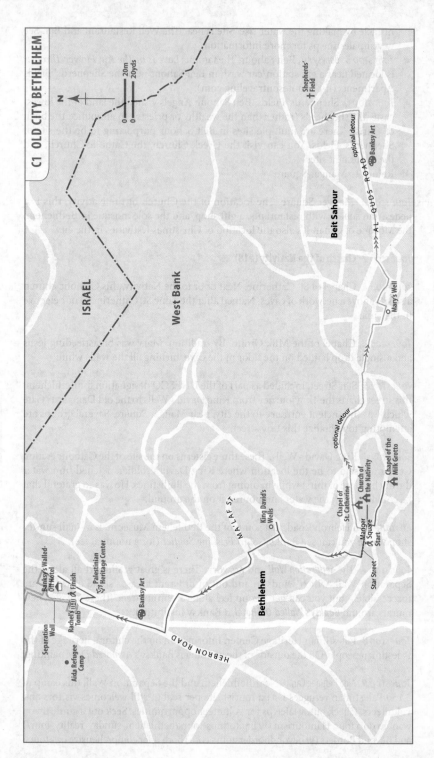

C1 OLD CITY BETHLEHEM

ISRAEL

West Bank

Bethlehem

Beit Sahour

Separation Wall

Aida Refugee Camp

Banksy's Walled-Off Hotel

Rachel's Tomb · Finish

Palestinian Heritage Center

Banksy Art

HEBRON ROAD

MA'I LAF ST.

King David's Wells

Chapel of St. Catherine

Church of the Nativity

Manger Square · Start

Star Street

Chapel of the Milk Grotto

AL QUDS ROAD

optional detour

Mary's Well

Banksy Art

Shepherds' Field

optional detour

N

0   20m
0   20yds

Tour stop 10 **Banksy's Walled-Off Hotel**.

Optional tour stop *Rachel's Tomb*: marking the boundary between Israel and Palestine, Rachel's Tomb is also the proposed burial site for the biblical matriarch Rachel. Considered the third-holiest site in Judaism, the site has religious significance to Muslims and Christians. Occasionally, Christians are allowed entry, but Muslims are usually not. Only Jews are allowed to walk in at the time of writing, so to visit you have to drive.

Ending point Cross over to the Israeli side at Rachel's Tomb for a bus or taxi, or double-back to your parked car in/around Manger Square.

TIPS
★ Bring your passport. This trip crosses borders.
★ Parking is available on the streets, but there's a covered lot just below Manger Square (tight fits; you'll have to leave your keys).
★ If you are visiting the area around Christmas, expect long waits and more activities – this could add several more hours to your day.
★ Visits to refugee camps require preplanning.

FOOD There are a number of restaurants, falafel shops, hummusiyas, etc. near Manger Square.

ACTIVITIES Obviously, if you can make it work, *Christmas Mass in Bethlehem* is a worthwhile adventure. The Church of the Nativity hosts a midnight mass at the site of Jesus' birth on the observed day of his birth, led by the Patriarch of Jerusalem on December 25, and led by the Orthodox community on Epiphany and Orthodox Christmas on January 6 and 7.

C2 SOUTHERN WEST BANK

Distance 100km north to south
Driving time 2½ hours
Completion time 3 days

Starting point From Jerusalem: 20km/35 minutes; from Tel Aviv: 75km/1¼ hours.

Tour stop 1 **Battir Hills**. If you want to visit the area of Battir, the best way to do so is through a walking tour, which will can take a good chunk of the day and incorporate **Bethlehem (#40)**. You can always coordinate a car or taxi picking you up at a certain spot. Best bet would be to drop your car in Bethlehem, then hire a taxi or guide to drop you in Battir, then walk back to Beit Jala. Check **w** walkpalestine.com and **w** welcometopalestine.com/destinations/bethlehem/battir/ for walking tour options.

Optional tour stop *Mar Elias Monastery* (6th century): in Kings 1, Elijah stayed here during his flight from Jezebel. On the road to Bethlehem, visits possible, handicrafts for sale.

Optional tour stop *Monastery of St. Theodosius* (6th century): said to be the location where the Three Wise Men took shelter after delivering their gifts to Joseph and Mary, denying the location of the Holy Family to King Herod. The monastery was

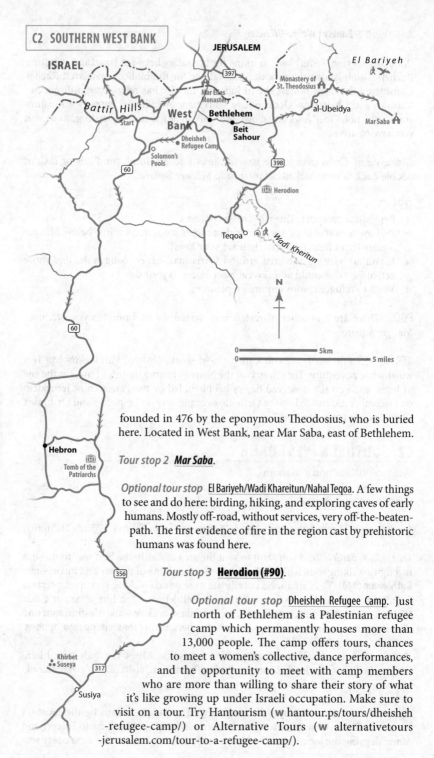

JERUSALEM

ISRAEL

397

Monastery of
St. Theodosius

El Bariyeh

Mar Elias
Monastery

al-Ubeidya

Battir Hills

**West
Bank**

Bethlehem

Start

**Beit
Sahour**

Mar Saba

Dheisheh
Refugee Camp

Solomon's
Pools

398

60

Herodion

Teqoa

Wadi Kheritun

N

0 ——————— 5km
0 ——————— 5 miles

60

Hebron

Tomb of the
Patriarchs

founded in 476 by the eponymous Theodosius, who is buried
here. Located in West Bank, near Mar Saba, east of Bethlehem.

Tour stop 2 **Mar Saba.**

Optional tour stop El Bariyeh/Wadi Khareitun/Nahal Teqoa. A few things
to see and do here: birding, hiking, and exploring caves of early
humans. Mostly off-road, without services, very off-the-beaten-
path. The first evidence of fire in the region cast by prehistoric
humans was found here.

Tour stop 3 **Herodion (#90).**

356

Optional tour stop Dheisheh Refugee Camp. Just
north of Bethlehem is a Palestinian refugee
camp which permanently houses more than
13,000 people. The camp offers tours, chances
to meet a women's collective, dance performances,
and the opportunity to meet with camp members
who are more than willing to share their story of what
it's like growing up under Israeli occupation. Make sure to
visit on a tour. Try Hantourism (w hantour.ps/tours/dheisheh
-refugee-camp/) or Alternative Tours (w alternativetours
-jerusalem.com/tour-to-a-refugee-camp/).

Khirbet
Suseya

317

Susiya

Tour stop 4 <u>Solomon's Pools</u>. These three pools are named after King Solomon who is traditionally cited as the creator of these spring-fed reservoirs, though they were likely built 900 years after his rule, around 100 BCE. Because they rest on hills where they collect the spring water, ancient aqueducts would send the water to Jerusalem to provide the city with water.

Tour stop 5 <u>Hebron</u>. Famous dishes in this southern West Bank city include *mahshi lift* (turnips stuffed with minced lamb and rice in a tamarind sauce), *al-qidrah* (a rice and lamb casserole served on Fridays), and falafel with eggplant. Downtown are the ruins of Tel Rumeida, perhaps the site of biblical Hebron. Hebron is the only West Bank city with a sizable Jewish and Arab population. Get both perspectives on Abraham Tours' "dual narrative" tour (**w** abrahamtours.com/tours/hebron-tour/).

Tour stop 6 **Tomb of the Patriarchs and Old Town of Hebron (#46)**.

Tour stop 7 <u>Khirbet Suseya</u>. Well-preserved 4th-century synagogue, with interesting mosaics, and some rooms being converted for Muslim use.

Ending point To Jerusalem: 85km/1½ hours back through West Bank, or 135km exiting West Bank and circling around on highways (less hassle, same travel time, but 50km more); to Tel Aviv: 135km/1¾ hours.

TIPS
★ Don't forget your passport for this trip. You're crossing recognized boundaries.
★ Visits to refugee camps require preplanning.
★ Driving directions are generally not available through traditional GPS due to the Israeli restrictions into and out of the West Bank for locals.
★ Avoid the area if there are reports of violence anywhere in the West Bank prior to your trip. Flash episodes of violence can spring up quickly and in multiple spots at once because of isolated incidents elsewhere in Israel or the Territories.

FOOD Street food in Hebron is legendary – see the Hebron tour stop.

C3 JERICHO AND WADI QELT

Distance 100km
Driving time 2¼ hours
Completion time 2 days

Starting point From Jerusalem: 15km/25 minutes; from Tel Aviv: 80km/1¼ hours.

Tour stop 1 <u>Monastery of St. Martyrius</u>. Martyrius served as patriarch of Jerusalem (a line of bishops which extends to the first bishop of Jerusalem, James the Just, Jesus' brother) from 478 to 486. Contemporaneous with the ruins close to Euthymius and damaged after Persian invasion in 614 CE. By prior arrangement only.

Tour stop 2 <u>Monastery of St. Euthymius</u>. An early church (428 CE) and later monastery, now in ruins, located in the West Bank town of Ma'ale Adumim. Named after the founder, Euthymius of Lesser Armenia, in 482. By prior arrangement only.

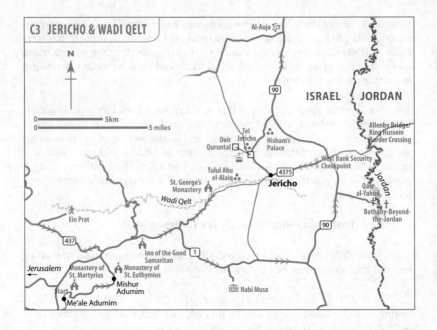

Al-Auja

N

0 ————————— 5km
0 ————————— 5 miles

ISRAEL JORDAN

90

Allenby Bridge/
King Hussein
Border Crossing

Deir
Quruntal

Tel
Jericho

Hisham's
Palace

West Bank Security
Checkpoint

4375

Tulul Abu
el-Alaiq

St. George's
Monastery

Jericho

Qasr
al-Yahud

Wadi Qelt

Bethany-Beyond-
the-Jordan

Ein Prat

90

437

Jerusalem
←

Monastery of
St. Martyrius

Inn of the Good
Samaritan

Monastery of
St. Euthymius

1

Mishur
Adumim

Start

Nabi Musa

Me'ale Adumim

Tour stop 3 **Ein Prat**. A variety of desert canyon walks, with the highlight being the hillside Faran Monastery, founded in 330 CE.

Tour stop 4 **Inn of the Good Samaritan**. Commemorates the parable of the Good Samaritan. Museum of Mosaics is now on site.

Tour stop 4 **St. George's Monastery and Wadi Qelt (#97)**.

Tour stop 5 **Nabi Musa**. Tomb of Moses, located in the West Bank (not to be confused with Mount Nebo, Moses' final resting place) and traditionally the destination of an annual pilgrimage of Palestinian Muslims starting in Jerusalem.

Tour stop 6 **Qasr al-Yahud**. Israel's answer to Jordan's claim to the true baptism site of Jesus (at **Bethany-Beyond-the-Jordan (#41)**). This site sits opposite the Jordanian marker and caters to far more tourists, though its authenticity as the true baptism site is in question. That said, it's linked to the location where the Israelites crossed the Jordan River.

Tour stop 7 **Jericho and Hisham's Palace (#26)**.

At site **Deir Quruntal**, **Tulul Abu el-Alaiq**.

Tour stop 8 **Al-Auja**. The Al-Auja Ecocenter offers a community center and ecolodge for a variety of one-day courses introducing guests or same-day visitors to Palestinian life, with food, hiking, political, historical, and ecologically focused itineraries (**w** aujaecocenter.org).

Ending point To Jerusalem: 60km/1 hour; to Tel Aviv: 115km/1¾ hours.

TIPS

★ Several of the sites require pre-authorization to visit. You can also call for admission when you arrive, though don't expect anyone to come running. Contact **w** dannythedigger.com for a combined trip.

★ Monasteries tend to be closed on Sundays.

★ Monasteries have dress codes. Women can't simply wear pants, but must actually wear a dress in St. George's Monastery, for instance.

★ You need a passport to enter Jericho. Much of the rest of this itinerary, though in the West Bank, is under Israeli control. The easiest entry is from the east, turning from Route 90 after Qasr al-Yahud.

FOOD Eat in downtown Jericho. Plenty of options.

ACTIVITIES For biking aficionados, try <u>Sugar Trail</u>, a 10km desert mountain-biking trail descending from 600m to 350m below sea level.

C4 NORTHERN WEST BANK: RAMALLAH REGION

Distance 110km one-way
Driving time 3 hours
Completion time 2 days

Starting point From Jerusalem: 9km/20 minutes; from Tel Aviv: 60km/1 hour; from Ramallah: 16km/35 minutes.

Tour stop 1 <u>Ramot Polin Apartments</u>, for bizarre egg-crate architecture.

Tour stop 2 <u>Nebi Samuel</u>. Burial site of the biblical prophet Samuel, the Tomb of Samuel sits in a crypt below a Crusader-era fortress which now sits underneath the Nebi Samuel (or Nabi Samwil) mosque.

[Pass a checkpoint]

Tour stop 3 **Ramallah (#68)**.

Tour stop 4 <u>Yasser Arafat Museum</u> (🕐 10.00–17.00 Tuesday–Sunday). A mausoleum in Ramallah to the former leader of the Palestinians, with information on Arafat's life and the Palestinian national movement.

Optional tour stop <u>Et-Tell, ancient Ai</u>: burned buildings from the site coincide roughly with the date of the biblical account when the Israelites attacked the ancient city of Ai.

Tour stop 5 <u>Taybeh Brewing Company</u> (🕐 08.00–16.00 Monday–Saturday). A small brewery northeast of Ramallah with a well-regarded series of Palestinian beers, sold globally.

Optional tour stop <u>The Palestinian Museum</u> (🕐 09.00–17.00 Sunday–Thursday): located in Birzeit, West Bank (7km north of Ramallah), this new museum, independently owned and beautifully constructed, was dubbed one of the "coolest new attractions of 2016" and seeks to promote Palestinian culture to Arab and international audiences.

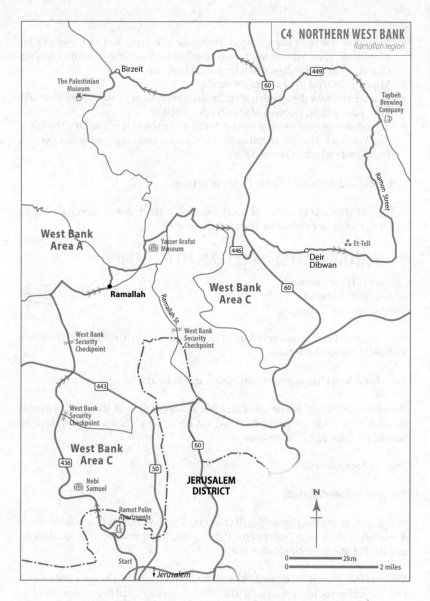

Birzeit

The Palestinian
Museum

449

60

Taybeh
Brewing
Company

Ramon Street

**West Bank
Area A**

Yasser Arafat
Museum

446

Et-Tell

Deir
Dibwan

**West Bank
Area C**

60

Ramallah

Ramallah St.

West Bank
Security
Checkpoint

West Bank
Security
Checkpoint

443

West Bank
Security
Checkpoint

**West Bank
Area C**

436

Nebi
Samuel

50

60

**JERUSALEM
DISTRICT**

N

Ramot Polin
Apartments

Start

Jerusalem

0   2km
0   2 miles

Ending point To Ramallah: 40km/1 hour; to Jerusalem: 40km/45 minutes; to Tel
Aviv: 45km/45 minutes.

TIPS

★   Bring your passport – you will be crossing borders.

★   You may want to overnight in Ramallah to experience its acclaimed nightlife.

FOOD Plenty of food options in Ramallah. Liquid lunch at Taybeh.

C5 NORTHERN WEST BANK: NABLUS REGION

Distance 140km one-way
Driving time 3 hours
Completion time 2 days

Starting point From Ramallah: 40km/1½ hours; from Jerusalem: 75km/1½ hours; from Tel Aviv: 75km/1½ hours.

Tour stop 1 <u>Shuqba/Natuf Caves</u>. Prehistoric cave highlighting the Stone Age Natufian culture. The origin of the term "Natufian culture" comes from this site, excavated in 1928, showcasing a hunter-gatherer culture that was transitioning to a sedentary lifestyle, perhaps evolving to the agricultural phase of human progression.

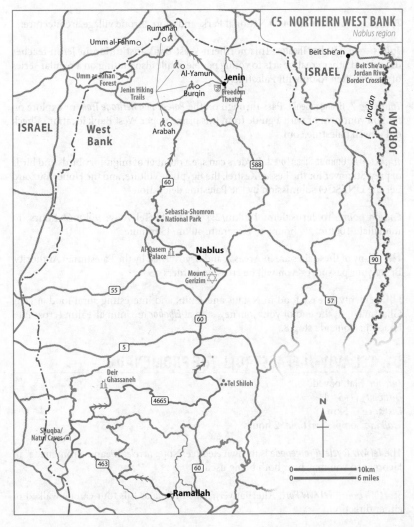

Tour stop 2 <u>Deir Ghassaneh</u>. One of the best preserved of the <u>Palestinian Throne Villages</u>, in a rural part of the West Bank, 30km northwest of Ramallah. For a walking tour of this region, check out w sufitrails.ps and its Deir Ghassaneh Trail.

Optional tour stop <u>Tel Shiloh</u>: here, ancient Israelites brought the Tabernacle. Visit the ancient home of the Tabernacle, mosaics of a Byzantine church, walls of the ancient city, and an ancient synagogue.

Tour stop 3 **Nablus (#61)**.

Tour stop 4 **Mount Gerizim**.

Optional tour stop <u>Al-Qasem Palace</u>: one of the Palestinian Throne Villages, located in Beit Wazan. It was threatened with destruction, but restored and rebuilt with a solid investment and plan, and now serves as a function hall.

Tour stop 5 **Sebastia-Shomron** National Park, and more throne village architecture.

Tour stop 6 <u>Freedom Theatre</u>. This northern West Bank institution in Jenin teaches drama and other creative arts to young people, while also putting on a regular series of shows, often to do with Palestine.

Tour stop 7 <u>Hiking in Jenin</u>. Pass through on the ***Palestinian Heritage Trail***, or explore on foot on your own or with a guide from this prime upper West Bank location. Check out w walkpalestine.com.

Tour stop 8 <u>Umm ar-Rihan Forest</u>. Birders can see a number of migratory birds and birds of prey. Stopover for the Lesser Kestrel, the Egyptian Vulture, and the Honey Buzzard per the UNESCO submission by the Palestine delegation.

Ending point To Jerusalem: 100km/2½ hours; to Tel Aviv: 90km/2 hours; to Ramallah: 100km/2½ hours; to Nazareth: 40km/45 minutes.

TIP Many of these sites are in Areas A and B, governed by the Palestinian Authority. Bring your passport – you will be crossing borders.

FOOD Plenty of easy food in Nablus and Jenin, and interesting rural food at Deir Ghassaneh. At the end of your journey, stop at ***Elbabor*** in Umm al-Fahm (cross into Israel) just outside stop 8.

D1 TEL AVIV-JAFFA: STROLL THE PROMENADE

Terrain Flat, paved
Difficulty (1–5) 1
Distance 7.5km
Walking/completion time 2 hours

The ***Tel Aviv Tayelet/Promenade*** is its own elective. Note: *tayelet* means "promenade" in Hebrew, so you may hear both being used.

Starting point **Tel Aviv Port**. Alternatively, start in Jaffa as this tour can be walked in either direction.

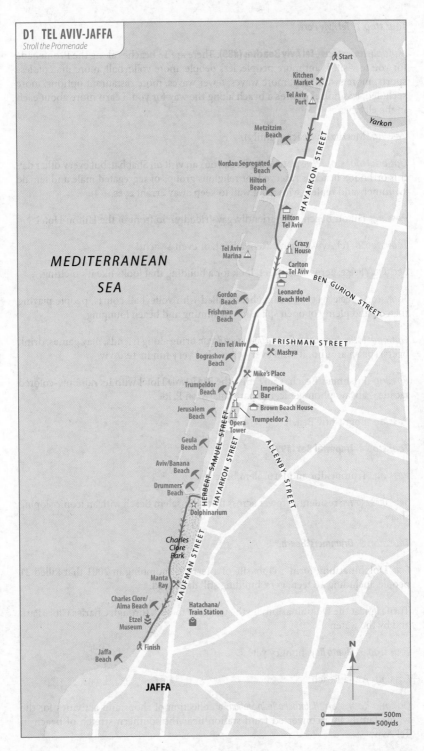

D1 TEL AVIV-JAFFA
Stroll the Promenade

↟ Start

Kitchen Market

Tel Aviv Port

Yarkon

Metzitzim Beach

HAYARKON STREET

Nordau Segregated Beach

Hilton Beach

Hilton Tel Aviv

Tel Aviv Marina

Crazy House

Carlton Tel Aviv

Leonardo Beach Hotel

BEN GURION STREET

MEDITERRANEAN SEA

Gordon Beach

Frishman Beach

FRISHMAN STREET

Dan Tel Aviv

Mashya

Bograshov Beach

Mike's Place

Imperial Bar

Trumpeldor Beach

Brown Beach House

Trumpeldor 2

Jerusalem Beach

Opera Tower

HERBERT SAMUEL STREET

HAYARKON STREET

ALLENBY STREET

Geula Beach

Aviv/Banana Beach

Drummers' Beach

Dolphinarium

Charles Clore Park

KAUFMAN STREET

Manta Ray

Charles Clore/ Alma Beach

Etzel Museum

Hatachana/ Train Station

Jaffa Beach

↟ Finish

JAFFA

N

| 0 | 500m |
| 0 | 500yds |

Tour stop 1 **Tel Aviv Port**.

Multiple tour stops **Tel Aviv Beaches (#89)**. There are 13 beaches along the Promenade for you to visit. Want more people, less people, more volleyball, more matcot, less sports, more swimming, more waves, fewer waves, more restaurant options, more secluded, less noise? There's a beach along the way for you. Learn more about each in the elective.

Passing Metzitzim Beach (family).

Optional tour stop Nordau Segregated Beach: you can visit on Shabbat, but every other day this orthodox beach is reserved for religious groups of segregated male and female swimmers and replete with a big wall to keep away errant eyes.

Passing Hilton Beach (dog-friendly/gay-friendly), in front of the Hilton Hotel.

Tour stop 2 Tel Aviv Marina. Rent a boat, or even a yacht!

See Crazy House: across the street, look for a building that looks like it's melting.

Tour stop 3 Gordon Beach: a huge beach filled with volleyball courts, people playing matcot, and plenty of open space for swimming and beach lounging.

Optional tour stop Group Fun at a Downtown Beach: bring along friends, play games, drink beers, splash around. It's fun everywhere, but very fun in Tel Aviv.

Passing Frishman Beach. Can't miss the Dan Tel Aviv Hotel with its rainbow-colored facade – always photogenic, but particularly on Pride.

Passing Bograshov Beach.

Tour stop 4 **Imperial Bar (#99)**.

Passing Trumpeldor and Jerusalem beaches.

See Opera Tower: residential tower across from Jerusalem Beach with an iconic sloping shape.

Tour stop 5 **Drummers' Beach**.

See Dolphinarium: former club, site of a terrorist bombing in 2001 that killed 21 people, including 16 teenagers; building still destroyed.

Turn right at the Dolphinarium on the walkway to walk through Charles Clore Park and by the water.

Tour stop 6 **Manta Ray**: hungry yet?

Passing Alma Beach.

Optional tour stop Hatachana Train Station: a collection of shops and activities for the whole family in a converted train station near the southern stretch of beach in Tel Aviv.

Optional tour stop Etzel Museum, commemorating the Irgun, a Zionist paramilitary group fighting for Israeli independence.

Tour stop 7 **Jaffa (#30)**.

Ending point Jaffa. From here, you can begin *D2: Jaffa*.

Alternative You can also do this same route via rented bicycle on the **Tel-O-Fun Bike Share** program, which offers one-day rentals and allows (encourages!) the use of different pickup/dropoff locations.

TIPS
★ The walk is great year-round, though busiest and warmest in the summer, of course.
★ Schedule for early afternoon so you don't miss sunset (which varies greatly depending on time of year – as early as 16.00, as late as 21.00). This will also prepare you for drinks and dinner options in the itinerary.
★ Lounge chairs are relatively inexpensive, so you can stake your claim for the whole day on one beach if it suits you.
★ This route is busiest on Fridays and Saturdays.

FOOD **Manta Ray** is a higher-end restaurant that is included as stop 6. **Mashya** offers more fine dining a block from the beach. If you cross the street from the beach, you'll find bakeries, falafel stands, and a variety of restaurants all along Herbert Samuel and HaYarkon Streets. The **Tel Aviv Port** has several restaurants, including Kitchen Market, or continue on to *D2: Jaffa*.

DRINK **Imperial Bar (#99)** doesn't open until 18.00, so you may want to circle back, or head here for happy hour before your dinner reservations.

STAY **Brown Beach House**, Dan Tel Aviv, and Leonardo Beach Hotel.

ACTIVITIES
★ Water Sports: kitesurfing, stand-up paddleboarding, traditional surfing, yachting, swimming are all popular
★ Playing Matcot on the beach: if you're looking to pick up an easy game while you pick up a few friends, try matcot, a game like table tennis without the table. Unmissable plops all along the water.
★ *Group Fun at a Downtown Beach*: nothing better than a bunch of friends and an entire afternoon to frolic in the sand, water, and sun.
★ *Tel Aviv Pride Celebration* in June (see *LGBTQ*, p. 540).

D2 JAFFA

Terrain Some steps and hills
Difficulty (1–5) 2
Distance 3km
Walking time 45 minutes–1 hour
Completion time 2 hours

For more on **Jaffa (#30)**, check out the elective.

Starting point Jaffa Clock Tower, or just before on the Promenade. You'll want to leave the Tayelet/Promenade and head up the steep hill for great views of Tel Aviv's skyline. This early-20th-century clock tower was built to celebrate the anniversary of the reign of an Ottoman sultan (whose empire would collapse shortly thereafter).

Tour stop 1 View to port and Andromeda's Rock. From a few areas – including Kedumim Square as well as the HaMidron Gardens, overlooking the Tel Aviv beaches – you can look towards the sea for boulders where legend has it that Andromeda (of Greek mythology) was chained up as sacrifice for a sea monster, but Perseus swooped in on Pegasus and saved her.

Tour stop 2 Kedumim Square visitor center provides free maps and walking tours.

Tour stop 3 St. Peter's Church was built in honor of St. Peter who resurrected Tabitha in Acts of the Apostles. The interior resembles European cathedrals and contains scenes from St. Peter's life.

Tour stop 4 House of Simon the Tanner, believed to be the location in Acts of the Apostles where Peter stays after resurrecting Tabitha.

Tour stop 5 Zodiac Fountain and Wishing Bridge. The streets of Jaffa are named after the signs of the zodiac and street names are often adorned with the corresponding symbol. Also in Kedumim Square.

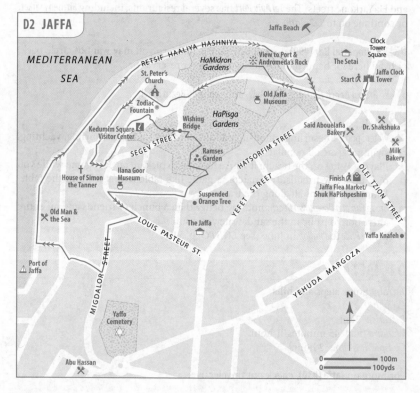

Tour stop 6 Ramses Garden. Circle back through the gardens behind Kedumim Square to Ramses Gate, which highlights a period of time when Jaffa was part of the Egyptian kingdom.

Tour stop 7 Suspended Orange Tree. This is one of the most photographed sites in town – literally a suspended orange tree. It's an artistic work by Ran Morin.

Tour stop 8 **Ilana Goor Museum**. You can't miss this beautifully constructed contemporary and eclectic sculpture and art museum, dedicated to the artist Ilana Goor.

Tour stop 9 Port of Jaffa. There are a number of restaurants, shops, and galleries along this stone-paved street. Walk to the end of the port and circle back around on the roads behind the water, making a couple of lefts. You'll run into the Smiling Whale statue.

Tour stop 10 **Jaffa Flea Market**/Shuk HaPishpeshim.

Ending point **Jaffa Flea Market** (grab a drink or dinner).

TIPS
★ This itinerary can be done in reverse.
★ As you wrap up around the port, don't miss out on the port-side walk.

FOOD Try Old Man and the Sea on the port for outdoor dining with freshly caught fish and nearly two dozen tiny sides to accompany your meal at a fixed price. **Abu Hassan** has one of the world's best and most famous hummus stands. Said Abouelafia Bakery serves a variety of great sweet and savory bread products, and is open all night. If you are seeking a filling breakfast (of eggs and tomatoes), you can't go wrong with **Shakshuka/Dr. Shakshuka**, a breakfast institution, open all day.

STAY Luxurious properties The Jaffa and The Setai are both here.

D3 TEL AVIV: CITY CENTER

Terrain Almost completely flat
Difficulty (1–5) 1
Distance 10km
Walking time 2½ hours
Completion time 6 hours

Starting point Banana Beach (southern end of long stretch of beaches), crossing the street to explore…

Tour stop 1 Kerem HaTeimanim/Yemenite Quarter: near the Carmel Market in Tel Aviv, this quarter is trying to resist gentrification as long as possible, but still has a lot of young-people-friendly restaurants (mainly Yemeni Jewish), bars, and cafés. Voted 15th coolest neighborhood in the world by *Time Out* in 2019. No specific route to take – wind your way through the streets.

Tour stop 2 **Carmel Market (#87)**.

Tour stop 3 The PhotoHouse (⏱ 10.00; w thephotohouse.co.il). This working Tel Aviv store has thousands of photos on archive from Tel Aviv, its people, and life from 1936 to the present.

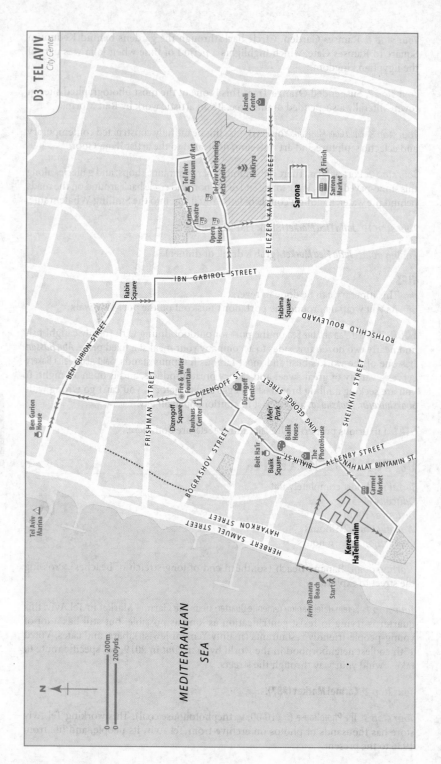

MEDITERRANEAN SEA

N

0 ——— 200m
0 ——— 200yds

Tel Aviv Marina

Ben Gurion House

BEN-GURION STREET

FRISHMAN STREET

Rabin Square

IBN GABIROL STREET

Tel Aviv Museum of Art

Cameri Theatre

Tel Aviv Performing Arts Center

Opera House

HaKirya

ELIEZER KAPLAN STREET

Azrieli Center

Finish

Sarona

Sarona Market

Habima Square

ROTHSCHILD BOULEVARD

SHEINKIN STREET

Dizengoff Square

Fire & Water Fountain

DIZENGOFF ST.

Dizengoff Center

Bauhaus Center

BOGRASHOV STREET

Meir Park

KING GEORGE STREET

Bialik House

Beit Ha'ir

Bialik Square

BIALIK ST.

The PhotoHouse

ALLENBY STREET

NAHALAT BINYAMIN ST.

Carmel Market

SHEINKIN STREET

HERBERT SAMUEL STREET

HAYARKON STREET

Kerem HaTeimanim

Start

Aviv/Banana Beach

Tour stop 4 Bialik Square.

At site **Bialik House** and Beit Ha'ir: Tel Aviv's former Town Hall which houses a number of visiting artists and scholars, also open for tourists, with a number of lectures and activities, along with a history of Tel Aviv and a reconstruction of the office of Tel Aviv's first mayor, Meir Dizengoff (☉ beit_hair_museum).

Tour stop 5 Dizengoff Center. Big mall, interesting layout – no straight edges, wide variety of food options on Thursday/Friday afternoons at food fair.

Tour stop 6 [and possible detour]: **Modern Movement (Bauhaus Architecture) (#16)**. Note: this is a loosely organized walking tour, but can be combined with *D5: Tel Aviv: Architecture*.

Optional tour stop *Bauhaus Center*, Dizengoff 77: pick up your White City walking tour here or grab a self-guided tour map, shop for some Bauhaus merch, and learn about the Bauhaus architecture movement in Tel Aviv (w bauhaus-center.com).

Tour stop 7 Dizengoff Square and the Fire and Water Fountain. This colorful sculpture moves and splays water and, if you catch it at the right time, will send flames into the air.

Tour stop 8 Ben Gurion House. The first prime minister's family home, with many of the rooms in their original condition (w bg-house.org).

Tour stop 9 Rabin Square. Now a public park, this is where the peace-seeker Prime Minister Yitzhak Rabin was giving a speech in support of the Oslo Accords (a peace process between Israelis and Palestinians) when he was assassinated by an Israeli ultra-nationalist.

Tour stop 10 **Tel Aviv Museum of Art (#95)**.

At site At the complex are the Tel Aviv Performing Arts Center, the Opera House, and the Cameri Theatre – the best-known theater production in Israel, with daily performances showing English and French (w cameri.co.il/eng/).

Optional tour stop HaKirya: located in central Tel Aviv, this is a space forever threatened to be taken over by development contractors and home to the Israel Defense Forces headquarters.

Optional tour stop Marganit Tower: a communications tower in the heart of a military district.

Optional tour stop Matcal Tower: Israel Defense Forces block glass building with a giant satellite on top and a huge pole running through the entrance.

Optional tour stop Azrieli Center: with a mall at the base, you just might find yourself in this complex, consisting of one circular, one triangular, and one square tower.

Tour stop 11 Sarona and Sarona Market. A newer, modern market in the heart of Tel Aviv with dozens of food vendors selling all kinds of international cuisine, from ramen to tacos and everything in between. A number of boutique vendors sell their gourmet foodstuffs and equipment here. You'll also find beer, wine, fresh fish, and other delicacies. Very popular!

Optional tour stop Azrieli Sarona Tower: the tallest building in Israel, located in the Sarona neighborhood of Tel Aviv, this complex was opened in 2017 and stands 238m (781ft) tall.

TIPS
★ Visit Carmel Market in the morning, the earlier the better but no later than 13.00.
★ Try to end your tour of Nahalat Binyamin at dusk, which is when bars start to open. Carmel also reopens.
★ Every summer, the city stays out all night for performances and spontaneous fun at Tel Aviv White Night. Well worth coordinating a visit to coincide with this event.

FOOD There are literally hundreds of options all along this route. Check out our food tour in *D6: Tel Aviv: Food and Drink*. For quick bites, try **Carmel Market (#87)**, Sabich Frishman, Falafel Gabai, or crowd favorite ***Miznon***; Cafe Xoho is a good café; and for restaurants try ***Pastel***, M25, Claro, Toto, Dok, Anastasia, and Brothers/Ha'achim.

DRINK Check out Tel Aviv Nightlife (#82).

STAY See D1, D2, D4, or maps in D6.

D4 TEL AVIV: ROTHSCHILD AND SOUTHERN NEIGHBORHOODS

Terrain Almost completely flat
Difficulty (1–5) 1
Distance 10km
Walking time 2–2½ hours
Completion time 4 hours

Starting point Habima Square

Optional tour stop Habima Theatre: Israel's national performing arts venue, with Hebrew-language productions (**w** habima.co.il).

Tour stop 1 **Rothschild Boulevard**.

Tour stop 2 Sheinkin Street. Tons of unique items on this road running from Nahalat Binyamin/Carmel Market to Rothschild Boulevard, with clothing boutiques, and stores selling jewelry, shoes, bikes, and dozens of other options.

Tour stop 3 **Modern Movement (Bauhaus Architecture) (#16)**. You'll find a variety of Bauhaus and other modern buildings to gaze upon in/around Rothschild Blvd. Walk along to D5 concurrently to this tour, as they are complementary.

En route Pagoda House. Considered "eclectic," this house was built in the 1924 as a merger of styles, including Bauhaus with some clear Eastern influences.

Optional tour stop Sommer Contemporary Art Museum: opened in 1999 at the southern end of Rothschild at Herzl 16, the goal with Sommer is promotion of Israeli artists to international audiences.

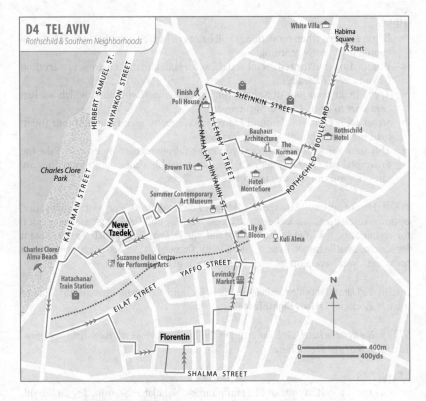

D4 TEL AVIV
Rothschild & Southern Neighborhoods

White Villa
Habima Square
Start
Rothschild Hotel
HERBERT SAMUEL ST.
HAYARKON STREET
SHEINKIN STREET
Finish
Poli House
Bauhaus Architecture
The Norman
ALLENBY STREET
NAHALAT BINYAMIN ST.
ROTHSCHILD BOULEVARD
Brown TLV
Hotel Montefiore
Charles Clore Park
Sommer Contemporary Art Museum
Neve Tzedek
Lily & Bloom
Kuli Alma
KAUFMAN STREET
Charles Clore/ Alma Beach
Suzanne Dellal Centre for Performing Arts
YAFFO STREET
Levinsky Market
Hatachana/ Train Station
EILAT STREET
N
Florentin
0   400m
0   400yds
SHALMA STREET

Tour stop 4 **Neve Tzedek** neighborhood.

At site <u>Suzanne Dellal Centre for Dance and Theatre</u>: contemporary dance theater.

Optional detour <u>Hatachana Train Station (D1)</u>: a family-friendly space with shopping and food.

Tour stop 5 <u>Florentin</u> neighborhood. Everything south of Derech Jaffa, west to Elifelet Street, south to Shalma Road, and east to HaAliya is considered the Florentin neighborhood. You're going to want to just weave in and out of streets here. Once voted by *Thrillist* e-mag as the second most hipster neighborhood in the world, this place has nightlife, fashion, coffee, graffiti, cocktails, and of course hipsters. Enjoy.

Tour stop 6 <u>Levinsky Market</u> (north Florentin). Located in the Florentin neighborhood, this unincorporated market spans several streets of vendors selling nuts, spices, pulses and grains, vegetables, tea and coffee, and lots of snacks of an international flavor, particularly Balkan and Iranian.

Tour stop 7 <u>Nahalat Binyamin</u>. Once just a garment district, but now a hip street with bars, restaurants, and lots of interesting clothing boutiques by Israel's coolest designers. Adjacent to the **Carmel Market (#87)**.

Ending point Anywhere you like in Florentin or Nahalat Binyamin. If it's late, head to <u>Kuli Alma</u> for a drink, the hippest spot in town.

★ Begin midday, when more things will be open. In fact, combine with D3, which should begin early morning.
★ Plan to drop into the restaurant you chose for later and make a dinner reservation (if you haven't already).
★ Try to make your tour of Nahalat Binyamin coincide with dusk, which is when bars start to open. Carmel also reopens.
★ Street art is famous in/around Florentin. We recommend a graffiti tour (often held in the afternoon); see *Activities* below.
★ This tour works much better if you don't follow each route exactly. Take the proverbial path less traveled, which is what neighborhoods are about. They are safe – so you can feel free to explore back alleys.

FOOD Lots of options! Also see *D6: Tel Aviv: Food and Drink*. For good beach/picnic options, stock up at Yom Tov Delicatessen; Meshek Barzilay and Cafe Kaymak are great cafés; for restaurants, try *Tzfon Abraxas*, *George and John Tel Aviv*, *Mashya*, *OCD*, *Popina*, Alena at The Norman, Dallal Restaurant, Habasta, Milgo & Milbar, Ouzeria, Port Said, Social Club, or Tenat; and for sweets, you have pastries from Dallal Bakery or gelato from Anita.

DRINK Kuli Alma, Par Derriere, Bellboy Bar, Butler Bar, and Suramare all live on this side of town. Check out **Tel Aviv Nightlife (#82)**.

STAYS *The Norman Hotel*, Lily & Bloom, Brown TLV, Poli House, White Villa Hotel, Hotel Montefiore, and Rothschild Hotel are all here.

ACTIVITIES
★ Organize a graffiti tour of Florentin and/or Nahalat Binyamin. Try Grafitiyul, Abraham Tours, or Be Tel Aviv Tours. Or follow along with an explanation of styles at w israel-in-photos.com/tel-aviv-florentin-graffiti.html.
★ Try to visit for *Purim in Tel Aviv* and be sure to get a fun costume (it's like a non-scary Halloween) so you can join revelers all night celebrating drink, merriment, and Esther saving the Jewish people from the evil Haman.

D5 TEL AVIV: ARCHITECTURE

Terrain Mostly flat
Difficulty (1–5) 1
Distance/walking time You decide!
Completion time 1+ days

ARCHITECTURAL STYLES IN TEL AVIV
Eclectic Many of these buildings were constructed in the 1920s, prior to the Modernist revolution and the arrival of Bauhaus, with the idea being to merge architectural styles from the East and the West to create a distinctly Israeli look.

Beit Ha'ir, 27 Bialik, 1925	Levin House, 46 Rothschild, 1924
Bialik House, 22 Bialik, 1926	Nordoy Hotel, 27 Nahalat Binyamin, 1925
Great Synagogue, 110 Allenby Street, 1926	Pagoda House, 12–20 Nachmani, 1924

Modern Movement (Bauhaus Architecture) (#16) This style emerged in Germany, with several architects who studied under the Bauhaus school emigrating to Palestine to create a practical and beautiful style perfect for this desert Mediterranean climate. "Form follows function," as they say in the Bauhaus school. Jews who studied under this school brought the design form to Tel Aviv in the 1930s and began constructing this "White City," now with more than 4,000 historic buildings, a quarter of which are being renovated. Some are stunning, but age, weather, and neglect have left thousands in a sad state.

24–26 Balfour, 1935
3 Mapu Street, 1937
61 Rothschild, 1932
Asia House, 2 Dafna Street, 1979
Avraham Soskin House, 12 Lillenblum, 1933
Bauhaus Center, 77 Dizengoff
Biggelman House, 11 Shaul HaMelekh, 1934
Braun-Rabinsky House, 82 Rothschild, 1932
Bruno House, 3 Strauss, 1933
Dizengoff Square, 1934
Dunkelblum House, 3 Yael, 1935
Ehrlich House, 79 Herzl, 1933
Engel House, 84 Rothschild, 1933
Esther Cinema, 12 Dizengoff Square, 1930
Felicja Blumental Music Center, 26 Bialik Square, 1931
Hotel Cinema, 1 Zamenhoff, Dizengoff Square, 1938
Jacobson's Building, 28 Levontin, 1937

Kabbalah Center, 14 Ben Ami, 1937
Kiper House, 32 Ben Gurion, 1936
Kiriyaty House, 12–14 Ruppin, 1938
Krieger House, 71 Rothschild, 1934
Max-Liebling House, 29 Idelson Street, 1936
The Norman Hotel, 23–25 Nachmani, 1920s
Poli House, 62 Allenby, 1934
Recanati House, 35 Menachem Begin, 1935
Reisfeld House, 96 HaYarkon, 1935
Rubinsky House, 65 Sheinkin, 1935
Shomo Yafe House/Bauhaus Museum, 21 Bialik, 1935
Thermometer House/Shami House, 5 Frug, 1936
Workers' Dormitory, 31, 33–35, 37 Frishman, 1934–36
Yitzhaki House apartment block, Rothschild 89–91, 1935
Zlatopolsky House, 9 Gordon, 1935

Brutalism Simply put: raw concrete buildings that became popular in the 1950s. With more detail: an architectural style that values function over beauty (the style is often referred to as "ugly," though it has plenty of admirers), often showcasing the construction materials and bringing structural elements into view. Brutalist structures are often made with concrete, seemingly heavy, but surprisingly cool in Israel summers. Tel Aviv and Beer Sheva have the best offerings:

Carlton Tel Aviv, 10 Eliezer Peri, 1981
El Al Building, 32 Ben Yehuda, 1963
Europe–Israel Tower, 35 Shaul HeMelech, 1979
Hilton Tel Aviv, 205 HaYarkon, 1965
Jabotinsky Institute, 38 King George, 1963

Marganit Tower, HaKirya, 1987
Renaissance Tel Aviv, 121 HaYarkon, 1971
Shalom Meir Tower, 9 Ehad Ha'am, 1965
Tel Aviv City Hall, 69 Ibn Gabirol, 1966

Postmodern

Azrieli Center, 1999
Crazy House, 181 HaYarkon, 1989
Cymbalista Synagogue, Tel Aviv University, 1998
Dan Tel Aviv, 99 HaYarkon, 1953
Dizengoff Tower, 50 Dizengoff, 1983

Hechal Yehuda Synagogue, 13 Ben Saruq, 1980
Isrotel Tower, HaYarkon 78, 1997
Opera Tower, 1 Allenby, 1993
2 Trumpeldor, 2005

Contemporary

Azrieli Sarona Tower, 121 Menachem Begin, 2017
Design Museum Holon, 2010
International Bank Building, 42 Rothschild, 2009
Matcal Tower, HaKirya, 2005
Meier on Rothschild, 36 Rothschild, 2017

Peres Center for Peace, 132 Kedem, Jaffa, 2010
Tel Aviv Museum of Art (#95), 27 Sha'ul HaMelech, 2010
Tel Aviv Port, 2003

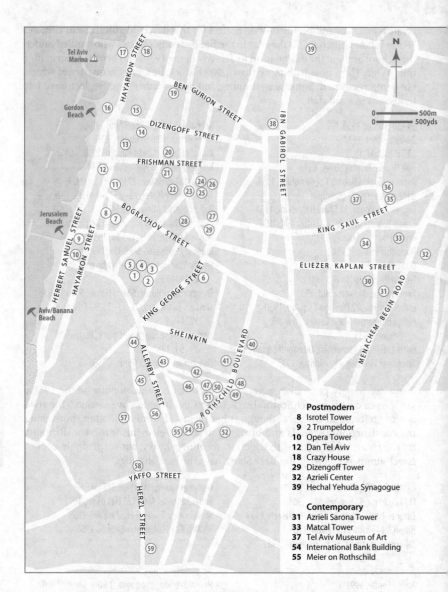

Postmodern

8 Isrotel Tower
9 2 Trumpeldor
10 Opera Tower
12 Dan Tel Aviv
18 Crazy House
29 Dizengoff Tower
32 Azrieli Center
39 Hechal Yehuda Synagogue

Contemporary

31 Azrieli Sarona Tower
33 Matcal Tower
37 Tel Aviv Museum of Art
54 International Bank Building
55 Meier on Rothschild

Regional The German neighborhood of Sarona deserves its own special mention, as it was first established in a different location in 1871, then relocated starting in 2003 to the present location where several of the old houses have been restored and turned into a shopping district and park.

WALKING TOUR Note: you can do as much of this tour as you please, breaking up the tour by each of the areas indicated below.

Starting point Hilton Beach/Tel Aviv Marina.
Tour area 1 Beachside and HaYarkon Street.
Tour area 2 Bialik Square.

D5 TEL AVIV
Architecture

Eclectic
2 Bialik House
4 Beit Ha'ir
45 Nordoy Hotel
46 Pagoda House
53 Levin House
56 Great Synagogue

International Style/Bauhaus
1 Shomo Yafe House/Bauhaus Museum
3 Felicja Blumental Music Center
5 Max-Liebling House
11 Reisfeld House
13 3 Mapu Street
14 Kiriyaty House
15 Zlatopolsky House
19 Kiper House
20 Workers' Dormitory
21 Thermometer House/Shami House
22 Kabbalah Center
23 Dizengoff Square
24 Esther Cinema
25 Hotel Cinema
26 Dunkelblum House
27 Biggelman House
28 Bauhaus Center
36 Asia House
40 Rubinsky House
41 Yitzhaki House apartment block
42 24–26 Balfour
43 Bruno House
44 Poli House
47 The Norman Hotel
48 Engel House
49 Braun-Rabinsky House
50 Krieger House
51 61 Rothschild
52 Jacobson's Building
58 Avraham Soskin House
59 Ehrlich House

Brutalism
6 Jabotinsky Institute
7 El Al Building
16 Renaissance Tel Aviv
17 Carlton Tel Aviv
34 Marganit Tower
35 Europe–Israel Tower
38 Tel Aviv City Hall
57 Shalom Meir Tower

Tour area 3 Dizengoff Square.
Tour area 4 HaKirya and Sarona.
Tour area 5 **Rothschild Boulevard**.
Tour area 6 **Neve Tzedek**.
Ending point Peres Center (beautiful walk along the beach south of Jaffa).

FOOD See *D6: Tel Aviv: Food and Drink* (below) to match your hunger with your location.

D6 TEL AVIV: FOOD AND DRINK

Terrain Mostly flat
Difficulty (1–5) 1
*Distance/walking
time* You decide!
Completion time 1+ days

Israeli Cuisine (#51) comes up quite a bit in our electives, and, while you can't try every single restaurant, you can make an excellent sampling from our suggestions. This is what we've done for you below, with you filling in your choice based on preference.

Starting point Jaffa.

Tour stop 1 Breakfast. We're going to start with the most important meal of the day. Whether you like savory or sweet, you're in luck. If you're staying at a hotel that provides a big Israeli breakfast (U), that's great, and also highly recommended – the options fall on the "parve" side of the menu, meaning dairy and no meat (fish/egg okay). Typical dishes include shakshuka, labneh yogurt, salads, hummus, baba ghanoush, and other chickpea/eggplant spreads, raw vegetables, pastries, and smoked/cured fish.

But skip it one morning and make your way to **Jaffa (#30)** so you can try shakshuka, a tomato-and-egg dish that is becoming a popular global staple, at **Shakshuka/Dr. Shakshuka**. If eggs are not your thing, you have two options: a variety of hummuses (also, *masabacha*) and the fluffiest pita on Earth at **Abu Hassan**; or, delectable treats such as the famed *rugelach* at Said Abouelafia Bakery (D2). You could also do all three. Get everything takeaway and bring to the beach to eat overlooking the water.

Optional If you're already desperate for a takeaway coffee, there's a Cafelix (best reviewed coffeeshop) in the American-German Colony just to the north of Jaffa.

Tour stop 2 Our next stop will be **Carmel Market (#87)**, with its made-on-the-spot juices, cheese shops, shawarma stands, produce vendors, fishmongers, kosher butchers, and sundries sellers. Carmel has a number of guided-tour options which you can review in the elective.

Tour stop 3 Coffee. You can't experience Tel Aviv without taking in its famous *Café Culture*. Starbucks didn't survive in Israel – as Israelis love to tell you – because the flavors are slightly different. Brewed coffee is uncommon. Italian-style espresso prevails, along with cappuccinos, lattes, and other espresso-based drinks. Most coffeeshops also serve salad fare. Check out *Do #15: Drink It!* (p. 93) for more on coffee and coffeehouses. Cafelix has three outlets and is by far the best regarded of all the Tel Aviv coffeehouses. Nahat, Cafe Xoho (D3), and *Bialik House* cafés all rank highly as well.

Tour stop 4 Lunch near Dizengoff Square. Decide for yourself: are you in the mood for something fresh or something sandwichy (pita)? There are a number of vegetarian-friendly cafés with salads and lighter fare, particularly Cafe Kaymak (D4) (Levinsky), Meshek Barzilay (D4) (Rothschild), Anastasia (D3) (Frishman), and Cafe Xoho (D3) (Gordon/Ben Yehuda). However, our recommendation is you go with a pita sandwich that'll blow your mind.

There's also the ubiquitous falafel, and you can't go wrong with these gems: Falafel Gabai (D3), Falafel Frishman (next door to Sabich Frishman (D3)), Razon, Mifgash Osher, **Miznon**, and HaKosem, all on major streets near Dizengoff.

But for something completely different: have you tried a **sabich** at *Sabich/Oved's* or Sabich Frishman (D3)? This unique vegetarian pita sandwich will not leave you wanting, with eggplant, boiled egg, salat, potatoes, and a variety of condiments, including amba, tahini, and zhug.

Miznon has something for everyone to die for (in a pita), plus world-famous roasted cauliflower. It's also become a beloved chain, available in five global cities. You could also go the carnivorous route at M25 (D3) in Carmel Market, with the Jerusalem mix being a firm favorite at this popular shawarma stand. Alternatively, you can eat two fancy meals today, visiting one of the modern Israeli cuisine restaurants referenced at dinner.

Tour stop 5 Head over to Sarona Market (D3). There are dozens of eateries to choose from. You likely won't be hungry at this point, so take a break to do some shopping at any of the cute and trendy sundry shops.

Burn off some of the calories as you walk towards the next market. Head west to Ibn Gabirol street, cross to Marmorek, and turn left on Rothschild. Stroll down this cute street, stopping at any of the coffeeshops lining the boulevard. Along the way, hopefully you will have decided upon a dinner option. Pop in to get a reservation if you haven't secured one already. You might have to try a few places if it's the weekend.

Tour stop 6 A bit more neighborhood-y than Carmel, Levinsky Market (D4) is found across a number of side streets that intersect with Levinsky Street in north Florentin (D4). Here, you can sample a variety of Greek, Balkan, Turkish, and Persian foods, including halva, olives, cured meats, dried fruits, pistachios and other nuts, and huge mounds of spices. Yom Tov Delicatessen (D4) is one of the most famous, selling wine, preserves, jams, olives and peppers, pickles, and a beautiful array of oils and condiments.

Optional For those wanting a truly authentic experience, HaTikva Market (D8) is a bit more off-the-beaten-path.

Tour stop 7 Dessert. You've been hard at work all day, so time to take a break. What's your poison? For Italian gelato and the best-reviewed of all dessert places in Tel Aviv, try Anita (D4), with rotating flavors such as pavlova, salted bagel, mille-feuille, and pistachio Bronte. If you happen to be in town during Hanukkah, the name Roladin (with several locations) will come up, particularly for their pillowy and enormous Sufganiyot, or donuts. For comfort dessert, try NOLA American Bakery for treats such as donuts, cookies, brownies, and milkshakes. Tamara Yogurt is for the weight-conscious. HaMalabiya specializes in *malabi*, a gelatinous milk and rose dessert you have to taste to understand. Try Bakery for French pastries (and tiramisu!), Milk Bakery for high-end decadence, Dallal Bakery (D4) for *halva babka* (and *bourekas*, if you're feeling peckish), and, for the beloved Arab *kanafeh*, you have two great options in Knafeh Bar in Florentin or Yaffo Knafeh in Jaffa.

Tour stop 8 Next up is happy hour. There's an establishment every 5m ready to serve you a beer on the beach, so you needn't go far to quench your thirst. If you want a lively scene, try Mike's Place, an American-style sports bar. Or, for something swanky, we have the internationally recognized **Imperial Bar (#99)**, with craft cocktail wizards ready to wow you.

D6 TEL AVIV
Food and Drink (south) – key

	Breakfast	5D	HaMalabiya		**Bars**
1A	Dr. Shakshuka	5E	Milk Bakery	8A	Kuli Alma
1B	Abu Hassan	5F	Dallal Bakery	8B	Par Derriere
1C	Said Abouelafia's Bakery	5G	Yaffa Knafeh	8C	Shpagat
1D	Cafelix	5H	Lehamim	8D	Teder.fm
1E	Leon Bakery	5I	Anita Gelato	8E	Sputnik
				8F	The Block
	Coffee and Cafés		**Casual Dinner**	8G	Bellboy & Butler Bars
2A	Basma	6A	Old Man and the Sea	8H	Aria Lounge
2B	Mae Cafe	6B	Tenat	8I	Pasáž
2C	Rothschild Coffee Kiosk	6C	Porter & Sons	8J	Abraham's Hostel
2D	EspressoBAR	6D	Hatraklin Meat & Wine Bistro	8K	Abraxas Bar
2E	Bucke Cafe	6E	Busi Grill	8L	Beit Maariv
2F	Cafe Kaymak			8M	Dalida
			Modern Israeli Cuisine	8N	Hoodna
	Lunch	7A	Tzfon Abraxas/North Abraxas	8O	The Space
3A	Meshek Barzilay	7B	Manta Ray	8P	Radio EPGB
3B	Falafel Razon	7C	George and John	8Q	Tasting Room
3C	Hummus Habait	7D	OCD	8R	Whiskey Bar
3D	Sabich	7E	Popina	8S	Dungeon Night Club
3E	Hummus HaCarmel	7F	Pastel		
3F	Shukshuka	7G	Habasta		**Stays**
3G	M25	7H	Milgo & Milbar	9A	The Jaffa
3H	Yom Tov Delicatessen	7I	Claro	9B	The Setai
		7J	Alena at The Norman	9C	The Norman
	Markets	7K	Toto	9D	Lily & Bloom
4A	Sarona Market	7L	Ouzeria	9E	Brown TLV
4B	Carmel Market	7M	Yaffo Tel Aviv	9F	Poli House
4C	Levinsky Market	7N	Dallal Restaurant	9H	Hotel Montefiore
4D	Hatikva Market	7O	Suramare	9H	Rothschild Hotel
		7P	Port Said		
	Bakeries and Dessert	7Q	Social Club		
5A	Halva Kingdom				
5B	Anita Gelato				
5C	Tamara Yogurt				*See overleaf for map*

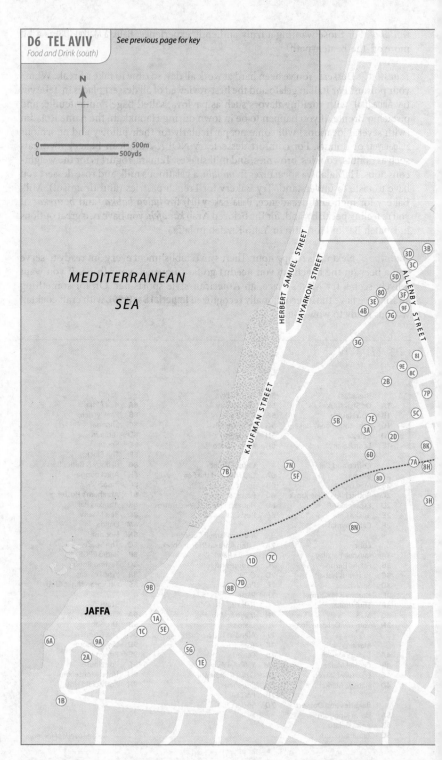

N

0 ———————— 500m
0 ———————— 500yds

MEDITERRANEAN

SEA

HERBERT SAMUEL STREET

HAYARKON STREET

ALLENBY STREET

KAUFMAN STREET

JAFFA

3D
3B
3C
5D
80
3F
3E
4B
9F
7G
3G
8I
9E
8C
2B
7P
5B
7E
5C
3A
2D
6D
8K
7N
7A
8H
7B
5F
8D
3H
8N
1D
7C
8B
7D
9B
1A
1C
5E
6A
9A
5G
2A
1E
1B

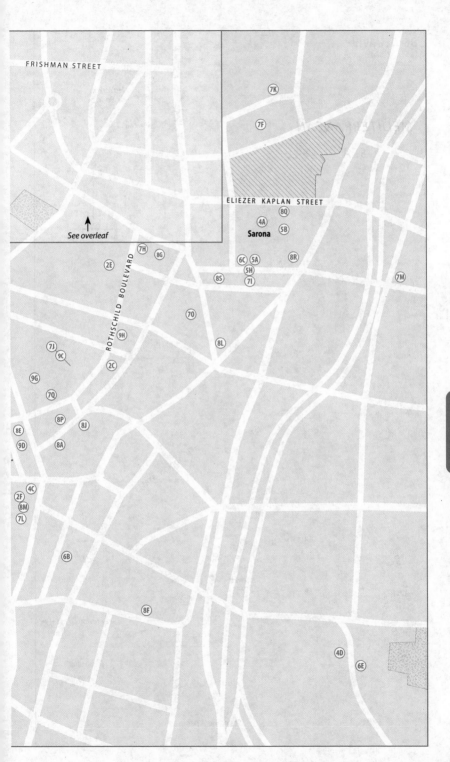

FRISHMAN STREET

7K

7F

ELIEZER KAPLAN STREET

8Q

4A

Sarona   5B

7H   8G

2E

6C   5A

5H

8R

8S   7I

7M

70

9H   8L

ROTHSCHILD BOULEVARD

7J

9C

2C

9G

7Q

8P   8J

8E

9D   8A

4C

2F

8M

7L

6B

8F

4D   6E

See overleaf

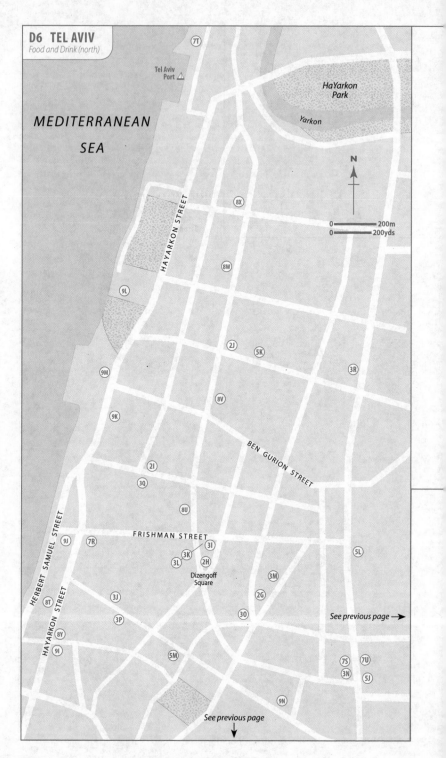

MEDITERRANEAN

SEA

Tel Aviv
Port

HaYarkon
Park

Yarkon

N

0   200m
0   200yds

7T

8X

8W

9L

2J   5K

3R

9M

8V

9K

BEN GURION STREET

2I

3Q

8U

FRISHMAN STREET

HERBERT SAMUEL STREET

9J   7R

3I
3K
3L   2H

Dizengoff
Square

5L

3M

2G

8T

3J

30

See previous page →

HAYARKON STREET

3P

8Y

9I

5M

7S   7U

3N   5J

9N

See previous page

	Coffee and Cafés
2G	Cafelix
2H	Nahat Cafe
2I	CafeXoho
2J	Loveat

	Lunch
3I	Anastasia
3J	Falafel Gabai
3K	Falafel Frishman
3L	Sabich Frishman
3M	Mifgash Osher
3N	Miznon
3O	HaKosem
3P	Mashawsha
3Q	Shakshukia
3R	Sabich Complete

	Bakeries and Dessert
5J	Roladin
5K	NOLA American Bakery
5L	Bakery
5M	Le Moulin

	Modern Israeli Cuisine
7R	Mashya
7S	Dok
7T	Kitchen Market
7U	Ha'achim/Brothers

	Bars
8T	Mike's Place
8U	Spicehaus
8V	Jasper John's
8W	223 Bar
8X	Double Standard
8Y	Imperial and La Otra

	Stays
9I	Brown Beach House
9J	Dan Tel Aviv
9K	Leonardo Beach Hotel
9L	Hilton Tel Aviv
9M	Carlton Tel Aviv
9N	White Villa

Tour stop 9 For dinner, we recommend **Modern Israeli Cuisine**, a food gourmand's bliss and a blend of Mediterranean and Arab flavors, sophistication, casualness, and tahini. There's usually tahini. You can't forget Israeli wine either, which is a whole separate conversation (see *Do #15: Drink It!*, p. 93).

BUCKET!'s own recommendation is **Tzfon Abraxas**, if you can get a table. It's trendy, delicious, and some of the dishes you'll be thinking about forever (mmm… cauliflower). Our other highly recommended options include **Manta Ray**, **George and John Tel Aviv**, **OCD**, **Popina**, **Mashya**, and **Pastel**. There are other options all over town, so perhaps start with the cuisine type that strikes you first, or else just go with whatever is closest to your hotel. Habasta (D4), Milgo & Milbar (D4), Claro (D3), Alena at The Norman (D4), Toto (D3), Dok (D3), HaSalon (D7), Turkiz (D7), Ouzeria (D4), Yaffo-Tel Aviv (D7), Kitchen Market (D1), Dallal Restaurant (D4), and Brothers/Ha'achim (D3) (our other favorite).

If you'd like your dinner to slip into your evening seamlessly, these spots incorporate well-regarded food into their hip aesthetic: Suramare (D4), Port Said (D4), and Social Club (D4). But there are other delicious options, particularly if you don't want to spend $100 each. **Busi Grill** is in the Hatikva district and serves grilled meats from lunch until very late. Old Man and the Sea (D2) marries Turkish, Arab, and seafood fare with whole grilled fish accompanied by 20 (!) little salads. With the number of Ethiopians in Tel Aviv, you'd expect the food to be good, and you'd be right – try Tenat (D4) (also vegetarian).

Tour stop 10 **Tel Aviv Nightlife (#82)** is legendary. Keep in mind that young locals don't go out until late, but your options are still vast. Check out *Do #15: Drink It!* (p. 93) for more on bars. The best-rated are Kuli Alma (D4) (off Rothschild, south), the sister-bars of Bellboy Bar (D4) and Butler Bar (D4) (off Rothschild, north), and Par Derriere (D4) (American-German Colony).

TIPS

★ You can *very* easily turn this into a 2–3-day adventure, without cramming so much food into one day.

★ Make reservations for dinner, ideally several weeks in advance. Lunch in fancier places also might require a reservation, though you can often get a booking in the same week if you're flexible on time.

★ Most restaurants have two seatings. Go with the later if you can handle it (you should after all the eating you've done today!) so you can merge effortlessly into your post-dinner plans.

★ Restaurants are mostly informal/casual, but check *Do #14: Eat It!* (p. 80).

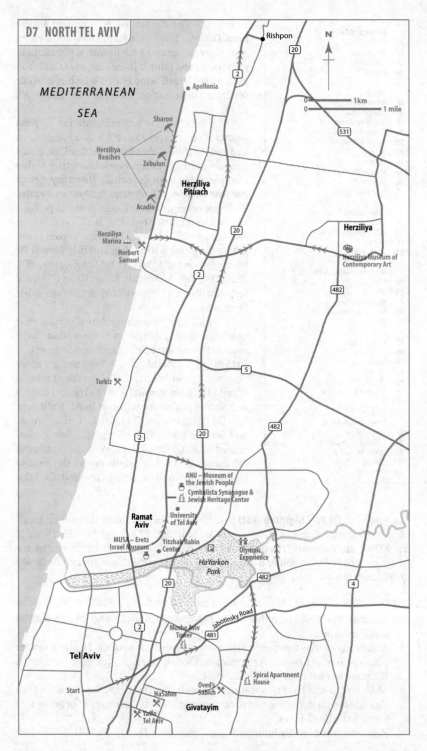

N

MEDITERRANEAN
SEA

0   1km
0   1 mile

Rishpon

20

2

Apollonia

531

Sharon

Herziliya
Beaches

Zebulon

Herziliya
Pituach

20

Acadia

Herziliya

2

Herziliya
Marina

Herbert
Samuel

Herziliya Museum of
Contemporary Art

482

5

Turkiz

482

20

2

ANU – Museum of
the Jewish People

Cymbalista Synagogue &
Jewish Heritage Center

University of Tel Aviv

Ramat
Aviv

MUSA – Eretz
Israel Museum

Yitzhak Rabin
Center

HaYarkon
Park

Olympic
Experience

482

4

20

Moshe Aviv
Tower

Jabotinsky Road

481

2

Tel Aviv

Start

Spiral Apartment
House

Oved's
Sabich

HaSalon

Givatayim

Yaffo
Tel Aviv

D7 NORTH TEL AVIV

Distance 9km
Driving time 25 minutes
Completion time 3 days

Starting point From Dizengoff Square: 5km/15 minutes.

Optional tour stop Moshe Aviv Tower. Also called City Gate, this Ramat Gan building houses both business and residences is the second-tallest building in Israel (and Tel Aviv).

Optional tour stop Spiral Apartment House in Ramat Gan. Seriously bizarre contemporary apartment building. Great photo op.

Tour stop 1 HaYarkon Park. A good place to go for a run, catch a musical act, see the diversity of geological formations in the Rock Garden, or to pick up some sun or grass in one of its six gardens. Picnicking is popular, with lots of kid activities (including a water park). You can rent a bike or paddleboat, and you can also exercise and play on the climbing walls, basketball court, or trampolines.

At site Olympic Experience: explore the history of Israel in the Olympics, test your merits, and meet some famed Olympians at the National Sports Center.

Tour stop 2 **MUSA – Eretz Israel Museum**.

Tour stop 3 Yitzhak Rabin Center. This institute seeks to share the work and life of Israel's peace-seeking fifth prime minister who was assassinated in 1995.

Tour stop 4 Cymbalista Synagogue and Jewish Heritage Center. A flat, square base with two giant flower-pot-resembling spiraling towers, designed in 1996 by Mario Botta and located in Tel Aviv University. Architectural marvel for being a contemporary design of a synagogue.

Tour stop 5 **ANU – Museum of the Jewish People (#77)**.

Optional tour stop The Herziliya Museum of Contemporary Art: more than 1,000 contemporary artworks.

Tour stop 6 **Herziliya Beaches**.

Tour stop 7 **Apollonia**.

Optional tour stop Rishpon: just north of Herziliya, this moshav has a water park and a downtown with a number of cafés.

Ending point To Dizengoff Square: 20km/30 minutes.

TIP Do some research. You don't need to see everything on this itinerary, or *D8: South Tel Aviv* (below). It's a combination of suggestions that all happen to be in the suburbs of Tel Aviv. Feel free to mix and match.

FOOD Every town has food options. ***Herbert Samuel*** is in the Ritz-Carlton in Herziliya. Turkiz is between Ramat Aviv and Herziliya, on the beach. ***Sabich/Oved's*** serves the most interesting sandwich in Ramat Gan. Yaffo-Tel Aviv and HaSalon are on the other side of the highway from the Azrieli Towers.

D8 SOUTH TEL AVIV

Distance 50km
Driving time 1½ hours
Completion time 2 days

Starting point From Dizengoff Square: 12km/20 minutes.

Tour stop 1 Kikar Levana/White Square sculpture at Wolfson Park. Start your morning by taking in a serene visual Bauhaus-inspired sculpture garden with a great view of Tel Aviv in the distance.

Tour stop 2 HaTikva Market. Often called "the poor man's Carmel," this Tel Aviv shuk has just about everything, with none of the tourists. It's a very diverse neighborhood, and there are plenty of foods to be sampled. Though it lacks much of the cosmopolitan energy of **Carmel Market (#87)** or **Mehane Yehuda Market (#67)**, it makes up for it in authenticity. Try the kibbeh (raw meat)!

Tour stop 3 Safari Park at Ramat Gan Park (🕘 09.00). A zoo with a drive-through component, several African species, open-air fenced areas, and a number of projects and activities to entertain the kids.

Tour stop 4 ***Design Museum Holon***.

Optional tour stop Israel Children's Museum: guided activities for kids involving speech, time, darkness, imaginary creatures, and more, in Holon outside Tel Aviv (w childrensmuseum.org.il/eng/).

Optional tour stop Rishon Letzion: just south of Tel Aviv is Israel's fourth-largest city, with its own interesting history. Visits include to its great synagogue (1889), a history museum, and a village park.

Optional tour stop Museum of Rishon Letzion: many "firsts" happened in this corner of greater Tel Aviv, established in 1882, and this museum documents the events.

Tour stop 5 ***Weizmann Institute of Science***.

Tour stop 6 White Mosque of Ramle. An Umayyad-era mosque completed in 720, described as even more beautiful than the Damascus mosque. Made of marble, the only piece left is the 27m-tall minaret, as the rest was destroyed during the earthquake of 1034, and rebuilt during subsequent Muslim dynasties.

Tour stop 7 Pool of the Arches/Al-Anazia. Underground reservoir from the Abbasid era (789 CE) in Ramle, with ancient inscriptions on the wall and a chance to row around the waters in a canoe.

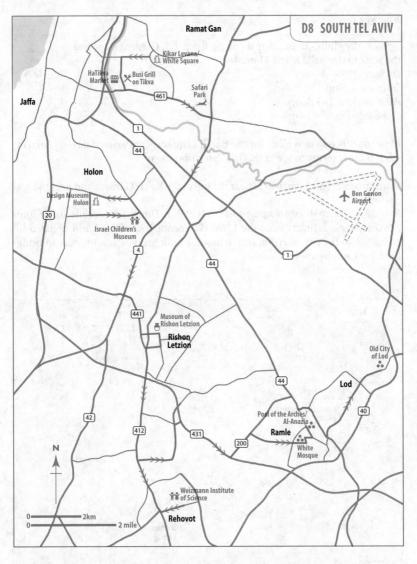

Ramat Gan

Kikar Levana/
White Square

HaTikva
Market

Busi Grill
on Tikva

Jaffa

Safari
Park

461

1

44

Holon

Design Museum
Holon

20

Israel Children's
Museum

4

Ben Gurion
Airport

1

44

441

Museum of
Rishon Letzion

**Rishon
Letzion**

Old City
of Lod

44

Lod

42

412

431

200

Pool of the Arches/
Al-Anazia

Ramle

White
Mosque

40

N

0   2km
0   2 mile

Weizmann Institute
of Science

Rehovot

Optional tour stop Old City of Lod: ancient Modi'im where the Maccabeans led their revolt and where still stands St. George's Church, named after the saint who refused to renounce Christianity and was killed in Lod in the 4th century CE.

Ending point To Dizengoff Square: 20km/30 minutes.

TIP You can add beaches to this itinerary: *Rishon Letzion* has a popular public beach. *Palmahim (E3)* beach is a national park, has a fee, but worth it.

FOOD You'll find food in all of these major towns.

E1 HAIFA

Terrain Very hilly, particularly if you do the Baháʼí Gardens steps and the walk to the Stella Maris Monastery
Difficulty (1–5) 4
Distance 7.5km
Walking time 2–3 hours
Completion time 6 hours

Most tourists pop into Haifa for the Baháʼí Gardens – understandably, it's amazing – but there is plenty to see in this laid-back port town.

Starting point Park somewhere near the top of the Baháʼí Gardens and near the zoo.

Tour stop 1 <u>Tikotin Museum of Japanese Art</u> (🕐 10.00). A Dutch-Jewish collector of some 7,000 Japanese artifacts from the 17th–19th centuries, Felix Tikotin donated his collection to the city of Haifa, with whom he built his museum in order to bridge the Israeli and Japanese cultures.

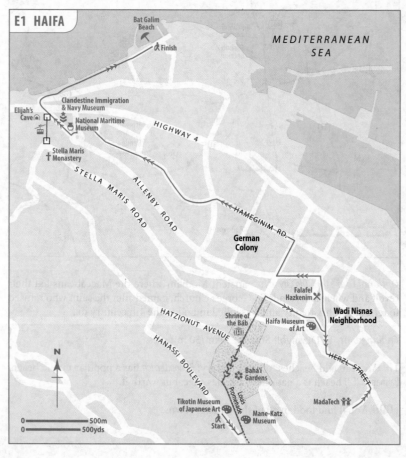

Optional tour stop _Mane-Katz Museum_: Mane Katz was an artist from the "School of Paris" who donated his works to the city of Haifa.

Tour stop 2 _Louis Promenade_: a great and rightly popular view of Haifa, the Bahá'í Gardens, and the sea.

Tour stop 3 **Baháʼí Gardens (#27)** and the Shrine of the Báb. English tours are at 10.00, 12.00, and 15.00 (closed Wednesdays).

Tour stop 4 Wadi Nisnas and _Falafel Hazkenim_: maybe the best falafel sandwich you'll ever have? You be the judge. Wadi Nisnas is a popular shopping/market district.

Optional tour stop _MadaTech_: More than 20 exhibits for kids covering a range of scientific fields, from chemistry to dentistry to aviation.

Tour stop 5 _German Colony_. The first neighborhood in the Holy Land set up by the German Templars in 1868, now a short stroll from the Baháʼí Gardens where you can stop for lunch, shopping, or coffee.

You can either walk to the monastery, taxi, or take the stunning cable car ride (entrance near the Clandestine Museum).

Tour stop 6 **Stella Maris** monastery.

Tour stop 7 _Clandestine Immigration & Naval Museum_/Ha'apala. A naval history museum in Haifa documenting the days of immigration by Jews into Palestine, before the declaration of the state of Israel.

Tour stop 8 Elijah's Cave and/or the National Maritime Museum. Depending on your time, take a tour of the cave where Elijah took shelter in 1 Kings and/or visit the archaeology findings at the Maritime Museum.

Tour stop 9 _Bat Galim Beach_ (or any of the south Haifa beaches – see *E7: Mediterranean Beaches*). Replete with boardwalk, cafés and restaurants, surfing, swimming, and beachfront.

Ending point Circle back to your starting point, either by cab or have someone pick you up. Walking will be an incline of 300m and about 1½ hours.

TIPS
★ You'll likely have to park your car and taxi back to it, or coordinate for someone to pick you up at the end of this itinerary. You will be starting at the top of a steep hill, and will likely not want to walk back up that hill at the end of the day.
★ Make use of the cable cars. You can go to/from the National Maritime Museum and the Stella Maris Monastery without expending too much energy.

FOOD Falafel is famous in the Wadi Nisnas area, and _Falafel Hazkenim_ the most famous. There are plenty of restaurant options in German Colony or near the beaches.

E2 AKKO

Terrain Flat, but for the city walls
Difficulty (1–5) 2
Distance 4km
Walking time 1–2 hours
Completion time 6 hours

Akko (#13) makes for a fantastic day trip.

Starting point Parking lot near the Templar Tunnel, or, if you can walk 5 minutes, there's a free parking lot along the northern stretch of wall.

Tour stop 1 Templar Tunnel. A 1,000-year-old, 350m passageway taking the resident Knights Templar military from the Citadel to the port/sea.

Tour stop 2 Old City Shuk and Hummus Said. Hope you came hungry. Hummus Said in the Old City Market is a fabulous, busy, everyman shop with extremely inexpensive plates of hummus and pita. Could it be the best hummus in the world?

Tour stop 3 Old Akko Walls, Treasures in the Wall Museum, and Akko's visitor center.

Tour stop 4 Citadel/Knights' Hall/Hospitaller Fortress/Underground Prisoners' Museum/Okashi Art Museum. Layers of history here, all right next to each other.
★ The Citadel is an Ottoman building on top of a Crusader citadel, part of the Knights Hospitallers' defensive structure.
★ The Hospitaller Fortress/Knights' Halls was an infirmary originally built for pilgrims to the Holy Land. Now, the great Crusader hall serves as an interesting museum to the Crusades and the Hospitaller Order that worked in Jerusalem and Akko.
★ The Underground Prisoners' Museum tells a later story – that of Jewish resistance fighters imprisoned here during the British rule in the early 1900s.
★ The Okashi Art Museum is in the same area and has contemporary art.

Tour stop 5 Hammam al-Pasha (Turkish bath). Ottoman-era Turkish bath museum, with extremely silly videos showing how 18th-century denizens used the baths.

Tour stop 6 Find souvenirs in the Turkish bazaar or plan a meal at the quaint seafood mini-restaurant Ma'adali.

Tour stop 7 Al-Jazzar Mosque, aka White Mosque, from the Ottoman era, is the largest mosque outside of Jerusalem and its Ottoman architectural style was modeled on the mosques of Istanbul.

Tour stop 8 Religious sites, including St. George Church, the House of 'Abbud, Ramhal Synagogue, and Al-Muallaq Mosque. Seek permission before entering sites where the doors are closed.

Tour stop 9 Akko Port and city walls. The history of Akko as a fortified city goes back a millennium, though the beautiful blocks currently in place date to the late Ottoman period. The walls helped ward off an attack by Napoleon's navy in 1799. They make for a great stroll – don't skip out walking the top of the wall.

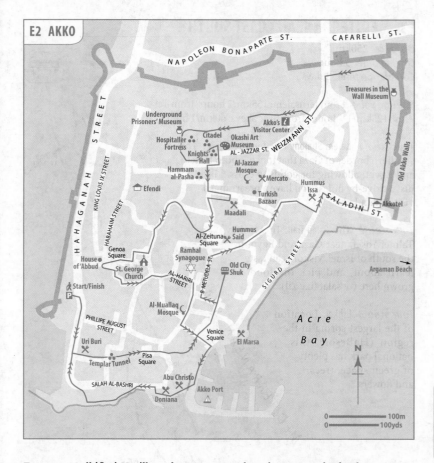

Inside the map:

NAPOLEON BONAPARTE ST.

CAFARELLI ST.

Treasures in the Wall Museum

HAHAGANAH STREET

KING LOUIS IX STREET

HABAHAIM STREET

Underground Prisoners' Museum

Citadel

Hospitaller Fortress

Knights' Hall

Okashi Art Museum

AL-JAZZAR ST.

Akko's Visitor Center

WEIZMANN ST.

Al-Jazzar Mosque

Hammam al-Pasha

Mercato

Hummus Issa

SALADIN ST.

Efendi

Turkish Bazaar

Old Akko Walls

Akkotel

Maadali

Al-Zeituna Square

Hummus Said

House of 'Abbud

Genoa Square

St. George Church

Ramhal Synagogue

AL-HARIRI STREET

B. METUDELA ST.

Old City Shuk

SIGURD STREET

Argaman Beach

Start/Finish

Al-Muallaq Mosque

PHILLIPE AUGUST STREET

Acre Bay

Uri Buri

Templar Tunnel

Pisa Square

Venice Square

El Marsa

N

SALAH AL-BASHRI

Abu Christo

Doniana

Akko Port

0 ——————— 100m
0 ——————— 100yds

Tour stop 10 **Uri Buri**. You'll need a reservation, but plan to spend a few hours at Uri Buri. Order the chef's selection of plates (they keep coming until you say stop). It's a seafood bonanza, fresh, interesting, and astonishingly good.

Ending point Parking lot.

TIPS

★ Make a reservation for lunch, especially if you're going to Uri Buri.
★ You can pay for the full tour at the Templar Tunnel entrance and get access to most places on this itinerary.
★ Don't sweat the directions here. You can get lost in Akko, which is very easy to do, but it's also small so you'll find your way back. There's no "right way" to see it.

FOOD *Uri Buri* and Hummus Said, as referenced above, but also Maadali, El Marsa, Mercato, Doniana, and Abu Christo, as well as Hummus Issa. This city is teeming with seafood and hummus joints.

STAY If you're staying the night, pick either the Efendi or Akkotel for extravagance.

BEACH *Argaman Beach* is across the bay with great views of the Old City walls.

E3 MEDITERRANEAN COAST SOUTH

Distance 250km
Driving time 3 hours
Completion time 2 days

Starting point From Jerusalem: 155km/2 hours; from Tel Aviv: 125km/1¾ hours; from Beer Sheva: 60km/1 hour.

Tour stop 1 Kerem Shalom border crossing. The southern border of Gaza that touches both Israel and Egypt, allowing for goods to cross. Likely just a drive-by unless you have a prearranged visit scheduled.

Tour stop 2 The Salad Trail. In Moshev Talmei Yosef, near Gaza and Egypt in the south of Israel, visitors can taste, learn about, and pick the food grown here (w salat4u.co.il).

Tour stop 3 Eshkol. Location of the largest spring in the region (HaBesor), this national park has plenty of green space, trees, and flowers.

Tel Aviv

Palmahim

Rishon Letzion

4

7

MEDITERRANEAN SEA

Ashdod Performing Arts Center
Ashdod

Ashdod Art Museum

3

Tel Ashkelon
Ashkelon

4

35

Erez Crossing

ISRAEL

34

Gaza

Shokeda Forest

Tomb of the Baba Sali

25

Beer Sheva

N

232

Eshkol National Park

EGYPT

Kerem Shalom Border Crossing

The Salad Trail

0 ———— 10km
0 ———— 10 miles

Optional tour stop <u>Scarlet South Festival</u>: fields of red anemones in the northern Negev, usually from late January to February. Try Shokeda Forest for carpets of flowers.

Optional tour stop <u>Tomb of the Baba Sali</u>: pilgrimage site in Netivot, Israel dedicated to the Sephardic rabbi who performed miracles through prayer.

Optional tour stop <u>Erez Crossing</u>: the one land crossing for people to get to/from Gaza (though only international aid workers are allowed in currently).

Tour stop 4 **<u>Tel Ashkelon</u>**.

Tour stop 5 <u>Ashdod Performing Arts Center</u>. Stunning cultural arts center with theater, music, and other diverse entertainment.

Optional tour stop <u>Ashdod Art Museum</u>: modern and contemporary art overlooking the marina.

Tour stop 6 <u>Palmahim</u> beach. A national park with lifeguards on duty, some eateries, and glorious beach for days.

Ending point To Jerusalem: 65km/1 hour; to Tel Aviv: 25km/30 minutes.

TIPS
★ If you want to catch a show, you can schedule the two Ashdod electives for the end of the day.
★ Ashkelon and Eshkol national parks are interesting to history buffs, and fine for a stroll, but do not require a heavy commitment.

FOOD You can find plenty of food in Ashdod, Ashkelon, and Beer Sheva.

E4 MEDITERRANEAN COAST CENTRAL

Distance 80km
Driving time 2 hours
Completion time 4 days

Starting point From Jerusalem: 110km/1¼ hours; from Tel Aviv: 40km/35 minutes.

Optional tour stop <u>Iris Reserve</u>. Found just south of **Netanya**, this reserve hosts visitors in February and March who come to view the rare purple iris.

Tour stop 1 **<u>Beit Yannai</u>** beach.

Tour stop 2 **<u>Caesarea (#25)</u>**.

Near site <u>Aqueduct Beach</u>: a Roman aqueduct serves as gorgeous backdrop to this pleasant beach.

Tour stop 3 <u>Nahal Taninim</u> nature reserve. Meaning "crocodile stream," this river hasn't hosted crocodiles in over 100 years, so it makes for a good camping and weekend nature getaway.

At site <u>Jisr az-Zarqa</u>. Much more rustic, local feel on this beach, part of a fishing village.

Tour stop 4 <u>Jabotinsky Park</u>. This park is sponsored by KKL-JNF and has a variety of historic sites of interest amid its green spaces.

Tour stop 5 <u>Ramat HaNadiv</u>. Fragrance gardens, moderate hikes, great Mediterranean views.

Tour stop 6 **Zichron Ya'akov**.

At site **Elma Arts Complex**.

Tour stop 7 **Dor HaBonim (#100)** beach.

Optional tour stop *Ralli Museums*: Jewry from Greece, Spain, and Portugal.

Tour stop 8 <u>Atlit Detention Camp</u>. Ships, planes, and residential barracks highlighting the immigration center (detention camp) that captured and imprisoned Jews trying to enter Israel during the British mandate period.

Nearby <u>Atlit Beach</u>.

Ending point To Jerusalem: 150km/1½ hours; to Tel Aviv: 75km/1 hour; to Haifa: 17km/20 minutes; to Rosh Pina: 100km/1¼ hours.

TIPS

★ Beit Yannai and Dor HaBonim are both fabulous beaches. You needn't visit both in one day unless you're trying to check boxes.

★ If you try to spend time at the beach and visit Caesarea in full, you'll already fill up a full day. In order to complete this day, the beach stops will have to be truncated.

E4 MEDITERRANEAN COAST
Central

★ The Iris Reserve is best viewed in February and March, so can be skipped outside those months.

FOOD Helena Banamal in Caesarea is a great lunch spot. ***Zichron Ya'akov*** has a number of restaurants, as do ***Netanya*** and other spots along the coast.

STAY The ***Elma Arts Complex*** is a gorgeous Brutalist architectural masterwork with great views.

ACTIVITIES Add a winery: Margalit Winery (E6) is right outside the Caesarea gates. ***Carmel Winery*** and Tishbi Winery (E6) are both within ***Zichron Ya'akov***. Recanati Winery (E6) is just south of Hadera. Vitkin Winery (E6) is due east of Beit Yanai. Amphorae Winery (E6) is the turnoff right before Nahal Me'arot on Highway 4.

E5 MEDITERRANEAN COAST NORTH

Distance 55km
Driving time 1½ hours
Completion time 3 days

Starting point From Jerusalem: 150km/1¾ hours; from Tel Aviv: 85km/1 hour; from Rosh Pina: 100km/1¼ hours.

Tour stop 1 **Haifa**.

At site See *E1: Haifa*. Priorities are **Bahá'í Gardens (#27)**, ***Stella Maris*** lighthouse, Tikotin Museum of Japanese Art (E1), German Colony (E1), Bat Galim Beach (E1), and the Clandestine Immigration & Naval Museum (E1).

Tour stop 2 Ein Afeq nature reserve. A preserved swamp with a pedestrian bridge built to observe the birds and plants along the pathway.

Tour stop 3 **Akko (#13)**.

At site See *E2: Akko*: walking tour can be done in 2–4 hours, or truncated.

Tour stop 4 **Shrine of Bahá'u'lláh**.

Tour stop 5 Nahariya. Ruins of a citadel dating to 1400 BCE with plans for it to be incorporated into a residential high-rise building.

Tour stop 6 **Akhziv Beach** and National Park.

Optional tour stop Akhzivland: considered a "micronation" by the one person who lives on this tiny enclave between Nahariya and Lebanon. The founder, Eli Avivi, died in 2018, but the nation lives on in the Akhzivland Museum, near the Akhziv National Park.

Tour stop 7 **Rosh HaNikra** (⊕ 09.00–18.00 summer, Saturday, and holidays; 09.00–16.00 winter, Friday, and holiday eves).

Ending point To Rosh Pina: 65km/1 hour; to Tel Aviv: 130km/1¾ hours; to Jerusalem: 185km/2¼ hours.

TIPS

★ English tours of the Baháʼí Gardens are limited, so you'll want to plan to be in Haifa at the time of your prescheduled tour. This might mean you don't begin your day in Haifa.

★ Rosh HaNikra activities require a ticket, so you have to arrive before closing.

★ Akko can be either truncated to just the perimeter walls, or you can take a tour of the whole city which could last all day. Make sure to check out **Akko (#13)**.

★ This tour can also be done north–south.

FOOD *Uri Buri* is a famous seafood restaurant in Akko. Maadali (E2) is also in Akko.

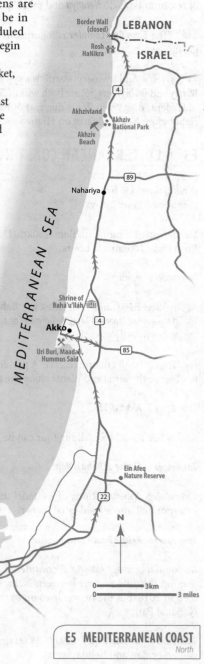

LEBANON

Border Wall (closed)

Rosh HaNikra

ISRAEL

4

Akhzivland

Akhziv National Park

Akhziv Beach

89

Nahariya

MEDITERRANEAN SEA

Shrine of Baháʼuʼlláh

Akko

4

85

Uri Buri, Maadali, Hummus Said

Ein Afeq Nature Reserve

22

Haifa

Baháʼí Gardens

N

0 ——— 3km
0 ——— 3 miles

South Haifa Beaches

2

E5 MEDITERRANEAN COAST
North

E6 CENTRAL ISRAEL WINERIES

Distance 50km
Driving time 1 hour
Completion time 2 days

Starting point From Jerusalem: 110km/1¼ hours; from Tel Aviv: 45km/45 minutes.

Tour stop 1 Vitkin Winery, Kfar Vitkin (⊕ 09.30–17.00 Sunday–Wednesday, 11.00–23.00 Thursday, 10.30–15.30 Friday; reservations recommended; w vitkin-winery.co.il). Specializing in blends and using a dozen interesting grapes to make its high-end (Shorashim) and budget (Israeli Journey) brands. Rogov gives the winery five stars.

Tour stop 2 Recanati Winery, Hefir Valley (⊕ 08.00–16.00 Sunday–Thursday, 09.00–13.00 Friday; w recanati-winery.com). Founded in 2000, Recanati hired a winemaker who had worked previously in Amphorae and Carmel. Its 2011 Cabernet Sauvignon is still the highest-ranked Israeli wine out of over 1,000 ranked wines.

Tour stop 3 Margalit Winery, Binyamina, organized visits by phone (w margalit-winery.com/en/contact-us/). A well-renowned brand which has maintained a "boutique" image, Margalit has a reputation as a Bordeaux-style producer of full-bodied reds with cherry and smoke aromas. Its wines are meant to be aged, with the Special Reserve Cabernet Sauvignon and Enigma blend usually scoring high with critics. Rogov gave Margalit wines five stars; Hugh Johnson gave it three stars.

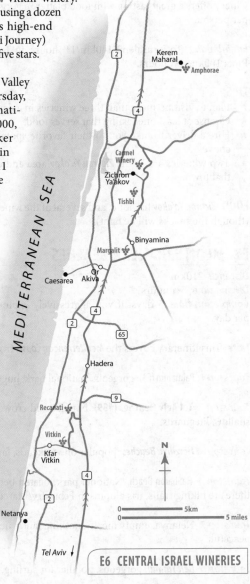

Tour stop 4 Tishbi Winery, Zichron Ya'akov (south) (⊕ 08.00–1700 Sunday–Thursday, 09.00–15.00 Friday; w tishbi.com/en/). A wine- and chocolate-tasting center, along with an interesting history, just outside of *Zichron Ya'akov*. Hugely popular, with a restaurant right downtown.

Tour stop 5 **Carmel Winery**, Zichron Ya'akov (⊕ 09.30–17.00 Sunday–Thursday, 09.00–14.00 Friday; reservations only).

Tour stop 6 Amphorae Winery, Kerem Maharal (predetermined time slots for tours every day; w amphoraewines.com/wine-sessions/). Twenty minutes south of Haifa, this winery offers a great tasting with food platter in gorgeous surroundings for 140 ILS per person.

Ending point To Jerusalem: 140km/1¾ hours; to Tel Aviv: 75km/1 hour; to Rosh Pina: 100km/1¼ hours.

TIPS
★ Plan to visit no more than three wineries in a day.
★ Choose at least one tasting that serves food.
★ Hire a driver to take you to their favorite spots and recommend some of the above.
★ Two wineries are in the *Zichron Ya'akov* area and can be visited on a day trip to that town.

FOOD *Zichron Ya'akov* has food, and several of the wineries offer food of various types (though the snacks will be light).

E7 MEDITERRANEAN BEACHES

Distance 210km
Driving time 5¼ hours
Completion time 5 days, if you aggressively explore three beaches per day

Note This itinerary covers the *Mediterranean Coast*, from south to north.

Tour stop 1 Palmahim (E3): gorgeous, national park, huge expanse of sand, great waves.

Tour stop 2 **Tel Aviv Beaches (#89)**: popular and crowded, great atmosphere, sports, shallow, lifeguards.

Tour stop 3 **Herziliya Beaches**: popular on weekends, family, clean, very soft sand.

Tour stop 4 HaSharon Beach. National park located between Netanya and Herziliya, there are hiking trails, iris blooms in February/March, but no facilities.

Tour stop 5 Netanya: empty mostly, nothing fancy, near city of *Netanya*, great waves, peaceful.

Tour stop 6 **Beit Yannai**: gorgeous, popular for surfing, but empty midweek.

Tour stop 7 Geder Beach. National park for a tiny beach north of **Netanya**, with a great view from the top of the adjacent cliff.

Tour stop 8 Aqueduct Beach (E4). In **Caesarea (#25)**, actually next to a Roman aqueduct!

Tour stop 9 Jisr az-Zarqa (E4). Empty beach between Dor and Caesarea, where **Israel National Trail** runs through, but few people are found here – accessible via the town of the same name.

Tour stop 10 **Dor HaBonim (#100)**: most beautiful in Israel? Camping, ship-wreck, hikes, archaeology, sand dunes, and hippies, plus gorgeous water.

Tour stop 11 Atlit Beach (E4). Three-kilometer beach, with one stretch being a nudist beach, the rest pretty family-friendly, framed to the south by a Crusader castle.

Tour stop 12 South Haifa Beaches. The beaches of Dado, Zamir, and Carmel all stretch south of Haifa before finding the great South Beach strip of white sand.

Tour stop 13 Bat Galim Beach (E1).

Tour stop 14 **Argaman Beach**: city beach, good views of Old City, least trashy of beaches up north?

Tour stop 15 **Akhziv Beach**: remote option, archaeo-logical ruins nearby.

Optional tour stop Solo Fun at a Wave-Filled Beach: techni-cally, if there's no lifeguard on duty,

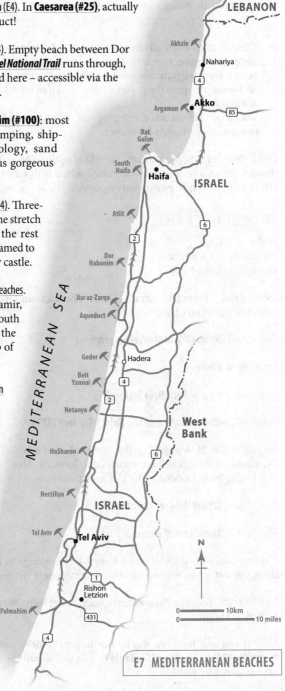

E7 MEDITERRANEAN BEACHES

you shouldn't be swimming. And you should be careful of undertow, so maybe bring a friend. But if you're a good swimmer and love waves, head to some of the northern Mediterranean beaches for some splashy fun. But be safe: make sure a lifeguard is present before throwing yourself at 3m waves.

TIPS

★ These beaches cover all kinds – popular and remote, urban and rural. But there are dozens more. Given that these are recommended by the hive, the word's out on these already. Seek local opinions if you're wanting something more off-the-beaten-path (hint: you'll never find it in a guidebook read by thousands of foreigners).
★ You can do almost this entire program with a tent. Wild camping for the win!
★ Lifeguards go off-duty for winter.

FOOD All of the major cities have great food options. Most beaches have restaurants, though the remote ones may be more limited with facilities. Also, some beaches (HaBonim) have grill pits so you can cook if you bring food with you.

F1 MOUNT CARMEL

Distance 50km
Driving time 1¼ hours
Completion time 1 day

Starting point From Jerusalem: 145km/1½ hours; from Tel Aviv: 75km/1 hour; from Rosh Pina: 100km/1 hour.

Tour stop 1 **Nahal Me'arot/Wadi el-Mughara**.

Tour stop 2 **Ein Hod**.

Optional tour stop South Haifa Beaches (E7).

Optional tour stop **Haifa** and the **Bahá'í Gardens (#27)**.

Tour stop 3 Hecht Museum. A private collection of artifacts from the Canaanite to Byzantine periods, as well as a variety of styles of art. Also on display is a 5th-century BCE fishing boat. Located at the University of Haifa.

Tour stop 4 **Carmel Hai-Bar** wildlife reserve.

Tour stop 5 **Mount Carmel** national park.

Optional tour stop Daliyat al-Karmel: largest Druze village in Israel with a downtown shopping district to soak up the unique atmosphere (warning: slightly touristy).

Ending point To Rosh Pina: 80km/1 hour; to Tel Aviv: 80km/1 hour; to Jerusalem: 120km/1½ hours.

TIPS If you only have one day up north, your priority should be **Haifa**, **Akko (#13)**, **Nazareth (#29)**, or the **Sea of Galilee (#7)**. This trip is really best for those with multiple days to spend up north.

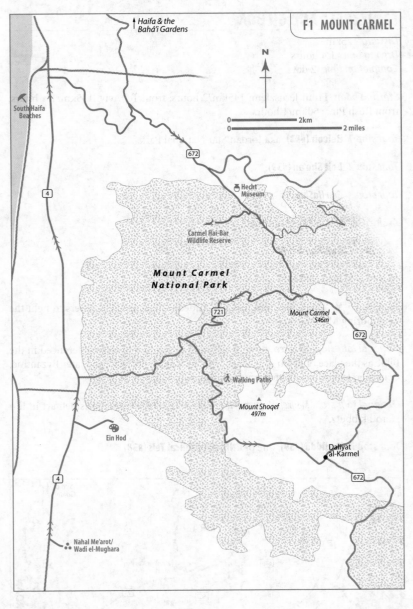

FOOD HaBeit Be'einhud is our recommendation in Ein Hod. You can also find good falafel in **Haifa**. Or drive to nearby **Elbabor**.

STAYS There's a popular spa, the Carmel Forest Spa Resort, here.

F2 JEZREEL AND GILBOA

Distance 75km
Driving time 1¾ hours
Completion time 2 days

Starting point From Jerusalem: 145km/2 hours; from Tel Aviv: 135km/1¾ hours; from Rosh Pina: 60km/1 hour.

Tour stop 1 **Belvoir (#93)**, aka Jordan Star National Park.

Tour stop 2 **Beit She'an (#39)**.

Tour stop 3 **Gan HaShlosha**.

At site Gan Garoo, a kangaroo petting zoo.

Tour stop 4 **Beit Alpha (#64)**.

Tour stop 5 **Mount Gilboa**.

Tour stop 6 Ma'ayan Harod. From this site, Gideon directed his followers to fight the neighboring Midianites.

Optional tour stop *Tel Jezreel*: biblical site in the Kingdom of Israel referenced in the Bible as the place of death of Jezebel, with an Israelite fortress, and later Byzantine, Crusader, Islamic, and Ottoman-era villages.

Optional tour stop *Mishkan Museum of Art*: a collection of Jewish and Israeli art in Ein Harod kibbutz.

Tour stop 7 **Megiddo (#59)**, one of **UNESCO's Biblical Tels (#38)**.

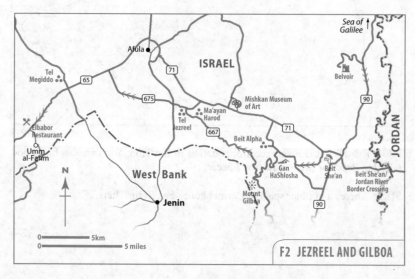

F2 JEZREEL AND GILBOA

Tour stop 8 **_Elbabor_** restaurant, Umm al-Fahm.

Ending point To Rosh Pina: 70km/1 hour; to Tel Aviv: 80km/1 hour; to Jerusalem: 120km/1¼ hours.

TIPS

★ You can start this trip in either direction, but beginning on the east allows you to end for lunch or dinner at **_Elbabor_**.

★ The drive through **_Mount Gilboa_** is the interesting part of that site, so though you may see the map and think it's not the most direct path, going to/from Ma'ayan Harod and Beit She'an will provide the right route.

★ Try to make it to your ending point before sunset – driving west through Gilboa at sunset will be blinding.

★ Bring your swimsuit for **_Gan HaShlosha_**.

FOOD Bring picnic food – it's not exactly a food desert, but there are a lot of parks with light concessions, at best. **_Nazarene Fusion Cuisine_** is nearby.

G1 NAZARETH

Terrain Hilly, particularly to get to the Basilica of Jesus the Adolescent
Difficulty (1–5) 3
Distance 4km, or 2.5km if you drive to the Basilica of Jesus the Adolescent
Walking time 1 hour
Completion time 3 hours

Nazareth and its Biblical Sites (#29) make for a great day of activities all on their own, though this can be combined with road trips *F2: Jezreel and Gilboa* (above) and *G2: Central Galilee* (below).

Starting point There is free parking (blue and white) or various garages on Paulus HaShlishi (Paul III), rounding the east of the Basilica.

Tour stop 1 **_Basilica of the Annunciation_** and grottoes.

Tour stop 2 St. Joseph's Church and Museum of Ancient Nazareth. In these underground caverns, adjacent to the massive Basilica, is believed to be the site where Joseph of Nazareth (Jesus' father) worked as a carpenter, as well as other parts of the ancient village.

Tour stop 3 International Center of Mary of Nazareth. A museum and religious site with multimedia displays, an archaeological site, and history of Mary, the mother of Christ.

Tour stop 4 Abu Ashraf. Stop for a snack at this local coffeehouse haunt. Famous for lunch, desserts, and Arab coffee.

Tour stop 5 Greek Catholic Church-Synagogue. Tradition has this synagogue, with a church built atop, as the location of Jesus of Nazareth's youthful learnings and early sermons.

Tour stop 6 Old City Market/Shuk. Lots of food, souvenirs, spices, and more to be had in this shopping district.

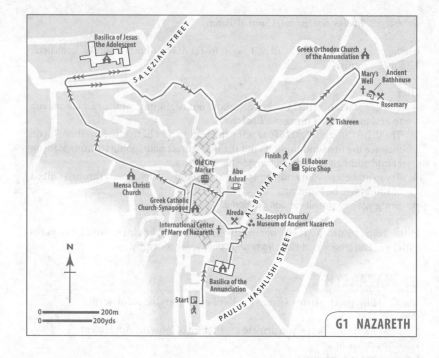

G1 NAZARETH

Tour stop 7 Mensa Christi Church. Place where Jesus ate with his disciples following his resurrection. The table survived, according to legend, and is located inside the church. Note: permission required from the Guardian of the Convent, opposite the church at the first door in the alleyway.

Tour stop 8 Basilica of Jesus the Adolescent. Beautiful church, but even more gorgeous views from the vantage on top of the hill.

Tour stop 9 Greek Orthodox Church of the Annunciation/St. Gabriel's Church. At the center of this church is a spring from where Mary and other Nazarenes drew water. Per Greek Orthodox belief, the church is built over the site where the Annunciation occurred (rather than the Catholic site at her home, over which the Basilica currently stands). The latest iteration of this Nazareth church dates to the Ottoman era.

Tour stop 10 Mary's Well. Another contender for the spot where Mary received notice from God that she would bear His son.

Tour stop 11 Ancient Bathhouse of Nazareth. Roman bathhouse, next to Mary's Well, discovered inside a souvenir shop! Fee required.

Tour stop 12 El Babour Spice Shop. Famous for a reason, this shop offers literally hundreds of spices of all kinds, for vegetables, meats, desserts, and soup.

Tour stop 13 Lunch. **Nazarene Fusion Cuisine** is quickly becoming a foodie haven for those in the know, combining local Galilean specialties with international style and ingredients. Some popular places include Rosemary, Tishreen, and Alreda.

TIPS

★ Many sites are closed Sundays.

★ The Basilica of Jesus the Adolescent is located up a steep hill. You may wish to take a drive or taxi in this part, if you aren't up for the walk. It'll save about 30 minutes and 1.5km.

FOOD Lunch is included on this tour.

G2 CENTRAL GALILEE

Distance 100km
Driving time 2½ hours
Completion time 2 days

Starting point From Jerusalem: 160km/2 hours; from Tel Aviv: 110km/1½ hours; from Rosh Pina: 60km/45 minutes.

Optional tour stop *Nahalal*: The first moshav was built – supposedly with the help of members of Degania Aleph, the first kibbutz – in 1921. This moshav became famous based on its interesting layout, like a spoke on a wheel. The center wheel contains all of the moshav's shared buildings, and each family of the community is entitled to one of the 80 spokes of land emanating out from the center.

Tour stop 1 **Tsipori (#56)**.

Tour stop 2 **Nazareth and its Biblical Sites (#29)**, including the ***Basilica of the Annunciation***.

Tour stop 3 ***Church of the Transfiguration***.

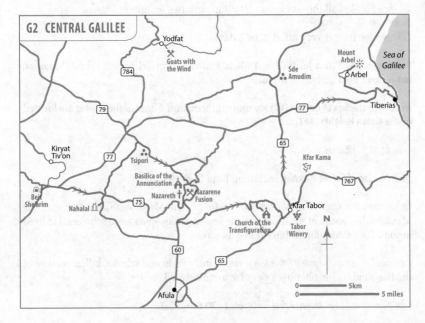

Tour stop 4 Kfar Kama. One of two Circassian towns in the Galilee, with a visitor center and museum to explain Circassian history and culture.

Tour stop 5 Sde Amudim (aka Khirbet Amodam). A national park in the Galilee with essentially only one extant pillar, presumably representing an ancient (3rd–4th centuries CE) synagogue, though the jury is out.

Tour stop 6 **Mount Arbel**.

Ending point To Rosh Pina: 40km/40 minutes; to Tel Aviv: 145km/1¾ hours; to Jerusalem: 185km/2 hours.

TIPS
★ DIY **Beit She'arim (#79)** on the front end and/or any of the *G3: Sea of Galilee* or *G4: Jesus Sites in the Galilee* sites (below) on the back end.
★ Following the *G1: Nazareth* city walk (above) will add a minimum of 2 hours to your itinerary. If in a rush, head to the ***Basilica of the Annunciation***.

FOOD Goats with the Wind is a great turnoff farm-to-table restaurant with superb cheeses and great picnic platters. The Arab-Israeli-modern style of **Nazarene Fusion Cuisine** is all the rage in Israel.

ACTIVITIES Tabor Winery is located on the eastern base of Mount Tabor, location of the **Church of the Transfiguration**. The new technology-focused Sanhedrin Trail offers a similar hike to the **Jesus Trail (#69)**, and both can be done in shorter portions to combine with other daily activities.

G3 SEA OF GALILEE
Distance 65km all the way around/100km with two lookouts
Driving time 1½ hours
Completion time 1 very full day, or 2 days

Starting point From Jerusalem: 180km/2 hours; from Tel Aviv: 135km/1½ hours; from Rosh Pina: 28km/30 minutes.

Note See the **Sea of Galilee (#7)** for more information. Some of these sites are located in the **Golan Heights (#62)**.

Tour stop 1 **Tiberias**.

Nearby **Sea of Galilee Beaches**, including Bora Bora Beach.

Optional tour stop Tomb of Maimonides: Moses ben Maimon, aka Rambam, aka Maimonides, is one of the most famous Jewish philosophers and scholars. He lived in the 12th century and is buried in Tiberias.

Optional tour stop Tomb of Rabbi Akiva: 1st-century rabbi and scholar, killed because of the Bar Kokhba Revolt, now a popular tomb site in Tiberias.

Optional tour stop **Mount Arbel** for view (+30 minutes).

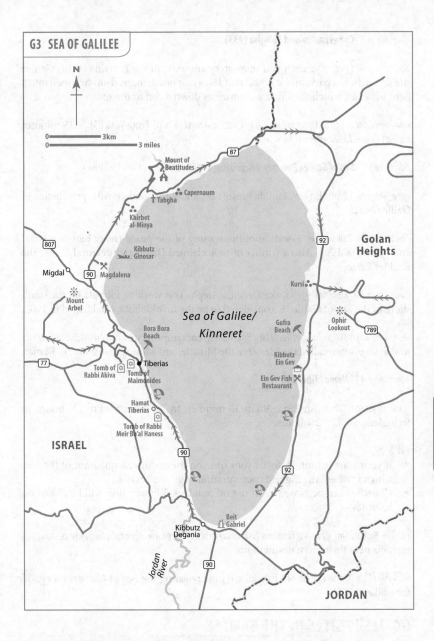

Tour stop 2 <u>Kibbutz Ginosar</u>. Popular museum where an ancient fishing boat from Jesus' time was unearthed from the muddy bank of the Kinneret at this kibbutz, mostly intact, and is now on display.

Tour stop 3 <u>Khirbet al-Minya</u>. Umayyad palace from the 8th century CE located on the northwest shore of the Sea of Galilee.

Tour stop 4 <u>***Mount of Beatitudes***</u>.

Tour stop 5 **Capernaum and Tabgha (#33)**.

Tour stop 6 Kursi. A church and monastery are some of the remains at this Galilee site and national park, and it is said that Jesus cast out demons from two men into a herd of swine, which then threw themselves down a cliff to the sea.

Optional tour stop Ophir Lookout (I3) (+25 minutes) and Peace Vista (I3) (+25 minutes more) – see *I3: Southern Golan*.

Tour stop 7 **Sea of Galilee Beaches**, including Gofra and Ein Gev (below).

Tour stop 8 Kibbutz Ein Gev. Holiday resort on a kibbutz, replete with private Sea of Galilee beach.

Tour stop 9 Beit Gabriel. Location of the signing of the peace treaty between Israel and Jordan in 1994. Also a winner of an acclaimed Israeli architectural honor, the Rechter Prize.

Tour stop 10 Kibbutz Degania, aka Degania Aleph. This working kibbutz on the south shore of the Sea of Galilee is considered to be the first kibbutz, established in 1909.

Optional tour stop Tomb of Rabbi Meir Ba'al Haness: contemporary of Rabbi Akiva, he was a Jewish sage, often called the Master of the Miracle, and whose grave is also in **Tiberias**.

Tour stop 11 **Hamat Tiberias**.

Ending point To Rosh Pina: 30km/35 minutes; to Tel Aviv: 140km/1¾ hours; to Jerusalem: 180km/2¼ hours.

TIPS

★ If your time is limited, focus your time on the northwest quadrant of the Sea, which is where the highest concentration of great sites lies.
★ Churches can be closed or in use on Sundays. Kibbutz sites will be closed on Saturdays.

FOOD Kibbutz Ein Gev has a famous fish restaurant. There are several roadside restaurant turnoffs near the tourist destinations.

ACTIVITIES Kinneret Trail: 60km trail circumnavigating the Sea of Galilee, also good for walkers.

G4 JESUS SITES IN THE GALILEE

Distance 100km
Driving time 2¾ hours
Completion time 2 days

Starting point From Jerusalem: 150km/1¾ hours; from Tel Aviv: 100km/1¼ hours; from Rosh Pina: 55km/45 minutes.

Note See **Sea of Galilee (#7)** for more information.

Tour stop 1 <u>Nain</u>: one of three episodes in the New Testament involving resurrection by Jesus – this time, a widow's dead child (Luke 7:11–17).

Tour stop 2 **Church of the Transfiguration**, on Mount Tabor, the site of the transfiguration of Christ as told in Matthew 17:1–8, Mark 9:2–8, and Luke 9:28–36, where Jesus encapsulates both Heaven and Earth when God causes Jesus to shine with light and declares him to be His son.

Tour stop 3 **Nazareth (#29)** and the **Basilica of the Annunciation**, marking the Annunciation – the place where Mary was visited by the Angel Gabriel telling her of her role as the mother of God's son, Jesus (Luke 1:26–38).

Optional tour stop <u>Kfar Kana</u>: Jesus attends a wedding and turns water into wine, his first miracle on a grand scale. There's a Catholic church in town known as the Wedding Church commemorating this event from John 2:1–11.

Optional tour stop <u>Migdala</u>: birth home of Mary Magdalene (Migdala is where "Magdalene" comes from, i.e., Mary of Migdala). Be sure to visit old Magdala (Khirbet Majdal) on the other side of Highway 90, where you can visit the ancient city ruins and eat in <u>Magdalena</u> (see below).

Tour stop 4 <u>Kibbutz Ginosar (G3)</u>.

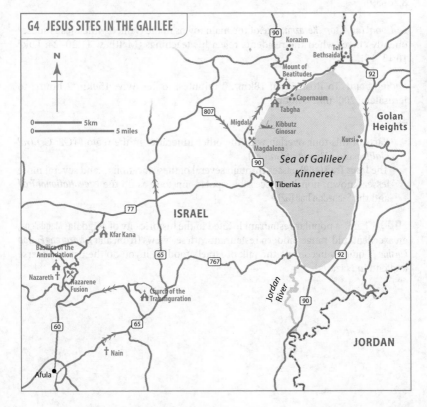

Tour stop 5 **Mount of Beatitudes**, where Jesus gave his Sermon on the Mount, a moral treatise which outlined the Beatitudes and introduced the Lord's Prayer (Matthew 5–7).

Tour stop 6 **Tabgha (#33)**, site of the Church of the Multiplication of Loaves and Fishes and the Church of the Primacy of St. Peter. In the former, Jesus fed the masses by multiplying five loaves of bread and two fish into a meal that served 5,000 as told in all four Gospels (Matthew 14:13–21; Mark 6:31–44; Luke 9:12–17; John 6:1–14). In the latter, Jesus appeared before his disciples after his resurrection for the third time (John 21:1–24) while also elevating Peter among the disciples and making him the most important of the 12 during the time of Christ.

Tour stop 7 **Capernaum (#33)**, home of St. Peter and a number of other apostles. Jesus heals a sick woman and a paralyzed man here, among others. Jesus also curses this town when it rejected his teaching. Referenced in Matthew, Mark, Luke, and John.

Tour stop 8 Tel Bethsaida: the birthplace of three apostles, including Peter, Philip, and Andrew. Jesus cures a man of blindness (Mark 8:22–26) and miraculously feeds 5,000 people (Luke 9:10–17). The exact location of this site is unknown but is generally presumed to be at et-Tell on the north coast of the Sea of Galilee.

Optional tour stop Kursi (G3), where Jesus exorcises demons from a man into a herd of pigs, who then throw themselves off a cliff (Matthew 8:28–34; Mark 5:1–20; Luke 8:26–39).

Optional tour stop **Korazim**, one of the main towns in the Galilee, which Jesus subsequently curses when the residents reject his teachings (Matthew 11:20–24; Luke 10:13–15).

Ending point To Rosh Pina: 18km/20 minutes; to Tel Aviv: 150km/2 hours; to Jerusalem: 200km/2¼ hours.

TIPS

★ Parts of this tour overlap with the other itineraries in the region (*G2: Central Galilee* and *G3: Sea of Galilee*).

★ The **Jesus Trail (#69)** passes through several of these locations – and several more lesser-known, non-bus-accessible spots – on foot, as do the ***Israel National Trail*** and the Sanhedrin Trail (G2).

FOOD There's a popular restaurant located in the historic city of Migdala, Magdalena, an excellent mid-range modern restaurant with sea views (from afar). ***Nazarene Fusion Cuisine*** is quickly becoming the talk of Israel's foodies, if you do the trip in reverse and end in Nazareth.

H1 UPPER GALILEE

Distance 90km
Driving time 1¾ hours
Completion time 2 days

Starting point From Jerusalem: 185km/2 hours; from Tel Aviv: 135km/1¾ hours; from Rosh Pina: 52km/50 minutes.

Tour stop 1 **Yehi'am**.

Tour stop 2 **Montfort**.

Tour stop 3 **Bar'am**.

Tour stop 4 **Tsfat/Safed (#58)**.

At site Ashkenazi Ari Synagogue, Caro Synagogue, Isaac Luria Synagogue, and HaAri (c16th century), one of the oldest extant synagogues still in use.

At site Memorial Museum of Hungarian Speaking Jewry. A Tsfat museum highlighting the daily life of eastern European Jews (w hjm.org.il).

Tour stop 5 Nahal Amud. Human remains from Neanderthal man and Mousterian culture were found in the caves at this nature reserve.

Optional tour stop Amirim is a moshav that specializes in vegetarian fare.

WALKS & DRIVES

H1 Upper Galilee

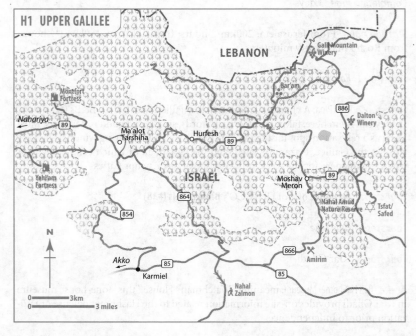

Tour stop 6 Nahal Zalmon. Easy hiking path (can be extended) in this national park along a year-round spring, passing the remains of 14 old flour mills.

Ending point To Rosh Pina: 30km/20 minutes; to Tel Aviv: 145km/1½ hours; to Jerusalem: 185km/2 hours.

TIPS
★ Safed gets cold in the winter.
★ Stay the night in Rosh Pina (H2) (Anchor), if you're interested in a pit stop. Lovely accommodations (if pricey) and good food. Great for friends.

FOOD Amirim, as above. Or you can find takeaway (falafel) and restaurants in Safed. Or if you're headed back to Jerusalem or Tel Aviv, stop at Goats with the Wind (G2) or **Elbabor** on your way out.

ACTIVITIES
★ Festival at ***Lag B'Omer at Moshav Meron*** (can be skipped elsewhen).
★ Try a *Druze Cooking Workshop* with Galileat (**w** galileat.com), including foraging greens, harvesting olives, and cooking Druze cuisine.

WINE Galil Mountain Winery is just outside of **Bar'am**. Dalton Winery is located 12km/15 minutes southeast of **Bar'am** and 11km/15 minutes north of Safed.

H2 GALILEE PANHANDLE

Distance 75km
Driving time 2 hours
Completion time 3 days

Starting point From Jerusalem: 200km/2 hours; from Tel Aviv: 150km/1½ hours; from Rosh Pina: 9km/9 minutes.

Tour stop 1 **Korazim**.

Tour stop 2 Rosh Pina. A charming mountain town filled with hotels, B&Bs (tzimmers, as they call them here, taking the German word), shops, and good restaurants. Most use it as a relaxation spot for the weekend, or as a base for touring wineries. It's very close to the Galilee, Nazareth, Safed, and the Golan, all of which can be day trips when staying here for the weekend. Also one of our Anchor Cities.

Tour stop 3 **Tel Hazor**, one of UNESCO's **Biblical Tels (#38)**.

Tour stop 4 **Hula Lake**.

Tour stop 5 Kfar Giladi.

At site Beit HaShomer Museum: meaning "Watchman's House," this stone-house museum in Kfar Giladi provides on-site information related to the Hashomer defense organization prior to independence.

H2 GALILEE PANHANDLE

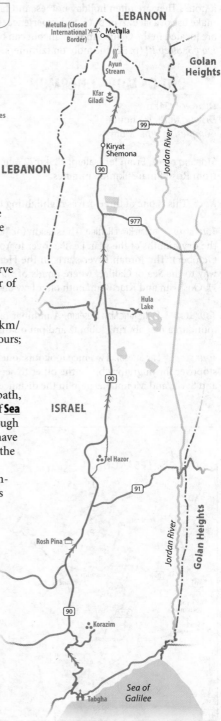

At site <u>Tel Hai Fort</u> (Roaring Lion Monument): commemorating one of the first battles (1920) between Jews and Arabs in the Upper Galilee following Jewish resettlement of the Holy Land.

Tour stop 6 <u>Ayun Stream</u>. A nature reserve in the Upper Galilee with a number of waterfalls flowing year-round.

Ending point To Rosh Pina: 39km/ 30 minutes; to Tel Aviv: 190km/2¼ hours; to Jerusalem: 240km/2½ hours.

TIPS

★ These sites are off the beaten path, and often skipped over in favor of **Sea of Galilee (#7)** or road trips through the **Golan Heights (#62)**. If you have multiple days, you can explore the area from Rosh Pina.

★ Rosh Pina is one of our recommended Anchor Cities. There's otherwise no strong reason to visit, other than fine dining.

★ Rosh Pina gets cold in the winter.

★ National Parks close at 15.00 in the winter.

FOOD Rosh Pina has the best options for good food.

STAYS Try a <u>Tzimmer</u>! With a named derived from the German word for "room," these guesthouses are very popular accommodation options among Israelis for weekend getaways, without having to stay in

a hotel. They are often holiday homes, and families and groups can use a kitchen, make use of a jacuzzi or pool, and experience the tranquility of the wilderness. Many are located in the Galilee and Golan, but can be found throughout Israel. Check out *Do #5: Sleep It!* (p. 52) for more on tzimmers.

I1 FOOT OF MOUNT HERMON

Distance 54km
Driving time 1½ hours
Completion time 1 day

Starting point From Jerusalem: 225km/2½ hours; from Tel Aviv: 185km/2¼ hours; from Rosh Pina: 30km/25 minutes.

Note This is one of three drives highlighting the **Golan Heights (#62)**.

Tour stop 1 Jordan River Rafting. The season for "kayaking" (really, rafting) runs during the dry months of the year, i.e. Passover to Yom Kippur (April/May to September/October). The Jordan River starts in the Hermon mountain range and winds its way to the Sea of Galilee, where rapids of varying degrees of difficulty await. Kfar HaGoshrim and Kfar Blum both offer lazy and "challenging" courses.

Tour stop 2 Prehistoric Man Museum. A number of prehistoric artifacts and bones were found in a neighboring kibbutz and put on display here.

Tour stop 3 Snir Stream. Two nice lookouts: one of the reservoir which has become a stopover for migratory birds; the other to see the northern borders with Lebanon and Syria, and Mount Hermon in the distance.

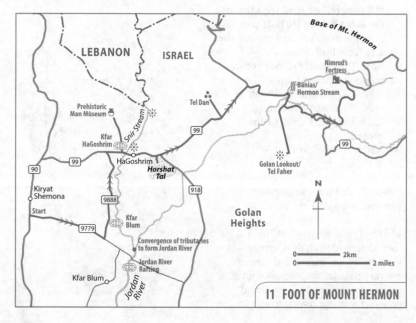

Tour stop 4 Horshat Tal. Visit the ancient oak forest or the orchid reserve. Swimming in the lake and camping are some of the options at this 700-acre park near Kiryat Shmona.

Tour stop 5 **Tel Dan (#63)**.

Tour stop 6 **Banias (#80)**.

Tour stop 7 Golan Lookout/Tel Faher. This site peers down to the valleys below and commemorates the battle between Israel and Syria during the Six-Day War which left the Golan Heights under Israeli control.

Tour stop 8 **Nimrod's Fortress (#85)**.

Ending point To Rosh Pina: 50km/50 minutes; to Tel Aviv: 210km/2½ hours; to Jerusalem: 250km/2¾ hours.

TIPS
★ We recommend using Rosh Pina as an Anchor City if you have multiple day or weekend trips planned, but you can also rent a tzimmer in the Galilee or Golan.
★ National Parks close at 15.00 in the winter.

FOOD There are a few options in some of the smaller towns. Majdal Shams (12) has excellent Druze cuisine. Otherwise, pack a lunch.

12 NORTHERN GOLAN

Distance 115km
Driving time 2¼ hours
Completion time 2 days

Starting point From Jerusalem: 265km/3¼ hours; from Tel Aviv: 220km/2¾ hours; from Rosh Pina: 65km/1¼ hours.

Note This is one of three drives highlighting the **Golan Heights (#62)**.

Tour stop 1 **Mount Hermon**.

Tour stop 2 Majdal Shams and The Shouting Hill. Better to refer to the town, Majdal Shams, rather than the "Shouting Hill," as the latter has been known since the 1960s. Technology has now rendered the hill a relic of a bygone era when family members, separated after the 1967 Six-Day War, would use bullhorns to communicate with one another. That practice is no more, but a visit to this Druze village is worth your time, as is the food.

Tour stop 3 Birkat Ram. A large crater lake in the Golan, inhabited by Druze and the subject of folklore – including having opened during Noah's Flood and being the teary eye of a scorned wife whose husband is Mount Hermon.

Tour stop 4 Mount Bental Lookout. Look out upon the Golan and the abandoned village of Quneitra, following the Israeli occupation of the Golan Heights, now a crossing for Syrian Druze living in the Golan who produce and distribute apples to Syria.

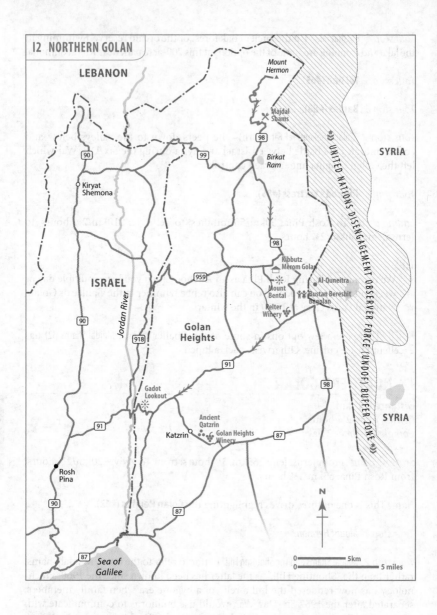

12 NORTHERN GOLAN

Tour stop 5 <u>Gadot Lookout</u>. Another Golan Heights military outpost, where you can visit Syrian bunkers and trenches that were overtaken by the Israeli Defense Forces in the Six-Day War, with views of the Hula Valley.

Tour stop 6 ***Ancient Qatzrin***.

Tour stop 7 **Golan Heights Winery (#75)**.

Ending point To Rosh Pina: 23km/25 minutes; to Tel Aviv: 185km/2 hours; to Jerusalem: 225km/2½ hours.

TIPS

★ This is a full-day itinerary, so if you plan on skiing you'll want to make it two days.

★ You can also hike at Mount Hermon if it's not ski season.

★ If driving more than 2 hours to get here, don't plan on making the trip in one day. Do yourself a favor: stay the night and tack on sites from *I1: Foot of Mount Hermon* (above) or *I3: Southern Golan* (below).

★ National parks close at 15.00 in the winter, but the rains bring clearer skies for the vistas.

★ This drive can go in either direction. If you're looking to stay in the region, consider camping, or taking more luxurious options in Rosh Pina.

FOOD Majdal Shams has great Arab-Druze cuisine.

STAYS Kibbutz Merom Golan: a resort inside a kibbutz where guests can stay in their own cabins, ride horses, swim and do other activities, as well as eat with the community in the Gaucho Restaurant (from $150/night).

ACTIVITIES If you have kids (or just like food), *Picking Fruit* in the Golan is a great activity – Bustan Bereshit Bagolan is popular near Merom Golan. If you're looking for adventure activities, you can hike some or all of the Golan Trail, which starts at Mount Hermon.

WINE Pelter Winery has a cult following, and is located in Ein Zivan just south of Merom Golan and near the Syrian border. Also, the 600+km Israel Bike Trail (U) begins at Mount Hermon and continues all the way to Eilat, with multiple trails for different types of riders and lots of signposts and welcome signs (**w** ibt.org.il).

I3 SOUTHERN GOLAN

Distance 110km
Driving time 2 hours
Completion time 2 days

Starting point From Jerusalem: 215km/2¼ hours; from Tel Aviv: 170km/2 hours; from Rosh Pina: 25km/25 minutes.

Note This is one of three drives highlighting the **Golan Heights (#62)**.

Tour stop 1 Meshushim Stream. A large natural pool in the Golan surrounded by stunning hexagonal basalt columns.

Optional tour stop Tel Bethsaida (G4).

Tour stop 2 Majrase-Betiha/Bethsaida Valley. A wet hike, with a number of routes requiring walking through these streams as they head towards the Sea of Galilee.

Tour stop 3 **Yehudiya**.

Tour stop 4 **Gamla**.

Tour stop 5 Nahal el-Al. A couple of waterfalls, some pool swimming, and a 4–5-hour round-trip walk.

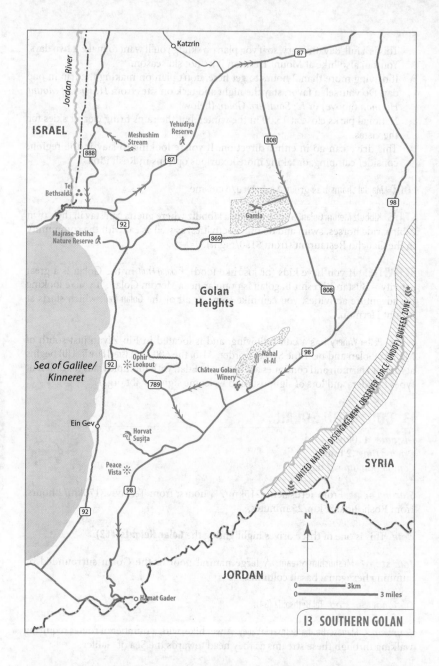

Tour stop 6 **Ophir Lookout**. From Highway 92 hugging the eastern seaboard of the Sea of Galilee, take Route 789 at Kursi National Park (away from the sea) until you see signs for Ophir lookout (מצפה אופיר).

Tour stop 7 **Horvat Suṣiṭa (Hippos)**. One of the Cities of the Decapolis (W3), Hippos advanced due to its strategic location on top of a plateau just east of the Sea of Galilee.

Tied to the Greeks from the 3rd century BCE and later the Romans, before Muslim conquest in the 7th century, Hippos was abandoned after the 749 CE earthquake.

Tour stop 8 Peace Vista. Mitzpe HaShalom, or Peace Vista, is off Route 98, 12km north of **Hamat Gader**, overlooking the Sea of Galilee.

Tour stop 9 **Hamat Gader**.

Ending point To Rosh Pina: 55km/45 minutes; to Jerusalem: 200km/2¼ hours; to Tel Aviv: 160km/1¾ hours.

TIPS
★ National parks close at 15.00 in the winter, but the rains bring clearer skies for the vistas.
★ This trip is heavy on walks in nature reserves, so just pick one or two if you want to do the rest of the stops.

FOOD Pack lunches.

ACTIVITIES Château Golan Winery is adjacent to the Nahal el-Al nature reserve.

J1 NORTHERN NEGEV

Distance 180km
Driving time 2¾ hours
Completion time 2 days

Starting point From Jerusalem: 120km/1½ hours; from Tel Aviv: 110km/1½ hours.

Tour stop 1 Beer Sheva. Capital of the Negev, this desert city grew up in the latter part of the 20th century from waves of immigrants from Arab countries, India, Ethiopia, and the former Soviet countries. Particularly famous for its shuk/market where you can buy Bedouin goods and its mosque-turned-Islamic-museum. Nearby are archaeological ruins, various national parks and reserves, and within the city itself is a fine collection of Brutalist architecture, particularly pleasant at the Negev Brigade Monument outside of town. Check out *Haaretz*'s Beersheva architecture article (**w** haaretz.com/israel-news/travel/.premium-1.633213).

Visit Negev Museum of Art: located in the former Ottoman Governor's Mansion, this museum focuses on Negev Israeli artists.

Visit Israeli Air Force Museum: hosts a number of decommissioned fighter jets to view on this former air base.

Tour stop 2 **Tel Beer Sheva**, one of UNESCO's **Biblical Tels (#38)**.

Tour stop 3 **Museum of Bedouin Culture**, aka Joe Alon Center (🕑 09.00–16.00 Sunday–Thursday).

Tour stop 4 Sidreh-Lakiya Negev Weaving. A visitor center in a Bedouin community that connects tourists directly to Bedouin women and increases their economic opportunities (**w** sidreh.org).

Tour stop 5 _**Tel Arad**_.

Tour stop 6 _**Yatir Winery**_.

Optional tour stop _Dimona_: this Negev city near Beer Sheva is known for being home to two unique populations – Indian Jews (7,500) and the Hebrew Israelite Community, or Black Hebrews (3,000).

Tour stop 7 _**Mamshit**_, part of the **Incense Route (#73)**.

Optional tour stop _Yeruham_: visit this park for the Yeruham Iris in February/March and return in October/November for the Yellow Crocus.

Optional tour stop _Little Makhtesh/HaMakhtesh HaKatan_: walk to the bed and to observation points in this smallest of the three major makhtesh (erosion craters).

Optional tour stop _Big Makhtesh/HaMakhtesh HaGadol_: start at the Colored Sands car park and take the half-day hike to sweeping desert landscapes.

**Ending point** To Jerusalem: 145km/1¾ hours; to Tel Aviv: 145km/1¾ hours; to Mitzpe Ramon: 55km/40 minutes.

TIPS

★ This itinerary ends near the starting point of *J2: Southern Negev* (below).
★ One could continue to the Dead Sea after **Tel Arad**/**Yatir Winery** and forego the other sites.
★ The Negev Wine Route (J2) includes **Yatir Winery**, among others.
★ Most everything is closed for Shabbat.
★ Outdoor sites in this desert region will be very hot during summer days.
★ Yeruham blossoms only occur certain times of the year.
★ You only save 30 minutes of driving by skipping the Pearl sites (your choice!).

FOOD Lots of options in Beer Sheva.

ACTIVITIES **Yatir Winery**, near Tel Arad, offers rare desert-produced wines.

J2 SOUTHERN NEGEV

Distance 80km
Driving time 1½ hours
Completion time 3 days

Starting point From Jerusalem: 200km/2¼ hours; from Tel Aviv: 190km/2 hours; from Eilat: 150km/1¾ hours.

Optional tour stop *Driving Through the Negev*: by driving from Tel Aviv to the Dead Sea (2 hours) or Tel Aviv to Eilat (4 hours), you'll get picturesque emptiness filled with interesting geological features.

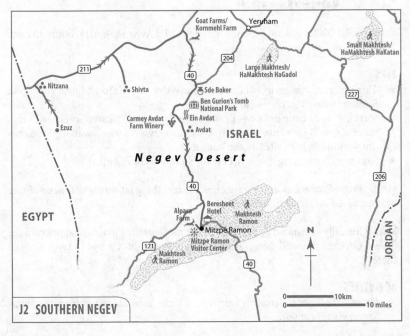

J2 SOUTHERN NEGEV

685

Optional stop Ezuz. Tiny town (fewer than 100 people) near the border with Egypt which offers tzimmer lodging, hiking tours, artistry, and agricultural products, such as honey and goat's cheese.

Tour stop 1 <u>Negev Goat Farms</u>. There are a variety of choices, surprisingly, letting you pet goats, work as a helper, buy cheese and milk, or eat in a fancy restaurant using goat products. Try Kornmehl Farm.

Tour stop 2 <u>Sde Boker</u>. Story of the life and death of the first prime minister of Israel, David Ben Gurion, in his home for the last 20 years of his life.

Tour stop 3 <u>Ben Gurion's Tomb</u>. The gravesite of David Ben Gurion and his wife, Paula, near Sde Boker.

Tour stop 4 **<u>Ein Avdat (#74)</u>**.

Tour stop 5 **<u>Avdat (#48)</u>**, part of the **<u>Incense Route (#73)</u>**.

Optional detour Other stops on the Incense Route nearby include ***<u>Halutza</u>***, ***<u>Nitzana</u>***, and ***<u>Shivta</u>***. See J3.

Tour stop 6 <u>Alpaca Farm</u>. Lots more to do at this farm than simply look at alpacas (and llamas). Activities include shearing, weaving, feeding, riding, and spinning wool. They are not local (they come from South America), but they are distantly related to camels. Best for kids.

Tour stop 7 ***<u>Mitzpe Ramon</u>*** visitor center.

Tour stop 8 **<u>Makhtesh Ramon (#28)</u>**.

Ending point To Jerusalem: 145km/1¾ hours; to Tel Aviv: 145km/1½ hours; to Eilat: 200km/2¼ hours.

TIPS

★ This itinerary can go in either direction. We've chosen to end near Makhtesh Ramon in case you choose to camp there.

★ Start hiking as early or late as possible (before sunset) to avoid overhead sun – there is very little shade here. Ein Avdat also involves much walking. You may not want to do both sites on the same day.

★ Summer is scorching in the Negev, and hardly recommended.

FOOD ***<u>Mitzpe Ramon</u>*** has a few easy choices, and the goat farms will have dining options based on locally produced cheese.

STAY Critically acclaimed <u>Beresheet Hotel</u> in ***<u>Mitzpe Ramon</u>*** is a glorious addition to the desert. On the other end, <u>Negev Camping</u> is also a highlight. Or end in <u>Ezuz</u> and sleep there.

ACTIVITIES

★ ***<u>Hiking in the Negev</u>*** is definitely worth your time. You can depart from the ***<u>Mitzpe Ramon</u>*** visitor center.

★ Check out Astronomy Israel: based in *Mitzpe Ramon*, this group organizes desert night sky tours, with and without telescopes (w astronomyisrael.com).

WINE Carmey Avdat Farm Winery is part of the Negev Wine Route: an unexpected group of wineries which have received critical acclaim in the heart of the desert. Spend a day or weekend visiting the Sde Boker, Yatir, Boker Valley, and Carmey Avdat wineries, sample the locally famous Merlot, during a visit to some of the famous Negev sites. Carmey Avdat's website has more information and maps (w carmeyavdat.com/negev-wine-route).

J3 INCENSE ROUTE

Distance 225km, some via 4x4
Driving time 6 hours
Completion time 2 days

For more on this elective, see **Incense Route (#73)**.

Tour stop 1 **Mamshit**.

Tour stop 2 **Halutza**. Despite it being the Incense Route city-site with the least amount of excavation, this city was actually the only one not abandoned after the Arabs took over the area in the 7th century. Before that and after the Nabataean period ended, the town was capital of Palaestina Tertia.

Tour stop 3 **Shivta**.

Tour stop 4 **Nitzana**.

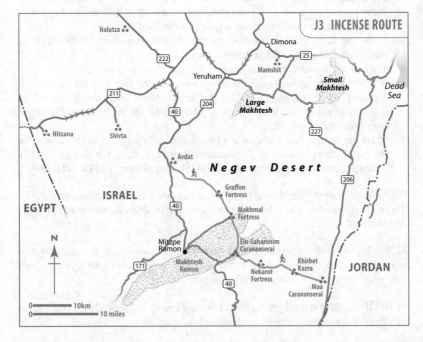

Tour stop 5 **Avdat (#48)**.

Tour stop 6 Graffon Fortress (hiking required). This small site includes two small towers, a residential complex, and a water reservoir.

Tour stop 7 Makhmal Fortress. This two-story fortress and water reservoir are located on the north side of **Makhtesh Ramon (#28)**.

Tour stop 8 Ein-Saharonim Caravanserai. Located near the Saharonim Stream, this $42m^2$ fortress may have been destroyed in a fire, as layers of ash have been found at the site.

Tour stop 9 Nekarot Fortress (hiking required). Another guard station, protecting the Incense Route and its travelers from robbers, this fort includes four structures, including a water reservoir, a Roman tower and hall, an observation tower, and a destroyed Nabataean complex.

Tour stop 10 Khirbet Kazra/Qasra (hiking required). This guard post has the remains of a tower and a water reservoir.

Tour stop 11 Moa Caravanserai. This transit station and castle are the most eastern Nabataean ruins in Israel, and were a stop after the journey from Petra.

TIPS

★ This tour includes all ten spots referenced in the UNESCO declaration of World Heritage, but there are other Nabataean spots you may want to add, or some you may want to skip.

★ Avdat is the best preserved, so should not be missed. **Shivta** and **Mamshit** are next, and **Halutza** is mostly buried under sand (which makes it interesting!).

★ We've packed the most important sites first, culminating with Avdat. The others can be skipped unless you are on a tour or a die-hard fan.

★ Three sites have no direct road access and require hiking through the Negev to reach them – Kazra, Nekarot, and Graffon.

★ 4x4 is recommended to reach most of the sites (except Avdat).

★ A few tour companies offer combination tours to visit everything on this itinerary, plus camping in Makhtesh Ramon. These tours usually go in the opposite direction, starting at Moa. Try Danny the Digger (w dannythedigger. com/tours/incense-route/).

★ There are several non-Nabataean sites nearby you may want to check out. See the *J1: Northern Negev* and *J2: Southern Negev* itineraries (above) for Ezuz (J2), *Dimona (J1)*, *Yeruham (J1)*, **Makhtesh Ramon (#28)**, *Mitzpe Ramon*, and **Ein Avdat (#74)**.

FOOD Very limited. You should bring all of your own rations for the many hikes. There are restaurants and a few places to stock up in **Mitzpe Ramon** or Beer Sheva (J1) further north.

STAYS We recommend staying in **Mitzpe Ramon** for the two overnights, but you may also want to camp. (Hire a guide and/or stay at a campground unless you are *very* prepared – you will need to carry all your own water.)

ACTIVITIES **Hiking in the Negev** is rustic, hot, and empty, but should give you a sense of what the same journey was like thousands of years ago.

K1 DEAD SEA (ISRAEL)

Distance 115km
Driving time 2½ hours
Completion time 3 days

Starting point From Jerusalem: 45km/35 minutes; from Tel Aviv: 105km/1¼ hours.

Driving Highway 90: Israel's longest road, running from Metula in the upper Galilee Panhandle all the way south, past the Sea of Galilee, West Bank and Jericho, the Dead Sea and Masada, and the Aravah, to Eilat where it terminates at the Red Sea. As you enter micro-region K1, it offers amazing views of the Dead Sea in the east and towering salt flats to the west. Look for sinkholes and old signposts showing the historic height of the Dead Sea.

Optional tour stop The north Dead Sea beaches of New Kalya Beach, Neve Midbar Beach, and Biankini/Siesta Beach are three of the remaining entryways for Dead Sea immersion, located next to one another and each requiring an entrance fee. These beaches are ideal if you are looking for a quick trip from Jerusalem, but better services can be found in **Ein Bokek** in the south of the Dead Sea.

Tour stop 1 **Qumran (#70)**.

Tour stop 2 Einot Tsukim Nature Reserve. This biosphere at the Dead Sea offers a viewpoint to see up close how far the Dead Sea has retreated.

Optional tour stop Wadi Daraja: considered hard by Israeli standards, which is saying something! You'll need rope. Passes the Muraba'at Caves and rappels down more than a dozen waterfalls.

Tour stop 3 Kibbutz Mitzpe Shalem. Ahava Dead Sea products, including facial masks, mud, bath salts, and lots of natural products sourced locally.

Former tour stop only Mineral Beach. **Important caveat:** One of the most popular beaches along the Dead Sea is now a cavernous hole in the ground thanks to water diversion tactics that have shrunk the Dead Sea and set off an irreversible cascade of damage by way of sinkholes. Though often referenced, this site is closed indefinitely.

Tour stop 4 **Ein Gedi (#50)**.

Tour stop 5 **Masada (#8)**.

Optional tour stop Masada's Snake Path: on the front side of Masada (facing the Dead Sea), you can take this windy path up the cliff to the plateau above. Most use the cable car, but plenty choose this more realistic historic path to the top – bring lots of water and hike early (path closes at 10.00).

Optional tour stop Masada's Roman Trails: on the back end of Masada are the ramps created by the Romans to ultimately penetrate the hilltop bastion of Jewish resistance, Masada. Walkers can hike the trail up and to the ancient town, but getting to the trailhead from this end requires a 4-hour detour through the desert with a 4x4.

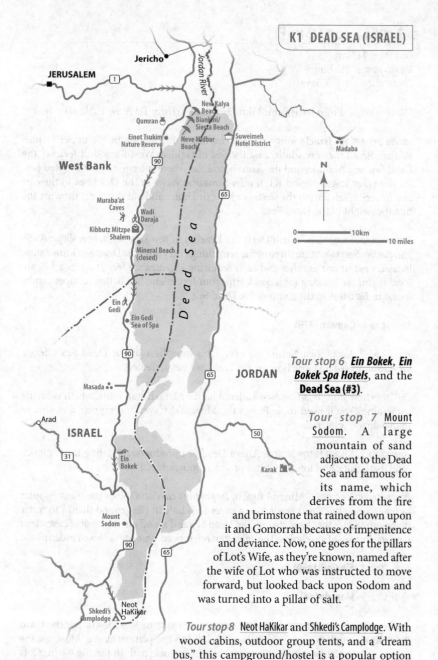

Tour stop 6 **Ein Bokek**, **Ein Bokek Spa Hotels**, and the **Dead Sea (#3)**.

Tour stop 7 **Mount Sodom**. A large mountain of sand adjacent to the Dead Sea and famous for its name, which derives from the fire and brimstone that rained down upon it and Gomorrah because of impenitence and deviance. Now, one goes for the pillars of Lot's Wife, as they're known, named after the wife of Lot who was instructed to move forward, but looked back upon Sodom and was turned into a pillar of salt.

Tour stop 8 **Neot HaKikar** and **Shkedi's Camplodge**. With wood cabins, outdoor group tents, and a "dream bus," this campground/hostel is a popular option for exploring the Dead Sea and desert wadis. Shkedi's provides details for hikes and mountain biking through the southern Dead Sea desert area which hugs the border with Jordan.

Ending point To Jerusalem: 140km/2 hours; to Tel Aviv: 180km/2½ hours; to Eilat: 190km/2¼ hours.

TIPS

★ The first beaches are optional if you plan to go all the way to *Ein Bokek*. Also, you can skip the *Ein Bokek Spa Hotels* if you plan to access the sea from one of the public entrances.

★ This route can be done in either direction.

★ If you plan to hike Masada, you'll want to be there before 10.00 due to heat restrictions.

★ Several guidebooks say that you can simply turn off or park by the highway and head to the Dead Sea – this is dangerous and to be avoided. There are sinkholes appearing every day due to the disappearance of the shoreline.

★ If you start in Eilat, you'll want to do this trip in reverse. If you drive from Tel Aviv, you can also do it in reverse if you take Highway 31 through the desert to arrive.

★ The last stop is a campground, but you can turn back at Mount Sodom if you don't want to stay the night.

FOOD *Ein Bokek* has a few options, and there's a good dining hall at **Masada (#8)**.

STAYS Review *Ein Bokek Spa Hotels*.

ACTIVITIES

★ Add in a canyoning trip to Wadi Qumran.

★ For something truly wild, take a *Powered Parachute Flight* and hover over Masada with the Dead Sea in the background – a glorious and exhilarating experience (w xn----zhcb4afbwe7a0dnem.co.il/extreme-activities-in-israel or book through Tourist Israel, w touristisrael.com/tours/powered-parachute-flights/).

L1 EILAT

Terrain Flat
Difficulty (1–5) 1
Distance 9km
Walking time 2 hours
Completion time 4 hours

Starting point Begin at your hotel. Have a nice breakfast, take a dip in the pool, enjoy yourself – you're (likely) on vacation!

Tour stop 1 Kings City. A biblical-themed amusement park that was closed in 2015. Do you like closed theme parks? Creepy, right? Here's one.

Tour stop 2 North Beach. The most popular choice in this Red Sea resort town, with lots of water activities to choose from, in addition to swimming and snorkeling. Stroll the promenade here, do some shopping, grab a drink – this is the quintessential spot of commercialism in Eilat.

Tour stop 3 Shopping. Pick a mall, any mall. Maybe Ice Mall with the big indoor ice rink? The seaside Mall Hayak Eilat? Big Eilat? Duty-free shopping is very popular in this area, a no-tax zone.

Tour stop 4 Marina. From here, you can go on a diving expedition or boating tour.

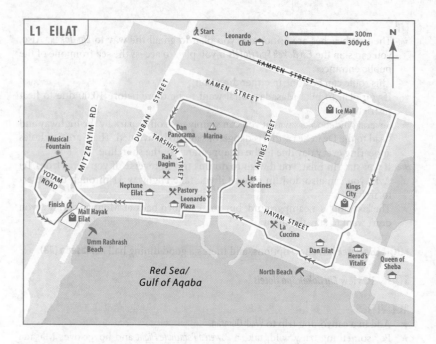

Tour stop 5 Musical Fountain. Evening performances, à la Bellagio Fountain in Vegas.

Tour stop 6 Umm Rashrash. Commemorates Israel's 1949 declaration of Eilat as the southernmost border.

Tour stop 7 Beach. Time to get in the water! This is the **Red Sea/Gulf of Aqaba (#10)**. Mosh Beach, just south of the city, is quite popular, but all of the beaches are sandy, hot, and popular.

Ending point Dinner/hotel.

TIPS

- ★ **Eilat (#78)** is not the most culture-rich city, but regardless – you may still find yourself here. If that's the case, the above itinerary will allow you to get out of your hotel zone a bit. If you don't feel like it, don't be bothered. Nothing on this itinerary is required.
- ★ If you have a car, the best options are all within a short drive. Skip this itinerary and do *L2: Israel's Red Sea and Egyptian Border* and *L3: Arabah Desert* (below) over a few days. Or take one day or two nights to go to **Petra (#2)**.

FOOD Tons of highly regarded places, including Pastory, Rak Dagim, Les Sardines, and La Cuccina.

STAY Plenty to choose from, including Isrotel Agamim.

ACTIVITIES Skydiving is a thing. Obviously so is diving. And water sports are popular – kitesurfing, stand-up paddleboarding, etc. Twice a year the city hosts the Red Sea Jazz Festival.

L2 ISRAEL'S RED SEA AND EGYPTIAN BORDER

Distance 30km
Driving time 30 minutes
Completion time 1 day

Starting point From Jerusalem: 315km/3½ hours; from Tel Aviv: 330km/4 hours; from Eilat: 25km/20 minutes.

Optional tour stop <u>Mount Karkom</u>/Har Karkom. A site in the southern Israeli Negev Desert that is revered by some as the true location of the biblical Mount Sinai, given the likelihood that the Israelites marched from Egypt towards Israel in a straight line (present-day Mount Sinai is roughly 400km south of the Mediterranean on the Sinai peninsula). Religious activity appears to have occurred here based on recent excavations, though roughly 1,000 years before modern-day estimates place the event of Moses' Exodus. Access via Route 10 requires pre-authorization (use a guide). Plenty of ancient inscriptions found on rocks throughout the region.

Tour stop 1 **<u>Red Canyon</u>**.

Optional tour stop <u>Wadi Ein Netafim</u>. Raptor watching from Mount Yoash.

Tour stop 2 <u>Dolphin Reef</u>. A theme park with pavilions to observe dolphins "in their natural habitat," swimming and diving with them in a controlled pool, and three heated relaxation pools for adults. The latter is paid separately and includes 2 hours in the pools and the option of working with a personal spa consultant. Beach Inspector's 2018 Awards for Best "WOW" Beach.

Optional tour stop **<u>Eilat (#78)</u>**.

Optional tour stop The International Birding and Research Center is a bird sanctuary north towards the Eilat/Wadi Araba border crossing.

Optional tour stop The Botanical Garden of Eilat is across the street from the birding center.

Optional tour stop Mosh Beach, just south of the city, is quite popular.

Tour stop 3 **<u>Coral Beach (#83)</u>**. For further information, also see **<u>Red Sea (#10)</u>**.

Tour stop 4 **<u>Underwater Observatory</u>**.

Ending point To Eilat: 9km/15 minutes.

TIPS
★ You'll want to spend the night in the area, as driving back for 4 hours in the dark in the desert after conducting all of those activities is not recommended.
★ If you're trying to save money, you could do worse than take your chances with border agents and staying the night in either <u>Taba (T1)</u> (dirt cheap) or **<u>Aqaba (#43)</u>** (half the price of Eilat).
★ Absurdly hot in the summer and extremely busy during Israeli holidays.
★ <u>Mount Karkom</u> can also be accessed through the desert via **<u>Mitzpe Ramon</u>**.

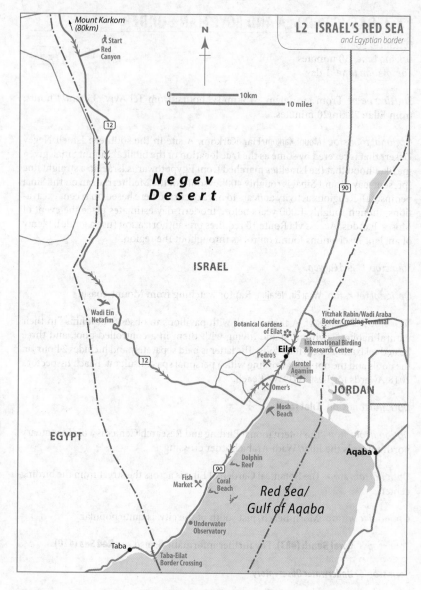

FOOD Some good options include Pedro's, Omer's, and Fish Market.

STAYS Just north of the city center, the highest-ranking hotel in this region is the Isrotel Agamim (L1).

L3 ARABAH DESERT

Distance 80km
Driving time 1¼ hours
Completion time 2 days

Starting point From Jerusalem: 265km/
3¼ hours; from Tel Aviv: 280km/3¼ hours;
from Eilat: 65km/45 minutes.

Tour stop 1 Kibbutz Neot Smadar. Offers tours
of this Negev community, including to
its art center, winery, and vegetarian
restaurant.

At site Neot Smadar Winery. The tiny
Negev town is represented well at
this winery, with a gift shop, art
center, restaurant (Pundak), and
of course winery. Very interesting
winemaking conditions with such
drastic changes in temperature.

Tour stop 2 Kibbutz Lotan.

Optional tour stop Kibbutz Ketura. Home
to the Arava Institute, where students
can study abroad to learn about
sustainable environmental practices.

Tour stop 3 Yotvata Hai-Bar.

Tour stop 4 Timna (#96).

Tour stop 5 Amram's Pillars.
An easy walk to visit these
five pillars, perceived to
be elaborately carved
columns but actually
a completely natural
phenomenon of
water erosion in the
Eilat Mountain
region.

Kibbutz Neot Smadar
Neot Smadar Winery
40
Kibbutz Ketura
Kibbutz Lotan
90
ISRAEL
JORDAN

Negev Desert

Yotvata Hai-Bar

90

Mount Timna 447m
Timna Park
65
Ramon International Airport

Amram's Pillars

ISRAEL
90
JORDAN
Yitzhak Rabin/ Wadi Araba Border Crossing

12
EGYPT
Eilat
Aqaba

N

Red Sea/ Gulf of Aqaba

Taba

L3 ARABAH DESERT

0 — 5km
0 — 5 miles

Ending point To Eilat: 18km/20 minutes; to Tel Aviv: 355km/4 hours; to Jerusalem: 320km/4 hours.

TIPS

★ If traveling from the Dead Sea, you can consider spending the night before at <u>Shkedi's Camplodge (K1)</u> in <u>Neot HaKikar (K1)</u> to be closer to the first stop.

★ Stay in **Eilat (#78)** or, if you arrive early enough, cross to either <u>Taba (T1)</u> or **Aqaba (#43)**.

FOOD The kibbutzim will all have food options, as does Timna.

M1 AQABA

Terrain Mostly flat
Difficulty (1–5) 1
Distance 5km, round trip
Walking time 1 hour
Completion time 2 hours

Starting point Hotel.

Tour stop 1 Scuba. This is what makes the **Red Sea/Gulf of Aqaba (#10)** famous! Do your research and pick a dive shop that suits your interest and skill level, and head out first thing for a half-day dive.

Tour stop 2 Ancient Church. Considered the oldest "purpose-built" Christian church in the world, from the 3rd century, predating the **Church of the Holy Sepulchre (#9)** and **Church of the Nativity (#18)** by 20–30 years.

Tour stop 3 Ayla. The ruins of an ancient Umayyad (later Abbasid, then Fatimid) city that existed prior to the establishment of Aqaba.

Tour stop 4 Sharif Hussein Bin Ali Mosque. Named after an emir of Mecca until 1917, this large, white mosque downtown is lit up at night for your viewing pleasure. Non-Muslims not allowed entry.

Tour stop 5 Aqaba Museum (⊕ 08.00–17.00 Sunday–Thursday, 10.00–17.00 Friday and Saturday, closes one hour earlier in summer). Archaeological museum with pieces from many of the periods of this city's long history. Former house of Sharif Hussein Bin Ali (see mosque above).

Tour stop 6 Aqaba Castle. Built by the Mamluks, this castle served as a major battleground during World War I when Arab nationalists fought against the Ottoman Empire, and was memorialized in the movie *Lawrence of Arabia*.

Tour stop 7 Flagpole. On the coast stands a 130m-high flagpole commemorating the Arab Revolt, the flag of which currently serves as the Palestinian flag – the same as the Jordanian flag, but without the star in the red triangle.

Tour stop 8 Marina. End the day with a glass-bottom boat ride, a dip in the sea, a snorkel, or a dive.

Ending point Dinner/hotel.

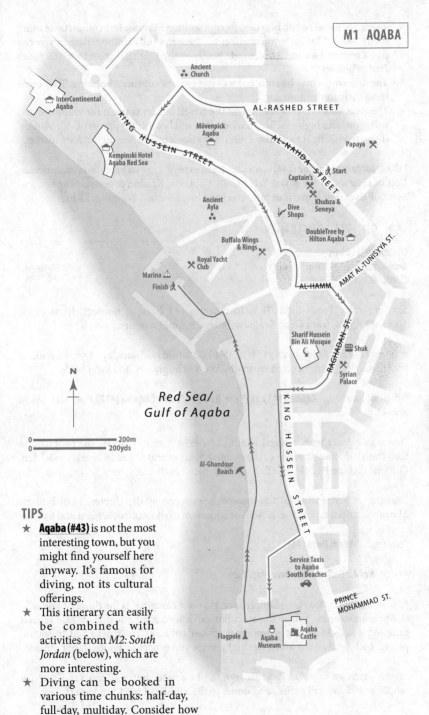

InterContinental Aqaba

Ancient Church

KING HUSSEIN STREET

Kempinski Hotel Aqaba Red Sea

AL-RASHED STREET

Mövenpick Aqaba

AL-NAHDA STREET

Papaya ✕

Start ⚓

Captain's ✕

Ancient Ayla

Khubza & Seneya ✕

Dive Shops

DoubleTree by Hilton Aqaba

Buffalo Wings & Rings ✕

AMAT AL-TUNISYYA ST.

Royal Yacht Club ✕

Marina △

Finish 🚶

AL-HAMM

Sharif Hussein Bin Ali Mosque ☪

RAGHADAN ST.

Shuk 🏛

Syrian Palace ✕

N ↑

Red Sea/ Gulf of Aqaba

0 ——— 200m
0 ——— 200yds

Al-Ghandour Beach ⚓

KING HUSSEIN STREET

Service Taxis to Aqaba South Beaches 🚗

PRINCE MOHAMMAD ST.

Flagpole ⚑

Aqaba Museum

Aqaba Castle

TIPS

★ **Aqaba (#43)** is not the most interesting town, but you might find yourself here anyway. It's famous for diving, not its cultural offerings.

★ This itinerary can easily be combined with activities from *M2: South Jordan* (below), which are more interesting.

★ Diving can be booked in various time chunks: half-day, full-day, multiday. Consider how much time and money you want to spend.

★ There are some public beaches, though women may not feel comfortable using them. Many Muslim women will enter the water fully clothed. Rather, you can pay a nominal fee to visit a private beach on the southern coast (see *M2: South Jordan* below).

★ The dive shops may be chill, but will still require advanced booking. They often leave early in the morning.

★ The Ayla Oasis development near the Israeli border is not quite complete, but will soon offer high-end accommodations and beachfront properties for visitors.

★ If you're visiting on a Friday evening, try Souk by the Sea, an outdoor market.

FOOD **Jordanian Cuisine (#44)** is something to experience – its breakfasts in particular. Lots of reviews on the Royal Yacht Club, Captain's, Khubza & Seneya, Papaya, and Syrian Palace. For American fare, everyone loves Buffalo Wings and Rings.

M2 SOUTH JORDAN

Distance 110km
Driving time 1¾ hours, one-way
Completion time 3 days

Starting point From Eilat: 7km/10 minutes (+1 hour at border); from Petra: 130km/2 hours; from Dead Sea/Suweimeh: 280km/3¼ hours.

Tour stop 1 *Aqaba Bird Observatory* (🕐 08.00–15.00 Saturday–Thursday). Offers a walking trail through 0.5km² of territory to observe 390 migratory and local birds.

Optional tour stop **Aqaba (#43)** and the **Red Sea/Gulf of Aqaba (#10)** (see *M1: Aqaba* above).

Tour stop 2 South Beach. Several beach clubs exist here to regulate the people (and thus trash), making this one of the cleanest beaches and places to snorkel in Jordan. Options include B12 Beach Club and Berenice Beach Club.

Tour stop 3 Marine Science Station Aquarium. Sponsored by the University of Jordan's Marine Science Station, this is Aqaba's aquarium to show off local plant and fish life.

Tour stop 4 **Wadi Rum (#4)**.

At site *Hot Air Balloon Ride Over Wadi Rum*.

At site *Glamping in Wadi Rum*: glamping, or glamour camping, is for those of you who don't mind sleeping under the stars but can afford a little luxury. While regular camping is $20–30 a night, glamping is upwards of $200. You'll get a bed, breakfast, private bath, and all the amenities and service you expect in a hotel… but outside!

At site *Sandboarding in Wadi Rum*: no snow to be found, but you can sand-surf (or sandboard) down tall ochre sand dunes in the middle of the Rum Desert.

Ending point To Petra/Wadi Musa: 110km/1¾ hours; to Aqaba: 72km/1¼ hours; to Amman: 320km/4¼ hours.

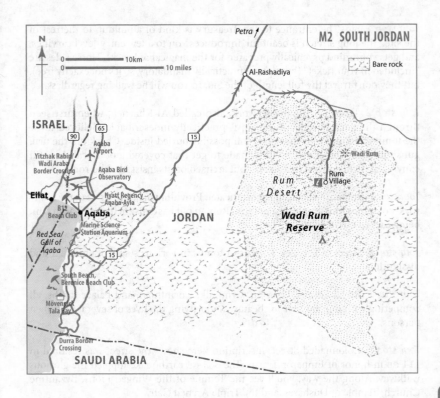

TIPS

★ If you are planning to snorkel or dive, then you'll want to add in *M1: Aqaba* (above). Otherwise, you may choose to skip Aqaba.

★ This itinerary can be done in either direction.

★ Staying the night in Wadi Rum and "glamping" may afford you more time the next day for activities, in addition to the desert park adventure.

★ Most snorkel/dive trips require an 08.00–09.00 departure, if you are doing this trip in reverse.

★ Birding is best done outside of summer months (as is Wadi Rum, honestly).

FOOD Aqaba has plenty of food options.

ACTIVITIES Rock Climbing in Wadi Rum is popular, with lots of routes mapped by adventurists (w mountainproject.com).

N1 PETRA HIGHLIGHTS

Terrain Rocky, dusty, descent on way in, a bit of a climb on the way out
Difficulty (1–5) 2
Distance 8.5km
Walking time 2 hours, but you'll stop a lot so plan for the whole day
Completion time 6 hours

Starting point **Petra (#2)** visitor center: buy your tickets.

Tour stop 1 Siq. The entrance to the Treasury is kind of a buildup to the rest of the site. The long stretch is beautiful, introduces you to a few entry-level carvings, and gets your mind psychically prepared for the magical red rocks. Horse rides are "included in your ticket" (but tips are practically mandatory, so it's not exactly free), but they don't travel the full length of the Siq, so you will be walking regardless.

Tour stop 2 Treasury. The masterwork, also called Al Khazneh, when first seen through the narrow walls of the Siq is practically indescribable. Believed to be the tomb of a king, with the spoils still possibly buried inside. Check out the urn: gunshots show the efforts bandits made to get that coveted loot. Locals are still convinced it's filled with treasures… but archaeologists insist it's solid rock.

Tour stop 3 Roman/Nabataean Amphitheater. Providing majestic views of the many rock-cut tombs, this amphitheater looks Roman but has a distinctly Nabataean flair, being carved out of rock.

Tour stop 4 Street of Façades. Dozens of tombs in various stages of grandeur and dissolution.

Tour stop 5 Royal Tombs. Uneishu, Urn, Silk, Corinthian, and Palace tombs, all competing with one another for beauty in glorifying the lives of several unknown persons.

Tour stop 6 Colonnaded Street. Inscription here shows the street was restored in 114 CE in honor of Emperor Trajan. The 363 CE earthquake toppled the glorious walkway. Along the way, you'll see the Temple of the Winged Lions, Byzantine Church, Temple of Dushares, and the Triple Arched Gate.

Tour stop 7 Great Temple. "Mabruk" to Brown University (plaques show the honors) for restoring this massive structure.

Tour stop 8 Qasr al-Bint, aka Temple of Dushares. Dushara was the name of the principal Nabataean god. This is the building with the largest facade but, unlike many

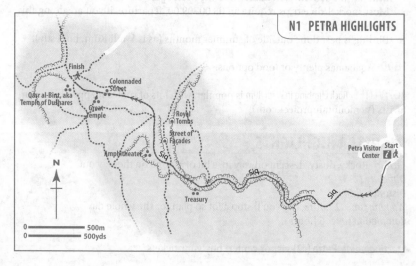

of its neighbors, was *not* carved from mountains. Rather, it was constructed from stone, leading archaeologists to the conclusion that it may be the most important temple in Petra.

Ending point Petra visitor center.

TIPS
★ Arrive early. Site opens at 06.00 and you want to be the first to the Treasury.
★ You can skip the "free" horses.
★ Tacking on a hike (see *N2: Petra's Best Hikes* below) will add an additional 2 hours, unless you hoof it.
★ If you only have one day total, we recommend you add a hike, but it'll be an exhausting day.

FOOD Limited food options in the park itself. Plan to carry snacks.

ACTIVITIES **Petra by Night** is another way to enter: at dark to candlelight. **Little Petra** is 9km north of Wadi Musa.

N2 PETRA'S BEST HIKES

Terrain Dusty, some broken paths along the hike, the al-Khubtha trail involves easy scrambling, lots of stairs on the others, steep elevation changes
Difficulty (1–5) 4, if doing all of them
Distance 20km
Walking/completion time 6–8 hours, highly dependent on your speed

Starting point Walk from the **Petra (#2)** visitor center through the Siq to the Treasury.

Tour stop 1 <u>Jabal al-Khubtha</u> (2–3 hours). This is the famed Indiana Jones view of the Treasury, and it's a more-than-worthwhile hike. Start at the Treasury and take in the majestic building first from ground level. Then, continue to the back side of the Royal Tombs. Follow the signs that take you to the green trail, and look for directional arrows leading you to a tea shop. There's a man (sometimes sleeping) perched precariously over the best viewing platform, but there are good views before and after him too. Once there, you'll get a spectacular view of the Treasury from above. Bonus: very few travelers make this hike.

Tour stop 2 <u>High Place of Sacrifice</u> (1–3 hours). Eight hundred steps to the top! Beautiful steps, beautiful scenery. The rewarding view makes this worthwhile. The actual "high place" requires a bit of imagination, but the altar where animals (and maybe humans? children?) were sacrificed is easy to recognize. Look around – many of the mountaintops have sacrificial altars like this one. Once you finish, you can turn back around for an easier descent, or continue on towards Qasr al-Bint where you'll pass a variety of interesting carvings and monuments, including the Lion Fountain, Garden Triclinium, Roman Soldier's Tomb, the Renaissance Tomb, and an excavation site called as-Zantur.

Tour stop 3 <u>Ad-Deir, aka the Monastery</u> (2 hours). Another 800-step, 4km uphill trail at the end of the Siq leads to this masterful temple, the largest on the site at 40m wide, and

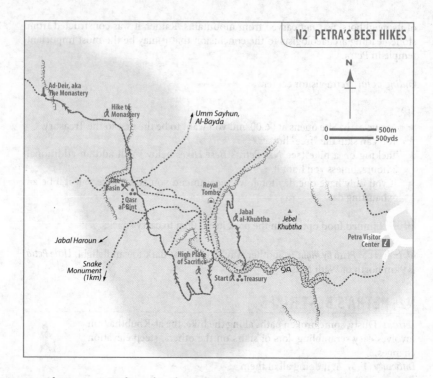

a worthy venture. Dedicated to the god Obodos, it's called the Deir ("Monastery"). Walk a bit further to the viewpoint from opposite the Monastery for a great long-distance shot.

Ending point Walk back to the entrance, another 6km/1½–2 hours from the farthest point at the Monastery.

TIPS

★ Each hike takes about 2 hours, though the official site (**w** visitpetra.jo) recommends longer.

★ Don't forget the walk between the entrance and Treasury is 30–40 minutes one-way.

★ The hikes can be done in any order.

★ There are a few carvings along the way, so be sure to carry your Petra map to spot the various sites.

★ There are other hikes to choose from: Jabal Haroun, Snake Monument, and Al-Beidha, along with some unstructured options that allow you to enter Petra without traversing the Siq. You'll likely need a guide; inquire at the visitor center.

FOOD One restaurant – the Basin.

N3 PETRA AND WADI MUSA

Terrain Hilly, plus hikes in Petra
Difficulty (1–5) 4, including the hike to *Little Petra*
Distance 13km
Walking time 6–8 hours
Completion time 3 days

Note You will need to coordinate *Petra by Night* and *Petra Kitchen (#84)* in advance.

Starting point Wadi Musa.

Day 1
★ *Tour stop 1 Petra by Night*. Try to arrive by mid-afternoon and confirm a tour of the same night to visit Petra by moonlight and candles. The official guided tour starts at the Petra visitor center at 20.30 and ends with a ceremony at the Treasury at 22.30. Operates Monday, Wednesday, and Thursday, canceled for rain; 17 JD for ages 10+.
   Alternative option If it's not taking place today, swap places with Petra Kitchen and add *N1: Petra Highlights* (above) to the afternoon.

Day 2
★ *Tour stop 2 Petra (#2)*. Get a big breakfast at your hotel and head out early. If you haven't already, take in the sites in *N1: Petra Highlights*. Plan on doing two hikes from *N2: Petra's Best Hikes* (above) today: the Ad-Deir, aka the Monastery (N2) and the High Place of Sacrifice (N2) (if you are up for it). Once finished, turn back and drive to…
★ *Tour stop 3 Little Petra*.
   Alternative option If you are driving north out of Wadi Musa, you can drive here on your way out of town.
★ *Tour stop 4 Petra Kitchen (#84)*: on main street near entrance to Petra, a cooking class where you make and eat a delicious Jordanian dinner (35 JD, 18.00–21.00, may start later in summer).

Day 3 Plan to arrive at the Petra gates at 06.00, when they open. Walk briskly down to the Treasury to get unobstructed views and photos of Petra's most famous building. Then do another hike from *N2: Petra's Best Hikes* – we recommend *Jabal al-Khubtha*. You should still have time to make breakfast at your hotel.

Ending point Wadi Musa.

TIPS
★ **Petra Kitchen (#84)** and *Petra by Night* both occur at the same time, so you will need to plan at least two nights in Wadi Musa in order to experience both.
★ *Petra by Night* only operates three nights a week. Plan accordingly!
★ You can drive to *Little Petra* in lieu of walking; 18km round-trip.

FOOD **Petra Kitchen (#84)** is a dinner. There are plenty of other restaurants, including one in the park, but packing lunch is a good idea, as is gorging on your hotel's breakfast buffet before heading out.

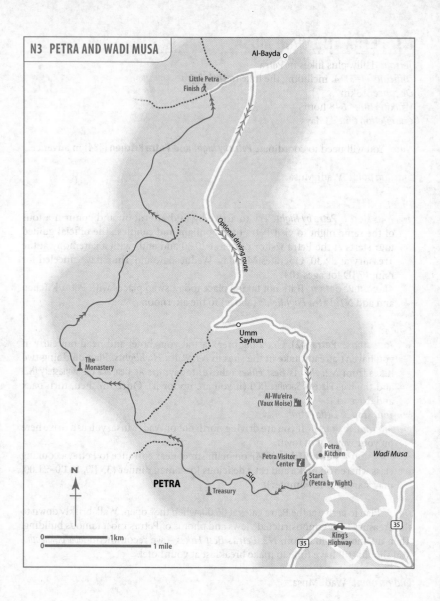

01 KING'S HIGHWAY

Distance 310km
Driving time 6 hours
Completion time 5 days, plus Petra

For more information on this elective, see **King's Highway (#31)**.

Starting point Begin your trip by exploring Petra for 2–3 days.

Tour stop 1 **Petra (#2)**.

Tour stop 2 *Shobak*.

Tour stop 3 **Dana Biosphere Reserve (#21)**.

At site **Feynan Ecolodge (#86)** – note that you may need to park your car in town and arrange separate transportation with the guesthouse.

At site Nawatef Camp: Bedouin eco-tourism camp in Dana reserve.

At site Khirbet Feynan. Copper mining has been going on here for thousands of years, but the Romans expanded the practice to create a huge operation.

Tour stop 4 Wadi al-Hassa. A 40km-long river north of Petra, with walks and year-round water flow.

Optional tour stop *Khirbet et-Tannur*: a Nabataean sanctuary and temple dedicated to a fertility goddess, located in Jebel Tannur.

Optional tour stop *Mu'tah*: Muhammad fought (and lost to) the Eastern Roman Empire. Can visit gravesites to Muhammad's companions.

Tour stop 5 **Karak (#49)**.

At site Karak Town: shrines to several of Muhammad's followers in and around Karak Castle.

Tour stop 6 Viewpoints of **Wadi Mujib (#23)**. On Highway 35, has a number of good viewpoint turnoffs right around the Mujib Dam, about 45km north of Karak. One is called the Grand Canyon viewpoint (there are usually cafés that advertise the stop) and another 13km further north called the Mujib Valley Panorama.

Optional tour stop Qasr Bashir. Small Roman fort an hour south of Amman.

Tour stop 7 **Umm ar-Rasas (#81)**.

Tour stop 8 **Madaba (#19)**.

Optional tour stop *Wadi Jadid*: home to Bronze Age dolmens (burial stones).

Ending point To Amman: 38km/45 minutes; to Suweimeh: 38km/45 minutes.

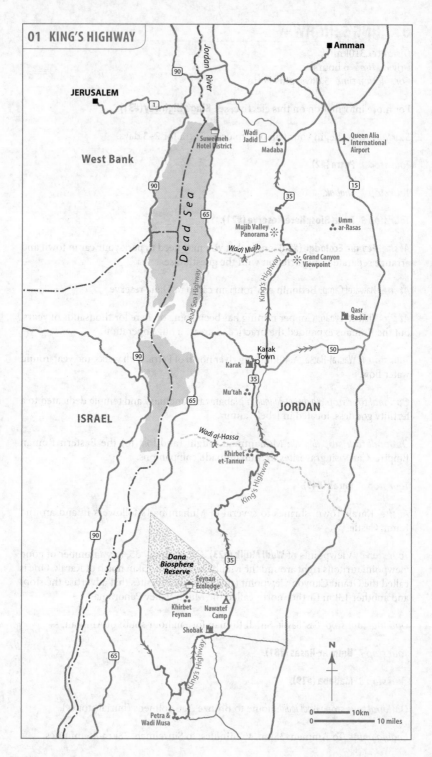

Amman

Jordan River

JERUSALEM

90

1

West Bank

Suweimeh
Hotel District

Wadi
Jadid

Madaba

Queen Alia
International
Airport

90

65

Dead Sea

Dead Sea Highway

15

35

Mujib Valley
Panorama

Wadi Mujib

Grand Canyon
Viewpoint

Umm
ar-Rasas

King's Highway

Qasr
Bashir

90

65

Karak
Town

Karak

35

Mu'tah

50

ISRAEL

JORDAN

Wadi al-Hassa

Khirbet
et-Tannur

King's Highway

Dana
Biosphere
Reserve

Feynan
Ecolodge

35

90

Khirbet
Feynan

Nawatef
Camp

Shobak

King's Highway

65

90

N

Petra &
Wadi Musa

King's Highway

0   10km
0   10 miles

TIPS

★ This itinerary does not take into account the time required to explore Petra. We recommend an additional 2–3 days.

★ You can skip Qasr Bashir, which will allow you to continue on Highway 35 towards Umm ar-Rasas, saving about 45 minutes. (It generally tends to be faster to detour east towards Highway 15, the Desert Highway.)

★ The ancient highway included Aqaba, Amman, Jerash, and sites in Syria, though the physical highway has long since worn away. The King's Highway of today ends in Madaba, though Highway 35 continues to Amman and Jerash and further north under differing names.

FOOD Hotels are the best spot for food in these areas – start with a giant breakfast in Petra. You may want some picnic food, but you'll find restaurants near all the major sites.

STAYS There are good places to stay in Petra, Dana, Madaba, and Ma'in. Everywhere else is a bit of a struggle, though there are options. Two of our electives are places to stay in Dana: **Feynan Ecolodge (#86)** and Nawatef Camp.

P1 DEAD SEA HIGHWAY

Distance 120km
Driving time 2¼ hours
Completion time 1 day

Starting point From Wadi Rum: 240km/3 hours; from Aqaba: 180km/2 hours; from Petra: 95km/1½ hours.

Dead Sea Highway: the alternative north–south route (Highway 65) from King's Highway affords its own picturesque look at this country, passing some lesser-known sites all along the country's western border, including – as the name implies – the Dead Sea.

Tour stop 1 Fifa Nature Reserve. Some 23km^2 that highlight salt and tropical plant species in west Jordan, with an elevation as low as –420m.

Tour stop 2 **Lot's Cave**.

At site Lowest Point on Earth Museum.

Tour stop 3 Zikra Initiative. Offering local tours of the Dead Sea area, cooking classes, and guided hikes, all in support of the Bedouin community. Based in Gawr al-Mazraah.

Tour stop 4 **Wadi Mujib and Mujib Biosphere Reserve (#23)**.

Tour stop 5 **Hammamat Ma'in Hot Springs**.

Optional tour stop Dead Sea Panorama Complex: great view from a high-up plateau overlooking the sea.

Tour stop 6 **Dead Sea (#3)**.

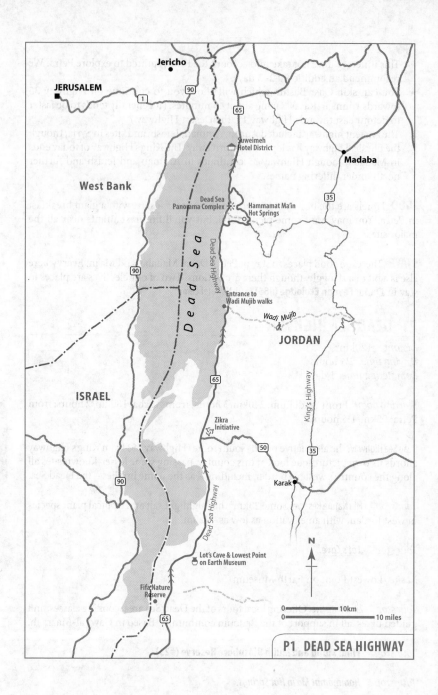

Tour stop 7 **Suweimeh Spa Hotels**.

Ending point Ideally Suweimeh, an Anchor City; to Amman: 50km/50 minutes; to Aqaba: 280km/3½ hours.

TIPS

★ For the full Dead Sea Highway experience, drive north from Aqaba on Route 65. Note: it's very empty, so make sure you have a full tank, lots of water, and pack a lunch.

★ If coming from Petra, you can take a mountainous route to the Dead Sea Highway instead of the more traditional King's Highway path (preferred).

★ If you drive from Aqaba, you will see a lot more of the Desert Highway – 180km more to be exact.

★ Given the Dead Sea doesn't make an appearance until several hours from Aqaba, the road is also called the Jordan Valley Highway.

★ Alternative plan: stay the night (or a few nights) in **Feynan Ecolodge (#86)**, and then start this itinerary.

★ The Mujib Reserve is only open certain months of the year.

FOOD You'll want to eat a big breakfast and take some snacks along the way. There's plenty of food in each hotel once you arrive in Suweimeh.

P2 CHRISTIAN JORDAN

Distance 110km
Driving time 2½ hours
Completion time 1 day

Starting point From Jerusalem: 45km/40 minutes to border, 1–1½ hours at border crossing, then 16km/20 minutes to site; from Amman: 55km/50 minutes; from Suweimeh: 22km/25 minutes.

Tour stop 1 **Bethany-Beyond-the-Jordan (#41)**.

Tour stop 2 **Mount Nebo (#24)**.

Tour stop 3 **Madaba and the Madaba Map (#19)**.

At site Church of the Beheading of John the Baptist. This Madaba church, near the Madaba Map, is interesting in its own right for being built atop a functioning Moabite well. Great views from the bell tower.

Tour stop 4 **Mukawir**.

Note The road to Mukawir is challenging, so times are much slower than you might think.

Ending point Ideally Suweimeh, an Anchor City, where you can soak again in the **Dead Sea (#3)**; to Amman: 55km/1 hour; to Aqaba: 275km/3¼ hours; to Jerusalem: 26km/30 minutes to border, 1–1½ hours at border crossing, then 45km/40 minutes to Jerusalem.

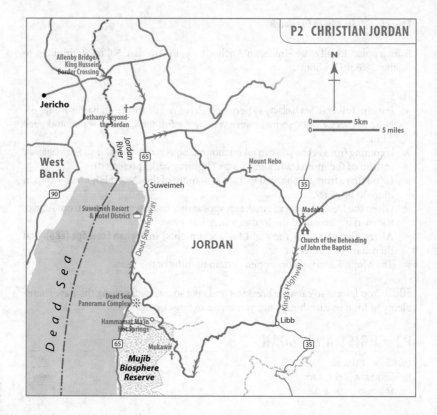

TIPS

★ This tour can be done in either direction.

★ Afternoon is best for Nebo – or doing the drive down the cliff face from Mukawir to Ma'in – as the sunset is stunning. There are a few places to pull over for views or a drink.

★ The Jordan Pass covers most of these sites, in case you bought one for Petra.

★ Border crossing times are approximates – arrive early, don't return late.

FOOD Eat breakfast in your hotel. You'll pass through a few towns along the way which will have snack and lunch options.

Q1 ANCIENT AMMAN

Terrain Uphill/steep incline if you're walking to/from the Citadel, otherwise it's flat
Difficulty (1–5) 3
Distance 6km, one-way
Walking time 1½ hours
Completion time 4 hours

Starting point Taxi to the Citadel.

Tour stop 1 Amman Citadel. Check out **Ancient Amman (#37)** for more information about the history of this multilayered site. Formerly the site of ancient Rabbath Ammon, this area, called Jabal al-Qal'a (Citadel Hill), is the highest hill in the city, and now holds a collection of impressive ruins from Roman, Byzantine, and Umayyad times. Don't miss the Umayyad Palace, the Temple of Hercules, and a Byzantine church.

Tour stop 2 **Jordan Archaeological Museum**. Located at the site of the Citadel, this museum contains artifacts from all over Jordan dating from the first settlers up to the 15th century.

Tour stop 3 Roman Theater (Hashemite Plaza). Built in the 2nd century, this Roman-era theater could seat 6,000 visitors and has been restored to beautiful glory, and its location right in the downtown heart of Amman makes it even more appealing.

Tour stop 4 Roman Odeon (Hashemite Plaza). A smaller version of the Roman Theater, located just adjacent, with a seating capacity of 500.

Tour stop 5 Roman Nymphaeum. Also built in the 2nd century, this public fountain is not completely restored, but it provides an interesting contrast to the encroaching city buildings from the hilltop above. From its grand fountain once flowed a natural spring, now wholly underground.

Ending point Rainbow Street (Q2), for food or drinks.

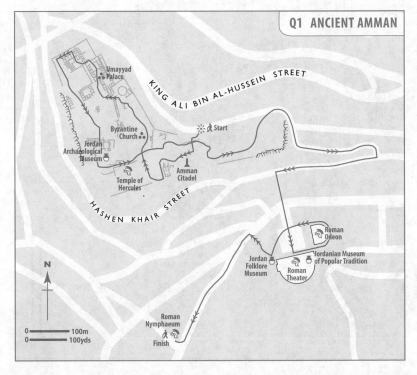

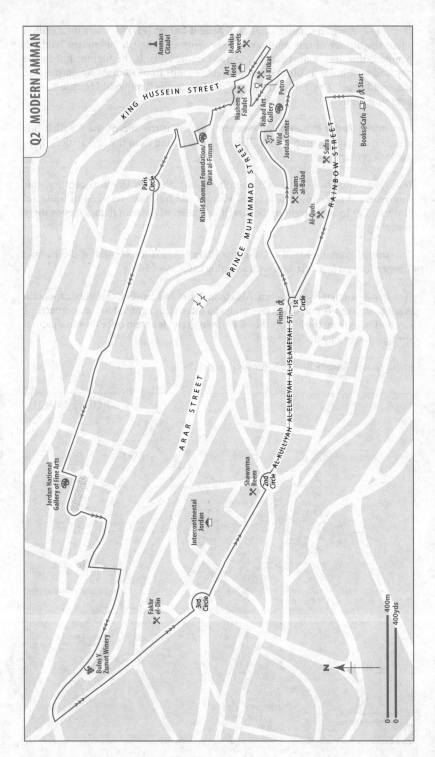

Amman Citadel

Habiba Sweets

Art Hotel

Al-Kitkat

KING HUSSEIN STREET

Hashem Falafel

Nabad Art Gallery

Petro

Wild

Jordan Center

Shams al-Balad

Sufra

Al-Quds

RAINBOW STREET

Books@Cafe

Start

Khalid Shoman Foundation/ Darat al-Funun

Paris Circle

PRINCE MUHAMMAD STREET

Finish

1st Circle

AL-KULLIYAH AL-ELMEYAH AL-ISLAMEYAH ST.

ARAR STREET

Jordan National Gallery of Fine Arts

Shawarma Reem

2nd Circle

Intercontinental Jordan

3rd Circle

Fakhr el-Din

Bulos / Zumot Winery

N

0   400m
0   400yds

TIPS

★ Taxiing to the top of the Citadel hill is recommended unless you really want the exercise (it's very steep).

★ The Citadel itself has a number of interesting ruins atop, so you'll be spending the majority of your time there.

★ If you're in a hurry, you can combine this itinerary with *Q2: Modern Amman* (below).

★ Admission to the Citadel is included in the Jordan Pass.

★ The Jordan Folklore Museum (Q3) and the Jordan Museum of Popular Traditions (Q3) are both located in the Roman Theater plaza. You can visit these now, particularly if you combine with *Q2: Modern Amman*.

★ You can taxi to the *Jordan Museum (Q3)* and make things even easier (it's a 1km walk).

FOOD Al-Quds Falafel (Q2) is located near the *Jordan Museum (Q3)* and provides a great stopping point for refueling.

Q2 MODERN AMMAN

Terrain A bit hilly, but manageable
Difficulty (1–5) 2
Distance 8km
Walking time 2 hours
Completion time 8 hours

We have two **Modern Amman (#36)** walking tours, this one focusing on food, cafés, art, and wine.

Starting point If connecting from *Q1: Ancient Amman* (above), we start you on Rainbow Street at Books@Cafe.

Tour stop 1 Books@Cafe. Coffeeshop in downtown Amman with an extensive menu and a place to buy and read a wide variety of books.

Tour stop 2 Rainbow Street. Amman's hippest, most pedestrian-friendly street offers a variety of restaurants, bars, shops, hostels, and hotels.

Tour stop 3 Falafel and sweets. You can't come to Jordan without eating falafel! Try the famous Al-Quds Falafel on Rainbow Street or Hashem Falafel, en route to Darat al-Funun. Then cross the street and take in knafeh, the beloved phyllo dessert, at Habiba Sweets.

Tour stop 4 **Wild Jordan Center**.

Tour stop 5 Nabad Art Gallery. A contemporary art gallery.

Tour stop 6 Khalid Shoman Foundation/Darat al-Funun. A contemporary art gallery, in a glorious complex, dedicated to Arab art. Arab artists take residencies and fellowships here, while visitors view exhibitions and listen to talks (w daratalfunun.org).

Tour stop 7 Jordan National Gallery of Fine Arts. More than 3,000 works from regional and international artists, mostly from the developing world, located in downtown Amman.

Tour stop 8 Bulos Y Zumot Winery. A Jordanian winery (!), this group is the first Jordanian producer to be recognized in the *1000 Wines of the World Guide*, with several medals given to its St. George brand.

Ending point Dinner. Maybe Fakhr el-Din for something a bit more upscale?

TIPS

★ This tour can be combined with *Q1: Ancient Amman* (above) and/or *Q3: Cultural Amman* (below).

★ Skip the walking portion at the end and just cab to Bulos Y Zumot and/or the restaurant of your choice. You'll save about 45 minutes of walking time.

FOOD Lots of options: Hashem Falafel (en route between Grand Husseini and Darat al Funun), Fakhr el-Din, Shams al-Balad, and Al-Kitkat are all excellent options.

DRINK Petro has a dedicated fan base.

STAY Art Hotel and Intercontinental Jordan have both received acclaim.

Q3 CULTURAL AMMAN

Terrain Mostly flat, except ascent to Abu Darwish
Difficulty (1–5) 2
Distance 9km
Walking time 2¼ hours
Completion time 8 hours

This **Modern Amman (#36)** walking tour focuses on religion, markets, cooking, customs, and tradition.

Starting point Roman Theater Plaza.

Tour stop 1 Jordan Folklore Museum. Opposite the Popular Traditions Museum is this museum showcasing the clothing, music, and culture of Jordanians.

Tour stop 2 Jordan Museum of Popular Traditions. Don't skip this museum at the Roman amphitheater in Amman, with lots of great exhibits on the Jordanian people.

Tour stop 3 Abu Darwish Mosque. A standout, with its layered, almost LEGO black-and-white look. A Circassian building.

Optional tour stop Jordan Museum. Premiere Jordanian museum showcasing the country's history and culture. Now the largest in the country since its opening in 2005, the site covers some 1.5 million years of history. Contains artifacts from the *Ain Ghazal (Q4)* site found in northeast Amman (little of the site is left, nor is it set up for visitors) which has several artifacts from a Neolithic (c8000-year-old) community.

Tour stop 4 Grand Husseini Mosque. Built in 1924 atop a 7th-century mosque, this pink-and-white Ottoman-era building has four photo-worthy minarets.

Tour stop 5 Al-Pasha Turkish Bath. Amman has a number of Turkish baths (hammams) offering scrubs and soaks with separate entry for men and women. Many hotels offer similar spa experiences, but Al-Pasha is probably the most famous.

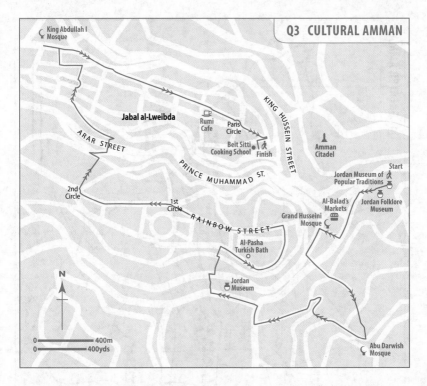

King Abdullah I Mosque

Jabal al-Lweibda

ARAR STREET

Rumi Cafe

Paris Circle

Beit Sitti Cooking School

Finish

KING HUSSEIN STREET

Amman Citadel

Start

Jordan Museum of Popular Traditions

2nd Circle

1st Circle

PRINCE MUHAMMAD ST.

RAINBOW STREET

Al-Balad's Markets

Jordan Folklore Museum

Grand Husseini Mosque

Al-Pasha Turkish Bath

Jordan Museum

N

0 ——— 400m
0 ——— 400yds

Abu Darwish Mosque

Tour stop 6 Al-Balad's markets. An old/new neighborhood with lots of nice places you can stop, including the Gold Market, the Sugar Market, spices, nut roasters, and lots of little shops promoting the tradecraft that families have been practicing for generations.

Tour stop 7 *King Abdullah I Mosque*. A turquoise-domed mosque that can manage 10,000 visitors, and allows non-Muslims entry.

Tour stop 8 Paris Circle and cooking school. Part of Jabal al-Lweibda, a contemporary art and just plain contemporary neighborhood. Visitors love Rumi Cafe and ***Beit Sitti*** cooking school, which starts classes in the late afternoon and evening to coincide with dinner.

Ending point Hotel, or dinner if you're not partaking in ***Beit Sitti***.

TIPS
★ There are several Hammams. If you're running short on time, or Al-Pasha is full, there are plenty of other city hammams to choose from. With a car, you can get to Alf Layla wa Layla, the other famous hammam in Amman.
★ ***Beit Sitti*** cooking school has only periodic classes, which can be found on its website (w beitsitti.com), but it also has a restaurant.
★ The walking portion is about 1½ hours, but doing both a Turkish bath and the cooking school will take up most of your day.
★ If you taxi to King Abdullah mosque, and then return to Beit Sitti by taxi, you'll shave off about 4km/1 hour walking.
★ If you cab to Abu Darwish, you'll save 1.5km/40 minutes walking.

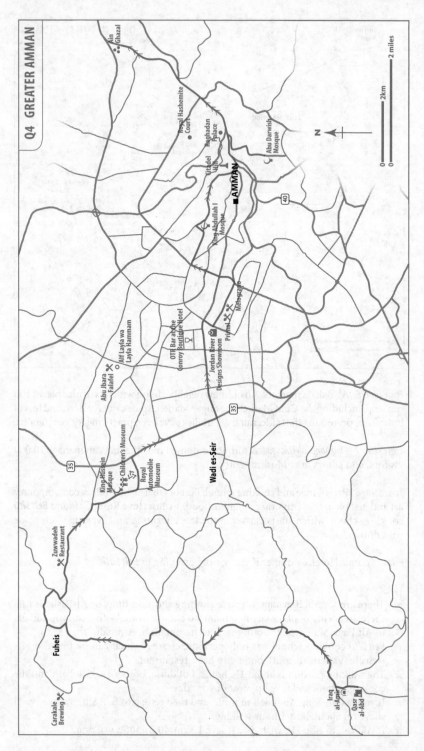

N

0   2km
0   2 miles

Ain Ghazal

Royal Hashemite Court

Raghadan Palace

Abu Darwish Mosque

Citadel Hill

■ AMMAN

King Abdullah I Mosque

40

Mehyar

Prime

Jordan River Designs Showroom

OTI Bar at the Conroy Boutique Hotel

Alf Layla wa Layla Hammam

Abu Jbara Falafel

Children's Museum

King Hussein Mosque

Royal Automobile Museum

35

Wadi es-Seir

35

Zuwwadeh Restaurant

Fuheis

Carakale Brewing

Iraq al-Amir

Qasr al-Abd

FOOD *Beit Sitti* is a restaurant and cooking school. Otherwise, see *Q2: Modern Amman* (above) for food options.

Q4 GREATER AMMAN

Distance 70km
Driving time 1½ hours
Completion time 2 days

Note Includes several sites referenced in **Modern Amman (#36)**.

Starting point From Amman Citadel: 23km/40 minutes.

Tour stop 1 **_Qasr al-Abd_**. Iraq al-Amir is nearby, with a series of caves from the Roman era.

Tour stop 2 Fuheis, on the outskirts of Amman, is a foodie destination with several renowned restaurants including Carakale Brewing and Zuwwadeh.

Tour stop 3 King Hussein Mosque, Dabouq. The largest mosque in Jordan, and created in the Umayyad style.

Tour stop 4 Children's Museum of Jordan. For children of all ages, this museum has activities themed from flight, space, water conservation, the human body, and archaeological digs (w cmj.jo).

Tour stop 5 Royal Automobile Museum. Amman's famed car museum, including more than 100 years of imported cars.

Tour stop 6 Jordan River Designs Showroom. Shop handicrafts for a good cause supporting opportunities for Jordanian youth.

Optional tour stops If you haven't completed *Q3: Cultural Amman* (above), which includes the *King Abdullah I Mosque (Q3)* and the Abu Darwish Mosque (Q3), then add them in here.

Optional tour stop Jordan's Royal Guards. Visit the Circassian guards of Jordan's King at the Raghadan Palace in the Royal Hashemite Court.

Optional tour stop Ain Ghazal. Unlikely you'll be able to enter but, at 2km from Queen Alia Airport, this is one of the earliest farming villages of the area, dating to more than 10,000 years ago.

Ending point To Amman Citadel: 8km/15 minutes.

TIPS
★ Traffic in Amman can dramatically alter travel times.
★ Mosques require strict dress codes, and you still may not be allowed in.

FOOD See Fuheis (Stop 2), or try Primal or Melograno near the Jordan River Designs Showroom.

DRINK OTR in the Conroy Boutique Hotel has a speakeasy vibe.

ACTIVITIES Visit one of Amman's hammam's. Alf Layla wa Layla is a popular option.

R1 EASTERN DESERT

Distance 575km (with Burqu) or 275km (without)
Driving time 7½ hours or 4 hours, respectively
Completion time 3 days

Starting point From Amman: 70km/1 hour; from Suweimeh: 135km/2 hours.

Tour stop 1 **Umm el-Jimal**.

Optional tour stop Burqu (+300km/3½ hours total). Like **Feynan Ecolodge (#86)** in Dana, this is an environmentally friendly lodge from which to explore another (future) nature reserve and birding area in Jordan's far eastern desert. Qasr Burqu (W1) on site.

Tour stop 2 **Qasr Azraq**.

Tour stop 3 **Azraq Wetlands (#55)**.

Tour stop 4 Wadi al-Dahik. Hiking close to the Saudi border through the "White Desert."

Tour stop 5 **Shaumari** wildlife reserve.

Tour stop 6 **Qasr Amra (#20)**, most famous of the Desert Palaces.

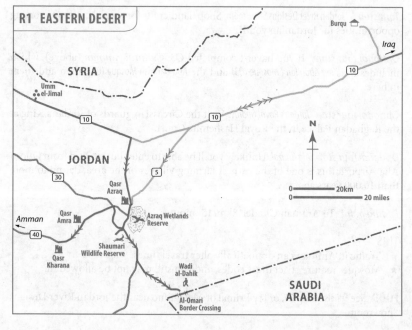

Tour stop 7 **Qasr Kharana**.

Ending point To Amman: 70km/1 hour; to Suweimeh: 105km/1½ hours.

TIPS

★ This is the desert – be prepared with tires that won't melt, sunscreen, and plenty of water if you're going anytime other than winter.

★ There are plenty of other castles to view. Check out *W1: Umayyad Castles* for more ideas.

★ Go to **w** rscn.org.jo for maps of this remote region.

★ If you make the drive to Burqu, plan to stay the night in the ecolodge there.

FOOD Pack a lunch.

S1 NORTH JORDAN

Distance 120km
Driving time 3 hours
Completion time 2 days

Starting point From Amman: 50km/50 minutes; from Suweimeh: 90km/1½ hours.

Tour stop 1 **Jerash (#14)**.

Tour stop 2 **Umm Qais (#45)**.

Tour stop 3 Yarmouk Forest. This park across from Umm Qais has a number of moderate hikes around its forests and lakes. Start at the visitor center.

Tour stop 4 Abila, aka Raphana. A site that dates to the Bronze Age, Abila has evidence of buildings from Greek, Roman, Byzantine, and Muslim eras, with churches, temples, theaters, baths, and renowned megalithic columns that were possibly repurposed into a basilica.

Tour stop 5 Irbid Museum of Jordanian Heritage (🕐 08.00–17.00 Sunday–Thursday). Located at Yarmouk University, this museum details Jordan's history, from the hunter-gatherer periods through the Islamic times.

Ending point To Amman: 85km/1½ hours; to Suweimeh: 125km/2 hours.

TIPS

★ Roads in Jordan can become plagued with traffic in/around cities.

★ Travel times are very approximate.

★ Some "highways" may have inexplicable speed bumps or other physical barriers to slow you down.

★ You can go to Irbid first (it's on the way), but Umm Qais is the more important site.

FOOD Jerash and Irbid have plenty of food options.

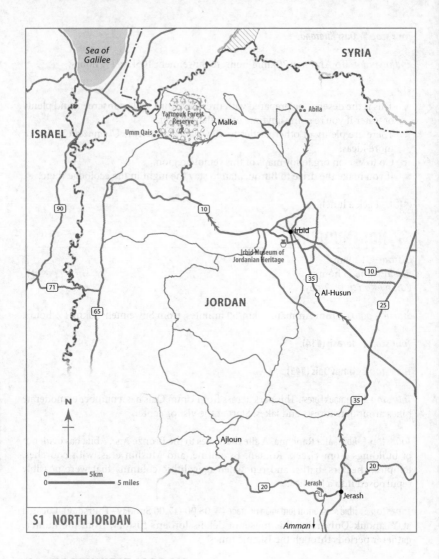

Sea of Galilee

SYRIA

Yarmouk Forest Reserve

Malka

Abila

Umm Qais

ISRAEL

Irbid

Irbid Museum of Jordanian Heritage

90

10

10

71

65

JORDAN

Al-Husun

35

25

N

35

Ajloun

20

Jerash

Jerash

20

Amman ↓

0 — 5km
0 — 5 miles

S1 NORTH JORDAN

S2 NORTHWEST JORDAN

Distance 140km
Driving time 3¼ hours
Completion time 2 days

Starting point From Amman: 65km/1¼ hours; from Suweimeh: 100km/1¾ hours.

Tour stop 1 <u>Dibeen Forest</u>. This reserve covers a bit over 8km² of forested mountains known for their Aleppo pine, the southernmost limits of this tree.

Tour stop 2 **Ajloun Fortress (#76)**.

Tour stop 3 **Ajloun Forest (#57)**.

At site **_Al-Ayoun Trail_** (12km, strenuous).

Tour stop 4 **_Pella_**.

Optional tour stop **_Damiya Dolmen Field_**: hundreds of megalithic blocks cut from sandstone were arranged as burial tombs for Bronze Age (3600–3000 BCE) inhabitants of this Jordan Valley site. The dolmens stand up to 1m tall and up to 7m long.

Tour stop 5 **_As-Salt_**.

Ending point To Amman: 28km/45 minutes; to Suweimeh: 45km/45 minutes.

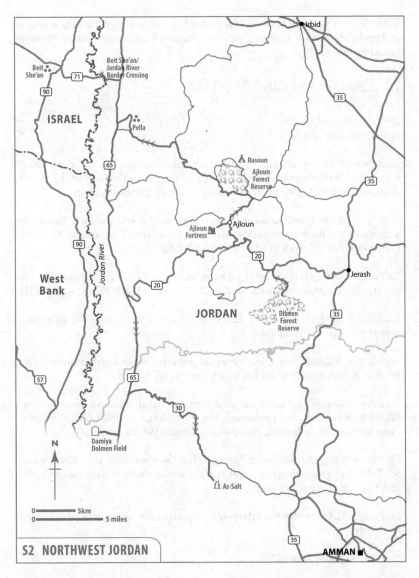

★ Roads in Jordan can become plagued with traffic in/around cities.
★ Travel times are very approximate.
★ Some "highways" may have inexplicable speed bumps or other physical barriers to slow you down.

FOOD Each of the small towns you'll encounter will have basic food options, though not necessarily a solid tourism industry – so you may want to pack a lunch.

STAY A popular camping option at Ajloun Forest Reserve is Rasoun Camping, with various adventure activities.

ACTIVITIES If you're in town in March/April, a visit to any of the nature reserves will provide you with sweeping views of glorious blossoming Jordanian Wildflowers, including the Black Iris.

T1 SINAI ON THE GULF OF AQABA

Distance 450km
Driving time 6½ hours
Completion time 7 days

Security note Do not attempt this itinerary unless deemed safe by your country's authorities. Terrorism incidents have been on the rise in the Sinai in the past few years, so check with your foreign ministry before attempting this trip.

Note You will likely not be able to drive this yourself unless you fly to Sharm, rent a car there, and do the tour backwards. There are no rental car companies in Taba. Otherwise, you will need to take buses and/or hire a driver.

Tour stop 1 Taba. This is the overland entry to the Sinai from Israel/Eilat where you can stay in luxe properties for a fraction of the costs of **Eilat (#78)** and **Aqaba (#43)**.

Tour stop 2 Pharaoh's Island Citadel. This once Crusader, then Ayyubid castle can be visited on a side trip from Taba.

Tour stop 3 Coloured Canyon. Near Nuweiba are these multi-hued sandstone rocks running approximately 800m long, with some as tall as 30m.

Tour stop 4 Nuweiba Beach Camps. Between Taba and Dahab is this no-longer-a-resort-town which features a few restaurants, but mostly beach camps, which allow you to sleep outdoors on little more than a straw mattress ($8–15 per person).

Optional activity Drive through Wadi Nasb. The 4x4 route from the coastal Sinai to St. Catherine's gets high marks, though make sure to check with competent authorities to ensure the passage is safe.

Tour stop 5 **St. Catherine's Monastery (#22)**, organized through your hotel in Nuweiba or Dahab.

Tour stop 6 **Mount Sinai (#15)**.

Tour stop 7 <u>St. Catherine's Mount</u>. The highest point in Egypt at 2,629m, 4 miles/5.5km south of St. Catherine's Monastery. Overnights are common, but can be achieved in a day.

Tour stop 8 **Red Sea (#10)**.

Tour stop 9 **Dahab (#54)**. You have your pick – from nice hotels to bamboo huts for a few dollars.

Optional tour stop *Blue Hole*: popular dive site near Dahab in the Sinai with the unfortunate moniker (whether true or not) of "deadliest dive site in the world." Divers get confused, likely from a combination of nitrogen narcosis, which can impair judgment, having only one oxygen tank,

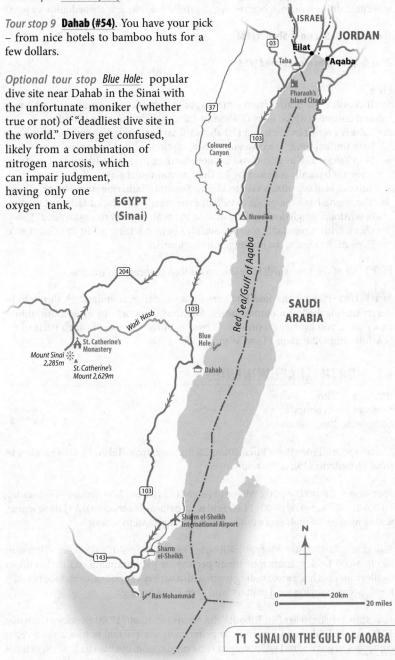

T1 SINAI ON THE GULF OF AQABA

and going beyond the 30m limit ("the arch" which beckons divers is much deeper, but appears closer). At any rate, the fish and coral are the real attraction here and can be seen aplenty right from the shore.

Optional tour stop *The Bedouin Way*: offering day safaris from Dahab in the Sinai and mountain dinners of goat, beef, or veg (**f** thebedouinway; **w** thebedouinway.com).

Tour stop 10 **Sharm el-Sheikh (#88)**.

Tour stop 11 **Ras Mohammad (#53)**.

TIPS
★ If crossing the border from Israel to get to Taba, factor in an hour for borders and customs (which doesn't occur in Taba itself, but further inland).
★ Taba is a resort location, but Dahab and Sharm are the better options. Still, if you have limited time, Taba is a good, cheap option for Red Sea access.
★ Skip Taba and Nuweiba if you are not planning to stay in either of those places. They are basically noteworthy for their accommodations.
★ You can also organize a visit to Mount Sinai/St. Catherine from Sharm.
★ The region has been prone to violent extremists who attack tourists: at the time of writing, though doable, a trip driving in the Sinai is not recommended. Always check with a reputable touring outfitter before setting off in the desert solo. Repeat: the region can be dangerous for tourists.

FOOD All of the towns will have dining options that cater to tourists.

ACTIVITIES Pick up the ***Sinai Trail*** here for an exciting multiday trek through the desert among Bedouin communities. For those wanting an even more unique experience, you can also coordinate a two- or three-day trek through parts of the blissfully empty Sinai on a <u>Camel Safari</u>.

U1 NORTH ISRAEL WINERIES

Distance 175km
Driving time 3 hours
Completion time 2 days

Starting point From Rosh Pina: 20km/20 minutes; from Tel Aviv: 170km/2 hours; from Jerusalem: 215km/2½ hours.

Tour stop 1 <u>Dalton Winery (H1)</u>, Merom Hagalil (⊕ 10.00–17.00 Sunday–Wednesday, 10.00–21.00 Thursday, 10.00–14.00 Friday; **w** dalton-winery.com). A Galilee winery with a number of high-end brands, and a tasting room to sample.

Tour stop 2 <u>Galil Mountain Winery (H1)</u>, Kibbutz Yiron (⊕ 09.00–17.00 Sunday–Thursday, 09.00–14.00 Friday; tours four times per day; **w** galilmountain.co.il). This upper Galilee vineyard has a great tasting room with a variety of options, to include tastings, tours, accompanying food platters, and even blind tastings.

Tour stop 3 <u>Pelter Winery (I2)</u>, Kibbutz Ein Sivan (⊕ 10.00–17.00 Sunday–Thursday, 10.00–16.00 Friday and Saturday; **w** pelter.co.il). At 150,000 bottles a year, Pelter continues to grow – and not just in its wine production, but also its liquors, as it has

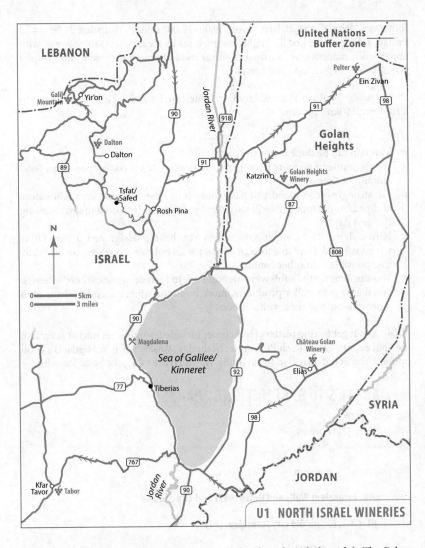

begun embracing spirits (eau du vie, gin, majhoul, and apple brandy). The Pelter wines are non-kosher and the Matar label is kosher. Great tasting room; 50 ILS will get you a sampling of wines and cheeses.

Tour stop 4 **Golan Heights Winery (#75)** (⏲ 08.30–17.30 Sunday–Thursday, 08.30–14.00 Friday; **w** golanwines.co.il/en).

Tour stop 5 <u>Château Golan Winery (l3)</u>, Eliad (⏲ 10.30–15.30 daily; **w** chateaugolan.com). A non-kosher winery where all the wines take a bit of new oak aging, from a few months to a year, no additional yeasts are added outside of the natural processes, and harvesting is done by hand. Production is about 75,000 bottles a year (small). Daniel Rogov gives this winery five stars, and the Touriga Nacional Reserve 2008 received 93 points from him. The Eliad Royal Reserve 2012 received 92 points from the Wine Advocate. Hugh Johnson says this is a two- to three-star winery.

Tour stop 6 Tabor Winery (G2), Kfar Tavor (09.00–17.00 Sunday–Thursday, 09.00–14.00 Friday; w taborwinery.co.il). Highly awarded for its great value Galilee wines, with upper-level competitions awarding its Shiraz and Cabernet Sauvignon, and a helpful visitor center to purchase and sample.

Ending point To Rosh Pina: 45km/35 minutes; to Tel Aviv: 115km/1½ hours; to Jerusalem: 150km/2 hours.

TIPS

★ This trip can be done in any order.

★ We recommend no more than three wineries in a day, if you're spending a good amount of time in each.

★ We strongly recommend you base yourself in Rosh Pina for the night before and/or after the tour (this will also afford you the ability to do more wine tasting the next day).

★ Hire a driver to be super safe, unless you have a designated driver. Don't wine-taste and drive in a foreign country – it's not safe anywhere, but it's really irresponsible in another country.

★ You can sign up for a full wine tour and ask to include some of these wineries. You'll also get smaller producers, more boutique wineries, and perhaps even more one-on-one time with vintners.

FOOD You'll get tasting platters (sometimes included, sometimes not) at several of the above spots. Eat in Rosh Pina or near Tiberias (Magdalena (G4) in Migdal is a good option). You could also plan to eat in the Syrian Druze village of Majdal Shams (I2).

U2 ISRAEL'S 10 BEST NATIONAL PARKS

Distance 850km
Driving time 11¼ hours
Completion time 9 days

Starting point Jerusalem.

Tour stop 1 **Jerusalem Walls and Gates (#47)** and *City of David*.

At site BUCKET! Site **Old City Jerusalem (#1)**.

Tour stop 2 **Ein Gedi (#50)**.

Tour stop 3 **Masada (#8)**.

En route BUCKET! Site **Dead Sea (#3)**.

Tour stop 4 **Avdat (#48)**.

Tour stop 5 **Makhtesh Ramon (#28)**.

Tour stop 6 **Caesarea (#25)**.

Tour stop 7 **Megiddo (#59)**.

Tour stop 8 **Tsipori (#56)**.

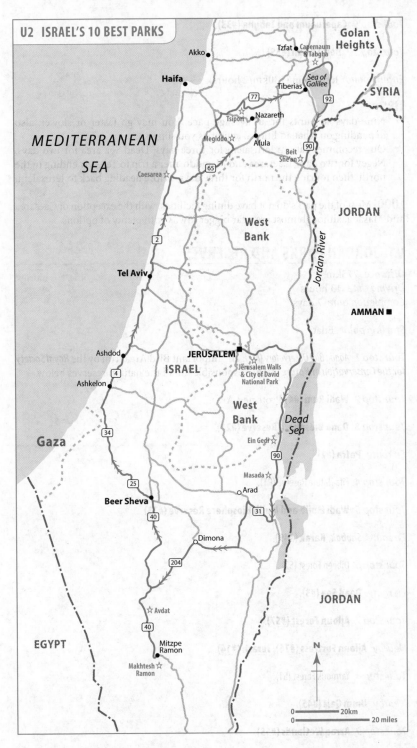

U2 ISRAEL'S 10 BEST PARKS

Golan Heights

Akko

Tzfat
Capernaum & Tabgha

Haifa

Sea of Galilee

Tiberias

SYRIA

92

77

Tsipori
Nazareth

Megiddo
Afula

Beit She'an

90

Caesarea

65

MEDITERRANEAN SEA

West Bank

JORDAN

2

Tel Aviv

AMMAN

Ashdod

JERUSALEM

ISRAEL

Jerusalem Walls & City of David National Park

4

Ashkelon

West Bank

Dead Sea

Gaza

34

Ein Gedi

90

Masada

25

Arad

Beer Sheva

31

40

Dimona

204

JORDAN

Avdat

N

EGYPT

40

Mitzpe Ramon

Makhtesh Ramon

0   20km
0   20 miles

Jordan River

Tour stop 9 **Capernaum and Tabgha (#33)**.

Tour stop 10 **Beit She'an (#39)**.

Ending point Jerusalem (130km/2 hours).

TIPS

★ Nine days accounts for an average pace. You may go faster or slower, also depending on what additional activities you slip in.

★ Our recommendation: Jerusalem for three days, Dead Sea area for two days, Negev for two days, Caesarea and Megiddo after a trip to Tel Aviv ending in the north, then touring the north for three days, before heading back to Jerusalem.

FOOD Most of the parks do not have dining facilities, with the exception of Caesarea and Masada, although most are near bigger towns with plenty of options.

V1 JORDAN PARKS AND RESERVES

Distance 775km
Driving time 13 hours
Completion time 7 days

Starting point Eilat.

Tour stop 1 <u>*Aqaba Bird Observatory (M2)*</u>: an "Important Bird Area" run by the ***Royal Society for the Conservation of Nature (RSCN)***, responsible for all the natural reserves below.

Tour stop 2 **Wadi Rum (#4)** Protected Area.

Tour stop 3 **Dana Biosphere Reserve (#21)**.

En route **Petra (#2)**.

Tour stop 4 Fifa Nature Reserve (P1).

Tour stop 5 **Wadi Mujib and Mujib Biosphere Reserve (#23)**.

En route ***Shobak***, **Karak (#49)**.

Tour stop 6 Dibeen Forest (S2).

En route **Dead Sea (#3)**.

Tour stop 7 **Ajloun Forest (#57)**.

Nearby **Ajloun Fortress (#76)**, **Jerash (#14)**.

Tour stop 8 Yarmouk Forest (S1).

Nearby **Umm Qais (#45)**.

Tour stop 9 **Azraq Wetlands (#55)**.

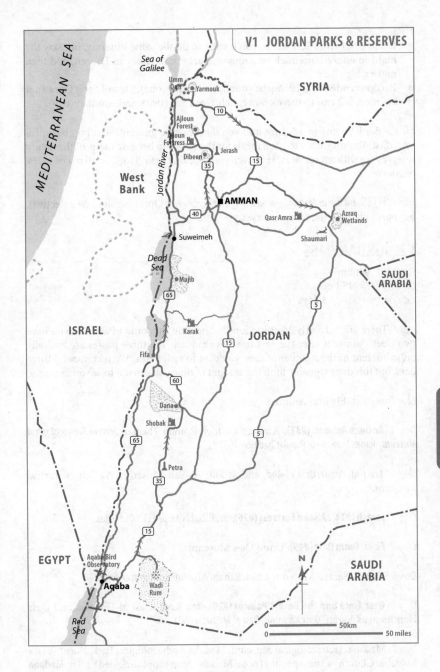

MEDITERRANEAN SEA

Sea of Galilee

SYRIA

Umm Qais
Yarmouk

Ajloun Forest
Ajloun Fortress

Dibeen

Jerash

West Bank

Jordan River

AMMAN

Qasr Amra

Azraq Wetlands

Suweimeh

Shaumari

Dead Sea

Mujib

SAUDI ARABIA

ISRAEL

Karak

JORDAN

Fifa

Dana

Shobak

Petra

EGYPT

Aqaba Bird Observatory

Aqaba

Wadi Rum

SAUDI ARABIA

Red Sea

N

0   50km
0   50 miles

En route **Qasr Amra and the Desert Palaces (#20).**

Tour stop 10 ***Shaumari.***

Ending point To Amman: 100km/1½ hours; to Aqaba: 375km/4½ hours.

TIPS

* If you enter from Jerusalem, you'll want to do the same itinerary, but stay the night in either Suweimeh or Amman, start the itinerary in Dibeen, and then make a big circle.
* Recommended nights: Aqaba (one), Wadi Rum (one), Dana (one), Petra (not counted, but two to three), Suweimeh/Dead Sea (two), and Amman (two).

FOOD Book rooms in advance and you'll at least be guaranteed a big, beautiful breakfast. You may want to pack meals for the road trip because many of the nature reserves are without services. However, you'll be able to find food in all major cities, of course.

ACTIVITIES *Hiking in Jordan* is a worthwhile endeavor. Options galore (see elective), but particularly in the forest reserves.

V2 JORDAN PASS

Distance 900km
Driving time 15 hours
Completion time 13 days

Note There are currently 36 attractions included in the Jordan Pass, and you have two weeks to use it after the first time it's scanned. The three passes are basically only different in the number of days you plan to visit Petra. We recommend three days, but this does arguably limit the amount of time you can use to see other places.

Starting point Fly into Amman.

Day 1 **Ancient Amman (#37)**: Amman Citadel, Roman Theater, **Jordan Archaeological Museum**, Jordan Museum of Popular Traditions (Q3).

Day 2 Iraq al-Amir/**Qasr al-Abd**, and **As-Salt**: As-Salt Museum, As-Salt Historical Museum.

Day 3 **Jerash (#14)**, **Ajloun Fortress (#76)**, St. Elijah's Hill/Tel Mar Elias.

Day 4 **Pella**, **Umm Qais (#45)**, Umm Qais Museum.

Day 5 Dar Al-Saraya Museum Irbid, Rihab/Al-Mafraq, **Umm el-Jimal**.

Day 6 **Qasr Amra and the Desert Palaces (#20)**, **Qasr Azraq**, Qasr al-Hallabat and Qasr Hammam as-Sarah, **Qasr Kharana**, Qasr al-Mushatta (W1).

Day 7 Madaba Archaeological Museum, Madaba Archaeological Park, Burnt Palace Madaba, Church of the Apostles (note: Madaba Map is not included), all in **Madaba (#19)**; **Umm ar-Rasas (#81)**.

Day 8 **Karak (#49)**, Karak Museum, **Shobak**, Lowest Place on Earth Museum.

Days 9–11 **Petra (#2)**.

Day 12 Al-Humaymah (note: 45km south of Petra and the turn is just north of the Desert Castle Bazar souvenir store), **Wadi Rum (#4)**.

Day 13 **Aqaba (#43)**: Aqaba Museum, Aqaba Castle.

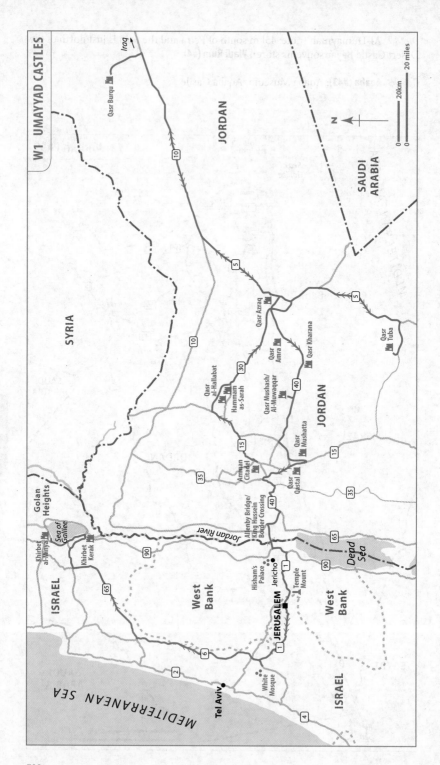

W1 UMAYYAD CASTLES

MEDITERRANEAN SEA

Tel Aviv

ISRAEL

White Mosque

JERUSALEM

Temple Mount

Jericho

Hisham's Palace

West Bank

West Bank

Dead Sea

Jordan River

Allenby Bridge/ King Hussein Border Crossing

Khirbet al-Minya

Sea of Galilee

Golan Heights

Khirbet Kerak

SYRIA

Amman Citadel

Qasr Qastal

Qasr Mushatta

Qasr Mushash/ Al-Muwaqqar

Hammam as-Sarah

Qasr al-Hallabat

Qasr Amra

Qasr Kharana

Qasr Azraq

Qasr Tuba

JORDAN

Qasr Burqu

Iraq

SAUDI ARABIA

N

0   20km
0   20 miles

732

TIPS

★ We've left *one* day to take it easy! You choose!
★ Accommodation is completely up to you. You may not want to camp in Wadi Rum, and might prefer to hang out at our Anchor City on the Dead Sea, Suweimeh, instead of staying in different towns every night.

W1 UMAYYAD CASTLES

Distance 600km in Jordan, 275km in Israel
Driving time Jordan: 8 hours; Israel: 6 hours; border crossing: 1 hour;
total time = 15 hours
Completion time 6 days (3 in each country)

Starting point Amman.

Part 1: Jordan

★ *Tour stop 1* Amman Citadel, part of **Ancient Amman (#37)**.
★ *Tour stop 2* Qasr al-Hallabat and Hammam as-Sarah. A double site, with mosque and bathhouse (3km east). Originally a Roman fortress from the 2nd century, you can see arches, cisterns, a palace, and mosaics.
★ *Tour stop 3* Qasr Burqu. Situated next to a seasonal lake in the middle of the desert, this fort was originally Roman, and now is more known as a stopping ground for migrating birds.
★ *Tour stop 4* **Qasr Azraq**.
★ *Optional tour stop* Qasr Tuba (+180km/2 hours, returning to Azraq). Of limestone and brick construction, this palace contains the remains of some walls and towers. It's a bit out of the way and requires a desert vehicle to access.
★ *Tour stop 5* **Qasr Amra (#20)**.
★ *Tour stop 6* **Qasr Kharana**.
★ *Tour stop 7* Qasr Mushash/Al-Muwaqqar. Not much left here, though it was once grandiose. There are a few capitols, cisterns, and walls. You'll need a desert-ready vehicle to access the site.
★ *Tour stop 8* Qasr al-Mushatta. Unfinished desert palace, just north of the airport.
★ *Tour stop 9* Qasr al-Qastal. Possibly the earliest Umayyad settlement, located now in a residential area near the airport. This 68m² palace and adjacent complex, including a mosque with minaret, has some nice mosaics, and is a tentative entry on the UNESCO World Heritage List.
★ Border crossing at Allenby/King Hussein Bridge, near Jericho (+ 50km/1 hour).

Part 2: Israel and Palestine

★ *Tour stop 10* **Jericho and Hisham's Palace (#26)**.
★ *Optional tour stop* Jerusalem's **Temple Mount (#12)**, with the Umayyad-built structures of **Dome of the Rock (#6)**, *Dome of the Chain*, and **Al-Aqsa Mosque (#65)**.
★ *Tour stop 11* White Mosque (D8) of Ramle.
★ *Tour stop 12* Al-Sinnabra/Khirbet Kerak, Sea of Galilee. Commissioned by the same person who built the Dome of the Rock in Jerusalem, not much remains of this site on the shores of the Galilee. Likely home to the earliest Umayyad complex.
★ *Tour stop 13* Khirbet al-Minya (G3), Sea of Galilee.

Ending point To Rosh Pina: 17km/20 minutes; to Tel Aviv: 150km/1¾ hours; to Jerusalem: 190km/2¼ hours.

★ Many of these stops can also be found in *R1: Eastern Desert*.
★ If you skip Burqu, you'll save 300km/3½ hours.

FURTHER AFIELD None of the following Umayyad sites has a ruin score better than 1, but they might be worth seeking out for die-hards:

★ ***Umm el-Jimal*** has Umayyad ruins, but they mostly renovated extant structures.
★ Ayla (Aqaba – Mamluk castle, or Aqaba Castle now stands over the ruins).
★ Khirbet Khann al-Zabib.
★ Qasr Bayir.
★ Qasr Uweinid.
★ Qasr al-Fudayn.
★ Qasr Ain as-Sil.
★ Qasr Aseikhin.
★ Be'er Ora Qiblatain Mosque, Israel.

Also note: the below sites are *Ayyubid*, not to be confused with the earlier-period Umayyad.

★ ***Ajloun Fortress (#76)*** (a rare Ayyubid Castle).
★ Ayyubid Medieval Watchtower on Amman's Citadel Hill.

W2 NABATAEAN RUINS

Distance 350km in Jordan, 400km in Israel
Driving time 6 hours in Jordan, 6 hours in Israel
Completion time 7 days (2 days in Israel, 1 day crossing, 4 days in Jordan)

Israel See *J3: Incense Route*.

Cross the border at either Allenby or Eilat.

Jordan
★ *Tour stop 1* Ayla, see **Aqaba (#43)**.
★ *Tour stop 2* **Wadi Rum (#4)**. Near Wadi Rum village, a Nabataean Temple gets some interested visitors: walk towards Jebel Rum, behind the Rest House.
★ *Tour stop 3* Humayma (⊕ 29°57′0″N 35°20′49″E). Several layers of ruins here, as it also served as home to the Abbasid Caliphate some 500 years after the Nabataeans left.
★ *Tour stop 4* **Petra (#2)**.
★ *Tour stop 5* ***Little Petra***.
★ *Tour stop 6* Sela (⊕ 30°45′0.78″N 35°43′35.97″E). After a hike to the top of Jebel Sela, you'll find caves, high points of sacrifice, inscriptions, and other rarely visited Nabataean and Edomite sites.
★ *Tour stop 7* Khirbet ed-Dharieh (⊕ 30°54′26.6″N 35°42′10.7″E). Interesting Nabataean settlement, some 100km north of Petra, with expansive ruins, mostly looted.
★ *Tour stop 8* *Khirbet et-Tannur (01)*.

Ending point To Aqaba: 230km/3 hours; to Amman: 165km/2½ hours; to Allenby/ King Hussein Bridge: 150km/2½ hours.

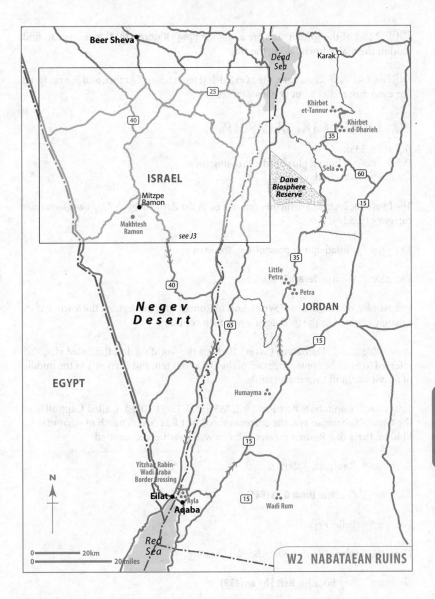

TIPS

★ Spend as much time in Petra as possible. This is the most famous site, and for good reason.

★ You'll likely need to organize trips to Humeima, Sela, Khirbet et-Tannur, and Khirbet ed-Dharieh with a special-interest tour group; these are not set up for tourists. Try Jordan Select Tours (w select.jo) or check with your hotel.

★ At the end of the trip, you will have to circle back to the same border crossing point, unless given permission earlier (usually requires much advanced planning).

FOOD Most of the Jordan sites are along the **King's Highway (#31)** and you can find food in the major towns along the way.

FURTHER AFIELD Gaza City; Meda'in Saleh (Hegra), Saudi Arabia; and Bosra, Syria. For even more, check out **w** nabataea.net.

W3 CITIES OF THE DECAPOLIS

Distance 235km
Driving time 5 hours, plus border crossing time
Completion time 3 days

The Cities of the Decapolis are further referenced in the *Archaeology – City Conglomerates* category (p. 512).

Tour stop 1 Philadelphia: present-day Amman.

Tour stop 2 Gerasa: **Jerash (#14)**.

Impossible stop A Qanawat (Syria). Lots of Roman sites throughout the town, unfortunately situated in the middle of a war-torn country.

Impossible stop B Damascus (Syria). Perhaps the world's oldest inhabited city, also referred to as an honorary member of the Decapolis ten, and currently in the middle of a civil war, and thus inaccessible.

Tour stop 3 Capitolias: Beit Ras (32°35′55″N 35°51′30″E). Called Capitolias in the Greek/Nabataean era, the current city of Beit Ras covers much of what may be hidden. Parts of a Roman theater and city wall have been excavated.

Tour stop 4 Raphana: Abila (S1).

Tour stop 5 Gadara: **Umm Qais (#45)**

Tour stop 6 Pella: *Pella*

Cross the border at Jordan River Border Crossing.

Tour stop 7 Scythopolis: **Beit She'an (#39)**

Tour stop 8 Hippos: Horvat Suṣiṭa (32°46′44.0″N 35°39′34.0″E).

Ending point To Rosh Pina: 40km/40 minutes; to Tel Aviv: 160km/2¼ hours; to Jerusalem: 175km/2½ hours; to Amman: 160km/3 hours (plus border crossing time).

TIP Crossing at the Beit She'an/Jordan River Border Crossing makes this trip a breeze, but make sure you read about the border first in *Do #10: Enter It!* (p. 66). It will likely require a guide.

FOOD Shouldn't be a problem in most of these sites.

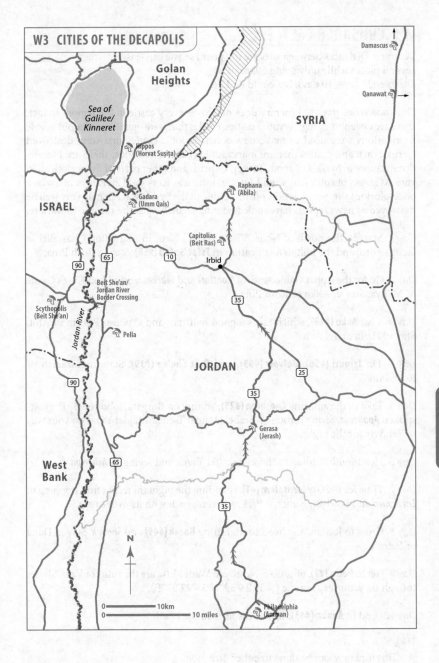

W3 CITIES OF THE DECAPOLIS

Golan Heights

SYRIA

ISRAEL

Sea of Galilee/ Kinneret

Hippos (Horvat Suṣita)

Gadara (Umm Qais)

Raphana (Abila)

Capitolias (Beit Ras)

Irbid

Beit She'an/ Jordan River Border Crossing

Scythopolis (Beit She'an)

Jordan River

Pella

JORDAN

Damascus

Qanawat

90

65

10

35

35

25

35

Gerasa (Jerash)

West Bank

65

N

Philadelphia (Amman)

| 0 | 10km |
| 0 | 10 miles |

Distance Distances between sites are not great, so you can feasibly visit several places while only going 50km or so
Completion time 10 days, but could be 13+

Our *Crusader Castle Hopping* itinerary does not cover every castle in the region. In fact, there are dozens missing: Ayyubid castles, castles that were once Crusader but whose foundations were used to make new constructions, castles that were destroyed (Jerusalem), and castles that are inaccessible (Gaza City). Plus, there are literally dozens more in Syria, Lebanon, Turkey, Cyprus, and other parts of the region, all in various stages of ruin. Our would-be-32nd site was Krak des Chevaliers in Syria, a once-glorious site, which is now off-limits due to the Syrian war – it may very well be destroyed as news reports have indicated intense shelling at the site due to warfare.

Day 1 Start in the north of Israel. Visit Château Neuf in Margaliot, Chastellet at Jacob's Ford, and the hilltop fortification in **Tsfat/Safed (#58)**. Stay in Rosh Pina.

Day 2 Go for the Upper Galilee sites of *Montfort* and *Yehi'am*, and add on King's Castle in Mi'ilya. Stay in Akko or Rosh Pina.

Day 3 Visit **Akko (#13)**, which takes a good half-day, and Château Pèlerin in Atlit. Stay in Haifa or Tel Aviv.

Day 4 Do **Tsipori (#56)**, **Belvoir (#93)**, and **Beit She'an (#39)**. Stay in Nazareth or Rosh Pina.

Day 5 Take in the amazing **Caesarea (#25)**, adding on Burgata, followed by the soft-spoken *Apollonia*. Swing through Mirabel (Mijdal Tsedek/Majdal Yaba) on your way to Tel Aviv for the night.

Day 6 Head south, adding in Ibelin near Tel Yavne and seeing *Tel Ashkelon*.

Day 7 Time for **Old City Jerusalem (#1)**, spending the night there, but first stopping in *Ein Hemed* and Castel (B1) National Park, adjacent, each with its own castle.

Day 8 Cross to Jordan, and head south hitting **Karak (#49)** and *Shobak*. Stay in Dana or Petra.

Day 9 Get to **Petra (#2)**, of course. Nearby in Wadi Musa are the ruins of Vaux Moise, though they are very remote (⊕ 30°19'59"N 35°27'57"E).

Day 10 End in **Aqaba (#43)**, whose castle is on the beach.

TIPS

★ This itinerary can be done in either direction.
★ Included are well-preserved sites and some with mere foundations of once-great buildings. You'll get a variety of perspectives, but mostly great-looking buildings.

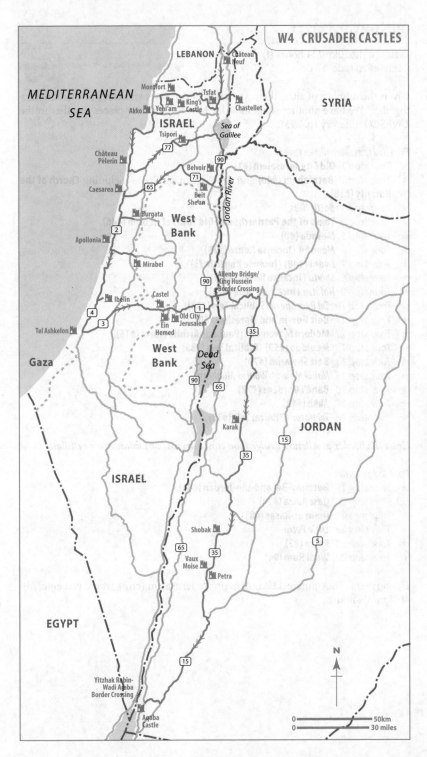

W5 UNESCO SITES

Distance 1,650km/24 hours (!)
Completion time 18 days

Given the number of sites, there are a number of ways you can put this itinerary together. We have another suggestion for how to put these places together in the *UNESCO* itinerary (p. 795).

Part 1: Jerusalem/Palestine
★ *Tour stop 1* **Old City Jerusalem (#1)**.
★ *Tour stop 2* **Bethlehem (#40)** and the Pilgrimage Route including **Church of the Nativity (#18)**.
★ *Tour stop 3* *Battir Hills*.
★ *Tour stop 4* **Tomb of the Patriarchs and Old Town of Hebron (#46)**.
★ *Tour stop 5* **Masada (#8)**.
★ *Tour stop 6* *Mamshit* (**Incense Route (#73)**).
★ *Tour stop 7* **Avdat (#48)** (**Incense Route (#73)**).
★ *Tour stop 8* *Shivta* (**Incense Route (#73)**).
★ *Tour stop 9* *Halutza* (**Incense Route (#73)**).
★ *Tour stop 10* *Tel Beer Sheva* (**Biblical Tels (#38)**).
★ *Tour stop 11* **Beit Guvrin and Maresha (#60)**.
★ *Tour stop 12* **Modern Movement (Bauhaus Architecture) (#16)**.
★ *Tour stop 13* **Megiddo (#59)** (**Biblical Tels (#38)**).
★ *Tour stop 14* **Beit She'arim (#79)**.
★ *Tour stop 15* *Nahal Me'arot/Wadi el-Mughara*.
★ *Tour stop 16* **Bahá'í Gardens (#27)**.
★ *Tour stop 17* **Akko (#13)**.
★ *Tour stop 18* *Tel Hazor* (**Biblical Tels (#38)**).

Cross the border at Allenby Bridge (you can also cross at Jordan River or Eilat).

Part 2: Jordan
★ *Tour stop 19* **Bethany-Beyond-the-Jordan (#41)**.
★ *Tour stop 20* **Qasr Amra (#20)**.
★ *Tour stop 21* **Umm ar-Rasas (#81)**.
★ *Tour stop 22* *Little Petra*.
★ *Tour stop 23* **Petra (#2)**.
★ *Tour stop 24* **Wadi Rum (#4)**.

Ending point To Amman: 325km/4 hours; to Jerusalem (cross where you entered): 400km/5½ hours.

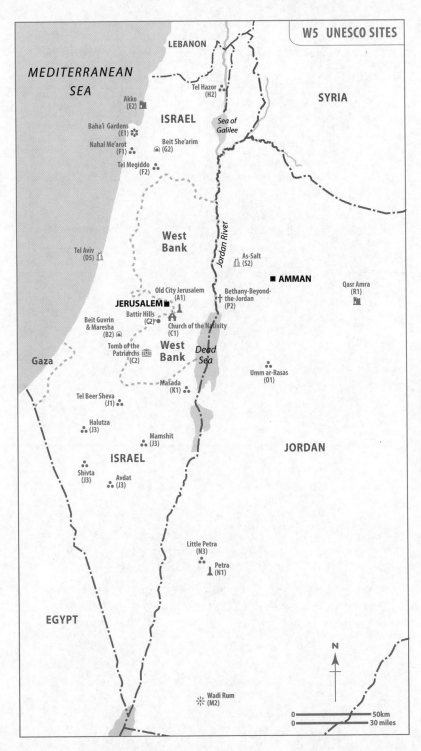

MEDITERRANEAN
SEA

LEBANON

SYRIA

Tel Hazor
(H2)

Akko
(E2)

ISRAEL

Sea of
Galilee

Baha'i Gardens
(E1)

Beit She'arim
(G2)

Nahal Me'arot
(F1)

Tel Megiddo
(F2)

West
Bank

Jordan River

Tel Aviv
(D5)

As-Salt
(S2)

AMMAN

Qasr Amra
(R1)

Old City Jerusalem
(A1)

JERUSALEM

Bethany-Beyond-
the-Jordan
(P2)

Beit Guvrin
& Maresha
(B2)

Battir Hills
(C2)

Church of the Nativity
(C1)

Tomb of the
Patriarchs
(C2)

West
Bank

Dead
Sea

Umm ar-Rasas
(O1)

Gaza

Masada
(K1)

Tel Beer Sheva
(J1)

Halutza
(J3)

Mamshit
(J3)

JORDAN

ISRAEL

Shivta
(J3)

Avdat
(J3)

Little Petra
(N3)

Petra
(N1)

EGYPT

N

Wadi Rum
(M2)

0   50km
0   30 miles

Part 10

Itineraries by BUCKET!

INTRODUCTION

Not everyone has the stamina, time, or desire to create their own unique travel experience. If you fall into this camp, these itineraries are for you. The following chapters offer a variety of options from "helpful guidance" to "completely preplanned." And you can take your pick as you go along.

A note on how these itineraries work: there is no one-size-fits-all option. You might open the first recommendation – BUCKET! sites – and think, "But where are all the details?" The point of each individual itinerary is to allow you room to adapt based on your own situation. When was the last time you used a guidebook itinerary exactly as written?

Keep in mind that if the itinerary says "BUCKET! Itinerary" then our goal is to tell you how to hit those three sites, and it's your job to fill in the rest of your time with sites that are in or around those sites. For that information, you'll want to explore themes, regions, and rankings to find other sites that will be of interest to you.

Alternatively, you can review Part 9, *Walks and Drives*, where you'll find city tours, half- to full-day excursions, and multiday trips with lots of point-to-point recommendations.

Keep in mind that these itineraries will not tell you, "… then you should stay in this hotel, and eat at this restaurant…" If that's what you're looking for, we highly recommend you hire a travel agent to help you plan your trip. You can still use this book, and these itineraries in particular, to help you narrow down the options – and we hope that you will. But we've rarely been satisfied at food or lodging "highlights" from other guidebooks, and have foregone those recommendations here. To pick the right hotel for you, start with *Do #5: Sleep It!* (p. 48) for experiential lodging options. In *Do #14: Eat It!* (p. 80), you'll learn about the types of foods you'll find in each country. Specific recommendations for each can be found in their respective themes: *Accommodation* (p. 565) and *Food and Drink* (p. 561).

ITINERARY OPTIONS

TIME-SPECIFIC Only a short trip planned? You'll still want to make the most of your time. We've got ideas for you if you've got only a few hours, a few days, or a few weekends.

HIGH SCORE Interested in structuring your trip around the highest-scoring electives in the Holy Land? Or perhaps you're interested in just the best of Israel or Jordan?

MORE SUPERLATIVES In each of our principal electives, we provide scales that give you a quick assessment of a site's popularity and entertainment, as well as the extent of ruins you're likely to find at archaeological sites. Here, we provide itineraries that send you to the highest ranked in those superlative categories.

COUNTRY-SPECIFIC These are the classic itineraries of guidebooks from yesteryear that provide country-specific itinerary options (i.e., you're in Israel for ten days, so here's your itinerary). What we have done is slightly different: we give you all the highest-rated electives in each of our four main states: Israel, Palestine, Jordan, and the Sinai. Depending on your pace, will tell you how much time you need to see everything. You can add and discard as necessary.

MACRO-REGIONS We set out itineraries for each of our macro-regions: A–W.

OFF THE BEATEN PATH Here you'll find itineraries for Israel/Palestine and Jordan incorporating exceptional sites worthy of your attention, but which you may have missed as they are ranked #51–100.

THEMATIC We've also created super-simple, easy-to-follow itineraries that can help you put together a trip relevant to your preferred type of activity. Maybe you're looking for a religious-themed trip or maybe something that covers the major landmarks. Perhaps you want something that gets your heartbeat up or that gives you thrills from the experience. Each of our themed itineraries will cover your needs. There are plenty of sample itineraries to use, or you can build your own, based on the number of days you have available.

COMPLETISTS For those focused on checking boxes, we have a few itineraries that are sure to wow, mostly because these named sites are all part of a world-renowned designation system, such as UNESCO, national parks, and Wonders of the World.

CROSS-GENRE This group explores broader topics which bring together categories from various themes, like "gourmet" or "modernity."

BUDGET If you're saving money or blowing money, we have ways to cater to your budget needs.

COMPANIONS You may require itineraries that cater to groups with specific needs: elderly parents, kids, family-friendly, and group-friendly locales, among others.

TIME-UNLIMITED Perhaps you needn't be bound to itineraries. Taking a sabbatical? Going around the world for a year? Or just like to take your time on trips? These itineraries are meant to merely give you ideas as to how you can organize your many weeks and months.

CLASSIC Perhaps you're not interested in reinventing the wheel? People have been making pilgrimages, crusades, traveling – whatever you want to call it – to the Holy Land for thousands of years. You can follow in those footsteps.

TAILORED Or, if all else fails, find an expert to show you the way. Full disclosure: we hope these are your last choice. Yes, by all means, we want you to support local business, using local tour guides whenever possible who can provide their own unique perspectives, advice, and anecdotes to color your trip. However, you should still be able to construct your own itinerary first – you did buy this guide to help you do so, after all!

Time-Specific

STOPOVER/LAYOVER

What are the chances you are going to have a **layover** in Ben Gurion Airport? None – Israel does not serve as a transit hub for anywhere else in the region. However, you may have a long layover in Amman on your way to another destination. **Stopovers** are more likely. For instance, you may find yourself in Israel on a business trip where you have tiny fragments of time in which to accomplish tourism between meetings, business dinners, and/or early/late flights.

A few ideas for 1–3-hour breaks (not including transit times):

From Ben Gurion Airport Head straight to Jerusalem's Old City to get the most bang for your buck. Follow *City Walk A1* for highlights of the Old City, which lasts 3 hours. Most of the sites in the Old City don't close, with the exception of Temple Mount – but you can still see the golden dome from a number of places along the walk.

From Queen Alia Airport Follow our Amman city walks, either *Q1: Ancient Amman* or *Q2: Modern Amman*.

Tel Aviv, summer If you're around in the summer (liberal definition: April to September), you'll want to take in a sunset at the beach and possibly more, such as swimming, volleyball, or sunbathing. Just take a walk along the Promenade – north to the port or south to Jaffa – if you can't change clothes. Plenty of food/drink options along the way.

Tel Aviv/Jerusalem evening (summer or winter) On a hefty per diem? Take in one of the city's fancy restaurants. The table will be yours all evening if you book ahead. See the *Food* theme (p. 561). On your own dime? Try a mid-level place, or street falafel or shawarma. Are drinks in order? Bars can be a bit scattered, so check out *Do #18: Late Nit!* (p. 107).

Tel Aviv essence Pick any of the Tel Aviv city walks – maybe *D6: Tel Aviv: Food and Drink* if you're hungry, or *D5: Tel Aviv: Architecture* if you're feeling sophisticated.

Jerusalem essence Prioritize: first comes the Old City. Once that's complete, visit the surrounding hills. Then you can either take in one of Jerusalem's amazing museums such as Israel Museum or Yad Vashem, or follow *A7: Jerusalem: New City and Neighborhoods* through pedestrian boulevards towards Mehane Yehuda Market, day or night.

THREE-DAY CITY IMMERSIONS: THREE CITIES

If you've only got two to three full days, you have three viable, good options to keep you busy without having to move around the country/region. We'll assume you've flown into Ben Gurion or Amman International and are staying in either Tel Aviv, Jerusalem, or Amman.

JERUSALEM IMMERSION

Day 1 Arrive at Ben Gurion (airport, around 30 minutes) or Allenby (land border, around 1 hour), head directly to your hotel, and unload. If it's Friday, the whole city will be shut down, so you may be relying on your hotel for services (food, water, snacks, etc.). Don't expect much unless you're staying at a large international brand.

That afternoon/evening, you'll want to get your bearings – start with *A7: Jerusalem: New City and Neighborhoods*. Nosh on yummies at the **Mehane Yehuda Market (#67)**, open late (except Fridays). Fancier restaurants are open Friday evenings, if that's your arrival day. Ask your hotel for recommendations and reservation assistance, which will be necessary.

Day 2 After breakfast (ideally in your hotel, but you can find cafés and patisseries open everywhere), head early in the morning to the Old City. Depending on your energy level and interest, plan to do *City Walks A1* or *A2* in the morning. These cover the main sites, though the second tour is far more comprehensive. If you go it on your own, at the very least, your priorities are the **Dome of the Rock (#6)**, **Western Wall (#11)**, and **Church of the Holy Sepulchre (#9)**, though you needn't squeeze all of them into the morning. You could spend all day visiting these three sites.

The Dome of the Rock is not accessible on Saturday mornings, so, if you are visiting on a weekend, you may have to save that one piece for Sunday morning.

Eat in a falafel and hummus shop for lunch. Or you might try shawarma, but really you can't leave Israel without eating falafel and hummus.

If you have time in the afternoon, start *City Walk A5*. The three hills will mostly be drive-by stops given the time crunch. You could alternatively visit just one more thoroughly: *City of David*, **Mount Zion (#92)**, or **Mount of Olives (#34)**.

If by some miracle you still have time left, you can walk the perimeter of the Old City from the rafters on *City Walk A3* or go on a deep dive of the *Jewish Quarter* in *City Walk A4*.

If walking is not your bag, you can alternatively visit one of the two New City museums (**Israel Museum (#17)** or **Yad Vashem (#35)**, the Holocaust Museum), depending on your interest.

For dinner, either eat cheaply in **Mehane Yehuda Market (#67)** or seek assistance in reserving one of Jerusalem's sleek, new restaurants. The most well regarded is **Machneyuda (#98)** – not to be confused with the market!

Day 3 Depart your hotel following breakfast. You can leave your luggage at the front desk so you can get around much easier. Three recommended options for this day: 1) Catch up on whatever you missed yesterday, e.g., Dome of the Rock. 2) Visit the other museum in West Jerusalem (New City). 3) Explore some of the special activities that require a separate ticket, such as **Ramparts Walk (#91)**, **Western Wall Tunnels (#94)**, *City of David*, and **Jerusalem Archaeological Park (#71)**.

You'll find that's a pretty exceptional weekend.

TEL AVIV IMMERSION

Day 1 Arrive at Ben Gurion and head to your hotel (around 45 minutes, traffic-dependent). If you are staying close to **Tel Aviv Beaches (#89)**, spend your first afternoon walking along the Promenade, following *City Walk D1*. Have your hotel reception make reservations for you in one of Tel Aviv's modern restaurants – check out "Top Restaurants" in the *Food and Drink* theme (p. 561) for our recommendations. For your **Tel Aviv Nightlife (#82)**: dinner starts late here, and nightclubs start even later, so feel free to take a nap now (or head to the beach to do it there).

Along the stretch, stop for a snack at one of the restaurants facing the water (you may have to cross to the other side of the road) and order a falafel in pita. Load it up with your favorite condiments and then park yourself on a bench or the sand (you can also rent a chair, but go ahead and just sit on the sand – it's super-soft).

Get in the water if you're feeling up for it – there are changing rooms in a few spots along the boardwalk. You won't want to miss the sunset facing the Mediterranean, which is glorious 365 days a year. In the summer, it sets quite late, so check the sunset time on your phone.

At dinner, be sure to sample Israel's wine region; the waiting staff will be happy to give you recommendations. If you're going to a lounge/musical venue, you can arrive around 22.00, but most regular bars won't pick up until midnight.

Day 2 Now that you're deeply immersed in the scene, you'll probably wake up late. Get another dinner reservation. Grab a pastry (boureka or rugelach, recommended), a filling takeaway hummus (yes, for breakfast!), or some hearty shakshuka. Check out *Do #14: Eat It!* (p. 80).

Then commence your walking tours of **Tel Aviv (#5)** and **Jaffa (#30)**. Depending on your energy level, we recommend three back to back, but you can cut out parts that don't interest you. Depending on where you're sleeping, you can tackle these in any order.

We have two full-city tours that take in the major attractions. *City Walk D3* includes sites and neighborhoods north of **Rothschild Boulevard**, itself a bustling street with shopping, eclectic architecture, restaurants, and cafés. The tour includes walks through some of the historic parts of town, including the primary **Modern Movement (Bauhaus Architecture) (#16)** districts. The other walking tour for sites and neighborhoods is *City Walk D4*, which includes hipster and Arab neighborhoods south of Rothschild.

If you're visiting midweek, lots of Tel Aviv's best restaurants have *prix fixe* menus with two- or three-course lunches at deeply discounted prices. You can also have a range of options by visiting one of Tel Aviv's diverse food markets – **Carmel Market (#87)** (street food), Sarona Market (D3) (food hall), and **Tel Aviv Port** (food hall) provide the best range. Check out *Do #14: Eat It!* (p. 80) for more information.

If you're up for a third walk, head over to Jaffa and commence *City Walk D2*. Alternatively, you can skip all the walking and just go right to the beach! There's plenty of activity here: lounging, bars, mellow music, volleyball, paddleball (matcot), stand-up paddleboarding, kitesurfing, swimming, running, and lots of chatter.

Definitely nap if you plan on going out later. And/or grab a coffee. Dinner's about 21.00. If you're looking for a show, visit the *Entertainment* theme (p. 557). Check out *Do #18: Late Nit!* (p. 107) for party options after.

Day 3 Take in a big Israeli Breakfast (U) from your hotel before checking out, and if not provided, you already know your local coffeeslinger, shakshuka shack, and hummusiya.

If you did three walks yesterday, get yourself to the beach! You need a break. Otherwise, take some time to walk around Jaffa or the other neighborhoods.

For lunch, try Jaffa's Old Man and the Sea (D2), which tosses 20 salads on your table before taking your (whole) fish order. You can also go with one of the delicious pocket sandwich options, such as shawarma, mixed grill, falafel, or sabich (eggplant/egg).

If you missed picking up souvenirs, you can buy (duty-free-priced) Dead Sea products, Israeli wine, and Toblerone (of course) at the airport on your departure.

AMMAN IMMERSION Huge caveat: you can certainly entertain yourself in Amman for a weekend, as there are plenty of options to keep you entertained. However, if you only have three total days in Jordan, you need to leave Amman and go immediately to **Petra (#2)** – our second-highest-ranked site in the region and a can't-miss. If you're set on staying in Amman, here are our recommendations:

Day 1 Assuming you fly in on this day, first head to your hotel for rest and splashing water on your face. Amman is not the greatest walking city, but it is certainly an interesting experience – and we're going to do it all day tomorrow. You can feel free to wander around unescorted, or head for Rainbow Street (Q2) for food or drink. Spend the afternoon sucking on a hookah, if that's to your liking. It is definitely customary around these parts.

Day 2 Follow the *Q1: Ancient Amman* walking tour during the morning before it gets too warm. The first stop (Citadel) is very impressive on its hilltop perch, but is a very steep climb. Either start early or take a cab to the top. This part of the tour will allow you to see much of ancient Amman and its downtown ruins. Then, wander over to Rainbow Street (Q2) for lunch. Visit a gallery, stop in a bar for a refreshment, and shop for spices, daggers, Dead Sea salt, olive wood carvings, and other souvenirs. There are several modern bars and restaurants, and you can get a feel for them in our Amman chapter. Alternatively, begin the *Q2: Modern Amman* walking tour.

Day 3 If you haven't visited already, you should head to the **Dead Sea (#3)**, one of our BUCKET! sites, and buy a day pass at one of the local hotels to take a dip in the near-saltiest of saltwater seas. Alternatively (and if you're leaving late), you can organize a day tour to **Jerash (#14)**, the region's best Roman ruins and only an hour north of town (though traffic can make this time very variable).

ANCHOR CITIES: DAYS 1–10 PRIORITIES

Looking for *general* guidance for plotting out your trip? Look no further. You simply have to decide which of the following four Anchor Cities is going to be your home base. Once you know that detail, you can structure the days however you like. Thus, if you have seven days and are staying in Jerusalem, you don't have to do the Tel Aviv portion of your trip on day 5. You can move around the itineraries however you like.

In general: if you are spending only one day at the site/activity, then you'll be returning back to your Anchor City for the night, and not checking out of your hotel. However, if you add a second day, it's probably more economical both time- and money-wise to stay the night at that site (e.g., Tel Aviv).

Note: "If you have…" implies *full days*. Unless you arrive very early or very late, don't count your arrival/departure day. In the following table, alphanumerics in parentheses (e.g., "A1") refer to the walks and drives described in Part 9.

If you have…	Jerusalem	Tel Aviv	Dead Sea Jordan or Amman
1 day	Jerusalem, Old City (A1, A2) *if time*: A3, A4	Tel Aviv, Jaffa (D1, D2)	Skip Amman, go to Dead Sea: relax, no itinerary
2 days	+ Jerusalem, Old City (unfinished) *and/or* + Jerusalem, New City (A7)	+ Tel Aviv walks (D3, D4) or beach *if time*: D2	+ Amman (Q1, Q2)
3 days	+ Dead Sea, Masada (K1)	+ Jerusalem, Old City (A1)	– Day 1–2 itineraries + Petra (N1) *if self-drive*: O1, P1
4 days	+ Jerusalem: museum or activity	same, less hurried *and/or* add in new Jerusalem itineraries (A2, A5, A7, A8)	+ Dead Sea (add back in) *if time*: + holy sites around Dead Sea, Madaba, Mount Nebo, Bethany-Beyond-the-Jordan (P2)
5 days	+ Tel Aviv (D1, D2)	– Day 4 activities, above +2 days in Petra, ideally via flight to Eilat	+ Wadi Rum, including overnight
6 days	–1 day in Tel Aviv or Jerusalem, you decide +2 days Petra, flying 1 evening earlier to Eilat or afternoon taxi from Allenby (5 hours)	+ Dead Sea, Masada (K1)	+ Jerash, north sites (S1)
7 days	+1 more day in Jerusalem, Petra, or Tel Aviv	+ Bethlehem (C1, C2)	+ Jerusalem, Old City (A1)
8 days	+ Sea of Galilee for Jesus sites (G4) *if time*: Nazareth (G1)	+ Caesarea, Haifa, *and/or* Akko (E1, E2)	+1 more day in Jerusalem (A2–A8)
9 days	+ Palestine sites: Bethlehem, Jericho (C1, C3)	+ Sea of Galilee for Jesus sites (G4) *if time*: Nazareth (G1)	+ Red Sea for diving *or* + Dana Biosphere Reserve
10 days	+ Caesarea, Haifa, *and/or* Akko (E1, E2)	+ Jerusalem: museum or activity	+ the other Day 9 activity *or* + Desert Palaces (R1)

WEEKENDS: FIFTEEN TRIPS

Long live long weekends! If you're spending a few weeks or months in Israel for work, and don't have all day to meander around but do have some weekends to get away, this section is for you. Of course, some of this will depend on where you're stationed, but we've ranked them more or less in order of importance, with the Jordan sites at the end since they are more logistically complicated. For Jordan, you'll want to make sure you have a multiple-entry visa to Israel and Jordan or you might get questioned from one or both border patrols for going in and out so frequently.

W/end	Location	See/do	Stay	Region
1	Jerusalem	Old City, New City	luxe options	A
2	Dead Sea + Masada	including morning sunrise hike and a spa day	resort	K
3	Petra	main sites, including three walks, + Wadi Rum in a pinch	downtown Wadi Musa	N
4	Tel Aviv + Jaffa	restaurants, cafés, beaches, bars	beachside, boutique	D
5	Sea of Galilee	biblical sites, circuit around the lake	Rosh Pina resort	G
6	Mediterranean highlights	Roman ruins, Bahá'í gardens, Crusader towns, beaches	boutique-luxe	E
7	Golan	national parks, skiing, forests, hikes	kibbutz or tzimmer	I
8	Lower Galilee	national park circuit	Rosh Pina, kibbutz, or tzimmer	F
9	Wineries	Judean Hills or Golan or Galilee or north coast	spa, resort, tzimmer, hotel	U
10	Negev	hiking, craters, Ben Gurion's resting place	ecolodge, camping, tukul, mud hut	J
11	Red Sea	snorkeling, scuba	hotel, Eilat or Aqaba	L, M
12	Jordan north	Roman ruins, forest hikes, Amman	hotel	S
13	Jordan west	Dead Sea, Christian sites	resort in Suweimeh	P
14	Jordan south	Crusader castles (Kerak, Shobak), Wadi Rum	ecolodge (Feynan Ecolodge)	M, O
15	Jordan east	Desert Castles	hotel in Amman	R

High Score

BUCKET! ITINERARY

We start first with the three BUCKET! items, two sites and one experience. In case you skipped the entire beginning of this book, the two BUCKET! sites that should be at the top of your list are: **Old City Jerusalem (#1)** and **Petra (#2)**, and the experience you need to try is the **Dead Sea (#3)**. These sites are the best bang-for-your-buck, most impressive, fun-for-everyone, eye-dropping, and superlative-central must-see spots. If you're starting from scratch with no other plans in place, then you need to begin with these three sites.

Minimum time 3 full days starting in Jerusalem; 5 full days starting in Amman.

Starting point This itinerary works fine flying into either Ben Gurion or Amman, but the order in which you see the sites will change, as will our recommendation for the Dead Sea.

ARRIVING TO BEN GURION/TEL AVIV AIRPORT

1–3 days in the Old City Sleep anywhere in Jerusalem. It's important you start early if your time is limited. Start your morning in the Old City, with the goal of doing one of our Old City Jerusalem walks (to include **Dome of the Rock (#6)**, **Church of the Holy Sepulchre (#9)**, **Western Wall (#11)**, and **Temple Mount (#12)** at a minimum: see *City Walk A1*). Review **Old City Jerusalem (#1)** to determine the amount of time you want to spend there. To run through the highlights, you need 4 hours, but to get a great overview, visit sites with entrance ticket requirements, walk through the four quarters, shop and eat, you'll need three days.

½–1 day at the Dead Sea Take a day trip to the Dead Sea from Jerusalem. This can be arranged from your hotel, you can take a bus, or you can rent a car and head there yourself. There are a few beaches on the north side of the Dead Sea (45 minutes) that have an entry fee, or there's a good public beach on the southern end of the Dead Sea at **Ein Bokek** (1½ hours from Jerusalem). Either way, it only takes 15 minutes to bob in the sea to capture this amazing experience, though you might want to take advantage of the many spa options and spend a half- or full day. Check out **Dead Sea (#3)** for more details on timing.

1–2 days in Petra To get to Petra, you can take a day trip, if you're short on time (many do this), or you can plan to spend a longer amount of time. If you go the day-trip route, you have two options:

1. Fly from Ben Gurion to Eilat (perhaps early in the morning, perhaps the night before and stay in a hotel in Eilat), get picked up by a tour company and be escorted across the southern border (1 hour) before heading north (2 hours) to Petra.
2. Cross from the Allenby border, 1 hour from Jerusalem. There aren't public buses running to Petra, so you'll have to organize a cab on the other side, which will be pricey and long – the trip takes about 4 hours – but will save you the plane ride.

With a day trip, you'll have time to walk the Siq (main causeway) and see the sites in the valley itself. If you want to do a hike, you'll have to hoof it – it's 2 hours to the Monastery and back if you're fit and fast.

If you can afford more time, spend more time. Petra is worthy. If you arrive the night before, it is essential to be at the entry gate by 06.00 to be among the first to catch a glimpse of the Treasury at the end of the Siq. Then you can take your time with the hikes and spend the night again, if you like. You can participate in one of the two recommended evening activities: *Petra by Night* and **Petra Kitchen (#84)**. You can also tack on *Little Petra* (5km to the north) if you have a free morning or afternoon.

ARRIVING TO AMMAN

2–3 days in Petra/Wadi Musa Head south from Amman to Wadi Musa (3 hours), the town where Petra is located, by bus, car, or taxi. As you likely have a Jordan-focused itinerary, plan to spend at least one night in Petra and get a two- or three-day pass to the park (only 5 JD more per day). You should be able to do two hikes in addition to all the ground-level sites, plus the three other recommended activities: *Petra by Night*, **Petra Kitchen (#84)**, and *Little Petra*.

1 day at the Dead Sea The order of your trip is going to vary here, depending on whether you have plans to cross at the southern border or not. Let's assume you're going to cross at Allenby/King Hussein Bridge (1 hour west of Amman and 1 hour east of Jerusalem). In this case, you'll want to drive 2 hours north from Petra to Suweimeh, the "town" with all of the cheap (but luxurious enough) hotels on the north side of the Jordanian side of the Dead Sea. Inside the hotel, you will gain access to private beaches to reach the sea. It will be much quieter than the Israeli side, likely with mud pits for you to use, and a great Jordanian breakfast to boot! You can also just pay for a day pass if you don't want to stay the night, though bear in mind that the border can close early.

2–3 days in Old City, Jerusalem Crossing the border first thing in the morning, you can head to the Old City, or your hotel, and begin that itinerary. You won't want to cross the Allenby border twice in one day as the sheer amount of time it takes would not make the trip to Jerusalem worth it, so plan on spending at least one night in Jerusalem. Plan to spend as much time as you have in Jerusalem, which is really the star of the show in the Holy Land.

DEPARTING FROM EITHER AIRPORT
We'd never recommend that you try to cross an international border on the same day as you have an international flight – that sounds like travel trouble waiting to happen. That said, you can technically get from Jerusalem to Queen Alia Airport in Amman in the same day, but should plan on starting the journey at least 7 hours before your scheduled flight, as you can get stuck in lines at the border. Wait times of 1 hour on both the Israeli and Jordanian sides are not irregular. It's 1½ hours from Allenby Bridge to Ben Gurion Airport, and 1 hour from the King Hussein Bridge (same bridge, different name in Jordan) to Queen Alia Airport. You should arrive 3 hours before any international flight in this region. That's not a joke: security can be intense and lines long.

TOP TEN

If you're looking to hit the top ten sites in the region, you're going to need a good plan as the sites are fairly spread out (and span two countries!).

A reminder on rank: **Wadi Rum (#4)**, about 2 hours south of Petra; **Tel Aviv (#5)**, about 1 hour west of Jerusalem; **Dome of the Rock (#6)** (Jerusalem's Old City); **Sea of Galilee (#7)**, about 2 hours north of Jerusalem/Tel Aviv; **Masada (#8)**, about 2 hours southeast of Jerusalem; **Church of the Holy Sepulchre (#9)** (again, in the Old City); and **Red Sea/Gulf of Aqaba (#10)** (4 hours south of Jerusalem/Tel Aviv; 2 hours south of Petra). And don't forget our BUCKET! sites, which are the priority here. So we're going to add time for **Old City Jerusalem (#1)**, **Petra (#2)**, and **Dead Sea (#3)**.

Minimum time 6 very packed days (you can do it in less, but it won't be enjoyable and you'll be glossing over a lot); 10 days preferred.

Starting point This itinerary works from either entryway (Israel's Ben Gurion Airport or Jordan's Queen Alia Airport), and will require crossing several borders.

1–2 days (2–3 nights) in the Old City, Jerusalem The Old City is listed as our #1 site, and for good reason – there are tons of things to do there. Four of our other top 12 sites are co-located in the Old City, and you can easily hit all four in one day, though you may be inclined to spend longer. To figure out a good plan of attack, visit *City Walks A1–A4*.

1 day (1–2 nights) in Tel Aviv Tel Aviv is best known for **Israeli Cuisine (#51)**, **Tel Aviv Beaches (#89)**, **Tel Aviv Nightlife (#82)**, climate, and **Modern Movement (Bauhaus Architecture) (#16)**. You can squeeze all of that into a day but, if you're looking to relax, you should add more time in Tel Aviv. At the least, you'll want to spend two nights in Tel Aviv as a base for your trip to the Galilee. (You could also use Jerusalem.)

1 day (0 nights) to Sea of Galilee Follow *Road Trips G2* or *G3*, which loop around the Sea and stop at the many biblically relevant spots along the way. Head back to Tel Aviv, or stay in Nazareth, Rosh Pina, or Tiberias if you're planning on seeing more of the north (i.e., Golan or Lower Galilee).

1 Day (0 Nights) in Masada and the Dead Sea Start your morning driving south from Tel Aviv to **Masada (#8)**, the city on the mountain plateau (2 hours). After hiking around the site, you can cool off in the **Dead Sea (#3)** after a short drive south to the free public beaches at *Ein Bokek*. Either drive 2 hours south to Eilat or stay the night in one of the *Ein Bokek Spa Hotels*.

1 day (1–2 nights) in Eilat or Aqaba for the Red Sea Use either Eilat (Israel) or cross the border to Aqaba (Jordan) as your base for exploring the **Red Sea/Gulf of Aqaba (#10)**. If you are more interested in snorkeling, Israel makes more sense. The diving sites in Jordan are better, and should be coordinated in advance.

2–4 days (2–3 nights) in Jordan You have two top ten sites to see in Jordan: **Petra (#2)** and **Wadi Rum (#4)**. You can also visit the **Red Sea/Gulf of Aqaba (#10)** and the **Dead Sea (#3)** here, too, where accommodations are often cheaper (and sometimes nicer) than on the Israeli side. You can do these sites in either order. From Aqaba, you can reach Petra in 2 hours or Wadi Rum in about 1 hour.

If you visit Wadi Rum first, you can either sleep under the stars in one of the Bedouin camp facilities, or leave the park before sunset and head directly to Petra. You'll need at least half a day in Wadi Rum, but 24 hours is normal.

Or visit Petra first, and drive by Wadi Rum on the way back to Aqaba. Plan to spend at least one full day in Petra. If you arrive after noon, don't even think about cramming the whole park into one afternoon – you'll miss all the exceptional hikes.

Cross the border in the morning, and drive 4 hours to Tel Aviv or Jerusalem. Spend the night or take a late-night flight home.

HIGH BUCKET! SCORES: 7+

Our BUCKET! *scores* are slightly different than the *rankings* of each of our individual electives. For a full explanation, see *BUCKET! Scores* (p. 14). Here's how to put together an itinerary that hits all of BUCKET!'s highly rated sites, including all sites with a rating of 7–10. You can pick and choose from the below for shorter itineraries.

Recommended time 22–28 days.

2–3 days in Jerusalem If you're going to do anything in the Holy Land, your trip has to include the **Old City Jerusalem (#1)**. There are so many amazing spots – touching the ground where Christ's cross was hoisted at the **Church of the Holy Sepulchre (#9)**, gazing at the golden **Dome of the Rock (#6)**, watching all kinds of Jewish followers praying and inserting notes into the **Western Wall (#11)**, exploring the underground history of Jerusalem at the **Western Wall Tunnels (#94)**, walking among Jerusalem history at the **Citadel/Tower of David (#32)**, visiting the sad but triumphant **Yad Vashem (#35)**, exploring 10,000 years of anthropologic history at the **Israel Museum (#17)**, and following Jesus' last steps on the **Via Dolorosa (#42)**. You can't go wrong here. Set aside one meal for our highest-ranked restaurant, **Machneyuda (#98)**.

1 day in Bethlehem Take a day trip south to **Bethlehem (#40)**, primarily to visit the **Church of the Nativity (#18)** for its grotto which marks the spot where Jesus was born. On your way back to Jerusalem, stop by the *Separation Wall*.

½–1 day in Jericho The world's oldest walled city, **Jericho (#26)** comes with all sorts of history at its main site, but nearby *Deir Quruntal* and **Hisham's Palace (#26)** make this triply interesting.

1–2 days at the Dead Sea and Masada We prefer the *Suweimeh Spa Hotels* on the Jordanian side of the **Dead Sea (#3)** for their nicer (and much less expensive) resorts, private access to the sea, and tanks of readily available mud to lather yourself in (which you can rarely find in public spaces). **Masada (#8)** is another must-see for its views and interesting history.

2–3 days in Tel Aviv There's plenty to keep yourself busy in **Tel Aviv (#5)**, despite its mostly lackluster "site" offerings. Our Tel Aviv walking itineraries (*City Walks D1–D6*) will provide you with a great overview of the city, including gems such as the UNESCO-declared **Modern Movement (Bauhaus Architecture) (#16)**, the glorious stretches of fine-white-sand **Tel Aviv Beaches (#89)** (particularly Gordon Beach (D1)), and, for the gastronome, the beautiful 6km *Tel Aviv Tayelet/Promenade*, and a spectrum of modern **Israeli Cuisine (#51)** restaurants, with our favorite being *Tzfon Abraxas*. **Imperial**

Bar (#99) is the most awarded of Tel Aviv's many bars. Don't skip breakfast (try: bourekas, rugelach, shakshuka, or a *Hummus* breakfast at *Abu Hassan*). Take an extra day and set yourself up for a kitesurfing lesson, stand-up paddleboarding, or regular surfing – your choice. And if you're around in June, *Tel Aviv Pride Celebration (D1)* is a must-see event.

1 long day at Mediterranean coast sites If you start early, you can leave Tel Aviv early and squeeze in a morning visit to the Roman ruins of **Caesarea (#25)**, an English-language tour of the **Bahá'í Gardens (#27)** in *Haifa*, and an afternoon visit to the Crusader town of **Akko (#13)**, followed by a pre-reserved dinner at the country's best seafood restaurant, *Uri Buri*.

1 day in the Nazareth region (plus more if you want to hike longer) **Nazareth (#29)** was Jesus' hometown and houses the imposing and beautiful *Basilica of the Annunciation*, a church within a church within a church. Stop at **Beit She'an (#39)** for some under-appreciated Roman ruins. You can also take in the sites on foot, with a variety of visit stops along the **Jesus Trail (#69)**, passing historically relevant and tourist-empty sites along the way. If you have the energy, spend up to 44 days hiking the *Israel National Trail*, traversing the country from the Golan Heights to the Red Sea.

1 day at the Sea of Galilee Spend a day on the **Sea of Galilee (#7)**, beginning your counterclockwise journey from *Tiberias*. Follow *G4: Jesus Sites in the Galilee* or circumnavigate the whole lake with a drive through parts of the Golan. On your way in or out of the region, a stop at *Elbabor* in Umm al-Fahm is recommended for delicious Arab-Israeli cuisine.

1 day at wineries (or your whole trip, who are we kidding) There are a number of places you can do a *Winery Tour*, with easy circuits and nearby wineries present in the Judean Hills (outside Jerusalem), along the Mediterranean coast, the Galilee, and the Golan. Organizing a tour is easy, or drive yourself (with a designated driver), but keep in mind you'll need reservations for most wineries, and that many don't have public cellar doors.

1 day in the Negev Unless you're visiting in the summer, spend time at **Makhtesh Ramon (#28)**, the erosion crater in the Negev Desert providing some spectacular views.

2–3 days in Petra **Petra (#2)** is magical. We recommend sleeping over at least one night so you can arrive at the entrance gate promptly at 06.00, to be the first soul at the Treasury. The Monastery hike is our favorite, but a close second goes to the *Jabal al-Khubtha (N2)* trail, which takes you to the top of the cliffs above and opposite the Treasury for a spectacular "Indiana Jones" view.

1–2 days in Wadi Rum **Wadi Rum (#4)** is gorgeous, but how do you make the experience even better? A *Hot Air Balloon Ride Over Wadi Rum* from above, of course. You can continue the luxury by *Glamping in Wadi Rum (M2)* in a chic outdoor tent (with bathroom and bed), or save your cash and sleep under the stars with the Bedouins.

1 day in Jerash The best Roman ruins in the region are found at **Jerash (#14)**. The sheer scale will impress you more than you could think possible.

1 day in Mujib Jordan's best hikes (maybe after Petra) can be found at **Wadi Mujib and Mujib Biosphere Reserve (#23)**. More *Hiking in Jordan* options exist if this interests you.

1 day at the Desert Palaces You'll need a rental car or driver to get to Jordan's Eastern Desert to visit **Qasr Amra (#20)** and the other Umayyad palaces.

Eating (no extra days necessary) There are dozens of great restaurants in the Holy Land, and even more great options for fast food, dessert, coffee, bread, and other snacks (**Jordanian Cuisine (#44)** and **Israeli Cuisine (#51)**). *Modern Israeli Cuisine* can be found in Tel Aviv, Jerusalem, Nazareth, Akko, and Rosh Pina. Street food is everywhere, and falafel is king. (Perhaps hummus is queen?)

1 night at an ecolodge Don't miss a true Bedouin experience, with stargazing, cooking demos, tea ritual, walking through the Dana reserve, and homemade cuisine – all at **Feynan Ecolodge (#86)**.

1 day to weeks/months at a kibbutz, including volunteering and Ulpan Visiting a kibbutz can sound a bit intimidating. They are, after all, closed communities. For true immersion, though, you'll want to be a ***Kibbutz Volunteer***. You'll work six days a week, make little to no money, and your bones will ache at the end of each day, but you'll meet lots of interesting people, debate Zionism, work with crops and animals, and eat local.

1 day on the Mediterranean beaches Spend a day stopping at a few of the ***Mediterranean Coast*** highlights to get different perspectives. **Dor HaBonim (#100)**, *Beit Yannai*, **Tel Aviv Beaches (#89)** – all different strokes for different blokes (swimming pun). See *Road Trip E7* for a north-to-south review of the best Mediterranean beaches.

2 days in the Sinai Yes, it's dangerous and mostly off-limits. But if the region opens back up, spend some time doing absolutely nothing in the laid-back not-resort-town of **Dahab (#54)** and snorkeling or scuba diving at **Ras Mohammad (#53)**.

More Superlatives

MOST POPULAR

If you're a glutton for punishment, or have an immense FOMO, you'll want to make sure you pack these sites into your itinerary, each with more than a million visitors per year. As you might expect, they are mostly religious sites.

Start your trip in the Old City Jerusalem and plan to spend one or two days visiting the main sites: **Temple Mount (#12)**, the **Western Wall (#11)**, **Via Dolorosa (#42)**, and the **Church of the Holy Sepulchre (#9)** – all part of *City Walk A1*. Cross east to **Mount of Olives (#34)** to visit the many holy sites there and capture a beautiful shot of the Old City. Take a bus to **Bethlehem (#40)** to take in the **Church of the Nativity (#18)** and other sites on the Pilgrimage Route. Spend another day at the **Dead Sea (#3)**, soaking in the salty waters.

Before leaving Jerusalem, schedule time at **Yad Vashem (#35)**, the Holocaust Museum, then head west to the Mediterranean coastal town of **Tel Aviv (#5)**. You'll want to eat, drink, swim, and relax in this secular town – plan at least a couple of days. Don't forget to walk the Promenade to **Jaffa (#30)**, the ancient Arab town, now a lively hub of activity.

Then spend a few days in the north, first visiting the **Baháʾí Gardens (#27)** in *Haifa*, then over to the **Sea of Galilee (#7)**, with its most visited sites being the combined national park sites of **Capernaum and Tabgha (#33)**.

Days required Jerusalem: 1 day; Mount of Olives: ½ day plus ½ day in Bethlehem; Dead Sea: 1 day; Yad Vashem: ½ day; Tel Aviv/Jaffa: 1½ days; Baháʾí Gardens and some popular spots on the Sea of Galilee: 1 day.

COMPLETE RUINS

The following itinerary incorporates ruins that rate as a 5 on our *Ruin Score* (p. 19). This means the sites are mostly complete, and contain large and impressive monuments that are easy on the eyes and require little imagination.

Everything begins with the **Old City Jerusalem (#1)**, which itself is a living monument, a 1km² fortress city, whose walls (**Ramparts Walk (#91)**) are a testament to its millennia of history, containing within them the spectacular **Dome of the Rock (#6)** and the long-standing (though renovated) **Al-Aqsa Mosque (#65)** on **Temple Mount (#12)**, along with the *Dome of the Chain* and the *Fountain of Sultan Qaytbay*. Part of Temple Mount is, of course, the **Western Wall (#11)**, the Jewish monument to their lost Temple. The Crusader-designed **Church of the Holy Sepulchre (#9)** and the Armenians' *St. James' Cathedral* each dominate their respective quarters.

Two more sites that are famous for their sheer grandiosity are **Petra (#2)** and **Caesarea (#25)**, both of which are very well preserved and testament to their former glory. Part of Israel's recent history (1930s), several of the more than 4,000 **Modern Movement (Bauhaus Architecture) (#16)** buildings around Tel Aviv are in various states of glory and disrepair. And the **Church of the Nativity (#18)** in **Bethlehem (#40)**, celebrating Jesus' birth, has been more or less in its present form since the 500s!

Days required Jerusalem: 2 days; Petra: 2 days; Caesarea, Tel Aviv, and Bethlehem: ½ day each.

MOST ENTERTAINING

For our most entertaining electives, we considered all of our 4s and 5s, which gave us quite an assortment of activities.

While the Old City doesn't lead the rankings for once, Jerusalem's western neighborhoods (**Jerusalem, New City (#72)**) provide plenty of shopping, dining, and interesting happenings on the several pedestrian-only streets. Jerusalem's museums also get high marks for their engaging displays: both **Israel Museum (#17)** and **Yad Vashem (#35)** aim to impress. Further west, **ANU – Museum of the Jewish People (#77)** also has displays to fascinate all age levels. You can't miss **Tel Aviv (#5)** or the **Tel Aviv Nightlife (#82)**, which provide endless fun in the sun, excellent **Israeli Cuisine (#51)**, music, dancing, bars, and entertainment.

Watch the ruins come alive in **Petra (#2)**, where the site itself provides enough visual stimulation to please everyone. When you're done, don't miss Jordanian cooking lessons at **Petra Kitchen (#84)**. If you have time, add in a night or two at **Feynan Ecolodge (#86)** where you'll interact with the local Bedouin community.

The **Dead Sea (#3)** is another crowd-pleaser, with its surprisingly buoyant waters never failing to shock new visitors.

The **Red Sea/Gulf of Aqaba (#10)** is a holiday zone, so it gets high marks pretty much everywhere. **Ras Mohammad (#53)** in the Sinai has some of the world's best diving and snorkeling opportunities. **Eilat (#78)** was redesigned as a resort town, with beachfront, dolphins, aquaria, snorkeling, shopping, and hotel boardwalks.

Akko (#13) has incorporated immersive technology into several of its Crusader ruins. **Caesarea (#25)**, too, has really considered the visitor to make sure the site comes alive. And don't miss **Golan Heights Winery (#75)**, Israel's first successful commercial winery, which actually has a tasting room that requires no reservation.

Days required Jerusalem: 2 days; Tel Aviv: 2 days; Petra: 2 days; Dana/Feynan: 2 days; Dead Sea: 1 day; Red Sea: 2 days; Akko/Caesarea: 1 day; winery: ½ day.

Country-Specific

BEST OF ISRAEL

If you're looking to skip the hassle of international borders, look no further than the Best of Region itineraries that follow. Note: these itineraries only take into account Gold electives.

Minimum time 15 full days, but you'll be sprinting.
Recommended time 18+ full days.

Starting point Jerusalem, but you could easily make this Tel Aviv and put Jerusalem later in your itinerary.

Base You can use a series of Anchor Cities here, starting in Jerusalem, moving to Tel Aviv, then sleeping up north if you want in Rosh Pina. But it could just as easily be done all from Tel Aviv, if you don't mind driving 1½–2 hours on the way home. (You can always stop at a new beach on the *Mediterranean Coast*!) That said, this makes for a quintessential road trip: pack the car, stop when you're ready, camp when you want, hotel when you need.

3–5 days in Jerusalem

★ *Day 1* You'll start your Best of Israel tour in Jerusalem, where you get the most bang for your buck. Your first day or two should be spent in **Old City Jerusalem (#1)**, with the goal of seeing a litany of sites. Start with the **Dome of the Rock (#6)** and **Al-Aqsa Mosque (#65)** on **Temple Mount (#12)**. Visit the **Western Wall (#11)**, **Western Wall Tunnels (#94)**, and the **Jerusalem Archaeological Park (#71)** on the southern portion of the Wall. Next, head to the Christian Quarter for the **Church of the Holy Sepulchre (#9)**, the **Via Dolorosa (#42)**, and the **Citadel/Tower of David (#32)**.

★ *Day 2* Start the day walking around and atop the Old City walls, beginning with the **Ramparts Walk (#91)** and circumnavigate the walls, all part of the Jerusalem Walls National Park. Outside the Old City walls, you'll venture to the **Mount of Olives (#34)** for captivating views and stunning churches. En route, there are various interesting neighborhoods, including *City of David*, **Mount Zion (#92)**, and *Yemen Moshe*, among others. Of particular note in **Jerusalem, New City (#72)**, the neighborhood of **Mea She'arim (#66)** is where Hasidic Jewry live a conservative lifestyle amid a modernizing city. You can end your trip at the enticing **Mehane Yehuda Market (#67)**. Don't forget dinner reservations at **Machneyuda (#98)**, Israel's best-reviewed restaurant.

★ *Day 3* This is museum day, with the **Israel Museum (#17)** and **Yad Vashem (#35)** (Holocaust Museum) both near one another in the western part of central Jerusalem.

½ day in Greater Jerusalem

On your way to Tel Aviv, stop through **Beit Guvrin and Maresha (#60)**, a fascinating UNESCO site.

1–3 days in Tel Aviv

You can really plow through all that **Tel Aviv (#5)** has to offer in a day, though it won't be terribly relaxing, which defeats the purpose: this town is meant to be enjoyed, so maximize your time here. For those that like itineraries, select any or all of our Tel Aviv tours (*City Walks D1–D6*) to capture the essence of this Mediterranean city, its **Modern Movement (Bauhaus Architecture) (#16)**, and the ancient (now Arab) seaport of **Jaffa (#30)**. Plan for at least one beach day (**Tel Aviv Beaches (#89)**), which might morph into a typical Tel Aviv night (**Tel Aviv Nightlife (#82)**). Begin at **Imperial Bar (#99)** – voted best bar in the Middle East – for happy hour. Don't forget to sample some of the famous **Israeli Cuisine (#51)** at a street falafel or shawarma stall at **Carmel Market (#87)**, or, if your budget can handle it, one of Tel Aviv's fancy restaurants. If you need to get out of the sun, don't miss **ANU – Museum of the Jewish People (#77)** and the **Tel Aviv Museum of Art (#95)**.

2–3 days on the Mediterranean coast (day trip from Tel Aviv, or side trip to Anchor City) Drive north from Tel Aviv to **Caesarea (#25)**, site of some majestic and seaside Roman ruins. If the weather is nice, don't miss **Dor HaBonim (#100)**, considered by many to be Israel's finest beach, though you might cancel the rest of your plans once you get there. Venture further north to the **Bahá'í Gardens (#27)** of *Haifa*, and continue on to **Akko (#13)** for a quaint and functional Arab town nestled in an old Crusader fortress. Return to Tel Aviv each night or you can sleep in Rosh Pina (Anchor in the north) or Nazareth.

3–4 days in the Lower Galilee (day trip from Tel Aviv or Anchor City) Start the day in **Nazareth (#29)** with a visit to the *Basilica of the Annunciation*, and follow it up with lunch (or dinner) in one of Nazareth's tasty fusion restaurants. UNESCO has designated three distant towns as **Biblical Tels (#38)**, a collection of Iron Age city ruins which includes **Megiddo (#59)**. **Beit She'an (#39)** is a sinfully under-appreciated Roman site. Not to be confused with **Beit She'arim (#79)**, a site with a number of Jewish sarcophagi discovered in caves. To the south of the Sea of Galilee you'll find **Beit Alpha (#64)**, an ancient synagogue with an amusing mosaic, and **Belvoir (#93)**, a well-preserved Crusader castle. This is pure road-trip gold, but you can anchor from Tel Aviv or Rosh Pina and do a series of day trips, in any order.

1–2 days at the Sea of Galilee (day trip from Tel Aviv, or spend the night in Nazareth, Rosh Pina, or Tiberias) Use *Road Trips G2 or G3* as your guide, visiting the biblical sites of the **Sea of Galilee (#7)**, to include **Capernaum and Tabgha (#33)** – this will take you a day. You can pick up a walk on the **Jesus Trail (#69)** from here, or anywhere along the way to **Nazareth (#29)**. **Tsfat/Safed (#58)**, the spiritual center of the north, is a short drive from the *Mount of Beatitudes*.

2–3 days in the Golan Heights (long day trip from Tel Aviv, or spend the night in Rosh Pina or a tzimmer) Depending on your goal for this region, you can either do a highlights reel to get the Golani feeling, or spend more time by sleeping in Rosh Pina or a tzimmer for a few days. Check out **Golan Heights (#62)** to narrow down your options. Some of the popular sites include the ancient **Tel Dan (#63)**, the forested **Banias (#80)**, and the mystical **Nimrod's Fortress (#85)**. Don't forget a stop at the place that put Israeli wine on the map: **Golan Heights Winery (#75)**.

1–2 days in the Negev (day trip from Tel Aviv) No tour of the Negev would be complete without a hike through **Makhtesh Ramon (#28)**, easily approachable from the visitor center at *Mitzpe Ramon*, but obviously much better by way of a hike. Close by are the ruins of **Avdat (#48)**, the most extensive Israeli ruins of the ancient Nabataean people – the same group that built Petra. Take an extra day to seek out other spots along the

Incense Route (#73), including *Mamshit*, *Shivta*, *Halutza*, and maybe even far-off *Nitzana*. The UNESCO **Biblical Tels (#38)** city of *Tel Beer Sheva* is also nearby.

1–2 days at the Dead Sea (day trip from Jerusalem or Tel Aviv) You can do a quick overview of the four popular spots here in one day, but you'll seriously be hustling. At the north end of the sea is the national park of **Qumran (#70)**, where the Dead Sea Scrolls were discovered. **Ein Gedi (#50)** offers lots of interesting hikes, though there are a few flatter options with good facilities if your goal is not "up." **Masada (#8)** can be cut short by taking the cable car (rather than hiking the front or back cliffs) and doing a quick circuit of the site's ruins, but you should try to spend time here – the view is fantastic. The **Dead Sea (#3)** has a number of access points but, if you're short on time, you may want to pay to enter from the northernmost spots (Biankini/Siesta Beach (K1) or New Kalya Beach (K1)) and take 15–30 minutes to wade around in the salt water. Or, if you're heading south to Eilat, you can seek out the free beach at *Ein Bokek*, on the southern banks of the Dead Sea.

1 day in Eilat If you're at all interested in snorkeling the **Red Sea/Gulf of Aqaba (#10)**, then you'll have to make the trek down to **Eilat (#78)**. You'll have to overnight in order to see its several sites, including **Coral Beach (#83)**, and on your way back up you can stop by an ancient copper mine and theme park, **Timna (#96)**.

From here you can cross over to Jordan and start the Best of Jordan itinerary (below). Or visit just the sites you have time for – at a minimum, Petra – before heading back home.

BEST OF THE WEST BANK/PALESTINE

If you're looking for a best-of tour of the West Bank (aka Palestine), here are our recommendations from the Gold and Silver electives.

Minimum time 5 full days.
Recommended time 8 full days.

Starting point Jerusalem.

1–3 days in Jerusalem While technically still under Israel authority, East Jerusalem is mostly Arab/Muslim, and you may consider it to be a part of Palestine. There are a number of sites in East Jerusalem worthy of a visit, including the **Mount of Olives (#34)**, while **Temple Mount (#12)** with the **Dome of the Rock (#6)** and the various Muslim sites are all worthy of your attention. Check out *City Walk A6* for a comprehensive look.

1–2 days in Bethlehem Cross south from Jerusalem into the West Bank (bring your passport!) and be in **Bethlehem (#40)** within 10 minutes. Take a tour of the **Church of the Nativity (#18)** and other sites in Bethlehem's Old City. Walk or drive to see some of Banksy's art on various buildings, including the imposing *Separation Wall*. If you have a car (rental cars from Israel are not allowed), you can see the rolling green *Battir Hills* – beautiful olive and grape territory. Spend the night in the wacky but modern *Banksy's Walled-Off Hotel*.

1–2 days in the southern West Bank Head out early the next morning to Herod's final resting place, **Herodion (#90)**, before taking in the **Tomb of the Patriarchs (#46)** in Hebron. Add on a hike to **Mar Saba**, one of the cliffside monasteries. Return to Bethlehem, or cross back to Jerusalem. Alternatively, take an extra day to hike the **Palestinian Heritage Trail**, Abraham's old stomping grounds, and a community-based Bedouin experience that goes through Palestinian cities/towns while engaging with Bedouin communities.

1 day in Jericho Head east towards the border where you'll find **Jericho (#26)**, the oldest walled city in the world. **Deir Quruntal** (aka Monastery of Temptation), accessible via cable car, and **Tulul Abu el-Alaiq** are recommended stops. A walk through **Wadi Qelt (#97)** will take you to another cliff-hanging monastery, St. George's.

1–3 days in north Palestine **Ramallah (#68)** offers vibrant nightlife and is the largest Palestine city (also considered the de facto capital). Drive north and coordinate a visit to **Sebastia-Shomron** and its national park to view Throne Village architecture. You'll want to visit **Nablus (#61)** for its khanafe dessert, its several archaeological sites, and **Mount Gerizim** – center of the universe according to the Samaritans who live here. You can fly through these sites in a day (see *Road Trip C4*), or base yourself in Ramallah and visit the northern sites from there.

BEST OF JORDAN

Either tackle this in one fabulous, off-the-beaten-path trek, or tack it onto your Israel experience. The following sites are all the Jordan Gold electives.

Minimum time 10 full days, but you're skimping on time in Petra and blowing through just about everything.
Recommended time 15 full days.

Starting/ending point Amman.

1–2 days in Amman Fly into Amman and spend the night. Depending on your arrival time, you may be able to squeeze the highlights into your arrival day. Check out the walking tours for **Ancient Amman (#37)** (*City Walk Q1*) and **Modern Amman (#36)** (*City Walk Q2*) – four hours each.

1 day at the Desert Palaces (day trip from Amman) From Amman, hire a car or take a taxi to **Qasr Amra (#20)**, one of the Desert Palaces in the eastern Jordanian desert, and the most impressive. There are over a dozen you can pick and choose from, but the other three significant ruins are **Qasr al-Abd**, **Qasr Kharana**, and **Qasr Azraq**. See *Road Trip R1* for more details. Also on the circuit are **Azraq Wetlands (#55)**, a wildlife oasis amid the sea of sand.

2 days in north Jordan (day trip from Amman, or overnight) From Amman, head north an hour to **Jerash (#14)** for the region's most impressive Roman ruins, swinging through **Ajloun Forest (#57)** and a visit to **Ajloun Fortress (#76)**. Head up to the Israel–Syria border to spend the night near **Umm Qais (#45)**, one of the Cities of the Decapolis (*Road Trip W3*), or plan a separate day trip up north.

2–3 days on the King's Highway There's a lot to see on the **King's Highway (#31)**, which was a historic trade route and offers spectacular views of Jordan's Rift Valley (V). You can visit the biblical sites of **Madaba (#19)** and **Mount Nebo (#24)** along the way, but we've saved them for later. The drives here are long, so you'll want to get to the **Dana Biosphere Reserve (#21)** before dark. Along the way, you'll pass the castle at **Karak (#49)**. Spend the night at **Feynan Ecolodge (#86)** to break up the drive, but if you do, plan to stay at least one full day for the included activities with Bedouins.

1–3 days in Petra Next, we're heading to **Petra (#2)**, a BUCKET! site and a spectacular one at that. If you arrive early enough, you can breeze through Petra's highlights in a long and tough day, but there are plenty of things to see and do here, including *Little Petra*, *Petra by Night*, and **Petra Kitchen (#84)**, in addition to the many hikes inside the park itself.

1–2 days in Wadi Rum On your way out of Petra, stop by **Wadi Rum (#4)**, either for a day trip through its beautiful red rock mountains, and ending the night either under the stars in a Bedouin camp (+1 day), or in a hotel in **Aqaba (#43)**. Spend the afternoon (or next day) snorkeling the **Red Sea (#10)** waters.

1–2 days on the Dead Sea Highway On your way back up to Amman, take Highway 65 along the Israeli border and you'll pass the Mujib Nature Reserve with the famous **Wadi Mujib (#23)** wet hike. Continue on to one of the inexpensive resort hotels in Suweimeh, lather in mud, and take a soak in the salty waters of our BUCKET! experience: the **Dead Sea (#3)**. Stay another day or two for relaxation.

1–2 days on the biblical circuit The next morning, from the Dead Sea, drive the Christian Jordan (*Road Trip P2*) circuit to take in **Bethany-Beyond-the-Jordan (#41)**, making sure to visit the famous **Madaba Map (#19)**, and **Mount Nebo (#24)** where Moses was said to have died. UNESCO treasure **Umm ar-Rasas (#81)** has a superior collection of mosaics found buried away for millennia. Spend the night back at the Dead Sea or in Amman.

BEST OF THE SINAI

Add this piece on to your Eilat trip, if you have time. Though maybe the least-considered locale in the region, and hard to do yourself given the inability to take cars over the border, if you can manage it you'll get a number of unforgettable locations along the way. Gold electives below.

Minimum time 5 full days.
Recommended time 7 full days.

Starting point Taba.

1 day in Taba If you haven't spent any time yet on the Red Sea, you are welcome to a night in Taba (T1) – the cheaper cousin to Eilat and Aqaba. Though nothing spectacular, it does have nice hotels with good food, and access to the **Red Sea (#10)**, which will get you started with your snorkeling adventure (diving comes later).

2–3 days in Dahab Take a load off in **Dahab (#54)**, a relaxing beach town with dirt-cheap beach camp accommodations. You can take diving trips from here (to the mysterious *Blue Hole (T1)*) and arrange a visit to **Mount Sinai (#15)** for a sunrise hike, as well as **St. Catherine's Monastery (#22)**, which carries a prestigious collection of ancient literature. If you're keen, you can take part in a short- or long-distance hike on the

**Sinai Trail** that continues west; the trail passes through Mount Sinai, St. Catherine's, and Jebel Katharina, the highest peak on the Sinai.

2–3 days in Sharm el-Sheikh Continue the relaxation trend by heading to the resort town of **Sharm el-Sheikh (#88)**. You can arrange a diving trip to one of the most revered coral reefs on the planet at **Ras Mohammad (#53)**, and visit a variety of other Red Sea diving spots.

Macro-Regions

For maps see p. 572. In the following itineraries, alphanumerics in parentheses (e.g., "A1") refer to micro-regions and the corresponding walks and drives described in Part 9.

A JERUSALEM

Jerusalem is centrally located, straddling between Israel and the West Bank, with the Old City sitting right on the border. We also cover East Jerusalem (Palestine) and West Jerusalem (Israel).

Highlights Jerusalem has more highly ranked sites than any of the other regions.
Anchor Jerusalem is an Anchor City.
Electives BUCKET! (1); Gold (18); Silver (12).
Highest-ranked elective **Old City Jerusalem (#1)**.
BUCKET! Score 7+ **Old City Jerusalem (#1)**, **Dome of the Rock (#6)**, **Church of the Holy Sepulchre (#9)**, **Western Wall (#11)**, **Israel Museum (#17)**, **Citadel/Tower of David (#32)**, **Yad Vashem (#35)**, **Via Dolorosa (#42)**.
One-day itinerary Combine A1 + A5.
Multiday itinerary A1 → A5 → A3 → A8 + A7 → A2 → A4 → A6.
Itinerator! tip You probably don't want to see a bunch of museums in the same day, so mix and match sites from A7 and A8 over a couple of days, or just pick a few highlights to fill one day.

B GREATER JERUSALEM

This region covers the areas just outside of West Jerusalem, circling to the south, west, and north (within Israel's borders) and all the way to the Tel Aviv limits, south to Beit Guvrin, and north to the airport.

Highlights There's a great variety of sites here, from the UNESCO site of Beit Guvrin to a gorgeous synagogue, hikes, hummus, monasteries, a stalactite cave, a variety of wineries, and a zoo.
Anchor/road trip This region can be visited using Jerusalem or Tel Aviv as an Anchor City, or passing through on your way from Jerusalem to Tel Aviv (or vice versa).
Electives Gold (1); Silver (6).
Highest-ranked elective **Beit Guvrin and Maresha (#60)**.
BUCKET! Score 7+ Judean Hills Wineries (B3).
Half-day itinerary Beit Guvrin.
One-day itinerary Do a half-day at your preferred highlights and spend the rest of your time at Beit Guvrin.
Multiday itinerary B2 → B1 → B3.

C WEST BANK

The West Bank is far-reaching and inclusive of some of the iconic names associated with Palestine: Bethlehem, Jericho, Ramallah, Hebron, and Nablus.

Highlights In addition to the famous cities, there's a variety of geography here, including a holy mountain, cliff-hanging monasteries in dry wadis, and ancient UNESCO-designated terraced hills.

Anchor/road trip This region can be visited using Jerusalem as an Anchor City, exploring the northern portions over a day and the southern over another day. Bethlehem and Jericho might require their own separate day trips.

Electives Gold (8); Silver (9).

Highest-ranked elective **Church of the Nativity (#18)**.

BUCKET! Score 7+ **Church of the Nativity (#18)**, **Jericho and Hisham's Palace (#26)**, **Bethlehem (#40)**, *Separation Wall*.

Half-day itinerary Take a bus to Bethlehem to see the Church of the Nativity.

One-day itinerary C1, and drive to either Herodion or Hebron if you've got wheels and the energy.

Multiday itinerary C1 → C3 → C2 → C5 → C4.

D TEL AVIV

Tel Aviv sits on the Mediterranean, northwest of Jerusalem and roughly halfway between the border with Egypt and Lebanon. Gush Dan, representing Tel Aviv and its suburbs, holds about half of Israel's population.

Highlights Sun, fun, and yum. Lots of relaxation in Tel Aviv, with some hedonism mixed in, if that's what you're after.

Anchor Tel Aviv is an Anchor City.

Electives Gold (9); Silver (28).

Highest-ranked elective **Tel Aviv (#5)**.

BUCKET! Score 7+ **Tel Aviv (#5)**; **Modern Movement (Bauhaus Architecture) (#16)**; **Tel Aviv Beaches (#89)**; *Tzfon Abraxas*; Water Sports (D1); Gordon Beach (D1); *Tel Aviv Pride Celebration (D1)*; *Group Fun at a Downtown Beach (D1)*.

Half-day itinerary D1.

One-day itinerary D1 + D2, plus make a reservation at one of the many great restaurants (D6).

Multiday itinerary Incorporate D6 throughout; D1 + D2 → D3 → D5 → D4.

E MEDITERRANEAN COAST

We cover everything between Gaza and Lebanon, as well as the skinny part of Israel in the middle from Highway 2 to Highway 6 (west of the West Bank).

Highlights As evidenced by the title, there are a lot of beach options here, but there is so much more to be found. From Caesarea, Haifa, and Akko to lesser-known sites like Nahal Me'arot, Zichron Ya'akov, and Dor HaBonim.

Anchor/road trip If you're visiting for the day, use Tel Aviv as an Anchor. If you plan to spend multiple days up north, road-trip through, landing in Rosh Pina, Nazareth, or Akko.

Electives Gold (4); Silver (15).

Highest-ranked elective **Akko (#13)**.
BUCKET! Score 7+ **Akko (#13)**; **Caesarea (#25)**; **Bahá'í Gardens (#27)**; *Mediterranean Coast*; *Uri Buri*.
Half-day itinerary E2.
One-day itinerary Parts of E1 + E2.
Multiday itinerary E5 → E4 → E7 → E6 → E3.

F MOUNT CARMEL AND JEZREEL VALLEY

Mount Carmel is located just south of Haifa, and we continue the region as it expands eastwards towards the Jordan River. The area adjacent to the northern border with the West Bank is the Jezreel Valley, including Mount Gilboa.

Highlights This area has more important sites than you're probably aware (or have heard) of, but is worthy of your time, particularly the ruins covering many thousands of years of history: Megiddo, Belvoir, Beit Alpha, and Beit She'an, among many others.
Anchor/road trip Anchor from Tel Aviv, or road-trip through and overnight in Rosh Pina (also an Anchor City).
Electives Gold (5); Silver (6).
Highest-ranked elective **Beit She'an (#39)**.
BUCKET! Score 7+ **Beit She'an (#39)**.
Half-day itinerary All of Beit She'an.
One-day itinerary F2.
Multiday itinerary F2 → F1.

G LOWER GALILEE AND KINNERET

The "Kinneret" is another name for the Sea of Galilee. The sites of the Lower Galilee are just north of Mount Carmel.

Highlights This area includes Nazareth and other famous New Testament sites.
Anchor/road trip You can drive to/from Tel Aviv in one day, or spend the night in Rosh Pina on your way to the Golan.
Electives Gold (5); Silver (8).
Highest-ranked elective **Sea of Galilee (#7)**.
BUCKET! Score 7+ **Sea of Galilee (#7)**; **Nazareth and its Biblical Sites (#29)**; **Jesus Trail (#69)**; *Basilica of the Annunciation*.
Half-day itinerary G1.
One-day itinerary G4.
Multiday itinerary G2 + G1 → G4 + G3.

H UPPER GALILEE

The northerly parts of Israel bordering Lebanon from the coast to the Golan are all part of the Upper Galilee, including the Galilee Panhandle, which separates historic Israel from the Golan Heights.

Highlights These sites are mostly under-explored, but there are several national parks and Crusader castles to explore, as well as the highest-elevated city in Israel, Tsfat.
Anchor/road trip Rosh Pina, with its excellent lodging and food options, is one of our Anchor Cities from which to explore the region.

Electives Gold (1); Silver (7).
Highest-ranked elective **Tsfat/Safed (#58)**.
BUCKET! Score 7+ *Druze Cooking Workshops (H1)*.
Half-day itinerary **Hula Lake** and/or **Bar'am**.
One-day itinerary H1.
Multiday itinerary H1 → H2.

I GOLAN HEIGHTS

Making up the northeastern portion of the country, this territory has been under Israeli control since 1967.

Highlights The Golan is a completely unique geography compared with the rest of Israel, with big forests, colder weather, and even a snow-capped mountain (sometimes). Syrian Druze still live in this area, and remnants of the 1967 war are everywhere. And lots of national parks!
Anchor/road trip You can make a day trip to the Golan, but manage expectations as it's a lot of driving both to the territory and within (sites are mostly distant from one another, and there is no public transportation). Stay in Rosh Pina or a tzimmer if you have plans to spend more than a day.
Electives Gold (5); Silver (5).
Highest-ranked elective **Golan Heights (#62)**.
BUCKET! Score 7+ n/a.
Half-day itinerary **Banias (#80)** and/or **Nimrod's Fortress (#85)**.
One-day itinerary I1.
Multiday itinerary I1 → I2 → I3.

J NEGEV

The Negev Desert makes up the lower half of Israel, from Beersheva to Eilat.

Highlights Here we find the world's largest erosion crater, the Nabataean Incense Route, and amazing views and hikes.
Anchor/road trip Visit from Jerusalem or Tel Aviv. Or stop in Mitzpe Ramon on your way to Eilat.
Electives Gold (4); Silver (10).
Highest-ranked elective **Makhtesh Ramon (#28)**.
BUCKET! Score 7+ **Makhtesh Ramon (#28)**.
Half-day itinerary Easy/moderate hike and visitor center at Makhtesh Ramon.
One-day itinerary J2.
Multiday itinerary J2 (+J3, if interested) → J1.

K DEAD SEA (ISRAEL)

Covers the area on the western shore of the Dead Sea. Half of it is technically in the West Bank, but it's all under Israeli control.

Highlights A BUCKET! site alone makes this area worth exploring, but you also have hiking, Dead Sea Scrolls, and a town built on top of a mountain (with great views).
Anchor/road trip Very quick trips are possible from Jerusalem, but even trips from Tel Aviv are possible if you commit to a very full day. For longer trips, stay in Ein Bokek on the south lake.

Electives BUCKET! (1); Gold (3); Silver (3).
Highest-ranked elective **Dead Sea (#3)**.
BUCKET! Score 7+ **Dead Sea (#3)**; **Masada (#8)**; *Powered Parachute Flight above Dead Sea/ Masada (K1)*.
Half-day itinerary Pop down for a quick dip, either on the north shore at Kalia/Neve Midbar Beach (K1) or the south lake at **Ein Bokek** (+1 hour one-way).
One-day itinerary Masada early morning → **Ein Bokek Spa Hotels** + Dead Sea *or* K1 (highlights only).
Multiday itinerary All K1 (each break is one potential overnight): stops 1–3 → stops 4–5 → stop 6, either Snake Path or Roman Trails → stop 7 → stops 8–9.

L EILAT AND ARABAH

Eilat sits on the southernmost point of Israel on the Red Sea, spitting distance from Taba, Egypt, and Aqaba, Jordan. The Arabah is the desert south of the Dead Sea that forms the Jordan Rift Valley (V) between Israel and Jordan.

Highlights Eilat is a resort town with plenty for family of all ages. It's hot, but there is a variety of water and indoor activities in Eilat and the surrounds. Timna Park is a popular excursion.
Anchor/road trip Day trips are not recommended, so plan to overnight – probably in Eilat, Mitzpe Ramon (if stopping halfway), or one of the campgrounds.
Electives Gold (4); Silver (4).
Highest-ranked elective **Red Sea/Gulf of Aqaba (#10)**.
BUCKET! Score 7+ n/a.
Half-day itinerary Snorkeling is not great here, but can be done. Have a visit to the **Underwater Observatory** or skip Eilat and drive up to **Timna (#96)**.
One-day itinerary L2.
Multiday itinerary L2 → L3 → L1.

M SOUTH JORDAN

Though mostly desert and empty, we include everything south of Petra.

Highlights Wadi Rum's majestic red desert is definitely worth a stop, if not an overnight. A visit to the Red Sea will fulfill all your snorkeling and scuba dreams in a way that the Mediterranean might not.
Anchor/road trip Day trips are not recommended, so plan to overnight: in Aqaba if crossing from Israel, or Wadi Rum if you're going straight there.
Electives Gold (4); Silver (1).
Highest-ranked elective **Wadi Rum (#4)**.
BUCKET! Score 7+ **Wadi Rum (#4)**; *Hot Air Balloon Ride Over Wadi Rum*.
Half-day itinerary Wadi Rum, not spending the night, doing a short excursion.
One-day itinerary Wadi Rum *or* scuba via Aqaba.
Multiday itinerary M2 → M1.

N PETRA

Petra is located in the small town of Wadi Musa. All the sites are within 10km.

Highlights This is the second-highest-scoring individual site, and easily worth three days of your time, which makes it easier to coordinate trips to nearby sites.

Anchor/road trip We recommend a road trip here, stopping in Petra for however long you can spend (three days is ideal). Visit Wadi Rum before and the Dead Sea/Suweimeh after (or vice versa), visiting King's Highway and biblical sites along the journey.
Electives BUCKET! (1); Gold (1); Silver (2).
Highest-ranked elective **Petra (#2)**.
BUCKET! Score 7+ **Petra (#2)**.
One-day itinerary N1 + one hike from N2 if you can hurry.
Multiday itinerary N3 + N2.

O KING'S HIGHWAY

Highway 35 from Petra north to Amman, with a few detours.

Highlights Castles, mosaics, nature, and ecolodges all along a gorgeously scenic route.
Anchor/road trip Perfect road trip, departing from or ending in Petra.
Electives Gold (6); Silver (1).
Highest-ranked elective **Madaba and the Madaba Map (#19)**.
BUCKET! Score 7+ **Feynan Ecolodge (#86)**.
Half-day itinerary Driving the road, but no time for stopping other than a scenic pass.
One-day itinerary Depending on time, focus on **Karak (#49)**, **Umm ar-Rasas (#81)**, and/or Madaba. (Not enough time for **Dana Biosphere Reserve (#21)** or **Feynan Ecolodge (#86)**.)
Multiday itinerary O1.

P DEAD SEA (JORDAN)

The Dead Sea Highway runs from Aqaba, but the first sites of interest aren't until the actual Dead Sea. We also consider the elevated area directly east of the Dead Sea.

Highlights In addition to the Dead Sea, there are a number of biblical sites of interest within a short drive of the Anchor City of Suweimeh.
Anchor/road trip Base yourself in Suweimeh, on the north coast of the Dead Sea. There are resorts and it's less chaotic than Amman.
Electives BUCKET! (1); Gold (4); Silver (4).
Highest-ranked elective **Dead Sea (#3)**.
BUCKET! Score 7+ **Dead Sea (#3)**; **Wadi Mujib and Mujib Biosphere Reserve (#23)**.
Half-day itinerary If you haven't visited the Dead Sea yet, buy a day pass from a hotel. Otherwise, stop through **Madaba and the Madaba Map (#19)** or **Umm ar-Rasas (#81)**.
One-day itinerary P2.
Multiday itinerary P1 → P2.

Q AMMAN

Amman is approximately 1 hour east of the Israeli border.

Highlights Amman has several interesting Roman ruins right in the heart of downtown, and can be coupled with its rising modernity – new restaurants, bars, and hotels are popping up everywhere.
Anchor/road trip You can anchor in Amman or visit on a day trip from Suweimeh.

Electives Gold (2); Silver (4).
Highest-ranked elective **Modern Amman (#36)**; **Ancient Amman (#37)**.
BUCKET! Score 7+ n/a.
Half-day itinerary Q1.
One-day itinerary Q1 + Q2.
Multiday itinerary Q1 + Q2 → Q3 → Q4.

R EAST JORDAN

Everything to the east of Amman, through the peninsula that borders Syria, Iraq, and Saudi Arabia.

Highlights The Desert Palaces are the highlight, but there are bird zones, a wildlife reserve, and some oasis areas which make a nice break from the dry desert.
Anchor/road trip Road trip/day trip from Amman.
Electives Gold (2); Silver (4).
Highest-ranked elective **Qasr Amra and the Desert Palaces (#20)**.
BUCKET! Score 7+ n/a.
Half-day itinerary Drive to/from Qasr Amra.
One-day itinerary R1 (without Burqu).
Multiday itinerary R1 (with Burqu).

S NORTH JORDAN

From Amman northwards to the Israeli and Syrian borders, with Highway 15 as the eastern limit.

Highlights Despite its high ranking, Jerash is criminally overlooked in terms of regional travel.
Anchor/road trip Use Amman as your Anchor.
Electives Gold (4); Silver (3).
Highest-ranked elective **Jerash (#14)**.
BUCKET! Score 7+ **Jerash (#14)**.
Half-day itinerary Jerash.
One-day itinerary S1.
Multiday itinerary S1 → S2.

T SINAI

The Sinai peninsula flanks the entire west coast of Israel's land border, but you'll find mostly desert and militants here. We review only the portion that stretches along the Gulf of Aqaba, from Taba to Ras Mohammad.

Highlights The Sinai is not always the safest place for travelers but, if you can make it work, you'll find some amazing spots at Mount Sinai, Dahab, and Ras Mohammad's reefs, among other places.
Anchor/road trip Road trip is okay when agreed upon by government authorities. Otherwise, fly to Sharm and hire a company to shuttle you around.
Electives Gold (5); Silver (1).
Highest-ranked elective **Mount Sinai (#15)**.
BUCKET! Score 7+ **Ras Mohammad (#53)**; **Dahab (#54)**.

One-day itinerary Not really possible, but if you're going to pick only one activity, visit Dahab.
Multiday itinerary T1.

U CROSS-ISRAEL/PALESTINE

Covers electives that span across the entire country, or are not region-based.

Highlights From food to hikes to UNESCO sites, there is a lot to cover.
Anchor/road trip Up to you – review the individual itineraries.
Electives Gold (2); Silver (4).
Highest-ranked elective **Biblical Tels (#38)**.
BUCKET! Score 7+ **Israeli Cuisine (#51)**; *Modern Israeli Cuisine*; *Winery Tour*; *Kibbutz Volunteer*; Israeli Breakfast (U); Ulpanim (U); Beaches (U).
Electives without a micro-region *Israel National Trail*.

V CROSS-JORDAN

Top-to-bottom Jordan.

Highlights Food, hikes, and meeting the Jordanian people.
Anchor/road trip Up to you – review the individual itineraries.
Electives Gold (2); Silver (3).
Highest-ranked elective **Jordanian Cuisine (#44)**.
BUCKET! Score 7+ **Jordanian Cuisine (#44)**.
Electives without a micro-region **Jordan Trail (#52)**; *Hiking in Jordan*; *Jordanian Hospitality*; *Royal Society for the Conservation of Nature (RSCN)*.

W WHOLE HOLY LAND

Electives that can be found in Israel, Palestine, Jordan, and Egypt.

Highlights From hummus to camel riding, you'll find many similarities tying these cultures, countries, and nations together.
Anchor/road trip Up to you – review the individual itineraries.
Electives Gold (0); Silver (5).
Highest-ranked elective **Hummus**.
BUCKET! Score 7+ **Hummus**.
Electives without a micro-region **Argila/Hookah/Shisha**; *Bedouin Tents and Coffee*; *Café Culture*; *Camel Riding*; *Hummus*.

Off the Beaten Path

ISRAEL AND PALESTINE

Most everyone knows that Jerusalem and Tel Aviv are great spots in Israel. In fact, most of our top 50 ranked sites are well-trodden stops on the tourist trail. But there are still hidden gems located throughout the country when we look at some of the lesser-known (but *worthy!*) sites ranked #51–100.

If multilayered history is what you're after, and you've already been to **Megiddo (#59)** and **Jericho (#26)**, **Tsipori (#56)** might be right up your alley, with mosaics, Crusader forts, and early churches.

The biblical sites at the **Sea of Galilee (#7)** are rightfully popular, but have you ever considered visiting them on foot? The **Jesus Trail (#69)** allows you to do just that – in day-trip chunks or over several days.

Also up north are two interesting "Beit"s with similar names. **Beit She'arim (#79)** is a UNESCO World Heritage site highlighting ancient Jewish necropolis and accompanying sarcophagi. **Caesarea (#25)** has the most recognizable Roman ruins, but the ones at **Beit She'an (#39)** are equally impressive and much quieter.

The Crusader ruins at **Akko (#13)** are very impressive, but the best-preserved fort in Israel would have to be **Belvoir (#93)**, south of the Kinneret. Often confused as a Crusader castle but actually dating years later to the Ayyubids is **Nimrod's Fortress (#85)**, a sprawling mountaintop castle located in the Golan with sweeping views. **Banias (#80)** is a lush park nearby replete with Greek ruins and a waterfall.

Some of the region's desert sites are also worth visiting. You don't want to miss the hanging **St. George's Monastery (#97)** in the Wadi Qelt, near **Jericho (#26)**, perched right on the side of a mountain and still in use after one-and-a-half millennia.

Timna (#96), an ancient copper mine, is a great day trip from **Eilat (#78)** for those who need some education to coincide with their vacation.

Further afield in the Negev is the **Incense Route (#73)**. **Petra (#2)** may be the most popular Nabataean town, but there are ruins of Nabataean towns and way stations stretching from Saudi Arabia to the Mediterranean, including the Israeli Negev. **Avdat (#48)** is the best preserved and is right off the highway; **Ein Avdat (#74)**, a desert oasis, is right up the street.

Tel Aviv Beaches (#89) are to die for, but they are never not busy. Try **Dor HaBonim (#100)**, considered by many to be the best beach in Israel, if you're looking for beauty and solace.

Should you have a few days to spare after visits to **Jericho (#26)** and **Bethlehem (#40)**, you may want to consider a trip to the final resting place of King Herod (who ordered the construction of the Second Temple and Caesarea, among other grand works) at **Herodion (#90)**, just south of Bethlehem. Continue a bit further to visit the shared city of Hebron (C2), the only city where Jews and Arabs live together in the West Bank. There, you'll want to see the **Tomb of the Patriarchs (#46)**, Abraham and family's burial spot. Don't skip a night in **Ramallah (#68)**, which is quickly becoming the hippest city in Palestine. Further north is **Nablus (#61)**, with interesting food, history, and Samaritan culture.

JORDAN

With the exception of perhaps **Petra (#2)** and **Amman (#36/#37)**, almost everything feels off-the-beaten-path in Jordan. With its **Red Sea (#10)** access on the south shore, **Aqaba (#43)** has the best diving out of the three Gulf of Aqaba cities (Taba (T1) and **Eilat (#78)**). **Wadi Rum (#4)** is also popular, but often too far for quick visits.

Forget Jordan-specific "bests": **Jerash (#14)** contains the best Roman ruins in the whole region. Dueling sites, the **Ajloun Forest (#57)** and **Ajloun Fortress (#76)**, can be found near Jerash.

There's a whole circuit of **Qasr Amra and the Desert Palaces (#20)** in the eastern Jordan desert which can be done on an aggressive day trip or overnight. Nearby you can walk over the **Azraq Wetlands (#55)** on its boardwalk and learn about the animals and plants that have made this land their home.

The **Dana Biosphere Reserve (#21)** is home to unique flora and fauna, as well as the reputed **Feynan Ecolodge (#86)**, where interacting with the Bedouin community is part of the experience. **Wadi Mujib and Mujib Biosphere Reserve (#23)** will not leave you wanting for nature either, and will even get you soaked on one of the knee-deep trails.

Everyone who passes through Amman rightfully visits its ancient sites, but there's a lot more to Amman than history. See **Modern Amman (#36)** to ensure you're getting both pictures.

Popular with the Christian set and very close to the border, **Bethany-Beyond-the-Jordan (#41)** is the presumed location of Jesus' baptism. Another very popular site is **Madaba (#19)**, with its famed mosaic map and churches. Once you're finished there, check out the stunning mosaics at UNESCO site **Umm ar-Rasas (#81)**.

Way up north near the Israeli and Syrian borders is **Umm Qais (#45)**, a multilayered archaeological site amid greenery and rugged hills.

Thematic

No matter your itinerary, you have hopefully budgeted time for our three BUCKET! sites of the **Old City Jerusalem (#1)**, **Petra (#2)**, and the **Dead Sea (#3)**. There's plenty more to see besides these sites, though. Below, find the top experiences: our BUCKET! sites, yes, but also UNESCO World Heritage sites, unique spots, and places that make you go "wow."

Jerusalem 2–3 days. *Consider*: City Walks A1, A7. *Electives*: **Old City Jerusalem (#1)**; **Church of the Holy Sepulchre (#9)**; **Western Wall (#11)**; **Mea She'arim (#66)**. The number-one site in the Holy Land, as ranked by us and the world, is the Old City in Jerusalem. Of particular note: the Church of the Holy Sepulchre, for its many sites referenced in the last days of Jesus Christ, including the place where he was crucified and buried. The Western Wall is a monolithic reminder of the tension between Jews and Arabs, but the site itself is also interesting as a cultural melange of Jews that come to pray. Step back in time with a short visit to Mea She'arim, one of **Jerusalem, New City (#72)**'s ultra-orthodox neighborhoods.

Greater Jerusalem 1 day. *Consider*: Road Trip B1. *Electives*: **Beit Guvrin and Maresha (#60)**. The UNESCO site of Beit Guvrin and Maresha lets you explore the bizarre underground world of its early residents.

West Bank/Palestine 1 day. *Consider*: City Walk C1; Road Trip C2. *Electives*: **Church of the Nativity (#18)**; **Bethlehem (#40)**; *Battir Hills*; *Separation Wall*. Just south of Jerusalem, spend a day wandering through Bethlehem's alleys, check out the Church of the Nativity and wait in line to see the very spot where Jesus was said to have been born. Then check out some anti-establishment art (including Banksy's) on the imposing *Separation Wall*. As you're driving back, look for the terraced hills in the Battir region, also a UNESCO site.

Tel Aviv 1 day. *Consider*: City Walk D5. *Electives*: **Modern Movement (Bauhaus Architecture) (#16)**. You don't want to miss out on Tel Aviv's thousands of buildings designated by UNESCO as part of the Modern Movement in the "White City" of Tel Aviv.

Mediterranean coast 1 day. *Consider*: City Walks E1, E2, Road Trip E5. *Electives*: **Akko (#13)**; **Baha'í Gardens (#27)**. Be sure to time your visit to Haifa to coincide with the Baha'í Gardens tour (otherwise you'll only be able to see the terraced cliffside from the street). Explore the underground Crusader tunnels and knights' halls in the walled city of Akko.

Galilee and Jezreel 1–2 days. *Consider*: Road Trip F1. *Electives*: **Beit She'arim (#79)**; **Biblical Tels (#38)**; **Jesus Trail (#69)**; **Megiddo (#59)**; *Nahal Me'arot/Wadi el-Mughara*; *Tel Hazor*. Megiddo is the site of the biblical story of Armageddon, and you'd think it accurate if you consider the 20+ civilizations that are buried one on top of another (there's a good explanation for this). One of the other UNESCO-designated Biblical Tels, *Tel Hazor*, is located north of the Sea of Galilee (the third is outside Beersheva). Beit She'arim, also a UNESCO site, holds dozens of Jewish sarcophagi and catacombs, many still untouched. If you've got a few days, or just an afternoon, walk through time by trekking the Jesus Trail, a unique experience that puts Biblophiles in touch with many of the earliest recorded places in the Holy Land. En route to these famous sites, visit the Neolithic caves called Nahal Me'arot and Wadi el-Mughara which chart the very rise of civilization and spread of humanity.

Golan 1 day. *Consider*: Road Trips I1–I2. *Electives*: **Golan Heights (#62)**; *Israel National Trail*. The Golan Heights are truly a unique experience – the geography, residents, weather, and history are all different from the rest of the country because of its historic association to Syria (Israel annexed the land in 1980). You can begin the long journey to the Red Sea from here – on the country's popular Israel National Trail.

Negev 1–2 days. *Consider*: Road Trips J2, J3. *Electives*: **Avdat (#48)**; **Incense Route (#73)**; **Makhtesh Ramon (#28)**; *Mitzpe Ramon*. The Nabataean passage to the sea is now called the Incense Route, commemorating the spices that were carried from the east all the way to the Mediterranean. Visit Avdat, the biggest of the Incense Route sites. Mitzpe Ramon is also a great spot to stare out across the vast expanse of the Makhtesh Ramon crater.

Dead Sea and Masada 1–2 days. *Consider*: Road Trip K1. *Electives*: **Dead Sea (#3)**; **Masada (#8)**; *Ein Bokek Spa Hotels*. Start your morning on a hike up the Snake Path of Masada, catching the sun rise over Jordan and the Dead Sea. As one of our BUCKET! experiences, the Dead Sea is unlike anything you've done before. Lather yourself in mud, soak up the UV-less rays, and then read a book while lounging on nothing more than your keister out in the salty sea. Stay the night and do it again tomorrow at one of the resorts at *Ein Bokek* or day spas up the road.

Jordan 3–6 days. *Consider*: Road Trips M2, O1, P1, P2, Q3, R1, S1. *Electives*: **Bethany-Beyond-the-Jordan (#41)**; **Qasr Amra and the Desert Palaces (#20)**; **Feynan Ecolodge (#86)**; **Petra (#2)**; **Umm ar-Rasas (#81)**; **Wadi Rum (#4)**; *Little Petra*. There is so much of interest in Jordan, and it remains so unfortunately (though sometimes refreshingly) void of tourists in parts. Its UNESCO sites include the baptism site of Bethany-Beyond-the-Jordan, the mosaic site of Umm ar-Rasas, the red sands of Wadi Rum, and the Umayyad palaces out in the eastern desert. And of course the shining star (usually with lots of tourists), Petra and its little neighbor, Little Petra. Plan a stop in Dana for a Bedouin experience (with more luxe environs) at the Feynan Ecolodge.

Egypt 1–2 days. *Consider*: Road Trip T1. *Electives*: **Dahab (#54)**; **Mount Sinai (#15)**; **Ras Mohammad (#53)**; **St. Catherine's Monastery (#22)**. If you cross into Egypt from Israel, you'll want to visit St. Catherine's Monastery for its famed relics, and its strategic location to Mount Sinai – a strenuous but popular sunrise hike. Spend the night (or two or three) on ultra-cheap outdoor accommodation (they have hotels too) at the super-relaxed Dahab, then head south for one of the world's finest diving sites, Ras Mohammad.

Minimum travel time 14 days, bare minimum.

Routing option 1) Start in Jerusalem. The Old City can be done in a day, if you are in a hurry. 2) Take a day trip to Bethlehem. 3) Take a day trip to the Dead Sea. 4) Head west through Beit Guvrin on your way to Tel Aviv, where you should stay the night. 5) Take a day trip (returning to Tel Aviv), visiting the Mediterranean highlights. 6) Then drive back to the Galilee the next day. Or you can stay in Rosh Pina for the night, visiting Galilee sites one day and Golan sites the next. 7) On a long day trip south from Tel Aviv or Jerusalem, you can pass through a few of the Incense Route sites, and stop to gaze at the majesty of Makhtesh Ramon. Or, spend the night there. 8) Either head back north to Jerusalem to cross over to Jordan, or head south to Eilat and cross to Jordan from that border. 9) Either way, you can follow our Jordan driving itineraries, as many of the sites are in multiple locations spread around the country. 10) Finally, if you want to fly to Sharm, or hoof it on bus to the Sinai, you can end your trip with some sun, some morning hiking, and a straw mat in Dahab… or a five-star resort in Sharm – your choice.

RELIGION

Want a great overview of the world's three great monotheistic religions? Well, look no further than the Holy Land. We've combined the best from our *Religion* theme (p. 487) to present sites celebrating great historical figures, commemorating moments in the holy books, and pick the most interesting and relevant houses of religion. Feel free to mix and match from the following options based on your current plan, or, if you want to focus your trip specifically on these places, we've indicated minimum times for each regional location.

Old City Jerusalem 1–2 days. *Consider*: City Walks A1, A2, A5, A7. *Electives*: **Al-Aqsa Mosque (#65)**; **Church of the Holy Sepulchre (#9)**; **Dome of the Rock (#6)**; **Mount of Olives (#34)**; **Via Dolorosa (#42)**; **Western Wall (#11)**. *Combine with*: Garden Tomb (A6); Kidron Valley (A5); *Church of St. Anne and the Pools of Bethesda*; *Monastery of Abu Ghosh*; Ethiopian Quarter (A7). Many of our highest-ranked sites are located all within a short walking distance of one another. Use our walking tours to find your way around.

Palestine 1–2 days. *Consider*: Road Trip C2. *Electives*: **Bethlehem (#40)**; **Church of the Nativity (#18)**; **Tomb of the Patriarchs and Old Town of Hebron (#46)**; **St. George's Monastery and Wadi Qelt (#97)**; *Deir Quruntal*; *Mar Saba*; *Mount Gerizim*. *Combine with*: Road Trips C3, C4. The birthplace of Jesus in Bethlehem is one of the most popular attractions in the Holy Land. Less well known are the cliffside monasteries in the Wadi Qelt region, the Samaritan site of Mount Gerizim, and the burial tombs of the patriarchs and matriarchs of the Abrahamic religions.

Galilee 1–2 days. *Consider*: Road Trip G2. *Electives*: **Beit She'arim (#79)**; **Nazareth and its Biblical Sites (#29)**; **Church of the Transfiguration**; *Tel Arad*. *Combine with*: **Megiddo (#59)**; Kfar Kama (G2); **Tsipori (#56)**. There are several sites to be visited for Christian tourists in the greater Galilee (with a high concentration on the Sea itself, as mentioned below). Tel Arad houses the only known House of Yahweh in Israel. Beit She'arim was an ancient burial site, replete with recovered sarcophagi.

Sea of Galilee 1 day. *Consider*: Road Trips G3, G4. *Electives*: **Capernaum and Tabgha (#33)**; **Sea of Galilee (#7)**; *Mount of Beatitudes*. *Combine with*: Kibbutz Ginosar (G3); Korazim; Kursi (G3). If you are interested in the life and times of Jesus Christ, this Sea of Galilee tour will tickle your fancy.

Jordan 1–2 days. *Consider*: Road Trip P2. *Electives*: **Bethany-Beyond-the-Jordan (#41)**; **Mount Nebo (#24)**; *Mukawir*; *Petra by Night*. Moses died atop Mount Nebo, Jesus was baptized near Bethany-Beyond-the-Jordan, and John the Baptist was executed at Mukawir. For a more spiritual experience, try Petra by Night.

Egypt 1–2 days. *Consider*: Road Trip T1. *Electives*: **Mount Sinai (#15)**; **St. Catherine's Monastery (#22)**. Moses received the Ten Commandments atop Mount Sinai, and St. Catherine's Monastery – at the base of the mountain – serves as both historical and practical jumping-off point for understanding the biblical Sinai.

Minimum travel time 6 days, plus travel time.

Routing option 1) Start with the Old City Jerusalem itinerary – it contains the most important sites for Islam, Judaism, and Christianity. 2) Add in Palestine sites, as Bethlehem is only 30 minutes south of Jerusalem. 3) Head to the Sea of Galilee next, if you have an interest in seeing New Testament sites affiliated with Jesus' life and ministry. 4) Then continue to the Galilee for visits to Nazareth and surrounding sites. 5) If you have plans to visit Jordan (Petra!), be sure to add time for their biblical sites. 6) If the security situation allows, make time for Mount Sinai and St. Catherine's Monastery, located in Egypt's Sinai peninsula.

ARCHAEOLOGY

In many ways, history was recorded, in its many iterations, in the Holy Land. Archaeological sites continually show evidence of an *even older* synagogue, an *earlier* village, the *oldest known* human remains, and *even earlier* population movements out of Africa through this region. There are many stories in our written and oral histories, and this region will provide a history lover with plenty of opportunities to get into the proverbial weeds trying to decipher a mark on this stone and anachronistic iconography on that rubble building. Prepare to be awed.

Jerusalem 2–3 days. *Electives*: **Israel Museum (#17)**; **Jerusalem Archaeological Park (#71)**; **Bible Lands Museum**; **City of David**. *Combine with*: City Walk A1. Here, you can start with the City of David for an excellent overview of the history of the Old City. To ramble around ruins and active excavations, head just south of the Western Wall for the Jerusalem Archaeological Park. The Israel Museum and Bible Lands Museums in Central Jerusalem require a cab, but are worth a visit, particularly the Israel Museum, in which you can spend an entire day and not get bored.

Palestine 1–2 days. *Electives*: **Herodion (#90)**; **Jericho and Hisham's Palace (#26)**; **Sebastia-Shomron**. Jericho is one of our two major sites that showcase the literally dozens of civilizations that have made the Holy Land home over the past millennia. The first major Islamic caliphate, the Umayyads, established a site at Jericho that is well worth a visit. Herodion is the deathplace of the great builder during the Roman/Jesus era, Herod. Sebastia is a site similar to Caesarea or Jerash, located near Nablus.

Mediterranean coast 1–2 days. *Electives*: **Akko (#13)**; **Caesarea (#25)**; **Apollonia**; **Nahal Me'arot/Wadi el-Mughara**. If you start in Tel Aviv and work your way north, you'll first run into Apollonia, with some surprisingly interesting Crusader ruins hanging in some cases precipitously off nearby cliffs. Caesarea is the mother of Roman sites, with Herod as the chief constructor to bring it to its zenith. The earliest known human settlements (though this changes frequently) were found at the UNESCO site, Nahal Me'arot, on the way to Akko, site of a Crusader castle that was later fortified as an Arab fort.

Galilee and Jezreel 2–3 days. *Electives*: **Belvoir (#93)**; **Biblical Tels (#38)**; **Megiddo (#59)**; **Sea of Galilee (#7)**; **Tsipori (#56)**; *Bar'am*; *Korazim*; *Montfort*; *Yehi'am*. Many of the sites in this region span multiple time periods, particularly Megiddo, with more than 20 layers of civilization buried on top of one another on its small hills. Megiddo and Tel Hazor are two early Iron Age sites that make up the UNESCO site of Biblical Tels, along with Tel Beer Sheva in the Negev. There are several "historical" sites as told in the Bible in this region, relating to Jesus' life and ministry. Several Roman and Crusader ruins round out the entertainment.

Golan 1–2 days. *Electives*: **Banias (#80)**; **Nimrod's Fortress (#85)**; **Tel Dan (#63)**. If you continue a bit further from the Galilee you'll reach the Golan, whose sites span millennia. Tel Dan is one of the oldest known cities in the region, while Banias pays homage to Pan, the Greek god of the wild and nymphs. Nimrod is one of the most enjoyable fortresses, commonly mistaken for a Crusader castle, but actually attributable to Saladin's Ayyubid Empire which was trying to ward off the Sixth Crusade.

Masada 1 day. *Elective*: **Masada (#8)**. Visit this ancient Jewish outpost on top of a cliff, overlooking the Dead Sea, and contemplate the last moments of the Jewish rebels who, according to legend, committed mass suicide rather than suffer Roman rule.

Negev 2 days. *Electives*: **Avdat (#48)**; **Incense Route (#73)**; **Timna (#96)**; *Mamshit*; *Tel Beer Sheva*. Near Eilat, Timna Park shows the prehistoric period when copper mining was common. Further north, Tel Beer Sheva is the third of UNESCO's Biblical Tels, highlighting the first golden age of Jewish rule. The famous Nabataeans that created Petra were also involved in an important trade route through the Negev, and the Incense Route contains multiple sites highlighting stops on the way from Petra to the Mediterranean, including Avdat and Mamshit.

Jordan 3–4 days. *Electives*: **Ajloun Fortress (#76)**; **Karak (#49)**; **Petra (#2)**; **Qasr Amra and the Desert Palaces (#20)**; *Little Petra*; *Shobak*. Start in Petra, of course, as it's a BUCKET! site and never ceases to amaze. The Nabataeans established several sites during their pinnacle period in history, which can be seen at Little Petra as well as the Incense Route sites mentioned under "Negev" above. The Desert Palace loop allows you to see several structures in various states of repair, several with beautiful and unusual murals of the first caliph period, the Umayyads. Both Karak and Shobak have great big castles to explore from the Crusader era. The Ajloun Fortress is one of Saladin's strategic Ayyubid forts from the 12th century.

Minimum travel time 13 days, if hitting every region. At least 8 days if you plan to hit just one or two sites in each region.

Routing option 1) All itineraries should begin in Jerusalem. 2) The Palestine sites are good for folks who have lots of time and interest. 3) For those who want to do the Mediterranean sites quickly, skip Apollonia, but Caesarea, Nahal Me'arot, and Akko are all worth a visit, for different reasons. 4) In the Galilee, you may want to pick one site from each period, such as Megiddo (Iron Age), Tsipori (Roman), Belvoir (Crusader), and any of the Sea of Galilee sites – perhaps Nazareth and/or Kibbutz Ginosar (where a Jesus-era boat was discovered). 5) The Golan sites are nice, though out of the way. If you have to pick only one, go for Nimrod. 6) The Negev sites are often stones in the sand, though Timna is set up for families, and Avdat has the most preserved and well-placed ruins. 7) If you're heading into Jordan – and you should, for Petra – we recommend dedicating some time there. At a minimum, you should see Petra, the Nabataean masterpiece.

STRUCTURE

Just want to see pretty buildings? Impressive feats? Lucky for you, there is a lot of beauty to be found in the millennia-old buildings and carved facades, as well as the infrastructure projects and modern monuments. Amid the desert backdrop, admire the variety and antiquity of the structures that still stand, many after dozens of successive wars and conquering parties. The following are just a few of the highlights.

Jerusalem 2–3 days. *Consider*: City Walks A1, A2, A5, A6, A7. *Electives*: **Dome of the Rock (#6)**; **Jerusalem Walls and Gates (#47)**; **Mount of Olives (#34)**; **Temple Mount (#12)**; **Western Wall (#11)**; *City of David*; *Hezekiah's Tunnel*; *Yemen Moshe*; *YMCA*. Some of the most iconic sites are found right next to each other. Start your journey at the epicenter of the struggle over Jerusalem – Temple Mount, site of the Dome of the Rock, the Fountain of Sultan Qaytbay, and the Dome of the Chain. The Western Wall is one of the last of the retaining walls of Temple Mount, and a sight to behold. The walls of Jerusalem themselves are worthy of a circumnavigation, and while you take your stroll right outside the Old City, you can catch glimpses of Montefiore's Windmill, the YMCA, the onion domes of the Mount of Olives, and the oldest part of Jerusalem, the City of David, including Hezekiah's Tunnel.

Greater Jerusalem ½ day for museums; ½ day for Beit Guvrin. *Consider*: Road Trips A8, B1. *Electives*: **Beit Guvrin and Maresha (#60)**; **Israel Museum (#17)**; **Yad Vashem (#35)**; *Bridge of Strings*. Jerusalem may be old, but modern architecture is still redefining the skyline. The Israel Museum's Shrine of the Dome, Yad Vashem's precipitous placement, and famous architect Calatrava's landmark Bridge of Strings all add to the environment. Outside of town, UNESCO site Beit Guvrin will introduce you to underground living such that you will never think of pigeon-rearing in the same way.

Palestine ½ day each. *Electives*: **Wadi Qelt (#97)**; *Battir Hills*. Two of the most eye-pleasing engineering developments are each located in the West Bank, just outside Jerusalem. Visit Wadi Qelt for cliff-hanging monasteries and the Battir Hills for the use of the original terraced earth and irrigation systems.

Tel Aviv 1 day. *Consider*: City Walk D5. *Electives*: **Modern Movement (Bauhaus Architecture) (#16)**; **Tel Aviv Museum of Art (#95)**; *Design Museum Holon*. Tel Aviv's known as the White City because of its large concentration of buildings constructed in the Modern Movement style, known commonly as Bauhaus. The Museum of Art is a play on that theme, and worth a visit for photo opportunities. Outside of town, the Design Museum in Holon is also photo-worthy with its beautifully colored curved facade.

North Israel 1 day. *Electives*: **Bahá'í Gardens (#27)**; **Nazareth and its Biblical Sites (#29)**; *Basilica of the Annunciation*. Perhaps on par with Versailles in terms of their attention to manicured lawns and symmetry, the Bahá'í Gardens are a gorgeous cliffside monument to the Bahá'í faith. Then, head east to Nazareth to catch a glimpse of the striking Basilica of the Annunciation, where Mary was proclaimed the Mother of God.

Petra 1–3 days. *Elective*: **Petra (#2)**. No trip to the region would be complete without a stop at this glorious, formerly hidden gem. The engineering is still fascinating: how *did* they build an entire town out of mountainside?

Minimum travel time 7 days, plus travel time.

Routing option 1) Start with the Old City, then move to the hills outside the Old City Walls, followed by the museums in New City. 2) Add in Palestine sites of interest. 3) Spend time in Tel Aviv soaking up modern architecture. 4) Take a day trip from Tel Aviv to see Haifa and Nazareth. 5) Add Petra, anywhere.

NATURE AND SCENIC

Rocky deserts and lush forests, glorious beaches and hills of salt, fresh water, salt water, and *really* salty water, the lowest place on Earth, and even a mountain with snow: the Holy Land may be small in area, but it is rich in geographic diversity and natural beauty. Though you needn't go too far outside of Jerusalem to find nature (and no matter your journey, we recommend you spend 2–3 days in Jerusalem, regardless), it's true that the farther you go, the more natural the environment.

Tel Aviv 1 day. *Electives*: **Jaffa (#30)**; **Tel Aviv (#5)**. Tel Aviv's a big city, but its white-sand beaches will mentally transport you to a tropical island paradise. (And, when the fun in the sun ends, you have great restaurants and bars to attend to.) Head to Jaffa for great Tel Aviv photo opportunities.

Mediterranean coast 1–2 days. *Electives*: **Bahá'í Gardens (#27)**; **Dor HaBonim (#100)**; **Mount Carmel**; **Rosh HaNikra**. All along the Mediterranean coast, you can find beautiful spots of nature at remote beaches such as Dor, or go with something more manicured for your moments of deep contemplation, such as the Bahá'í Gardens in Haifa. Mount Carmel, just outside of Haifa, surrounds you with trees, wildlife, and parks. Rosh HaNikra on the border with Lebanon has wonderfully carved rocks where bright blue water splashes through – great photo opportunities abound.

Galilee and Jezreel 1–2 days. *Electives*: **Jesus Trail (#69)**; **Gan HaShlosha**; **Hula Lake**; **Israel National Trail**; **Mount Arbel**; **Tiberias**. You're bound to see and experience lots of natural beauty on the Jesus Trail and the Israel National Trail in this area. Hula Lake will put you in touch with your inner ornithologist. Gan HaShlosha has tidal pools amid a lush grove. And the Sea of Galilee, from the vantage points of Tiberias and Mount Arbel, provides a lovely picture of the region. There are lots of roadside vistas on the eastern side of the Sea.

Golan 2–3 days. *Electives*: **Banias (#80)**; **Golan Heights (#62)**; **Tel Dan (#63)**; **Gamla**; **Hamat Gader**; **Yehudiya**. This is where you truly get into the wilder areas of this region. Unlike the other geographical regions of Israel, the Golan Heights have Mount Hermon (snow!), green national parks in Tel Dan and Banias, the Yehudiya Forest, and Gamla Nature Reserve. Hamat Gader warms you with sulfur pools and crocodiles.

Negev 1 day. *Electives*: **Ein Avdat (#74)**; **Makhtesh Ramon (#28)**. More natural beauty in the south. Don't miss the glorious views of the canyon (really a makhtesh, a naturally eroding crater) from the Mitzpe Ramon visitor center. Go camping and see some glorious stars. Ein Avdat is a rare oasis in the desert nearby.

Dead Sea and Masada 1–2 days. *Electives*: **Dead Sea (#3)**; **Ein Gedi (#50)**; **Masada (#8)**. Go from the lowest point on Earth and one of the saltiest bodies of water to the adjacent mountain which housed a rebel Jewish community for years atop its perilous cliffs. Nearby Ein Gedi will give you a different desert hiking experience – one with waterfalls.

Eilat/Aqaba 1–2 days. *Electives*: **Coral Beach (#83)**; **Red Sea (#10)**; **Timna (#96)**; **Underwater Observatory**; **Yotvata Hai-Bar**. Further south, you can find a desert animal park at Yotvata, mineral caves in Timna Park, diving in the Red Sea (at Eilat, Aqaba, or Taba), and snorkeling and fish-viewing opportunities at Coral Beach and the Underwater Observatory in Aqaba.

Petra 1–3 days. *Electives*: **Petra (#2)**; **Little Petra**. Petra's a wild experience. You take the 1km path from the main gates just to the beginning of the site, and then the beauty really starts to set in. Gorgeous rocks of pink, orange, and red highlight the monolithic carved motifs of the ancient Nabataean civilization.

Jordan 2–3 days. *Electives*: **Ajloun Forest (#57)**; **Azraq Wetlands (#55)**; **Dana Biosphere Reserve (#21)**; **King's Highway (#31)**; **Qasr Amra and the Desert Palaces (#20)**; **Wadi Mujib and Mujib Biosphere Reserve (#23)**; **Wadi Rum (#4)**. "Wild Jordan" as they call it. After Petra, you should explore the even more stunning Wadi Rum (by hot air balloon, maybe?), with its rolling red desert sands and mountain backdrop. (With stargazing at night!) Jordan's nature reserves are home to many endangered animals and plants, and many require guides – well worth the trouble to plan. King's Highway has a number of spots for gorgeous photo opportunities.

Egypt 1 day. *Electives*: **Ras Mohammad (#53)**; **Sharm el-Sheikh (#88)**. Perhaps the best diving in the world, the Ras Mohammad National Park at the southern tip of the Sinai peninsula will get you quickly acquainted with the non-terrestrial world.

Minimum travel time 5 days to see mountains, desert, beaches, forests, craters, caves, rivers, lakes, and seas; and a minimum 12 days to see everything.

Routing option 1) Soak up the sun in Tel Aviv, unless you have plans to do beaches elsewhere along the Mediterranean. 2) Head north, stopping in Dor, Haifa, and Rosh HaNikra. 3) Go east towards the Sea of Galilee, where you'll have to make some choices about sites because few are right next to one another. If you're hiking, that's a whole different itinerary. If not, you can see Gan HaShlosha first (along with the other Lower Galilee attractions), head north towards Tiberias, and swing through Hula Lake on your way to the Golan. 4) Past Hula, you can make stops at Tel Dan, Banias, and Nimrod's Fortress on your way to Mount Hermon (if you like skiing or, in the summer, hikes). Then south from there to Gamla and Yehudiya for more hikes, eagle watching, and river trekking. 5) Drive south on Highway 90 past Jerusalem to Ein Gedi, Masada, and the Dead Sea (3 hours). 6) Keep going south, making pit stops at Timna and Yotvata, as you like. If you spend the day in Eilat, you can swim, dive, and explore the Underwater Observatory. 7) Cross the border to either Taba (to head to Sinai's tip) or Aqaba. If the latter, then you have a jumping-off point for the rest of Jordan. 8) Head north from Aqaba to Wadi Rum, spend the night under the stars, and head to Petra. Again, start early and have the place to yourself in the morning. 9) Visit any of the biosphere reserves – Dana, Mujib, Azraq, or Ajloun – depending on how your itinerary works out. 10) Head back to Israel, or visit Sinai from here.

SOCIETY AND PEOPLE

There's an incredible diversity in this region that often goes unrecognized. We include glimpses of the wide array of ethnicities, language families, national origins, and religious groups you might find – from those living like it's still the 1800s (Mea She'arim) to a mostly secular, almost hedonistic society (Tel Aviv).

Jerusalem 3–4 days. *Consider*: City Walks A1–A7. *Electives*: **Jerusalem, New City (#72)**; **Old City Jerusalem (#1)**. Jerusalem can offer you a little of everything. In the Old City, catch Orthodox Jews praying at the Western Wall, devout Muslims praying at Al-Aqsa, and six Christian denominations vying for praying opportunities (peacefully) at the Church of the Holy Sepulchre. Each of the four quarters offers you a glimpse of a different slice of life – Christian, Muslim, Jewish, and Armenian. Outside the walls, other "quarters" have been named after their historic residents, including the Russian and Ethiopian quarters. The Mea She'arim neighborhood houses several groups of ultra-Orthodox Jews, some of whom appear to have walked out of 19th-century Europe. East Jerusalem is where the Arabs of the town live. Here, you can also find Christian devotees at any of the several churches on Mount Zion. In the New City, the bustling streets of Nakhalat Shiva and Ben Yehuda will give you a taste of the non-sacramental Jerusalemite lifestyle.

West Bank/Palestine 2 days. *Electives*: **Nablus (#61)**; **St. George's Monastery and Wadi Qelt (#97)**; *Deir Quruntal*; *Mount Gerizim*; *Separation Wall*. It's a different world in the West Bank, where many residents don't have access to Jerusalem, let alone Israel or other countries. For a big dose of reality, head right to the Separation Wall and see how these two societies are, quite literally, still divided. At the Monastery of St. George of Chobiza in Wadi Qelt and the Monastery of Temptation (or Deir Quruntal) nearby, observe Greek monks living dangerously on the edge. Samaritans can still be found in Nablus and nearby Mount Gerizim. On just the outskirts of Jerusalem, you'll find a variety of closed communities comprised of Jewish "settlers" who've transformed the land into thriving townships. You can also meet Palestinian refugees in Jenin and in camps outside Bethlehem.

Tel Aviv 1 day. *Consider*: City Walks D1, D2. *Electives*: **Jaffa (#30)**; **Tel Aviv (#5)**. Far more secular than the rest of the region, Tel Aviv can surprise you with its laid-back dress, lax open-bottle policies, and smells of Mary Jane wafting in every neighborhood. Jaffa has been an Arab town (now incorporated as Tel Aviv-Jaffa) for millennia, and still retains that vibe, though in a relaxed sense, much like Tel Aviv. Stroll down Rothschild Boulevard and through Neve Tzedek to feel even more hip. And, if you're in town in June, you certainly won't want to miss the Tel Aviv Pride Celebration – the largest in the Middle East.

Mediterranean coast 1 day. *Consider*: City Walks E1, E2. *Electives*: **Akko (#13)**; *Haifa*. The two northern cities of Haifa and Akko are each known for the Jewish and Arab populations who coexist peacefully. The German Colony in Haifa is an old European neighborhood.

Golan 1 day. *Elective*: **Golan Heights (#62)**. Israel annexed the Golan Heights from Syria in 1981, separating families on either side of the border. The Druze community can choose whether to take up Israeli citizenship (many remain non-citizen residents), and many still have connections to family members on the other side of the demarcation line.

Negev 1 day. *Electives*: **Mamshit**; **Museum of Bedouin Culture**. Explore Bedouin culture at the eponymous museum in Beersheva, and sleep under an Ethiopian tukul in Mamshit.

Jordan 2–3 days. *Electives*: **Feynan Ecolodge (#86)**; **Modern Amman (#36)**; **Wadi Rum (#4)**; **Jordanian Hospitality**. Soak up Arab culture in the cafés of Amman, Bedouin culture under the stars at Wadi Rum, and local community ways at the eco-friendly Feynan Ecolodge in Dana, and everywhere you sit or stand you'll be met with an inevitable smile, as Jordan is also well known for its hospitality.

Egypt 1 day. *Electives*: **Dahab (#54)**; **St. Catherine's Monastery (#22)**. Stay with other Christian pilgrims at the famed UNESCO site, St. Catherine's Monastery, in the foothills of Mount Sinai. And find the travelers who don't want to be found in Dahab.

Minimum travel time 13 days minimum if you go to Egypt and Jordan. You can soak up a lot of culture in Jerusalem alone, though.

Routing option 1) Start with the Old City, visiting each of the four quarters. Head to East Jerusalem and the Mount of Olives, then circle back around the Old City towards Jaffa Gate. From there, head west on foot through the New City neighborhoods. 2) Visiting the West Bank will give you another perspective on the Holy Land, assuredly. If you're so inclined, you can coordinate a trip to a refugee center. Or, Christian tourists can hike to cliff-hugging monasteries in the desert. 3) Pop over to Jordan, if you're including it in your itinerary. You can sleep in Amman, Wadi Rum, or Dana (Feynan Ecolodge) for comfy accommodations. (Don't miss Petra, though.) 4) Head back to Israel and make your way to Tel Aviv for some very nonreligious shenanigans. 5) Observe what could be the possible future of a one- or two-state solution if Palestinian and Israeli leaders ever negotiate a deal – peaceful coexistence (perhaps?). Haifa and Akko both seem to be faring well in that regard. 6) In the Galilee and Golan, you'll encounter minority Druze populations. 7) Then head all the way south (or skip the north, if not of interest) to the Negev to meet up with Bedouins, Ethiopians, black Israelites, and other communities. 8) Pilgrims may wish to cross the border at Eilat (towards Taba) and organize a trip to St. Catherine's (and, while there, hike up Mount Sinai) in Egypt.

CULTURE

The Holy Land might not be the first place you consider when thinking of world-class museums, modern art, sculpture, design, and performance, but it really holds its own. Not only does it have an outstanding collection of ancient artifacts for you to view and learn about, but it has an interesting array of modern history, art, and anthropology museums as well. This itinerary is general because "culture" is fairly general, and can be combined with other "cultural" activities, such as holidays, special events, or people. Refer to *Society and People* (p. 784) for more specifics on the types of people you can meet, and check *Noteworthy* (p. 776) if you want to combine any of this itinerary with more traditional tourism activities.

Jerusalem 2–3 days. *Electives*: **Citadel/Tower of David (#32)**; **Israel Museum (#17)**; **Jerusalem, New City (#72)**. With the exception of the Citadel and the Wohl Archaeological Museum, all of these sites are outside the Old City. The Israel Museum alone can eat up your whole day with its exquisite exhibits, and you can catch a talk or performance at the Yitzhak Rabin Center inside. For intimate archaeology, try the Rockefeller Archaeological Museum or, for biblical history and artifacts, try the Bible Lands Museum. The Hadassah Synagogue has a modern-era stained-glass window designed by Marc Chagall that is worth a stop. And while in the Old City, start your journey at the Citadel, or the Tower of David, at Jaffa Gate to orient yourself to the many layers of history you're about to unpack. In the New City, find playful art installations in the Nakhalat Shiva neighborhood and street musicians on Ben Yehuda.

Tel Aviv 2–3 days. *Electives:* **ANU – Museum of the Jewish People (#77)**; **Jaffa (#30)**; **Tel Aviv Museum of Art (#95)**; *Bialik House*; *Drummers' Beach*; *MUSA – Eretz Israel Museum*; *Neve Tzedek*; *Weizmann Institute of Science*. There are plenty of artists and wannabes in the Tel Aviv area, so, if you're looking for an artsy vibe, this is the place to be. Neighborhoods such as Neve Tzedek, Jaffa, and Florentin each have their own distinguished character. The museums in and around Tel Aviv all offer something different, and are rightly popular. Drummers' Beach is for those drum-circle-loving travelers, while the Israel Philharmonic and Suzanne Delal Center are for those wanting something a bit fancier (just a bit). Lots of places for concerts. There's plenty to choose from here: art, sculpture, performance, and architecture.

Mediterranean coast 1 day. *Electives:* **Akko (#13)**; *Ein Hod*; *Haifa*; *Zichron Ya'akov*. Ein Hod is an artists' colony outside of Haifa, while Haifa itself has a reputable Japanese art collection (and the Bahá'í Gardens). Zichron Ya'akov also has art (as does Tsfat a bit further afield). Plus, check out several millennia of history, with lots of good Crusader reenactments at the Knights' Hall in Akko.

Jordan 2–3 days. *Electives:* **Madaba (#19)**; **Modern Amman (#36)**; **Umm ar-Rasas (#81)**. Find art and artists at the Darat al Funun workshop in Amman, glorious mosaic floors in Umm ar-Rasas and Madaba (including the famed Madaba Map), and Jordanian culture at the museums of Popular Culture, Folkore, and Archaeology.

Minimum travel time 7 days.

Routing option 1) In Jerusalem, you probably want to start with the Old City, and then pick one or two museums. 2) Next head to Tel Aviv, where you can spend days if not months soaking up the music, dance, and art, not to mention all the sun. Plan to spend several days here. 3) Then you can really go in several directions. Head to the north, south, or east to Jordan.

ACTIVE

With great infrastructure and weather (for the most part…), you can keep up your active lifestyle in any number of ways in Israel, Jordan, and Egypt. Keep in mind that merely visiting the Old City, Petra, and/or Tel Aviv will send you well beyond your 10,000 steps a day. So this section is for those who like walking for the sake of walking, are interested in water activities such as surfing on boards and kites, and enjoy extreme sports spelled "X-TREME." There's an activity here for everyone who likes to get their heart racing.

Jerusalem 1 day. *Electives:* **Jerusalem Walls and Gates (#47)**; **Mount of Olives (#34)**; **Old City Jerusalem (#1)**; **Ramparts Walk (#91)**. At a minimum, walk the Old City, a BUCKET! site. Hike the Rampart Walk, around Jerusalem's walls, or the Mount of Olives to get your heart rate up.

Greater Jerusalem ½ day. *Elective*: **Sataf**. To the west of town is this nature park, with jogging paths through the Jerusalem hills.

Tel Aviv 1–2 days. *Electives*: **Tel Aviv Beaches (#89)**; *Tel Aviv Tayelet/Promenade*; *Tel-O-Fun Bike Share*. There are lots of sports and exercise options in Tel Aviv, from wandering the Promenade, stopping at free exercise facilities, volleyball nets, and matcot sessions (aggressive paddleball). Plus, tons of runners and walkers. And those that prefer bike riding, you share the same lanes, but everyone seems fine with it – and you can rent by the hour or day with the popular and ubiquitous Tel-O-Fun Bike Share service. If you plan well enough in advance, you can organize a surfing or stand-up paddleboarding lesson. Obviously, swimming is free!

Mediterranean coast ½ day. *Electives*: **Mediterranean Coast**; **Mount Carmel**. Good hiking and walking paths in Mount Carmel. Of course, there's also a dozen great beaches to choose from, if you want to surf or swim.

Galilee 2–3 days. *Electives*: **Jesus Trail (#69)**; *Sea of Galilee Beaches*. The Jordan River produces some rapids that allow you to kayak in the Galilee. The Jesus Trail also begins in this area and provides great multiday hikes through this part of the Holy Land. There's also the option to kitesurf on the Sea of Galilee.

Golan 1 day. *Electives*: **Golan Heights (#62)**; *Israel National Trail*; *Mount Hermon*; *Yehudiya*. Skiing on Mount Hermon, walking through Yehudiya Forest, and the multi-week Israel National Trail (which starts in the Golan and ends in Eilat) are all great excursions in this area, but there are plenty of off-trail options for your exploration fun as well (though be careful of land mines).

Negev 1–2 days. *Electives*: **Ein Avdat (#74)**; **Makhtesh Ramon (#28)**; *Hiking in the Negev*. Hiking through the Ramon Crater (Makhtesh Ramon) is extremely popular, and for great reason – it's gorgeous (though it's dangerously hot several months of the year). Ein Avdat has some waterfall walks if you want a break from the desert sun.

Dead Sea and Masada 1–2 days. *Electives*: **Ein Gedi (#50)**; **Masada (#8)**. More hiking opportunities abound in Ein Gedi (with great views of the Dead Sea). Masada offers great hiking opportunities – entering from three different hiking paths.

Red Sea 1–2 days. *Electives*: **Aqaba (#43)**; **Coral Beach (#83)**; **Eilat (#78)**; **Red Sea (#10)**. Get your scuba on in the Red Sea – Eilat, Taba, and Aqaba are all good options. Snorkeling options galore at Eilat's Coral Beach Reserve.

Petra 1–3 days. *Elective*: **Petra (#2)**. The main path in Petra is rocky and sloped, but doable for most travelers. Exploring the rest of the site requires leg power – most of the popular hikes involve hiking hundreds of steps, but the rewards are always worth the calorific expense. There are a few full-day hikes in the region as well. A new path has opened between Petra and Little Petra.

Jordan 1–2 days. *Electives*: **Ajloun Forest (#57)**; **Dana Biosphere Reserve (#21)**; **Wadi Mujib and Mujib Biosphere Reserve (#23)**. Several of Jordan's nature reserves are renowned for their half- and full-day hikes, replete with rivers, forests, and unique flora and fauna. Check out Dana, Wadi Mujib, and Ajloun Forest Reserve. The recently minted Jordan Trail also offers 40 days of hiking throughout this country.

Egypt 1–2 days. *Electives:* **Dahab (#54)**; **Ras Mohammad (#53)**; **Sharm el-Sheikh (#88)**. Scuba fanatics already know that Ras Mohammad National Park, at the bottom tip of the Sinai in Egypt, is considered one of the world's best scuba spots. There are a number of other spots to explore from Sharm and Dahab.

Minimum travel time 12 days.

Routing option 1) Start in the Old City, because it's an important BUCKET! site. Walk the Ramparts Walk for some good exercise. 2) Head to Tel Aviv and take a surfing lesson. You will likely need to book in advance, particularly in high season (surfing is regulated during busy seasons). 3) Start with a goal of swimming in all the seas: Dead, Red, and Med. The Sea of Galilee has some beaches, but boating or kitesurfing are more interesting. 4) Kayak on the Jordan River. 5) If you are visiting in the winter, head right to Mount Hermon at the tippy-top of Israel in the Golan for some skiing action. 6) Tackle a piece or all of one of the long hikes: Israel Trail, Jordan Trail, or the Jesus Trail. 7) Hike through Makhtesh Ramon, the largest Negev crater (or visit one of the nearby makhteshim). 8) Trek through a canyon and do some rock scrambling. Add rappelling, and the Dead Sea area on the Israel side is a good option – you can do both in Ein Gedi and Wadi Daraja – and they both run by Route 90. Soak in the Dead Sea (BUCKET!) at the end of the day. 9) Scuba in the Red Sea – you have your choice, with the Sinai arguably the finest. Snorkelers will find the Red Sea sufficient, and visiting a clean beach is essential – try the Coral Beach Reserve. 10) Cross to Jordan: visiting the nature reserves is still an off-the-beaten-path activity, but they are ready for tourists. Just be sure to book in advance – often required. 11) Finally, don't forget Petra (BUCKET!). Do all three major hikes.

LEISURE

Active itinerary too much for you? Let's try the opposite – how about you reward yourself with some R&R activities: spas, beaches, thermal pools, weekend getaways, peace and quiet. We've picked the finest.

Tel Aviv 1–2 days. *Electives:* **Tel Aviv Beaches (#89)**; **Tel Aviv Nightlife (#82)**; *Herziliya Beaches*. You've got beaches and more beaches. And, once you're done with your leisure time, you have restaurants, bars, and nightclubs to choose from.

Mediterranean coast 1–2 days. *Electives:* **Dor HaBonim (#100)**; *Akhziv Beach*; *Beit Yannai*; *Mediterranean Coast*. Some of the finest beaches in Israel can be found just north and south of Tel Aviv – same white sand but far fewer crowds. If you want to avoid crowds, try Dor Beach or Beit Yannai.

Golan 1 day. *Elective:* *Hamat Gader*. After your strenuous hike or your ski adventure, relax those tired bones in the hot springs of Hamat Gader.

Dead Sea and Masada 1 day. *Electives:* **Dead Sea (#3)**; *Ein Bokek Spa Hotels*; *Ein Bokek*. There are several access points to the Dead Sea still open (many have closed, such as Mineral Beach, due to sinkholes), and one good public beach (Ein Bokek). But we suggest you splurge at a Dead Sea resort – the Sea of Spa is inexpensive and offers mineral pools, mud baths, and access to the Dead Sea via a semi-private beach.

Egypt 1–2 days. *Elective*: **Dahab (#54)**. For an off-the-beaten-path destination, skip Sharm and try Dahab – you'll find utter peace, a bohemian charm, and dirt-cheap accommodation.

Minimum travel time 5 days.

Routing option 1) If you fly into Ben Gurion, you can head right to Tel Aviv and start your trip off with beach, beach, and more beach. 2) Those looking for fewer crowds should try Dor or Beit Yannai – on a weekday. 3) It's a 2-hour drive to the Dead Sea (BUCKET!) from Tel Aviv. The sand is never great (and often you're walking on rocks) so don't expect much from the beach experience. Rather, you go for the chill of floating in the waters. Add on a spa experience for true pleasure. 4) If you happen to find yourself in the Golan or the Sinai, feel free to follow our recommendations there, as well.

ENTERTAINMENT

After you've explored the Old City, Dead Sea, and Petra (required!), it's time to get to the business of entertainment.

Jerusalem 1–2 nights. *Electives*: **Citadel/Tower of David (#32)**; **Jerusalem, New City (#72)**; **Mehane Yehuda Market (#67)**; **Old City Jerusalem (#1)**. Plenty of shopping to be done in the Old City, from pottery in the Armenian quarter to spices in the Muslim quarter and tons of souvenirs in the Christian quarter just beyond the Jaffa Gate. Jerusalem may not be thought of as a nightlife city, but it holds its own. The Mehane Yehuda Market is bumping at night, with lots of young people, beer gardens, food stands, and live music. The areas just to the west of the Old City have a vibrant second life on the streets after dark. You can also check out an after-hours sound and light show at the Citadel/Tower of David.

West Bank/Palestine 1–2 nights. *Electives*: **Old Town of Hebron (#46)**; **Nablus (#61)**; **Ramallah (#68)**; *Argila/Hookah/Shisha*. The West Bank has much to offer – from nightlife options in Ramallah to the world's oldest city in Jericho and the birth site of Jesus of Nazareth in Bethlehem. Under-appreciated are Nablus, for its craftsmen's handmade soaps and the plethora of street food options in Hebron. Ramallah's evening scene is becoming hipper year by year. With local breweries, hipsters, and plenty of shisha shops, you'd easily forget you're in Palestine behind the walls.

Tel Aviv 2–3 nights. *Electives*: **Jaffa (#30)**; **Tel Aviv Nightlife (#82)**; *Drummers' Beach*; *Neve Tzedek*; *Tel Aviv Port*. Tel Aviv is where it's at. Jaffa's port is happening, but shops turn into restaurants, bars, and just cool outdoor spaces in the flea market area just east of/behind the port area. Find shopping on Sheinkin, Rothschild, and Nahalat Binyamin. Get shopping and food in Jaffa, the Tel Aviv Port, and Sarona. Florentin and Neve Tzedek have lots of bars. Drummers' Beach allows hippies and friends-of to listen to smooth beats while watching the sunset. Some of the most popular bars, Kuli Alma and/or Bellboy, should definitely be on your hit list. After midnight, you can begin your plans for how you're going to dance the rest of your night away.

Mediterranean coast 1 day. *Electives*: **Ein Hod**; **Zichron Ya'akov**. Ein Hod is an artists' colony near Haifa where you can buy all sorts of crafts. Same in Zichron Ya'akov, with the added benefit of visiting big and small wine producers.

Galilee/Golan 1 day. *Elective*: **Tsfat/Safed (#58)**. Lots of artists put their work on display in the old Jewish town of Tsfat.

Dead Sea 1 day. *Elective*: **Dead Sea (#3)**. Looking for great souvenirs that everyone will love – religious or not? Check out Ahava's outlet at Kibbutz Mitzpe Shalem and load up on brand-name Dead Sea mud and spa products.

Petra 1–3 nights. *Electives*: **Petra (#2)**; **Petra Kitchen (#84)**; *Petra by Night*. Petra requires a full 2–3 days to explore properly, but don't forget to save some energy (or nap beforehand) for the candlelit hike down the Siq to the Treasury during the Petra by Night ceremony and the cooking night at Petra Kitchen.

Minimum travel time 8 days.

Routing option 1) Spend your day at the Old City. Then, start your explorations of evening bars and restaurants in the New City. 2) The West Bank offers a ton of opportunities in shopping and nightlife. Head there from Jerusalem. 3) Take a trip to the Dead Sea. 4) Cross over to Jordan to visit Petra. Check dates and information so you don't miss Petra by Night. Spend another night to cook with Petra Kitchen. 5) Then cross back at Aqaba and drive up to Tel Aviv, where you'll base yourself for your trip/s to the north. 6) Complete your whirlwind of fun with bar-hopping in Tel Aviv through hotspots around the city.

FOOD AND DRINK

You want to splurge a little? Stay someplace fancy, or crazy, something new? Eat at the hot restaurants, drink at the coolest bars, and sip coffee at the hippest coffeeshops? Well why didn't you say so? Here you go.

Jerusalem 1–2 days. *Electives*: **Machneyuda (#98)**; *Café Culture*. When you're done with all your sightseeing, check out the most popular restaurant in the country – Machneyuda (be sure to book a table in advance). Then wind through pedestrian alleys and take in some of the country's coffee scene.

Greater Jerusalem ½ day. *Electives*: **Hummus**; Abu Ghosh (B1). Abu Ghosh is famous for its dozens of hummusiyas, or hummus restaurants.

Tel Aviv 3 days. *Consider*: City Walk D6. *Electives*: **Carmel Market (#87)**; **Israeli Cuisine (#51)**; *Abu Hassan*; *Modern Israeli Cuisine*; *Sabich/Oved's*; *Shakshuka/Dr. Shakshuka*; *Tzfon Abraxas*. Epicenter of the cuisine blowing up the world: modern Israeli. The Carmel, Levinsky, Hatikva, and Sarona markets all offer different experiences. Don't miss street food or the modern Israeli restaurants sprouting up everywhere. And don't you ever, ever, miss breakfast. You'll be making shakshuka for all your friends when you get home. Check out *City Walk D6* and the *Top Restaurants* category (p. 561) for more recommendations.

Mediterranean coast 1 day. *Electives*: **Akko (#13)**; *Elbabor*; *Haifa*; *Uri Buri*. Amazing restaurants are to be found in Akko (best: Uri Buri), while Haifa is perhaps the best spot on Earth for falafel (begin: debates). Elbabor is also excellent.

Galilee/Golan 1–2 days. *Electives*: **Golan Heights Winery (#75)**; *Nazarene Fusion Cuisine*. Nazareth is quickly becoming known for its Arab fusion cuisine. See below for wineries.

Negev 1 day. *Electives:* **Yatir Winery**; Negev Wine Route (J2). Yes, even the Negev – with its more than 40°C weather – has a wine scene. Tour Yatir and other places before starting your hike or camping expedition.

Jordan 2+ days. *Electives:* **Feynan Ecolodge (#86)**; **Jordanian Cuisine (#44)**; **Modern Amman (#36)**; **Wild Jordan Center**. Jordanian food is not universally understood, but you'll understand it when you dive into one of the better hotel breakfasts. Make sure you start your day off right with a piping bowl of fuul. As you head around the country, touring magical sites, be sure to stop in the Wild Jordan Center or Books@Cafe to catch your breath and have some tea, a national pastime. Off the beaten path, get to Dana Reserve where you can enjoy coffee, food, and cooking, all in a nature reserve home to Bedouin villagers.

Wineries 1+ days. *Elective:* **Winery Tour**. Don't forget to add a winery tour to your list of things to do – the Golan region produces some of the most recognizable bottles, including Golan Heights Winery, which put Israeli wine on the map. Take your pick from our three customized day trips (bookings required): in the Judean Hills (*Road Trip B3*), Mediterranean (*Road Trip E6*), or Galilee/Golan (*Road Trip U1*).

Minimum travel time 11 days.

Routing option 1) Visit the country's most revered restaurant in Jerusalem. 2) Stop by a hummus restaurant in West Jerusalem. 3) Wine and dine in style in Tel Aviv. 4) Head north to visit Haifa and Akko for their sites and food. 5) Organize a winery tour. 6) While in the neighborhood, swing by a series of desert-climate wineries. 7) Then Jordan for coffee (still a win) and great breakfasts.

ACCOMMODATION

There is a wide array of accommodation to choose from for your trip. If you're more interested in where you're staying than what you're doing, you could do worse than the following schedule.

Jerusalem 1+ days. *Elective:* **King David Hotel**; **Mamilla Hotel**. Explore the Old City by day and rest in one of the region's nicest hotels by night.

West Bank 1–2 days. *Elective:* **Banksy's Walled-Off Hotel**. Visit Bethlehem and see one of its most iconic sites up close: the Separation Wall.

Tel Aviv 1+ days. *Elective:* **The Norman Hotel**; **Brown Beach House**. Plop your head on a pillow at one of the resplendent boutique beachside hotels.

Northern Israel 1+ days. *Electives:* **Elma Arts Complex**; **Tiberias** or Rosh Pina (H2); Tzimmers (H2). Head north for a few days, stopping first at the Bauhaus-inspired Elma. On your way around the Sea of Galilee or touring the Golan, you can stay in one of Tiberias' resorts (though we prefer Rosh Pina, nearby).

Southern Israel 2–3 days. *Electives:* **Eilat (#78)**; **Kibbutz Lotan**; **Mitzpe Ramon**; Negev Camping (J2). Stop in Mitzpe Ramon for a killer view, perhaps even from your hotel: Beresheet Hotel (J2). Or camp in the Negev Desert under the stars. Then chillax in Eilat. Resorts and beach galore.

Jordan 3+ days. *Electives*: **Feynan Ecolodge (#86)**; **Petra (#2)**; *Glamping in Wadi Rum (M2)*; resort hotel in Suweimeh (Anchor) on the Dead Sea. Crossing at Eilat, you can work your way from south to north at Jordan's best accommodation.

Egypt 2+ days. *Electives*: **Dahab (#54)**; **Sharm el-Sheikh (#88)**; Nuweiba Beach Camps (T1). Need even more resort? Sharm el-Sheikh is popular, and close to one of the world's great diving spots. Dahab and Nuweiba each have dirt-cheap options that might entice you.

Minimum travel time 11 days, though this itinerary can be split up based on interest.

Routing option 1) Use Jerusalem as an anchor to explore the West Bank. 2) Tel Aviv is famous for its small, modern boutique hotels. 3) A few fancy options in Zichron Ya'akov and Akko. 4) Stay in Rosh Pina (Anchor) to visit the Galilee/Golan, or Tiberias, or rent a tzimmer. 5) Sleep under the stars in the Negev. 6) Resort time on the Red Sea. 7) Glamping in Wadi Rum. 8) Hoteling in Petra. 9) Don't skip Feynan in Dana, a Bedouin experience well worth the time. 10) End on the Dead Sea in one of Suweimeh's resort hotels.

ORGANIZED

Looking for something structured? We have corralled the best options for events that require your interest and presence to be pulled off effectively (not you? – see *Leisure* above), but they will also give you easy and great exposure to the sights, sounds, smells, and tastes of the Holy Land. These itineraries are for those that want to be led and/or want some guidance on how to DIY. We've got scenic drive itineraries, walking tours, and participatory activities, such as cooking workshops or petting zoos.

Jerusalem 2–3 days. *Consider*: City Walks A1–A7. *Electives*: **Citadel/Tower of David (#32)**; **Israel Museum (#17)**; **Jerusalem, New City (#72)**; **Old City Jerusalem (#1)**; **Mehane Yehuda Market (#67)**; **Western Wall Tunnels (#94)**; **Yad Vashem (#35)**. Jerusalem provides a plethora of options to those looking for a guided experience. We have created a number of walking-tour itineraries that may be of interest to you DIYers. Otherwise, check out our various Jerusalem chapters to learn of guide options. Several of the museums also offer times for English-language tours. Note the Western Wall Tunnels requires advance booking (which you may be able to do on the day if you're lucky, but we highly recommend prebooking).

Greater Jerusalem 1 day. *Consider*: Road Trips B2, B3. *Electives*: **Beit Guvrin and Maresha (#60)**; Judean Hills Wineries (B3). Take part in an active archaeological dig at Beit Guvrin/Maresha, a UNESCO World Heritage Site. You can also follow our DIY driving tour for ideas on putting together a Judean Hills winery tour.

Tel Aviv 1–2 days. *Consider*: City Walks D1–D6. *Electives*: **ANU – Museum of the Jewish People (#77)**; **Modern Movement (Bauhaus Architecture) (#16)**; **Carmel Market (#87)**; **Jaffa (#30)**; **Tel Aviv (#5)**. Like Jerusalem, Tel Aviv offers much for the semi-DIY traveler. There are a number of great walking tours (ours included!) around Jaffa, through the Bauhaus neighborhoods, in the Carmel Market, and around some of Tel Aviv's super-hip neighborhoods.

Mediterranean coast 1–2 days. *Consider*: City Walks E1, E2; Road Trips E4, E5. *Electives*: **Akko (#13)**; **Bahá'í Gardens (#27)**; *Haifa*; *Mediterranean Coast*. Akko is renowned for a few great restaurants, and you can walk about town, stopping in at world-renowned hummusiyas, a home-style Arab restaurant serving family-secret dishes, exquisite seafood, and a great market. Haifa's Bahá'í community offers guided tours in multiple languages of its gorgeous hillside garden. Afterwards, walk yourself over to the Arab part of town for falafel. If you'd like to drive, we have a number of full-day trip ideas.

Galilee and Jezreel 1–2 days. *Consider*: Road Trips F1, F2, G2–G4, H1, City Walk G1. *Electives*: **Jesus Trail (#69)**; **Nazareth and its Biblical Sites (#29)**; *Basilica of the Annunciation*; *Mount Gilboa*; *Druze Cooking Workshops (H1)*. In between your tour of the Basilica of the Annunciation in Nazareth (where you can volunteer!), stop at some of Nazareth's famed fusion restaurants, markets, spice shops, and coffee spots. Hire a guide to help you through part or all of the Jesus Trail, pointing out historical reference points along the way. Drivers may like the established stopping points along the scenic Mount Gilboa. Everyone will love the introduction to Druze culture and food at a half-day cooking class.

Sea of Galilee 1 day. *Consider*: Road Trips G3, G4. *Electives*: **Sea of Galilee (#7)**. Step into the New Testament with sites referenced throughout the period of Jesus' life and ministry right next door to one another. We offer a couple of road-tripping ideas, though you can also reference our suggestions for guided tours.

Golan 1–2 days. *Consider*: Road Trips I1–I3. *Electives*: **Golan Heights (#62)**. The Golan Heights offer lots of opportunities to the traveler, including nature, sport, views, and activities. We think they makes an excellent multi-stop-itinerary day trip, but you could easily spend a weekend. Kibbutz Merom Golan has horseback riding. There are several nearby sites offering pick-your-own and all-you-can-eat fruit farms. Check out our full-day tour suggestions.

Negev 1 day. *Consider*: Road Trips J1–J3. *Electives*: **Incense Route (#73)**; **Makhtesh Ramon (#28)**; *Museum of Bedouin Culture*. If you want to see the "Grand Canyon" of Israel, hire a guide to take you through Makhtesh Ramon. Or take a jeep tour! If you're looking for culture, a local Bedouin will escort you through Beersheva's Museum of Bedouin Culture. And those looking for a good road trip in the hinterlands can find 20 obscure stopping points along the ancient Nabataean Incense Route.

Dead Sea 1 day. *Consider*: Road Trip K1. *Elective*: **Dead Sea (#3)**. The Dead Sea region packs a punch, with a number of highly ranked stops within a short distance of one another. Added bonus: the drive down Highway 90 is stunning.

Eilat and Arabah 1–2 days. *Consider*: City Walk L1, Road Trips L2, L3. *Electives*: **Eilat (#78)**; *Kibbutz Lotan*; *Yotvata Hai-Bar*. Volunteers ready to work can head to Kibbutz Lotan for 3–6-month "green" apprenticeships. Those with just an afternoon (and kids!) can drive through Yotvata Nature Reserve to see desert wildlife up close. And swim with dolphins in Eilat.

Petra 1–3 days. *Consider*: City Walk N1, N2, Road Trips N3, M2. *Electives*: **Petra (#2)**; **Petra Kitchen (#84)**; **Wadi Rum (#4)**. There's no lack of guides at the entrance to Petra (and throughout the park) ready to regale you with stories of the lost Nabataean civilization. Be sure to set up your cooking class at Petra Kitchen. Spoil yourself with a guided drive through Wadi Rum. And top it off with a camel ride in either Petra or Wadi Rum.

Other Jordan 4–6 days. *Consider*: Road Trips O1, R1. *Electives*: **Dana Biosphere Reserve (#21); Qasr Amra and the Desert Palaces (#20); King's Highway (#31); Wadi Mujib and Mujib Biosphere Reserve (#23)**. Confirm one of the excellent guides for a riveting hike through the interesting Dana and Mujib reserves. Two great multi-stop drives in this region: the Desert Palaces to the east of Amman, and the King's Highway which runs from Amman south through some of the country's best spots, including Petra, and provides a beautiful backdrop along the way.

Egypt 2–3 days. *Electives*: **Camel Riding; Sinai Trail.** And for something completely off the beaten path, try a multiday camel safari or long-distance hike through the Sinai.

Minimum travel time 11 days without Jordan or Egypt, or 18 days with, but you can easily pick and choose with this itinerary.

Routing option 1) Get your fill of history in Jerusalem with a guided tour through the Old City and/or one of the many museums. 2) Do a dig at Beit Guvrin on your way to Tel Aviv. 3) You'll use your camera as much as your brain on one of Tel Aviv's many walking tours. 4) Drive north and do a food sampling – Haifa, Akko, and Nazareth each offer their own unique spin on Levantine cuisine. A Druze cooking school is an option too. 5) Driving tours abound when you head to the northeast of Israel – through the Golan, around the Sea of Galilee, or through the national parks of the southern Galilee. 6) Similarly, with a car, the Dead Sea and Negev regions open up to you. 7) Get to Jordan from Eilat. Head first to Wadi Rum, swing by Petra, then head north through the sites along the King's Highway. 8) With time, check out the Desert Palaces east of Amman.

Completists

WONDERS OF THE WORLD

Creating an itinerary from the new "Wonders of the World" selections should not be terribly difficult; two of our Holy Land BUCKET! sites achieved this prestigious title. **Petra (#2)** and the **Old City Jerusalem (#1)** were named Wonders of the World by the New7Wonders Foundation and *USA Today/Good Morning America*, respectively. The only remaining wonder of the *ancient* world still standing is the Great Pyramid of Khufu in Giza, Egypt, which you can tack onto your Holy Land trip, if you want to do a larger regional trip.

UNESCO

There are a number of UNESCO sites in this area of the world (forgetting that there are dozens more nominated and not yet accepted by the committee). You can absolutely mix and match whatever is of interest to you in this itinerary. Every site here is among our highest-rated sites, and all are recommended.

The easiest way to approach such an itinerary would be to break it up by borders, after which you can go in whatever order suits your plans best.

Minimum time 13 full days, but 18 days is more realistic.

Part 1: Jerusalem/Palestine
★ *Starting point* Jerusalem
★ *Jerusalem* 1–2 days. *Consider*: City Walks A1, A3. Highlights of **Old City Jerusalem (#1)**, per UNESCO, are the **Dome of the Rock (#6)**, the **Church of the Holy Sepulchre (#9)**, the **Western Wall (#11)**, and the walls, which you can approach from the **Ramparts Walk (#91)** or the outside along the **Jerusalem Walls and Gates (#47)**. All of this can be rushed through in a day, or you can space it out over two days.
★ *Bethlehem and Battir Hills* 1 day. *Consider*: City Walk C1, Road Trip C2. Visit the **Church of the Nativity (#18)** and **Bethlehem (#40)** on a day trip from Jerusalem. En route or on your way out, drive through the *Battir Hills*, northwest of Bethlehem.
★ *Hebron* 1 day. *Consider*: Road Trip C2. In a pinch, you can combine this with the Bethlehem day, but that's a fair bit of driving and hard to predict the wait times in either Bethlehem or the **Tomb of the Patriarchs (#46)**.

Part 2: Israel
★ *Starting point* Jerusalem
★ *Masada* 1 day. *Consider*: Road Trip K1. Just a couple of hours south of Jerusalem, you can add on the **Dead Sea (#3)** to this excursion, and hit the only BUCKET! site not a UNESCO designate.
★ *Beit Guvrin and Maresha* 1 day. On your way out of Jerusalem, stop at the underground human caves of **Beit Guvrin (#60)** and across the way to the sister site of Maresha.

- ★ *Starting point (also consider anchoring)* Tel Aviv
- ★ *Tel Aviv* 1 day. *Consider*: City Walk D5. Check out **Modern Movement (Bauhaus Architecture) (#16)** for information on White City tours (note: "Bauhaus" is not specifically referenced by UNESCO, but rather the larger "Modern Movement" in architecture).
- ★ *Mediterranean coast* 2 days. *Consider*: Road Trips E4, E5, F1. Over two days, you can check out any of these four sites, in really any grouping, as they are all pretty close to one another: the **Bahá'í Gardens (#27)** in *Haifa* with its 13.00 English language tour; **Akko (#13)**; **Megiddo (#59)**, of the **Biblical Tels (#38)**; and the *Nahal Me'arot* caves.
- ★ *Galilee* 1 day. *Consider*: City Walk G1, Road Trips G2–G4, H1. **Tel Hazor** is not the most exciting site, and makes up one of three of the Biblical Tels. If you've seen Megiddo, you've seen the most interesting. Regardless, you can see this and the **Beit She'arim (#79)** sarcophagi in a day. You may want to add some Jesus sites around the **Sea of Galilee (#7)**, or in **Nazareth (#29)**, which are between these two sites.
- ★ *Negev* 1–2 days. *Consider*: Road Trip J3. If you're very interested in the Biblical Tels, you can visit the third one at **Tel Beer Sheva**, outside present-day Beer Sheva. Otherwise, it is skippable. The **Incense Route (#73)** has roughly 20 sites, but many are loosely organized and buried in sand. The most developed site is **Avdat (#48)**, with other desert Nabataean towns a few hours apart. There are other pit stops on this journey, but you will be very unlikely to hit them all in one day.

Part 3: Jordan

- ★ *Dead Sea west* 1 day. *Consider*: Road Trip P2. Cross the border at Allenby/King Hussein east of Jerusalem and head north for a short drive to **Bethany-Beyond-the-Jordan (#41)**, the site of Jesus' baptism. Stay in Amman or at the **Dead Sea (#3)**.
- ★ *Eastern Desert* 1 day. *Consider*: Road Trips R1, then O1. You can put the two 8th-century sites of the Muslim fort of **Qasr Amra (#20)** and Christian **Umm ar-Rasas (#81)** together, being roughly 1½ hours apart. Drive south to Petra.
- ★ *Petra* 1–3 days. *Consider*: City Walks N1, N2, Road Trip N3. Follow the itinerary for **Petra (#2)**, completing as many of the hikes there as you can muster – referenced are the many tombs, the Monastery, and the Point of High Sacrifice, as well as *Little Petra*.
- ★ *Wadi Rum* 1–2 days. *Consider*: Road Trip M2. **Wadi Rum (#4)** is our only mixed cultural and natural site, according to UNESCO. Plan to spend a day walking through its red sea of desert and a night under the stars.

ENDANGERED

See these sites before they disappear forever! Some suffer from susceptibility to weather, earthquakes, or development, while others are deteriorating while waiting for government or external funding. Check out the *Spotlight* category (p. 482) for more information on these sites. We'll break these sites up again by borders.

Minimum time 12 full days, but 15 days is more realistic.

Part 1: Jerusalem/Palestine

- ★ *Old City Jerusalem* 1–2 days. *Consider*: City Walk A1. As the epicenter of three religious movements, fighting breaks out fairly regularly in **Old City Jerusalem (#1)**, and one can never predict when exactly violence and destruction will occur.

Stabbings have occurred at the city gates, tensions often flair near Temple Mount, and Dome of the Rock sits atop the most important site in Judaism (several monuments that have occupied this spot have been the cause of regional wars over the millennia).

★ *Southern West Bank* 1 day. *Consider*: City Walk C1, Road Trip C2. Held up by an elaborate arrangement of rods, poles, and buttresses, you'll want to visit the **Church of the Nativity (#18)** in Bethlehem before it comes crumbling down – doable on a day trip from Jerusalem. En route or on your way out, drive through the *Battir Hills*, northwest of Bethlehem, whose ancient terraced agricultural land was at risk of destruction by way of the *Separation Wall*. Tack on Hebron, if time, to catch the **Tomb of the Patriarchs (#46)**, considered a World Heritage Site in Danger due to the periodic conflict that erupts there.

★ *Northern West Bank/Nablus* 1 day. *Consider*: Road Trip C5. Head north towards **Nablus (#61)** for a stop at the Tel Balatah, an ancient Canaanite and later Greek site with problems of vandalism and regional violence bringing it to the attention of the World Monuments Watch. Head west from here to *Al-Qasem Palace (C5)* for an important example of Palestinian Throne Village architecture, restored in 2011.

Part 2: Israel

★ *Dead Sea and Masada* 1 day. *Consider*: Road Trip K1. See the **Dead Sea (#3)** before it evaporates and/or giant sinkholes remove all its access points. **Masada (#8)** also could suffer from earthquake damage or the rare torrential downpour, which happened two years in a row recently.

★ *En route to Tel Aviv* 1 day. When you leave Jerusalem, stop first right north of **Mehane Yehuda Market (#67)** at the depopulated city of *Liftah (B1)*. Your next stop is the *Old City of Lod (D8)*, requiring a lot of excavation work, near the airport. Swing by Ramle's *White Mosque (D8)* before its minaret falls over! Spend the night in Tel Aviv.

★ *Tel Aviv* 1 day. *Consider*: City Walk D5. Do a **Modern Movement (Bauhaus Architecture) (#16)** walking tour through the streets of **Tel Aviv (#5)** where you'll see some of the well-preserved and not-so-well-preserved modernist style buildings from the 1930s–50s.

★ *Mediterranean coast* 1 day. *Consider*: Road Trips E4, E5. Just north of Tel Aviv is the national park of *Apollonia*, which could slide off a cliff with any more erosion or as a result of an intense earthquake. Head further north to *Haifa* to visit the historic German Colony, much of which has been restored since its declaration on the World Monuments Watch list. End the day in **Akko (#13)**, a wonderful Arab site always at risk of violence and maintenance-related decay.

★ *Galilee and Golan* 1 day. *Consider*: Road Trip W3. The layered ruins of **Beit She'arim (#79)**, and particularly its hilltop portion, are threatened by erosion and a lack of maintenance. **Tel Dan (#63)**, 1 hour northeast and bordering Lebanon, is constantly in the line of attack from weather, violence, and government bureaucracy. Additionally, several ancient Roman and Mamluk sites – called Cities of the Decapolis – are threatened by pollution, erosion, sewage, and mismanagement throughout the Jordan River valley.

Part 3: Jordan

★ *North of Amman* 1 day. Abila (S1), in the far north of the country, has suffered from looting, so go quick to see this mostly unvisited Roman site. You can stop by the mostly unmarked and unguarded *Damiya Dolmen Field (S2)* near Damia, Jordan, on the Jordan River, on your way south to stay the night in the Dead Sea town of Suweimeh or Amman.

★ *Amman and east* 1 day. *Consider*: Road Trip R1. Just outside of Amman, stop by *Ain Ghazal (Q4)*, a Neolithic site in an Amman neighborhood suffering from urban development and erosion. Then head east towards the Desert Palace site of **Qasr Amra (#20)**, which has undergone recent upgrades highlighting its 1,300-year-old Islamic paintings. Stay again in Amman or back in the Dead Sea.

★ *Petra* 1–3 days. If you head south from Amman or the Dead Sea, on your way to **Petra (#2)**, you can swing through *Khirbet et-Tannur (01)*, an ancient Nabataean site that has experienced much looting. Petra, as you'll notice, can become very crowded quickly. High ticket prices have not served as a deterrent, so try to plan your trips during off-seasons to allow for better maintenance and upkeep… and to have the site mostly to yourself.

Part 4: Gaza 1 day. If you find yourself in Gaza with some free time, swing by Tel Umm el-Amr for a visit to St. Hilarion's Monastery, which is regularly at risk of being destroyed by rockets in the conflict between Palestine and Israel.

NATIONAL PARKS AND RESERVES

With more than 70 declared national parks and reserves in Israel, and a half-dozen nature reserves in Jordan, you will have a wide assortment of both scenery and activities to choose from. You will likely not be able to put together an itinerary that encompasses the millions of dunams these sites collectively represent!

We've crafted a series of itineraries to give you the best of the national parks and nature reserves, based on their location. However, you can mix and match according to your preferred itinerary. For instance, you may want to see Masada, Caesarea, Dana, and Beit She'an – all in different locations. That's okay – see below for how long you should expect to spend in places and, while you make stopovers, see the "combine with" line for suggestions on what else you can do to fill the time.

Note Be sure to invest in the Israel National Park Pass and the Jordan Pass if your itinerary warrants it (it probably will) – see *Discount Cards/Passes* in *Do #7: Money It!* (p. 60).

Jerusalem and hills Consider: City Walk A3, Road Trips B1, B2; + **Jerusalem Walls and Gates (#47)** and *City of David* (½–1 day) circumnavigates the 4km of walls around the city, and adds the Iron Age capital of Israel; + **Beit Guvrin and Maresha (#60)** (½ day) underground caves showcasing a whole civilization established below the earth. *Combine with*: **Hadassah Synagogue and Chagall Windows**, Judean Hills Wineries (B3), Stalactite Caves (B2), Abu Ghosh (B1).

Dead Sea parks Consider: Road Trip K1; + **Masada (#8)** (½ day) ruins on top of a mountain; + **Ein Gedi (#50)** (½ day) oasis with hiking in the middle of the desert; + **Qumran (#70)** (1–2 hours) historic site of the Dead Sea Scrolls, with museum. *Combine with*: **Dead Sea (#3)**.

Negev parks Consider: Road Trip J2; + **Avdat (#48)** (1 hour) best Nabataean ruins in the Negev; + **Makhtesh Ramon (#28)** (1 hour to 1 day) a giant crater with hikes and views; + **Incense Route (#73)** (includes Avdat, seeing the other sites could take a whole day) a group of sites representing the trade route the Nabataeans established from Petra to the Mediterranean. *Combine with*: Negev Wine Route (J2), Negev Camping (J2), and Negev Goat Farms (J2).

Mediterranean parks/reserves Consider: Road Trip E3; + **Caesarea (#25)** (2 hours–½ day) ancient Roman ruins (the best in Israel); + **Dor HaBonim (#100)** (½ day (beach) to overnight) gorgeous beaches, sand dunes, camping; + *Nahal Me'arot/ Wadi el-Mughara* (1–2 hours) Neolithic caves. *Combine with*: **Bahá'í Gardens (#27)**, **Akko (#13)**, Central Israel Wineries (*Road Trip E6*).

Galilee Consider: Road Trips F1, F2; + **Megiddo (#59)** (1–2 hours) layers and layers of history at the ancient biblical town of Armageddon; + **Tsipori (#56)** (2 hours) Roman ruins, ancient Jewish synagogue, mosaics; + **Beit She'arim (#79)** (1–2 hours) necropolis carved out of mountainside; + **Beit She'an (#39)** (2 hours) impressive Roman ruins, mosaics, hill of ancient civilizations; + **Beit Alpha (#64)** (1 hour) unearthed synagogue with hilarious mosaic floor; + *Gan HaShlosha* (2 hours) natural water pools. *Combine with*: **Nazareth (#29)**, **Sea of Galilee (#7)**.

Golan Consider: Road Trips H2, I1, I2; + **Tel Dan (#63)** (2 hours) park where history meets water fun; + **Nimrod's Fortress (#85)** (2–3 hours) Ayyubid castle involving hiking to summit, great views; + *Hula Lake* (2 hours) seasonal bird-watching, bikes and carts. *Combine with*: **Golan Heights Winery (#75)**, *Mount Hermon*.

Jordan reserves Consider: Road Trip V1; + **Dana Biosphere Reserve (#21)** (½ day or 2–3 days) unique species of animals, including wild cats and dogs, plus hiking, camping, and ecolodges; + **Wadi Mujib and Mujib Biosphere Reserve (#23)** (½–1 day) mountain climbing, rapids, hiking; + **Ajloun Forest (#57)** (½ day) woodlands, hiking; + *Shaumari* (½ day) wildlife reserve with oryx/antelope, among other animals; + **Azraq Wetlands (#55)** (1–2 hours) wetland walking paths, bird-watching. *Combine with*: **Petra (#2)**, **Feynan Ecolodge (#86)**, **Karak (#49)**, **Qasr Amra and the Desert Palaces (#20)**.

Cross-Genre

COMMUNITY

Focus Villages, neighborhoods, streets, crafts, activities that interact with local population, volunteering opportunities, rural life, minority groups, language learning.

Sub-themes and categories Cool Neighborhoods; Streets, Squares, and Ports; Towns; Cooperatives; Identity; Ethnic Groups; Community Celebration; Markets; Handmade; Nightlife; Volunteer; Language School.

Time commitment 1–10 days.

Villages What's a Samaritan? Try **Nablus (#61)**. And Druze? Try one of their four villages in the **Golan Heights (#62)**. For extra credit, meet the Circassians in Kfar Kama (G2).

Community centers Al-Auja (C3) in the West Bank has a popular community center. The Black Hebrew community in the town of *Dimona (J1)* in the Negev offers tours as well.

Kibbutzim Spend a few weeks or months with members of Kibbutzim (U), helping with their work chores, meeting people from all over the world, and learning about these uniquely Israeli communal groups in the process.

Refugees There are a number of refugee centers in Israel. Two popular ones to visit in the West Bank are Dheisheh Refugee Camp (C2) and Aida Refugee Camp (C1).

Small towns **Zichron Ya'akov** and *Ein Hod*, both near *Haifa*, give you the chance to chat with locals while buying wine, art, and other handmade items.

The way things were Step back in time to an Eastern European Jewish village in the 1800s at **Mea She'arim (#66)**, a neighborhood west of the Old City Jerusalem.

Bustling areas Feel the energy of the masses! Try **Jaffa (#30)**, *Rothschild Boulevard*, *Ben Yehuda Street*, and Manger Square in **Bethlehem (#40)**.

Markets Want to see how real people shop? Don't miss **Carmel Market (#87)** in Tel Aviv, **Mehane Yehuda Market (#67)** in Jerusalem, or any of their other markets.

Rural people Some Bedouin still practice the old art of nomadism, though many have settled into small collectives. Participating in Bedouin activities is a unique opportunity, available at the *Museum of Bedouin Culture* in Beer Sheva, **Feynan Ecolodge (#86)** in **Dana Biosphere Reserve (#21)**, and in the Negev and **Wadi Rum (#4)**.

Urban people What's more urban than a hipster? Check out the Florentin (D4) neighborhood in Tel Aviv for cool bars, graffitied buildings, coffee all day, and skinny jeans galore.

Crafts Most Jerusalem "handicraft" isn't handmade at all, but rather machine-made junk from China. There's still hope: there remains an artistic history and locality embedded in the pottery found in the Armenian Quarter (A2) in Jerusalem.

Interactive Try a Hebrew language program in one of the Ulpanim (U), a cooking class at **Petra Kitchen (#84)**, a one-on-one session learning the winemaking process in one of Israel's many wineries, participate in a Friday seder with a local Jewish friend, or join your Muslim friend in an iftar ceremony during Ramadan.

Nightlife **Tel Aviv (#5)** is famous for its evening scene, but the nightlife in Jerusalem and **Ramallah (#68)** have a surprisingly robust fan base as well. Soak up local atmosphere by sipping on *Argila/Hookah/Shisha* at a bar in the West Bank or Jordan.

Volunteer There are tons of opportunities to get to know local communities, from assisting with African refugees to helping victims of terror to teaching.

FINE ARTS

Focus Performances, art museums, sculptures, performance centers.

Sub-themes and categories Architecture; Meet Locals; Museums of Art; Music; Performance; Visual Arts.

Time commitment 1–10 days.

Architecture In **Tel Aviv (#5)**, you can find two interesting schools of modern architecture, done in the international style for which the city has earned UNESCO World Heritage status: Bauhaus and Brutalism (**Modern Movement (Bauhaus Architecture) (#16)**). But both styles can be found throughout Israel. Throne Village Architecture in the West Bank and Arab Eclecticism in the town of *As-Salt* in Jordan also provide interesting opportunities to see unique architectural styles.

Concerts and festivals There are lots of interesting venues for concerts in Israel, including musical acts in the ancient Roman amphitheater in **Caesarea (#25)**, a large outdoor space in HaYarkon Park (D7) in north Tel Aviv, and lots of tiny venues throughout town. The Oud Festival (A7) is a popular celebration of this Middle Eastern stringed instrument. The Red Sea Jazz Festival (L1) is a biannual gathering of talent in the southernmost region in Israel, and the music/dance Israel Festival (A7) is held in Jerusalem each spring.

Music Israel has a dedicated music scene worth exploring. Drummers and hippies might like to check out *Drummers' Beach* at sunset on the weekend.

Opera Though it hasn't taken place in a few years, **Masada (#8)** once provided the stunning backdrop to an annual, one-night opera festival, usually occurring in September.

Sculpture The finest sculpture garden in the country can be found at the **Israel Museum (#17)** in Jerusalem. A love-it-or-hate-it attraction in Tel Aviv is the Fire and Water Fountain (D3) in Dizengoff Square – decide for yourself.

Frescoes From the frescoes in the **Desert Palaces (#20)** of eastern Jordan to art collections at the **Israel Museum (#17)** and **Tel Aviv Museum of Art (#95)**, there will be plenty to suit your tastes.

Graffiti Take a walk through Florentin (D4), a suburb of Tel Aviv, checking out its various graffitied buildings along the way. The **Separation Wall** in Bethlehem has a lot of interesting tags, including some famous Banksy ones.

Theater Several theater options, including two in Tel Aviv – the Cameri Theatre (D3) and the Suzanne Dellal Centre for Dance and Theatre (D4). There's also the widely regarded Freedom Theatre (C5) in an unexpected location: Jenin in the northern West Bank.

Design **Design Museum Holon**, in southern Tel Aviv, gives you all you need and want from a museum dedicated to design and contemporary culture.

Artists' towns **Ein Hod** and **Zichron Ya'akov**, both near **Haifa**, have dozens of shops available for folks looking to support local artists and empty living room walls. **Jaffa (#30)** also has an artists' quarter and a weekly art market, as well as numerous galleries and art-focused bars.

ON THE ROAD

Note The network of buses and trains is pretty expansive in Israel, but that doesn't mean you can get everywhere. In order to see some more remote places, or at least to see fewer tourists, you're going to need your own wheels.

Focus Lookouts, scenic drives, driving tours, vistas, off the beaten path.

Sub-themes and categories Exploration; Off the Beaten Path; Geography; Vistas; Scenic Drives; Multi-Stop/Self-Directed.

Time commitment 1–10 days.

Scenic drives Simply driving the highways of Israel and Jordan is a thrillingly beautiful experience. The gold standard is **King's Highway (#31)** in Jordan, the historic trade route that passed through Aqaba on to Damascus through Transjordan. The alternative north–south Jordan route is the Dead Sea Highway (P1), also a stunner. Highway 90, along Israel's eastern border, is another beautiful road, as is Highway 40, meandering through the craters and Negev Desert.

Beaches To reach some of the more remote locations, you'll need a car, and some good sneakers for walking. We list several options in **Mediterranean Coast**.

Escapes The wine region of the Judean Hills Wineries (B3) is a stark contrast to the metropolises of Tel Aviv and Jerusalem. North of Bethlehem, check out the UNESCO-designated **Battir Hills** for beautiful vistas of the ancient land of olives and wine, and feel a million miles away. The **Golan Heights (#62)** can also feel quite remote with its population of 40,000 living among several dozen villages.

Vistas There are tons of turnoff points to revel in throughout Jordan and Israel. Look for tall hills near bodies of water: ***Mount Arbel*** at the Sea of Galilee, **Ein Gedi (#50)** or

Mount Sodom (K1) at the Dead Sea, or even **Jaffa (#30)** overlooking Tel Aviv. Don't miss the **Makhtesh Ramon (#28)** lookout at *Mitzpe Ramon*.

Geography Salt mountains, a shrinking blue sea, and the world's lowest place on Earth, the **Dead Sea (#3)** makes for one interesting destination. Enjoy the spectacular twists and turns along Highway 90 in Israel and along the Dead Sea Highway (P1) in Jordan. A drive to **Wadi Rum (#4)** will also afford you a magnificent look at otherworldly red rock formations.

Classic routes The ancient **King's Highway (#31)** route winds you past the Jordanian sites of **Karak (#49)**, *Shobak*, **Dana Biosphere Reserve (#21)**, **Madaba (#19)**, and **Jerash (#14)**, among other famous locales. You can make a weekend of visiting the Cities of the Decapolis (*Road Trip W3*), stops along the Nabataean **Incense Route (#73)** (*Road Trip W2*), the **Desert Palaces (#20)** loop, or take a trip to see various Crusader-era castles in the north of Israel (*Road Trip W4*).

Winery hopping A trip to Israel is not complete without a day bopping between exquisitely local wineries. There are a number of wine regions to choose from: Golan, including the trend-setting **Golan Heights Winery (#75)**, the Galilee, the Judean Hills, and there's even a Negev wine route (*Road Trips B3, E6, and U1*).

RELAXATION

Focus Beach, hotel, staying local, loosely planned activities, spas, sun, water, parks.

Sub-themes and categories Rivers, Lakes, and Waterfalls; Parks; The Great Outdoors; Sunrise/Sunset; People-Watching; Small Towns; Water Sports; Beaches; Sea Access; Thermal Waters; Spas and Massage; Peaceful; Vacation Resorts and Hotels.

Time commitment 1–10 days.

Resorts You have your choice of big resorts at *Ein Bokek Spa Hotels* or *Suweimeh Spa Hotels* at the **Dead Sea (#3)**, **Eilat (#78)**, **Sharm el-Sheikh (#88)**, as well as specific sites such as the Carmel Forest Spa.

Small towns For quaint, easy-going attitudes (which can sometimes be hard to find in this Sabra culture!), try either *Zichron Ya'akov* or Rosh Pina (H2) (Anchor).

Massage Sure, expensive hotels will offer traditional spa services (and charge you beaucoup for them) but you can get a great, cheap massage at one of the many Turkish baths around **Modern Amman (#36)**, **Petra (#2)**, **Akko (#13)**, and **Nablus (#61)**.

Thermal waters *Hamat Gader*, south of the Sea of Galilee, offers sulfur pools and an ancient hammam amid its repurposed Roman ruins. In the Lower Galilee, *Gan HaShlosha* has naturally warm outdoor pools that make for crowded times on weekends, but you'll have them to yourself during weekdays. The *Hammamat Ma'in Hot Springs* near the Dead Sea in Jordan also has natural heated pools on its complex.

Beaches You will not want for beaches in the Holy Land. From **Sharm el-Sheikh (#88)** in the south of Egypt's Sinai to the entire strip of *Mediterranean Coast* in Israel to the famous **Tel Aviv Beaches (#89)**, there are dozens and dozens of great options.

Sunset Given that the sun sets in the west, and the Mediterranean is on the west, pretty much the entire western side of Israel is a convenient spot to pull up some sand and get cozy at sundown to see beautiful skies and listen to the waves lapping ashore.

Doing nothing If you have a friend, meet up for a coffee. It'll take all day to finish – that's the Middle Eastern coffee culture in a nutshell. You'll find endless places to practice this important pastime.

Gardens The serene **Bahá'í Gardens (#27)** will put you in a meditative space in no time.

Parks Watching birds for hours could perhaps do the same for you – *Hula Lake* offers twice-annual migrations and the opportunity to see thousands of thirsty avians lay over at once. There are plenty of peaceful hikes to be done in the network of national parks in Israel in Jordan.

Waterfalls *Yehudiya*, *Gamla*, Nahal el-Al (I3) in the Golan, and Wadi al-Hassa (O1) in western Jordan all provide access to nature's most beautiful geological formation, the waterfall.

Swimming Just south of **Eilat (#78)**'s downtown area, you'll find the entry-fee-required sanctuary called Dolphin Reef (L2), replete with "relaxation pools" to keep parents entertained while their kids go off and frolic.

Luxury Sometimes a little pampering can go a long way to rejuvenation – check out our *Luxury* itineraries below (p. 812).

ANCIENT HISTORY

Focus Museums, ruins, sites of antiquity, digs.

Sub-themes and categories Ruins by Period; City Conglomerates; Walls; Historic Battlefields; Active Excavations; Impressive Structural Remains; Technological Advancement; Infrastructure; Museums of History; Museums of Archaeology; Digs.

Time commitment 5–10 days.

Human advancement To find out how humans left Africa and found their way to the Middle East, start with *Nahal Me'arot*, a UNESCO World Heritage Site that recognizes the locality where humans may have begun to settle down from their foraging ways and commence an agrarian lifestyle. **Timna (#96)** contains ancient mines that were worked during the prehistoric Bronze Age.

First settlements On the south side of the Old City's walls lies the original settlement of Jerusalem, though it was then called the *City of David*. Here you will find all sorts of discoveries related to these original Jewish settlers. *Hezekiah's Tunnel* is an ancient manmade aqueduct and water source that has since been converted into a wet hiking adventure.

Mounds (tels) One of the most surprising parts of many trips to archaeological sites in Israel is the bizarre fact that cities were built on top of other cities. The UNESCO **Biblical Tels (#38)** of **Megiddo (#59)**, *Tel Hazor*, and *Tel Beer Sheva* are three recognized sites where so many successive layers of civilization were built on top of one another that the sites eventually became huge mounds of earth. Visiting now, you will see what look like hills but, when you approach the site, you'll learn that more than 20 layers of civilization are buried one on top of another.

Ancient cities Similar to the story of the tels, there are places that have shown up in history again and again. **Jericho (#26)**, often called the world's oldest walled city, is just one of those places – with history that spans each of our eras. **Megiddo (#59)** and **Tel Ashkelon** have both withstood the test of time and now present their history in various successive layers. And nothing competes with **Old City Jerusalem (#1)** for historical value.

Rise of empires This region has been conquered by dozens of foreign powers, each leaving its mark on Levantine society through cultural, architectural, or religious influences. Visit the *Archaeology* theme (p. 499) to move forward through time and discover how the Holy Land has changed over the millennia.

Excavations As you might envision, there are active excavations going on everywhere. Even today, the government may want to build a new highway through an area, will begin construction, and then stumble upon an ancient treasure trove which gets immediately reprogrammed as an archaeological dig. Some of our more popular sites, such as **Petra (#2)**, **Masada (#8)**, and **Jaffa (#30)**, all have ongoing excavations in various stages of completion.

Participate in a dig Maybe *you* can uncover the next great archaeological find! **Beit Guvrin (#60)**, Emek Tzurim (A6), and Tel Gezer Archaeological Project (B2), all near Jerusalem, offer regular digs for earnest participants.

Museums What better place than a museum to get your fill of archaeological discoveries? The **Israel Museum (#17)** has a wonderful collection on the advancement of human civilization. Visit the **Citadel/Tower of David (#32)** museum at Jaffa Gate in the Old City for wonderful background on the origin and history of this great city. And if you're into Palestinian art and artifacts, try the *Rockefeller Archaeological Museum* in East Jerusalem.

MEMORIAL

Focus Modern monuments, historical markers, museums, burial place, cemeteries.

Sub-themes and categories Religious Figures; Burial; Historic Battlefields; Historic Monuments; Memorial; Land; Holidays; Festivals and Events; Museums of Culture, Ethnicity, Nationality; Museums of Important Persons.

Time commitment 4–5 days.

Holidays Israel recognizes Holocaust Remembrance Day (Yom HaShoah) and Memorial Day (Yom Hazikron) each year. The latter is a somber holiday that remembers Israel's fallen soldiers. Many religious holidays are also days of remembrance, such as Eid-al-Adha (Festival of the Sacrifice) and Easter, among others.

Religious figures You could do worse than **Old City Jerusalem (#1)** for your fill of memorial sites, many of which are highly rated and ranked. King David's tomb is located in **Mount Zion (#92)**. Moses is believed to have died on **Mount Nebo (#24)** in Jordan. Christians visit the **Via Dolorosa (#42)** to follow along Jesus Christ's final moments, culminating at the **Church of the Holy Sepulchre (#9)** where they pay homage to the crucifixion and burial spots of Jesus. Also part of the history of Christianity are the sites of **Nazareth (#29)** and **Bethlehem (#40)**, including the **Church of the Nativity (#18)** where visitors can set foot in the grotto where Jesus was believed to be born. Muslims believe the **Dome of the Rock (#6)** sits over the spot where Muhammad ascended to Heaven.

Political figures David Ben Gurion, the first prime minister of Israel, spent his final days in Sde Boker (J2), where you can visit his home and learn about his very interesting life. His burial site is its own national park just outside of Sde Boker.

Peace, war, and the in-between The remains at **Masada (#8)** tell the story of the Jews who refused to resign to Roman rule and instead chose self-sacrifice. In modern times, the ***Separation Wall*** that cleaves the West Bank from Israel proper continues to remind the residents who can't cross the border that there remain many literal and figurative obstacles to cross before these two cultures can find peace.

Museums **Yad Vashem (#35)** is a great memory museum, highlighting not only the horrors of the Holocaust (which is what most Holocaust museums do), but also bringing light and hope in the stories of those that survived and those that fought back. **ANU – Museum of the Jewish People (#77)** in Tel Aviv tells the story of how Jews ended up all over the globe, and came back to Israel.

Tombs Kidron Valley (A5), located between the Old City and Mount of Olives, has several well preserved and monumental tombs to visit. **Mount of Olives (#34)** and **Mount Zion (#92)** are both home to famous graves. The **Church of the Holy Sepulchre (#9)** marks the spot where, according to Scripture, Jesus died, was buried, and rose again. The founding fathers of Judaism are buried in the **Tomb of the Patriarchs (#46)** in Hebron. Be wowed at the hidden caves of **Beit She'arim (#79)**, which kept dozens of sarcophagi from looters and destroyers until its rediscovery in the late 19th century. The Bahá'í people dedicate the Shrine of the Báb to their founder at the **Bahá'í Gardens (#27)** in *Haifa*.

GOURMET

Focus Restaurants, local cuisine, drinks, markets, street food, tours of wineries, breweries, farms.

Sub-themes and categories Cuisine; Food; Top Restaurants; Culinary Capitals; Great Wine; Wineries; Cooking School/Food Activities; Food and Market Tours.

Time commitment 1–10 days.

Wine tours Discover Israel's fledgling wine industry on a day tour or weekend trip to a wine region. With wine regions from as far north as the Golan and as far south as the Negev, you'll have dozens of options. Just remember to book in advance.

Markets Foodies will love the variety of greens, spices, and produce on display at the neighborhood outdoor markets. **Carmel Market (#87)** is Tel Aviv's largest market, and offers a "Bite Card" which allows you to sample as you browse. The **Mehane**

Yehuda Market (#67) is Israel's finest, though considerably smaller. It too offers a "Bite Card," as well as an entirely new and different experience in the evening time, when musicians come out and bars open along the street. If you prefer something a little more sterile, Tel Aviv offers several bustling choices, including Sarona Market (D3) and the *Tel Aviv Port*, each replete with exotic dining options, unique gift stores, and vendors of local goods and foodstuffs.

Cooking classes Renowned cooking school **Petra Kitchen (#84)** is an excellent evening activity in Wadi Musa (especially because there is little else to do in town after dark), offering a cooking demo/practice, fabulous dinner, and recipes to take home over a 3-hour experience. **Feynan Ecolodge (#86)** offers cooking classes twice a week with Bedouin chefs. *Druze Cooking Workshops (H1)* offer a taste of Druze cuisine, while providing a glimpse of how this interesting ethnic group lives.

Modern restaurants Jordan's famous restaurant Fakhr el-Din (Q2) is located inside an elegant home. **Machneyuda (#98)** provides casual-cool elegance and excellent modern Israeli fare. Helena Banamal (E4) serves refined but filling plates from its waterfront property in Caesarea. But **Tel Aviv (#5)** stands out for its breadth of options, with new chefs and their restaurants regularly being favorably reviewed by international food connoisseurs and critics.

Farms Interested in local cheeses, yogurt, and other dairy products? Several options can be found in the Negev at your friendly neighborhood goat farm. There are lots of just-off-the-road restaurants in the Galilee as well.

Breakfast One doesn't often associate breakfast with "gourmet," but gourmands will nonetheless appreciate the vast spreads associated with Israeli Breakfast (U) and its Jordanian counterpart (which are similar in their love of spreads, pickles/olives, savories, breads, and salads). Fancier hotels, such as those in Rosh Pina, the Dead Sea, Eilat, and Petra, will offer the broadest variety. The Mövenpick and Dan line of hotels, as well as the *King David Hotel* in Jerusalem, are well known for their morning spreads.

MODERNITY

Focus Modern art, modern cuisine, modern performance, modern architecture.

Sub-themes and categories Architectural Styles; Modern Architecture; Beautiful Structures; Skyline; Impressive Feats; Principal Cities; Cool Neighborhoods; Streets, Squares, and Ports; Museums of Art; Museums of History; Museums of Science and Learning; Performance; Visual Arts; Top Restaurants; Highly Recommended Accommodation; Experiential Lodging; Vacation Resorts and Hotels.

Time commitment 1–10 days.

Cities No city in Israel is more modern than **Tel Aviv (#5)**. It's under a constant state of construction and reimagining. Sleek new buildings by famous architecture firms are going up all over town, in and around the layers of Bauhaus antiquity and desert landscaping that otherwise makes the city so famous.

Buildings In Jerusalem, the **Israel Museum (#17)** and **Yad Vashem (#35)** both stand out for their exquisite collections and curation, but are equally laudable for their beautiful architectural designs. The ***Rockefeller Archaeological Museum***, ***Design Museum Holon***, and the Museum for Islamic Art (A7) also have noteworthy facades.

Architectural styles We might no longer think of the building styles as "modern," but they certainly fall into the "International Style" of **Modern Movement (Bauhaus Architecture) (#16)** – Bauhaus, Brutalism, Art Deco, and their modernist spins are on display all throughout Israel.

Monuments Odes to a time when power represented progress, Montefiore's Windmill (A7) in *Yemen Moshe* still represents "awe," though it has long since ceased to function. The Fire and Water Fountain (D3) in Tel Aviv is a hymn to the Art Deco period of the city's past.

Art **Tel Aviv Museum of Art (#95)**, the **Israel Museum (#17)** in Jerusalem, and a number of galleries in and around both cities showcase local talent.

History **Yad Vashem (#35)** tells the story of the Holocaust, **ANU – Museum of the Jewish People (#77)** tells how Jews came to Israel and where they are in the world today, the Beit HaShomer Museum (H2) provides the history of the relatively nascent Israel Defense Forces, and the *MUSA – Eretz Israel Museum* tells the story of the founding of Israel from a variety of interesting perspectives, including cars, stamps, and coins.

Technology Get the latest on science and technology from the ***Weizmann Institute of Science*** with fun, interactive gadgets to enlighten your kids' imaginations about science and its practical uses.

Performance Check out the Israel Festival (A7) for modern dance interpretations year after year. For more regular performances, check out the Cameri Theatre (D3) of Tel Aviv, Suzanne Dellal Centre for Dance and Theatre (D4) in Neve Tzedek, or the Freedom Theatre (C5) in Jenin.

Food We have several electives and whole sections dedicated to this topic! Of particular note are the **Israeli Cuisine (#51)** revolution, **Tel Aviv (#5)**'s fantastic restaurant scene, and *Nazarene Fusion Cuisine*.

Lodging You'll find plenty of sleek, modern accommodations throughout Israel, Jordan, and Egypt. The pleasure will cost you: prices for hotels can be exorbitant, even during off-season. The Beresheet Hotel (J2) in Mitzpe Ramon, *The Norman Hotel* in Tel Aviv, the ***Brown Beach House***, and the ***Elma Arts Complex*** near Zichron Ya'akov have all received press for their shiny interiors.

ROMANTIC

Focus Nice restaurants, good hotels, spas, massage, private beach, pack a picnic/hike, beach, thoughts for good candlelit dinners.

Sub-themes and categories Sunrise/Sunset; Easy Hikes and Trails; Remote Beaches; Thermal Waters; Spas and Massage; Peaceful; Top Restaurants; Great Wine; Wineries; Highly Recommended Accommodation; Vacation Resorts and Hotels.

Time commitment 2–3 days.

Meals Try **Machneyuda (#98)** in Jerusalem or ***Tzfon Abraxas*** in Tel Aviv for special occasions (and make a reservation!). They may be casual chic, but the food is exceptional and worthy of a romantic date where you can share plates. Also, check out our section on dining in *Do #14: Eat It!* (p. 80), and look for buzzy/romantic restaurants when you're out and about.

Fancy hotels Two highly rated boutique hotels in Tel Aviv are ***The Norman Hotel*** and the **Brown Beach House**. Other hot stays include ***Elma Arts Complex*** in Zichron Ya'akov, the ***Mamilla Hotel*** and Waldorf Astoria (A7) in Jerusalem, Brown TLV (D4) and Poli House (D4) in Tel Aviv, and Efendi (E2) in Akko. You can check out other options and recommendations in *Do #5: Sleep It!* (p. 48).

Spas Head to the ***Ein Bokek*** at the **Dead Sea (#3)** for a spa resort to pamper yourself and your loved one. In addition to being new and beautiful with great views, the Beresheet Hotel (J2) in Mitzpe Ramon also has a well-regarded spa.

Weekends away Lots of people will rent a house (tzimmer) in the **Golan Heights (#62)** and Galilee regions to decompress from city life. You can alternatively find a cute B&B in Rosh Pina (H2) (Anchor) before beginning your weekend of pampering and wine-ing. In the winter, **Eilat (#78)** is a popular destination, and has a variety of (expensive) hotels to choose from. Or take a flight to **Sharm el-Sheikh (#88)** in the Sinai for some holiday luxury.

Private beaches Though Tel Aviv and other metropolitan beaches can get very crowded during high season (and even low season), fret not – there are plenty of options along the ***Mediterranean Coast*** to suit your desires for seclusion. **Dor HaBonim (#100)** is a great choice, where you just may find a few others also camping under the stars.

Sunset Pull up some sand anywhere on the **Tel Aviv Beaches (#89)** for a gorgeous and romantic display.

Wineries Book a wine tour in advance and get an intimate outing at a boutique winery. You needn't travel far, as the Judean Hills Wineries (B3) between Tel Aviv and Jerusalem offer delicious tastings, often paired with cheese boards.

Quick hikes If you're willing to work a little bit for your love, consider one of the under-2-hour hikes, such as **Ein Gedi (#50)** near the Dead Sea, ***Mount Carmel*** near Haifa, and ***Yehudiya*** in the Golan.

UNDER THE SUN

Focus Beach, amusement park, outdoor concert, cafés, dining al fresco.

Sub-themes and categories Parks; The Great Outdoors; Walks and Hikes; Water Sports; Beaches; Sea Access; Amusement Parks; Street Food and Quick Bites; Vacation Resorts and Hotels; Coffee, Tea, and Coffeeshops; Petting Zoos and Animal Rides.

Time commitment 2–3 days.

Beaches First, pick your body of water – the **Mediterranean Coast**, the **Dead Sea (#3)**, the **Sea of Galilee (#7)**, or the **Red Sea (#10)** – these are all great options for getting your fill of vitamin D.

Beach towns **Tel Aviv (#5)** is the quintessential beach town (with restaurants and bars to counterbalance the sunny days). But you'll find just as much enthusiasm from proponents of **Eilat (#78)**, **Aqaba (#43)**, **Herziliya Beaches**, as well as **Dahab (#54)** and **Sharm el-Sheikh (#88)** in the Sinai.

Soaking the healthy rays The **Dead Sea (#3)** is believed by many to avoid any deleterious effects of UV due to its below-sea-level elevation. Soak up those rays at **Ein Bokek** or any of the other access points from Israel or Jordan.

Amusement parks and zoos You won't want for sun in the Negev, so bring your sunscreen as you explore **Timna (#96)** or the **Yotvata Hai-Bar** animal reserve. Other animal parks include the Gan Garoo (F2) petting zoo, the Dolphin Reef (L2), **Camel Riding**, and an Alpaca Farm (J2) in the Negev, which will each provide lots of outdoor exposure.

Parks Grab some sun on the slopes of Haifa at the **Bahá'í Gardens (#27)**, in HaYarkon Park (D7) in Tel Aviv, or any of the dozens of national parks (see *Road Trip U2*), most of which have lawns and space for laying out a blanket under a tree or even… under the sun.

Cafés Spend some time doing nothing, sitting on the street drinking a cup of joe, watching people pass by. You can do this really anywhere, but **Tel Aviv (#5)** and **Jerusalem, New City (#72)** provide the greatest people-spotting vantages. **Rothschild Boulevard** in Tel Aviv, **Ben Yehuda Street** in Jerusalem, and the Florentin (D4) neighborhood of Tel Aviv are just a few examples of great café culture. See *Do #15: Drink It!* (p. 93) for more on coffee and wine, and *Do #14: Eat It!* (p. 80) for more on cafés and outdoor eateries.

Dining al fresco Almost every restaurant has outdoor eating space. The restaurants in **Jaffa (#30)** are pretty reliable in this way, as are the restaurants all along the **Tel Aviv Tayelet/Promenade** up to the **Tel Aviv Port**.

Budget

SHOESTRING

Cities Though they are all big cities, you can maintain a semi-shoestring lifestyle while in **Tel Aviv (#5)**, **Jerusalem, New City (#72)**, and **Modern Amman (#36)**. The other cities may be harder to find budget accommodations, activities, and dining options, but the big cities offer cheap, if not free, options in all of these categories.

Activities Two of our three BUCKET! sites are actually free – lucky you! (**Petra (#2)** is pricey.) But there are plenty of other options that are free, such as beach activities in **Tel Aviv (#5)**, the **Bahá'í Gardens (#27)** tour, and many of the religious sites in various parts of Israel – Bethlehem, Nazareth, etc. Note that sites in Jordan generally charge a fee, but the Jordan Pass can be a great money-saver and covers just about everything you'd want to see.

Walking Walking is the cheapest option you have for activities, and we offer dozens of options to keep you entertained. Explore the city walks in Part 9 for tons of ideas.

Jerusalem Consider: City Walks A1–A7. **Old City Jerusalem (#1)** is free to enter and explore with no charge for most of the major sites, including the **Western Wall (#11)**, **Dome of the Rock (#6)**, and the **Church of the Holy Sepulchre (#9)**. The **Mount of Olives (#34)** is also free, though be aware that the **Ramparts Walk (#91)**, the *City of David*, and **Citadel/Tower of David (#32)** have separate entrance fees. Otherwise, wander empty-pocketed to your heart's content!

Dead Sea And though it's not free to get there, you can swim in the **Dead Sea (#3)** at the public beach of *Ein Bokek*, right on the southern part of the sea. And it's actually quite nice! Buses can get you there.

Parks Consider: Road Trip U2. National parks are not free but, if you buy a park pass, you can visit as many as you like. They include sites such as **Caesarea (#25)** and **Masada (#8)**, among lots of other hidden gems. Check out *Discount Cards/Passes* in *Do #7: Money It!* (p. 60).

Camping In Israel, most of the national parks have free or cheap campgrounds, and there's lots of wild camping on beaches, in the **Golan Heights (#62)**, and in the Negev at **Makhtesh Ramon (#28)**. If you're a hiker, you have other cheap camping options along the extensive *Israel National Trail*, *Jesus Trail (#69)*, Golan Trail (I2), and **Jordan Trail (#52)**, among others. The nature reserves in Jordan and a number of places in the Sinai, such as camping in **Dahab (#54)** and **St. Catherine's Monastery (#22)**, can also be done very cheaply.

Cheap lodging There are also a number of hostels to choose from in the major cities. Check out *Do #5: Sleep It!* (p. 48) for more information.

Food Find the cheapest food options on the street. **Israeli Cuisine (#51)** and **Jordanian Cuisine (#44)** have lots of great options for those on a budget, including the ubiquitous falafel and shawarma sandwiches. Markets are another great options, with **Mehane Yehuda Market (#67)** in Jerusalem, **Carmel Market (#87)** in Tel Aviv, and **Jaffa (#30)** having great street food options.

Transportation Buses are not Asia-level cheap, but they are still fairly affordable. Check out *Do #11: Transport It!* (p. 71) for more information on options that meet your budget.

LUXURY

Beach resorts If you want to spend a lot of money on beach resorts, you're in luck! There are plenty of options, though they aren't necessarily the highest-rated hotels we have. **Eilat (#78)**, for instance, is possibly the most popular resort area in Israel, with several popular hotel brands (Dan) offering rooms a more than $500 per night. **Tel Aviv (#5)** resorts are better bang for your buck.

Boutique hotels There are lots of beautiful new hotels opening up, and most are in the "boutique" category, rather than the glitzy resorts, à la Ritz-Carlton. Consider **The Norman Hotel**, the Brown TLV (D4), The Jaffa (D2), and The Setai (D2) while in Tel Aviv, or the **King David Hotel** or **Mamilla Hotel** in Jerusalem. All are excellent options with many accolades. Lots of options also exist in Rosh Pina (H2), a great Anchor City while you explore the Galilee and the Golan. See *Do #5: Sleep It!* (p. 48) for a bevy of options.

Spa hotels The **Elma Arts Complex** just outside **Zichron Ya'akov** and the Beresheet Hotel (J2) in **Mitzpe Ramon** are two gorgeous, newish complexes. You can find great options on the **Dead Sea (#3)** at **Suweimeh Spa Hotels** or at **Ein Bokek Spa Hotels**. Check out *Do #5: Sleep It!* (p. 48).

Sky Two adrenaline-rich and bird's-eye activities stand out for the hive: a **Hot Air Balloon Ride Over Wadi Rum** and a *Powered Parachute Flight above Dead Sea/Masada (K1)*. Neither are cheap.

Water If you're interested in learning water sports (kiteboarding, stand-up paddleboarding, and surfing) and have a few days to kill, you can get private lessons in several places along the **Mediterranean Coast**. There's also a fairly robust yachting community, and you can rent a boat for a day or join a club if you're around for a while. Scuba is also a costly activity, and you can spend a fair bit of time at the **Red Sea (#10)** exploring the underwater world.

Restaurants You do not have to spend a fortune to get a good meal, but it doesn't hurt. Israel can be extremely expensive, with shabby-chic restaurants charging upwards of $100 a person, including wine. There are plenty of high-end restaurants to choose from if you have a Black Card itching to be used. **Herbert Samuel**, Helena Banamal (E4), and others all feature in our *Top Restaurants* category (p. 561), though there are plenty to choose from depending on your preferences.

Companions

KID-FOCUSED

Beach fun You really can't go wrong with the beach. There's always a strip of sand with infinite possibilities for fun – in **Tel Aviv (#5)**, **Herziliya Beaches**, and other places along the **Mediterranean Coast**. Or, head south to the Negev for some fun on the **Red Sea (#10)**.

Fun for everyone The **Tel Aviv Port** is popular on Fridays and Saturdays for families. The Sarona Market (D3) area has lots of good eateries and shops, while the Hatachana Train Station (D1) adds entertainment many weekends. Both are in Tel Aviv.

Amusement parks and zoos In **Eilat (#78)**, you can't miss the **Underwater Observatory** which offers prime views of the coral reefs and other plant and animal life. Just north of Eilat is the **Yotvata Hai-Bar** nature reserve where endangered animals from the Bible are bred and roam freely. The **Carmel Hai-Bar** nature reserve in the Carmel National Park just outside of **Haifa** offers a similar experience, with a petting zoo to accompany. Other such animal-friendly places include the Alpaca Farm (J2) in **Mitzpe Ramon**, the Gan Garoo (F2) petting zoo in the Galilee, the Tisch Family Zoological Gardens (B1), and the Dolphin Reef (L2). Mini Israel (B2), between Jerusalem and Tel Aviv, is always a big (but miniature!) hit.

Kid-friendly museums The **Israel Museum (#17)** has plenty to offer young ones, particularly in its Youth Wing, while the **Weizmann Institute of Science** has lots of science and technology fun for your grade-school-aged kids. **Timna (#96)** is an enormous outdoor historical site that offers ample room to run and play while learning about ancient peoples in the region. Older kids will also love Beit Ha'ir (D3) which uses a variety of interesting technology to tell the story of Tel Aviv.

Exciting activities There are tons of options for your kids, including horseback riding at Kibbutz Merom Golan (I2) and Picking Fruit (I2), both in the **Golan Heights (#62)**. Or they can participate in an archaeological dig in **Beit Guvrin (#60)**, sleep under the stars with Astronomy Israel (J2), or visit a water park in Rishpon (D7).

Fun festivals Kids love Yom Kippur (U) when they can play on the street without the worry of cars. Purim in Tel Aviv (D4) is like Halloween when kids get to dress up in costume. The annual Israel Festival (A7) in Jerusalem often has lots of activities to keep the young ones occupied.

ALL AGES AND GENERATIONS

The following recommended sites are meant to complement the "kid-focused" sites above. These may still be kid-friendly, but are fun for the whole family.

Dead Sea The **Dead Sea (#3)** is a great adventure for everybody. While you do need to know how to swim, and you also need to know how not to get the water in your mouth or eyes, the salty waters can still provide lots of entertainment for the youngsters and older folks in your group. And if you visit a venue with more amenities, such as the *Ein Bokek Spa Hotels* or *Suweimeh Spa Hotels*, everyone can relax in the pool when they get tired of the salt water.

Cities to run around in The **Tel Aviv Beaches (#89)** and *Tel Aviv Tayelet/Promenade* provide ample opportunities for kids to run around and play while the adults soak up the sun or watch the waves roll in. **Akko (#13)** is another family-friendly destination, with interesting exhibits and walls your kids can run on top of (careful not to let them get too high – it's quite a drop). **Eilat (#78)** has beaches galore, an *Underwater Observatory*, Dolphin Reef (L2), snorkeling in **Coral Beach (#83)**, and other fun activities for the whole family. **Old City Jerusalem (#1)** has a number of activities for varied audiences, including the **Western Wall Tunnels (#94)** which take you several stories below the present-day level of the street, as well as *Hezekiah's Tunnel* which lets you traipse through knee-high water while learning about Jerusalem's ancient past.

Museums All of the museums in the region have plenty to offer a diverse group of interests. The **Israel Museum (#17)** has great historical exhibits, but an equally nice sculpture lawn and youth wing. **Yad Vashem (#35)** has plenty of exhibits to cater to all tastes. The **Citadel/Tower of David (#32)** museum gives great background on the Old City, but also provides a map to kids that gives context to their exploration of the Old City. The *Weizmann Institute of Science* has several exhibits for kids of all ages, and we mean you adults too.

Parks The National Park system in Israel does a great job of entertaining all of its audience members. **Beit Guvrin (#60)** is always filled with families exploring the caves, the pathways through the forest in **Banias (#80)** make walking to the waterfall painless, and *Hula Lake* offers bikes and trains to circle the lake and view the many visiting bird species. *Mount Carmel* and *Tel Ashkelon* have great green space.

Natural heritage **Rosh HaNikra** has caves that lap water high against its walls and provide lots of squeals of excitement. Looking out at an erosion crater from the visitor center at **Makhtesh Ramon (#28)**, hiking to the *Red Canyon* near Eilat, and **Timna (#96)** all showcase the interesting geography of Israel.

Resorts It might just be easiest to haul the whole family in a car or plane and settle into a resort for a weekend (or longer!). **Eilat (#78)**, **Aqaba (#43)**, and Taba (T1) all have dozens of hotel options at various price points. **Sharm el-Sheikh (#88)** is a beautiful getaway in the Sinai.

Beaches And of course any beach is going to provide all sorts of options for families and wide-ranging age groups. Pick anywhere along the *Mediterranean Coast*. *Tiberias* offers access to the *Sea of Galilee Beaches*, which contain parks, walkways, swimming, and surfing opportunities. Beach camping is a great way of keeping the fun going for multiple days.

BIG GROUP FRIENDLY

Taking a bus with a group of 30? Or just trying to coordinate a bunch of people and looking for a place where you don't have to continually check in through the buddy system?

Old City Jerusalem Our first suggestion, **Old City Jerusalem (#1)**, has lots of winding alleys and places to get lost – but it is an absolute must. There are plenty of big tour groups roaming around with flags and/or matching T-shirts, so you won't be out of place if this is you. Tour guides can be arranged at Jaffa Gate very easily. Inside, the **Western Wall (#11)** is a large open plaza and easy for groups to congregate. **Temple Mount (#12)** is also a large space, though harder to get into. There are lots of groups clamoring to get into the **Church of the Holy Sepulchre (#9)**, which was not designed to handle the millions of visitors each year, so there are regularly long lines and cramped rooms.

Petra You'll have a better time, honestly, if you can break up into smaller groups, but **Petra (#2)** is outdoors and much of the base can be done in a big tour group, if you are looking to split the cost of a guide among lots of people.

Dead Sea The **Dead Sea (#3)** tends to be fairly confined to the sea, with little place to lose your guests, so a visit to **Ein Bokek** or any of the towns on the north side can allow for masses to run around for a specified amount of time before meeting back up at the bus.

Masada **Masada (#8)** is a good option for many. Its site, atop a plateau overlooking the Dead Sea, lets the athletic types hike up the Snake Path while others can take the cable car. The site itself is open space that works well for tour groups. For those that don't like the heat, there are canopies, a museum, and a café to retreat to.

Roman ruins **Jerash (#14)**, **Caesarea (#25)**, and the sites of **Ancient Amman (#37)** all have big spaces that work well for tour groups.

Jerusalem museums The **Israel Museum (#17)**, **Yad Vashem (#35)**, the **Citadel/Tower of David (#32)**, the **Jerusalem Archaeological Park (#71)**, and *City of David* parks are all well equipped to handle larger groups.

Christian sites You might not enjoy the experience with so many people, but there are lots of groups traveling through the **Mount of Olives (#34)**, the Jesus sites in the **Sea of Galilee (#7)**, the *Basilica of the Annunciation* in **Nazareth (#29)**, and the **Church of the Nativity (#18)** in **Bethlehem (#40)**. The latter, in particular, is often very crowded, with long wait times particularly around Christmas.

National parks You can organize discounts for large groups (usually 20 or more) at several national parks. **Beit Guvrin (#60)** and **Beit She'arim (#79)** are both great for groups.

Time-Unlimited

TWELVE WEEKS

If you've got time, then we've got suggestions. This can, of course, go in any order, and the longer you're on the road, the more likely your trip will be more spontaneous. We have very loose suggestions for how to schedule your three-month sojourn. If you've got only eight weeks, you could squeeze everything into a shorter period, or with 16 weeks you could elongate the experience.

Week 1 Consider: City Walks A1–A7, Road Trip A8. Jerusalem! Spend three or four days roaming the Old City. It's only one square mile, and it's surrounded by walls, so you can explore every nook and cranny. Spend the other three or four days visiting the Jerusalem outside the Old City walls – **Mount of Olives (#34)**, **Mount Zion (#92)**, *City of David*, **Mea She'arim (#66)**, Nakhalat Shiva (A7) and *Ben Yehuda Street*, **Mehane Yehuda Market (#67)**, and the museums in Jerusalem's New City, for starters. Our walking tours will go a long way here – do one per day!

Week 2 Consider: Road Trips K1, L1. Take a couple of days to head south towards the **Dead Sea (#3)**, **Masada (#8)**, and **Ein Gedi (#50)** areas. There are a few hostels there to keep costs down. Work your way down to **Eilat (#78)**, through the Arabah and spend a few days snorkeling or doing scuba, hiking in the *Red Canyon* or to Amram's Pillars (L3). Maybe jaunt over to Har Karkom to see an alternative theory location for the biblical Mount Sinai.

Weeks 3–4 Consider: Road Trips M2, O1, P2, R1, S1, City Walks Q1, Q2. Cross over at **Eilat (#78)** to **Aqaba (#43)** in Jordan. Head to **Wadi Rum (#4)** and sleep under the stars, then plan to spend several days in **Petra (#2)**. If you want to complete all of the hikes, you'll need at least three days, and the longest hike will take you to *Little Petra*. After you get your fill of the Nabataean ruins, head north for walks through **Dana Biosphere Reserve (#21)**, traipse through **Karak (#49)** and *Shobak* castles, and coordinate guided hikes in **Wadi Mujib (#23)**. See the Christian sites around the **Dead Sea (#3)**. Spend a day or two in **Amman (#36/#37)**, with a day trip east to **Qasr Amra and the Desert Palaces (#20)**. Make a loop of the northern sites, including **Jerash (#14)**, **Ajloun Forest (#57)** and **Ajloun Fortress (#76)**, and **Umm Qais (#45)**, and anything else you have time for (*Pella*, *Damiya Dolmen Field (S2)*, and *As-Salt* are all under-visited).

Week 5 Consider: City Walks D1–D6, Road Trips B2, B3, E4. Cross back over to Israel (note: you will likely need to use whichever border crossing you used earlier) and head to **Tel Aviv (#5)**. Tel Aviv is not cheap, so you can use it either as a base (it has several nice hostels and lots of street food) for hopping around to other parts of the region, or just plan to spend a couple of days lounging on the beach drinking cheap beer. If you're looking for a few day trips, you can organize an expedition through the Judean Hills Wineries (B3), head to **Beit Guvrin (#60)** for UNESCO love, and check out the Roman ruins at **Caesarea (#25)**.

Week 6 Consider: Road Trip E5, City Walks E1, E2. Take the train up to *Haifa*, worthy of a couple of days to see the **Bahá'í Gardens (#27)** and sample the laid-back vibe (there are bars, cafés, museums, street food options, and beaches). Do **Akko (#13)** for a day or two, as there are plenty of spots in the walled city to linger happily. You can keep going north to the Lebanon border and *Rosh HaNikra*.

Week 7 Consider: Road Trips F1, F2, G2, G3, City Walk G1. Get east! Check out **Beit She'arim (#79)**, **Megiddo (#59)**, and **Tsipori (#56)**, then stop over in **Nazareth (#29)** for a few days (great food and Jesus sites). Head south to the Lower Galilee sites of **Belvoir (#93)**, **Beit She'an (#39)**, *Gan HaShlosha*, and **Beit Alpha (#64)**. Turn north towards the **Sea of Galilee (#7)**. You can circle the sea on foot, if that interests you, stopping along the way at the many biblical spots.

Week 8 Consider: Road Trips I1, I2, I3. Spend a week in the **Golan Heights (#62)**, climbing or skiing *Mount Hermon*, *Picking Fruit (I2)*, jungling through **Banias (#80)**, and hiking to **Nimrod's Fortress (#85)**. Get a buzz circling the borders with Lebanon, Syria, and Jordan (the only one open at present), but being sure to watch out for land mines (no off-roading).

Or skip the previous two weeks, and…

Go on a two-week hike or bike ride. Head from the Mediterranean straight to the **Sea of Galilee (#7)** or *Mount Hermon*, depending on which journey you choose – the *Israel National Trail*, **Jesus Trail (#69)**, Golan Trail (I2), or Israel Bike Trail (U). You can camp along the way, and get a more intimate view of off-the-beaten-path destinations along the trip.

Week 9 Consider: Road Trip J2. Either walk down, or take a car/bus, to *Mitzpe Ramon*. Spend a few days wandering through the various canyons in the desert region, principally **Makhtesh Ramon (#28)**, but also the Big Makhtesh (Makhtesh HaGadol) and Little Makhtesh (Makhtesh HaKatan).

Week 10 Consider: Road Trips C2–C5, City Walk C1. Time to head to Palestine. Commute back up to Jerusalem, which you can use as your base, or stay in Bethlehem. Visit **Bethlehem (#40)**, **Tomb of the Patriarchs and Old Town of Hebron (#46)**, and **Herodion (#90)** in the southern part of the West Bank. **Jericho (#26)** is just east of Jerusalem, close to the Jordanian border crossing. Highlights include hiking to **St. George's Monastery and Wadi Qelt (#97)**. **Ramallah (#68)**, **Nablus (#61)**, and *Mount Gerizim* are all located in the north part of the West Bank.

Weeks 11–12 Add one or more of the following:
★ *Option 1 Consider*: Road Trip T1. Cross over to the Sinai (or fly). If you're posh, base at **Sharm el-Sheikh (#88)** for some serious R&R. If you're backpacking, **Dahab (#54)** will suit you (and you can easily kill lots of time here as it's super chill and cheap). Add in a hike to **Mount Sinai (#15)**, a visit to **St. Catherine's Monastery (#22)**, and a scuba or snorkel adventure at **Ras Mohammad (#53)**.
★ *Option 2* Learn to [fill-in-the-blank water sport] and lounge on a Tel Aviv (or other!) beach, eating street snacks, meeting all sorts of folks after midnight, and spending the days alternating between sunbathing and caffeine injections with your new friends. Add in some Hebrew lessons at one of the Ulpanim (U) to make your forever friends. (Arabic language school is becoming popular too.)
★ *Option 3* Spend two weeks (or four, if you redesign weeks 3–4) in a cultural immersion: volunteer at a local NGO, work with your hands in the ground in a modern kibbutz, or literally dig up history at an archaeological site.

SLOW HOLY LAND

The secret to making your money stretch as long as possible is to not do too much each day. You'll quickly learn that it takes a lot of time to plan where you're going to sleep every night, how you're going to get from point A to point B, and talking to people to get recommendations. Much of this guidebook focuses on the short-term traveler, because that's most of us. Its goal is to teach you how to triage the enormous number of things to do into your two-day or two-week trip. But sometimes we take sabbaticals and can just take it easy, focusing on one site or event a day. If you're ready to take the plunge into slow travel, you surely won't be disappointed. Here are some of our travel tidbits for your consideration, in no particular order:

★ United States citizens get a three-month stay in Israel on entry, and a one-month stay in Jordan. These **visas** are obtained at ports of entry, and are not required to be obtained in advance. In Jordan, you can request to stay longer by registering with the Jordanian police before the expiration of the entry visa. Or you can obtain a visa prior to arrival at the Israel or Jordanian embassies. More information for US citizens can be found at w travel.state.gov. Other nationals should try their Ministries of Foreign Affairs for information.

★ **Rental cars** can't cross borders. **Taxis** aren't cheap in Israel, but are relatively inexpensive in Jordan (depending on where you want to go). **Buses** are pretty cheap.

★ **Camping** is free and permissible in many beaches and parks in Israel. The weather is amenable. Cheap hotels are easy to come by in Jordan. Camping can also be done in Jordan, but usually involves hiring a guide (typically Bedouin), as unregistered camping is not allowed, and registered campgrounds aren't plentiful.

★ If you like hiking and camping, you're in luck – Israel has a nation-long trail called the *Israel National Trail* which runs approximately 1,000km and takes 40–60 days to complete. It passes through a dozen geological zones, and has decent facilities along the way and lots of history and scenery.

★ There are dozens of shorter **hikes** that can take anywhere from a day to a weekend. Check out our *Walks and Hikes* categories (p. 548) for more information.

★ You can spend a lot of time working as a *Kibbutz Volunteer* in Israel, which can afford you free housing if you're okay with toiling away (quite literally), cooking, machinery, and community living. These once-socialist enclaves have mostly gone capitalist in order to best provide for the community members, but the spirit of once-in-a-lifetime adventure remains.

★ **Language school** will also keep you busy for as long as you may want to keep yourself learning. Hebrew schools, called Ulpanim (U), are free for new Olim ("Jewish immigrants"), so cash in if you're Jewish and have come to stay permanently. Everyone else: you'll experience total immersion in the land which brought Hebrew back from the dead only a little over 100 years ago. In Amman, you can find a number of Arabic programs for various types of students – from diplomats to wanderers.

★ Israel does not want for **holidays**. With six months or a year, you can capture the essence of culture through one of the monthly holidays or festivals that grace each calendar year. (Your best bet: make a new friend and get invited to something local, such as a seder or cultural event.)

★ **Outdoor** activities tend to be free and well attended, so you're bound to meet others, even if you have only pennies to spare.

- ★ Food can be cheap, if you don't mind **fast food**. And we're not talking about burgers. Falafel in pita, shawarma, sabich, hummus, masabacha, fuul – this is the heavy sustenance you'll need to keep you going all day long. Will you have some bad falafel? Yes. But there are shops everywhere: keep searching until you find the place that matches your budget and your liking.
- ★ As for evening activities, restaurant food is expensive. And bar prices are similar to the USA and Europe. Beer can be cheap, but you won't find cheaper prices at grocery stores. Duty free isn't anywhere near as "free" as you'd hope. Neither Israelis nor Jordanians drink heavily in their cultures. The influx of Russians to Tel Aviv and surroundings has changed the evening and focus of late nights for some. Mostly, you'll find friends nursing one drink for hours, or simply not drinking at all. That's all normal. For your vice fulfillment, you can always choke down the **local beer** varieties – as cheap as it comes – which don't win any prizes for taste, but are perfectly tolerable. As for smokers, you might find *Argila/Hookah/Shisha* a suitable alternative to tobacco, and it lasts much longer than a cigarette.
- ★ Cheap accommodation abounds. There are **hostels** and budget hotels in most cities and towns. Outside of free camping, the shores of the Red Sea on the Egyptian coast offer the cheapest options, with some no-frills mattresses-on-the-sand for just a few dollar equivalents. Some lodging options might strike you as more expensive than you were expecting, such as *Glamping in Wadi Rum (M2)* or **Feynan Ecolodge (#86)** in **Dana Biosphere Reserve (#21)**.

Places to Spend an Eternity, or at Least a Couple Weeks

Jerusalem You can easily spend a day in each of the three main religious sites. **Temple Mount (#12)** offers green space to spend time and sit, though keep in mind this is a Muslim site so women travelers may feel uncomfortable lingering for too long. The **Western Wall (#11)**, **Western Wall Tunnels (#94)**, and surrounding museums (*Wohl Archaeological Museum*) that discuss the Wall in greater detail can easily bide a day or longer. The **Church of the Holy Sepulchre (#9)** has a number of nooks and crannies to keep you interested, and people-watching in the two busiest spots (the upstairs spot where the cross stood, and the Sepulchre itself), as well as long waits to get in, can keep you occupied for the better part of a day anyhow. Instead of cramming a bunch of spots into one day, you can stretch out our city walks (see Part 9) into two or three days each. Spend the whole day at the **Citadel/Tower of David (#32)**. Walk slowly along the **Ramparts Walk (#91)**. Take your time at the **Mount of Olives (#34)**, and at **Mount Zion (#92)**, and at the *City of David*. You won't get bored people-watching in the *Jewish Quarter*. The tiny nooks and crannies can have you exploring new and historic Jerusalem for weeks.

Tel Aviv If you're into lounging, and can spare a week or two on the beach, you're in luck. There are plenty of hostels to choose from, and you can lounge to your heart's content. Pick up a game of matcot, surf, kiteboard, parasail, go yachting, bodyboarding, or stand-up paddleboarding – the options are really as endless as your bank account. When you need a break from the sun, you can wander down any of the pedestrian alleys and hang out, sipping coffee, while people-watching for hours.

Petra Taking your time with **Petra (#2)** is a real luxury, as most people arrive in a hurry, run to the Treasury, hike quickly to the High Point or Monastery, and leave completely exhausted. With a number of hikes to choose from, and no great hurry (though you will be limited by your ticket options – so purchase the three-day pass, which is only slightly more expensive than the one-day), you can slow down and enjoy each unique journey.

Red Sea The Israeli side would be too expensive to linger too long at the **Red Sea (#10)**, but you can make your Jordanian dinar last in Jordan, and your Egyptian pounds go on forever in Egypt. Buy your own snorkeling gear and entertain yourself for days with the plant and animal life off the shallow sea shelf.

WHOLE HOLY LAND SPRINT: GOLD

Interested in seeing every Gold elective in this region? That's quite a commitment, but it can be done. We have identified 100 sights and experiences that have been lauded by travelers, reviewers, travel agents, tour guides, writers, photographers, and Holy Land lovers. Let's be honest: they're all worth seeing.

Our macro-regions are organized A–T (with trans-boundary regions denoted by the letters U–Z). The regions adjacent to each other in the alphabet are also adjacent to each other geographically. Thus, you could start at A (Jerusalem) and work your way forward in the alphabet while simultaneously working your way through Israel, then Jordan, and lastly the Sinai. For maps see p. 572.

So, how to go about a full Holy Land tour in the most mathematically and logistically rational way possible (i.e., trying to hit everything, but starting with the regions that offer the most bang for your buck)?

★ There are 100 Gold electives, and Jerusalem (A) has 20 of them, which is 20% of the total. Tel Aviv (D) comes in next with nine electives, followed by the West Bank (C) with eight. The Lower Galilee and Kinneret (G) holds six, as does King's Highway (O).

★ For logistical reasons, it makes sense to start with Jerusalem (A) and then do the West Bank (C). You can hit Greater Jerusalem (B)'s one elective on your way to Tel Aviv (D) before working your way north.

★ The next important group is the Lower Galilee and Kinneret (G). On the way, you may want to visit the four electives at Mount Carmel and Jezreel (F). And, while you're up there, tack on the one site in the Upper Galilee (H). Finish up with a tour of the highlights of the Golan Heights (I).

★ Then work your way south, hitting the Mediterranean coastline (E), which has four electives.

★ The Negev (J), Dead Sea (Israel) (K), and Eilat and Arabah (L) all have four electives each and can be done successively.

★ You also have three electives that are related to broader Israel (U) and not tied to a region. You'll be able to tick those off as you go along.

★ At this point, you can go to the Sinai or go to Jordan. Jordan has more electives in total, but the Sinai (T) has a lot for one region: five.

★ Once in Jordan, either complete the three South Jordan (M) electives, or you can begin working your way north, which is where the bulk of the activity is. Either stop in Petra (N) now or save it for the end. Either way, drive along King's Highway (O) for its six electives.

★ Veer west to the Dead Sea (Jordan) (P) with its five electives, head to Amman (Q) and do its two plus the pair in the East Jordan (R).

★ North Jordan (S) has four more electives to entice you. If you haven't done southern Jordan yet, now's the time.

- ★ Like Israel, there are three electives in Jordan not tied to a region (V). Do these anytime.
- ★ Thus, the mathematical order of prioritization goes: A-C-B-D-F-G-H-I-E-J-K-L-T-M-N-O-P-Q-R-S. As you can see, it's practically the same as just following the alphabet.

WHOLE HOLY LAND CRAWL: GOLD, SILVER, BRONZE

We tout our 100 sites and activities as being the very best that the Holy Land has to offer. While true, our research uncovered thousands of other things to see and do in this area. Anytime a place received special mention – a star, a thumbs-up, etc. – we included it in our list of exceptional regional sites/activities. Those places which had multiple recommendations and reached a certain score achieved the coveted Gold status, while three rose high enough to become global BUCKET! sites and experiences. However, there are hundreds more highly recommended sites that are worthy of your time.

Our "whole Holy Land crawl" is essentially a rough guide to completing all of our electives: Gold, Silver, and Bronze. All 700+. This feat requires a systematic approach, one that arguably involves methodically pressing through micro-region by micro-region. To make this easy for you, every elective has a macro-region (ABC) and micro-region (123). Some electives have no micro-region and are classified by simply the macro-region, and those you can slot in as you deem fit.

So how do you put such a trip together? We'd recommend you start regionally. As we demonstrated in the *Whole Holy Land Sprint* above, you can start with A and work your way alphabetically for a perfectly logical trip.

Take a look in Part 9 at the city walks and road trips associated with that region. Every one of our electives has been incorporated into those tours. It would take you months of nonstop travel to complete, but it could be done, particularly for those who find themselves living short- or long-term in the region.

But is it really possible to finish off the entire list? No. You will likely not be able to volunteer for every referenced agency or eat in every restaurant (though that's a good challenge!). Plus, there are a number of places that are closed, inaccessible, or seasonal, because businesses are volatile, sites require upkeep, and border tensions flare 'round these parts.

How many have you completed? Let us know at #bucketholyland.

REGIONAL ADD-ONS

The historical Holy Land extends far beyond the borders of Israel, Jordan, Palestine, the Sinai, and any other present boundaries that we currently recognize. A couple of our regions (Gaza, X; Lebanon and Syria, Y) are off the map for the time being due to violence, war, and political problems. But the borders could extend even further, if we had unlimited space. (We do not.) The following are therefore a few ideas in keeping with the Holy Land spirit and offer ways to combine your Israel, Jordan, and Sinai tour with some other fascinating spaces nearby.

Egypt along the Nile From the Sinai (or Tel Aviv or Amman), you can fly to Cairo and begin a journey exploring the ancient world's most famous civilization, with a stunning array of sites and artifacts. Several more BUCKET! sites are here, from the Pyramids of Giza and Saqqara to Luxor and Abu Simbel. Additionally, there are biblical sites galore in Egypt. Moses grew up in Egypt, Mary and Joseph fled there, and the Exodus began from the Land of Goshen, east of present-day Cairo. There are a number of ancient churches and synagogues in Cairo, Alexandria, and along the western shore of the Red Sea.

Lebanon Lebanon's history is as rich as its southern neighbors, with a modern history arguably as tumultuous. Unlike Israel – a land that continues to struggle in adapting to diversity – Lebanon began its independence in a power-sharing arrangement among its five major ethnic/nationalist/religious groups. Strife still envelops the region at times, so visitors should always look to guidance provided by their embassies. If you do decide to visit, there is a rich array of activities and sites, accumulated from the region's various ruling parties since ancient times. The Canaanites and Phoenicians from the early Bible chapters resided in the area now known as Lebanon, so there are plenty of archaeological sites to visit. Tyre and Baalbek each offer very impressive displays. The site of Byblos is an amalgamation of successive cultures, dating from the Neolithic period. There are Umayyad palaces at Anjar, Monastic Christian settlements in the Holy Valley (Wadi Qadisha), and wineries in Bekaa. Beirut is a culinary powerhouse, as well as a cultural beacon for many Lebanese (and Arab) people. The nightlife rivals Tel Aviv in several cities. And the beaches are much less touristed. Lebanon is famous for cedar trees. There is also a walking trail, called the Lebanon Mountain Trail, in the south, as well as Beaufort Castle – a great Crusader fortress.

Turkey Several books of the New Testament reference places in Turkey, though it's not often thought of as part of the Holy Land. Tradition says Mary came here after the crucifixion and lived her remaining days. The Seven Churches of Asia, discussed in the Book of Revelation, are located in various parts of Turkey near the Aegean coast. Many believe Mount Ararat in Turkey to be the resting place of Noah's Ark. Istanbul is home to many of the world's great churches and mosques, including the BUCKET! sites of Hagia Sophia and the Blue Mosque.

Cyprus In the 1st century CE, while the island of Cyprus was under Roman rule, the Apostle Paul, Mark the evangelist, and Barnabas left the Holy Land to Cyprus in order to spread Christianity, founding one of the earliest churches around 45 CE. A few stories from the Book of Acts of the Apostles take place here. Cyprus has many impressive ruins combined with great food, gorgeous beaches, and UNESCO sites, making it well worth a visit while you are in the area.

Syria St. John the Baptist is said to be buried in a shrine in the Grand Mosque of Damascus. There are Umayyad Desert Castles in Syria, too, much like in eastern Jordan. However, having been under a constant state of siege for the better part of a decade, Syria is unfortunately inaccessible at the present time. One of the most famous Crusader castles is Krak des Chevaliers (our #32A: it would have been 32nd in our overall ranking had it not been off-limits for the last ten years). Near the epicenter of the violence (Homs), much remains unknown about the state of disrepair in Syria's ancient sites, including Krak des Chevaliers. Palmyra, an ancient Roman city, also faced irreparable damage when warring groups used it as a battleground.

Saudi Arabia If you somehow manage to find your way into Saudi Arabia (visas are hard to come by independently, but can be arranged with a tour), you will of course be in one of the world's most closed Muslim societies. Foreigners (read: non-Muslims) are not allowed to visit Mecca or Medina. However, you can visit Meda'in Saleh, a Nabataean sister city to Petra and UNESCO site since 2008.

The closest BUCKET! sites to tie your round-the-world trip together are the following:

Giza and Saqqara
Karnak and Luxor
Abu Simbel
The Cyclades and Santorini

The Acropolis and Athens
Sultanahmet, Istanbul
Cappadocia

Overland routes to reach several of these places have become inaccessible at the present time due to the Syrian war that has closed the cross-roads between Turkey and Jordan. Separately, ISIS has cells in the deserts of the Egyptian Sinai, so an overland journey from the Red Sea coast to Cairo may be possible, but it is not recommended. Ferries will no longer transport you across the Mediterranean. Your best bet will be to fly between all of these locations. Luckily for you, budget airlines from Europe are penetrating many markets.

You may also combine your Holy Land experience with one of our prospective BUCKET! guides:

The Two Lands (Upper and Lower Egypt)
Anatolia

Caucasus
The Aegean

Let us know on w buckettravelguides.com which book you'd like to see next.

Classic

HISTORIC

Travelers have been making pilgrimages to the Holy Land since at least the 4th century, which we know because the first surviving account dates from 333–4 CE in the *Itinerarium Bordigalense*. The traveler had come a long distance, traversing overland through to Tyre (a city in Lebanon) before heading south to Caesarea, and then curiously back north to Beit She'an and Nablus. At the time, Christians were seeking to cast eyes on the very places where Jesus had stood, preached, died, and transformed into God. The traveler stopped at Mount Gerizim on his way to Jerusalem. This would have been a very different Jerusalem than the one we know today – the Second Temple had been destroyed 300 years earlier, the Dome of the Rock had not yet been built, and the Church of the Holy Sepulchre (then a basilica built by Constantine) was still under construction. Constantine's Basilica would be consecrated the following year, 335 CE. In the *Itinerarium* we learn that Jews were already visiting Jerusalem once a year (the maximum allowed) to pray at the Western Wall, as they had been banned from entering the Temple Mount following the Bar Kokhba Revolt in the 2nd century. After Jerusalem, the traveler visited Jericho (historic), Bethany-by-the-Jordan (Christian), and Hebron (Judeo-Christian), putting together a diverse trip much like we do today.

Another early Christian traveler, called the Palestine Pilgrim, or Antoninus of Piacenza, wrote an account in or around 560/570 CE. His trip took him down the coast to Mount Carmel, before heading east towards Cana (where Jesus turned water into wine at a wedding), Nazareth, and Mount Tabor. He visited the various churches at the Sea of Galilee and continued to Banias before turning south to Umm Qais (then Gadara), Beit She'an, Nablus, and Sebastia. He traversed the Jordan Valley to Jericho, Bethany, the Mount of Olives, and finally Jerusalem. He makes little mention of the ruins on Temple Mount, but does talk of the Church of the Holy Sepulchre. He then headed to Hebron before turning west to the coast, passing Ashkelon, Gaza, and on to St. Catherine's Monastery and other sites in the Sinai before heading south along the Nile.

An Arab man, al-Muqaddasi, was born in Jerusalem in 945 CE and traveled extensively around the region to provide short descriptions of many familiar places in his account, *Description of the Province of Syria, including Palestine*. The references to the holy sites in Jerusalem, particularly the Dome of the Rock and other locations on Temple Mount, are worth the read. Several new "tourist spots" are mentioned, including Sodom and Gamorrah along the Dead Sea, Lydda, Amman, Jaffa, and the White Mosque of Ramle (particularly its minaret), which is referred to as the finest of its kind in all the land.

Jews were also known to travel to the Holy Land in medieval times, and Menachem ben Peretz of Hebron was one of these travelers in the 13th century. His tour incorporated several important Jewish tombs and holy places, beginning in Hebron and later the tombs of Jonah and Rachel near Bethlehem, before heading to Jerusalem. There, he wrote of the Western Wall and a large Jewish population. He would later visit a number of other historically significant tombs, including those of Zechariah and Absalom in the Kidron Valley, right outside the Jerusalem walls.

Richard Pococke visited the Holy Land from 1737–1741 and wrote *A Description of the East and other Countries*, detailing his time in Egypt, Palestine ("Palæstina or the Holy Land," as he titles it), Syria, and other parts of Mesopotamia, Turkey, and Greece. His account is fascinating if not solely for the great illustrations.

David Roberts was a lithographer who made the region famous through selling his landscapes, watercolors, and other images after a year-long trip to the Holy Land in 1838. He sailed through Alexandria, circling the southern part of the Sinai before visiting Aqaba and Petra, then heading to historic Palestine. He saw Hebron, Gaza, Ashkelon, Ashdod, Jaffa, Bethlehem, Jericho, Nablus, Nazareth, and Akko, before working his way through Lebanon and out through Beirut.

John Lloyd Stephens was an American explorer who wrote a series of books, most famously about the Mayans, but has a worthwhile read on the Holy Land entitled *Incidents of Travel in Egypt, Arabia Petraea, and the Holy Land* (1837). The book follows Stephens as he explores Egypt and the Sinai before heading north into the uncharted territories of "Edom" (the biblical name for the land in Israel and Jordan south of the Dead Sea). From Aqaba, he visited the bramble-walled and mysterious Petra, then headed on the road to Gaza through to Jaffa, Hebron, Bethlehem, and Jerusalem. He visited Jericho, Mar Saba, and went "out of Judea" to Mount Gerizim, Sebastia, Mount Tabor, and Nazareth. Stephens completed the Sea of Galilee circuit before heading west to Akko and Mount Carmel, ending his travels in Tyre.

There are plenty of great, free travel accounts throughout the centuries and millennia detailing these grand journeys through historic Palestine. You can find a good summary on Wikipedia (w en.wikipedia.org/wiki/Travelogues_of_Palestine). Then head over to w archive.org and Google Books to read many of these riveting accounts of Palestine, Israel, Jordan, Judea and Samaria, Edom, Aelia Capitolina, Greater Syria, and the Holy Land (all overlapping regions describing the same place we're covering) in full.

PILGRIMAGE

Religious pilgrimage is typically a spiritual journey, usually on foot, to a specific, sacred place as laid out in religious doctrine. Depending on the religion, the ranking and sanctity of a site can vary. For instance, Jerusalem is considered "the third-holiest site in Islam," one of "the four holy cities" in Judaism, though in Christianity the city of Jerusalem itself is not categorized. That said, the **Church of the Holy Sepulchre (#9)** *is* considered one of the holiest sites in Christianity. In practice, this means that religious pilgrims may or may not include certain stops on their spiritual (and physical) journeys.

Bahá'í Bahá'í have a nine-day pilgrimage that passes through holy spots in **Akko (#13)** and *Haifa*, including the **Bahá'í Gardens (#27)** and the *Shrine of Bahá'u'lláh* (w pilgrimage. bwc.org/pilgrimage/).

Christianity Christian pilgrims are not limited to, but may include any of the following:

★ **Old City Jerusalem (#1)**, the site of the last days of Jesus' life and resurrection.
★ **Bethlehem (#40)**, the birthplace of Jesus, particularly the **Church of the Nativity (#18)**.
★ **Nazareth (#29)**, the town where Jesus was raised, and where Mary received the Annunciation.

★ *Ein Kerem*, the birthplace of St. John the Baptist.
★ Bethany, location for the resurrection of Lazarus.
★ **Jericho (#26)**, site of *Deir Quruntal*, the Monastery of the Temptation.
★ Galilee region: *Kfar Kana (G4)*, site of the marriage at Cana where Jesus turned water to wine; *Tel Bethsaida (G4)*, the birthplace of three apostles; **Capernaum (#33)**, location of the House of St. Peter; **Tabgha (#33)**, location of the Church of the Multiplication of the Loaves and Fishes and the Church of the Primacy of St. Peter; Magdala, the birthplace of Mary Magdalene; the *Mount of Beatitudes*, where Jesus gave the Sermon on the Mount; and Mount Tabor, site of the Transfiguration and host to the *Church of the Transfiguration*.
★ Jordan: **Bethany-Beyond-the-Jordan (#41)**, where Jesus was baptized; *Mukawir*, site of the imprisonment and beheading of St. John the Baptist; and **Mount Nebo (#24)**, the place where Moses died and was presumed to be buried.

Judaism The holiest place for Jews is the **Western Wall (#11)**, which is the closest physical location to the **Temple Mount (#12)**, the location of the Islamic **Dome of the Rock (#6)**. Temple Mount once held the First and Second Temples, both of which were destroyed more than 2,000 years ago. Jews will make pilgrimages to a number of other important sites, such as the graves of rabbinical leaders. Places of pilgrimage in the Holy Land often include:

★ **Old City Jerusalem (#1)**, including the **Western Wall (#11)**, **Yad Vashem (#35)**, Tomb of David on **Mount Zion (#92)**, and *Rambam Synagogue (A4)*.
★ *Rachel's Tomb (C1)*, at the border between Israel and Palestine en route to Bethlehem.
★ Hebron for **Tomb of the Patriarchs (#46)** and Abraham's Oak.
★ Beer Sheva (J1) contains Abraham's Well.
★ **Nablus (#61)** is home to the Tomb of Joseph and *Mount Gerizim*.
★ *Tiberias* houses the *Tomb of Maimonides (G3)* and the *Tomb of Rabbi Meir Ba'al Haness (G3)*.
★ **Tsfat/Safed (#58)** has numerous ancient synagogues, as well as the Tomb of Haari Ashkenazi.

Samaritan **Mount Gerizim** is the holiest site for Samaritans. One of the four holy tenets of identification for the Samaritans is making an annual pilgrimage to the summit of Mount Gerizim for Pesach/Passover, Shavuot, and Sukkot.

Islam The focal point of Muslim pilgrimage is Mecca, Saudi Arabia. So important is Mecca to Islam and in the history of Muhammad that making a trip (*hajj*) there on foot is considered one of the five pillars of Islam. Two-and-a-half million people took part in the Hajj of 2019. Medina is the second-most important city in Islam, and **Old City Jerusalem (#1)** is third. Located on **Temple Mount (#12)**/Haram as-Sharif is the **Dome of the Rock (#6)**/Qubbat al-Sakhrah, the most recognizable building in Jerusalem and the oldest Muslim building in the world. Also located on Temple Mount is the **Al-Aqsa Mosque (#65)**, built to replace the mosque referred to by Muhammad in the Quran as "the farthest mosque," which is the translation of "al-aqsa."

Druze The Druze make an annual pilgrimage to the Tomb of Jethro, or Nabi Shu'ayb, located outside *Tiberias*.

CINEMATIC

Ever wonder where some of your favorite films were shot? Quite a few have used the Holy Land as backdrop.

Indiana Jones If one were so inclined to follow Indiana's sojourns, you'd indeed find yourself in the Holy Land at some point (along with India, China, Sri Lanka, Kauai, and Tunisia, among other destinations). **Petra (#2)** served as backdrop for the *Indiana Jones and the Last Crusade* film, as the Holy Grail was stashed within the Treasury complex. The film crew got a famous cut of the Treasury from above (and across), accessible now via trail (and highly recommended).

Lawrence of Arabia This famed film was shot in Spain, Morocco, California, and also Jordan. This time, **Wadi Rum (#4)** served to brighten the tones of the film, with its red rock cliffs. The long walks occurred amid black basalt geology near Jordan's border with Saudi Arabia in Jebel Tubayq, while the camel caravan took place in Jafr. **Karak (#49)**, Aqaba Fort, and *Qasr Azraq* were all part of Lawrence's original journey. Black Tomato, a travel agency based in the UK, used to run Lawrence of Arabia tours: check with them for personalizing a similar itinerary (**w** blacktomato.com).

Transformers: Revenge of the Fallen The second movie in the *Transformers* series used the Monastery of **Petra (#2)** as the "Tomb of the Primes." Other filming locations in Jordan included *As-Salt* and **Wadi Rum (#4)**. Egypt (the Pyramids, naturally) appears as well, along with various shots from the USA.

The Mummy Returns The *Mummy* sequel also features the Treasury building from **Petra (#2)**, as well as the Hijaz Railway, outside **Modern Amman (#36)**.

Kingdom of Heaven Based on the Crusades, this story is set in walled **Old City Jerusalem (#1)**, with parts in **Karak (#49)**. The scenery outside the walls of Jerusalem provides a stark contrast to its current level of development!

The Hurt Locker This movie about the Iraq War contained many desert scenes that were shot in Jordan, rather than Iraq, and **Modern Amman (#36)** was substituted for Baghdad.

The Martian Much of the red desert of Mars was shot in **Wadi Rum (#4)**.

Jesus Christ Superstar Shot in multiple locations throughout Israel, including **Avdat (#48)**, **Dead Sea (#3)**, **Beit Guvrin (#60)**, **Beit She'an (#39)**, and **Herodion (#90)**.

OVERLAND

Remember the days (mostly pre-September 11, 2001) when you could commute overland through the Middle East? Sigh, no more. Several popular overland routes from the 20th century used to include some iteration of overland travel via Europe to Istanbul, on through Anatolian Turkey, over to Aleppo and Damascus in Syria, down to Amman and through Jordan, into Israel and Palestine, and south towards Eilat before entering Egypt. Travelers could then amble down the Sinai's east coast (as we recommend – when safe to do so) before crossing over the Suez Canal to the African continent proper.

Classic

This entire itinerary had various iterations, depending on whether you had plans to visit Lebanon, of which the border with Israel has been closed for decades. It was unidirectional as well, since most Arab countries disallow access if you have evidence of travel to Israel. (This is no longer a major problem because Israel has stopped stamping passports, instead supplying paper entry and exit slips to track your arrival and departure from the country.)

Nowadays, this route has various issues. War has broken out everywhere, it seems, and once-saintly cities have been hobbled by terrorist attacks. Over the past decade, there have been attacks against tourists, civil war, terrorism, suicide bombings, uprisings, coups d'état, armed militias, proxy wars, and nonstop violence occurring throughout Turkey, Lebanon, Syria, and Iraq. Palestinians have launched several attacks against Israel from Gaza, and occasionally the Sinai, Lebanon, and Syria, which are responded to by Israel with even more force. These periodic flare-ups have led to rocket attacks, bus rammings, stabbings, and the occasional suicide bomb attack.

Perhaps one day travelers will be able to make this great overland trip through the Middle East again, but for now this route is not safe and is not recommended.

The Man in Seat 61 (w seat61.com) offers a few suggestions for how to do an overland trek to Israel which includes ships and ferries, but most of these are also currently nonoperational.

Our BUCKET! travel itinerary includes great backpacking and overland options between Israel, the West Bank, Jordan, and (cautiously) the Sinai. We hope to be able to offer expanded regional recommendations in the future.

Tailored

LOCAL TOUR GUIDES

You often see people walking around with tour guides, but where do they find them? Most people pick a tour-bus or travel agent who picks the tour guide for you behind the scenes. This is one option, and can be explored further in *Travel Agents and Specialists* below. If you prefer to find your own guide, there are a few options.

★ You can find a private tour **through a tour agency**. If this floats your boat, check out the trusty Tourist Israel (**w** touristisrael.com/type/private-tours/). They let you pick your requirements (transport/guide), number of days and sites/experiences you'd like to include, as well as hotels, meals, and other add-ons.

★ **Specialty guides** abound on the Touring Israel site (**w** touringisrael.com/guides/), all English-speaking, licensed by the Ministry of Tourism, and many with Master's degrees in a wide range of subjects.

★ **Hiking?** Try Tiuli (**w** tiuli.com/tour-guides), the site that coordinates trekkers, walkers, backpackers, and the like with experienced outdoors guides.

★ Two sites offer an assortment of options, with **prearranged itineraries and list prices**. There are a number of private tour guides who advertise directly on Viator (**w** viator.com), replete with customer feedback, or Tours by Locals (**w** toursbylocals.com).

If you are looking for a guide in Old City Jerusalem, Petra, or Wadi Rum (in addition to other sites, including Jericho, Jerash, and other smaller sites), you can skip the hassle of prearranging and coordinating, and simply pick a guide upon arrival.

★ Tour guides happily stand at the Jaffa Gate entrance to welcome visitors to the Old City.

★ At Petra, you'll inevitably be hounded by numerous guides from the Siq entrance to the start of the Monastery trail asking if you're interested.

★ In Wadi Rum, the "tour guides" are required, but can often serve as little more than jeep drivers, whisking you from tourist spot A to tourist spot B. Inquire at the visitor center/reception desk if you are seeking more interaction.

In any of these locations, when in doubt, you can ask to see a guide's credentials. Keep in mind that you may be shown a badge or paperwork, but how will you know if the documentation is legit? If you're after a guaranteed reputable, government-approved, licensed tour guide, you'll likely want to book in advance.

TOURISM BOARDS

Of course, BUCKET! is not the only source of trip planning out there. Though we highly recommend you design your own trip, or at least pick the style of itinerary that suits you best, you can also decide to follow one of the following suggestions, many of which were put together by professional tourism ministries.

Jordan **Jordan's Ministry of Tourism** offers a five-, eight-, and 11-day itinerary of its best selections (**w** issuu.com/visitjordan/docs/visitors-guide/26). The **Jordan Tourism Board** has produced several sleek brochures with itineraries referencing a few travel styles: fun and adventure, history and culture, eco and nature, leisure and wellness, and religion and faith, each with a mix-and-match type of setup (**w** myjordanjourney. com/brochures). You can then select specific sites and put them together to create your own tour through the Tourism Board (**w** myjordanjourney.com/build-my-jordan-journey). The **Jordan Pass** is a tourist pass/entry visa to Jordan that allows access to Petra and a bunch of other spots, all for the same price, and varies depending whether you stay in Petra for one, two, or three days. The website where you can buy the pass offers four suggested itineraries, "Biblical Trail," "UNESCO Enthusiasts," "Ancient Ruins," and "Museum Buffs" (**w** jordanpass.jo/Contents/Suggested_Itineraries.aspx).

Israel **Israel's Ministry of Tourism** sponsors the website **w** info.goisrael.com/en and offers an interactive set of criteria which allows you to narrow down tourist options based on attraction type (e.g., archaeology, beaches, wineries), region, suitability for children, among other categories (**w** info.goisrael.com/en/things-to-do).

TRAVEL AGENTS AND SPECIALISTS

Condé Nast Traveler gives names of specific Top Travel Specialists each year. In 2020, Jennifer Barnaby from Wild Frontiers, Jim Berkeley from Destinations & Adventures, and Jonathan Rose from Touring Israel all knew their way around a Jordan itinerary, while other Israel experts included Susan Weissberg from Wyllys Professional Travel and Joe Yudin from Touring Israel. Thirty-five agents claim some level of expertise in the Middle East, including cruise and activity specialists (**w** cntraveler.com/travel-specialists).

Travel + Leisure publishes a list of best special-interest travel agents each year. If you'd like to speak with a recognizable name and industry professional directly about your special interests (LGBT, foodies, honeymoon, sports, etc.), try **w** travelandleisure.com/a-list/best-special-interest-travel-agents.

Wendy Perrin has a WOW List on her website (**w** www.wendyperrin.com/wow-list/) and she singles out Joe Yudin, referenced above, and Jonathan Rose, whose trips start at $650 per day, and you can read excellent reviews on her website. Jonny Bealby of Wild Frontiers is also listed for work in Jordan, starting at $700/day. Wendy can also put you in touch with Jordan experts.

Speaking of Joe Yudin, he actually runs **Touring Israel**, which offers customized private tours of Israel, with very specific guides for your exquisite tastes, and everything catered to your requests (**w** touringisrael.com/tours/).

TOUR OPERATORS

As you may have surmised, there are dozens of travel agents who can book trips for you. A simple Google search can provide an endless list of names and agencies. So how do you narrow down all those options?

Your best bet is probably **budget**. The sticker price is sometimes shocking, but keep in mind that the price is often mostly inclusive, meaning all of your lodging, many of your meals, all the transportation, entrance fees, sometimes tips, and other priceless coordination and assistance pieces are included in the price. Not having to deal with those pieces of the jigsaw will give you peace of mind and allow you to relax on your vacation.

The following tour operators are widely regarded by travelers as reputable, organized, good value, and great experiences. Do you recognize one? Have you used one before? Many operators give discounts to repeat customers or special incentives for referrals. Sticker prices are often negotiable as well, depending on your needs and budget. So, if your budget is $400 a day, don't let $500 scare you away: they'll be willing to work with you. (Also, we haven't listed anything where the price wasn't specifically referenced online. You shouldn't have to pull teeth to find out approximate costs.)

Higher-budget trips (above $500/night)

★ *Artisans of Leisure* ($1,300/night) gives you personalized, private sightseeing tours in luxury accommodations. They have family, Jewish, Christian, and culinary-focused tour options (w artisansofleisure.com/tour/Israel_tours_luxury_travel.php).

★ *Cazenove+Loyd* ($900/night) sets you up with a licensed archaeologist (bio on the website!), great accommodations, beer/wine at dinner, visa and entrance fees, among other luxury assistance to justify the price, which includes a donation and visit to the King Hussein Cancer Foundation (w cazloyd.com/en).

★ *Abercrombie & Kent* ($600/night) is a popular high-end tour company, often highly regarded by tour guides themselves for providing thoughtful, exclusive, and complete itinerary packages for its clients. It offers several options through Israel and/or Jordan from eight to 14 days, or through a tailor-made package you can begin to develop on its website. Its lodging options are usually of the finest quality, so the prices match (w abercrombiekent.com).

★ *Wilderness Travel* ($570/night) prides itself on its dream trips in the adventure/active travel category. It has one Jordan itinerary, seven days, which incorporates several of the highlights, including Amman, Jerash, Petra, Wadi Rum, and the Dead Sea (w wildernesstravel.com/trip/jordan/jordan-private-journey/itinerary).

Mid-range trips ($200–500/night)

★ *Pomegranate* ($400+/night) is an Israel-specific high-end tour company with a variety of short- and long-tour options. Its private journeys include "Classic Israel," "Jewish Heritage," "Christian Heritage," and "Desert Indulgence." Small-group tours leave a few times a year. It also has biking, hiking, and family tour options (w pomegranate-travel.com).

★ *Journeys International* ($300–500/night) offers itineraries in small groups of 5–12, limited activity, and decent comfort. Its "Israel In-Depth" itinerary is quite comprehensive (w journeysinternational.com/destinations/middle-east/israel/israel-depth); the Jordan itinerary is equally fulfilling (w journeysinternational.com/destination/middle-east/jordan/).

★ *Cox & Kings* ($250–500/night) is the oldest travel company in the world. It is routinely ranked among the highest in traveler satisfaction surveys. In the Holy Land, it gives you superior group or luxury/superior private tour options, comprehensive itineraries and short breaks, and accommodation-only options (w coxandkings.co.uk/destinations/middle-east/).

★ *Black Tomato* ($250–500/night) caters in luxury holidays (and honeymoons!) with some premade itineraries in Jordan that may suit your fancy, including seven nights in luxury locations in Jordan, and eight nights on a "cultural odyssey." For a country that ranks medium on the development index, Jordan might not be the easiest swallow for DIY travelers, but it can be with a little assistance. The company also offers holidays and honeymoon in Israel (w blacktomato.com).

★ *Tauck* ($400/night) has penetrated just about every global market, and it has a small presence in Israel and Jordan as well. It offers a 13-day trip with most meals included, easy pace, and lots of BUCKET!-recommended activities (w tauck. co.uk/tours/israel-jordan-escorted-tour).

★ *Scott Dunn* (from $375/night, including flights from London) customizes Jordan itineraries for you, with great accommodation options, longer stays in remote areas (Wadi Rum, Dana Reserve), and can include a variety of activities, such as trekking, diving, and desert camping (w scottdunn.com).

★ *Intrepid Travel* ($225-300/night) has max-12 groups, and caters to independent-minded (but friendly!) backpacker types who want a little coordination and have some money to spend – it is not the cheapest outfitter. However, it is well regarded, and often has 25%-off sales (w intrepidtravel.com). It also offers women-only itineraries in Jordan (w intrepidtravel.com/us/jordan/jordan-womens-expedition-141148).

★ *Audley Travel* ($270/night) has several featured tours of Jordan, all tailor-made (w audleytravel.com/jordan).

Budget trips (below $200/night)
★ *Trailfinders* ($170-200/night) gives a few options for Jordan bike tours, private holidays, and small-group adventures. It also has a handful of "unmissable experiences" you can tack on to your adventure, such as ballooning in Wadi Rum, belly dancing, and local family visits (w trailfinders.com/tours/the-middle-east/jordan/).

★ *Responsible Travel* ($160-180/night) coordinates small-group tours that work to protect culture and wildlife, invest in the local economy, and to counter mass tourism. Trips include "Walking Palestine," eight days through Israel and Palestine, and a week in Jordan along the Desert and King's highways (w responsiblevacation.com).

★ *Explore!* ($100-150/night) offers nights in kibbutzim, group sizes of 12-18, and pretty active itineraries (w explore.co.uk/holidays/holy-land).

CRUISES

Lots of cruise companies offer stops in Israel, either at the Ashdod port (note: Ashdod itself is not on the traveler's circuit), Haifa, or Aqaba. Your best bet is to get immediately to Jerusalem or Petra, which are the most interesting sites on the itineraries, and make sure the Dead Sea is included for a BUCKET!-level experience. Let's rank the options based solely on their onshore excursion options. For now, we are ignoring any poor-quality websites that make finding shore excursions unnecessarily difficult.

★ *Silversea* Has ports in Aqaba, Sharm el-Sheikh, Haifa, and Ashdod, offering four port days in the Holy Land on its Athens-to-Dubai trip. Unique shore options include Beit Guvrin, a visit to a kibbutz and local winery, and a day at the Caesarea Golf Club.

★ *Seabourn* Offers multiday cruises through the Suez, with stops in Aqaba, Ashdod, and Haifa. Its excursions offer overnights, partnerships with UNESCO, and private drivers for 9-11 hours. Total days = 3, plus overnight options.

★ *Oceania* Offers several luxury cruises that touch Haifa (10+ days), and even more that touch Aqaba (20+ days). Its excursions are perhaps the most comprehensive, with options to visit Megiddo, Beit She'arim, Rosh HaNikra, Akko, the

Golan Heights, Tsfat, and other unique places on extended day trips (in addition to the expected locations). Total days in Holy Land = 3.

★ *Royal Caribbean* Offers a Suez Canal package that passes through Aqaba, Ashdod, and Haifa, offering day trips to Jerusalem, Petra, and the Baháʼí Gardens, which provides cursory but decent exposure to the Holy Land. Total days in Holy Land = 3.

★ *Azamara* Has an "Israel Intensive Voyage," with five days in country along with stops in Cyprus and Greece. The Haifa port-of-call offers excursions to a number of spots in Haifa, as well as Akko, Caesarea, and the Galilee. In Ashdod, you can see Ashdod, Jerusalem, Tel Aviv, Bethlehem, Masada, and the Dead Sea. In addition to the port of Aqaba, you can also visit Wadi Rum and Petra. Explorers Guides for each of these locations are available online.

★ *Cunard* Offers lots of excursion options, including to Nazareth, Haifa, Jerusalem, Caesarea, Galilee, Bethlehem, Masada, and the Dead Sea, though the ports of Haifa and Aqaba are only for cruise durations of 20 days or longer. Total days in Holy Land = 2.

★ *Holland America* Offers two destinations from its *Nieuw Statendam* ship: in Haifa, you can visit a number of northern destinations, including Golan, Nazareth, and Haifa; and in Ashdod, you can head to Bethlehem, Tel Aviv-Jaffa, and Jerusalem. Total days in Holy Land = 2.

★ *Princess Cruises* Visits Aqaba port and offers an array of opportunities to visit Petra, Wadi Rum, and Aqaba itself for scuba, cooking classes, or full-day tours by van or private car. Total days in Holy Land = 1.

Disclaimer We have not taken any of these cruises so cannot attest to their quality. Readers can let us know and we will adjust accordingly.

BUS TOURS

Are you looking for *only* a bus tour? Yes, they exist aplenty. Yes, you will see dozens if not hundreds of tourists pouring off of them at the Dead Sea, Jerusalem, Petra, etc.

But don't concentrate on the bus company itself. These are usually contracted by a tour guide or operator. Rather, focus on our earlier advice: find a tour operator that can help you plan your most ideal day trips. Let them make the arrangements for the land packages, to include activities and transportation. If you end up on a bus, so be it.

Bad guides will convince you to pay for things you don't need. Are you staying in Jerusalem? Then you don't need a bus to see the Old City. There are no vehicles allowed inside the city walls, so you will be walking either way! Thus, use a reputable source to make sure you don't pay for something you don't need.

If you don't know specifically what you want to see and do, that's okay. A good travel agent will help guide you, so don't just go mindlessly Googling. If you've picked up our book, we're already preaching to the choir. But just in case: do a little bit of research to find a reputable company or agent – you can start with our recommendations in this very chapter.

Part 11

Electives by Alphabet

Abila   719
Abu Ashraf   667
Abu Darwish Mosque   714
Abu Ghosh's hummusiyas   614
Abu Hassan   442
Ad-Deir, aka the Monastery   701
Aida Refugee Camp   619
Ain Ghazal   717
Ajloun Forest (#57)   373
Ajloun Fortress (#76)   403
Akhziv Beach   442
Akhzivland   659
Akko (#13)   216
Akkotel   655
Al-Anazia. See Pool of the Arches
Al-Aqsa Mosque (#65)   387
Al-Auja   624
Al-Ayoun Trail   442
Al-Jazzar Mosque   654
Al-Kitkat   714
Al-Pasha Turkish Bath   714
Al-Qasem Palace   628
Al-Quds Falafel   713
Alena at The Norman   647
Alpaca Farm   686
American Colony Hotel   605
Amirim   675
Amman, Ancient (#37)   310
Amman, Modern (#36)   307
Amphorae Winery   662
Amram's Pillars   695
Anastasia   642
Ancient Bathhouse of Nazareth   668
Anita   643
ANU – Museum of the Jewish People (#77)
   404
Apollonia   442
Aqaba (#43)   335
Aqaba Bird Observatory   698
Aqueduct Beach   657
Archaeological Seminars Dig-for-a-Day   615
Argaman Beach   443
Argila/Hookah/Shisha   443
Armenian Quarter   597
Art Hotel   714
As-Salt   443
Ashdod Art Museum   657
Ashdod Performing Arts Center   657
Ashkenazi Ari Synagogue   375
Astronomy Israel   687
Atlit Beach   658

Atlit Detention Camp   658
Avdat (#48)   353
Ayun Stream   677
Azraq Wetlands (#55)   371
Azrieli Center   635
Azrieli Sarona Tower   636

Bahá'í Gardens (#27)   271
Banias (#80)   409
Banksy Art   619
Banksy's Walled-Off Hotel   443
Bar'am   443
Basilica of the Agony   300
Basilica of the Annunciation   444
Bat Galim Beach   653
Battir Hills   444
Bauhaus Architecture. *See* Modern
   Movement
Bauhaus Center   635
Beaches   554
Bedouin Tents and Coffee   444
Bedouin Way, The   724
Beer Sheva   683
Beit Alpha (#64)   386
Beit Gabriel   672
Beit Guvrin and Maresha (#60)   378
Beit Ha'ir   635
Beit HaShomer Museum   676
Beit Jamal Monastery   615
Beit She'an (#39)   317
Beit She'arim (#79)   407
Beit Shmuel-Mercaz Shimshon   611
Beit Sitti   444
Beit Yannai   445
Bellboy Bar   647
Belvoir (#93)   429
Belz Great Synagogue   614
Ben Gurion House   635
Ben Gurion's Tomb   686
Ben Shemen Forest   616
Ben Yehuda Street   445
Beresheet Hotel   686
Bethany-Beyond-the-Jordan (#41)   326
Bethany and Lazarus' Tomb   301
Bethlehem (#40)   322
Bethphage   301
Bethsaida Valley. *See* Majrase-Betiha
Bialik House   445
Biankini/Siesta Beach   689
Bible Lands Museum   445
Biblical Museum of Natural History   615

Biblical Tels (#38) 314
Big Makhtesh/HaMakhtesh HaGadol 684
Birkat Ram 679
Bloomfield Science Museum 613
Blue Hole 723
Bonem House 608
Books@Cafe 713
Breakfast. *See* Israeli Breakfast
Bridge of Strings 446
Brothers/Ha'achim 647
Brown Beach House 446
Brown Jerusalem 611
Brown TLV 638
Bulos Y Zumot Winery 714
Burqu 718
Busi Grill 446
Buster's 618
Butler Bar 647

Caesarea (#25) 261
Café Culture 446
Cafe Kaymak 642
Cafe Xoho 642
Camel Riding 447
Camel Safari 724
Cameri Theatre 635
Capernaum and Tabgha (#33) 295
Cardo 447
Carmel Hai-Bar 447
Carmel Market (#87) 419
Carmel Winery 447
Carmey Avdat Farm Winery 687
Caro Synagogue 375
Castel 614
Chagall Windows. *See* Hadassah
    Synagogue
Chakra 611
Château Golan Winery 725
Children's Museum of Jordan 717
Chords Bridge. *See* Bridge of Strings
Christmas Mass in Bethlehem 621
Church of the Ascension 300
Church of the Beheading of John the Baptist
    709
Church of the Holy Sepulchre (#9) 189
Church of Mary Magdalene 300
Church of the Nativity (#18) 235
Church of the Paternoster 300
Church of St. Anne and the Pools of Bethesda
    448
Church of St. John the Baptist 596

Church of the Transfiguration 448
Citadel/Tower of David (#32) 292
Cities of the Decapolis 512
City of David 448
Clandestine Immigration & Naval Museum 653
Claro 647
Clos de Gat Winery 617
Coloured Canyon 722
Consulate General of Belgium/Villa Salameh
    607
Coral Beach (#83) 413
Crazy House 630
Crusader Castle Hopping 738
Cuisine. *See* Israeli Cuisine; Jordanian
    Cuisine; Modern Israeli Cuisine;
    Nazarene Fusion Cuisine
Cymbalista Synagogue 649

Dahab (#54) 370
Daliyat al-Karmel 664
Dallal Bakery 643
Dallal Restaurant 647
Dalton Winery 724
Damiya Dolmen Field 721
Dan Tel Aviv 630
Dana Biosphere Reserve (#21) 247
Dead Sea (#3) 145
Dead Sea Highway 707
Dead Sea Panorama Complex 707
Dead Sea Scrolls 232
Decapolis Cities. *See* Cities of the
    Decapolis
Deir Ghassaneh 628
Deir Quruntal 448
Desert Palaces. *See* Qasr Amra
Design Museum Holon 448
Dheisheh Refugee Camp 622
Dibeen Forest 719
Dimona 684
Dizengoff Center 635
Dok 647
Dolphin Reef 693
Domaine du Castel 449
Dome of the Chain 449
Dome of the Rock (#6) 170
Dor HaBonim (#100) 438
Dormition Abbey 427
Dr. Shakshuka. *See* Shakshuka
Driving Highway 90 689
Driving Through the Negev 686
Drummers' Beach 449

Druze Cooking Workshops   676

Ecce Homo Arch   596
Efendi   655
Eilat (#78)   405
Ein Afeq   659
Ein Avdat (#74)   400
Ein Bokek   449
Ein Bokek Spa Hotels   450
Ein Gedi (#50)   361
Ein Hemed   450
Ein Hod   450
Ein Kerem   450
Ein Prat   624
Einot Tsukim   689
El Bariyeh/Wadi Khareitun/Nahal Teqoa   622
El-Ghawanima Tower   595
Elbabor   451
Ella Valley Vineyards   618
Elma Arts Complex   451
Emek Tzurim   605
Emmaus Nicopolis   616
Erez Crossing   657
Eshkol   656
Et-Tell, ancient Ai   625
Ethiopian Quarter   609
Eucalyptus   611
Ezuz   686

Fakhr el-Din   714
Falafel Gabai   642
Falafel Hazkenim   653
Feynan Ecolodge (#86)   417
Fifa Nature Reserve   707
Fire and Water Fountain   635
Flam Winery   617
Florentin   637
Fountain of Sultan Qaytbay   451
Freedom Theatre   628
Fuheis   717

Gadot Lookout   680
Galil Mountain Winery   724
Gamla   451
Gan Garoo   666
Gan HaShlosha   452
Garden Tomb   605
Gatsby Cocktail Room ·   611
Geder Beach   663
George and John Tel Aviv   452
German Colony   653

Glamping in Wadi Rum   698
Goats with the Wind   670
Golan Heights (#62)   382
Golan Heights Winery (#75)   402
Golan Lookout/Tel Faher   679
Golan Trail   681
Goldstein Synagogue   613
Gordon Beach   630
Greek Orthodox Church of the Annunciation   668
Group Fun at a Downtown Beach   630
Gulf of Aqaba. *See* Red Sea

Ha'achim. *See* Brothers
Haas Promenade   613
Habasta   647
HaBeit Be'einhud   665
Habima Theatre   636
Hadassah Synagogue and Chagall Windows   452
Haifa   452
HaKirya   635
Halutza   452
Hamat Gader   453
Hamat Tiberias   453
Hammamat Ma'in Hot Springs   453
Hammams   715
Haram es-Sharif. *See* Temple Mount
HaSalon   647
HaSharon Beach   662
Hashem Falafel   713
Hatachana Train Station   630
HaTikva Market   650
HaYarkon Park   649
Hebrew University, Safra Campus   613
Hebron   623
Hecht Museum   664
Helena Banamal   659
Herbert Samuel   453
Herodion (#90)   423
Herziliya Beaches   454
Herziliya Museum of Contemporary Art, The   649
Herzl Museum   611
Hezekiah's Tunnel   454
High Place of Sacrifice   701
Hiking in Jenin   628
Hiking in Jordan   454
Hiking in the Negev   454
Hisham's Palace. *See* Jericho
Holy Trinity Cathedral   609
Holy Week in Jerusalem   603

Horshat Tal   679
Hospitaller Fortress/Knights' Halls   654
Hot Air Balloon Ride Over Wadi Rum   455
Hotel Montefiore   638
Hula Lake   455
Hummus   455
Hummus Said   654
Hurva Square and Synagogue   601
Hutzot Hayotzer Arts and Crafts Festival   611

Ilana Goor Museum   633
Imperial Bar (#99)   437
Incense Route (#73)   399
Inn of the Good Samaritan   624
Intercontinental Jordan   714
International Center of Mary of Nazareth   667
Irbid Museum of Jordanian Heritage   719
Iris Reserve   657
Isaac Luria Synagogue   375
Ishtabach   611
Israel Bike Trail   681
Israel Children's Museum   650
Israel Festival   611
Israel Museum (#17)   232
Israel National Trail   455
Israeli Air Force Museum   683
Israeli Breakfast   87
Israeli Cuisine (#51)   365
Isrotel Agamim   692

Jabal al-Khubtha   701
Jabotinsky Park   658
Jaffa (#30)   284
Jaffa, The   633
Jaffa Clock Tower   632
Jaffa Flea Market   456
Jerash (#14)   220
Jericho and Hisham's Palace (#26)   266
Jerusalem, New City (#72)   397
Jerusalem, Old City. *See* Old City
   Jerusalem
Jerusalem Archaeological Park (#71)
   396
Jerusalem Nightlife   611
Jerusalem Theatre   607
Jerusalem Walls and Gates (#47)   350
Jesus Trail (#69)   393
Jewish National Library   613
Jewish Quarter   456
Jisr az-Zarqa   658
Jordan Archaeological Museum   456

Jordan Folklore Museum   714
Jordan Museum   714
Jordan Museum of Popular Traditions   714
Jordan National Gallery of Fine Arts   713
Jordan River Designs Showroom   717
Jordan River Rafting   678
Jordan Trail (#52)   367
Jordanian Cuisine (#44)   339
Jordanian Hospitality   456
Jordanian Wildflowers   722
Jordan's Royal Guards   717
Judean Hills Wineries   616

Karaite Synagogue   601
Karak (#49)   357
Kerem HaTeimanim/Yemenite Quarter   633
Kerem Shalom   656
Kfar Kama   670
Kfar Kana   673
Khalid Shoman Foundation/Darat al-Funun   713
Khirbet al-Minya   671
Khirbet et-Tannur   705
Khirbet Feynan   705
Khirbet Suseya   623
Khirbet Umm el-Umdan Synagogue   616
Kibbutz Degania   672
Kibbutz Ein Gev   672
Kibbutz Ginosar   671
Kibbutz Ketura   695
Kibbutz Lotan   456
Kibbutz Merom Golan   681
Kibbutz Mitzpe Shalem   689
Kibbutz Neot Smadar   695
Kibbutz Volunteer   457
Kibbutzim   535
Kidron Valley   603
Kikar Levana/White Square   650
King Abdullah I Mosque   715
King David Hotel   457
King David's Tomb   428
King's Highway (#31)   288
Kinneret Trail   672
Kitchen Market   631
Knesset   611
Knights' Halls. *See* Hospitaller Fortress
Korazim   457
Kuli Alma   637
Kursi   672

Lag B'Omer at Moshav Meron   457
Latrun Monastery   616

INDEX

Leonardo Beach Hotel   631
Levinsky Market   642
Liftah   614
Lily & Bloom   638
Lina Hummusiya   597
Little Makhtesh/HaMakhtesh HaKatan   684
Little Petra   458
Lot's Cave   458
Louis Promenade   653
Lutheran Church of the Redeemer   596
Lutheran Guest House   597

M25   642
Maadali   655
Ma'ayan Harod   666
Machneyuda (#98)   436
Madaba and the Madaba Map (#19)   241
MadaTech   653
Magdalena   674
Majda   614
Majdal Shams and The Shouting Hill   679
Majrase-Betiha/Bethsaida Valley   681
Makhtesh Ramon (#28)   274
Mamilla Hotel   458
Mamluk Buildings   595
Mamshit   458
Mane-Katz Museum   653
Mansaf   561
Manta Ray   459
Mar Elias Monastery   621
Mar Saba   459
Margalit Winery   661
Marganit Tower   635
Marine Science Station Aquarium   698
Masada (#8)   182
Masada's Roman Trails   689
Masada's Snake Path   689
Mashya   459
Matcal Tower   635
Matcot   631
Mea She'arim (#66)   389
Mediterranean Coast   459
Megiddo (#59)   376
Mehane Yehuda Market (#67)   390
Meier on Rothschild   639
Mekudeshet. *See* Sacred Music Festival
Memorial Museum of Hungarian Speaking Jewry   675
Menachem Begin Heritage Center   607
Meshek Barzilay   642
Meshushim Stream   681

Migdala   673
Milgo & Milbar   647
Mini Israel   616
Mishkan Museum of Art   666
Mitzpe Ramon   460
Miznon   460
Modern Israeli Cuisine   460
Modern Movement (Bauhaus Architecture) (#16)   228
Monastery, The. *See* Ad-Deir
Monastery of Abu Ghosh   460
Monastery of the Flagellation   596
Monastery of St. Euthymius   623
Monastery of St. Martyrius   623
Monastery of St. Theodosius   621
Montefiore's Windmill   607
Montfort   461
Mordoch   611
Moshav Meron. *See* Lag B'Omer
Moshe Aviv Tower   649
Mosque of Omar   596
Mount Arbel   461
Mount of Beatitudes   462
Mount Bental Lookout   679
Mount Carmel   461
Mount Gerizim   461
Mount Gilboa   462
Mount Hermon   462
Mount Karkom   693
Mount Nebo (#24)   258
Mount of Olives (#34)   299
Mount Sinai (#15)   225
Mount Sodom   690
Mount Zion (#92)   427
Mujib Biosphere Reserve. *See* Wadi Mujib
Mukawir   462
Muristan   596
MUSA – Eretz Israel Museum   463
Museum of Bedouin Culture   463
Museum for Islamic Art   607
Museum of Rishon Letzion   650
Museum of Underground Prisoners   609
Muslim Quarter   595
Mu'tah   705

Nabi Musa   624
Nablus (#61)   381
Nahal Amud   675
Nahal el-Al   681
Nahal Me'arot/Wadi el-Mughara   463
Nahal Refaim   613

Nahal Taninim   657
Nahal Teqoa. *See* El Bariyeh
Nahal Zalmon   676
Nahalal   669
Nahalat Binyamin   637
Nahariya   659
Nain   673
Nakhalat Shiva   609
National Memorial Day   39
Nawatef Camp   705
Nazarene Fusion Cuisine   463
Nazareth and its Biblical Sites (#29)   279
Nebi Samuel   625
Negev Camping   686
Negev Goat Farms   686
Negev Museum of Art   683
Negev Wine Route   687
Neot HaKikar   690
Neot Kedumim Biblical Landscape   616
Neot Smadar Winery   695
Netanya   464
Neve Midbar Beach   689
Neve Tzedek   464
New Kalya Beach   689
Nimrod's Fortress (#85)   415
Nitzana   464
Nordau Segregated Beach   630
Norman Hotel, The   464
North Beach   691
Nuweiba Beach Camps   722

OCD   464
Old City Jerusalem (#1)   121
Old City of Lod   651
Old Man and the Sea   647
Olympic Experience   649
Opera Tower   630
Ophir Lookout   682
OTR   718
Oud Festival   607
Ouzeria   647
Oved's Sabich. *See* Sabich

Pagoda House   636
Palestinian Heritage Museum   605
Palestinian Heritage Trail   465
Palestinian Museum, The   625
Palestinian National Theatre   605
Palestinian Throne Villages   518
Palmahim   657
Par Derriere   647

Pastel   465
Peace Vista   683
Pella   465
Pelter Winery   724
Petra (#2)   135
Petra Kitchen (#84)   414
Petra by Night   465
Petro   714
Pharaoh's Island Citadel   722
PhotoHouse, The   633
Picking Fruit   681
Poli House   638
Pool of the Arches/Al-Anazia   650
Popina   466
Port Said   647
Powered Parachute Flight   691
Prehistoric Man Museum   678
Purim in Tel Aviv   638

Qasr al-Abd   466
Qasr Amra and the Desert Palaces (#20)   244
Qasr Azraq   466
Qasr Bashir   705
Qasr Burqu   733
Qasr Kharana   466
Qasr al-Mushatta   733
Qasr al-Qastal   733
Qasr al-Yahud   624
Qatzrin, Ancient   442
Qumran (#70)   394

Rabin Square   635
Rachel's Tomb   621
Rachmo   611
Rainbow Street   713
Ralli Museums   658
Ramallah (#68)   391
Ramat HaNadiv   658
Rambam Synagogue   601
Ramot Polin Apartments   625
Ramparts Walk (#91)   426
Ras Mohammad (#53)   368
Rasoun Camping   722
Recanati Winery   661
Red Canyon   466
Red Sea/Gulf of Aqaba (#10)   199
Red Sea Jazz Festival   692
Rift Valley   524
Rishon Letzion   650
Rishpon   649

INDEX

Rock Climbing in Wadi Rum   699
Rockefeller Archaeological Museum   467
Room of the Last Supper (Cenacle)   428
Rosh HaNikra   467
Rosh Pina   676
Rothschild Boulevard   467
Rothschild Hotel   638
Royal Automobile Museum   717
*Royal Society for the Conservation of Nature
   (RSCN)*   467
Russian Quarter   609

Sabich Frishman   642
Sabich/Oved's   468
Sacred Music Festival, aka Mekudeshet   614
Safari Park   650
Safed. *See* Tsfat
Said Abouelafia Bakery   641
Salad Trail   656
Sandboarding in Wadi Rum   698
Sanhedrin Trail   670
Sarona Market   642
Sataf   468
Scarlet South Festival   657
Schindler's Grave   428
Schocken Villa and Library   608
Sde Amudim   670
Sde Boker   686
Sea of Galilee (#7)   175
Sea of Galilee Beaches   468
Sea Horse Winery   618
Sebastia-Shomron   468
Separation Wall   469
Sephardic Synagogues   601
Setai, The   633
Shakshuka/Dr. Shakshuka   469
Shams al-Balad   714
Sharm el-Sheikh (#88)   420
Shaumari   469
Sheinkin Street   636
Shivta   469
Shkedi's Camplodge   690
Shobak   469
Shouting Hill, The. *See* Majdal Shams
Shrine of Bahá'u'lláh   470
Shuqba/Natuf Caves   627
Shushan Street   609
Sidreh-Lakiya Negev Weaving   684
Siesta Beach. *See* Biankini Beach
Sinai Trail   470
Snir Stream   678

Social Club   647
Solo Fun at a Wave-Filled Beach   663
Solomon's Pools   623
Solomon's Quarries. *See* Zedekiah's Cave
Sommer Contemporary Art Museum   636
South Beach   698
South Haifa Beaches   663
Spiral Apartment House   649
St. Catherine's Monastery (#22)   251
St. Catherine's Mount   722
**St. George's Monastery and Wadi Qelt
   (#97)**   434
St. James' Cathedral   470
Stalactite Caves   615
Stella Maris   470
Sufganiyot   643
Sugar Trail   625
Supreme Court of Israel   471
Suramare   647
Suweimeh Spa Hotels   471
Suzanne Dellal Centre for Dance and Theatre
   637

Taba   722
Tabgha. *See* Capernaum
Tabor House   609
Tabor Winery   726
Taybeh Brewing Company   625
Tel Arad   471
Tel Ashkelon   471
Tel Aviv (#5)   162
Tel Aviv Beaches (#89)   422
Tel Aviv Museum of Art (#95)   432
Tel Aviv Nightlife (#82)   412
Tel Aviv Port   472
Tel Aviv Pride Celebration   540
Tel Aviv Tayelet/Promenade   472
Tel Aviv White Night   636
Tel Beer Sheva   472
Tel Bethsaida   674
Tel Dan (#63)   385
Tel Faher. *See* Golan Lookout
Tel Gezer Archaeological Project   616
Tel Hai Fort   677
Tel Hazor   472
Tel Jezreel   666
Tel Lachish   615
Tel-O-Fun Bike Share   473
Tel Shiloh   628
Temple Mount (#12)   210
Temple Mount Sifting Project   606

Tenat   647
Tiberias   473
Ticho House   609
Tikotin Museum of Japanese Art   652
Timna (#96)   433
Tisch Family Zoological Gardens   614
Tishbi Winery   662
Tomb of the Baba Sali   657
Tomb of Maimonides   670
Tomb of the Patriarchs and Old Town of Hebron (#46)   345
Tomb of Queen Helena of Adiabene   605
Tomb of Rabbi Akiva   670
Tomb of Rabbi Meir Ba'al Haness   672
Tomb of the Virgin   300
Toto   647
Tower of David. *See* Citadel
Tsfat/Safed (#58)   375
Tsipori (#56)   372
Tulul Abu el-Alaiq   473
Turkiz   647
Twilight in Jerusalem   597
Tzfon Abraxas   473
Tzimmers   52
Tzora Winery   618

U. Nahon Museum of Italian Jewish Art   609
Ulpanim   568
Umm ar-Rasas (#81)   410
Umm ar-Rihan Forest   628
Umm el-Jimal   474
Umm Qais (#45)   341
Underwater Observatory   474
Uri Buri   474

Via Dolorosa (#42)   330
Villa Salameh. *See* Consulate General of Belgium
Vitkin Winery   661

Wadi al-Dahik   718
Wadi al-Hassa   705
Wadi Daraja   689
Wadi Ein Netafim   693

Wadi Jadid   705
Wadi Khareitun. *See* El Bariyeh
Wadi Mujib and Mujib Biosphere Reserve (#23)   255
Wadi Nasb   722
Wadi Qelt. *See* St. George's Monastery
Wadi Qumran   691
Wadi Rum (#4)   155
Waldorf Astoria   611
Water Sports   631
Weizmann Institute of Science   474
Western Wall (#11)   205
Western Wall Tunnels (#94)   430
White Mosque   650
White Square. *See* Kikar Levana
White Villa Hotel   638
Wild Jordan Center   475
Winery Tour   475
Wohl Archaeological Museum   475
Wolfson Museum of Jewish Art   607

Yad Ben Zvi Institute for Judaeo-Arab Studies   608
Yad Hashmona   614
Yad Vashem (#35)   303
Yaffo-Tel Aviv   647
Yarmouk Forest   719
Yasser Arafat Museum   625
Yatir Winery   475
Yehi'am   476
Yehudiya   476
Yemen Moshe   476
Yemenite Quarter. *See* Kerem HaTeimanim
Yeruham   684
Yitzhak Rabin Center   649
YMCA   476
Yom Kippur   36
Yom Tov Delicatessen   642
Yotvata Hai-Bar   477

Zedekiah's Cave/Solomon's Quarries   605
Zichron Ya'akov   477
Zikra Initiative   707

INDEX

NOTES